# CORPORATIONS
## LAW AND POLICY
## MATERIALS AND PROBLEMS
### Fourth Edition

By

**Lewis D. Solomon**

*Arthur Selwyn Miller Research Professor of Law*
*George Washington University National Law Center*

**Donald E. Schwartz**

*Late Professor of Law*
*Georgetown University Law Center*

**Jeffrey D. Bauman**

*Professor of Law*
*Georgetown University Law Center*

**Elliott J. Weiss**

*Charles E. Ares Professor of Law*
*University of Arizona College of Law*

**AMERICAN CASEBOOK SERIES®**

**WEST GROUP**

ST. PAUL, MINN., 1998

COPYRIGHT © 1982, 1988, 1994 WEST PUBLISHING CO.
COPYRIGHT © 1998 By WEST GROUP
        610 Opperman Drive
        P.O. Box 64526
        St. Paul, MN 55164–0526
        1–800–328–9352

**Library of Congress Cataloging-in-Publication Data**

Corporations, law and policy : materials and problems / by Lewis D.
  Solomon . . . [et al.]. — 4th ed.
     p.    cm. — (American casebook series)
  Includes index.
  ISBN 0–314–23148–X (hard)
  1. Corporation law—United States—Cases.  I. Solomon, Lewis, D.
II. Series.
KF1413.S63   1998
346.73'066—dc21                         98–3558
                                           CIP

**ISBN** 0–314–23148–X

*To Matt and Kira, to show to their grandchildren.*
J.D.B.

*To Peter, the other lawyer in my family,
and Loren, the other teacher.*
E.J.W.

*For Don, with love.*
J.D.B.
E.J.W.

\*

# Preface to the Fourth Edition

All students and teachers of corporate law realize that there are many valid and varied ways to present the subject. The case method, standing alone, cannot fully encompass the diverse influences which are brought to bear on the field. We believe that a casebook which uses the problem method as an organizing principle is more effective for the task than a more traditional casebook. Using such a method also permits greater use of non-case materials which illuminate the questions which invariably arise in the study of corporate law, regardless of the depth in which such study is undertaken. Thus the emphasis in this edition of the book, as it was in previous editions, is on the development of the skill of learning how to solve problems. Because corporate lawyers most often engage in counseling rather than litigation, we believe that our approach is especially suitable for a course in corporate law. Hopefully, it will also enable the student to appreciate where matters of judgment become paramount.

We appreciate that not all of our colleagues in the field share our view on the use of problems. We respect their approaches and we have designed the book so that it may be used in a more conventional form, making little or no use of the problems. We are aware of many splendid teachers who use the book in precisely that way.

We should also note that while cases do comprise the largest part of the materials, we also have made extensive use of other materials. To integrate problems of public policy, legal ethics, accounting and economic analysis, we rely heavily on non-case material, consisting of secondary sources or our own textual notes. All of these subjects are vital to the understanding of corporate law and its place in our legal, economic, political and cultural system.

The organizing principle of the book is to introduce certain basic themes in the first few chapters and develop those themes throughout the book with increasing depth and sophistication. Chapter 2 uses a simple fact pattern to present an economic analysis of a business enterprise. In basic terms, we look at questions of risk-bearing, monitoring and incentives as they affect the parties to the enterprise. The analysis of these questions provides a reference point to which recurrent use may be made. We remind students of that analysis when we study the financial structure of the corporation, the duties of directors and officers, the governance of the corporation, derivative suits and changes in control. Thus we use the lessons from this early chapter throughout the course. When we reach the study of publicly held corporations, we present additional materials on agency costs, market efficiency, and the debate over the concept of the corporation as a nexus of contracts among competing interests.

This is not advanced economics material. We do not employ sophisticated graphs or calculus. Rather we seek to present fundamental economic concepts in order to develop in our students a deeper understanding about the nature of the corporation and the role of law and lawyers. Some of the material, particularly in the later chapters, is controversial, and we have provided ample space to the trenchant criticisms of the law and economics viewpoint. Corporate law is increasingly influenced by these ideas; they may have contributed as much to the development of corporate law in recent years as the formal acts of lawmakers. That influence is manifested in actions by courts, legislators and regulators. It is also clear that lawyers in their practice apply the learning from several disciplines solving problems. Some particularly interesting examples of the latter are seen in two provocative articles: Gilson, *Value Creation by Business Lawyers: Legal Skills and Asset Pricing,* 94 Yale L.J. 239 (1984); Klein, *The Modern Business Organization: Bargaining Under Constraints,* 91 Yale L.J. 1521 (1982).

After this introduction, we deal with the fact that many students lack a basic understanding of corporations and how they function. The Chesapeake Marine Services problem in Chapter 3 presents some of the fundamental concepts in corporate law, including the duty of care, the business judgment rule and the duty of loyalty. The chapter also illustrates judicial attitudes toward the interaction between the common law and a corporate statute and, perhaps most important, provides the student with a basic understanding of the structure of the corporation. Chapters 4 and 5 discuss the corporation and the Constitution and the role of corporation in society in contexts that emphasize the representative nature of the corporate governance system, the centrality of the business judgment rule, the power of managers, and the mechanisms available to shareholders who disagree with managers' actions. These chapters provide students with a framework that will allow them to understand better the issues that arise in connection with choosing an organizational form, organizing a corporation, designing a capital structure, and allocating power between shareholders and managers—materials that otherwise often seem unrelated.

Chapters 6 and 7 introduce the student to the issues that arise in connection with the decision to incorporate and in the incorporation process itself. Chapters 8 and 9 deal with valuation and corporate finance. Taken together, these chapters are intended to show the interplay between a statutory regime, the economics of a business, and the needs of the parties to the venture. Chapter 13 revisits this theme in the specific context of close corporations; the chapter illustrates the tension between legal rules and the desire for private ordering.

This edition reflects the extensive developments in themes of corporate governance that have burgeoned in recent years. These themes begin in Chapter 12 which explores the theoretical governance structure of a corporation and the allocation of power among shareholders, directors and officers. It uses a reorganization transaction to demonstrate the potential conflicts that can arise from such allocation. Chapter 12 also highlights the increased importance that courts attach to shareholder voting, particularly in the election of directors.

Chapters 14 and 15 present a detailed discussion of the roles of individual shareholders, institutional investors and outside directors in the governance of the publicly held corporation. These chapters include a summary of the theory of the firm debate, discussion of the recently revised SEC proxy materials, and materials describing the emergence and increasing activism of institutional investors. They are intended to provide a working matrix for discussing the materials in subsequent chapters dealing with fiduciary duties, derivative suit litigation, and transactions involving corporate control.

The first edition of this book appeared as the American Bar Association was nearing the completion of the Revised Model Business Corporation Act and the American Law Institute was beginning serious deliberation of its Principles of Corporate Governance. The ABA completed the RMBCA in 1984, but has made, and continues to make, important and controversial changes to that statute. The ALI has published the final version of the Principles of Corporate Governance; the influence of that work on corporate law makers and lawyers is one of the themes that will be played out in the coming years. Both works are featured prominently in this edition.

There is another focus to this book that we have sought to retain: its concern for issues of public policy relating to corporations. All teachers of corporation law understand that this is not a course in corporate mechanics; we are not simply training technicians. Law students study corporation law, not simply because they intend to practice in that field (some would never dream of doing so) but because all lawyers need to be educated about the phenomenon of the corporation and how the law deals with its impact. We constantly raise policy questions with our students: why should the law provide limited liability; why should we delegate enormous powers over other people's money to agents over whom we exercise so little control; why should persons with minimal interests in a corporation be allowed to bring suit in its name; whether our systems of management accountability are adequate; why should insider trading be prohibited; and countless other questions that go to the core of the subject. We have included many recent materials to assist in this respect.

A corporate law casebook can be written from several perspectives; we have written this book to be helpful primarily to students. We have written many lengthy notes which are designed to provide a fuller understanding of discrete areas, especially where knowledge of the way in which the corporate world operates is needed in order for cases and statutes to make any sense. We have also found that students seek not mere recital of rules, but demand explanations for why things are the way they are and whether they should be that way. Our notes attempt to provide guidance in reaching those explanations. We find ourselves comfortable writing in that environment. While practitioners may also find our approach useful, the reader on whom we have focused our attention is the intelligent novice, no matter what his or her age.

This book is designed to be supplemented by the West Publishing's Corporations and other Business Associations Statutes, Rules and Forms in convenient form the Revised Model Business Corporation Act (with official comment at strategic places), the Delaware General Corporation Law, various other relevant statutes, applicable portions of the federal securities laws and rules, and sample articles of incorporation, by-laws, and other forms.

As to editorial details, citations in the texts of cases and other materials, as well as the footnotes of courts and commentators, have been omitted without so specifying. We use the pronoun "she" for "he or she" in most places out of concern for simplicity, not out of bias. The footnotes of decisions and excerpts from books and articles bear the original number; those of the authors are indicated by asterisks and similar symbols.

A teacher's manual for this edition is available from the publisher. It contains further details and suggestions as to how the book and the problems might be used.

We owe thanks to many people. This is the first edition of the book in which one of the original authors did not participate, and we hope we have been true to their original inspiration. The spirit of our late colleague, Don Schwartz, permeates the entire book. Russ Stevenson co-authored the first edition before moving from teaching to the "real world." Lew Solomon has been our valued friend and colleague throughout. Professors Warren Schwartz and Steve Salop of Georgetown were extremely helpful in reviewing the economics material, particularly in Chapter 2. Colleagues at various law schools have been generous with their praise, criticism and suggestions. To name some would be to slight others, but we thank all of them. Our classes have been our guinea pigs and their comments have assisted us in keeping our focus on our student users.

We also owe special thanks to former Justice Andrew G.T. Moore II of the Delaware Supreme Court. One of the authors had the privilege of teaching a seminar with Justice Moore for six years; both of us have benefited immeasurably from his insights into Delaware corporate law while he was on the bench and afterward. Justice Moore also taught some of the materials in this book in his own courses and provided us with invaluable comments. The remaining deficiencies, of course, are our own.

Finally, we have had invaluable assistance from our student research assistants. Erica Hashimoto and Laurel Watts of Georgetown displayed extraordinary creativity in developing the ideas in Chapters 16 and 17. Jeff Rothschild of Georgetown also provided invaluable research assistance. In providing Herculean support in the last-minute rush to publication, Jennifer Johnson and Janene Sohng of Georgetown showed a remarkable ability to make sure that the details of every chapter were correct. We have rarely seen such care taken on any project. Karen Summerhill, the Faculty Support Librarian of Georgetown was there at all hours of the day and night to answer questions, provide support, and see that it all came out alright. Without all of them, our work would have been far more difficult.

JEFFREY D. BAUMAN
ELLIOTT J. WEISS

May 1998

\*

# Acknowledgments

William T. Allen, Ambiguity in Corporation Law, 22 Del. J. Corp. L. 894, 894-898 (1997).

William T Allen, Independent Directors in MBO Transactions: Are They Fact or Fantasy?, 45 Bus.Law. 2055 (1990).

William T. Allen, Our Schizophrenic Conception of the Business Corporation, 14 Cardozo L.Rev. 261, 263-64, 278-79 (1992).

American Bar Association Committee on Corporate Laws, Changes in the Model Business Corporation Act—Amendments Pertaining to Indemnification and Advance for Expenses, 49 Bus. Law. 741 (1994). Copyright © 1994 by the American Bar Association. All rights reserved. Reprinted by permission of the American Bar Association.

American Bar Association, Model Rules of Professional Conduct, Rules 1.6, 1.7, 1.13, 2.1 and Comments (1983). Reprinted by permission of the American Bar Association. Copies of the Model Rules are available from Order Fulfillment, American Bar Association, 750 North Lake Shore Drive, Chicago, IL 60611.

American Law Institute, Principles of Corporate Governance: Analysis and Recommendations, Comment a to § 1.38; § 2.01; Comment e to § 2.01; Comment d(2)(a) to § 5.04; § 1.23 and Comment; § 3.02; § 5.02 and Comment to § 5.02(a)(2)(B); § 5.05; § 5.15(a)-(b) and Comment; Comment to § 7.01; and pp. 324, 587-89 (1994). Copyright © 1994 by The American Law Institute. Reprinted with the permission of The American Law Institute.

Adolf A. Berle, Jr., The Theory of Enterprise Entity, 47 Colum.L.Rev. 343, 348 (1947). This article originally appeared at 47 Colum.L.Rev. 343, 348 (1947). Reprinted by permission.

Reprinted with the permission of Macmillan Publishing Company from THE MODERN CORPORATION AND PRIVATE PROPERTY by Adolf A. Berle, Jr. and Gardiner C. Means. Copyright © 1932 by Macmillan Publishing Company, renewed 1960 by Adolf A. Berle, Jr. and Gardiner C. Means.

Sanjai Bhagat & Bernard Black, The Relationship Between Board Composition and Firm Performance, in Klaus Hopt, Mark Roe & Eddy Wymeersch, eds., Corporate Governance: The State of the Art and Emerging Research (Oxford University Press forthcoming 1998).

Bernard Black, Agents Watching Agents: The Promise of Institutional Investor Voice. Originally published in 38 UCLA L.Rev. 811, 821-22, 822-24 (1992). Copyright © (1992), The Regents of the University of California. All rights reserved. Reprinted with the permission of the author, The Regents of the University of California, and Fred B. Rothman & Co.

William W. Bratton, The Economic Structure of the Post-Contractual Corporation, 87 Nw.U.L.Rev. 180-197 (1992).

Victor Brudney, Contract and Fiduciary Duty in Corporate Law, 38 B.C. L. Rev. 595 (1997).

Victor Brudney & Marvin A. Chirelstein, A Restatement of Corporate Freezeouts, 87 Yale L.J. 1354, 1356-57 n. 9 (1977). Reprinted by permission of The Yale Law Journal Company and Fred B. Rothman & Company from The Yale Law Journal, vol. 87, pp. 1354, 1356-57 n. 9.

Warren Buffet, Letters to Shareholders from Berkshire Hathaway Inc. Annual Reports of 1978, 1983, 1984 and 1986. Reprinted by permission. Copyright © Warren Buffet and/or Berkshire Hathaway Inc. All rights reserved.

Henry N. Butler, The Contractual Theory of the Corporation, 11 George Mason L.Rev. 99 (1989).

Henry N. Butler and Larry E. Ribstein, Opting Out of Fiduciary Duties: A Response to the Anti-Contractarians, 65 Wash.L.Rev. 1, 12-18 (1990). Reprinted with permission of Washington Law Review and Fred B. Rothman & Co.

Robert Charles Clark, Agency Costs Versus Fiduciary Duties, in John W. Pratt and Richard J. Zeckhauser, Principals and Agents: The Structure of Business (1985) 55-64, 66-69. Reprinted by permission of the Harvard Business School Press.

Robert Charles Clark, Corporate Law 389-94 (1986). Reprinted by permission of the author.

John C. Coffee, Jr., Liquidity Versus Control: The Institutional Investor as Corporate Monitor, 91 Colum.L.Rev. 1277, 1281-89 (1991). This article originally appeared at 91 Colum.L.Rev. 1277 (1991). Reprinted by permission of the author and Columbia Law Review.

John C. Coffee, Jr., The Folklore of American Capitalism, 95 Mich. L. Rev. 1970 (1997).

James D. Cox, Insider Trading and Contracting: A Critical Response to the "Chicago School," 1986 Duke L.J. 628, 635, 646, 648.

James D. Cox & Harry Munsinger, Bias in the Boardroom: Psychological Foundations and Legal Implications of Corporate Cohesion, 48 L. & Contemp.Prob., Summer 1985, at 83, 103-4. Reprinted by permission of Duke University School of Law.

Developments in the Law—Conflicts of Interest in the Legal Profession, 94 Harv.L.Rev. 1244, 1339-42 (1981).

Frank H. Easterbrook and Daniel R. Fischel, Limited Liability and the Corporation, 52 U.Chi.L.Rev. 89 (1985), reprinted in The Economic Structure of Corporate Law, 41-44 (1991). Copyright © 1985, The University of Chicago Law Review. Reprinted with permission of University of Chicago Law Review.

Melvin Eisenberg, The Structure of the Corporation: A Legal Analysis 56-58 (1976).

Milton Friedman, Capitalism and Freedom 133-34 (1962).

Ronald Gilson & Reinier Kraakman, The Mechanics of Market Efficiency, 70 Va.L.Rev. 549, 549-50 (1984).

Roberto C. Goizueta, Letter to the Editor, Harvard Business Review, (Nov.-Dec. 1990).

James J. Hanks, Jr., Evaluating Recent State Legislation on Director and Officer Liability Limitation and Indemnification, 43 Bus.Law. 1207, 1231-36 (1988). Copyright © 1988 by the American Bar Association. Reprinted with permission.

Geoffrey C. Hazard, Jr., Ethics in the Practice of Law 58, 60-61, 63-68 (1978). Yale University Press. Copyright © 1978 by Seven Springs Farm Center, Inc.

John A.C. Hetherington, Bargaining For Fiduciary Duties: Preserving the Vulnerability of the Disadvantaged?, 70 Wash.U.L.Q. 341, 351 (1992).

John A.C. Hetherington and Michael P. Dooley, Illiquidity and Exploitation: A Proposed Statutory Solution to the Remaining Close Corporation Problem, 63 Va.L.Rev. 1, 26-27 (1977).

Michael C. Jensen, Eclipse of the Public Corporation, Harvard Business Review 61 (Sept.-Oct. 1989). Reprinted by permission of the Harvard Business Review. Copyright © 1989 by the President and Fellows of Harvard College; all rights reserved.

Michael C. Jensen, Letter to the Editor, Harvard Business Review (Nov.-Dec. 1990).

Laura Lin, The Effectiveness of Outside Directors as a Corporate Governance Mechanism: Theories and Evidence, 90 Nw. U. L.Rev. 898 (1996). Reprinted by special permission of Northwestern University School of Law, Northwestern University Law Review, vol. 90, no. 3, pp. 898-976.

Bayless Manning, A Taxonomy of Corporate Law Reform, in Commentaries on Corporate Structure and Governance, 120-122 (D. Schwartz ed. 1979); Copyright © 1979 by the American Law Institute. Reprinted with the permission of the American Law Institute-American Bar Assocation Committee on Continuing Professional Education.

Bayless Manning, The Business Judgment Rule and the Director's Duty of Attention: Time for Reality, 39 Bus.Law. 1477, 1481-92, 1492-95 (1984). Copyright © 1984 by the American Bar Association. All rights reserved. Reproduced with the permission of the American Bar Association and its Section of Corporation, Banking and Business Law.

Bayless Manning with James J. Hanks, Jr., Legal Capital 5-40 (3d ed. 1990).

David Millon, Redefining Corporate Law, 24 Ind.L.Rev. 223, 277 (1991).

Ira M. Milstein, Letter of the Editor, Harvard Business Review (Nov. Dec. 1990).

Report of the NACD Blue Ribbon Commission on Director Professionalism (1998). Reprinted from Report of the NACD Blue Ribbon Commission on Director Professionalism with permission of the publisher, National Association of Corporate Directors, 1707 L. St., N.W., Washington, DC 20036 - 202/775-0509 - Copyright © January 1998. All rights reserved.

Allan Nevins & Frank E. Hill, Ford: Expansion and Challenge, 97, 99-100 (1957).

William C. Norris, Letter to the Editor, Harvard Business Review (Nov.-Dec. 1990).

Charles R. O'Kelley, Jr., Filling Gaps in the Close Corporation Contract: A Transaction Cost Analysis, 87 Nw.U.L.Rev. 216, 231, 234-35, 238, 240-41 (1992).

Richard A. Posner, Economic Analysis of Law 392-93, 406-409 (4th ed. 1992). Reprinted by permission of Little, Brown and Company

Alfred Rappaport, The Staying Power of the Public Corporation, Harvard Business Review 96 (Jan.-Feb. 1990). Reprinted by permission of the Harvard Business Review. Copyright © 1990 by the President and Fellows of Harvard College; all rights reserved.

Norman Redlich, Lawyers, The Temple, and the Market Place, 30 Bus.Law. 65 (1975). Copyright © 1975 by the American Bar Association. All rights reserved. Reprinted by permission of the American Bar Association.

Edward B. Rock, The Logic and (Uncertain) Significance of Institutional Shareholder Activism, 79 Geo.L.J. 445, 469-76 (1991). Reprinted with the permission of the publisher. Copyright © 1991 The Georgetown Law Journal Association and Georgetown University.

Mark J. Roe, Chaos and Evolution in Law and Economics, 109 Harv. L. Rev. 641 (1996). Copyright © (1996) by the Harvard law Review Association.

Mark J. Roe, Strong Managers, Weak Owners: The Political Roots of the Separation of Ownership from Control (1994). Reprinted with the permission of the author.

Roberta Romano, Public Pension Fund Activism in Corporate Governance Reconsidered, 93 Colum.L.Rev. 795, 796-852 (1993). Reprinted by permission of Columbia Law Review and the author.

Carl W. Schneider, Joseph M. Manko & Robert S. Kant, Going Public-Practice Procedure and Consequences, 27 Vill.L.Rev. 1, 10-17, 19-20, 25-31, 33 (1981). Reprinted with permission from Villanova Law Review Volume 27, No. 1, pp. 1-51. Copyright © 1981 by Villanova University.

Thomas A. Smith, Institutions and Entrepreneurs in American Corporate Finance, 85 Calif. L. Rev. 1 (1997). © 1997, California Law Review, Inc. Reprinted with permission.

James Surowiecki, The Taming of the Barbarians: How a rapacious leveraged-buyout firm became a positive force in the corporate economy. First published in Slate, www.slate.com (2/5/98). Reprinted with permission.

E. Norman Veasey, Jesse A. Finkelstein & C. Stephen Bigler, Delaware Supports Directors with a Three-Legged Stool of Limited Liability, Indemnification and Insurance, 42 Bus.Law. 401, 404-12 (1987). Copyright © 1987 by the American Bar Association. All rights reserved. Reproduced with the permission of the American Bar Association and its Section of Corporation, Banking and Business Law.

Elliott J. Weiss, The Board of Directors, Management and Corporate Takeovers: "Opportunities and Pitfalls," in Arnold W. Sametz (ed.), The Battle for Corporate Control: Shareholder Rights, Stakeholder Interests and Managerial Responsibilities 36-38 (1991). (Leonard Stem School of Business, New York University).

Elliott J. Weiss, Social Regulation of Business Activity: Reforming the Corporate Governance System to Resolve an Institutional Impasse, 28 U.C.L.A. L.Rev. 343 (1981). Originally published in 28 U.C.L.A. L.Rev. 343. Copyright © 1981, The Regents of the University of California. All rights reserved.

Elliott J. Weiss, Whose Rules Should Govern Takeovers: Delaware's, the ALI's or Martin Lipton's?, 33 Ariz.L.Rev. 761 (1991). Copyright © 1991 by the Arizona Board of Regents. Reprinted by permission.

Elliott J. Weiss & John Beckerman, Let the Money do the Monitoring: How Institutional Investors Can Reduce Agency Costs in Securities Class Actions, 104 Yale L.J. 2053, 2072-74 (1995).

Ralph K. Winter, Jr., State Law, Shareholder Protection and the Theory of the Corporation, 6 J. Legal Studies 251, 256-57, 259, 275, 276 (1977).

*

# Summary of Contents

# Table of Contents

*

# Table of Cases

The principal cases are in bold type. Cases cited or discussed in the text are roman type. References are to pages. Cases cited in principal cases and within other quoted materials are not included.

# CORPORATIONS
## LAW AND POLICY
### MATERIALS AND PROBLEMS
#### Fourth Edition

*

# Chapter 1

# INTRODUCTION

## A. AN HISTORICAL SKETCH OF THE CORPORATION

All modern business corporations, be they giant, well-known firms like Exxon or Coca–Cola or local companies that operate a single taxicab or grocery market, have four basic attributes:

(1) Separate entity with perpetual existence. Every corporation is a legal entity with an unlimited life that exists separate from those who provide it with risk capital (generally called "shareholders" or "stockholders") and those who manage its business (its "directors" and "officers," sometimes referred to collectively as its "managers").

(2) Limited liability. While a corporation is liable for its debts and obligations, the corporation's shareholders are responsible for the corporation's debts and obligations only to the extent of the resources they have invested in the corporation. Put differently, liability for a corporation's debts and obligations is limited to the assets the corporation owns.

(3) Centralized management. Shareholders elect a corporation's directors, but are deemed to have delegated to those directors (operating collectively as a "board of directors") the power to manage the corporation's business.

(4) Transferability of ownership interests. Shareholders can transfer to others their ownership interests in a corporation.

The history of corporation law is largely a chronology of the evolution of these attributes. However, legal scholars disagree on the nature of that history and the importance of earlier business organizations to the modern business corporation. What seems most likely is that, as with other organisms, the evolution of the business corporation is an eclectic process in which those characteristics that reflect contemporary policies and needs survive, and those that do not gradually are discarded. Alfred F. Conard, CORPORATIONS IN PERSPECTIVE 126 (1976).

1

## 1. DEVELOPMENTS IN ENGLAND

Early English corporate law dealt with ecclesiastical, municipal and charitable bodies; only later did it focus on commercial associations. The early ecclesiastical corporation emerged partly as a device for the church to hold property. It was to these ecclesiastical, municipal and charitable bodies that the concession theory of corporate existence was first applied, i.e., that corporate existence could only be conferred by a grant of the sovereign.

The principal medieval commercial associations were the merchant guilds. Many of these guilds obtained royal charters as a means of obtaining special privileges, especially monopolies of trade. While the royal charter thus conferred privileges, it also served an important function to the sovereign. "The major impetus derived from the need of the national authority to assert itself and to establish its superiority in law over otherwise divisive local governments or interest groups." *Id.* at 3.

To a large extent, the merchant guilds served different purposes than modern corporations and lacked many of the characteristics that we commonly think of as essential to business corporations. Each member of a guild continued to trade on her own account, subject to the regulations of the guild, and remained individually liable for her own acts. The guilds functioned primarily to regulate trade by their members and to protect the monopoly against the intrusion of nonmembers.

During the period in which the guilds remained active, the Company of the Staple and the Company of the Merchant Adventurers were organized for trading overseas, the former handling the raw commodities of a town and the latter handling the export of manufactured products. These companies were virtually extensions of the guild principle to foreign trade. Their members remained individually liable and traded on their own accounts, subject to the regulations of the company, as enforced by a governor and assistants elected by the members. While royal charters for these early regulated companies have been found as early as the fourteenth century, they did not become common until the sixteenth century, with the expansion of foreign trade and settlement. Charters were obtained "largely because of the need to acquire a monopoly of trade for members of the company and governmental power over the territory for the company itself." *Id. See also,* Paul L. Davies, Gower's Principles of Modern Company Law 20 (6TH ED. 1997)

In the sixteenth and early seventeenth centuries, the principle of trading on joint stock, previously confined to partnerships, was introduced into regulated companies, which gradually became joint commercial enterprises rather than trade protection associations. The East India Company, first chartered in 1600, best typifies the transition to joint stock. Its members could subscribe to joint stock or could carry on trade privately. Initially, each voyage was separately funded, and the proceeds were divided at the end of each voyage. Beginning in 1614, subscriptions to joint stock were taken for a period of years rather than for each voyage, and in the 1650s permanent joint stock was introduced. The shares were freely transferable and individual liability was limited to the amount of shares owned. The Company kept a stock transfer book. The capital stock grew to an enormous size, and in 1709 the Company made a large loan to the English government. It appears that the Company was the first corporation engaged in large state operations with a perpetual charter and, most significantly, a permanent capital.

By 1692, England had three large joint stock companies, the East India Company, the Royal African Company, and the Hudson's Bay Company. They were treated as extensions of the state and expected to perform important public functions, notably trade. They were given a monopoly in carrying on a particular trade and the right to make regulations with regard to it. In 1692, private trading was finally forbidden to members of joint stock companies.

The transition from the early trading companies to the permanent joint stock company also involved a shift in the function served by incorporation. Hurst notes:

> From the late sixteenth century royal chartering of companies to develop foreign trade and colonies was a prominent feature of national policy. A royal charter was essential to such ventures. In times of political uncertainty merchants who combined for a foreign venture without explicit royal sanction risked prosecution for criminal conspiracy against the national interest. Moreover, the royal charter legitimized a range of public functions performed by such trading organizations in organizing terms of trade, setting up local governments, controlling customs, and, in effect, making foreign policy in their areas of operation. Thus, in this early phase such corporate privileges as served private profit seeking were an incidental return for the public jobs the corporation undertook. But throughout the late seventeenth century trade began to bulk larger than public functions in the activities of such companies. By the eighteenth century English lawmakers and businessmen alike had come to regard the corporation mainly as a structure useful to private trading operations; public responsibilities receded so far into the background as to become of secondary account.

Hurst, *supra*, at 4.

Trading on joint stock became increasingly frequent during the seventeenth century and was extended to companies for domestic operation. The practice of conducting business on a joint stock basis was not confined to incorporated companies. Unincorporated joint stock companies were able to obtain many of the advantages commonly associated with incorporation through the use of complex deeds of settlement, which provided for transferability of shares, continuity of life, and central management. Some writers have suggested that these unincorporated associations, rather than the monopolistic trading companies, were the real forerunners of the modern business corporation, *see, e.g.*, Henry W. Ballantine, BALLANTINE ON CORPORATIONS 33 (rev. ed. 1946); James D.

Cox et al., CORPORATIONS §§ 2.2 and 2.4 (1995), but it seems more likely that each form of association borrowed from the other as the two developed side by side. E. Merrick Dodd & Ralph J. Baker, CASES AND MATERIALS ON CORPORATIONS 14 (2d ed. 1951).

The beginning of the eighteenth century was characterized by a boom of promotion and speculation in both incorporated and unincorporated companies. This boom was stimulated by the grandiose scheme of the South Sea Company to acquire virtually the entire English national debt by buying out the debt holders or exchanging the Company's stock for their holdings. When the flood of speculative enterprises was at its height in 1720, Parliament enacted the famous "Bubble Act," "An Act to Restrain the Extravagant and Unwarranted Practice of Raising Money by Voluntary Subscriptions for Carrying on Projects Dangerous to the Trade and Subjects of this Kingdom." The Bubble Act was aimed at restricting unincorporated joint stock companies with transferable shares; it forbade individuals to act as a corporation without a charter. The Act permitted incorporation, and some companies succeeded in obtaining charters. But the Act reflected a general distrust of corporations and had the effect of making both the Crown and Parliament hesitant to grant charters. This, plus vagueness in the Bubble Act's prohibitions, encouraged formation of unincorporated associations of the kind the Act was designed to destroy. In particular, entrepreneurs began to use deeds of settlement. This device "pooled resources in the control of trustees to manage them for designated business purposes. Equity would recognize the transferability of shares in such a pool. By the early nineteenth century such an arrangement might even include limited liability for debts * * *." Hurst, *supra* at 3. By 1825, when it was repealed, the Bubble Act had become a dead letter.

## 2. DEVELOPMENTS IN THE UNITED STATES

The principles of the Bubble Act were extended to the American colonies, precluding the formation of unincorporated joint stock companies. Although the Act did not preclude the formation of duly chartered corporations, there was initial resistance to such entities which were perceived as instruments of royal prerogative and antithetical to the ideals of economic equality. In the late eighteenth century, however, corporations became more readily accepted. The earliest corporations were non-business entities such as charities, churches, cities and boroughs; these were followed shortly by the incorporation of banks, stage and navigation companies, turnpikes and canals and other financial and transportation businesses. During this period charters were granted by special acts of state legislatures, which, although the matter was not free from doubt, were tacitly understood to have acceded to the power of the Crown in the granting of corporate status.

By 1800 there were about 335 incorporated businesses, all of which had been created by such acts. For this reason, corporate policy during this period was shaped primarily by legislative practice. But the number of corporations formed in the early 1800s grew geometrically. To cope

with the increased legislative burden, charters became increasingly standardized. A corporate charter was also considered a valuable privilege,
and the legislative monopoly on the conferral of this privilege created
certain obvious temptations, to which some legislators and entrepreneurs inevitably yielded, to their mutual profit. Criticism of the resulting
corruption produced a growing feeling by the business community that
incorporation was a right rather than a privilege, not reserved for a
select few. More important, incorporation became a matter of economic
necessity. As industrial and manufacturing concerns grew, individuals no
longer had resources adequate to finance such enterprises. These factors
eventually led states to enact general corporation laws that allowed any
group of persons to organize themselves into a corporation by complying
with the prescribed conditions. New York was the pioneer; in 1811, it
enacted a law that gave the privilege of self-incorporation to the organizers of certain manufacturing companies, but limited the capital of those
companies to $100,000 and their existence to 20 years.

This rapid growth of corporations in size and number did not occur
without opposition. Throughout its history, some in America have feared
the aggregations of capital and the growing power in American society
that corporations seemed to represent. But this opposition did little to
stem the tide of corporate growth; other states soon followed New York's
lead and encouraged incorporation by enacting general corporation laws.
Many of the restrictions on size and duration were lifted. Because there
was no federal corporation law, a state had little incentive to enact
stringent laws, for they would only encourage would-be corporations to
seek charters in other states.

It was not uncommon in the early nineteenth century for states
themselves to become partners in corporate enterprises, in part because
many of the early corporations were involved in transportation and other
business that the state traditionally had conducted. In addition, joining a
corporation was a good way for a state to give financial support to an
enterprise while providing some public accountability. Lawrence M.
Friedman, A HISTORY OF AMERICAN LAW 192 (2d ed. 1985). State involvement fell off in the 1830s and '40s. Many of the states' investments went
bad in the Panic of 1837. In addition, the feeling grew that states had no
business meddling in what was properly the sphere of private enterprise.

Thus the period from 1800 to 1850 saw substantial changes in the
law of corporations. Unleashed from the constraints imposed by special
charters, corporations continued to flourish during the latter half of the
nineteenth century. The burgeoning of the railroad industry did much to
shape their growth. Management of a railway company required a larger
central organization, and capital requirements often exceeded the resources of any single individual. A variety of financial instruments, for
which the corporate form proved convenient, were devised to meet the
railways' capital requirements and corporations generally became more
dependent on the availability of an open market for their securities.

But once again the rapid growth of corporate power and the unchecked abuses which seemed to follow disturbed many Americans. Pressure grew to reform the internal corporate mechanism and to impose limits on corporations' power. By the 1860s, the device of the shareholder derivative suit had been developed to deal with managers' fraud, and other doctrines were emerging aimed at imposing greater control over corporate management. Railway regulation was a leading public issue in the 1870s, and in the 1880s the Interstate Commerce Commission was created, primarily for the purpose of controlling the railroads. In 1890 the Sherman Act was passed to combat "trusts" that dominated major industries. Thus, while during this period businesses by and large had a free hand to adapt the corporate instrument to their will, regulatory efforts also were initiated to circumscribe some of the power and impact of large corporations and their managers.

In 1888, New Jersey enacted an innovative new enabling statute, a general corporation law that authorized creation of corporations but included none of the traditional limitations on corporations' size, scope or duration. New Jersey further "modernized" its general corporation law in 1896.

Delaware entered the competition in 1899. A small state, Delaware passed an enabling statute with a view to attracting incorporations and thereby generating substantial franchise tax revenues. When New Jersey, under the leadership of Governor Woodrow Wilson, amended its corporation law in 1913 to reimpose a number of restrictive provisions, Delaware emerged as the venue of choice, at least for publicly traded corporations. It has retained that position ever since, and currently is the domicile of more than half the Fortune 500 companies and more than 40% of companies listed on the New York Stock Exchange.

More generally, the availability of enabling statutes in Delaware and elsewhere led other states to abjure efforts to use general corporation laws to regulate corporate activities. "Enablingism" became the dominant statutory mode. Today, state corporation laws almost universally allow any person to form a corporation, grant all corporations broad powers, and establish frameworks for corporate operations that include few regulatory restrictions. As one commentator has described it, these laws enable the organizers of a corporation to pour into an empty vessel the brew of their choice, free of almost all state-imposed constraints. Elvin R. Latty, *Why Are Corporation Laws Largely "Enabling?"* 50 CORN.L.Q. 599 (1965).

At this point, a student beginning the study of corporation law might well wonder about the role of federal law. After all, many corporations, especially publicly traded corporations, operate on a national or international basis. Doesn't it seem logical that federal law would regulate these national and multi-national organizations?

We address this question at greater length in Chapter 7. At this point, suffice it to say that almost all American corporations are creatures of state law. There is no general federal corporation law. However, certain provisions of the federal securities laws do regulate significant aspects of the relationship among participants in corporations, especially publicly owned corporations, largely by requiring the managers of publicly owned corporations to disclose to shareholders and prospective investors important information about those corporations and their activities.* See Chapters 10, 14, 18 and 19.

## B.   REGULATING THE MODERN CORPORATION: THE SEARCH FOR ACCOUNTABILITY

In the mid-twentieth century, the prevalence and increasing uniformity of state enabling laws led some to conclude that all interesting questions of corporation law had been answered. In 1962, then-Professor Bayless Manning wrote that "corporation law, as a field of intellectual endeavor, is dead in the United States. * * * We have nothing left but our great empty corporation statutes—towering skyscrapers of rusty girders, internally welded together and containing nothing but wind." Bayless Manning, *The Shareholder's Appraisal Remedy: An Essay for Frank Coker*, 72 YALE L.J. 223, 245 (1962).

### William T. Allen, *Our Schizophrenic Conception of the Business Corporation*
14 CARDOZO L.REV. 261, 263–65, 272–73 (1992).

* * * I doubt that Dean Manning's observation was far off the mark in 1962. Modern corporation law statutes were, and still are, "enabling" statutes in the broadest sense of that term. They are almost literally empty, and those few mandatory features that remain—such as the requirement of an annual meeting of shareholders, or a right to inspect the company's books and records for a proper corporate purpose—are themselves under attack from some quarters as paternalistic clogs on efficiency.

* * *

Two inconsistent conceptions have dominated our thinking about corporations since the evolution of the large integrated business corporation in the late nineteenth century. Each conception could claim dominance for a particular period, or among one group or another, but neither has so commanded agreement as to exclude the other from the discourses of law or the thinking of business people.

In the first conception, the corporation is seen as the private property of its stockholder-owners. The corporation's purpose is to advance the purposes of these owners (predominantly to increase their

---

* The federal government also regulates corporations through a variety of substantive laws, including antitrust, banking, civil rights, environmental, labor and product safety laws.

wealth), and the function of directors, as agents of the owners, is faithfully to advance the financial interests of the owners. I call this the property conception of the corporation, because it sees the corporation as the property of its stockholders. This model might almost as easily be called a contract model, because in its most radical form, the corporation tends to disappear, transformed from a substantial institution into just a relatively stable corner of the market in which autonomous property owners freely contract.

The second conception sees the corporation not as the private property of stockholders, but as a social institution. According to this view, the corporation is not strictly private; it is tinged with a public purpose. The corporation comes into being and continues as a legal entity only with governmental concurrence. The legal institutions of government grant a corporation its juridical personality, its characteristic limited liability, and its perpetual life. This conception sees this public facilitation as justified by the state's interest in promoting the general welfare. Thus, corporate purpose can be seen as including the advancement of the general welfare. The board of directors' duties extend beyond assuring investors a fair return, to include a duty of loyalty, in some sense, to all those interested in or affected by the corporation. This view could be labeled in a variety of ways: the managerialist conception, the institutionalist conception, or the social entity conception. All would be descriptive, since the corporation is seen as distinct from each of the individuals that happens to fill the social roles that its internal rules and culture define. The corporation itself is, in this view, capable of bearing legal and moral obligations. To law and economics scholars, who have been so influential in academic corporate law, this model is barely coherent and dangerously wrong.

These two, apparently inconsistent, conceptions have coexisted in our thinking over the last century. For most of the century the lack of agreement on the ultimate nature and purpose of the business corporation has not generated intense conflict. A host of macro-economic factors—secularly rising prosperity, a lack of global competition, and the absence of powerful shareholders—probably account for this placid status quo. By the 1980s however, emerging global competition, capital market innovation, and the growth and evolution of institutional investors, among other factors, made possible the takeover movement, which glaringly exposed our inconsistent thinking about the nature of the business corporation.

\* \* \*

The law "papered over" the conflict in our conception of the corporation by invoking a murky distinction between long-term profit maximization and short-term profit maximization. Corporate expenditures which at first blush did not seem to be profit maximizing, could be squared with the property conception of the corporation by recognizing that they might redound to the long-term benefit of the corporation and its shareholders. Thus, without purporting to abandon the idea that directors ultimately owe loyalty only to stockholders and their financial interests, the law was able to approve reasonable corporate expenditures for charitable or social welfare purposes or other actions that did not maximize current profit.

There is a utility in this long-term/short-term device. Though employment of this distinction is subject to obvious manipulation, it can nevertheless resolve the tension between these differing conceptions of the corporation in a way that offers the possibility of some judicial protection to shareholders, while affording substantial room to the multi-constituency, social entity conception to operate. With this distinction, judicial review of particular decisions is available under the fiduciary duty standard. But corporate directors are also afforded very considerable latitude to deal with all groups or institutions having an interest in, or who are affected by, the corporation. The long-term/short-term distinction preserves the form of the stockholders oriented property theory, while permitting, in fact, a considerable degree of behavior consistent with a view that sees public corporations as owing social responsibilities to all affected by their operation.

Thus, while early on much ink was spilled on the question to whom should directors be responsible, in practice the question of the nature of the corporation seemed essentially unproblematic until the emergence of the cash tender offer of the 1980s. The long-term/short-term distinction proved a serviceable, if an intellectually problematic way, for the corporation law to avoid choosing between the alpha of property and the omega of relationships.

———

The goals of corporation law include promoting the efficient operation of business corporations and providing fairly for the interests of those who participate in corporations. If every participant in a corporation had the same goals, had access to all relevant information, and was able to process that information in a perfectly rational fashion, little need would exist for a body of law to govern their relationships. The participants would reach agreement at every juncture, no matter what structure they used to reach those decisions, because their information and reasoning processes would be identical. *See* Kenneth J. Arrow, THE LIMITS OF ORGANIZATION 68–70 (1974).

But in the real world, participants in corporations operate in an environment characterized by uncertainty, limited information and "bounded rationality." Participants' goals also often differ. Consequently, the principal task of corporation law is to create a governance structure for corporations that promotes an appropriate degree of accountability among the participants. In addressing this task, the following questions must be considered.

    1.   To what extent is it reasonable to rely on market forces and contractual arrangements to promote management accountability to the shareholders and prevent overreaching?

2.  If legal intervention is desirable, should it be in the form of mandating structural devices, such as meetings and voting; imposing fiduciary obligations on those who hold positions of power; requiring disclosure of information; or providing additional protection to those, such as creditors, whose relationship with the corporation is primarily contractual?

3.  How is, and how should, responsibility for regulating corporations be divided between federal and state law?

Albert O. Hirschman, an economist, has developed a conceptual framework that is helpful when analyzing these questions. In EXIT, VOICE AND LOYALTY (1970), Hirschman addressed the problems posed by organizations that operate at less than peak efficiency, as almost all organizations do. He was concerned primarily with large organizations, but developed concepts that are relevant to small organizations as well.

Hirschman postulated that two fundamentally different strategies are available to a person who is dissatisfied with an organization. One strategy is "exit": the person can sever her connection with the organization. A motorist can decide not to buy the same brand of car again after having suffered with a "lemon;" a shareholder can sell her stock in a corporation that pays its executives compensation she believes is grossly excessive; a law student can move out of her parents' home to escape their incessant questions about why she spends so much time studying.

The other strategy is "voice": a person can remain within the organization and attempt to remedy the situation. The motorist can write a letter of complaint; the shareholder can attend the annual meeting and question the company's compensation arrangements; the law student can try to explain that her professors' demands are unreasonable.

Hirschman pointed out that a combination of exit and voice frequently will lead to greater improvement in the organization's performance than exclusive reliance on one or the other. However, a participant's willingness to rely on voice will depend heavily on her estimates of the prospects for success and:

> [W]hile exit requires nothing but a clearcut either-or decision, voice is essentially an *art* constantly evolving in new directions. The situation makes for an important bias in favor of exit when options are present: customer-members [or shareholders] will ordinarily base their decisions on *past* experience with the cost and effectiveness of voice even though the possible *discovery* of lower cost and greater effectiveness is of the very essence of voice. The presence of the exit alternative can therefore tend to *atrophy the development of the art of voice.*

*Id.* at 43.

Economists generally favor exit. They argue that either exit will force the organization to eliminate inefficiency or the organization will be replaced by a more efficient competitor. As applied to corporation law, this view implies that legal rules should be directed primarily at sustaining market forces and enforcing contractual arrangements, and that legal intervention to advance other goals generally is unnecessary and inefficient.

As the above quotation indicates, Hirschman suggests a different approach. In some circumstances, voice will be more effective, either eliciting a positive response from those who control the corporation or causing new leaders to be chosen. Moreover, Hirschman notes that if exit is the only available option, the most quality-conscious participants in the organization are likely to exit first. But those participants often will be more qualified to help the organization identify and overcome its problems than those who remain. Consequently, structuring the organization to promote voice may advance the socially important goal of preventing the organization's deterioration from becoming cumulative.

Hirschman also points out that a third factor, "loyalty," may determine whether a participant chooses to pursue exit or voice. People tend to have stronger feelings of loyalty toward social or political organizations, such as their family or political party, than toward economic organizations such as corporations. Thus, they generally are more reluctant to sever ties with their families or to change political parties than to trade-in a Chevy for a Toyota or to sell General Motors stock.

Loyalty is more intangible than exit and voice. But how an organization is structured and what strategy the organization employs to deal with participants' dissatisfactions can have a powerful influence over their feelings of loyalty and whether they choose exit or voice when they become dissatisfied.

For students of corporation law, Hirschman's analytic structure provides a useful frame of reference. To what extent does a given rule facilitate exit or voice? Does the law establish an appropriate balance between exit and voice? How might exit or voice operate in any given situation, and how should the availability of one or the other influence the rights and remedies of the participants? How does the size of the corporation (public or closely-held) affect the need to create different exit and voice mechanisms and the rules that facilitate each?

Hirschman's work also reminds us of the need to take account of intangibles such as loyalty. Although the extent to which they influence an individual's decision in any specific situation often are difficult to predict, Hirschman reminds us that intangibles often dominate an individual's decision making. Economic analysis has many virtues. But the analyst who treats every person as an interchangeable "rational utility maximizer" overlooks the fact that people differ in all sorts of very human ways. These differences should be taken into account in many contexts, of which corporate law is but one.

### William T. Allen, *Ambiguity in Corporation Law*

22 DEL.J.CORP.L. 894–897 (1997).

[Shortly after his retirement, Chancellor Allen took a somewhat different perspective from Hirschman.]

It is sometimes noted by an honoree attending a testimonial that the experience is a little like attending one's own funeral. On both occasions balance is out and appreciation alone is heard. The honoree, unlike the deceased, experiences this unusual treat as a bit strange, even if pleasant. But stranger still would be the experience of the honoree taking an active part in the process—for the body to sit up and speak. This is roughly my role on this occasion. As I completed my work as a judge in June 1997, I learned that the editorial staff of *The Delaware Journal of Corporate Law* desired to commemorate my passing, so to speak, with some commentary in one of its volumes. I was asked to add something to that which others might say. It seemed ungracious to decline, yet, like the fellow in the casket, my active participation seems a bit problematic.

I am, of course, deeply suspect as a judge of the usefulness of the work that occupied me, largely to the exclusion of all else, for twelve years. The flaws and limitations it reflects and the worthiness of any contributions that are embedded in it are for others to assess if they are so inclined. Nevertheless, perhaps I can contribute to this volume in two ways. Most importantly, I would like to employ this opportunity to note "for the record," so to speak, my professional debt to a number of Delaware judges and lawyers and to record the deep honor I felt in being able to serve for twelve years as Chancellor of Delaware. This I do at the conclusion of these comments.

I thought also that I might use this occasion to ruminate a bit about some basic aspects of the corporation law, the tension that occupies its core, and the judge's role in assisting the system to move along productively. More personally, I thought I could explain, if briefly and informally, some background perceptions concerning the judicial process when it deals with a certain kind of corporation law problem.

\* \* \*

Let me start with a general observation—the practice of corporation law and the adjudication of human conflict turning on questions of corporation law, when accomplished at its most expert level, entails more than technical knowledge. At its most sophisticated and accomplished level this activity ultimately takes on an artistic aspect. By this somewhat provocative statement I do not mean to deny that a great deal of technical knowledge, both of corporation, and securities law doctrine (and history) and of corporate finance is essential for even a competent performance as a corporate law advisor or judge. Indeed, I suppose that technical shortcomings—an incomplete or inaccurate understanding of the economic and the corporate finance underpinnings of corporate law doctrine—is perhaps the most frequent source of dysfunctional legal rulings in corporation law. In saying that expert practice of corporation law or corporate law judging ultimately entails artistic judgments, I do not mean to minimize the technical learning that plays a part in expertise. I do mean to emphasize that technical knowledge, whether financial or doctrinal, is not all that is necessary for mastery of this field. Mastery requires artistry. What this short essay tries to do in a nonacademic way, is to point out the underlying economic forces—the tension I referred to—inherent in the form of the publicly traded corporation that makes ambiguity a productive, if risky, condition of corporation law and makes imagination and artistry important ingredients to success in working in this area of law. That at least is the thesis.

The tension I refer to is the tension between the ways in which long-term wealth may be maximized through broad managerial discretion and the ways long-term wealth maximization may be thought to require protections that entail limitation on the power of management. This tension follows from the fundamental nature and the source of utility of the corporate form and it accounts in substantial part for the inability of the corporation law to deal clearly and decisively with its most difficult recurring problem—directorial duties in defending against a hostile takeover.

### Purpose of Corporate Law

Stated broadly, but I think accurately, the elemental purpose of corporation law is the facilitation of cooperative activity that produces wealth. A net increase in total wealth, other things remaining unchanged, is an absolute good. With increased wealth, all other things remaining the same, there is a greater ability to relieve human suffering and enhance life. That is an unqualified good. While we no longer take much notice of the fact, the corporate form is a powerful engine for wealth production. We no longer think of our legal forms of organization in such terms, but that is in part because we have lost sight of the profound effects that this form of organization produces.

### How the Corporate Form Increases Total Wealth

Corporation law facilitates wealth creation principally by creating a legal structure that makes it substantially cheaper for investors to commit their capital to risky ventures. It does this through the innovation of tradable share interests, centralized management, limited liability, and the entity concept itself. The interaction of these legal characteristics facilitates diversification of investments and centralization of management. This allows capital to subject itself to greater risk. It is the ability to increase the degree of risk that can be rationally accepted that provides the greatest source of the efficiency of the corporate form.

Much of this utility depends upon investors allowing themselves to be safely passive. In other words, corporation law, understood in the "big picture" sense, is chiefly about facilitating long-term capital growth. Owners of capital will commit their capital to a long-term investment with the characteristics of common stock offers—no maturity date and no promising return on capital—at a comparative low cost, only if assured that (1) some agency (centralized management) will be available to monitor changing markets, technology, and other environmental factors and to adjust the corporation's business plans continually in response to changes from those sources; and (2) despite the very broad discretion that that monitoring and timely acting requirement entails, that agency will be sufficiently constrained or incented to assure that investors' interests will be advanced over the term of an indefinite and unknown future, as responsive changes are made. *Thus much of the utility of the publicly traded corporate form derives from the fact that the shareholders will be passive and managements only loosely constrained in their exercise of discretionary judgment.* Therefore, it can be seen that the proper orientation of corporation law is the *protection of long-term value of capital* committed indefinitely to the firm. That protection is afforded not because the law has been captured by capitalist interests, but because the greatest production of goods and services is apt to be produced by a system that offers such protections.

### Core Corporate Law Protections of Capital

The corporate law provides a few vital sources of assurance to shareholders which allows investors, to a substantial extent, to be rationally passive in most circumstances. Primarily, corporate law affords common stock a right to vote. This right to vote is elemental. Most importantly, the vote includes the right to elect a board of directors annually; to vote on charter amendments; and to vote for certain fundamental corporate transactions. The shareholders' right to vote ultimately forces incumbent management to be attentive to investor concerns at the risk of ouster in a proxy contest.

The right of shareholders to sell their share interests without any corporate or management concurrence, is fundamental as well as an economic source of constraint on the exercise of management discretion. It makes possible the "takeover" market and in a similar way forces management to keep investor interests in mind as they manage the enterprise.

The third elementary right of shareholders is the right to hold management accountable under the developed law of fiduciary obligation. That duty constrain self dealing of various kinds, albeit quite imperfectly, and protects to some extent the right to vote and right to sell.

### Cross-Efficiency Effects of the Corporate Form

Each of these sources of constraint offer to owners of capital assurances that will tend to lower the cost at which capital will be made available to an enterprise. But in some respects these capital-protecting devices—especially the loosely defined fiduciary duty protection—do so at a cost. These unspecified commands to act with loyalty and care add uncertainty as well, which is costly. One way of looking at the fundamental tension of corporation law is to see how these two effects of the fiduciary duty may pull in opposite directions.

The costs that fiduciary obligations impose are easy to identify in a general way. Clear, "hard and fast" legal rules reduce uncertainty and allow business people to contract relatively efficiently. They allow parties to avoid undesirable consequences by contracting around them. There is utility in this and indeed a utility that proponents of the efficiency inducing properties of the Delaware General Corporation Law often claim for it, with some justification. But this ability that certainty in the boundaries of legal obligation creates also creates the risk that agents— such as corporate management—might deploy such well-defined rules cleverly (and technically correctly), but with the purpose in mind not to advance long-term interests of investors, but to pursue some different purpose. It could happen. Thus, at least in that corner of contract law occupied by corporation law, clarity itself may be thought to be a qualified good, not an unqualified good.

The fiduciary concept adds ambiguity. That ambiguity is capable of causing either a net cost (i.e., adding more certainty than is optimum to the governance system) or a net benefit. Whether the corporate law is at one end of this spectrum of economic effects or the other depends on the way the fiduciary duty is enforced. Unfortunately, there is no science currently available that permits the precise measurement of these cross-cutting efficiency effects in general (i.e., systemically) or in a particular firm. Thus I assert that, at its most sophisticated level, corporation law is presently an artistic enterprise.

# Chapter 2

# INTRODUCTION TO THE ECONOMICS
# OF THE FIRM

---

This chapter introduces economic concepts fundamental to the analysis of business ventures. Understanding those concepts will enable a lawyer to identify the potential tensions between the participants in such ventures and assist in their resolution. In a business setting, a lawyer performs most effectively when she can understand the economic stakes for each of the participants.

To facilitate the exploration of these fundamental concepts, this chapter makes the simplifying assumption that the venture in question involves only two parties: a person who owns the business but wishes to do little or no work in it, and a second person who will do most or all of the work. We will refer to the first person as the "owner" or "employer" and to the second person as the "employee," even though they may not have a traditional "employer-employee" relationship. The principles used to analyze their relationship, however, apply equally to more complex settings. You will have frequent occasion to recall them as you work with problems involving more complex ventures in succeeding chapters.

In any business venture, the parties have a shared interest in agreeing on a structure that produces the largest total return to the venture at the lowest cost. In the real world, however, such a structure is difficult to achieve because each of the parties probably will want to receive as large a share as possible of the venture's total profits. Moreover, the parties will not know what the future holds. They also may have different preferences concerning which risks of the business they are willing to bear as well as different capacities to bear or insure against those risks. In addition, if the employee does not receive all the profits of the business, she will not work as hard as she would if she owned the business herself. Because of these conflicts, the self-interest of each party, viewed from an *ex post* perspective (after the venture has begun or when it is finished) will not always coincide with the interest of the venture as a whole.

16

Despite these conflicts, both parties see gains from entering into the venture together. The goal of the analysis in this chapter is to understand how the parties try to minimize the effects of the conflicts and maximize the value of the transaction for each of them. To achieve those ends, they must decide how to distribute the risks of the future uncertainties of the business and how to create incentives that will encourage the employee to work for the best interest of the venture rather than exclusively for her own interest. As we shall see, there is a fundamental tension between these objectives that makes it impossible to achieve them completely. The owner will also have to obtain information so that she can see whether the employee is doing what she is supposed to, and establish sanctions for the employee's failure to do so (these supervisory procedures often are referred to as "monitoring"). All these steps must be taken *before* the venture begins; i.e., the problem must be viewed from an *ex ante* perspective. The parties are willing to take these steps because, as noted above, they believe that they will each gain more from working together than they would if they worked separately.

## PROBLEM

## OF WINE AND WINEMAKING*

Ann Jones has recently purchased a vineyard in the middle of California's Napa Valley. The vineyard produces grapes which she proposes to sell to winemakers throughout the area. She does not anticipate making wine on her own. She is unable to farm the land herself because she lives in Los Angeles. Ann is aware that growing grapes is a risky activity. Her crop yields and profits will depend on unpredictables such as the weather and the price of grapes at harvest time (which, in turn, will be influenced by the availability of grapes from other sources). The size and quality of her crop also will depend upon the effort and ability of the person who does the farming.

Ann has recently met Bill Smith, a young man who has the necessary equipment, expertise and inclination to do the work necessary to grow grapes. Ann and Bill wish to negotiate an advantageous contract whereby Bill will handle the farming at Ann's vineyard. For the moment, they intend to cover only the coming growing season in the contract; they are proceeding on the assumption that thereafter, they will not deal with each other again.

At the outset, a number of issues must be decided: the level of compensation to be paid to Bill, the structure of the compensation plan, and the nature and extent of Bill's duties. The first issue on which they intend to negotiate is the compensation structure, although they recognize that all the issues are closely related. Two alternatives have been proposed:

---

* We are indebted to Professors Steven C. Salop and Warren F. Schwartz of the Georgetown University Law Center. Professor Salop is the principal author of this problem. Both he and Professor Schwartz assisted us greatly in the following notes.

(i) *Employment*: Bill will be paid a monthly salary. Ann will retain the entire proceeds of the harvest less the salary to Bill.

(ii) *Tenancy*: Bill will lease the land from Ann for a yearly rent in exchange for the right to receive the entire proceeds of the harvest.

Although the subsequent sections of the chapter formally analyze the determinants of the structure which the parties might adopt, consider, as a matter of your own intuition and experience, how the following factors might influence Ann and Bill in choosing one of these plans or a variant of one of them.

(a) Ann is rich and Bill is poor or vice versa.

(b) Ann owns a number of other vineyards in the same area.

(c) Ann owns a number of other vineyards in other areas of the state or in different states.

(d) Bill is young and intends to grow grapes under annual arrangements like this one (but with other local owners) for the next 20 years.

(e) Ann has experience growing grapes herself and visits the area frequently.

(f) Growing grapes in this region is not difficult and requires little expertise or judgment—only hard work.

# A.  RISK

## 1.  INTRODUCTION

When someone other than the owner of an enterprise is brought in to do some or all of the work of the business, one question affecting the structure of their agreement is how they will allocate the various risks of the venture. Such risks can be broken down into two categories. One type is "non-controllable" risk. A non-controllable risk is one which, although it may affect some businesses more than others, is always present to some extent: the weather, the general state of the economy, the level of interest rates, market prices, war and peace, etc. These risks cannot be completely eliminated. The other type of risk is "controllable" risk, i.e., a risk which relates to the specific business: its competitive position, its product line, the quality of its management, the adequacy of its physical plant, etc. The extent to which such risks can be controlled depends on how well the people assigned to perform specific tasks in a business actually perform them. As we will see, successful performance depends in part on the incentives the performers have to act in the best interest of the business and in part on the monitoring and sanctioning devices which have been created to reduce the likelihood that they will not perform well.

## 2.  NON–CONTROLLABLE RISKS

When we refer to the non-controllable risks of a venture, we actually mean two things: those risks that are truly beyond control (war and peace) and those that will remain after all reasonable efforts at controlling them have been exercised.

The question of who should bear these non-controllable risks is best approached by first looking at the means available to each party to avoid bearing the risk. One such means is to pool the cost of the risk with others who bear the same risk—by purchasing insurance, for example. Essentially, risk pooling reduces the risk for the members of the pool because each member bears a pro rata share of the total loss suffered by the pool. The total loss likely to be suffered by a large number of people subject to the same or similar risk is easier to predict than the loss that any one of them is likely to suffer. A person growing grapes, for example, can limit her non-controllable risks by purchasing insurance against floods, tornados, hurricanes and drought.

A second means of limiting these risks is to invest in a number of ventures, each of which involves risks different from the others. A simple example of this kind of diversification is provided by considering an investor in the stock market. The investor can reduce the effect of a decline in the value of any given stock by diversifying the number and nature of the stocks which she owns. Although such diversification will not completely eliminate the risk of loss in any given stock, it will reduce the total risk because the performance of the entire portfolio is more likely to be balanced between gains and losses. Thus the diversified portfolio will offer a more certain return than can be obtained from any particular stock.

Diversification can take many forms. If the principal variable affecting the harvest in a vineyard is the amount of rainfall, an owner can diversify her risk by investing in ten vineyards, each of which is expected to have different rainfall. The owner also can diversify by investing her other capital in stocks and bonds, a strawberry patch (see Chapter 6), baseball trading cards and Impressionist paintings, each of which involves risks that are of a completely different nature from, and are independent of, the risks of a vineyard.

The third way of protecting against non-controllable risks is to place the burden of the risk on the person who is best able to bear it. For example, if A is richer than B, it may be desirable for A to bear the risk because a large loss will have less catastrophic consequences for her.

In thinking about the vineyard problem, also consider Bill's investment. Unlike Ann, Bill is investing human capital. Because he cannot work for more than one employer, he is not able to diversify his capital in the same way that Ann can. This inability to diversify may affect his attitude toward risk and his choice of how to arrange his relationship with Ann.

## 3.  RISK PREFERENCE

In determining the optimal allocation of risk, it also is important to take into account each party's subjective preference for risk.

An individual who is risk neutral makes decisions based solely on the expected return involved. (The "expected return" is the sum of each possible return multiplied by the probability of that return.) The magnitude of the risk is irrelevant to her decision. For example, suppose an individual is given a choice between Coin Toss A, in which she will receive $200 if the coin comes up heads but only $100 if the coin comes up tails *or* receiving a certain payment of $140 without tossing the coin. A risk neutral person would prefer Coin Toss A to the certain payment of $140 because the expected return would be greater.

|              | return | probability | expected return |
|--------------|--------|-------------|-----------------|
| Coin Toss A: | $100   | 0.5         | $ 50            |
|              | $200   | 0.5         | $100            |
|              |        |             | $150            |
| Payment:     | $140   | 1.0         | $140            |

In contrast, a risk averse person takes the magnitude of risk, as well as the expected return, into account when making a decision. In the previous example, a risk averse person would think: "Even though there is a 50% chance that I will get $200 if the coin comes up heads, there is also a 50% chance I will end up with only $100, if the coin comes up tails. Maybe I'm better off taking a certain $140 to risking ending up with only $100." The risk averse person then would decide whether the $10 greater expected return from Coin Toss A is enough to compensate her for the risk of receiving only $100, or $40 less than she would receive if she avoided the risks of Coin Toss A. Economists assume that people in general are risk averse and that, in this example, most people would think about their choice as described above. But economists also would acknowledge that the decision by any given person to take the certain $140 or participate in Coin Toss A would turn on how risk averse that person was.

One customary economic measure of risk aversion is the "risk premium." A risk premium is the amount of money a risk avoider would pay to obtain certainty. In Coin Toss A, a risk avoider would be prepared to pay $10 as a risk premium to obtain a certain $140.

The risk premium is one useful measure of risk aversion, but it indicates nothing about another potentially relevant factor, the expected variation of the returns. Consider Coin Toss B, described below:

|              | return | probability | expected return |
|--------------|--------|-------------|-----------------|
| Coin Toss B: | $ 0    | 0.5         | $ 0             |
|              | $300   | 0.5         | $150            |
|              |        |             | $150            |
| Payment:     | $140   | 1.0         | $140            |

A risk avoider prepared to pay $10 to avoid the risk involved in Coin Toss A presumably would be prepared to pay at least the same premium to avoid the risk of Coin Toss B. Clearly though, because of the greater variation ($300 or nothing, rather than $200 or $100), Coin Toss B involves more risk than Coin Toss A. Thus, we can predict with confidence that, if the choice was between Coin Toss A and Coin Toss B, a risk averse person would select Coin Toss A.

The opposite of risk aversion is risk loving. As does a risk avoider, a risk loving person takes the magnitude of the risk, as well as the expected return, into account. But neither Coin Toss example would pose any problem for a risk loving person; she would surely choose either Coin Toss A or Coin Toss B over a certain payment of $140. The issue would become difficult only if the amount of the certain payment was increased to more than $150. Then a risk lover would focus on the comparison between the certain return and the higher return available if the coin came up heads, rather than comparing the certain return to the lowest possible return, as would a risk averse person. But again, whether a risk lover will select the certain payment or the Coin Toss will depend on how large the certain payment is and how risk loving that person is. Here, too, variation may be significant. If the choice were between Coin Toss A and Coin Toss B, a risk lover would select Coin Toss B.

### 4.  CONTROLLABLE RISKS

What do we mean by a "controllable risk?" Generally, a risk is considered controllable when one of the parties, by acting or not acting, can cause good or bad things to happen to the venture. For example, if the size of the harvest depends in part on the willingness to get up before dawn to spray the vines with a chemical to prevent insect damage, the risk to the venture is that the employee will not expend the effort to do so.

The heart of the difficulty in distributing risk among the parties is that a party will have a greater incentive to control a risk which that party bears. Thus, in the spraying example, if the employee receives the same compensation no matter how many grapes are produced, she will have little incentive to rise early and spray the vines to prevent the insect damage. When a person does less than is optimal to control a risk, that failure is called "shirking." (More generally, the danger that a person who does not bear a risk will not take steps to control that risk is referred to as "moral hazard.") To avoid shirking, the owner (who *does* bear the risk) must monitor the employee to ensure that she takes risk reducing precautions. From a risk controlling perspective, it may be most efficient to place the risk on the employee so as to avoid the costs of monitoring.

At the same time, however, the party who is in the best position to control the risk may not (for reasons relating to risk preference) be the best person to bear it. If the owner is wealthier, less risk averse, or better able to diversify or insure against the risk, from a risk bearing perspective, she should bear the risk. Thus there is a clear tension between the risk controlling and the risk bearing perspectives.

The spraying example illustrates this general problem. We might place all the risk on the employer, thus requiring her to monitor the employee to reduce the shirking. In such case, the employer would bear the costs of monitoring and would have to come up with appropriate monitoring devices. These problems are discussed in Section B. However, because shirking *is* within the control of the employee, it may be better to have her bear the costs of her own shirking and thus avoid the necessity of monitoring. Neither of these allocations of risk is a perfect solution; each entails costs the parties would prefer to avoid and neither will eliminate completely the employee's shirking. What is required, therefore, is an arrangement that will be the best compromise between the conflicting risk controlling and risk bearing objectives of the parties. The possibilities for such an arrangement are discussed in the following sections.

## B.  ALLOCATING RISK TO THE OWNER

If the owner is less risk averse than the employee, the parties will not want the employee to bear the risk of the success or failure of the business. Instead, it will be preferable that the employee be paid a salary and the owner receive the profits or incur the losses. In this situation, the risk of the employee's shirking takes on greater significance for the owner who must now directly or indirectly monitor the employee. Such monitoring consists of two parts. First, the owner must decide what constitutes optimal performance by the employee. Second, having decided that, the owner must determine whether the desired level of performance is occurring or has occurred. The first part requires looking at shirking from an *ex ante* perspective, i.e., before the employee has begun to work. The second part examines the employee's conduct from an *ex post* perspective, i.e., after the employee has begun to work. In considering the costs and benefits of various monitoring devices, it is useful to keep these two perspectives in mind.

One solution would be for the owner to supervise the employee directly. This form of monitoring combines both perspectives: the owner is physically able both to prescribe optimal standards and observe whether they are being met. It also has obvious drawbacks. Deciding what the employee should do and obtaining the relatively detailed information about whether she did it would be time-consuming and costly and contrary to the principal reason the owner hired the employee, i.e., to enable the owner to spend relatively little time and effort on the business. Of course, if the owner did not want to directly supervise the employee, she could hire a supervisor. Doing that, however, would create an additional problem: Who would supervise the supervisor to ensure that she did not shirk? In a small business, the costs of such an arrangement would almost certainly outweigh the benefits, although you should keep this alternative in mind when you study publicly held corporations.

An alternative monitoring device would be an employment contract between the owner and the employee. Such a contract would contain elements of both parts of monitoring: it would specify the employee's duties and it would prescribe the sanctions to be imposed if the employee failed to perform those duties.

In deciding whether such a contract is desirable, let us examine each part separately. Some aspects of the employee's work can be satisfactorily defined in a contract; other aspects are more problematic. Consider a saleswoman for a clothing manufacturer whose job is to arrange for the clothing to be sold in stores in a given geographical area by meeting with buyers from those stores. A contract could be drafted with a provision specifying the number of hours the saleswoman was required to work and the number of stores she had to visit. Would such a provision be desirable? Where success is measured primarily by the quality of a person's effort, it is difficult to define the optimal level of that effort in a contract. The number of hours worked may not be as important as the way in which the hours were spent; the number of stores visited may not be as significant as what transpired in each store. Most important, a large number of hours spent working does not guarantee corresponding profits.

Because of the *ex ante* drafting difficulty, shirking may continue even if there is a contract. This shirking does not vitiate the desirability of a contract; it may simply cause us to bring an *ex post* perspective to bear on the drafting. In the example of the saleswoman, consider the following provision:

> Saleswoman will use her best efforts in selling employer's clothes. Any dispute over this issue will be resolved by an arbitrator mutually acceptable to the parties.

The term "best efforts" prescribes the saleswoman's efforts *ex ante*. In the terms we have used, it calls upon the employee to expend the same effort she would expend if she bore the entire risk. However, it does have the advantage of being given content after the fact by reference to the actual circumstances encountered by the employee and the steps she took to accomplish the task assigned to her.

From an *ex post* perspective, the enforcement mechanism of such a clause may be a useful monitoring device. In deciding whether to enforce the clause, the employer could use easily observable measures to alert her to the possibility that the employee was shirking. For example, the employer could compare the sales of the employee with those made in the previous year or by other salespeople. If, after such comparison, the owner also found that the venture's sales were high, she could infer that the saleswoman had used her best efforts. If, however, sales were low, the owner could then invoke the judicial settling-up process to determine whether the saleswoman had, in fact, used her "best efforts." Because the saleswoman could not know *ex ante* whether her employer would try to enforce the contract, her incentive to shirk would be reduced.

From an *ex ante* perspective, another problem encountered in devising an appropriate monitoring system is that the parties are unlikely to foresee all the contingencies that might arise over the life of the contract, particularly if the contract is for a long period of time. Moreover, some contingencies which are foreseeable may be so unlikely to occur that the costs of drafting provisions to deal with them would exceed the expected benefits. If, however, such a contingency did arise, how should the contract be construed? Some economists argue that a court should decide how the parties would have provided for the contingency if they had originally thought to do so.

At first blush, such a method of analysis may seem both impossible and unrealistic. But economists who support this approach would argue that, although each party may have been concerned primarily with maximizing her own return from the venture rather than with the venture's total return, it is fair to assume each party would recognize that her share is likely to increase if the total return is greater. Therefore, a court should assume the parties would have adopted the provision maximizing the overall return.

Other analysts, including some economists, question whether the provision that would maximize overall returns easily can be identified and suggest that, in any event, reasonable persons may well be more concerned with ensuring a fair division of returns than with maximizing total returns. (These arguments will recur, in a variety of contexts, throughout this book.)

Although less expensive than direct supervision by the owner, contracting is a costly method of specifying optimal performance for both parties. Information, negotiation and drafting costs all must be incurred (lawyers' time is not cheap). Moreover, the potential cost of enforcing contracts are high and cannot be disregarded, even if they never actually materialize. Finally, keep in mind that the use of a contract shifts the ultimate resolution of a dispute to a third party—the court—and thereby creates uncertainty for both parties to the contract.

## C.  ALLOCATING RISK TO THE EMPLOYEE

As we have seen, one organizational model places the risk of the employee's shirking entirely on the owner of the business. The owner then will find it necessary to provide incentives to the employee and to incur monitoring costs, which will reduce (but not eliminate completely) the employee's shirking.

The opposite extreme would be an organizational model that places the risk of shirking entirely on the employee. For example, the owner could rent the business to the employee for a fixed fee and allow the employee to retain all the profits. Such an arrangement would create gains for the owner by eliminating her monitoring costs; almost by definition, the only monitoring would be the employee's own self-monitoring. If the employee works less hard, it will be because she values her non-work activities more than her work; her reduced profits from the business will be counterbalanced by the value she places on those activities.

A less drastic way of allocating risk is to compensate the employee so as to reward her efforts or penalize her if her efforts do not produce satisfactory results. For example, in the previous example of the saleswoman, consider the following:

> Saleswoman is to be paid an annual salary of $x. However, if the net income to employer from the sale of clothing in stores for which saleswoman is responsible is less than $y, her annual salary shall be reduced by z percent.

Is such a provision desirable? The relationship between the employee's effort and the owner's ultimate profit depends on a number of factors. Some of them probably are beyond the control of either party; some that are within their control may not relate to the specific problem of shirking. If shirking is the owner's principal concern, it may make more sense to tie the salary reduction to the gross volume of clothing that the saleswoman negotiates in each store. On the other hand, to the extent that the profits of the venture *do* depend on the saleswoman's efforts, such a clause creates incentives for the saleswoman and reduces the need to monitor her performance.

Even when the risks of the venture during the period of employment are allocated to the employee, a need for monitoring may exist because the parties have differing time horizons. An employee whose compensation is based on a measure such as gross sales for the year will necessarily want to increase current sales. The owner, in contrast, may have a longer time horizon and be willing to forego higher sales this year if her firm is likely to be able to sell the same goods, at a significantly higher price, in the following year. Or, in the vineyard problem, the employee may wish to maximize the yield so as to obtain more immediate revenue from a higher harvest while the owner might choose to crop the vines more severely so as to improve the quality of the grapes they will bear in future years. In such cases, monitoring will be necessary to protect the longer-range interests of the owner.

Finally, consider the situation of the employee after she stops working for the owner. If she shirked, she may have damaged her reputation, thus reducing her value to people who may be interested in hiring her in the future. This reduction will occur because, in making hiring decisions, employers take into account the way in which people have performed in the past. Hence, evidence that an employee has worked diligently will be valuable to the employee, because it will provide a signal to a future employer that less monitoring of the employee's shirking will be necessary. Note that the use of reputation as a self-monitoring device does not involve any reallocation of the risks or returns of the venture. Thus, reputation is a useful element in both the employment and tenancy models.

## D.  IN SEARCH OF THE MIDDLE GROUND

We have already seen that under one polar model, the owner bears all the risks of the venture. Were risk the parties' only concern, this would be a desirable model, assuming, as is often the case, that the owner is the better risk bearer. But such risk allocation carries a price; the owner must incur monitoring costs and create incentives to reduce the likelihood of shirking. The profits of the venture will be reduced by these costs. Under the other polar model, the employee bears all the risks but realizes the gains resulting from her own efforts to control those risks. Again, if controlling risk were the parties' only concern, this would be a desirable model; it has the lowest monitoring and enforcement costs and it puts the risk on the person best able to control it. But this model also carries a price: the employee must bear risks which the employer is better able to bear.

Might there be a satisfactory middle ground? Suppose that the parties agreed to divide the profits 50–50 (or some other mutually agreeable percentage). The employee would still have some incentive to shirk. This incentive would be reduced, however, because the shirking would reduce the employee's own share of the profits. The owner would still need to monitor, but because of the employee's interest in the profits of the venture, the monitoring costs would be reduced. This reduction, however, is achieved by placing part of the risk on the party less able to bear it. The parties thus have to search for that distribution of risk that is best for them, taking into account the desire both to minimize monitoring costs and to place the risk on the party better able to bear it.

As we shall see, corporations involve a complex network of arrangements between owners and employees similar to those we have been discussing. What motivates all these arrangements are the choices the shareholders and managers of a corporation make about how to distribute the risks inherent in their particular business venture.

## E.  AN INTEGRATED APPROACH

William A. Klein and John C. Coffee, BUSINESS
ORGANIZATION AND FINANCE
5, 12–14, 20–24, 33–37 (6th Ed. 1996).

Suppose that a grocery store is owned by a person, Pamela, who devotes her full time to the management of the store. That is, she owns and operates the store. The two functions, ownership and management (operation), need not be combined in the same person. If Pamela hires a person to serve as manager in her place and delegates broad decision-making powers to that person, she is still the owner and is still called a sole proprietor. The possibility of specialization, or separation of functions, is an attribute of a sophisticated (and efficient) economic system; it also produces the kinds of problems that require the application of lawyer skills. But that gets ahead of our story.

\* \* \* To some considerable degree, the relationships among creditors, suppliers, employees, and owners are viewed here as ones involving contributors to a *joint economic enterprise*. A more customary approach would depict the owner as the core of the enterprise and the other elements as inputs hired by the owner and having only a very narrow interest in the enterprise. On this latter view, there is less jointness, less commonality of interest. Either view is permissible and both are useful. The joint-enterprise perspective seems to offer more fresh insights and a better understanding of economic functions. If we were concerned solely with traditional, established legal doctrine, the perspective in which the owner establishes the business and then hires capital, employees, and other inputs would probably be more appropriate, though some legal institutions may be evolving in the direction of the joint-undertaking model.

Suppose that Pamela hires Chuck, whose duties will be primarily to stock the shelves and keep the store clean. In a small business it is unlikely that there will be a written contract spelling out the mutual rights and obligations of Chuck and Pamela. Even though not spelled out in writing, however, a set of rights and obligations does exist. The terms of this implicit agreement can be found in part in common-law *doctrines of agency and contract,* and in part in modern legislation affecting the employment relationship. \* \* \*

In the common parlance, Chuck is an *"employee."* In legal terminology, Pamela is the *"principal"* and Chuck is an *"agent."* Within this category of principal and agent, the law of agency defines a subcategory that covers the Pamela–Chuck relationship, namely, *"master"* and *"servant."* Pamela is the "master" and Chuck is the "servant." These terms are used to describe a relationship in which one person (the master) "controls or has the *right to control* the physical conduct of the other" (the servant). (Quotation from Restatement of the Law of Agency (2d), Sec. 2.) This means that Pamela has the right not only to expect Chuck to perform particular tasks but also to tell him how to perform them. \* \* \* [T]he term "agent" has a broader scope in law than in common parlance; it includes any person who has agreed with another person (the "principal") to "act on his behalf and subject to his control." Restatement, Agency (2d), Sec. 1.

\* \* \*

Suppose that Pamela decides to withdraw from the active management of the business and to hire a general manager, Morris, to run the business. To some significant degree, Pamela will need to rely on Morris's judgment about how to manage the store—about such matters as prices, subordinate personnel, merchandise quality, and so on. These decisions will be much broader in scope and greater in impact on the success or failure of the business than the decisions made by lower-level employees such as Chuck. The delegation of decision-making authority is largely unavoidable; the purpose of hiring a general manager is to shift to that person the burden of making important decisions as problems arise. Many of those problems cannot be anticipated and, even if they could, the correct solution could not be specified in advance. Pamela must of necessity rely on Morris's competence and on his good faith. * * *

As an employee of Pamela, Morris will, like Chuck, be subject to her legal right to *control*. If all goes well, Pamela will not need to exercise control, but she may consider it very important to have the right to do so. It is, after all, her money (or assets) that will be at risk. Ordinarily, a person with money invested at substantial risk will want to have the right to review and control decisions that can materially affect the value of that investment. This kind of need for control is, of course, limited. Pamela's concern will be mostly with basic policy decisions and she need not be much concerned with minor, day-to-day decisions and routine operating decisions.

Pamela's relationship with Morris, like her relationship with Chuck, will be affected significantly by the ease with which Morris can be *replaced*. This will depend in part on general economic circumstances such as the number of grocery stores in the area and the number of trained managers. It will also depend, however, on the *specific training or knowledge* that Morris acquires in managing Pamela's store. As that specific training or knowledge increases, Morris becomes more and more valuable to Pamela and more and more difficult for her to replace. To that extent, Pamela will become dependent on Morris and will find it costly to replace him. But this is a two-way street. Morris will have acquired training that is valuable to Pamela, and to Pamela alone, and to this extent he is dependent on her. This kind of symbiotic relationship can obviously lead to discord over division of the gains from the joint endeavor. Part of the job of a lawyer is to anticipate such problems and to help provide, in advance, formulas for their resolution. * * *

Pamela's relationship with Morris will also be affected by how he is compensated. In order to provide Morris with proper incentives, Pamela may insist that part of his reward be contingent on the success of the business. Morris might, in fact, demand such an arrangement. At the same time, there is likely to be a limit to the risk Morris is willing to take and he will probably insist on some assured minimal level of compensation. Thus, the compensation "package" may consist of a salary (a fixed claim) plus a bonus based on profits (a residual claim). The presence of an element of incentive compensation like a bonus based on profits shifts some of the risk of the business to Morris; that is an attribute of any residual, as opposed to fixed, claim. It aligns Morris's objectives and interests with those of Pamela, and thereby allows her to be less concerned with the need for supervision, review, and control. But as Morris's rewards become increasingly dependent on the success of the business, he will become more concerned about control. If he is paid nothing but a fixed wage, he may be willing to follow any orders that Pamela wants to give him (though he may object because of concern for his future). If, on the other hand, his rewards are heavily dependent on the profits of the business, he may want some assurance of freedom from interference by Pamela in his operation of the business. Again, there arises a conflict that can be negotiated but may be extremely difficult to resolve to the satisfaction of both Morris and Pamela. Moreover, it should be noted that the formulation of an incentive compensation formula can be a formidable task. For example, Pamela and Morris may decide that Morris is to receive some portion of the net profits of the business. But the concept of "net profits" is not self-defining; it requires a determination, for example, of the appropriate rate of depreciation of assets used in the business. Beyond that, there is the very real possibility that profits will be affected by circumstances such as the behavior of competitors, which may or may not be related to Morris's performance. There may be good reasons for making the incentive compensation contingent on profits over a fairly long period of time—for example, five years—but then what happens if Pamela wants to sell out after three years? Problems like these, again, can be difficult to resolve in advance, and are fraught with potential antagonism. One can easily appreciate why Morris and Pamela may at the outset choose to pretend that they don't exist or why they may want to assume that mutually acceptable solutions will appear as concrete issues arise.

* * *

The problems of contingent reward (risk) and control, whose interrelationship we have just seen, are in turn related to the problem of the *duration* of the relationship—in other words, to the problem of termination. Like any other employee, Morris will want as much security of employment as he can get. He will want the option of keeping his job as long as he wants it, though he will have to accept the fact that in most private employment he cannot expect too much in this regard. Pamela may want to tie up Morris's services for as long as possible, without committing herself, though again she will not have much expectation of being able to do so. Where Morris's compensation is contingent to some significant degree on the success of the business, the issue of duration of the contract will take on added importance. At the outset Morris may consider that he will need a substantial period of time to achieve his profit-making expectations. Moreover, if he is to receive a portion of the yearly profits he may want to be able to remain in command in order to protect what he has been able to create. As the length of the contract period increases, however, it becomes increasingly difficult to anticipate and deal with the problems arising from changing circumstances. To a considerable extent it will be necessary to leave problems for resolution as they arise, relying on the proposition that by and large the outcomes prescribed by law, in the absence of explicit agreement, will be consistent with what the parties would have provided had they tried to anticipate and resolve all conceivable issues. But in some circumstances, the failure to resolve issues in some detail in advance will lead to acrimony and costly litigation. That is a risk that perhaps the parties should try to take into account, however vaguely, at the beginning of their association; it is questionable whether many people do so.

\* \* \*

\* \* \* The duty of loyalty is, of course, a more general obligation of employees (and other agents and fiduciaries). Problems of Morris's faithfulness, loyalty, and devotion to duty are especially troublesome because they are difficult to define and even more difficult to monitor. Viewing the matter negatively, Pamela will be concerned about the possibilities of stealing, cheating, and shirking and how to prevent or limit them. For convenience, we can refer to stealing, cheating, shirking and other such volitional or controllable conduct as *self-dealing*. By a variety of techniques, an employer can control the incidence of self-dealing by employees, but not without costs in time or money. There is likely, therefore, to be a residual loss to the employer from the employee's self-dealing that it is not worthwhile to try to prevent. For example, to detect stealing by Morris (and others) Pamela probably will rely on such negative sanctions as the threat of dismissal, bad references, and even criminal action. To detect criminal behavior she will need to spend her own time in reviewing operations or hire others to do so. This is part of the cost of hiring managers. It is a cost that does not occur when Pamela manages the business herself. And no matter how great the expenditure on prevention and detection, there will remain some possibility of undetected theft.

Stealing by managers is not likely to be a central concern of many business firms. Shirking, and other forms of self-serving behavior such as lavish use of expense accounts, are more pervasive and significant problems. Control of shirking may take the form of observation (with varying degrees of care) of performance or results, followed by reward (e.g., bonus or promotion) or punishment (e.g., demotion or discharge). But observation is costly and often inaccurate and rewards and punishments are imperfect, though useful, tools for controlling self-dealing. To illustrate and expand on this observation, suppose that Pamela moves to a distant place and must, of necessity, give Morris broad discretion in the operation of the business. Now consider the question of how many hours a week he is to work. Suppose that when Pamela managed the business herself she worked 60 hours a week. Further, let's suppose that if Morris owned the business himself he would work 60 hours a week. It does not follow that Morris will work 60 hours a week as manager of Pamela's business, since the benefit to him from doing so may not be sufficient to induce that level of effort. Pamela may recognize that there is no point in trying to specify that Morris will work a set number of hours per week at some specified level of effort. Even if it were possible to prescribe unambiguously an appropriate number of hours and level of effort, it might be too difficult for Pamela to determine the number of hours actually put in by Morris, much less the level of his effort. Pamela may be better off to rely on the threat of discharge for inadequate performance (which means that she will incur costs in observing performance and in gathering information about other managers with whom she might replace Morris) and on the use of rewards based on results that tend to flow from effort.

\* \* \*

In the Pamela–Morris kind of situation there is a form of economic specialization, with Pamela supplying risk-bearing capital and Morris supplying managerial skill. If, in the customary mode, we think of Pamela as the owner, there is a separation of ownership and control. Morris must have considerable decision-making freedom. Specification of how he should react to all possible issues is not feasible. Given the need to vest in Morris the power to exercise business judgment or discretion, self-dealing by Morris becomes possible. The duty of loyalty prescribes— in some situations with clarity and in others only with considerable ambiguity—how Morris is supposed to behave, but this code of conduct is not self-executing. Moreover, it is impossible to design a system of sharing of rewards that will make Morris's interests identical to those of Pamela. Pamela will of necessity spend some of her time or her money, or both, trying to determine how faithfully Morris is serving her interests.

Economists (and others) often seem to think of the costs of defining, detecting, and preventing self-dealing as a sort of waste. Similarly, they find waste to the extent that a benefit that Morris takes for himself, such as leisure, is worth less to him than its cost to Pamela (for example, in lost profits). (The residual loss to Pamela from self-dealing that cannot feasibly be prevented is not an economic waste since Pamela's loss is Morris's gain.) That concept of waste is, however, a peculiar one when examined closely. The possibility of self-dealing is an inevitable product of the decision to hire a manager to run a business. One can cope with this possibility in a variety of ways, like hiring monitors such as detectives or outside auditors. The cost of doing so is certainly a departure from what Pamela might hope for and from what she could achieve if she ran the business herself. But this cost is an inevitable outcome of the facts that she has chosen to retire from active management and that in our imperfect world the people on whom she must rely may not be entirely trustworthy and loyal. It is unfortunate that people are not all perfectly trustworthy and loyal; it is unfortunate that people are not all perfect in all respects. But we must learn to live with the fact of imperfection and the costs thereby imposed. A violation of the duty of loyalty may be more galling than a violation of other obligations because the violation is likely to involve a sneaky act—an act that the employee knows is wrong but expects to be able to get away with because of problems of detection. Violation of the duty of loyalty may, therefore, be seen as unethical or immoral (as contrasted, for example, with a violation of the duty of care). This might justify the imposition of punitive damages or other special remedies (though by and large the law has not proceeded in that direction) or the incurring of extraordinary costs for detection. Still, there is no more sense in bemoaning the costs of disloyalty than there is in bemoaning the costs of friction in an engine. We lubricate engines to reduce friction, but we are willing to accept some residual level of friction. We continue to use engines, despite the cost of lubrication, and despite the residual friction, because we conclude we are better off by doing so than we would be otherwise. People with capital, like Pamela, hire managers, despite the monitoring costs, because they feel they are better off than they would be with any alternative investment or venture. This observation is, of course, a tautology. It is a useful tautology in that it reminds us of the silliness of worrying about unavoidable departures from unattainable ideals. While the point may seem obvious in the present context, it is often ignored in the context of large, complex economic organizations such as publicly held corporations.

In other words, we must be careful about comparing the actual situation, with division of ownership and management, to the *mythical ideal of the owner-managed firm*. Once Pamela decides, for whatever reason, that she does not want to manage the business, the standard of an owner-managed firm is unattainable. Morris simply cannot be expected to act as he would if he were the owner. He is not an owner; and he is a human being. Pamela is not a manager any longer; she is an investor. Both think that they are better off with the other than without. If that were not so, they would not have made the deal they made. It seems more useful to compare their actual position to what they would have if they could not combine their resources (services and capital) than to what they would have in the unattainable combined-owner-manager situation. In the actual position, with separation of management from ownership of capital, both can be expected to try to bargain for as much as possible in the way of contributions by the other and returns to themselves. It is fatuous to expect that Morris will behave selflessly, as if all the returns to his efforts were his. Pamela might hope for something close to that result, but she would be silly to expect to achieve it. All of this may, again, seem obvious in the small-firm context. For large firms it is also valid but frequently ignored both by lawyers and economists.

Suppose, however, that when Pamela hires Morris, she says, either explicitly or implicitly, that she expects him, as manager, to behave just as she would behave, or as he would behave if he were the owner. And suppose that Morris accepts the job on those terms. To a considerable extent the legal system seems to infer, and even to impose, such bargains. This is what is contemplated by the law when it refers to a duty of loyalty or a *fiduciary obligation*. That duty or obligation is like a golden rule, a broad, vague constraint applied to employment relationships (a one-way rule in favor of the employer). It is the kind of duty associated not only with employees but with trustees, brokers, and a whole host of other kinds of people (fiduciaries) who undertake to accomplish some objective for another person. The need to rely on a vague concept such as the duty of loyalty stems from the difficulty of specifying precisely what it is that the employer expects of the employee (on the need, that is, for discretion in the employee). The rule of law that embodies the duty of loyalty is a useful one. Without it, mutually advantageous economic relationships might not be feasible. As we have seen, however, violations of the duty of loyalty may be extremely difficult to detect. To that extent, and given the infirmities of human nature, the duty of loyalty may to a significant extent embody an unattainable ideal. It is wholly unrealistic to expect that all employees will as a matter of conscience consistently act as faithful retainers, selflessly pursuing the interests of their employers even at their own expense, or that we can be fully effective in efforts to force them to do so. We can publicly deplore the departures from the ideal. It may be useful to do so—to establish ethical standards and use deprivation of respect as a tool for enforcing the loyalty aspect of the business agreement. But we must be careful not to refuse to recognize the reality and cope with it.

# Chapter 3

## AN INTRODUCTION TO THE LAW
## OF CORPORATIONS

---

### A.  INTRODUCTION

This chapter introduces some of the basic terms and concepts of the traditional law of corporations. In approaching the problems and materials that follow, you should be particularly conscious that they intentionally cast you in the role of planner and counselor to your client, a role to which the usual first-year law school course does not expose students more than casually. However, that is the role corporate (and most other) lawyers play most of the time. These materials emphasize the use of corporate law to plan transactions.

At first, you are apt to find the role of planner somewhat uncomfortable. A real client would expect her lawyer to structure a transaction so as to maximize benefits and minimize legal and business risks. But business transactions go forward in a world fraught with uncertainty and often involve doing things that have never been done before. Such transactions raise novel and difficult legal questions. Rarely will there be case law directly on point, if there is any case law at all. The client, however, is interested in more than the arguments that can be made on either side. She is paying (often at very high rates) for the benefits of her lawyer's legal expertise, experience and, most of all, judgment.

In this book, we frequently ask you to recommend a course of action to a client. Trying to make such recommendations should help you develop the intangible qualities that allow business lawyers to make sound judgments. It also may provide you with opportunities to show some creativity by generating alternative approaches to a problem that will allow your client to surmount some legal or business obstacle to achieving her objectives. Clients do not want to be told "That is illegal," or "You cannot do it." They are paying their lawyers to figure out, within the constraints of ethical conduct, how *to* do something. The experienced, creative lawyer frequently can chart out a lawful strategy that will allow the client to accomplish her objectives.

# B.  SOME BASIC TERMS AND CONCEPTS

To help you understand the problems and the materials in this chapter, we will first outline some basic terms and concepts and explain their role in the standard framework of corporate law. We explore these terms and concepts in greater detail in later chapters.

## 1.  CORPORATE STATUTES

The statute to which we refer most often is the Revised Model Business Corporation Act (RMBCA). The RMBCA is a product of the Committee on Corporate Laws of the Section of Business Law of the American Bar Association. The Committee adopted the RMBCA in 1984 and has amended it many times since. Thirty-five states have enacted corporation statutes modeled on the RMBCA or its predecessor, the Model Business Corporation Act.

We also refer frequently to the Delaware General Corporation Law (DGCL). More publicly-held corporations are organized in Delaware than in any other state and Delaware's courts have issued a large number of important corporate law decisions. Edward S. Adams and John H. Matheson, Selected Corporations and Other Business Associations Statutes, Rules and Forms (West) includes relevant sections of the RMBCA, official comments to certain sections, and relevant sections of the DGCL and other statutes. For a full discussion of the RMBCA, see the four-volume Model Business Corporation Act Annotated (3d ed. 1985).

## 2.  ORGANIC DOCUMENTS

The provisions of a state's corporation statute govern all corporations organized pursuant to its terms. Every corporation statute requires that each corporation have its own *articles of incorporation* (sometimes called the *charter* or the *certificate of incorporation*), which represents, in a sense, the constitution of that corporation. The articles contain certain provisions required by statute (such as the name of the corporation) and other provisions that regulate the internal affairs of the corporation. Every corporation also has *bylaws*, which usually set forth the details of the corporation's internal governance arrangements (such as procedures for calling meetings). A corporation's articles cannot conflict with the statute under which the corporation is organized and a corporation's bylaws cannot conflict with the statute or the articles.

## 3.  THE CORPORATE ACTORS

The *stockholders* (or *shareholders*) of a corporation "own" the corporation in that they own its stock. Unlike owners of other assets, however, stockholders do not control directly the corporation that they own. Rather, they elect a *board of directors*, which is responsible for managing or supervising the corporation's business. In addition, stockholders' approval must be obtained before a corporation can engage in certain fundamental transactions, such as a merger or the sale of all its assets, and before the articles of incorporation can be amended. Stockholders also can amend the bylaws and can vote on matters that corporate management asks them to approve.

As indicated, the board of directors has legal responsibility for managing or supervising the corporation's business. Boards include "inside" directors—individuals who are corporate employees and affiliates—and "outside" directors—individuals who generally have no other affiliation with the corporation. When directors act in their capacity as directors, they are supposed to represent the interests of shareholders and are not considered employees of the corporation.

The *officers* of the corporation, who usually include a president, one or more vice-presidents, a secretary, and a treasurer, run the corporation's day-to-day business. Corporation statutes and by-laws generally impose few specific duties on officers.

This model reflects corporate statutes. Corporate reality sometimes differs. Some boards actively manage or oversee their corporation's business; others act more like "rubber stamps," approving whatever management places before them. In corporations with a relatively small number of stockholders ("close corporations"), there often is a substantial overlap among shareholders, directors and officers, and it is common for one or more people to fill all three roles.

## 4. CORPORATE SECURITIES

Stockholders' ownership of a corporation is evidenced by shares of *stock*, which represents their residual ownership interest in the corporation. There is always *common stock*. There may be one or more classes of *preferred stock*, which represent ownership interests with certain priorities over the common stock. A corporation's articles of incorporation specify how many shares of common and preferred stock the corporation is *authorized* to issue. More stock can be issued only if the articles are amended. The portion of the authorized stock that has been sold and remains in the hands of stockholders is the stock *outstanding*. A corporation's board of directors generally is free to sell *authorized but unissued stock* on whatever terms it decides are reasonable.

Stock, whether common or preferred, is considered an *equity security*, a term that derives from the "equity of redemption" of a mortgagor and relates to the fact that stockholders stand at the end of the line when it comes to distributions of corporate funds. *Debt securities* represent claims on a corporation's assets that have priority over the claims represented by equity securities. Debt securities include *bonds, debentures* and *notes*.

## 5. FIDUCIARY PRINCIPLES

The relationships among the various corporate actors are governed in part by express legal rules and in part by *fiduciary principles* drawn originally from the law of trusts. The basic fiduciary duties that officers and directors owe to the corporation are the *duty of care* and the *duty of loyalty*. Another fiduciary duty that implicates both care and loyalty is the *duty of disclosure*.

## PROBLEM
### CHESAPEAKE MARINE SERVICES—PART I

The Chesapeake Marine Services Company, Inc., ("Chesapeake") is incorporated in the state of Columbia[1] [Delaware]. Its business consists principally of the provision of barge and towing services. It also maintains a small shipyard in which it services its own vessels and does repair work for others. Its articles of incorporation and by-laws are substantially the same as those in the Corporation Forms section of Adams & Matheson, SELECTED CORPORATIONS AND OTHER BUSINESS ASSOCIATIONS STATUTES, RULES AND FORMS. The articles authorize the issuance of 1,000 shares of common stock; and also contain the following provision:

> Wherever a vote of the shareholders is required by statute to approve an amendment to these Articles of Incorporation or a merger or sale of all or substantially all of the assets of the corporation, such approval shall be by the holders of two-thirds of the outstanding stock.

All 1,000 authorized shares have been issued. John Apple, Chesapeake's largest shareholder, owns 350 shares. Fourteen other shareholders, many affiliated with the Lambert family, own the remaining 650 shares, but none of them individually owns more than 200 shares.

The Chesapeake board consists of five directors: Apple, James Lambert (the president of the company), two other members of the Lambert family, and Nancy Carter, another substantial shareholder.

Apple, who has been in the marine transport business for many years, acquired his Chesapeake stock in a series of purchases over the last few years. Members of the Lambert family, the other principal shareholders of Chesapeake, expressed concern about Apple's more recent acquisitions and told Apple that they were strongly opposed to his trying to gain control of Chesapeake.

Apple also owns a half interest in United Harbor Services, Inc. ("United"), a somewhat smaller firm that competes with Chesapeake. Apple acquired his interest in United about three years ago, after a dispute with Chesapeake over the continuation of leases on two tugboats he owned and had leased to Chesapeake for several years. Chesapeake's board of directors refused to renew the leases and Apple conveyed the tugboats to United in exchange for half of its stock.

For the past few years, Chesapeake's management has been concerned about a perceived shortage of capital. The firm's business has been growing; it needs to expand the shipyard, and the board believes it could make profitable use of one or two more tugboats. Moreover, within

---

**1.** Columbia is a fictitious United States jurisdiction that has adopted the RMBCA. Alternative references to Delaware and the DCGL are provided for those who choose to deal with this or subsequent Problems as questions of Delaware law.

the last year Chesapeake has experienced temporary shortages of cash. It has occasionally had to delay payments to suppliers, causing it to lose the usual trade discounts for prompt payment. A year ago Chesapeake's bank rejected Chesapeake's request for a loan because Chesapeake had already borrowed as much as the bank believed was prudent and because the bank had doubts about the future growth of Chesapeake's business.

James Lambert then decided that the best course for Chesapeake was to raise additional equity capital. At the last board meeting, he recommended an amendment to the articles of incorporation to double the number of authorized shares of common stock. Apple opposed the amendment, stating that, in his opinion, Chesapeake should not seek additional capital. Apple also indicated that he would do everything he could to block the amendment. Chesapeake's board of directors decided not to act on James Lambert's proposal, but to ask your firm for advice as to the following:

1. What risk of liability, if any, would the directors run if they recommended that the shareholders amend the articles of incorporation so as to permit Chesapeake to raise additional capital by selling new stock?

2. What actions, if any, can the board take to ensure that the proposed amendment to Chesapeake's articles of incorporation is adopted?

The partner in charge has suggested that, in developing responses to the board's questions, you consider the following:

a. What alternatives are available to a company in Chesapeake's position when it needs to raise new capital?

b. Why do the articles of incorporation contain a limit on the number of shares of common stock that can be issued? See RMBCA §§ 2.02 and 6.01(a) [DGCL § 102(a)(4) ].

c. The provision of the articles of incorporation quoted above puts Apple, who owns more than one-third of Chesapeake's common stock, in a position to block any amendment to the articles. Is the quoted provision consistent with RMBCA §§ 2.02, 7.27, 10.01, and 10.03 [DGCL §§ 102, 216, and 242]? What purpose does that provision serve?

d. RMBCA §§ 10.03, 11.03, and 12.02 [DGCL §§ 242, 251 and 271] require shareholder approval, by a majority of the shares, for certain "fundamental changes" in the corporate structure, such as amendments to the articles, sales of substantially all of a corporation's assets, and mergers. How do you reconcile these provisions with RMBCA § 8.01(b) [DGCL § 141(a)]?

e. If Apple votes his stock against a proposed amendment that all the other directors believe would benefit the corporation, could Chesapeake successfully challenge Apple's action? Would it matter whether Apple was motivated by a good faith belief that it would not be in Chesapeake's best interest to sell more stock or simply by his desire to make it more difficult for Chesapeake to compete with United?

# BAYER v. BERAN

49 N.Y.S.2d 2 (Sup.Ct.1944).

SHIENTAG, JUSTICE.

These derivative stockholders' suits present for review two transactions upon which plaintiffs seek to charge the individual defendants, who are directors, with liability in favor of the corporate defendant, the Celanese Corporation of America. * * * Before taking up the specific transactions complained of, I shall consider generally certain pertinent rules to be applied in determining the liability of directors of a business corporation such as is here involved. * * *

Directors of a business corporation are not trustees and are not held to strict accountability as such. Nevertheless, their obligations are analogous to those of trustees. Directors are agents; they are fiduciaries. The fiduciary has two paramount obligations: responsibility and loyalty. Those obligations apply with equal force to the humblest agent or broker and to the director of a great and powerful corporation. They lie at the very foundation of our whole system of free private enterprise and are as fresh and significant today as when they were formulated decades ago. The responsibility—that is, the care and the diligence—required of an agent or of a fiduciary, is proportioned to the occasion. It is a concept that has, and necessarily so, a wide penumbra of meaning—a concept, however, which becomes sharpened in its practical application to the given facts of a situation.

The concept of loyalty, of constant, unqualified fidelity, has a definite and precise meaning. The fiduciary must subordinate his individual and private interests to his duty to the corporation whenever the two conflict. In an address delivered in 1934, Mr. Justice, now Chief Justice, Stone declared that the fiduciary principle of undivided loyalty was, in effect, "the precept as old as Holy Writ, that 'a man cannot serve two masters.' More than a century ago equity gave a hospitable reception to that principle and the common law was not slow to follow in giving it recognition. No thinking man can believe that an economy built upon a business foundation can long endure without loyalty to that principle." He went on to say that "The separation of ownership from management, the development of the corporate structure so as to vest in small groups control of resources of great numbers of small and uninformed investors, make imperative a fresh and active devotion to that principle if the modern world of business is to perform its proper function." Stone, *The Public Influence of the Bar*, 48 HARVARD LAW REVIEW 1, 8.

A director is not an insurer. On the one hand, he is not called upon to use an extraordinary degree of care and prudence; and on the other hand it is established by the cases that it is not enough for a director to be honest, that fraud is not the orbit of his liability. The director may not act as a dummy or a figurehead. He is called upon to use care, to exercise judgment, the degree of care, the kind of judgment that one would give in similar situations to the conduct of his own affairs.

The director of a business corporation is given a wide latitude of action. The law does not seek to deprive him of initiative and daring and vision. Business has its adventures, its bold adventures; and those who in good faith, and in the interests of the corporation they serve, embark upon them, are not to be penalized if failure, rather than success, results from their efforts. The law will not permit a course of conduct by directors, which would be applauded if it succeeded, to be condemned with a riot of adjectives simply because it failed. Directors of a commercial corporation may take chances, the same kind of chances that a man would take in his own business. Because they are given this wide latitude, the law will not hold directors liable for honest errors, for mistakes of judgment. The law will not interfere with the internal affairs of a corporation so long as it is managed by its directors pursuant to a free, honest exercise of judgment uninfluenced by personal, or by any considerations other than the welfare of the corporation.

To encourage freedom of action on the part of directors, or to put it another way, to discourage interference with the exercise of their free and independent judgment, there has grown up what is known as the "business judgment rule". "Questions of policy of management, expediency of contracts or action, adequacy of consideration, lawful appropriation of corporate funds to advance corporate interests, are left solely to their honest and unselfish decision, for their powers therein are without limitation and free from restraint, and the exercise of them for the common and general interests of the corporation may not be questioned, although the results show that what they did was unwise or inexpedient." *Pollitz v. Wabash R. Co.*, 207 N.Y. 113, 124, 100 N.E. 721, 724. Indeed, although the concept of "responsibility" is firmly fixed in the law, it is only in a most unusual and extraordinary case that directors are held liable for negligence in the absence of fraud, or improper motive, or personal interest.

The "business judgment rule", however, yields to the rule of undivided loyalty. This great rule of law is designed "to avoid the possibility of fraud and to avoid the temptation of self-interest." Conway, J., in *Matter of Ryan's Will*, 291 N.Y. 376, 406, 52 N.E.2d 909, 923. It is "designed to obliterate all divided loyalties which may creep into a fiduciary relation * * *." Thacher, J., in *City Bank Farmers Trust Co. v. Cannon*, 291 N.Y. 125, 132, 51 N.E.2d 674, 676. "Included within its scope is every situation in which a trustee chooses to deal with another in such close relation with the trustee that possible advantage to such other person might influence, consciously or unconsciously, the judgment of the trustee * * *." Lehman, Ch. J., in *Albright v. Jefferson County National Bank*, 292 N.Y. 31, 39, 53 N.E.2d 753, 756. The dealings of a director with the corporation for which he is the fiduciary are therefore viewed "with jealousy by the courts." *Globe Woolen Co. v. Utica Gas & Electric Co.*, 224 N.Y. 483, 121 N.E. 378, 380. Such personal transactions of directors with their corporations, such transactions as may tend to produce a conflict between self-interest and fiduciary obligation, are, when challenged, examined with the most scrupulous care, and if there is any evidence of improvidence or oppression, any indication of unfairness or undue advantage, the transactions will be voided. "Their dealings with the corporation are subjected to rigorous scrutiny and where any of their contracts or engagements with the corporation are challenged the burden is on the director not only to prove the good faith of the transaction but also to show its inherent fairness from the viewpoint of the corporation and those interested therein." *Pepper v. Litton*, 308 U.S. 295, 306, 60 S.Ct. 238, 245, 84 L.Ed. 281.

While there is a high moral purpose implicit in this transcendent fiduciary principle of undivided loyalty, it has back of it a profound understanding of human nature and of its frailties. It actually accomplishes a practical, beneficent purpose. It tends to prevent a clouded conception of fidelity that blurs the vision. It preserves the free exercise of judgment uncontaminated by the dross of divided allegiance or self-interest. It prevents the operation of an influence that may be indirect but that is all the more potent for that reason. The law has set its face firmly against undermining "the rule of undivided loyalty by the 'disintegrating erosion' of particular exceptions." *Meinhard v. Salmon*, 249 N.Y. 458, 464, 164 N.E. 545, 546.

The first, or "advertising", cause of action charges the directors with negligence, waste and improvidence in embarking the corporation upon a radio advertising program beginning in 1942 and costing about $1,000,000 a year. It is further charged that they were negligent in selecting the type of program and in renewing the radio contract for 1943. More serious than these allegations is the charge that the directors were motivated by a noncorporate purpose in causing the radio program to be undertaken and in expending large sums of money therefor. It is claimed that this radio advertising was for the benefit of Miss Jean Tennyson, one of the singers on the program, who in private life is Mrs. Camille Dreyfus, the wife of the president of the company and one of its directors; that it was undertaken to "further, foster and subsidize her career"; to "furnish a vehicle" for her talents.

Eliminating for the moment the part played by Miss Tennyson in the radio advertising campaign, it is clear that the character of the advertising, the amount to be expended therefor, and the manner in which it should be used, are all matters of business judgment and rest peculiarly within the discretion of the board of directors. Under the authorities previously cited, it is not, generally speaking, the function of a court of equity to review these matters or even to consider them. Had the wife of the president of the company not been involved, the advertising cause of action could have been disposed of summarily. Her connection with the program, however, makes it necessary to go into the facts in some detail.

[The court reviews the history of the decision to launch a program of radio advertising.]

So far, there is nothing on which to base any claim of breach of fiduciary duty. Some care, diligence and prudence were exercised by these directors before they committed the company to the radio program. It was for the directors to determine whether they would resort to radio advertising; it was for them to conclude how much to spend; it was for them to decide the kind of program they would use. It would be an unwarranted act of interference for any court to attempt to substitute its judgment on these points for that of the directors, honestly arrived at. The expenditure was not reckless or unconscionable. Indeed, it bore a fair relationship to the total amount of net sales and to the earnings of the company. The fact that the company had offers of more business than it could handle did not, in law, preclude advertising. Many corporations not now doing any business in their products because of emergency conditions advertise those products extensively in order to preserve the good will, the public interest, during the war period. The fact that the company's product may not now be identifiable did not bar advertising calculated to induce consumer demand for such identification. That a program of classical and semiclassical music was selected, rather than a variety program, or a news commentator program, furnishes no ground for legal complaint. True, variety programs have a wider popular appeal than do musicals, but it would be a very sad thing if the former were the only kind of radio programs to be used. Some of the largest industrial concerns in the country have recognized this and have maintained fine musical programs on the radio for many years.

Now we have to take up an unfortunate incident, one which cannot be viewed with the complacency displayed by some of the directors of the company. This is not a closely held family corporation. The Doctors Dreyfus and their families own about 135,000 shares of common stock, the other directors about 10,000 shares out of a total outstanding issue of 1,376,500 shares. Some of these other directors were originally employed by Dr. Camille Dreyfus, the president of the company. His wife, to whom he has been married for about twelve years, is known professionally as Miss Jean Tennyson and is a singer of wide experience.

Dr. Dreyfus, as was natural, consulted his wife about the proposed radio program; he also asked the advertising agency, that had been retained, to confer with her about it. She suggested the names of the artists, all stars of the Metropolitan Opera Company, and the name of the conductor, prominent in his field. She also offered her own services as a paid artist. All of her suggestions as to personnel were adopted by the advertising agency. While the record shows Miss Tennyson to be a competent singer, there is nothing to indicate that she was indispensable or essential to the success of the program. She received $500 an evening. It would be far-fetched to suggest that the directors caused the company to incur large expenditures for radio advertising to enable the president's wife to make $24,000 in 1942 and $20,500 in 1943.

Of course it is not improper to appoint relatives of officers or directors to responsible positions in a company. But where a close relative of the chief executive officer of a corporation, and one of its dominant directors, takes a position closely associated with a new and expensive field of activity, the motives of the directors are likely to be questioned. The board would be placed in a position where selfish, personal interests might be in conflict with the duty it owed to the corporation. That being so, the entire transaction, if challenged in the courts, must be subjected to the most rigorous scrutiny to determine whether the action of the directors was intended or calculated "to subserve some outside purpose, regardless of the consequences to the company, and in a manner inconsistent with its interests." *Gamble v. Queens County Water Co.*, 123 N.Y. 91, 99, 25 N.E. 201, 202.

After such careful scrutiny I have concluded that, up to the present, there has been no breach of fiduciary duty on the part of the directors. The president undoubtedly knew that his wife might be one of the paid artists on the program. The other directors did not know this until they had approved the campaign of radio advertising and the general type of radio program. The evidence fails to show that the program was designed to foster or subsidize "the career of Miss Tennyson as an artist" or to "furnish a vehicle for her talents". That her participation in the program may have enhanced her prestige as a singer is no ground for subjecting the directors to liability, as long as the advertising served a legitimate and a useful corporate purpose and the company received the full benefit thereof.

The musical quality of "Celanese Hour" has not been challenged, nor does the record contain anything reflecting on Miss Tennyson's competence as an artist. There is nothing in the testimony to show that some other soprano would have enhanced the artistic quality of the program or its advertising appeal. There is no suggestion that the present program is inefficient or that its cost is disproportionate to what a program of that character reasonably entails. Miss Tennyson's contract with the advertising agency retained by the directors was on a standard form, negotiated through her professional agent. Her compensation, as well as that of the other artists, was in conformity with that paid for comparable work. She received less than any of the other artists on the program. Although she appeared with greater regularity than any other singer, she received no undue prominence, no special build-up. Indeed, all of the artists were subordinated to the advertisement of the company and of its products. The company was featured. It appears also that the popularity of the program has increased since it was inaugurated.

It is clear, therefore, that the directors have not been guilty of any breach of fiduciary duty, in embarking upon the program of radio advertising and in renewing it. It is unfortunate that they have allowed themselves to be placed in a position where their motives concerning future decisions on radio advertising may be impugned. The free mind should be ever jealous of its freedom. "Power of control carries with it a trust or duty to exercise that power faithfully to promote the corporate interests, and the courts of this State will insist upon scrupulous performance of that duty." Lehman, Ch. J., in *Everett v. Phillips*, 288 N.Y. 227, 232, 43 N.E.2d 18, 19. Thus far, that duty has been performed and with noteworthy success. The corporation has not, up to the present time, been wronged by the radio advertising attacked in the complaints.

[The court also found no merit in plaintiffs' second cause of action.]

### Note on the Business Judgment Rule

Note that the court followed very different approaches in evaluating plaintiffs' "advertising" claim—that it was imprudent for Celanese to spend $1,000,000 a year to advertise on a classical music program—and plaintiffs' self-dealing claim—that Celanese had incurred those expenses primarily to advance Ms. Tennyson's career as a singer. The court gave short shrift to the "advertising" claim because the *business judgment rule* protected the board's decision concerning where to advertise Celanese's products.

The business judgment rule (BJR) plays a central role in the American system of corporate law. The BJR has both structural and substantive aspects. Substantively, the BJR creates a presumption that, absent evidence of self-dealing or the directors not being fully informed, all board decisions are intended to advance the interests of the corporation and its shareholders. Consequently, courts will not entertain shareholder suits that challenge the wisdom of such decisions. Structurally, the BJR implements the basic corporate attribute of centralized management by insulating the board's decision-making prerogatives from shareholder (and judicial) second guessing.

This chapter and the next several chapters illustrate several contexts in which the BJR comes into play. The BJR was already well established in at the time of *Bayer v. Beran*. However, the BJR has become a much more prominent part of corporate law in recent years. One indicator of this change is that the number of judicial decisions that refer to the business judgment rule has roughly quadrupled in each of the past two decades.

## GAMBLE v. QUEENS COUNTY WATER CO.

123 N.Y. 91, 25 N.E. 201 (1890).

[Mullins built a system of water pipes, known as the "Rockaway Beach Extension," at an out-of-pocket cost of about $69,000. He then contracted to sell the "Rockaway Beach Extension" to the Queens County Water Co., of which he was a shareholder, for $60,000 in bonds and $50,000 in stock. The water company's shareholders, with Mullins participating, voted to approve the transaction and a dissident shareholder then brought suit to set it aside.]

PECKHAM, J.

* * * The so-called "Rockaway Beach Extension" was not built by defendant Mullins under any contract with the defendant corporation. * * * Upon its completion, Mullins was the sole and absolute owner thereof, with power to operate it himself, or to sell it to others, or, in

brief, to exercise such acts of ownership over the property as any other owner might have exercised. This is not the case of a trustee entering into a contract with himself, or purchasing from himself, where the contract is liable to be repudiated at the mere will, or even whim, of the *cestui que trust.* Having the rights of an absolute owner of this extension, Mullins was at liberty to make such contract in regard to its disposal as he should see fit, so long of course as he did not, while acting in his own interest on the one side, also act on the other in the capacity of trustee or representative, so that his interest and his duty might conflict. In this case, Mullins did not so act. He bases his right to the stock and bonds of the company defendant upon the vote of the majority of its shareholders taken at a regularly convened meeting, to purchase the property at the price named in the resolution adopted at such meeting, the price being $60,000 in bonds, and $50,000 in the stock of such company. * * * There were a majority of shareholders, and a majority of shares voted upon, in favor of such resolution, without counting the defendant Mullins or his shares, although he voted upon them in favor of such resolution. In so doing, he committed no legal wrong. A shareholder has a legal right at a meeting of the shareholders to vote upon a measure, even though he has a personal interest therein separate from other shareholders. In such a meeting, each shareholder represents himself and his own interests solely, and he in no sense acts as a trustee or representative of others. The law of self-interest has at such time very great and proper sway. There can be little doubt, too, that at such meetings those who do vote upon their own stock vote upon it in the light solely of their own interest, or at least in what they conceive to be their own interest. Their action resulting from such votes must not be so detrimental to the interests of the corporation itself as to lead to the necessary inference that the interests of the majority of the shareholders lie wholly outside of and in opposition to the interests of the corporation, and of the minority of the shareholders, and that their action is a wanton or a fraudulent destruction of the rights of such minority. * * *

I think that where the action of the majority is plainly a fraud upon, or, in other words, is really oppressive to the minority shareholders, and the directors or trustees have acted with and formed part of the majority, an action may be sustained by one of the minority shareholders suing in his own behalf * * *. It is not, however, every question of mere administration or of policy in which there is a difference of opinion among the shareholders that enables the minority to claim that the action of the majority is oppressive, and which justifies the minority in coming to a court of equity to obtain relief. Generally the rule must be that in such cases the will of the majority shall govern. The court would not be justified in interfering, even in doubtful cases, where the action of the majority might be susceptible of different constructions. To warrant the interposition of the court in favor of the minority shareholders in a corporation or joint stock association, as against the contemplated action of the majority, where such action is within the corporate powers, a case must be made out which plainly shows that such action is so far opposed

to the true interests of the corporation itself as to lead to the clear inference that no one thus acting could have been influenced by any honest desire to secure such interests, but that he must have acted with an intent to subserve some outside purpose, regardless of the consequences to the company and in a manner inconsistent with its interests. Otherwise the court might be called upon to balance probabilities of profitable results to arise from the carrying out of the one or the other of different plans proposed by or on behalf of different shareholders in a corporation, and to decree the adoption of that line of policy which seemed to it to promise the best results, or at least to enjoin the carrying out of the opposite policy. This is no business for any court to follow.
\* \* \*

[The court ruled in favor of defendants and ordered a new trial.]

## C.  EQUITABLE LIMITATIONS ON LEGAL POSSIBILITIES

### PROBLEM

### CHESAPEAKE MARINE SERVICES—PART II

Prevented by Apple's opposition from authorizing additional Chesapeake's stock, James Lambert came to your firm for advice about how Chesapeake might raise the equity capital it needs. After discussing the matter with one of the partners, Lambert proposed the following plan. Chesapeake will organize a new corporation, CMS Shipyard, Inc. ("Shipyard"), with authorized capital of 10,000 shares of common stock, and will transfer the assets of its shipyard division to Shipyard in exchange for 2,000 shares of its common stock. Then Shipyard will sell another 1,500 shares of common stock, for $100 per share, half to members of the Lambert family and half to a few outside investors. Shipyard will not offer any stock to Apple. Finally, Shipyard will use about $100,000 of the cash it expects to receive to expand its ship repair business and will lend the remaining $50,000 to Chesapeake.

The partner has sent you a memo describing the proposed transaction and continuing as follows:

I don't see any problems with the mechanics of the proposed transaction. Chesapeake clearly has the power, under RMBCA § 3.02, to create Shipyard and to purchase some of its stock. Chesapeake's board does not need shareholder approval to transfer the assets of the shipyard division, because they constitute far less than "substantially all" of Chesapeake's assets. (See RMBCA § 12.02.) In fact, the division has generated only about 15 percent of Chesapeake's profits over the past few years and the book value[1] of

---

**1.** "Book value" of an asset is the value at which it is carried on the accounts of a business. According to standard accounting practice, book value is generally equal to the cost of the asset or, in the case of a depreciable asset, cost less an allowance for depreciation arrived at by a more-or-less arbitrary formula. As a result of this practice, the "real" value of an asset may depart significantly from its book value. The

the division's assets is $200,000, or about 10 percent of the total book value of Chesapeake's assets. The fair market value of the division is more, probably about $375,000, but that still is less than 20 percent of Chesapeake's estimated total fair market value.

On the other hand, the transaction looks like an "end run" around the two-thirds majority provision in Chesapeake's articles, and Apple probably will challenge it. Most likely, he will claim that the transaction (i) is unwise, (ii) is unfair, and, (iii) in any event, is unlawful because Chesapeake "is doing indirectly what it could not do directly." Is a court likely to view any of these claims as meritorious? Does Chesapeake have good responses to these claims? Is evidence relating to Lambert or Apple's motives likely to affect a court's evaluation? Finally, if any of these claims appears to have merit, can you think of a way to restructure the proposed transaction to eliminate the problem and still attain most or all of Chesapeake's objectives? Our client wants to raise money, not get bogged down in litigation.

In answering these questions, first reconsider *Bayer v. Beran*. Then consider the following.

## SCHNELL v. CHRIS–CRAFT INDUSTRIES, INC.

285 A.2d 437 (Del.Sup.1971).

[Plaintiffs, a group of Chris–Craft shareholders, were dissatisfied with the company's economic performance. They resolved to seek control by electing a new board of directors at Chris–Craft's next annual shareholders' meeting. On October 16, 1971, as required by federal law, they filed documents announcing their intentions with the Securities and Exchange Commission. On October 18, Chris–Craft's board met and amended the corporation's by-laws, which had previously fixed January 11 as the date of the annual meeting, to authorize the board to set an annual meeting date at any time in December or January. The board then proceeded to schedule the upcoming meeting for December 8, thereby reducing by more than a month the time available to the insurgents to solicit the support of other shareholders. The board also set the place of the meeting in Cortland, New York, a small town far from any transportation hubs. The board said it changed the meeting date because weather conditions made it difficult to get to Cortland in January and because holding the meeting well before Christmas would reduce problems with the mail. Meanwhile, however, the board took a number of other actions to impede the insurgents, including resisting providing them with the list of stockholders to which they were entitled under Delaware law. The trial court found that the defendants' actions, including the change in the date of the annual meeting, were designed to obstruct the plaintiffs' efforts to gain control. But the court declined to

book value of a corporation is the aggregate       ties.
of the book value of its assets less its liabili-

reschedule the meeting on its original date, holding that the plaintiffs had delayed too long in seeking judicial relief. On appeal, the Supreme Court reversed.]

HERRMANN, JUSTICE (for the majority of the Court):

It will be seen that the Chancery Court considered all of the reasons stated by management as business reasons for changing the date of the meeting; but that those reasons were rejected by the Court below in making the following findings:

> I am satisfied, however, in a situation in which present management has disingenuously resisted the production of a list of its stockholders to plaintiffs or their confederates and has otherwise turned a deaf ear to plaintiffs' demands about a change in management designed to lift defendant from its present business doldrums, management has seized on a relatively new section of the Delaware Corporation Law for the purpose of cutting down on the amount of time which would otherwise have been available to plaintiffs and others for the waging of a proxy battle. Management thus enlarged the scope of its scheduled October 18 directors' meeting to include the by-law amendment in controversy after the stockholders committee had filed with the S.E.C. its intention to wage a proxy fight on October 16.

> Thus plaintiffs reasonably contend that because of the tactics employed by management (which involve the hiring of two established proxy solicitors as well as a refusal to produce a list of its stockholders, coupled with its use of an amendment to the Delaware Corporation Law to limit the time for contest), they are given little chance, because of the exigencies of time, including that required to clear material at the S.E.C., to wage a successful proxy fight[1] between now and December 8. * * *

In our view, those conclusions amount to a finding that management has attempted to utilize the corporate machinery and the Delaware Law for the purpose of perpetuating itself in office; and, to that end, for the purpose of obstructing the legitimate efforts of dissident stockholders in the exercise of their rights to undertake a proxy contest against management. These are inequitable purposes, contrary to established principles of corporate democracy. The advancement by directors of the by-law date of a stockholders' meeting, for such purposes, may not be permitted to stand.

When the by-laws of a corporation designate the date of the annual meeting of stockholders, it is to be expected that those who intend to contest the reelection of incumbent management will gear their campaign to the by-law date. It is not to be expected that management will

---

**1.** Shareholders in public companies rarely attend annual meetings. They vote by granting a proxy—a written authority to vote their shares—to some other person. In the event of a contest for control, both management and dissident shareholders solicit proxies from shareholders.

attempt to advance that date in order to obtain an inequitable advantage in the contest.

Management contends that it has complied strictly with the provisions of the new Delaware Corporation Law in changing the by-law date. The answer to that contention, of course, is that inequitable action does not become permissible simply because it is legally possible.

Accordingly, the judgment below must be reversed and the cause remanded, with instructions to nullify the December 8 date as a meeting date for stockholders; to reinstate January 11, 1972 as the sole date of the next annual meeting of the stockholders of the corporation; and to take such other proceedings and action as may be consistent herewith regarding the stock record closing date and any other related matters.

### *Note: Independent Legal Significance*

A number of other cases, most of them involving mergers[1] or recapitalizations,[2] have taken what seems, on the surface at least, to be a rather different view of actions that comply with all relevant statutory provisions. In these cases, plaintiffs have argued that defendants were making use of a mechanism provided in one section of the statute to accomplish a result that they could not have accomplished had they pursued it in an arguably more straightforward fashion. In *Bove v. Community Hotel Corp. of Newport*, R.I., 105 R.I. 36, 249 A.2d 89 (1969), for example, holders of preferred stock had the right to receive 24 years of unpaid dividends before the corporation could pay any dividends on its common stock. Management wanted to eliminate the preferred stockholders' claim so that the corporation could sell new common stock and raise needed capital. Under Rhode Island law, the dividend claims could be eliminated by amending the charter, but such an amendment required unanimous approval of the preferred stockholders, which would not be forthcoming.

Consequently, management decided to pursue another alternative. It created a new corporation with nominal assets and proposed to merge the old corporation into it in a transaction that would eliminate the old preferred stock and the associated claims for dividends. The merger required the approval of two-thirds, rather than all, of the preferred stock. If the merger was approved, preferred stockholders who voted against it had the option of demanding to be paid a judicially determined "fair value" for their stock, rather than accepting stock in the surviving

---

**1.** A merger is a statutory technique for combining two or more corporations into one. The surviving corporation acquires all of the assets and assumes all of the liabilities of the merging corporations. The shareholders of the surviving corporation normally continue to hold their stock. The shareholders of the acquired corporation or corporations exchange their stock for stock of the surviving corporation or other consideration, such as debt securities or cash.

**2.** A recapitalization involves a change in the capital structure of a corporation, usually accomplished by an amendment to the articles, as a result of which some or all of the corporation's securities are converted into securities having different characteristics.

corporation. Some preferred stockholders, however, sought to enjoin the merger. Denying relief, the Rhode Island Supreme Court stated:

> Concededly, unanimity of the preferred stockholders is unobtainable in this case, and plaintiffs argue, therefore, that to permit the less restrictive provisions of the merger statute to accomplish indirectly what otherwise would be incapable of being accomplished directly by the more stringent amendment procedures of the general corporation law is tantamount to sanctioning a circumvention or perversion of that law.
>
> The question, however, is not whether recapitalization by the merger route is a subterfuge, but whether a merger which is designated for the sole purpose of cancelling the rights of preferred stockholders with the consent of less than all has been authorized by the legislature. The controlling statute is § 7–5–2. Its language is clear, all-embracing and unqualified. It authorizes any two or more business corporations *which were or might have been organized* under the general corporation law to merge into a single corporation; and it provides that the merger agreement shall prescribe " * * * the terms and conditions of consolidation or merger, the mode of carrying the same into effect * * * *as well as the manner of converting the shares of each of the constituent corporations into shares or other securities of the corporation resulting from or surviving such consolidation or merger*, with such other details and provisions as are deemed necessary." (emphasis ours) Nothing in that language even suggests that the legislature intended to make *underlying purpose* a standard for determining permissibility. Indeed, the contrary is apparent since the very breadth of the language selected presupposes a complete lack of concern with whether the merger is designed to further the mutual interests of two existing and nonaffiliated corporations or whether alternatively it is purposed solely upon effecting a substantial change in an existing corporation's capital structure.
>
> Moreover, that a possible effect of corporate action under the merger statute is not possible, or is even forbidden, under another section of the general corporation law is of no import, it being settled that the several sections of that law may have independent legal significance, and that the validity of corporate action taken pursuant to one section is not necessarily dependent upon its being valid under another. *Hariton v. Arco Electronics, Inc.*, 40 Del.Ch. 326, 182 A.2d 22, aff'd, 41 Del.Ch. 74, 188 A.2d 123.
>
> We hold, therefore, that nothing within the purview of our statute forbids a merger between a parent and a subsidiary corporation even under circumstances where the merger device has been resorted to solely for the purpose of obviating the necessity for the unanimous vote which would otherwise be required in order to cancel the priorities of preferred shareholders.

Similarly, *In Matter of Hesston Corp.*, 254 Kan. 941, 870 P.2d 17 (1994) adopted the doctrine of "independent legal significance" and upheld a merger that cashed out holders of preferred stock at price lower than they were entitled to received if their stock was redeemed.

### Notes and Questions

1.   In both *Schnell* and *Bove*, plaintiffs argued that a transaction that complied with the statute should be enjoined because the transaction was improperly motivated. In the former case, the allegedly improper purpose was to obstruct a contest for control. In the latter, the motive was allegedly to circumvent a provision of the statute designed to protect the plaintiffs' claim to dividends. Why might a court grant relief in one case and not in the other?

2.   There is no doubt that the bylaw change in *Schnell* was authorized by the applicable statute. Indeed, although the trial court's opinion, quoted by the Supreme Court, stated that "management has seized on a relatively new section of the Delaware Corporation Law," the change would also have complied with the old provision. What, then, is the source of the law that the Supreme Court found defendants to have violated?

3.   Would the *Schnell* court have reached the same result had management made the bylaw change before learning of the insurgents' plans? In other words, is a detrimental effect on plaintiffs sufficient to justify judicial relief, or is an improper purpose required as well?

4.   For an analysis of the *Schnell* doctrine and the role of improper motive, see Douglas M. Branson, *The Chancellor's Foot in Delaware:* Schnell *and its Progeny*, 14 J. Corp. L. 515 (1989).

## D.   LITIGATION BY SHAREHOLDERS

A corporation's managers owe fiduciary duties to the corporation and its shareholders. Managers who breach those duties can be held liable for any losses they have caused. However, fashioning a remedy to enforce managers' fiduciary duties often involves conceptually difficult issues. We explore those issues at length in Chapter 20.

The corporation itself unquestionably has the right to sue unfaithful managers. More often than not, though, the managers whose conduct is at issue control the corporation and are not likely to initiate a suit against themselves. Moreover, in the ordinary course, shareholders are not authorized to act directly for the corporation, and thus cannot enforce a corporate claim against the managers.

The *derivative suit* was developed to alleviate this problem. The derivative suit is an action in equity brought by a shareholder on behalf of the corporation. The action is brought against the corporation for failure to bring an action in law against some third party, most often an unfaithful or careless manager, and against the third party herself. The corporation (the real party at interest) is a nominal defendant and the plaintiff-shareholder controls prosecution of the suit. Any recovery belongs to the corporation for whose benefit the suit has been brought.

Occasionally, a shareholder's financial interest in a corporation is sufficiently large to make it attractive for her to finance, out of her own pocket, the cost of initiating and maintaining a derivative action. More commonly, the principal party in interest is not the nominal plaintiff-shareholder but her attorney who typically is awarded an attorney's fee, paid by the corporation, if some relief is awarded or agreed to in settlement. The fee is awarded in consideration for the benefits rendered to the corporation. The prospect of receiving this fee can make it economically attractive for an attorney to represent a shareholder on a contingent fee basis. But this prospect also raises the possibility that a derivative suit may be initiated primarily to generate an attorney's fee for plaintiff's counsel.

Today, either statutory provisions, court rules, or both, govern this combination of equity and legal actions, establish the right of shareholders to bring derivative suits, and regulate the manner in which they are prosecuted. See RMBCA §§ 7.40–7.47.

# Chapter 4

# THE CORPORATION AND THE CONSTITUTION

## A. INTRODUCTION

A corporation is an artificial being, a collective entity. It is not a natural person, although it is created by natural people. Nevertheless, it is endowed with some of the legal attributes of a natural person. It can own property, enter into contracts, sue and be sued in its own name. It can be held liable for its debts while, except in unusual circumstances, those who gave it life—its officers, directors and shareholders—are not liable for those same debts.

Because a corporation is considered a "person" for some purposes does not mean that it is a "person" for all purposes. In constitutional law, the issue is often framed as whether a corporation is entitled to the same treatment as a natural person. The Supreme Court first discussed this issue in *Trustees of Dartmouth College v. Woodward*, 17 U.S. (4 Wheat.) 518, 4 L.Ed. 629 (1819). In 1769, the British Crown had granted articles of incorporation to the trustees of Dartmouth College. After the American Revolution, New Hampshire, as successor to the Crown, enacted three laws amending Dartmouth's charter so as to give state officials a major role in the governance of the college. Dartmouth sued to invalidate the amendments, claiming they violated the contract clause of the U.S. Constitution (Art. I, § 10). The New Hampshire Supreme Court rejected Dartmouth's claim, and the college appealed to the Supreme Court.

The Court, in an opinion by Chief Justice Marshall, held New Hampshire's action was invalid because the charter constituted a contract between the state and the college that was "within the letter of the Constitution and within its spirit also * * *." 17 U.S. at 644. The Chief Justice described a corporation's basic attributes in terms suggesting that a corporation is both a fictional entity created by the state and the product of a contract among private parties:

> A corporation is an artificial being, invisible, intangible, and existing only in contemplation of law. Being the mere creature of

law, it possesses only those properties which the charter of its creation confers upon it, either expressly, or as incidental to its very existence. These are such as are supposed best calculated to effect the object for which it was created. Among the most important are immortality, and, if the expression may be allowed, individuality; properties, by which a perpetual succession of many persons are considered as the same, and may act as a single individual. They enable a corporation to manage its own affairs, and to hold property, without the perplexing intricacies, the hazardous and endless necessity, of perpetual conveyances for the purpose of transmitting it from hand to hand. It is chiefly for the purpose of clothing bodies of men, in succession, with these qualities and capacities, that corporations were invented, and are in use. By these means, a perpetual succession of individuals are capable of acting for the promotion of the particular object, like one immortal being. But this being does not share in the civil government of the country, unless that be the purpose for which it was created. Its immortality no more confers on it political power, or a political character, than immortality would confer such power or character on a natural person. It is no more a state instrument, than a natural person exercising the same powers would be.

*Id*. at 636–37.

Subsequent to *Dartmouth College*, the Court has examined the extent to which a corporation is entitled to the rights and privileges that the Constitution provides to natural persons. *Santa Clara County v. Southern Pacific Railroad Co.*, 118 U.S. 394, 6 S.Ct. 1132, 30 L.Ed. 118 (1886), the most important of these cases, held that a corporation is entitled to equal protection of the law under the Fourteenth Amendment. *Minneapolis & St. Louis Railway Co. v. Beckwith*, 129 U.S. 26, 9 S.Ct. 207, 32 L.Ed. 585 (1888), decided two years later, extended the holding of *Santa Clara* and ruled that a corporation also is entitled to due process of law. *Hale v. Henkel*, 201 U.S. 43, 26 S.Ct. 370, 50 L.Ed. 652 (1906), subsequently established that a corporation is protected against unreasonable searches and seizures by the Fourth Amendment, but also held that the Fifth Amendment's protection against self-incrimination is not available to a corporation.

Questions about the personhood of a corporation lead inevitably to the broader questions raised in Chapter 1 that occupy us throughout the book. What *is* the corporation? Is it private in nature or does it also serve some public ends? Is it essentially contractual in nature or is it a creature of the state which created it and to which it is responsible? What devices are available to make it "accountable?" To whom is it accountable? What is the nature of its accountability?

Consider these questions in reading the following cases involving the application of the First Amendment to corporate speech.

# B.  THE FIRST AMENDMENT

## PROBLEM

## REGULATING CORPORATE LOBBYING—PART I

You are the legislative assistant to Kathleen Bruin, who recently was elected a Columbia State Senator. In recent years, there were frequent reports that corporations exert tremendous influence on the Columbia Legislature, and Sen. Bruin campaigned heavily on the claim that, if elected, she would work to reduce corporations' political influence. Now in office, Sen. Bruin wants to propose legislation that would make it unlawful for "any business corporation, by itself or through any agent, employee or other person, to communicate, other than in a public hearing, directly with any member or employee of the Legislature of Columbia to secure or defeat the passage of any pending or proposed legislation by said Legislature."

Senator Bruin anticipates that opponents of this legislation will contend that it is both unconstitutional and unwise. As the following materials make clear, a court almost surely would hold the proposed legislation violated the First Amendment if it were directed at individuals. The more relevant question, on which the Senator is seeking your advice, is whether the fact the legislation regulates only business corporations would lead a court to hold it was not unconstitutional. Sen. Bruin also has asked you to consider whether, as a matter of public policy, it makes sense to limit corporate lobbying of the Columbia Legislature.

In developing your responses to these questions, consider:

1.  Is there any difference between the political activity of corporations and that of individuals?

2.  What are the interests of shareholders in the political expenditures made by their corporations? By what mechanisms are those interests protected? Are those mechanisms sufficient?

3.  Who actually decides what positions a corporation should take on political issues? What criteria are relevant to the decision? Does the business judgment rule protect such decisions?

4.  What does it mean to say that "the corporation" supports a particular issue?

5.  If there are valid reasons for concern about corporate political activities, do they arise from the size of the corporation or are the reasons more closely related to the characteristics of a corporation? Is there something about corporate status alone that makes corporate political activities more troublesome?

### Note: Regulation of Political Speech

Political speech lies at the core of the First Amendment, but the Supreme Court has not held every limitation on participation in the political process to be unconstitutional. The Corrupt Practices Act has long barred corporate and union contributions to candidates in federal elections; the Court has never ruled directly on the Act, but has treated it with considerable deference. Most notably, in *United States v. United Automobile Workers*, 352 U.S. 567, 588–90, 77 S.Ct. 529, 540, 1 L.Ed.2d 563 (1957), the Court reinstated an indictment of the U.A.W. for sponsoring a broadcast, directed at the general public, endorsing candidates for federal office, in the face of claims that so construing the Act would create significant First Amendment problems.

As concerns lobbying, the Court has upheld the Lobbying Act, which requires registration of lobbyists and disclosure of payments made to lobbyists. See *United States v. Harriss*, 347 U.S. 612, 74 S.Ct. 808, 98 L.Ed. 989 (1954). The Court first construed rather general language, describing who must register under the Act as limited to persons who engage in "direct communication with members of Congress on pending or proposed federal legislation." *Id.* at 620, 74 S.Ct. at 813. It continued:

> Present-day legislative complexities are such that individual members of Congress cannot be expected to explore the myriad pressures to which they are regularly subjected. Yet full realization of the American ideal of government by elected representatives depends to no small extent on their ability to properly evaluate such pressures. Otherwise the voice of the people may all too easily be drowned out by the voice of special interest groups seeking favored treatment while masquerading as proponents of the public weal. This is the evil which the Lobbying Act was designed to help prevent.

> Toward that end, Congress has not sought to prohibit these pressures. It has merely provided for a modicum of information from those who for hire attempt to influence legislation or who collect or spend funds for that purpose. It wants only to know who is being hired, who is putting up the money, and how much. It acted in the same spirit and for a similar purpose in passing the Federal Corrupt Practices Act—to maintain the integrity of a basic governmental process.

> Under these circumstances, we believe that Congress, at least within the bounds of the Act as we have construed it, is not constitutionally forbidden to require the disclosure of lobbying activities. To do so would be to deny Congress in large measure the power of self-protection.

*Id.* at 625, 74 S.Ct. at 816.

Similarly, the Court has rejected challenges to legislation that denies corporations and individuals business expense deductions for lobbying activities, *Cammarano v. United States*, 358 U.S. 498, 79 S.Ct. 524, 3 L.Ed.2d 462 (1959), and that bars lobbying by organizations that receive tax-deductible charitable contributions, *Regan v. Taxation With Representation*, 461 U.S. 540, 103 S.Ct. 1997, 76 L.Ed.2d 129 (1983). In both cases, the Court reasoned that deductions and tax-exempt status are matters of grace, not of right, and that Congress has no obligation to subsidize political speech. The Court also upheld the Hatch Act, which deters federal Civil Service employees from participating in political campaigns. *See United Public Workers v. Mitchell*, 330 U.S. 75, 67 S.Ct. 556, 91 L.Ed. 754 (1947).

On the other hand, the Court has been considerably less tolerant of express limitations on political speech by individuals and unincorporated associations. In *Buckley v. Valeo*, 424 U.S. 1, 96 S.Ct. 612, 46 L.Ed.2d 659 (1976), the Court drew a fundamental distinction between campaign contributions and expenditures. Contributions are entitled to only limited First Amendment protection, because they convey undifferentiated expressions of support, not specific ideas. Thus, Congress's interest in reducing corruption and the appearance of corruption is sufficient to support a limitation on the amount any individual can contribute to a candidate for federal office.

Expenditures, by contrast, relate directly to the expression of political views and are entitled to greater protection.

> A restriction on the amount of money an individual can spend on political communication during a campaign necessarily reduces the quantity of expression by restricting the number of issues discussed, the depth of their exploration, and the size of the audience reached. This is because virtually every means of communicating in today's mass society requires the expenditure of money.

*Id.* at 19, 96 S.Ct. at 634.

A limit on how much an individual can spend to support a campaign for office will be subjected to "exacting scrutiny." The strict limits Congress imposed in the Federal Election Campaign Act, as amended, did not survive such scrutiny because they would have materially restricted dissemination of ideas in the political marketplace.

Relying on similar arguments, the Court subsequently held unconstitutional a local ordinance that limited individuals' expenditures of their own money on political speech, *Citizens Against Rent Control/ Coalition for Fair Housing v. City of Berkeley*, 454 U.S. 290, 102 S.Ct. 434, 70 L.Ed.2d 492 (1981), and a federal regulation barring independent expenditures by political action committees to support presidential candidates, *Federal Election Commission v. National Conservative Political Action Committee*, 470 U.S. 480, 105 S.Ct. 1459, 84 L.Ed.2d 455 (1985) (NCPAC). In the latter case, the Court explained:

> We held in *Buckley* and reaffirmed in *Citizens Against Rent Control* that preventing corruption or the appearance of corruption are the only legitimate and compelling government interests thus far identified for restricting campaign finances. * * *

> Corruption is a subversion of the political process. Elected officials are influenced to act contrary to their obligations of office by the prospect of gains to themselves or their campaigns. The hallmark of corruption is the *quid pro quo*: dollars for political

favors. But here the conduct proscribed is not contributions to the candidate, but independent expenditures in support of the candidate.

*Id.* at 496–97, 105 S.Ct. at 1468.

In two cases, the Court has considered directly the validity of restrictions on political speech by business corporations.

## FIRST NATIONAL BANK OF BOSTON v. BELLOTTI
435 U.S. 765, 98 S.Ct. 1407, 55 L.Ed.2d 707 (1978).

MR. JUSTICE POWELL delivered the opinion of the Court.

In sustaining a state criminal statute that forbids certain expenditures by banks and business corporations for the purpose of influencing the vote on referendum proposals, the Massachusetts Supreme Judicial Court held that the First Amendment rights of a corporation are limited to issues that materially affect its business, property, or assets. The court rejected appellants' claim that the statute abridges freedom of speech in violation of the First and Fourteenth Amendments. The issue presented in this context is one of first impression in this Court. * * * We now reverse.

* * *

### I

The statute at issue prohibits appellants, two national banking associations and three business corporations, from making contributions or expenditures "for the purpose of * * * influencing or affecting the vote on any question submitted to the voters, other than one materially affecting any of the property, business or assets of the corporation." The statute further specifies that "[no] question submitted to the voters solely concerning the taxation of the income, property or transactions *of individuals* shall be deemed materially to affect the property, business or assets of the corporation."

Appellants wanted to spend money to publicize their views on a proposed constitutional amendment that * * * would have permitted the legislature to impose a graduated tax on the income of individuals. * * * The parties' statement of agreed facts reflected their disagreement as to the effect that the adoption of a personal income tax would have on appellants' business; it noted that "[there] is a division of opinion among economists as to whether and to what extent a graduated income tax imposed solely on individuals would affect the business and assets of corporations." Appellee did not dispute that appellants' management believed that the tax would have a significant effect on their businesses.

* * *

### III

If the speakers here were not corporations, no one would suggest that the State could silence their proposed speech. It is the type of speech indispensable to decisionmaking in a democracy, and this is no less true because the speech comes from a corporation rather than an individual. * * *

The question in this case, simply put, is whether the corporate identity of the speaker deprives this proposed speech of what otherwise would be its clear entitlement to protection. * * *

[A]ppellee suggests that First Amendment rights generally have been afforded only to corporations engaged in the communications business or through which individuals express themselves. * * *

But the press does not have a monopoly on either the First Amendment or the ability to enlighten. Cf. *Buckley v. Valeo*, 424 U.S. at 51 n. 56. Similarly, the Court's decisions involving corporations in the business of communication or entertainment are based not only on the role of the First Amendment in fostering individual self-expression but also on its role in affording the public access to discussion, debate, and the dissemination of information and ideas. Even decisions seemingly based exclusively on the individual's right to express himself acknowledge that the expression may contribute to society's edification.

We thus find no support in the First or Fourteenth Amendment, or in the decisions of this Court, for the proposition that speech that otherwise would be within the protection of the First Amendment loses that protection simply because its source is a corporation that cannot prove, to the satisfaction of a court, a material effect on its business or property. * * *

In the realm of protected speech, the legislature is constitutionally disqualified from dictating the subjects about which persons may speak and the speakers who may address a public issue. If a legislature may direct business corporations to "stick to business," it also may limit other corporations—religious, charitable, or civic—to their respective "business" when addressing the public. Such power in government to channel the expression of views is unacceptable under the First Amendment. Especially where, as here, the legislature's suppression of speech suggests an attempt to give one side of a debatable public question an advantage in expressing its views to the people,[22] the First Amendment is plainly offended. * * *

## IV

The constitutionality of § 8's prohibition of the "exposition of ideas" by corporations turns on whether it can survive the exacting scrutiny necessitated by a state-imposed restriction of freedom of speech. Especially where, as here, a prohibition is directed at speech itself, and the speech is intimately related to the process of governing, "the State may prevail only upon showing a subordinating interest which is compel-

---

**22.** Our observation about the apparent purpose of the Massachusetts Legislature is not an endorsement of the legislature's factual assumptions about the views of corporations. * * * Corporations, like individuals or groups, are not homogeneous. * * * It is arguable that small or medium-size corporations might welcome imposition of a graduated personal income tax that might shift a greater share of the tax burden onto wealthy individuals.

ling," *Bates v. Little Rock*, 361 U.S. 516, 524 (1960), "and the burden is on the government to show the existence of such an interest." *Elrod v. Burns*, 427 U.S. 347, 362 (1976). * * *

Appellee nevertheless advances two principal justifications for the prohibition of corporate speech. The first is the State's interest in sustaining the active role of the individual citizen in the electoral process and thereby preventing diminution of the citizen's confidence in government. The second is the interest in protecting the rights of shareholders whose views differ from those expressed by management on behalf of the corporation. However weighty these interests may be in the context of partisan candidate elections, they either are not implicated in this case or are not served at all, or in other than a random manner, by the prohibition in § 8.

### A

According to appellee, corporations are wealthy and powerful and their views may drown out other points of view. If appellee's arguments were supported by record or legislative findings that corporate advocacy threatened imminently to undermine democratic processes, thereby denigrating rather than serving First Amendment interests, these arguments would merit our consideration. But there has been no showing that the relative voice of corporations has been overwhelming or even significant in influencing referenda in Massachusetts, or that there has been any threat to the confidence of the citizenry in government.

Nor are appellee's arguments inherently persuasive or supported by the precedents of this Court. Referenda are held on issues, not candidates for public office. The risk of corruption perceived in cases involving candidate elections, e.g., *United States v. Automobile Workers*, supra; simply is not present in a popular vote on a public issue. To be sure, corporate advertising may influence the outcome of the vote; this would be its purpose. But the fact that advocacy may persuade the electorate is hardly a reason to suppress it: The Constitution "protects expression which is eloquent no less than that which is unconvincing." *Kingsley Int'l Pictures Corp. v. Regents*, 360 U.S. at 689. We noted only recently that "the concept that government may restrict the speech of some elements of our society in order to enhance the relative voice of others is wholly foreign to the First Amendment. * * * " *Buckley*, 424 U.S. at 48–49. * * *

### B

Finally, appellee argues that § 8 protects corporate shareholders, an interest that is both legitimate and traditionally within the province of state law. *Cort v. Ash*, 422 U.S. 66, 82–84 (1975). The statute is said to serve this interest by preventing the use of corporate resources in furtherance of views with which some shareholders may disagree. This purpose is belied, however, by the provisions of the statute, which are both underinclusive and overinclusive.

The underinclusiveness of the statute is self-evident. Corporate expenditures with respect to a referendum are prohibited, while corporate activity with respect to the passage or defeat of legislation is permitted, even though corporations may engage in lobbying more often than they take positions on ballot questions submitted to the voters. Nor does § 8 prohibit a corporation from expressing its views, by the expenditure of corporate funds, on any public issue until it becomes the subject of a referendum, though the displeasure of disapproving shareholders is unlikely to be any less.

The fact that a particular kind of ballot question has been singled out for special treatment undermines the likelihood of a genuine state interest in protecting shareholders. It suggests instead that the legislature may have been concerned with silencing corporations on a particular subject. * * *

The overinclusiveness of the statute is demonstrated by the fact that § 8 would prohibit a corporation from supporting or opposing a referendum proposal even if its shareholders unanimously authorized the contribution or expenditure. Ultimately shareholders may decide, through the procedures of corporate democracy, whether their corporation should engage in debate on public issues.[34] Acting through their power to elect the board of directors or to insist upon protective provisions in the corporation's charter, shareholders normally are presumed competent to protect their own interests. In addition to intracorporate remedies, minority shareholders generally have access to the judicial remedy of a derivative suit to challenge corporate disbursements alleged to have been made for improper corporate purposes or merely to further the personal interests of management.

Assuming, *arguendo*, that protection of shareholders is a "compelling" interest under the circumstances of this case, we find "no substantially relevant correlation between the governmental interest asserted and the State's effort" to prohibit appellants from speaking.

V

Because that portion of § 8 challenged by appellants prohibits protected speech in a manner unjustified by a compelling state interest, it must be invalidated. The judgment of the Supreme Judicial Court is *Reversed*.

MR. JUSTICE WHITE, with whom MR. JUSTICE BRENNAN and MR. JUSTICE MARSHALL join, dissenting.

---

**34.** Appellee does not explain why the dissenting shareholder's wishes are entitled to such greater solicitude in this context than in many others where equally important and controversial corporate decisions are made by management or by a predetermined percentage of the shareholders. * * *

[Moreover,] no shareholder has been "compelled" to contribute anything. Apart from the fact, noted by the dissent, that compulsion by the State is wholly absent, the shareholder invests in a corporation of his own volition and is free to withdraw his investment at any time and for any reason. * * *

I

There is now little doubt that corporate communications come within the scope of the First Amendment. This, however, is merely the starting point of analysis, because an examination of the First Amendment values that corporate expression furthers and the threat to the functioning of a free society it is capable of posing reveals that it is not fungible with communications emanating from individuals and is subject to restrictions which individual expression is not. Indeed, what some have considered to be the principal function of the First Amendment, the use of communication as a means of self-expression, self-realization, and self-fulfillment, is not at all furthered by corporate speech. It is clear that the communications of profitmaking corporations are not "an integral part of the development of ideas, of mental exploration and of the affirmation of self." They do not represent a manifestation of individual freedom or choice. * * * Shareholders in such entities do not share a common set of political or social views, and they certainly have not invested their money for the purpose of advancing political or social causes or in an enterprise engaged in the business of disseminating news and opinion. In fact, as discussed *infra*, the government has a strong interest in assuring that investment decisions are not predicated upon agreement or disagreement with the activities of corporations in the political arena.

Of course, it may be assumed that corporate investors are united by a desire to make money, for the value of their investment to increase. Since even communications which have no purpose other than that of enriching the communicator have some First Amendment protection, activities such as advertising and other communications integrally related to the operation of the corporation's business may be viewed as a means of furthering the desires of individual shareholders. This unanimity of purpose breaks down, however, when corporations make expenditures or undertake activities designed to influence the opinion or votes of the general public on political and social issues that have no material connection with or effect upon their business, property, or assets. Although it is arguable that corporations make such expenditures because their managers believe that it is in the corporations' economic interest to do so, there is no basis whatsoever for concluding that these views are expressive of the heterogeneous beliefs of their shareholders whose convictions on many political issues are undoubtedly shaped by considerations other than a desire to endorse any electoral or ideological cause which would tend to increase the value of a particular corporate investment. * * *

The self-expression of the communicator is not the only value encompassed by the First Amendment. One of its functions, often referred to as the right to hear or receive information, is to protect the interchange of ideas. * * * This proposition does not establish, however, that the right of the general public to receive communications financed by means of corporate expenditures is of the same dimension as that to hear other forms of expression. * * * Even the complete curtailment of corporate communications concerning political or ideological questions not integral to day-to-day business functions would leave individuals, including corporate shareholders, employees, and customers, free to communicate their thoughts. Moreover, it is unlikely that any significant communication would be lost by such a prohibition. These individuals would remain perfectly free to communicate any ideas which could be conveyed by means of the corporate form. Indeed, such individuals could even form associations for the very purpose of promoting political or ideological causes.

The governmental interest in regulating corporate political communications, especially those relating to electoral matters, also raises considerations which differ significantly from those governing the regulation of individual speech. Corporations are artificial entities created by law for the purpose of furthering certain economic goals. In order to facilitate the achievement of such ends, special rules relating to such matters as limited liability, perpetual life, and the accumulation, distribution, and taxation of assets are normally applied to them. States have provided corporations with such attributes in order to increase their economic viability and thus strengthen the economy generally. It has long been recognized, however, that the special status of corporations has placed them in a position to control vast amounts of economic power which may, if not regulated, dominate not only the economy but also the very heart of our democracy, the electoral process. Although *Buckley v. Valeo*, 424 U.S. 1 (1976), provides support for the position that the desire to equalize the financial resources available to candidates does not justify the limitation upon the expression of support which a restriction upon individual contributions entails, the interest of Massachusetts and the many other States which have restricted corporate political activity is quite different. It is not one of equalizing the resources of opposing candidates or opposing positions, but rather of preventing institutions which have been permitted to amass wealth as a result of special advantages extended by the State for certain economic purposes from using that wealth to acquire an unfair advantage in the political process, especially where, as here, the issue involved has no material connection with the business of the corporation. The State need not permit its own creation to consume it. Massachusetts could permissibly conclude that not to impose limits upon the political activities of corporations would have placed it in a position of departing from neutrality and indirectly assisting the propagation of corporate views because of the advantages its laws give to the corporate acquisition of funds to finance such activities. Such expenditures may be viewed as seriously threatening the role of the First Amendment as a guarantor of a free marketplace of ideas. Ordinarily, the expenditure of funds to promote political causes may be assumed to bear some relation to the fervency with which they are held. Corporate political expression, however, is not only divorced from the convictions of individual corporate shareholders, but also, because of the ease with which corporations are permitted to accumulate capital, bears no relation to the conviction with which the ideas expressed are held by the communicator.

This Nation has for many years recognized the need for measures designed to prevent corporate domination of the political process. The Corrupt Practices Act, first enacted in 1907, has consistently barred corporate contributions in connection with federal elections. This Court has repeatedly recognized that one of the principal purposes of this prohibition is "to avoid the deleterious influences on federal elections resulting from the use of money by those who exercise control over large aggregations of capital." *United States v. Automobile Workers*, 352 U.S. 567, 585 (1957). * * *

## II

There is an additional overriding interest related to the prevention of corporate domination which is substantially advanced by Massachusetts' restrictions upon corporate contributions: assuring that shareholders are not compelled to support and financially further beliefs with which they disagree where, as is the case here, the issue involved does not materially affect the business, property, or other affairs of the corporation. The State has not interfered with the prerogatives of corporate management to communicate about matters that have material impact on the business affairs entrusted to them, however much individual stockholders may disagree on economic or ideological grounds. Nor has the State forbidden management from formulating and circulating its views at its own expense or at the expense of others, even where the subject at issue is irrelevant to corporate business affairs. But Massachusetts has chosen to forbid corporate management from spending corporate funds in referenda elections absent some demonstrable effect of the issue on the economic life of the company. In short, corporate management may not use corporate monies to promote what does not further corporate affairs but what in the last analysis are the purely personal views of the management, individually or as a group.

* * *

The Court assumes that the interest in preventing the use of corporate resources in furtherance of views which are irrelevant to the corporate business and with which some shareholders may disagree is a compelling one, but concludes that the Massachusetts statute is nevertheless invalid because the State has failed to adopt the means best suited, in its opinion, for achieving this end. It proposes that the aggrieved shareholder assert his interest in preventing the expenditure of funds for nonbusiness causes he finds unconscionable through the channels provided by "corporate democracy" and purports to be mystified as to "why the dissenting shareholder's wishes are entitled to such greater solicitude in this context than in many others where equally important and controversial corporate decisions are made by management or by a predetermined percentage of the shareholders." *Ante*, at 794, and n. 34. It should be obvious that the alternative means upon the adequacy of which the majority is willing to predicate a constitutional adjudication is [not] able to satisfy the State's interest * * *.

* * *

There is no apparent way of segregating one shareholder's ownership interest in a corporation from another's. It is no answer to respond, as the Court does, that the dissenting "shareholder is free to withdraw his investment at any time and for any reason." Ante, at 794 n. 34. * * * Clearly the State has a strong interest in assuring that its citizens are not forced to choose between supporting the propagation of views with which they disagree and passing up investment opportunities.

Finally, even if corporations developed an effective mechanism for rebating to shareholders that portion of their investment used to finance political activities with which they disagreed, a State may still choose to restrict corporate political activity irrelevant to business functions on the grounds that many investors would be deterred from investing in corporations because of a wish not to associate with corporations propagating certain views. The State has an interest not only in enabling individuals to exercise freedom of conscience without penalty but also in eliminating the danger that investment decisions will be significantly influenced by the ideological views of corporations. While the latter concern may not be of the same constitutional magnitude as the former, it is far from trivial. Corporations, as previously noted, are created by the State as a means of furthering the public welfare. One of their functions is to determine, by their success in obtaining funds, the uses to which society's resources are to be put. A State may legitimately conclude that corporations would not serve as economically efficient vehicles for such decisions if the investment preferences of the public were significantly affected by their ideological or political activities. It has long been recognized that such pursuits are not the proper business of corporations. The common law was generally interpreted as prohibiting corporate political participation. * * *

I would affirm the judgment of the Supreme Judicial Court for the Commonwealth of Massachusetts.

Mr. Justice Rehnquist, dissenting.

* * *

The question presented today, whether business corporations have a constitutionally protected liberty to engage in political activities, has never been squarely addressed by any previous decision of this Court. However, the General Court of the Commonwealth of Massachusetts, the Congress of the United States, and the legislatures of 30 other States of this Republic have considered the matter, and have concluded that restrictions upon the political activity of business corporations are both politically desirable and constitutionally permissible. The judgment of such a broad consensus of governmental bodies expressed over a period of many decades is entitled to considerable deference from this Court. * * *

Early in our history, Mr. Chief Justice Marshall described the status of a corporation in the eyes of federal law [in *Dartmouth College v. Woodward*].

The appellants herein either were created by the Commonwealth or were admitted into the Commonwealth only for the limited purposes described in their charters and regulated by state law. Since it cannot be disputed that the mere creation of a corporation does not invest it with all the liberties enjoyed by natural persons, our inquiry must seek to determine which constitutional protections are "incidental to its very existence." *Dartmouth College, supra*, at 636.

There can be little doubt that when a State creates a corporation with the power to acquire and utilize property, it necessarily and implicitly guarantees that the corporation will not be deprived of that property absent due process of law. Likewise, when a State charters a corporation for the purpose of publishing a newspaper, it necessarily assumes that the corporation is entitled to the liberty of the press essential to the conduct of its business. * * *

It cannot be so readily concluded that the right of political expression is equally necessary to carry out the functions of a corporation organized for commercial purposes. A State grants to a business corporation the blessings of potentially perpetual life and limited liability to enhance its efficiency as an economic entity. It might reasonably be concluded that those properties, so beneficial in the economic sphere, pose special dangers in the political sphere. Furthermore, it might be argued that liberties of political expression are not at all necessary to effectuate the purposes for which States permit commercial corporations to exist. So long as the Judicial Branches of the State and Federal Governments remain open to protect the corporation's interest in its property, it has no need, though it may have the desire, to petition the political branches for similar protection. Indeed, the States might reasonably fear that the corporation would use its economic power to obtain further benefits beyond those already bestowed. I would think that any particular form of organization upon which the State confers special privileges or immunities different from those of natural persons would be subject to like regulation, whether the organization is a labor union, a partnership, a trade association, or a corporation. * * *

It is true, as the Court points out, that recent decisions of this Court have emphasized the interest of the public in receiving the information offered by the speaker seeking protection. The free flow of information is in no way diminished by the Commonwealth's decision to permit the operation of business corporations with limited rights of political expression. All natural persons, who owe their existence to a higher sovereign than the Commonwealth, remain as free as before to engage in political activity.

I would affirm the judgment of the Supreme Judicial Court.

# AUSTIN v. MICHIGAN CHAMBER OF COMMERCE

494 U.S. 652, 110 S.Ct. 1391, 108 L.Ed.2d 652 (1990).

[The Michigan Campaign Finance Act, § 54(1), prohibited corporations from using corporate funds for contributions or independent expenditures in support of or in opposition to any candidate in elections for state office. The Michigan State Chamber of Commerce, a nonprofit Michigan corporation with more than 8,000 members, three-quarters of which were for-profit corporations, alleged that the statute unconstitutionally barred it from running an advertisement in support of a candidate in a special election for the Michigan House of Representatives.

The Chamber's status as a non-profit corporation added a complicating element to the case. In *Federal Election Comm'n v. Massachusetts Citizens for Life, Inc.*, 479 U.S. 238 (1986) (MCFL), the Court had held unconstitutional a federal regulation barring independent campaign expenditures by a non-profit membership corporation "formed for the express purpose of promoting political ideas" and supported entirely by individuals. Thus, even if the Court concluded that the Michigan statute was not unconstitutional with regard to business corporations, it had to consider whether the Chamber more closely resembled a business corporation or an advocacy group like MCFL.]

Justice Marshall delivered the opinion of the Court.

## II

To determine whether Michigan's restrictions on corporate political expenditures may constitutionally be applied to the Chamber, we must ascertain whether they burden the exercise of political speech and, if they do, whether they are narrowly tailored to serve a compelling state interest. *Buckley v. Valeo*, 424 U.S. 1, 44–45 (1976) (*per curiam*). Certainly, the use of funds to support a political candidate is "speech"; independent campaign expenditures constitute "political expression 'at the core of our electoral process and of the First Amendment freedoms.' "Id., at 39. The mere fact that the Chamber is a corporation does not remove its speech from the ambit of the First Amendment. See, e.g., *First National Bank of Boston v. Bellotti*, 435 U.S. 765, 777 (1978).

## B

The State contends that the unique legal and economic characteristics of corporations necessitate some regulation of their political expenditures to avoid corruption or the appearance of corruption. State law grants corporations special advantages—such as limited liability, perpetual life, and favorable treatment of the accumulation and distribution of assets—that enhance their ability to attract capital and to deploy their resources in ways that maximize the return on their shareholders' investments. These state-created advantages not only allow corporations to play a dominant role in the nation's economy, but also permit them to use "resources amassed in the economic marketplace" to obtain "an unfair advantage in the political marketplace." *MCFL*, 479 U.S., at 257. As the Court explained in *MCFL*, the political advantage of corporations is unfair because

> "[t]he resources in the treasury of a business corporation * * * are not an indication of popular support for the corporation's political ideas. They reflect instead the economically motivated decisions of investors and customers. The availability of these resources may make a corporation a formidable political presence, even though the power of the corporation may be no reflection of the power of its ideas." *Id.* at 258.

We therefore have recognized that "the compelling governmental interest in preventing corruption support[s] the restriction of the influence of political war chests funneled through the corporate form." *NCPAC*, *supra*, 470 U.S. at 500–501.

The Chamber argues that this concern about corporate domination of the political process is insufficient to justify restrictions on independent expenditures. Although this Court has distinguished these expenditures from direct contributions in the context of federal laws regulating individual donors, *Buckley*, 424 U.S. at 47, it has also recognized that a legislature might demonstrate a danger of real or apparent corruption posed by such expenditures when made by corporations to influence candidate elections, *Bellotti*. * * * Michigan's regulation aims at a different type of corruption in the political arena: the corrosive and distorting effects of immense aggregations of wealth that are accumulated with the help of the corporate form and that have little or no correlation to the public's support for the corporation's political ideas. * * * We emphasize that the mere fact that corporations may accumulate large amounts of wealth is not the justification for § 54; rather, the unique state-conferred corporate structure that facilitates the amassing of large treasuries warrants the limit on independent expenditures. Corporate wealth can unfairly influence elections when it is deployed in the form of independent expenditures, just as it can when it assumes the guise of political contributions. We therefore hold that the State has articulated a sufficiently compelling rationale to support its restriction on independent expenditures by corporations.

[The Court also found that the Act was "precisely targeted to eliminate the distortion caused by corporate spending while also allowing corporations to express their political views" because it permitted corporations to make independent political expenditures through separate segregated funds. The Court reasoned that "persons contributing to such funds understand that their money will be used solely for political purposes, [so] the speech generated accurately reflects contributors' support for the corporation's political views."

The Court also rejected the Chamber's claim that the Campaign Finance Act, even if constitutional with respect to for-profit corporations, could not be applied to a non-profit corporation such as the Chamber. It distinguished the Chamber from MCFL on three grounds.

First, MCFL was formed solely to promote political ideas, while the Chamber had more varied purposes. Second, members of the Chamber were more like shareholders in a corporation than members of MCFL, in that they had incentives to remain involved with the Chamber even if they disagreed with its political positions. Third, "[b]ecause the Chamber accepts money from for-profit corporations, it could * * * serve as a conduit for corporate political spending."]

JUSTICE STEVENS, concurring.

In my opinion the distinction between individual expenditures and individual contributions that the Court identified in *Buckley v. Valeo*, 424 U.S. 1, 45–47 (1976), should have little, if any, weight in reviewing corporate participation in candidate elections. In that context, I believe the danger of either the fact, or the appearance, of quid pro quo relationships provides an adequate justification for state regulation of both expenditures and contributions. Moreover, as we recognized in *First National Bank of Boston v. Bellotti*, 435 U.S. 765 (1978), there is a vast difference between lobbying and debating public issues on the one hand, and political campaigns for election to public office on the other. Accordingly, I join the Court's opinion and judgment.

JUSTICE SCALIA, dissenting.

"Attention all citizens. To assure the fairness of elections by preventing disproportionate expression of the views of any single powerful group, your Government has decided that the following associations of persons shall be prohibited from speaking or writing in support of any candidate: _____" In permitting Michigan to make private corporations the first object of this Orwellian announcement, the Court today endorses the principle that too much speech is an evil that the democratic majority can proscribe. I dissent because that principle is contrary to our case law and incompatible with the absolutely central truth of the First Amendment: that government cannot be trusted to assure, through censorship, the "fairness" of political debate.

## I

### A

The Court's opinion says that political speech of corporations can be regulated because "[s]tate law grants [them] special advantages," and because this "unique state-conferred corporate structure * * * facilitates the amassing of large treasuries." This analysis seeks to create one good argument by combining two bad ones. Those individuals who form that type of voluntary association known as a corporation are, to be sure, given special advantages—notably, the immunization of their personal fortunes from liability for the actions of the association—that the State is under no obligation to confer. But so are other associations and private individuals given all sorts of special advantages that the State need not confer, ranging from tax breaks to contract awards to public employment to outright cash subsidies. It is rudimentary that the State cannot exact as the price of those special advantages the forfeiture of

First Amendment rights. The categorical suspension of the right of any person, or of any association of persons, to speak out on political matters must be justified by a compelling state need. See *Buckley v. Valeo*, 424 U.S. 1, 44–45 (1976). Which is why the Court puts forward its second bad argument, the fact that corporations "amas[s] large treasuries." But that alone is also not sufficient justification for the suppression of political speech, unless one thinks it would be lawful to prohibit men and women whose net worth is above a certain figure from endorsing political candidates. Neither of these two flawed arguments is improved by combining them and saying, as the Court in effect does, that "since the State gives special advantages to these voluntary associations, and since they thereby amass vast wealth, they may be required to abandon their right of political speech."

As for the second part of the Court's argumentation, the fact that corporations (or at least some of them) possess "massive wealth": Certain uses of "massive wealth" in the electoral process—whether or not the wealth is the result of "special advantages" conferred by the State—pose a substantial risk of corruption which constitutes a compelling need for the regulation of speech. Such a risk plainly exists when the wealth is given directly to the political candidate, to be used under his direction and control. We held in *Buckley v. Valeo*, supra, however, that independent expenditures to express the political views of individuals and associations do not raise a sufficient threat of corruption to justify prohibition. * * *

*Buckley v. Valeo* should not be overruled, because it is entirely correct. The contention that prohibiting overt advocacy for or against a political candidate satisfies a "compelling need" to avoid "corruption" is easily dismissed. * * * I expect I could count on the fingers of one hand the candidates who would generally welcome, much less negotiate for, a formal endorsement by AT & T or General Motors. The advocacy of such entities that have "amassed great wealth" will be effective only to the extent that it brings to the people's attention ideas which—despite the invariably self-interested and probably uncongenial source—strike them as true.

The Court does not try to defend the proposition that independent advocacy poses a substantial risk of political "corruption," as English-speakers understand that term. * * * "Michigan's regulation," we are told, "aims at a different type of corruption in the political arena: the corrosive and distorting effects of immense aggregations of wealth that are accumulated with the help of the corporate form and that have little or no correlation to the public's support for the corporations's political ideas." Under this mode of analysis, virtually anything the Court deems politically undesirable can be turned into political corruption—by simply describing its effects as politically "corrosive," which is close enough to "corruptive" to qualify. It is sad to think that the First Amendment will ultimately be brought down not by brute force but by poetic metaphor.

\* \* \* But it can be said that I have not accurately quoted today's decision. It does not endorse the proposition that government may ensure that expenditures "reflect actual public support for the political ideas espoused," but only the more limited proposition that government may ensure that expenditures "reflect actual public support for the political ideas espoused *by corporations*." Ante, at 1397 (emphasis added). The limitation is of course entirely irrational. Why is it perfectly all right if advocacy by an individual billionaire is out of proportion with "actual public support" for his positions? There is no explanation, except the effort I described at the outset of this discussion to make one valid proposition out of two invalid ones: When the vessel labeled "corruption" begins to founder under weight too great to be logically sustained, the argumentation jumps to the good ship "special privilege"; and when that in turn begins to go down, it returns to "corruption." Thus hopping back and forth between the two, the argumentation may survive but makes no headway towards port, where its conclusion waits in vain.

### B

But even if the object of the prohibition could plausibly be portrayed as the protection of shareholders ( [which Justice Brennan argued in a concurring opinion], but which the Court's opinion, at least, does not even assert), that would not suffice as a "compelling need" to support this blatant restriction upon core political speech. A person becomes a member of that form of association known as a for-profit corporation in order to pursue economic objectives, i.e., to make money. Some corporate charters may specify the line of commerce to which the company is limited, but even that can be amended by shareholder vote. Thus, in joining such an association, the shareholder knows that management may take any action that is ultimately in accord with what the majority (or a specified supermajority) of the shareholders wishes, so long as that action is designed to make a profit. That is the deal. The corporate actions to which the shareholder exposes himself, therefore, include many things that he may find politically or ideologically uncongenial: investment in South Africa, operation of an abortion clinic, publication of a pornographic magazine, or even publication of a newspaper that adopts absurd political views and makes catastrophic political endorsements. His only protections against such assaults upon his ideological commitments are (1) his ability to persuade a majority (or the requisite minority) of his fellow shareholders that the action should not be taken, and ultimately (2) his ability to sell his stock. \* \* \* It seems to me entirely fanciful, in other words, to suggest that the Michigan statute makes any significant contribution towards insulating the exclusively profit-motivated shareholder from the rude world of politics and ideology.

\* \* \*

### II

\* \* \*

Despite all the talk about "corruption and the appearance of corruption"—evils that are not significantly implicated and that can be avoided in many other ways—it is entirely obvious that the object of the law we have approved today is not to prevent wrongdoing but to prevent speech. Since those private associations known as corporations have so much money, they will speak so much more, and their views will be given inordinate prominence in election campaigns. This is not an argument that our democratic traditions allow—neither with respect to individuals associated in corporations nor with respect to other categories of individuals whose speech may be "unduly" extensive (because they are rich) or "unduly" persuasive (because they are movie stars) or "unduly" respected (because they are clergymen). The premise of our system is that there is no such thing as too much speech—that the people are not foolish but intelligent, and will separate the wheat from the chaff. As conceded in Lincoln's aphorism about fooling "all of the people some of the time," that premise will not invariably accord with reality; but it will assuredly do so much more frequently than the premise the Court today embraces: that a healthy democratic system can survive the legislative power to prescribe how much political speech is too much, who may speak and who may not.

\* \* \*

Because today's decision is inconsistent with unrepudiated legal judgments of our Court, but even more because it is incompatible with the unrepealable political wisdom of our First Amendment, I dissent.

JUSTICE KENNEDY, with whom JUSTICE O'CONNOR and JUSTICE SCALIA join, dissenting.

II

\* \* \*

A

Our cases acknowledge the danger that corruption poses for the electoral process, but draw a line in permissible regulation between payments to candidates ("contributions") and payments or expenditures to express one's own views ("independent expenditures"). Today's decision abandons this distinction and threatens once protected political speech. \* \* \*

The majority almost admits that, in the case of independent expenditures, the danger of a political quid pro quo is insufficient to justify a restriction of this kind. Since the specter of corruption, which had been "the only legitimate and compelling government interest[s] thus far identified for restricting campaign finances," *NCPAC*, supra, at 496–497, is missing in this case, the majority invents a new interest: combatting the "corrosive and distorting effects of immense aggregations of wealth," ante at 1397, accumulated in corporate form without shareholder or public support. The majority styles this novel interest as simply a different kind of corruption, but has no support for its assertion. \* \* \*

A similar argument to that made by the majority was rejected in *Bellotti*. There, we rejected the assumption that "corporations are wealthy and powerful and their views may drown out other points of view" or "exert an undue influence" on the electorate in the absence of a showing that the relative voice of corporations was significant. 435 U.S. at 789. * * *

The speech suppressed in this case was directed to political qualifications. The fact that it was spoken by the Michigan Chamber of Commerce, and not a man or woman standing on a soapbox, detracts not a scintilla from its validity, its persuasiveness, or its contribution to the political dialogue.

### B

The majority relies on the state interest in protecting members from the use of nonprofit corporate funds to support candidates whom they may oppose. We should reject this interest as insufficient to save the Act here, just as we rejected the argument in *Bellotti*, 435 U.S. at 792–793.

The Court takes refuge in the argument that some members or contributors to nonprofit corporations may find their own views distorted by the organization * * *. One need not become a member of the Michigan Chamber of Commerce or the Sierra Club in order to earn a living. To the extent that members disagree with a nonprofit corporation's policies, they can seek change from within, withhold financial support, cease to associate with the group, or form a rival group of their own. Allowing government to use the excuse of protecting shareholder rights to stifle the speech of private, voluntary organizations undermines the First Amendment.

\* \* \*

### IV

The Court's hostility to the corporate form used by the speaker in this case and its assertion that corporate wealth is the evil to be regulated is far too imprecise to justify the most severe restriction on political speech ever sanctioned by this Court. * * *

By constructing a rationale for the jurisprudence of this Court that prevents distinguished organizations in public affairs from announcing that a candidate is qualified or not qualified for public office, the Court imposes its own model of speech, one far removed from economic and political reality. It is an unhappy paradox that this Court, which has the role of protecting speech and of barring censorship from all aspects of political life, now becomes itself the censor. In the course of doing so, the Court reveals a lack of concern for speech rights that have the full protection of the First Amendment. I would affirm the judgment.

### Note: Bellotti and Austin

1. It is hard to dispute the *Austin* dissenters' claims that the Court's opinion cannot be reconciled with *Bellotti*. In fact, the Court

made no real effort to do so. Perhaps that is because the six-member majority in *Austin* included the four dissenters in *Bellotti*. A lawyer charged with interpreting the Court's opinions in these two cases must decide what weight, if any, to give to this fact.

2.   In *Bellotti* and *Austin*, different Justices describe the nature of the corporation in different terms. How do their characterizations differ? Which characterization seems to be the most accurate? Why do the Justices care? Do certain characteristics make corporations unique? How, if at all, should those characteristics affect the permissible limits on state regulation of corporate speech?

3.   Jill Fisch suggests that the *Austin* Court's concerns about corporations' political influence derive largely from concerns about the separation of ownership and control in public corporations. She argues that the limitations on political speech that *Austin* upholds cannot be reconciled with traditional First Amendment values. A better policy, she suggests, would be to make managers more accountable to shareholders for political expenditures. Jill E. Fisch, *Frankenstein's Monster Hits the Campaign Trail: An Approach to Regulation of Corporate Political Expenditures*, 32 WM. & MARY L.REV. 587 (1991). Meir Dan–Cohen, by contrast, suggests that individual speech is valued for its expressive content, but that "a corporation's right to free speech * * * is derivative of and parasitic to the listener's interests." Regulation of corporate speech thus may be justified because large corporations' disproportionate input might lead to "congestion that would otherwise be detrimental to listeners' interests." Meir Dan–Cohen, *Freedoms of Collective Speech: A Theory of Protected Communications by Organizations, Communities, and the State*, 79 CAL. L.REV. 1229 (1991).

## C.   REGULATING CORPORATIONS' INTERNAL AFFAIRS

### PROBLEM
### REGULATING CORPORATE LOBBYING—PART II

Senator Bruin has reconsidered her proposed legislation because of concerns that a court might find it unconstitutional and criticism about the restrictions that it would impose on small, closely-held corporations. She would prefer to restrict lobbying only by large, publicly-held corporations and to do so indirectly. Accordingly, she proposes to amend the Columbia Business Corporation Law to allow any shareholder to recover from the directors of a Columbia corporation in a derivative suit "any corporate funds or other resources used, directly or indirectly, to communicate, other than in a public hearing, directly with any member or employee of the Legislature of Columbia to secure or defeat the passage of any pending or proposed legislation by said legislature, unless such use of corporate funds has been expressly authorized, after full disclosure of the position the corporation intends to advance, by a vote of the holders of 80 percent of said corporation's voting stock."

Sen. Bruin has asked for your opinion as to whether this revised legislation:

1. Is likely to limit effectively large corporations' influence on the Columbia Legislature?

2. Violates the Commerce Clause of the U.S. Constitution?

3. Raises serious First Amendment issues?

In thinking about these questions, consider how the proposed legislation differs from the legislation Sen. Bruin originally proposed and whether the courts are likely to attach significance to those differences.

———

In *Dartmouth College, supra,* the Court held that a state could not unilaterally amend the provisions of a corporate charter it had granted. Justice Story, concurring, suggested that states could avoid this problem by granting charters subject to a reserved right to amend them. 17 U.S. at 712. States seized upon this suggestion and began to include in all corporate charters a clause reserving the state's power to amend or repeal any authority granted to the corporation. When general corporation laws came into vogue, states added similar reserved powers clauses to their constitutions, their general corporation laws, or both. Currently, all states reserve the power to amend the corporate charters they issue.

When states attempt to regulate foreign corporations (i.e., corporations chartered by other states), the situation becomes a bit more complex. Several provisions of the U.S. Constitution are relevant, but the obligations they impose have not all been defined precisely. A state may not impair obligations under a contract made in a sister state. (Art. I, § 10.) A state must give full faith and credit to the laws and judicial proceedings of a sister state. (Art. IV, § 1.) Under the Fourteenth Amendment, as noted previously, a state must provide all corporations with equal protection of the law and due process of law. A widely-observed conflict of laws principle, the "internal affairs doctrine," captures the principal operative thrust of these obligations: the law of the state in which a corporation is incorporated controls disputes among participants in that corporation, such as disputes between shareholders and directors and disputes between shareholder groups. *See* RESTATEMENT (SECOND) OF CONFLICT OF LAWS §§ 296–310 (1971); Ralph K. Winter, Jr., *State Law, Shareholder Protection, and the Theory of the Corporation*, 6 J. LEGAL STUDIES 251, 252 (1977). See Chapter 7 for a more detailed discussion of the doctrine, which has profound consequences for the remainder of the materials in the book.

Two other Constitutional provisions frequently implicated by state efforts to regulate corporations are the supremacy clause (Art. VI), which nullifies state constitutions and laws that conflict with the U.S. Constitution or federal law, and the commerce clause (Art. I, § 8), which limits a state's power to regulate transactions that involve interstate commerce. Whether state antitakeover laws conflict with these Constitutional provisions has been the focus of much recent litigation.

### Introduction to CTS Corp. v. Dynamics Corp. of America

Responding to the takeover wave of the late 1970s and 1980s, a number of states adopted laws designed to protect local corporations from uninvited takeover bids.* During the 1980s, the Supreme Court passed on claims that two state antitakeover laws violated the Supremacy Clause and the Commerce Clause of the U.S. Constitution.

The Supremacy Clause claims were based on the Williams Act, a measure Congress adopted in 1968 to regulate tender offers. Pub. L. No. 90–439, 82 Stat. 454 (1968), codified at 15 U.S.C. §§ 78m(d)-(e), 78n(d)-(f) (1991), §§ 13(d)-(e), 14(d)-(f) of the Securities Exchange Act of 1934. The Act was intended to ensure that when a public company becomes the target of a tender offer, its shareholders will receive adequate information about the bid and have sufficient time to evaluate that information. Although the Act imposed some burdens on bidders, Congress attempted to limit those burdens and to take "extreme care to avoid tipping the scales in favor of management or in favor of the person making the takeover bid." 113 Cong. Rec. 24664 (1967) (remarks of Sen. Williams).

*Edgar v. MITE Corp.*, 457 U.S. 624, 102 S.Ct. 2629, 73 L.Ed.2d 269 (1982), involved an Illinois law regulating tender offers for any corporation 10 percent or more of whose shares were owned by Illinois residents, if the corporation also was organized under Illinois law, had its principal office in Illinois, *or* had 10 percent of its assets in Illinois. MITE made a takeover bid for Chicago Rivet, which satisfied all three conditions.

The law required MITE to give Chicago Rivet and the Illinois Secretary of State 20 days advance notice of its bid. During that period, MITE would be barred from communicating with Chicago Rivet's shareholders. In addition, the Secretary of State could schedule a hearing on the fairness of MITE's offer, establish a timetable for that hearing, and hold MITE's offer in abeyance until the hearing was completed. If the Secretary then concluded the offer was unfair, she could block MITE from proceeding with its offer. Rather than comply with the law; MITE sued to have it declared unconstitutional.

The six Justices that considered the merits (three Justices opined only that the case was moot) all voted to hold the Illinois law unconstitutional on one or more grounds. Three concluded that the law was preempted because it conflicted with the Williams Act's "policy of neutrality;" four concluded the Illinois law violated the Commerce

---

* An uninvited takeover bid frequently involves an offer (called a *"tender offer"*), made directly to a corporation's shareholders, to purchase all or a large portion of that corporation's stock. If a person seeks to gain control of a corporation against the opposition of the target company's management, a tender offer often is attractive because the offer can succeed if a sufficient number of shareholders accept and tender their stock at the offered price. (See Chapter 22 for a discussion of other aspects of the law relating to takeover bids.)

Clause because it directly regulated interstate commerce; and five concluded the law violated the Commerce Clause because the burdens it imposed on interstate commerce were excessive in comparison to the local benefits the law produced. The Court rejected Illinois's claim that the internal affairs doctrine protected the law from constitutional attack, noting that the law was not limited to Illinois corporations but also covered foreign corporations that had the requisite proportion of Illinois shareholders and either their principal office or 10 percent of their assets in Illinois.

In an effort to avoid the impact of *MITE*, several states enacted "second generation" antitakeover laws that purported to regulate the internal affairs of corporations incorporated in that state. Indiana's statute, the Indiana Control Share Acquisitions law (ICSA), was the first to be challenged. ICSA differed from the Illinois law involved in *MITE* in that it amended to the Indiana Business Corporation Law and applied only to Indiana corporations.* ICSA provided that any person who acquired sufficient stock to pass one of three thresholds—set at 20, 33–1/3 and 50 percent of the stock of a corporation to which the Act applied and defined as "control shares"—would not be entitled to vote that stock unless a majority of that corporation's disinterested shareholders voted to approve the acquisition. An acquiror could ensure the shareholder vote would take place within 50 days by filing certain information, requesting a shareholder meeting, and agreeing to pay the meeting expenses.

ICSA thus effectively extended to 50 days the time a target company's managers had to defeat a hostile bid, since no potential acquiror would purchase stock in a target company unless it was sure it would be able to vote that stock. Thus the statute represented a substantial extension of the 20 business day period that the Williams Act allowed. But ICSA also made it easier for a target company's shareholders to protect themselves against certain tactics that might coerce them into accepting a bid that they preferred to reject.

Dynamics, the owner of 9.6 percent of CTS, an Indiana corporation covered by ICSA, announced a tender offer for sufficient shares to increase its ownership interest to 27.5 percent, thus potentially triggering ICSA. Dynamics simultaneously sued to enjoin enforcement of ICSA, claiming it was preempted by the Williams Act and violated the Commerce Clause. The Seventh Circuit, relying on *MITE*, agreed that ICSA was unconstitutional on both grounds. *See Dynamics Corp. of America v. CTS Corp.*, 794 F.2d 250 (7th Cir.1986).

## CTS CORP. v. DYNAMICS CORP. OF AMERICA
481 U.S. 69, 107 S.Ct. 1637 95 L.Ed.2d 67 (1987).

JUSTICE POWELL delivered the opinion of the Court.

[The Supreme Court first reversed the Seventh Circuit's holding that ICSA was preempted. The Court noted that it was not bound by

---

* As an attempt to regulate only the internal affairs of Indiana corporations, ICSA was further limited to corporations that had: (1) at least 100 shareholders; (2) at least 10% of their stock owned by Indiana residents; and (3) their principal place of business or substantial assets in Indiana.

*MITE*'s plurality holding that the Williams Act implicitly preempts state laws that conflict with a "policy of neutrality," but observed that the Indiana law "passes muster even under the broad interpretation of the Williams Act articulated * * * in *MITE*." 481 U.S. at 81. The Court then stated: (1) ICSA did not necessarily impose any delay on tender offers or preclude an offeror from purchasing shares as soon as the Williams Act permits; (2) even if ICSA did impose some delay, the delay was not unreasonable; and (3) "[t]he longstanding prevalence of state regulation in this area suggests that, if Congress intended to preempt all state laws that delay the acquisition of voting control following a tender offer, it would have said so explicitly." *Id.* at 86. It is unclear which of these statements represents the Court's holding and which are *dicta*.]

### III

As an alternative basis for its decision, the Court of Appeals held that the Act violates the Commerce Clause of the Federal Constitution. We now address this holding. On its face, the Commerce Clause is nothing more than a grant to Congress of the power "[t]o regulate Commerce * * * among the several States * * *," Art. I, § 8, cl. 3. But it has been settled for more than a century that the Clause prohibits States from taking certain actions respecting interstate commerce even absent congressional action. The Court's interpretation of "these great silences of the Constitution," *H.P. Hood & Sons, Inc. v. Du Mond*, 336 U.S. 525, 535, 69 S.Ct. 657, 663, 93 L.Ed. 865 (1949), has not always been easy to follow. Rather, as the volume and complexity of commerce and regulation have grown in this country, the Court has articulated a variety of tests in an attempt to describe the difference between those regulations that the Commerce Clause permits and those regulations that it prohibits.

### A

The principal objects of dormant Commerce Clause scrutiny are statutes that discriminate against interstate commerce. The Indiana Act is not such a statute. It has the same effects on tender offers whether or not the offeror is a domiciliary or resident of Indiana. Thus, it "visits its effects equally upon both interstate and local business," *Lewis v. BT Investment Managers, Inc.*, [447 U.S. 27, 36, 100 S.Ct. 2009, 2015–2016, 64 L.Ed.2d 702 (1980)].

Dynamics nevertheless contends that the statute is discriminatory because it will apply most often to out-of-state entities. This argument rests on the contention that, as a practical matter, most hostile tender offers are launched by offerors outside Indiana. But this argument avails Dynamics little. "The fact that the burden of a state regulation falls on some interstate companies does not, by itself, establish a claim of discrimination against interstate commerce." *Exxon Corp. v. Governor of*

*Maryland*, 437 U.S. 117, 126, 98 S.Ct. 2207, 2214, 57 L.Ed.2d 91 (1978). Because nothing in the Indiana Act imposes a greater burden on out-of-state offerors than it does on similarly situated Indiana offerors, we reject the contention that the Act discriminates against interstate commerce.

### B

This Court's recent Commerce Clause cases also have invalidated statutes that may adversely affect interstate commerce by subjecting activities to inconsistent regulations. The Indiana Act poses no such problem. So long as each State regulates voting rights only in the corporations it has created, each corporation will be subject to the law of only one State. No principle of corporation law and practice is more firmly established than a State's authority to regulate domestic corporations, including the authority to define the voting rights of shareholders. See RESTATEMENT (SECOND) OF CONFLICT OF LAWS § 304 (1971) (concluding that the law of the incorporating State generally should "determine the right of a shareholder to participate in the administration of the affairs of the corporation"). Accordingly, we conclude that the Indiana Act does not create an impermissible risk of inconsistent regulation by different States.

### C

The Court of Appeals did not find the Act unconstitutional for either of these threshold reasons. Rather, its decision rested on its view of the Act's potential to hinder tender offers. We think the Court of Appeals failed to appreciate the significance for Commerce Clause analysis of the fact that state regulation of corporate governance is regulation of entities whose very existence and attributes are a product of state law. * * * See *First National Bank of Boston v. Bellotti*, 435 U.S. 765, 822–824, 98 S.Ct. 1407, 1439–1441 (1978) (Rehnquist, J., dissenting). Every State in this country has enacted laws regulating corporate governance. By prohibiting certain transactions, and regulating others, such laws necessarily affect certain aspects of interstate commerce. This necessarily is true with respect to corporations with shareholders in States other than the State of incorporation. Large corporations that are listed on national exchanges, or even regional exchanges, will have shareholders in many States and shares that are traded frequently. The markets that facilitate this national and international participation in ownership of corporations are essential for providing capital not only for new enterprises but also for established companies that need to expand their businesses. This beneficial free market system depends at its core upon the fact that a corporation—except in the rarest situations—is organized under, and governed by, the law of a single jurisdiction, traditionally the corporate law of the State of its incorporation.

These regulatory laws may affect directly a variety of corporate transactions. Mergers are a typical example. In view of the substantial effect that a merger may have on the shareholders' interests in a corporation, many States require supermajority votes to approve mergers. See, e.g., 2 MBCA § 73 (requiring approval of a merger by a majority of all shares, rather than simply a majority of votes cast); RMBCA § 11.03 (same). By requiring a greater vote for mergers than is required for other transactions, these laws make it more difficult for corporations to merge. State laws also may provide for "dissenters' rights" under which minority shareholders who disagree with corporate decisions to take particular actions are entitled to sell their shares to the corporation at fair market value. See, e.g., 2 MBCA §§ 80, 81; RMBCA § 13.02. By requiring the corporation to purchase the shares of dissenting shareholders, these laws may inhibit a corporation from engaging in the specified transactions.[12]

It thus is an accepted part of the business landscape in this country for States to create corporations, to prescribe their powers, and to define the rights that are acquired by purchasing their shares. A State has an interest in promoting stable relationships among parties involved in the corporations it charters, as well as in ensuring that investors in such corporations have an effective voice in corporate affairs.

There can be no doubt that the Act reflects these concerns. The primary purpose of the Act is to protect the shareholders of Indiana corporations. It does this by affording shareholders, when a takeover offer is made, an opportunity to decide collectively whether the resulting change in voting control of the corporation, as they perceive it, would be desirable. A change of management may have important effects on the shareholders' interests; it is well within the State's role as overseer of corporate governance to offer this opportunity. The autonomy provided by allowing shareholders collectively to determine whether the takeover is advantageous to their interests may be especially beneficial where a hostile tender offer may coerce shareholders into tendering their shares.

Appellee Dynamics responds to this concern by arguing that the prospect of coercive tender offers is illusory, and that tender offers generally should be favored because they reallocate corporate assets into the hands of management who can use them most effectively. As indicated [in our discussion of Dynamics' preemption claim,] Indiana's concern with tender offers is not groundless. Indeed, the potentially coercive aspects of tender offers have been recognized by the SEC, and by a number of scholarly commentators. The Constitution does not

---

**12.** Numerous other common regulations may affect both nonresident and resident shareholders of a corporation. Specified votes may be required for the sale of all of the corporation's assets. See 2 MBCA § 79; RMBCA § 12.02. The election of directors may be staggered over a period of years to prevent abrupt changes in management. See 1 MBCA § 37; RMBCA § 8.06. Various classes of stock may be created with differences in voting rights as to dividends and on liquidation. See 1 MBCA § 15; RMBCA § 6.01(c). Provisions may be made for cumulative voting. See 1 MBCA § 33, ¶ 4; RMBCA § 7.28. Corporations may adopt restrictions on payment of dividends to ensure that specified ratios of assets to liabilities are maintained for the benefit of the holders of corporate bonds or notes. See 1 MBCA § 45 (noting that a corporation's articles of incorporation can restrict payment of dividends); RMBCA § 6.40 (same). Where the shares of a corporation are held in States other than that of incorporation, actions taken pursuant to these and similar provisions of state law will affect all shareholders alike wherever they reside or are domiciled. * * *

require the States to subscribe to any particular economic theory. We are not inclined "to second-guess the empirical judgments of lawmakers concerning the utility of legislation," *Kassel v. Consolidated Freightways Corp.*, 450 U.S., at 679, 101 S.Ct., at 1321 (Brennan, J., concurring in judgment). In our view, the possibility of coercion in some takeover bids offers additional justification for Indiana's decision to promote the autonomy of independent shareholders.

Dynamics argues in any event that the State has " 'no legitimate interest in protecting the nonresident shareholders.' "Dynamics relies heavily on the statement by the *MITE* Court that "[i]nsofar as the * * * law burdens out-of-state transactions, there is nothing to be weighed in the balance to sustain the law." 457 U.S. at 644, 102 S.Ct. at 2641. But that comment was made in reference to an Illinois law that applied as well to out-of-state corporations as to in-state corporations. We agree that Indiana has no interest in protecting nonresident shareholders of *nonresident corporations*. But this Act applies only to corporations incorporated in Indiana. We reject the contention that Indiana has no interest in providing for the shareholders of its corporations the voting autonomy granted by the Act. Indiana has a substantial interest in preventing the corporate form from becoming a shield for unfair business dealing. * * *

### D

Dynamics' argument that the Act is unconstitutional ultimately rests on its contention that the Act will limit the number of successful tender offers. There is little evidence that this will occur. But even if true, this result would not substantially affect our Commerce Clause analysis. We reiterate that this Act does not prohibit any entity—resident or nonresident—from offering to purchase, or from purchasing, shares in Indiana corporations, or from attempting thereby to gain control. It only provides regulatory procedures designed for the better protection of the corporations' shareholders. We have rejected the "notion that the Commerce Clause protects the particular structure or methods of operation in a * * * market." *Exxon Corp. v. Governor of Maryland*, 437 U.S. at 127, 98 S.Ct. at 2215. The very commodity that is traded in the securities market is one whose characteristics are defined by state law. Similarly, the very commodity that is traded in the "market for corporate control"—the corporation—is one that owes its existence and attributes to state law. Indiana need not define these commodities as other States do; it need only provide that residents and nonresidents have equal access to them. This Indiana has done. Accordingly, even if the Act should decrease the number of successful tender offers for Indiana corporations, this would not offend the Commerce Clause.

### IV

On its face, the Indiana Control Share Acquisitions Chapter evenhandedly determines the voting rights of shares of Indiana corporations. The Act does not conflict with the provisions or purposes of the Williams Act. To the limited extent that the Act affects interstate commerce, this is justified by the State's interests in defining the attributes of shares in its corporations and in protecting shareholders. Congress has never questioned the need for state regulation of these matters. Nor do we think such regulation offends the Constitution. Accordingly, we reverse the judgment of the Court of Appeals.

*It is so ordered.*

————

### Developments Following CTS

Professor Roberta Romano, *The Future of Hostile Takeovers: Legislation and Public Opinion*, 57 U.Cin.L.Rev. 457 (1988), describes the impact of *CTS* as follows:

> Although more than twenty states enacted second generation statutes in the years between the *MITE* and *CTS* decisions, legislators and lobbyists were often reluctant to promote legislation for fear of constitutional infirmities. The most frequently adopted version of a second generation statute was therefore one with limited regulatory scope. After the *CTS* decision, however, the pace and scope of legislation changed: fourteen new statutes were adopted within approximately six months. More important, several of the new statutes strengthened less restrictive second generation statutes by using Indiana as a model, and many test *CTS*'s limits by mandating constraints on bidders that go further than the Indiana statute. * * *

> Perhaps the most important reaction to *CTS* * * * is that Delaware, the leading incorporation state, enacted a [third] generation statute. * * * Part of the impetus for [Delaware's] effort stemmed from the threat of some Delaware corporations to reincorporate in states that had second generation statutes if no bill was forthcoming. Delaware feared, rightly or wrongly, that inaction would hurt its preeminence in the incorporation business.

Courts subsequently relied on *CTS* to uphold Delaware's antitakeover law and all other antitakeover laws framed as regulations of domestic corporations' internal affairs against Commerce Clause and preemption claims. Examples of such laws are control share laws and "business combination" laws, which gave a target company's incumbent directors the right for several years to block certain transactions that an aspiring acquiror was likely to want to consummate. Another example is "constituency statutes," which authorized a target company's directors to resist any takeover bid they believed would affect adversely the interests of constituencies of the corporation other than its shareholders—such as employees, customers, and communities in which the company operated. *See* Elliott J. Weiss, *What Lawyers Do When the Emperor Has No Clothes: Evaluating CTS Corp. v. Dynamics Corp. of America and Its Progeny—Part II*, 79 Geo. L.J. 211, 238–264 (1990).

On the other hand, no third generation law that regulates takeover bids for foreign corporations has survived a challenge based on the

Commerce Clause, even where the law's substantive provisions closely track ICSA. Relying on *CTS*, courts have reasoned that such laws subject corporations to potentially inconsistent state regulation, i.e., between the laws of the state of incorporation and the antitakeover statute. See Weiss, *supra*, at 218–225.

## AMANDA ACQUISITION CORP. v. UNIVERSAL FOODS CORP.

877 F.2d 496 (7th Cir.1989), cert. denied, 493 U.S.
955, 110 S.Ct. 367, 107 L.Ed.2d 353 (1989).

EASTERBROOK, CIRCUIT JUDGE.

* * * Wisconsin has a third-generation takeover statute. Enacted after *CTS*, it postpones the kinds of transactions that often follow tender offers (and often are the reason for making the offers in the first place). Unless the target's board agrees to the transaction in advance, the bidder must wait three years after buying the shares to merge with the target or acquire more than 5% of its assets. We must decide whether this is consistent with the Williams Act and Commerce Clause.

I

[Amanda Acquisition Corp., a shell company formed to acquire Universal Foods Corp., a diversified firm incorporated in Wisconsin and traded on the New York Stock Exchange, made a tender offer for all outstanding shares of Universal and also brought suit claiming the Wisconsin law, Wis. Stat. § 180.726, which covered Universal, was unconstitutional. The court described the Wisconsin law and noted that, "[a]s a practical matter, Wisconsin prohibits any offer contingent on a merger between bidder and target, a condition attached to about 90% of contemporary tender offers."]

II

A

If our views of the wisdom of state law mattered, Wisconsin's takeover statute would not survive. Like our colleagues who decided *MITE* and *CTS*, we believe that antitakeover legislation injures shareholders. Managers frequently realize gains for investors via voluntary combinations (mergers). If gains are to be had, but managers balk, tender offers are investors' way to go over managers' heads. If managers are not maximizing the firm's value—perhaps because they have missed the possibility of a synergistic combination, perhaps because they are clinging to divisions that could be better run in other hands, perhaps because they are just not the best persons for the job—a bidder that believes it can realize more of the firm's value will make investors a higher offer. Investors tender; the bidder gets control and changes things. The prospect of monitoring by would-be bidders, and an occasional bid at a premium, induces managers to run corporations more efficiently and replaces them if they will not.

Premium bids reflect the benefits for investors. * * * Only when the bid exceeds the value of the stock (however investors compute value) will it succeed. A statute that precludes investors from receiving or accepting a premium offer makes them worse off. It makes the economy worse off too, because the higher bid reflects the better use to which the bidder can put the target's assets. (If the bidder can't improve the use of the assets, it injures itself by paying a premium.)

* * *

## B

Skepticism about the wisdom of a state's law does not lead to the conclusion that the law is beyond the state's power, however. We have not been elected custodians of investors' wealth. States need not treat investors' welfare as their *summum bonum*. Perhaps they choose to protect managers' welfare instead, or believe that the current economic literature reaches an incorrect conclusion and that despite appearances takeovers injure investors in the long run. Unless a federal statute or the Constitution bars the way, Wisconsin's choice must be respected.

[The Wisconsin law is not preempted by the Williams Act.]

## C

The Commerce Clause grants Congress the power "[t]o regulate Commerce * * * among the several States". * * *

When state law discriminates against interstate commerce expressly—for example, when Wisconsin closes its border to butter from Minnesota—the negative Commerce Clause steps in. The law before us is not of this type: it is neutral between inter-state and intra-state commerce. Amanda therefore presses on us the broader, all-weather, be-reasonable vision of the Constitution. Wisconsin has passed a law that unreasonably injures investors, most of whom live outside of Wisconsin, and therefore it has to be unconstitutional, as Amanda sees things. * * *

Illinois's law, held invalid in *MITE*, regulated sales of stock elsewhere. Illinois tried to tell a Texas owner of stock in a Delaware corporation that he could not sell to a buyer in California. By contrast, Wisconsin's law, like the Indiana statute sustained by *CTS*, regulates the internal affairs of firms incorporated there. Investors may buy or sell stock as they please. * * *

Buyers of stock in Wisconsin firms may exercise full rights as investors, taking immediate control. No interstate transaction is regulated or forbidden. True, Wisconsin's law makes a potential buyer less willing to buy (or depresses the bid), but this is equally true of Indiana's rule. Many other rules of corporate law—supermajority voting requirements, staggered and classified boards, and so on—have similar or greater effects on some persons' willingness to purchase stock. *CTS*, 481 U.S. at 89–90, 107 S.Ct. at 1649–50. States could ban mergers outright, with even more powerful consequences. Wisconsin did not allow mergers among firms chartered there until 1947. We doubt that it was violating the Commerce Clause all those years. Every rule of corporate law affects investors who live outside the state of incorporation, yet this has never been thought sufficient to authorize a form of cost-benefit inquiry through the medium of the Commerce Clause. * * *

Wisconsin could exceed its powers by subjecting firms to inconsistent regulation. Because § 180.726 applies only to a subset of firms incorporated in Wisconsin, however, there is no possibility of inconsistent regulation. * * * This leaves only the argument that Wisconsin's law hinders the flow of interstate trade "too much". *CTS* dispatched this concern by declaring it inapplicable to laws that apply only to the internal affairs of firms incorporated in the regulating state. States may regulate corporate transactions as they choose without having to demonstrate under an unfocused balancing test that the benefits are "enough" to justify the consequences.

To say that states have the power to enact laws whose costs exceed their benefits is not to say that investors should kiss their wallets goodbye. States compete to offer corporate codes attractive to firms. Managers who want to raise money incorporate their firms in the states that offer the combination of rules investors prefer. Laws that in the short run injure investors and protect managers will in the longer run make the state less attractive to firms that need to raise new capital. If the law is "protectionist", the protected class is the existing body of managers (and other workers), suppliers, and so on, which bears no necessary relation to state boundaries. States regulating the affairs of domestic corporations cannot in the long run injure anyone but themselves. * * *

The long run takes time to arrive, and it is tempting to suppose that courts could contribute to investors' welfare by eliminating laws that impose costs in the short run. The price of such warfare, however, is a reduction in the power of competition among states. Courts seeking to impose "good" rules on the states diminish the differences among corporate codes and dampen competitive forces. Too, courts may fail in their quest. How do judges know which rules are best? Often only the slow forces of competition reveal that information. Early economic studies may mislead, or judges (not trained as social scientists) may misinterpret the available data or act precipitously. Our Constitution allows the states to act as laboratories; slow migration (or national law on the authority of the Commerce Clause) grinds the failures under. No such process weeds out judicial errors, or decisions that, although astute when rendered, have become anachronistic in light of changes in the economy. * * *

* * * A state with the power to forbid mergers has the power to defer them for three years. Investors can turn to firms incorporated in states committed to the dominance of market forces, or they can turn on legislators who enact unwise laws. The Constitution has room for many economic policies. "[A] law can be both economic folly and constitutional." *CTS*, 481 U.S. at 96–97, 107 S.Ct. at 1653–54 (Scalia, J., concur-

ring). Wisconsin's law may well be folly; we are confident that it is constitutional.

### Notes on Amanda Acquisition

1. In arguing that takeovers are beneficial, Judge Easterbrook assumes corporations should operate solely to increase shareholders' wealth. David Millon contends that this assumption, while widely accepted, is not immutable. There is an argument that corporations should operate to advance broader social purposes. Professor Millon notes that this argument has had little impact on the development of corporation law during most of the twentieth century, but suggests that concerns about the social and economic impact of hostile takeovers have reawakened interest in it. See David Millon, *Theories of the Corporation*, 1990 DUKE L.J. 201, 227–28:

> State legislators have responded to these concerns by enacting increasingly bold legislation designed to curb hostile takeovers. Some have suggested that the legislators who pass these laws are acting as toadies to locally influential corporate managers who stand to lose their positions if their companies are taken over. The statutes themselves, however, reveal clearly that they address a quite different set of concerns. For example, a recent amendment to North Carolina's corporate statute refers expressly to a broad range of issues, including lost employment, tax revenues, and community service activities. Similarly, Wisconsin's anti-takeover statute [held constitutional in *Amanda Acquisition*] candidly declares that Wisconsin corporations "encompass, represent and affect, through their ongoing business operations, a variety of constituencies including shareholders, employees, customers, suppliers and local communities and their economies," and the statute states further that it is intended "to promote the welfare of these constituencies" and "should allow for the stable, long-term growth of resident domestic corporations."

2. Judge Easterbrook makes a second controversial claim—that competition among states will promote development of efficient corporation laws. Some commentators who share his assumption that corporations should operate solely to increase shareholders' wealth nonetheless suggest that decisions concerning the state in which a firm should be incorporated (or reincorporated) reflect not market forces but managers' preference for laws that tolerate self-aggrandizing behavior. (These issues are considered at greater length in Chapter 7.) Lucian Bebchuk observes that the proliferation of state antitakeover laws, which clearly have the potential to benefit managers at shareholders' expense, represents strong evidence that, at least with regard to certain issues, competition among the states does not lead to laws that maximize shareholder wealth. See Lucian A. Bebchuk, *Federalism and the Corporation: The Desirable Limits on State Competition in Corporate Law*, 105 HARV. L. REV. 1435, 1467–70 (1992). Judge Easterbrook seems to have accepted Bebchuck's claim insofar as it relates to antitakeover laws. See Frank H.

Easterbrook & Daniel R. Fischel, The Economic Structure of Corporate Law 221–22 (1991). However, he minimizes this failure of competition as an isolated phenomenon. Other commentators suggest that if competition among the states has not produced efficient results with respect to antitakeover laws, there is little reason to believe competition is any more effective with respect to rules defining managers' fiduciary duties.

3.    Professor Bebchuk also points out that to the extent one believes corporation laws should further the interests of persons other than shareholders, competition among states will not produce optimal results. "[S]hareholders, managers and entrepreneurs who seek to maximize shareholder value will ignore [the interests of non-shareholder constituencies] in evaluating corporate law rules. Consequently, if states seek to attract incorporations by offering rules that enhance shareholder value, the offered rules may well differ from the socially desirable ones. In particular, the rules produced by state competition will be systematically less favorable to non-shareholder parties than the socially desirable ones." Bebchuk, *supra*, at 1485.

4.    Since *Amanda Acquisition* dealt with an antitakeover law, the court had no occasion to consider another issue relating to the scope of the internal affairs doctrine. Even if states are free, as *Amanda Acquisition* suggests, to adopt whatever laws they wish regulating economic relationships within domestic corporations, do they have similar freedom to adopt laws that have the effect of restricting activities that otherwise would be protected by the First Amendment if those laws are framed as regulations of corporations' internal affairs?

# Chapter 5

## THE CORPORATION AND SOCIETY

### A. INTRODUCTION

Controversy has ebbed and flowed over the years about the role large corporations play in American society. As we saw in Chapter 4, those corporations represent independent concentrations of economic power and, many would say, social and political power as well. Critics claim large corporations lack "legitimacy"—that their managers function as a sort of economic oligarchy making decisions that significantly affect not only shareholders but employees, consumers, suppliers, and communities, without being accountable to any of them. Edward Mason made this point cogently forty years ago:

> * * * [W]e are all aware that we live not only in a corporate society but a society of large corporations. The management—that is, the control—of these corporations is in the hands, at most, of a few thousand men.* Who selected these men, if not to rule over us, at least to exercise vast authority, and to whom are they responsible? The answer to the first question is quite clearly: they selected themselves. The answer to the second is, at best, nebulous. This, in a nutshell, constitutes the problem of legitimacy.

Edward S. Mason, *Introduction to* THE CORPORATION IN MODERN SOCIETY 5 (Edward S. Mason, ed. 1959).

Some critics have argued that corporations should be more "responsible," that they should take account of all the constituencies their operations affect and even that they should assume responsibility for broader societal problems, such as the quality of inner city life, which they affect only tangentially. Other critics stress the need to assure that managers are "accountable" (whatever that may mean), that shareholders or others be given the authority to monitor managers' performance effectively. Defenders of existing rules, however, argue that corporations should be concerned exclusively with maximizing the profits they can earn within the law, and that market forces, government regulation and

---

* And women? See Chapter 15. [Ed.]

the mechanisms of the corporate governance system do constrain managers' discretion effectively.

This controversy raises two broad classes of questions. First, whose interests should corporations seek to serve, those of their shareholders, or those of society at large? Second, by what mechanisms should managers' discretion be harnessed? Are market forces, government regulation, and the corporate governance system sufficient, or are changes in one or another of these mechanisms necessary or desirable? If so, how should they be made?

In the early 1930s, two leading corporate law scholars, Adolf A. Berle, Jr. and E. Merrick Dodd, debated the role of corporate management and of the corporation. Berle's view was that corporate powers were held in trust "at all times exercisable only for the ratable benefit of all the shareholders * * *." Adolf A. Berle, Jr., *Corporate Powers as Powers in Trust*, 44 HARV.L.REV. 1049 (1931). Dodd's thesis was that the business corporation was properly seen "as an economic institution which has a social service as well as a profit making function." E. Merrick Dodd, *For Whom Are Corporate Managers Trustees?*, 45 HARV. L.REV. 1145, 1148 (1932).

Twenty years later, the New Jersey Supreme Court seemed to vindicate both points of view. In *A.P. Smith Manufacturing Co. v. Barlow*, 13 N.J. 145, 98 A.2d 581 (1953), *appeal dismissed* 346 U.S. 861, 74 S.Ct. 107, 98 L.Ed. 373 (1953), it upheld the validity of a corporate gift to Princeton University. But in reaching this conclusion, the court accepted the company's argument that its gift at least arguably advanced its long-run business interests. As Professor Berle astutely observed, the effect of the decision was to recognize that "[m]odern directors are not limited to running business enterprise for maximum profit, but are in fact and recognized in law as administrators of a community system." Adolf A. Berle, *Foreword to* THE CORPORATION IN MODERN SOCIETY xii (Edward S. Mason, ed. 1959).

In 1954, Professor Berle conceded that Dodd had won the argument, at least for the moment. Adolf A. Berle, Jr., THE 20TH CENTURY CAPITALIST REVOLUTION 169 (1954). However, he did not acknowledge that Dodd had been correct. See THE CORPORATION IN MODERN SOCIETY xii (E. Mason, ed. 1959). See also, A.A. Sommer, Jr., *Whom Should the Corporation Serve? The Berle–Dodd Debate Revisited Sixty Years Later*, 16 DEL. J. CORP. L. 33 (1991); Joseph L. Weiner, *The Berle–Dodd Dialogue on the Concept of the Corporation*, 64 COLUM. L. REV. 1458 (1964).

Professor Dodd's thesis may be viewed as managerialism because it treats corporate managers as professionals whose duties require the exercise of almost statesmanlike responsibility. Professor Berle's view became associated with notions of "corporate democracy," although he never meant to apply literally the political analogy that term suggests. Others, however, have relied on that analogy more strongly. Robert Dahl, a political scientist, described the corporation as a political entity, imposing its will on affected citizens who have no voice in its policies, unless they are stockholders. Professor Dahl's remedy was to provide representation to the affected constituencies of the corporation, perhaps by allowing them to vote or by providing representation on the board of directors for special constituencies. Robert Dahl, AFTER THE REVOLUTION? 115 et seq. (1970). Abram Chayes urged that a "rule of law" be applied to corporations that would allow all constituencies affected by corporate activities to participate in the election of corporate directors. Abram Chayes, *The Modern Corporation and the Rule of Law, in* THE CORPORATION IN MODERN SOCIETY 25 (Edward S. Mason, ed. 1959). Of course, the members of these other constituencies might be considerably less concerned than a corporation's shareholders with the long-term profitability of the corporation's operations.

In the 1960s and 1970s, attention shifted to "externalities" generated by corporate activities, such as environmental pollution and workplace hazards, which market forces did not control effectively and which, at least early in that period, government did little to regulate. Concern also was aroused by reports that many large corporations had made illegal political contributions to President Nixon's 1972 reelection campaign and had paid large amounts in bribes and kickbacks to officials of foreign governments. Demands were made that the corporate governance system be strengthened to ensure, at a minimum, that corporate activities in areas of public concern were not unlawful.

At that time, boards of directors of most public companies included some "outside directors"—persons who were not full-time employees of the company. In addition, boards generally included the company's chief executive officer (CEO) and several other high-ranking officers. The outside directors were predominantly white men (still true today) busily engaged in their primary occupations as senior officers of other corporations. They devoted relatively small amounts of time to the boards on which they sat as outside directors and relied principally on information furnished to them by managers. In form, they were elected by the shareholders, but in fact they were nominated by the CEO and faced no opposition for election. For the most part, it was safe to say that directors were self-selected, self-perpetuating, loyal to management, and inclined to devote relatively little time to their directorships. They also generally were paid fairly nominal sums for their efforts, at least in comparison to their earnings from other sources.

Eventually, a consensus of sorts emerged: that the board of directors had the potential to operate as an effective disciplinary force within the corporation; that a board could ensure management was pursuing a coherent business strategy which could take account of the corporation's external and internal environment; that a board could encourage managers to take account of the social effects of business operations that pressure to meet short-run profit targets otherwise might lead managers to ignore. It also seemed clear that a board of directors would be more likely to play these roles, all of which involve monitoring managers' performance, only if a majority of directors were outsiders. This latter point has received increasing emphasis. *See, e.g.,* ALI, PRINCIPLES OF COR-

PORATE GOVERNANCE (1994) § 3A.01. Nevertheless, there still is considerable controversy over whether a change in board structure will affect corporate performance. Chapter 15 deals with these issues in more detail.

During the takeover boom of the 1980s, takeover-related litigation subjected the decisionmaking processes of many large companies' boards of directors to unprecedented scrutiny. Some boards clearly operated with considerable independence, pressuring managers to promote shareholders' interest and taking positions different from those management preferred. Other boards appeared to acquiesce uncritically in whatever management proposed, apparently unconcerned about how their decisions would affect shareholders' well-being. The takeover movement also raised the question of precisely what that well-being consisted: the ability to receive an immediate large premium for their stock, or a concern for the long-term viability of the corporation. Chapter 22 examines those issues more fully.

As Chancellor Allen noted in Chapter 1, takeovers also stimulated renewed interest in an idea that seemed to have lost currency: the notion that managers should be allowed, or even required, to take explicit account of the interests of non-shareholder constituencies when managing a corporation's business. Whether the constituency statutes that many states adopted in response to takeover pressures (see Section C.3 of this Chapter) will lead to broader board concern for such constituencies remains to be seen.

## B.  CORPORATE CHARITABLE GIVING AND SOCIAL RESPONSIBILITY

It is easy to get caught up in generalizations and emotional responses when discussing "corporate responsibility." While it is important not to submerge value systems in technical legal analysis, such discussions demand careful analysis of the nature of the "responsibility," to whom it is owed, and how it should be fulfilled. To focus these issues, we examine one narrow topic, charitable giving, in the context of both the older doctrine of *ultra vires* and modern limitations on such giving.

### 1.  INTRODUCTION: CORPORATE PURPOSES AND CORPORATE POWERS: THE DOCTRINE OF ULTRA VIRES

The statutory charter that created early corporations included as one of its principal provisions a statement of the purposes for which the corporation was to be formed. According to the common law doctrine of *ultra vires* (literally, "beyond the power"), a corporation may not engage in activities outside the scope of the purposes thus defined. In a famous English case, for example, the House of Lords held that a corporation whose charter authorized it to "sell or lend all kinds of railway plant, to carry on the business of mechanical engineers and general contractors, etc." exceeded its purposes in purchasing a concession to construct and operate a railway line in Belgium. The corporation had contracted with one Riche to do the construction, but after Riche had done some of the work, the corporation repudiated the contract. The House of Lords rejected Riche's suit on the contract on the ground that the corporation lacked the power to build a railroad and thus to bind itself to the contract. *Ashbury Railway Carriage & Iron Co. v. Riche*, 33 N.S.Law Times Rep. 450 (1875).

The doctrine of *ultra vires* found its roots principally in a suspicion of concentrations of economic power. A second reason was to enable investors to limit their economic exposure to the risks of a defined business undertaking. The legal mechanisms available to challenge an allegedly *ultra vires* act took the form of either a *quo warranto* (literally, "by what authority") proceeding instituted by the state for the forfeiture of the corporate charter or the assertion of the corporate incapacity in various forms in the context of private lawsuits. That a corporate act was unauthorized and therefore void was often asserted as a defense to an action against the corporation on a corporate obligation, as in the *Ashbury Railway Carriage* case.

The *ultra vires* doctrine also could be asserted affirmatively in a shareholder action against a corporation's managers who caused the corporation to suffer a loss by engaging in activity outside its authority. In at least one relatively modern case, the shareholders of a corporation were held personally liable as partners on a contract found to be outside the purposes specified in the articles of incorporation (although there were other factors that contributed to the result). *Lurie v. Arizona Fertilizer & Chemical Co.*, 101 Ariz. 482, 421 P.2d 330 (1966).

In the nineteenth century, a large portion of the law of corporations was devoted to the resolution of disputes arising under the *ultra vires* doctrine; today, the issue is rarely seen in the courts. Clearly, the original purpose of the doctrine, the curbing of the powers of the large corporation, was a failure and it has been largely replaced by expanding fiduciary duties.

## 2. THE MODERN DOCTRINE OF ULTRA VIRES

Once states began to enact general incorporation statutes, it became a simple matter to circumvent the limitations of the *ultra vires* doctrine by drafting the articles of incorporation in as broad terms as the attorney could imagine. Purpose clauses often went on for pages, listing—or at least attempting to list—every conceivable activity in which a corporation might engage, even if the intention of the promoters was to undertake only the first activity on the list. Today, corporate statutes often provide, as does DGCL § 102(a)(3), "It shall be sufficient to state, either alone or with other businesses or purposes, that the purpose of the corporation is to engage in any lawful act or activity for which corporations may be organized under the General Corporation Law of Delaware, and by such statement all lawful acts and activities shall be within the purpose of the corporation, except for express limitations, if any." Since DGCL § 101(b) also provides that "[a] corporation may be incorporated or organized under this chapter to conduct or promote any lawful business or purposes, except as may otherwise be provided by the constitution or other law of this State" the organic documents of the corporation provide no limitation on corporate purposes. *See* RMBCA § 3.04.

There is a conceptual distinction to be drawn between corporate *purposes* and corporate *powers*, although it is one that often is ignored by corporate lawyers. It would be *ultra vires* for a corporation either to engage in a business not included within the statement of purposes set forth in its charter or, in carrying on its business, to exercise a power that the charter or the statute prohibited. Articles of incorporation formerly contained a lengthy list of both "powers" and "purposes." In practice, however, it is often difficult to distinguish between the two, and in an excess of caution, attorneys often listed "powers" among what were, properly conceived, simply "purposes" of a corporation. For example the "purposes" clauses found in many form books included acquiring or dealing in real property. For most corporations this would not be a purpose but simply the "power" to acquire real estate in the normal course of affairs. But dealing in real property would clearly be a "purpose" of a corporation organized to engage in the real estate business. Today, statutes such as RMBCA § 3.02, which grants extremely broad powers to a business corporation, renders most of this learning irrelevant.

In addition to adopting a permissive approach both to the definition of corporate purposes and to the statutory grant of powers, modern corporate statutes often limit the uses to which the doctrine of *ultra vires* can be put, most importantly by precluding a corporation from using the defense of *ultra vires* against an otherwise valid obligation. *See, e.g.*, RMBCA § 3.04. There are, however, three areas in which the doctrine continues to have some vitality, although even in those areas, both case law and statutes have narrowed their scope. First, at common law a corporation was prohibited from becoming a member of a partnership, on the theory that to do so exposed the assets of the corporation to risks created by decisions of the other partners. *See Whittenton Mills v. Upton*, 76 Mass. (10 Gray) 582 (1858). Most statutes today contain express authorization for corporations to become partners, and even where the statute does not so provide, a corporation can validly include such a power in its articles of incorporation.

Corporations also were not generally authorized to guarantee the obligations of others on the theory that such guarantees could not be in the interest of the shareholders. *See Brinson v. Mill Supply Co., Inc.*, 219 N.C. 498, 14 S.E.2d 505 (1941). This limitation also has largely disappeared, as a result of case law and modern statutory provisions (although the latter are sometimes subject to qualification).

The third, and most significant, area in which the *ultra vires* doctrine was of concern, (and, indeed, remains so) relates to the "waste" of corporate assets by their use for other than corporate purposes. Although shareholders have sought to show that their corporations have "given away" or "wasted" assets in a variety of different ways, the most common charge has been that a corporate charitable donation was *ultra vires*. A simple illustration of the concept of waste in another context is that, while it is legal for a corporation to pay salaries to its officers, if those salaries become too high, they may become "wasteful" and therefore *ultra vires. See, e.g., Rogers v. Hill*, 289 U.S. 582, 53 S.Ct. 731, 77 L.Ed. 1385 (1933) (Chapter 17). Thus, if corporate managers overdo "their" largess to themselves or others, they may be guilty of wasting corporate assets.

Modern statutory provisions, such as RMBCA § 3.02(13) and DGCL § 122(9), together with a number of cases similar to those set forth below, have gone a long way toward eliminating any doubts about the power of corporations to make *some* charitable contributions. The establishment of the basic principle that corporations may use their assets for ends that are unrelated—or at least not *directly* related—to the financial well-being of the shareholders, does not put an end to the legal issues, however. It is clear that at some point, a gift that is valid in principle can become so large as to constitute a waste of corporate assets. Drawing that line, however, is another matter.

## 3. MODERN LIMITATIONS ON CORPORATE CHARITABLE GIVING

### PROBLEM

### UNION AIRLINES

You are general counsel for Union Airlines, Inc., a major U.S. domestic air carrier headquartered in Georgetown, Columbia. The company has $1 billion in assets and generates $700 million in annual revenues. Due to increased competition and higher fuel prices, Union's profits have declined steadily for the last several years, and it has posted large losses for the last three.

Wright, the company's chief executive officer just telephoned and told you that Union intends to make a corporate donation of $500,000 to the Georgetown Opera Company to help it survive a financial crisis that threatens to prevent the Opera from opening the current season.

1. Wright would like your opinion on the legality of the gift. What should you tell him? Consider RMBCA §§ 3.02 and 3.04 [DGCL §§ 122 and 124] and the materials that follow.

2. Would your opinion change if you learned that Wright had been trying for years to join the board of directors of the Opera, perhaps the most socially prestigious board in Georgetown, and that the proposed gift appeared to be a *quid pro quo* for an invitation to Wright to join that board?

# THEODORA HOLDING CORP. v. HENDERSON

257 A.2d 398 (Del.Ch.1969).

[For many years, Girard Henderson dominated the affairs of Alexander Dawson, Inc., through his controlling interest in that corporation. In 1955, he transferred shares to his then wife, Theodora Henderson, as part of a separation agreement. In 1967, Mrs. Henderson formed the Theodora Holding Corporation and transferred to it 27 percent of the outstanding stock of Alexander Dawson, Inc. During that year, the combined dividends paid by Alexander Dawson, Inc. to Mrs. Henderson and her corporation totalled $286,240.

From 1960 to 1966, Girard Henderson had caused Alexander Dawson, Inc. to make annual corporate contributions ranging from $60,000 to more than $70,000 to the Alexander Dawson Foundation ("the Foundation"), which Henderson had formed in 1957. All contributions were unanimously approved by the shareholders. In 1966, Alexander Dawson, Inc. donated to the Foundation a large tract of land valued at $467,750 for the purpose of establishing a camp for under-privileged boys. In April 1967, Mr. Henderson proposed that the board approve a $528,000 gift of company stock to the Foundation. One director, Theodora Ives, objected and suggested that the gift be made instead to a charitable corporation supported by her mother (Girard Henderson's ex-wife) and herself. Girard Henderson responded by causing a reduction in the Alexander Dawson, Inc. board of directors from eight members to three. The board thereafter approved the gift of stock to the Foundation.

Theodora Holding Corp. then brought suit against certain individuals, including Girard Henderson, challenging the gift and seeking an accounting and the appointment of a liquidating receiver for Alexander Dawson, Inc.]

Marvel, Vice Chancellor.

* * * Title 8 Del.C. § 122 provides as follows:

Every corporation created under this chapter shall have power to—

* * * (9) Make donations for the public welfare or for charitable, scientific or educational purposes, and in time of war or other national emergency in aid thereof.

There is no doubt but that the Alexander Dawson Foundation is recognized as a legitimate charitable trust by the Department of Internal Revenue. It is also clear that it is authorized to operate exclusively in the fields of " * * * religious, charitable, scientific, literary, or educational purposes, or for the prevention of cruelty to children or animals * * * ". Furthermore, contemporary courts recognize that unless corporations carry an increasing share of the burden of supporting charitable and educational causes that the business advantages now reposed in corporations by law may well prove to be unacceptable to the representatives of an aroused public. The recognized obligation of corporations towards philanthropic, educational and artistic causes is reflected in the statutory law of all of the states, other than the states of Arizona and Idaho.

In *A.P. Smith Mfg. Co. v. Barlow*, 13 N.J. 145, 98 A.2d [581], appeal dismissed, 346 U.S. 861, 74 S.Ct. 107, 98 L.Ed. 373, a case in which the corporate donor had been organized long before the adoption of a statute authorizing corporate gifts to charitable or educational institutions, the Supreme Court of New Jersey upheld a gift of $1500 by the plaintiff corporation to Princeton University, being of the opinion that the trend towards the transfer of wealth from private industrial entrepreneurs to corporate institutions, the increase of taxes on individual income, coupled with steadily increasing philanthropic needs, necessitate corporate giving for educational needs even were there no statute permitting such gifts, and this was held to be the case apart from the question of the reserved power of the state to amend corporate charters. The court also noted that the gift tended to bolster the free enterprise system and the general social climate in which plaintiff was nurtured. And while the court pointed out that there was no showing that the gift in question was made indiscriminately or to a pet charity in furtherance of personal rather than corporate ends, the actual holding of the opinion appears to be that a corporate charitable or educational gift to be valid must merely be within reasonable limits both as to amount and purpose. * * *

I conclude that the test to be applied in passing on the validity of a gift such as the one here in issue is that of reasonableness, a test in which the provisions of the Internal Revenue Code pertaining to charitable gifts by corporations furnish a helpful guide. The gift here under attack was made from gross income and had a value as of the time of giving of $528,000 in a year in which Alexander Dawson, Inc.'s total income was $19,144,229.06, or well within the federal tax deduction limitation of 5% of such income. The contribution under attack can be said to have "cost" all of the stockholders of Alexander Dawson, Inc. including plaintiff, less than $80,000, or some fifteen cents per dollar of contribution, taking into consideration the federal tax provisions applicable to holding companies as well as the provisions for compulsory distribution of dividends received by such a corporation. In addition, the gift, by reducing Alexander Dawson, Inc.'s reserve for unrealized capital gains taxes by some $130,000, increased the balance sheet net worth of stockholders of the corporate defendant by such amount. It is accordingly obvious, in my opinion, that the relatively small loss of immediate income otherwise payable to plaintiff and the corporate defendant's other stockholders had it not been for the gift in question, is far outweighed by the overall benefits flowing from the placing of such gift in channels where it serves to benefit those in need of philanthropic or educational support, thus providing justification for large private holdings, thereby benefiting plaintiff in the long run. Finally, the fact that the interests of the Alexander Dawson Foundation appear to be increasingly directed towards the rehabilitation and education of deprived but deserving young people is peculiarly appropriate in an age when a large segment of youth is alienated even from parents who are not entirely satisfied with our present social and economic system. * * *

On notice, an order in conformity with the holdings of this opinion may be presented.

## KAHN v. SULLIVAN
594 A.2d 48 (Del.1991).

Holland, Justice:

This is an appeal from the approval of the settlement of one of three civil actions brought in the Court of Chancery by certain shareholders of Occidental Petroleum Corporation ("Occidental"). Each civil action challenged a decision by Occidental's board of directors (the "Board"), through a special committee of Occidental's outside directors ("the Special Committee"), to make a charitable donation. The purpose of the charitable donation was to construct and fund an art museum.

The shareholder plaintiffs in this litigation, Joseph Sullivan and Alan Brody, agreed to a settlement of their class and derivative actions subject to the approval of the Court of Chancery. The settlement was authorized, on behalf of Occidental, by the Special Committee. The shareholder plaintiffs in the other two civil actions, Alan R. Kahn ("Kahn") and Barnett Stepak ("Stepak"), appeared in the Sullivan action and objected to the proposed settlement. California Public Employees Retirement System ("CalPERS") was permitted to intervene as a shareholder plaintiff in the Kahn action and also appeared in opposition to the proposed settlement in the Sullivan action. * * *

### Facts

Occidental is a Delaware corporation. According to the parties, Occidental has about 290 million shares of stock outstanding which are held by approximately 495 thousand shareholders. For the year ending December 31, 1988, Occidental had assets of approximately twenty billion dollars, operating revenues of twenty billion dollars and pre-tax earnings of $574 million. Its corporate headquarters are located in Los Angeles, California.

At the time of his death on December 10, 1990, Dr. Hammer was Occidental's chief executive officer and the chairman of its board of directors. Since the early 1920's, Dr. Hammer had been a serious art collector. When Dr. Hammer died, he personally and The Armand Hammer Foundation (the "Foundation"), owned three major collections of art (referred to in their entirety as "the Art Collection"). The Art Collection, valued at $300–$400 million included: "Five Centuries of Art," more than 100 works by artists such as Rembrandt, Rubens, Renoir and Van Gogh; the Codex Hammer, a rare manuscript by Leonardo da Vinci; and the world's most extensive private collection of paintings, lithographs and bronzes by the French satirist Honore Daumier.

For many years, the Board has determined that it is in the best interest of Occidental to support and promote the acquisition and exhibition of the Art Collection. Through Occidental's financial support and sponsorship, the Art Collection has been viewed by more than six million people in more than twenty-five American cities and at least eighteen foreign countries. The majority of those exhibitions have been in areas where Occidental has operations or was negotiating business contracts. * * *

Dr. Hammer enjoyed an ongoing relationship with the Los Angeles County Museum of Art ("LACMA") for several decades. In 1968, Dr. Hammer agreed to donate a number of paintings to LACMA, as well as funds to purchase additional art. For approximately twenty years thereafter, Dr. Hammer both publicly and privately expressed his intention to donate the Art Collection to LACMA. However, Dr. Hammer and LACMA had never entered into a binding agreement to that effect. Nevertheless, LACMA named one of its buildings the Frances and Armand Hammer Wing in recognition of Dr. Hammer's gifts.

Occidental approved of Dr. Hammer's decision to permanently display the Art Collection at LACMA. In fact, it made substantial financial contributions to facilitate that display. In 1982, for example, Occidental paid two million dollars to expand and refurbish the Hammer Wing at LACMA.

In 1987, Dr. Hammer presented Daniel N. Belin, Esquire ("Belin"), the president of LACMA's Board of Trustees, with a thirty-nine page proposed agreement which set forth the terms upon which Dr. Hammer would permanently locate the Art Collection at LACMA. LACMA and Dr. Hammer tried, but were unable to reach a binding agreement. Consequently, Dr. Hammer concluded that he would make arrangements for the permanent display of the Art Collection at a location other than at LACMA. On January 8, 1988, Dr. Hammer wrote a letter to Belin which stated that he had "decided to create my own museum to house" the Art Collection.

On January 19, 1988, at a meeting of the executive committee of Occidental's board of directors ("the Executive Committee"), Dr. Hammer proposed that Occidental, in conjunction with the Foundation, construct a museum for the Art Collection. After discussing Occidental's history of identification with the Art Collection, the Executive Committee decided that it was in Occidental's best interest to accept Dr. Hammer's proposal. * * *

The art museum concept was announced publicly on January 21, 1988. On February 11, 1988, the Board approved the Executive Committee's prior actions. * * *

On December 15, 1988, the Board was presented with a detailed plan for the Museum proposal. The Board approved the concept and authorized a complete study of the proposal. Following the December 15th Board meeting, the law firm of Dilworth, Paxson, Kalish & Kauffman ("Dilworth") was retained by the Board to examine the Museum proposal and to prepare a memorandum addressing the issues relevant to the Board's consideration of the proposal.[6] The law firm of Skadden, Arps, Slate, Meagher & Flom ("Skadden Arps") was retained to represent the new legal entity which would be necessitated by the Museum proposal. Occidental's public accountants, Arthur Andersen & Co. ("Arthur Andersen"), were also asked to examine the Museum proposal.

On or about February 6, 1989, ten days prior to the Board's prescheduled February 16 meeting, Dilworth provided each member of the Board with a ninety-six page memorandum. It contained a definition of the Museum proposal and the anticipated magnitude of the proposed charitable donation by Occidental. It reviewed the authority of the Board to approve such a donation and the reasonableness of the proposed donation. The Dilworth memorandum included an analysis of the donation's effect on Occidental's financial condition, the potential for good will and other benefits to Occidental, and a comparison of the proposed charitable contribution by Occidental to the charitable contributions of other corporations.

The advance distribution of the Dilworth memorandum was supplemented on February 10, 1989 by a tax opinion letter from Skadden Arps. * * *

During the February 16 Board meeting, a Dilworth representative personally presented the basis for that law firm's analysis of the Museum proposal, as set forth in its February 6 written memorandum. * * * Following the Dilworth presentation, the Board resolved to appoint the Special Committee, comprised of its eight independent and disinterested outside directors, to further review and to act upon the Museum proposal * * *. The Board then adjourned to allow the Special Committee to meet.

The Special Committee consisted of individuals who collectively had approximately eighty years of service on Occidental's board of directors. * * * Those Board members were not officers of Occidental, and were not associated with the Museum or the Foundation. * * *

The minutes of the February 16, 1989 meeting of the Special Committee outline its consideration of the Museum proposal. Those minutes reflect that many questions were asked by members of the Special Committee and were answered by the representatives of Dilworth, Skadden Arps, or Arthur Andersen. As a result of its own extensive discussions, and in reliance upon the experts' opinions, the Special Committee concluded that the establishment of the Museum, adjacent to Occidental's corporate offices in Los Angeles, would provide benefits to Occidental for at least the thirty-year term of the lease. The Special Committee also concluded that the proposed museum would establish a new cultural landmark for the City of Los Angeles.

On February 16, 1989, the Special Committee unanimously approved the Museum proposal, [which committed Occidental to spend

6. At the time of its selection, Dilworth also represented Dr. Hammer personally.

more than $85 million for a museum, to be identified as "The Armand Hammer Museum of Art and Cultural Center," to which the Art collection would be transferred. Occidental would receive public recognition for its role in establishing the Museum by the naming of the courtyard, library, *or* auditorium of the museum for Occidental.] * * *

On April 25, 1989, Occidental reported the Special Committee's approval of the Museum proposal to its shareholders in the proxy statement for its annual meeting to be held May 26, 1989. On May 2, 1989, the first shareholder action ("the Kahn action") was filed, challenging Occidental's decision to establish and fund the Museum proposal. The Sullivan action was filed on May 9, 1989. * * *

Settlement negotiations were entered into almost immediately between Occidental and the attorneys for the plaintiffs in the Sullivan action. * * *

On June 3, 1989, the parties to the Sullivan action signed a Memorandum of Understanding that set forth a proposed settlement in general terms. The proposed settlement was subject to the right of the plaintiffs to engage in additional discovery to confirm the fairness and adequacy of the proposed settlement.

On June 9, 1989, the plaintiffs in the Kahn action moved for a preliminary injunction to enjoin the proposed settlement in the Sullivan action and also for expedited discovery. * * *

In denying the motion for injunctive relief, the Court of Chancery * * * identified six issues to be addressed at any future settlement hearing:

(1) the failure of the Special Committee appointed by the directors of Occidental to hire its own counsel and advisors or even to formally approve the challenged acts; (2) the now worthlessness of a prior donation by Occidental to the Los Angeles County Museum; (3) the huge attorney fees which the parties have apparently decided to seek or not oppose; (4) the egocentric nature of some of Armand Hammer's objections to the Los Angeles County Museum being the recipient of his donation; (5) the issue of who really owns the art; and (6) the lack of any direct substantial benefit to the stockholders.

On July 20, 1989, the Special Committee met to discuss the Museum proposal. * * *

At its July 20 meeting, the Special Committee also reviewed the July 19, 1989 decision and order of the Court of Chancery denying Kahn's request for injunctive relief in the Sullivan action. In response to one of the concerns expressed by the Court of Chancery, the Special Committee resolved to retain independent Delaware counsel with no prior connection to Occidental or its officers. * * *

On October 6, 1989, Occidental's Board of Directors, by unanimous written consent, delegated full authority to the Special Committee to settle the shareholder litigation filed in Delaware on Occidental's behalf. * * *

The Special Committee met again on November 16, 1989. * * * Prior to that meeting, the Special Committee received a draft of the Stipulation of Settlement of the Sullivan action, a revised Transfer Agreement in accordance with its September 20 request, and an abstract and analysis of the Transfer Agreement prepared by Morris James [the law firm the Special Committee had retained]. At the meeting on November 16, all of these documents were discussed with Brown of Morris James. The form of a stipulation of settlement was approved unanimously by the Special Committee.

The parties to the Sullivan action presented the Court of Chancery with a fully executed Stipulation of Compromise, Settlement and Release agreement ("the Settlement") on January 24, 1990. This agreement was only slightly changed from the June 3, 1989 Memorandum of Understanding. The Settlement, *inter alia*, provided:

(1) The Museum building shall be named the "Occidental Petroleum Cultural Center Building" with the name displayed appropriately on the building.

(2) Occidental shall be treated as a corporate sponsor by the Museum for as long as the Museum occupies the building.

(3) Occidental's contribution of the building shall be recognized by the Museum in public references to the facility.

(4) Three of Occidental's directors shall serve on the Museum's Board (or no less than one-third of the total Museum Board) with Occidental having the option to designate a fourth director.

(5) There shall be an immediate loan of substantially all of the art collections of Dr. Hammer to the Museum and there shall be an actual transfer of ownership of the collections upon Dr. Hammer's death or the commencement of operation of the Museum—whichever later occurs.

(6) All future charitable contributions by Occidental to any Hammer-affiliated charities shall be limited by the size of the dividends paid to Occidental's common stockholders. At current dividend levels, Occidental's annual contributions to Hammer-affiliated charities pursuant to this limitation could not exceed approximately three cents per share.

(7) Any amounts Occidental pays for construction of the Museum in excess of $50 million and any amounts paid to the Foundation upon Dr. Hammer's death must be charged against the agreed ceiling on limitations to Hammer-affiliated charities.

(8) Occidental's expenditures for the Museum construction shall not exceed $50 million, except that an additional $10 million may be expended through December 31, 1990 but only if such additional expenditures do not enlarge the scope of construction and if such expenditures are approved by the Special Committee. Amounts in excess of $50 million must be charged against the limitation on donations to Hammer-affiliated charities.

(9) Occidental shall be entitled to receive 50% of any consideration received in excess of a $55 million option price for the Museum property or 50% of any consideration the Museum receives from the assignment or transfer of its option or lease to a third party.

(10) Plaintiffs' attorneys' fees in the Sullivan action shall not exceed $1.4 million. * * *

On April 4, 1990, the settlement hearing in the Sullivan action was held.[22]

On August 7, 1990, the Court of Chancery found the Settlement to be reasonable under all of the circumstances. The Court of Chancery concluded that the claims asserted by the shareholder plaintiffs would likely be dismissed before or after trial. While noting its own displeasure with the Settlement, the Court of Chancery explained that its role in reviewing the proposed Settlement was restricted to determining in its own business judgment whether, on balance, the Settlement was reasonable.[23] The Court opined that although the benefit to be received from the Settlement was meager, it was adequate considering all the facts and circumstances.

## STANDARD OF REVIEW

* * * In an appeal from the Court of Chancery, following the approval of a settlement of a class action, the function of this Court is more limited in its nature. This Court does not review the record to determine the intrinsic fairness of the settlement in light of its own business judgment. This Court reviews the record "solely for the purpose of determining whether or not the Court of Chancery abused its discretion by the exercise of its business judgment." * * *

## CLAIMS AND DEFENSES

* * * The proponents of the Settlement argued that the business judgment rule could undoubtedly have been invoked successfully by the defendants as a complete defense to the shareholder plaintiffs' claims. * * * The Objectors presented several alternative arguments in support of their contention that the shareholder plaintiffs would have been able

---

**22.** In the interim, the Special Committee met on March 29, 1990 to consider a request to approve the expenditure of an additional ten million dollars on the construction of the Museum. * * * [T]he Special Committee approved the expenditure * * *.

**23.** The Court of Chancery noted:

Despite this Court's expressed displeasure with the settlement efforts, as set forth in its July 19, 1989 opinion in Kahn, the settlement now before the Court is only slightly changed from the June 3, 1989 Memorandum of Understanding.

[Therefore] * * * the settlement in the Court's opinion leaves much to be desired. The Court's role in reviewing the proposed Settlement, however, is quite restricted. If the Court was a stockholder of Occidental it might vote for new directors, if it was on the Board it might vote for new management and if it was a member of the Special Committee it might vote against the Museum project. But its options are limited in reviewing a proposed settlement to applying Delaware law to the facts adduced in the record and then determining in its business judgment whether, on balance, the settlement is reasonable.

to rebut the defense based on the protection which the presumption of the business judgment rule provides. * * *

First, the Objectors submitted that the business judgment rule would probably not protect the actions of the Special Committee because the independence of the Special Committee was questionable. In support of that argument, the Objectors assert that at least four members of the Special Committee had close ties to Dr. Hammer and personal business dealings with him. After examining the record, the Court of Chancery found that the Objectors had not established any facts that the Special Committee had any self-interest in the transaction either from a personal financial interest or from a motive for entrenchment in office. The Court of Chancery also concluded that there was no evidence in the record indicating that any of the members of the Special Committee were in fact dominated by Dr. Hammer or anyone else.

Second, in a related argument, the Objectors argued that the presumption of the business judgment rule would have been overcome because the Special Committee proceeded initially without retaining independent legal counsel. * * * However, in approving the Settlement, the Court of Chancery noted that the Special Committee had retained independent counsel, and "subsequently, and for the first time, formally approved the challenged charitable contributions." Thus, the Court of Chancery specifically found that the Special Committee had the advice of independent legal counsel before it finally approved the Museum proposal. * * *

The Court of Chancery carefully considered each of the Objectors' arguments in response to the merits of the suggested business judgment rule defense. It concluded that if the Sullivan action proceeded, it was highly probable in deciding a motion to dismiss, a motion for summary judgment, or a post-trial motion, the actions of "the Special Committee would be protected by the presumption of propriety afforded by the business judgment rule." Specifically, the Court of Chancery concluded that it would have been decided that the Special Committee, comprised of Occidental's outside directors, was independent and made an informed decision to approve the charitable donation to the Museum proposal. These conclusions by the Court of Chancery are supported by the record and are the product of an orderly and logical deductive process.

Following its analysis and conclusion that the business judgment rule would have been applicable to any judicial examination of the Special Committee's actions, the Court of Chancery considered the shareholder plaintiffs' claim that the Board and the Special Committee's approval of the charitable donation to the Museum proposal constituted a waste of Occidental's corporate assets. In doing so, it recognized that charitable donations by Delaware corporations are expressly authorized by 8 Del.C. § 122(9). It also recognized that although § 122(9) places no limitations on the size of a charitable corporate gift, that section has been construed "to authorize any reasonable corporate gift of a charitable or educational nature." *Theodora Holding Corp. v. Henderson,*

Del.Ch., 257 A.2d 398, 405 (1969). Thus, the Court of Chancery concluded that the test to be applied in examining the merits of a claim alleging corporate waste "is that of reasonableness, a test in which the provisions of the Internal Revenue Code pertaining to charitable gifts by corporations furnish a helpful guide." Id. We agree with that conclusion.

The Objectors argued that Occidental's charitable contribution to the Museum proposal was unreasonable and a waste of corporate assets because it was excessive. The Court of Chancery recognized that not every charitable gift constitutes a valid corporate action. Nevertheless, the Court of Chancery concluded, given the net worth of Occidental, its annual net income before taxes, and the tax benefits to Occidental, that the gift to the Museum was within the range of reasonableness established in *Theodora Holding Corp. v. Henderson*, Del.Ch., 257 A.2d 398, 405 (1969). Therefore, the Court of Chancery found that it was "reasonably probable" that plaintiffs would fail on their claim of waste. That finding is supported by the record and is the product of an orderly and logical deductive process.

### ADEQUACY OF THE SETTLEMENT

In examining the Settlement, the Court of Chancery * * * evaluated not only the nature of the shareholder plaintiffs' claims but also the possible defenses to those claims. * * * After carefully evaluating the parties' respective legal positions, the Court of Chancery opined that "the [shareholder plaintiffs'] potential for ultimate success on the merits [in the Sullivan action] is, realistically, very poor."

Second, * * * after considering the legal and factual circumstances of the case *sub judice*, the Court of Chancery examined the value of the Settlement. The proponents of the Settlement argued that the monetary value of having the Museum building called the "Occidental Petroleum Cultural Center Building" was approximately ten million dollars. The Court of Chancery noted that, in support of their valuation arguments, the proponents also argued that the Settlement: (1) reinforced and assured Occidental's identification with and meaningful participation in the affairs of the Museum; (2) reinforced and protected the charitable nature and consequences of Occidental's gifts by securing the prompt delivery and irrevocable transfer of the Art Collection to the Museum; (3) imposed meaningful controls upon the total construction costs that Occidental will pay, which had already forced the reduction of the construction budget by $19.4 million; (4) placed meaningful restrictions upon Occidental's future charitable donations to "Hammer" affiliated entities and avoided increases in posthumous payments to the Foundation or any other designated recipient after Dr. Hammer's death; (5) restored to Occidental an equitable portion of any appreciation of the properties in the event the Museum exercised its option and disposed of the properties or transferred its option for value; and (6) guaranteed that the Art Collection would continue to be located in the Los Angeles area and remain available for the enjoyment of the American public rather than dissipated into private collections or sold abroad.

The Court of Chancery characterized the proponents' efforts to quantify the monetary value of most of the Settlement benefits as "speculative." The Court of Chancery also viewed the estimate that naming the building for Occidental would have a ten million dollar value to Occidental with "a good deal of skepticism." Nevertheless, the Court of Chancery found that Occidental would, in fact, receive an economic benefit in the form of good will from the charitable donation to the Museum proposal. It also found that Occidental would derive an economic benefit from being able to utilize the Museum, adjacent to its corporate headquarters, in the promotion of its business.

Finally, the Court of Chancery applied its own independent business judgment in deciding whether the Settlement was fair and reasonable. * * * The Court of Chancery found that "the benefit [of the Settlement] to the stockholders of Occidental is sufficient to support the Settlement and is adequate, if only barely so, when compared to the weakness of the plaintiffs' claims." The Court of Chancery concluded that "although the Settlement is meager, it is adequate considering all the facts and circumstances." * * *

CONCLUSION

The reasonableness of a particular class action settlement is addressed to the discretion of the Court of Chancery, on a case by case basis, in light of all of the relevant circumstances. In this case, we find that all of the Court of Chancery's factual findings of fact are supported by the record. We also find that all of the legal conclusions reached by the Court of Chancery were based upon a proper application of well established principles of law. Consequently, we find that the Court of Chancery did not abuse its discretion in deciding to approve the Settlement in the Sullivan action. Therefore, the decision of the Court of Chancery is Affirmed.

### Notes on Kahn v. Sullivan

1. Dr. Hammer's decision to renege on his oral promise to donate the Art Collection to LACMA was precipitated by LACMA's rejection of his insistence that an entire floor of LACMA's Frances and Armand Hammer Building be remodeled to house the Art Collection and that the names of other donors, currently inscribed over galleries on that floor, be removed. Consequently, LACMA and Dr. Hammer never discussed other demands that LACMA found objectionable, such as that the main entrance to the floor be outfitted with a full length portrait of Hammer, that each work in the Collection be separately identified as donated by Hammer, that LACMA never sell any of the works in the Collection, that the collection be exhibited together on the special floor, and that no other works be exhibited with the Collection. See Robert A. Jones, Battle of the Masterpieces; The Armand Hammer–County Museum Deal: A Saga of Art, Power and Big Understandings, L.A. Times Magazine 8 (May 22, 1988).

2. Dr. Hammer dominated Occidental from the time he took control of the company until his death at age 92. Until 1980, when the SEC discovered the practice and objected to it, Dr. Hammer required that every person elected to Occidental's board sign and deliver to him an undated letter of resignation. At least five of the eight members of the Special Committee joined the board prior to the time he discontinued this practice. Dr. Hammer also apparently viewed himself as indispensible to Occidental's success. He dismissed four experienced executives hired by Occidental as his potential successor, concluding that none of them were up to the job.

3. While Occidental agreed to pay counsel fees to the *Sullivan* plaintiffs of up to $1.4 million, the Vice–Chancellor awarded a fee of only $800,000, reflecting, to some degree, his skepticism about the merits of the settlement. See *Sullivan v. Hammer*, [CCH] Fed. Sec. L. Rep. ¶ 95,415, 1990 WL 114223 (Del.Ch. 1990). Counsel for the other plaintiffs, however, were awarded no fees for their efforts.

4. In November 1994, the UCLA/Hammer Museum sold the Codex Hammer for $30.8 million at auction to William Gates, CEO of Microsoft Corp. Suzanne Muchnic, *Microsoft's Gates Revealed as Leonardo's Mystery Buyer*, L.A. TIMES, p. A20, col. 1 (Nov. 13, 1994).

### *Note: Corporations and Charitable Contributions*

While individuals tend to contribute between 2 and 3 percent of their income to charities, the average corporate gift is in the range of 1 to 2 percent of pretax income. A survey of the Fortune 500 manufacturing companies, the Fortune 500 service companies, and certain other corporations, indicated that for 1995, median contributions represented 1.24 percent of United States pretax income. Internal Revenue Service data show that contributions by all corporations represented 1.97 percent of total corporate income. American Association of Fund-Raising Counsel, GIVING U.S.A.: THE ANNUAL REPORT ON PHILANTHROPY FOR THE YEAR 1994 90 (1995). The Reasons for Corporate Generosity are not Exclusively Altruistic. The Internal Revenue Code Allows Corporations to Deduct Charitable Contributions up to 10 Percent of Their Taxable Income When They Calculate Their Taxes.

Advocates of at least some corporate philanthropy, including the managements of most major corporations, typically argue that charitable giving is in the best long-run interest of the corporation. That view is not universal, however. Critics, including many shareholders, protest that such giving deprives shareholders of money they might otherwise receive as dividends. They urge that management should not give away money that properly belongs to the shareholders. If the shareholders wish to make such gifts, they should make that decision themselves.

These critics also argue that corporate charitable contributions often result from the primary goal of maximizing the corporation's profits rather than benefiting the "community." *See, e.g.*, Hayden W. Smith, *If Not Corporate Charity, Then What?*, 41 N.Y.L.SCH.L. REV. 757, 762

(1997). They contend that such contributions also reflect the directors' personal motives and a desire for "increased power, status, and prestige." Faith Stevelman Kahn, *Pandora's Box: Managerial Discretion and the Problem of Corporate Philanthropy*, 44 UCLA L.Rev. 579, 616 (1997). *See also*, Jayne W. Barnard, *Corporate Philanthropy, Executives' Pet Charities and the Agency Problem*, 41 N.Y.L.Sch.L.Rev. 1147, 1164–1165 (1997).

The problem of accountability for charitable contributions is exacerbated by the fact that neither the federal securities laws nor state corporate law require that such contributions be disclosed to the shareholders. This lack of disclosure, coupled with the broad standards of a decision such as *Theodora Holding*, gives corporate managers broad discretion with relatively little effective monitoring when they exercise that discretion.

One public corporation, Berkshire Hathaway, Inc., has attempted to bridge the gap between these competing views by allowing each shareholder to direct the corporation to donate a certain amount per share owned to a charity or charities of the shareholder's choice. See Berkshire Hathaway Inc., 1990 Annual Report, 54–55. In one of his annual letters to shareholders, Warren Buffet, Chairman of Berkshire Hathaway,* explained:

> When A takes money from B to give to C and A is a legislator, the process is called taxation. But when A is an officer or director of a corporation, it is called philanthropy. We continue to believe that contributions, aside from those with quite clear benefits to the company, should reflect the charitable preferences of owners rather than those of officers or directors.

Berkshire Hathaway Inc., 1987 Annual Report.

Interestingly, well over 90% of the shareholders participate annually in the program.

For an analysis of many of the issues involving charitable contributions, in addition to the articles cited above, *see* Symposium, *Corporate Philanthropy: Law, Culture, Education and Politics*, 41 N.Y.L.Sch.L.Rev. 753 (1997).

## C.  CORPORATE SOCIAL RESPONSIBILITY TRENDS

### PROBLEMS

The three problems that follow all involve corporate actions that could have significant social consequences. You should approach them

---

* Mr. Buffet is considered by many to be a unique figure in the American business community. He acquired control of Berkshire Hathaway in 1965, when it had a book value of less than $20 per share and a real value of even less, and through the acquisition of several successful businesses and investments in others, he built Berkshire into a conglomerate with a market value, at the end of 1997, of $42,000 per share.

Mr. Buffet's annual letters to shareholders "have drawn a sophisticated following" in the business and financial community. Andrew Tobias, *Letters From Chairman Buffet*, Fortune 137 (Aug. 22, 1983). They discuss, in pointed but accessible language, numerous issues relating to investing in and managing business corporations. Excerpts from Buffet's letters appear at several points in this book.

as outside counsel whom the corporation has asked for advice. Keep in mind the distinction between legal advice, which the corporation surely wants, and policy advice, which the corporation may or may not be seeking. Also consider what your professional and ethical responsibilities are in advising your client.

In analyzing the problems, think about the following:

1. Does the board have a fiduciary duty to choose one course of action, or might more than one course of action be consistent with its duty? To the extent that profit maximization is relevant or dispositive, is it helpful to frame the board's decisions in terms of long-term, rather than short-run, profitability?

2. What interests, if any, besides those of shareholders may or must the board consider? Is there a way in which the board can appropriately take account of non-shareholder interests without unreasonably increasing its exposure to liability?

3. To the extent that the board may or must consider interests other than those of the shareholders, how should it determine what those interests are? Should it look to federal legislation, for example, to ascertain national public policy? To the individual consciences of board members about what is "right", "just" or "fair?"

4. How, if at all, would your advice change if the corporation was organized under a general corporation law that allowed or required boards of directors to take account of the interests of non-shareholder constituencies?

## A.  MORRILL, DEW, INC.

Morrill, Dew, Inc. is a consumer products and pharmaceutical company. A researcher in Morrill, Dew's pharmaceutical laboratory realized about two years ago that MD–379, a compound Morrill, Dew had been developing as a treatment for ulcers, had considerable potential as an abortifacient (a drug that causes a woman to spontaneously abort a fetus). About a year ago, Morrill, Dew quietly began human trials of MD–379 in a government-approved program in China. The results were very positive. When taken as instructed, MD–379 caused more than 98% of the pregnant women who used it to abort. The only adverse side effects were comparable to the effects generally experienced by women experiencing spontaneous miscarriages at early stages of pregnancy.

Information about Morrill, Dew's work with MD–379 recently was leaked to the press. Pro-choice groups began to press Morrill, Dew to submit the drug for approval by the U.S. Food and Drug Administration ("FDA"), with a view to making it available for sale in the United States. Pro-life groups, on the other hand, are threatening to organize a boycott of other Morrill, Dew products if it seeks FDA approval. Management's best estimate is that, aside from the boycott threat, MD–379 could be a modestly profitable product, adding earnings of about $20 million per year to Morrill, Dew's current annual earnings of about $850 million. Management, however, fears that losses caused by a boycott of other Morrill, Dew products by pro-life groups could exceed the profits that MD–379 would generate. Of course, it also is possible that pro-choice groups will mount a boycott if Morrill, Dew does not proceed.

The board of directors is scheduled to decide at its next meeting whether to seek FDA approval or to announce that Morrill, Dew will not attempt to market the drug in the United States. Several members of the board have strong opinions, pro and con, on the morality of marketing an abortifacient. The board has asked you to make a presentation, at the start of its meeting, as to the possibility directors will be held liable should the board either seek FDA approval or abandon further work on MD–379.

## B.   INTERNATIONAL ELECTRONICS INC.

International Electronics Inc. ("IEI"), has a large assembly plant located in West Lyme, a small town in New Hampshire. With over 1,000 workers, IEI is the town's major employer. For the last several years, the West Lyme plant has been only marginally profitable, in part because of its size and in part because of high labor costs. IEI believes this situation is likely to continue. Its management has recommended that the plant be closed and that IEI build a new, larger plant, employing 3,000 people, in Malaysia. Because the going wage rate in Malaysia is only one-fifth that in West Lyme, management expects IEI would earn close to twenty percent per annum on its investment in the new plant, considerably in excess of IEI's average return on capital.

Closing the plant is likely to have a devastating effect on West Lyme. Building the new plant in Malaysia, on the other hand, will provide employment for a large number of people who now live in extreme poverty. To what extent can and should the board take these and other relevant "non-economic" factors into account in deciding what to do?

## C.   U.S. DRUGS, INC.

U.S. Drugs, Inc., produces a broad line of pharmaceutical products. It has recently developed a new drug that is extremely effective in treating certain serious liver disorders, but that, in human trials, has apparently led to heart failure in a small, but statistically significant, number of cases. As a consequence, the FDA has refused to license sale of the new drug in the United States. U.S. Drugs has invested a substantial amount of money in the development and testing of the drug, and would like to recoup that investment if possible. Its international division has developed a plan to manufacture and sell the new drug in certain Latin American countries whose drug laws are substantially more tolerant of drugs with potentially serious side effects than those of the United States, so long as adequate information is provided about those side effects to prescribing physicians and druggists. U.S. Drugs' board of directors has asked your advice on whether the company should proceed to manufacture and sell the new drug in Latin America.

## 1. JUDICIAL APPROACHES

### DODGE v. FORD MOTOR CO.

204 Mich. 459, 170 N.W. 668 (1919).

[Although the principal issue in this famous case was whether the corporation could be compelled to pay a dividend, the case is best remembered for its discussion of the role of a corporation in society, a discussion that was elicited by Henry Ford's insistence in describing his motives for business decisions in terms of social rather than economic values.

This action was brought by the Dodge brothers, two minority shareholders, against the Ford Motor Company, Henry Ford, and other members of the board of directors, to compel the payment of a dividend, to enjoin construction of the River Rouge plant, and for other relief. The lower court granted all relief requested by plaintiffs.

Ford Motor Company was organized in 1903 with an initial capital of $150,000. Henry Ford took 225 of the 1,500 shares authorized, the Dodge brothers took 50 shares each, and several others subscribed to a few shares each. At the time the suit was brought, the company's capital was $2,000,000, the plaintiffs owned 10% of the outstanding stock, and Ford owned 58% and completely dominated the company.

The company paid regular quarterly dividends amounting to $1,200,-000 per year and, in addition, had paid during the years 1911 through 1915 a total of $41 million in "special dividends." The plaintiffs alleged that Ford had "declared it to be the settled policy of the company not to pay in the future any special dividends, but to put back into the business for the future all of the earnings of the company other than the regular dividend * * *."

The defendants appealed from a lower court order directing the corporation to pay a dividend of $19 million, enjoining it from building a smelter at the River Rouge plant and restraining it from "increasing of the fixed capital assets," or "holding of liquid assets * * * in excess of such as may be reasonably required in the proper conduct and carrying on of the business and operations" of the corporation.]

OSTRANDER, C.J.

* * * To develop the points now discussed, and to a considerable extent they may be developed together as a single point, it is necessary to refer with some particularity to the facts.

When plaintiffs made their complaint and demand for further dividends, the Ford Motor Company had concluded its most prosperous year of business. The demand for its cars at the price of the preceding year continued. It could make and could market in the year beginning August 1, 1916, more than 500,000 cars. Sales of parts and repairs would necessarily increase. The cost of materials was likely to advance, and perhaps the price of labor; but it reasonably might have expected a profit for the year of upwards of $60,000,000. * * * In justification [of their dividend policy and business plan], the defendants have offered testimony tending to prove, and which does prove, the following facts: It had been the policy of the corporation for a considerable time to annually reduce the selling price of cars, while keeping up, or improving, their quality. As early as in June, 1915, a general plan for the expansion of the productive capacity of the concern by a practical duplication of its plant had been talked over by the executive officers and directors and agreed upon; not all of the details having been settled, and no formal action of directors having been taken. The erection of a smelter was considered, and engineering and other data in connection therewith secured. In consequence, it was determined not to reduce the selling price of cars for the year beginning August 1, 1915, but to maintain the price and to accumulate a large surplus to pay for the proposed expansion of plant and equipment, and perhaps to build a plant for smelting ore. It is hoped, by Mr. Ford, that eventually 1,000,000 cars will be annually produced. The contemplated changes will permit the increased output.

The plan, as affecting the profits of the business for the year beginning August 1, 1916, and thereafter, calls for a reduction in the selling price of the cars. It is true that this price might be at any time increased, but the plan called for the reduction in price of $80 a car. The capacity of the plant, without the additions thereto voted to be made (without a part of them at least), would produce more than 600,000 cars annually. This number, and more, could have been sold for $440 instead of $360, a difference in the return for capital, labor, and materials employed of at least $48,000,000. In short, the plan does not call for and is not intended to produce immediately a more profitable business, but a less profitable one; not only less profitable than formerly, but less profitable than it is admitted it might be made. The apparent immediate effect will be to diminish the value of shares and the returns to shareholders.

It is the contention of plaintiffs that the apparent effect of the plan is intended to be the continued and continuing effect of it, and that it is deliberately proposed, not of record and not by official corporate declaration, but nevertheless proposed, to continue the corporation henceforth as a semi-eleemosynary institution and not as a business institution. In support of this contention, they point to the attitude and to the expressions of Mr. Henry Ford.

Mr. Henry Ford is the dominant force in the business of the Ford Motor Company. No plan of operations could be adopted unless he consented, and no board of directors can be elected whom he does not favor. One of the directors of the company has no stock. One share was assigned to him to qualify him for the position, but it is not claimed that he owns it. A business, one of the largest in the world, and one of the most profitable, has been built up. It employs many men, at good pay.

"My ambition," said Mr. Ford, "is to employ still more men, to spread the benefits of this industrial system to the greatest possible number, to help them build up their lives and their homes. To do this we are putting the greatest share of our profits back in the business."

"With regard to dividends, the company paid sixty per cent on its capitalization of two million dollars, or $1,200,000, leaving $58,000,000 to reinvest for the growth of the company. This is Mr. Ford's policy at present, and it is understood that the other stockholders cheerfully accede to this plan."

He had made up his mind in the summer of 1916 that no dividends other than the regular dividends should be paid, "for the present."

"Q.  For how long? Had you fixed in your mind any time in the future, when you were going to pay? A. No.

"Q.  That was indefinite in the future? A. That was indefinite; yes, sir."

The record, and especially the testimony of Mr. Ford, convinces that he has to some extent the attitude towards shareholders of one who has dispensed and distributed to them large gains and that they should be content to take what he chooses to give. His testimony creates the impression, also, that he thinks the Ford Motor Company has made too much money, has had too large profits, and that, although large profits might be still earned, a sharing of them with the public, by reducing the price of the output of the company, ought to be undertaken. We have no doubt that certain sentiments, philanthropic and altruistic, creditable to Mr. Ford, had large influence in determining the policy to be pursued by the Ford Motor Company—the policy which has been herein referred to.

It is said by his counsel that—

Although a manufacturing corporation cannot engage in humanitarian works as its principal business, the fact that it is organized for profit does not prevent the existence of implied powers to carry on with humanitarian motives such charitable works as are incidental to the main business of the corporation.

And again:

As the expenditures complained of are being made in an expansion of the business which the company is organized to carry on, and for purposes within the powers of the corporation as hereinbefore shown, the question is as to whether such expenditures are rendered illegal because influenced to some extent by humanitarian motives and purposes on the part of the members of the board of directors.

* * * [The cases referred to by counsel], after all, like all others in which the subject is treated, turn finally upon the point, the question, whether it appears that the directors were not acting for the best interests of the corporation. We do not draw in question, nor do counsel

for the plaintiffs do so, the validity of the general proposition stated by counsel nor the soundness of the opinions delivered in the cases cited. The case presented here is not like any of them. The difference between an incidental humanitarian expenditure of corporate funds for the benefit of the employees, like the building of a hospital for their use and the employment of agencies for the betterment of their condition, and a general purpose and plan to benefit mankind at the expense of others, is obvious. There should be no confusion (of which there is evidence) of the duties which Mr. Ford conceives that he and the stockholders owe to the general public and the duties which in law he and his codirectors owe to protesting, minority stockholders. A business corporation is organized and carried on primarily for the profit of the stockholders. The powers of the directors are to be employed for that end. The discretion of directors is to be exercised in the choice of means to attain that end, and does not extend to a change in the end itself, to the reduction of profits, or to the nondistribution of profits among stockholders in order to devote them to other purposes.

There is committed to the discretion of directors, a discretion to be exercised in good faith, the infinite details of business, including the wages which shall be paid to employees, the number of hours they shall work, the conditions under which labor shall be carried on, and the price for which products shall be offered to the public.

It is said by appellants that the motives of the board members are not material and will not be inquired into by the court so long as their acts are within their lawful powers. As we have pointed out, and the proposition does not require argument to sustain it, it is not within the lawful powers of a board of directors to shape and conduct the affairs of a corporation for the merely incidental benefit of shareholders and for the primary purpose of benefiting others, and no one will contend that, if the avowed purpose of the defendant directors was to sacrifice the interests of shareholders, it would not be the duty of the courts to interfere.

We are not, however, persuaded that we should interfere with the proposed expansion of the business of the Ford Motor Company. In view of the fact that the selling price of products may be increased at any time, the ultimate results of the larger business cannot be certainly estimated. The judges are not business experts. It is recognized that plans must often be made for a long future, for expected competition, for a continuing as well as an immediately profitable venture. The experience of the Ford Motor Company is evidence of capable management of its affairs. It may be noticed, incidentally, that it took from the public the money required for the execution of its plan, and that the very considerable salaries paid to Mr. Ford and to certain executive officers and employees were not diminished. We are not satisfied that the alleged motives of the directors, in so far as they are reflected in the conduct of the business, menace the interests of shareholders. It is enough to say, perhaps, that the court of equity is at all times open to complaining shareholders having a just grievance. * * *

The decree of the court below fixing and determining the specific amount to be distributed to stockholders is affirmed. In other respect, * * * the said decree is reversed.

### Note: Dodge v. Ford

Henry Ford asserted on numerous occasions that he wanted only a small profit from his venture:

> I hold this [view] because it enables a large number of people to buy and enjoy the use of a car and because it gives a larger number of men employment at good wages. Those are the two aims I have in life. But I would not be counted a success * * * if I could not accomplish that and at the same time make a fair amount of profit for myself and the men associated with me in the business.

* * *

> And let me say right here, that I do not believe that we should make such an awful profit on our cars. A reasonable profit is right, but not too much. So it has been my policy to force the price of the car down as fast as production would permit, and give the benefits to users and laborers, with resulting surprisingly enormous benefits to ourselves.

Allan Nevins & Frank E. Hill, FORD: EXPANSION AND CHALLENGE 1915–1933, 97 (1957).

Mr. Ford was challenged on cross-examination by counsel for the Dodge brothers, Ellicott G. Stevenson, producing the following colloquy:

STEVENSON: Now, I will ask you again, do you still think that those profits were "awful profits?"
FORD: Well, I guess I do, yes.
STEVENSON: And for that reason you were not satisfied to continue to make such awful profits?
FORD: We don't seem to be able to keep the profits down.
STEVENSON: * * * Are you trying to keep them down? What is the Ford Motor Company organized for except profits, will you tell me, Mr. Ford?
FORD: Organized to do as much good as we can, everywhere, for everybody concerned.

* * *

What, demanded Stevenson, was the purpose of the company? "To do as much as possible for everybody concerned," replied Ford. " * * * To make money and use it, give employment, and send out the car where the people can use it." He added, "And incidentally to make money."

STEVENSON: Incidentally make money?
FORD: Yes, sir.
STEVENSON: But your controlling feature * * * is to employ a great army of men at high wages, to reduce the selling price of your car, so that a lot of people can buy it at a cheap price, and give everybody a car that want one.

FORD:              If you give all that, the money will fall into your hands;
                   you can't get out of it.

*Id.* at 99–100.

## SHLENSKY v. WRIGLEY

95 Ill.App.2d 173, 237 N.E.2d 776 (1968).

SULLIVAN, JUSTICE.

This is an appeal from a dismissal of plaintiff's amended complaint on motion of the defendants. The action was a stockholders' derivative suit against the directors for negligence and mismanagement. The corporation was also made a defendant. Plaintiff sought damages and an order that defendants cause the installation of lights in Wrigley Field and the scheduling of night baseball games.

Plaintiff is a minority stockholder of defendant corporation, Chicago National League Ball Club (Inc.), a Delaware corporation with its principal place of business in Chicago, Illinois. Defendant corporation owns and operates the major league professional baseball team known as the Chicago Cubs. The corporation also engages in the operation of Wrigley Field, the Cubs' home park, the concessionaire sales during Cubs' home games, television and radio broadcasts of Cubs' home games, the leasing of the field for football games and other events and receives its share, as visiting team, of admission moneys from games played in other National League stadia. The individual defendants are directors of the Cubs and have served for varying periods of years. Defendant Philip K. Wrigley is also president of the corporation and owner of approximately 80% of the stock therein.

Plaintiff alleges that since night baseball was first played in 1935 nineteen of the twenty major league teams have scheduled night games. In 1966, out of a total of 1620 games in the major leagues, 932 were played at night. Plaintiff alleges that every member of the major leagues, other than the Cubs, scheduled substantially all of its home games in 1966 at night, exclusive of opening days, Saturdays, Sundays, holidays and days prohibited by league rules. Allegedly this has been done for the specific purpose of maximizing attendance and thereby maximizing revenue and income.

The Cubs, in the years 1961–65, sustained operating losses from its direct baseball operations. Plaintiff attributes those losses to inadequate attendance at Cubs' home games. He concludes that if the directors continue to refuse to install lights at Wrigley Field and schedule night baseball games, the Cubs will continue to sustain comparable losses and its financial condition will continue to deteriorate.

Plaintiff alleges that, except for the year 1963, attendance at Cubs' home games has been substantially below that at their road games, many of which were played at night.

Plaintiff compares attendance at Cubs' games with that of the Chicago White Sox, an American League club, whose weekday games were generally played at night. The weekend attendance figures for the two teams was similar; however, the White Sox week-night games drew many more patrons than did the Cubs' weekday games.

Plaintiff alleges that the funds for the installation of lights can be readily obtained through financing and the cost of installation would be far more than offset and recaptured by increased revenues and incomes resulting from the increased attendance.

Plaintiff further alleges that defendant Wrigley has refused to install lights, not because of interest in the welfare of the corporation but because of his personal opinions "that baseball is a 'daytime sport' and that the installation of lights and night baseball games will have a deteriorating effect upon the surrounding neighborhood." It is alleged that he has admitted that he is not interested in whether the Cubs would benefit financially from such action because of his concern for the neighborhood, and that he would be willing for the team to play night games if a new stadium were built in Chicago.

Plaintiff alleges that the other defendant directors, with full knowledge of the foregoing matters, have acquiesced in the policy laid down by Wrigley and have permitted him to dominate the board of directors in matters involving the installation of lights and scheduling of night games, even though they knew he was not motivated by a good faith concern as to the best interests of defendant corporation, but solely by his personal views set forth above. It is charged that the directors are acting for a reason or reasons contrary and wholly unrelated to the business interests of the corporation; that such arbitrary and capricious acts constitute mismanagement and waste of corporate assets, and that the directors have been negligent in failing to exercise reasonable care and prudence in the management of the corporate affairs.

The question on appeal is whether plaintiff's amended complaint states a cause of action. It is plaintiff's position that fraud, illegality and conflict of interest are not the only bases for a stockholder's derivative action against the directors. Contrariwise, defendants argue that the courts will not step in and interfere with honest business judgment of the directors unless there is a showing of fraud, illegality or conflict of interest.

The cases in this area are numerous and each differs from the others on a factual basis. However, the courts have pronounced certain ground rules which appear in all cases and which are then applied to the given factual situation. The court in *Wheeler v. Pullman Iron and Steel Company*, 143 Ill. 197, 207, 32 N.E. 420, 423, said:

> It is, however, fundamental in the law of corporations, that the majority of its stockholders shall control the policy of the corporation, and regulate and govern the lawful exercise of its franchise and business. * * * Every one purchasing or subscribing for stock in a

corporation impliedly agrees that he will be bound by the acts and proceedings done or sanctioned by a majority of the shareholders, or by the agents of the corporation duly chosen by such majority, within the scope of the powers conferred by the charter, and courts of equity will not undertake to control the policy or business methods of a corporation, although it may be seen that a wiser policy might be adopted and the business more successful if other methods were pursued. The majority of shares of its stock, or the agents by the holders thereof lawfully chosen, must be permitted to control the business of the corporation in their discretion, when not in violation of its charter or some public law, or corruptly and fraudulently subversive of the rights and interests of the corporation or of a shareholder.

* * * Plaintiff argues that the allegations of his amended complaint are sufficient to set forth a cause of action under the principles set out in *Dodge v. Ford Motor Co.*, 204 Mich. 459, 170 N.W. 668. * * *

From the authority relied upon in that case it is clear that the court felt that there must be fraud or a breach of that good faith which directors are bound to exercise toward the stockholders in order to justify the courts entering into the internal affairs of corporations. This is made clear when the court refused to interfere with the director[s'] decision to expand the business. * * *

Plaintiff in the instant case argues that the directors are acting for reasons unrelated to the financial interest and welfare of the Cubs. However, we are not satisfied that the motives assigned to Philip K. Wrigley, and through him to the other directors, are contrary to the best interests of the corporation and the stockholders. For example, it appears to us that the effect on the surrounding neighborhood might well be considered by a director who was considering the patrons who would or would not attend the games if the park were in a poor neighborhood. Furthermore, the long run interest of the corporation in its property value at Wrigley Field might demand all efforts to keep the neighborhood from deteriorating. By these thoughts we do not mean to say that we have decided that the decision of the directors was a correct one. That is beyond our jurisdiction and ability. We are merely saying that the decision is one properly before directors and the motives alleged in the amended complaint showed no fraud, illegality or conflict of interest in their making of that decision. * * *

Finally, we do not agree with plaintiff's contention that failure to follow the example of the other major league clubs in scheduling night games constituted negligence. Plaintiff made no allegation that these teams' night schedules were profitable or that the purpose for which night baseball had been undertaken was fulfilled. Furthermore, it cannot be said that directors, even those of corporations that are losing money, must follow the lead of the other corporations in the field. Directors are elected for their business capabilities and judgment and the courts cannot require them to forego their judgment because of the decisions of directors of other companies. Courts may not decide these questions in the absence of a clear showing of dereliction of duty on the part of the specific directors and mere failure to "follow the crowd" is not such a dereliction.

For the foregoing reasons the order of dismissal entered by the trial court is affirmed.

## 2.  WHAT IS CORPORATE RESPONSIBILITY?: OTHER VIEWS

### Milton Friedman, CAPITALISM & FREEDOM

#### 133–34 (1962).

The view has been gaining widespread acceptance that corporate officials * * * have a "social responsibility" that goes beyond serving the interest of their stockholders * * *. This view shows a fundamental misconception of the character and nature of a free economy. In such an economy, there is one and only one social responsibility of business—to use its resources and engage in activities designed to increase its profits so long as it stays within the rules of the game, which is to say, engages in open and free competition, without deception or fraud. * * * It is the responsibility of the rest of us to establish a framework of law such that an individual in pursuing his own interest is, to quote Adam Smith again, "led by an invisible hand to promote an end which was no part of his intention. Nor is it always the worse for the society that it was no part of it. By pursuing his own interest, he frequently promotes that of the society more effectually than when he really intends to promote it. I have never known much good done by those who affected to trade for the public good."

Few trends could so thoroughly undermine the very foundations of our free society as the acceptance by corporate officials of a social responsibility other than to make as much money for their stockholders as possible. This is a fundamentally subversive doctrine. If businessmen do have a social responsibility other than making maximum profits for stockholders, how are they to know what it is? Can self-selected private individuals decide what the social interest is? Can they decide how great a burden they are justified in placing on themselves or their stockholders to serve that social interest? Is it tolerable that these public functions of taxation, expenditure, and control be exercised by the people who happen at the moment to be in charge of particular enterprises, chosen for those posts by strictly private groups? If businessmen are civil servants rather than the employees of their stockholders then in a democracy they will, sooner or later, be chosen by the public techniques of election and appointment.

Elliott J. Weiss, *Social Regulation of Business Activity:
Reforming the Corporate Governance System to
Resolve an Institutional Impasse*

28 UCLA L.Rev. 343, 418–32 (1981).

Corporations are creations of law, and have as their ultimate purpose the welfare of society. In an earlier era, when resources were abundant, technology simple and affluence uncommon, corporations could promote societal welfare by single-mindedly promoting their own financial well-being. But changes in society have led to a geometric increase in the number of situations in which corporate pursuit of financial objectives seems inconsistent with public welfare, and to a commensurate increase in social regulation of corporate activity. This regulatory splurge has failed, largely because government lacks the capacity to regulate effectively without the cooperation of the regulated. Consequently, society now needs to reconsider the stated objective of corporate activity. * * *

The standard that * * * can best promote social welfare is "altruistic capitalism." This standard would require corporate directors to exercise reasonable care to ensure that management operates the business: (1) as if the firm were a pure competitor concerned with long-term profitability; (2) as if the firm paid all the external costs and captured all the external benefits of its operation; (3) as if the firm's customers and competitors shared all relevant information that the firm possessed; and (4) as if the firm were liable for all acts of its employees and agents.

Several aspects of this standard warrant amplification. First, the standard governs directors and contemplates that they will monitor the performance of corporate executives rather than involve themselves in the nuts and bolts of corporate decision making. * * *

Second, altruistic capitalism gives continuing prominence to corporations' financial performance; it requires that corporations temper, but not abandon, their quest for profits. A firm's compliance with this standard would not threaten its financial viability since all of its significant competitors would be operating under the same standard. * * *

Third, altruistic capitalism strikes an appropriate balance between public and private authority. * * *

Finally, substituting altruistic capitalism for the current standard of profit maximization would alter the atmosphere surrounding corporate decision making, but would not really increase corporate directors' discretionary power. Even under existing law, corporate directors have broad latitude to promote social values. * * *

Still, the existing profit maximization standard requires directors to frame and justify their decisions in financial terms. * * *

Adopting altruistic capitalism as the legal standard for corporate behavior would change the corporate decision-making environment.

\* \* \* Altruistic capitalism would not, however, be a self-executing standard. It would allow directors considerable discretion, since the business judgment rule would continue to insulate directors' reasonable decisions from judicial second-guessing. Consequently, directors governed by the standard of altruistic capitalism would be free to reach the same decisions now reached by directors pursuing traditional financial objectives, albeit after engaging in a somewhat different decision-making process.

Thus, corporate law reform should not be limited to restating the objective of corporate activity. Adoption of the suggested new legal standard is likely to have little effect on corporate behavior unless directors are committed to a policy of social responsiveness \* \* \*.

[Professor Weiss proposes that Congress create a National Directors Corps, the members of which would be appointed by the President with the advice and consent of the Senate, and that large corporations be required to draw at least two-thirds of their directors from the National Directors Corps. He contends that "[s]election procedures, community and peer pressure, and their own views of their social roles all should lead National Directors to behave diligently and responsibly \* \* \*." To promote accountability, he also suggests that "shareholders and outsiders affected by corporate actions \* \* \* be allowed to sue National Directors for failure to exercise reasonable care in monitoring corporate performance. Negligent National Directors could be put on probation, or suspended or expelled from the Corps."]

## ALI, PRINCIPLES OF CORPORATE GOVERNANCE: ANALYSIS AND RECOMMENDATIONS (1994)

### § 2.01 THE OBJECTIVE AND CONDUCT OF THE CORPORATION

(a) Subject to the provisions of Subsection (b) \* \* \*, a corporation should have as its objective the conduct of business activities with a view to enhancing corporate profit and shareholder gain.

(b) Even if corporate profit and shareholder gain are not thereby enhanced, the corporation, in the conduct of its business:

(a) Is obliged, to the same extent as a natural person, to act within the boundaries set by law;

(2) May take into account ethical considerations that are reasonably regarded as appropriate to the responsible conduct of business; and

(3) May devote a reasonable amount of resources to public welfare, humanitarian, educational, and philanthropic purposes.

### COMMENT

e.  *Corporate objective and corporate conduct.*  The subject matter of these Principles is the governance of business corporations. The business corporation is an instrument through which capital is assembled for the activities of producing and distributing goods and services and making investments. These Principles take as a basic proposition that a business corporation should have as its objective the conduct of such activities with a view to enhancing corporate profit and shareholder gain. This objective, which will hereafter be referred to as "the economic objective," is embodied in Subsection (a). The basic proposition is qualified in the manner stated in Subsection (b), which speaks to the conduct of the corporation. The provisions of Subsection (b) reflect a recognition that the corporation is a social as well as an economic institution, and accordingly that its pursuit of the economic objective must be constrained by social imperatives and may be qualified by social needs.

*f. The economic objective.* In very general terms, Subsection (a) may be thought of as a broad injunction to enhance economic returns, while Subsection (b) makes clear that certain kinds of conduct must or may be pursued whether or not they enhance such returns (that is, even if the conduct either yields no economic return or entails a net economic loss). In most cases, however, the kinds of conduct described in Subsection (b) could be pursued even under the principle embodied in Subsection (a). Such conduct will usually be consistent with economic self-interest, because the principle embodied in Subsection (a)—that the objective of the corporation is to conduct business activities with a view to enhancing corporate profit and shareholder gain—does not mean that the objective of the corporation must be to realize corporate profit and shareholder gain in the short run. Indeed, the contrary is true: long-run profitability and shareholder gain are at the core of the economic objective. Activity that entails a short-run cost to achieve an appropriately greater long-run profit is therefore not a departure from the economic objective. An orientation toward lawful, ethical, and public-spirited activity will normally fall within this description. The modern corporation by its nature creates interdependencies with a variety of groups with whom the corporation has a legitimate concern, such as employees, customers, suppliers, and members of the communities in which the corporation operates. The long-term profitability of the corporation generally depends on meeting the fair expectations of such groups. Short-term profits may properly be subordinated to recognition that responsible maintenance of these interdependencies is likely to contribute to long-term profitability and shareholder gain. The corporation's business may be conducted accordingly.

For comparable reasons, the economic objective does not imply that the corporation must extract the last penny of profit out of every transaction in which it is involved. Similarly, under normal circumstances the economic objective is met by focusing on the business in which the corporation is actually engaged.

Although a corporate decisionmaker needs to meet a standard of care in making decisions, that standard can be satisfied even when, as is often the case, a prospective profit cannot be particularized. Recurring instances of this sort include those in which the object of a corporate action is to maintain the confidence of business organizations with which the corporation deals, to foster the morale of employees, or to encourage favorable or forestall unfavorable government regulation—as by abstaining from conduct that would engender unfavorable public reaction against the corporation, providing lawful assistance in connection with lobbying or referenda activities, or voluntarily adopting a course of conduct so as to forestall legislation that would instead mandate such conduct. There is also no conflict with the economic objective when a corporation takes an action that will generate profit (or reduce the level of losses) not only for itself but also for other firms, if the corporation's benefit is likely to exceed the corporation's costs. In general, if the corporate officials who authorize a decision satisfy the test of the business judgment rule, the decision itself would satisfy § 2.01.

### 3.  OTHER CONSTITUENCY STATUTES

*a.  Introduction.* While corporate law traditionally has focused on the relationship between the board of directors and the shareholders, almost thirty state legislatures have adopted statutes that permit, and in one case require, a board of directors to consider the effect of any corporate action on non-shareholder interests. These interests may include the corporation's employees, customers, creditors, suppliers, the economy of the state/region/nation, community and societal interests, and the long-term and short-term interests of the corporation.

Constituency statutes were typically enacted together with anti-takeover legislation to protect corporate directors who oppose a hostile bid for control. While several of these statutes apply in the limited context of takeovers or control transactions, the majority are not so limited.

Ohio's statute, Ohio Rev. Code Ann. § 1701.59(E), which is typical, provides:

> [A]  director, in determining what he reasonably believes to be in the best interests of the corporation, shall consider the interests of the corporation's shareholders and, in his discretion, may consider any of the following:
>
> (1) The interests of the corporation's employees, suppliers, creditors, and customers;
>
> (2) The economy of the state and nation;
>
> (3) Community and societal considerations;
>
> (4) The long-term as well as short-term interests of the corporation and its shareholders, including the possibility that these interests may be best served by the continued independence of the corporation.

Variations abound. Some statutes impose mandatory requirements on directors. For example, insofar as a decision relates to the sale of all or substantially all of a corporation's assets, Connecticut *requires* a director of a publicly held corporation to consider the standard list of factors "in determining what he reasonably believes to be in the best interests of the corporation." Conn. Stock Corp. Act § 33–313(e). The

Connecticut statute does not require that such mandatory consideration of other constituencies apply to any other decision.

The Indiana and Pennsylvania statutes do *not* require directors to consider other constituencies, but *permit* directors to subordinate shareholders' interests to those of other constituencies. Pa. Bus. Corp. L. § 1715(a) states that "directors * * * shall not be required, in considering the best interests of the corporation or the effects of any action, to regard any corporate interest or the interests of any group affected by such action as a dominant or controlling interest or factor." *See also* Ind. Bus. Corp. L. § 23–1–35–1(f)). Thus, directors of Indiana and Pennsylvania corporations can claim that they acted in the best interests of a corporation even when they knowingly disregarded shareholders' economic interests.

To preclude claims by constituencies that feel their interests were not properly taken into account, the Indiana and Pennsylvania statutes also include what has been labeled a conclusive presumption of validity provision. Ind. Bus. Corp. L. § 23–1–35–1(g); Pa. Bus. Corp. L. § 1715(d). Specifically, they provide that any determination based on a disinterested board's discretionary consideration of the long-term corporate interests or the interests of "the other [enumerated] corporate constituent groups * * * shall conclusively be presumed to be valid unless it can be demonstrated that the determination was not made in good faith after reasonable investigation." Ind. Bus. Corp. L. § 23–1–35–1(g).

*b.   The Future of Constituency Statutes.* In 1990, the Committee on Corporate Laws of the American Bar Association studied constituency statutes. Finding them "an inappropriate way to regulate corporate relationships or to respond to unwanted takeovers and that an expansive interpretation of the other constituencies statutes cast in the permissive mode is both unnecessary and unwise," it declined to include a constituency statute in the Revised Model Business Corporation Act. American Bar Association Committee on Corporate Laws, *Other Constituencies Statutes: Potential for Confusion*, 45 Bus. Law. 2253, 2270–2271 (1990). The Committee concluded that constituency statutes may be interpreted "to impose new powers and duties on directors" and "they may radically alter some of the basic premises upon which corporation law has been constructed in this country without sufficient attention having been given to all the economic, social, and legal ramifications of such a change in the law." Id. at 2253. Although the Committee believed that the statutes could create opportunities for misunderstanding and potential mischief, the debate continues; however, no serious effort has been mounted to repeal any constituency statute.

In contrast to the approach of the Committee on Corporate Laws, David Millon, *Redefining Corporate Law*, 24 Ind. L. Rev. 223,277 (1991) concludes:

> It is conceivable that the directors' duty [i.e., constituency] statutes herald the beginnings of a radically different understanding

of corporate law and corporate purpose. If they are manifestations of a deeper design to enhance the status of nonshareholders within the corporate enterprise, several lines of development are possible. One could imagine greater nonshareholder involvement in the decision-making process, through voting rights, for example. More radically, we might revise our notion of corporate governance so as to replace the present hierarchical structure with one in which significant decision-making authority spreads downwards, from management into the hands of those most directly affected. And if nonshareholders are to have powers of control, perhaps new ownership structures should be considered as well.

---

For more detailed background on constituency statutes and the arguments in favor of and against them, see Symposium: *Corporate Malaise—Stakeholder Statutes: Cause or Cure?*, 21 STETSON L. REV. 1 (1991); Lawrence E. Mitchell, *A Theoretical and Practical Framework for Enforcing Corporate Constituency Statutes*, 70 TEX. L. REV. 579 (1992); Steven M. H. Wallman, *Corporate Constituency Statutes: Placing the Corporation's Interests First*, 11 BUS. L. UPDATE 1 (Nov./Dec. 1990); A.A. Sommer Jr., *Whom Should the Corporation Serve? The Berle–Dodd Debate Revisited Sixty Years Later*, 16 DEL. J. CORP. L. 33 (1991); Charles Hansen, *Other Constituency Statutes: A Search for Perspective*, 46 BUS. LAW. 1355 (1991); James J. Hanks, *Non–Stockholder Constituency Statutes: An Idea Whose Time Should Never Come*, 3 INSIGHTS 20 (Dec. 1989); David Millon, *Redefining Corporate Law*, 24 IND. L. REV. 223 (1991).

### 4. THE ROLE OF COUNSEL

Counseling a client who wants to take some potentially controversial action also can raise difficult issues for an attorney. Consider, by way of example, a client who wants to relocate a factory whose employees are on strike. *Abrams v. Allen*, 297 N.Y. 52, 74 N.E.2d 305 (1947), makes clear that a decision to relocate so as to consolidate manufacturing operations represents a presumptively valid business judgment, while a decision to relocate based solely on a desire to punish striking employees may subject directors to liability. A lawyer clearly should not advise a client to misrepresent her reasons for deciding to relocate so as to bring her decision within the protection of the business judgment rule. On the other hand, is it troublesome if the lawyer, before the client announces her decision, explains the holding of *Abrams* as to the reasons for relocating a factory that a court is and is not likely to treat as valid?

Norman Redlich, Lawyers, The Temple,<br>and the Market Place<br>30 BUS.LAW. 65, 65–67 (1975).

\* \* \* We may sometimes resent the fact that the public is pointing to the lawyers and holding us responsible for many of the moral shortcomings of the country, but there is no way that the legal profession can avoid bearing this burden. We play too crucial a role in government and corporate life to avoid this responsibility. * * *

Let me state the problem. Lawyers, including house counsel, are both a part of, and also professionally removed from, corporate and governmental entities which have engaged, and will continue to engage, in actions which may be illegal and immoral. These entities require our advice and are entitled to our services. Moreover, society has a profound interest in having a corps of professionals giving competent legal advice to these corporate and governmental entities.

The question we face is this. How does that corps of professionals— we lawyers—so carry out our mission that we can hold our heads high and say to the public, "We have done all that we can to prevent the wrongdoings of our clients consistent with our responsibility to advise them as to the law"? * * *

First, let us talk about our clear professional responsibility to say, "No." We all operate under a canon which commands us to " * * * exercise independent professional judgment on behalf of a client." I know how difficult it sometimes is, when an important and powerful client is embarking on some course of action which everyone is convinced is in the best interests of the company only to have the lawyer insist on some step-such as disclosure—which he feels is legally required. * * *

A lawyer can be under enormous pressure to "go along" with a transaction when he knows that the facts are simply not as they are portrayed to a government agency or to another private party. We have all heard the seductive serpent-like song. It has many refrains: "Who will ever know?" "You're not the judge, you're only the lawyer." "I didn't hire you to tell me what I can't do." "Whose lawyer are you, anyway?" You've heard these and many more. Often nothing at all needs to be said. Everyone is going along on the basis of certain assumptions, and it is so difficult to speak up and announce, as in the famous fable, "Look, the Emperor has no clothes."

But if there is anything which is clear, it is our professional duty to refuse to approve of, or participate in, transactions which we believe to be unlawful, even if it means that we have to delay or thwart a major program of a client, or cause a considerable loss of money, or embarrass management—or even cause us to lose a major client. * * *

Moreover, lawyers in this situation are constantly underestimating their own power. They speak not from weakness but from strength. Very often the client wants the lawyer's stamp of approval and will not proceed without it. Despite all of the pressuring, and occasional bullying, the lawyer does hold the passkey and only he can turn it. In the final analysis, we cannot expect the public to respect lawyers as independent professionals if they run for cover when a powerful client wants them to go along with a shady transaction on grounds that "everyone is doing it" or that "no one will find out."

## AMERICAN BAR ASSOCIATION, MODEL RULES
## OF PROFESSIONAL CONDUCT (1983)

### Rule 2.1  Advisor

In representing a client, a lawyer shall exercise independent professional judgment and render candid advice. In rendering advice, a lawyer may refer not only to law but to other considerations such as moral, economic, social and political factors, that may be relevant to the client's situation.

### COMMENT

### Scope of Advice

A client is entitled to straightforward advice expressing the lawyer's honest assessment. Legal advice often involves unpleasant facts and alternatives that a client may be disinclined to confront. In presenting advice, a lawyer endeavors to sustain the client's morale and may put advice in as acceptable a form as honesty permits. However, a lawyer should not be deterred from giving candid advice by the prospect that the advice will be unpalatable to the client.

Advice couched in narrowly legal terms may be of little value to a client, especially where practical considerations, such as cost or effects on other people, are predominant. Purely technical legal advice, therefore, can sometimes be inadequate. It is proper for a lawyer to refer to relevant moral and ethical considerations in giving advice. Although a lawyer is not a moral advisor as such, moral and ethical considerations impinge upon most legal questions and may decisively influence how the law will be applied.

A client may expressly or impliedly ask the lawyer for purely technical advice. When such a request is made by a client experienced in legal matters, the lawyer may accept it at face value. When such a request is made by a client inexperienced in legal matters, however, the lawyer's responsibility as advisor may include indicating that more may be involved than strictly legal considerations.

\* \* \*

### Offering Advice

In general, a lawyer is not expected to give advice until asked by the client. However, when a lawyer knows that a client proposes a course of action that is likely to result in substantial adverse legal consequences to the client, duty to the client \* \* \* may require that the lawyer act if the client's course of action is related to the representation. A lawyer ordinarily has no duty to initiate investigation of a client's affairs or to give advice that the client has indicated is unwanted, but a lawyer may initiate advice to a client when doing so appears to be in the client's interest.

# Chapter 6

# THE CHOICE OF ORGANIZATIONAL FORM

## PROBLEM

## PRECISION TOOLS—PART I

This is the first part of a multi-part Problem that will give you the opportunity to address a number of important issues that arise when a group of clients attempt to acquire and operate an existing business, including: (1) deciding on the legal form they should use to operate that business (this Chapter); (2) resolving issues that arise in connection with organizing a corporation to operate that business (Chapter 7); (3) evaluating the business they plan to purchase (Chapter 8); and (4) designing a capital structure for their new corporation (Chapter 9). Part I of the Problem includes background information about (1) the principal participants in the proposed business venture and (2) the business they plan to acquire. Keep this information in mind; you will need to use it in subsequent parts of the Problem.

For many years, Precision Tools, Inc. ("PT") has been producing precision components for manufacturers of different kinds of communication equipment. PT has a staff of highly skilled machinists capable of producing components that meet demanding specifications. Large companies often find it more efficient to contract with PT than to set up special, in-house departments to produce these components. PT's largest customer, from whom it derives over a third of its business, is Majestic Radio Corp., a major producer of two-way radio equipment. Harry Stern and John Starr founded PT and continue to own and manage it. Stern and Starr are now contemplating retirement and are seeking to sell PT.

Jessica Bacon, 30, is a writer and researcher for business publications. While working on a story about the small companies that contributed to the success of IBM-compatible personal computers, she became interested in learning more about other small businesses in the country, their importance to the economy, their profitability and the kind of people who owned and operated them. Precision Tools was one of the companies she studied.

Jessica has discussed PT with Michael Lane, 32, an engineer employed by a large computer company. Michael believes rapid growth is likely in the telecommunications business, and that large companies increasingly will come to rely on dependable producers of small precision components. Michael thinks PT is well positioned to capitalize on this trend; its employees are highly skilled in fabricating a wide variety of precision components and its production machinery is state of the art. Michael and Jessica believe that with new and aggressive management, PT could grow rapidly.

Michael and Jessica's plans, if they acquire PT, include designing an expanded product line that will enable PT to compete for new telecommunications business and more aggressively marketing PT's current line of products. To carry out these plans, they will need to purchase additional equipment for PT and provide it with increased working capital. Michael comes from a financially modest background, is married, has two young children and owns his home. Aside from $100,000 he plans to invest in PT, Michael has little capital. Jessica, who is not married, plans to invest $200,000 in PT. She also has a stock portfolio worth about $175,000 and stands to inherit several hundred thousand dollars on the death of her father, who is retired.

Michael and Jessica's mutual friend, Bernie Gould, has told them he would be willing to invest about $600,000 in their new business if Jessica and Michael acquire PT. Bernie, 62 years old, is a partner in an insurance brokerage business with two other individuals of about the same age. Bernie is thinking of retiring from that business in a few years. He is married and has a son, Bill, who is presently a college junior. Bill is not sure what he wants to do when he graduates but is sure he does not want to be an insurance broker. Bill is a computer buff and is very enthusiastic about his father's involvement in the PT venture. Bernie is equally excited about the project, but he says that he is too busy with other affairs to spend much time helping with day-to-day management. However, he would like to make his substantial business experience available where it could be helpful and he also insists on having some voice on the new directions in which Michael and Jessica plan to take PT's business.

Michael, Jessica and Bernie have agreed that Michael has the experience and skills to serve as the chief executive officer and manage the operational side of the business and that Jessica, who obtained an M.B.A. before becoming a reporter, is well qualified to serve as the chief financial officer. Michael and Jessica plan to be full-time employees of the new business.

Because they are purchasing a going concern, Jessica, Michael and Bernie think their new venture may be profitable from the beginning. However, they recognize the real possibility that it will experience losses in the first few years due to the costs involved in expanding PT's business, borrowing at higher than prime interest rates, and sowing some marketing seeds that will not bear fruit immediately.

When Michael first came to you about this transaction, one of the things he said was, "We want you to set up a corporation for us." After reflecting on the matter, would you advise Michael, Jessica and Bernie form a corporation to acquire PT? Would it be more advantageous for them to use another form of business organization? How would you explain this choice to them?

# A.  INTRODUCTION

In planning a new business, the owners must decide which organizational form best suits their needs. This decision is by no means simple. The choice of organizational form will depend largely upon the economics of the venture, the preferences of the individual owners and tax considerations. The balance that the owners strike will dictate their choice among the three primary forms of business organization available to joint owners: the partnership, the corporation and the limited liability company.

Before the recent development of the limited liability company, the choice of organizational form was confined to a choice between the partnership and the corporation. In their default forms—the form of organization that exists by operation of law in the absence of agreement to the contrary by the owners—partnerships and corporations are polar opposites. A partnership is an entity in which all the participants have unlimited liability, an equal voice in management, and the ability to act as agents for the partnership and incur obligations that will be binding on all the partners. In contrast, a corporation is based upon principles of centralized management and limited liability for the participants.

Although the major attributes of each form are antithetical, the law affords the parties considerable flexibility to agree on an organizational structure that deviates considerably from the the norms of the default models. This flexibility means that the theoretical distinctions between these two forms may not be as great as they appear. Moreover, the advent of the limited liability company—an entity that provides limited liability for the participants with the tax advantages of a partnership— provides the owners of a business with even more flexibility to adopt an organizational form tailored to their particular needs.

Partnerships may be either general partnerships or limited partnerships. In virtually all states, partnerships are governed by uniform statutes. General partnerships are subject to the Uniform Partnership Act ("UPA") in all states but Louisiana. Limited partnerships in virtually every jurisdiction are regulated either by the Uniform Limited Partnership Act ("ULPA") or the Revised Uniformed Limited Partnership Act ("RULPA"). These statutes allow considerable flexibility and informality in the organization and operation of partnerships.

The UPA defines a partnership as "an association of two or more persons to carry on as co-owners a business for profit." § 6(1). In a general partnership, each partner possesses an equal voice in management and the authority to act as agent for the partnership. See § 18(e) and § 9(1). Each partner is subject to unlimited liability for the debts of the partnership, as well as the torts of her partners committed within the course of the partnership's business. §§ 13–15. However, most states have recently adopted statutes providing for the creation of limited liability partnerships ("LLPs") and limiting the liability of partners in these entities.

The RULPA defines a limited partnership as a "partnership formed by two or more persons * * * and having one or more general partners and one or more limited partners." § 101(7). In a limited partnership, a limited partner has no voice in the active management of the partnership, which is conducted by the general partner. *See* RULPA § 403. Additionally, the limited partner's liability is limited to her initial contribution to the partnership, while the general partner is subject to unlimited liability. §§ 9(1), 17(1). However, some states have recently adopted statutes providing for the creation of limited liability limited partnerships ("LLLPs") and limiting the liability of general partners in such entities.

At the opposite end of the continuum, corporations are entities that are distinct from their owners. The principal differences between a corporation and a partnership lie in the management structure and liability provisions. In contrast to the general partnership, the management of the corporation is centralized in a board of directors. RMBCA § 8.01. An attractive feature of the corporate form is that a shareholder of a corporation is not personally liable for the debts of the corporation. RMBCA § 6.22.

Between these two poles are hybrid forms of ownership, the most important of which is the limited liability company ("LLC"). The LLC is a relatively new form of business organization. Like the corporation, a limited liability company is an entity separate from its owners, who are called "members." Members, like shareholders in a corporation, receive the benefits of limited liability. Management arrangements generally are specified in an "operating agreement." State LLC statutes vary much more than do state corporation and partnership statutes. However, in 1995 the Commissioners of Uniform State Laws promulgated a Uniform Limited Liability Company Act which, while controversial in many respects, seems likely to produce a greater degree of uniformity among state LLC statutes than is now the case.

In this chapter, we contrast the principal non-tax features of both forms of partnership, the limited liability company, and the corporation. We discuss the primary distinctions between the default modes of operation and the principal ways in which these defaults can be varied. Finally, we consider the principal tax consequences of the choice of organizational form.

# B.  NON–TAX ASPECTS

## 1.  FORMATION

The formation of a corporation requires formal action with the state. In order to incorporate, the persons creating the corporation, or incorporators, must file articles of incorporation containing certain information about the company and its incorporators, such as the corporate name, the number of authorized shares, and the name and address of each incorporator. The articles may also contain certain other information, such as corporate purpose, provisions regarding management and regulation of the corporation, and limitations on the powers of the corporation and the shareholders, officers and directors. See RMBCA § 2.02; Del. Gen. Corp. L. § 102. Under the RMBCA, corporate existence begins when the articles of incorporation are filed. Failure to comply with the legal formalities of incorporation can result in the failure to recognize the existence of the corporation as a legal entity.

Forming a general partnership, on the other hand, requires no filing with the state. A partnership may arise in two ways. The most common method is consensual formation. It occurs when two or more individuals enter into a contractual relationship, usually embodied in a partnership agreement which governs the the relationship of the partners, including such matters as managerial rights, distribution rights, interests in profits and losses, and rights upon dissolution of the enterprise. Because of the definition of a partnership in UPA § 6(1), a partnership may also arise by operation of law. A non-consensual partnership often results in undesirable and unforeseen consequences to the partners, such as unlimited liability for debts of the partnership.

A limited partnership, like a corporation, requires the filing with the state of a certificate setting forth the rights and duties of the partners among themselves and identifying the general partners. RULPA § 201. Typically, the general and limited partners also execute a written partnership agreement. If new general partners are added, amended filings are necessary.

The formation of an LLC also requires the filing of *articles of organization*, which must include the name of the LLC and the address of its registered agent, with the appropriate state agency. The members also enter into an *operating agreement* (which some statutes call the "regulations" of the LLC, the "limited liability company agreement," or the "member control agreement") that sets forth the members' rights and duties. Some statutes require that the operating agreement be written; others allow oral operating agreements to govern some or all aspects of the members' relationship. Some statutes allow an operating agreement to override provisions of the articles of organization; others provide that, in the case of conflict, the articles of organization govern.*

---

* To form an LLP (or LLLP), the partners must file a certificate with a designat-

## 2. LIMITED LIABILITY

Limited liability is the key non-tax feature of a corporation. A corporation is a separate legal entity which is responsible for its own debts and other liabilities. A shareholder's liability is limited to her original investment in the corporation. There are three major exceptions to shareholder limited liability. Shareholders will be personally liable: 1) where the corporation is not properly formed (*see* Chapter 7); 2) for unpaid capital contributions that they have agreed to make (*see* Chapter 9); and 3) where the veil of limited liability is pierced (*see* Chapter 11). In addition, shareholders in many small corporations increase their financial exposure by personally guaranteeing loans made to the corporation.

A partnership differs from a corporation in that the general partners, in their individual capacities, are subject to unlimited liability for the obligations of the partnership. UPA § 15. Partnership liability for the torts of the partnership is joint and several. Partners are exposed only to joint liability for the partnership's contractual obligations. With respect to both contractual obligations and tort liability, each partner may bind the partnership, and thus the other partners, provided that the act giving rise to liability is performed in the ordinary course of business. UPA § 9(1); § 13.**

In a limited partnership, the general partner faces the same unlimited liability as a partner in a general partnership. A limited partner, on the other hand, is shielded by the same limited liability rule as a corporate shareholder. The limited partner's liability is limited to her investment in the enterprise, provided that she does not participate in the management of the firm. Courts have struggled to determine what constitutes "participation in management," but the cases have painted no bright lines. RULPA § 303 provides limited guidance in defining "participation." It states that certain activities, such as advising the general partner with respect to the business and voting on critical transactions, are not to be considered "participation." Thus, the statute allows a limited amount of participation in certain activities without denying limited partners the protection of limited liability.

To further insulate the participants in a limited partnership from personal liability, the law allows the general partner to be a corporation. That corporation is liable for the claims against the partnership, but its shareholders will be shielded from liability for claims arising from the corporate general partner's debts.

All limited liability company statutes provide for limited liability for the entity's members and managers. For example, Delaware's statute provides, " * * * [n]o member or manager of a limited liability company

---

ed state office. *See, e.g.*, 6 Del. C. Ann. § 1544 (partnership must file application with Secretary of State, who registers firm).

** Some state LLP statutes exempt partners in an LLP from liability for torts other than those they or employees they super-

vise have committed. *See, e.g.*, 6 Del. C. Ann. § 1515. Other LLP statutes provide that partners in an LLP have no liability for any partnership debts merely on account of their status as partners. *See, e.g.*, Minn. Stat. Ann. § 323.14.

shall be obligated for any * * * liability of the limited liability company solely by reason of being a member or acting as a manager of the limited liability company." 6 Del. C. Ann. § 18–303. Thus, unlike a limited partner, a member of a limited liability company can participate in management and still receive this protection. However, as is the case with the shareholders of a corporation, members of a limited liability corporation may be held liable where the entity is not properly formed, for unpaid capital contributions, and where the veil of limited liability is pierced.

### 3. MANAGEMENT AND CONTROL

The management of a corporation is centralized in the board of directors. Under the traditional statutory model, shareholders generally elect the board of directors who oversee the day-to-day operations of the business. RMBCA § 7.28 provides that, absent special provisions in the articles of incorporation, directors are elected by a plurality of shares entitled to vote. Unless the articles provide otherwise, each share is entitled to one vote.

Corporate owners often vary this model in the articles of incorporation. For example, in a close corporation, where there often is substantial overlap between owners and managers, the articles may provide for guaranteed board representation for each owner and may also specify some details of how the corporation is to be managed.

In a general partnership, absent contrary provisions in the partnership agreement, the management functions are vested in all the partners. Each partner has an equal voice, regardless of the amount of her capital contribution. UPA § 18(e). Decisions generally are made on the basis of a majority vote of the partners, but major changes, such as modification of a partner's decision making authority, cannot be made without the unanimous consent of the partners. UPA § 18(h).

As with a corporation, partners often modify these rules through the partnership agreement. Partnership agreements frequently provide that a partner's voice in management will be in proportion to her capital contribution. Thus, a partner who contributes 60% of a partnership's capital will be entitled to 60% of the voting power. Some partnership agreements assign exclusive management responsibility over various functions to one or more partners.

In a limited partnership, as noted, the limited partners may not participate in the management of the business without losing the protection of limited liability. The general partners thus have responsibility for most management decisions. However, RULPA gives limited partners the right to vote on certain major decisions, including dissolution, changing the nature of the business, the removal of a general partner and certain other extraordinary events. *See* RULPA §§ 302, 303(b).

In an LLC, the basic document controlling management of the entity is its operating agreement. Most jurisdictions provide that absent an agreement to the contrary, members have a voice in management in proportion to their capital contributions. See, e.g., 6 Del. C. Ann. § 18–402. Some jurisdictions, such as Texas, vest management responsibilities in a designated board of managers. Texas Ann. Civ. St. Art. 1528n, art. 2.12. Where the statute vests management in the firm's members, the members may appoint a manager to oversee the operation of the firm. See, e.g., 6 Del. C. Ann. § 18–402.

An LLC can be either *member-managed* or *manager-managed*. In a member-managed LLC, all members have the authority to make management decisions and to act as agents for the LLC. In a manager-managed LLC, members are not agents of the entity and make only major decisions. The *managers*, who do not have to be members, make most ordinary business decisions and have the authority to act as agents of the LLC.

### 4. CONTINUITY OF EXISTENCE

Most states provide, either by statute or common law, that a corporation has perpetual existence. The articles of incorporation may provide for a shorter term. RMBCA § 3.02; DGCL § 102(b)(5). The parties also may agree in advance that the corporation will be dissolved in specified circumstances, such as the death or disability of one of the key participants.

In the absence of contrary provisions in the partnership agreement, a general partnership is dissolved upon the death, bankruptcy or withdrawal of a partner. UPA §§ 31–32. Most partnership agreements provide that, upon the death of a partner, the surviving partners will continue the business and pay the estate of the deceased partner the value of her partnership interest.

A partner may withdraw at any time and thereby dissolve the partnership, even if that act violates a provision of the partnership agreement. If a partner causes the dissolution of the firm "in contravention of the partnership agreement" (UPA § 31(d)(2)), the partner causing the dissolution is subject to various penalties, including liability to the other partners for damages resulting from her wrongful act (UPA § 38(2)(a)(II)). The other partners also have the option of continuing the partnership's business without the consent or participation of the partner causing the dissolution (UPA § 38(2)(b)) and of buying out that partner's interest, thus avoiding sale of the assets and termination of the partnership's business.

The business of a limited partnership generally continues upon the death, bankruptcy or voluntary withdrawal of a limited partner. Most limited partnership agreements restrict a limited partner's right to withdraw her capital. In the absence of contrary agreement, it is only when a general partner withdraws that a limited partnership is dissolved. RULPA § 801.

In order to allow LLCs to qualify to be taxed as partnerships, LLC statutes initially did not allow LLCs to have perpetual existence. Recent changes in federal tax regulations (discussed below) now allow an LLC to be taxed as a partnership whether or not it has perpetual existence. Many states have revised their LLC statutes to allow an LLC to have this corporate characteristic.

## 5. TRANSFERABILITY OF INTERESTS

One of the distinctive features of a corporation is that its stock is freely transferable without the consent of the other shareholders. This feature of ownership is often troublesome to owners of a close corporation because the success of the venture depends upon the ability of owners to work together. Therefore, the articles of incorporation of a close corporation often will contain restrictions on the transferability of stock. Even without such restrictions, free transferability may be of little practical value because of the lack of a ready market for the stock.

In a general partnership, because each partner possesses the authority to bind the partnership and subject the other partners to personal liability, it is critically important that a partner not have a new unwanted partner thrust upon her without her consent. Thus, the default rule is that the admission of a new partner requires the unanimous consent of the partners. UPA § 18(g). A partnership interest has limited transferability. A partner may freely assign her interest in the partnership but her assignee may only share in the partnership's profits; she will not have a voice the management of the partnership unless the other partners admit her as a partner. UPA § 27.

Limited partners also may freely assign their interests, but the assignee may only exercise the rights of a limited partner with the consent of all the remaining partners. Because limited partners do not participate actively in the management of the partnership, however, these restrictions on the rights of an assignee are less important.

Most LLC statutes provide that, absent contrary provisions in the articles of organization or the operating agreement, members are free to transfer their economic interests in distributions of assets and earnings by the LLC but may transfer their interests in management (the right to vote or to act as an agent of the LLC) only with the consent of all other members. However, recent LLC statutes allow members to agree in advance that management rights in an LLC are freely transferable. Because transferability of interests is no longer relevant to the tax classification of an LLC, many older LLC statutes have been amended to allow for free transferability of management rights.

## 6. FINANCING MATTERS

The corporate form provides financing flexibility because there are a variety of well recognized financing devices available to a corporation, including the ability to issue stock.

Partnerships face more substantial hurdles in raising capital. Apart from injections of equity capital by existing partners, the sole method of raising equity capital in a partnership is the creation of new partnership interests. This process may be more cumbersome than the issuance of stock in a corporation because it requires the unanimous consent of the partners. While a partnership may borrow funds with the same facility as a corporation, borrowing in a partnership produces the undesirable consequence of exposing the partners to additional personal liability.

Because of the limited liability protections afforded to limited partners and the tax advantages discussed in Section D of this chapter, the limited partnership is an easier vehicle for raising capital than is the general partnership. Accordingly, it is often the form used in large enterprises organized as a partnership.

The limited liability company operating agreement may provide for various classes of members with such rights and duties as contained in the agreement. This flexibility facilitates raising capital.

## C. PLANNING CONSIDERATIONS

### 1. BALANCING OWNERSHIP INTERESTS

In choosing a form of organization, the owners must consider how their choice will affect the delicate balance between majority and minority owners. This balance differs, depending upon the owners' choice between corporation and partnership. In a partnership, a dissatisfied partner or group of partners can dissolve the partnership unilaterally. Charles O'Kelley notes the advantages and counterbalancing risks associated with this dissolution mechanism:

> The at-will dissolution mechanism protects both individual and collective adaptive needs. For example, if because of changed circumstances, a partner's capital will have a higher value when invested in some other endeavor, she may simply dissolve the old partnership and reinvest her human and money capital elsewhere. Moreover, this unilateral withdrawal mechanism may be used by the majority to achieve needed team changes that, absent unanimous consent, cannot be directly accomplished within the existing partnership. Thus, if a partner's human capital has become obsolete, but the partner will not retire, the majority may simply dissolve the old partnership, purchase the firm's assets at a judicial sale, and form a new partnership that does not include the former partner. On the other hand, the dissolution process is not without cost and uncertainty, both of which operate to constrain good-faith adaptive acts, unless they are clearly necessary.

\* \* \*

> Partnership form thus exposes majority partners to two risks: the risk that a minority partner will extort unfair changes in team rules by opportunistically threatening to dissolve the partnership and the risk that a minority partner will shirk, content in the belief that the majority will be unwilling to expel her for fear that a court might label the resulting dissolution wrongful.

Charles R. O'Kelley, Jr., *Filling Gaps in the Close Corporation Contract: A Transaction Cost Analysis*, 87 Nw. U. L.Rev. 216, 238 (1992).

Consequently, in planning the partnership, the partners should consider contractual provisions focusing on wrongful dissolution to reduce the risk of opportunism. Professor O'Kelley notes:

> * * * For example, the risk of opportunistic dissolution by the majority and opportunistic threats of dissolution by the minority may be greatly reduced by a simple agreement among the partners that the partnership will endure for a specified term or undertaking. Any dissolution of the partnership before completion of the agreed undertaking or term would be in contravention of the partnership agreement, and therefore, an act causing wrongful dissolution.

> On the other hand, if the partners' greatest concern is potential shirking by minority partners, the risk of this type of opportunism may be reduced by a contractual agreement among the partners providing that the majority may expel a partner under specified conditions. If a partner is expelled pursuant to such contractual power, then dissolution will not be considered wrongful. The expelling partners may continue the partnership's business, and need only pay to the expelled partner the "net amount due her from the partnership."

*Id*. at 234–35.

In contrast to the partnership default rules, which tend toward protection of the minority, corporate law provisions tend to favor the majority shareholders. In contrasting the management and continuity of existence features of a corporation with partnership default rules, Professor O'Kelley states:

> * * * The corporation's adaptive mechanism is the board of directors acting by majority rule. Such mechanism enables the majority to insist on a change in the duties or compensation of a minority owner without incurring significant costs. If the minority shareholder is unhappy with her new status she may withdraw her human capital from the team (if not already discharged) and sell her shares. Alternatively, she may bring a petition for involuntary dissolution on the grounds that the majority's actions are oppressive or that equitable relief is necessary to protect the minority's reasonable expectations or interests. [See, e.g., RMBCA § 14.30(2)(ii).] Each of these protective devices is imperfect. If the minority shareholder sells her shares, she is likely to receive substantially less than she would if the corporation were dissolved and its assets sold as a going concern. If she seeks equitable relief, she must carry the burden of proving predicate facts entitling her to relief.

> The downsides of corporate statutory governance norms, especially when compared to partnership statutory governance rules, are the relative lack of assurance that individual adaptive needs will be satisfied and the relatively greater risk of majority opportunism

posed because minority shareholder[s] may not withdraw their money capital from the firm. If a partner finds it value-maximizing to withdraw her capital from the firm and invest it elsewhere, the at-will dissolution mechanism insures that she will be able to do so. In a corporation, a minority shareholder has no similar adaptive rights. On the other hand, the corporation law preference for majority adaptability combines with the lack of a unilateral minority withdrawal right to insulate the majority from the threat of minority opportunism. A minority shareholder simply has no ability to withdraw unilaterally, and thus, no ability to extort an objectively unjustifiable change in terms from the majority.

*Id.* at 240–41.

Of course, maintaining an optimal balance between majority and minority owners often is not the parties' exclusive concern. The attraction of limited liability, standing alone, may be sufficient to lead prospective investors to choose the corporate form, even though they might other wise prefer a partnership governance structure. This has lead some commentators to speculate that the advent of the limited liability company, which easily can be structured much like a partnership (and which is taxable as a partnership), may spell the death knell of the partnership form of organization. *See* Larry E. Ribstein, *The Deregulation of Limited Liability and the Death of Partnership*, 70 Wash U. L.Q. 417 (1992).

## 2.  THE ECONOMICS OF THE CHOICE

### Richard A. Posner, Economic Analysis of Law
392–393 (4th ed. 1992).

#### Problems in Financing Business Ventures

The theory of the firm tells us why so much economic activity is organized in firms but not why most of those firms are corporations. A clue is that firms in which the inputs are primarily labor rather than capital often are partnerships or individual proprietorships rather than corporations. The corporation is primarily a method of solving problems encountered in raising substantial amounts of capital.

How does the impecunious entrepreneur who has a promising idea for a new venture go about raising the necessary capital? Borrowing *all* of the needed capital is probably out of the question. If the riskless interest rate is 6 percent but the venture has a 50 percent chance of failing and having no assets out of which to repay the loan, the lender, if risk neutral, will charge an interest rate of 112 percent.[2] The high interest charge, plus amortization, will impose a heavy fixed cost on the venture from the outset. This will increase the danger of failure * * *—and in turn the interest rate.

---

**2.**  Suppose the loan is for $100 and is to be repaid at the end of a year. The lender must charge an interest rate that will yield an expected value of $106, given a 50 percent probability of repayment. Solving the equation .5x = $106 for x yields $212–i.e., $100 in principal plus $112 in interest.

These difficulties could in principle be overcome by careful and imaginative drafting of the loan agreement, but the transaction costs might be very high. An alternative is for the entrepreneur to admit a partner to the business who is entitled to receive a portion of the profits of the venture, if any, in exchange for contributing the necessary capital to it. The partner's compensation is determined automatically by the fortunes of the business. There is no need to compute an interest rate although this is implicit in the determination of the fraction of any future profits that he is to receive in exchange for his contribution. Most important, there are no fixed costs of debt to make the venture even riskier than it inherently is; the partner receives his profits only if earned.

But there are still problems. A partnership can be dissolved by, and is automatically dissolved on the death of, any partner. The impermanence of the arrangement may deter the commitment of large amounts of money to an enterprise in which it may be frozen for years. The partners may be able to negotiate around this hurdle but not without incurring transaction costs that may be high. Moreover, to the extent that they agree to limit the investing partner's right to dissolve the partnership and withdraw his money, the liquidity of his investment is reduced and * * * he may be placed at the mercy of the active partner. * * *

Further, since each partner is personally liable for the debts of the partnership, a prospective investor will want to figure out the likely extent of the enterprise's potential liability, or even to participate in the actual management of the firm to make sure it does not run up huge debts for which he would be liable. And still a risk of indefinite liability would remain. In principle, the enterprise could include in all of its contracts with customers and suppliers a clause limiting its liability to the assets of the enterprise * * *. But the negotiation of such waivers would be costly. And it would be utterly impracticable to limit most tort liability in this way. Nor, * * * is insurance a complete answer.

### The Corporation as a Standard Contract

The corporate form is the normal solution that the law and business practice have evolved to solve the problems discussed in the preceding section. The corporation's perpetual existence obviates the need for a special agreement limiting withdrawal or dissolution, although such an agreement may turn out to be necessary for other reasons to be discussed. The shareholder's liability for corporate debts is limited to the value of his shares (limited liability). Passive investment is further encouraged by (1) a complex of legal rights vis-à-vis management and any controlling group of shareholders, and (2) the fact that equity interests in a corporation are broken up into shares of relatively small value that can be, and in the case of the larger corporations are, traded in organized markets. The corporate form enables an investor to make small equity investments, to reduce risk through diversification * * *, and to liquidate his investment quickly and cheaply. Notice that without limited liability a shareholder would not even be allowed to sell his shares without the other shareholders' consent, since if he sold them to someone poorer than he, the risk to the other shareholders would be increased.

# D. THE TAX CONSEQUENCES OF BUSINESS ORGANIZATIONS: A BRIEF EXAMINATION

Because different forms of doing business result in different tax consequences, the choice of the form of enterprise often turns on those consequences. The major tax implications of that choice are summarized below, in terms that are intended to be understandable to students who have not yet studied tax.* Some of the more troublesome or complicated points are touched on only lightly or omitted altogether. Consequently, this survey should not be mistaken for a comprehensive statement of the relevant tax law.

## 1. PARTNERSHIP VS. CORPORATION

The principal difference in the tax treatment of business organizations is the treatment of the entity. Under the Internal Revenue Code, the corporation is a taxpayer separate from its shareholders. Corporations, and not the persons who own stock, pay taxes or deduct losses, based on the results of the corporation's operations. A partnership, by contrast, is considered an aggregate of individuals rather than a separate entity; hence, it is not a taxpayer. The partnership files an information return, but the purpose is essentially to determine how much tax the individual partners will pay on the income or loss attributable to them from the operation of the partnership. Both the income and expenses of the partnership are said to "flow-through" to the partners in proportion to their ownership interests.

This difference is significant because of the different tax rates for individuals and corporations. As of the date of this book, individual tax rates vary from 15 percent to 39.6 percent, although the effective rate may be higher because of the treatment of individual exemptions and deductions. Corporate rates are lower. Internal Revenue Code § 11 provides that the rate is 15 percent on the first $50,000 of taxable income, 25 percent on the next $25,000 of taxable income, 34 percent on taxable income from $75,000 to $10 million, and 35 percent on taxable income above $10 million.

Fluctuations in tax rates, as well as the particular circumstances of both the participants and the venture, point to the futility of generalizing about the advisability, from a tax standpoint, of choosing one form of business over another. All that can be said is that the planner should

---

* This discussion focuses on income taxes and does not consider the impact of payroll taxes, which can be substantial.

consider, among other things, the extent of non-business income and deductions, the number of dependents, the possibility of early business losses and ultimate success, the individual's needs for cash from the operations of the business, and the nature of the business itself.

The difference in tax treatment between corporations and partnerships has focused attention on what has somewhat loosely (and inaccurately) been called "double taxation." The corporation pays a tax on income it earns. When that income is distributed to shareholders as dividends, it is taxed again in the hands of the shareholders with no account taken of the tax the corporation paid earlier. In contrast, the partnership itself pays no tax. The income from the business is taxed only to the partners, regardless of whether or not the income is distributed. The following example illustrates the basic difference between taxation of partnerships and corporations.

Assume that Jessica Bacon and Michael Lane form a partnership that generates revenues and expenses similar to those generated by Precision Tools. At the end of each year, the partnership will compute its net income and file an information return. The partnership may pay "salaries" to Jessica and Michael and at the end of the year it will retain some of its profits in the business and distribute some portion to each partner. (There is an incongruity which must be recognized in a partnership paying a "salary" to an owner, but the Internal Revenue Code permits the payment to be deducted just as if it were paid to an employee who is not an owner.) The partnership, as noted above, will pay no tax on its net income. Jessica and Michael will pay taxes, at their respective individual tax rates, on the "salaries" which they received as well as on the amounts distributed to them. They will also be taxed on their proportionate share of the remainder of the net income that was not distributed to them. Significantly, if the partnership operates at a loss, each will be entitled to claim her proportionate share of that loss as deduction against income from other sources.

The partnership will compute its net income in much the same manner as an individual. To determine how much of the profit or the loss is attributed to each of the partners, reference is made initially to the partnership agreement. In the absence of a formal partnership agreement, or if the agreement is incomplete as to a particular point, the tax law makes certain assumptions. For example, if the partners neglect to state how much of the profits each is entitled to receive, the law presumes that they are equal partners.

If Jessica and Michael form a corporation, at the end of the year, the corporation will again pay salaries to Jessica and Michael, distribute some portion of the profits to them, and retain the balance. Unlike a partnership, the corporation will pay taxes, although, as with a partnership, the corporation also can deduct their salaries as a business expense. Jessica and Michael will pay taxes on those salaries and on any amounts that the corporation distributes to them. Unlike a partnership, they will *not* pay taxes on any profits that the corporation retains in the business, nor will they be entitled to claim a deduction if the corporation operates at a loss.

The choice of the corporate form, however, raises an additional tax question that affects the economics of the venture. When Jessica and Michael form the corporation, they must decide what securities—stock or debt—the corporation will issue in exchange for the capital that it needs. The tax significance of this choice is significant. As noted above, when a corporation distributes dividends to its shareholders, the corporation receives no deduction for the amount distributed to its shareholder. By contrast, when the corporation pays interest on indebtedness, even if the creditor is a shareholder, the corporation receives a deduction for the interest it pays. In both cases, Jessica and Michael will be taxed on what they receive; the difference is that because interest is deductible to the corporation and dividends are not, the use of debt will reduce the corporation's taxable income and may even eliminate all so-called double taxation.

This last example illustrates what may be the most important point about the tax aspects of doing business in corporate form; namely, that individuals by forming a corporation have created a tax-paying entity. If the business earned as much money as it did when operated in a partnership form, the owners will be worse off financially if they distribute all profits to themselves as dividends. They may, of course, reduce the corporation's profits by taking personal salaries, and if their salaries are equal to the entire amount of the company's profits, the corporation ordinarily will have no profits. Under these circumstances the consequences of operating in either partnership or corporate form would produce no tax differences. The Internal Revenue Code, as noted above, permits the deduction of "ordinary and necessary" business expenses. The amount allowed as a deduction for salaries is limited to a reasonable amount. The salaries paid to owner-employees will be carefully scrutinized if the returns are audited. If a business grows to substantial proportions, it may become difficult to deduct as "reasonable salaries" sums which fully equal the profits of the company. Thus, if the business grows, the likelihood is that the corporation will be taxed on at least some of its income, and if that income is then distributed to the shareholders, it will be taxed again.

The difference in the personal circumstances of the partners suggests some interesting thoughts for planning a business enterprise. For example, assume that Jessica, in addition to being a participant in the business, also receives income as the beneficiary of a family trust in the amount of $25,000 a year. Michael, on the other hand, has no income. They decide that the business will pay each of them an annual salary of $50,000 per annum in the first two years during which they expect the business to operate at a loss of $120,000 each year, including the deduction for their salaries.

If the venture is a partnership, Jessica will have income of $25,000 from the trust plus $50,000 received as salary for a total of $75,000 and may claim as a deduction the $60,000 loss that constitutes her share of the partnership's loss. Thus, the total income she will report is $15,000. Michael will have income of only $50,000, against which he may deduct $60,000; hence he will pay no tax. This will leave him with $10,000 of undeducted loss which he may carry back against income reported in earlier years and obtain a refund; if some loss still remains undeducted, he may carry that loss forward and apply it against income received in subsequent years. Whether he has such prior income or subsequent income will depend upon his personal circumstances. Jessica receives immediate benefit from the fact the partnership initially operates at a loss and can enjoy a substantial income at a low tax cost. The ability to directly offset personal income with losses from a business in which the partner is active is one of the attractive tax features of the partnership form of doing business; the business functions as a tax shelter. If the parties cannot use such benefits, or if the differential in tax rates is significant, the corporate form would become more attractive than would the partnership.

The inclination of the tax advisor is therefore to seek means of avoiding double taxation. In order to do so, a tax advisor may recommend the formation of a partnership or a hybrid organization, such as a limited liability company. Within the corporate form, double taxation can be reduced by retention of earnings. In fact, if Jessica and Michael expected to reinvest all income in the business for a number of years, operating as a corporation might save them taxes. With income of $120,000, for example, the corporation would pay federal income tax of $29,050, representing less than 25% of its income. Jessica and Michael in all likelihood would have to pay considerably more in taxes if $120,000 in income were attributed to them, as would be the case if they were partners.

If earnings are to be distributed, the tax advisor will try to minimize the effect of double taxation by increasing the corporation's business deductions and reducing its taxable income. As we have noted, income is taxed both to the corporation and the shareholder when it is distributed to the shareholder as a dividend. If it is distributed to the shareholder in the form of a salary, it is still taxed to the shareholder, but it reduces the corporation's tax since it constitutes a deductible expense. The same is true of interest on a loan from shareholders. So, if the shareholder is an employee, she will have no need for dividends if the amount which would otherwise be distributed as a dividend is paid to her as a salary. Similarly, if part of her investment in the corporation is in the form of a bond or a note, the interest paid to her will be an acceptable substitute for dividends. This type of corporate structuring for tax purposes is tricky business, however. The Internal Revenue Service is alert to the possibility that a taxpayer may seek to disguise dividends as salary or interest and may challenge the corporation's asserted deductions.

## 2. S CORPORATIONS

An S corporation is a corporation which has elected to be taxed under the provisions of Subchapter S of the Internal Revenue Code and which pays no tax itself. Its income is taxed to the shareholders at their individual rates. While this bears resemblance to partnership taxation, there are sufficient differences to make it inaccurate to say that such corporation is taxed as a partnership. In short, an S corporation has all the corporate attributes without being subject to "double taxation" on the corporate earnings.

## A.  Operation of an S Corporation

To qualify for Subchapter S treatment, a corporation must be a domestic corporation and cannot have more than thirty-five shareholders. The shareholders themselves must be individuals, estates or qualified trusts. The corporation can have only one class of stock. Shares that have different voting rights may be considered as belonging to the same class as long as they are otherwise alike. Finally, the corporation must elect to be treated under Subchapter S. In order to make a Subchapter S election all of the shareholders of the corporation must consent to be taxed as an S corporation.

Generally, an S corporation is taxed in a flow-through approach based on the partnership model. Corporate income, losses and credits, flow through to shareholders on a per share basis. This means that income is allocated to a shareholder according to the number of shares held and the number of days during the year the shareholder owned her stock. In the earlier example, if the entity were an S Corporation, the tax consequences would be the same for Jessica and Michael as if it were a partnership; Jessica still would have taxable income of $15,000 and Michael would still have no taxable income and a $10,000 loss carryover to be taxed at their individual rates.

Another advantage of electing Subchapter S (assuming that the shareholders are active participants in the business so that they are not subject to the passive loss rules) is the ability to offset income from other sources by any loss generated by the corporation.

## B. Termination of a Subchapter S Election

A Subchapter S election terminates if over any three year period more than 25 percent of the corporation's gross receipts constitute passive investment income. A Subchapter S election will also terminate if the number of shareholders exceeds thirty-five, or if any of the shareholders are nonresident aliens, or are not an individual, estate or qualified trust. Thus a transfer by an existing qualified shareholder to an unqualified entity or individual will automatically terminate the Subchapter S election. If a second class of stock is issued, the election will also be terminated. A Subchapter S also election can be revoked by the consent of holders of a majority of the corporation's stock.

Once the Subchapter S election is terminated or revoked, the corporation cannot make another Subchapter S election before the fifth taxable year beginning after the first year for which the termination or revocation was effective. If the IRS determines the termination was inadvertent or accidental and the disqualifying event is corrected within a reasonable time after discovery, then the corporation will not be disqualified.

### 3. LIMITED LIABILITY COMPANIES, PARTNERSHIPS AND LIMITED PARTNERSHIPS

LLCs, LLPs and LLLPs, all relatively new forms of business entities, are attractive to many investors because they can be taxed as partnerships but have the key corporate attribute of affording limited liability to their owners. All states had adopted legislation authorizing LLCs and most have authorized LLPs.

Until recently, determination of the tax treatment of an unincorporated entity was made under Treasury regulations, known as the "Kintner" regulations, which looked to four factors to determine whether an unincorporated entity would be taxed as a partnership or as an "association taxable as a corporation" pursuant to Internal Revenue Code § 7701(a): (1) limited liability of owners; (2) centralized management; (3) free transferability of interests; and (4) continuity of life. In 1988, the Internal Revenue Service ruled that an LLC organized under Wyoming law could be taxed as a partnership even though the liability of its members was limited. Rev. Rul. 88–76, 1988 Cum. Bull. 360. This led many states to adopt LLC (and LLP and LLLP) statutes that provided limited liability for the owners of these entities but not for centralized management, free transferability of interests or continuity of life.

Unincorporated entities with limited liability began to proliferate, as did questions relating to the tax classification of such entities. This led the Treasury to reconsider the Kintner regulations and to adopt, in 1997, a radically new and simplified approach to classifying unincorporated entities. Treasury's new "check the box" regulations provide that every unincorporated entity will be taxed as a partnership unless its owners check a box (on I.R.S. Form 8832) electing to have the entity taxed as a corporation. *See* Treas. Reg. § 301.7701. Thus, every entity organized under an LLC (or LLP or LLLP) statute now is taxed as a partnership unless it elects to be taxed as a corporation.

If only the rest of the tax code could so easily be simplified!

# Chapter 7

# THE INCORPORATION PROCESS

### PROBLEM
### PRECISION TOOLS—PART II

Jessica, Michael and Bernie have decided to operate Precision Tools as a corporation and have asked you to handle the incorporation process. You are now confronted with the following questions:

1. You have represented Michael in past business dealings, and it was at his suggestion that the three of them called upon you. All three have now asked you to handle the legal work in forming the corporation. Is there any reason why you should not proceed with this representation?

2. Assuming that you have selected Columbia as the place of incorporation, what are the formalities with which you must comply? Consider RMBCA §§ 2.01–2.07.

3. Assume you prepare the articles of incorporation, review them with all three parties, have them signed by the incorporator, and, since you are leaving town on vacation, you give them to Michael who agrees to file them the next day. He forgets to do so, but on that day two events occur:

   a. He places a large order for new office furniture from a local merchant for the account of the "corporation."

   b. The worker who delivers the merchandise slips on a slick surface on the "corporation's" premises which were not properly cleaned, and is injured. If the "corporation," for some reason is unable to pay for the merchandise or the injury, are Jessica, Michael, or Bernie personally liable? Consider the question under common law and RMBCA § 2.04. Read the Official Comment to RMBCA § 2.04. Contrast DGCL § 329.

4. As you are working on the incorporation papers, Michael calls to say that he has just talked with a supplier of important new equipment that the business will need and that will require special installation. The supplier can offer the company a special price on purchase and

prompt installation if they sign a contract and begin work on Monday. Your clients want to go ahead. Your experience tells you that it will be impossible to complete the incorporation of Precision Tools by that time, because some details need to be resolved. How should the contract be handled?

5. Should the business be incorporated in Columbia, in Delaware, or in some other jurisdiction?

6. The selection of the state of incorporation, having the consequences that it does, should cause you to reflect on the purpose of corporate law in a larger sense than the immediate impact on your clients. In that vein, consider the purposes of a corporation law:

   a. Is it designed to protect shareholders by imposing constraints on corporate managers? If so, what other constraints might achieve the same result?

   b. Is it designed to protect the best interests of the shareholders by giving maximum flexibility to corporate managers in running the business?

   c. Is it designed to allow market forces to best protect the shareholders' interests? Which markets?

   d. Are there interests other than shareholders that the corporate law is intended to protect? What are those interests? How does, or how can, corporate law protect those interests?

   e. Is corporate law designed to reduce the transaction costs inherent in beginning a business venture by providing standard arrangements among the parties to the venture and facilitating private variations from those standards?

## A. LAWYERS' PROFESSIONAL RESPONSIBILITIES: WHO IS THE CLIENT?

At first blush, determining who is the "client" would not seem to be a difficult task. An attorney-client relationship is either formed explicitly by a formal contractual agreement or implicitly by the client requesting, and the attorney performing, legal services for the client. In practice, however, a situation such as Precision Tools in which more than one person is requesting legal services, often arises and, when it does, the issues are more complex than might initially appear.

When Jessica, Michael and Bernie appear in the lawyer's office, why should the lawyer not incorporate their business? If all that were to be done were to comply with the simple mechanics described in Part B of this Chapter, there might be no reason why the lawyer should not perform the work. But if more is required, as it usually is, problems immediately arise. The parties often have little idea of what form of business organization is most desirable for them or what legal issues will arise in structuring their business. They will look to the lawyer to guide them through the choices they must make. If the parties wish, issues such as the choice of securities, voting rights, and control (to name only a few) can and often should, be resolved at the time of incorporation. These issues may create actual or potential conflicts between the parties that will be clear to the lawyer but not to the parties. Moreover, when these conflicts have been identified, the parties may ask the lawyer to suggest the most desirable way of resolving them. How should the lawyer respond? To whom, if anyone, at this stage (before there even is a corporation), does the lawyer owe her loyalty?

These problems may be compounded if the enterprise is relatively small. The parties want to minimize their organizational expenses before the business has begun, and the cost of each party retaining her own lawyer at this stage may seem excessive. After all, they will say, all we want you, the lawyer, to do is to get us up and running and make sure that we won't have any major problems in the future. Why should we pay all that money to lawyers before we have even begun the business? Faced with these questions, a lawyer will have a natural tendency to proceed. Whether she should is the subject of this section.

Given the frequency with which such a situation arises, it is surprising that there is relatively little guidance available to the lawyer. Consider the extent to which the following materials are helpful. Consider also the unanswered questions that the lawyer must resolve for herself. Finally, bear in mind the practical consequences of the answer to the question of who is the client: only those who are clients can assert the attorney-client privilege, seek disqualification of the attorney in litigation because of the attorney's conflict of interest, or sue for malpractice.

## AMERICAN BAR ASSOCIATION MODEL RULES OF PROFESSIONAL CONDUCT

(1983).

### Rule 1.6  Confidentiality of Information

(a) A lawyer shall not reveal information relating to representation of a client unless the client consents after consultation, except for disclosures that are impliedly authorized in order to carry out the representation, and except as stated in paragraph (b).

(b) A lawyer may reveal such information to the extent the lawyer reasonably believes necessary:

(1) to prevent the client from committing a criminal act that the lawyer believes is likely to result in imminent death or substantial bodily harm; or

(2) to establish a claim or defense on behalf of the lawyer in a controversy between the lawyer and the client, to establish a defense

to a criminal charge or civil claim against the lawyer based upon conduct in which the client was involved, or to respond to allegations in any proceeding concerning the lawyer's representation of the client.

## COMMENT

The lawyer is part of a judicial system charged with upholding the law. One of the lawyer's functions is to advise clients so that they avoid any violation of the law in the proper exercise of their rights.

The observance of the ethical obligation of a lawyer to hold inviolate confidential information of the client not only facilitates the full development of facts essential to proper representation of the client but also encourages people to seek early legal assistance.

Almost without exception, clients come to lawyers in order to determine what their rights are and what is, in the maze of laws and regulations, deemed to be legal and correct. The common law recognizes that the client's confidences must be protected from disclosure. Based upon experience, lawyers know that almost all clients follow the advice given, and the law is upheld.

A fundamental principle in the client-lawyer relationship is that the lawyer maintain confidentiality of information relating to the representation. The client is thereby encouraged to communicate fully and frankly with the lawyer even as to embarrassing or legally damaging subject matter.

The principle of confidentiality is given effect in two related bodies of law, the attorney-client privilege (which includes the work product doctrine) in the law of evidence and the rule of confidentiality established in professional ethics. The attorney-client privilege applies in judicial and other proceedings in which a lawyer may be called as a witness or otherwise required to produce evidence concerning a client. The rule of client-lawyer confidentiality applies in situations other than those where evidence is sought from the lawyer through compulsion of law. The confidentiality rule applies not merely to matters communicated in confidence by the client but also to all information relating to the representation, whatever its source. A lawyer may not disclose such information except as authorized or required by the Rules of Professional Conduct or other law.

\* \* \*

### Disclosure Adverse to Client

The confidentiality rule is subject to limited exceptions. In becoming privy to information about a client, a lawyer may foresee that the client intends serious harm to another person. However, to the extent a lawyer is required or permitted to disclose a client's purposes, the client will be inhibited from revealing facts which would enable the lawyer to counsel against a wrongful course of action. The public is better protected if full and open communication by the client is encouraged than if it is inhibited.

Several situations must be distinguished.

First, the lawyer may not counsel or assist a client in conduct that is criminal or fraudulent. See Rule 1.2(d). Similarly, a lawyer has a duty under Rule 3.3(a)(4) not to use false evidence. This duty is essentially a special instance of the duty prescribed in Rule 1.2(d) to avoid assisting a client in criminal or fraudulent conduct.

\* \* \*

Third, the lawyer may learn that a client intends prospective conduct that is criminal and likely to result in imminent death or substantial bodily harm. As stated in paragraph (b)(1), the lawyer has professional discretion to reveal information in order to prevent such consequences. The lawyer may make a disclosure in order to prevent homicide or serious bodily injury which the lawyer reasonably believes is intended by a client. It is very difficult for a lawyer to ''know'' when such a heinous purpose will actually be carried out, for the client may have a change of mind.

The lawyer's exercise of discretion requires consideration of such factors as the nature of the lawyer's relationship with the client and with those who might be injured by the client, the lawyer's own involvement in the transaction and factors that may extenuate the conduct in question. Where practical, the lawyer should seek to persuade the client to take suitable action. In any case, a disclosure adverse to the client's interest should be no greater than the lawyer reasonably believes necessary to the purpose. A lawyer's decision not to take preventive action permitted by paragraph (b)(1) does not violate this Rule.

### Rule 1.7  Conflict of Interest: General Rule

(a) A lawyer shall not represent a client if the representation of that client will be directly adverse to another client, unless:

> (1) the lawyer reasonably believes the representation will not adversely affect the relationship with the other client; and

> (2) each client consents after consultation.

(b) A lawyer shall not represent a client if the representation of that client may be materially limited by the lawyer's responsibilities to another client or to a third person, or by the lawyer's own interests, unless:

> (1) the lawyer reasonably believes the representation will not be adversely affected; and

> (2) the client consents after consultation.

When representation of multiple clients in a single matter is undertaken, the consultation shall include explanation of the implications of the common representation and the advantages and risks involved.

## COMMENT

### *Loyalty to a Client*

Loyalty is an essential element in the lawyer's relationship to a client. An impermissible conflict of interest may exist before representation is undertaken, in which event the representation should be declined. If such a conflict arises after representation has been undertaken, the lawyer should withdraw from the representation. See Rule 1.16. Where more than one client is involved and the lawyer withdraws because a conflict arises after representation, whether the lawyer may continue to represent any of the clients is determined by Rule 1.9. See also Rule 2.2(c). As to whether a client-lawyer relationship exists or, having once been established, is continuing, see Comment to Rule 1.3 and Scope. * * *

### *Other Conflict Situations*

Conflicts of interest in contexts other than litigation sometimes may be difficult to assess. Relevant factors in determining whether there is potential for adverse effect include the duration and intimacy of the lawyer's relationship with the client or clients involved, the functions being performed by the lawyer, the likelihood that actual conflict will arise and the likely prejudice to the client from the conflict if it does arise. The question is often one of proximity and degree.

For example, a lawyer may not represent multiple parties to a negotiation whose interests are fundamentally antagonistic to each other, but common representation is permissible where the clients are generally aligned in interest even though there is some difference of interest among them.

* * *

A lawyer for a corporation or other organization who is also a member of its board of directors should determine whether the responsibilities of the two roles may conflict. The lawyer may be called on to advise the corporation in matters involving actions of the directors. Consideration should be given to the frequency with which such situations may arise, the potential intensity of the conflict, the effect of the lawyer's resignation from the board and the possibility of the corporation's obtaining legal advice from another lawyer in such situations. If there is material risk that the dual role will compromise the lawyer's independence of professional judgment, the lawyer should not serve as a director.

### Rule 1.13   Organization as Client

(a) A lawyer employed or retained by an organization represents the organization acting through its duly authorized constituents.

* * *

(d) In dealing with an organization's directors, officers, employees, members, shareholders or other constituents, a lawyer shall explain the identity of the client when it is apparent that the organization's interests are adverse to those of the constituents with whom the lawyer is dealing.

(e) A lawyer representing an organization may also represent any of its directors, officers, employees, members, shareholders or other constituents, subject to the provisions of Rule 1.7. If the organization's consent to the dual representation is required by Rule 1.7, the consent shall be given by an appropriate official of the organization other than the individual who is to be represented, or by the shareholders.

## COMMENT

### The Entity as the Client

An organizational client is a legal entity, but it cannot act except through its officers, directors, employees, shareholders and other constituents.

Officers, directors, employees and shareholders are the constituents of the corporate organizational client. * * *

When one of the constituents of an organizational client communicates with the organization's lawyer in that person's organizational capacity, the communication is protected by Rule 1.6. * * * This does not mean, however, that constituents of an organizational client are the clients of the lawyer. The lawyer may not disclose to such constituents information relating to the representation except for disclosures explicitly or impliedly authorized by the organizational client in order to carry out the representation or as otherwise permitted by Rule 1.6.

* * *

### Clarifying the Lawyer's Role

There are times when the organization's interest may be or become adverse to those of one or more of its constituents. In such circumstances the lawyer should advise any constituent, whose interest the lawyer finds adverse to that of the organization of the conflict or potential conflict of interest, that the lawyer cannot represent such constituent, and that such person may wish to obtain independent representation. Care must be taken to assure that the individual understands that, when there is such adversity of interest, the lawyer for the organization cannot provide legal representation for that constituent individual, and that discussion between the lawyer for the organization and the individual may not be privileged.

Whether such a warning should be given by the lawyer for the organization to any constituent individual may turn on the facts of each case.

*Dual Representation*

Paragraph (e) recognizes that a lawyer for an organization may also represent a principal officer or major shareholder.

————

Model Rule 1.13 and EC 5–18 of the Model Code of Professional Responsibility which is followed in some jurisdictions that have not adopted some form of the Model Rules adopt the "entity theory" of the corporation. Under that theory, the lawyer represents the corporation, and not its officers, directors, employees and shareholders. The corporation is an individual, standing apart from its constituents, and hence, any attorney hired to represent the corporation represents the corporation as a distinct legal entity and not its constituents. As such, the entity theory recognizes the corporation's lawyers, along with its officers and directors, as agents of the entity. The Disciplinary Rules of the Model Code do not adopt the entity theory. They rely on the more general rules concerning confidentiality and conflicts of interest. See DR 4–101, DR 5–101, DR 5–105.

The entity theory presupposes that the constituent parts of the corporation are essentially different (and identifiable) people; it appears to adopt the paradigm of the publicly-held corporation. Where, however, the corporation is in the process of being formed, or where the same people are likely to constitute all or a majority of the stockholders, directors and officers (as in a close corporation), the theory may present serious problems.

## JESSE BY REINECKE v. DANFORTH

169 Wis.2d 229, 485 N.W.2d 63 (1992).

[In 1985, Drs. Danforth and Ullrich were part of a group of twenty-three physicians who retained Douglas Flygt (Flygt), an attorney with the law firm of DeWitt, Porter, Huggett, Schumacher & Morgan, S.C. (DeWitt). The physicians asked DeWitt to assist them in creating a corporation for the purpose of purchasing and operating a magnetic resonance imaging machine (MRI). Flygt incorporated MRIGM in 1986 and continued to serve as its corporate counsel. The twenty-three physicians became the shareholders of MRIGM, and Dr. Danforth became president of the corporation.

In May 1988, the Jesse family sued Drs. Danforth and Ullrich for medical malpractice unrelated to the activities of MRIGM. The plaintiffs retained Eric Farnsworth, also an attorney with DeWitt. Farnsworth had conducted an internal conflict of interest check at DeWitt, but had not found the defendants listed as clients of the firm. Drs. Danforth and Ullrich moved to disqualify DeWitt, alleging that the firm had a conflict of interest. They argued that they were clients of DeWitt because of Flygt's pre-incorporation of the twenty-three physicians and because of other advice that Flygt had provided to the defendants.]

DAY, JUSTICE:

We begin with SCR 20:1.7, the conflict of interest rule [which parallels Model Rule 1.7]. Subsection (a) states: "A lawyer shall not represent a client if the representation of that client will be directly adverse to another, unless. * * *" Thus, the question is, who did or does DeWitt represent, *i.e.*, who were and are DeWitt's clients?

It is undisputed that DeWitt, through Farnsworth, represents Jean Jesse in this case. What remains disputed is whether Drs. Danforth or Ullrich were ever or are currently clients of DeWitt.

The entity rule contemplates that where a lawyer represents a corporation, the client is the corporation, not the corporation's constituents. * * *

[T]he clear purpose of the entity rule was to enhance the corporate lawyer's ability to represent the best interests of the corporation without automatically having the additional and potentially conflicting burden of representing the corporation's constituents.

If a person who retains a lawyer for the purpose of organizing an entity is considered the client, however, then any subsequent representation of the corporate entity by the very lawyer who incorporated the entity would automatically result in dual representation. This automatic dual representation, however, is the very situation the entity rule was designed to protect corporate lawyers against.

We thus provide the following guideline: where (1) a person retains a lawyer for the purpose of organizing an entity and (2) the lawyer's involvement with that person is directly related to that incorporation and (3) such entity is eventually incorporated, the entity rule applies retroactively such that the lawyer's pre-incorporation involvement with the person is deemed to be representation of the entity, not the person.

In essence, the retroactive application of the entity rule simply gives the person who retained the lawyer the status of being a corporate constituent during the period before actual incorporation, as long as actual incorporation eventually occurred.

This standard also applies to privileged communications under SCR 20:1.6. Thus, where the above standard is met, communications between the retroactive constituent and the corporation are protected under SCR 20:1.6. And, it is the corporate entity, not the retroactive constituent, that holds the privilege. This tracks the Comment to SCR 20:1.13 which states in part: "When one of the constituents of an organizational client communicates with the organization's lawyer in that person's organizational capacity, the communication is protected by Rule 1.6."

However, where the person who retained the lawyer provides information to the lawyer not directly related to the purpose of organizing an entity, then it is the person, not the corporation which holds the privilege for that communication.

Applying the above standard to the case at hand, we observe that the evidence cited and quoted by the defendants demonstrates that the above standard is met and that DeWitt represented MRIGM, not Drs. Danforth or Ullrich.

For example, defendants Drs. Danforth and Ullrich point to Flygt's affidavit wherein Flygt states that he was contacted *"to assist a group of physicians in Milwaukee in organizing an entity to own and operate one or more * * * facilities * * *."* (Emphasis added.)

Dr. Danforth points to a January 29, 1986 letter from Flygt to Dr. Danforth wherein Flygt stated:

I would suggest that the *corporation* come to a quick resolution of the subchapter S corporation question. * * * (Emphasis added).

Drs. Danforth and Ullrich point to a May 5, 1986 letter from Flygt to Dr. Danforth which states that "to the extent that there are common expenses of the partnership, such as drafting documents, etc., *it would be appropriate to have the entity pay those fees while the attorneys fees of each individual group are its own cost."* (Emphasis added).

[Drs.] Danforth and Ullrich point to a May 13, 1987 memorandum Flygt wrote to the "Shareholders" of MRIGM. This memorandum begins, "The purpose of this letter is to advise you as to a decision *which must be made by the corporation* at this time." (Emphasis added). * * *

This evidence overwhelmingly supports the proposition that the purpose of Flygt's pre-incorporation involvement was to provide advice with respect to organizing an entity and the Flygt's involvement was directly related to the incorporation. Moreover, that MRIGM was eventually incorporated is undisputed.

In addition, with respect to Flygt's advice concerning the structure of the entity, the fact that a particular corporate structure may benefit the shareholders or the fact that there was communication between Flygt and the shareholders concerning such structuring does not mean that Drs. Danforth and Ullrich were the clients of the law firm. Again, the very purpose of the entity rule is to preclude such automatic dual representation.

Drs. Danforth and Ullrich also contend that they provided certain confidential information to attorney Flygt that should disqualify DeWitt under SCR 20:1.6, the confidential information rule. Defendants point to questionnaires Flygt provided to the physicians involved in the MRI project which inquire, in part, as to the physicians' personal finances and their involvement in pending litigation.

Because MRIGM, not the physician shareholders, was and is the client of DeWitt, and because the communications between Drs. Danforth and Ullrich were directly related to the purpose of organizing MRIGM, we conclude that Drs. Danforth or Ullrich cannot claim the privilege of confidentiality.

*Jesse* leaves open the question of whether the entity theory is retroactive if the pre-incorporation activities are not successful. Does the same rationale apply to this situation? A related issue is presented when, during the pre-incorporation stage each party retains her own lawyer, with each lawyer representing her individual client and no lawyer representing the corporation directly. If, during the initial stages of operation, after the corporation has been only formally created, a conflict arises, it would be technically correct to say that any of the lawyers represents the corporation. However, commentators argue that it may be more realistic to say that each lawyer continues to represent her individual client and that only when the corporation begins to exist in a truer sense should one say that any of the lawyers may represent the corporation. Geoffrey C. Hazard, Jr. & William Hodes, The Law of Lawyering: A Handbook on the Model Rules of Professional Conduct 398–99 (2d ed. 1990).

At least one court has taken a different view of the entity theory. In *Opdyke v. Kent Liquor Mart*, 40 Del.Ch. 316, 181 A.2d 579 (1962), the plaintiff, one of three original shareholders, asserted that the lawyer who incorporated the company breached his duty to the plaintiff by purchasing stock in the corporation from the other stockholders, a transaction adverse to the plaintiff, who had wanted to buy the stock himself. In holding that the lawyer had breached his duty to the plaintiff, the court acknowledged the entity theory, but stated:

> * * * [I]n determining the existence or non-existence of the important relationship of attorney and client a broader approach is required. The question is, What in fact was the relationship between Brown [the attorney] and the three men? * * *

> It is clear to us that Brown was, at the beginning of the venture, and also at its end, the attorney for the three men. The corporation was simply a form for the carrying on of a joint venture. For our present purpose Brown must be regarded as the attorney for three joint adventurers. When they fell out he undertook to resolve their differences. He very properly told them that he could not represent any one of them against another. This was so, not because of the corporate form of the enterprise, but because of the well-settled rule that if a lawyer is retained by two clients and they get into a dispute he cannot ordinarily represent either. Indeed, Brown's justifiable insistence on this neutrality was a recognition, conscious or not, of his fiduciary duty to all three men. That he was acting in his capacity as a lawyer admits of no doubt. Why were they discussing the matter in his office if not to obtain his help and counsel in their difficulty? * * *

> But by these very acts he had emphasized his role of counselor to the three men. In suggesting the settlement he was discharging a characteristic function of the legal adviser. He could not escape the

fiduciary obligations of this relationship by insisting that he was acting only for a corporation.

181 A.2d at 583–84.

The modern test for determining who is or is not the client is the "reasonable expectations" test, as set forth in *Westinghouse Elec. Corp. v. Kerr–McGee Corp.*, 580 F.2d 1311 (7th Cir.1978). Under that test, if an attorney leads an individual or entity to believe that they are a client and the belief is reasonable under the circumstances, an attorney-client relationship will be created, whether or not the client pays the attorney any money or enters into a formal retainer agreement. Because of courts' reliance on the entity theory, the reasonable expectations test is usually limited to close corporations.

*Rosman v. Shapiro*, 653 F.Supp. 1441 (S.D.N.Y.1987), involved the disqualification of counsel for the corporation in litigation between the corporation's two shareholders. The court noted that although normally, corporate counsel does not also become counsel for the shareholders "where, as here, the corporation is a close corporation consisting of only two shareholders with equal interests in the corporation, it is indeed reasonable for each shareholder to believe that the corporate counsel is in effect his own individual attorney." *Id.* at 1445. In so finding, the court relied upon evidence which established that Rosman and Shapiro jointly consulted the attorney for legal advice concerning the creation of a corporation through which they would conduct their business. Apparently relying upon the belief that both partners and their partnership are jointly represented by the partnership attorney, the court held that "it would exalt form over substance to conclude that [the attorneys] only represented [the company], solely because Rosman and Shapiro chose to deal * * * through a corporate entity." *Id.*

After deciding that the shareholders were both clients of the "corporation's" attorneys, the court held that the law firm would not be disqualified pursuant to Canon 4 of the former American Bar Association Code of Professional Responsibility (relating to confidential information). Canon 4 was inapplicable because, "in this case, Rosman could not reasonably have expected that any information imparted to [the law firm] would have been withheld from Shapiro during the course of that representation because [the law firm] represented Shapiro and Rosman jointly. Given the prior joint representation, [the law firm] simply could not have possessed any information which Rosman intended to be held in 'confidence' or as a 'secret' from Shapiro." *Id.* at 1446.

The court ultimately did disqualify the law firm pursuant to Canon 9 (relating to the appearance of professional impropriety). Such a decision was warranted because "the obvious appearance of impropriety stemming from [the law firm]'s representation of Shapiro against its former client, Rosman" was too great. *Id.* The court concluded by noting that a contrary holding "would undermine the loyalty and trust upon which the attorney-client relationship is based." *Id.*

Another factor which some courts consider is how closely held the corporation is and whether the corporation resembles a partnership in function. This may be an important factor because some courts have held that a lawyer representing a partnership, which in itself may not be recognized as a legal person, "represents all the partners as to matters of partnership business" as joint clients. *Wortham & Van Liew v. Superior Court (Clubb)*, 188 Cal.App.3d 927, 932, 233 Cal.Rptr. 725, 728 (1987). If then, a court determines that a corporation functions, at its heart, as a partnership (however that may be determined), it may also decide that the attorney represents the corporation's constituents.

Such was the case in *Hecht v. Superior Court (Ferguson)*, 192 Cal.App.3d 560, 237 Cal.Rptr. 528 (2d Dist.1987), involving the joint client exception to the attorney-client privilege. The court noted that prior to incorporation, the parties had run the business for many years as if it were a partnership and had viewed each other as partners. In addition, they had formed the corporation solely for tax reasons and not to change the nature of their working relationship. Indeed, as the court noted, the new corporation had been "formed as a statutory close corporation, which is akin to a partnership in its informality." 199 Cal.App.3d at 565, 237 Cal.Rptr. at 531. Under those circumstances, it was reasonable for the plaintiff to believe that she was being represented by the "corporation's" attorney. *But see, Hoiles v. Superior Court (Freedom Newspapers)*, 157 Cal.App.3d 1192, 204 Cal.Rptr. 111 (1984) in which the court found that the existence of a close corporation did not provide a basis for an exception to the attorney-client privilege.

Courts also have considered other factors in determining the existence of the attorney-client relationship. One of these is the capacity in which the constituent acted when dealing with the attorney. If the court determines that the constituent sought legal advice on personal affairs or that the attorney represented her in a personal matter, the court may be more likely to find that a attorney-client relationship exists. *See Bobbitt v. Victorian House, Inc.*, 545 F.Supp. 1124, 1126–27 (N.D.Ill.1982). Likewise, the absence of such personal representation may indicate to the court that no attorney-client relationship exists. *See e.g., Professional Serv. Industr. v. Kimbrell*, 758 F.Supp. 676, 682–683 (D.Kan.1991); *Wayland v. Shore Lobster & Shrimp Corp.*, 537 F.Supp. 1220, 1223 (S.D.N.Y.1982). Often, in examining the nature of the relationship, the courts will look to any previous association between the possible client and the attorney in order to determine whether there was any past personal representation before the lawyer became counsel for the corporation. *See Hecht, supra.*

The significance of who paid the lawyer's fees is an issue upon which the courts seem divided. Some courts have stated that the payment of the attorney's fees by the corporation and not the potential client does not disprove the existence of the attorney-client relationship. *See e.g., Westinghouse Elec. Corp. v. Kerr–McGee Corp.*, 580 F.2d at 1317 and *In re Brownstein*, 288 Or. 83, 602 P.2d 655, 656 (1979). Other courts have implied that the corporation's payment is inconsistent with the conclusion that an attorney-client relationship exists between the corporate counsel and the individual. *See e.g., Wayland*, 537 F.Supp. at 1223 and *Dalrymple v. National Bank & Trust Co.*, 615 F.Supp. 979, 983 (W.D.Mich.1985). Still other courts have stated that the method of payment, while not dispositive of the existence of the attorney-client relationship, may be indicative of who the client is. *Hecht, supra.*

A court also may find that it was unreasonable for the constituent to believe himself to be a client if, at the time of the alleged representation, he was actually a "target" or "potential adversary" of the attorney in matters regarding the latter's representation of the entity. In *Dalrymple*, the court found that no attorney-client relationship had ever arisen between the director/defendants and the bank's attorney. There, the law firm was hired by a committee formed by the board of directors to investigate claims by a shareholder that the officers and directors were mismanaging the bank. Because the law firm was retained to represent the bank exclusively and because the directors were advised to seek their own, separate counsel, the court found that it was not reasonable for the directors to believe they were clients of the law firm. Therefore, no attorney-client relationship was formed, and the firm was not disqualified from representing a new client against the directors.

Even if no attorney-client relationship has been established between the constituents and the closely held corporation's attorney, some courts have held that the attorney may have a fiduciary duty to each of the individual shareholders. Whether such a duty exists can be either a question of law or of fact. If such a fiduciary relationship is found to exist, the corporate attorney could be responsible to a third party for a variety of duties, including negligence or fraud. *See Skarbrevik v. Cohen, England & Whitfield*, 231 Cal.App.3d 692, 282 Cal.Rptr. 627 (1991); *Fassihi v. Sommers, Schwartz, Silver, Schwartz & Tyler*, P.C., 107 Mich.App. 509, 309 N.W.2d 645, 648 (1981).

*See generally*, Note, *An Expectations Approach to Client Identity*, 106 HARV. L. REV. 687 (1993); Peter Jarvis, *Knowing Who Is and Isn't Your Client*, THE AM. LAW., Sept. 1991, at 41; *Developments in the Law—Conflicts of Interest In the Legal Profession*, 94 HARV. L. REV. 1244 (1981).

Geoffrey C. Hazard, Jr., ETHICS IN THE PRACTICE OF LAW
58, 60–61, 63–68 (1978).

The problem of deciding who is the client arises when a lawyer supposes that a conflict of interest prevents him from acting for all the people involved in a situation. That is, if the interests of the potential clients were in harmony, or could be harmonized, no choice would have to be made between them and the lawyer could act for all. When the lawyer feels that he can act for all, it can be said simply that he has several clients at the same time. When the clients are all involved in a single transaction, however, the lawyer's responsibility is rather different from what it is when he represents several clients in transactions that have nothing to do with each other. This difference is suggested by the proposition that a lawyer serving more than one client in a single transaction represents "the situation."

The term is the invention of Louis D. Brandeis, Justice of the United States Supreme Court and before that practitioner of law in Boston. It emerged in a hearing in which Brandeis's professional ethics as a lawyer had been questioned.

\* \* \*

The transactions complained of included the following: First, Brandeis had at one time represented one party in a transaction, later represented someone else in a way that impinged on that transaction. Second, he had acted in situations where those he served had conflicting interests, for example by putting together the bargain between parties to a business deal. Third, he had acted for a family business and continued so to act after a falling out among the family required reorganization of the business arrangement. Fourth, over a course of several years he had mediated and adjusted interests of the owners and creditors of a business in such a way as to keep the business from floundering.

The objections to Brandeis's conduct in all these situations were twofold. One was that his conduct was unethical per se because he represented conflicting interests. The other was that he had not adequately made clear to the clients that their interests were in conflict. On the second point, Brandeis acknowledged that at least in some instances he may not have adequately explained the situation to the clients and adequately defined his role as he saw it. Having acknowledged this, he defended his conduct not only on the ground of its being common practice but also on the ground that it was right. In the instances questioned, he said, he did not regard himself as being lawyer for one of the parties to the exclusion of the others, but as "lawyer for the situation." Eventually, the charge did not so much collapse as become submerged in concessions from other reputable lawyers that they had often done exactly as Brandeis.

\* \* \*

"Situations" can arise in different ways. Two or more people who have not been clients may bring a "situation" to a lawyer. Sometimes a client who has a lawyer will become involved in a transaction with a third party who does not, and the transaction is one that ought to be handled as a "situation." Most commonly, perhaps, a lawyer may find himself in a "situation" involving clients that he has previously served in separate transactions or relationships. In this circumstances the lawyer, if he properly can, will intercede before the transaction between his clients reaches counterposed positions. Doing so is in his interests, because that way he can retain both clients.

Having a lawyer act for the situation is also in the clients' interests, if adjustment on fair terms is possible, because head-on controversy is expensive and aggravating. A lawyer who failed to avoid a head-on controversy, given reasonable opportunity to do so, will have failed in what his clients generally regard as one of his chief functions—"preventive" legal assistance.

If Brandeis was wrong, then "lawyering for the situation" is marginally illicit professional conduct because it violates the principle of unqualified loyalty to client. But if Brandeis was right, and the record of good practitioners testifies to that conclusion, then what is required is not interdiction of "lawyering for the situation" but reexamination of what is meant by loyalty to client. That is, loyalty to client, like loyalty to country, may take different forms.

It is not easy to say exactly what a "lawyer for the situation" does. Clearly, his functions vary with specific circumstances. But there are common threads. The beginning point is that no other lawyer is immediately involved. Hence, the lawyer is no one's partisan and, at least up to a point, everyone's confidant. He can be the only person who knows the whole situation. He is an analyst of the relationship between the clients, in that he undertakes to discern the needs, fears, and expectations of each and to discover the concordances among them. He is an interpreter, translating inarticulate or exaggerated claims and forewarnings into temperate and mutually intelligible terms of communication. He can contribute historical perspective, objectivity, and foresight into the parties' assessment of the situation. He can discourage escalation of conflict and recruitment of outside allies. He can articulate general principles and common custom as standards by which the parties can examine their respective claims. He is advocate, mediator, entrepreneur, and judge, all in one. He could be said to be playing God.

Playing God is a tricky business. It requires skill, nerve, detachment, compassion, ingenuity, and the capacity to sustain confidence. When mishandled, it generates the bitterness and recrimination that results when a deep trust has been betrayed. Perhaps above all, it requires good judgment as to when such intercession can be carried off without unfairly subordinating the interests of one of the parties or having later to abort the mission.

When a relationship between the clients is amenable to "situation" treatment, giving it that treatment is perhaps the best service a lawyer can render to anyone. It approximates the ideal forms of intercession suggested by the models of wise parent or village elder. It provides adjustment of difference upon a wholistic view of the situation rather than bilaterally opposing ones. It rests on implicit principles of decision that express commonly shared ideals in behavior rather than strict legal right. The basis of decision is mutual assent and not external compulsion. The orientation in time tends to be a hopeful view of the future rather than an angry view of the past. It avoids the loss of personal autonomy that results when each side commits his cause to his own advocate. It is the opposite of "going to law."

One would think that the role of "lawyer for the situation" would have been idealized by the bar in parity with the roles of partisan advocate and confidential adviser. The fact that it has not been may itself be worth exploring.

It is clear that a "lawyer for the situation" has to identify clearly his role as such, a requirement that Brandeis conceded he might not always have fulfilled. But beyond saying that he will undertake to represent the best interests of all, a lawyer cannot say specifically what he will do or what each of the clients should do in the situation. (If the outcome of the situation were clearly foreseeable, presumably the lawyer's intercession would be unnecessary.) Moreover, he cannot define his role in the terms of the direction of his effort, for his effort will not be vectored outward toward third persons but will aim at an interaction among the clients. Hence, unlike advocacy or legal counselling involving a single client, lawyering for a situation is not provided with a structure of goals and constraints imposed from outside. The lawyer and the clients must create that structure for themselves, with the lawyer being an active participant. And like the other participants he cannot reveal all that is on his mind or all that he suspects the others may have on their minds, except as doing so aids movement of the situation along lines that seem productive.

A lawyer can proceed in this role only if the clients trust him and, equally important, he trusts himself. Trust is by definition ineffable. It is an acceptance of another's act without demanding that its bona fides be objectively provable; to demand its proof is to confess it does not exist. It is a relationship that is uncomfortable for the client but perhaps even more so for the lawyer. Experienced as he is with the meanness that people can display to each other, why should the lawyer not doubt his own susceptibility to the same failing? But trust is involved also in the role of confidential adviser and advocate. Why should lawyers regard their own trustworthiness as more vulnerable in those roles than in the role of "lawyer for the situation"?

Perhaps it is because the legal profession has succeeded in defining the roles of confidential adviser and advocate in ways that substantially reduce the burden of being trustworthy in these roles. The confidential adviser is told that he may not act to disclose anything about the client, except an announced intention to commit a crime. Short of this extremity, the rules of role have it that the counsellor has no choices to make between the interests of his client and the interest of others. His commitment is to the client alone. Correlatively, the advocate is told that he may assert any claim on behalf of a client except one based on fabricated evidence or one empty of any substance at all. Short of this extremity, the advocate also has no choices to make.

The "lawyer for the situation," on the other hand, has choices to make that obviously can go against the interests of one client or another, as the latter perceives it. A lawyer who assumes to act a intercessor has to evoke complete confidence that he will act justly in the circumstances. This is to perform the role of the administered justice itself, but without the constraints inherent in that process (such as the fact that the rules are written down, that they are administered by independent judges, and that outcomes have to be justified by references to reason and precedent). The role of lawyer for the situation therefore may be too prone to abuse to be explicitly sanctioned. A person may be entrusted with it only if he knows that in the event of miscarriage he will have no protection from the law. In this respect, acting as lawyer for the situation can be thought of as similar to a doctor's "authority" to terminate the life of a hopeless patient: It can properly be undertaken only if it will not be questioned afterwards. To this extent Brandeis's critics may have been right.

Yet it seems possible to define the role of intercessor, just as it has been possible to define the role of the trustee or guardian. The role could be defined by contrast with those of confidential counsellor and advocate, perhaps to the advantage of clarity in defining all three. At minimum, a recognition of the role of lawyer for the situation could result in a clearer perception by both clients and lawyers of one very important and socially estimable function that lawyers can perform and do perform.

## B.  THE PROCESS OF INCORPORATION

The process of forming a corporation is simple and quick. Although the procedure differs slightly from state to state, the provisions of RMBCA §§ 2.01–2.04 illustrate the procedure generally required.

The organization is formally accomplished by an "incorporator" who, after incorporation, plays no other role in the corporation. The incorporator signs and files the articles of incorporation with the Secretary of State or another designated official, and in some cases also files with a county official in the county where the principal place of business of the corporation in that state will be located. Sometimes the corporation will not have a place of business in the state, in which case the registered address will function as the office where service of process or other official notice is sent.

The drafting of the articles of incorporation may be a relatively complex undertaking because the promoters wish to embody some or all of the terms of a complex arrangement in the articles. On the other hand, it is possible, and probably more common, to create a corporation with a simple, one page document. The filing of the articles of incorporation is accompanied by the payment of a fee, part of which is usually calculated on the basis of the number of authorized shares or the aggregate legal capital of the company, as is more specifically described in Chapter 9. Note the minimal filing requirements contained in RMBCA § 1.20.

In RMBCA jurisdictions, formal corporate existence commences with the filing of the articles of incorporation with state officials. RMBCA § 2.03. In some other states, the corporation's existence commences with the issuance of a certificate of incorporation by the Secretary of State or other official.

After the corporation has come into legal existence, the statute requires that an organizational meeting be held, either by the incorporators, who select the first members of the board of directors, or, where the initial board is named in the articles of incorporation, by the board members so named. RMBCA § 2.05. At its first meeting, the board typically accomplishes a number of standard tasks, including the election of additional members, if any, to the board, the adoption of by-laws, the appointment of officers, the adoption of a corporate seal, the designation of a bank as depository for corporate funds, and often the sale of stock to the initial shareholders. Review the sample by-laws and minutes of an organizational meeting of the board of directors that are included in CORPORATIONS AND OTHER BUSINESS ASSOCIATIONS STATUTES: RULES AND FORMS (Edward S. Adams & John Matheson, eds. 1997 ed.). *See also*, RMBCA § 2.06.

In many cases, the routine legal work associated with the incorporation process is not performed directly by the attorney but, under the attorney's instruction, by a corporation service company, which performs the clerical work for a relatively modest fee. The result is a standard form of corporation, not a handcrafted one, but one that is often sufficient for ordinary situations. In addition to providing "standard" articles of incorporation, by-laws, and forms of stock certificate and handling the filing of the necessary documents with the state, service companies perform a variety of other routine tasks such as handling the qualification of the corporation to do business in other jurisdictions, acting as "registered agent" for the corporation, and assisting in the filing of annual and other reports required by the jurisdiction of incorporation and the states in which the corporation is registered as a foreign corporation. On the doors of the Wilmington, Delaware offices of the major service companies there can be found a veritable "who's who" of American industry.

## C. DEFECTIVE INCORPORATION

### 1. AT COMMON LAW

Under modern statutes, the incorporation process is extremely simple, and there should be no reason for doing it incorrectly. Nevertheless, a slip occasionally occurs (more frequently under older statutes) and the intended corporation does not come into legal existence—at least not when the parties expected. Defects can arise from a wide variety of circumstances. The incorporators may have neglected to make any filing at all, which is the most serious omission, or they may have filed but made a relatively small error, e.g., improper notarization, shortfall on the filing fee, a neglected signature or the like. They may have failed to make a required second filing, e.g., to file with both the state and county where the principal office is to be located. Most of these defects are technical in the most Pickwickian sense: they go to the heart of nothing (which is why the RMBCA has eliminated many prior technical requirements). Does not "justice" demand that third parties be denied access to the personal resources of the shareholders should the business become unable to pay its debts, if: (1) the investors in the would-be corporation believed that they had taken all the steps necessary to create a corporation and had instructed their lawyer to file the necessary papers; (2) the lawyer thought she had filed all the necessary papers; and (3) the persons with whom the organization dealt believed they were doing business with a corporation and expected to look only to that organization for payment of any debt? Of course, there is some state interest in having parties comply with the formalities required for incorporation, but the threat to that interest seems remote when the failure of the parties to comply with some technical requirement was inadvertent. Acting on this perception, courts of equity developed the concept that the business association could, in a proper case, be a *"de facto"* corporation, even if it was not a corporation *"de jure."* Courts also developed the concept of *corporation by estoppel* to achieve results deemed "just" where the de facto corporation doctrine could not be used.

## CRANSON v. INTERNATIONAL BUSINESS MACHINES CORP.

234 Md. 477, 200 A.2d 33 (1964).

HORNEY, JUDGE.

On the theory that the Real Estate Service Bureau was neither a *de jure* nor a *de facto* corporation and that Albion C. Cranson, Jr., was a partner in the business conducted by the Bureau and as such was personally liable for its debts, the International Business Machines Corporation brought this action against Cranson for the balance due on electric typewriters purchased by the Bureau. At the same time it moved for summary judgment and supported the motion by affidavit. In due course, Cranson filed a general issue plea and an affidavit in opposition to summary judgment in which he asserted in effect that the Bureau was a *de facto* corporation and that he was not personally liable for its debts.

The agreed statement of facts shows that in April 1961, Cranson was asked to invest in a new business corporation which was about to be created. Towards this purpose he met with other interested individuals and an attorney and agreed to purchase stock and become an officer and director. Thereafter, upon being advised by the attorney that the corporation had been formed under the laws of Maryland, he paid for and received a stock certificate evidencing ownership of shares in the corporation, and was shown the corporate seal and minute book. The business of the new venture was conducted as if it were a corporation, through corporate bank accounts, with auditors maintaining corporate books and records, and under a lease entered into by the corporation for the office from which it operated its business. Cranson was elected president and all transactions conducted by him for the corporation, including the dealings with I.B.M., were made as an officer of the corporation. At no time did he assume any personal obligation or pledge his individual credit to I.B.M. Due to an oversight on the part of the attorney, of which

Cranson was not aware, the certificate of incorporation, which had been signed and acknowledged prior to May 1, 1961, was not filed until November 24, 1961. Between May 17 and November 8, the Bureau purchased eight typewriters from I.B.M., on account of which partial payments were made, leaving a balance due of $4,333.40, for which this suit was brought.

Although a question is raised as to the propriety of making use of a motion for summary judgment as the means of determining the issues presented by the pleadings, we think the motion was appropriate. Since there was no genuine dispute as to the material facts, the only question was whether I.B.M. was entitled to judgment as a matter of law. The trial court found that it was, but we disagree.

The fundamental question presented by the appeal is whether an officer of a defectively incorporated association may be subjected to personal liability under the circumstances of this case. We think not.

Traditionally, two doctrines have been used by the courts to clothe an officer of a defectively incorporated association with the corporate attribute of limited liability. The first, often referred to as the doctrine of *de facto* corporations, has been applied in those cases where there are elements showing: (1) the existence of law authorizing incorporation; (2) an effort in good faith to incorporate under the existing law; and (3) actual use or exercise of corporate powers. The second, the doctrine of estoppel to deny the corporate existence, is generally employed where the person seeking to hold the officer personally liable has contracted or otherwise dealt with the association in such a manner as to recognize and in effect admit its existence as a corporate body.

\* \* \*

I.B.M. contends that the failure of the Bureau to file its certificate of incorporation debarred *all* corporate existence. But, in spite of the fact that the omission might have prevented the Bureau from being either a corporation *de jure* or *de facto,* we think that I.B.M. having dealt with the Bureau as if it were a corporation and relied on its credit rather than that of Cranson, is estopped to assert that the Bureau was not incorporated at the time the typewriters were purchased. In 1 Clark and Marshall, PRIVATE CORPORATIONS, § 89, it is stated:

> The doctrine in relation to estoppel is based upon the ground that it would generally be inequitable to permit the corporate existence of an association to be denied by persons who have represented it to be a corporation, or held it out as a corporation, or by any persons who have recognized it as a corporation by dealing with it as such; and by the overwhelming weight of authority, therefore, a person may be estopped to deny the legal incorporation of an association which is not even a corporation *de facto*.

In cases similar to the one at bar, involving a failure to file articles of incorporation, the courts of other jurisdictions have held that where one has recognized the corporate existence of an association, he is estopped to assert the contrary with respect to a claim arising out of such dealings.

Since I.B.M. is estopped to deny the corporate existence of the Bureau, we hold that Cranson was not liable for the balance due on account of the typewriters.

Judgment reversed; the appellee to pay the costs.

## 2.  THE IMPACT OF THE REVISED MODEL BUSINESS CORPORATION ACT

The de facto corporation and corporation by estoppel doctrines created, in the eyes of some commentators, "uncertainties" about corporate existence, although it is by no means clear what harm these uncertainties did to anyone. In the typical situation, of which *Cranson* is a good example, the plaintiff must be pleasantly surprised to find that what he thought was a corporation was never validly incorporated. The de facto corporation doctrine only restores the plaintiff to the position which he originally anticipated. But the desire for predictability is strongly felt by those who plan business transactions. Sections 56 and 146 of the previous version of the RMBCA reflected the legislative attempt to provide this certainty. Those sections were interpreted in *Robertson v. Levy*, 197 A.2d 443 (D.C.App.1964) to have abolished the de facto corporation and corporation by estoppel doctrines. Levy and Robertson had entered into a contract under which Levy was to form a corporation to purchase Robertson's business. Levy filed articles of incorporation and six days later Robertson transferred his business to the "corporation" which gave its note in exchange. In the meantime, however, the articles of incorporation had been returned as defective, and refiled, but the certificate, denoting official corporateness, was not issued until nine days after the delivery of the note. The company later failed, and Robertson sued Levy on the note, which he had signed as "president" of the "corporation."

After reviewing the historical development of de facto corporation and corporation by estoppel doctrines, the court concluded that the Sections 56 and 146, which had been adopted in the District of Columbia, were intended "to eliminate problems inherent in the de jure, de facto and, estoppel concepts." Courts were thus no longer to inquire into equities but were to recognize corporate existence only when the appropriate authorities have issued a certificate of incorporation; individuals who presume to act as a corporation are jointly and severally liable for "its" acts. That Robertson intended to look only to the "corporation" for payment of the note, and had accepted a note from the "corporation," did not, therefore, estop him from recovering from Levy personally.

RMBCA § 2.04 modifies this unequivocal position by imposing liability only on those persons who act "as or on behalf of a corporation" "knowing" that no corporation actually exists. See Official Comment to § 2.04. Seemingly, RMBCA § 2.04 preserves some semblance of the de facto doctrine because knowledge encompasses "good faith." Official

Comment to RMBCA § 2.04 (next to last paragraph). In other words, if some steps have been taken to bring about the corporation, liability will not be imposed on the parties who do not know that the steps to achieve corporateness were not completed.

But consider three people who do not consult an attorney, decide to call themselves a corporation, have a good faith belief that a corporation exists and do not actually know that no corporation has been formed. Under RMBCA § 2.04, the Official Comment to RMBCA § 2.04, and the common law, are they personally liable or is there still some vestige of corporateness?

One final question that you might wish to ponder, albeit with some fear in your heart, is the liability of the lawyer who fails to effect incorporation for her client and who fails to constrain the client's business dealings until full compliance with statutory requirements has been achieved.

## D. PRE–INCORPORATION ACTIVITIES OF PROMOTERS

There may be occasions when it is necessary for the promoters of a corporation to execute contracts on behalf of the corporation before the formalities of incorporation are completed and the corporation has come into legal existence. This is less of a problem than it once was; incorporation formalities have been simplified and can now generally be completed in a few days (or upon filing, under RMBCA § 2.03(a)). Nevertheless there are still times when it is necessary to execute a contract with a third party before incorporation is completed. Since at the time of such a transaction there is no corporation capable of becoming a party to the contract, the application of traditional principles of contract and agency law presents certain conceptual questions: Can the corporation subsequently become bound by the contract, and if so, under what theory? Is the promoter who executes the contract liable on the contract if the corporation never comes into existence? Or if it fails? If the corporation does come into existence and adopts the contract as its own, can the corporation sue on the contract?

The leading English case held that a pre-incorporation contract executed by the promoters bound only the promoters and that the corporation could not subsequently become a party after it came into existence. *Kelner v. Baxter*, L.R. 2 P.C. 174 (1866). The underlying theory was that under traditional agency law a contract could be ratified by a principal only if the principal was in existence at the time the contract was executed. The result was that, although the corporation might become liable for benefits it received under the contract, it did not, by accepting those benefits, ratify the contract and so become liable. Neither, in fact, could the corporation adopt the contract, even by explicit vote of its board of directors. Although a few early American decisions accepted this doctrine, *e.g., Abbott v. Hapgood*, 150 Mass. 248,

22 N.E. 907; 908 (1889), it has by now been almost completely repudiated in this country. Now, it is generally accepted that after a corporation comes into existence, it may adopt and so become liable on the contract.

In *McArthur v. Times Printing Co.*, 48 Minn. 319, 51 N.W. 216 (1892), a contract was enforced against a corporation although execution occurred prior to corporate existence. The contract sprung into being upon the formation of the corporation and adoption by the board. Ratification was impossible, since the contract could not relate back to the time prior to corporate existence, at least insofar as the corporation was affected.

Against the background of the theoretical hurdles suggested by *Kelner v. Baxter*, the American courts had some difficulties finding a rational basis to justify the conclusion in *McArthur* that a corporation can become bound by a contract executed before it had any life of its own. There have been at least four different conceptual bases advanced to support this result: (1) ratification, (2) adoption, (3) the acceptance of a continuing offer, and (4) novation or the creation of a new contract based upon mutual agreement of the parties. *See* Henry Winthrop Ballantine, BALLANTINE ON CORPORATIONS 108 (rev. ed. 1946); James D. Cox et. al., Corporations § 5.4 at § 5.8 (1995). None of these is wholly satisfying. Perhaps the best explanation is that pre-incorporation agreements are *sui generis* and need not be strait-jacketed by the traditional common law principles of agency and contracts.

As a general rule, when a promoter contracts for the benefit of a corporation which is contemplated but has not been organized, she is personally liable on it in the absence of an agreement to the contrary. Furthermore, the promoter is not discharged from liability merely because the corporation is later organized and receives the benefits of the contract, even where the corporation adopts the contract. However, the parties may agree specifically to discharge the liability of the promoter.

Although the parties may incorporate into the contract an express agreement that the promoter would not be held personally liable, pre-incorporation contracts typically do not expressly address promoter liability. Thus, the intentions of the parties, as deduced from the contract and the facts and circumstances of the parties' dealings, determine whether the promoter is personally liable. Factors used in analyzing whether a promoter will be held liable for a pre-incorporation contract include: (1) form of signature—did the promoter sign as an agent of the corporation? (2) action of seller—did the seller intend to look only to the corporation for payment? (3) partial performance—did the promoter's partial performance of the contract indicate an intent to be held personally liable? (4) novation—did action taken by the parties discharge the promoter's liability?

The intention of the contracting parties is the principal focus of judicial opinions on the question. The promoter may claim that it was "intended" that once the contemplated corporation was brought into existence her own liability would fall by the wayside and the corporation would substitute for her. This is clear enough if the contract contains a novation provision stating that the promoter's liability terminates if the corporation is formed and manifests a willingness to become a party to the contract. As you may recall from your Contracts course, a novation is a three-party arrangement in which a new corporation assumes all of a promoter's rights and liabilities under a pre-incorporation contract thereby discharging the promoter. *See* RESTATEMENT (SECOND) OF CONTRACTS § 280 (1981). To be effective, the third party must assent to the substitution of the new corporation for the promoter who agrees to abandon her status as an original party to the contract.

If an express advance assent to a novation is not explicit in the pre-incorporation contract, courts utilize rules of contractual interpretation, as well as the parties' dealings, to determine the parties' intentions. For example, if the third party looked first to the promoter and then, exclusively, to the corporation, a court may infer an intent to create a novation. Thus, even without a specific novation provision, the promoter may argue that she fulfilled her promise by creating the corporation which is able to step into her shoes and giving the corporation the opportunity to pay its debt. It has been held, however, that creating the corporation is not enough, and that the corporation must adopt the contract by some affirmative act before it becomes bound and the promoter is released. *RKO–Stanley Warner Theatres, Inc. v. Graziano*, 467 Pa. 220, 355 A.2d 830 (1976); *Herbert v. Boardman*, 134 Vt. 78, 349 A.2d 710 (1975).

How is adoption accomplished? More than the creation of the corporation is needed, even though its promoter possesses knowledge of the contract. Where that promoter becomes a member of the board of directors of the corporation, at least, it is fair to impute her knowledge of the contract to the corporation, and subsequent acts by the corporation—with such knowledge—may constitute adoption. *See Peters Grazing Association v. Legerski*, 544 P.2d 449 (Wyo.1975). The corporation may also, of course, adopt the contract by express action of its directors.

If the corporation never comes into existence or comes into existence and subsequently becomes unable to perform its obligations under the contract, the third party may sue the individuals who signed the contract on its behalf. If the promoters do not disclose to the third party that the corporation does not exist at the time of the execution of the contract, they may be liable on a theory of breach of an implied warranty that the corporate principal exists and that the promoter has the authority to act for the corporation. When the third party relies on this implied representation to her detriment, she can sue to hold the promoter individually liable on the contract.

But what if the third party knows of the nonexistence of the corporation? How should a court construe a contract signed, to take a well known example, "D.J. Geary, for a bridge company to be organized and incorporated"? *O'Rorke v. Geary*, 207 Pa. 240, 56 A. 541 (1903). There are several possible interpretations: (1) The parties intend that

Geary is to use his best efforts to bring a corporation into existence and to have it adopt the contract as its own. There is no intention that Geary will ever be bound personally. (2) The parties intend that Geary will be liable on the contract until such time as he successfully incorporates the corporation and has it adopt the contract. (3) The parties intend that Geary will be bound on the contract and will remain bound even if the corporation comes into existence and adopts the contract.

The rule stated in the RESTATEMENT (SECOND) OF AGENCY § 326 (1958) provides: "Unless otherwise agreed, a person who, in dealing with another, purports to act as agent for a principal whom both know to be non-existent or wholly incompetent, becomes a party to such contract." Under this rule, of course, Geary would be bound on the contract and would remain bound even if the corporation were ultimately to adopt it.

Also, the considerations of fairness may support a different result. The pre-incorporation contract may provide evidence of the parties' intentions. Thus, the to-be-formed corporation may be designated as the performing party or the promoter's signature may indicate that she did not intend to bind herself personally. While the signature format standing alone is seldom dispositive, because it applies to the whole context of the agreement, if additional contract terms indicate that the third party intended to look solely to the corporation for satisfaction, the promoter may not be held personally liable.

The third party's intentions are also a factor to be considered. In *Quaker Hill, Inc. v. Parr*, 148 Colo. 45, 364 P.2d 1056 (1961), for example, the plaintiff sold nursery stock to the defendants. The plaintiff's salesman insisted on executing the contract before the corporation was formed. At the suggestion of the plaintiff, the contract of sale named as purchaser a corporation that did not yet exist. The defendants did ultimately organize a corporation (using a different name than that in the contract because the original name was already in use in the state). The corporation, however, never functioned as a going concern, and the nursery stock (all of which died) remained unpaid for. The court held that the defendants were not liable for the purchase price as the evidence suggested that the plaintiffs had intended to look only to the corporation and not to the individual defendants for payment.

The third party may also argue, often successfully based on the precedents, that partial performance by the promoter during the preincorporation period gives rise to an inference that the promoter intended to be personally bound. That was, in fact, the holding of O'Rorke v. Geary. *See also White & Bollard, Inc. v. Goodenow*, 58 Wash.2d 180, 361 P.2d 571 (1961).

Ultimately, the problem is one of adequate drafting: there is no reason why any specific interpretation should not be spelled out explicitly in the contract and given effect by the courts. For example, the promoter may take an option, which can be assigned to the corporation after its formation. In this manner, the promoter never becomes an obligee. However, there will inevitably be cases in which the parties do not or are unable to arrange their affairs neatly, and the courts are left to struggle with the resulting problems.

# E. CHOICE OF THE STATE OF INCORPORATION

## 1. INTRODUCTION: THE LAW APPLICABLE TO CORPORATIONS

What turns on the decision of where to incorporate? Until you know the answer to that question, you cannot intelligently choose the state of incorporation.

As we saw in Chapter 4, a corporation is a legal person and has certain constitutional rights, including equal protection of the law and the right not to be deprived of property without due process of law. Under early doctrine, a state could exclude out-of-state corporations altogether from engaging in intrastate business within its borders. *See*, e.g., *Bank of Augusta v. Earle*, 38 U.S. (13 Pet.) 519, 10 L.Ed. 274 (1839); *Paul v. Virginia*, 75 U.S. (8 Wall.) 168, 19 L.Ed. 357 (1868); *Railway Express Agency v. Virginia*, 282 U.S. 440, 51 S.Ct. 201, 75 L.Ed. 450 (1931), and thus could subject foreign corporations to conditions on doing business within the state. More recently, the Supreme Court has concluded that it is "now established that whatever the extent of a state's authority to exclude foreign corporations from doing business within its boundaries, that authority does not justify imposition of more onerous taxes or other burdens on foreign corporations than those imposed on domestic corporations, unless the discrimination between foreign and domestic corporations bears a rational relation to a legitimate state purpose." *Western & Southern Life Insurance Co. v. State Board of Equalization of California*, 451 U.S. 648, 101 S.Ct. 2070, 68 L.Ed.2d 514 (1981). *See Watson v. Employers Liability Assurance Corp., Ltd.*, 348 U.S. 66, 74, 75 S.Ct. 166, 171, 99 L.Ed. 74, 83 (1954) (Frankfurter, J., concurring). In practice, states do not exclude foreign corporations, but seek to assert some control, mainly for revenue raising purposes. Thus, if a company is to engage in "local" business* in a foreign state, it must register within the state so as to qualify to do business there as a foreign corporation. But if the corporation's intrastate activities are an inseparable part of an interstate transaction, it may not be required to qualify as a foreign corporation because of the constitutional prohibition against interference with interstate commerce. *Eli Lilly & Co. v. Sav–On–Drugs*, 366 U.S. 276, 81 S.Ct. 1316, 6 L.Ed.2d 288 (1961); *Allenberg Cotton Co. v. Pittman*, 419 U.S. 20, 95 S.Ct. 260, 42 L.Ed.2d 195 (1974).

---

* What constitutes "doing business" has generated countless court opinions but remains, nevertheless, an unusually unrefined area of the law of corporations. It should be noted that "doing business" for the purpose of requiring a corporation to register as a foreign corporation is not necessarily "doing business" for the purposes of jurisdiction of the courts or amenability to service of process, and that both are different from "doing business" for the purpose of imposing state taxes.

Originally, the main purpose of the registration requirement was to assure that foreign corporations would be subject to the jurisdiction of the courts of the state and amenable to service of process in the state, objectives that have been largely achieved by the expansion of long-arm jurisdiction. Today, sanctions for a failure to qualify to do business are relatively mild; they generally entail little more than a temporary bar of access to local courts. This may be embarrassing when the corporation is sued and is unable to file an answer or a counterclaim; but under most statutes, registration even after the suit is filed removes this bar. RMBCA § 15.02.

Registration (also known as qualification) of a foreign corporation involves filing with a jurisdiction's secretary of state a formal application for a certificate of authority together with other requisite documents and paying a filing fee. RMBCA §§ 15.01, 15.03. Typically, a foreign corporation must appoint a local resident agent or designate the secretary of state to receive service of process for lawsuits brought in that state. RMBCA § 15.07. Qualification means that the foreign corporation is authorized to transact business in the state. It also becomes subject to service of process within the jurisdiction and to applicable taxes.

The principles embodied in the full faith and credit clause of the Constitution and the idea of comity require a state which hosts a foreign corporation to respect the legislative enactments and judicial decisions of the state of incorporation of the foreign corporation. When a corporation incorporated in one state does business in another it carries with it whatever rights were conferred by the act of incorporation and the applicable law of its state of incorporation.

The law of the state of incorporation also ordinarily determines the rules that govern the "internal affairs" of a corporation. RESTATEMENT (SECOND) OF CONFLICTS OF LAWS §§ 296–310 (1971). Recall Chapter 4, Section C. Although the term "internal affairs" has no clear definition, it generally is deemed to include matters bearing on the relationship between owners (shareholders) and managers (officers and directors). The internal affairs rule also applies to the relationships between different classes of shareholders, between shareholders and creditors, and between shareholders and employees. For example, under the internal affairs rule, the law of the state of incorporation governs the right of shareholders to vote, to receive distributions of corporate property, to receive information from the management about the affairs of the corporation, to limit the powers of the corporation to specifically chosen fields of activity, and to bring suit on behalf of the corporation when the managers refuse to do so. It also determines the procedures by which the board of directors will act, the managers' right to be indemnified by the corporation when they are sued for their conduct, and the corporation's right to issue stock and to merge with other companies. Perhaps most importantly, the internal affairs rule applies to rules defining the duties that the managers of a corporation, as fiduciaries, owe to shareholders.

This list, by no means exhaustive, suggests the impossibility of administering any other rule, at least if the corporation is a multi-state venture. How could it be decided, for example, which stockholders were entitled to vote at an annual meeting if it were necessary to refer to the potentially conflicting law of every state in which the corporation did business? Obviously with respect to such questions a choice must be made; the internal affairs rule makes it by deciding them according to the law of the state of incorporation.

Of course, the "external affairs" of a corporation are generally governed by the law of the place where the activities occur and by federal and state regulatory statutes rather than by the place of incorporation. For example, a state's labor laws govern conditions of employment and minimum wages of the operations of all businesses within the state, wherever the businesses might be incorporated. State tax laws generally apply to activities of any corporation within the state, especially those that are imposed on corporate real estate and income. (Franchise taxes, which are collected by the state of incorporation from companies incorporated there, do not depend on the situs of a corporation's activities or property.)

Some activities are governed by both internal and external rules. For example, state corporation law controls the right to merge and the procedure to be followed, but mergers are also independently subject to anti-trust laws and securities laws.

The internal affairs doctrine is a choice-of-law rule and, like other such rules is amenable to change by a particular jurisdiction (subject always to the requirements of the U.S. Constitution). Thus in an effort to protect its citizens, a state, in principle at least, is free to apply some or all of its own corporate law rules to corporations that have substantial contacts with the state even though they are incorporated elsewhere. New York and California have chosen to exercise this power over what have been called "pseudo-foreign" corporations, meaning corporations that carry on most of their activities or have a majority of their shareholders in the state but are incorporated in another state. Calif. Corp. Code § 2115, N.Y.B.C.L. § 1320.

The California statute makes certain provisions of California law governing corporate affairs applicable to a foreign corporation if (1) more than 50 percent of its property, payroll, and sales are within California and (2) more than 50 percent of its voting securities are held of record by persons with California addresses. A corporation falling within this class becomes subject to, among others, the California provisions on dividends and other distributions of corporate property, election and removal of directors, directors' standard of care, indemnification of officers and directors, and the regulation of mergers and sales of assets. One of the provisions made applicable by the statute is a requirement that "cumulative" voting (a procedure discussed in greater detail in Chapter 13) be used in the election of directors rather than "straight" voting. This provision thus makes mandatory a form of voting which is at least optional in most other states.

Suppose a corporation is incorporated in a state that allows "straight" voting for directors but it meets the California tests for pseudo-foreign corporations. How are directors elected? A California appellate court has held that the California voting provisions govern, rejecting a constitutional challenge to § 2115. *Wilson v. Louisiana–Pacific Resources*, Inc., 138 Cal.App.3d 216, 187 Cal.Rptr. 852 (1982). A corporation meeting all the tests of § 2115, but incorporated under Utah law, challenged the requirement that directors be elected by cumulative voting, asserting that the statute violated the full faith and credit, the commerce and contract clauses, impaired property without due process of law, and deprived the corporation of equal protection of the law. All the challenges were rejected. Among other things, the court found that a state need only have a significant contact in order to apply its law, a test that was clearly met under the legislative standard. The generally applied "internal affairs rule," the court observed, is a common law test that the legislature rejected, and it is not a constitutional requirement. The spectre of conflicting rules, which might result from differences between California and the other states was viewed as minimal. The nature of the California tests necessarily excludes claims by other states to govern the affairs of the corporation (except that the court does not mention the conflicting claim of the incorporating state which need have *no* physical contact), but in any event the burden is not so substantial.

A constitutional challenge to § 2115 could result from the Supreme Court's decision in *CTS Corp. v. Dynamics Corp. of America*, *supra* Chapter 4, upholding an Indiana statute dealing with corporate takeovers. The Court observed that, "No principle of corporation law and practice is more firmly established than a state's authority to regulate domestic corporations, including the authority to define voting rights of shareholders." 481 U.S. at 89, 107 S.Ct. at 1649. The Court also stated, "It is thus an accepted part of the business landscape in this country for States to create corporations, to prescribe their powers, and to define the rights that are acquired by purchasing their shares." 481 U.S. at 91, 107 S.Ct. at 1650.

In *McDermott Inc. v. Lewis*, 531 A.2d 206 (Del.1987), the court applied Panama law to permit the shares of a Panamanian parent corporation to be voted by its subsidiary, a Delaware corporation. Under DGCL § 160(c), the shares could not be voted. In contrast to *Wilson*, *supra*, the Delaware Supreme Court observed that "application of the internal affairs doctrine is not merely a principle of conflicts of law. It is also one of serious constitutional proportions—under due process, the commerce clause and the full faith and credit clause—so that the law of one state governs the relationships of a corporation to its stockholders, directors and officers in matters of internal corporate governance. The alternatives present almost intolerable consequences to the corporate enterprise and its managers. With the existence of multistate and multinational organizations, directors and officers have a significant right, under the fourteenth amendment's due process clause, to know what law will be applied to their actions. Stockholders also have a right to know by what standards of accountability they may hold those managing the corporation's business and affairs." *Id.* at 216–27.

For analyses of pseudo-foreign corporation statutes and the constitutional limitations on applying the law of the forum state to the internal affairs of a foreign corporation, *see* Norton P. Beveridge, *The Internal Affairs Doctrine: The Proper Law of a Corporation*, 44 BUS. LAW. 693, 702–15 (1989); Deborah A. DeMott, *Perspectives on Choice of Law for Corporate Internal Affairs*, 48 LAW. & CONTEMP. PROBS. 161 (Summer 1985).

## 2. PRACTICAL CONSIDERATIONS

Before making an intelligent judgment as to the state of incorporation, it is first necessary to understand the nature and scope of the business that is to be incorporated. The lawyer must know where the company intends to operate and what kinds of activity it intends to conduct in particular locations. For most businesses, particularly smaller ones, there should be a strong presumption in favor of incorporating where the principal operations are to be conducted. If operations are confined to a single state, incorporating in that state will reduce filing, reporting and tax burdens. But if a company intends to operate in more than one state (which is often the case), it may be required to qualify to do business as a foreign corporation in other jurisdictions.

If the lawyer concludes that the corporation is not required to qualify as a foreign corporation in any state because all of its activities are local, local incorporation is usually most desirable. Counsel will generally recommend foreign incorporation only if particular provisions of the corporation law of the local jurisdiction are especially burdensome to the owners or managers of the corporation or the administration of the local statute is inefficient. Such a situation would be unusual for most small businesses.

Some of the other factors to be considered in deciding where to incorporate are:

1.  The organization tax rates and the franchise tax rates.

2.  The simplicity of operation of the corporation. For example, some jurisdictions, but not all, permit: (1) a corporation's board of directors to act by unanimous consent without a meeting or by means of a conference telephone call, and (2) a corporation to dispense with stockholder meetings and shareholders to act by the consent of the holders of a sufficient number of shares.

3.  Restrictions on dividends and other distributions. These may be important for a number of reasons, and the directors may be liable personally for dividends or other distributions that are not permitted under state law.

4.   Shareholder rights. Some jurisdictions severely limit the participatory rights of shareholders. Such limitations may reflect majoritarian principles rather than an anti-shareholder attitude (an issue we will consider in greater depth in Chapter 12).

5.   Indemnification. Officers and directors are entitled to be indemnified for their expenses in connection with a law suit if they satisfy the statutory standard of conduct. Indemnification provisions vary among the states (an issue we will consider again in Chapter 16). Ordinarily, this consideration is more relevant to a publicly held company than to a close corporation.

6.   Provisions for close corporations. A number of states provide easier operational arrangements and a relaxing of the corporate norms to accommodate the private bargain that participants in a close corporation may want to strike, which in some cases deviates from the statutory pattern.

7.   Liability for wages. Although limited liability for shareholders is the general rule, there are occasional statutory exceptions. For example, New York and Wisconsin impose some personal liability on the shareholders for unpaid wages to employees. N.Y.B.C.L. § 630 provides that the ten largest shareholders of a company are jointly and severally liable for all "debts, wages or salaries due or owing to any of its laborers, servants or employees other than contractors, for services performed by them for such corporation." The statute does not apply to corporations whose securities are publicly traded.

Wis. Stat. § 180.0622 imposes a more limited personal liability on shareholders in by making the shareholders of every corporation, other than railroad corporations, personally liable for all debts (not to exceed six months' service in any case) owing to employees, up to the amount equal to the par value of their shares, or the consideration paid for their no par shares. As we shall soon see, this may be only a token amount. Unlike New York, however, the Wisconsin provision applies to shareholders of foreign corporations. *Joncas v. Krueger*, 61 Wis.2d 529, 213 N.W.2d 1 (1973).

## 3.   POLICY CONSIDERATIONS

### a.   *Introduction*

The public policy issues that grow out of the selection of the state of incorporation flow from the internal affairs rule. Should the participants in a corporation, or some group of those participants, have the freedom to select the body of law that will govern the corporation's internal affairs? Is there a danger that some states, in an effort to attract incorporations so as to generate franchise tax revenues, will adopt laws that treat certain participants unfairly? Which participants makes the decision on where to incorporate, and what factors influence their decisions?

As noted in Chapter 1, all state corporation laws are essentially enabling laws. They provide for an organizational framework in which a business can operate and abjure regulatory goals. Things were not always so. The following excerpt from Mr. Justice Brandeis' famous dissenting opinion in *Liggett Co. v. Lee* recounts some of the historical development.

## LIGGETT CO. v. LEE

288 U.S. 517, 53 S.Ct. 481, 77 L.Ed. 929 (1933).

Mr. Justice Brandeis (dissenting in part).

[The case, itself, was a challenge to the constitutionality of a tax imposed by Florida on chain stores. The Court struck down the tax. Brandeis' dissenting view was that "Whether the corporate privilege shall be granted or withheld is always a matter of state policy * * *. If a state believes that adequate protection * * * can be secured, without revoking the corporate privilege, by imposing * * * upon corporations the handicap of higher, discriminatory license fees as compensation for the privilege, I know of nothing in the Fourteenth Amendment to prevent it from making the experiment."]

Second. The prevalence of the corporation in America has led men of this generation to act, at times, as if the privilege of doing business in corporate form were inherent in the citizen; and has led them to accept the evils attendant upon the free and unrestricted use of the corporate mechanism as if these evils were the inescapable price of civilized life, and, hence, to be borne with resignation. Throughout the greater part of our history a different view prevailed. Although the value of this instrumentality in commerce and industry was fully recognized, incorporation for business was commonly denied long after it had been freely granted for religious, educational, and charitable purposes. It was denied because of fear. Fear of encroachment upon the liberties and opportunities of the individual. Fear of the subjection of labor to capital. Fear of monopoly. Fear that the absorption of capital by corporations, and their perpetual life, might bring evils similar to those which attended mortmain. There was a sense of some insidious menace inherent in large aggregations of capital, particularly when held by corporations. So at first the corporate privilege was granted sparingly; and only when the grant seemed necessary in order to procure for the community some specific benefit otherwise unattainable. The later enactment of general incorporation laws does not signify that the apprehension of corporate domination had been overcome. The desire for business expansion created an irresistible demand for more charters; and it was believed that under general laws embodying safeguards of universal application the scandals and favoritism incident to special incorporation could be avoided. The general laws, which long embodied severe restrictions upon size and upon the scope of corporate activity, were, in part, an expression of the desire for equality of opportunity.

* * *

The removal by the leading industrial states of the limitations upon the size and powers of business corporations appears to have been due, not to their conviction that maintenance of the restrictions was undesirable in itself, but to the conviction that it was futile to insist upon them; because local restriction would be circumvented by foreign incorporation. Indeed, local restriction seemed worse than futile. Lesser states, eager for the revenue derived from the traffic in charters, had removed safeguards from their own incorporation laws. Companies were early formed to provide charters for corporations in states where the cost was lowest and the laws least restrictive. The states joined in advertising their wares. The race was one not of diligence but of laxity. Incorporation under such laws was possible; and the great industrial States yielded in order not to lose wholly the prospect of the revenue and the control incident to domestic incorporation.

### b.  History of State Competition for Corporations

New Jersey was the first state to depart from the early philosophy of strict limitations on corporations beginning with its 1888 incorporation statute, which was followed by a revision in 1896. With its 1899 statute, Delaware entered the competition, and eventually succeeded in becoming the leading state for the incorporation of large businesses. Charles Beard, the noted historian, described how this came about in testimony before a Senate Committee considering federal corporate legislation in 1937:

> Under the leadership of Woodrow Wilson, after he was challenged by Theodore Roosevelt to reform his own state, the legislature of New Jersey passed a series of laws doing away with corporate abuses and applying high standards to corporations. What was the result? The revenues of the State from taxes on corporations fell. Malefactors moved over into other states. In time the New Jersey Legislature repealed its strict and prudent legislation, and went back, not quite, but almost to old ways. * * *

*Federal Licensing of Corporations:* Hearings on S. 10 Before a Subcommittee of the Senate Committee on the Judiciary, 75th Cong., 1st Sess. 74 (1937).

Another commentator observed that:

> The sovereign state of Delaware is in the business of selling its corporation law. This is profitable business, for a corporation law is a good commodity to sell. The market is large, and relatively few producers compete on a national scale. The consumers of this commodity are corporations. * * * Delaware, like any other good businessman, tries to give the consumer what he wants. In fact, those who will buy the product are not only consulted about their preferences, but are also allowed to design the product and run the factory.

Comment, *Law for Sale: A Study of the Delaware Corporation Law of 1967*, 117 U. PA. L.REV. 861, 861–862 (1969).

### c. The "Race for the Bottom" Debate

#### i. The Interventionist View: Federal Minimum Standards and Federal Chartering

Delaware corporate law has always been the subject of great controversy. In his seminal article, *Federalism and Corporate Law: Reflections Upon Delaware*, 83 YALE L.J. 663, 705 (1974), Professor William L. Cary argued that in its attempt to maintain its primacy as the home of large corporations, Delaware led a "race for the bottom" of corporate law. He contended that Delaware systematically had eliminated or reduced shareholder protections. As evidence, he pointed to statutory provisions reducing the shareholder vote required to approve a merger from two-thirds to a majority. He also cited numerous decisions which he interpreted as giving an overly liberal application to the business judgment rule and making it easier for corporate managers to resist hostile tender offers.

Cary's argument is based on the existence of the federal system that we have already noted. Because managers can choose where to incorporate, no state can use its corporate law to impose policies or governance structures on corporations that those managers would find antithetical. If the legislature were to do so, managers would simply reincorporate in a more hospitable jurisdiction. Accordingly, Cary proposed that Congress adopt a federal minimum standards law, applicable to larger public companies, that would impose federal fiduciary standards and other restrictions on corporate officers and directors.

Other proposals for federal intervention have gone much further. A task force under the direction of consumer activist Ralph Nader urged federal incorporation of all large corporations, not to supplement state law or be superimposed on state law as Professor Cary urged, but to replace state corporation law. Ralph Nadar, et al., CONSTITUTIONALIZING THE CORPORATION: THE CASE FOR FEDERAL CHARTERING OF GIANT CORPORATIONS (1976). *See also* Donald E. Schwartz, *A Case for Federal Chartering of Corporations*, 31 BUS.LAW. 1125 (1976). These proposals, unlike Professor Cary's, urged reform of corporation law not only to protect shareholder but as a means of enhancing corporate social responsibility.

#### ii. The Law and Economics View: The Benefits of Competition

It is possible to disagree with Professor Cary on a number of levels. His choice of cases to support his arguments is clearly selective. The reduction of the required shareholder vote in a merger transaction can be viewed as supporting majority rule and preventing a small minority from blocking a transaction that is advantageous to the corporation rather than as a means of exploiting shareholders. Nevertheless, his arguments and criticisms had considerable force and they have influenced Delaware lawyers and judges to this day.

The most significant intellectual disagreement comes from those who argue that market forces rather than legal doctrine will align the interests of shareholders and managers. They also contend that competition among states will ultimately benefit investors. The principal response to Cary came from Professor (now Judge) Ralph K. Winter, Jr.

### Ralph K. Winter, Jr., *State Law, Shareholder Protection, and the Theory of the Corporation*
6 J. LEGAL STUD. 251, 256–257, 259, 275, 276 (1977).

[Professor Cary's] claim, it is absolutely critical to note, is not that an overriding social goal is sacrificed by state law, but simply that Delaware is preventing *private* parties from optimizing their *private* arrangements. With all due respect both to Professor Cary and to the almost universal academic support for his position, it is implausible on its face. The plausible argument runs in the opposite direction: (1) If Delaware permits corporate management to profit at the expense of shareholders and other states do not, then earnings of Delaware corporations must be less than earnings of comparable corporations chartered in other states and shares in the Delaware corporations must trade at lower prices. (2) Corporations with lower earnings will be at a disadvantage in raising debt or equity capital. (3) Corporations at a disadvantage in the capital market will be at a disadvantage in the product market and their share price will decline, thereby creating a threat of a takeover which may replace management. To avoid this result, corporations must seek out legal systems more attractive to capital. (4) States seeking corporate charters will thus try to provide legal systems which optimize the shareholder-corporation relationship.

The conclusion that Delaware shares sell for less is implicit in Professor Cary's analysis, for if a "higher" legal standard for management conduct will increase investor confidence, investor confidence in Delaware stock must have been less than in stocks of other states for more than a generation. This lack of confidence would have long been reflected in the price of Delaware shares. Moreover, a reduction in the earnings of a corporation will affect its ability to raise debt capital, as well as equity, since the risk of a lender is thereby increased and a higher interest rate will be charged. Delaware corporations, therefore, not only face a lower share price but also must pay higher interest rates.

\* \* \*

Intervention in private transactions which impose no social cost can be justified only as a means of reducing the costs to the private parties. Thus, a prime function of state corporation codes is to supply standard terms which reduce the transaction costs, and thereby increase the benefits, of investing by eliminating costly bargaining which might otherwise accompany many routine corporate dealings. But substituting a mandatory legal rule for bargaining also may impose a cost in the form of the elimination of alternatives which the parties might prefer.

\* \* \*

Much of the legal literature calling for further federal regulation either assumes that no costs will fall upon shareholders or merely undertakes a cursory "eyeballing" of the potential costs. To be sure, self-dealing and fraud exist in corporate affairs and their elimination is desirable. But at some point the exercise of control by general rules of law may impose costs on investors which damage them in both quantity and quality quite as much as self-dealing or fraud. A paradox thus results: maximizing the yield to investors generally may, indeed almost surely will, result in a number of cases of fraud or self-dealing; and eliminating all fraud or self-dealing may decrease the yield to shareholders generally.

\* \* \*

A state which rigs its corporation code so as to reduce the yield to shareholders will spawn corporations which are less attractive as investment opportunities than comparable corporations chartered in other states or countries, as well as bonds, savings accounts, land, etc. Investors must be attracted before they can be cheated, and except for those seeking a "one shot," "take the money and run," opportunity to raid a corporation, management has no reason to seek out such a code. \* \* \* The chartering decision, therefore, so far as the capital market is concerned, will favor those states which offer the optimal yield to both shareholders and management.

\* \* \*

So far as the capital market is concerned, it is not in the interest of management to seek out a corporate legal system which fails to protect investors, and the competition between states for charters is generally a competition as to which legal system provides an optimal return to both interests. Only when that competition between legal systems exists can we perceive which legal rules are most appropriate for the capital market. Once a single legal system governs that market, we can no longer compare investor reaction. Ironically, in view of the conventional wisdom, the greater danger is not that states will compete for charters but that they will not.

———

### iii.   Analysis of Interventionist and Market–Oriented Perspectives

Proponents of the view that market forces shape corporate law often point to a study by two University of Chicago economists to support their theoretical arguments. Peter Dodd & Richard Leftwich, *The Market for Corporate Charters: "Unhealthy Competition" Versus Federal Regulation*, 55 J.Bus.L. 259 (1980), found no statistically significant changes in the price of the stock of companies that announced their intent to reincorporate in Delaware. However, the "events" analyzed in their study were ambiguous. Among other points, reincorporation usually is prompted by other circumstances and events, such as a proposed merger, which may have influenced the stock market's reaction more than the announced intent to reincorporate. Other commentators have pointed out that Dodd and Leftwich's results do not clearly repudiate the theory that a stockholder's position is worsened when a corporation reincorporates in Delaware.

Weiss and White examined the effect on investors, as measured by the impact on stock prices, of seemingly significant changes in corporate law doctrines by Delaware courts. They determined that investors did not react to judicial opinions that significantly changed state corporate law and suggested that these results called into question the existence of an investor-dominated market for corporate law. Elliott J. Weiss & Lawrence J. White, *Of Econometrics and Indeterminacy: A Study of Investors' Reactions to "Changes" in Corporate Law*, 75 CAL. L. REV. 551 (1987).

Judge Easterbrook and Professor Fischel support the "thesis that competition creates a powerful tendency for states to enact laws that operate to the benefit of investors * * *." Frank H. Easterbrook & Daniel R. Fischel, THE ECONOMIC STRUCTURE OF CORPORATE LAW 222 (1991). However, they characterize the market for state corporate law as less than efficient. They conclude that state competition for investors does not eliminate opportunistic behavior by managers. Similarly, competition for incorporation does not eliminate opportunistic behavior by states— even Delaware has enacted an antitakeover statute. Ultimately, though, Easterbrook and Fischel oppose a federal corporate law "because Federal laws face less competition * * *." *Id.* at 223.

Other commentators question whether state competition is truly effective. Lucian A. Bebchuk, *Federalism and the Corporation: The Desirable Limits on State Competition in Corporate Law*, 105 HARV. L. REV. 1435 (1992) argues that managerial opportunism and externalities may lead states to undesirable corporate statutory provisions. Professor Bebchuk concludes that state competition is likely to fail to maximize shareholder value in the following three areas: 1) issues involving the potential transfer of significant value from shareholders to managers, such as self-dealing transactions; 2) issues that directly affect the strength of market discipline, such as the regulation of takeover bids; 3) issues that involve potential transfers between controlling shareholders and public shareholders, such as the regulation of parent-subsidiary transactions. According to Bebchuck: "With respect to all of these issues, state competition can be expected systematically to produce rules that favor managers and dominant shareholders more than would the value-maximizing rules. This conclusion * * * follows from a recognition of the structural forces at work in the state charter competition." *Id.* at 1484. One of the key premises underlying Bebchuk's analysis is his belief that market discipline (namely, the market for corporate control, the managerial labor market, the market for additional capital, and the product market) probably will not discharge managers from seeking inefficient (nonshareholder value maximizing) rules with respect to issues involving the significant redistribution of wealth from shareholders to managers.

Bebchuk also points to the presence of significant adverse impacts on parties other than managers and shareholders, so-called externalities, in areas such as the regulation of takeover bids and corporate disclosure, noting that "if the rule is designed by the states, then the competition among them will lead state officials to exclude consideration of [third party] interests." *Id.* at 1485.

Because of the failure of state competition to deal with the problem of managerial opportunism and externalities, Bebchuk advocates an expansion of federal regulation, at least in the form of federal minimum standards to govern a number of areas. These would include managers' fiduciary duties, the fiduciary duties of controlling shareholders in freezeouts, dividend restrictions, and various aspects of takeover bids now governed by state law. He concludes, "Because federal law officials would not be affected by incorporation decisions in the same way that state law officials are, the federal law process would not suffer from the above two structural biases [managerial opportunism and externalities]." *Id.* at 1501.

### d. The Preeminence of Delaware

Stepping back from the welter of theoretical and empirical studies, the "race," whether for the bottom, as Cary described it or the top, as portrayed by Winter may be over. History has given Delaware an insurmountable lead.

Commentators generally agree on the reasons why Delaware has become preeminent. Roberta Romano, *The State Competition Debate in Corporate Law*, 8 CARDOZO L. REV. 709 (1987), notes that when publicly traded firms choose to reincorporate—move from one state where they are already incorporated to another—they choose Delaware 82% of the time. Firms tend to choose Delaware because of what Romano calls the "first mover advantage." Firms feel relatively confident that Delaware will respond promptly to the concerns of corporate managers in the future, because it has done so in the past.

Three factors bolster this belief. First, Delaware relies heavily on franchise taxes and therefore would have much to lose by failing to amend its statute in order to provide firms with advantages offered elsewhere. Second, the Delaware state constitution requires a two-thirds vote of both houses of the legislature to change its corporate code. The supermajority requirement makes it particularly difficult for the legislature to deprive corporations of benefits they currently enjoy. Finally, Delaware has tremendous assets in terms of "legal capital" which includes a massive body of corporate case law, judicial expertise, and an administrative body that is geared to rapidly process corporate filings.

In another article, Romano attaches particular importance to Delaware's judicial system. Courts in other jurisdictions increasingly look to and rely upon Delaware case law. Romano concludes:

> The value of a Delaware domicile to firms is more than an up-to-date code; Delaware also offers a comprehensive body of case law, which is not easily replicated by another state, and a handful of experienced judges. These factors afford firms greater predictability of the legal outcomes of their decisions, facilitating planning and reducing the costs of doing business. Indeed, the large number of

corporations domiciled in Delaware contributes to the development of its case law, for the sheer numbers make it more likely that a particular issue will have been litigated.

Roberta Romano, Law as a Product: *Some Pieces of the Incorporation Puzzle*, 1 J. L. Econ. & Org. 225, 280 (1985).

Professors Macey and Miller agree that Delaware is winning the race and is likely to continue to do so for reasons similar to those cited by Professor Romano. Jonathan R. Macey & Geoffrey P. Miller, *Toward an Interest–Group Theory of Delaware Corporate Law*, 65 Tex. L. Rev. 469 (1987). They note that Delaware corporate law provides incentives to incorporate in Delaware to all the major parties in corporate decision-making, including shareholders, managers, attorneys, and investment bankers. The Delaware code allows corporations to devise private arrangements to "contract around" its statute thereby providing for opportunities to enhance the value of the firm and thus benefit its shareholders. Managers are lured by preferential statutory provisions including those dealing with obtaining personal benefits, managerial compensation, allowing self-dealing contracts, and corporation indemnification of managers. Attorneys, especially corporate counsel, are "seduced" by Delaware corporate law, as is evidenced by the overwhelming majority of reincorporating firms who stated that their counsel suggested the move. Finally, investment bankers tend to prefer Delaware, perhaps because of case law which leads to hefty profits for its industry. Macey and Miller agree with Romano that Delaware is likely to continue winning the "race to the bottom" because it effectively guarantees corporations a continuation of favorable treatment in the future. Delaware "bonds" its promise that its corporate law will remain attractive by providing extraordinarily knowledgeable lawyers and judges and because political factors militate in favor of the continued guarantee. Various interest groups within the state, notably the bar, have a tremendous stake in preserving the primacy of Delaware.

It is easy to become simplistic in thinking about the effect of providing a legal climate managers and their lawyers find conducive. Consider the effect of a provision like DGCL § 228, which permits a majority of a corporation's shareholders to act by written consent. Professor Cary criticized this provision, because the managers of a public corporation can rely on it to avoid holding an annual meeting, at which they will be expected to respond to shareholders' questions and complaints. But does this provision clearly favor the interests of managers *as opposed to shareholders* ? As we will see in Chapter 12, shareholders may benefit because the consent procedure makes it easier for shareholders to act in situations where no meeting is on the horizon and no provisions has been made to allow shareholders to call such a meeting. Thus, § 228 appears to have some benefits for shareholders as well as involving some potential costs.

### e.  *The ALI and the ABA*

In the 1980s, the American Law Institute and the American Bar Association's Committee on Corporate Laws emerged as important forces in the field of corporate law. The Committee on Corporate Laws, is unique within the ABA: its membership is by invitation only and is limited to 25, and it has authority to make final decisions without reference to any higher authority within the ABA. In 1954, the Committee published the first Model Business Corporation Act, which it modelled on the Illinois corporate statute. The Committee's purpose was to produce a statute that was responsive to changing business practices and that state legislatures could use as a model when updating their corporate laws. However, when it produced and updated the Model Act and when it drafted the RMBCA in the early 1980s, the Committee largely avoided taking positions on controversial issues.

That changed in the late 1980s. The Committee proposed Subchapter F of the RMBCA, dealing with director's conflicting interest transactions, and identified its work as embodying an "entirely new approach" to that subject. Committee on Corporate Laws, *Changes in the Model Business Corporation Act—Amendments Pertaining to Director's Conflicting Interest Transactions*, 43 Bus. Law. 691 (1988). Similarly, in 1989 the Committee proposed new rules relating to derivative litigation that specifically addressed a number of issues that were surrounded by "[a] great deal of controversy * * *." Introductory Comment to RMBCA Subchapter D. Why the Committee adopted this new approach is unclear, but because so many states have based their corporate statutes on the RMBCA, it seems likely the Committee's more recent innovations will receive serious attention from many state legislatures.

The ALI is an independent organization made up of prominent jurists, practitioners and academics. Its principal product has been the various Restatements of the Law. In 1978, the ALI decided to proceed with a project dealing with corporate governance issues, the premise of which was to "preserve and enhance the effectiveness of corporations as the vehicles of the free-enterprise system." Roswell B. Perkins, *The Genesis and Goals of the ALI Corporate Governance Project*, 8 Cardozo L.Rev. 661 (1987). The Corporate Governance Project proved to be quite controversial. Some commentators believed the reporters' recommendations largely reflected the views of academic ideologues and were at variance with corporate practice and generally accepted principles of corporate law. *See, e.g.*, Jonathan R. Macey, *The Transformation of the American Law Institute*, 61 Geo. Wash. L.Rev. 1212 (1993). Others defended both the work of the reporters and the scope of the Project. Roswell B. Perkins, *Thanks, Myth and Reality*, 48 Bus. Law. 1313 (1993). In any event, courts began to take account of the Project's work even as it appeared in draft form. The Project's final product, ALI, Principles of Corporate Governance: Analysis and Recommendations (1994), thus seems likely to exert a major influence on developments in corporate law, even though the Principles have been heavily criticized by commentators at all points along the ideological spectrum. *See* Symposium, *The American Law Institute's Principles of Corporate Governance*, 61 Geo. Wash. L.Rev. 871 (1993).

# Chapter 8

# AN INTRODUCTION TO FINANCIAL ACCOUNTING AND VALUATION

---

## PROBLEM
### PRECISION TOOLS—PART III

The following is the most recent financial statement of Precision Tools, Inc. ("PT"), the company whose business Michael Lane, Jessica Bacon and Bernie Gould are interested in purchasing. Michael, Jessica and Bernie have asked you to review these financial statements with a view to helping them decide whether to purchase PT and what price to offer. Currently, you are the only professional advising them.

Consider the following:

1.   What information in PT's financial statements should be of the greatest interest to Michael, Jessica and Bernie? In particular, what do those statements tell you about the profitability of PT's operations, the value of PT's assets, and whether PT should be able to meet its financial obligations as they fall due?

2.   After analyzing PT's liquidity, debt coverage, equity and cash flow, what additional questions should Michael, Jessica and Bernie ask before deciding whether to purchase PT and how much to offer and pay for it?

## PRECISION TOOLS, INC.
### BALANCE SHEET
#### (As of December 31)

| Assets | 1997 | 1996 |
|---|---|---|
| **Current Assets** | | |
| Cash | 150,000 | 275,000 |
| Accounts receivable (less allowance for doubtful accounts) | 1,380,000 | 1,145,000 |
| Inventories | 1,310,000 | 1,105,000 |
| Prepaid expenses | 40,000 | 35,000 |
| Total Current Assets | 2,880,000 | 2,560,000 |
| | | |
| **Fixed Assets** | | |
| Land [1] | 775,000 | 775,000 |
| Buildings | 2,000,000 | 2,000,000 |
| Machinery | 1,000,000 | 935,000 |
| Office equipment | 225,000 | 205,000 |
| Total property, plant and equipment | 4,000,000 | 3,915,000 |
| Less accumulated depreciation | 1,620,000 | 1,370,000 |
| Net Fixed Assets [2] | 2,380,000 | 2,545,000 |
| | | |
| Total Assets | 5,260,000 | 5,105,000 |
| | | |
| **Liabilities and Equity** | | |
| **Current Liabilities** | | |
| Accounts payable | 900,000 | 825,000 |
| Notes payable | 600,000 | 570,000 |
| Accrued expenses payable | 250,000 | 235,000 |
| Total Current Liabilities | 1,750,000 | 1,630,000 |
| | | |
| **Long Term Liabilities** | | |
| Notes payable, 12.5%, due 12/15/03 | 2,000,000 | 2,000,000 |
| Notes payable, 11%, due 7/1/93 | — | 355,000 |
| Total Liabilities | 3,750,000 | 3,985,000 |
| | | |
| **Stockholders' Equity** | | |
| Common stock (1,000 shares authorized and outstanding) | | |
| Paid-in capital | 200,000 | 200,000 |
| Retained earnings | 1,310,000 | 920,000 |
| Total Equity | 1,510,000 | 1,120,000 |
| | | |
| **Total Liabilities and Equity** | 5,260,000 | 5,105,000 |

1. The land is in a modern industrial park, and was purchased for the price shown on the balance sheet fifteen years ago. Comparable nearby property recently sold for $975,000.

2. The machinery and equipment is in good repair. Depreciation is on a level (straight line) basis over the estimated life of the equipment. The building and equipment have a fair market value of approximately $200,000 in excess of the amounts shown on the balance sheet.

## STATEMENT OF INCOME
### (Year Ended December 31)

|  | 1997 | 1996 | 1995 |
|---|---|---|---|
| Net sales | 7,500,000 | 7,000,000 | 6,800,000 |
| Operating Expenses |  |  |  |
|   Cost of goods sold | 4,980,000 | 4,650,000 | 4,607,000 |
|   Depreciation | 250,000 | 240,000 | 200,000 |
|   Selling and administrative expense [1] | 1,300,000 | 1,220,000 | 1,150,000 |
|   Research and development | 50,000 | 125,000 | 120,000 |
| Operating income | 920,000 | 765,000 | 723,000 |
|   Interest expense | 320,000 | 375,000 | 375,000 |
| Income before taxes | 600,000 | 390,000 | 348,000 |
|   Income taxes | 210,000 | 136,000 | 122,000 |
| Net Income | 390,000 | 254,000 | 226,000 |

[1]. Includes salaries paid to Stern and Starr totaling $130,000 in 1997, $120,000 in 1996, and $100,000 in 1995, and bonuses totaling $120,000 in 1997, $100,000 in 1996, and $80,000 in 1995.

## STATEMENT OF CASH FLOWS
### (Year Ended December 31)

|  | 1997 | 1996 |
|---|---|---|
| From Operating Activities |  |  |
| Net Income | 390,000 | 254,000 |
| Decrease (Increase) in accounts receivable | (235,000) | ( 34,000) |
| Decrease (Increase) in inventories | (205,000) | ( 28,000) |
| Decrease (Increase) in prepaid expenses | ( 5,000) | ( 3,000) |
| Increase (Decrease) in accounts payable | 75,000 | 25,000 |
| Increase (Decrease) in accrued expenses payable | 15,000 | 7,000 |
| Depreciation | 250,000 | 240,000 |
| Total from Operating Activities | 285,000 | 461,000 |
| From Investing Activities |  |  |
| Sales (Purchases) of machinery | ( 65,000) | (378,000) |
| Sales (Purchases) of office equipment | ( 20,000) | ( 27,000) |
| Total from Investing Activities | ( 85,000) | (405,000) |
| From Financing Activities |  |  |
| Increase (Decrease) in short-term borrowings | 30,000 | ( 40,000) |
| Increase (Decrease) in long-term borrowings | (355,000) | — |
| Total from Financing Activities | (325,000) | ( 40,000) |
| Increase (Decrease) in Cash Position | (125,000) | 16,000 |

## A.  FINANCIAL ACCOUNTING DEMYSTIFIED

"Omigosh, accounting! Isn't this what I went to law school to avoid? If I wanted to learn accounting, I would have gone to B-school. Why do I have to understand this stuff?"

Don't panic! The authors appreciate that this statement may reflect the feelings of many law students—especially those with no background in accounting or finance—when they reach this Chapter. Nonetheless, this book includes materials designed to introduce basic accounting concepts. We believe most students will find that obtaining some grasp of basic accounting concepts will help them better understand what gives a business value. Clients value lawyers who can read and analyze financial statements. It is difficult for a lawyer to competently negotiate or draft documents for a transaction unless she understands both the transaction and her client's goals. Even more valuable is the lawyer who can help her client better understand the transaction. Moreover, appreciating where value lies in any given business setting, in turn, will help students better understand what is at stake in many of the cases and problems included in this book. In short, "[a] business client's favorite lawyer is the one about whom the client would say: 'This lawyer thinks like me!' "Robert C. Boehm, *Dealing from strength: 15 winning tips for business lawyers*, 2 Bus. Lawyer Today 58 (Nov./Dec. 1992).

Contrary to common belief, understanding basic accounting concepts does not require expertise in mathematics or a degree in finance. True, as PT's financial statements evidence, accounting information is presented largely in numerical form. But the materials that follow emphasize that, while the numbers in financial statements always appear precise, in fact (i) they are the product of a highly conceptual process that involves many subjective judgments; (ii) they reflect that process and those judgments, not some sort of scientific truth; and (iii) they tell only part of what is important about a firm's business and finances.

This last point is significant. The goal of financial statements is to convey information to the user, whether she be an investor, a lender, or a corporate manager. But the information that these statements give is not the entire story of the business. As you read the following materials, ask yourself what additional information you would want in order to understand the stories that lie behind the numbers. In so doing, you will begin to perform one of a lawyer's most important functions in a business transaction: helping the client ask the right questions.

### 1.  INTRODUCTION TO ACCOUNTING PRINCIPLES

The two basic financial statements are the balance sheet and the income statement. The relationship of these two statements often is described using the analogy of a snapshot and a motion picture. A balance sheet—the "snapshot"—presents a picture of the firm at some given moment, listing all property it owns (its "*assets*"), all amounts it owes (its *"liabilities"*), and the value, at least conceptually, of the owners' interest in the firm (its *"equity"*). An income statement—the "motion picture"—presents a picture of the results of the firm's operations during the period between the dates of successive balance sheets.

Financial statements are produced through a three-stage process. First, a company enters on its books information concerning every transaction in which it is involved—the recording and controls stage. Next comes the audit stage; the company, sometimes with the assistance of independent public accountants, verifies the information recorded on its books. Finally, in the accounting stage, the company classifies and analyzes the audited information and presents it in a set of financial statements.

RMBCA § 16.20 requires corporations to furnish their shareholders with annual balance sheets and income statements, but allows corporations to decide what principles to use when preparing those statements. Most firms, and all public corporations, use Generally Accepted Accounting Principles, or *GAAP*, when they prepare financial statements. GAAP are promulgated—or, more accurately, legislated—by a quasi-public body, the Financial Accounting Standard Board (FASB). The rules adopted by the FASB embody not immutable scientific or mathematical truths, but the (often controversial) judgments and policy preferences of a group of highly-qualified accounting professionals. Moreover, as the perceptions, judgments and preferences of the members of the FASB change over time, so do GAAP concerning how information about various kinds of transactions should be presented. This provides our first important insight about accounting: the need to keep in mind the difference between actual events and how information about those events is presented in financial statements. Events themselves are real. How to describe them often is problematic. But if information about an event is to be included in a financial statement, GAAP control how it is presented.

A simple hypothetical illustrates this point. Assume Exco purchased land and a building for $100,000 on January 1, immediately rented the property to a tenant, who paid rent during the year in an amount exactly equal to Exco's out-of-pocket costs, and that these were the only transactions in which Exco engaged during the year. On December 31 of that year, Smith offered to purchase the land and building for $105,000, but Exco decided not to sell. Did Exco earn a profit for the year?

The answer to this question depends on what is meant by "profit." If profit means being better off at the end of the year than at the beginning, a person might argue that Exco earned a profit. It started the year with $100,000 and ended the year owning property which, assuming Smith's offer was genuine, had a fair market value of at least $105,000. In essence, Exco was at least $5,000 better off on December 31 than it had been on January 1. The $5,000 could be viewed as Exco's profit, because Exco could have realized that profit had it chosen to sell.

An economist might well respond that to determine whether Exco earned a profit depends on the rate of inflation. If inflation was less than 5 percent, Exco made a profit because on December 31 it could have exchanged the property for $105,000, which could have been used to purchase more in the way of goods and services than Exco could have purchased with $100,000 on January 1. But if inflation exceeded 5 percent, Exco should be deemed to have incurred a loss, because the $105,000 it could have received would not allow it to purchase as much in the way of goods and services as it could have purchased with $100,000 on January 1.

An accountant preparing an income statement in accordance with GAAP would report that Exco incurred a loss. GAAP require Exco to treat as an "expense" both its out-of-pocket expenditures and some portion of the cost of the building it used to generate rental income during the year. (The accountant would call this a *depreciation expense*— a charge against income not tied to any outlay of cash.) In addition, GAAP would prohibit the accountant from recording the apparent gain in the value of the property because the property had not been sold; that Smith had made a *bona fide* offer to buy the property would be deemed irrelevant.

In short, there are different meanings to "profit," of which GAAP provides but one. But it is the one that is used in preparing financial statements. Thus, unless one understands the more important assumptions and fundamental principles underlying GAAP, it is difficult to appreciate the information in those statements. The most important assumptions and principles include the following:

**Separate Entity Assumption**: A business enterprise is viewed as an accounting unit separate and distinct from its owners, whether or not it has a separate legal existence.

**Continuity Assumption**: A business enterprise is viewed as a going concern that is expected to continue in operation for the foreseeable future.

**Unit of Measure Assumption**: Financial statements report the results of business activity in terms of money and assume that the value of the relevant unit of money—the dollar—remains constant.

**Time Period Assumption**: To produce useful financial information, the results of economic activities must be allocated to discrete time periods, generally not longer than one year in duration, even though such activities often extend over or affect several time periods.

**Cost Principle**: Historic cost provides the best basis for recording a transaction, because it can be determined objectively and is verifiable.

**Consistency Principle**: A firm should consistently apply the same accounting concepts, standards and procedures from one period to the next.

**Full Disclosure Principle**: Financial statements should include sufficient information, in the statements or in explanatory notes, to ensure full understanding of all significant economic information about a firm.

**Modifying Principles**: (a) *Materiality*—Accounting only needs to be concerned with the accuracy of information that a reasonable decision-maker would consider to be important; where information is immaterial, strict adherence to GAAP is not required. (b) *Conservatism*—Accounting counteracts managers' assumed tendency to present financial information about a firm in the most favorable light possible by mandating, in general, that profits not be anticipated and that probable losses be recognized as soon as possible.

The goals of the accounting process (and of GAAP) include presenting information about a firm's financial position and the results of its operations that (i) is as accurate as possible, (ii) is as reliable as possible, and (iii) can be prepared at reasonable cost. As the Exco hypothetical makes clear, trade-offs between these goals often are required. For example, one might argue that Exco's balance sheet should report the value of its property as $105,000, because Smith offered to pay that much. But before accepting this argument, one would need to consider a host of additional questions. How can a firm determine whether an offer is *bona fide* ? Assuming it is *bona fide*, should the firm be required to determine whether the property is worth more than the offer? Should a determination of current market value be required whether or not an offer to purchase has been received? How should the market value of property with unique characteristics be determined? Is market value information sufficiently important and sufficiently reliable to justify the cost of obtaining such information? Does that depend on whether the firm intends to hold the property or sell it? Should value be reported in terms of constant dollars or constant units of purchasing power? If the property is revalued, should the same thing be done for Exco's other assets and liabilities? Etc., etc., etc.

Three points emerge. First, GAAP consists of a series of conventions, none of which is immediately intuitive. These conventions are designed to resolve potential differences as to the appropriate method of presenting financial information. Second, whatever the shortcomings of GAAP, developing better accounting rules involves complex problems to which there are no easy answers. Finally, a person who understands GAAP can better appreciate the limitations of the information presented in a firm's financial statements and the additional information that one may need to make decisions relating to that firm.

## 2.  THE FUNDAMENTAL EQUATION

In a conceptual sense, the accounting process involves no more than elaboration of what is known as *the fundamental equation* :

## ASSETS = LIABILITIES + EQUITY

Consider, first, the terms used in the fundamental equation. "Assets" refers to all property, both tangible and intangible, owned by the reporting firm. "Liabilities" refers to all amounts that firm owes to others, whether pursuant to written evidence of indebtedness or otherwise. "Equity" represents, at least in concept, the interest of the firm's owners. Equity initially includes the value of the property (including money) the owners contribute when they organize the firm. Since the owners bear the risk of the firm's operations, equity increases thereafter whenever the firm earns a profit and decreases when it incurs a loss. Equity also increases whenever the owners contribute additional property to the firm and decreases whenever they withdraw property from it. In sum, equity is the owner's residual interest, assuming (which is never the case) that all the assets and liabilities on the balance sheet could be liquidated for the amounts shown there.

The fundamental equation often is presented as a sort of magic incantation, but it is easier to understand why assets always equal liabilities plus equity (especially if one is unfamiliar with accounting) by envisioning the firm in more concrete terms. Only one abstraction is necessary: the assumption that the firm is an entity separate from its owners. Visualize the firm as an empty jar, beginning its life with no assets, no liabilities and no equity.* The firm's balance sheet, at the moment of formation, will be as follows:

$$\text{ASSETS} = \text{LIABILITIES} + \text{EQUITY}$$
$$\$0 \quad = \quad \$0 \quad + \quad \$0$$

1. Now assume that the owner of the firm invests $12 (i.e., puts $12 in the jar). The firm's balance sheet will be:

$$\text{ASSETS} = \text{LIABILITIES} + \text{EQUITY}$$
$$\$12 \quad = \quad \$0 \quad + \quad \$12$$

2. Next assume the firm borrows an additional $10 (i.e., puts $10 in the jar and records an IOU for $10). Its balance sheet will be:

$$\text{ASSETS} = \text{LIABILITIES} + \text{EQUITY}$$
$$\$22 \quad = \quad \$10 \quad + \quad \$12$$

Note that each of these transaction had two effects on the balance sheet. The first increased assets and also increased equity; the second increased assets ($10 went into the jar) and also increased liabilities (the jar—i.e., the firm—incurred a debt in that amount). The same will be true of every transaction in which the firm is involved—it will always

---

* Students for whom the following discussion proves difficult to follow may find it helpful to begin with an empty jar or other container and physically act out each of the transactions described. When doing so, keep in mind that "equity" will be equal to the *net* value of the contents of the jar—the value, computed in accordance with GAAP, of all assets less all liabilities.

affect two balance sheet accounts. Moreover, because any profit or loss will always be reflected in the equity account, *the balance sheet will always remain in balance*.

3.   Assume the firm buys two felt-tip pens for $2 each (i.e., the firm takes $4 in cash, an asset, out of the jar and puts $4 worth of pens— remember the cost principle—into the jar). Because one asset is exchanged for another, the balance sheet remains unchanged.

$$ASSETS = LIABILITIES + EQUITY$$
$$\$22 = \$10 + \$12$$

4.   Next the firm buys a scissors on credit for $5 (i.e., it puts scissors worth $5 in the jar and incurs a liability of $5, which can be envisioned as a bill for $5 placed in the jar).

$$ASSETS = LIABILITIES + EQUITY$$
$$\$27 = \$15 + \$12$$

5.   Then the firm sells one of the felt-tip pens for $3 (i.e., it exchanges a pen that cost $2 for $3 in cash. The $1 profit results in a $1 increase in equity.)

$$ASSETS = LIABILITIES + EQUITY$$
$$\$28 = \$15 + \$13$$

See if you can figure out the accounting for the following three transactions without further explanation.

6.   The firm then pays the bill for the scissors.

$$ASSETS = LIABILITIES + EQUITY$$
$$\$23 = \$10 + \$13$$

7.   Next the firm pays $2.00 in rent for the use of the jar.

$$ASSETS = LIABILITIES + EQUITY$$
$$\$21 = \$10 + \$11$$

8.   Finally, the owner takes $5.00 out of the jar so she can go to the movies.

$$ASSETS = LIABILITIES + EQUITY$$
$$\$16 = \$10 + \$6$$

Although many business transactions are much more complex, and accounting for them is considerably more complicated, the entries made above reflect the essence of all financial accounting. Viewed conceptually, the accounting process involves no more than adjusting entries in a firm's asset, liability and equity accounts. A firm could keep an accurate set of books simply by updating, after every transaction, a balance sheet that contained only an asset, a liability and an equity account.

So proceeding, however, would not produce much *useful* financial information. Managers, investors and creditors are interested in two basic categories of financial information: (a) data about a firm's financial status at a given time, including data about the nature of its assets and liabilities; and (b) information about the results of the firm's operations (i.e., whether it has been profitable). Clearly, balance sheet #8 does not provide this kind of information, even if we compare it with balance sheet #1. One can tell that the firm's assets increased from $12 to $16, its liabilities increased from $0 to $10, and its equity declined from $12 to $6. But one cannot determine anything about the nature of the firm's assets (how much cash does it have? how much merchandise?), the due dates of the liabilities (must they be repaid tomorrow or in five years?), or whether the firm's operations were profitable.

GAAP attempt to respond to these questions by requiring every firm (1) to assign its assets, liabilities and equity to more particularized sub-accounts and (2) to prepare an income statement reporting the results of the firm's operations for the period between the dates of its balance sheets. Most problems that arise in financial accounting relate to one of these processes: (1) Deciding what asset, liability and equity accounts any given transaction affects; and (2) Determining whether a transaction involves current operations and thus should be reflected in the firm's income statement, or whether the transaction should only affect the firm's balance sheet accounts.

## 3. FINANCIAL STATEMENT TERMS AND CONCEPTS

### a. How Different Financial Statements Relate

As noted above, the balance sheet often is described as a "snapshot" and the income statement as a "motion picture." The income statement also can be viewed as a "bridge" between successive balance sheets. That is, the income statement records whether the firm realized a profit (or incurred a loss) during the period between successive balance sheets. That profit (or loss) then is reflected on the firm's balance sheet as of the end of that period by increasing (or decreasing) the owners equity account by the amount of that profit (or loss).

The fundamental equation, and thus the balance sheet, represents the conceptual core of a firm's financial statements. Investors and creditors, however, often are more interested in a firm's income statement. They view information about the results of past operations as the best available indicator of a firm's ability to generate profits in the future. Moreover, investors seem to place a very high value on firms whose profits rise steadily.* As one commentator has observed, "if a company reports six straight years of rising profits, Wall Street will cheer. But if it reports five up years and one year of earnings falling only

---

* Recall, from Chapter 2, that most people are risk averse. The more volatile a firm's income, the greater the risk premium investors are likely to demand before investing in that firm. This gives managers an economic incentive to "manage" the income their firm reports.

1%, the company may find itself friendless." Roger Lowenstein, *How to Be a Winner in the Profits Game*, THE WALL ST. J. C1 (April 3, 1997).

Managers, not surprisingly, are sensitive to the way in which many investors evaluate income statements. Moreover, because of the flexibility inherent in GAAP, it is not uncommon for a firm's managers to "massage" their firms' income statement so as to report steady profits or, better yet, steadily rising profits.* For example, as discussed in the next section, GAAP permits managers to choose one of several methods to value a firm's inventory. The discussion of financial statement terms and concepts in this and the following section notes other aspects of GAAP that facilitate such "massaging" of income statement numbers.

The GAAP requirement that most firms use *accrual accounting* to prepare their financial statements is central here. In addition, the *Realization Principle* requires a firm to recognize revenue in the period that services are rendered or goods are sold, even if payment is not received in that period. Consider how these requirements would affect a lawyer who provided $1,000 in services in Year 1 and was not paid until Year 2. In which year did she "earn" the $1,000? Most individuals compute their income, at least when preparing their income tax returns, using *cash accounting* ; they would report the $1,000 as earned in Year 2, when payment was received. Accrual accounting, in contrast, focuses not on the movement of cash, but on the lawyer's performance of the services. Thus, a lawyer using accrual accounting would treat the $1,000 as earned in Year 1.

The other side of the accrual accounting coin, so to speak, is the *Matching Principle*. It requires a firm to allocate to the period in which revenues are earned the expenses it incurs to generate those revenues. Thus, if the lawyer transmitted materials to her client in Year 1 via Federal Express, but did not pay the Federal Express bill until Year 2, she still would account for the Federal Express charges as an expense incurred in Year 1.

Taken together, the Realization and Matching Principles go a long way toward ensuring that an income statement prepared using accrual accounting presents a conceptually sound computation of the economic results of a firm's operations for the period it covers. Those principles also limit substantially a firm's ability to manipulate its payment and receipt of cash so as to "manage" the income it reports. But because recognition of revenues and recording of expenses are tied to events more difficult to measure than the movement of cash, the Realization and Matching Principles also increase substantially the subjectivity of information reported in income statements.

---

* David Burgstahler & Ilia Dichev, *Earnings management to avoid earnings decreases and losses*, 24 J. ACCTG. & ECON. 99 (1997), "provides compelling empirical evidence that earnings decreases and losses are frequently managed away." *Id.* at 124. Their data suggest that managers of 8% to 12% of firms that otherwise would report small decreases in earnings use the discretion provided by GAAP to report earnings increases and that managers of 30% to 44% of "firms with slightly negative pre-managed earnings [*i.e.*, small losses] exercise discretion to report positive earnings." *Id.*

GAAP deal with this problem of subjectivity, at least in part, by requiring firms to prepare a third financial statement—a *statement of cash flows*—in addition to a balance sheet and an income statement. A firm must use cash, not "income," to pay its bills, repay its debts, and make distributions to its owners. Cash, not "income," must be on hand when the firm needs it. Over a period of many years, say 10 or 15, a firm's total income and cash flow usually will be very similar. But over shorter periods, income and cash flow often will differ substantially.

The statement of cash flows, as its name suggests, reports on the movement of cash into and out of a firm. The statement reflects all transactions that involve the receipt or disbursement of cash, whether they relate to operations or involve only balance sheet transactions such as investments in plant and equipment, new borrowings, repayment of loans, equity investments, or distributions to equity holders. It does not reflect non-cash charges such as depreciation, discussed in the next section.

### b. Balance Sheet Terms and Concepts

What follows are brief descriptions of the most important balance sheet accounts. The descriptions also point out instances where the accounting treatment of certain balance sheet accounts has an impact on a firm's income statement. As you read these descriptions, consider PT's balance sheet and, where relevant, PT's income and cash flow statements at the beginning of the chapter ..

1. *Assets* are listed in the balance sheet in order of decreasing liquidity, i.e., their ability to be converted to cash.

(A) *Current assets* include cash and other assets which in the normal course of business will be converted into cash in the reasonably near future, generally within a year of the date of the balance sheet. More specifically:

(1) *Cash* is money in the till and money in demand deposits in the bank.

(2) *Marketable securities* are investments of cash not needed for current operations. Most firms invest surplus cash in very liquid securities, such as commercial paper and treasury bills, with a view to generating interest income.

(3) *Accounts receivable* are amounts not yet collected from customers to whom goods have been shipped or services delivered. Recognizing that some customers will not to pay their bills, GAAP require that accounts receivable be adjusted by deducting an allowance (or "reserve") for bad debts. Firms often compute this allowance on the basis of past experience. But when dramatic changes occur in the nature of a firm's customers, the nature of its business, or relevant economic conditions, past experience may not prove to be an accurate predictor of future trends. The balance sheet sometimes shows accounts receivable as a net figure without indicating the amount of the reserve.

Losses from extending credit to customers also represent a cost of doing business. Consequently, GAAP also require a firm to treat any increase in its allowance for bad debts as a charge against income, in the form of a "bad debt expense."

Most of the assets of a firm engaged in a financing business are represented by *notes or loans receivable*, which constitute a kind of account receivable. Consequently, relatively small increases or decreases in the percentage of debts the firm estimates will not be repaid are likely to have a major impact on the firm's reported earnings. Many of the banks that failed in recent years reported robust annual earnings almost up to the time they failed. Relying on past experience, they grossly underestimated the portion of outstanding loans that borrowers would not repay. Only when large numbers of borrowers began to default did it become obvious that the banks were (and for some time had been) insolvent.

(4) *Inventory* represents goods held for use in production or for sale to customers. GAAP require inventory to be valued at the lower of cost or market. Firms that hold a relatively small number of identifiable items in inventory often use the *specific identification method*. They value each inventory item at cost, unless its market value is lower than cost.

Most firms, though, find it impractical to keep track of the cost of each item in their inventory. Those firms use different methods to account for inventory. Every firm will know how much it paid for all items added to inventory during any given period, even though it often will have purchased those items at different times for different prices. By conducting a physical count at the end of the accounting period, the firm can determine the number of items remaining in inventory—known as the *closing inventory*. The accounting problem then reduces to how to value the closing inventory. This value will affect both the firm's balance sheet and its income statement. Items sold from inventory, called *cost of goods sold* ("COGS"), often represents a firm's largest single expense. To compute COGS, a firm adds its purchases to its opening inventory and then subtracts the value of its closing inventory.

Most firms use one of three accounting methods to compute the value of closing inventory (and, indirectly, COGS). GAAP allows all three. Brief descriptions of the three methods illustrate how GAAP deals with this difficult and important conceptual problem.

The *average cost method* visualizes inventory as being sold at random from a bin: a firm computes the average cost of all items purchased as inventory and values the closing inventory (i.e., the items "remaining in the bin") at that average cost.

The *first in, first out (FIFO) method* visualizes inventory as flowing through a pipeline: the items purchased first are assumed to be the first sold; the items purchased most recently are assumed to comprise the closing inventory (i.e., those items "remain in the pipeline").

The *last in, first out (LIFO) method* visualizes inventory as sold from the top of a stack: the items purchased most recently are assumed to be the first items sold; the items purchased first are assumed to comprise the closing inventory (i.e., those items "remain at the bottom of the stack").

In periods of changing prices, the inventory method a firm uses can have a material impact on the value of the inventory account, on COGS. and hence its reported profits. With LIFO, the inventory value will be lower, profits will be lower and, significantly, taxes will be lower than if FIFO were used. Because it gives value to the oldest inventory in stock, it is more conservative than FIFO. In an inflationary economy, because inventory replacement will cost more, the profits on each item sold will be lower; hence, LIFO more accurately reflects the economic results of the corporation. By contrast, if FIFO were used, the profit would be higher but much of that profit would be attributable to the inflationary rise in the cost of the inventory. These profits, in turn, might not be replicated when all the old inventory is sold.

(5) *Prepaid expenses* are payments a firm has made in advance for services it will receive in the coming year, such as the remaining value of a one-year insurance policy that a firm purchased and paid for two months before a year ended.

*Deferred charges*, such as payments made to promote the introduction of a new product, represent a type of asset similar to prepaid expenses. Deferred charges sometimes are treated as current assets because the firm expects them to produce benefits in the next year; sometimes they are treated as long-term assets because the firm will not use them up in one year. Sometimes firms inflated their reported profits by treating as deferred charges payments that they should record as current expenses. The effect of such treatment is to reduce expenses on the firm's income statement, and thus to increase net income. A large deferred charge account, and especially a large and growing deferred charge account, often should provoke further inquiry.

(B) *Fixed assets*, sometimes referred to as *property, plant and equipment*, are the assets a firm uses to conduct its operations (as opposed to those it holds for sale). Under GAAP, when a firm acquires a fixed asset, it records the asset on its balance sheet at cost. However, because the firm uses the fixed asset to generate revenue, the Matching Principle requires the firm to charge a portion of the asset's cost against that revenue.* This charge, which can be computed using one of several formulas, is recorded on the firm's income statement as a *depreciation expense*. This expense, which is not actually paid in cash, is based on the assumption that an asset ultimately will wear out. The depreciation charge is designed to match against operating income the cost of the asset over its useful life. GAAP requires a firm to add up all the

---

* No depreciation expenses are charged in connection with land a firm uses to produce revenues, because land has an unlimited life and consequently is not used up in the production process.

depreciation expenses it has charged in connection with all fixed assets it continues to own and to record the total, on the asset side of its balance sheet, as a reduction in the value of those fixed assets. This account is called the *allowance for depreciation* or *accumulated depreciation*.

The balance sheet value (or *book value*) of a firm's fixed assets—cost less the allowance for depreciation—is not intended to reflect, and usually does not reflect, either the current market value of those assets or what the firm would have to pay to replace them. In times of inflation, book value often is much lower than either current or replacement value. As technology changes, or when a company is still using a fully depreciated asset, book value may exceed market value because fixed assets have become obsolete even though they are still being used.

(C) *Intangible assets* have no physical existence, but often have substantial value—a cable TV franchise granting a company the exclusive right to service certain areas, for example, or a patent or trade name. GAAP require firms to carry intangible assets at cost, less an allowance for *amortization* (the equivalent of depreciation, applied to intangibles). However, GAAP do not allow a firm to record as an asset the value of an intangible asset the firm has developed or promoted, rather than purchased. Consequently, the value of many extremely well-known intangible assets, such as the brand names "Coke" and "Pepsi," does not appear on the balance sheets of the firms that own them.

Similarly, when a firm incurs expenditures for research and development (R & D), it must treat those expenditures as current expenses and match them against current revenues. It cannot record them as intangible assets or deferred charges even if a firm's R & D activities produce discoveries or lead to products that will enable the firm to generate substantial revenues in future years.

Financial statements sometimes report an intangible asset called *goodwill*. An entry for goodwill reflects the fact that the reporting company purchased another firm for a price that exceeded the fair market value of the acquired firm's tangible and identifiable intangible assets. GAAP require firms to amortize goodwill over a period of not more than 40 years.

2. *Liabilities* usually are divided into current liabilities and long-term liabilities.

(A) *Current liabilities* are the debts a firm owes that must be paid within one year of the balance sheet date. Current liabilities often are evaluated in relation to current assets which, in a sense, are the source from which current liabilities must be paid.

(B) *Long-term liabilities* are debts due more than one year from the balance sheet date. Balance sheets usually list fixed liabilities, such as mortgages and bonds, by their maturities and the interest rates they bear. Some long-term liabilities must be estimated. An insurance company, for example, can only estimate the amounts it will have to pay out on the policies it has written. Those estimates usually have a material impact on both the company's balance sheet and its income statement.

In recent years, business firms have developed a variety of techniques for engaging in *off balance sheet financing*—transactions that involve long-term financial obligations, but which, because of their form, are not recorded as liabilities on the balance sheet. GAAP require firms to report certain off balance sheet financing arrangements, such as long-term operating leases, in footnotes to their financial statements. Others, however, do not have to be disclosed. Moreover, only occasionally must a firm record contingent liabilities, such as claims by regulatory agencies or plaintiffs in civil suits, on its balance sheet. Where such claims have not yet been asserted, GAAP often does not require even footnote disclosure.

3.  *Equity* represents the owners' interest in a firm. The terminology used for equity accounts will vary, depending on whether the firm is a sole proprietorship, a partnership or a corporation. Whatever the form, the amount of a firm's equity (also known as its *net worth*) will equal the difference between the book values of the firm's assets and liabilities.* If a firm's liabilities exceed its assets, equity will be a negative figure.

Corporations' books divide equity among two or three accounts. Some state laws require corporations to issue stock with some *stated* or *par value*. As explained in more detail in Chapter 9, these values are established arbitrarily, but once established, have legal and accounting significance. When a corporation issues stock with a par or stated value, its balance sheet will include a *stated capital* or *legal capital* account for each class of such stock. The amounts in those accounts is calculated by multiplying the par value of that class of stock by the number of shares issued and outstanding. In a jurisdiction that does not require stock to have par or stated value, no stated capital or legal capital account is necessary.

In economic terms, a corporation's equity can be divided between two categories. One, termed *paid-in capital*, reflects all amounts received by the corporation from purchasers of its stock.** The other, called *retained earnings* or *earned surplus*, reflects the cumulative results of the corporation's operations over the period since it was formed. Each year, this account is increased by an amount equal to net income or decreased by an amount equal to net loss. In addition, any distributions the corporation makes to its shareholders, in the form of *dividends*, are subtracted from the retained earnings account.

## 4.  INTRODUCTION TO FINANCIAL ANALYSIS

Managers, investors and creditors use the information in financial statements to engage in financial analysis of the reporting company.

---

* This follows from the fundamental equation. That is, if ASSETS = LIABILITIES + EQUITY, then ASSETS – LIABILITIES = EQUITY.

** A corporation with par value stock often will divide its paid-in capital between accounts titled "stated capital" and "capital surplus." Terminology varies though, and other account titles sometimes are used.

Such analysis involves consideration of the relationship between certain data in a firm's current and prior financial statements. It also involves comparison of data derived from a given firm's financial statements with comparable data drawn from the financial statements of other firms engaged in the same or similar businesses. Consider the following types of analyses in connection with PT's financial statements.

### a.  Liquidity Analysis

One focus of analysis is liquidity: does a firm have sufficient cash, or assets it is likely to convert into cash, to meet its financial obligations as they come due? Three commonly used indicators of a firm's liquidity are its *working capital*, defined as the difference between current assets and current liabilities; its *current ratio*, computed by dividing current assets by current liabilities; and its *liquidity ratio,* computed by dividing "quick assets" by current liabilities. Quick assets are cash, marketable securities, and accounts receivable.

As a rule of thumb, analysts prefer current assets to be at least twice as large as current liabilities. But this is a generalization. A firm with a small inventory and easily collectible accounts receivable can operate safely with a lower current ratio.

A gradual increase in a firm's current ratio, based on a comparison of successive balance sheets, is a sign of financial strength. Too large a ratio, however—4:1 or 5:1—may signal that the firm is not managing current assets efficiently.

The liquidity ratio provides a more sophisticated evaluation of liquidity than the current ratio. A company with a high current ratio nonetheless may find it difficult to meet its current obligations if most of its current assets are inventory. Quick assets can be converted into cash without selling goods from inventory.

### b.  Debt Coverage Analysis

Creditors, in particular, are interested in a firm's ability to pay its debts on time. They frequently will compute a firm's *debt:equity ratio*, dividing a firm's long-term debt by the book value of its equity. A ratio of more than 1:1 indicates the firm is relying principally on borrowed capital. This poses some danger for debtholders, especially where the ratio is much higher than 1:1, because if the firm's business falters, it may find itself unable to generate sufficient revenues to pay the interest due on its debt. In effect, the firm's debtholders may be bearing some of the risk ordinarily borne by equity investors.

Creditors also often are interested in the *interest coverage ratio*. They compare a firm's annual earnings to the annual interest payments due on the firm's long-term debt. Most analysts consider debt a safe investment if earnings are at least three or four times interest payments.

### c. *Equity Analysis*

In valuing the firm, analysts tend to focus on its equity accounts and income statement. One common, but frequently unreliable, indicator is the firm's *net book value*. Profitable companies often show a very low net book value and very substantial earnings, especially if they generate income largely by developing or exploiting intangible assets. Examples of such companies are service businesses such as advertising agencies, whose profitability depends primarily on a continuing flow of customers rather than on their tangible assets. Companies engaged in capital-intensive businesses, such as railroads, often show a high net book value for their equity but have low or irregular earnings. The assets of insurance companies and banks are largely liquid (cash, accounts receivable, and marketable securities); the net book value of such a company often is a fair indication of its true value (so long as the company has accurately estimated its reserve for liabilities or its allowance for bad debts).

In evaluating a firm's income statement, analysts frequently look for trends in revenues and earnings. Are they increasing, decreasing, or relatively stable? Do they fluctuate dramatically or change at a relatively steady pace?

Analysts also evaluate the ratio of various expense items to revenues, both over time and in relation to the ratios of other firms in the same line of business. An income statement generally reports net sales (gross sales less returns) on the top line, and then subtracts cost of goods sold, other operating expenses, interest expenses and taxes. Operating income and income before taxes often are reported as sub-totals. Look at PT's income statement again.

One can easily calculate what percentage of net sales each category of expenses represents. These calculations often produce useful insights about trends in a company's business or additional inquiries one should make. Consider, for example, the significance of an increase in *profit margin*—the difference, stated as a percentage of net sales, between net sales and operating expense. Changes in profit margin can reflect changes in efficiency, in product line or in type of customer served. Where a company's profit margin is very low compared to other firms in the same business, profits might improve if management improves. If profit margins of all firms in a given line of business are low, competition probably is intense and increasing a firm's profit margin may well prove to be difficult.

Similar inferences can be drawn from other income statement data. What, for example, would you conclude if a firm reported an increase in *fixed costs*—depreciation and other overhead, including interest expense—as a percentage of sales? What if it reported a decrease in "discretionary" expenses, such as R & D, advertising and promotion, which a firm often can reduce without causing proportionate increases in current income?

Finally, analysts usually compute *return on equity* by dividing equity as reported on a firm's balance sheet for the previous year (*not* the current year) into the net income the firm has reported for the current year. Analysts then compare the resulting percentage to the return available on alternative investments. For example, if return on a firm's equity is less than the return available on a risk-free investment such as U.S. Treasury notes (and if reported income accurately reflects the results of the firm's operations), an analyst is likely to conclude that the firm is worth considerably less than its net book value. After all, why bear the risks of purchasing equity if one can earn a larger return on a risk-free investment?

Similarly, if a firm's return on equity greatly exceeds the returns available from risk-free investments, an analyst might conclude (subject to the *caveat* noted above and the risks associated with the firm's business) that the firm is worth considerably more than its net book value. In essence, the analyst would imply that a significant portion of the firm's earning power is attributable to the value of intangible assets that, due to GAAP, is not reflected on the firm's balance sheet.

### d.  *Cash Flow Analysis*

As should be clear by now, "income" is a concept, and computation of a firm's income generally depends on numerous subjective judgments and is heavily influenced by the assumptions underlying GAAP. Cash, on the other hand, is tangible; one can touch, smell and even taste it. Moreover, a company needs cash to pay its bills, repay its debts, and make distributions to its owners.

The sources and uses of a given firm's cash can include its operations, its purchases and sales of fixed assets, and its financing activities. The statement of cash flows reports how much cash a firm has generated and how much it has used in connection with each of these three activities. PT's statement of cash flows shows how that firm has generated and used cash during the prior two years.

Firms frequently report significantly different amounts of income and cash flow for any given year. The disparity most often is attributable, at least in part, to GAAP requirements relating to accounting for fixed assets. Recall the Exco hypothetical. GAAP require Exco to account for its purchase of the property as an exchange of one asset, $100,000 in cash, for another asset, property worth $100,000. That transaction would have no direct impact on Exco's income statement. But GAAP also would require Exco to report a depreciation expense, say $5,000 a year, in each year it used the property to generate rental income. That "expense," however, does not reflect any current disbursement of cash.

In the year Exco purchased the property, it would report cash flow much lower than its income (or, more accurately, negative cash flow much larger than the loss it would report).* In each subsequent year,

---

* Assuming all other expenses were paid and all rental income was received during

Exco would report cash flow in excess of its income, because reported income would be reduced by a depreciation expense that would not involve any contemporaneous disbursement of cash. More specifically, Exco's statement of cash flows would report the amount of each year's depreciation expense as an addition to cash flow from operations. (Note the similar entry on PT's statement of cash flows.)

Changes in the amounts of cash a firm used to provide financing to customers (increases or decreases in accounts receivable), to carry inventory, and to prepay expenses, also will affect cash flow from operations, as will increases or decreases in current liabilities. The statement of cash flows also reflects investing activities: how much the firm paid for fixed assets and received from the sale of such assets. Finally, the statement reports financing activities: increases and decreases in short-and long-term borrowing, sales and repurchases of equity interests, and distributions to equity holders.

Comparison of a firm's income and cash flow statements often will provide insights into the direction of its business or suggest further inquiries that one might make. Consider the implications when cash flow from operations lags income, for example. Is the shortfall due to rapid growth in the firm's business? If so, is substantial additional financing necessary to sustain that growth? Do increases in inventory and accounts receivable reflect long-term growth in the firm's business, or a short-term effort to pump up reported earnings? If accounts receivable and inventory decreased, does that suggest the firm is managing its current assets more efficiently or that its business is declining? Note again that the financial statements simply provide raw data. By asking these and similar questions, one can obtain a better understanding of a firm's business than would be the case if one analyzed that firm's income statement alone.

# B.　VALUING THE ENTERPRISE

## PROBLEM
### PRECISION TOOLS—PART IV

Michael, Jessica and Bernie have decided to try to purchase PT. They have asked you to assist them in deciding how much to offer. You should consider:

(1) What techniques are the purchasers and sellers likely to use to value PT?

(2) Is there a price (or range of prices) that both the purchasers and the sellers are likely to find acceptable?

## 1.　THE OLD MAN AND THE TREE: A PARABLE OF VALUATION

Once there was a wise old man who owned an apple tree. The tree was a fine tree, and with little care it produced a crop of apples each year

---

Year 1, Exco would report a loss of $5,000
and negative cash flow of $100,000.

which he sold for $100. The man was getting old, wanted to retire to a different climate and he decided to sell the tree. He enjoyed teaching a good lesson, and he placed an advertisement in the Business Opportunities section of the Wall Street Journal in which he said he wanted to sell the tree for "the best offer."

The first person to respond to the ad offered to pay the $50 which, the offeror said, was what he would be able to get for selling the apple tree for firewood after he had cut it down. "You are a very foolish person," said the old man. "You are offering to pay only the salvage value of this tree. That might be a good price for a pine tree or perhaps even this tree if it had stopped bearing fruit or if the price of apple wood had gotten so high that the tree was more valuable as a source of wood than as a source of fruit. But my tree is worth much more than $50."

The next person to come to see the old man offered to pay $100 for the tree. "For that," said she, "is what I would be able to get for selling this year's crop of fruit which is about to mature."

"You are not quite so foolish as the first one," responded the old man. "At least you see that this tree has more value as a producer of apples than it would as a source of firewood. But $100 is not the right price. You are not considering the value of next year's crop of apples, nor that of the years after. Please take your $100 and go elsewhere."

The next person to come along was a young man who had just started business school. "I am going to major in marketing," he said. "I figure that the tree should live for at least another fifteen years. If I sell the apples for $100 a year, that will total $1,500. I offer you $1,500 for your tree."

"You, too, are foolish," said the man. "Surely the $100 you would earn by selling the apples from the tree fifteen years from now cannot be worth $100 to you today. In fact, if you placed $41.73 today in a bank account paying 6% interest, compounded annually, that small sum would grow to $100 at the end of fifteen years. Therefore the present value of $100 worth of apples fifteen years from now, assuming an interest rate of 6%, is only $41.73, not $100. Pray," said the old man, "take your $1,500 and invest it safely in high-grade corporate bonds until you have graduated from business school and know more about finance."

Before long, there came a wealthy physician, who said, "I don't know much about apple trees, but I know what I like. I'll pay the market price for it. The last fellow was willing to pay you $1,500 for the tree, and so it must be worth that."

"Doctor," advised the old man, "you should get yourself a knowledgeable investment adviser. If there were truly a market in which apple trees were traded with some regularity, the prices at which they were sold would be a good indication of their value. But there is no such market. And the isolated offer I just received tells very little about how much my tree is really worth—as you would surely realize if you had heard the other foolish offers I have heard today. Please take your money and buy a vacation home."

The next prospective purchaser to come along was an accounting student. When the old man asked "What price are you willing to give me?" the student first demanded to see the old man's books. The old man had kept careful records and gladly brought them out. After examining them the accounting student said, "Your books show that you paid $75 for this tree ten years ago. Furthermore, you have made no deductions for depreciation. I do not know if that conforms with generally accepted accounting principles, but assuming that it does, the book value of your tree is $75. I will pay that."

"Ah, you students know so much and yet so little," chided the old man. "It is true that the book value of my tree is $75, but any fool can see that it is worth far more than that. You had best go back to school and see if you can find some books that will show you how to use your numbers to better effect."

The next prospective purchaser was a young stockbroker who had recently graduated from business school. Eager to test her new skills she, too, asked to examine the books. After several hours she came back to the old man and said she was now prepared to make an offer that valued the tree on the basis of the capitalization of its earnings.

For the first time the old man's interest was piqued and he asked her to go on.

The young woman explained that while the apples were sold for $100 last year, that figure did not represent profits realized from the tree. There were expenses attendant to the tree, such as the cost of fertilizer, the expense of pruning the tree, the cost of the tools, expenses in connection with picking the apples, carting them into town and selling them. Somebody had to do these things, and a portion of the salaries paid to those persons ought to be charged against the revenues from the tree. Moreover, the purchase price, or cost, of the tree was an expense. A portion of the cost is taken into account each year of the tree's useful life. Finally, there were taxes. She concluded that the profit from the tree was $50 last year.

"Wow!" exclaimed the old man. "I thought I made $100 off that tree."

"That's because you failed to match expenses with revenues, in accordance with generally accepted accounting principles," she explained. "You don't actually have to write a check to be charged with what accountants consider to be your expenses. For example, you bought a station wagon some time ago and you used it part of the time to cart apples to market. The wagon will last a while and each year some of the original cost has to be matched against revenues. A portion of the amount has to be spread out over the next several years even though you expended it all at one time. Accountants call that depreciation. I'll bet you never figured that in your calculation of profits."

"I'll bet you're right," he replied. "Tell me more."

"I also went back into the books for a few years and I saw that in some years the tree produced fewer apples than in other years, the prices varied and the costs were not exactly the same each year. Taking an average of only the last three years, I came up with a figure of $45 as a fair sample of the tree's earnings. But that is only half of what we have to do so as to figure the value."

"What's the other half?" he asked.

"The tricky part," she told him. "We now have to figure the value to me of owning a tree that will produce average annual earnings of $45 a year. If I believed that the tree was a one year wonder, I would say 100% of its value—as a going business—was represented by one year's earnings. But if I believe, as both you and I do, that the tree is more like a corporation, in that it will continue to produce earnings year after year, then the key is to figure out an appropriate rate of return. In other words, I will be investing my capital in the tree, and I need to compute the value to me of an investment that will produce $45 a year in income. We can call that amount the capitalized value of the tree."

"Do you have something in mind?" he asked.

"I'm getting there. If this tree produced entirely steady and predictable earnings each year, it would be like a U.S. Treasury bond. But its earnings are not guaranteed. So we have to take into account risk and uncertainty. If the risk of its ruin was high, I would insist that a single year's earnings represent a higher percentage of the value of the tree. After all, apples could become a glut on the market one day and you would have to cut the price and increase the costs of selling them. Or some doctor could discover a link between eating an apple a day and heart disease. A drought could cut the yield of the tree. Or, heaven forbid, the tree could become diseased and die. These are all risks. And of course we do not know what will happen to costs that we know we have to bear."

"You are a gloomy one," reflected the old man. "There are treatments, you know, that could be applied to increase the yield of the tree. This tree could help spawn a whole orchard."

"I am aware of that," she assured him. "We will include that in the calculus. The fact is, we are talking about risk, and investment analysis is a cold business. We don't know with certainty what's going to happen. You want your money now and I'm supposed to live with the risk. That's fine with me, but then I have to look through a cloudy crystal ball, and not with 20/20 hindsight. And my resources are limited. I have to choose between your tree and the strawberry patch down the road. I cannot do both and the purchase of your tree will deprive me of alternative investments. That means I have to compare the opportunities and the risks."

"To determine a proper rate of return," she continued, "I have looked at investment opportunities that are comparable to the apple tree, particularly in the agribusiness industry, where these factors have been taken into account. I have concluded that 20% would be an appropriate rate of return. In other words, assuming that the average earnings from the tree over the last three years (which seems to be a representative period) are indicative of the return I will receive, I am prepared to pay a price for the tree that will give me a 20% return on my investment. I am not willing to accept any lower rate of return because I don't have to; I can always buy the strawberry patch instead. Now, to figure the price, we simply divide 45 by .20."

"Long division was never my long suit. Is there a simpler way of doing the figuring?" he asked hopefully.

"There is," she assured him. "We can use an approach we Wall Street types prefer, called using a price-earnings (or P–E) ratio. To compute the ratio, we divide 100 by the rate of return we are seeking. If I was willing to settle for an 8% return, I would use a P–E ratio of 12.5 to 1. But since I want to earn 20% on my investment, I divided 100 by 20 and came up with a P–E ratio of 5:1. In other words, I am willing to pay five times the tree's estimated annual earnings. Multiplying $45 by 5, I get a value of $225. That's my offer."

The old man sat back and said he greatly appreciated the lesson. He would have to think about her offer, and he asked if she could come by the next day.

When the young woman returned she found the old man emerging from a sea of work sheets, small print columns of numbers and a calculator. "Glad to see you," he said. "I think we can do some business."

"It's easy to see how you Wall Street smarties make so much money, buying people's property for less than its true value. I think I can get you to agree that my tree is worth more than you figured."

"I'm open minded," she assured him.

"The number you worked so hard over my books to come up with was something you called profits, or earnings that I earned in the past. I'm not so sure it tells you anything that important."

"Of course it does," she protested. "Profits measure efficiency and economic utility."

"Maybe," he mused, "but it sure doesn't tell you how much money you've got. I looked in my safe yesterday after you left and I saw I had some stocks that hadn't ever paid much of a dividend to me. And I kept getting reports each year telling me how great the earnings were, but I sure couldn't spend them. It's just the opposite with the tree. You figured the earnings were lower because of some amounts I'll never have to spend. It seems to me these earnings are an idea worked up by the accountants. Now I'll grant you that ideas, or concepts as you call them, are important and give you lots of useful information, but you can't fold them up, and put them in your pocket."

Surprised, she asked, "What is important, then?"

"Cash flow," he answered. "I'm talking about dollars you can spend, or save or give to your children. This tree will go on for years yielding revenues after costs. And it is the future, not the past, that we're trying to figure out."

"Don't forget the risks," she reminded him. "And the uncertainties."

"Quite right," he observed. "I think we can deal with that. Chances are that you and I could agree, after a lot of thought, on the possible range of future revenues and costs. I suspect we would estimate that for the next five years, there is a 25% chance that the cash flow will be $40, a 50% chance it will be $50 and a 25% chance it will be $60. That makes $50 our best guess, if you average it out. Then let us figure that for ten years after that the average will be $40. And that's it. The tree doctor tells me it can't produce any longer than that. Now all we have to do is figure out what you pay today to get $50 a year from now, two years from now, and so on for the first five years until we figure what you would pay to get $40 a year for each of the ten years after that. Then, throw in the 20 bucks we can get for firewood at that time, and that's that."

"Simple," she said. "You want to discount to the present value of future receipts including salvage value. Of course you need to determine the rate at which you discount."

"Precisely," he noted. "That's what all these charts and the calculator are doing." She nodded knowingly as he showed her discount tables that revealed what a dollar received at a later time is worth today, under different assumptions of the discount rate. It showed, for example, that at an 8% discount rate, a dollar delivered a year from now is worth $.93 today, simply because $.93 today, invested at 8%, will produce $1 a year from now.

"You could put your money in a savings bank or a savings and loan association and receive 5% interest, insured. But you could also put your money into obligations of the United States Government and earn 8% interest.* That looks like the risk free rate of interest to me. Anywhere else you put your money deprives you of the opportunity to earn 8% risk free. Discounting by 8% will only compensate you for the time value of the money you invest in the tree rather than in government securities. But the cash flow from the apple tree is not riskless, sad to say, so we need to use a higher discount rate to compensate you for the risk in your investment. Let us agree that we discount the receipt of $50 a year from now by 15%, and so on with the other deferred receipts. That is about the rate that is applied to investments with this magnitude of risk. You can check that out with my cousin who just sold his strawberry patch

* These numbers will vary with prevailing interest rates. The principle remains the same.

yesterday. According to my figures, the present value of the anticipated annual net revenues is $268.05, and today's value of the firewood is $2.44, making a grand total of $270.49. I'll take $270 even. You can see how much I'm allowing for risk because if I discounted the stream at 8%, it would come to $388.60.

After a few minutes reflection, the young woman said to the old man, "It was a bit foxy of you yesterday to let me appear to be teaching you something. Where did you learn so much about finance as an apple grower?"

"Don't be foolish, my young friend," he counseled her. "Wisdom comes from experience in many fields. Socrates taught us how to learn. I'll tell you a little secret; I spent a year in law school."

The young woman smiled at this last confession. "I have enjoyed this little exercise but let me tell you something that some of the financial whiz kids have told me. Whether we figure value on the basis of the discounted cash flow method or the capitalization of earnings, so long as we apply both methods perfectly we should come out at exactly the same point."

"Of course!" the old man exclaimed. "Some of the wunderkinds are catching on. But the clever ones are looking not at old earnings, but doing what managers are doing and projecting earnings into the future. The question is, however, which method is more likely to be misused. I prefer to calculate by my method because I don't have to monkey around with depreciation. You have to make these arbitrary assumptions about useful life and how fast you're going to depreciate. Obviously that's where you went wrong in your figuring."

"You are a crafty old devil," she rejoined. "There are plenty of places for your calculations to go off. It's easy to discount cash flows when they are nice and steady, but that doesn't help you when you've got some lumpy expenses that do not recur. For example, several years from now that tree will require some extensive pruning and spraying operations that simply do not show up in your flow. The labor and chemicals for that once-only occasion throw off the evenness of your calculations. But I'll tell you what, I'll offer you $250. My cold analysis tells me I'm overpaying, but I really like that tree. I think the psychic rewards of sitting in its shade must be worth something."

"It's a deal," said the old man. "I never said I was looking for the highest offer, but only the *best* offer."

MORAL: There are several. Methods are useful as tools, but good judgment comes not from methods alone, but from experience. And experience comes from bad judgment.

Listen closely to the experts, and hear those things they don't tell you. Behind all the sweet sounds of their confident notes, there is a great deal of discordant uncertainty. One wrong assumption can carry you pretty far from the truth.

Finally, you are never too young to learn.

## 2. NOTE: OTHER THOUGHTS ON VALUING A BUSINESS

### a. *Context and Valuation*

In response to the question, "How much is a business worth?", one must ask "Why do we want to know?" Valuation of a business is best viewed as a process directed to a particular end. The nature of that process, and the result it achieves, may vary according to the purpose for which a value is sought. It is one thing to negotiate the selling of a going business (or a flowering apple tree); it is quite another to appraise the business for estate tax purposes and still another matter to determine the value of a business when the owner of 80% of the business wants to buy out the other 20%.

The old man in the parable was able to sell the entire interest in the apple tree to a buyer. The buyer knew she would be able to make all decisions about the care and use of the apple tree without having to consult anybody, without having to share profits with anybody and without having to worry about any conflict of interests she might have. Suppose, however, the parable involved the old man's young partner who had a one-third interest in the apple tree. Would the value of his interest simply be one-third of the value of the tree? Or would his interest be worth a lesser percentage because he lacked the ability to convey control over the tree? That is, presumably the tree would be worth the same whether it was owned by one person or by twenty, but the value of each person's interest might not be proportionate because of the consequences of majority rule. Or, as George Orwell put it, "all animals are created equal, but some animals are more equal than others."

### b. *Buying a Dream*

The decision to buy a small business often represents the embodiment of a life-long dream. Many prospective purchasers, however, tend to become preoccupied with their dreams, in the view of James E. Schrager, a businessman who also teaches entrepreneurship at the University of Chicago Graduate School of Business. They then ignore important facts relating to businesses they have become interested in purchasing. Mr. Schrager suggests that, before even discussing price, a prospective purchaser get a feel for the business by asking the current owners open-ended questions such as: "How did they start the business? What have been their most difficult hurdles? How have they kept their customers happy? Why do people buy their product? What production problems have they had? How did they locate sales and production staff? What has been their biggest success? How do they see the future?" James E. Schrager, *How Much Should You Pay for a Dream*? THE WALL ST. J. A6 (Aug. 17, 1992).

Mr. Schrager also advises prospective purchasers to evaluate a business's products themselves and learn how other people use them and what they think of them. A business's competition also should be assessed: Is it strong or weak? Is it well financed and profitable or struggling to remain afloat? What does the state of the competition imply about prospects that the target business can be made more profitable?

The best way to price a business often is to determine what people are paying for similar businesses. But the potential target company's financial statements are a source of important information, too. Mr. Schrager suggests that prospective purchasers look behind financial statement numbers. "Find out what makes up the cost of goods sold, investigate factory overhead charges, understand the selling and market-ing expenses, and so on." Attempt to determine whether receivables really are collectible and whether inventory is obsolete. In addition, inquire into contingent liabilities, such as possibly costly environmental claims. He posits three numbers "as upper limits for the target's price: Rarely is a small business worth more than one times sales; four times book value; or eight times earnings." Of course, there are exceptions, but a price above these limits usually should be considered too rich.

Mr. Schrager concludes: "[W]hen its your net worth on the line, you need more than just dreams. You need to remember that arriving at the right price for a small business requires as much work with your head as with your heart."

### c.   *Valuing a Business: Thoughts of Chairman Warren*

[As Chairman of Berkshire Hathaway, Inc. Warren Buffet has amassed a fortune of more than $30 billion dollars by investing in and purchasing other companies. The following excerpts from Mr. Buffet's annual letters to the shareholders of Berkshire Hathaway suggest his approach to valuing businesses.]

### Appendix to the 1983 Annual Report (concerning valuing a business's "goodwill"):

When a business is purchased, accounting principles require that the purchase price first be assigned to the fair value of the identifiable assets that are acquired. Frequently, the sum of the fair values put on the assets (after the deduction of liabilities) is less than the total purchase price of the business. In that case, the difference is assigned to an asset account entitled "excess of cost over equity in net assets acquired" [i.e., "Goodwill."] * * *

When [the purchase of a business] create[s] Goodwill, it must be amortized over not more than 40 years through charges—of equal amount in every year—to the earnings account. Since 40 years is the maximum period allowed, 40 years is what managements (including us) usually elect. * * *

That's how accounting Goodwill works. To see how it differs from economic reality, let's look at an example close at hand. We'll round some figures, and greatly oversimplify, to make the example easier to follow. We'll also mention some implications for investors and managers.

Blue Chip Stamps bought See's [Candy Shops, Inc.] early in 1972 for $25 million, at which time See's had about $8 million of net tangible assets. * * * This level of tangible assets was adequate to conduct the business without use of debt, except for short periods seasonally. See's was earning about $2 million after tax at the time, and such earnings seemed conservatively representative of future earning power in constant 1972 dollars.

Thus our first lesson: businesses logically are worth far more than net tangible assets when they can be expected to produce earnings on such assets considerably in excess of market rates of return. The capitalized value of this excess return is economic Goodwill.

In 1972 (and now) relatively few businesses could be expected to consistently earn the 25% after tax on net tangible assets that was earned by See's—doing it, furthermore, with conservative accounting and no financial leverage. It was not the fair market value of the inventories, receivables or fixed assets that produced the premium rates of return. Rather it was a combination of intangible assets, particularly a pervasive favorable reputation with consumers based upon countless pleasant experiences they have had with both product and personnel.

Such a reputation creates a consumer franchise that allows the value of the product to the purchaser, rather than its production cost, to be the major determinant of selling price. Consumer franchises are a prime source of economic Goodwill. Other sources include governmental franchises not subject to profit regulation, such as television stations, and an enduring position as the low cost producer in an industry.

Let's return to the accounting in the See's example. Blue Chip's purchase of See's at $17 million over net tangible assets required that a Goodwill account of this amount be established as an asset on Blue Chip's books and that $425,000 be charged to income annually for 40 years to amortize that asset. By 1983, after 11 years of such charges, the $17 million had been reduced to about $12.5 million. * * *

But what are the economic realities? One reality is that the amortization charges that have been deducted as costs in the earnings statement each year since acquisition of See's were not true economic costs. We know that because See's last year earned $13 million after taxes on about $20 million of net tangible assets—a performance indicating the existence of economic Goodwill far larger than the total original cost of our accounting Goodwill. In other words, while accounting Goodwill regularly decreased from the moment of purchase, economic Goodwill increased in irregular but very substantial fashion.

Another reality is that annual amortization charges in the future will not correspond to economic costs. It is possible, of course, that See's economic Goodwill will disappear. But it won't shrink in even decrements or anything remotely resembling them. What is more likely is that the Goodwill will increase—in current, if not in constant, dollars—because of inflation.

* * *

\* \* \* Any unleveraged business that requires some net tangible assets to operate (and almost all do) is hurt by inflation. Businesses needing little in the way of tangible assets simply are hurt the least.

And that fact, of course, has been hard for many people to grasp. For years the traditional wisdom—long on tradition, short on wisdom—held that inflation protection was best provided by businesses laden with natural resources, plants and machinery, or other tangible assets ("In Goods We Trust"). It doesn't work that way. Asset-heavy businesses generally earn low rates of return—rates that often barely provide enough capital to fund the inflationary needs *of* the existing business, with nothing left over for real growth, for distribution to owners, or for acquisition of new businesses.

In contrast, a disproportionate number of the great business fortunes built up during the inflationary years arose from ownership of operations that combined intangibles of lasting value with relatively minor requirements for tangible assets. In such cases earnings have bounded upward in nominal dollars, and these dollars have been largely available for the acquisition of additional businesses. This phenomenon has been particularly evident in the communications business. That business has required little in the way of tangible investment—yet its franchises have endured. During inflation, Goodwill is the gift that keeps giving.

But that statement applies, naturally, only to true economic Goodwill. Spurious accounting Goodwill—and there is plenty of it around—is another matter. When an overexcited management purchases a business at a silly price, the same accounting niceties described earlier are observed. Because it can't go anywhere else, the silliness ends up in the Goodwill account. Considering the lack of managerial discipline that created the account, under such circumstances it might better be labeled "No–Will." Whatever the term, the 40–year ritual typically is observed and the adrenalin so capitalized remains on the books as an "asset" just as if the acquisition had been a sensible one.

\* \* \*

We believe managers and investors alike should view intangible assets from two perspectives:

(1) In analysis of operating results—that is, in evaluating the underlying economics of a business unit—amortization charges should be ignored. What a business can be expected to earn on unleveraged net tangible assets, excluding any charges against earnings for amortization of Goodwill, is the best guide to the economic attractiveness of the operation. It is also the best guide to the current value of the operation's economic Goodwill.

(2) In evaluating the wisdom of business acquisitions, amortization charges should be ignored also. They should be deducted neither from earnings nor from the cost of the business. This means forever viewing purchased Goodwill at its full cost, before any amortization. Further-

more, cost should be defined as including the full intrinsic business value—not just the recorded accounting value—of all consideration given. * * *

Operations that appear to be winners based upon perspective (1) may pale when viewed from perspective (2). A good business is not always a good purchase—although it's a good place to look for one.

We will try to acquire businesses that have excellent operating economics measured by (1) and that provide reasonable returns measured by (2). Accounting consequences will be totally ignored.

### From the 1978 Annual Report (concerning investment in a low-margin business):

Earnings of $1.3 million in 1978, while much improved from 1977, still represent a low return on the $17 million of capital employed in [Berkshire's textile] business. Textile plant and equipment are on the books for a very small fraction of what it would cost to replace such equipment today. And, despite the age of the equipment, much of it is functionally similar to new equipment being installed by the industry. But despite this "bargain cost" of fixed assets, capital turnover is relatively low * * *.

The textile industry illustrates in textbook style how producers of relatively undifferentiated goods in capital intensive businesses must earn inadequate returns except under conditions of tight supply or real shortage. As long as excess productive capacity exists, prices tend to reflect direct operating costs rather than capital employed. Such a supply-excess condition appears likely to prevail most of the time in the textile industry, and our expectations are for profits of relatively modest amounts in relation to capital.

We hope we don't get into too many more businesses with such tough economic characteristics.

### From the 1986 Annual Report (concerning the value of a business to its owners):

[W]hat may be called "owner earnings" * * * represent (a) reported earnings plus (b) depreciation, depletion, amortization, and certain other non-cash charges * * * less (c) the average annual amount of capitalized expenditures for plant and equipment, etc. that the business requires to fully maintain its long-term competitive position and its unit volume. (If the business requires additional working capital to maintain its competitive position and unit volume, the increment also should be included in (c). * * *

Our owner-earnings equation does not yield the deceptively precise figures provided by GAAP, since (c) must be a guess—and one sometimes very difficult to make. Despite this problem, we consider the owner earnings figure, not the GAAP figure, to be the relevant item for valuation purposes—both for investors in buying stocks and for managers in buying entire businesses. We agree with Keynes's observation: "I would rather be vaguely right than precisely wrong." * * *

[C]alculations of this sort usually do not provide * * * pleasant news. * * * Most managers probably will acknowledge that they need to spend something more than (b) on their businesses over the longer term just to hold their ground in terms of both unit volume and competitive position. When this imperative exists—that is, when (c) exceeds (b)— GAAP earnings overstate owner earnings. Frequently this overstatement is substantial. The oil industry has in recent years provided a conspicuous example of this phenomenon. Had most major oil companies spent only (b) each year, they would have guaranteed their shrinkage in real terms.

All of this points up the absurdity of the "cash flow" numbers that are often set forth in Wall Street reports. These numbers routinely include (a) plus (b)—but do not subtract (c). Most sales brochures of investment bankers also feature deceptive presentations of this kind. These imply that the business being offered is the commercial counterpart of the Pyramids—forever state-of-the-art, never needing to be replaced, improved or refurbished. * * *

"Cash Flow," true, may serve as shorthand of some utility in descriptions of certain real estate business or other enterprises that make huge initial outlays and only tiny outlays thereafter. A company whose only holding is a bridge or an extremely long-lived gas field would be an example. But "cash flow" is meaningless in such businesses as manufacturing, retailing, extractive companies, and utilities because, for them, (c) is always significant. To be sure, businesses of this kind may in a given year be able to defer capital spending. But over a five-or ten-year period, they must make the investment—or the business decays.

Why, then, are "cash flow" numbers so popular today? In answer, we confess our cynicism: we believe these numbers are frequently used by marketers of businesses and securities in attempts to justify the unjustifiable (and thereby to sell what should be the unsalable). When (a)—that is, GAAP earnings—looks by itself inadequate to service debt of a junk bond or justify a foolish stock price, how convenient it becomes for salesmen to focus on (a) + (b). But you shouldn't add (b) without subtracting (c): though dentists correctly claim that if you ignore your teeth they'll go away, the same is not true for (c). The company or investor believing that the debt-servicing ability or the equity valuation of an enterprise can be measured by totalling (a) and (b) while ignoring (c) is headed for certain trouble. * * *

Questioning GAAP figures may seem impious to some. After all, what are we paying the accountants for if it is not to deliver us the "truth" about our business. But the accountants' job is to record, not to evaluate. The evaluation job falls to investors and managers.

Accounting numbers, of course, are the language of business and as such are of enormous help to any one evaluating the worth of a business and tracking its progress. [We] would be lost without these numbers:

they invariably are the starting point for us in evaluating our own businesses and those of others. Managers and owners need to remember, however, that accounting is but an aid to business thinking, never a substitute for it.

———

For additional insightful analysis, see William A. Klein & John C. Coffee, BUSINESS ORGANIZATION AND FINANCE 302–324 (6th ed. 1996).

# Chapter 9

# FINANCIAL STRUCTURE OF
# THE CORPORATION

---

## PROBLEM

### PRECISION TOOLS—PART V

Michael Lane, Jessica Bacon and Bernie Gould have agreed to organize Precision Tools Corporation ("PTC") as a Columbia corporation and to have PTC acquire all of the assets, tangible and intangible, of Precision Tools, Inc. ("PT") and assume all of PT's liabilities. Stern and Starr have agreed to sell PT to PTC for $2 million. In addition to financing the purchase of PT's business by PTC, Michael, Jessica and Bernie want to provide PTC with an additional $150,000 to finance an expansion of its business. Thus, they need to raise a total of $2,150,000.

Michael and Jessica each are prepared to commit $200,000 to PTC. Jessica can provide that amount in cash, but Michael cannot raise more than $100,000 in cash. However, he is prepared to give PTC a note for the additional $100,000. In exchange for their investments, Michael and Jessica each expect to receive 40% of PTC's common stock.

Bernie is prepared to invest $600,000 in PTC. In exchange for $100,000 of his investment, he will receive 20% of PTC's common stock. Bernie is prepared to use the remaining $500,000 either to purchase preferred stock or to make a long-term loan to PTC. Whatever the form of that investment, Bernie wants to be assured that he will receive at least $50,000 in income from PTC every year before any payments (other than salary) are made to Michael and Jessica and that, if PTC is liquidated, the $500,000 will be repaid before any payments are made with respect to PTC's common stock.

In addition to the $900,000 in cash that Michael, Jessica and Bernie are prepared to invest, PTC has arranged to borrow $500,000 from Columbia National Bank ("Bank"). PTC has agreed to repay that sum in five annual installments of $100,000 each, the first of which will be due in five years, and to pay interest at 12 percent per annum on the unpaid principal. The bank will not have any right to participate in the management of PTC or any right to receive payments other than those just described. However, the bank has required PTC and Bernie to agree that, whatever form Bernie's $500,000 investment takes, Bernie's funds will remain committed to PTC until the bank's loan has been repaid in full and, in the event PTC is liquidated, Bernie's claims will be subordinated to those of the bank.

Stern and Starr have agreed to provide the additional $750,000 that PTC needs by accepting a note for $750,000 of the $2 million purchase price. Consequently, PTC will be required to pay them only $1.25 million in cash. The note will require PTC to make annual interest payments of $90,000 (equal to 12% of the face value of the note) and to pay the principal of $750,000 to Stern and Starr in 10 years. If PTC fails to make any interest payment when due, the $750,000 in principal will become due immediately. Stern and Starr will not have any right to participate in the management of PTC or any right to receive payments other than those just described.

In considering the following questions, you may find it helpful to recall the material you studied in Chapter 2, Introduction to the Economics of the Firm.

1. Michael, Jessica and Bernie have tentatively agreed on a capital structure that is fairly typical for a corporation such as PTC. They will own 40%, 40% and 20% of PTC's common stock, respectively. Bernie also will own preferred stock or a debt security. The Bank and Stern and Starr will hold debt securities that provide them with no right to participate in the general management of PTC.

What are the interests of each of these the parties with regard to (a) participating in the management of PTC, (b) receiving current income with respect to their investments and (c) recovering the capital they are committing to PTC? Consider, in this regard, the risks involved in this venture and the parties' attitudes toward bearing those risks. How does the form of the parties' proposed investments advance and protect their interests? How does it allocate risk-bearing among the parties? Consider, in particular, the options open to Stern and Starr to protect their interests as creditors of PTC.

2. Would it be better for Bernie to receive preferred stock or a debt security in exchange for the $500,000 of his proposed investment that will not be allocated to common stock?

a. What business and legal risks does the choice entail for PTC and the three investors? Keep in mind the importance of not jeopardizing the legal and tax advantages of any debt securities they may use, or the possibility that they may elect to have PTC classified as a Subchapter S corporation.

b. What risks and benefits does the choice entail for Bernie? If Bernie elects to purchase preferred stock, how should the terms of that stock be structured to protect Bernie's interest in receiving income of $50,000 a year with respect to this portion of his investment?

3. How would you advise Michael, Jessica and Bernie were they to advise you that Bernie's accountant has proposed that they invest $100,000 in the common stock of PTC rather than the $500,000 they had originally contemplated. Their percentage ownership would remain 40–40–20. She suggested that they use the remaining $400,00 to purchase PTC notes with a face amount of $400,000. The notes (1) would be repaid only after PTC had made all payments due to Stern and Starr, Bank and Bernie; (2) would bear interest at the rate of 5% a year, payable only if PTC has earnings of at least $50,000 in any given year; and (3) would mature in 30 years.

4. Assume Bernie is concerned that Michael and Jessica may, at some future time, seek to reduce his 20% interest in profits and control by issuing additional shares of stock to themselves or to others or to finance expansion of PTC's business.

a. Could Bernie's concerns be met by including a preemptive rights provision in PTC's articles of incorporation? See RMBCA § 6.30 [DGCL § 1.02(b)(3)].

b. Why might Michael and Jessica be wary of such a provision?

c. Could Bernie's concerns be met by limiting the amount of stock PTC is authorized to issue? Would some other action be necessary to make such a limitation effective?

# A. CORPORATE SECURITIES

## 1. INTRODUCTION

Those who finance a corporation or any other economic enterprise generally are interested in the (i) power to exercise control over the management of the enterprise; (ii) right to receive income from the firm's operations; (iii) right to share in the firm's assets if the firm becomes insolvent or liquidates voluntarily; and (iv) need to protect their investment from the inevitable risks of the business. Partnership and corporation law rely on different contractual mechanisms to allocate these interests. In a partnership, investors' interests are determined by the partnership agreement. In a corporation, the terms of investors' interests are embodied in the securities they own. That is, corporate securities are the vehicles by means of which those who provide capital to the firm specify their interests in the firm's management, income stream and assets and protect themselves against risk. The choice of securities in a corporation, therefore, reflects the trade-offs between control, profit and risk that each participant must make.

Corporate securities can be divided into two broad categories: equity securities and debt securities. In general, equity securities represent more or less permanent commitments of capital to a corporation, while debt securities represent capital invested for a limited number of years. Holders of equity securities bear more risk because their claims to income are contingent on the corporation earning a profit. In addition, their rights in the corporation's assets are subordinated to the claims of both trade creditors and holders of the corporation's debt securities. Holders of equity securities, because they have the power to elect the corporation's board of directors, typically exert more control over the risks of the corporation's business.

Holders of debt securities bear less risk. Their claims to income are fixed, and the corporation is obligated to repay their capital at some future date certain. Moreover, debtholders' rights can be secured by a lien on some or all of the firm's assets or by contractual covenants restricting the firm's operations. Apart from such covenants, however, debtholders ordinarily play no role in the management of the firm.

The distinction between equity and debt securities is not as sharp and well defined as the foregoing summary might suggest. Corporate statutes and case law impose few limitations on planners' ability to design both types of securities with a wide variety of characteristics. In any given corporation, control, profit and risk can be allocated however the investors desire. For example, DGCL § 221 allows corporations to issue debt securities that have voting rights, while DGCL § 151 allows corporations to issue stock with no voting rights (so long as at least one class of stock has voting rights). See, also, RMBCA § 6.01. Nonetheless, to facilitate understanding and discussion, the following sections describe securities within the two basic categories of equity and debt. For more extended discussion of the characteristics of different securities, see William A. Klein and John C. Coffee, Jr., Business Organizations and Finance 235–301 (6th ed. 1996).

## 2.  EQUITY SECURITIES

Although the RMBCA no longer does so, we use the terms *common stock* and *preferred stock* to describe the two basic kinds of equity securities. Corporate statutes require that at least one class of equity security must have voting rights and the right to receive the net assets of the corporation in the event the corporation is dissolved or liquidated. These rights usually are assigned to common stock.

### a.  Common Stock

Common stock is the most basic of all corporate securities. All corporations have common stock, and many small corporations issue no other kind of security. Common stock usually holds the exclusive power to elect a corporation's board of directors. In a few corporations one or more classes of common stock is non-voting and in many corporations preferred stock has limited voting rights (see below).

A corporation must first use its income to satisfy the claims of the holders of its more senior securities (debt and preferred stock). All income that remains "belongs," in a conceptual sense, to the holders of common stock. Whether a corporation distributes that income to its shareholders, in the form of a *dividend*, or reinvest it in the corporation's business, is largely within the discretion of its board of directors. See Section C. At least in theory, a board of directors should reinvest a corporation's income only if it believes that the corporation can generate more income from those funds than can the corporation's shareholders.

Common stock also represents a *residual claim* on the assets of a corporation, in the sense that, if the corporation is liquidated, its assets first must be used to pay the claims of creditors and holders of preferred stock. What remains belongs to the common stock. As a consequence, the common stock bears the greatest risk of loss if the corporation experiences economic difficulties and embodies the greatest potential for gain if the corporation is successful.

As a practical matter, though, except when they experience financial difficulty, corporations rarely are liquidated. Consequently, common stock represents a more or less permanent commitment of capital to a corporation. If a firm is successful, holders of its common stock frequently can realize financial gains by selling their stock to other investors, who will buy at a price that reflect the firm's increased value. Shareholders often realize such gains even though a corporation is paying out none or only a small portion of its income as dividends, because their firm is reinvesting its income profitably.

Two mechanisms protect the interests of holders of common stock. First, common stock generally has voting rights, which allows holders to participate in a firm's management to a greater degree than holders of any other type of corporate security. Holders of common stock often have the exclusive right to elect the board of directors. Holders of common stock also customarily have the right to remove directors and their approval must be secured before the articles of incorporation are amended or the corporation engages in certain fundamental transactions, such as mergers.

Second, holders of common stock are protected by the fiduciary obligations imposed on the board of directors. As we have seen, courts defer to a considerable degree to directors' business judgments, but they do so on the assumption that directors will exercise reasonable care when making business decisions and will act in shareholders' best interest. These assumptions (and obligations) extend to decisions concerning whether a corporation should reinvest its profits or distribute them as dividends. In addition, directors have a duty to refrain from engaging in transactions that will provide them with unfair profits at the corporation's expense. In short, directors have broad discretion to manage, but must bear in mind that they are managing other people's money and that they have obligations to do so carefully and loyally.

### b. Preferred Stock

Absent specific provisions in a company's articles of incorporation, courts generally presume that "stock is stock"—that all equity securities have the same voting rights, right to dividends, and equity of redemption. Stock is classified as preferred stock when the articles of incorporation assign to it economic rights senior to those customarily assigned to common stock. Preferred stocks vary widely, depending on the attributes they are assigned.

Preferred stock usually has dividend rights senior to those of common stock. The seniority of preferred stock arises out of provisions limiting the payment of dividends on common stock until dividends due on preferred stock have been paid. This dividend preference often is stated as a fixed amount that must be paid annually or quarterly. Such a preference may expire if the dividend due for a given period is not paid. Alternatively, it may be *cumulative*; if a dividend is not paid when due, the right to receive it accrues and all accumulated dividend arrearages must be paid before any dividends are paid on common stock.

Preferred stock also may be made "participating." In that event, preferred stock will receive dividends whenever they are paid on common stock, either in the same amount or as a multiple of the amount paid on common stock. Indeed, operating on the principle that "stock is stock" unless a corporation's articles of incorporation specify to the contrary, some courts have interpreted preferred stock clauses to require such participation unless a contrary intent is clearly spelled out.

In addition to a dividend preference, preferred stock often is entitled to a preference on liquidation, through which the preferred stockholders have a right to receive a specified amount before any distributions are made with respect to common stock. The amount of this preference most often is the amount that the corporation received when it sold the preferred stock plus, in the case of cumulative preferred, any accumulated dividends. In some instances, a small "liquidation premium" also must be paid. However, as is the case with common stock, the preferred stock's equity of redemption is subordinate to the claims of creditors. Consequently, when a corporation does not have assets sufficient to pay its debts, the preferred stockholders receive nothing in the event of liquidation.

Preferred stock sometimes represents a permanent commitment of capital to a corporation and sometimes does not. In the latter event, the stock will be "redeemable" for some specified amount. The right to require redemption may be held by the stockholder, by the corporation, or by both. The amount for which stock is to be redeemed generally is equal to the preference to which it is entitled in the event of liquidation.

Preferred stock can have voting rights, and will be deemed to have voting rights equal to those of common stock unless the articles of incorporation provide otherwise. But the voting rights of preferred stock often are limited to specified issues and circumstances. Preferred stock usually has a statutory right to vote on changes in the corporate structure that affect adversely its rights and preferences. In addition, preferred stock often is given the right to elect some or all of a corporation's directors if dividends due on such stock are not paid for some designated period. Such provisions reflect the nature of the contract that holders of preferred stock often make with a corporation: they relinquish the right to participate in control in exchange for a priority claim to periodic dividends; only if the corporation fails to pay those dividends does the preferred stock reassert its claim to participate in (or exert) control.

The standard features of preferred stock described above may be supplemented by a variety of others, including the right to convert preferred stock into common stock at some specified ratio, the right to vote on certain transactions, or the right to require the corporation to redeem preferred stock if and when specified events should occur. All of these rights are essentially contractual in nature. That is, they must be spelled out in the articles of incorporation. Moreover, courts, influenced by the adage that "no man can serve two masters," have taken the position that, with respect to issues where the interests of preferred and common stock conflict, directors' fiduciary duties run solely to the common stock. Preferred stock is entitled only to the contractual protection spelled out in the provisions of the articles of incorporation that authorize such stock.

Corporations often sell preferred stock in lieu of debt. The two have obvious similarities. The price at which a company can sell preferred stock is influenced by factors similar to those that determine the price at which it can borrow—the dividend rate, the redemption features, whether the preferred can be converted into common stock and, if so, at what price. Consequently, the requirement that the terms of preferred stock be spelled out in the articles of incorporation can pose real timing problems, especially in the case of a publicly-held company. It usually takes a minimum of 30 days to obtain shareholder approval of an amendment to the articles of incorporation authorizing new preferred stock: during that period economic conditions are likely to change enough so that the terms of the preferred initially specified no longer reflect current market conditions.

To deal with this problem, most corporation statutes permit shareholders to authorize "blank check preferred stock," the essential characteristics of which—rights to dividends, preferences in the event of liquidation, redemption rights, voting rights, and the right to be converted into common stock—can be set by the board of directors at the time the stock is sold. See RMBCA § 6.02. Such an authorization may facilitate the sale of preferred stock, but it also enhances substantially the power of a corporation's board of directors by allowing it to issue preferred stock for a variety of purposes without first seeking explicit shareholder approval.

## 3. DEBT SECURITIES

Debt securities—usually denominated as "bonds" or "debentures"—represent liabilities of a corporation. However, they differ from other liabilities, such as the claims of trade creditors, who sell goods and services with the expectation of being paid within a short period of time (30 to 90 days) or the claims of financial institutions that lend money to corporations on a short-term basis. Debt securities constitute a part of a corporation's long-term capital structure; as such, they reflect an ongoing interest in the corporation's financial fortunes.

As a definitional matter, bonds differ from debentures in that they are secured by a mortgage on corporate assets, whereas debentures are backed only by the general credit of the corporation. Bonds also generally have longer maturities (20 years or more) than debentures (usually 10–20 years), although there is no rigid rule in this regard. However, to simplify discussion, we use the term "bond" in this chapter to refer generically to both bonds and debentures.

The terms of a bond often are fixed by a complex contract known as an "indenture." Whether or not an indenture is used, it is fundamental that the debt contract set forth a fixed obligation to repay a fixed amount of *principal* on a particular date. The instrument should also require that *interest* in a fixed amount be paid at periodic intervals. The interest obligation is not dependent on the corporation's having earned a profit; a corporation that fails to pay interest on a bond when due will be in default. Often, the entire principal will immediately become due and payable and the bondholders will be entitled to pursue all legal remedies for which they have bargained, including the right to initiate bankruptcy proceedings.

If a bond is secured, the debt contract also must specify the terms of the security arrangement. The debt contract also may include provisions, known as *covenants* or *negative covenants*, that require the borrower to refrain from taking certain actions that might jeopardize the position of the bondholders. A corporation may agree, for example, not to pay any dividends or to repurchase any of its own shares unless it meets certain financial conditions.

Bonds may be made redeemable or "callable" at a fixed price at the option of the borrower. This right can be valuable to a corporation; if interest rates decline, it can borrow the money needed to repay outstanding high-interest bonds at a lower interest rate and then use it to finance a redemption of those high-interest bonds. To compensate bondholders for their loss of income, a bond's redemption price usually is set at something above the principal that the bondholders would be entitled to receive when the bonds mature.

Because the terms and conditions of debt securities are fixed entirely by contract and often are the result of extensive negotiations, many other provisions may be included in a debt contract. Provisions allowing bonds to be converted into stock are one example. Requirements that borrowers make payments into a "sinking fund" that will be used to repay part of the principal prior to the bond's maturity date are another.

Bonds usually do not carry the right to vote. Moreover, a borrower corporation's directors owe bondholders only such obligations as are spelled out in the debt contract. They are not fiduciaries for the bondholders. *See Metropolitan Life Ins. Co. v. RJR Nabisco, Inc.*, 716 F.Supp. 1504 (S.D.N.Y.1989) (holding that RJR Nabisco did not have an implied duty to deal fairly with bondholders and could implement refinancing that greatly increased bondholders' risk, so long as bond indenture did not expressly bar such activity). Consequently, their interests are protected only to the extent that they have negotiated appropriate covenants as part of their debt contracts. Bondholders generally do not have standing to maintain a derivative suit. See Chapter 20.

Unless the articles of incorporation provide to the contrary, a corporation's board of directors has the authority to issue debt securities without shareholder approval. The board decides whether the corporation should incur new debt, in what amount, and on what terms and conditions. The board must involve shareholders only if it decides to issue bonds that will be convertible into stock and the corporation does not have enough stock authorized to satisfy the bonds' conversion rights. In such a case, the board must seek shareholder approval of an amendment to the articles of incorporation increasing the number of authorized shares. However, shareholders do not approve the actual issuance of the convertible debt securities.

The use of long-term debt as part of a corporation's capital structure creates a tension between debt and equity investors. Both have stakes in the long term health of the corporation and both benefit if the corporation accumulates funds in excess of the amount it needs for current operations. But holders of debt and equity have agreed to different trade-offs between risk and reward, and each thus has a different perspective on the degree of risk that a corporation should assume. Unless she has bargained for a right to convert her debt into stock, a bondholder has accepted rights to fixed payments of interest and repayment of her capital in lieu of the possibly higher, but uncertain, returns available to holders of equity securities, especially common stock. The holder of common stock has assumed more risk, but also can exercise more control over the conduct of the corporation's business. Concomitantly, a debt holder is viewed as an outsider entitled only to the protection specified in her contract. The holder of common stock, on the other hand, is protected by directors' fiduciary obligations, including their obligation to deal with holders of debt securities (and preferred stock) in whatever fashion advances the interests of the common stockholders. Despite the obvious differences between debt and equity securities, because of the potential to customize the terms of each security, it is often helpful to think of them as falling along a continuum rather than as being polar extremes.

## 4.  DESIGNING A CORPORATION'S CAPITAL STRUCTURE

### a.  *In General*

As we have seen, the capital structure that any given corporation chooses—the mix of common stock, preferred stock, and long-term debt—allocates among investors rights to participate in managing the firm, claims on the firm's income, risks of insolvency, and potential financial rewards. Since investing is a voluntary act, persons organizing a corporation cannot simply select some capital structure and then impose it on potential investors. They must design the capital structure of the firm in general, and the terms of specific securities in particular, so that investors find those securities more attractive than other investments they can make.

Within the limits imposed by market forces, however, persons organizing a corporation generally have the ability to select among different capital structures that reflect differing allocations of control, risk, and claims on the corporation's income and assets. As is the case when choosing an organizational form, federal income tax considerations often will influence the organizers' choice.

### b.  Tax Considerations

The Internal Revenue Code, on its face, provides a corporation with a powerful incentive to rely as heavily as possible on debt financing. Under section 163 of the Internal Revenue Code, a corporation can deduct from its taxable income interest paid on bonds it has issued, but not dividends paid on its preferred or common stock. Consider how this affects a company whose annual income, before payment of taxes, interest or dividends, is $50,000. If the company pays a $10,000 dividend on its preferred stock, its taxable income will remain $50,000. But if the company replaces the preferred stock with bonds and pays $10,000 interest on those bonds, its taxable income will be reduced to $40,000. Moreover, repayment of the principal of a bond generally will constitute a tax-free return of capital to the recipient.

While a variety of tax wrinkles may affect the use of stock and debt in particular circumstances, the fact that debt is tax-advantaged raises two questions: Why don't corporations always issue bonds rather than preferred stock? And why don't corporations raise as much of their capital as possible by selling debt to persons who might otherwise purchase common stock?

The first question is provoked by the fact that preferred stock and bonds are both senior securities and have many similar characteristics. Both entitle the holder to priority over the common stock in receiving periodic distributions (in the form of dividends or interest) and to priority claims to the corporation's assets in the event of liquidation. However, payment of preferred stock dividends rests in the discretion of the board of directors, who may choose to omit a dividend if the company is experiencing hard times. In contrast, the holder of a debt security is a creditor and is entitled to interest payments and the timely repayment of principal whether the company prospers or not. This provides one reason for a corporation to favor preferred stock over bonds. Failure to pay interest or to repay principal when due constitutes a default which can lead to bankruptcy proceedings. Failure to pay preferred stock dividends may have painful consequences, such as allowing the preferred stock to elect some portion of a corporation's board, but they are unlikely to be as drastic.

In addition, while interest payments are always deductible by the payor corporation, they also always constitute taxable income to the recipient (unless it is a tax-exempt entity). Dividends on preferred stock are not deductible by the payor, but corporations can claim a deduction equal to 70% of the dividends they receive from unrelated companies and thus pay tax on only 30% of those dividends. As a consequence, corporations are prepared to purchase preferred stock paying less in annual dividends than the interest they would receive on on investments of comparable amounts in corporate bonds.

### c.  *Leverage and the Allocation of Risk*

Financing a corporation largely with borrowed money involves substantial business risks. A corporation will find it profitable to finance business activities with borrowed money whenever it can earn more income from those activities than it will pay in interest on the borrowed money. This concept is known as "*leverage.*" Whatever the corporation earns in excess of its interest costs will increase the corporation's income and benefit its shareholders. In effect, the corporation is using the borrowed money as a lever to increase its (and its shareholders') income.

But leverage also increases shareholders' risk. If a corporation earns less from the activities being financed than the interest on the borrowed money, the corporation's income will decline. Interest must be paid whether or not the new investment is profitable. Consequently, corporations often are reluctant to rely on borrowed money unless they are quite confident that leverage will work to their advantage.

To illustrate, assume Ann Jones has $2 million to invest and wants to purchase a business that will cost $5 million. Ann believes she can raise the additional $3 million she needs either by selling 60% of the equity to other investors for $3 million or by borrowing $3 million from a bank. If Ann is confident the business will generate at least $1 million a year in profits, which would represent a 20% return on a $5 million investment, and Ann can borrow $3 million at less than 20% annual interest, she will prefer to borrow the money. Assuming an interest rate of 15%, her calculation will be as follows:

|  | Borrow $3 million | Sell equity |
| --- | --- | --- |
| Income before interest | $1,000,000 | $1,000,000 |
| (Interest) | ( 450,000) | — |
| Net income | 550,000 | 1,000,000 |
| Income allocated to other investors | — | 600,000 |
| Income allocated to Ann | 550,000 | 400,000 |

In other words, if the business performs as Ann expects, Ann will end up with $550,000 if she borrows the $3 million and with only $400,000 if she sells equity. Moreover, this calculation does not take account of taxes. Let's assume that the $1 million profit Ann expects is an after-tax figure and that Ann believes the business will generate $1.5 million in income before taxes and interest. Interest can deducted from income in calculating a business's taxable income. Consequently, if we again assume an interest rate of 15%, Ann's calculation will be as follows:

|  | Borrow $3 million | Sell equity |
| --- | --- | --- |
| Income before interest and taxes | $1,500,000 | $1,500,000 |
| (Interest) | ( 450,000) | — |
| Pre-tax income | 1,050,000 | 1,500,000 |
| Taxes (@ 33%) | 350,000 | 500,000 |
| Net income | 700,000 | 1,000,000 |
| Income allocated to other investors | — | 600,000 |
| Income allocated to Ann | 700,000 | 400,000 |

In other words, due to what is often described as the "tax kicker," Ann will be $300,000 better off if she borrows the $3 million she needs rather than selling additional equity, assuming, again, that the business performs as well as Ann expects.

At this point, you may well be wondering why people who own or want to buy businesses don't always borrow most of the funds they need, rather than selling equity to other investors. Leverage clearly has the potential to increase the profit that one can realize from an investment. But leverage also has a down side. Most businesses involve substantial risks. Outcomes often vary from what people expect. And, as discussed in Chapter 2, people have different attitudes towards risk. Consequently, leveraging one's investment may not work well and may not appear attractive. Consider, for example, how Ann would fare if the business she wants to buy earns only $300,000 before interest and taxes.

|  | Borrow $3 million | Sell equity |
| --- | --- | --- |
| Income before interest and taxes | $ 300,000 | $ 300,000 |
| (Interest) | ( 450,000) | — |
| Pre-tax income | ( 150,000) | 300,000 |
| Taxes (@ 33%) | — | 100,000 |
| Net income | — | 200,000 |
| Income allocated to other investors | — | 120,000 |
| Income allocated to Ann | ( 150,000) | 80,000 |

If Ann spreads the risk of buying the business among herself and other investors, she still ends up with $80,000. That might not seem like much of a return on a $2 million investment, but it is a lot better than the $150,000 loss Ann would have to absorb if she borrows the funds she needs.

For many years, it was conventional wisdom that, aside from situations in which the same persons held a corporation's equity and debt securities, common stock should comprise at least one-third, and more often one-half, of a corporation's long-term capital. During the 1980s, that belief was challenged, and many public corporations adopted highly-leveraged capital structures. Some had debt to equity ratios in excess of 9:1; *i.e.*, more than 90% of their long-term capital was debt. Highly-leveraged capital structures have controversial implications for corporate governance, which we discuss in Section D.

### d.  *Other Risks of Excessive Debt*

Two other considerations may limit investors' willingness to allocate capital to debt rather than to equity. One relates to the tax treatment of their investments, the other to how putative debt may be treated in a bankruptcy proceeding.

#### i.  *Tax Risks*

The Internal Revenue Service (IRS) is keenly aware that investors, particularly in the case of a closely-held corporation, may be tempted to abuse the right to deduct interest payments. If a corporation's share-holders attempt to treat a large portion of their investment as "debt," so as to generate large interest deductions and minimize the corporation's taxable income, the IRS may seek to characterize as equity all debt those shareholders hold. If the IRS succeeds, all "interest" payments the corporation has made with respect to the shareholders' "debt" will be treated as dividends and the deductions the corporation has claimed for those "interest" payments will be disallowed.

*Slappey Drive Industrial Park v. United States*, 561 F.2d 572, 580–582 (5th Cir.1977), reviews the principles on which courts rely to determine whether to classify an instrument as equity or debt.

> The tax code provides widely disparate treatment of debt and equity. * * * [T]he classification as debt or equity may affect the taxation of the original transaction, the resulting bases and hence the taxation of subsequent transfers, and the taxation of payments the corporation makes to the shareholder with respect to the instrument. * * *

> Unfortunately, the great disparity in the tax treatment of debt and equity does not derive from a clear distinction between those concepts. The problem is particularly acute in the case of close corporations, because the participants often have broad latitude to cast their contributions in whatever form they choose. Taxpayers

have often sought debt's advantageous tax treatment for transactions that in substance more closely resembled the kind of arrangement Congress envisioned when it enacted the equity provisions. Thus the labels that parties attach to their transactions provide no guarantee of the appropriate tax treatment.

Articulating the essential difference between the two types of arrangement that Congress treated so differently is no easy task. Generally, shareholders place their money "at the risk of the business" while lenders seek a more reliable return. That statement of course glosses over a good many considerations with which even the most inexperienced investor is abundantly familiar. A purchaser of General Motors stock may bear much less risk than a bona fide lender to a small corporation.

Nevertheless, the "risk of the business" formulation has provided a shorthand description that courts have repeatedly invoked. Contributors of capital undertake the risk because of the potential return, in the form of profits and enhanced value, on their underlying investment. Lenders, on the other hand, undertake a degree of risk because of the expectancy of timely repayment with interest. Because a lender unrelated to the corporation stands to earn only a fixed amount of interest, he usually is unwilling to bear a substantial risk of corporate failure or to commit his funds for a prolonged period. A person ordinarily would not advance funds likely to be repaid only if the venture is successful without demanding the potential enhanced return associated with an equity investment.

These considerations provide only imperfect guidance when the issue relates to a shareholder's purported loan to his own corporation, the usual situation encountered in debt-equity cases. It is well established that shareholders may loan money to their corporations and achieve corresponding tax treatment. When making such loans they could hardly be expected to ignore their shareholder status; their motivations will not match those of potential lenders who have no underlying equity interest. The "risk of the business" standard, though, continues to provide a backdrop for our analysis. While we should not expect a creditor-shareholder to evidence motivations and behavior conforming perfectly to those of a mere creditor, neither should we abandon the effort to determine whether the challenged transaction is in substance a contribution to capital masquerading as debt.[15]

Rather than attempt to measure concrete cases against an abstract formulation of the overriding test, we have identified numerous observable criteria that help place a given transaction on

---

**15.** In emphasizing the usefulness of comparing a challenged transaction to the type of arrangement that a disinterested lender would have entered, the Third Circuit has noted that disregard of the shareholder-lender's personal interest in his own corporation is fairer than presumptively construing all such transactions adversely to the shareholder. *See Fin Hay Realty Co. v. United States*, 398 F.2d 694, 697 (3d Cir.1968).

one side of the line or the other. We have always recognized, however, that the various factors are not equally significant. "The object of the inquiry is not to count factors, but to evaluate them." *Tyler v. Tomlinson*, 414 F.2d 844, 848 (5th Cir.1969). Each case turns on its own facts; differing circumstances may bring different factors to the fore.

With that preliminary caveat, we note the factors that prior cases have identified:

(1) the names given to the certificates evidencing the indebtedness;

(2) The presence or absence of a fixed maturity date;

(3) The source of payments;

(4) The right to enforce payment of principal and interest;

(5) participation in management flowing as a result;

(6) the status of the contribution in relation to regular corporate creditors;

(7) the intent of the parties;

(8) "thin" or adequate capitalization;

(9) identity of interest between creditor and stockholder;

(10) source of interest payments;

(11) the ability of the corporation to obtain loans from outside lending institutions;

(12) the extent to which the advance was used to acquire capital assets; and

(13) the failure of the debtor to repay on the due date or to seek a postponement.

*Estate of Mixon v. United States*, 464 F.2d 394, 402 (5th Cir.1972).[16] As indicated above, these factors are but tools for discerning whether a transaction more closely resembles the type arrangement for which Congress provided debt or equity treatment.

### ii.   Bankruptcy Risks

Another peril of a debt-heavy capital structure is that a court may treat putative debt as equity in a bankruptcy proceeding. Under the "Deep Rock Doctrine," named for a bankrupt company involved in the leading case of *Taylor v. Standard Gas & Electric Co.*, 306 U.S. 307, 59 S.Ct. 543, 83 L.Ed. 669 (1939), bankruptcy courts have exercised their equity jurisdiction to subordinate the claims of shareholder creditors to those of other creditors when they conclude the shareholder creditors have not invested adequate equity capital in a corporation. *See also*

---

**16.** The list is not exhaustive; our cases undoubtedly mention considerations that have yet to take a number. * * *

*Pepper v. Litton*, 308 U.S. 295, 60 S.Ct. 238, 84 L.Ed. 281 (1939). When the Deep Rock Doctrine is invoked, shareholder-creditors usually receive no repayment with respect to the "debt" they hold.

In *In re Fett Roofing & Sheet Metal Co., Inc.*, 438 F.Supp. 726 (E.D.Va.1977), *aff'd* 605 F.2d 1201 (4th Cir.1979), Donald Fett formed Fett Roofing and Sheet Metal Co., Inc. in 1965 to take over the roofing business he had operated as a sole proprietor and transferred assets worth $4,914.85 to it in exchange for all of its stock. In 1974, 1975 and 1976, Mr. Fett borrowed$7,500, $40,000 and $30,000, respectively from a bank, transferred those sums to the corporation and took back demand promissory notes. On April 6, 1976, at a time when the corporation had become insolvent, Mr. Fett recorded three deeds of trust intended to secure these notes with the corporation's realty, inventory, equipment and accounts receivable. He backdated the deeds to the dates on which the money had actually been borrowed.

On November 8, 1976, an involuntary petition in bankruptcy was filed. As of that date, the debts the corporation owed to secured creditors alone stood at $413,000, while no additional equity ever had been invested by Mr. Fett. The court observed that while a debt-equity ratio of more than 80 to 1 would not, by itself, serve to convert what was otherwise a *bona fide* shareholder loan into a contribution to capital, it did cast serious doubt on whether Mr. Fett's alleged loans should be treated as debt rather than equity. The absence of evidence that the corporation ever formally authorized the "borrowings" in question or ever paid interest on them, coupled with the undisputed day-in-and-day-out control over the corporation's affairs wielded by Mr. Fett, left the court with little doubt that Mr. Fett, ignoring corporate formalities, had infused new capital into the corporation to finance its acquisition of equipment and material necessary for the functioning of its business. Consequently, the court set aside the deeds of trust purporting to secure Mr. Fett's advances to the corporation and subordinated Mr. Fett's claims to those of other creditors.

On the other hand, in *In re Trimble Co.*, 479 F.2d 103 (3d Cir.1973), the court found that the corporation in question was adequately capitalized to begin with, but subsequently suffered overwhelming losses. In that situation, the test it used to decide whether a contribution by a shareholder was a loan or an additional injection of capital was whether the advance was made at a time when a bank or other ordinary commercial agency would be willing to lend it funds.

In *In re Branding Iron Steak House*, 536 F.2d 299, 301–2 (9th Cir.1976), the court stated:

> A creditor's claim cannot be subordinated to the claims of other creditors simply because the claimant is an officer, director, or controlling shareholder in a bankrupt corporation. * * * However, when it would be inequitable to permit such a creditor to share equally with other creditors, the Bankruptcy Judge may subordinate

his claim. *Costello v. Fazio*, 256 F.2d 903 (9th Cir.1958); Anno. 51 A.L.R.2d 989, 993.

In *Costello, supra*, three individuals engaged in a partnership for the operation of a plumbing company. The partnership capital consisted of $51,620.78, of which each of the three partners had invested unequal amounts. After four years of operation the business was undergoing serious financial difficulties, and the decision was made to incorporate. In the year preceding incorporation net losses totalled $22,521.34. In anticipation of incorporation, all of the partnership capital except $6,000 was withdrawn and converted into debt evidenced by promissory notes issued to two of the partners. An expert testified that there was little hope of financial success at that time in view of the recent business reverses. The business was incorporated, and the partnership debts, including the two promissory notes issued to the former partners, were assumed by the corporation. Two years later, when the corporation filed a voluntary petition in bankruptcy, the two former partners made claims on their promissory notes. The Bankruptcy Referee refused to subordinate their claims, finding that the corporation was adequately capitalized and that the claimants had not acted for their own personal or private benefit to the detriment of the corporation. The District Court affirmed, but our Court reversed, holding that both of the critical findings of the Bankruptcy Referee were clearly erroneous.

Here, the Bankruptcy Judge concluded that the present case is controlled by *Costello*. Because of the result we reach we can assume without deciding that the Bankruptcy Judge was correct in concluding that the restaurant was undercapitalized. Nevertheless, given this assumption, undercapitalization is the only significant fact common to both our present case and *Costello*.

In *Costello*, the claimants argued that mere undercapitalization should not, in and of itself, be sufficient to require subordination of their claims. We responded that "much more" than mere undercapitalization had been shown. 256 F.2d at 910. It seems virtually undeniable that the facts in *Costello* reflect a calculated maneuver by the investors, met with consistent business reverses, to attempt to reduce their risk to the detriment of other creditors. The *Costello* court found it significant that the partners "stripped the business of 88% of its stated capital at a time when it had a minus working capital and had suffered substantial business losses." 256 F.2d at 910.

In contrast, here the bankrupt did not begin to suffer business losses until several years after its incorporation. There was thus no clear intention by Richmond and Alexander to shift their risk to other creditors in the face of business reverses. Indeed, there was no stripping away of the restaurant's capitalization at all. Richmond held promissory notes for money loaned to the restaurant from the outset. At no time was existing capital withdrawn and converted into debt.

Moreover, it is not disputed that Richmond was not at all active in the operation of the enterprise. Before the legitimate claim of an officer, director, or shareholder of a bankrupt corporation may be subordinated to the claims of other creditors, not only must that person have the ability and intent to control the corporation, but he must in fact exercise that control to the detriment of other creditors. The record is devoid of any evidence whatsoever that Richmond exercised such control.

In our view, mere undercapitalization, standing alone, is not enough to justify the subordination of the legitimate claims of officers, directors, and shareholders of a bankrupt corporation to those of other creditors. We acknowledge that a claim may be subordinated even in the absence of fraud or mismanagement, * * * Nevertheless, a Bankruptcy Court is a court of equity, and subordination requires some showing of suspicious, inequitable conduct beyond mere initial undercapitalization of the enterprise. * * *

## B.  AUTHORIZATION AND ISSUANCE OF EQUITY SECURITIES

First some terminology: *"Authorized"* shares are those shares of stock created by an appropriate clause in the articles of incorporation. Until shares are first sold to stockholders, they are *"authorized but unissued."* When sold, they are *"authorized and issued"* or *"authorized and outstanding."* If they are repurchased by the corporation, they become *"authorized and issued, but not outstanding."* Shares that are authorized and issued, but not outstanding are commonly referred to as *"treasury shares"* (a term not used in the RMBCA but used in other statutes).

Corporation statutes do not dictate how many or what kind of shares are authorized; the statutes do require that the articles of incorporation include the number of shares that a corporation is authorized to issue and describe certain characteristics of those shares. RMBCA §§ 2.02(a)(2), (b)(2)(iv); DGCL § 102(a)(4). *See also* Article Four of the Model Articles of Incorporation in Adams & Matheson, CORPORATIONS AND OTHER BUSINESS ASSOCIATIONS: STATUTES, RULES AND FORMS.

If a corporation issues all the shares authorized in its articles of incorporation, it must amend the articles to authorize additional shares before it can issue more stock. An amendment must be recommended by the board of directors and approved by holders of at least a majority of its outstanding stock. (RMBCA § 10.03; DGCL § 242.) Recall that in the Chesapeake Marine Services Problem in Chapter 3, the corporation had sold all of its authorized stock and could not itself sell any more because a minority shareholder held sufficient stock to veto any amendment to the articles of incorporation.

## 1.  THE SIGNIFICANCE OF AUTHORIZING STOCK

Should the organizers of a corporation authorize more shares than they initially plan to issue? The corporation may want to issue additional shares at a later date to raise new money, to use for employee benefit plans, or to acquire other companies. As a practical matter, it may seem tempting to authorize a large number of shares at first so the corporation can issue additional shares in the future without the bother of amending the articles.

However, when deciding how many shares to authorize, one should consider more than questions of convenience. A corporation's board of directors normally has sole power to decide whether additional shares should be issued. Consequently, if a corporation's original shareholders "authorize" more shares than they initially plan to purchase, they also delegate to the board of directors authority to decide if and when additional shares should be issued.

In a close corporation where there is often a substantial overlap between shareholders and directors, the decision on how much stock to authorize requires some thought. Shareholders may wish to retain control over the issuance of new shares by limiting the original authorization to the number of shares contemplated to be issued immediately. The issuance of any new shares will then require an amendment of the articles and thus a shareholder vote. Recall that it was just such a requirement that gave Apple the power to veto an increase in the authorized capital of Chesapeake Marine Services. Such a limitation can protect minority shareholders and will preserve existing control relationships. *See* Chapter 13.

In large corporations, however, shareholders have relatively little influence over day-to-day management, and yielding the power to issue common stock may not constitute the surrender of much real power. Convenience usually decides the question in favor of an initial authorization of a large number of shares. Shareholders do retain some power over the issuance of additional shares of common stock if the corporation is incorporated in a state whose laws require shareholder approval for the issuance of a large number of shares, *see, e.g.,* 15 Ohio Rev.Code Ann. § 1701.83(A), or is listed on the New York Stock Exchange, whose rules require listed companies to obtain shareholder approval before they increase outstanding stock by more than 18.5%. *See* N.Y.S.E. COMPANY MANUAL, § 312.00.

### Note: Blank Check Preferred Stock and Poison Pills

Recall "blank check preferred" stock described in Section A.2.b. Such stock was often used as consideration in corporate mergers. As you will see in other chapters, in the mid–1980s, however, corporations developed "*poison pill*" plans which constituted relatively powerful defenses against uninvited takeover bids. Many such plans were based on the availability of authorized but unissued blank check preferred. A corporation's board of directors would create a new class of preferred stock with unusual features, such as a right to require the corporation to redeem the preferred at a price equal to twice its fair market value. Then the corporation would distribute to its shareholders "rights" to purchase shares of the newly-created preferred, usually by exchanging their shares of common stock for the preferred. Shareholders could exercise the rights only if some triggering event occurred, such as the announcement of an uninvited takeover bid. Until such an event occurred, the corporation would have the option of redeeming the rights for a nominal payment, usually no more than $0.05 per share. But while the rights remained outstanding, they were a powerful deterrent to uninvited takeover bids because, combined with the newly-created preferred stock, they had the potential to make a takeover prohibitively expensive.

In *Moran v. Household International, Inc.*, 500 A.2d 1346 (Del.1985), the court held that nothing in the Delaware statute made adoption of a poison pill plan unlawful and that a decision to adopt such a plan would be reviewed under the enhanced business judgment rule applicable to defensive tactics in tender offers. *See* Chapter 22. After *Moran*, many state legislatures explicitly authorized the creation of poison pill plans. Consequently, shareholders in publicly-held corporations must think twice before approving proposals to authorize blank check preferred because of the varied uses to which it can be put.

## 2. PREEMPTIVE RIGHTS AND OTHER DUTIES IN THE ISSUANCE OF SHARES

The precise number of shares that a shareholder owns in a corporation at a particular time determines her position relative to other stockholders. What is important, however, is not the absolute *number* of shares the stockholder owns, but the *percentage* of the corporation's outstanding stock those shares represent. Consider two corporations that are otherwise identical, except that A has 200 shares of common stock outstanding and B has 1,000 shares outstanding. Fifty shares of A, representing 25% of its outstanding stock, clearly have greater proportionate voting power than 50 shares of B, representing 5% of its outstanding stock.

A shareholder may be concerned that if additional shares are sold to other investors, her interest in the corporation will be diminished or "diluted." This concern will be valid if the shareholder is interested primarily in maintaining her proportionate ownership interest because, for example, it allows her to exercise a degree of control. (Again, recall Chesapeake Marine Services.) We will refer to this as a concern about "equity dilution."

A shareholder also may be concerned about "economic dilution"— the possibility that sales of additional shares will reduce the value of the shares she holds. This concern is most salient in two situations. First, other shareholders, particularly if they control the board of directors, may arrange to purchase additional shares at less than fair market value and thus appropriate to themselves a portion of the value of the corporation's assets. Second, the board of directors may sell shares to unrelated persons at prices that the board believes to be fair, but that the non-controlling shareholders believe is too low.

On the other hand, if a corporation sells additional shares at a price that reflects their fair market value, and if the corporation uses the funds received for those shares to produce income at a rate at least equal to the return it is generating on its existing capital, shareholders' economic interests will not be diluted. For example, if a company with 1000 shares of common stock issued and outstanding has a fair market value of $10,000, then the fair market value of each share will be $10. The sale of 500 additional shares at $10 per share will not dilute the economic value of existing shareholders' stock, if the fair market value of *all* the shares, after investing the additional $5,000, is at least $10 per share. If, however, the company sold new shares for less than $10, or if the company's fair value was more than $10,000, there would be economic dilution.

The common law doctrine of *"preemptive rights"* addressed concerns about equity dilution. Courts held a shareholder had an inherent right to maintain her interest in a corporation by purchasing a proportionate share of any new stock issued for cash; i.e., a shareholder who owned 100 shares in a corporation with 1,000 shares issued and outstanding would be entitled to purchase 10% of any new issue of stock by that corporation. *See Stokes v. Continental Trust Co.*, 186 N.Y. 285, 78 N.E. 1090 (1906). The doctrine worked reasonably well for corporations with few shareholders and simple capital structures. It became problematic where a corporation had several classes of stock outstanding, or sought to issue stock in exchange for property to be used in its business. Preemptive rights also were of questionable value in publicly-held corporations: a typical public shareholder, owning far less than 1% of the outstanding stock, presumably would care little that a new issue would reduce her proportionate interest in the firm from 0.001% to 0.0009%. Moreover, if she believed the firm was selling new stock at too low a price, she could protect herself by purchasing additional shares on the open market.

Courts and legislatures both addressed the problems posed by preemptive rights. Courts developed several exceptions to the rule that shareholders always were entitled to preemptive rights. Legislatures modified state corporate laws to provide corporations with the option of abolishing preemptive rights.

RMBCA § 6.30 adopts an "opt-in" approach. To provide shareholders with preemptive rights, a corporation must include an appropriate provision in its articles of incorporation. A simple declaration, such as "The corporation elects to have preemptive rights," will do. But absent such a declaration, no preemptive rights exist. RMBCA § 6.30(a). Delaware law no longer explicitly addresses preemptive rights. *See* DGCL § 161. However, DGCL § 157 authorizes a corporation to issue rights to purchase its stock. These could include preemptive rights, and a provision requiring such rights could be included in the articles of incorporation. *See* DGCL § 102(b)(1).

The RMBCA also addresses some of the problems associated with preemptive rights. Unless the articles provide otherwise, no preemptive rights exist with respect to shares issued to compensate executives, shares issued within six months after a company is organized, or shares sold for other than for money. RMBCA § 6.30(b). Similarly, preemptive rights are limited in corporations with multiple classes of stock. *Id.*

Most public corporations have abolished preemptive rights; a shareholder who wishes to maintain her proportionate interest can do so by purchasing additional shares in the market. In a closely held corporation, however, preemptive rights can provide significant protection to minority shareholders. A lawyer organizing a close corporation should consider and discuss with her clients, when preparing the articles of incorporation, whether preemptive rights should be adopted and, if so, what the terms of those rights should be. For an excellent discussion of relevant considerations, *see* F. Hodge O'Neal & Robert B. Thompson, O'NEAL'S CLOSE CORPORATIONS § 3.39 (3d. ed. 1992).

At times, preemptive rights alone are not sufficient to protect minority shareholders' interests. In *Katzowitz v. Sidler*, 24 N.Y.2d 512, 301 N.Y.S.2d 470, 249 N.E.2d 359 (1969), two of the three shareholders in a corporation with preemptive rights hatched a plan to eliminate the third, who was short of funds. Although the corporation's stock was worth $1300 per share, they approved a new issue at par value of $100 a share. The cash-short shareholder, who could not afford to purchase any additional stock, sued to enjoin the offer, claiming that the new issue was designed to dilute his interest. The court granted the requested relief, stating: "The price was not so much a bargain as it was a tactic, conscious or unconscious on the part of the directors, to place Katzowitz in a compromising situation." 249 N.E.2d at 365. *See, also, Bennett v. Breuil Petroleum Corp.*, 34 Del.Ch. 6, 99 A.2d 236 (1953) (holding shareholder with preemptive rights also had "right not to purchase" stock, which was wrongfully impaired by offering at substantially less than stock's fair value); *but see Hyman v. Velsicol Corp.*, 342 Ill.App. 489, 97 N.E.2d 122 (1951) (holding preemptive rights adequately protected minority shareholder's interests and declining to inquire into fairness of stock issue).

Courts also have shown a willingness to intervene, in situations where preemptive rights do not apply, to protect shareholders' proportionate interests in the control of close corporations. In *Schwartz v. Marien*, 37 N.Y.2d 487, 373 N.Y.S.2d 122, 335 N.E.2d 334 (1975), control of the corporation was divided between two family groups, each of which owned 50 shares of stock and had two seats on the board. When one director died, the two directors representing the other (Marien) family elected a third director to fill the vacancy on the board. The board then approved the sale of one share each to the two Marien directors and the new director and two shares to a long-time corporate employee.

Schwartz, the surviving director from the other family, sought to buy five additional shares so as to maintain her family's 50% interest. The board refused.

The court held that directors of a close corporation have a fiduciary duty to protect shareholders' proportionate equity interests when they issue stock, whether or not shareholders have preemptive rights. Shares can be issued in a manner that treats existing shareholders differently only to advance a bona fide business purpose. Moreover, the board has the burden of proving not only that the stock issue was approved "to achieve a bona fide independent business objective, but as well that such objective could not have been accomplished substantially as effectively by other means which would not have disturbed proportionate stock of ownership." 335 N.E.2d at 338.

On the other hand, *Yasik v. Wachtel*, 25 Del.Ch. 247, 17 A.2d 309 (1941), denied cancellation of shares that allegedly had been issued to shift control of a close corporation. There, however, the complaining shareholder could not alone exercise control and had never combined with others to exercise control.

For discussion of similar issues, as they relate to contests for control of public corporations, see Chapter 22.

## C.  REGULATION OF LEGAL CAPITAL

As we have seen, a creditor's claims against a corporation's income and assets have priority over the claims of equity securityholders. This priority is valuable, however, only if (1) the debtor corporation has received all amounts it claims to have been paid for its equity securities, and (2) the corporation is barred from jeopardizing the creditor's interests by distributing to its equity securityholders, in the form of dividends or otherwise, assets that it needs to satisfy the creditor's claims. Creditors, not surprisingly, usually seek to protect their interests by contract. But state corporation laws also provide some protection for creditors by regulating *legal capital*—the terms and conditions on which a corporation is permitted to sell stock and pay dividends.

In fact, protecting creditors was a major preoccupation of corporate law during the 19th century and most of the 20th century. However, by the 1970s, if not earlier, it became clear that the legal capital rules no longer protected creditors and probably never had. Bayless Manning's Legal Capital played a leading role in debunking these rules. California was the first state to revise its statute to take account of this new learning. Many others followed, stimulated by the revision of the legal capital provisions of the RMBCA. But in many others, including Delaware, the traditional rules remain in force.

Lawyers need to understand these rules, both the old and the new, for two reasons. First, as a condition of many financing transactions, a corporation's lawyer will be asked to opine that all of a corporation's stock is "validly issued, fully paid and nonassessable." To render such an opinion, a lawyer must review all transactions in which the corporation issued stock and to see whether they were effectuated in compliance with the governing statutory provisions.

Second, most corporation statutes explicitly provide that directors can be held liable if they approve issuance of stock or distribution of a dividend in violation of applicable statutory standards. These provisions heighten directors' concerns about their personal liability, and often lead them to seek advice of counsel in connection with decisions that might otherwise seem to involve no more than garden variety business judgments. Indeed, today the principal purpose of the legal capital rules is to provide a benchmark for the propriety of the declaration of dividends.

## PROBLEM
### PRECISION TOOLS—PART VI

Recall that Michael, Jessica and Bernie have agreed to pay a total of $500,000 for the common stock of PTC. They also have agreed that PTC initially will issue 5,000 shares of common stock. Jessica will pay $200,000 in cash for 2,000 shares (*i.e.*, $100 per share). Michael will pay $100,000 in cash and give PTC a note for $100,000 in exchange for another 2,000 shares. Bernie will pay $100,000 in cash for the remaining 1,000 shares. Bernie also will invest an additional $500,000 in 20–year subordinated notes.

1.  Prepare a balance sheet for PTC that reflects its financial position after Bernie, Jessica and Michael make their investments and the bank completes its loan to PTC. Then prepare a balance sheet that reflects PTC's financial position after it completes the acquisition of PT's business for $2 million.

2.  Prepare answers to the following questions on the assumption that PTC is organized under Delaware law. *See* DGCL §§ 102(a)(4), 152–154.

   a.  Is it necessary for PTC to set a par value for its common stock?

   b.  What would be the consequence of setting the par value of PTC's stock at $100 per share—the price for which the stock will be sold—or at some lower value, such as $1 per share? Does the statute limit PTC's choice? How would PTC reflect the transaction on its balance sheet if it sets the par value at $100 per share? At $1 per share?

   c.  If PTC decides to issue no par stock, is its board of directors required to take any further action? Would any such action be desirable?

   d.  Can PTC accept Michael's note as partial payment for the 2,000 shares he will receive? Does your answer depend on whether the par value is $100 per share or $1 per share? Could any problem with the note be remedied by substituting Michael's promise to serve as president of PTC for the next five years?

3. Prepare answers to the following questions on the assumption that PTC is organized under Columbia law. *See* RMBCA §§ 6.21–6.22.

    a. Is it necessary for PTC to set a par value for its common stock?

    b. How would PTC account on its balance sheet for the proposed sale of stock?

    c. Can PTC accept Michael's note as partial payment for some of the 2,000 shares he will receive? Could PTC also issue stock in exchange for Michael's promise to serve as president of PTC for the next five years?

## 1.  A CONCISE HISTORY OF LEGAL CAPITAL AND PAR VALUE

### Bayless Manning with James J. Hanks, Jr., LEGAL CAPITAL
#### (3d ed. 1990) pp. 5–40.

The ideal world as conceived by the creditor of the corporation is a world that is normally wholly unacceptable to the shareholder. The investor who buys shares of stock in the incorporated enterprise and the investor who lends money to the incorporated enterprise, are, as a matter of economics, engaged in the same kind of activity and are motivated by the same basic objectives. They are both making capital investment; they both expect or hope to get their money back in the long run, either by liquidating pay-out or by sale of the security; and they both expect and hope to receive income from their investment in the interim before their capital is returned to them in full. In the stereotypic model transaction, the investor who chose to take a shareholder's position rather than a creditor's position in a particular transaction, simply made a calculated economic judgment that was different from the creditor's. The shareholder estimated that he could make more money by relinquishing to creditor investors a "prior" claim for interest and a fixed principal payment on maturity, and, by opting for uncertain "dividends" and the residual claim to the assets of the enterprise that would remain after all creditors, with their fixed claims, had been paid off. The shareholder is willing to admit the "priority" of the creditor's interest claim and claim for principal payment on maturity. That does *not* imply, however, that the shareholder is willing to stand by chronologically until such time as the creditors have been paid in full. The shareholder will usually insist, that if, as he hopes, the enterprise makes money (and perhaps even if it does not), the shareholders will receive some return on (or of) their investment from time to time, regardless of the fact that there are creditor claims outstanding. Such periodic payments to shareholders are characterized as "dividends;" and, in the usual and normal case of the healthy incorporated enterprise, it is assumed that some assets will be regularly distributed out from the corporate treasury to the shareholder investors in dividend form.

Simple as this observation may be, its implications are far-reaching. If it were the case that all creditors had to be paid off before *any* payment could be made to shareholder investors, and if shareholders received nothing until ultimate liquidation of the enterprise when they would divide the residuum left after payment of all creditors—if, in other words, the terms "prior" and "before" were chronological as well as hierarchical—the creditor would not have to worry about assets being drained away into the hands of junior claimants and he would sleep better at night. But that arrangement would be wholly unacceptable to shareholders. Shareholders insist—and ultimately creditors must concede—that *during the life* of the creditor's claims, assets may be passed out to an investing group that hierarchically ranks below the creditors. The question becomes unavoidable: How much of the assets in the treasury of the incorporated enterprise may be distributed to shareholders, when and under what circumstances?

* * *

The nineteenth century pattern of corporate financing provided a ready suggestion to judges and statutory draftsmen for a way to gauge the quantity of assets that shareholders had, at some time or another, put into the corporate treasury. According to that pattern of corporate practice, an entrepreneurial organizer, the "promoter" who had conceived of an idea for a new business would make the rounds of people who had money to invest ("capitalists" all, whether little grey widows or sturdy yeomen), and seek to persuade them to invest in stock of the proposed enterprise. If the idea had appeal, and if the promoter was persuasive, * * * the subscriber, would, on call of the future board of directors of the corporation when organized, put in a set amount of money, or other assets, and would receive a set number of shares of the newly formed corporation. Given this practice, it was to be expected, and was perhaps inevitable, that in drawing up the subscription agreements for any single enterprise, a fixed mathematical relationship would be set between the amount of dollars to be invested by a subscriber and the number of shares he would receive: so many dollars to be put in for each share issued. That relationship produced the concept of the "par value" of the stock to be issued. In the normal situation, no equity investor could expect to obtain a share of stock for less than the par value of it, since presumably all other purchasers were paying that amount. Similarly, no share subscriber could be persuaded to agree to pay more than the par value for a share since other investors were receiving a similar share by paying in the par value. * * *

* * * In time, the par value of the stock was required by statute to be stated as a provision in the corporate charter.

The essentially arbitrary character of this number must be understood. If, for example, each of three investors agreed to invest $10,000 in stock of a new company, the number of shares to be issued, N, and the par value $P, could be anything—could be any number that the promoters might set so long as N × $P = $30,000. Further, so far as the shareholders in this case were concerned, it was immaterial what "par" was so long as each one received the same number of shares for his $10,000 investment.

Against this familiar background of practice, however, it was easy for the courts—and legislatures—to take a next assumption, and it early became a matter of common understanding, that the "par value" was what the shareholder *ought* to have paid for his stock. Stock which was issued without a corresponding pay-in of assets valued at an amount equal to par was called "watered stock"—stock issued not against assets but against water. (The term also echoed an ancient sharp practice in another field, the aquatizing of livestock before weighing them in for sale.) * * *

It will be clear to the reader that the development of the "par" concept just described arose as a response to the problems of assuring equitable contribution among shareholders. But development of the shareholder's par payment obligation served, in a somewhat fortuitous and naive way, to further the corporate creditor's interest in seeing shareholder assets committed to the enterprise. One can spin at least a hypothetical argument as to why this should be and how it came to be.

The argument would go in this wise: If a creditor extends credit immediately after the incorporation of the new enterprise and if he has been informed that the par value of the shares is $P and the number of shares that have been issued is N, it is not unreasonable for him to assume that the shareholders have collectively contributed into the corporate treasury an amount of dollars equal to the par value of the shares issued multiplied by the number of shares that were issued, or $PN. In a kind of rough and ready way, assuming that there have been no other transactions, the creditor might infer that the number $PN is an approximation of the total assets of the corporation, and on that basis might conclude that he could safely lend a certain amount of funds to the enterprise.

Did any rational creditor ever in fact act that way or extend credit on such a naive basis? The answer has to be "no." But * * * in time, this much became clear:

(1) The courts came to recognize that purchasers of shares from the corporation have some obligation to invest in the corporate enterprise;

(2) It came to be understood (perhaps "assumed" is a better word) that the measure of the investment liability of such a shareholder was the number of shares issued to him times the par value of the shares; and

(3) It came to be recognized that at least some creditors could in at least some circumstances enforce this obligation of the purchasing shareholder in some way. * * *

In the nineteenth century pattern of corporate financing, it was simply assumed that good companies—respectable companies—solid investments—would have stock with a high par value. * * * Nonetheless, eventually the practical argument prevailed and the invariable practice of using high par value common stock gradually gave way to the use of low par common stock. * * *

* * * [T]he separation of par and purchase price has the effect of opening a chasm between the lawyer's perspective and economist's concept of the entrepreneur's capital investment. If there are ten subscribers in a newly incorporated enterprise each of whom buys 10 shares of stock at a price of $50 per share, the economist, or the businessman would say that the company's beginning "capital" is $5,000. But the lawyer (and later the accountant) will tell the economist or the businessman that the "capital" is determined by par, and in this case is the number of issued shares, 100, multiplied by the par value of each share, $10, for a total of $1,000; the other $4,000 is something else about which we will hear more later. With the evolution of low par stock, came the evolution of that strange lawyer's convention * * *—"legal capital"— the $1,000 in the example just given. * * *

It was not until 1912 that analysis of the matter had reached a sufficiently wide circle to produce statutory authorization of no par stock. The advent of no par stock did not, however, have the effect of eliminating the concept of legal capital. It was, and still is, statutorily necessary to designate some dollar number on the corporate balance sheet as "capital." * * * The responsibility for making that statement, and the power to make it, is placed by corporation statutes with the board of directors, and the dollar number declared by them made in the customary form of a board resolution, is the "stated capital" of the corporation. * * *

What does the law do to prevent shareholders of a distressed company from pulling assets out of the corporate treasury just when the creditor needs them? * * *

Two basic propositions slowly emerged: (1) The measuring rod for judging the propriety or impropriety of the distributions to equity holders is the corporation's "capital"; and (2) "capital" refers not to assets but to that abstract number that is obtained by multiplying the number of shares of stock outstanding by the par value assigned to each share. * * *

The general idea of the legal capital scheme is that no distribution may be made to shareholders unless, after the distribution, the corporation has not only enough assets to pay its creditors but also an additional specified amount. This amount is called "stated capital". Anything over the sum of stated capital and liabilities is known as "surplus." * * *

The following statements may now be made about "legal capital."

a.   Legal capital is a number expressed in dollars.

b.   That number is initially the product of par value—itself an arbitrary dollar amount printed on the stock certificate and recited in the certificate of incorporation—multiplied by the number of shares "outstanding."

c.  Legal capital is a number that appears on the *right-hand,* or claimant's side of the balance sheet, *not* on the left-hand asset side. "Legal capital" is *not* an asset, a fund, or a collection of assets. And it does not refer to an asset, a fund, or a collection of assets. (The same is true of "surplus.")

d.  Legal capital is a number that implies that a valuation of at least that amount was placed upon some indeterminate assets that were transferred to the corporation at some indeterminate past time in exchange for shares then issued. Legal capital can at best be read to convey a message by implication—a message about a historical event.

Legal capital is entirely a legal invention, highly particularized in its meaning, historical in reference, *and not relatable in any way to the ongoing economic condition of the enterprise.* For most purposes, it is best thought of simply as a dollar number—a number having certain consequences and derived by specified statutory procedures, but just a number.

The law makes use of the concept of "legal capital" in two ways:

a.  It is the maximum number of dollars up to which someone might in certain circumstances be able sometime to hold some shareholders liable if the implied statement in [a-d] above could be proved to be false.

b.  It is a datum line, or water table, or bench mark, or nock on a measuring stick laid alongside the total number on the asset side of the balance sheet, on the basis of which lawyers will—or will not—sign an opinion that a proposed distribution of corporate assets to shareholders is valid, legal, and generates no liabilities either for the board of directors that declares it or the shareholders who receive it.

And here is the real bite. In the world of corporate finance, the closure of any significant transaction is utterly dependent upon opinions of legal counsel that are delivered at the closing, stating that the transaction is valid and legally enforceable. Whenever a corporate financial transaction requires the lawyers to inquire into a company's legal capital position, the impact of the statutory schemes of legal capital is enormously magnified by the Go/No-go function performed by opinions of counsel. The lawyers, in turn, are compelled to develop an understanding of the statutory scheme and of its application. From that state of affairs "legal capital" draws its perverse vitality. * * *

## 2.  THE ISSUANCE OF STOCK AND STOCKHOLDERS' LIABILITY

### a.  *Quantity of Consideration*

Under a regime of legal capital characterized by sales of stock at par, corporation law was much consumed with questions relating to "watered stock." Promoters frequently acquired stock in exchange for property worth less than the par value of the shares they received and then sought to mislead other investors about the value of their contributions. Knowing that capital must be equal to the par value of all shares issued and outstanding, promoters would report the property they contributed as an asset equal in value to the par value of the shares they received. That is, a promoter who contributed land worth $5,000 to a newly-formed corporation in exchange for 100 shares of $100 par value common stock would record the transaction as follows:

| Assets | | Liabilities and Equity | |
|--------|--------|------------------------|--------|
| Land | $10,000 | Capital (100 shares common stock, $100 par value) | $10,000 |
| Total | $10,000 | Total | $10,000 |

Courts, operating on the flawed premise that investors and creditors deal with a corporation on the basis of its stated capital, focused their attention on the right-hand side of the balance sheet and held promoters liable for "watering" the capital account. But "capital," of course, was computed mechanically—by multiplying the number of shares issued and outstanding by the par value of those shares. The real fraud was on the left-hand side of the balance sheet—in the overvaluation of the property contributed by the promoter.

States that retain traditional legal capital rules all have now adopted statutory provisions governing shareholders' liability for watered stock. DGCL § 162 is typical. It provides that shareholders are liable for "the sum necessary to complete the amount of the unpaid balance of the consideration for which shares were issued or are to be issued by the corporation." Interesting interpretative questions relating to this section can be posed, but in practice they virtually never arise. Corporate lawyers avoid the problems associated with watered stock by setting the par value far below the price at which the corporation plans to sell its stock and by monitoring carefully transactions in which stock is issued. The most salient question today often is whether to use low-par or no-par stock. The choice usually depends on the manner in which the relevant jurisdiction calculates the tax or "franchise fee" payable on incorporation. That fee frequently is calculated on the basis of the aggregate authorized capital of the corporation, with no-par stock "deemed" to have some arbitrary par value for this purpose.

Another reason valuation problems rarely arise in this context is that most statutes now provide that the board's judgment as to the value of property exchanged for stock is conclusive, absent fraud, or, as in DGCL § 152, absent "actual fraud." This language suggests that courts should treat as dispositive any good faith determination by a board of directors concerning the value of property. The last important case holding shareholders liable for watered stock was *Bing Crosby Minute Maid Corp. v. Eaton, 46 Cal.2d 484, 297 P.2d 5 (1956).*

### b. *Quality of Consideration*

A question closely related to the quantity of consideration is the quality or type of consideration for which stock may validly be issued. Cash is always acceptable. Services rendered and real or personal property are also permissible because they are either convertible to cash (property) or they have already contributed to the corporation's assets (services).

Under many state statutes (e.g. DGCL § 152), however, an executory contract to render *future* services is invalid consideration. Professor David Herwitz explains:

> The traditional concern about future services as consideration for stock lies chiefly in the fact that such services can prove valuable to a business only as a going concern and are totally devoid of realizable value for creditors or stockholders in the event of a liquidation of the enterprise. While of course other intangible items, notably goodwill, may prove worthless upon the failure of an enterprise, promised future services are subject to the special objection that they have no realizable value from the outset.

David R. Herwitz, *Allocation of Stock Between Services and Capital in the Organization of a Close Corporation*, 75 HARV.L.REV. 1098, 1105–6 (1962).

But a corporation certainly can pay a substantial salary advance to a person with some particular skill to induce her to come to work for the enterprise. And it also can pay her a bonus to acquire her services. If such an advance payment or bonus could be then used by the employee to purchase stock, why not just short-circuit the process and allow the corporation to issue the stock directly in exchange for the promise of future services? *Petrishen v. Westmoreland Finance Corp.*, 394 Pa. 552, 147 A.2d 392 (1959), relied on that analogy to approve stock issued for future services under a traditional statute. *Rooney v. Paul D. Osborne Desk Co., Inc.*, 38 Mass. App. 82, 645 N.E.2d 50 (1995), adopted a more straightforward approach. The court refused to allow a corporation to void an agreement to issue stock for future services where plaintiff had accepted a job with the corporation in reliance on that agreement and issuing the stock did not harm any creditor of the corporation.

Many states also prohibit corporations from accepting promissory notes as consideration for stock, especially unsecured notes signed by a purchaser-shareholder. Suppose the note is secured? Calif.Corp.Code § 409(a)(1) provides that a promissory note "adequately secured by collateral other than the shares acquired * * * "is good consideration for the purchase of shares. Suppose the note is unsecured, but guaranteed? The court in *Eastern Oklahoma Television Co., Inc. v. Ameco, Inc.*, 437 F.2d 138 (10th Cir.1971) held a personal guarantee of an obligation of the corporation was, in part, adequate consideration for the issuance of stock. *See also Citizens Bank of Windsor v. Landers*, 570 S.W.2d 756 (Mo.App.1978).

Whether a note is given for par value, or only the excess of the purchase price over par value, may be critical. In *Shoen v. Shoen*, 167 Ariz. 58, 804 P.2d 787 (App.1990), certain "key employees" of a Nevada corporation were allowed to purchase stock by making cash down payments equal to par value, which was less than 4% of the price for which the shares were issued, and giving the corporation non-recourse notes for the balance. Thus, if the purchasers defaulted, the corporation's only remedy was to return the down payments and recover the stock. Other shareholders sued to have the stock issuance declared unlawful because the corporation could not recover from the key employees "the unpaid balance of the consideration for which the shares were issued." The court rejected this claim, pointing out that the key employees had paid cash equal to the par value of the shares they purchase, the notes were legally enforceable obligations and it was not inconsistent with the Nevada statute (which is virtually identical to Delaware law in this respect) to treat the notes as valid consideration for stock.

### c. *Legal Capital Under the Revised Model Act*

The RMBCA jettisons the traditional approach to legal capital. RMBCA § 6.21 abolishes the concepts of "par value" and "stated value," although a corporation may retain par value if it so elects in its articles of incorporation. RMBCA § 2.02. Shares may be issued for such consideration as the board may authorize, at a fixed price, a minimum price, a formula price or any other method of price determination. Business conditions—and not the artificial notion of par value—determine the price for which shares may be issued. According to the Official Comment to RMBCA § 6.21, "there is no minimum price at which specific shares must be issued and therefore there can be no 'watered stock' liability for issuing shares below an arbitrarily fixed price." Clearly, the drafters believed that the old system of legal capital did not protect creditors' interests. What remains unclear is whether any system is needed, whether a fiduciary approach provides greater protection than the outmoded legal capital regime, or whether creditors are better protected through their own ability to contract rather than through a corporate law mechanism.

The issuance of shares still requires valid consideration, but the board of directors no longer needs to translate the consideration into dollars (for corporate law purposes, anyway) nor must it declare the consideration adequate. According to the Official Comment, shareholders' interests are protected by the business judgment of the board of directors rather than by formal statutory and accounting rules.

The RMBCA also abandons traditional restrictions on the quality of consideration. RMBCA § 6.21 permits sale of stock for future services or promissory notes. Again, the statutory scheme relies on the directors' judgment that the values exist. § 6.21(c) makes clear that shares are fully paid and non-assessable after the corporation has received the bargained-for consideration. The Official Comment notes that whether shares are validly issued depends solely on whether proper corporate procedures have been followed.

Of course, in addition to satisfying the requirements of the RMBCA, a corporation ultimately will have to prepare a financial statement. Then, if not before, it will have to place a dollar value on the property paid for stock. If those values are inflated, no liability will result under the RMBCA, but liability may exist under common law fraud or under the federal securities laws. (See Chapters 10 and 19.)

Liability of shareholders for payment of their shares is similar to that under Delaware law, except that there is no requirement that shareholders pay at least par value. RMBCA § 6.22 limits shareholders' liability to "payment of the consideration for which the shares were authorized to be issued or specified in the subscription agreement."

For a good explanation of the Model Act's approach, *see* the Official Comments to RMBCA §§ 6.21 and 6.22, reprinted in Adams & Matheson, CORPORATIONS AND BUSINESS ASSOCIATIONS: STATUTES, RULES AND FORMS.

## 3. DIVIDENDS AND OTHER DISTRIBUTIONS

### PROBLEM

### PRECISION TOOLS—PART VII

After three years of operations, the relevant entries on PTC's balance sheet, prior to the payment of any dividend, are as follows:

| Assets | | Liabilities and Equity | |
|---|---|---|---|
| Cash | $ 200,000 | Current Liabilities | 2,650,000 |
| Other Current Assets | 3,135,000 | Long–Term Liabilities | 3,750,000 |
| Total Current Assets | 3,335,000 | Total Liabilities | 6,400,000 |
| Net Fixed Assets | 3,481,750 | Common Stock (5,000 shares authorized and outstanding | 500,000 |
| Good Will | 83,250 | | |
| Note Receivable | 100,000 | Retained Earnings | 100,000 |
| | | Total Equity | 600,000 |
| Total Assets | 7,000,000 | Total Liabilities and Equity | 7,000,000 |

PTC earned net profits of $90,000 in its most recent year.

How would you answer the following questions under each of the following assumptions:

(a) PTC is organized under Delaware law and its common stock is $100 par value;

(b) PTC is organized under Delaware law and its common stock is $1 par value; and

(c) PTC is organized under Columbia law.

See DGCL §§ 160, 170, 172–174, 242(a)(3), 244; RMBCA §§ 6.31, 6.40 and Official Comment to § 6.40.

1. Can PTC pay a dividend of $200,000 to its shareholders at this time? What steps, if any, could it take to make lawful any dividend that otherwise would be unlawful?

2. A dispute has arisen between Bernie and the other shareholders over the continued employment of Bill Gould. The parties have decided to resolve their differences by having the company repurchase Bernie's 1,000 shares for $500,000. Assuming that the corporation can borrow sufficient money on a long term basis to finance the purchases, can it buy the stock?

3. Assume the balance sheet shown above is for a date five years after the organization of PTC and that PTC has paid no dividends and has never repurchased any of its stock. Michael, Jessica and Bernie continue to own their stock, but Michael and Jessica actually control PTC. Michael and Jessica are paid substantial salaries; Bernie receives no salary. Michael and Jessica would like to accumulate income in PTC with a view to buying the business of one of PTC's major customers. Bernie wants PTC to pay some dividend. Is it likely that Bernie would succeed in a suit to compel payment of a dividend?

### a. the Rationale for Regulating Dividends

Investors purchase a corporation's stock in the hope that they will realize gains in the form of dividends received while they hold that stock, capital appreciation when they sell it, or some combination of the two. For various reasons shareholders may be willing, or even eager, to forego dividends and realize most of their gain in the form of capital appreciation, particularly in closely-held corporations where shareholders are employees and can take out profits in the form of salaries and other compensation. In the case of publicly-held corporations, however, many investors are reluctant to rely entirely on capital gains; changes in the fortunes of a particular company, in business conditions generally, and the tenor of the stock market make such reliance too risky. Moreover, many investors, depend on dividends from their investments for current income, and try to invest in companies with stable businesses, such as public utilities, that pay regular and substantial dividends.

When a corporation seeks to raise capital by selling stock, it must compete with alternative uses of prospective investors' funds—including consumption, the purchase of gold bars, savings accounts, money market funds, government debt obligations, real estate, and wagering at a casino—to mention just a few. Consequently, corporations try to maximize the appeal of their stock, and thus to minimize their cost of capital, by paying careful attention to their dividend policies.

Corporate law does not leave decisions concerning the payment of dividends entirely to the workings of the market place and the discretion of corporate managers. As Dean Manning points out, shareholders and creditors have sharply conflicting interests with regard to the size and frequency of dividend payments. Because directors are elected by and are accountable to shareholders, they clearly would be inclined to favor shareholders' interests if their power to declare dividends was unrestricted. To counter this tendency, corporate law traditionally has sought to protect creditors' interests with regard to dividend payments, as it has with regard to issuance of stock. Recognizing that preferred stockholders also can be jeopardized by overly-generous dividend payments, corporate law also has sought to protect their interests.

### b.  the Traditional Approach to Regulating Dividends

The traditional approach to restricting dividend payments relied on the concept of legal capital and the associated notion of "surplus." Some states permit dividends to be paid only to the extent that a corporation has "earned surplus." This term is generally defined to mean a surplus which arises from the accumulation of profits during the life of the enterprise. While there are difficult interpretive questions involved in the meaning of the operative terms, the policy is plain enough. Dividends are supposed to be the fruit of the tree, and unless fruit has been borne, nothing can be picked.

More common are statutes that allow dividends to be paid out of "surplus," without regard to whether it is "earned" or not. *See, e.g.,* DGCL § 170, N.Y.B.C.L. § 510. The theory underlying such provisions is that the only cushion on which creditors can rely is a corporation's "stated" or "legal" capital. The rest of the shareholders' equity account is "surplus" (usually called either "earned" or "capital" surplus) and is at the disposition of the shareholders.

In addition to the payments that might be made under one of the foregoing provisions, some states also permit the payment of dividends whenever a corporation has current earnings. *See* DGCL § 170. Their statutes define current earnings in various ways, sometimes looking only to the most recent fiscal year, and sometimes looking to the preceding year, either alone or in combination with the current year. Such so-called "nimble dividend" provisions in effect allow the payment of dividends by currently profitable corporations even where such payments impair stated capital.

As should be clear by now, restrictions on dividends based on the concept of legal capital are unlikely to be effective. The Delaware and New York statutes, which limit the protection for senior security holders to legal capital, can be easily manipulated. For example, a corporation can reduce the par value of its outstanding stock by amending its articles of incorporation, thereby reducing stated capital and increasing surplus in an account usually called "reduction surplus." This increases the amount of dividends the corporation lawfully can pay.

Courts may go even further in weakening restrictions on dividend payments based on the concept of legal capital. Suppose a corporation's real estate increases in value. Can the corporation reflect the higher value on its balance sheet? If it does, the corporation will have to match the increase on the left-hand (asset) side of its balance sheet with an equivalent increase on the right-hand-side of its balance sheet. The account it will increase is shareholders' equity—more specifically, "surplus." It probably will call this increase "revaluation surplus," rather than "earned surplus." But whatever the label, surplus, and the corporation's dividend paying power, will be increased. The celebrated case of *Randall v. Bailey*, 23 N.Y.S.2d 173 (Sup.Ct.1940), *aff'd* 288 N.Y. 280, 43 N.E.2d 43 (1942), sustained payment of a dividend based on the existence of a revaluation surplus created in this manner. *Klang v. Smith's Food & Drug Centers, Inc.* 702 A.2d 150 (Del. 1997), involved a similar issue. Smith's Food & Drug ("SFD") had repurchased a large block of its stock through a tender offer. Prior to authorizing the tender offer, SFD's board had revalued the corporation's assets and liabilities. Absent that revaluation, the repurchase would have caused a deficit in surplus in violation of DGCL § 160. The Delaware Supreme Court affirmed a trial court decision rejecting a shareholder's challenge to the repurchase, stating:

> * * * In cases alleging impairment of capital under Section 160, the trial court may defer to the board's measurement of surplus unless a plaintiff can show that the directors "failed to fulfill their duty to evaluate the assets on the basis of acceptable data and by standards which they are entitled to believe reasonably reflect present values." In the absence of bad faith or fraud on the part of the board, courts will not "substitute [our] concepts of wisdom for that of the directors." Here, plaintiff does not argue that the SFD Board acted in bad faith. Nor has he met his burden of showing that the methods and data that underlay the board's analysis are unreliable or that its determination of surplus is so far off the mark as to constitute actual or constructive fraud. Therefore, we defer to the board's determination of surplus, and hold that SFD's self-tender offer did not violate 8 *Del.C.* § 160.

As we saw in Chapter 6, generally accepted accounting principles stress historic cost and would not allow such an upward revaluation. But statutes based on legal capital do not require corporations to employ generally accepted accounting principles (GAAP). They can keep separate and completely legal sets of books to compute the amount available for distribution to shareholders. However, consistent with GAAP, a corporation that based its dividend payments on such books almost surely is obliged to write-down the book value of any assets worth significantly less than their cost (or cost less accumulated depreciation).

### c. Protection Against Excessive Dividends Under the Model Act

The RMBCA abandons restrictions based on legal capital or surplus tests altogether. Instead, unless the articles provide otherwise, RMBCA

§ 6.40(c) simply prohibits "distributions," as defined in § 1.40(6), if after the distribution (1) "the corporation would not be able to pay its debts as they become due in the usual course of its business," or (2) "the corporation's total assets would be less than its total liabilities plus" any sum needed to satisfy the claims of preferred stockholders in the event of dissolution. The Official Comment to § 6.40 characterizes these as the "equity insolvency test" and the "balance sheet test." Neither test can be applied mechanically; both require the exercise of judgment. That judgment is exercised by a corporation's board of directors.

Dean Manning calls this provision "the big bomb" because directors face personal liability if they judge wrong. The RMBCA, and more specifically the Official Comment to § 6.40, recognizes this danger and attempts to reduce it by stating that decisions concerning distributions should be evaluated as would any other exercise of business judgment.

In evaluating the corporation's ability to meet its obligations as they come due, directors generally can assume that the company will remain a going concern. The Official Comment suggest several benchmarks directors may wish to consider, but no bright line tests. Where solvency appears to be a matter of concern, directors may find it helpful to analyze a company's liquidity and cash flows, using both reports on the results of operations and any forecasts or budgets management has prepared.

The balance sheet test is to be made on the basis of (1) specified financial statements or (2) fair valuation or other reasonable methods. The RMBCA leaves this determination to the directors and does not mandate the use of GAAP. Of course, directors can protect themselves by relying on financial reports prepared in accordance with GAAP. *See* RMBCA § 8.30. California law involves similar tests, but does require use of GAAP. *See* Calif.Corp.Code §§ 114 and 500(b).

Clearly a policy that turned on concepts of par value provided little protection to creditors because of the ease with which restrictions could be circumvented. The law as now reflected in RMBCA § 6.40 seems more realistic, but does it furnish meaningful protection to creditors? Directors cannot render the corporation insolvent by approving a distribution, but the RMBCA does not preclude them from going to the edge. No cushion is required. By contrast, consider Calif. Corp. Code § 500 which requires that a corporation's liquid and hard assets (total assets less certain intangibles) after a distribution equal at least 125% of liabilities and that directors employ GAAP in making this computation. One explanation for the different approaches is that the drafters of the RMBCA appear to have decided that corporate law is not the vehicle through which creditors should be protected. They can rely on contract, or on fraudulent conveyance law, such as the Uniform Fraudulent Conveyance Act. A similar attitude is reflected in other aspects of corporate law, which provides that managers' fiduciary duties run only to shareholders, allow only shareholders to bring derivative actions and rarely allow creditors to "pierce the corporate veil" and reach the assets of shareholders of insolvent corporations. For an excellent discussion of these issues, see Robert C. Clark, CORPORATE LAW, Chap. 2 (1986).

### d.  *Stock Dividends*

Not all dividends involve the distribution of cash to stockholders. Corporations occasionally pay what are known as "stock dividends" in which additional shares of stock are distributed. In economic terms, such a dividend produces no meaningful change in the financial status of the corporation or its shareholders. It merely divides shareholders' ownership interests in the corporation into a greater number of shares while leaving each shareholder's proportionate interest unchanged. Indeed, the reason for paying such a "dividend" often is to produce the appearance that shareholders are receiving something when the corporation is not in a position to pay a dividend in cash.

Since a stock dividend does not result in the distribution of any of the corporation's assets, there is no need to place limitations on it for the protection of creditors. Indeed, because the par value (if any) of the shares distributed must be added to stated capital (see, e.g., DGCL § 173) a stock dividend can actually benefit creditors. RMBCA § 6.23 recognizes that a stock dividend involves the issuance of shares "without consideration." RMBCA § 1.40(6) excludes such a dividend from the definition of a "distribution."

### e.  *Repurchase of Shares*

A corporation may want to repurchase some of its outstanding stock for a variety of reasons. If the repurchase is pro rata from all shareholders, it will have almost exactly the same effect as a dividend; the only difference will be a reduction in the number of shares outstanding. But whether a repurchase is pro rata or from less than all shareholders, its impact on creditors will be the same as if the corporation paid a dividend. Consequently, corporation statutes generally impose restraints on the repurchase of stock similar to those imposed on dividends. N.Y.B.C.L. § 513 for example, generally permits repurchases only out of surplus, although it allows repurchase or redemption of redeemable shares out of capital. DGCL § 160 prohibits the repurchase of common stock if it would impair capital, which amounts to essentially the same thing. The RMBCA defines the repurchase of shares as a "distribution" in § 1.40(6) and subjects it to the limitations contained in § 6.40.

Traditional statutes classify reacquired shares as "treasury stock." Treasury stock remains "issued," but is not "outstanding." If treasury shares are resold (technically they are "sold" and not "issued" although there seems to be little or no practical distinction), the restriction imposed on surplus when they were purchased is eliminated. On the other hand, preemptive rights ordinarily do not extend to sales of treasury shares and a corporation generally may not vote treasury shares. *See, e.g.*, DGCL § 160(c).

The RMBCA eliminates the concept of treasury shares. § 6.31 provides that reacquired shares automatically revert to the status of authorized but unissued stock, thereby avoiding the complexity of prior law.

### f. Liability for Unlawful Distributions

When a corporation makes an unlawful distribution to shareholders, creditors' interests usually are placed in jeopardy. When an unlawful distribution results in actual losses to creditors, the directors who authorized that distribution can be held liable. *See, e.g.*, RMBCA § 8.33 which imposes liability on the directors who voted for a dividend, distribution, or repurchase of stock that violates the restrictions of the Act. *See also* DGCL § 174; and N.Y.B.C.L. § 719.* A director held liable for an unlawful distribution has an action for contribution against shareholders who received a distribution knowing that it was improper. RMBCA § 8.33(b); DGCL § 174(c). While shareholders of a Delaware corporation can exculpate directors from liability for many breaches of the duty of due care, they cannot provide such exculpation for unlawful distributions. *See* DGCL § 102(b)(7).

## D. CORPORATE DIVIDEND POLICY: LEGAL AND ECONOMIC ISSUES

Decisions as to whether dividends lawfully can be paid arise only when corporations are in financial difficulty. In solvent corporations, decisions relating to dividends involve a basic financial policy issue: should cash not needed for current operations be reinvested in the business or distributed to shareholders? Professors Klein and Coffee observe that, apart from changing the corporation's capital structure,

> there is no necessary connection between the dividend decision and the investment decision. If a corporation lacks spare cash, because it has paid dividends or for any other reason, it can still take advantages of investment opportunities as long as it is able to finance those investments by selling new securities.

William A. Klein & John C. Coffee, Jr., BUSINESS ORGANIZATION AND FINANCE 375–76 (6th ed. 1996). Nonetheless, courts traditionally have examined the investment opportunities available to a corporation when evaluating a challenge to its dividend policy.

### 1. CLOSE CORPORATIONS

### DODGE v. FORD MOTOR CO.
204 Mich. 459, 170 N.W. 668 (1919).

[The factual background of this famous action is set forth in Chapter 5, as is the portion of the court's decision refusing to enjoin Ford's plans

---

* New York also makes the violation of the restrictions on distributions a criminal offense under some circumstances. See N.Y.Penal Law § 190.35.

to expand production and lower the price of its cars, even though demand at current prices exceeded Ford's production capacity. The following portion of the opinion deals with the Dodge brothers' request, which the trial court granted, for an order compelling Ford to pay a special dividend of $19 million—an amount equal to one-half of Ford's cash surplus—in addition to the $1.2 million regular dividend Ford had declared.]

* * * [T]he case for plaintiffs must rest upon the claim * * * that in any event the withholding of the special dividend asked for by plaintiffs is arbitrary action of the directors requiring judicial interference.

The rule which will govern courts in deciding these questions is not in dispute. It is, of course, differently phrased by judges and by authors, and, as the phrasing in a particular instance may seem to lean for or against the exercise of the right of judicial interference with the actions of corporate directors, the context, or the facts before the court, must be considered. This court, in *Hunter v. Roberts, Throp & Co.*, 83 Mich. 63, 71, 47 N.W. 131, 134, recognized the rule in the following language:

> It is a well-recognized principle of law that the directors of a corporation, and they alone, have the power to declare a dividend of the earnings of the corporation, and to determine its amount. Courts of equity will not interfere in the management of the directors unless it is clearly made to appear that they are guilty of fraud or misappropriation of the corporate funds, or refuse to declare a dividend when the corporation has a surplus of net profits which it can, without detriment to its business, divide among its stockholders, and when a refusal to do so would amount to such an abuse of discretion as would constitute a fraud, or breach of that good faith which they are bound to exercise towards the stockholders.

In COOK ON CORPORATIONS (7th Ed.) § 545, it is expressed as follows:

> The board of directors declare the dividends, and it is for the directors, and not the stockholders, to determine whether or not a dividend shall be declared.

> When, therefore, the directors have exercised this discretion and refused to declare a dividend, there will be no interference by the courts with their decision, unless they are guilty of a willful abuse of their discretionary powers, or of bad faith or of a neglect of duty. It requires a very strong case to induce a court of equity to order the directors to declare a dividend, inasmuch as equity has no jurisdiction, unless fraud or a breach of trust is involved. There have been many attempts to sustain such a suit, yet, although the courts do not disclaim jurisdiction, they have quite uniformly refused to interfere. The discretion of the directors will not be interfered with by the courts, unless there has been bad faith, willful neglect, or abuse of discretion.

> Accordingly, the directors may, in the fair exercise of their discretion, invest profits to extend and develop the business, and a

reasonable use of the profits to provide additional facilities for the business cannot be objected to or enjoined by the stockholders.

\* \* \*

When plaintiffs made their complaint and demand for further dividends, The Ford Motor company had completed its most prosperous year of business [and had earned a profit of almost $60 million]. \* \* \* It had assets of more than $132,000,000, a surplus of almost $112,000,000, and its cash on hand and municipal bonds were nearly $54,000,000. Its total liabilities, including capital stock, was a little over $20,000,000. \* \* \* Considering only these facts, a refusal to declare and pay further dividends appears to be not an exercise in discretion on the part of the directors but an arbitrary refusal to do what the circumstances required to be done. \* \* \*

[The court reviewed Ford's plans to finance an major expansion of its business.]

Assuming the general plan and policy of expansion and the details of it \* \* \* were for the best ultimate interest of the company and therefore of its shareholders, what does it amount to in justification of a refusal to declare and pay a special dividend or dividends? The Ford Motor Company was able to estimate with nicety its income and profit. It could sell more cars than it could make. Having ascertained what it would cost to produce a car and to sell it, the profit upon each car depended upon the selling price. That being fixed, the yearly income and profit was determinable, and, within slight variations, was certain.

There was appropriated—voted—for the smelter $11,325,000. \* \* \* [A]ssuming that the plans required an expenditure sooner or later of $9,895,000 for duplication of the plant, and for land and other expenditures $3,000,000, the total is $24,220,000. The company was continuing business, at a profit—a cash business. If the total cost of proposed expenditures had been immediately withdrawn in cash from the cash surplus (money and bonds) on hand August 1, 1916, there would have remained nearly $30,000,000.

Defendants say, and it is true, that a considerable cash balance must be at all times carried by such a concern. But, as has been stated, there was a large daily, weekly, monthly, receipt of cash. The output was practically continuous and was continuously, and within a few days, turned into cash. Moreover, the contemplated expenditures were not to be immediately made. The large sum appropriated for the smelter plant was payable over a considerable period of time. So that, without going further, it would appear that, accepting and approving the plan of the directors, it was their duty to distribute on or near the 1st of August, 1916, a very large sum of money to stockholders. \* \* \*

The decree of the court below fixing and determining the specific amount to be distributed to stockholders is affirmed. In other respects, \* \* \* the said decree is reversed.

### Note: Dividend Decisions in Close Corporations

As the authorities cited in *Dodge v. Ford* suggest, shareholders face an uphill battle when they bring an action to compel a corporation's board of directors to declare a dividend. Rare indeed is the corporation that is so flush with cash and so clearly profitable that a court will find a board's refusal to declare a dividend reflects "bad faith" or "an abuse of discretion." In assessing the precedential force of *Dodge v. Ford*, one also should keep in mind the business struggle in which that case played a part. Ford's business then principally involved assembling cars using parts supplied by others. The Dodge brothers, in addition to owning 22% of Ford's stock, were among Ford's largest suppliers. In addition, the Dodge brothers had begun manufacturing cars in competition with Ford. Ford's decision to withhold dividends deprived the Dodge brothers of cash they needed to finance the expansion of their manufacturing operations, and Ford's plan to reduce the selling price of its cars placed additional competitive pressure on those operations.

Most attempts by shareholders to compel boards of directors to declare dividends have involved closely-held companies (as was Ford Motor Company at the time of the case). *Gottfried v. Gottfried*, 73 N.Y.S.2d 692 (Sup.Ct.1947), is typical. The plaintiff-shareholders alleged that (1) there was bitter animosity between the directors (who were the majority shareholders) and the plaintiffs (the minority shareholders); (2) the majority shareholders sought to coerce the minority shareholders to sell their stock to them at a grossly inadequate price; (3) the majority shareholders wanted to avoid heavy personal income taxes on any dividends that might be declared; (4) the majority shareholders, who were on the corporation's payroll, paid themselves excessive salaries and bonuses and borrowed money from the corporation; and (5) the nonpayment of dividends was designed to compel the minority shareholders, who were not on the corporation's payroll, to sell their stock to the majority shareholders.

Although the court expressed sympathy for the minority shareholders, who had been discharged from the corporate payroll, it did not find that the hostility and dissension among shareholders provided a sufficient basis on which to conclude that the refusal to pay dividends was due to the directors' "bad faith." According to the court "The essential test of bad faith is to determine whether the policy of the directors is dictated by their personal interests rather than corporate welfare. Directors are fiduciaries. Their [beneficiaries] are the corporation and the stockholders as a body. Circumstances appraised in the light of the financial condition and requirements of the corporation, will determine the conclusion as to whether the directors have or have not been animated by personal, as distinct from corporate considerations." Id. at 695.

The court found that bonuses and corporate loans to the majority shareholders were a long-standing company practice. In addition, the remuneration to one defendant could not be considered excessive because he had played an important role in the "tremendous expansion" of the company's subsidiary, Hanscom Baking Corporation, between 1933 and 1946. In dismissing the complaint and directing judgment for the defendants, the court concluded:

> The testimony discloses that many general considerations affected the policy of the Board of Directors in connection with dividend payments. Some of the major factors were as follows: The recognition that earnings during the war years might be abnormal and not representative of normal earning capacity; the pressing need for heavy expenditures for new equipment and machinery, replacement of which had been impossible during the war years; heavy expenditures required to finance the acquisition and equipment of new Hanscom stores in harmony with the steady growth of the business; the increased initial cost of opening new stores because, under present conditions, it has become difficult to lease appropriate sites necessitating actual acquisition by ownership of locations; the erection of a new bakery for Hanscom at a cost of approximately $1,000,000 inasmuch as the existing plant is incapable of producing the requirements of Hanscom sales which are running at the rate of approximately $6,000,000 per annum; unstable labor conditions with actual and threatened strikes; several pending actions involving large sums of money under the Federal Fair Labor Standards Act; a general policy of financing expansion through earnings requiring long-term debt.

> The plaintiffs oppose many of these policies of expansion. There is no evidence of any weight to the effect that these policies of the Board of Directors are actuated by any motives other than their best business judgment. If they are mistaken, their own stock holdings will suffer proportionately to those of the plaintiffs. With the wisdom of that policy the court has no concern. It is this court's conclusion that these policies and the expenditures which they entail are undertaken in good faith and without relation to any conspiracy, scheme and plan to withhold dividends for the purpose of compelling the plaintiffs to sell their stock or pursuant to any other sinister design. 73 N.Y.S.2d at 700–01.

*Zidell v. Zidell, Inc.*, 277 Or. 413, 560 P.2d 1086 (1977), further exemplifies courts' reluctance to compel the declaration of a dividend. Corporations owned mainly by two brothers paid no dividends while both brothers were employees. After the plaintiff resigned his position because of an internal dispute about compensation, small dividends were declared. Plaintiff protested that they were unreasonably small. The court noted:

> Plaintiff had the burden of proving bad faith on the part of the directors in determining the amount of corporate dividends. In the present case, plaintiff has shown that the corporations could afford to pay additional dividends, that he has left the corporate payroll, that those stockholders who are working for the corporations are

receiving generous salaries and bonuses, and that there is hostility between him and the other major stockholders.

560 P.2d at 1089.

Nonetheless, because the defendants were able to point to credible explanations for a conservative dividend policy—future needs for expensive improvements, accumulating large inventory, renovation of the plant—the court refused to find that the low dividends were due to bad faith.

Only occasionally have courts been prepared to intervene. In *Miller v. Magline, Inc.*, 76 Mich.App. 284, 256 N.W.2d 761 (1977), the corporation's board of directors had adopted a management compensation scheme providing for a low base salary plus a generous incentive bonus program, with any remaining profits to be retained by the corporation as working capital. The court ruled that defendant directors had breached their fiduciary duty to plaintiffs by not declaring a dividend:

> It is our opinion that under all of the circumstances of the case, that the directors of the management group were placed in the impossible situation of trying to give an impartial answer to the determination as to whether dividends should be granted. They already were taking a profit distribution via a percentile of profits before taxes. Therefore, we deem it an untenable position to argue that nonpayment of dividends is justified on the basis that such a concept of profit distribution would imperil the continued well being of the corporation. If such retention of profits were indicated they should have been more diligent in seeing that distributions based upon percentage of profits also should be curtailed.

256 N.W.2d at 770.

As these cases suggest, a shareholder in a close corporation often is well advised to enter into an agreement requiring dividends be paid under appropriately defined circumstances. A shareholder in a close corporation generally cannot easily sell her stock; if she is not employed by the company and receives no dividends (whether labelled as such or disguised as salary or bonus payments), she receives no meaningful economic return from her investment. As we shall see in Chapter 13, courts have become increasingly sensitive to such situations. They tend to uphold agreements relating to the payment of dividends and otherwise extend protections to a minority shareholders who they conclude have been exploited.

## 2.   PUBLIC CORPORATIONS

### KAMIN v. AMERICAN EXPRESS CO.

86 Misc.2d 809, 383 N.Y.S.2d 807 (1976), aff'd on opinion below
54 A.D.2d 654, 387 N.Y.S.2d 993 (1st Dept.1976).

[In 1972, American Express purchased almost 2 million shares of stock in Donaldson, Lufkin & Jenrette, Inc. (DLJ), for $29.9 million. By

1975, the stock had declined in value to approximately $4 million. American Express announced that it would distribute the DLJ stock as a dividend. Two shareholders sued to enjoin distribution of the dividend. They argued that American Express would be better off selling the DLJ stock.

The shareholders pointed out that a distribution of the DLJ stock would not have any impact on American Express's liability for income taxes. On the other hand, if American Express sold the DLJ stock, it could reduce otherwise taxable capital gains by an amount equal to its roughly $26 million loss on the DLJ stock and thus save approximately $8 million in taxes. In effect, the shareholders' argument was that rather than distribute $4 million in DLJ stock as a dividend, American Express could sell the stock, save $8 million in taxes, and then (if it wished) distribute $12 million (the sale price plus the tax savings) as a dividend.

The American Express board of directors considered the shareholders' argument at a meeting on October 17, 1975, and decided to proceed with the dividend. The board had previously been advised by its accountants that if the DLJ stock was distributed as a dividend, rather than sold, American Express would not have to reduce its reported income for 1975 to reflect its loss on its investment. Rather, it could bypass its income statement and simply reduce retained earnings by $29.9 million—the book value of the stock it would be distributing.]

EDWARD J. GREENFIELD, JUSTICE.

Examination of the complaint reveals that there is no claim of fraud or self-dealing, and no contention that there was any bad faith or oppressive conduct. The law is quite clear as to what is necessary to ground a claim for actionable wrongdoing. * * *

More specifically, the question of whether or not a dividend is to be declared or a distribution of some kind should be made is exclusively a matter of business judgment for the Board of Directors.

> * * * Courts will not interfere with such discretion unless it be first made to appear that the directors have acted or are about to act in bad faith and for a dishonest purpose. It is for the directors to say, acting in good faith of course, when and to what extent dividends shall be declared * * * The statute confers upon the directors this power, and the minority stockholders are not in a position to question this right, so long as the directors are acting in good faith * * *.

Thus, a complaint must be dismissed if all that is presented is a decision to pay dividends rather than pursuing some other course of conduct. * * * The directors' room rather than the courtroom is the appropriate forum for thrashing out purely business questions which will have an impact on profits, market prices, competitive situations, or tax advantages. * * *

* * * The affidavits of the defendants and the exhibits annexed thereto demonstrate that the objections raised by the plaintiffs to the

proposed dividend action were carefully considered and unanimously rejected by the Board at a special meeting called precisely for that purpose at the plaintiffs' request. The minutes of the special meeting indicate that the defendants were fully aware that a sale rather than a distribution of the DLJ shares might result in the realization of a substantial income tax saving. Nevertheless, they concluded that there were countervailing considerations primarily with respect to the adverse effect such a sale, realizing a loss of $25 million, would have on the net income figures in the American Express financial statement. Such a reduction of net income would have a serious effect on the market value of the publicly traded American Express stock. This was not a situation in which the defendant directors totally overlooked facts called to their attention. They gave them consideration, and attempted to view the total picture in arriving at their decision. While plaintiffs contend that according to their accounting consultants the loss on the DLJ stock would still have to be charged against current earnings even if the stock were distributed, the defendants' accounting experts assert that the loss would be a charge against earnings only in the event of a sale, whereas in the event of distribution of the stock as a dividend, the proper accounting treatment would be to charge the loss only against surplus. While the chief accountant for the SEC raised some question as to the appropriate accounting treatment of this transaction, there was no basis for any action to be taken by the SEC with respect to the American Express financial statement.

The only hint of self-interest which is raised, not in the complaint but in the papers on the motion, is that four of the twenty directors were officers and employees of American Express and members of its Executive Incentive Compensation Plan. Hence, it is suggested, by virtue of the action taken earnings may have been overstated and their compensation affected thereby. Such a claim is highly speculative and standing alone can hardly be regarded as sufficient to support an inference of self-dealing. There is no claim or showing that the four company directors dominated and controlled the sixteen outside members of the Board. * * *

---

### Note: Dividend Decisions in Public Corporations

To assess the merits of the American Express board's decision to distribute the DLJ stock as a dividend requires consideration of two questions. First, was the board correct in its belief that stock market investors are more interested in the accounting treatment of American Express's divestiture of its interest in DLJ than in that transaction's financial impact on American Express? Second, even if the board's assessment was correct, was it appropriate for the board to seek to increase the market price of American Express stock by abjuring a transaction (selling the DLJ stock and recording the loss) that would have produced greater economic benefits for the company. In this regard, see Henry T.C. Hu, *Risk, Time and Fiduciary Principles in Corporate Investment*, 38 U.C.L.A. L.REV. 277, 281 (1990), arguing that managers' fiduciary duty should be reformulated to require maximization of the "intrinsic value" (i.e., the discounted cash flow value) of a corporations' stock, and that managers should disregard "evidence that stock market pricing of shares is, to a disturbing extent, ill-informed and irrational."

The result in *Kamin* in any event underlines courts' propensity to extend to dividend decisions by public corporations, even more so than closely-held firms, the protection of the business judgment rule. Note the *Kamin* court's pithy observation that the appropriate battleground for such decisions is the boardroom, not the courtroom.

Economists traditionally have found the payment of dividends mysterious. Merton Miller and Franco Modigliani, two Nobel laureates, have pointed out that shareholders effectively can declare their own dividends by selling stock or borrowing money collateralized by their stock, while allowing the company to accumulate capital. Dividends seem especially puzzling when a firm simultaneously goes into the market to raise fresh capital. Merton Miller & France Modigliani, *Dividend Policy, Growth and the Valuation of Shares*, 34 J. BUSINESS 411 (1961). Other economists have found that "changes in dividends have an effect upon share prices, apparently because the changes communicate unique information to investors about management's perception of the corporation's future profitability." Richard O. Kummert, *State Statutory Restrictions on Financial Distributions by Corporations to Shareholders, Part I*, 55 WASH.L.REV. 359, 366 (1980). Professor Kummert believes that empirical evidence shows that corporate boards also believe that dividend policy affects share prices.

Other commentators suggest a tie between dividends and agency costs. Frank Easterbrook, *Two Agency–Cost Explanations of Dividends*, 74 AMER.ECON.REV. 650 (1984) argues that shareholders may prefer dividends because when they are paid, managers must resort more frequently to the market place for new capital. Thus managers subject themselves to closer monitoring by investment bankers and new investors, who will demand both fidelity and the proper adjustment between risk and prudence. Warren Buffet offers the following observations about corporations' dividend policies:

Warren Buffet, *Letter to Shareholders,*
*Berkshire Hathaway Inc.*

1984 ANNUAL REPORT.

[A]llocation of capital is crucial to business and investment management. Because it is, we believe managers and owners should think hard about the circumstances under which earnings should be retained and under which they should be distributed.

The first point to understand is that all earnings are not created equal. In many businesses—particularly those that have high asset/profit ratios—inflation causes some or all of the reported earnings to become ersatz. The ersatz portion—let's call these earnings "restricted"—cannot, if the business is to retain its economic position, be distributed as dividends. Were these earnings to be paid out, the business would lose ground in one or more of the following areas: its ability to maintain its unit volume of sales, its long-term competitive positions, its financial strength. No matter how conservative its payout ratio, a company that consistently distributes restricted earnings is destined for oblivion unless equity capital is otherwise infused.

Restricted earnings are seldom valueless to owners, but they often must be discounted heavily. In effect, they are conscripted by the business, no matter how poor its economic potential. * * *

Let's turn to the much-more-valued unrestricted variety. These earnings may, with equal feasibility, be retained or distributed. In our opinion, management should choose whichever course makes greater sense for the owners of the business.

This principle is not universally accepted. For a number of reasons managers like to withhold unrestricted, readily distributable earnings from shareholders—to expand the corporate empire over which the managers rule, to operate from a position of exceptional financial comfort, etc. But we believe there is only one valid reason for retention. Unrestricted earnings should be retained only when there is a reasonable prospect—backed preferably by historical evidence or, when appropriate, by a thoughtful analysis of the future—that *for every dollar retained by the corporation, at least one dollar of market value will be created for owners*. This will happen only if the capital retained produces incremental earnings equal to, or above, those generally available to investors.

To illustrate, let's assume that an investor owns a risk-free 10% perpetual bond with one very unusual feature. Each year the investor can elect either to take his 10% coupon in cash, or to reinvest the coupon in more 10% bonds with identical terms; i.e., a perpetual life and coupons offering the same cash-or-reinvest option. If, in any given year, the prevailing interest rate on long-term, risk-free bonds is 5%, it would be foolish for the investor to take his coupon in cash since the 10% bonds he could instead choose would be worth considerably more than 100¢ on the dollar. Under these circumstances, the investor wanting to get his hands on cash should take his coupon in additional bonds and then immediately sell them. By doing that, he would realize more cash than if he had taken his coupon directly in cash. Assuming all bonds were held by rational investor, no one would opt for cash in an era of 5% interest rates, not even those bondholders needing cash for living purposes.

If, however, interest rates were 15%, no rational investor would want his money invested for him at 10%. Instead, the investor would choose to take his coupon in cash, even if his personal cash need were nil. The opposite course—reinvestment of the coupon—would give an investor additional bonds with market value far less than the cash he could have elected. If he should want 10% bonds, he can simply take the cash received and buy them in the market, where they will be available at a large discount.

An analysis similar to that made by our hypothetical bondholder is appropriate for owners in thinking about whether a company's unrestricted earnings should be retained or paid out. Of course, the analysis is much more difficult and subject to error because the rate earned on reinvested earnings is not a contractual figure, as in our bond case, but rather a fluctuating figure. Owners must guess as to what the rate will average over the intermediate future. However, once an informed guess is made, the rest of the analysis is simple: you should wish your earnings to be reinvested if they can be expected to earn high returns, and you should wish them paid to you if low returns are the likely outcome of reinvestment.

\* \* \*

In judging whether managers should retain earnings, shareholders should not simply compare total incremental earnings in recent years to total incremental capital because that relationship may be distorted by what is going on in a core business. During an inflationary period, companies with a core business characterized by extraordinary economics can use small amounts of incremental capital in that business at very high rates of return \* \* \*. But, unless they are experiencing tremendous unit growth, outstanding businesses by definition generate large amounts of excess cash. If a company sinks most of this money in other businesses that earn low returns, the company's overall return on retained capital may nevertheless appear excellent because of the extraordinary returns being earned by the portion of earnings incrementally invested in the core business. The situation is analogous to a Pro–Am golf event: even if all of the amateurs are hopeless duffers, the team's best-ball score will be respectable because of the dominating skills of the professional.

Many corporations that consistently show good returns both on equity and on overall incremental capital have, indeed, employed a large portion of their retained earnings on an economically unattractive, even disastrous, basis. Their marvelous core businesses, however, whose earnings grow year after year, camouflage repeated failure in capital allocation elsewhere (usually involving high-priced acquisitions of businesses that have inherently mediocre economics). The managers at fault periodically report on the lessons they have learned from the latest disappointment. They then usually seek out future lessons. (Failure seems to go to their heads.)

In such cases, shareholders would be far better off if earnings were retained only to expand the high-return business, with the balance paid in dividends or used to repurchase stock (an action that increases the owners' interest in the exceptional business while sparing them participation in subpar businesses). Managers of high-return businesses who consistently employ much of the cash thrown off by those businesses in other ventures with low returns should be held to account for those allocation decisions, regardless of how profitable the overall enterprise is.

Nothing in this discussion is intended to argue for dividends that bounce around from quarter to quarter with each wiggle in earnings or in investment opportunities. Shareholders of public corporations understandably prefer that dividends be consistently predictable. Payments, therefore, should reflect long-term expectations for both earnings and returns on incremental capital. Since the long-term corporate outlook changes only infrequently, dividend patterns should change no more often. But over time distributable earnings that have been withheld by managers should earn their keep. If earnings have been unwisely retained, it is likely that managers, too, have unwisely retained.

———

In recent years, there has been considerable debate about the relationship between public corporations' dividend policies and their capital structure. Saul Levmore, *Monitors and Freeriders in Commercial and Corporate Settings*, 92 YALE L.J. 49 (1982), noted that a corporation's capital structure provides a device for monitoring management. Professor Levmore argues that debt holders, in pursuing their need to guard the security of their capital, provide signals to shareholders about the financial stability of the firm and about managerial performance and misconduct. As Professor Levmore notes, this early warning system enables a firm to reduce its agency costs and thereby lower its capital costs. Thus, while too much debt in the capital structure crowds the safety of the equity holders, and reduces shareholder values, the presence of some permanent debt benefits the stockholders and enhances share values.

The debate about public corporations' capital structure became quite heated in the late 1980s, following a decade in which many public corporations became the targets of hostile takeovers financed by high-yield debt and many others, perhaps to fend off takeover bids, adopted highly leveraged capital structures. A discussion of these issues in late 1980s articles in and letters to the editor of the Harvard Business Review suggests that the debate had a political as well as an economic dimension.

Michael Jensen, *Eclipse of the Public Corporation*

HARV. BUS. REV. 61 (Sept.–Oct. 1989).

The publicly held corporation, the main engine of economic progress in the United States for a century, has outlived its usefulness in many sectors of the economy and is being eclipsed. New organizations are emerging in its place—organizations that are corporate in form but have no public shareholders and are not listed or traded on organized exchanges. These organizations use public and private debt, rather than public equity, as their major source of capital. Their primary owners are not households but large institutions and entrepreneurs that designate agents to manage and monitor on their behalf and bind those agents with large equity interests and contracts governing the use and distribution of cash.

* * * [T]his organizational innovation should be encouraged. By resolving the central weakness of the public corporation—the conflict between owners and managers over the control and use of corporate resources—these new organizations are making remarkable gains in operating efficiency, employee productivity, and shareholder value. Over the long term, they will enhance U.S. economic performance relative to our most formidable international competitor, Japan, whose companies are moving in the opposite direction. * * * [C]ompanies increasingly resemble U.S. companies of the mid–1960s and early 1970s—an era of gross corporate waste and mismanagement that triggered the organizational transformation now under way in the United States.

* * * The forces behind the decline of the public corporation differ from industry to industry. But its decline is real, enduring, and highly productive. It is not merely a function of the tax deductibility of interest. Nor does it reflect a transitory LBO phase through which companies pass before investment bankers and managers cash out by taking them public again. Nor, finally, is it premised on a systematic fleecing of shareholders and bondholders by managers and other insiders with superior information about the true value of corporate assets.

The current trends do not imply that the public corporation has no future. The conventional twentieth-century model of corporate governance—dispersed public ownership, professional managers without substantial equity holdings, a board of directors dominated by management-appointed outsiders—remains a viable option in some areas of the economy, particularly for growth companies whose profitable investment opportunities exceed the cash they generate internally. * * * Companies choosing among a surplus of profitable projects are unlikely to invest systematically in unprofitable ones, especially when they must regularly turn to the capital markets to raise investment funds.

The public corporation is not suitable in industries where long-term growth is slow, where internally generated funds outstrip the opportunities to invest them profitably, or where downsizing is the most productive long-term strategy. In the tire industry, the shift to radials, which last three times longer than bias-ply tires, meant that manufacturers needed less capacity to meet world demand. Overcapacity inevitably forced a restructuring. The tenfold increase in oil prices from 1973 to 1981, which triggered worldwide conservation measures, forced oil producers into a similar retrenchment.

Industries under similar pressure today include steel, chemicals, brewing, tobacco, television and radio broadcasting, wood and paper products. In these and other cash-rich, low-growth or declining sectors, the pressures on management to waste cash flow through organizational slack or investments in unsound projects is often irresistible. It is in precisely these sectors that the publicly held corporation has declined most rapidly. Barring regulatory interference, the public corporation is also likely to decline in industries such as aerospace, automobiles and auto parts, banking, electric power generation, food processing, industrial and farm implements, and transportation equipment.

The public corporation is a social invention of vast historical importance. Its genius is rooted in its capacity to spread financial risk over the diversified portfolios of millions of individuals and institutions and to allow investors to customize risk to their unique circumstances and predilections. By diversifying risks that would otherwise be borne by owner-entrepreneurs and by facilitating the creation of a liquid market for exchanging risk, the public corporation lowered the cost of capital. These tradable claims on corporate ownership (common stock) also allowed risk to be borne by investors best able to bear it, without requiring them to manage the corporations they owned.

From the beginning, though, these risk-bearing benefits came at a cost. Tradable ownership claims create fundamental conflicts of interest between those who bear risk (the shareholders) and those who manage risk (the executives.) The genius of the new organizations is that they eliminate much of the loss created by conflicts between owners and managers, without eliminating the vital functions of risk diversification and liquidity once performed exclusively by the public equity markets. * * *

A central weakness and source of waste in the public corporation is the conflict between shareholders and managers over the payout of free cash flow—that is, cash flow in excess of that required to fund all investment projects with positive net present values when discounted at the relevant cost of capital. For a company to operate efficiently and maximize value, free cash flow must be distributed to shareholders rather than retained. But this happens infrequently; senior management has few incentives to distribute the funds, and there exist few mechanisms to compel distribution. * * *

Managers have incentives to retain cash in part because cash reserves increase their autonomy vis-à-vis the capital markets. Large cash balances (and independence from the capital markets) can serve a competitive purpose, but they often lead to waste and inefficiency. Consider a hypothetical world in which companies distribute excess cash to shareholders and then must convince the capital markets to supply funds as sound economic projects arise. Shareholders are at a great advantage in this world, where management's plans are subject to enhanced monitoring by the capital markets. Wall Street's analytical, due diligence, and pricing disciplines give shareholders more power to quash wasteful projects.

Managers also resist distributing cash to shareholders because retaining cash increases the size of the companies they run—and managers have many incentives to expand company size beyond that which maximizes shareholder wealth. Compensation is one of the most important incentives. Many studies document that increases in executive pay are strongly related to increases in corporate size rather than value.

The tendency of companies to reward middle managers through promotions rather than annual performance bonuses also creates a cultural bias toward growth. Organizations must grow in order to generate new positions to feed their promotion-based reward systems.

Finally corporate growth enhances the social prominence, public prestige, and political power of senior executives. Rare is the CEO who wants to be remembered as presiding over an enterprise that makes fewer products in fewer plants in fewer countries than when he or she took office—even when such a course increases productivity and adds hundreds of millions of dollars of shareholder value. The perquisites of the executive suite can be substantial, and they usually increase with company size.

The struggle over free cash flow is at the heart of the role of debt in the decline of the public corporation. Bank loans, mezzanine securities, and high-yield bonds have fueled the wave of takeovers, restructurings, and going-private transactions. The combined borrowings of all nonfinancial corporations in the United States approached $2 trillion in 1988, up from $835 billion in 1979. The interest charges on these borrowings represent more than 20% of corporate cash flows, high by historical standards.

This perceived "leveraging of corporate America" is perhaps the central source of anxiety among defenders of the public corporation and critics of the new organizational forms. But most critics miss three important points. First, the trebling of the market value of public-company equity over the last decade means that corporate borrowing had to increase to avoid a major *de*leveraging.

Second, debt creation *without retention of the proceeds of the issue* helps limit the waste of free cash flow by compelling managers to pay out funds they would otherwise retain. Debt is in effect a substitute for dividends—a mechanism to force managers to disgorge cash rather than spend it on empire-building projects with low or negative returns, bloated staffs, indulgent perquisites, and organizational inefficiencies. * * *

Borrowing allows for no such managerial discretion. Companies whose managers fail to make promised interest and principal payments can be declared insolvent and possibly hauled into bankruptcy court. In the imagery of G. Bennett Stewart and David M. Glassman, "Equity is soft, debt hard. Equity is forgiving, debt insistent. Equity is a pillow, debt a sword." Some may find it curious that a company's creditors wield far more power over managers than its public shareholders, but it is also undeniable.

Third, debt is a powerful agent for change. For all the deeply felt anxiety about excessive borrowing, "overleveraging" can be desirable and effective when it makes economic sense to break up a company, sell off parts of the business, and refocus its energies on a few core operations. Companies that assume so much debt they cannot meet the debt service payments out of operating cash flow force themselves to rethink their entire strategy and structure. Overleveraging creates the crisis atmosphere managers require to slash unsound investment programs, shrink overhead, and dispose of assets that are more valuable outside the company. The proceeds generated by these overdue restructurings can then be used to reduce debt to more sustainable levels, creating a leaner, more efficient and competitive organization. * * *

Critics of leverage also fail to appreciate that insolvency in and of itself is not always something to avoid—and that the costs of becoming insolvent are likely to be much smaller in the new world of high leverage than in the old world of equity-dominated balance sheets. * * *

How can insolvency be less costly in a world of high leverage? Consider an oversimplified example. Companies A and B are identical in every respect except for their financial structures. Each has a going-concern value of $100 million (the discounted value of its expected future cash flows) and a liquidation or salvage value of $10 million. Company A has an equity-dominated balance sheet with a debt ratio of 20%, common for large public companies. Highly leveraged Company B has a debt ratio of 85%, common for LBOs.

Now both companies experience business reversals. What happens? Company B will get in trouble with its creditors much sooner than Company A. After all, Company B's going-concern value doesn't have to shrink very much for it to be unable to meet its payments on $85 million of debt. But when it does run into trouble, its going-concern value will be nowhere near its liquidation value. If the going-concern value shrinks to $80 million, there remains $70 million of value to preserve by avoiding liquidation. So Company B's creditors have strong incentives to preserve the remaining value by quickly and efficiently reorganizing their claims outside the courtroom.

No such incentives operate on Company A. Its going-concern value can fall dramatically before creditors worry about their $20 million of debt. By the time creditors do intervene, Company A's going-concern value will have plummeted. And if Company A's value falls to under $20 million, it is much more likely than Company B to be worth less than its $10 million salvage value. Liquidation in this situation is the likely and rational outcome, with all its attendant conflicts,dislocations, and costs.

### Alfred Rappaport, *The Staying Power of the Public Corporation*
HARV. BUS. REV. 96 (Jan–Feb 1990).

Reports of the "eclipse of the public corporation" underestimate its institutional staying power and unique capacity for renewal. In his recent HBR article, Michael C. Jensen, a distinguished scholar of corporate finance and governance, argues for a revolution in the structure of ownership and control in the U.S. economy.

I share many of his criticisms of large public companies, especially their dismal performance over the past 20 years. But I disagree profoundly with his advocacy of the "LBO Association" as a superior organizational form. A program of radical and comprehensive reform of the public company—a program based on new approaches to how executives are paid, companies governed, business strategies evaluated, and excess resources distributed to shareholders—can inspire an unprecedented rejuvenation of this vital institution. Indeed, the renewal process is already under way.

Let's be clear: The publicly held corporation is worth saving. As an organizational form, it is inherently flexible and capable of renewal—properties that are crucial to stability and progress in a market-driven economy and that transitory organizations like LBOs cannot replicate. A company's institutional permanence is essential to customers expecting long-term satisfaction on service and product upgrades, suppliers making investment decisions about next-generation components, and employees whose planning horizons and commitments extend for decades. This is not to argue blindly in favor of the organizational status quo or against hardheaded and continual evaluations of business units. But public companies are more than collections of assets to be traded or taken private for one-time gain. They are vibrant, dynamic institutions—capable of long periods of underperformance, to be sure, but also fully capable of self-correction.

Moreover, the driving force behind efficiency and value creation in LBOs—taking on a mountain of debt that rewards shareholders and disciplines management—can impose real costs on business strategy and flexibility. As Jensen readily acknowledges, buyout companies do get in financial trouble more frequently than public companies do. He assures us that troubled private companies are reorganized quickly and efficiently, often under new management, and without entering formal court proceedings—an innovation he calls the "privatization of bankruptcy."

Jensen may be right that leverage in and of itself is not an invitation to Chapter 11 or liquidation. But the prospect of frequent voluntary reorganizations among buyout companies should not be dismissed lightly. In a world of fierce global competition, distinctions between reorganization and liquidation are not particularly meaningful. Either way, the weakened company has almost surely lost the competitive battle. Today's environment puts a premium on rapid response to change—the capacity to adapt quickly to new technologies in production or distribution, unanticipated shifts in consumer tastes, or major economic dislocations. That requires the financial flexibility of a public company not burdened with extraordinary debt.

Finally, and rather ironically, the very act of going private in the interest of shareholders abolishes the single best source of information about corporate value: the daily stock price. Managers of public companies receive continuous feedback on their performance from the collective judgment of objective investors who have a compelling interest to be accurate in their assessments of the future. Imperfect as it may be (and as unwilling as some public company managers may be to concede the point), there is no better barometer of a company's long-term prospects than how much investors are willing to pay for its shares. Incorporating the stock market's signals into strategic deliberations is an advantage enjoyed only in the public company structure.

### Letters to the Editor of the Harvard Business Review
HARV. BUS. REV. 182 et seq. (Nov–Dec 1989).

[*From William C. Norris, former Chairman and CEO of Control Data Corp.*:] An American business system driven by hostile takeovers and the threat of takeovers, featuring highly efficient allocation of assets among LBO companies, won't be competitive in the long run. Even if it were, I believe that it would not be acceptable to most Americans because it fails to provide the degree of social justice that we want. * * *

[*From Ira Millstein, private attorney and counsel to The Business Roundtable*:] We don't need to eclipse public corporations by relying on LBO Associations to achieve the management excellence and congruity of interests between management and owners sought by Mr. Jensen. Such excellence can be achieved by relying on the factors he writes off as lost causes—boards of directors and competitive product markets—both of which are alive and getting well. * * *

Jensen seeks managers who will operate their corporations as world-class competitors, slim and trim, and who are ready to pay out free cash flow or excess assets value to the shareholders * * *. Wall Street can do the job, he notes, that markets and boards have failed to do, by substituting a few owners, like institutions, who will work with astute deal makers, like the LBO boutiques. Together they can "actively" manage, using high-yield junk bonds for financing.

But what happens if there is no public market to reliquify the frozen investment? Are the institutions and the deal makers forever investors? If so, they may not be too astute. We have no significant evidence that most LBO Associations will not go public again. Only time will tell.

How many corporations can be managed by Wall Street, by truly astute managers and earnest institutions? Haven't the transaction costs begun to outweigh the asserted benefits? These problems and flaws in and of themselves make panacean enthusiasm for reliance on Jensen's model highly questionable. * * *

[*From Roberto C. Goizueta, Chairman and CEO, Coca–Cola Company*:] "Eclipse of the Public Corporation" is a good academic exercise and thought provoking, but that is all.

Corporate legitimacy * * * derives from the fact that in the context of our democratic and capitalistic system the publicly held company, its faults notwithstanding, *has proven to be* the most effective instrument for creating the products, services, jobs, and earnings by which the members of society can improve their lives. These corporations will remain large and successful only to the extent that they continue to serve the public well. * * *

Corporations' profitability cannot become secondary without endangering our national economic well-being. But this is not the same as requiring maximum profits and cash flows to the disregard of public-interest issues that government regulations do not mandate.

The current climate that engenders larger and larger LBOs runs contrary to everything I have said. When a corporation gets "mortgaged," the interests of lenders takes precedence over everything else, paying down debt become the number one goal. In such circumstances, it is nearly impossible to serve the public interest well, to be socially, as well as fiscally, responsible. Furthermore, the need to service the huge debt load virtually eliminates any margin for error in management's decision-making process. Risk taking and the entrepreneurial spirit, therefore, as well as investments for the long term, * * * get wiped out rather than enhanced.

[*Professor Jensen's response*:] * * * A shareholder-driven company doesn't ignore its stakeholders. What it does is to invest resources to benefit each of these constituencies to the point where the additional benefits to the company (measured in terms of real cash flows in the short and long term) exceed the additional cost. * * *

If the champions of stakeholders mean something else, if they argue for spending corporate funds on constituencies without any expectation of long-term benefit to the company, then they're advocating the waste of corporate resources. In some cases, the expenditures might generate social benefits that exceed their cost, even if the private benefits to the corporation are less than their cost. In these cases, the corporation would be subsidizing others, but the expenditure would be socially desirable.

There are, however, no forces in such a system to ensure that resources are spent where the social benefits exceed the costs. Resources are spent in ways that reflect the preferences of top management * * *. This means that to the extent we have CEOs who run their companies without regard for shareholders and efficiency, we are likely to cripple the economy. The solution to social problems emanating from the presence of externalities such as air or water pollution, poor education, crime or poverty is to establish proper rules of the game through the political and legal systems * * *. The advocates of stakeholder theory would have us depend on the beneficence of self-appointed corporate top management spending someone else's money—a solution that history reveals will not work.

––––––––

A recent appraisal of the results obtained by Kohlberg, Kravis, Roberts ("KKR"), whose takeover of RJR-Nabisco ("RJR") was the focus of the best selling book, BARBARIANS AT THE GATES, provides a different perspective on leverage and leveraged buyouts.

James Surowiecki, *The Taming of the Barbarians: How*
*a rapacious leveraged-buyout firm became a*
*positive force in the corporate economy*

http://www.slate.com/motleyfool/98–02–05/motleyfool.asp

KKR is a private partnership rather than a corporation. In essence, what the firm does is raise money from investors—primarily pension funds, closed-end mutual funds, and banks—and then put that money to use in the hope of getting those investors better returns than they could have found in the stock or bond markets. KKR does so by buying and selling companies, which is to say that the firm never makes a deal to buy a company without plans to sell it eventually or to take it public or both. * * *

The obvious conclusion [many] draw from this is that KKR must be hurting these companies' long-term prospects by trying to maximize their short-term value. If you're buying a company knowing that some-where down the line you'll want to sell it, the argument goes, you'll shortchange research and development, cut back on long-term invest-ment and sell off slow-performing parts of the business in an effort to make the company look better in the present. As a result, KKR gets richer while the country as a whole ends up poorer.

The problem with this analysis is that it assumes that KKR is smart while everyone else is dumb. * * * [I]f you think that markets are even relatively good at determining a fair price for assets, then KKR can't hurt its companies' long-term prospects without hurting itself.

What about the question of debt, though? In part, what KKR did when it purchased companies in the 1980s was replace those companies' dividend payments to shareholders with debt payments to creditors. In principle, one is no better or worse for a company's health than the other. But there is one big difference between dividends and debts, which is that if you fail to pay the first, your stock price get punished, but the company stays in business—while if you fail to pay the second, the company goes under. And there's no question that the LBO craze led to the destruction of a series of companies that took on more debt, often in the form of junk bonds, than they could handle. * * * The near-collapse of [the RJR] deal almost sent [KKR] out of business, in addition to making Kravis a poster boy for unrestrained greed.

In retrospect, though, two things seem clear. First, the RJR deal was atypical of KKR's broader strategy. Second, the whole fiasco was the best thing that could have happened to the firm. The death of LBO fervor, which in practical terms meant the death of banks' willingness to lend freely to almost anyone, forced KKR to refocus its business around the strongest deals possible. * * *

The results have been striking. Duracell, bought by KKR in 1988 for $350 million, was sold to Gillette for $3.7 billion in 1996. In that same year, it sold American Re, a reinsurer, to a German company for a profit of $1.8 billion, and Stop & Shop to a Dutch company for a profit of $1.4 billion. All these were companies that KKR had owned for an extended period of time during which all had expanded, improved productivity, and—in the case of Duracell—benefited from increases in R & D spending. * * *

One familiar interpretation of KKR's success is that it illustrates the disciplining power of debt. Becoming highly leveraged has forced managers to think seriously about costs, trim overhead, and improve productivity. * * * But the truth is that KKR's success illustrates a more mundane—but even more important—point, which is that managers of a company perform better when they're held accountable by the owners of that company. KKR has not succeeded because of the discipline of debt or even the promise of untold riches. Rather, it has succeeded because it brought a relentless focus on the bottom line to the corporations it has owned, and established standards its managers have had to live up to. For most of this century, U.S. corporations featured rubber-stamp boards of directors handpicked by management and uninterested in rocking the boat. What these boards have allowed managers to do is, simply, play with other people's money. And in some very basic sense, what KKR has done best is get managers to take other people's money seriously.

# Chapter 10

## THE REGULATION OF SECURITIES ISSUANCE

### A. INTRODUCTION: WHY SECURITIES REGULATION?

The purchasers of securities—from the largest banks, insurance companies, and other "institutional investors" to the most modest householder looking for a more profitable place than a savings account to invest a small nest egg—are, in a sense, consumers. In that respect the securities laws, state and federal, constitute an enormously complex and comprehensive consumer protection scheme—one of the earliest such schemes to find its way into the American legal system. Why, it might be asked, was it that laws designed to protect purchasers of securities came so long before any similar effort was made to protect purchasers of consumer products; and why do those laws remain, for the most part, more far-reaching and often better enforced?

There is, to be sure, more than one reason. But certainly the most important is to be found in the central role played by the market for securities in a capitalist economy. Since the early part of the century it has been the perception of lawmakers (a perception to which some critics now take exception) that without the kind of protection furnished investors by the securities laws, the capital markets—and ultimately the economy—would be far less healthy. This probably is the case, at least in part, because securities are different from most other kinds of property. Securities are intangible; they have value only insofar as they represent an interest in the entity that issued them. Consequently, a "consumer" cannot determine the value of a security as easily as he can the value of a house or a television set.

The federal securities laws reflect this fact. Throughout these statutes, "there is the recurrent theme * * * of disclosure, again disclosure, and still more disclosure." 1 Louis Loss and Joel Seligman, SECURITIES REGULATION 27 (3d ed. 1989). This surely is true of the Securities Act of 1933. Taking its cue from Justice Brandeis's famous dictum that "sunlight is the best disinfectant, electric light the best policeman," Louis D.

Brandeis, OTHER PEOPLE'S MONEY AND HOW THE BANKERS USE IT 92 (1914), Congress passed laws—the Securities Act of 1933 and the Securities Exchange Act of 1934—that depend largely on disclosure. They require issuers to file disclosure documents with the Securities and Exchange Commission before offering or selling securities and to update those documents periodically.

PROBLEM

PRECISION TOOLS—PART VIII

Michael and Jessica believe PTC should expand its product line substantially. Such action, they believe, will help PTC by achieve economies of scale that will allow it to compete more effectively with larger rivals.

Michael and Jessica estimate that it will take $3 million in new capital to finance the expansion they would like to undertake. Given PTC's heavily leveraged capital structure and modest profits, Michael and Jessica doubt that PTC will be able to borrow that $3 million at a reasonable rate of interest. Moreover, they are reluctant to incur the risks that would be involved in increasing PTC's debt load dramatically. Consequently, Michael and Jessica would like to investigate whether PTC can raise the capital it needs by selling either convertible preferred stock or low-interest notes convertible into stock.

Michael and Jessica have asked you to advise them of their securities law obligations and options if PTC decides to offer such stock or notes.

## B.   FEDERAL REGULATION OF SECURITIES OFFERINGS

### 1.   OVERVIEW

*Securities and Exchange Commission,* THE WORK OF THE SEC

7–10 (1997).

#### Securities Act of 1933

This "truth in securities" law has two basic objectives:

- to require that investors are provided with material information concerning securities offered for public sale; and

- to prevent misrepresentation, deceit, and other fraud in the sale of securities.

A primary means of accomplishing these objectives is disclosure of financial information by registering offers and sales of securities. Most offerings of debt and equity securities issued by corporations, limited partnerships, trusts, and other issuers must be registered. Federal and most other domestic government debt securities are exempt. Certain transactions qualify for exemptions from registration provisions; these exemptions are discussed below.

### Purpose of Registration

Registration is intended to provide adequate and accurate disclosure of material facts concerning the company and the securities it proposes to sell. Thus, investors may make a realistic appraisal of the merits of the securities and then exercise informed judgment in determining whether to purchase them.

Registration requires, but does not guarantee, the accuracy of the facts represented in the registration statement and prospectus. However, the law does prohibit false and misleading statements under penalty of fine, imprisonment, or both. Investors who purchase securities and suffer losses have important recovery rights under the law if they can prove that there was incomplete or inaccurate disclosure of material facts in the registration statement or prospectus. If such misstatements are proven, the following could be liable: the issuing company, its responsible directors and officers, the underwriters, controlling interests, the sellers of the securities, and others. These rights must be asserted in an appropriate federal or state court (not before the Commission, which has no power to award damages).

Registration of securities does not preclude the sale of stock in risky, poorly managed, or unprofitable companies. In fact, it is unlawful to represent that the Commission approves or disapproves of securities on their merits. The only standard which must be met when registering securities is adequate and accurate disclosure of required material facts concerning the company and the securities it proposes to sell. The fairness of the terms, the issuing company's prospects for successful operation, and other factors affecting the merits of investing in the securities (whether price, promoters' or underwriters' profits, or otherwise) have no bearing on the question of whether or not securities may be registered.

### The Registration Process

The Commission has registration forms for different types of companies. These provide essential facts while minimizing the burden and expense of complying with the law. In general, registration forms call for

- a description of the company's properties and business;
- a description of the security to be offered for sale and its relationship to the company's other capital securities;
- information about the management of the company; and
- financial statements certified by independent public accountants.

Registration statements and prospectuses on securities become public immediately after filing with the SEC. However, it is unlawful to sell the securities until the effective date. The act provides that most registration statements shall become effective on the 20th day after filing (or on the 20th day after filing the last amendment). At its discretion, the Commission may advance the effective date if it benefits the interests of investors and the public, the adequacy of publicly available information, and the ease with which the facts about the new offering can be disseminated and understood.

Registration statements are subject to examination for compliance with disclosure requirements. If a statement appears to be incomplete or inaccurate, the company usually is informed by letter and given an opportunity to file correcting or clarifying amendments. * * *

### Exemptions From Registration

In general, registration requirements apply to securities of both U.S. and foreign companies or governments sold in U.S. securities markets. There are, however, certain exemptions. Among these are:

- private offerings to a limited number of persons or institutions who have access to the kind of information that registration would disclose and who do not plan to redistribute the securities;

- offerings restricted to residents of the state in which the issuing company is organized and doing business;

- securities of municipal, state, federal, and other domestic governmental instrumentalities as well as charitable institutions and banks;

- "small issues" not exceeding certain specified amounts made in compliance with SEC regulations; and

- offerings of "small business investment companies" made in accordance with SEC regulations.

Whether or not the securities are registered, antifraud provisions apply to all sales of securities involving interstate commerce or the mails.

The "small issue" exemption was adopted by Congress primarily as an aid to small business. The law provides that offerings of certain sizes may be exempt from full registration, subject to provisions designed to protect investors. The Commission's Regulation A permits certain U.S. and Canadian companies to make exempt offerings. A similar regulation is available for offerings under $5 million by small business investment companies licensed by the Small Business Administration. Regulation D permits certain companies to make exempt offerings under $1 million with only minimal federal restrictions; more extensive disclosure requirements and other conditions apply for offerings exceeding that amount.

Exemptions are available when certain specified conditions are met. These conditions include use of an offering circular containing certain basic information in the sale of the securities. * * *

## 2.   THE REGISTRATION PROCESS

The centerpiece of the 1933 Act is Section 5. That section, to oversimplify a bit, makes it unlawful for any person to offer any security unless a registration statement regarding that security has been filed with the S.E.C. Section 5 also prohibits the sale of the security unless the registration statement is in effect. Finally, Section 5 requires that a "statutory prospectus" (in the jargon of the profession), which includes the most important information in the registration statement, be delivered to the buyer prior to or at the same time as the security is sold. Schedule A to the 1933 Act, as amplified and interpreted by SEC regulations, sets forth the information that an issuer must include in the registration statement.

Carl W. Schneider, Joseph M. Manko & Robert S. Kant, *Going Public—Practice, Procedures and Consequences*

27 Vill.L.Rev. 1, 10–17 (1981).

The registration statement is the disclosure document required to be filed with the SEC in connection with a registered offering. It consists physically of two principal parts. Part I of the registration statement is the prospectus, which is the only part that normally goes to the public offerees of the securities. It is the legal offering document. Part II of the registration statement contains supplemental information which is available for public inspection at the office of the SEC.

The registration forms contain a series of detailed "items" and instructions, in response to which disclosures must be made. But they are not forms in the sense that they have blanks to be completed like a tax return. Traditionally, the prospectus describes the company's business and responds to all the disclosures required in narrative rather than item-and-answer form. It is prepared as a brochure describing the company and the securities to be offered. The usual prospectus is a fairly stylized document, and there is a customary sequence for organizing the material.

* * *

In the typical first public offering, the items to which it is most difficult to respond, and which require the most creative effort in preparation, deal with the description of the company's business, properties, material transactions with insiders, and use of proceeds. Other matters required to be disclosed in the prospectus deal with the details of the underwriting, the plan for distributing the securities, capitalization, pending legal proceedings, competition, description of securities being registered, identification of directors and officers and their remuneration, options to purchase securities, and principal holders of securities. There are also detailed requirements concerning financial statements and financial information concerning the company's business segments.

The cost of a public offering usually is substantial. It includes fees paid to the attorneys for the issuer, who usually draft most of the registration statement, fees paid to accountants, fees paid to the underwriter, and fees paid to the underwriter's attorneys. In addition, the issuer's senior managers usually are heavily involved in, and devote a considerable amount of time to, preparation of the registration statement.

The Draconian liability provisions of the 1933 Act motivate the issuer, its directors and senior executives, and the underwriter to exercise a high degree of care in preparing the registration statement. The most significant of these provisions is Section 11, which allows any person who purchased a security covered by a registration statement to sue the issuer, all other persons who signed the registration statement, the issuer's directors, the underwriters, and all accountants, engineers, appraisers and other experts named as having prepared or certified some portion of the registration statement. If a purchaser can prove that there was a material misstatement or omission in the registration statement and that she lost money on the purchase, she can recover her loss from the issuer. She also can recover from the other defendants unless they succeed in demonstrating that they exercised "due diligence" in the preparation of the registration statement.* This means that all those who might be liable under Section 11 must show that they reviewed the registration statement and conducted a reasonable investigation to satisfy themselves that was accurate. *See In re Software Toolworks Inc.*, 50 F.3d 615 (9th Cir.1994); *Escott v. BarChris Const. Corp.*, 283 F.Supp. 643 (S.D.N.Y.1968).

Section 12 of the 1933 Act complements Section 11. Section 12(a)(1) provides that any person who purchases a security that should have been registered and was not may rescind the transaction at any time within one year of the purchase. This is true regardless of whether the buyer knew that the security should have been registered. Section 12(a)(2) provides that any person who sells a security by means of a prospectus that is materially false or misleading may be liable unless he is able to prove that he did not know, and in the exercise of reasonable care could not have known, that the prospectus was materially false or misleading.

To avoid the costs associated with the registration process, firms often attempt to raise capital without going through that process. Some do this by attempting to structure the transactions in which they raise

* With respect to those portions of the statement prepared or certified by experts (in the jargon of the profession the "expertised" portions), such as the financial statements, the non-expert defendants are not liable if they can show that they had no reasonable ground to believe and did not believe that the portion in question was materially false. Section 11(b)(3)(C). With respect to the "unexpertised" portions of the registration statement (or the liability of the expert for the portion he "expertised"), a defendant must show that he "had, after reasonable investigation, reasonable ground to believe and did believe" that there was no material misstatement or omission. Section 11(b)(3)(A) and (B).

capital so that they do not involve a "security." Others attempt to sell securities in transactions that are exempt from registration.

## 3.  DEFINITION OF A SECURITY

Section 2(a)(1) of the 1933 Act provides

When used in this title, unless the context otherwise requires—

(1) The term "security" means any note, stock, treasury stock, bond debenture, evidence of indebtedness, certificate of interest or participation in any profit-sharing agreement, collateral-trust certificate, preorganization certificate or subscription, transferable share, investment contract, * * * or, in general, any interest or instrument commonly known as a "security" * * *.

Numerous promoters have attempted to raise capital (and, at times, to exploit unsophisticated investors) by selling interests in property as part of arrangements that the promoters claimed did not involve a "security." In *SEC v. W.J. Howey Co.*, 328 U.S. 293, 301, 66 S.Ct. 1100, 1104, 90 L.Ed. 1244 (1946), the Supreme Court held that interests in orange groves that the Howey Company sold to investors were "investment contracts"—and thus "securities"—because they involved "[1] an investment of money [2] in a common enterprise [3] with profits to come solely from the efforts of others." Subsequent Supreme Court and lower federal court decisions have refined the various parts of this definition. Most significantly, some cases held that interests in some schemes were investment contracts even though profits depended primarily, but not "solely," on the efforts of persons other than the investors. Among these have been cases involving pyramid schemes, *see SEC v. Glenn W. Turner Enterprises, Inc.*, 474 F.2d 476 (9th Cir.1973), *cert. denied* 414 U.S. 821, 94 S.Ct. 117, 38 L.Ed.2d 53 (1973), and programs in which investors agreed to buy, raise and resell chinchillas, *see Miller v. Central Chinchilla Group, Inc.*, 494 F.2d 414 (8th Cir.1974), and earthworms, *see Smith v. Gross*, 604 F.2d 639 (9th Cir.1979).

## REVES v. ERNST & YOUNG

494 U.S. 56, 110 S.Ct. 945, 108 L.Ed.2d 47 (1990).

JUSTICE MARSHALL delivered the opinion of the Court.

This case presents the question whether certain demand notes issued by the Farmers Cooperative of Arkansas and Oklahoma (Co–Op) are "securities" within the meaning of § 3(a)(10) of the Securities Exchange Act of 1934. We conclude that they are.

I

The Co–Op is an agricultural cooperative that, at the time relevant here, had approximately 23,000 members. In order to raise money to support its general business operations, the Co–Op sold promissory notes payable on demand by the holder. Although the notes were uncollateralized and uninsured, they paid a variable rate of interest that was adjusted monthly to keep it higher than the rate paid by local financial institutions. The Co–Op offered the notes to both members and non-members, marketing the scheme as an "Investment Program." Advertisements for the notes, which appeared in each Co-Op newsletter, read in part: "YOUR CO–OP has more than $11,000,000 in assets to stand behind your investments. The Investment is not Federal [sic ] insured but it is ... Safe ... Secure ... and available when you need it." App. 5 (ellipses in original). Despite these assurances, the Co–Op filed for bankruptcy in 1984. At the time of the filing, over 1,600 people held notes worth a total of $10 million.

After the Co–Op filed for bankruptcy, petitioners, a class of holders of the notes, filed suit against Arthur Young & Co., the firm that had audited the Co-Op's financial statements (and the predecessor to respondent Ernst & Young). Petitioners alleged, *inter alia*, that Arthur Young had intentionally failed to follow generally accepted accounting principles in its audit, specifically with respect to the valuation of one of the Co–Op's major assets, a gasohol plant. Petitioners claimed that Arthur Young violated these principles in an effort to inflate the assets and net worth of the Co–Op. Petitioners maintained that, had Arthur Young properly treated the plant in its audits, they would not have purchased demand notes because the Co–Op's insolvency would have been apparent. On the basis of these allegations, petitioners claimed that Arthur Young had violated the antifraud provisions of the 1934 Act as well as Arkansas' securities laws.

Petitioners prevailed at trial on both their federal and state claims, receiving a $6.1 million judgment. Arthur Young appealed, claiming that the demand notes were not "securities" under either the 1934 Act or Arkansas law, and that the statutes' antifraud provisions therefore did not apply. A panel of the Eighth Circuit, agreeing with Arthur Young on both the state and federal issues, reversed. We granted certiorari to address the federal issue and now reverse the judgment of the Court of Appeals.

## II

### A

This case requires us to decide whether the note issued by the Co–Op is a "security" within the meaning [of § 3(a)(10)] of the 1934 Act. * * *

The fundamental purpose undergirding the Securities Acts is "to eliminate serious abuses in a largely unregulated securities market." *United Housing Foundation, Inc. v. Forman*, 421 U.S. 837 849 (1975). In defining the scope of the market that it wished to regulate, Congress painted with a broad brush. It recognized the virtually limitless scope of human ingenuity, especially in the creation of "countless and variable schemes devised by those who seek the use of the money of others on the promise of profits," *SEC v. W.J. Howey Co.*, 328 U.S. 293, 299 (1946), and determined that the best way to achieve its goal of protecting investors was "to define 'the term' security 'in sufficiently broad and general terms so as to include within that definition the many types of instruments that in our commercial world fall within the ordinary concept of a security.' " *Forman, supra,* 421 U.S. at 847–848 (quoting H.R.Rep. No. 85, 73d Cong., 1st Sess., 11 (1933)). Congress therefore did not attempt precisely to cabin the scope of the Securities Acts.[1] Rather, it enacted a definition of "security" sufficiently broad to encompass virtually any instrument that might be sold as an investment.

Congress did not, however, "intend to provide a broad federal remedy for all fraud." *Marine Bank v. Weaver,* 455 U.S. 551, 556 (1982). Accordingly, "[t]he task has fallen to the Securities and Exchange Commission (SEC), the body charged with administering the Securities Acts, and ultimately to the federal courts to decide which of the myriad financial transactions in our society come within the coverage of these statutes." *Forman, supra,* 421 U.S. at 848. In discharging our duty, we are not bound by legal formalisms, but instead take account of the economics of the transaction under investigation. * * *

A commitment to an examination of the economic realities of a transaction does not necessarily entail a case-by-case analysis of every instrument, however. Some instruments are obviously within the class Congress intended to regulate because they are by their nature investments. In *Landreth Timber Co. v. Landreth,* 471 U.S. 681 (1985), we held that an instrument bearing the name "stock" that, among other things, is negotiable, offers the possibility of capital appreciation, and carries the right to dividends contingent on the profits of a business enterprise is plainly within the class of instruments Congress intended the securities laws to cover. *Landreth Timber* does not signify a lack of concern with economic reality; rather, it signals a recognition that stock is, as a practical matter, always an investment if it has the economic characteristics traditionally associated with stock. Even if sparse exceptions to this generalization can be found, the public perception of common stock as the paradigm of a security suggests that stock, in whatever context it is sold, should be treated as within the ambit of the Acts. *Id.* at 687, 693.

We made clear in *Landreth Timber* that stock was a special case, explicitly limiting our holding to that sort of instrument. *Id.* at 694. Although we refused finally to rule out a similar per se rule for notes, we intimated that such a rule would be unjustified. Unlike "stock," we said, " 'note' may now be viewed as a relatively broad term that encompasses instruments with widely varying characteristics, depending on whether issued in a consumer context, as commercial paper, or in some other investment context." *Ibid.* While common stock is the quintessence of a security and investors therefore justifiably assume that a sale of stock is covered by the Securities Acts, the same simply cannot be said of notes, which are used in a variety of settings, not all of which involve invest-

---

**1.** We have consistently held that "[t]he definition of a security in § 3(a)(10) of the 1934 Act, ... is virtually identical [to the definition in the Securities Act of 1933] and, for present purposes, the coverage of the two Acts may be considered the same." *United Housing Foundation, Inc. v. Forman,* 421 U.S. 837, 847, n. 12 (1975) (citations omitted). We reaffirm that principle here.

ments. Thus, the phrase "any note" should not be interpreted to mean literally "any note," but must be understood against the backdrop of what Congress was attempting to accomplish in enacting the Securities Acts.

Because the *Landreth Timber* formula cannot sensibly be applied to notes, some other principle must be developed to define the term "note." A majority of the Courts of Appeals that have considered the issue have adopted, in varying forms, "investment versus commercial" approaches that distinguish, on the basis of all of the circumstances surrounding the transactions, notes issued in an investment context (which are "securities") from notes issued in a commercial or consumer context (which are not).

The Second Circuit's "family resemblance" approach begins with a presumption that any note with a term of more than nine months is a "security." *See, e.g., Exchange Nat. Bank of Chicago v. Touche Ross & Co.*, 544 F.2d 1126, 1137 (C.A.2 1976). Recognizing that not all notes are securities, however, the Second Circuit has also devised a list of notes that it has decided are obviously not securities. Accordingly, the "family resemblance" test permits an issuer to rebut the presumption that a note is a security if it can show that the note in question "bear[s] a strong family resemblance" to an item on the judicially crafted list of exceptions, *id.* at 1137–1138, or convinces the court to add a new instrument to the list.

In contrast, the Eighth and District of Columbia Circuits apply the test we created in *SEC v. W.J. Howey Co.*, 328 U.S. 293 (1946), to determine whether an instrument is an "investment contract" to the determination whether an instrument is a "note." * * *

We reject the approaches of those courts that have applied the *Howey* test to notes; *Howey* provides a mechanism for determining whether an instrument is an "investment contract." The demand notes here may well not be "investment contracts," but that does not mean they are not "notes." To hold that a "note" is not a "security" unless it meets a test designed for an entirely different variety of instrument "would make the Acts' enumeration of many types of instruments superfluous," *Landreth Timber*, 471 U.S. at 692, and would be inconsistent with Congress' intent to regulate the entire body of instruments sold as investments.

The other two contenders—the "family resemblance" and "investment versus commercial" tests—are really two ways of formulating the same general approach. Because we think the "family resemblance" test provides a more promising framework for analysis, however, we adopt it. The test begins with the language of the statute; because the Securities Acts define "security" to include "any note," we begin with a presumption that every note is a security. We nonetheless recognize that this presumption cannot be irrebuttable. As we have said, Congress was concerned with regulating the investment market, not with creating a general federal cause of action for fraud. In an attempt to give more content to that dividing line, the Second Circuit has identified a list of instruments commonly denominated "notes" that nonetheless fall without the "security" category. *See Exchange Nat. Bank, supra*, at 1138 (types of notes that are not "securities" include "the note delivered in consumer financing, the note secured by a mortgage on a home, the short-term note secured by a lien on a small business or some of its assets, the note evidencing a 'character' loan to a bank customer, short-term notes secured by an assignment of accounts receivable, or a note which simply formalizes an open-account debt incurred in the ordinary course of business (particularly if, as in the case of the customer of a broker, it is collateralized)"); *Chemical Bank*, [726 F.2d at] 939 (adding to list "notes evidencing loans by commercial banks for current operations").

We agree that the items identified by the Second Circuit are not properly viewed as "securities." More guidance, though, is needed. It is impossible to make any meaningful inquiry into whether an instrument bears a "resemblance" to one of the instruments identified by the Second Circuit without specifying what it is about those instruments that makes them non-"securities." * * *

An examination of the list itself makes clear what those standards should be. In creating its list, the Second Circuit was applying the same factors that this Court has held apply in deciding whether a transaction involves a "security." First, we examine the transaction to assess the motivations that would prompt a reasonable seller and buyer to enter into it. If the seller's purpose is to raise money for the general use of a business enterprise or to finance substantial investments and the buyer is interested primarily in the profit the note is expected to generate, the instrument is likely to be a "security." If the note is exchanged to facilitate the purchase and sale of a minor asset or consumer good, to correct for the seller's cash-flow difficulties, or to advance some other commercial or consumer purpose, on the other hand, the note is less sensibly described as a "security." Second, we examine the "plan of distribution" of the instrument, *SEC v. C.M. Joiner Leasing Corp.*, 320 U.S. 344, 353 (1943), to determine whether it is an instrument in which there is "common trading for speculation or investment," *id.* at 351. Third, we examine the reasonable expectations of the investing public: The Court will consider instruments to be "securities" on the basis of such public expectations, even where an economic analysis of the circumstances of the particular transaction might suggest that the instruments are not "securities" as used in that transaction. Finally, we examine whether some factor such as the existence of another regulatory scheme significantly reduces the risk of the instrument, thereby rendering application of the Securities Acts unnecessary. *See, e.g., Marine Bank*, 455 U.S. at 557–559, and n. 7.

We conclude, then, that in determining whether an instrument denominated a "note" is a "security," courts are to apply the version of the "family resemblance" test that we have articulated here: A note is presumed to be a "security," and that presumption may be rebutted only by a showing that the note bears a strong resemblance (in terms of the four factors we have identified) to one of the enumerated categories of instrument. If an instrument is not sufficiently similar to an item on the list, the decision whether another category should be added is to be made by examining the same factors.

B

Applying the family resemblance approach to this case, we have little difficulty in concluding that the notes at issue here are "securities." Ernst & Young admits that "a demand note does not closely resemble any of the Second Circuit's family resemblance examples." Brief for Respondent 43. Nor does an examination of the four factors we have identified as being relevant to our inquiry suggest that the demand notes here are not "securities" despite their lack of similarity to any of the enumerated categories. The Co–Op sold the notes in an effort to raise capital for its general business operations, and purchasers bought them in order to earn a profit in the form of interest. Indeed, one of the primary inducements offered purchasers was an interest rate constantly revised to keep it slightly above the rate paid by local banks and savings and loans. From both sides, then, the transaction is most naturally conceived as an investment in a business enterprise rather than as a purely commercial or consumer transaction.

As to the plan of distribution, the Co–Op offered the notes over an extended period to its 23,000 members, as well as to nonmembers, and more than 1,600 people held notes when the Co–Op filed for bankruptcy. To be sure, the notes were not traded on an exchange. They were, however, offered and sold to a broad segment of the public, and that is all we have held to be necessary to establish the requisite "common trading" in an instrument.

The third factor—the public's reasonable perceptions—also supports a finding that the notes in this case are "securities." We have consistently identified the fundamental essence of a "security" to be its character as an "investment." The advertisements for the notes here characterized them as "investments" and there were no countervailing factors that would have led a reasonable person to question this characterization. In these circumstances, it would be reasonable for a prospective purchaser to take the Co–Op at its word.

Finally, we find no risk-reducing factor to suggest that these instruments are not in fact securities. The notes are uncollateralized and uninsured. * * *

The court below found that "[t]he demand nature of the notes is very uncharacteristic of a security," 856 F.2d, at 54, on the theory that the virtually instant liquidity associated with demand notes is inconsistent with the risk ordinarily associated with "securities." This argument is unpersuasive. Common stock traded on a national exchange is the paradigm of a security, and it is as readily convertible into cash as is a demand note. The same is true of publicly traded corporate bonds, debentures, and any number of other instruments that are plainly within the purview of the Acts. The demand feature of a note does permit a holder to eliminate risk quickly by making a demand, but just as with publicly traded stock, the liquidity of the instrument does not eliminate risk altogether. Indeed, publicly traded stock is even more readily liquid than are demand notes, in that a demand only eliminates risk when, and if, payment is made, whereas the sale of a share of stock through a national exchange and the receipt of the proceeds usually occur simultaneously.

We therefore hold that the notes at issue here are within the term "note" in § 3(a)(10). * * *

## 4.  EXEMPTIONS FROM REGISTRATION

Sections 3 and 4 of the 1933 Act exempt certain *securities* and *transactions* from the registration requirements of § 5. The broadest of the exemptions is found in Section 4(1), which exempts "[t]ransactions by any person other than the issuer, underwriter, or dealer." This provision eliminates from the coverage of the 1933 Act most transactions in which investors trade previously issued securities. It does not relate to the initial offer or sale of securities by a corporation such as PTC.

### a.  Intrastate Offering Exemption

§ 3(a)(11), the "intrastate offering" exemption, exempts from registration any security that is part of an issue *offered and sold* exclusively to "persons resident within" one state by a corporation "incorporated by and doing business within" that state. Although cast as a securities exemption, it more closely resembles a transaction exemption.

For many years, the lack of a clear definition of many key terms in § 3(a)(11) gave pause to careful lawyers. For example, while § 3(a)(11) requires the issuer to be "doing business within" the state in which the offer is made, it gives no indication of how much business is required. Similarly, the SEC took the position that a person who has her principal residence in a state does not qualify as a "resident" if she is domiciled elsewhere. *See* Securities Act Rel. 33–4434 (Dec. 6, 1961). This uncertainty was significant because if an issuer sold any portion of an issue in a manner inconsistent with the requirements of § 3(a)(11), it could be held liable for recision, under 12(1), to every person who purchased securities any of the securities in that issue.

The SEC eliminated much of this uncertainty when it adopted Rule 147, which simplifies compliance with § 3(a)(11). As a consequence, the utility of the intrastate offering exemption now depends largely on local conditions. It obviously is riskier to attempt an intrastate offering in a metropolitan area that encompasses more than one state. Moreover, in some states the failure to register an offering under the 1933 Act increases the burden of complying with the local blue sky law, with the result that there is little or no net saving in time and expense.

### b. Private Offering Exemption

Section 4(2), the so-called "private offering exemption," which exempts "transactions by an issuer not involving any public offering," is much more important to small corporations. Without it, the smallest closely-held corporation could be required to go through the costly and time consuming process of filing a registration statement when it first issued stock. For larger offerings, especially when securities are sold to investors who are not active participants in the business, whether this exemption is available often is not always clear. As the following case illustrates, defining the limits of the private offering exemption has proved a difficult task for the courts and the SEC.

## DORAN v. PETROLEUM MANAGEMENT CORP.

545 F.2d 893 (5th Cir.1977).

GOLDBERG, CIRCUIT JUDGE:

[Plaintiff Doran purchased a "special participant" interest in a limited partnership, formed to drill for oil. He agreed to contribute $25,000 in cash to the partnership and to assume a promissory note, payable by the organizers of the partnership, for about $114,000. His share of the production payments from the partnership's wells was to be used to make the payments on the note.

Due to difficulties with the Wyoming Oil and Gas Conservation Commission, the production payments declined and were not sufficient to service the note. When Doran defaulted on his obligation to pay the note, the holder obtained a state court judgment against him. Doran then sued seeking damages for breach of contract, recision of his purchase of the partnership interest, and a declaration that the organizers of the partnership were liable for the state court judgment. The district court concluded that the sale of the partnership interest to Doran qualified as a private offering and entered a judgment in favor of defendants.]

### II. THE PRIVATE OFFERING EXEMPTION

No registration statement was filed with any federal or state regulatory body in connection with the defendants' offering of securities.[4] Along with two other factors that we may take as established—that the defendants sold or offered to sell these securities, and that the defendants used interstate transportation or communication in connection with the sale or offer of sale—the plaintiff thus states a prima facie case for a violation of the federal securities laws.

The defendants do not contest the existence of the elements of plaintiff's prima facie case but raise an affirmative defense that the relevant transactions came within the exemption from registration found

---

4. The district court correctly concluded that the limited partnership interest was a "security" as that term is defined by the Securities Act of 1933 and the Securities and Exchange Act of 1934.

in § 4(2). Specifically, they contend that the offering of securities was not a public offering. The defendants, who of course bear the burden of proving this affirmative defense, must therefore show that the offering was private.

This court has in the past identified four factors relevant to whether an offering qualifies for the exemption. * * * The relevant factors include the number of offerees and their relationship to each other and the issuer, the number of units offered, the size of the offering, and the manner of the offering. Consideration of these factors need not exhaust the inquiry, nor is one factor's weighing heavily in favor of the private status of the offering sufficient to ensure the availability of the exemption. Rather, these factors serve as guideposts to the court in attempting to determine whether subjecting the offering to registration requirements would further the purposes of the 1933 Act.

The term, "private offering," is not defined in the Securities Act of 1933. The scope of the § 4(2) private offering exemption must therefore be determined by reference to the legislative purposes of the Act. In *SEC v. Ralston Purina Co.*, [346 U.S. 119 (1953),] the SEC had sought to enjoin a corporation's offer of unregistered stock to its employees, and the Court grappled with the corporation's defense that the offering came within the private placement exemption. The Court began by looking to the statutory purpose:

> Since exempt transactions are those as to which "there is no practical need for ... (the bill's) application," the applicability of (§ 4(2)) should turn on whether the particular class of persons affected need the protection of the Act. An offering to those who are shown to be able to fend for themselves is a transaction "not involving any public offering."

346 U.S. at 124. According to the Court, the purpose of the Act was "to protect investors by promoting full disclosure of information thought necessary to informed investment decisions." *Id.* at 124. It therefore followed that "the exemption question turns on the knowledge of the offerees." *Id.* at 126–27. That formulation remains the touchstone of the inquiry into the scope of the private offering exemption. It is most nearly reflected in the first of the four factors: the number of offerees and their relationship to each other and to the issuer.

In the case at bar, the defendants may have demonstrated the presence of the latter three factors. A small number of units offered, relatively modest financial stakes, and an offering characterized by personal contact between the issuer and offerees free of public advertising or intermediaries such as investment bankers or securities exchanges—these aspects of the instant transaction aid the defendants' search for a § 4(2) exemption.

Nevertheless, with respect to the first, most critical, and conceptually most problematic factor, the record does not permit us to agree that the defendants have proved that they are entitled to the limited sanctuary afforded by § 4(2). We must examine more closely the importance of demonstrating both the number of offerees and their relationship to the issuer in order to see why the defendants have not yet gained the § 4(2) exemption.

### A.  The Number of Offerees

Establishing the number of persons involved in an offering is important both in order to ascertain the magnitude of the offering and in order to determine the characteristics and knowledge of the persons thus identified.

The number of offerees, not the number of purchasers, is the relevant figure in considering the number of persons involved in an offering. A private placement claimant's failure to adduce any evidence regarding the number of offerees will be fatal to the claim. The number of offerees is not itself a decisive factor in determining the availability of the private offering exemption. Just as an offering to few may be public, so an offering to many may be private. Nevertheless, "the more offerees, the more likelihood that the offering is public." *Hill York Corp. v. American International Franchises, Inc.*, 448 F.2d 680, 688 (5th Cir. 1971). In the case at bar, the record indicates that eight investors were offered limited partnership shares in the drilling program a total that would be entirely consistent with a finding that the offering was private.

[The court rejected defendants' claim that Doran was the only offeree because he purchased a partnership interest different from that purchased by the other offerees.]

In considering the number of offerees solely as indicative of the magnitude or scope of an offering, the difference between one and eight offerees is relatively unimportant. Rejecting the argument that Doran was the sole offeree is significant, however, because it means that in considering the need of the offerees for the protection that registration would have afforded we must look beyond Doran's interests to those of all his fellow offerees. Even the offeree-plaintiff's 20–20 vision with respect to the facts underlying the security would not save the exemption if any one of his fellow offerees was in a blind.

### B.  The Offerees' Relationship to the Issuer

Since *SEC v. Ralston*, courts have sought to determine the need of offerees for the protections afforded by registration by focusing on the relationship between offerees and issuer and more particularly on the information available to the offerees by virtue of that relationship. Once the offerees have been identified, it is possible to investigate their relationship to the issuer.

\* \* \*

### 1.  The role of investment sophistication

The lower court's finding that Doran was a sophisticated investor is amply supported by the record, as is the sophistication of the other offerees. Doran holds a petroleum engineering degree from Texas A & M

University. His net worth is in excess of $1,000,000. His holdings of approximately twenty-six oil and gas properties are valued at $850,000.

Nevertheless, evidence of a high degree of business or legal sophistication on the part of all offerees does not suffice to bring the offering within the private placement exemption. We clearly established that proposition in *Hill York Corp. v. American International Franchises, Inc.*, 448 F.2d at 690. We reasoned that "if the plaintiffs did not possess the information requisite for a registration statement, they could not bring their sophisticated knowledge of business affairs to bear in deciding whether or not to invest...." Sophistication is not a substitute for access to the information that registration would disclose. As we said in *Hill York*, although the evidence of the offerees' expertise "is certainly favorable to the defendants, the level of sophistication will not carry the point. In this context, the relationship between the promoters and the purchasers and the 'access to the kind of information which registration would disclose' become highly relevant factors." 448 F.2d at 690.

In short, there must be sufficient basis of accurate information upon which the sophisticated investor may exercise his skills. Just as a scientist cannot be without his specimens, so the shrewdest investor's acuity will be blunted without specifications about the issuer. For an investor to be invested with exemptive status he must have the required data for judgment.

### 2.  *The requirement of available information*

The interplay between two factors, the relationship between offerees and issuer and the offerees' access to information that registration would disclose, has been a matter of some conceptual and terminological difficulty. For purposes of this discussion, we shall adopt the following conventions: We shall refer to offerees who have not been furnished registration information directly, but who are in a position relative to the issuer to obtain the information registration would provide, as having "access" to such information. By a position of access we mean a relationship based on factors such as employment, family, or economic bargaining power that enables the offeree effectively to obtain such information. When offerees, regardless of whether they occupy a position of access, have been furnished with the information a registration statement would provide, we shall say merely that such information has been disclosed. When the offerees have access to or there has been disclosure of the information registration would provide, we shall say that such information was available.

The requirement that all offerees have available the information registration would provide has been firmly established by this court as a necessary condition of gaining the private offering exemption. * * *

More specifically, we shall require on remand that the defendants demonstrate that all offerees, whatever their expertise, had available the information a registration statement would have afforded a prospective investor in a public offering. Such a showing is not independently sufficient to establish that the offering qualified for the private placement exemption, but it is necessary to gain the exemption and is to be weighed along with the sophistication and number of the offerees, the number of units offered, and the size and manner of the offering. Because in this case these latter factors weigh heavily in favor of the private offering exemption, satisfaction of the necessary condition regarding the availability of relevant information to the offerees would compel the conclusion that this offering fell within the exemption.

\* \* \*

### IV. CONCLUSION

An examination of the record and the district court's opinion in this case leaves unanswered the central question in all cases that turn on the availability of the § 4(2) exemption. Did the offerees know or have a realistic opportunity to learn facts essential to an investment judgment? We remand so that the trial court can answer that question.

This opinion focuses on facts because the Securities Act focuses on facts—facts disclosed, facts known, or access to facts. "Insider" or "outsider" labels are not determinative. Traditional forms are not determinative. In adjusting the generalities of § 4(2) to the realities of the contemporary market, we have seized on the availability to all offerees of pertinent facts. We have conditioned the private offering exemption on either actual disclosure of the information registration would provide or the offerees' effective access to such information. If the issuer has not disclosed but instead relies on the offerees' access, the privileged status of the offerees relative to the issuer must be shown.

We are conscious of the difficulty of formulating black letter law in this area in light of the multiplicity of security transactions and their multifarious natures. \* \* \* We do not want the private offering exemption to swallow the Securities Act, and we must resolve doubtful cases against the private placement claimant and in favor of the Act's paramount value of disclosure. By the same token, we must heed the existence and purposes of the exemption, and be cautious lest we discourage private avenues for raising capital. Our present emphasis on the availability of information as the *sine qua non* of the private offering is an attempt to steer a middle course.

We must reverse in part the judgment of the district court and remand for proceedings not inconsistent with this opinion.

#### c. *Regulation D Offerings*

The SEC promulgated Regulation D to facilitate smaller offerings and eliminate some of the uncertainties created by cases such as *Doran*. Regulation D is based in part on § 3(b) of the 1933 Act, which authorizes the SEC to exempt from registration issues of securities that do not exceed $5,000,000, and in part on the § 4(2) private offering exemption. The Regulation consists of eight rules, designated Rules 501–508. Rules 501–503 and 507–508 set forth definitions and conditions that apply to all the exemptions. Rules 504–506 define three classes of offerings that are exempt from the registration requirements of the Act.

*Rule 504*, issued pursuant to § 3(b), creates an exemption for "small" offerings. This exemption is available only to companies that are not publicly held. They may sell up to $1,000,000 in securities, during a 12–month period. Rule 504 imposes no limit on the number of investors to whom the securities can be sold, no requirements as to those investors' sophistication, and no disclosure requirements under federal law. (However, issues exempted by Rule 504 are subject to the disclosure requirements of state "blue sky" laws, discussed in Section C of this chapter). In addition, Rule 504 allows for the general solicitation of investors and imposes no restrictions on resales of securities offered under the rule.

*Rule 505*, also issued pursuant to § 3(b), exempts offerings of up to $5,000,000 which meet the following conditions. First, the issuer can not sell more than $5,000,000 in securities under Regulation D in a 12–month period. Second, sales can be made to an unlimited number of accredited investors, but to no more than 35 non-accredited investors. Rule 501(a) defines accredited investors to include institutional investors, wealthy individuals (regardless of investment sophistication), and key executives of the issuer. Third, the issuer must disclose the information set forth in Rule 502(b)(2)—information roughly comparable to that required in a registration statement. Fourth, the offering must not involve any general advertising or solicitation. Fifth, resales of securities purchased in a Rule 505 offering are restricted.

*Rule 506*, issued pursuant to § 4(2), has no dollar limitation. The requirements of Rule 506 otherwise are the same as those of Rule 505, with one significant difference. Sales in a Rule 506 offering cannot be made to any non-accredited investor unless the issuer reasonably believes that investor has "such knowledge and experience in financial and business matters that he is capable of evaluating the merits and risks of the prospective investment." However, securities can be sold to an unsophisticated purchaser in a rule 506 offering if he is represented by an advisor—a "purchaser representative"—who meets the investor sophistication requirements set forth in Rule 501(h).

Neither § 11 or § 12(2) of the 1933 Act applies to offerings made pursuant to Regulation D. Thus, an issuer who loses money in a Regulation D offering has no right to recover if his loss is caused by the issuer's negligent misrepresentation of a material fact. However, an investor in a Regulation D offering who proves that an issuer misrepresented material facts with the intent to defraud has a right to recover his losses in a private action brought under under Section 10(b) of the 1934 Act and SEC Rule 10b–5.

### d.  Regulation A Offerings

Another alternative available to an issuer is to make an offering pursuant to Regulation A, which creates a sort of "mini-registration" process. Regulation A, issued pursuant to § 3(b), allows an issuer to make a public offering of up to $5,000,000. (Existing shareholders also may sell up to $1,500,000 in securities under Regulation A, subject to certain restrictions. However, their sales count against the issuer's $5,000,000 limit.) The issuer is required to file an *Offering Statement* with a regional office of the SEC before commencing a Regulation A offering. The content requirements for an Offering Statement are easier to satisfy than the requirements for a registration statement.

In addition, Rule 254 allows an issuer to "test the waters" to determine whether there is investor interest in a planned offering before incurring the cost of preparing an Offering Statement. This rule, issued in 1992, represented a significant innovation in securities regulation. The SEC determined that a major impediment to small companies who sought to raise capital was that, if they had no established market for their securities, they were forced to incur the cost of preparing an offering statement before they could contact investors. *See* Rel. No. 33–6949 (July 20, 1992). Rule 254 allows an issuer to contact investors, prior to filing an Offering Statement, to determine whether they are interested in the possibility of investing in the securities a company plans to offer.

## C.  STATE BLUE SKY LAWS

From 1870 to 1930, the public sale of corporate stocks and bonds increased dramatically, and so did the incidence of securities fraud. To counter the predation practiced by peddlers of securities on innocent investors, state legislatures began enacting securities laws. Better known as "blue sky" laws after an early judicial opinion condemning "speculator schemes which have no more basis than so many feet of 'blue sky,'" these statutes regulate the sales of securities to purchasers within the jurisdiction.

Generally speaking these laws contain some form of one or more of three basic regulatory devices: (1) anti-fraud provisions which made it unlawful to make a false or misleading statement or to omit a material fact in connection with the sale of a security; (2) registration or licensing of certain persons engaged in the securities business prior to their trading in securities within a state; (3) registration or licensing of securities prior to any dealing in the securities, which frequently involves procedures and standards for an affirmative administrative approval of the merits of a particular issue.

Each of the three regulatory devices represents a somewhat different philosophical approach toward the same end of protecting the investing public. Antifraud provisions are intended to enable the administrator to issue public warnings, to investigate suspected fraudulent activities, to take injunctive or other steps to stop them, and as a last resort to punish them. Registration of brokers, dealers, agents and investment advisers is intended to prevent dishonest or unqualified persons from entering the securities business, to supervise their activities within the state once registration has been achieved, and to remove them from registration if they fall below any of the statutory standards. Registration of securities is intended to give the investor 'a run for his money' by excluding from the state those securities which do not satisfy the statutory standards.

1 Louis Loss and Joel Seligman, SECURITIES REGULATION 61 (3d ed. 1989).

Prior to 1996, blue sky laws often had an important impact on securities offerings. In large public offerings in which securities were sold in many states, it was necessary for someone, usually counsel for the underwriters, to "blue sky" the issue to assure compliance with the requirements of the laws of every state in which it was to be offered. Section 18 of the Securities Act of 1933 expressly preserved the effect of the state securities laws.

In 1996, Congress amended § 18 to preempt state blue sky law requirements for many securities offerings. More specifically, § 18 now prohibits states from imposing registration requirements for offerings of securities that are listed or will be listed on the New York Stock Exchange, the American Stock Exchange, or the NASD's National Market System or that are exempt from registration under § 4(2). However, § 18 still allows states to bring antifraud proceedings, to collect fees with respect to securities offerings made within their jurisdiction, and to require filing of documents solely for notice purposes. Section 18 also preserves states' right to require registration of intrastate offerings.

This change in § 18 was made in response to claims that, as concerned offerings regulated by federal law, state registration served no useful purpose and imposed substantial costs on issuers. *See* Rutherford B. Campbell, *An Open Attack on the Nonsense of Blue Sky Regulation*, 10 J.CORP.L. 553 (1985).

# Chapter 11

# PROTECTION OF CREDITORS: LIMITATIONS ON LIMITED LIABILITY

## A. OVERVIEW OF LIMITED LIABILITY

A principal advantage of the corporate form is that a shareholder's potential loss is limited to the amount that she has invested in the enterprise. This follows from the general rule that a corporation is liable for its own obligations and that creditors are entitled to look only to the corporation's assets to recover their claims.

There are exceptions to this rule, however, as there are to most others. In certain circumstances, courts allow claimants to disregard the corporate entity and recover directly from its shareholder(s). This result is described metaphorically as allowing a plaintiff to "pierce the corporate veil." Courts use other colorful phrases in these cases, describing corporations as the "agent," "alias," "alter ego," "corporate double," "dummy," or "instrumentality" of their shareholders. None of these terms, however, is particularly instructive. Judge Cardozo's observation in *Berkey v. Third Avenue Railway Co.*, 244 N.Y. 84, 94, 155 N.E. 58, 61 (1926), remains relevant: "The whole problem of the relation between [shareholder and corporation] is one that is still enveloped in a mist of metaphor. Metaphors in law are to be narrowly watched, for starting as devices to liberate thought, they end often by enslaving it."

Whether a corporation's veil should be pierced is the most litigated issue in corporate law. *See* Robert B. Thompson, *Piercing the Corporate Veil: An Empirical Study*, 76 CORNELL L. REV. 1036 (1991). Situations in which a corporation's assets are inadequate to fulfill its obligations to a claimant arise with some frequency. A useful perspective on this question is to see it as a matter of allocation of losses. The economic norm of a limited liability regime is that a substantial portion of the risk of business failure shifts to creditors and away from shareholders. When the assets of a corporation are inadequate to fulfill its obligations, under what circumstances should the court shift the risk back to the shareholders? A number of factors have led courts to make such a shift: (1)

insufficient attention to corporate formalities; (2) "abuse" of the corporate entity by pushing its advantages to extremes; and (3) whether the corporation is "undercapitalized."

In addition to these factors, courts have considered the nature of the creditor seeking to pierce the corporate veil. There are two principal types of creditors: voluntary creditors who contract with the corporation, and involuntary creditors—mainly tort victims. The difference between them appears to be their ability to bargain with the corporation. Yet even this distinction may become blurred; the contract creditor who sells merchandise or services over the telephone to a corporation generally does not engage in more investigation or bargaining than does the tort victim. What then is an appropriate standard for determining when the risk should be shifted from the shareholders to the creditors?

As you will see from the materials that follow, there is considerable indeterminacy in the case law in this area. Thus participants in a venture may have difficulty knowing what steps to take in order to ensure the benefits of limited liability and attorneys involved in a lawsuit may find it difficult to predict when a court will "pierce the corporate veil."

## 1. THE ECONOMIC JUSTIFICATION FOR LIMITED LIABILITY

Frank H. Easterbrook and Daniel R. Fischel, THE
ECONOMIC STRUCTURE OF CORPORATE LAW
41–44 (1991).

Publicly held corporations dominate other organizational forms when the technology of production requires firms to combine both the specialized skills of multiple agents and large amounts of capital. Limited liability reduces the costs of this separation and specialization of functions in a number of respects.

First, limited liability decreases the need to monitor agents. To protect themselves, investors could monitor their agents more closely. The more risk they bear, the more they will monitor. But beyond a point extra monitoring is not worth the cost. * * * Limited liability makes * * * passivity a more rational strategy and so potentially reduces the cost of operating the corporation.

Second, limited liability reduces the costs of monitoring other shareholders. Under a rule exposing equity investors to unlimited liability, the greater the wealth of other shareholders, the lower the probability that any one shareholder's assets will be needed to pay a judgment. Thus existing shareholders would have incentives to engage in costly monitoring of other shareholders to ensure that they do not transfer assets to others or sell to others with less wealth. Limited liability makes the identity of other shareholders irrelevant and thus avoids these costs.

Third, by promoting free transfer of shares, limited liability gives managers incentives to act efficiently. Although individual shareholders lack the expertise and incentive to monitor the actions of specialized agents, the ability of investors to sell creates opportunities for investors as a group to and constrains agents' actions. * * * [The] potential for displacement gives existing managers incentives to operate efficiently in order to keep share prices high.

With limited liability, the value of shares is set by the present value of the income stream generated by a firm's assets. The identity and wealth of other investors is irrelevant. Shares are fungible; they trade at one price in liquid markets. Under a rule of unlimited liability shares would not be fungible. Their value would be a function of the present value of future cash flows and the wealth of shareholders. Their lack of fungibility would impede their acquisition. * * * Limited liability allows a person to buy a large bloc without any risk of being surcharged, and thus it facilitates beneficial control transactions. A rule that facilitates transfers of control also induces managers to work more effectively to stave off such transfers, and so it reduces the costs of specialization whether or not a firm is acquired.

Fourth, limited liability makes it possible for market prices to reflect additional information about the value of firms. With unlimited liability, shares would not be homogeneous commodities and would no longer have one market price. Investors would be required to expend greater resources analyzing the prospects of the firm to know whether "the price is right." When all can trade on the same terms, though, investors trade until the price of shares reflect the available information about a firm's prospects. Most investors need not expend resources searching for additional information.

Fifth, * * * limited liability allows more efficient diversification. Investors can cut risk by owning a diversified portfolio of assets. Firms can raise capital at lower costs because investors need not bear the special risk associated with nondiversified holdings. This applies only under a rule of limited liability or some good substitute. * * *

Sixth, limited liability facilitates optimal investment decisions. When investors hold diversified portfolios, managers maximize investors' welfare by investing in any project with a positive net present value. * * * In a world of unlimited liability managers * * * would reject as "too risky" some projects with positive net present values. Investors would want them to do this because it would be the best way to reduce risks. By definition this would be a social loss, because projects with net present value are beneficial uses of capital. * * * The increased availability of funds for projects with positive net values is the real benefit of limited liability.

———————

Do economic efficiency considerations adequately explain the doctrine of limited liability? Stephen Presser asserts that, while Easterbrook and Fischel's six factors were important in the evolution of the doctrine, they do not provide a full explanation. Stephen B. Presser, *Thwarting the Killing of the Corporation: Limited Liability, Democracy, and Economics*, 87 Nw. U. L.Rev. 148, 155–156 (1992).

Presser disagrees with Easterbrook and Fischel's assertion that unlimited liability produces high monitoring costs that discourage investment. He contends that even in an unlimited liability regime, shareholders would still invest if the return on their investment were high enough; they would simply base their investment on the corporation's proven business strategies or the self-monitoring abilities of management. *Id.* at 158–59.

Presser also notes that monitoring would be required only where unlimited liability was joint and several. He believes that if limited liability were not the rule, the most likely alternative regime would be to hold shareholders liable pro rata for the proportion that their investments bore to the total investment in the firm. Under such a system, the need to monitor other shareholders would disappear because the wealth of other shareholders would be irrelevant. *Id.* at 160–61.

Finally, Presser notes that the benefits of diversified investments, such as the increased incentives for managers to invest in risky projects and a concomitant decrease in investment costs, could be obtained in other ways. For example, diversification could be achieved at the firm level, if firms had sufficient capital to invest in a wide range of opportunities. *Id.* at 162.

Presser concludes that, as a matter of history, "the imposition of limited liability was perceived as a means of encouraging the small-scale entrepreneur, and of keeping entry into business markets competitive and democratic." That may be true, but it also can be argued that limited liability primarily benefits the wealthy. The "small-scale entrepreneur" who invests most of her assets in a corporation reaps few benefits from limited liability because she has few other assets against which a creditor can claim. A person of wealth, on the other hand, might be very reluctant to invest a small portion of her assets in an entrepreneurial venture if all her other assets would be placed at risk. At a minimum, a wealthy person would be inclined to insist that the venture purchase more liability insurance, which would cause it to incur higher costs than a venture owned by shareholders who had invested virtually all their assets in its business.

## 2. VOLUNTARY CREDITORS

The justifications for limited liability are strongest when considering contract creditors such as employees, consumers, trade creditors and commercial lenders. Easterbrook and Fischel argue that limited liability is appropriate with respect to contract creditors because they can bargain for a risk premium to protect themselves.

> Limited liability's greatest effect is on the probability that any given creditor will be paid *ex post*. Even if firms pay for engaging in

risky activities, and thus take the right precautions, creditors of failed businesses are less likely to receive full compensation under a rule of limited liability. This is not an "argument" against limited liability, however, unless distributional concerns dominate. There is little role for distributional arguments when all of the parties are in privity, for they can strike their own bargains and are apt to contract around any unwelcome rule purportedly designed for their benefit. More to the point, they can choose to hold, under any rule, a different proportion of debt and equity which alters the risk. At all events * * * insurance makes distributional concerns much less serious than they might at first appear. The ability of potential victims to protect themselves against loss through insurance is a strong reason for disregarding distributional concerns in choosing among liability rules.

Easterbrook & Fischel, *supra*, at 52. See also Robert C. Clark, *The Duties of the Corporate Debtor to Its Creditors*, 90 HARV.L.REV. 505, 543 (1977).

Is this argument as persuasive with respect to trade creditors, who are less likely to seek information relevant to determination of the risk they will not be paid?

## 3. TORT CLAIMANTS

Another area of critical inquiry focuses on whether courts should treat tort claimants differently from contract creditors. In a contractual arrangement, a creditor can adjust her prices to account for the risk she will not be paid. This means of self-protection is not available to tort claimants. Thus, one might expect that courts would provide more protection to tort claimants than to contract creditors in "piercing" cases.

Robert Thompson's analysis of 1600 "piercing" cases casts considerable doubt on that expectation. He found that courts pierced the corporate veil more often in contract cases (about 42% of the cases) than in a tort actions (about 31% of the cases). Thompson, *supra*. One explanation of this result, he noted, was that many contract cases involve misrepresentations that effectively obviate the basis for the parties' contract. However, his study still showed that courts pierce in 34% of the contract cases that do not involve misrepresentation claims and in only 27% of the tort cases that do not involve misrepresentation claims. Thompson, *supra*, at 1069.

Professors Hansmann and Kraakman advocate disregarding limited liability in cases involving involuntary tort creditors. Henry Hansmann & Reinier Kraakman, *Toward Unlimited Shareholder Liability for Corporate Torts*, 100 Yale L.J. 1879 (1991). They claim that limited liability gives corporate managers incentives to incur too much risk because they know that the corporation can not be held liable for some costs its activities might generate. This will lead managers to invest in projects whose total social costs exceed their total social benefits.

Hansmann and Kraakman would replace limited liability with a rule that subjects shareholders to pro-rata liability for tort damages in excess of the firm's assets. Share prices should then decline to reflect the potential additional personal liability. That would give managers a greater incentive to consider the full expected social costs of the firm's torts and adjust their decisions accordingly.

Hansmann and Kraakman's argument has not achieved wide acceptance, even by those who criticize a limited liability regime. Professor Leebron agrees that investors would tolerate unlimited pro-rata liability in tort, and that such liability would lead to greater efficiency. However, he asserts that the argument that shareholders are necessarily better loss bearers than tort victims only applies in the absence of insurance markets. If, for instance, there are few shareholders and the injuries to tort victims are not severe, shareholders will be comparably inefficient risk bearers. Similarly, if insurance is available to tort victims, but not to shareholders, tort victims may be in a better position to bear the risk. Because the availability of shareholder liability insurance would be a function of both expected tort liability and business risks, it would be difficult to obtain. Leebron suggests that this problem would be mitigated by obtaining liability insurance at the enterprise level. He concludes that limited liability should be allowed only where the company obtains reasonable insurance. *See* David W. Leebron, *Limited Liability, Tort Victims, and Creditors*, 91 COL. L. REV. 1565 (1991).

Professor Grundfest, on the other hand, argues that any attempt to eliminate limited liability would fail because participants in the capital market would design options and other instruments that would allow them to obtain the benefits of equity ownership without exposing themselves to liability as shareholders. *See* Joseph A. Grundfest, *The Limited Future of Unlimited Liability: A Capital Markets Perspective*, 102 YALE L.J. 387 (1992).

## 4. CLOSE CORPORATIONS

Easterbrook and Fischel note that their economic efficiency rationale for limited liability begins to break down when applied to close corporations.* In companies owned by a small number of investors who also are managers, there is much less separation of management and risk bearing than in a public corporation and the absence of a market for close corporations' stock makes irrelevant the fact that limited liability increases the efficiency of the market for a corporation's stock. In

---

* However, "cases where courts have allowed creditors to reach the assets of shareholders have almost always involved close corporations." *Birbara v. Locke*, 99 F.3d 1233 (1st Cir.1996). Moreover, recently created forms of limited liability entities, such as LLCs, usually are closely held. Commentators assume that courts will use pretty much the same approach to decide whether to hold the members of an LLC liable for the LLC's debts as they do to decide whether to pierce the corporate veil. *See, e.g.*, Robert B. Thompson, *The Limits of Liability in the New Limited Liability Entities*, 32 WAKE FOREST L.REV. 1 (1997); Karin Schwindt, *Comment, Limited Liability Companies: Issues in Member Liability*, 44 UCLA L.REV. 1541 (1997). The first reported decision to address the issue relied on traditional piercing factors. *See Ditty v. CheckRite, Ltd., Inc.*, 973 F.Supp. 1320, 1335–36 (D.Utah 1997).

addition, limited liability is more likely to generate external costs because the shareholder-managers of a close corporation have more to gain personally by taking risks that may shift losses to creditors than do the managers of a public company. Easterbrook and Fischel conclude that a court can reduce the extent to which third parties bear these costs by disregarding limited liability in close corporations when there has been an abuse of the corporate privilege.

Presser does not agree that the argument for piercing the corporate veil is stronger for close corporations than publicly held corporations. He contends that Easterbrook and Fischel ignore the principal historical justification for limited liability—promoting individual investment in smaller firms. Thus, it is precisely in the context of such firms that limited liability should be most protected. Presser, *supra*, at 164, 171–72. David Leebron takes a middle position. He suggests that limited liability should exist for close corporation shareholders subject to two conditions: (1) shareholders should not be allowed to reduce capital available for involuntary creditors by using personally guaranteed debt rather than equity to finance the corporation and (2) shareholder-managers should be required to carry adequate insurance for foreseeable tort liabilities. Leebron asserts that these conditions would protect against the major abuses that typically concern the advocates of unlimited liability for shareholders of close corporations. Leebron, *supra*, at 1636.

## 5. PARENT AND SUBSIDIARY CORPORATIONS

The original conception of a corporation was of an entity whose assets, liabilities and operations—the entire "enterprise"—was all one entity. Adolf A. Berle, Jr., *The Theory of Enterprise Entity*, 47 Col. L. Rev. 343 (1947). Where a corporation operated through subsidiaries that were more or less indistinguishable parts of a larger enterprise, courts employed *ad hoc* approaches to hold parent corporations responsible for the liabilities of their subsidiaries, using terms such as "agency" and "mere instrumentality" to justify their decisions. As Berle described this judicial development,

> The courts disregard the corporate fiction specifically because it has parted company with the enterprise-fact, for whose furtherance the corporation was created; and having got that far, they then take the further step of ascertaining what is the actual enterprise-fact and attach the consequences of the acts of the component individuals or corporations to the enterprise entity, to the extent that the economic outlines of the situation warrant or require * * *. [These cases] suggest that to preserve the independence of an enterprise which is needed to support the continuance of separate legal personality, the stockholders must provide the entity with separate assets sufficient to give it at least a reasonable business chance to carry out its asserted functions.

*Id.* at 348–49.

### Richard A. Posner, AN ECONOMIC ANALYSIS OF LAW

4th ed. 1992.

### § 14.5   PIERCING THE CORPORATE VEIL

Although limited liability serves an important function in making equity investments attractive to individuals, disregarding it—piercing the corporate veil, in the jargon of corporation law—may promote efficiency in two situations.

1. Consider the taxi enterprise whose owners incorporate each taxicab separately in order to limit tort liability to accident victims. If such liability were a negotiated obligation, the creditor-victim would charge a higher interest rate to reflect the increased risk of a default; but it is not and cannot be. The result of separate incorporation is therefore to externalize a cost of taxi service.

Yet piercing the veil may not be optimal even in this situation. Permitting tort victims to reach the shareholders' assets would be a source of additional risk to the shareholders—and an increase in risk is a real cost to people who are risk averse. Although the company could insure itself against its torts, this would not be a completely satisfactory alternative. The managers might fail to take out adequate insurance; the insurance company might for a variety of reasons refuse or be unable to pay a tort judgment against the insured (the insurance company might, for example, become insolvent); the particular tort might be excluded from the coverage of the insurance policy. All this may sound pretty remote—until one replaces taxicab collisions by nuclear reactor accidents or asbestos-caused lung disease. * * *

A simple alternative to piercing the corporate veil is to require any corporation engaged in dangerous activity to post a bond equal to the highest reasonable estimate of the probable extent of its tort liability. Shareholders would be protected (in what sense?) and accident costs internalized.

2. A stronger case for piercing the corporate veil is warranted where separate incorporation misleads creditors. Corporations permitted to represent that they have greater assets to pay creditors than they actually have increase the costs that creditors must incur to ascertain the true credit worthiness of the corporations with which they deal.

* * *

Often a shareholder is a corporation rather than an individual, and it might seem that the policy of risk shifting that underlies the principle of limited liability would not apply in that case. If a parent corporation is made liable for its subsidiary's debts, the exposure of the parent's shareholders to liability, although greater than if the subsidiary enjoyed limited liability, is limited to their investment in the parent and can be further reduced by their holding a diversified portfolio of equities. * * *

[W]here a large, publicly held corporation operates through wholly owned subsidiaries, it may seem artificial in the extreme to treat these as separate entities for purposes of deciding what assets shall be available to satisfy creditors' claims. The question can be evaluated by dividing affiliated firms into two groups: firms in unrelated businesses and firms in closely related businesses. In the first group, maximization of the parent corporation's profits will require that the profits of each subsidiary be maximized separately; so the assets, costs, etc. of each subsidiary should be the same as they would be if they were separate firms. True, the common owner could take measures that concealed or distorted the relative profitability of his different enterprises, as by allocating capital among them at arbitrary interest rates. But such measures are costly; they reduce the information available to the common owner about the efficiency with which his various corporations are being managed. * * *

Even when the activities of affiliated corporations are closely related—when for example they produce complementary goods—each corporation normally will be operated as a separate profit center in order to assure that the profits of the group will be maximized. It is true that if there are substantial cost savings from common ownership, as in some cases where the affiliated corporations operate at successive stages in the production of a good, the two corporations will be managed differently from separately owned corporations in the same line of business; their operations will be more closely integrated than would be those of independent corporations. But it would be perverse to penalize such a corporation for its superior efficiency by withdrawing from it the privilege of limited liability that its nonintegrated competitors enjoy. Moreover, in this case as well, the common owner has a strong incentive to avoid intercorporate transfers that, by distorting the profitability of each corporation, make it more difficult for the common owner to evaluate their performance. That is why the price at which one division of a vertically integrated firm will "sell" its output to another division is normally the market price for the good in question (less any savings in cost attributable to making an intrafirm transfer compared to a market transaction) rather than an arbitrary transfer price designed to increase the profits of one division at the expense of the other.

The important difference between a group of affiliates engaged in related businesses and one engaged in a number of unrelated businesses is not that the conduct of the corporations in the first group will differ from that of nonaffiliated corporations in the same business but that the creditor dealing with a group of affiliates in related businesses is more likely to be misled into thinking that he is dealing with a single corporation. * * * The misrepresentation principle, however, seems adequate to deal with these cases. Indeed, where there is no misrepresentation, a rule abrogating the limited liability of affiliated corporations would not reduce the risks of any class of creditors but would increase their information costs. Although the creditor of A Corporation would know that if A defaulted he could reach the assets of its affiliate B, he would also know that if B defaulted, B's creditors might have a claim on the assets of A that might cause A to default on the debt to him. So to know how high an interest rate to charge, he would have to investigate B's financial situation as well as A. And B might be in a completely unrelated business.

————

The primary rationale for limited liability—investors are more willing to fund new business ventures when their liability is limited to the amount they invest—has been criticized as not applying fully when the investor is a parent corporation. See Phillip I. Blumberg, *Limited Liability and Corporate Groups,* 11 J. CORP. LAW 573 (1986). Limited liability originally protected the ultimate investors in an enterprise, the shareholders. Blumberg argues that the advantages of limited liability disappear when extended to the parent or affiliate of a subsidiary. For example, while it may seem unjust to hold shareholders liable for corporate actions ordered by the directors and managers, this unfairness argument does not apply to a parent that most likely controls and directs its subsidiary. Additionally, the need to attract thousands of investors to fund a large corporate enterprise by assuring them that their liability is limited is not a factor when one corporation provides most or all the capital for a subsidiary. As a result, eliminating limited liability for corporate groups will not affect the capital markets.

## PROBLEM
### PRECISION TOOLS—PART IX

PTC was a supplier of tools and components to Higgins Corporation, a manufacturer of smoke alarm systems for industrial use. Although these systems were generally considered high quality, Higgins found itself in great difficulty because it was inefficiently managed. Higgins was heavily indebted to PTC for merchandise purchased. In order to protect both its investment in Higgins, and its market, PTC made every effort to keep Higgins afloat, by extending payment terms and waiving interest costs. It even offered consulting services.

Ultimately, all efforts failed and Higgins went into bankruptcy. In the subsequent auction, Michael, Jessica and Bernie purchased Higgins' assets for $100,000—a price well below market value. They formed a new Columbia corporation called New Higgins Corporation to continue Higgins' existing business and for $25,000 purchased all the stock in proportion to their stock ownership of PTC. Counsel advised them that the separate corporate structure would be desirable so as to avoid jeopardizing PTC's assets by adding the risks of a new venture.

As part of its initial financing, in addition to selling its stock, New Higgins borrowed $75,000 from PTC's regular bank; the loan was guaranteed by the three stockholders and PTC. Jessica arranged the loan in her capacity as chief financial officer of New Higgins, the same position she holds at PTC. Finally, Michael, Jessica and Bernie loaned

New Higgins $50,000 as working capital and took back a three-year note, bearing an annual interest rate of 2% over the prime rate.

Michael and Jessica, who are directors of PTC, became the directors and, together with Shawn Nelson, who they hired to manage the company, were the officers of New Higgins. Shawn is the only salaried officer of New Higgins.

At counsel's insistence, after the annual shareholders' meeting to elect directors, New Higgins holds a formal board meeting to elect officers and ratify prior decisions. In order to reduce overhead, New Higgins consolidated its office with PTC's, and they now share bookkeeping and accounting personnel. New Higgins maintains its own bank account and pays PTC $300 per month for rent and "administrative services" that are performed by PTC employees.

One of the cost advantages that Michael, Jessica and Bernie anticipated in owning New Higgins was that PTC could share a common sales force with the new corporation since there was a big overlap in their customer base. As a consequence, the New Higgins sales force has been pared substantially.

In its first two years of existence, New Higgins lost money and, to provide working capital, PTC loaned New Higgins $25,000 after the first year and an additional $50,000 after the second year. These loans were two-year notes at prevailing interest rates. In the third and fourth years, the business prospered and, because of prior losses, New Higgins paid no taxes. After paying interest on its various notes, New Higgins then distributed all of its profits as a dividend to Michael, Jessica and Bernie.

Six months ago a factory that had purchased a New Higgins system burned down in a tragic fire in which three people were killed. The alarm system proved to be defective, resulting in a crucial delay in calling the firefighters. The families of the victims and the owner of the factory brought suit against New Higgins, alleging gross negligence in the manufacture and installation of the equipment. Because it was clear that the assets of the company and its insurance would not be sufficient to cover the losses, plaintiffs also sought recovery from PTC, Michael, Jessica and Bernie, asserting various theories that disregard the separate incorporation of New Higgins.

Prior to the fire, as part of its expanding business, New Higgins purchased the principal components for its systems from Acme Electronics, generally paying within 60 days of receiving Acme's invoice. At the time of the fire, New Higgins had unpaid invoices of $500,000 and subsequently received invoices for an additional $250,000. None of those invoices had been paid. Acme seeks to hold PTC, Michael, Jessica and Bernie liable for the entire $750,000.

Plaintiffs' counsel in both suits have approached you, as counsel for all the defendants, about a settlement of the claims. The plaintiffs' lawyers say they are confident that the court will pierce the corporate veil and hold your clients liable. Advise PTC, Michael, Jessica and Bernie as to the likelihood that a court will impose liability on any or all of them for each of the claims against New Higgins.

# B.  TORT CREDITORS

## WALKOVSZKY v. CARLTON

18 N.Y.2d 414, 276 N.Y.S.2d 585, 223 N.E.2d 6 (1966).

FULD, JUDGE.

This case involves what appears to be a rather common practice in the taxicab industry of vesting the ownership of a taxi fleet in many corporations, each owning only one or two cabs.

The complaint alleges that the plaintiff was severely injured four years ago in New York City when he was run down by a taxicab owned by the defendant Seon Cab Corporation and negligently operated at the time by the defendant Marchese. The individual defendant, Carlton, is claimed to be a stockholder of 10 corporations, including Seon, each of which has but two cabs registered in its name, and it is implied that only the minimum automobile liability insurance required by law (in the amount of $10,000) is carried on any one cab. Although seemingly independent of one another, these corporations are alleged to be 'operated * * * as a single entity, unit and enterprise' with regard to financing, supplies, repairs, employees and garaging, and all are named as defendants. The plaintiff asserts that he is also entitled to hold their stockholders personally liable for the damages sought because the multiple corporate structure constitutes an unlawful attempt 'to defraud members of the general public' who might be injured by the cabs.

The defendant Carlton has moved * * * to dismiss the complaint on the ground that as to him it 'fails to state a cause of action'. The court at Special Term granted the motion but the Appellate Division, by a divided vote, reversed, holding that a valid cause of action was sufficiently stated. * * * The law permits the incorporation of a business for the very purpose of enabling its proprietors to escape personal liability (*see, e.g., Bartle v. Home Owners Co-op.*, 309 N.Y. 103, 106, 127 N.E.2d 832, 833) but, manifestly, the privilege is not without its limits. Broadly speaking, the courts will disregard the corporate form, or, to use accepted terminology, 'pierce the corporate veil', whenever necessary 'to prevent fraud or to achieve equity'. (*International Aircraft Trading Co. v. Manufacturers Trust Co.*, 297 N.Y. 285, 292, 79 N.E.2d 249, 252.) In determining whether liability should be extended to reach assets beyond those belonging to the corporation, we are guided, as Judge Cardozo noted, by 'general rules of agency'. (*Berkey v. Third Ave. Ry. Co.*, 244 N.Y. 84, 95, 155 N.E. 58, 61, 50 A.L.R. 599.) In other words, whenever anyone uses control of the corporation to further his own rather than the corporation's business, he will be liable for the corporation's acts 'upon the principle of respondeat superior applicable even where the agent is a natural person'. (*Rapid Tr. Subway Constr. Co. v. City of New*

*York*, 259 N.Y. 472, 488, 182 N.E. 145, 150.) Such liability, moreover, extends not only to the corporation's commercial dealings * * * but to its negligent acts as well. * * *

* * *

In the case before us, the plaintiff has explicitly alleged that none of the corporations "had a separate existence of their own" and, as indicated above, all are named as defendants. However, it is one thing to assert that a corporation is a fragment of a larger corporate combine which actually conducts the business. (*See* Berle, *The Theory of Enterprise Entity*, 47 COL.L.REV. 343, 348—350.) It is quite another to claim that the corporation is a "dummy" for its individual stockholders who are in reality carrying on the business in their personal capacities for purely personal rather than corporate ends. Either circumstance would justify treating the corporation as an agent and piercing the corporate veil to reach the principal but a different result would follow in each case. In the first, only a larger corporate entity would be held financially responsible * * * while, in the other, the stockholder would be personally liable. * * * Either the stockholder is conducting the business in his individual capacity or he is not. If he is, he will be liable; if he is not, then it does not matter—insofar as his personal liability is concerned— that the enterprise is actually being carried on by a larger "enterprise entity". (*See* Berle, *The Theory of Enterprise Entity*, 47 COL.L.REV. 343.)

* * *

The individual defendant is charged with having "organized, managed, dominated and controlled" a fragmented corporate entity but there are no allegations that he was conducting business in his individual capacity. Had the taxicab fleet been owned by a single corporation, it would be readily apparent that the plaintiff would face formidable barriers in attempting to establish personal liability on the part of the corporation's stockholders. The fact that the fleet ownership has been deliberately split up among many corporations does not ease the plaintiff's burden in that respect. The corporate form may not be disregarded merely because the assets of the corporation, together with the mandatory insurance coverage of the vehicle which struck the plaintiff, are insufficient to assure him the recovery sought. If Carlton were to be held individually liable on those facts alone, the decision would apply equally to the thousands of cabs which are owned by their individual drivers who conduct their businesses through corporations organized pursuant to section 401 of the Business Corporation Law, * * * and carry the minimum insurance required by [the Vehicle and Traffic Law]. These taxi owner-operators are entitled to form such corporations, and we agree with the court at Special Term that, if the insurance coverage required by statute "is inadequate for the protection of the public, the remedy lies not with the courts but with the Legislature." It may very well be sound policy to require that certain corporations must take out liability insurance which will afford adequate compensation to their potential tort victims. However, the responsibility for imposing conditions on the privilege of incorporation has been committed by the Constitution to the Legislature * * * and it may not be fairly implied, from any statute, that the Legislature intended, without the slightest discussion or debate, to require of taxi corporations that they carry automobile liability insurance over and above that mandated by the Vehicle and Traffic Law.

This is not to say that it is impossible for the plaintiff to state a valid cause of action against the defendant Carlton. However, the simple fact is that the plaintiff has just not done so here. While the complaint alleges that the separate corporations were undercapitalized and that their assets have been intermingled, it is barren of any "sufficiently particular(ized) statements" * * * that the defendant Carlton and his associates are actually doing business in their individual capacities, shuttling their personal funds in and out of the corporations "without regard to formality and to suit their immediate convenience." (*Weisser v. Mursam Shoe Corp.*, 2 Cir., 127 F.2d 344, 345) Such a "perversion of the privilege to do business in a corporate form" (*Berkey v. Third Ave. Ry. Co.*, 244 N.Y. 84, 95, 155 N.E. 58, 61, supra) would justify imposing personal liability on the individual stockholders. Nothing of the sort has in fact been charged, and it cannot reasonably or logically be inferred from the happenstance that the business of Seon Cab Corporation may actually be carried on by a larger corporate entity composed of many corporations which, under general principles of agency, would be liable to each other's creditors in contract and in tort.[3]

In point of fact, the principle relied upon in the complaint to sustain the imposition of personal liability is not agency but fraud. Such a cause of action cannot withstand analysis. If it is not fraudulent for the owner-operator of a single cab corporation to take out only the minimum required liability insurance, the enterprise does not become either illicit or fraudulent merely because it consists of many such corporations. The plaintiff's injuries are the same regardless of whether the cab which strikes him is owned by a single corporation or part of a fleet with ownership fragmented among many corporations. Whatever rights he may be able to assert against parties other than the registered owner of the vehicle come into being not because he has been defrauded but because, under the principle of respondeat superior, he is entitled to hold the whole enterprise responsible for the acts of its agents.

In sum, then, the complaint falls short of adequately stating a cause of action against the defendant Carlton in his individual capacity.

The order of the Appellate Division should be reversed * * *.

KEATING, JUDGE (dissenting).

**3.** In his affidavit in opposition to the motion to dismiss, the plaintiff's counsel claimed that corporate assets had been 'milked out' of, and 'siphoned off' from the enterprise. Quite apart from the fact that these allegations are far too vague and conclusory, the charge is premature. If the plaintiff succeeds in his action and becomes a judgment creditor of the corporation, he may then sue and attempt to hold the individual defendants accountable for any dividends and property that were wrongfully distributed * * *.

The defendant Carlton, the shareholder here sought to be held for the negligence of the driver of a taxicab, was a principal shareholder and organizer of the defendant corporation which owned the taxicab. The corporation was one of 10 organized by the defendant * * *. The sole assets of these operating corporations are the vehicles themselves and they are apparently subject to mortgages.*

From their inception these corporations were intentionally undercapitalized for the purpose of avoiding responsibility for acts which were bound to arise as a result of the operation of a large taxi fleet having cars out on the street 24 hours a day and engaged in public transportation. And during the course of the corporations' existence all income was continually drained out of the corporations for the same purpose.

The issue presented by this action is whether the policy of this State, which affords those desiring to engage in a business enterprise the privilege of limited liability through the use of the corporate device, is so strong that it will permit that privilege to continue no matter how much it is abused, no matter how irresponsibly the corporation is operated, no matter what the cost to the public. I do not believe that it is.

Under the circumstances of this case the shareholders should all be held individually liable to this plaintiff for the injuries he suffered. * * * At least, the matter should not be disposed of on the pleadings by a dismissal of the complaint. "If a corporation is organized and carries on business without substantial capital in such a way that the corporation is likely to have no sufficient assets available to meet its debts, it is inequitable that shareholders should set up such a flimsy organization to escape personal liability. The attempt to do corporate business without providing any sufficient basis of financial responsibility to creditors is an abuse of the separate entity and will be ineffectual to exempt the shareholders from corporate debts. It is coming to be recognized as the policy of law that shareholders should in good faith put at the risk of the business unencumbered capital reasonably adequate for its prospective liabilities. If capital is illusory or trifling compared with the business to be done and the risks of loss, this is a ground for denying the separate entity privilege." (Ballantine, CORPORATIONS (rev.ed., 1946), § 129, pp. 302–303.)

In *Minton v. Cavaney*, 56 Cal.2d 576, 15 Cal.Rptr. 641, 364 P.2d 473, the Supreme Court of California had occasion to discuss this problem in a negligence case. The corporation of which the defendant was an organizer, director and officer operated a public swimming pool. One afternoon the plaintiffs' daughter drowned in the pool as a result of the alleged negligence of the corporation.

Justice Roger Traynor, speaking for the court, outlined the applicable law in this area. "The figurative terminology 'alter ego' and 'disregard of the corporate entity'," he wrote, 'is generally used to refer to the various situations that are an abuse of the corporate privilege. * * * The

---

* It appears that the medallions, which are of considerable value, are judgment proof. (Administrative Code of City of New York § 436–2.0.)

equitable owners of a corporation, for example, are personally liable when they treat the assets of the corporation as their own and add or withdraw capital from the corporation at will * * *; when they hold themselves out as being personally liable for the debts of the corporation * * *; Or *when they provide inadequate capitalization and actively participate in the conduct of corporate affairs.*" (56 Cal.2d, p. 579, 15 Cal.Rptr., p. 643, 364 P.2d p. 475; italics supplied.)

Examining the facts of the case in light of the legal principles just enumerated, he found that "(it was) undisputed that there was no attempt to provide adequate capitalization. (The corporation) never had any substantial assets. It leased the pool that it operated, and the lease was forfeited for failure to pay the rent. Its capital was 'trifling compared with the business to be done and the risks of loss.' " (56 Cal.2d, p. 580, 15 Cal.Rptr., p. 643, 364 P.2d p. 475.)

It seems obvious that one of 'the risks of loss' referred to was the possibility of drownings due to the negligence of the corporation. And the defendant's failure to provide such assets or any fund for recovery resulted in his being held personally liable.

* * *

The defendant Carlton claims that, because the minimum amount of insurance required by the statute was obtained, the corporate veil cannot and should not be pierced despite the fact that the assets of the corporation which owned the cab were "trifling compared with the business to be done and the risks of loss" which were certain to be encountered. I do not agree.

The Legislature in requiring minimum liability insurance of $10,-000, no doubt, intended to provide at least some small fund for recovery against those individuals and corporations who just did not have and were not able to raise or accumulate assets sufficient to satisfy the claims of those who were injured as a result of their negligence. It certainly could not have intended to shield those individuals who organized corporations, with the specific intent of avoiding responsibility to the public, where the operation of the corporate enterprise yielded profits sufficient to purchase additional insurance. Moreover, it is reasonable to assume that the Legislature believed that those individuals and corporations having substantial assets would take out insurance far in excess of the minimum in order to protect those assets from depletion. Given the costs of hospital care and treatment and the nature of injuries sustained in auto collisions, it would be unreasonable to assume that the Legislature believed that the minimum provided in the statute would in and of itself be sufficient to recompense "innocent victims of motor vehicle accidents * * * for the injury and financial loss inflicted upon them".

The defendant, however, argues that the failure of the Legislature to increase the minimum insurance requirements indicates legislative acquiescence in this scheme to avoid liability and responsibility to the public. In the absence of a clear legislative statement, approval of a scheme having such serious consequences is not to be so lightly inferred.

The defendant contends that the court will be encroaching upon the legislative domain by ignoring the corporate veil and holding the individual shareholder. This argument was answered by Mr. Justice Douglas in *Anderson v. Abbott, supra,* [321 U.S.] 366–367, 64 S.Ct. p. 540, where he wrote that: "In the field in which we are presently concerned, judicial power hardly oversteps the bounds when it refuses to lend its aid to a promotional project which would circumvent or undermine a legislative policy. To deny it that function would be to make it impotent in situations where historically it has made some of its most notable contributions. If the judicial power is helpless to protect a legislative program from schemes for easy avoidance, then indeed it has become a handy implement of high finance. *Judicial interference to cripple or defeat a legislative policy is one thing; judicial interference with the plans of those whose corporate or other devices would circumvent that policy is quite another.* Once the purpose or effect of the scheme is clear, once the legislative policy is plain, we would indeed forsake a great tradition to say we were helpless to fashion the instruments for appropriate relief." (Emphasis added.)

The defendant contends that a decision holding him personally liable would discourage people from engaging in corporate enterprise.

What I would merely hold is that a participating shareholder of a corporation vested with a public interest, organized with capital insufficient to meet liabilities which are certain to arise in the ordinary course of the corporation's business, may be held personally responsible for such liabilities. Where corporate income is not sufficient to cover the cost of insurance premiums above the statutory minimum or where initially adequate finances dwindle under the pressure of competition, bad times or extraordinary and unexpected liability, obviously the shareholder will not be held liable * * *.

The only types of corporate enterprises that will be discouraged as a result of a decision allowing the individual shareholder to be sued will be those such as the one in question, designed solely to abuse the corporate privilege at the expense of the public interest.

For these reasons I would vote to affirm the order of the Appellate Division.

DESMOND, C.J., and VAN VOORHIS, BURKE and SCILEPPI, JJ., concur with FULD, J.

KEATING, J., dissents and votes to affirm in an opinion in which BERGAN, J., concurs.

———

On remand, the court upheld an amended complaint against the shareholder as sufficiently alleging that the defendants conducted business in their individual capacities. 29 A.D.2d 763, 287 N.Y.S.2d 546 (2d

Dept.1968), *aff'd mem.* 23 N.Y.2d 714, 296 N.Y.S.2d 362, 244 N.E.2d 55 (1968). The case later settled.

## RADASZEWSKI v. TELECOM CORP.

981 F.2d 305 (8th Cir.1992), *cert. denied* 508 U.S. 908, 113 S.Ct. 2338, 124 L.Ed.2d 248 (1993)

RICHARD S. ARNOLD, CHIEF JUDGE.

This is an action for personal injuries filed on behalf of Konrad Radaszewski, who was seriously injured in an automobile accident on August 21, 1984. Radaszewski, who was on a motorcycle, was struck by a truck driven by an employee of Contrux, Inc. The question presented on this appeal is whether the District Court had jurisdiction over the person of Telecom Corporation, which is the corporate parent of Contrux. This question depends, in turn, on whether, under Missouri law, Radaszewski can "pierce the corporate veil," and hold Telecom liable for the conduct of its subsidiary, Contrux, and Contrux's driver. * * *

### I.

In general, someone injured by the conduct of a corporation or one of its employees can look only to the assets of the employee or of the employer corporation for recovery. The shareholders of the corporation, including, if there is one, its parent corporation, are not responsible. This is a conscious decision made by the law of every state to encourage business in the corporate form. Obviously the decision has its costs. Some injuries are going to go unredressed because of the insolvency of the corporate defendant immediately involved, even when its shareholders have plenty of money. To the general rule, though, there are exceptions. There are instances in which an injured person may "pierce the corporate veil," that is, reach the assets of one or more of the shareholders of the corporation whose conduct has created liability. In the present case, the plaintiff seeks to hold Telecom Corporation liable for the conduct of an employee of its wholly owned subsidiary, Contrux, Inc.

Under Missouri law, a plaintiff in this position needs to show three things. * * *

(1) Control, not mere majority or complete stock control, but complete domination, not only of finances, but of policy and business practice in respect to the transaction attacked so that the corporate entity as to this transaction had at the time no separate mind, will or existence of its own; and

(2) Such control must have been used by the defendant to commit fraud or wrong, to perpetrate the violation of a statutory or other positive legal duty, or dishonest and unjust act in contravention of plaintiff's legal rights; and

(3) The aforesaid control and breach of duty must proximately cause the injury or unjust loss complained of.

*Collet v. American National Stores, Inc.*, 708 S.W.2d 273, 284 (Mo.App. 1986).

[Because Telecom, as such, has had no contact with Missouri, whether Missouri courts have jurisdiction over Telecom depends on whether the corporate veil of Contrux can be pierced. The parties have argued the case as one of jurisdiction, and so will we, but in fact the underlying issue is whether Telecom can be held liable for what Contrux did.]

\* \* \*

## II.

[To satisfy] the second element of the *Collet* formulation, \* \* \* plaintiff cites no direct evidence of improper motivation or violation of law on Telecom's part. He argues, instead, that Contrux was undercapitalized.

Undercapitalizing a subsidiary, which we take to mean creating it and putting it in business without a reasonably sufficient supply of money, has become a sort of proxy under Missouri law for the second *Collet* element. \* \* \* The reason, we think, is not because undercapitalization, in and of itself, is unlawful (though it may be for some purposes), but rather because the creation of an undercapitalized subsidiary justifies an inference that the parent is either deliberately or recklessly creating a business that will not be able to pay its bills or satisfy judgments against it. This point has been made clear by the Supreme Court of Missouri. In *May Department Stores Co. v. Union Electric Light & Power Co.*, 341 Mo. 299, 327, 107 S.W.2d 41, 55 (1937), the Court found an improper purpose in a case where a corporation was "operating it without sufficient funds to meet obligations to those who must deal with it." Similarly, in *Consolidated Sun Ray, Inc. v. Oppenstein*, 335 F.2d 801 (8th Cir.1964), we said:

> Making a corporation a supplemental part of an economic unit and operating it without sufficient funds to meet obligations to those who must deal with it would be circumstantial evidence tending to show either an improper purpose or reckless disregard of the rights of others.

*Id.* at 806–07.

Here, the District Court held, and we assume, that Contrux was undercapitalized in the accounting sense. Most of the money contributed to its operation by Telecom was in the form of loans, not equity, and, when Contrux first went into business, Telecom did not pay for all of the stock that was issued to it. \* \* \* Telecom in effect concedes that Contrux's balance sheet was anemic, and that, from the point of view of generally accepted accounting principles, Contrux was inadequately capitalized. Telecom says, however, that this doesn't matter, because Contrux had $11,000,000 worth of liability insurance available to pay judgments like the one that Radaszewski hopes to obtain. No one can say, therefore, the argument runs, that Telecom was improperly motivated in setting up Contrux, in the sense of either knowingly or recklessly establishing it without the ability to pay tort judgments.

In fact, Contrux did have $1,000,000 in basic liability coverage, plus $10,000,000 in excess coverage. This coverage was bound on March 1, 1984, about five and one-half months before the accident involving Radaszewski. Unhappily, Contrux's insurance carrier became insolvent two years after the accident and is now in receivership. * * * But this insurance, Telecom points out, was sufficient to satisfy federal financial-responsibility requirements [applicable to interstate carriers such as Contrux].

The District Court rejected this argument. Undercapitalization is undercapitalization, it reasoned, regardless of insurance. The Court said:

> The federal regulation does not speak to what constitutes a properly capitalized motor carrier company. Rather, the regulation speaks to what constitutes an appropriate level of *financial responsibility*.

*Konrad Radaszewski v. Contrux, Inc.*, No. 88–0445–CV–W–1 (W.D.Mo. Oct. 26, 1990), slip op. 7 n. 6 (emphasis in original). This distinction escapes us. The whole purpose of asking whether a subsidiary is "properly capitalized," is precisely to determine its "financial responsibility." If the subsidiary is financially responsible, whether by means of insurance or otherwise, the policy behind the second part of the *Collet* test is met. Insurance meets this policy just as well, perhaps even better, than a healthy balance sheet.

At the oral argument, counsel for Radaszewski described the insurance company in question as "fly-by-night." He pointed out, and this is in the record, that the insurance agency that placed the coverage, Dixie Insurance Agency, Inc., was, like Contrux, a wholly owned subsidiary of Telecom. (Apparently the $1,000,000 primary policy is still in force. It is only the $10,000,000 excess policy that is inoperative on account of the insolvency of the excess carrier, Integrity Insurance Co.) Plaintiff argues that if the case went to trial he could show that the excess carrier "was an insurance company with wobbly knees for years before its receivership." Reply Brief of Appellant 9. He also says that the excess carrier was not strong enough even to receive a minimum rating in the Best Insurance Guide. Finally, plaintiff suggests that Contrux bought "its insurance from a financially unsound company which most certainly charged a significantly lower premium." Reply Brief of Appellant 10.

\* \* \*

Insurance is unquestionably relevant on the issue of "undercapitalization." The existence of insurance goes directly to the question of the subsidiary's financial responsibility. * * * Here, it is beyond dispute that Contrux had insurance, and that it was considered financially responsible under the applicable federal regulations. We see nothing sinister in the fact that the insurance was purchased through an agency wholly owned by Telecom. This is a common business practice. The assertion that a reduced premium was paid is wholly without support in the record. It is based on speculation only. There is no evidence that Telecom or Contrux knew that the insurance company was going to become insolvent, and no reason, indeed, that we can think of why anyone would want to buy insurance from a company that he thought would become insolvent.

\* \* \*

[I]nformation [that Integrity had operated for several years at a loss], in our view, supports at most an inference that Contrux may have made an error in business judgment in placing its excess coverage with Integrity. It furnishes no genuine support for an inference of improper purpose.

The doctrine of limited liability is intended precisely to protect a parent corporation whose subsidiary goes broke. That is the whole purpose of the doctrine, and those who have the right to decide such questions, that is, legislatures, believe that the doctrine, on the whole, is socially reasonable and useful. We think that the doctrine would largely be destroyed if a parent corporation could be held liable simply on the basis of errors in business judgment. Something more than that should be shown, and *Collet* requires something more than that. In our view, this record is devoid of facts to show that "something more."

\* \* \*

HEANEY, SENIOR CIRCUIT JUDGE, dissenting.

I respectfully dissent. The record is more than sufficient to support a prima facie showing that personal jurisdiction over Telecom exists.

\* \* \* In every respect on the basis of the record now before us, Contrux was nothing but a shell corporation established by Telecom to permit it to operate as a nonunion carrier without regard to the consequences that might occur to those who did business with Contrux or those who might be affected by its actions.

\* \* \*

The majority asks why anyone would want to buy insurance from an insolvent company. An answer readily comes to mind. The purchase was a cheap way of complying with federal regulations and furthered the illusion to all concerned that Contrux was a viable company able to meet its responsibilities. \* \* \*

As the matter now stands, the innocent victim may have to bear most of the costs of his disabling injuries without having the opportunity to prove that Contrux was intentionally undercapitalized. I believe this is wrong and inconsistent with Missouri law. I would thus remand for trial.

### Note: Undercapitalization

Courts using undercapitalization as a test for veil-piercing usually focus on whether, when the the corporation began its activities, it had sufficient financial resources to satisfy any losses likely to be generated its business, activities, given the risks associated with that business. The first question is what, precisely, counts as "capital"? Typically, capital consists of shareholder equity, although, in a tort context, it also may include insurance coverage. Moreover, it is not uncommon for one or more of the principal shareholders to lend the corporation substantial amounts of money; whether such loans will be considered capital depends on the totality of the circumstances, including the risks of the new venture and the proportion that the loans bear to the total capital of the corporation.

In *O'Hazza v. Executive Credit Corp.*, 246 Va. 111, 431 S.E.2d 318 (1993), the O'Hazza family contributed $10,000 in initial equity capital to the corporation and subsequently lent it approximately $140,000 over a two-year period. In reversing the trial court's decision to hold the individual shareholders personally liable for an unpaid corporate loan, the Virginia Supreme Court stated:

> Initial capitalization of a corporation can be an indicator of whether a corporation was created and operated as a sham or as the alter ego for another corporation or person. If, from its inception, a corporation is unable to pay its costs of doing business because of grossly inadequate capitalization, its legitimacy is suspect. Under such circumstances, stock holders may not be entitled to the corporate shield. Thus, the court in *Re County Green Ltd. Partnership*, 438 F.Supp. 701 (W.D.Va.1977), held that initial capitalization of $100, accompanied by a situation in which the controlling shareholder drained the corporation's earnings and increased the corporation's financial dependency, were factors used to justify a decision to pierce the corporate veil.

> In the instant case, the creditor produced no evidence to show what an appropriate level of capitalization would have been for a business that installed sound equipment. Consequently, a determination that $10,000 was insufficient initial capitalization is questionable, particularly in light of the $9,412 profit shown on the corporation's federal tax return for 1987, its first year of operation.

> We note also that, to gain certain tax advantages, small corporations increasingly, and legitimately, choose to initially capitalize the entity with a small portion of the investment represented by stock and with the larger portion of capital set up as loans to the corporation. If the corporation fails, these loans are subordinated to those of other creditors. And, as pointed out by the O'Hazzas, federal courts, in distinguishing between corporate debt and risk capital, have considered a loan made to a corporation by stockholders without expectation of repayment as an indication that the transaction involved venture capital, not a true loan.

431 S.E.2d at 321.

Logic suggests that rather than focus on whether a corporation had adequate capital when it was formed, courts also should require a corporation to increase its capital as the risks associated with its business grow. However, this logic has not been widely accepted. Courts generally have not required shareholders to increase a corporation's capital simply because the corporation has lost money. William P. Hackney and Tracey G. Benson, *Shareholder Liability for Inadequate Capital*, 43 U. PITT. L. REV. 837, 898–99 (1982). On the other hand, *Klokke Corp. v. Classic Exposition, Inc.*, 139 Or.App. 399, 912 P.2d 929 (Or.App.1996), held that a shareholder who contributed to the deliberate undercapitalization of a corporation could be held liable for its debts, with the caveat that his liability might be limited to the amount of capital he had wrongfully withdrawn from the corporation.

Professor Thompson, *supra*, argues that undercapitalization is not a significant factor in veil-piercing cases. He finds that undercapitalization was present in only 19% of the contract cases and 13% of the tort cases in which the corporate veil was pierced. These data suggest that when considering undercapitalization, context does not matter greatly. Nevertheless, undercapitalization may affect the outcome when it is present; in the cases in which undercapitalization was found, the corporate veil was pierced almost three-quarters of the time. The Ninth Circuit, interpreting California law, has stated that "undercapitalization alone will justify piercing the corporate veil." *Nilsson v. Louisiana Hydrolec*, 854 F.2d 1538, 1544 (9th Cir.1988). Presser suggests this statement is inaccurate. *See* Stephen B. Presser, PIERCING THE CORPORATE VEIL §§ 1.05[2] n.16, 2.05 (1993). However, in *Slottow v. American Cas. Co. of Reading, Pa.*, 10 F.3d 1355, 1360 (9th Cir.1993), the Ninth Circuit reiterated its view that, under California law, undercapitalization alone constitutes an "excellent argument" for piercing the corporate veil.

# C.   CONTRACT CREDITORS

## FREEMAN v. COMPLEX COMPUTING CO., INC.

119 F.3d 1044 (2d Cir.1997).

MINER, CIRCUIT JUDGE:

\* \* \*

### BACKGROUND

While pursuing graduate studies under a fellowship at Columbia University in the early 1990s, [defendant Jason] Glazier co-developed computer software with potential commercial value and negotiated with Columbia to obtain a license for the software. Columbia apparently was unwilling to license software to a corporation of which Glazier was an officer, director, or shareholder. Nonetheless, Columbia was willing to license the software to a corporation that retained Glazier as an independent contractor. The licensed corporation then could sublicense the product to others for profit.

Accordingly, in September of 1992, [Complex Computing Co., Inc. ("C3")] was incorporated, with an acquaintance of Glazier's as the sole shareholder and initial director, and Seth Akabas (a partner of Glazier's counsel in this action) as the president, treasurer and assistant secretary. In November of 1992, another corporation, Glazier, Inc., of which Glazier was the sole shareholder, entered into an agreement with C3 (the "consulting agreement").[1] Under the consulting agreement, Glazier, Inc. was retained as an independent contractor (titled as C3's "Scientific Advisor") to develop and market Glazier's software, which was licensed from Columbia, and to provide support services to C3's clients. Glazier was designated the sole signatory on C3's bank account, and was given a written option to purchase all of C3's stock for $2,000.

In September of 1993, C3 entered into an agreement with [plaintiff Daniel Freeman (the "C3–Freeman Agreement"), under which Freeman agreed to sell and license C3's computer software products for a five-year term. In exchange, C3 agreed to pay Freeman commissions on the revenue received by C3 over a ten-year period from the client-base developed by Freeman, including the revenue received from sales and licensing, maintenance and support services. The C3–Freeman Agreement included provisions relating to Freeman's compensation if C3 terminated the agreement prior to its expiration, or if C3 made a sale that did not result in revenues because of a future merger, consolidation, or stock acquisition. The agreement included an arbitration clause * * *.

Schedule 1 of the C3–Freeman Agreement listed the customers from whom Freeman would receive commissions. Although C3's president signed the C3–Freeman Agreement, Glazier personally signed the periodic amendments to Schedule 1. On March 24, 1994, Glazier signed an amended Schedule 1 that listed as customers, among numerous others, Thomson Financial, Banker's Trust and Chemical Bank. The amendment provided that "[t]o date, Dan Freeman has performed—and will continue to perform—material marketing services" as regards these customers.

On August 22, 1994, C3 and Thomson Investment Software, a unit or affiliate of Thomson [Trading Services, Inc. ("Thomson")], entered into a licensing agreement that granted Thomson exclusive worldwide sales and marketing rights of C3's products. Freeman contends that the licensing agreement resulted from efforts made by him over approximately nine months to bring the transaction to fruition.

In October of 1994, C3 gave Freeman the requisite 60–days notice of the termination of its agreement with him. The letter of termination, signed by Glazier, explained that C3's exercise of its option to terminate Freeman's employment was "an action to combat the overly generous termination clause we committed to, and to force a renegotiation of your sales contract."

---

**1.** Although the consulting agreement was between C3 and Glazier, Inc., numerous provisions in the agreement made express reference to Glazier personally. For example, the consulting agreement provided that it was terminable if Glazier himself was unable to perform or supervise performance of Glazier, Inc.'s obligations.

Glazier was hired in January of 1995 as Thomson Investment Software's Vice President and Director of Research and Development at a starting salary of $150,000 plus additional payments of "incentive compensation" based in part upon the revenues received by Thomson in connection with the sale or license of products developed by Glazier. On the same day, Thomson and C3 entered into an assets purchase agreement (the "Thomson Agreement" or "assets purchase agreement"). As part of the transaction, Thomson assumed C3's intellectual products, trademarks and tradenames. It also assumed most of the liabilities and obligations of existing agreements involving C3, including agreements with C3 customers such as Banker's Trust and Chemical Bank. The Thomson Agreement set forth a list of C3 agreements assumed by Thomson, but expressly excluded the C3–Freeman Agreement. Thomson paid a total of $750,000, from which Glazier was paid $450,000 as a "signing bonus" in connection with his new employment contract; and C3 was paid $300,000, $100,000 of which was held by Thomson in an escrow account to indemnify Thomson for legal expenses in defending itself against claims arising from the assets purchase agreement, as well as for other expenses.

In May of 1995, Freeman commenced the action giving rise to this appeal. * * * He estimated that he was due more than $100,000, and that the moneys due him in the future under the agreement would be in excess of $5 million.

\* \* \*

In a memorandum opinion dated June 28, 1996, the district court found that both C3 and Glazier should be compelled to arbitrate their disputes with Freeman in accordance with the C3–Freeman Agreement. The district court found that Glazier was subject to the arbitration clause of the C3–Freeman Agreement because he "did not merely dominate and control C3—to all intents and purposes, he was C3" and because he held the "sole economic interest of any significance" in the corporation. *Freeman v. Complex Computing Co., Inc.*, 931 F.Supp. 1115, 1120 (S.D.N.Y.1996). The district court intended the judgment to "dispose[ ] of all claims asserted herein between and among [Freeman, C3 and Glazier]." *Id.* at 1124.

\* \* \*

DISCUSSION

\* \* \*

## II. Piercing the Corporate Veil

Glazier argues on appeal that the district court erred in piercing the corporate veil to compel him to arbitrate Freeman's claims pursuant to the arbitration provision of the C3–Freeman Agreement. First, he contends that he cannot be held liable on a veil-piercing theory because he is neither a shareholder, officer, director or employee of C3. Second,

Glazier argues that the district court's determination that he controlled C3 does not justify piercing the corporate veil in the absence of a factual finding that he used his control over C3 to wrong Freeman. We reject the former contention, but agree that the district court erred in piercing the corporate veil before finding that Glazier used his domination of C3 to wrong Freeman.

Neither party disputes that New York law applies to these issues. We review de novo the district court's legal conclusions.

### A. Glazier's Equitable Ownership of C3

Glazier contends that he should not be held personally liable under a veil-piercing theory because he is not a shareholder, officer, director, or employee of C3. We reject this argument.

New York courts have recognized for veil-piercing purposes the doctrine of equitable ownership, under which an individual who exercises sufficient control over the corporation may be deemed an "equitable owner", notwithstanding the fact that the individual is not a shareholder of the corporation. As the Appellate Division explained in *Lally v. Catskill Airways, Inc.*, a nonshareholder defendant may be, "in reality," the equitable owner of a corporation where the nonshareholder defendant "exercise[s] considerable authority over [the corporation] . . . to the point of completely disregarding the corporate form and acting as though [its] assets [are] his alone to manage and distribute." 198 A.D.2d 643, 603 N.Y.S.2d 619, 621 (3d Dep't 1993).

\* \* \*

Because Glazier "exercised considerable authority over [the corporation] . . . to the point of completely disregarding the corporate form and acting as though [its] assets were his alone to manage and distribute," *see Lally*, 603 N.Y.S.2d at 621, he is appropriately viewed as C3's equitable owner for veil-piercing purposes. If there were board meetings, no minutes were kept from August 1994 through May 1995. Glazier agreed to personally indemnify C3's sole shareholder and director against any liability arising from the performance of his duties as C3's director. The president of C3 never attended a meeting of the Board of Directors. No shareholder received dividends or other distributions, despite the corporate income of $563,257 in 1994 and $200,000 from the assets sale to Thomson.

Glazier used C3 to sell his intellectual product and powers, including the software that he had co-developed at Columbia and which Columbia licensed to C3. Through payments from C3 to Glazier, Inc., he received the vast majority of the resulting revenues.[5] Both Glazier, Inc. and C3 were located at Glazier's apartment, and Glazier was the sole signatory

---

**5.** The consulting agreement provided that C3 would not pay anyone compensation unless Glazier, Inc. had first received its share in full. The consulting agreement obligated C3 to pay Glazier, Inc. annual compensation of $150,000, with "cost-of-living" adjustments. In addition, it was to pay Glazier, Inc. a bonus for each calendar year equal to 60% of the first $200,000 in revenues received by C3, 70% of the next $200,-000, 80% of the third $200,000, and 85% of all revenues received thereafter.

on C3's bank account. Glazier, Inc.'s consulting agreement with C3 expressly provided that it was terminable if Glazier himself was unable to perform or supervise the performance of Glazier, Inc.'s obligations to C3, which were described as "marketing [C3's] software products, developing new software products, enhancing [C3's] existing software products, and providing support services to [C3's] clients." These obligations essentially described C3's entire business.

Glazier himself gave Thomson a resume stating that from 1992 to the present, Glazier was the principal, owner and manager of C3, and that Glazier, Inc. was the predecessor to C3. C3 paid over $8000 to the law firm that represented Glazier personally in his negotiations with Thomson. These negotiations resulted in Thomson employing Glazier and paying him a $450,000 signing bonus. C3 then paid Glazier, through Glazier, Inc., an additional $210,000 out of the proceeds of the assets and other funds that were in the C3 bank account following the assets purchase. After payment of taxes and other expenses, this left only $10,000 in C3's account. Freeman contends that this balance renders C3 unable to fulfill its alleged obligations to him. Additionally, Glazier had an option to purchase all the shares of C3 from its sole shareholder for $2000. Thus, at his discretion, he could have become the sole shareholder for a small payment.

The district court found that "[t]o regard [Glazier] as anything but the sole stockholder and controlling person of C3 would be to exalt form over substance." *Freeman*, 931 F.Supp. at 1120. Under the unique facts of the instant case, viewed in their totality, we agree that it is appropriate to treat Glazier as an "equitable owner" for veil-piercing purposes. *See Lally*, 603 N.Y.S.2d at 621.

### B. Piercing the C3 Veil

The presumption of corporate independence and limited shareholder liability serves to encourage business development. *See Wm. Passalacqua Builders, Inc. v. Resnick Developers S., Inc.*, 933 F.2d 131, 139 (2d Cir.1991). Nevertheless, that presumption will be set aside, and courts will pierce the corporate veil under certain limited circumstances. Specifically, such "[l]iability ... may be predicated either upon a showing of fraud or upon complete control by the dominating [entity] that leads to a wrong against third parties." *Wm. Passalacqua Builders*, 933 F.2d at 138. As we explained in *Wm. Passalacqua Builders*, to pierce the corporate veil under New York law, a plaintiff must prove that "(1) [the owner] ha[s] exercised such control that the [corporation] has become a mere instrumentality of the [owner], which is the real actor; (2) such control has been used to commit a fraud or other wrong; and (3) the fraud or wrong results in an unjust loss or injury to plaintiff." *Id.* (internal quotation omitted).

To the extent that we have restated this test in cases such as *Carte Blanche (Singapore) Pte., Ltd. v. Diners Club International, Inc.*, 2 F.3d 24 (2d Cir.1993), in which we stated that veil-piercing will be allowed "in two broad situations: to prevent fraud or other wrong, or where a parent dominates and controls a subsidiary," *id.* at 26, the element of domination and control never was considered to be sufficient of itself to justify the piercing of a corporate veil. Unless the control is utilized to perpetrate a fraud or other wrong, limited liability will prevail. *See Wm. Passalacqua Builders*, 933 F.2d at 138. As we explained in *Electronic Switching Industries, Inc. v. Faradyne Electronics Corp.*, even if a plaintiff showed that the dominator of a corporation had complete control over the corporation so that the corporation "had no separate mind, will, or existence of its own," New York law will not allow the corporate veil to be pierced in the absence of a showing that this control "was used to commit wrong, fraud, or the breach of a legal duty, or a dishonest and unjust act in contravention of plaintiff's legal rights, and that the control and breach of duty proximately caused the injury complained of." 833 F.2d 418, 424 (2d Cir.1987).

In determining whether "complete control" exists, we have considered such factors as: (1) disregard of corporate formalities; (2) inadequate capitalization; (3) intermingling of funds; (4) overlap in ownership, officers, directors, and personnel; (5) common office space, address and telephone numbers of corporate entities; (6) the degree of discretion shown by the allegedly dominated corporation; (7) whether the dealings between the entities are at arms length; (8) whether the corporations are treated as independent profit centers; (9) payment or guarantee of the corporation's debts by the dominating entity, and (10) intermingling of property between the entities. *See Wm. Passalacqua Builders*, 933 F.2d at 139. No one factor is decisive. In this case, there is little question that Glazier exercised "complete control" over C3.

As discussed in the context of equitable ownership, the record is replete with examples of Glazier's control over C3. Therefore, the district court's finding of control was not erroneous. However, the district court erred in the decision to pierce C3's corporate veil solely on the basis of a finding of domination and control. "While complete domination of the corporation is the key to piercing the corporate veil, ... such domination, standing alone, is not enough; some showing of a wrongful or unjust act toward plaintiff is required." *Morris v. New York State Dep't of Taxation & Fin.*, 82 N.Y.2d 135, 603 N.Y.S.2d 807, 811, 623 N.E.2d 1157, 1161 (1993) (citation omitted); *see Wm. Passalacqua Builders*, 933 F.2d at 138. Thus, while we accept the district court's factual finding that Glazier controlled C3, we remand to the district court the issue of whether Glazier used his control over C3 to commit a fraud or other wrong that resulted in unjust loss or injury to Freeman. Though there is substantial evidence of such wrongdoing, a finding on this issue must be made in the first instance by the district court before veil-piercing occurs. * * *

GODBOLD, SENIOR CIRCUIT JUDGE, concurring in part, dissenting in part.

* * *

I concur in affirming the district court's holding that Glazier was in total control of C3. I see no need, however, to remand the case to the district court for it to determine whether "Glazier used his control over C3 to commit a fraud or other wrong that resulted in an unjust loss or injury to Freeman." The record before us discloses fraud or other wrong by Glazier, through C3, resulting in an unjust loss or injury to Freeman. Consequently C3's corporate veil is to be pierced, and, without more, arbitration should proceed against Glazier as well as C3.

In some "corporate veil" cases one must search the record for evidence shedding light on whether an individual's control of the corporation has been used to commit a fraud or wrong resulting in unjust loss or injury. Not in this case. Here it all hangs out.

C3 is Glazier's creature, subject to his "complete control" ("he [Glazier] was C3"). C3 agreed with Freeman for him to sell and license C3's software products for five years and to receive commissions for ten years on revenue received from Freeman's clients. Plus, if C3 merged or consolidated, Freeman was to receive an additional payment of 10% percent of the total consideration conveyed. The agreement contained a termination clause. C3 could terminate on sixty days notice, but Freeman was entitled to receive all compensation for services previously rendered as well as the commissions that accrued over a ten year period (presumably to include 10% percent of the consideration for a buy out or merger).

An arbitration clause was included: "Any controversy or claim arising out of or related to this Agreement or any breach thereof ... shall be settled by arbitration."

Approximately a year after the C3–Freeman agreement was made C3 entered into an agreement with Thomson Trading Services, Inc., an account developed by Freeman, to make Thomson its exclusive worldwide marketer. * * * Thomson took over existing C3 agreements, but not C3's agreement with Freeman. That agreement remained C3's responsibility. But C3 has paid Freeman nothing.

It remained for C3 to get rid of Freeman. It did so by a purported termination of the C3–Freeman agreement. C3 recited that it was exercising its option to terminate as "an action to combat the overly generous termination clause we committed to, and to force a renegotiation of your sales contract." In short, Freeman was not to receive the benefits guaranteed him by the termination clause; the termination was to force him to give up the "overly generous" termination benefits he was entitled to receive. The asserted termination was not to implement the provision for termination but in derogation of it.

By this Tinker-to Evans-to Chance play:

—C3's business has gone to Thomson.

—Thomson has handsomely rewarded Glazier.

—Thomson, in acquiring C3, has not assumed responsibility for the Freeman agreement.

—Glazier is enjoying the generous fruits of the C3–Thomson deal while C3 has been reduced to a shell.

—Freeman has been stripped of his benefits, paid nothing, and hung out to dry, on the asserted ground that benefits (past and future) agreed to be paid to him by C3 were too generous.

This is fraud by Glazier—a fully revealed rip off. But if one shrinks from the word "fraud" it is at least a "wrongful injury." We should not hesitate to say so at the appellate level, for the record is clear.\*

## KINNEY SHOE CORP. v. POLAN

939 F.2d 209 (4th Cir.1991).

CHAPMAN, SENIOR CIRCUIT JUDGE:

Plaintiff-appellant Kinney Shoe Corporation ("Kinney") brought this action \* \* \* against Lincoln M. Polan ("Polan") seeking to recover money owed on a sublease between Kinney and Industrial Realty Company ("Industrial"). Polan is the sole shareholder of Industrial. The district court found that Polan was not personally liable on the lease between Kinney and Industrial. Kinney appeals asserting that the corporate veil should be pierced, and we agree.

### I.

The district court based its order on facts which were stipulated by the parties. In 1984 Polan formed two corporations, Industrial and Polan Industries, Inc., for the purpose of re-establishing an industrial manufacturing business. The certificate of incorporation for Polan Industries, Inc. was issued by the West Virginia Secretary of State in November 1984. The following month the certificate of incorporation for Industrial was issued. Polan was the owner of both corporations. Although certificates of incorporation were issued, no organizational meetings were held, and no officers were elected.

In November 1984 Polan and Kinney began negotiating the sublease of a building in which Kinney held a leasehold interest. The building was owned by the Cabell County Commission and financed by industrial revenue bonds issued in 1968 to induce Kinney to locate a manufacturing plant in Huntington, West Virginia. Under the terms of the lease, Kinney was legally obligated to make payments on the bonds on a semi-annual basis through January 1, 1993, at which time it had the right to purchase the property. Kinney had ceased using the building as a manufacturing plant in June 1983.

The term of the sublease from Kinney to Industrial commenced in December 1984, even though the written lease was not signed by the parties until April 5, 1985. On April 15, 1985, Industrial subleased part

---

\* On remand, the court found that Glazier's actions constituted fraudulent or other wrongful behavior because they left Freeman as "a general creditor of an essentially defunct corporation with virtually no assets." *Freeman v. Complex Consulting Co., Inc.*, 979 F.Supp. 257, 260 (S.D.N.Y. 1997). The court entered an order compelling Glazier to arbitrate plaintiff's claim. [—Ed.]

of the building to Polan Industries for fifty percent of the rental amount due Kinney. Polan signed both subleases on behalf of the respective companies.

Other than the sublease with Kinney, Industrial had no assets, no income and no bank account. Industrial issued no stock certificates because nothing was ever paid in to this corporation. Industrial's only income was from its sublease to Polan Industries, Inc. The first rental payment to Kinney was made out of Polan's personal funds, and no further payments were made by Polan or by Polan Industries, Inc. to either Industrial or to Kinney.

Kinney filed suit against Industrial for unpaid rent and obtained a judgment in the amount of $166,400.00 on June 19, 1987. A writ of possession was issued, but because Polan Industries, Inc. had filed for bankruptcy, Kinney did not gain possession for six months. Kinney leased the building until it was sold on September 1, 1988. Kinney then filed this action against Polan individually to collect the amount owed by Industrial to Kinney. Since the amount to which Kinney is entitled is undisputed, the only issue is whether Kinney can pierce the corporate veil and hold Polan personally liable.

The district court held that Kinney had assumed the risk of Industrial's undercapitalization and was not entitled to pierce the corporate veil. Kinney appeals, and we reverse.

## II.

We have long recognized that a corporation is an entity, separate and distinct from its officers and stockholders, and the individual stockholders are not responsible for the debts of the corporation. *See, e.g., DeWitt Truck Brokers, Inc. v. W. Ray Flemming Fruit Co.*, 540 F.2d 681, 683 (4th Cir.1976). This concept, however, is a fiction of the law " 'and it is now well settled, as a general principle, that the fiction should be disregarded when it is urged with an intent not within its reason and purpose, and in such a way that its retention would produce injustices or inequitable consequences.' " *Laya v. Erin Homes, Inc.*, 352 S.E.2d 93, 97–98 (W.Va.1986) (quoting *Sanders v. Roselawn Memorial Gardens, Inc.*, 152 W.Va. 91, 159 S.E.2d 784, 786 (1968).

Piercing the corporate veil is an equitable remedy, and the burden rests with the party asserting such claim. DeWitt Truck Brokers, 540 F.2d at 683. A totality of the circumstances test is used in determining whether to pierce the corporate veil, and each case must be decided on its own facts. The district court's findings of facts may be overturned only if clearly erroneous. *Id.*

Kinney seeks to pierce the corporate veil of Industrial so as to hold Polan personally liable on the sublease debt. The Supreme Court of Appeals of West Virginia has set forth a two prong test to be used in determining whether to pierce a corporate veil in a breach of contract case. This test raises two issues: first, is the unity of interest and ownership such that the separate personalities of the corporation and the individual shareholder no longer exist; and second, would an equitable result occur if the acts are treated as those of the corporation alone. *Laya*, 352 S.E.2d at 99. Numerous factors have been identified as relevant in making this determination.

The district court found that the two prong test of *Laya* had been satisfied. The court concluded that Polan's failure to carry out the corporate formalities with respect to Industrial, coupled with Industrial's gross undercapitalization, resulted in damage to Kinney. We agree.

It is undisputed that Industrial was not adequately capitalized. Actually, it had no paid in capital. Polan had put nothing into this corporation, and it did not observe any corporate formalities. As the West Virginia court stated in Laya, " '[i]ndividuals who wish to enjoy limited personal liability for business activities under a corporate umbrella should be expected to adhere to the relatively simple formalities of creating and maintaining a corporate entity.' " *Laya*, 352 S.E.2d at 100 n. 6 (quoting *Labadie Coal Co. v. Black*, 672 F.2d 92, 96–97 (D.C.Cir. 1982)). This, the court stated, is " 'a relatively small price to pay for limited liability.' " *Id*. Another important factor is adequate capitalization. "[G]rossly inadequate capitalization combined with disregard of corporate formalities, causing basic unfairness, are sufficient to pierce the corporate veil in order to hold the shareholder(s) actively participating in the operation of the business personally liable for a breach of contract to the party who entered into the contract with the corporation." *Laya*, 352 S.E.2d at 101–02.

In this case, Polan bought no stock, made no capital contribution, kept no minutes, and elected no officers for Industrial. In addition, Polan attempted to protect his assets by placing them in Polan Industries, Inc. and interposing Industrial between Polan Industries, Inc. and Kinney so as to prevent Kinney from going against the corporation with assets. Polan gave no explanation or justification for the existence of Industrial as the intermediary between Polan Industries, Inc. and Kinney. Polan was obviously trying to limit his liability and the liability of Polan Industries, Inc. by setting up a paper curtain constructed of nothing more than Industrial's certificate of incorporation. These facts present the classic scenario for an action to pierce the corporate veil so as to reach the responsible party and produce an equitable result. Accordingly, we hold that the district court correctly found that the two prong test in *Laya* had been satisfied.

In *Laya*, the court also noted that when determining whether to pierce a corporate veil a third prong may apply in certain cases. The court stated: "When, under the circumstances, it would be reasonable for that particular type of a party [those contract creditors capable of protecting themselves] entering into a contract with the corporation, for example, a bank or other lending institution, to conduct an investigation of the credit of the corporation prior to entering into the contract, such party will be charged with the knowledge that a reasonable credit investigation would disclose. If such an investigation would disclose that the corporation is grossly undercapitalized, based upon the nature and the magnitude of the corporate undertaking, such party will be deemed to have assumed the risk of the gross undercapitalization and will not be permitted to pierce the corporate veil." *Laya*, 352 S.E.2d at 100. The district court applied this third prong and concluded that Kinney "assumed the risk of Industrial's defaulting" and that "the application of the doctrine of 'piercing the corporate veil' ought not and does not [apply]." While we agree that the two prong test of Laya was satisfied, we hold that the district court's conclusion that Kinney had assumed the risk is clearly erroneous.

Without deciding whether the third prong should be extended beyond the context of the financial institution lender mentioned in *Laya*, we hold that, even if it applies to creditors such as Kinney, it does not prevent Kinney from piercing the corporate veil in this case. The third prong is permissive and not mandatory. This is not a factual situation that calls for the third prong, if we are to seek an equitable result. Polan set up Industrial to limit his liability and the liability of Polan Industries, Inc. in their dealings with Kinney. A stockholder's liability is limited to the amount he has invested in the corporation, but Polan invested nothing in Industrial. This corporation was no more than a shell—a transparent shell. When nothing is invested in the corporation, the corporation provides no protection to its owner; nothing in, nothing out, no protection. If Polan wishes the protection of a corporation to limit his liability, he must follow the simple formalities of maintaining the corporation. This he failed to do, and he may not relieve his circumstances by saying Kinney should have known better.

### III.

For the foregoing reasons, we hold that Polan is personally liable for the debt of Industrial, and the decision of the district court is reversed and this case is remanded with instructions to enter judgment for the plaintiff.

Reversed and Remanded With Instructions.

### *Note: Piercing to Benefit Contract Creditors*

*Freeman* and *Polan* are exceptions to the general rule of limited liability. More typical, if less interesting to discuss, are cases such as *Paul Steelman, Ltd. v. Omni Realty*, 110 Nev. 1223, 885 P.2d 549 (Nev. 1994), and *Theberge v. Darbro, Inc.*, 684 A.2d 1298 (Me.1996). *Steelman* held that absent evidence that the original capital of a corporate general partner of a limited partnership was a sham, the fact that the corporation was undercapitalized would not support a decision to pierce the corporate veil. The court noted: "It is unfortunate that Steelman's recovery is limited to the assets of two insolvent entities; but Steelman alone is responsible for not protecting against the eventuality that occurred [i.e., the insolvency of the general partner] by insisting on individual guarantees from shareholders who were financially capable of satisfying its claims...." *Id.* at 551.

*Theberge* refused to hold the sole shareholder of a corporation to which plaintiffs had loaned money liable for the corporation's debt, even though the shareholder had assured plaintiffs orally that he would "stand behind" the corporation's obligations. Reversing a trial court judgment in favor of plaintiffs, the court stated:

> The [trial] court found, and the record supports, that the defendants did not act illegally or fraudulently, but, rather, conducted themselves 'shrewdly' and employed 'sharp business practices.' The court determined that defendants did not formally, personally, guarantee the transaction and that the plaintiffs were sophisticated real estate professionals who understood the significance of a personal guarantee. * * *
>
> [Others who had advanced funds to this real estate venture took action to secure the amounts they were owed.] The plaintiffs, by contrast, failed to obtain any such guarantee from any of the defendants and instead opted to proceed with the transaction. We decline to reconstruct the agreement negotiated between the parties to effect a result beyond the plain meaning of that bargain.

*Id.* at 1301.

# D.  PARENT–SUBSIDIARY CORPORATIONS

The division of a business enterprise into multiple corporations is done for the convenience and profit maximization of the owners. Sometimes the relationship is that of parent and subsidiary: one corporation owns the stock of another. Sometimes one corporation owns the stock of many corporations, all of whom are subsidiaries of the parent and affiliates of each other. In the first case, a plaintiff who asserts an injury caused by a corporate subsidiary will seek to reach the assets of the parent to satisfy the judgment. In the second instance, the plaintiff will attempt to recover from the affiliates if neither the corporation that caused the injury or the parent corporation have sufficient assets. While it may be appropriate to respect the limited liability of the shareholders of the *parent* corporation, does it make sense to allow all the related corporations that comprise a single enterprise to be treated as separate entities?

## In re SILICONE GEL BREAST IMPLANTS PRODUCTS LIABILITY LITIGATION
### 887 F.Supp. 1447 (N.D.Ala.1995).

POINTER, CHIEF JUDGE.

[This multidistrict proceeding involved cases filed in, or removed to, federal courts in virtually every state, the District of Columbia, Puerto Rico, and the Virgin Islands, by women who claimed they had been injured by breast implants produced by Medical Equipment Corp. ("MEC"), a wholly-owned subsidiary of Bristol–Myers Squibb Co. ("Bristol"). Bristol itself never manufactured or distributed breast implants, but plaintiffs claimed that Bristol could be held liable by piercing MEC's corporate veil. After discovery was substantially complete, Bristol moved for summary judgment on plaintiffs' piercing claim.

The court noted that it was bound to use the choice of law rules of the states in which these cases had been filed to determine whether MEC's corporate veil should be pierced, that many states would apply the law of Delaware, where Bristol and MEC were incorporated, and that other states would apply their own law. Consequently, summary judgment could be proper in some cases while not warranted in others.]

### III. FACTS

For purposes of Bristol's summary judgment motion, the court treats the following facts as established, either because they are not in genuine dispute or because they are supported by evidence viewed in the light most favorable to the plaintiffs.

MEC was incorporated in Wisconsin in 1969, with its principal place of business in Racine. It was an independent, privately-held corporation manufacturing a variety of medical and plastic surgery devices, including breast implants.

In 1982, after an extensive due diligence review that included information regarding capsular contracture, rupture, and gel bleed, Bristol * * * purchased MEC's stock for $28 million * * * [and transferred MEC's business to] MEC, a Delaware corporation * * * [that] has been a wholly-owned subsidiary of Bristol, operated by Bristol as part of its Health Care Group.

In 1988 Bristol expanded its breast implant business by purchasing from the Cooper Companies two other breast-implant manufacturers, Natural Y Surgical Specialties, Inc. and Aesthetech Corporation. Though executed in the name of MEC and the Cooper Companies, the purchase was negotiated between Bristol and the Cooper Companies, and the purchase price of $8.7 million was paid from a Bristol account (though charged to MEC). The due diligence review, which indicated potential hazards and possible liability relating to polyurethane-coated breast implants, was conducted jointly by MEC and Bristol.

Documents reflect that MEC has had, at least in form, a board of three directors, generally consisting of the Bristol Vice President then serving as President of Bristol's Health Care Group, another Bristol executive, and MEC's president. Bristol's Health Care Group President, who reported to Bristol's president or chairman, could not be outvoted by the other two MEC board members. Several of the former MEC presidents did not recall that MEC had a board, let alone that they were members; and one of these stated that he did not attend, call, or receive notice of board meetings in his five years of service because he had a designated Bristol officer to contact. The few resolutions that were adopted by MEC's board were apparently prepared by Bristol officials.

MEC prepared "significant event" reports for Bristol's Corporate Policy Committee. These reports included information on breast implant production, such as publicity, testing, expenses, lawsuit settlements, and backorders caused by sterilization difficulties. Neither Bristol managers nor MEC Presidents recall any orders or recommendations being issued by Bristol as a result of these reviews. Bristol also required MEC to prepare and submit a five-year plan for its review.

MEC submitted budgets for approval by Bristol's senior management. * * * Bristol had the authority to modify this budget, though it rarely, if ever, actually did so.

Cash received by MEC was transferred to an account maintained by Bristol. This money was credited to MEC, but the interest earned was credited to Bristol. Bristol was MEC's banker, providing such loans as it determined MEC needed. Bristol required MEC to obtain its approval for capital appropriations, though most, if not all, of these requests were approved.

Bristol set the employment policies and wage scales that applied to MEC's employees. Before hiring a top executive or negotiating the salary, MEC was required to seek Bristol's approval. Before hiring a vice president of MEC, MEC's president and his superior at Bristol interviewed the candidate. Key executive employees were rated on the Bristol schedule. Bristol set a target for salary increases below the key executive level and approved those for employees above that level. Key executives of MEC received stock options for Bristol stock. MEC employees could participate in Bristol's pension and savings plans.

Bristol provided various services to MEC. * * * Bristol's scientific experts researched the hazards of breast implants and polyurethane foam. * * * Bristol funded tests on breast implants. Another Bristol subsidiary, ConvaTec, assisted MEC in developing its premarket approval application (PMAA) regarding breast implants for the FDA. In addition to this assistance, Bristol hired an outside laboratory to verify ConvaTec's analysis. Bristol also conducted post-market surveillance at the request of the FDA.

Some of Bristol's in-house counsel acted as MEC attorneys. These attorneys advised MEC on virtually every aspect of its business including budgets, price increases, new product development, package inserts, liability, compliance with FDA regulations, and negotiated settlements with individuals claiming damages from breast implants. They also developed the system for handling complaints about MEC products. They reviewed all breast implant promotional materials and responses to allegations of harm and liability.

Bristol's Technical Evaluation and Service Department ("TESD") performed auditing and review functions for MEC once or twice a year. They performed all Good Manufacturing Practices (GMP) audits at MEC. These audits were designed to ensure consistent quality of MEC's products. Bristol expected MEC to comply with any manufacturing deficiencies TESD found. A number of the conditions listed as needing corrective action regarded breast implants. TESD also audited MEC's sterilization and lab companies.

Bristol's public relations department issued statements regarding the allegations of TDA production and cancer in rats implanted with polyurethane implants. Bristol's corporate communication department prepared question and answer scripts for MEC employees for use in responding to questions about breast implant safety. Bristol's public affairs department developed a strategic plan to address concerns about the MEME implant and to respond to questions and concerns about the safety of breast implants in general. Bristol's press releases consistently represented that Bristol was researching breast implant safety. For example, in a release dated July 9, 1991, Bristol stated that tests underway would "confirm the well-established safety profile of polyure-thane coated breast implants" and that Bristol completed testing which showed that earlier findings concerning the production of TDA from the breakdown of polyurethane were the result of inappropriate testing conditions. * * *

Bristol's name and logo were contained in the package inserts and promotional products regarding breast implants, apparently as a market-ing tool to increase confidence in the product. Bristol's name was used in all sales and promotional communications with physicians.

MEC posted a profit every year between 1983 and 1990. Total sales increased from approximately $14 million in 1983 to $65 million in 1990. Bristol never received dividends from MEC. Bristol prepared consolidat-ed federal income tax returns but MEC prepared its own Wisconsin tax forms. Bristol also purchased insurance for MEC under its policy. This insurance has a face value of over $2 billion.

Bristol's executive vice president suspended MEC's sales of polyure-thane coated breast implants on April 17, 1991, and determined not to submit a PMAA for the implants to the FDA. MEC ceased its breast implant business in 1991 and later that year MEC ceased all operations by selling its urology division. This sale could not have occurred without Bristol's approval, and proceeds from the sale were turned over to Bristol, which then executed a low-interest demand note for $57,518,888 payable to MEC. MEC's only assets at this time are this demand note and its indemnity insurance.

## IV. Analysis

The various theories of recovery made by plaintiffs against Bristol can be generally divided between those involving "corporate control" and those asserting direct liability. The corporate control claims deal with piercing the corporate veil to abrogate limited liability and hold Bristol responsible for actions of MEC. * * *

### A. "Corporate Control" Claims

The potential for abuse of the corporate form is greatest when, as here, the corporation is owned by a single shareholder. The evaluation of corporate control claims cannot, however, disregard the fact that, no different from other stockholders, a parent corporation is expected— indeed, required—to exert some control over its subsidiary. Limited liability is the rule, not the exception. However, when a corporation is so controlled as to be the alter ego or mere instrumentality of its stockholder, the corporate form may be disregarded in the interests of justice. So far as this court has been able to determine, some variation of this theory of liability is recognized in all jurisdictions.

An initial question is whether veil-piercing may ever be resolved by summary judgment. Ordinarily the fact-intensive nature of the issue will require that it be resolved only through a trial. Summary judgment, however, can be proper if * * * the evidence presented could lead to but one result. Because the court concludes that a jury (or in some jurisdictions, the judge acting in equity) could—and, under the laws of many states, probably should—find that MEC was but the alter ego of Bristol, summary judgment must be denied.

The totality of circumstances must be evaluated in determining whether a subsidiary may be found to be the alter ego or mere instrumentality of the parent corporation. Although the standards are not identical in each state, all jurisdictions require a showing of substantial domination. Among the factors to be considered are whether:

- the parent and the subsidiary have common directors or officers
- the parent and the subsidiary have common business departments
- the parent and the subsidiary file consolidated financial statements and tax returns
- the parent finances the subsidiary
- the parent caused the incorporation of the subsidiary
- the subsidiary operates with grossly inadequate capital
- the parent pays the salaries and other expenses of the subsidiary
- the subsidiary receives no business except that given to it by the parent
- the parent uses the subsidiary's property as its own
- the daily operations of the two corporations are not kept separate
- the subsidiary does not observe the basic corporate formalities, such as keeping separate books and records and holding shareholder and board meetings.

*United States v. Jon–T Chemicals, Inc.*, 768 F.2d 686, 691–92 (5th Cir.1985), *cert. denied* 475 U.S. 1014 (1986).

The fact-finder at a trial could find that the evidence supports the conclusion that many of these factors have been proven: two of MEC's three directors were Bristol directors; MEC was part of Bristol's Health Care group and used Bristol's legal, auditing, and communications departments; MEC and Bristol filed consolidated federal tax returns and Bristol prepared consolidated financial reports; Bristol operated as

MEC's finance company, providing loans for the purchase of Aesthetech and Natural Y, receiving interest on MEC's funds, and requiring MEC to make requests for capital appropriations; Bristol effectively used MEC's resources as its own by obtaining interest on MEC's money and requiring MEC to make requests for capital appropriations to obtain its own funds; some members of MEC's board were not aware that MEC had a board of directors, let alone that they were members; and the senior Bristol member of MEC's board could not be out-voted by the other two directors. These facts, even apart from evidence that might establish some of the other factors listed above, would provide significant support for a finding at trial that MEC is Bristol's alter ego.

Bristol contends that a finding of fraud or like misconduct is necessary to pierce the corporate veil. Despite Bristol's contentions to the contrary, Delaware courts—to which Bristol would have this court look—do not necessarily require a showing of fraud if a subsidiary is found to be the mere instrumentality or alter ego of its sole stockholder. *See Geyer v. Ingersoll Publications Co.*, 621 A.2d 784, 793 (Del.Ch.1992), *Mabon, Nugent & Co. v. Texas American Energy Corp.*, 16 Del.J.Corp.L. 829, 838, 1990 WL 44267 (Del.Ch.1990), and *Skouras v. Admiralty Enterprises, Inc.*, 386 A.2d 674, 681 (Del.Ch.1978). In addition, many jurisdictions that require a showing of fraud, injustice, or inequity in a contract case do not in a tort situation. *See Jon–T Chemicals*, 768 F.2d at 692. A rational distinction can be drawn between tort and contract cases. In actions based on contract, "the creditor has willingly transacted business with the subsidiary" although it could have insisted on assurances that would make the parent also responsible. *Id.* at 693. In a tort situation, however, the injured party had no such choice; the limitations on corporate liability were, from its standpoint, fortuitous and non-consensual.

There is, however, evidence precluding summary judgment even in jurisdictions that require a finding of fraud, inequity, or injustice. This conclusion is not based merely on the evidence that, even accepting Bristol's contentions regarding the amount of insurance available to MEC, MEC may have insufficient funds to satisfy the potential risks of responding to, and defending against, the numerous existing and potential claims of the plaintiffs. Equally significant is the fact that Bristol permitted its name to appear on breast implant advertisements, packages, and product inserts to improve sales by giving the product additional credibility. Combined with the evidence of potentially insufficient assets, this fact would support a finding that it would be inequitable and unjust to allow Bristol now to avoid liability to those induced to believe Bristol was vouching for this product.

Because the evidence available at a trial could support—if not, under some state laws, perhaps mandate—a finding that the corporate veil should be pierced, Bristol is not entitled through summary judgment to dismissal of the claims against it.

\* \* \*

# FLETCHER v. ATEX, INC.

68 F.3d 1451 (2d Cir.1995).

JOSE A. CABRANES, CIRCUIT JUDGE:

\* \* \*

## I.  BACKGROUND

The \* \* \* plaintiffs filed their respective complaints on December 4, 1992, and February 25, 1994, seeking recovery from Atex and Kodak, among others, for repetitive stress injuries that they claim were caused by their use of Atex computer keyboards. From 1981 until December 1992, Atex was a wholly-owned subsidiary of Kodak. \* \* \* In December 1992, Atex sold substantially all of its assets to an independent third party \* \* \*, [changed its name, and holds the proceeds from the sale.]

After extensive discovery, Kodak moved for summary judgment \* \* \* . The plaintiffs opposed Kodak's motion, arguing that genuine issues of material fact existed as to Kodak's liability under [the theory] \* \* \* that Atex was merely Kodak's alter ego or instrumentality \* \* \*.

On August 17, 1994, the district court rejected each of the plaintiffs' theories of Kodak's liability and granted Kodak's motion for summary judgment in both actions. [*Fletcher v. Atex, Inc.*, 861 F.Supp. 242 (S.D.N.Y. 1994] \* \* \*

## II.  DISCUSSION

\* \* \*

The district court correctly noted that "[u]nder New York choice of law principles, '[t]he law of the state of incorporation determines when the corporate form will be disregarded and liability will be imposed on shareholders.'" *Fletcher*, 861 F.Supp. at 244 (quoting *Kalb, Voorhis & Co. v. American Fin. Corp.*, 8 F.3d 130, 132 (2d Cir.1993)). Because Atex was a Delaware corporation, Delaware law determines whether the corporate veil can be pierced in this instance.

Delaware law permits a court to pierce the corporate veil of a company "where there is fraud or where [it] is in fact a mere instrumentality or alter ego of its owner." *Geyer v. Ingersoll Publications Co.*, 621 A.2d 784, 793 (Del.Ch.1992). Although the Delaware Supreme Court has never explicitly adopted an alter ego theory of parent liability for its subsidiaries, lower Delaware courts have applied the doctrine on several occasions, as has the United States District Court for the District of Delaware. *See Geyer*, 621 A.2d at 793; *Mabon, Nugent & Co. v. Texas Am. Energy Corp.*, No. CIV.A. 8578, 1990 WL 44267, at \*5, (Del.Ch. Apr.12, 1990); *Harper v. Delaware Valley Broadcasters, Inc.*, 743 F.Supp. 1076, 1085 (D.Del.1990), *aff'd*, 932 F.2d 959 (3d Cir.1991). Thus, under an alter ego theory, there is no requirement of a showing of fraud. *Id.* at 1085. To prevail on an alter ego claim under Delaware law, a plaintiff must show (1) that the parent and the subsidiary "operated as a single economic entity" and (2) that an "overall element of injustice or unfairness ... [is] present." *Id.* (internal quotation marks omitted).

\* \* \*

To prevail on an alter ego theory of liability, a plaintiff must show that the two corporations " 'operated as a single economic entity such that it would be inequitable ... to uphold a legal distinction between them.' " *Harper*, 743 F.Supp. at 1085 (quoting *Mabon*, 1990 WL 44267, at \* 5). Among the factors to be considered in determining whether a subsidiary and parent operate as a "single economic entity" are:

> "[W]hether the corporation was adequately capitalized for the corporate undertaking; whether the corporation was solvent; whether dividends were paid, corporate records kept, officers and directors functioned properly, and other corporate formalities were observed; whether the dominant shareholder siphoned corporate funds; and whether, in general, the corporation simply functioned as a facade for the dominant shareholder."

*Harco*, 1989 WL 110537, at \*4 (quoting *United States v. Golden Acres, Inc.*, 702 F.Supp. 1097, 1104 (D.Del.1988)). As noted above, a showing of fraud or wrongdoing is not necessary under an alter ego theory, but the plaintiff must demonstrate an overall element of injustice or unfairness. *Harco*, 1989 WL 110537, at \*5.

A plaintiff seeking to persuade a Delaware court to disregard the corporate structure faces "a difficult task." *Harco*, 1989 WL 110537, at \*4. Courts have made it clear that "[t]he legal entity of a corporation will not be disturbed until sufficient reason appears." *Id.* Although the question of domination is generally one of fact, courts have granted motions to dismiss as well as motions for summary judgment in favor of defendant parent companies where there has been a lack of sufficient evidence to place the alter ego issue in dispute.

Kodak has shown that Atex followed corporate formalities, and the plaintiffs have offered no evidence to the contrary. Significantly, the plaintiffs have not challenged Kodak's assertions that Atex's board of directors held regular meetings, that minutes from those meetings were routinely prepared and maintained in corporate minute books, that appropriate financial records and other files were maintained by Atex, that Atex filed its own tax returns and paid its own taxes, and that Atex had its own employees and management executives who were responsible for the corporation's day-to-day business. The plaintiffs' primary arguments regarding domination concern (1) the defendant's use of a cash management system; (2) Kodak's exertion of control over Atex's major expenditures, stock sales, and the sale of Atex's assets to a third party; (3) Kodak's "dominating presence" on Atex's board of directors; (4) descriptions of the relationship between Atex and Kodak in the corporations' advertising, promotional literature, and annual reports; and (5) Atex's assignment of one of its former officer's mortgage to Kodak in order to close Atex's asset-purchase agreement with a third party. The plaintiffs argue that each of these raises a genuine issue of material fact about Kodak's domination of Atex, and that the district court therefore erred in granting summary judgment to Kodak on the plaintiffs' alter ego theory. We find that the district court correctly held that, in light of the undisputed factors of independence cited by Kodak, "the elements identified by the plaintiffs ... [were] insufficient as a matter of law to establish the degree of domination necessary to disregard Atex's corporate identity." *Fletcher*, 861 F.Supp. at 245.

First, the district court correctly held that "Atex's participation in Kodak's cash management system is consistent with sound business practice and does not show undue domination or control." *Id.* at 244. The parties do not dispute the mechanics of Kodak's cash management system. Essentially, all of Kodak's domestic subsidiaries participate in the system and maintain zero-balance bank accounts. All funds transferred from the subsidiary accounts are recorded as credits to the subsidiary, and when a subsidiary is in need of funds, a transfer is made. At all times, a strict accounting is kept of each subsidiary's funds.

Courts have generally declined to find alter ego liability based on a parent corporation's use of a cash management system. *See, e.g., In re Acushnet River & New Bedford Harbor Proceedings*, 675 F.Supp. 22, 34 (D.Mass.1987) (Without "considerably more," "a centralized cash management system ... where the accounting records always reflect the indebtedness of one entity to another, is not the equivalent of intermingling funds" and is insufficient to justify disregarding the corporate form.); *United States v. Bliss*, 108 F.R.D. 127, 132 (E.D.Mo.1985) (cash management system indicative of the "usual parent-subsidiary relationship"); [*Japan Petroleum Co. (Nigeria) v. Ashland Oil Inc.*, 456 F.Supp. 831, 846 (D.Del.1978)], (finding segregation of subsidiary's accounts within parent's cash management system to be "a function of administrative convenience and economy, rather than a manifestation of control"). The plaintiffs offer no facts to support their speculation that Kodak's centralized cash management system was actually a "complete commingling" of funds or a means by which Kodak sought to "siphon[ ] all of Atex's revenues into its own account."

Second, the district court correctly concluded that it could find no domination based on the plaintiffs' evidence that Kodak's approval was required for Atex's real estate leases, major capital expenditures, negotiations for a sale of minority stock ownership to IBM, or the fact that Kodak played a significant role in the ultimate sale of Atex's assets to a third party. Again, the parties do not dispute that Kodak required Atex to seek its approval and/or participation for the above transactions. However, this evidence, viewed in the light most favorable to the plaintiffs, does not raise an issue of material fact about whether the two corporations constituted "a single economic entity." Indeed, this type of conduct is typical of a majority shareholder or parent corporation. In [*Akzona, Inc. v. Du Pont*, 607 F.Supp. 227 (D.Del.1984)], the Delaware district court noted that a parent's "general executive responsibilities" for its subsidiary's operations included approval over major policy decisions and guaranteeing bank loans, and that that type of oversight was insufficient to demonstrate domination and control. *Akzona*, 607 F.Supp. at 238 (internal quotation marks omitted). Similarly, the district court in the instant case properly found that the presence of Kodak employees at periodic meetings with Atex's chief financial officer and comptroller to be "entirely appropriate." *Fletcher*, 861 F.Supp. at 245 (citing *Akzona*, 607 F.Supp. at 238).

The plaintiffs' third argument, that Kodak dominated the Atex board of directors, also fails. Although a number of Kodak employees have sat on the Atex board, it is undisputed that between 1981 and 1988, only one director of Atex was also a director of Kodak. Between 1989 and 1992, Atex and Kodak had no directors in common. Parents and subsidiaries frequently have overlapping boards of directors while maintaining separate business operations. In *Japan Petroleum*, the Delaware district court held that the fact that a parent and a subsidiary have common officers and directors does not necessarily demonstrate that the parent corporation dominates the activities of the subsidiary. 456 F.Supp. at 841. Since the overlap is negligible here, we find this evidence to be entirely insufficient to raise a question of fact on the issue of domination.

Fourth, the district court properly rejected the plaintiffs' argument that the descriptions of the relationship between Atex and Kodak and the presence of the Kodak logo in Atex's promotional literature justify piercing the corporate veil. *Fletcher*, 861 F.Supp. at 245. The plaintiffs point to several statements in both Kodak's and Atex's literature to evidence Kodak's domination of its subsidiary. For example, plaintiffs refer to (1) a promotional pamphlet produced by EPPS (a/k/a Atex) describing Atex as a business unit of EPPS and noting that EPPS was an "agent" of Kodak; (2) a document produced by Atex entitled "An Introduction to Atex Systems," which describes a "merger" between Kodak and Atex; (3) a statement in Kodak's 1985 and 1986 annual reports describing Atex as a "recent acquisition[ ]" and a "subsidiar[y] ... combined in a new division"; and (4) a statement in an Atex/EPPS document, "Setting Up TPE 6000 on the Sun 3 Workstation," describing Atex as "an unincorporated division of Electronic Pre–Press Systems, Inc., a Kodak company." They also refer generally to the fact that Atex's paperwork and packaging materials frequently displayed the Kodak logo.

It is clear from the record that Atex never merged with Kodak or operated as a Kodak division. The plaintiffs offer no evidence to the contrary, apart from these statements in Atex and Kodak documents that they claim are indicative of the true relationship between the two companies. Viewed in the light most favorable to the plaintiffs, these statements and the use of the Kodak logo are not evidence that the two companies operated as a "single economic entity." *See Coleman v. Corning Glass Works*, 619 F.Supp. 950, 956 (W.D.N.Y.1985) (upholding corporate form despite "loose language" in annual report about "merger" and parent's reference to subsidiary as a "division"), *aff'd*, 818 F.2d 874 (1987); *Japan Petrol.*, 456 F.Supp. at 846 (noting that representations made by parent in its annual reports that subsidiary serves as an agent "may result from public relations motives or an attempt at simplification"); *American Trading & Prod. Corp. v. Fischbach & Moore, Inc.*, 311 F.Supp. 412, 416 (N.D.Ill.1970) ("boastful" advertising and consideration of subsidiaries as "family" do not prove that corporate identities were ignored).

Fifth, the plaintiffs contend that Atex's assignment of its former CEO's mortgage to Kodak in order to close the sale of Atex's assets to a third party is evidence of Kodak's domination of Atex. We reject this argument as well. The evidence is undisputed that Kodak paid Atex the book value of the note and entered into a formal repayment agreement with the former CEO. Formal contracts were executed, and the two companies observed all corporate formalities.

Finally, even if the plaintiffs did raise a factual question about Kodak's domination of Atex, summary judgment would still be appropriate because the plaintiffs offer no evidence on the second prong of the alter ego analysis. The plaintiffs have failed to present evidence of an "overall element of injustice or unfairness" that would result from respecting the two companies' corporate separateness. *See Harper*, 743 F.Supp. at 1085 (holding that plaintiff cannot prevail on alter ego theory "because he has failed to allege any unfairness or injustice which would justify the court in disregarding the [companies'] separate legal existences"). In the instant case, the plaintiffs offer nothing more than the bare assertion that Kodak "exploited" Atex "to generate profits but not to safeguard safety." There is no indication that Kodak sought to defraud creditors and consumers or to siphon funds from its subsidiary. The plaintiffs' conclusory assertions, without more, are not evidence, *see Quinn*, 613 F.2d at 445, and are completely inadequate to support a finding that it would be unjust to respect Atex's corporate form.

For all of the foregoing reasons, the district court's order entering summary judgment on the plaintiffs' alter ego theory of liability is affirmed.

### *Note: Choice of Law in Piercing Cases*

The courts in *Silicone Gel Breast Implants* and *Fletcher v. Atex* adopted different, though not necessarily conflicting, approaches to the question of whether the law of the state in which a corporation is organized or the law of the state in which an injury occurs governs when a plaintiff seeks to pierce the corporate veil. *Silicone Gel* concluded that states choice of law rules on this issue were not uniform. *Fletcher* held that, under New York law, the law of the state in which the corporation was chartered would govern.

*Yoder v. Honeywell, Inc.*, 104 F.3d 1215 (10th Cir.1997), *cert. denied* ___ U.S. ___, 118 S.Ct. 55, 139 L.Ed.2d 19 (1997), also involved an attempt to pierce the corporate veil of a wholly-owned subsidiary and hold the parent corporation, Honeywell, liable for repetitive stress injuries. The court in *Yoder* disagreed with *Fletcher*'s application of New

York choice of law rules. Plaintiffs, who were domiciled in Colorado, had sued Honeywell in federal district court in New York. Although the suit was transferred to Colorado, it was governed by the choice of law rules of the state in which the transferor court sits—*i.e.*, New York. New York applies the substantive law of the state that has the greatest interest in the litigation. *See Schultz v. Boy Scouts of America, Inc.*, 65 N.Y.2d 189, 491 N.Y.S.2d 90, 480 N.E.2d 679 (1985). The court concluded this was Colorado because, even though Honeywell and its subsidiary were Delaware corporations, plaintiff's theory was that Honeywell, acting through its alter ego, had tortiously injured her in Colorado. However, the court also concluded that plaintiff had not demonstrated any basis for piercing the veil under Colorado law and that summary judgment properly had been entered in favor of Honeywell.

# E.   ALTERNATIVES TO LIMITED LIABILITY

## 1.  IMPOSING SHAREHOLDER LIABILITY UNDER FEDERAL LAW

Although state law generally governs corporate issues, a growing body of federal law allows federal courts to find shareholders personally liable for corporate activities that violate federal mandates. One study found that federal courts were inconsistent in deciding whether to pierce the corporate veil, but that they more frequently pierced to give force to federal policies. Note, *Piercing the Corporate Law Veil: The Alter Ego Doctrine Under Federal Common Law*, 95 HARV. L. REV. 853 (1982).

Perhaps the leading expression of veil piercing by a federal court to effectuate federal policies is *Anderson v. Abbott*, 321 U.S. 349, 64 S.Ct. 531, 88 L.Ed. 793 (1944). The Court, relying on federal statutory provisions that have since been repealed, disregarded the corporate entity to hold shareholders liable for amounts equal to double their investments. The court held that a state may not endow its "corporate creatures with the power to place themselves above the Congress of the United States and defeat the federal policy * * * which Congress has announced." 321 U.S. at 365, 64 S.Ct. at 539.

In *Chicago v. Matchmaker Real Estate Sales Center, Inc.*, 982 F.2d 1086 (7th Cir.1992), the court pierced the veil of a real estate agency, even though the applicable federal statute did not specifically so direct, to insure that limited liability did not interfere with federal policy. The court held the corporation's chief executive officer, who was also the corporation's sole shareholder, liable for compensatory damages resulting from "racial steering" by corporate employees when showing houses for sale, which violated two federal statutes, the Civil Rights Act of 1866 and the Fair Housing Act of 1968. The court noted that "where common ownership and management exists, corporate formalities must not be rigidly adhered to when inquiry is made of civil rights violations." However, the court also stressed that it was holding liable the person who also was the sole shareholder and principal manager of the corporation.

The most important federal statute that leads to shareholder liability, at least in financial terms, is the Comprehensive Environmental Response, Compensation and Liability Act (CERCLA), 42 U.S.C. § 9601 *et seq.*, which imposes financial responsibility for cleaning up hazardous waste sites on, among others, any person who owned or operated such a site at the time of disposal of such wastes. In *Lansford–Coaldale Joint Water Auth. v. Tonolli Corp.*, 4 F.3d 1209, 1222 (3d Cir.1993), the court observed that:

> "[t]o be an operator requires more than merely complete ownership and the concomitant general control that comes with ownership. At a minimum it requires active involvement in the activities of the subsidiary." [*United States v. Kayser–Roth Corp.*, 910 F.2d 24, 27 (1st Cir.1990), *cert. denied*, 498 U.S. 1084, 111 S.Ct. 957, 112 L.Ed.2d 1045 (1991)]. Whereas a corporation's "mere oversight" of the subsidiary * * * corporation's business in a "manner consistent with the investment relationship" does not ordinarily result in operator liability, a corporation's "actual participation and control" over the other corporation's decision-making does.

Other courts of appeal have taken similar positions and some even have imposed liability under CERCLA on shareholders who simply had the capacity to control a corporation responsible for toxic pollution. Recently, however, the Sixth Circuit adopted a different approach. In *United States v. Cordova Chemical Co. of Michigan*, 113 F.3d 572 (6th Cir.1997) (*en banc*), it held (7–5) that a parent corporation could be held liable under CERCLA only if traditional state law requirements for piercing could be met. The Supreme Court has agreed to review that decision. ___ U.S. ___, 118 S.Ct. 621, 139 L.Ed.2d 506 (1997).

## 2. FRAUDULENT CONVEYANCE AND EQUITABLE SUBORDINATION CONCEPTS

Apart from veil piercing, courts use other methods to protect creditors' interests. One such method is to set aside certain conveyances that are fraudulent to creditors under the Uniform Fraudulent Conveyance Act (UFCA), codified in the U.S. Bankruptcy Code and many state statutes. The UFCA protects creditors from two general types of transfers: (1) transfers with the intent to defraud creditors, and (2) transfers that constructively defraud creditors. In order to support a finding of intentional fraud, the court must usually find an actual intent by the debtor to "hinder, delay or defraud." A finding of constructive fraud generally involves a transfer by the debtor while insolvent or near insolvency that is not made for fair consideration.

In the bankruptcy context, the UFCA could be utilized in place of veil piercing to set aside a fraudulent transfer that the corporation has made to its shareholders when it has outstanding debts to creditors. Thus, a court could set aside the transfer and apply it against the corporation's debts to its creditors. For example, the UFCA could be used to set aside an "excess" salary payment from a corporation to its sole shareholder that far exceeds the value of the shareholder's services to the corporation.

The UFCA background may illuminate the attention courts pay to the observance of corporate formalities and the intermingling of corporate and personal assets in deciding veil piercing cases. A disregard of corporate formalities often provides indirect evidence of a fraudulent conveyance. The intermingling of corporate and personal assets may provide direct evidence of a fraudulent conveyance.

Limits exist on the use of the UFCA in lieu of veil piercing. First, the UFCA requires a specific finding of a fraudulent transaction, which may be difficult to establish. Second, unlike veil piercing, which may impose unlimited liability on shareholders, the UFCA allows a court to set aside only the amount of the fraudulent conveyance, which may not satisfy a creditor's entire claim. Third, the fraudulent conveyance may be unrelated to a creditor's claim.

The doctrine of equitable subordination (discussed in Chapter 9) represents a second method to protect the interests of creditors. This doctrine is applicable only in federal bankruptcy proceedings. Under equitable subordination, certain creditors' claims, particularly those of corporate insiders, are subordinated to other creditors to reach an equitable result. Subordination thus allows outside creditors to receive payment before insiders. The result achieved by the equitable subordination doctrine is significant because priority in a federal bankruptcy proceeding often determines which creditors will get paid.

However, in contrast to veil piercing and application of fraudulent conveyance principles, equitable subordination does not increase the resources from which a creditor may satisfy her claim. It does not disregard the corporate form or hold a shareholder personally liable for the corporation's obligations. The doctrine only alters the normal priority of certain creditors' claims against the corporation's available resources. Nevertheless, it improves the chances that the corporation will be able to satisfy the creditors' debts. If a corporation is insolvent, the claims of outside creditors will likely exhaust the corporation's assets and the shareholder-officer probably will receive nothing.

Before the court will invoke the equitable subordination doctrine, there must be a showing of fraudulent conduct, mismanagement, or inadequate capitalization. Some cases explicitly reject inadequate capitalization as the sole basis for subordination. See, e.g., *In re Branding Iron Steak House*, 536 F.2d 299 (9th Cir.1976). As a baseline, courts generally look to whether a claimant engaged in some form of "inequitable conduct" and whether the misconduct resulted in injury to the bankrupt's creditor or conferred an unfair advantage on the claimant. *In re Mobile Steel Co.*, 563 F.2d 692, 699–700 (5th Cir.1977). Some courts have abandoned the insider misconduct standard. See, e.g., *Burden v. United States*, 917 F.2d 115, 119–20 (3d Cir.1990).

# Chapter 12

## MANAGEMENT AND CONTROL OF THE CORPORATION

### A. THE CORPORATE ACTORS: SHAREHOLDERS, DIRECTORS, AND OFFICERS

Three sets of actors—shareholders, directors, and officers—play important roles in the corporate governance system. Statutes generally stipulate the same basic governance structure for all corporations, regardless of their size or number of shareholders, although, as we will see in Chapter 13, many statutes now also allow closely-held corporations to adopt governance structures that deviate from this statutory norm.

In the standard governance system, the board of directors has the central role in, and bears ultimate responsibility for, the conduct of the corporation's business. RMBCA § 8.01(b), for example, provides: "All corporate powers shall be exercised by or under authority of, and the business and affairs of a corporation shall be managed under the direction of its board of directors * * *."

This statutory mandate does not mean the board of directors, acting as such, must manage a corporation's day-to-day business. Rather, the board may, and often does, delegate responsibility for day-to-day operations to the corporation's officers and employees. Some statutes, in fact, require a corporation to have certain officers, usually a president, one or more vice presidents, a secretary, and a treasurer. *See, e.g.*, N.Y.B.C.L. § 715. Most modern statutes, though, allow a corporation to designate the officers it will have, either in its bylaws or by action of its board of directors. RMBCA § 8.40. The Official Comment to RMBCA § 8.40 explains: "Experience has shown * * * that little purpose is served by a statutory requirement that there be certain officers, and statutory requirements may sometimes create problems of implied or apparent authority or confusion with nonstatutory offices the corporation desires to create."

Modern statutes generally say little about officers' duties and powers. *See e.g.*, RMBCA § 8.41. Implicit in the statutory scheme, however, is the notion that all power exercised by a corporation's officers derive from the power that the statute assigns to the board of directors and, consequently, must be delegated by the board to the officers.

Even though shareholders are considered to be a corporation's ultimate owners, corporate statutes do not authorize shareholders to manage the corporation's business directly. Rather, statutes make shareholders responsible for electing the corporation's directors. "Directors are elected at the first annual shareholders meeting and at each annual meeting thereafter * * *." RMBCA § 8.03(d). Shareholder meetings are to be held annually. RMBCA § 7.01. If an annual meeting has not been held in the previous 15 months, any holder of voting stock can require the corporation to convene an annual meeting, at which new directors can be elected. RMBCA § 7.03(a). Statutes also generally authorize shareholders to remove directors with or without cause, unless a corporation's articles of incorporation provide that directors can be removed only for cause. RMBCA § 8.08. Shareholders' power to remove directors for cause cannot be restricted.

In sum, corporate statutes establish a basic governance structure in which shareholders elect (and have the power to remove) a corporation's directors; directors are charged with managing the corporation's business; and officers and employees carry on day-to-day operations using powers that the board of directors has delegated to them. But this structure is subject to two important caveats. First, before effectuating certain *fundamental transactions* specified in the statute such as mergers or sale of substantially all of a corporation's assets (or amending the articles of incorporation in some significant fashion), the board must secure the approval of a majority of the shares entitled to vote. Put differently, one could say that shareholders have the power to veto such fundamental transactions and amendments. Second, shareholders also generally can amend a corporation's bylaws and may be able to make recommendations to the board concerning some matters within the board's sphere of responsibility.

This chapter focuses on the issues that arise as a consequence of the division of authority among a corporation's officers, directors, and shareholders. The chapter also reviews briefly the procedures that boards of directors and shareholders must follow when exercising their powers. The first section considers questions relating to the authority of a corporation's officers and employees, questions that turn largely on principles of agency law. The next section addresses the procedures a board of directors must follow in order to exercise its authority. Issues relating to the substance of directors' responsibilities are the focus of several subsequent chapters.

The largest part of the chapter deals with shareholders' rights with respect to the governance of the corporation. Issues involving shareholders' rights arise most frequently when some or most of a corporation's shareholders disagree with a policy or decision that the board supports. In such a situation, the board may seek to implement the policy or decision it favors without triggering shareholders' veto rights, while shareholders may attempt to participate in or otherwise influence the board or try to alter its membership. This chapter's discussion of shareholder rights addresses several issues relating to these conflicts. First, it outlines how statutes and courts have defined shareholders' rights with regard to corporate combinations, perhaps the most important class of fundamental transactions. Next, it addresses shareholders' rights with respect to sales of a substantial portion of a corporation's assets. Then it considers shareholders' rights to influence the decisions or alter the membership of a corporation's board of directors, and how courts limit boards of directors' ability to avoid or frustrate shareholders' exercise of those rights. Finally, it reviews the procedures shareholders must follow to exercise their voting rights and related issues involving shareholders' rights to inspect corporate books and records. The issue of shareholder participation in the governance of publicly-held corporations is treated again in Chapter 14.

## B.   ACTION BY EXECUTIVES: AGENCY PRINCIPLES AND THE AUTHORITY OF CORPORATE OFFICERS

### 1.   INTRODUCTION TO SOME BASIC AGENCY CONCEPTS

The corporation, an incorporeal entity, can act only through the agency of flesh and blood human beings. An understanding of the law of corporations, therefore, requires some knowledge of the law of agency. If you have not already had a formal course in agency law, you have by now at least been exposed to some agency principles in other basic courses. We review those principles here before examining their operation in the corporate context.

An agency is a consensual relationship between two parties, the *principal* and the *agent*. The principal selects the agent, who then must agree to act on the principal's behalf. The principal has the power to terminate the agency relationship unilaterally and can dictate to the agent how the agent will perform her duties. The relationship between principal and agent is of a *fiduciary* character which, oversimplifying a bit, means that the agent owes to the principal a duty of loyalty and obedience. The agent is bound not to act contrary to a reasonable order of the principal given within the scope of the agent's employment. Also, within the scope of the employment, the agent must always put the interests of the principal above her own. Perhaps of greatest relevance to the material in this chapter, the existence of an agency relationship confers on the agent a legal *power* to create rights in the principal's favor and, correlatively, to subject the principal to liability to third parties.

There are several possible sources of an agent's power to bind her principal in a legal relationship with a third party. First, the agent may have been granted *actual authority* to bind the principal. According to the RESTATEMENT SECOND OF AGENCY, § 7 (1958), this authority "is the power of the agent to affect the legal relations of the principal by acts done in accordance with the principal's manifestations of consent to [her]." "Actual authority" describes what the principal causes the agent to believe is the scope of her authority. Actual authority may be *express*, growing out of explicit words or conduct granting the agent power to do the act, or may be *implied* from words or conduct taken in the context of the relations between the principal and the agent. In either case, the authority "can be created by written or spoken words or other conduct of the principal which, reasonably interpreted, causes the agent to believe that the principal desires [her] so to act on the principal's account." *Id.* § 26.

Although it sounds paradoxical, an agent also may bind her principal even though she lacks the actual authority to do so. A principal, for example, may create *apparent authority* "by written or spoken words or any other conduct * * * which, reasonably interpreted, causes the third person to believe that the principal consents to have the act done on [her] behalf by the person purporting to act for [her]." *Id.* § 27. Note that the existence of *actual* authority depends upon communications between the principal and the agent, whereas the existence of *apparent* authority depends on communications between the principal and the third party.* In other words, to create apparent authority the principal must do or say something that induces the third party to believe that the agent has authority.

An agent also may bind her principal by what the Restatement calls "*inherent agency power.*" *Id.* § 8A. The clearest example of such power (which, using the terminology of the Restatement, is not "authority") is the rule that a principal is liable for the *torts* of her servant under the doctrine of *respondeat superior*. Since a principal normally would not authorize an agent to commit a tort, it is clear that this rule cannot be based on any theory of delegation of power. Instead, the rule embodies the concept that it is fair to charge the principal with the costs of a tort committed by an agent who was acting on behalf of the principal in the ordinary course of the principal's business.

Finally, a principal may become obligated to a third party by *ratifying* the act of another who, at the time of the act, lacked the power to bind the principal. The RESTATEMENT OF AGENCY (SECOND) § 8 (1958) defines ratification as "the affirmance by a person of a prior act which did not bind [her] but which was done or professedly done on [her] account, whereby the act, as to some or all persons, is given effect as if originally authorized by [her]." When someone ratifies an unauthorized act done by another in her name, it is said that the ratification "relates back" so as to leave the resulting state of affairs precisely as it would have been had the authority been conferred before the act. The ratifica-

---

* The principle of *estoppel* is often used to impose liability on the principal in situations in which apparent authority might have been used. The technical distinction is that for the principal to be estopped from denying the agent's authority, the third party must have changed position in reliance on some representation by the principal. *See* RESTATEMENT, SECOND OF AGENCY § 31 (1958).

tion creates an agency relationship regardless of whether such a relationship existed at the time of the act in question.

Ratification may be inferred from "any act, words or conduct which reasonably tend to show intention to ratify." *Myers v. Cook*, 87 W.Va. 265, 104 S.E. 593 (1920). It is probably enough in many instances that the incipient principal acquiesces in the transaction without raising objection to it. The ratifier's decision to accept the act need not be communicated. According to Professor Seavey, "Affirmance does not require a manifestation of consent to the agent, to the other party or any one." Warren Seavey, HANDBOOK OF THE LAW OF AGENCY 67 (1964).

A hypothetical may help illustrate these concepts. Suppose that Priscilla Principal, a horse breeder, says to her employee, Andrew Agent, "Andy, please go down to the stables, put up a sign, 'HORSES FOR SALE,' and sell all of my horses for $500 apiece." Andrew has *express authority* to sell the horses. He also probably has *implied authority* to accept an apparently valid check in payment since, as long as Priscilla had not previously demanded cash in such transactions, it is reasonable to assume that she intended that Andrew accept checks. He may or may not have implied authority to accept a used car or a hogshead of tobacco worth $500, depending on what would be reasonably understood from the circumstances (such as the normal practices in the trade or in the locality) and from the prior dealings between him and Priscilla.

Suppose, now that Priscilla gives him the same instructions but adds, "except Secretariat. Whatever you do, don't sell Secretariat." She also sends out letters to prospective buyers saying, "I am selling off my horses. If you are interested, please see Andrew Agent at the stables. He is authorized to act for me." If Andrew sells Secretariat to a recipient of the letter, Priscilla may not recover the horse. By communicating what would appear to a reasonable person to be an intention to give Andrew the authority to sell Secretariat, she has clothed him with *apparent authority* and is bound by his act, even though it was directly contrary to her instructions.

Now suppose that Priscilla has delegated the management of her horse farm to Andrew, who regularly buys and sells horses according to his own judgment. Under these circumstances, if he sells Secretariat to a stranger who has not received Priscilla's letter (and who thus has no basis for believing in Andrew's apparent authority), the sale is binding on Priscilla by virtue of Andrew's *inherent agency power*.

Another view of this situation is that Andrew has apparent authority by virtue of his position. If it is assumed that Andrew is a general agent with broad customary authority to sell any horse on the farm, the third person has a basis for believing in Andrew's authority and the letter does not add anything.

Finally, suppose that Andrew has never before sold any horses for Priscilla (and thus has no inherent power), but he nevertheless purports to sell Secretariat to the stranger. When Priscilla learns of the sale, she declares, "Well I guess that's okay. Five hundred dollars is a pretty good price for that nag anyway." She has *ratified* the transaction and becomes bound as if Andrew had been authorized to accomplish it in the first place. Indeed, she ratifies the transaction even if she says nothing but takes no steps to rescind it.

## 2. SPECIAL PROBLEMS OF AGENCY IN A CORPORATE CONTEXT: THE INHERENT AUTHORITY OF OFFICERS

### PROBLEM
### AGENCY RELATIONS—PART I

In order to test your understanding of agency concepts, consider on what basis, if any, the principal would be bound if the parties executed a contract in the following circumstances:

1.  The board of directors of Precision Tools Corporation passes a resolution directing Michael Lane, the president of the corporation, to contract for the construction of a new building.

2.  Jessica Green, the vice president of PTC, purchases $1000 worth of equipment. She frequently purchases materials used in PTC's operations, but the board has never explicitly authorized her to do so.

3.  Will Wright is a foreman in the plant. He has been instructed not to purchase any machinery or equipment without first asking Michael or Jessica, and he has never done so. One day while Michael and Jessica are away at a business conference, a representative of a wholesale machinery dealer visits the plant and tells Wright that he has a temporary oversupply which he is willing to sell at a substantial discount. Wright signs a purchase order for $1000 of equipment.

4.  Wright goes to an auto dealer (who has never seen him before) and signs a contract to purchase a new pickup truck for Precision Tools. He signs, "Precision Tools Corp., by Will Wright." When he tells Michael what he has done, Michael responds, "You really shouldn't have done that without asking us, Will. But I guess you're right, we do need the truck." They accept delivery without protest.

### AGENCY RELATIONS—PART II

Harold Hawks entered into a contract a little over a year ago with Acoustics Incorporated, a small manufacturer of high fidelity speakers, under the terms of which he was to become the exclusive regional distributor for Acoustics' products for a period of three years. The contract provided that Hawks was to purchase speakers from the corporation at its listed wholesale prices and resell them to his customers at a 15% markup. It also contained the somewhat unusual provision that if Hawks' purchases in any given year exceeded $500,000, he would be paid a "commission" at the end of the year of 2% of *all* his purchases.

Hawks negotiated the contract with Acoustics' president, James Huston, whose signature appeared at the bottom of the document thus:

Acoustics, Incorporated

By /s/James Huston

James Huston, President

A few months after the contract was signed there was a management shakeup at Acoustics and Huston was dismissed.

During the first year of the contract, Hawks purchased $650,000 worth of speakers from the firm. He wrote the new president, Margo Pickford, asking for his 2% commission. Her letter of response said that she knew nothing of the contract and denied any liability under it. Furthermore, she said, while Acoustics would be happy to continue with Hawks as a distributor, it did not consider the arrangement exclusive, and was in fact in the process of working out an arrangement with another distributor in the same region.

There was a second exchange of correspondence, in which Hawks sent Pickford a copy of the contract, and she wrote back that even if Huston had signed it, he had not been authorized to do so.

1. You have been retained to advise Hawks as to his legal rights. You are considering whether to file a breach of contract action. On what theories might you proceed? What additional information would you like to have? How would you get it?

2. You represent the corporation in an action brought by Hawks. Would you advise settling the claim?

## AGENCY RELATIONS—PART III

You represent the Third National Bank and Trust Company which is about to loan a substantial amount of money to Universal Widgets, Inc., a wholly owned subsidiary of Universal Inc. The loan is to be secured by a mortgage on Universal Widgets' plant, and because Universal Widgets is a relatively new company with a short operating history, the bank has also insisted on a guarantee executed by the parent corporation. You have been asked by the bank to handle the closing of the deal, at which you will be asked to provide an opinion that the mortgage, note, and guarantees are "valid, binding, and enforceable in accordance with their terms."

What documents will you need from Universal and Universal Widgets in order for you to render your opinion?

––––––

Some uncertainty exists as to the nature and extent of the authority possessed by corporate officers. The officer with the greatest authority—the senior officer in any given corporation—generally is designated the chief executive officer or *CEO*. At one time, a corporation's president usually was the CEO. More recently, though, titles have become less uniform. In some companies, the president still is the CEO. In others, especially large corporations, the CEO is likely to hold no other title beside chair of the board (unless someone other than the CEO chairs board meetings).

In addition to the CEO, corporations generally have a chief financial officer, or *CFO*, who sometimes holds the title of treasurer. The same person can be the CEO and the CFO and, in the case of small companies, often is. A corporation also usually is required to charge one officer with responsibility for preparing minutes of directors' and shareholders' meetings and authenticating the corporation's books and records. RMBCA § 8.40(c). That person often has the title of secretary.

Corporations, especially large firms, usually have a number of other officers. In recent years, titles have proliferated, although not to the same extent as in government. We are not aware of any corporate official holding a title equivalent to Deputy Assistant to the Special Assistant to the Deputy Assistant Undersecretary for [Whatever]. However, corporate titles such as "Senior Executive Vice-President" or "Chief Operating Officer and Member of the Office of the President" are far from uncommon.

Courts often have been less than meticulous in specifying the agency theory on which they were relying to hold a corporation liable as a consequence of the act of some officer holding one of these or some other title. In some given situation, an officer might be held to possess express authority as a consequence of the board of directors having appointed that person to a particular corporate office. Alternatively, a court could find the officer to have apparent authority, i.e., the power that a reasonable person dealing with the corporation would believe that officer to possess. Or, authority could be held to arise by implication, as a consequence of prior dealings between an officer and a third party that the board never sought to challenge.

Driven by pragmatic concerns, courts have developed rules of thumb designed to facilitate dealings between third parties and corporations. The court observed in *Moyse Real Estate Co. v. First National Bank of Commerce*, 110 Miss. 620, 70 So. 821 (1916):

> Nearly all of the big business and a large part of the small business is now conducted by corporations, and if it be the law that persons dealing with the president of a corporation about matters of business clearly within the powers of the corporation to transact must deal at arm's length, and demand that the president exhibit his credentials before entering into contracts with him, it seems to us that not only the corporation, but also those dealing with corporations, will be seriously hampered. * * *

> If it be true that the president did not possess the authority assumed by him in the present case, the proof of his lack of authority was in the possession of the corporation, and there would have been no difficulty in the way of its production. On the other hand, it might be very difficult and expensive for the plaintiff to have secured the evidence to show his authority.

70 So. at 822.

Since some corporeal person must carry on the corporation's business, courts assume that the CEO, whether known as the president or by some other title, has authority to bind the corporation in transactions entered into in the ordinary course of business. However, that authority does not extend to "extraordinary" transactions, which must be approved by the board of directors. *See Lee v. Jenkins Brothers*, 268 F.2d 357 (2d Cir.1959) *infra*.

Generalization is more difficult with respect to subordinate officers. Their authority depends on the how a board or CEO has elected to delegate responsibility within the company's management structure; it cannot be inferred from some inherent characteristic of the corporate governance system. Thus, any given case is likely to turn on a court's assessment of the facts and circumstances of the transaction at issue. A third party who deals with a corporation's subordinate officers generally bears the burden of demonstrating that an act was within the officer's authority. Moreover, courts require a third party who knows that a given transaction will benefit some officer personally to inquire in greater depth as to whether the officer has valid authority to enter into the transaction at issue. In *Branding Iron Motel, Inc. v. Sandlian Equity, Inc.*, 798 F.2d 396 (10th Cir.1986), the court held that a lender could not rely on what would otherwise be adequate evidence that a motel president had apparent authority to enter into a mortgage, where the lender knew the president was the ultimate beneficiary of the mortgage. In *Schmidt v. Farm Credit Services*, 977 F.2d 511 (10th Cir.1992), the court held that a lender could not rely on a board resolution authorizing the president to sign a loan agreement, but had to make further inquiries, where the lender knew the president would benefit personally from the loan. *See also*, *Squaw Mountain Cattle Co. v. Bowen*, 804 P.2d 1292 (Wyo.1991) (president lacked authority to agree to settlement that provided him with large personal monetary benefit.)

## LEE v. JENKINS BROTHERS

268 F.2d 357 (2d Cir.1959), cert. denied 361 U.S.
913, 80 S.Ct. 257, 4 L.Ed.2d 183 (1959).

[Lee sued Jenkins Brothers, a corporation, to recover pension payments allegedly due him under an oral contract made in 1920 on behalf of the corporation by Yardley. The Court of Appeals affirmed the District Court's dismissal of the case, ruling that Lee had not produced sufficient evidence of the alleged agreement to present a jury question. The court went on to discuss whether there was evidence sufficient to present a jury question as to whether Yardley had apparent authority to bind the corporation to the alleged agreement assuming, *arguendo*, a finding that there was an agreement.]

MEDINA, J.:

Our question on this phase of the case then boils itself down to the following: can it be said as a matter of law that Yardley as president, chairman of the board, substantial stockholder and trustee and son-in-law of the estate of the major stockholder, had no power in the presence of the company's most interested vice president to secure for a "reasonable" length of time badly needed key personnel by promising an experienced local executive a life pension to commence in 30 years at the age of 60, even if Lee were not then working for the corporation, when the maximum liability to Jenkins under such a pension was $1500 per year.

A survey of the law on the authority of corporate officers does not reveal a completely consistent pattern. For the most part the courts perhaps have taken a rather restrictive view on the extent of powers of corporate officials, but the dissatisfaction with such an approach has been manifested in a variety of exceptions such as ratification, estoppel, and promissory estoppel. For the most part also there has been limited discussion of the problem of apparent authority, perhaps on the assumption that if authority could not be implied from a continuing course of action between the corporation and the officer, it could not have been apparent to third parties either.

Such an assumption is ill-founded. The circumstances and facts known to exist between officer and corporation, from which actual authority may be implied, may be entirely different from those circumstances known to exist as between the third party and the corporation. The two concepts are separate and distinct even though the state of the proofs in a given case may cause considerable overlap.

The rule most widely cited is that the president only has authority to bind his company by acts arising in the usual and regular course of business but not for contracts of an "extraordinary" nature. The substance of such a rule lies in the content of the term "extraordinary" which is subject to a broad range of interpretation.

The growth and development of this rule occurred during the late nineteenth and early twentieth centuries when the potentialities of the corporate form of enterprise were just being realized. As the corporation became a more common vehicle for the conduct of business it became increasingly evident that many corporations, particularly small closely held ones, did not normally function in the formal ritualistic manner hitherto envisaged. While the boards of directors still nominally controlled corporate affairs, in reality officers and managers frequently ran the business with little, if any, board supervision. The natural consequence of such a development was that third parties commonly relied on the authority of such officials in almost all the multifarious transactions in which corporations engaged. The pace of modern business life was too swift to insist on the approval by the board of directors of every transaction that was in any way "unusual."

The judicial recognition given to these developments has varied considerably. Whether termed "apparent authority" or an "estoppel" to deny authority, many courts have noted the injustice caused by the practice of permitting corporations to act commonly through their executives and then allowing them to disclaim an agreement as beyond the authority of the contracting officer, when the contract no longer suited its convenience. Other courts, however, continued to cling to the past with little attempt to discuss the unconscionable results obtained or the doctrine of apparent authority. Such restrictive views have been generally condemned by the commentators.

The summary of holdings pro and con in general on the subject of what are and what are not "extraordinary" agreements is inconclusive at best * * *. But the pattern becomes more distinct when we turn to the more limited area of employment contracts.

It is generally settled that the president as part of the regular course of business has authority to hire and discharge employees and fix their compensation. In so doing he may agree to hire them for a specific number of years if the term selected is deemed reasonable. But employment contracts for life or on a "permanent" basis are generally regarded as "extraordinary" and beyond the authority of any corporate executive if the only consideration for the promise is the employee's promise to work for that period. Jenkins would have us analogize the pension agreement involved herein to these generally condemned lifetime employment contracts because it extends over a long period of time, is of indefinite duration, and involves an indefinite liability on the part of the corporation.

It is not surprising that lifetime employment contracts have met with substantial hostility in the courts, for these contracts are often oral, uncorroborated, vague in important details and highly improbable. * * *

However, at times such contracts have been enforced where the circumstances tended to support the plausibility of plaintiff's testimony. Thus when the plaintiff was injured in the course of employment and he agreed to settle his claim of negligence against the company for a lifetime job, authority has been generally found and the barrage of other objections adequately disposed of. And where additional consideration was given such as quitting other employment, giving up a competing business, or where the services were "peculiarly necessary" to the corporation, the courts have divided on the enforceability of the contract.

What makes the point now under discussion particularly interesting is the failure of the courts denying authority to make lifetime contracts to evolve any guiding principle. More often than not we find a mere statement that the contract is "extraordinary" with a citation of cases which say the same thing, without giving reasons. * * *

Where reasons have been given to support the conclusion that lifetime employments are "extraordinary," and hence made without authority, a scrutiny of these reasons may be helpful for their bearing on the analogous field of pension agreements. It is said that: they unduly restrict the power of the shareholders and future boards of directors on questions of managerial policy; they subject the corporation to an inordinately substantial amount of liability; they run for long and indefinite periods of time. Of these reasons the only one applicable to pension agreements is that they run for long and indefinite periods of time. There the likeness stops. Future director or shareholder control is in no way impeded; the amount of liability is not disproportionate; the agreement was not only not unreasonable but beneficial and necessary to the corporation; and pension contracts are commonly used fringe benefits in employment contracts. Moreover, unlike the case with life employment contracts, courts have often gone out of their way to find pension promises binding and definite even when labeled gratuitous by the employer. The consideration given to the employee involved is not at all dependent on profits or sales, nor does it involve some other variable suggesting director discretion.

Apparent authority is essentially a question of fact. It depends not only on the nature of the contract involved, but the officer negotiating it, the corporation's usual manner of conducting business, the size of the corporation and the number of its stockholders, the circumstances that give rise to the contract, the reasonableness of the contract, the amounts involved, and who the contracting third party is, to list a few but not all of the relevant factors. In certain instances a given contract may be so important to the welfare of the corporation that outsiders would naturally suppose that only the board of directors (or even the shareholders) could properly handle it. It is in this light that the "ordinary course of business" rule should be given its content. Beyond such "extraordinary" acts, whether or not apparent authority exists is simply a matter of fact.

Accordingly, we hold that, assuming there was sufficient proof of the making of the pension agreement, Connecticut, in the particular circumstances of this case, would probably take the view that reasonable men could differ on the subject of whether or not Yardley had apparent authority to make the contract, and that the trial court erred in deciding the question as a matter of law. We do not think Connecticut would adopt any hard and fast rule against apparent authority to make pension agreements generally, on the theory that they were in the same category as lifetime employment contracts. * * *

———

In *Joseph Greenspon's Sons Iron & Steel Co. v. Pecos Valley Gas Co.*, 34 Del. 567, 156 A. 350 (1931), the president of a gas company signed a contract to purchase 45 miles of gas pipe for approximately $145,000 without having obtained express authority from the gas company's board of directors. The court charged the jury that the president had implied authority to enter into contracts in the usual course of the corporation's business and stated that it was for the jury to decide whether the pipe order was such a contract.

The court also noted that a corporation's president could have the power to enter into a contract not in the ordinary course of business as a consequence of (1) some provision of statutory law, (2) the articles of incorporation, (3) a bylaw of the company, (4) a resolution of the board of directors, or (5) evidence that the corporation had allowed the president to act in similar matters and had recognized, approved and ratified the president's actions.

In *Scientific Holding Co., Ltd. v. Plessey Inc.*, 510 F.2d 15 (2d Cir.1974), a contract for Plessey to purchase International Scientific Ltd. (ISL), a predecessor to Scientific, was amended at the closing, when it became clear that ISL could not satisfy a financial condition to the purchase agreement. Kovar, ISL's president and chief operating officer, expressed concern about whether he was authorized to sign the amendment, but eventually agreed to do so. Several months later, Plessey sought to enforce the amendment. Scientific then attempted to repudiate it.

The court said that whether Kovar had authority to sign to the amendment was unclear. However, it ruled, even assuming Kovar lacked such authority, "Scientific's failure to repudiate the amendment for lack of authorization [from March] until mid-July estopped it from doing so later." Plessey prevailed.

## FIRST INTERSTATE BANK OF TEXAS v. FIRST NATIONAL BANK OF JEFFERSON

928 F.2d 153 (5th Cir.1991).

[In February 1982, New Orleans Property Development (NOPD) asked First National Bank of Jefferson (FNJ) to purchase $3 million in industrial revenue bonds. FNJ obtained a commitment from First Interstate to purchase $1 million of the bonds, then agreed to buy the entire $3 million. First Interstate and FNJ subsequently reached an oral agreement that First Interstate would purchase $2 million of the bonds if FNJ committed to repurchase those bonds on demand. Attorneys for the banks then prepared a draft Bond Purchase Agreement (BPA) and sent a copy to FNJ Senior Vice President John Boyd. Boyd discussed the BPA with FNJ President Arceneaux, who left Boyd with the impression that execution of the BPA was an "acceptable approach."

On July 29, 1982, First Interstate and FNJ purchased the NOPD bonds and executed the BPA. Boyd signed the BPA for FNJ.

In August 1988, First Interstate asked FNJ to repurchase its NOPD bonds pursuant to the BPA. FNJ refused, asserting that Boyd had not been authorized to sign the BPA. At the trial of First Interstate's suit to enforce the BPA, the district court held that First Interstate had not produced sufficient evidence to present a jury question as to whether Boyd had authority to sign the BPA and directed a verdict in favor of FNJ.]

W. EUGENE DAVIS, CIRCUIT JUDGE:

First Interstate argues that the district court erroneously directed a verdict for FNJ on the issue of Boyd's authority. * * * Our review of the record persuades us that reasonable, fair-minded jurors could reach different conclusions about whether Boyd had actual or apparent authority to bind FNJ.

The parties agree that Louisiana law governs our analysis. Louisiana agency law recognizes two types of authority, actual and apparent. We begin with a discussion of actual authority.

### A.

Actual authority can be express or implied. The district court held that a jury was not entitled to find that Boyd had express actual authority to execute the BPA because no corporate resolution or by-law specifically authorized the transaction. A principal, however, can confer actual authority orally. The following testimony could convince a jury that FNJ likely gave Boyd express actual authority to sign the BPA.

Boyd testified that FNJ authorized him to sign the BPA. Boyd said that he discussed the NOPD transaction, including the BPA, with Arceneaux and other FNJ officers. Arceneaux denied having such discussions. The district court weighed Boyd's testimony, but "considered [it] very weak." Given the corroborating evidence, we are persuaded that it was sufficiently strong for a reasonable jury to credit it.

Boyd's position in the FNJ hierarchy lends credence to his assertion that the bank authorized him to sign the BPA. Boyd was one of only four FNJ senior vice presidents, an office of considerable responsibility. He was hired by and reported directly to President Arceneaux. Not only did Boyd handle loans himself, [including the NOPD loan,] he also supervised several FNJ vice presidents. * * * A juror could surmise that a person who held the position of senior vice president, who was responsible for handling the NOPD loan account, and who supervised other loan officers was the type officer FNJ would have authorized to sign the interbank agreement at issue here. * * *

The record demonstrates that the BPA did not obligate FNJ any further than its March 12 commitment letter to NOPD. On that date, FNJ committed to buy the entire $3 million bond issue. President Arceneaux conceded that the letter bound FNJ to take the entire issue. The commitment letter does not condition the bond purchase on FNJ's ability to find a co-lender. Thus, the July 29 BPA did not extend FNJ's obligation on the bonds beyond its March 12 commitment. Both agreements made FNJ the principal lender on a $3 million loan. The fact that the BPA did not expand FNJ's exposure supports Boyd's assertion that FNJ authorized him to sign the BPA.

In sum, we conclude that the evidence presented a jury question whether FNJ gave Boyd express actual authority to execute the BPA.

### B.

We now turn briefly to the issue of implied actual authority. " 'Implied authority' is actual authority which is inferred from the circumstances and nature of the agency. An agent is vested with the implied authority to do all of those things necessary or incidental to the agency assignment." *Demolle v. Horace Mann Ins. Co.*, 491 So.2d 695, 698

(La.App. 5th Cir.1986), writ denied, 496 So.2d 1041 (La.1986). "Implied authority connotes permission from the principal for the agent to act, though that permission is not expressly set forth orally or in writing." *AAA Tire & Export, Inc. v. Big Chief Truck Lines*, 385 So.2d 426, 429 (La.App. 1st Cir.1980).

First Interstate argues that a juror might infer from the nature of the bank's business and Boyd's position in that business that Boyd had implied actual authority to sign the BPA. [However, Article 2997 of the Louisiana Civil Code, which provides that the power of an agent to sell, to buy, to contract a loan or to acknowledge a debt must be express, defeats this argument.] * * * The district court correctly declined to submit this theory to the jury. We turn finally to First Interstate's apparent authority argument.

## C.

A corporation will be liable to a third party even for the unauthorized acts of its agent under the doctrine of apparent authority if (1) the corporation manifests the agent's authority to the third party, and (2) the third party reasonably relies on the agent's purported authority as a result of the manifestation. We conclude that First Interstate also introduced sufficient evidence to create a jury question on Boyd's apparent authority to bind FNJ.

When FNJ hired Boyd as a senior vice president, it manifested to the public that Boyd had the authority to bind the bank in agreements necessary to conduct the bank's business. See *Cook v. Ruston Oil Mills & Fertilizer*, 170 La. 10, 127 So. 347, 353 (1930) ("[T]he corporation, by the very fact of the appointment of such manager, holds him out to the public as the person authorized to bind it by contracts necessary in the prosecution of its business."). On the day of the NOPD closing, FNJ specifically manifested to First Interstate that Boyd was authorized to execute the necessary closing papers on behalf of FNJ. FNJ sent Boyd and one of its trust officers to the closing with a certification that Boyd was its senior vice-president and that he was acting on behalf of FNJ's Board of Directors. The BPA was signed by the parties at the closing. The jury was entitled to conclude that when FNJ sent Boyd to the closing with a certificate of his authority, the bank was also manifesting Boyd's authority to sign the BPA, without which First Interstate would not have agreed to buy the NOPD bonds.

FNJ also implicitly manifested Boyd's authority when its president, Arceneaux, sent Boyd to consummate a deal that Arceneaux himself helped negotiate. LaRue, the loan officer representing First Interstate in the NOPD transaction, testified that he spoke to Arceneaux about the deal. LaRue said that he and Ken Anderson, First Interstate's executive vice president, agreed with Arceneaux in a telephone conversation that First Interstate would buy $2 million in bonds if FNJ acquiesced in a buy-out provision. If a jury accepts this testimony, it could conclude that Arceneaux's conversation with Anderson and LaRue was a specific manifestation of FNJ's willingness to commit to the BPA. The jury could also view this evidence as a manifestation by FNJ that Boyd, the FNJ senior vice president in charge of this transaction, was authorized to sign the BPA. * * *

FNJ argues that the doctrine of apparent authority does not apply in this case because First Interstate did not inquire into the extent of Boyd's authority. * * * We disagree. A third party can rely on the apparent authority of an agent until something occurs that would cause a reasonable person to inquire further into the circumstances. The cases cited by FNJ in which courts found a duty to inquire are distinguishable. In those cases, the agent was either not an officer or even an employee of the purported principal; thus, a reasonable person would have inquired about the agent's authority.

A jury could conclude that First Interstate need not have made further inquiry. * * * Because a reasonable jury could conclude that Boyd had apparent authority to bind FNJ on the BPA, a directed verdict was inappropriate. * * *

Affirmed in part, Reversed in part, and Remanded.

## 3.  THE CREATION OF EXPRESS AUTHORITY

Given the existence of questions as to the authority of corporate officers, including the CEO, careful counsel representing a party involved in a major transaction with a corporation usually will insist on receiving adequate evidence that the individuals who purport to act for the corporation are authorized to do so.

In essence, what is required is evidence that the board of directors has delegated authority to the officer to act on behalf of the corporation. The best evidence of a board decision is a copy of the minutes of the board of directors' meeting at which the resolution formalizing the decision was adopted. The resolution, in addition to approving the transaction in question, should designate the CEO or some other officer to execute the documents and do the other acts necessary to consummate the transaction. In the case of a particularly significant transaction, the minutes might include, as an attachment, a copy of the contract that the board has authorized the officer to sign.

Somewhat less important transactions may be covered by more general delegations of authority. For example, a board might authorize the CEO or some other officer to enter into contracts of a certain type or up to a certain value. If a party to a transaction with the corporation has doubts as to the authority of the official with whom she is dealing, she can request a copy of the resolution delegating such authority and the minutes of the board meeting at which the resolution was adopted.

But a question remains: how can a third party be sure the minutes and resolution are genuine? Customary practice is to have the secretary of the corporation (or other officer charged with maintaining the corporation's books and records) certify the minutes and resolution. The secretary has been held to have express authority to certify such documents, so that a corporation is bound by the secretary's certification. This holding allows inquiry into an officer's authority to enter into a contract to stop short of requiring a majority of the directors to swear in person that, yes, they did vote to authorize the officer to act. *See In the Matter of Drive–In Development Corp.*, 371 F.2d 215 (7th Cir.1966), cert. denied 387 U.S. 909, 87 S.Ct. 1691, 18 L.Ed.2d 626 (1967). It is also why some statutes do not permit the same person to be both president and secretary.

## C.  FORMALITIES OF ACTION BY THE BOARD OF DIRECTORS

### PROBLEM

### WIDGET CORPORATION

You are counsel to the Widget Corporation, which is incorporated in a jurisdiction that has adopted the RMBCA, and which has articles and bylaws similar to the Model Articles of Incorporation and Model Bylaws in Edward S. Adams and John H. Matheson, SELECTED CORPORATIONS AND OTHER BUSINESS ASSOCIATIONS STATUTES, RULES AND FORMS (West). Article III, Section 2 of Widget's bylaws provides for an eight-member board of directors. Widget's president advises you that she has just negotiated a sale of one of the corporation's plants on advantageous terms that will provide desperately needed working capital for the corporation. The sale agreement requires board authorization; the president hopes to close the sale and receive the proceeds within 36 hours. One of Widget's directors is in a local hospital for minor surgery, one is in London on business, one is mountain climbing in Nepal, and one is sailing in the Caribbean.

1.  Would a unanimous vote by the four available directors at a special meeting of the board be effective? Consider RMBCA §§ 8.20, 8.22, 8.23, and 8.24 [DGCL § 141] and Article III of the Model Bylaws.

2.  Suppose the president visits the ailing board member in the hospital, explains the sale fully, and has her execute a proxy authorizing the president to cast the director's vote in favor of the sale at the board meeting. The transaction subsequently receives the unanimous vote of the four available directors at a special meeting. Is this valid board action?

3.  What other alternatives are available for the board to authorize the sale? Consider RMBCA §§ 8.20, 8.21 and 8.23 [DGCL § 141] and Article III of the Model By-laws.

4.  How could the articles of incorporation and by-laws be modified to deal with some future crisis where it is not possible to assemble a majority of directors at a board meeting? Consider RMBCA §§ 8.22, 8.24 and 8.25 [DGCL § 141].

## 1. ACTION BY THE BOARD AT A MEETING

The board of directors traditionally takes formal action by vote at a meeting. Each director has one vote and may not vote by proxy. *Lippman v. Kehoe Stenograph Co.*, 11 Del.Ch. 80, 95 A. 895 (1915). Unless the articles or by-laws provide otherwise, the vote of a majority of the directors present at a board meeting at which there is a quorum is necessary to pass a resolution. RMBCA § 8.24(c).

One reason for the requirement that the board come together at a meeting to act is the view that the board is a collegial body. By consulting together, board members may draw on each other's knowledge and experience. More ideas and points of view are likely to be considered in the formulation of decisions, which may produce better results than if the directors act without consultation.

On a less pragmatic level, the directors have authority to act only as a body, not as individuals. In *Baldwin v. Canfield*, 26 Minn. 43, 1 N.W. 261 (1879), which involved the validity of a deed that all of a corporation's directors signed but that the board never approved at a meeting, the court stated:

> As we have already seen, the court below finds that, by its articles of incorporation, the government of the [corporation], and the management of its affairs, was vested in the board of directors. The legal effect of this was to invest the directors with such government and management *as a board,* and not otherwise. This is in accordance with the general rule that the governing body of a corporation, as such, are agents of the corporation only as a board, and not individually. Hence it follows that they have no authority to act, save when assembled at a board meeting. The separate action, individually, of the persons comprising such governing body, is not the action of the constituted body of men clothed with the corporate powers.

Courts have refused to uphold informal action by directors without a meeting when the board's alleged authority to bind the corporation was challenged by the corporation (*Peirce v. Morse–Oliver Bldg. Co.*, 94 Me. 406, 47 A. 914 (1900)), the directors of the corporation (*Schuckman v. Rubenstein*, 164 F.2d 952 (6th Cir.1947), cert. denied 333 U.S. 875, 68 S.Ct. 905, 92 L.Ed. 1151 (1948)), the corporation's trustee in bankruptcy (*Hurley v. Ornsteen*, 311 Mass. 477, 42 N.E.2d 273 (1942)), or pledgees of the corporation's stock (*Baldwin v. Canfield*, 26 Minn. 43, 1 N.W. 261 (1879)). Although courts frequently fail to articulate their reasons for requiring formal board action, "underlying almost all of the decisions * * * is a single policy: to protect shareholders and their investment from arbitrary, irresponsible or unwise acts on the part of the directors. When presented with informal director action, the courts will decline to apply the general rule when the shareholders, by their actions, indicate that they do not wish the protection or when such application will not afford them any greater protection." Matthew N. Perlstein, Note, *Corpo-*

*rations: When Informal Action by Corporate Directors Will Be Permitted to Bind the Corporation*, 53 B. U.L.REV. 101, 101 (1973).

Courts nonetheless are not blind to the fact that informal board action, particularly in close corporations, is extremely common. This reality has led courts to seek to protect innocent third parties from the strict application of the traditional rule permitting board action only at a meeting. Thus, courts have relied on numerous justifications to hold corporations liable on agreements never approved at formal board meetings.

a. *Unanimous Informal Agreement by the Directors*. In *Gerard v. Empire Square Realty Co.*, 195 App.Div. 244, 249, 187 N.Y.S. 306, 310 (1921) the court noted, "if all the directors are of one mind * * * discussion is futile * * *." In all probability there will be no discussion at all; the directors, being in agreement, will simply act, and, as a result, there will be no opportunity to further the corporate purpose.

b. *Emergency*. Situations arise where the board must make very quick decisions to prevent great harm or to take advantage of great opportunity. In such a situation, it may be impossible to assemble the board at a meeting. The corporation must proceed on the opinions of those directors who can be contacted in whatever manner contact may be made.

c. *Representation of the Interests of All Shareholders*. A conclusion reached at a meeting at which all the shareholders of the corporation are present will likely bind the corporation. *See e.g., Brainard v. De La Montanya*, 18 Cal.2d 502, 116 P.2d 66 (1941); *In re Kartub*, 7 Misc.2d 72, 152 N.Y.S.2d 34 (1956), aff'd 3 A.D.2d 896, 163 N.Y.S.2d 938 (1957). Courts have also held the corporation bound if the directors who participate in the informal action constitute a majority of the board and own a majority of the corporation's issued and outstanding shares. *See, e.g., Air Technical Development Co. v. Arizona Bank*, 101 Ariz. 70, 416 P.2d 183 (1966); *Phillips Petroleum Co. v. Rock Creek Mining Co.*, 449 F.2d 664 (9th Cir.1971). *But see, McDonald v. Dalheim*, 114 Ohio App.3d 543, 683 N.E.2d 447 (action invalid when participating directors owned a majority of the shares but did not constitute a quorum).

To buttress these common law exceptions to the general rule, a majority of states have enacted statutory provisions allowing informal director action under some conditions. RMBCA § 8.21, for example, allows action to be taken without a meeting on the unanimous written consent of the directors. The Official Comment notes: "Under section 8.21 the requirement of unanimous consent precludes the possibility of stifling or ignoring opposing argument. A director opposed to an action that is proposed to be taken by unanimous consent, or uncertain about the desirability of that action, may compel the holding of a directors' meeting to discuss the matter simply by withholding his consent." RMBCA § 8.20(b) permits board action to be taken by a conference telephone call. The Official Comment to RMBCA § 8.20 states: "The advantage of the traditional meeting is the opportunity for interchange that is permitted by a meeting in a single room at which members are physically present. If this opportunity for interchange is thought to be available by the board of directors, a meeting may be conducted by electronic means although no two directors are physically present at the same place * * *."

However, modern statutes also have led some courts to take a harder line towards corporations that disregard statutory requirements governing board actions. These courts reason that the more liberal statutory approaches to informal director action should pre-empt the common law doctrines described above. *Village of Brown Deer v. Milwaukee*, 16 Wis.2d 206, 114 N.W.2d 493 (1962), cert. denied 371 U.S. 902, 83 S.Ct. 205, 9 L.Ed.2d 164 (1962), involved a corporation whose president and majority shareholder had customarily made decisions without involving the board. The president signed a petition on behalf of the corporation for municipal annexation of land. The Wisconsin statute permitted a board to act by unanimous written consent without a meeting, but the president had not obtained the directors' consent. The court reasoned:

> * * * Corporations owe their existence to the statutes. Those who would enjoy the benefits that attend the corporate form of operation are obliged to conduct their affairs in accordance with the laws which authorized them. * * *

> The legislature having specified the means whereby corporations could function informally, it becomes incumbent upon the courts to enforce such legislative pronouncements. The legislature has said that the corporation could act informally, without a meeting, by obtaining the consent in writing of all of the Directors. In our opinion, this pronouncement has preempted the field and prohibits corporations from acting informally without complying with [the statute].

114 N.W.2d at 497.

In contrast to *Village of Brown Deer*, *White v. Thatcher Financial Group, Inc.*, 940 P.2d 1034 (Colo.Ct.App.1996) illustrates how far some courts will go in upholding informal board action in a close corporation even if such action appears to violate the applicable corporate statute. In *White*, the board approved payment of certain expenses to its outgoing president. Because of vacancies that had gone unfilled for several years, the board, which had consisted of four members had only two members which was less than the then statutory requirement of three. The court found that these two directors constituted a quorum of the statutory minimum and upheld the validity of the payments. In reaching this conclusion, the court drew on the fact that it was "the custom and practice of the corporation to operate with fewer than the required number of directors, but still with a quorum of the board, and the jury here apparently so found." *Id.* at 1038. The court noted that the purpose of the "custom and practice" doctrine was to protect innocent third parties in dealing with a close corporation and that the president was not such a person. Nevertheless, the court accorded no weight to the difference.

## 2. NOTICE AND QUORUM

Notice and quorum requirements apply to board meetings. The notice requirement makes personal attendance at a meeting reasonably possible. Directors know when regularly scheduled board meetings will be held. RMBCA § 8.22(a) acknowledges this fact by permitting directors to waive notice of regular meetings unless a company's articles of incorporation or bylaws require that notice be given. For special meetings, RMBCA § 8.22(b) requires that two days' notice be given of the date, time and place of meeting, unless the articles of incorporation or bylaws impose different requirements. Many companies provide directors with notice of the purpose of all meetings, so that directors will be better prepared to discuss the matters that will be on the agenda. RMBCA § 8.22 does not require such notice, but permits it to be included in the articles of incorporation or bylaws. Action taken at a board meeting held without the required notice is invalid. *Schmidt v. Farm Credit Services*, 977 F.2d 511 (10th Cir.1992).

Any director who does not receive proper notice may waive notice by signing a waiver before or after the meeting, RMBCA § 8.23(a), or by attending or participating in the meeting and not protesting the absence of notice. RMBCA § 8.23(b). However, a director who attends a meeting solely to protest the manner in which it was convened is not deemed to have waived notice. RMBCA § 8.23(b).

The quorum requirement helps preclude action by a minority of the directors. The statutory norm for a quorum is a majority of the total number of directors, although the articles of incorporation or bylaws may increase the quorum requirement or reduce it to no less than one-third of the board. RMBCA § 8.24. Action taken in the absence of a quorum is invalid. *Schoen v. Consumers United Group*, 670 F.Supp. 367 (D.D.C.1986).

## 3. COMMITTEES OF THE BOARD

Boards that have large numbers of members, such as the boards of many large, publicly-held companies, are unwieldy and often find it difficult, when acting as a whole, effectively to discharge all of their responsibilities. The trend in recent years toward increasing the proportion of outside directors has exacerbated this problem. Many companies have responded by delegating responsibility for many board functions to committees empowered to exercise, in defined areas, the authority of the board. *See generally* John A. McMullen, *Committees of the Board of Directors*, 29 Bus.Law. 755 (1974). This practice now is authorized explicitly in nearly every state. RMBCA § 8.25.

The executive committee is a common board committee because it can have the full authority of the board in all but a few essential transactions such as the declaration of a dividend or approval of a merger. RMBCA § 8.25 (e). Thus the executive committee often is the vehicle through which the board acts between meetings on less important matters of corporate housekeeping which, for technical reasons, require board approval.

The audit committee is another common board committee, particularly in publicly-held corporations. Its functions usually include selection of the company's auditors, specification of the scope of the audit, review of audit results, and oversight of internal accounting procedures. In the mid-'70s, disclosure that many large companies had used millions of dollars to pay bribes and make unlawful contributions increased the visibility of audit committees. Both the New York Stock Exchange and the National Association of Securities Dealers now require publicly-held companies to have audit committees.

Other relatively common committees include finance (usually responsible for giving advice on financial structure, the issuance of new securities, and the management of the corporation's investments), nomination (responsible for nominating new directors and officers), and compensation (responsible for fixing the salaries and other compensation of executives). Boards often create specialized committees to deal with specific problems. See Chapter 20 for a discussion of special litigation committees in connection with derivative suits.

A board committee can be permanent or temporary. Its functions can be active—making decisions on behalf of the board—or passive—doing research and presenting information so the full board can make more informed decisions. Case law and statutes increasingly reflect the view that committees are desirable because directors who are committee members have more incentive to develop expertise in the area of the committee's responsibility. RMBCA § 8.30(b) recognizes the expanding use of committees and permits a director to rely on the reports or actions of a committee on which she does not serve, so long as the committee reasonably merits her confidence.

# D. ACTION BY SHAREHOLDERS

## 1. INTRODUCTION

Shareholders meet at a regularly scheduled annual meeting, and also may meet at special meetings convened for particular purposes. Unless a corporation's articles of incorporation provide otherwise, each share is entitled to one vote.

Election of directors is the most important item of business at the annual meeting. Shareholders elect directors annually unless the articles of incorporation provide for staggered terms, in which event shareholders elect directors for terms of two or three years. RMBCA §§ 8.05, 8.06. The shareholders' power to elect directors is exclusive, except when a board seat is vacant in which case, unless the articles provide otherwise, either shareholders or the remaining directors can fill the vacancy. RMBCA § 8.10.

No matter other than the election of directors is required to be considered at an annual meeting. However, boards of directors often seek shareholder approval of other matters, such as the appointment of auditors, the adoption of management compensation plans, or the ratification of decisions that a board has made.

Most modern statutes also permit shareholders to act by means of written consent in lieu of a meeting. Under RMBCA § 7.04, action by written consent requires the approval of *all* the shareholders. This requirement effectively limits use of the consent procedure to closely held corporations. DGCL § 228 differs significantly; it allows holders of a *majority* of a company's voting stock to act by means of written consent. Consequently, shareholders holding a majority of the stock in a Delaware corporation can act without providing advance notice to the company's management or to other shareholders. As with most such statutory provisions, a company can include a provision in its articles of incorporation eliminating or restricting this power.

The general principle governing shareholder voting is that action taken by the "affirmative vote of the majority of shares present in person or represented by proxy at the meeting and entitled to vote on the subject matter shall be the act of the stockholders * * *." DGCL § 216. Most statutes require more than simple majority approval of certain transactions. See e.g. RMBCA § 11.03(e) (requiring majority of all shares entitled to vote to approve a merger). Statutes also generally allow a corporation to include in its articles of incorporation a provision requiring that a greater number of shares approve all shareholder actions or some particular actions.

Unlike directors, shareholders may vote by proxy. RMBCA § 7.22. A proxy is simply a limited form of agency power by which a shareholder authorizes another, who will be present at the meeting, to exercise the shareholder's voting rights. A proxy may give the proxy holder discretion to vote as she pleases or may direct her to vote in a particular way. In public corporations, management typically solicits from shareholders proxies authorizing one or more members of management to vote the shareholder's stock at the meeting. This proxy solicitation process is regulated primarily by the federal securities laws, a subject we consider in detail in Chapter 14.

## 2. SHAREHOLDERS' VETO AND EXIT RIGHTS

### PROBLEM

### LAFRANCE COSMETICS—PART I

LaFrance Cosmetics, Inc., a Columbia corporation, manufactures a line of cosmetics. Its articles of incorporation authorize two million shares of common stock, of which one million shares are issued and outstanding. Mimi LaFrance, who founded LaFrance and continues to chair the board, owns 400,000 shares. Her son, Pierre, the president and CEO, owns 100,000 shares, as does her daughter, Margaret, who is not otherwise involved in the business. The remaining 400,000 shares were bequeathed by Mimi's late husband, Maurice, to the Columbia Museum of Modern Art and are held in trust by the Third National Bank. The board of LaFrance consists of Mimi, Pierre, Margaret, Victor Gauguin, a retired businessman, and Lauren Miller, the senior vice-president responsible for the bank's trust department.

Pierre, with Mimi's support, has been seeking to expand LaFrance's business into related lines. He recently approached Sweet Violet, Inc. another Columbia corporation, about a business combination. Sweet Violet, which manufactures perfume and related toiletries, has about 250 shareholders, none of whom owns more than 10% of the 100,000 shares of Sweet Violet common stock currently outstanding. After extensive negotiations, Pierre and Sweet Violet's management agreed in principle on a transaction in which LaFrance would acquire Sweet Violet for 400,000 shares of LaFrance common stock.

Pierre then sought the LaFrance board of directors' approval of the proposed acquisition. Margaret objected strongly. In recent years, LaFrance has reinvested most of its income in an effort to become a more effective competitor of the large, publicly-held companies that dominate the cosmetics business. Margaret, dissatisfied with the relatively modest dividends LaFrance has been paying, has urged Pierre and Mimi to abandon this effort and sell LaFrance to one of those companies. She argued that the acquisition of Sweet Violet was inconsistent with her preferred strategy. LaFrance's other two directors, however, supported the proposed acquisition, Victor Gauguin strongly and Lauren Miller more moderately. Lauren also remarked that, while she favored the move, some other members of the Bank's investment committee had questioned whether this was a good time for LaFrance to expand. The LaFrance board then voted 4–1 to approve the proposed acquisition of Sweet Violet for 400,000 shares of LaFrance stock.

As counsel to LaFrance, Pierre has asked you to advise him on how to structure the proposed acquisition of Sweet Violet. Pierre is concerned about the possibility that Margaret, and perhaps the Bank, will vote against the transaction and seek to obtain the fair value of their shares by exercising dissenters' rights. The latter possibility would be particularly troublesome, because LaFrance already is strapped for cash. Pierre's preference is to avoid a vote by LaFrance's shareholders and, in all events, to avoid giving those shareholders dissenters' rights. Pierre also has advised you that Sweet Violet's management is indifferent as to how the proposed transaction is structured, so long as Sweet Violet's shareholders end up with 400,000 shares of LaFrance stock.

The proposed acquisition could be structured as either (1) a statutory merger of Sweet Violet into LaFrance, (2) a "triangular" merger of Sweet Violet into a subsidiary of LaFrance, (3) a statutory share exchange, or (4) an exchange of LaFrance stock for Sweet Violet's assets, followed by the dissolution of Sweet Violet.

1.  For each of these alternatives, determine:

(a) The applicable statutory requirements, including whether a vote by LaFrance's shareholders would be required (consider RMBCA §§ 11.01, 11.02, 11.03, 12.02, and 10.03);

(b) Whether LaFrance's shareholders would be entitled to dissenters' rights (consider RMBCA § 13.02);

(c) Whether Margaret is likely to succeed in a suit to block the transaction if LaFrance's shareholders are not given the right to vote or to assert dissenter's rights.

2. How would your answers to these questions differ if LaFrance were a Delaware corporation.

## A. BACKGROUND

As noted above, corporate statutes condition a board of directors' power to effectuate certain fundamental changes in a firm's form, scope or continuity of existence on the board's first obtaining shareholders' approval. Transactions subject to this requirement vary from state to state, but generally include most amendments to the articles of incorporation, significant mergers, the sale of all or substantially all of a corporation's assets, and dissolution. Shareholders' rights with respect to these matters can most accurately be described as *veto rights*, in that shareholders' authority is limited to blocking such changes by withholding their approval. Put differently, shareholders have no power to initiate fundamental changes.

It is important to note that the shareholders' veto power is limited to those fundamental changes prescribed in the statute. Many transaction which could be viewed as involving a fundamental change in the corporation's business, such as the acquisition of a new division for cash, do not require shareholder approval, notwithstanding the impact of such a transaction on the shareholders' investment.

At common law, one shareholder in a corporation could block all others from making any fundamental change in the corporation's business or charter, even a change as simple as extending the life of a corporation beyond its expiration date. *See* William J. Carney, *Fundamental Corporate Changes, Minority Shareholders, and Business Purposes*, 1980 AM. BAR. FOUNDATION RSCH. J. 69, 77–82. This rule was based on the idea that the charter was was a contract, both among the corporations's shareholders and between the corporation and the state, in which every shareholder had vested rights. *Id.* at 78 & n. 32. Majority shareholders were powerless to overcome a dissenter's opposition, except by buying her out.

State legislatures began to recognize that the unanimous consent requirement created the potential for tyranny by the minority. Situations arose in which an entrepreneurial investor apparently purchased stock in a company after some fundamental change had been proposed in order to veto that change and thus force the majority to repurchase her shares at a premium. *See, e.g., Windhurst v. Central Leather Co.,* 101 N.J.Eq. 543, 551–52, 138 A. 772, 776 (Ch.1927), *aff'd per curiam* 107 N.J.Eq. 528, 153 A. 402 (1931) ("while I cannot say that Windhurst is a *'professional* privateer,' * * * it would seem * * * that his venture was not entirely free of a piratical character.") Legislatures responded by amending corporation statutes to allow fundamental changes that were approved by a corporation's board of directors and a majority or super-majority of its shareholders. *See, e.g.,* Act of May 27, 1896, ch. 932, §§ 57, 58, 1896 N.Y. Laws 994 (voluntary dissolution and merger). Recall Professor Cary's argument in Chapter 7.

Concurrent with this weakening of minority shareholders' voice, legislatures granted shareholders a right, in effect, to "opt out" of a transaction involving a fundamental change in which their vote was required. A shareholder can dissent from the transaction and require the corporation to pay her in cash the value of her shares as determined by a court in an appraisal proceeding, if the transaction nonetheless is supported by the requisite majority of the corporation's shareholders. RMBCA § 13.02. In *Chicago Corp. v. Munds,* 20 Del.Ch. 142, 149, 172 A. 452, 455 (1934), a Delaware court described this development as follows:

> * * * At common law it was in the power of any single stock-holder to prevent a merger. When the idea became generally accept-ed that, in the interest of adjusting corporate mechanisms to the requirements of business and commercial growth, mergers should be permitted in spite of the opposition of minorities, statutes were enacted in state after state which took from the individual stock-holder the right theretofore existing to defeat the welding of his corporation with another. In compensation for the lost right a provision was written into the modern statutes giving the dissenting stockholder the option completely to retire from the enterprise and receive the value of his stock in money.

Some scholars rely on such explanations to argue that appraisal statutes were enacted to substitute an exit right for the veto rights that individual shareholders previously possessed. *See* Carney, *supra.* Others point out that this account fails to explain differences between appraisal statutes or certain significant features of appraisal statutes. *See* Hideki Kanda & Saul Levmore, *The Appraisal Remedy and the Goals of Corporate Law,* 32 UCLA L.Rev. 429, 434 (1985).

Whatever the rationale underlying appraisal statutes, three points remain clear. First, different states' corporation statutes provide share-holders with veto rights and dissenter's rights with regard to different sets of transactions. Second, shareholders are not entitled to assert dissenters' rights with respect to every transaction on which they are entitled to vote. Third, every corporation statute authorizes shareholders to dissent from certain transactions involving fundamental changes and to require the corporation to repurchase their stock for its fair value.

## B. THE MECHANICS OF CORPORATE COMBINATIONS

Questions relating to voting and appraisal rights arise most often in connection with corporate combinations—transactions that place the business operations of two or more companies under the control of one management. Corporate combinations raise numerous legal issues and are the basis of a great deal of corporate litigation. In subsequent chapters, we consider many of those issues, including whether the boards of directors of constituent corporations exercised reasonable care in approving a combination (see Chapter 16), whether constituent corporations made adequate disclosure of relevant facts to their shareholders (see Chapter 18), what tactics the board of directors of a target company can employ to resist an uninvited takeover bid (see Chapter 22), and what constitutes fair dealing in a combination involving a parent corporation and a controlled subsidiary and whether appraisal is the exclusive remedy available to shareholders in connection with such a transaction (see Chapter 23). Our concern in this chapter is limited to two narrower issues. This section discusses how corporate statutes define the availability of voting and appraisal rights in connection with different forms of corporate combinations. The next section considers whether the form or the substance of a combination should determine the availability of voting and appraisal rights.

Corporations can use a number of different transactional techniques to combine the operations of two or more companies in one firm. Business and tax considerations often dominate the choice of which technique to use. If selling rights in certain property would trigger significant financial or tax obligations, for example, the firms involved probably will try to structure the combination so that the entity holding title to those rights either survives the transaction or is extinguished by operation of law. Similarly, if the management of the post-combination firm would prefer to operate acquired firms as divisions, so as to avoid the administrative burden of maintaining subsidiary corporations, those planning the combination will liquidate or otherwise eliminate all but one of the corporations that survive the combination. But whatever transactional technique is used, and whatever the structure of the resulting business enterprise, the functional result largely will be the same: what were two or more separate business enterprises now will operate as parts of the same business entity, under the control of one board of directors and one management team.

The transactional technique used to effectuate a corporate combination can have dramatically different effects, though, on the voting and appraisal rights of the shareholders of the corporate parties to the combination. To illustrate, we will consider the transactional dynamics and impact on voting and appraisal rights of four basic techniques for bringing two (or more) corporations under the control of one management in a negotiated transaction: (1) a statutory merger, (2) a triangular merger, (3) a statutory share exchange, and (4) an acquisition by one corporation of the assets of another. We will also briefly consider the mechanics of a tender offer. In the following discussion, we designate the principal corporation surviving the combination—the parent corporation—as P, any subsidiary of P as S, and the corporation to be acquired—the target corporation—as T. To illustrate the differences between different states' laws, we outline the statutory requirements applicable to each of these transactions under the RMBCA and DGCL. For a full treatment, see 2 Martin D. Ginsburg & Jack S. Levin, MERGERS, ACQUISITIONS AND LEVERAGED BUYOUTS ¶ 1502 (1997).

## 1. STATUTORY MERGER

In a statutory merger,* as in all the other forms of corporate combination, P and T begin as separate legal entities. To effectuate a statutory merger, the boards of directors of P and T first adopt a plan of merger that (a) designates which corporation (here P) is to survive the merger, (b) describes the terms and conditions of the merger, (c) describes the basis on which shares of T will be converted into shares of P (or other property, such as cash or bonds), and (d) sets forth any amendments to P's articles of incorporation necessary to effectuate the plan of merger. RMBCA § 11.01; DGCL § 251(a). The plan of merger then is submitted to the shareholders of both P and T. A majority of the shares of both P and T entitled to vote on the merger must vote in favor. RMBCA § 11.03; DGCL § 251(b).

However, if the transaction qualifies as a so-called *"small scale merger"*—one that does not increase by more than 20 percent P's outstanding voting stock—no vote by P's shareholders is required.** RMBCA § 11.03(g); DGCL § 251(f). According to the Official Comment to RMBCA § 11.03(g): "The theory behind this subsection is that shareholders' votes should be required only if the transaction fundamentally alters the character of the enterprise or substantially reduces the shareholders' participation in voting or profit distribution." Similarly, if P owned at least 90 percent of the stock of T prior to the merger, the transaction can proceed as a *"short form"* merger and no vote by the shareholders of P or T is required. RMBCA § 11.04; DGCL § 253.

After any required shareholder approval is secured, the plan of merger is filed with an appropriate state office and the merger becomes

---

* Statutory merger means a combination effected pursuant to a corporate statute's merger provision, as distinguished from other forms of business combinations often described by the generic term "merger".

** We assume, wherever relevant, that P has authorized sufficient shares to effectuate the transaction in question. If sufficient shares of stock are not authorized, P's articles of incorporation will have to be amended, and P's shareholders will be entitled to vote on that amendment. In addition, if P is publicly held, as a practical matter the rules of the New York Stock Exchange (NYSE) or the National Association of Securities Dealers (NASD) may require a shareholder vote even though no vote is required by state law. NYSE and NASD rules require shareholder approval of any transaction in which a corporation will issue additional shares that exceed by more than 18.5 percent the number of shares outstanding before the transaction. Absent such a vote, the new shares will not be listed on the Exchange or traded through the NASD's automated quotation system (NASDAQ).

effective. By operation of law, T immediately ceases to exist, the assets of T become the assets of P, and the liabilities of T become the liabilities of P. No formal conveyances or assignments need to be executed. All shares of T are converted into shares of P (unless the plan of merger provides for use of cash or other property). Former shareholders of T automatically become shareholders of P; they also lose all rights they had as shareholders of T, unless they dissent and seek appraisal of their shares. RMBCA § 11.06; DGCL § 259. Shareholders of P retain their rights as shareholders of the surviving corporation, but they, too, are entitled to exercise dissenter's rights. RMBCA § 13.02; DGCL § 262. However, if the constituent corporations in a merger are widely held public corporations and the merger consideration is stock, dissenter's rights are not available to shareholders of P or T. DGCL § 262(b)(1)–(2). Similarly, dissenter's rights are not available to shareholders of P, if the transaction qualifies as a small scale or short form merger. RMBCA § 13.02, DGCL § 262(b)(1).

## 2. TRIANGULAR MERGER

Sometimes an acquiring corporation will want to use the statutory merger technique because of the relative ease with which assets can be transferred and liabilities assumed, but will seek to avoid certain legal or business consequences of a statutory merger. For example, P may be concerned about subjecting its own assets to unknown or contingent liabilities associated with T's business. Lawyers often employ a "triangular merger" to deal with such a situation.

A triangular merger is a variant form of statutory merger. The principal difference is that, after negotiating the terms of the combination with T, P creates a subsidiary corporation, S, and transfers to S, in exchange for 100% of its stock, the consideration that T's shareholders are to receive. (In the case of LaFrance's proposed acquisition of Sweet Violet, that would be 400,000 shares of LaFrance common stock.) Then, S and T follow the steps necessary to effectuate a statutory merger: the boards of S and T adopt the plan of merger; the shareholders of S and T vote to approve the merger; and T then is merged into S by operation of law. The only differences are that, rather than having S distribute its own shares to the shareholders of T, S distributes shares of P (or other property) to the shareholders of T,* and S, rather than P, becomes the owner of T's property and assumes T's liabilities.**

From the point of view of T's shareholders, it makes little difference whether a combination is structured as a statutory merger or a triangular merger. In either case, they vote on the transaction and, if they wish to exit, they can exercise dissenter's rights. Structuring a combination as a triangular merger, however, has a major impact on the rights of P's shareholders. In both cases they end up as shareholders of a corporation

---

* RMBCA § 11.01(b)(3) explicitly authorizes use of stock of a non-party corporation as consideration in a merger, as does DGCL § 251(b).

** The transaction could also be structured as a reverse triangular merger in which S is merged into T.

that controls the businesses formerly operated by P and T. But in the case of a triangular merger, it is the shareholders of S, not the shareholders of P, who vote on the merger and who can exercise dissenter's rights. S, of course, has only one shareholder—P. And P's board of directors, not P's shareholders, has the power to exercise P's rights as a shareholder of S. In short, if one looks no further than the four corners of the relevant statutes, by using the triangular merger technique, P's board can eliminate P's shareholders' right to vote on a corporate combination and to seek appraisal of their shares. RMBCA § 13.02.

## 3. EXCHANGE OF SHARES

Results that are functionally identical to those achieved by a statutory merger or a triangular merger can be achieved using a third form of combination—a statutory share exchange. As with a statutory merger, the boards of P and T first must approve an agreement, here called a plan of exchange, that spells out the terms on which shares of T will be exchanged for shares of P (or cash or other property). *See* RMBCA § 11.02.* Shareholders of T, but not those of P, then must approve the plan of exchange. RMBCA § 11.03.

Once approved, the plan of exchange is filed and shares of P are issued to the shareholders of T (unless the plan calls for use of cash or other property). T's former shareholders thereby become shareholders of P; they have no further rights as shareholders of T, unless they dissent and seek appraisal of their stock. RMBCA § 11.06. The status of P's shareholders is unchanged. Upon the effectuation of the exchange, T becomes a subsidiary of P, creating a corporate structure identical to that which would result from a triangular merger. If P does not want to operate T as a subsidiary, but wishes to end with precisely the same structure as would result from merging T into P, it can follow the exchange of shares by 1) dissolving T, distributing all of its assets to P and having P assume all of its liabilities, or 2) merging T into P in a "short form" merger.

## 4. EXCHANGE OF STOCK FOR ASSETS

In the fourth type of combination, P uses its stock (or some combination of stock, cash and other securities) to buy the assets of T. As with all the other forms of combination (except the tender offer), the first step in such a transaction is approval of an agreement of sale by the boards of directors of P and T. RMBCA § 12.02; DGCL § 271. The shareholders of T, the selling corporation, but not the shareholders of P, the acquiring corporation, then must approve the terms of the sale agreement. Under RMBCA § 13.02(a)(3), T's shareholders will have dissenter's rights if they vote against the transaction. If T is a Delaware corporation, though, dissenter's rights will not be available. DGCL § 262.

* Delaware law contains no provision for a statutory share exchange.

If a combination is structured as an exchange of stock for assets, T's assets will have to be transferred by deed or other form of conveyance, a process that can generate a good deal of paperwork. P may, but need not, also assume some or all of T's liabilities. Alternatively, T may retain sufficient liquid assets to pay off its liabilities. In a few jurisdictions (notably California and Pennsylvania), statutory requirements or common law principles relating to transferee liability may result in P being held responsible for certain of T's obligations.

If T is dissolved following sale of its assets (and assumption or payment of its liabilities), a stock for asset exchange will result in a corporate structure functionally identical to that produced by a statutory merger. P will own all of the assets of T, and usually will be responsible for all of T's liabilities. P, in turn, will be owned by its shareholders and the former shareholders of T.

## 5. TENDER OFFERS

P can also seek to acquire T by offering to purchase T's shares directly from the T shareholders, either for P stock or for cash or other property. Through such a *tender offer*, P can acquire control of T without a vote of the T board of directors. Unlike the other forms of acquisition, T shareholders "approve" the transaction by accepting P's offer rather than through a formal vote. Similarly, there are no dissenters' rights; T shareholders who wish to disapprove do so by refusing to tender their shares. If holders of a majority of T's shares tender their stock (and no state antitakeover law or provision of T's articles of incorporation prevents P from voting the shares it acquires), P will control T after the exchange of shares is completed. P then often will seek to acquire the remaining shares of T in some form of "second-step" transaction so as to avoid problems in managing the businesses of P and T as part of an integrated whole that may arise due to the presence of a minority interest in T.

P can make a tender offer without any vote by its shareholders, unless P does not have sufficient stock authorized to effectuate a proposed share exchange. P's shareholders also will not have dissenters' rights in the tender offer. Whether either company's shareholders have dissenter's rights in connection with the second step will depend on the form of that transaction.

## 6. SUMMARY

In short, these basic techniques, and numerous combinations and permutations of them, are available to effectuate a transaction that will combine the business operations of two or more corporations under the control of one management group. If stock of P, the surviving corporation, is the only consideration to be paid to the shareholders of T, the acquired corporation, each technique will result in the former shareholders of P and T emerging as the shareholders of P, and in P emerging as the owner, directly or through a wholly owned subsidiary, of its assets and the assets of T. As suggested by the following charts summarizing the statutory rules, the RMBCA and DGCL provide that, despite this near identity of result, whether the shareholders of P and T are entitled to vote on or dissent from a corporate combination will turn on the technique used to effectuate that combination.

## RMBCA

| | P (Surviving corporation) | | T (Acquired corporation) | |
|---|---|---|---|---|
| | Vote | Dissent | Vote | Dissent |
| Statutory Merger | Yes § 11.03 | Yes § 13.02 | Yes § 11.03 | Yes § 13.02 |
| Triangular Merger | No | No | Yes § 11.03 | Yes § 13.02 |
| Statutory Share Exchange | No § 11.03 | No § 13.02 | Yes § 11.03 | Yes § 13.02 |
| Stock for Assets | No | No | Yes § 12.02 | Yes § 13.02 |

## Del.Gen.Corp.L.

| | P (Surviving corporation) | | T (Acquired corporation) | |
|---|---|---|---|---|
| | Vote | Dissent | Vote | Dissent |
| Statutory Merger | Yes § 251 | Yes § 262* | Yes § 251 | Yes § 262* |
| Triangular Merger | No | No | Yes § 251 | Yes § 262* |
| Statutory Share Exchange | N.A. | N.A. | N.A. | N.A. |
| Stock for Assets | No | No | Yes § 271 | No |

\* Unless DGCL § 262(b)(1) applies.

## C.  DE FACTO AND DE JURE APPROACHES

Where the structure of a corporate combination is such that the applicable statute does not provide for voting or appraisal rights, a shareholder seeking to veto the combination or to assert dissenter's rights often will ask a court to treat the combination as if it were a merger, i.e., a *de facto merger*, even though it is cast in some other form. In *Irving Bank Corp. v. Bank of New York Co., Inc.*, 140 Misc.2d 363, 530 N.Y.S.2d 757 (1988), the court observed that "A study of those cases in which courts have found de facto merger demonstrates that the factual situation of each case must be independently studied, without 'slavish adherence to determinations made in other cases, where there are similarities and also degrees of difference.' " *Id.* at 760 (citing *Applestein v. United Board & Carton Corp.*, 60 N.J.Super. 333, 351, 159 A.2d 146, 156 (1960), *aff'd* 33 N.J. 72, 161 A.2d 474 (1960)). The court summarized cases finding de facto mergers as follows:

In *Lirosi v. Elkins*, 89 A.D.2d 903, 453 N.Y.S.2d 718 (2d Dep't 1982), the court held that a transfer of assets from one corporation to another, and the subsequent dissolution of the former corporation, constituted a de facto merger. In *Gilbert v. Burnside*, 197 N.Y.S.2d 623 (1959), rev'd 13 A.D.2d 982, 216 N.Y.S.2d 430 (2d Dep't 1961) aff'd 11 N.Y.2d 960, 229 N.Y.S.2d 10, 183 N.E.2d 325 (1962), the court held a "reorganization agreement" to be a de facto merger where the agreement provided for the sale of all of the assets of a corporation and its subsequent dissolution. In both cases, the Court found that the dissolution of the acquired corporation was an imminently expected occurrence.

There have been decisions in other jurisdictions finding de facto mergers in situations similar to those above. *See, e.g.*, *Applestein v. United Board & Carton Corp.*, 60 N.J.Super. 333, 159 A.2d 146 (1960), aff'd 33 N.J. 72, 161 A.2d 474 (1960) (where the agreement provided for a sale of assets, the dissolution of the seller and for the acquirer to assume all the debts of the acquired corporation, a de facto merger existed); *Rath v. Rath Packing Company*, 257 Iowa 1277, 136 N.W.2d 410 (1965) ("Plan of Reorganization" agreement held de facto merger where agreement provided for sale of all assets, assumption of all debts and liabilities, cessation of business of acquired corporation under its name; and acquiring company to change name to "Rath–Needham"); *Farris v. Glen Alden Corporation*, 393 Pa. 427, 143 A.2d 25 (1958) ("Reorganization Agreement" held de facto merger, where agreement provided for acquirer to immediately acquire all the assets of the target; acquirer to assume all of target's liabilities; target is to be dissolved).

Most recent decisions, however, have adopted a de jure approach to evaluating corporate combinations.

Our concern here is with shareholders' voting and appraisal rights. Persons with claims against corporations that have sold their assets and dissolved also often urge courts to apply the de facto merger doctrine, especially when their claims arise after the period in which claims can be asserted against former shareholders of those corporations. Some courts have been receptive to these claims, *see, e.g.*, *Ray v. Alad Corp.*, 19 Cal.3d 22, 136 Cal.Rptr. 574, 560 P.2d 3 (1977), but "most * * * state courts, and federal courts interpreting state law, have declined to adopt the 'product line' theory when faced with the issue." *Giraldi v. Sears, Roebuck & Co.*, 687 F.Supp. 987 (D.Md.1988).

530 N.Y.S.2d at 759.

# HARITON v. ARCO ELECTRONICS, INC.

40 Del.Ch. 326, 182 A.2d 22 (1962), aff'd 41 Del.Ch. 74, 188 A.2d 123 (1963).

SHORT, VICE CHANCELLOR.

Plaintiff is a stockholder of defendant Arco Electronics, Inc., a Delaware corporation. The complaint challenges the validity of the purchase by Loral Electronics Corporation, a New York corporation, of all the assets of Arco. Two causes of action are asserted, namely (1) that the transaction is unfair to Arco stockholders, and (2) that the transaction constituted a de facto merger and is unlawful since the merger provisions of the Delaware law were not complied with. * * *

Plaintiff now concedes that he is unable to sustain the charge of unfairness. The only issue before the court, therefore, is whether the transaction was by its nature a de facto merger with a consequent right of appraisal in plaintiff.

Prior to the transaction of which plaintiff complains Arco was principally engaged in the business of the wholesale distribution of components or parts for electronics and electrical equipment. * * *

Loral was engaged, primarily, in the research, development and production of electronic equipment. * * *

In the summer of 1961 Arco commenced negotiations with Loral with a view to the purchase by Loral of all of the assets of Arco in exchange for shares of Loral common stock. * * * [A]n agreement for the purchase was entered into between Loral and Arco on October 27, 1961. This agreement provides, among other things, as follows:

1.   Arco will convey and transfer to Loral all of its assets and property of every kind, tangible and intangible; and will grant to Loral the use of its name and slogans.

2.   Loral will assume and pay all of Arco's debts and liabilities.

3.   Loral will issue to Arco 283,000 shares of its common stock.

4.   Upon the closing of the transaction Arco will dissolve and distribute to its shareholders, pro rata, the shares of the common stock of Loral.

5.   Arco will call a meeting of its stockholders to be held December 21, 1961 to authorize and approve the conveyance and delivery of all the assets of Arco to Loral.

6.   After the closing date Arco will not engage in any business or activity except as may be required to complete the liquidation and dissolution of Arco.

Pursuant to its undertaking in the agreement for purchase and sale Arco caused a special meeting of its stockholders to be called for December 27, 1961. * * * At the meeting 652,050 shares were voted in favor of the sale and none against. The proposals to change the name of the corporation and to dissolve it and distribute the Loral stock were also approved. The transaction was thereafter consummated.

Plaintiff contends that the transaction, though in form a sale of assets of Arco, is in substance and effect a merger, and that it is unlawful because the merger statute has not been complied with, thereby depriving plaintiff of his right of appraisal.

Defendant contends that since all the formalities of a sale of assets pursuant to 8 Del.C. § 271 have been complied with the transaction is in fact a sale of assets and not a merger. In this connection it is to be noted that plaintiffs nowhere allege or claim that defendant has not complied to the letter with the provisions of said section.

The question here presented is one which has not been heretofore passed upon by any court in this state. In *Heilbrunn v. Sun Chemical Corporation*, Del., 150 A.2d 755, the Supreme Court was called upon to determine whether or not a stockholder of the *purchasing* corporation could, in circumstances like those here presented, obtain relief on the theory of a de facto merger. The court held that relief was not available to such a stockholder. It expressly observed that the question here presented was not before the court for determination. It pointed out also that while Delaware does not grant appraisal rights to a stockholder dissenting from a sale, citing *Argenbright v. Phoenix Finance Co.*, 21 Del.Ch. 288, 187 A. 124, and *Finch v. Warrior Cement Corp.*, 16 Del.Ch. 44, 141 A. 54, those cases are distinguishable from the facts here presented, "because dissolution of the seller and distribution of the stock of the purchaser were not required as a part of the sale in either case." In speaking of the form of the transaction the Supreme Court observes:

> The argument that the result of this transaction is substantially the same as the result that would have followed a merger may be readily accepted. As plaintiffs correctly say, the Ansbacher enterprise [seller] is continued in altered form as a part of Sun [purchaser]. This is ordinarily a typical characteristic of a merger. *Sterling v. Mayflower Hotel Corp.*, 33 Del.Ch. 293, 303, 93 A.2d 107, 38 A.L.R.2d 425 (Sup.1952), . Moreover the plan of reorganization *requires* the dissolution of Ansbacher and the distribution to its stockholders of the Sun stock received by it for the assets. As a part of the plan, the Ansbacher stockholders are compelled to receive Sun stock. From the viewpoint of Ansbacher, the result is the same as if Ansbacher had formally merged into Sun.

> This result is made possible, of course, by the overlapping scope of the merger statute and the statute authorizing the sale of all the corporate assets. This possibility of overlapping was noticed in our opinion in the *Mayflower* case.

> There is nothing new about such a result. For many years drafters of plans of corporate reorganization have increasingly resorted to the use of the sale-of-assets method in preference to the method by merger. Historically at least, there were reasons for this quite apart from the avoidance of the appraisal right given to stockholders dissenting from a merger.

* * * The doctrine of de facto merger in comparable circumstances has been recognized and applied by the Pennsylvania courts, both state and federal, *Lauman v. Lebanon Valley Railroad Co.*, 30 Pa. 42; *Marks v. Autocar Co.*, D.C., 153 F.Supp. 768; *Farris v. Glen Alden Corporation*, 393 Pa. 427, 143 A.2d 25. * * * The *Farris* case demonstrates the length

to which the Pennsylvania courts have gone in applying this principle. It was there applied in favor of a stockholder of the purchasing corporation, an application which our Supreme Court expressly rejected in *Heilbrunn*.

The right of appraisal accorded to a dissenting stockholder by the merger statutes is in compensation for the right which he had at common law to prevent a merger. *Chicago Corporation v. Munds*, 20 Del.Ch. 142, 172 A. 452. * * *

While plaintiff's contention that the doctrine of de facto merger should be applied in the present circumstances is not without appeal, the subject is one which, in my opinion, is within the legislative domain. * * * The argument underlying the applicability of the doctrine of de facto merger, namely, that the stockholder is forced against his will to accept a new investment in an enterprise foreign to that of which he was a part has little pertinency. The right of the corporation to sell all of its assets for stock in another corporation was expressly accorded to Arco by § 271 of Title 8, Del.C. The stockholder was, in contemplation of law, aware of this right when he acquired his stock. He was also aware of the fact that the situation might develop whereby he would be ultimately forced to accept a new investment, as would have been the case here had the resolution authorizing dissolution followed consummation of the sale. * * *

There is authority in decisions of courts of this state for the proposition that the various sections of the Delaware Corporation Law conferring authority for corporate action are independent of each other and that a given result may be accomplished by proceeding under one section which is not possible, or is even forbidden under another. * * *

In a footnote to Judge Leahy's opinion [in *Langfelder v. Universal Laboratories*, 68 F.Supp. 209, 211 n. 5 (D.Del.1946), aff'd 163 F.2d 804 (3d Cir.1947)] the following comment appears:

> The text is but a particularization of the general theory of the Delaware Corporation Law that action taken pursuant to the authority of the various sections of that law constitute acts of independent legal significance and their validity is not dependent on other sections of the Act. * * *

I conclude that the transaction complained of was not a de facto merger, either in the sense that there was a failure to comply with one or more of the requirements of § 271 of the Delaware Corporation Law, or that the result accomplished was in effect a merger entitling plaintiff to a right of appraisal.

Defendant's motion for summary judgment is granted. Order on notice.

### Note

One commentator offers the following perspective on *Hariton*:

> The basic premise implicitly adopted in *Hariton* may perhaps be stated more affirmatively. One does not invest in a unique corporate

entity or even a particular business operation, but rather in a continuous course of business which changes over a long period of time. Certainly the best investments are growth investments— investments in enterprises which change with time, technology, business opportunities, and altered demand; and the worst investments are those which diminish in value because the type of business has lost importance and the corporation has been unable to adapt to the changed conditions. Although a shareholder's enthusiasm dwindles when an enterprise changes internally for the worst, no one suggests that he should have an option to compel the return of his investment. Viewed this way, the fact that the change—for better or for worse—comes through marriage, whether by merger or assets sale, seems purely incidental. The fact that the corporate entity in which one invested disappears as a result of a merger or of a sale of assets coupled with dissolution is also beside the point. One's investment may gain immortality when it takes a new form, i.e., a share in a successor enterprise.

Ernest Folk, *De Facto Mergers in Delaware: Hariton v. Arco Electronics, Inc.*, 49 VA.L.REV. 1261, 1280–81 (1963).

## TERRY v. PENN CENTRAL CORP.

668 F.2d 188 (3d Cir.1981).

ADAMS, CIRCUIT JUDGE.

[Penn Central Corporation ("Penn Central") sought to acquire Colt Industries Inc. ("Colt"), by merging Colt with PCC Holdings, Inc. ("Holdings"), a wholly-owned subsidiary of Penn Central. Howard L. Terry and W.H. Hunt, shareholders of Penn Central, sought to enjoin the transaction on the ground that they were entitled to dissenter's rights.]

Terry and Hunt contend that * * * the proposed merger between Holdings and Colt constitutes a *de facto* merger between Colt and Penn Central, and that the Penn Central shareholders are therefore entitled to the protections for dissenting shareholders that Pennsylvania corporate law provides for shareholders of parties to a merger. Although this reasoning, with its emphasis on the substance of the transaction rather than its formal trappings, may be attractive as a matter of policy, it contravenes the language employed by the Pennsylvania legislature in setting out the rights of shareholders.

Section 908 of the Pennsylvania Business Corporation Law (PBCL), 15 P.S. § 1908, provides that shareholders of corporations that are parties to a plan of merger are entitled to dissent and appraisal rights, but adds that for an acquisition other than such a merger, the only rights are those provided for in Section 311 of the PBCL, 15 P.S. § 1311 (Purdon 1967 & Supp.1981–82). Section 311, in turn, provides for dissent and appraisal rights only when an acquisition has been accomplished by "the issuance of voting shares of such corporation to be outstanding immediately after the acquisition sufficient to elect a majority of the directors of the corporation." In this case the shares of Penn Central stock to be issued in the Colt transaction do not exceed the number of shares already existing, and thus the transaction is not covered by Section 311. Any statutory dissent and appraisal rights for Penn Central shareholders are therefore contingent upon Penn Central's status as a party to the merger within the meaning of Section 908. And as the district court points out, the PBCL describes the parties to a merger as those entities that are *actually* combined into a single corporation. \* \* \* At the consummation of the proposed merger plan here, both Holdings and Penn Central would survive as separate entities, and it would therefore appear that Penn Central \* \* \* is not a party to the merger.

Appellants argue that Penn Central is nevertheless brought into the amalgamation by the *de facto* merger doctrine as set out in Pennsylvania law in *Farris v. Glen Alden Corp.*, 393 Pa. 427, 143 A.2d 25 (1958). \* \* \*

None of these cases persuades us that a Pennsylvania court would apply the *de facto* merger doctrine to the situation before us. Although [*In re Jones & Laughlin Steel Corp.*, 488 Pa. 524, 412 A.2d 1099 (1980)] suggests that dissent and appraisal rights might be available if fraud or fundamental unfairness were shown, we are not faced with such a situation. No allegation of fraud has been advanced, and the only allegation of fundamental unfairness is that the appellants will, if the merger is consummated, be forced into what they consider a poor investment on the part of Penn Central without the opportunity to receive an appraised value for their stock. Even if appellants' evaluation of the merits of the proposed merger is accurate, poor business judgment on the part of management would not be enough to constitute unfairness cognizable by a court. And the denial of appraisal rights to dissenters cannot constitute fundamental unfairness, or the *de facto* merger doctrine would apply in every instance in which dissenters' rights were sought and the 1959 amendments by the legislature would be rendered nugatory.[7] \* \* \*

In the absence of any explicit guidance to the contrary by the Pennsylvania courts, we conclude that the language of the legislature in 1959 precludes a decision that the transaction in this case constitutes a *de facto* merger sufficient to entitle Penn Central shareholders to dissent and appraisal rights. We therefore hold that appellants do not possess such rights if a transaction such as the one involved here is consummated. \* \* \*

---

The American Law Institute has adopted a functional approach to determining a shareholder's right to vote on or dissent from a corporate

---

**7.** A different result might be reached if here, as in *Farris,* the acquiring corporation were significantly smaller than the acquired corporation such that the acquisition greatly transformed the nature of the successor corporation. But in this situation we do not have such a case: after the merger Penn Central would remain a major, diversified corporation, and would continue on the course of acquiring other corporations.

combination modelled largely on Chapter 12 of the California Corporations Code. A shareholder is entitled to vote on any transaction that qualifies as a "Transaction in Control," *see* ALI, PRINCIPLES OF CORPORATE GOVERNANCE § 6.01(b) (1994), and is entitled to appraisal rights in connection with any business combination, whatever its form, "unless those persons who were shareholders of the corporation immediately before the combination own 60 percent or more of the total voting power of the surviving * * * corporation immediately thereafter * * *." Id., § 7.21(a).

## ALI, PRINCIPLES OF CORPORATE GOVERNANCE (1994)

### § 1.38.  TRANSACTION IN CONTROL

(a) Subject to Subsection (b), a "transaction in control" with respect to a corporation means:

(1) A business combination effected through (i) a merger, (ii) a consolidation, (iii) an issuance of voting equity securities to effect an acquisition of the assets of another corporation which acquisition would constitute a transaction in control under Subsection (a)(2) with respect to the other corporation, or (iv) an issuance of voting equity securities in exchange for at least a majority of the voting equity securities of another corporation, in each case whether effected directly or by means of a subsidiary;

(2) A sale of assets that would leave the corporation without a significant continuing business; or

(3) An issuance of securities or any other transaction by the corporation (other than pursuant to a transaction described in Subsection (a)(1)) that, alone or in conjunction with other transactions or circumstances, would cause a change in control of the corporation;

(b) A transaction is not a transaction in control within § 1.38(a) if the transaction consists of:

(3) A transaction described in Subsection (a)(1) if those persons who were the holders of voting equity securities in the corporation immediately before the transaction would own immediately after the transaction at least 75 percent of the surviving corporation's voting equity securities, in substantially the same proportions in relation to other preexisting shareholders of the corporation.

**Comment:**

*a.  Comparison with existing law.* * * *

A central theme of § 1.38 is that the mere form in which a transaction is cast should not determine the manner in which the transaction is characterized. A continuing problem in corporation law is to identify those transactions that are so different from the day-to-day operation of the corporation's business that a different decisionmaking process, appraisal rights for shareholders who disapprove, or both, are appropriate. The traditional approach to this problem has been to specify the covered transactions by reference to the form in which those planning the transactions have cast them. * * *

This approach has resulted in an important problem. From the perspective of the managers who plan commercial transactions, the transaction often can be cast in a variety of forms without altering its economic substance. Thus, * * * the assertion of something akin to what has become to be called the de facto merger doctrine was inevitable. * * *

There are substantial difficulties associated with each of the four approaches to the de facto merger problem. The provision of different shareholder approval and appraisal procedures for substantially identical transactions is difficult to justify, whether accomplished by statute or through judicial deference to the equal dignity the legislature may have accorded different transactional forms. Judicial efforts to identify the essential characteristics of a merger may result in the imposition of the most restrictive procedures on all transactions because sales of assets and triangular mergers are substantially identical to two-party mergers. Finally, legislative efforts to incorporate the de facto merger doctrine into the corporate statute have reduced the problem, but not eliminated it. Although the net is cast more broadly, its reach is still determined by transaction form, leaving planners room to recast transactions to avoid shareholder approval and appraisal procedures. * * *

[Section 6.01] follows the approach of * * * treating all transactions in control alike, regardless of the form in which they are cast, and also follows the approach of those states that do not require approval of a merger agreement by shareholders of a corporation that is party thereto whose rights are not diluted by more than 25 percent. Section 1.38 seeks to avoid the difficulties encountered by courts and legislatures in dealing with the de facto merger problem by defining the range of transactions of concern by reference to their substance rather than their form.

## 3. TRANSACTION SIZE AND SHAREHOLDERS' RIGHTS

### PROBLEM

### LAFRANCE COSMETICS—PART II

Five years have passed since LaFrance acquired Sweet Violet. LaFrance's board of directors is unchanged; its stock is held as follows:

| | | |
|---|---|---|
| Mimi LaFrance | 400,000 | shares |
| Pierre LaFrance | 100,000 | shares |
| Margaret LaFrance | 100,000 | shares |
| Third National Bank, Trustee | 400,000 | shares |
| Former shareholders of Sweet Violet and others | 400,000 | shares |
| Total | 1,400,000 | shares |

LaFrance has invested heavily in the perfume business; the Sweet Violet division now accounts for nearly two-thirds of the book value of LaFrance's assets. LaFrance's investment produced a sharp increase in perfume sales; they have accounted for about 70% of LaFrance's total sales last year. But this investment has not produced the profits Mimi and Pierre anticipated. The perfume business has become more competitive, profit margins have declined, and LaFrance has had difficulty integrating perfume into its cosmetics business. Despite increased sales, the Sweet Violet division produced only 20% of LaFrance's net income last year. These disappointing results have depressed the price of LaFrance stock, for which a limited trading market has developed. Most recent sales have been at about $40 per share.

LaBelle, S.A., a large French perfume manufacturer, recently approached LaFrance with an offer to buy the Sweet Violet division for $50 million in cash, which is slightly more than the division's book value. Mimi and Pierre are anxious to accept the offer. Margaret continues to believe the entire company should be sold. She opposes the sale of Sweet Violet alone, fearing that Mimi and Pierre will use the proceeds to finance another ill-advised expansion effort. Lauren Miller now supports Margaret's position, but Victor Gauguin continues to side with Mimi and Pierre.

While a majority of LaFrance's directors thus will vote to accept LaBelle's offer, it is unclear whether a majority of LaFrance's shareholders would concur. Margaret and the bank almost certainly would oppose selling Sweet Violet to LaBelle. The views of the remaining shareholders are unknown, but many of them no doubt have been disappointed with LaFrance's results in recent years. Consequently, they might well be inclined to support Margaret's proposal that the entire company, not merely Sweet Violet, be sold.

Pierre has asked for your advice in connection with two conditions of LaBelle's offer. The first is that, at the closing, LaFrance deliver an unqualified opinion of counsel to the effect that LaFrance has complied with all applicable provisions of Columbia law in effectuating the sale of Sweet Violet. The other is that the closing occur within 120 days of today.

Pierre has asked what procedures LaFrance must follow to effectuate the sale of the Sweet Violet division. He wants to know, in particular, (i) if you are prepared to opine that shareholder approval is not required and (ii) assuming you reach that conclusion, how likely is it that Margaret or some other shareholder nonetheless could assert a claim that would survive a motion to dismiss for failure to state a claim and/or a motion for summary judgment, thus preventing the sale from closing within 120 days. In developing your response, consider RMBCA §§ 12.01 and 12.02, and the Official Comment to RMBCA § 12.01.

# GIMBEL v. SIGNAL COMPANIES, INC.

316 A.2d 599 (Del.Ch.1974), aff'd per curiam 316 A.2d 619 (Del.1974).

[On December 21, 1973, at a special meeting, the board of directors of Signal Companies, Inc. ("Signal") approved a proposal to sell its wholly owned subsidiary Signal Gas & Oil Co. ("Signal Oil") to Burmah Oil Inc. ("Burmah") for a price of $480 million. Based on Signal's books, Signal Oil represented 26% of Signal's total assets, 41% of its net worth, and produced 15% of Signal's revenues and earnings. The contract provided that the sale would take place on January 15, 1974 or upon obtaining the necessary governmental consents, whichever was later, but, in no event, after February 15, 1974, unless mutually agreed.

On December 24, 1973, plaintiff, a Signal shareholder, sued for a preliminary injunction to prevent consummation of the sale. The plaintiff, among other contentions, alleged that approval only by Signal's board was insufficient and that a favorable vote from a majority of the outstanding shares of Signal was necessary to authorize the sale].

QUILLEN, CHANCELLOR.

I turn first to the question of 8 Del.C. § 271(a) which requires majority stockholder approval for the sale of "all or substantially all" of the assets of a Delaware corporation. A sale of less than all or substantially all assets is not covered by negative implication from the statute. Folk, THE DELAWARE GENERAL CORPORATION LAW, Section 271, p. 400, ftnt. 3; 8 Del.C. § 141(a).

It is important to note in the first instance that the statute does not speak of a requirement of shareholder approval simply because an independent, important branch of a corporate business is being sold. The plaintiff cites several non-Delaware cases for the proposition that shareholder approval of such a sale is required. But that is not the language of our statute. Similarly, it is not our law that shareholder approval is required upon every "major" restructuring of the corporation. Again, it is not necessary to go beyond the statute. The statute requires shareholder approval upon the sale of "all or substantially all" of the corporation's assets. That is the sole test to be applied. While it is true that test does not lend itself to a strict mathematical standard to be applied in every case, the qualitative factor can be defined to some degree notwithstanding the limited Delaware authority. But the definition must begin with and ultimately necessarily relate to our statutory language.

In interpreting the statute the plaintiff relies on *Philadelphia National Bank v. B.S.F. Co.*, 41 Del.Ch. 509, 199 A.2d 557 (1964), *rev'd on other grounds*, 42 Del.Ch. 106, 204 A.2d 746 (Sup.1964). In that case, B.S.F. Company owned stock in two corporations. It sold its stock in one of the corporations, and retained the stock in the other corporation. The Court found that the stock sold was the principal asset B.S.F. Company had available for sale and that the value of the stock retained was declining. The Court rejected the defendant's contention that the stock sold represented only 47.4% of consolidated assets, and looked to the actual value of the stock sold. On this basis, the Court held that the stock constituted at least 75% of the total assets and the sale of the stock was a sale of substantially all assets. * * *

The key language in the Court of Chancery opinion in *Philadelphia National Bank* is the suggestion that "the critical factor in determining the character of a sale of assets is generally considered not the amount of property sold but whether the sale is in fact an unusual transaction or one made in the regular course of business of the seller." (41 Del.Ch. at 515, 199 A.2d at 561). Professor Folk suggests from the opinion that "the statute would be inapplicable if the assets sale is "one made in furtherance of express corporate objects in the ordinary and regular course of the business' "(referring to language in 41 Del.Ch. at 516, 199 A.2d at 561). Folk, *supra,* Section 271, p. 401.

But any "ordinary and regular course of the business" test in this context obviously is not intended to limit the directors to customary daily business activities. Indeed, a question concerning the statute would not arise unless the transaction was somewhat out of the ordinary. While it is true that a transaction in the ordinary course of business does not require shareholder approval, the converse is not true. Every transaction out of normal routine does not necessarily require shareholder approval. The unusual nature of the transaction must strike at the heart of the corporate existence and purpose. As it is written at 6A FLETCHER, CYCLOPEDIA CORPORATIONS (Perm.Ed.1968 Rev.) § 2949.2, p. 648:

> The purpose of the consent statutes is to protect the shareholders from fundamental change, or more specifically to protect the shareholder from the destruction of the means to accomplish the purposes or objects for which the corporation was incorporated and actually performs.

It is in this sense that the "unusual transaction" judgment is to be made and the statute's applicability determined. If the sale is of assets quantitatively vital to the operation of the corporation and is out of the ordinary and substantially affects the existence and purpose of the corporation, then it is beyond the power of the Board of Directors. With these guidelines, I turn to Signal and the transaction in this case.

Signal or its predecessor was incorporated in the oil business in 1922. But, beginning in 1952 Signal diversified its interests. In 1952, Signal acquired a substantial stock interest in American President lines. From 1957 to 1962 Signal was the sole owner of Laura Scudders, a nationwide snack food business. In 1964, Signal acquired Garrett Corporation which is engaged in the aircraft, aerospace, and uranium enrichment business. In 1967, Signal acquired Mack Trucks, Inc., which is engaged in the manufacture and sale of trucks and related equipment. Also in 1968, the oil and gas business was transferred to a separate division and later in 1970 to the Signal Oil subsidiary. Since 1967, Signal has made acquisition of or formed substantial companies none of which are involved or related with the oil and gas industry. As indicated previously, the oil and gas production development of Signal's business is now carried on by Signal Oil, the sale of the stock of which is an issue in this lawsuit. * * *

Based on the company's figures, Signal Oil represents only about 26% of the total assets of Signal. While Signal Oil represents 41% of the Signal's total net worth, it produces only about 15% of Signal's revenues and earnings. * * *

While it is true, based on the experience of the Signal–Burmah transaction and the record in this lawsuit, that Signal Oil is more valuable than shown by the company's books, even if, as plaintiff suggests in his brief, the $761,000,000 value attached to Signal Oil's properties by the plaintiff's expert Paul V. Keyser, Jr., were substituted [for $376.2 million] as the asset figure, the oil and gas properties would still constitute less than half the value of Signal's total assets. Thus, from a straight quantitative approach, I agree with Signal's position that the sale to Burmah does not constitute a sale of "all or substantially all" of Signal's assets.

In addition, if the character of the transaction is examined, the plaintiff's position is also weak. While it is true that Signal's original purpose was oil and gas and while oil and gas is still listed first in the certificate of incorporation, the simple fact is that Signal is now a conglomerate engaged in the aircraft and aerospace business, the manufacture and sale of trucks and related equipment, and other businesses besides oil and gas. The very nature of its business, as it now in fact exists, contemplates the acquisition and disposal of independent branches of its corporate business. Indeed, given the operations since 1952, it can be said that such acquisitions and dispositions have become part of the ordinary course of business. The facts that the oil and gas business was historically first and that authorization for such operations are listed first in the certificate do not prohibit disposal of such interest. As Director Harold M. Williams testified, business history is not "compelling" and "many companies go down the drain because they try to be historic."

It is perhaps true, as plaintiff has argued, that the advent of multi-business corporations has in one sense emasculated § 271 since one business may be sold without shareholder approval when other substantial businesses are retained. But it is one thing for a corporation to evolve over a period of years into a multi-business corporation, the operations of which include the purchase and sale of whole businesses, and another for a single business corporation by a one transaction revolution to sell the entire means of operating its business in exchange for money or a separate business. In the former situation, the processes of corporate democracy customarily have had the opportunity to restrain or otherwise control over a period of years. Thus, there is a chance for some shareholder participation. The Signal development illustrates the difference. For example, when Signal, itself formerly called Signal Oil and Gas Company, changed its name in 1968, it was for the announced "need for a new name appropriate to the broadly diversified activities of Signal's multi-industry complex." * * *

I conclude that measured quantitatively and qualitatively, the sale of the stock of Signal Oil by Signal to Burmah does not constitute a sale of "all or substantially all" of Signal's assets. * * * Accordingly, insofar as the complaint rests on 8 Del.C. § 271(a), in my judgment, it has no reasonable probability of ultimate success. * * *

––––––

In *Katz v. Bregman*, 431 A.2d 1274 (Del.Ch.1981), the court held that a corporation's sale of assets that constituted more than 51 percent of its total assets and generated approximately 45 percent of its net sales in the previous year, and that would cause the corporation to de[part radically from its historically successful line of business, constituted a sale of substantially all of the corporation's assets.

The Official Comment to RMBCA § 12.01 also contains an extensive discussion of what constitutes "all or substantially all" under both § 12.01 and other state statutes whose language differs from § 12.01.

## 4.  SHAREHOLDERS' POWER TO INITIATE ACTION

### PROBLEM
### LAFRANCE COSMETICS—PART III

The sale of the Sweet Violet Division still is pending. LaBelle is prepared to accept your opinion that shareholder approval is not required. However, Margaret, who seems to have the support of the Third National Bank, is investigating what actions she might take, as a shareholder, to block the sale. Pierre has asked you to prepare an analysis of the actions LaFrance's shareholders have the power to initiate; the procedures they would need to follow; and what LaFrance's board of directors might do to counter any such initiatives. More specifically, Pierre has asked you to respond to the following questions:

1.   Do LaFrance's shareholders have a right to have a special meeting of shareholders called to adopt a resolution compelling the board to abandon the sale of Sweet Violet? Alternatively, can the shareholders adopt a resolution recommending that the board abandon the sale of Sweet Violet? What would be the probable effect of such a resolution? Consider *Auer v. Dressel*.

2.   Can LaFrance's shareholders act other than at a properly called meeting?

3.   Could the shareholders remove the directors who support the sale and replace them with new directors who oppose the sale? Consider RMBCA §§ 7.02, 7.04, 7.05, 7.25, 8.05, 8.08, and 8.10, and Model By-laws, Article III § 9 and Article II §§ 2, 4, 7, and 11. Would your answer be different if the articles contained the a provision stating: "A director may be removed only for cause?" Consider *Auer v. Dressel* and *Campbell v. Loew's*.

4. Could those shareholders "pack" the board by amending the articles of incorporation or the by-laws (or both) and adding new directors who would vote against the sale? Assume that the by-laws of LaFrance are similar to the Model By-laws but provide for a board of five directors. Assume further that the articles of incorporation of LaFrance contain no provisions regarding the number of directors. Alternatively, assume that the articles provide for a five member board. Consider RMBCA §§ 10.20, 10.02, 10.03, 8.03, and 8.10, and Model By-laws, Article III §§ 2 and 9, and Article XI. Consider *Auer v. Dressel* and *Campbell v. Loew's.*

5. If LaFrance's shareholders request that a shareholders' meeting be called to consider proposals that would alter the membership of the LaFrance board, what discretion, if any, could LaFrance's board or management exercise in responding to that demand? What other tactics might the board employ to counter the shareholders' initiative? Reconsider *Schnell v. Chris–Craft Indus., Inc.* (Chapter 3); consider *Blasius Industries, Inc. v. Atlas Corp.*

6. To what extent would your answers to the foregoing questions change if LaFrance were a Delaware corporation? Consider DGCL §§ 141 and 228.

## A. SHAREHOLDER MEETINGS; PROCEDURAL CONCERNS

As in the case of action by directors, certain procedural requirements must be satisfied for shareholders to act, whether at an annual meeting, a special meeting, or by means of written consents.

### 1. THE CALL

A corporation's bylaws usually fix the date of the annual meeting. RMBCA § 7.01(a); Model By-laws, Article II § 1. Most corporation statutes provide that the board of directors, owners of 10 percent of the shares, or any person so authorized by the articles of incorporation or bylaws may call a special meeting of shareholders. RMBCA § 7.02(a); Model By-laws, Article II § 2. DGCL § 211(d) excludes stock ownership as a qualification for calling such a meeting.

The Delaware courts never have addressed the question of whether a given percentage of a corporation's shareholders have inherent power to call a special meeting. One could argue that shareholders have such power, at least if the purpose of the meeting is to take some action, such as removal of a director for cause, that itself is within shareholders' inherent power. *See Auer* v. *Dressel, infra.* On the other hand, the statutory power to act by written consent pursuant to DGCL § 228 may provide an effective mechanism for shareholders to exercise their power, without having the inherent power to call a special meeting.

### 2. NOTICE

A corporation must give written notice of an annual or special meeting to all shareholders entitled to vote at the meeting. RMBCA

§ 7.05; Model By-laws, Article II § 4. Only matters "within the purpose or purposes described in the meeting notice" may be considered at a special meeting. RMBCA § 7.02(c). However, shareholders can waive notice, either in writing or by attending the meeting and not objecting to the absence of notice. RMBCA § 7.06.

To satisfy the notice requirement, a board must set a "record date" prior to the meeting and provide that only shareholders "of record" as of that date will be entitled to vote at the meeting. RMBCA § 7.07; Model Bylaws, Article II § 5. The board, not the shareholders who called the meeting, has the exclusive power to set the record date and send out notices, unless the articles provide otherwise. *Young v. Janas*, 103 A.2d 299 (Del.Ch.1954). This power can have tactical significance, because a meeting generally can be set for anywhere between 10 and 60 days after notice is sent. RMBCA § 7.05(a).

On occasion, timing requirements relating to shareholder action take on great significance. That was the case when Bendix, a Delaware corporation, attempted to take over Martin Marietta, which was incorporated in Maryland. Bendix made a cash tender offer that, if successful, would have allowed it to purchase a majority of Martin Marietta's stock on September 17, 1982. Martin Marietta responded by offering to purchase a majority of Bendix stock. However, because its offer was made six days later, federal law prevented Martin Marietta from purchasing Bendix stock until September 23.

Differences between Delaware and Maryland law nonetheless seemed to give Martin Marietta the upper hand. Using Delaware's consent procedure, Martin Marietta could remove a majority of the Bendix board and replace it with new directors as soon as it acquired a majority of Bendix' shares—i.e., on September 23. Bendix, on the other hand, was powerless to compel a special meeting of Martin Marietta shareholders any earlier than 10 days after it became a 10 percent shareholder and filed a call—*i.e.*, September 27. By that date, assuming no judicial intervention, Martin Marietta would already control Bendix and would cause Bendix to desist from all actions directed at changing the make-up of the Martin Marietta board.

In the event, both Bendix and Martin Marietta succeeded in acquiring a majority of the other's stock, Bendix on September 17 and Martin Marietta on September 23. Before the courts could resolve the welter of litigation that surrounded their competing takeover bids, though, Allied Corporation appeared on the scene. It reached an agreement to purchase all of Bendix and to sell back to Martin Marietta most of the shares that Bendix had purchased. Thus Bendix, the original bidder, ended up as a subsidiary of Allied, and Martin Marietta, the original target, succeeded in remaining an independent (but much more heavily leveraged) company.

## 3. QUORUM

A quorum must be represented at a shareholders meeting, either in person or by proxy, for an action taken at the meeting to be effective. A quorum usually consists of a majority of the shares entitled to vote, unless the articles of incorporation provide otherwise. RMBCA § 7.25(a). The RMBCA sets no minimum or maximum quorum but requires an amendment establishing (or reducing) a supermajority quorum requirement to meet that same requirement. RMBCA §§ 7.25(a), 7.27. DGCL § 216 allows a majority of shares to amend a corporation's articles of incorporation or bylaws to increase the quorum requirement or to reduce it to as little as one-third of the shares entitled to vote, unless the articles or bylaws require some greater vote.

## 4. ACTION BY WRITTEN CONSENT

As discussed above, both the RMBCA and DGCL allow shareholders to act by written consent rather than at a meeting. However, the two statutes vary considerably.

RMBCA § 7.04(a) requires the consent in writing of all shareholders entitled to vote on an action. Consequently, all voting shareholders also must receive advance notice of the action to be taken. Unless the bylaws provide otherwise, the record date for determining which shareholders must consent to an action is the date the first shareholder consents in writing to that action. RMBCA § 7.04(b).

DGCL § 228 allows a majority of the shareholders entitled to vote on an action to act by means of written consent. Prompt notice that action has been taken by consent must be given to nonconsenting shareholders, but no advance notice is required. DGCL § 228(c). Every consent must be dated when signed, and the period during which consents can be signed is effectively limited to 60 days from the date the first consent delivered to the corporation was signed. DGCL § 228(c). That date also serves as the record date for a consent solicitation initiated by shareholders; if the board is soliciting consents, it may set a record date. DGCL § 213(b). We will examine the significance of DGCL § 228 in contests for control in Chapter 22.

## B. WHAT ACTIONS CAN SHAREHOLDERS INITIATE?

*Gimbel* is noteworthy not merely for its discussion of what constitutes "all or substantially all" of a corporation's assets, but for what it says about board and shareholder power. The court implicitly held that, absent some statutory requirement for shareholder approval, a board is authorized to take all actions it deems necessary in managing a corporation's business. By construing the Signal shareholders' reelection of the directors who converted Signal into a multi-business corporation as a tacit ratification of that strategy, the court also implied that the shareholders' most appropriate vehicle for expressing disapproval of directors' business judgments is the election of new directors. That philosophy also underlies RMBCA §§ 12.01 and 12.02 and the Official Comment to § 12.01.

*In re Time Inc. Shareholder Litigation*, Fed.Sec.L. Rep. ¶ 94,514 (Del.Ch.1989), *aff'd Paramount Communications Inc. v. Time, Inc*, 571 A.2d 1140 (Del.1989), (Chapter 22), reflects a similar point of view. The boards of Time and Warner Communications Inc. (WCI) had approved a plan for a triangular, stock-for-stock merger of WCI into a Time subsidiary. To comply with New York Stock Exchange rules, the plan provided for a vote of approval by Time's shareholders, as well as those of WCI. Before the shareholder meetings could be held, Paramount made a cash tender offer, at a substantial premium over the market price, for all outstanding shares of Time, subject to the condition that Time abandon its merger with WCI. Time's board responded by restructuring the WCI transaction as a cash tender offer by Time for 51% of WCI's stock, to be followed by a merger of WCI into a Time subsidiary. The first stage of this plan did not call for any vote by Time's shareholders.

Time shareholders sued to enjoin Time's cash tender offer. The court held that, under Delaware law, Time's shareholders had no right to vote on either the proposed cash tender offer or the proposed triangular merger. Chancellor Allen then observed:

> The value of a shareholder's investment, over time, rises or falls chiefly because of the skill, judgment and perhaps luck—for it is present in all human affairs—of the management and directors of the enterprise. When they exercise sound or brilliant judgment, shareholders are likely to profit; when they fail to do so, share values likely will fail to appreciate. In either event, the financial vitality of the corporation and the value of the company's shares is in the hands of the directors and managers of the firm. The corporation law does not operate on the theory that directors, in exercising their powers to manage the firm, are obligated to follow the wishes of a majority of shares. In fact, directors, not shareholders, are charged with the duty to manage the firm.

> In the decision they have reached here, the Time board may be proven in time to have been brilliantly prescient or dismayingly wrong. In this decision, as in other decisions affecting the financial value of their investment, the shareholders will bear the effects for good or ill. That many, presumably most, shareholders would prefer the board to do otherwise than it has done does not * * * in my opinion, afford a basis to interfere with the effectuation of the board's business judgment.

## AUER v. DRESSEL

306 N.Y. 427, 118 N.E.2d 590 (1954).

[The plaintiffs, who owned a majority of the Class A stock of R. Hoe & Co., Inc., brought an action for an order to compel the president of the corporation to call a special shareholders' meeting pursuant to a by-law provision requiring such a meeting when requested by holders of a majority of the stock. The articles of incorporation provided for an eleven-member board, nine of whom were to be elected by the Class A stockholders and two of whom were to be elected by the Common stockholders. The purposes of the special meeting were:

A.   To vote on a resolution endorsing the administration of Joseph L. Auer, the former President and demanding his reinstatement;

B.   to amend the articles of incorporation and by-laws to provide that vacancies on the board of directors arising from the removal of a director by the shareholders be filled only by the shareholders;

C.   to consider and vote on charges to remove four Class A directors for cause and to elect their successors;

D.   to amend the by-laws to reduce the quorum requirement for board action.

The president refused to call the meeting on the ground, among others, that the foregoing purposes were not proper subjects for a Class A shareholder meeting.]

DESMOND, JUDGE.

* * * The obvious purpose of the meeting here sought to be called (aside from the indorsement and reinstatement of former president Auer) is to hear charges against four of the class A directors, to remove them if the charges be proven, to amend the by-laws so that the successor directors be elected by the class A stockholders, and further to amend the by-laws so that an effective quorum of directors will be made up of no fewer than half of the directors in office and no fewer than one third of the whole authorized number of directors. No reason appears why the class A stockholders should not be allowed to vote on any or all of those proposals.

The stockholders, by expressing their approval of Mr. Auer's conduct as president and their demand that he be put back in that office, will not be able, directly, to effect that change in officers, but there is nothing invalid in their so expressing themselves and thus putting on notice the directors who will stand for election at the annual meeting. As to purpose (B), that is, amending the charter and by-laws to authorize the stockholders to fill vacancies as to class A directors who have been removed on charges or who have resigned, it seems to be settled law that the stockholders who are empowered to elect directors have the inherent power to remove them for cause, *In re Koch*, 257 N.Y. 318, 321, 322, 178 N.E. 545, 546 * * *. Of course, as the *Koch* case points out, there must be the service of specific charges, adequate notice and full opportunity of meeting the accusations, but there is no present showing of any lack of any of those in this instance. Since these particular stockholders have the right to elect nine directors and to remove them on proven charges, it is not inappropriate that they should use their further power to amend the by-laws to elect the successors of such directors as shall be removed after hearing, or who shall resign pending hearing. Quite pertinent at this point is *Rogers v. Hill*, 289 U.S. 582, 589, 53 S.Ct. 731, 734, 77 L.Ed. 1385, which made light of an argument that stockholders, by giving power to the directors to make by-laws, had lost their own power to make them; quoting a New Jersey case, *In re A.A. Griffing Iron Co.*, 63 N.J.L. 168, 41 A. 931, the United States Supreme Court said: " 'It would be preposterous to leave the real owners of the corporate property at the mercy of their agents, and the law has not done so' ". Such a change in the by-laws, dealing with the class A directors only, has no effect on the voting rights of the common stockholders, which rights have to do with the selection of the remaining two directors only. True, the certificate of incorporation authorizes the board of directors to remove any director on charges, but we do not consider that provision as an abdication by the stockholders of their own traditional, inherent power to remove their own directors. Rather, it provides an additional method. Were that not so, the stockholders might find themselves without effective remedy in a case where a majority of the directors were accused of wrongdoing and, obviously, would be unwilling to remove themselves from office.

We fail to see, in the proposal to allow class A stockholders to fill vacancies as to class A directors, any impairment or any violation of paragraph (h) of article Third of the certificate of incorporation, which says that class A stock has exclusive voting rights with respect to all matters "other than the election of directors". That negative language should not be taken to mean that class A stockholders, who have an absolute right to elect nine of these eleven directors, cannot amend their by-laws to guarantee a similar right, in the class A stockholders and to the exclusion of common stockholders, to fill vacancies in the class A group of directors.

\* \* \* Any director illegally removed can have his remedy in the courts, see *People ex rel. Manice v. Powell*, 201 N.Y. 194, 94 N.E. 634.

The order should be affirmed, with costs, and the Special Term directed forthwith to make an order in the same form as the Appellate Division order with appropriate changes of dates.

[VAN VOORHIS, J., dissented on the grounds that none of the cited purposes were appropriate subjects for action by shareholders at the requested meeting. Proposal A, the indorsement of Auer's tenure as president, was only "an idle gesture." The second proposal was improper because the articles of incorporation authorized the directors to fill vacancies on the board, and the change sought would have denied the common stockholders their rights to a voice in the replacement of directors through their two representatives on the board. Such a change, it was argued could be made only through special voting procedures. Proposal C, the removal of directors, was improper because a shareholders meeting was "altogether unsuited to the performance of duties which partake of the nature of the judicial function." Since most shareholders would vote by proxy, their decision would have to be made before the meeting at which the charges against the directors would be made and discussed. The fourth proposal was treated as irrelevant without action on the other three.]

## CAMPBELL v. LOEW'S, INC.

36 Del.Ch. 563, 134 A.2d 852 (1957).

[This case involved a battle for control of Loew's Inc., by two factions, one headed by its President, Vogel, and the other by Tomlinson. At the February, 1957 shareholders' meeting the two factions effected a compromise; each faction was to have 6 directors and a neutral director would complete the 13 member board. In July, 1957, two of the Vogel directors, one Tomlinson director and the neutral director resigned. On July 30, 1957 there was a board meeting attended only by the five Tomlinson directors, who attempted to fill two vacancies. These elections were ruled invalid for lack of a quorum. *Tomlinson v. Loew's Inc.*, 36 Del.Ch. 516, 134 A.2d 518 (1957) aff'd, 37 Del.Ch. 8, 135 A.2d 136 (Del.Supr.1957). Meanwhile, on July 29, 1957, Vogel, as president, sent out a notice calling a special shareholders' meeting for September 12, 1957 for the following purposes:

1.  to fill director vacancies;

2.  to amend the by-laws to increase the number of board members from 13 to 19; to increase the quorum from 7 to 10; and to elect six additional directors;

3.  to remove Tomlinson and Stanley Meyer as directors and to fill the vacancies thus created.

The plaintiff brought an action to enjoin this special shareholder's meeting and for other relief. The court first considered plaintiff's claim that the Vogel, as president, lacked the power to call a stockholders' meeting to amend the bylaws and fill vacancies on the board. Relying on a bylaw explicitly granting the president power to call special meetings of stockholders "for any purpose," the court rejected this claim.]

SEITZ, CHANCELLOR.

\* \* \*

Plaintiff next argues that the stockholders have no power between annual meetings to elect directors to fill newly created directorships.

Plaintiff argues in effect that since the Loew's by-laws provide that the stockholders may fill "vacancies", and since our Courts have construed "vacancy" not to embrace "newly created directorships" (*Automatic Steel Products v. Johnston*, 31 Del.Ch. 469, 64 A.2d 416, 6 A.L.R.2d 170), the attempted call by the president for the purpose of filling newly created directorships was invalid.

Conceding that "vacancy" as used in the by-laws does not embrace "newly created directorships", that does not resolve this problem. I say this because in *Moon v. Moon Motor Car Co.*, 17 Del.Ch. 176, 151 A. 298, it was held that the stockholders had the inherent right between annual meetings to fill newly created directorships. See also *Automatic Steel Products v. Johnston*, above. There is no basis to distinguish the *Moon* case unless it be because the statute has since been amended to provide that not only vacancies but newly created directorships "may be filled by a majority of the directors then in office * * * unless it is otherwise provided in the certificate of incorporation or the by-laws * * * ". 8 Del.C. § 223. Obviously, the amendment to include new directors is not worded so as to make the statute exclusive. It does not prevent the stockholders from filling the new directorships. * * *

I therefore conclude that the stockholders of Loew's do have the right between annual meetings to elect directors to fill newly created directorships.

Plaintiff next argues that the shareholders of a Delaware corporation have no power to remove directors from office even for cause and thus the call for that purpose is invalid. The defendant naturally takes a contrary position.

While there are some cases suggesting the contrary, I believe that the stockholders have the power to remove a director for cause. This power must be implied when we consider that otherwise a director who is guilty of the worst sort of violation of his duty could nevertheless remain on the board. It is hardly to be believed that a director who is disclosing the corporation's trade secrets to a competitor would be immune from removal by the stockholders. Other examples, such as embezzlement of corporate funds, etc., come readily to mind.

But plaintiff correctly states that there is no provision in our statutory law providing for the removal of directors by stockholder action. In contrast he calls attention to § 142 of 8 Del.C., dealing with officers, which specifically refers to the possibility of a vacancy in an office by removal. He also notes that the Loew's by-laws provide for the removal of officers and employees but not directors. From these facts he argues that it was intended that directors not be removed even for cause. I believe the statute and by-law are of course some evidence to support plaintiff's contention. But when we seek to exclude the existence of a power by implication, I think it is pertinent to consider whether the absence of the power can be said to subject the corporation to the possibility of real damage. I say this because we seek intention and such a factor would be relevant to that issue. Considering the damage a director might be able to inflict upon his corporation, I believe the doubt must be resolved by construing the statutes and by-laws as leaving untouched the question of director removal for cause. This being so, the Court is free to conclude on reason that the stockholders have such inherent power.

I therefore conclude that as a matter of Delaware corporation law the stockholders do have the power to remove directors for cause. I need not and do not decide whether the stockholders can by appropriate charter or by-law provision deprive themselves of this right. * * *

I turn next to plaintiff's charges relating to procedural defects and to irregularities in proxy solicitation by the Vogel group.

Plaintiff's first point is that the stockholders can vote to remove a director for cause only after such director has been given adequate notice of charges of grave impropriety and afforded an opportunity to be heard. * * *

I am inclined to agree that if the proceedings preliminary to submitting the matter of removal for cause to the stockholders appear to be legal and if the charges are legally sufficient on their face, the Court should ordinarily not intervene. The sufficiency of the evidence would be a matter for evaluation in later proceedings. But where the procedure adopted to remove a director for cause is invalid on its face, a stockholder can attack such matters before the meeting. This conclusion is dictated both by the desirability of avoiding unnecessary and expensive action and by the importance of settling internal disputes, where reasonably possible, at the earliest moment. Otherwise a director could be removed and his successor could be appointed and participate in important board action before the illegality of the removal was judicially established. This seems undesirable where the illegality is clear on the face of the proceedings. * * *

Turning now to plaintiff's contentions, it is certainly true that when the shareholders attempt to remove a director for cause, " * * * there must be the service of specific charges, adequate notice and full opportunity of meeting the accusation * * * ". See *Auer v. Dressel*, * * * above. While it involved an invalid attempt by directors to remove a fellow director for cause, nevertheless, this same general standard was recognized in *Bruch v. National Guarantee Credit Corp.* [13 Del.Ch. 180, 116 A. 738], above. The Chancellor said that the power of removal could not "be exercised in an arbitrary manner. The accused director would be entitled to be heard in his own defense".

Plaintiff asserts that no specific charges have been served upon the two directors sought to be ousted; that the notice of the special meeting fails to contain a specific statement of the charges; that the proxy statement which accompanied the notice also failed to notify the stockholders of the specific charges; and that it does not inform the stockholders that the accused must be afforded an opportunity to meet the accusations before a vote is taken.

Matters for stockholder consideration need not be conducted with the same formality as judicial proceedings. The proxy statement specifically recites that the two directors are sought to be removed for the reasons stated in the president's accompanying letter. Both directors involved received copies of the letter. Under the circumstances I think it must be said that the two directors involved were served with notice of the charges against them. * * *

I next consider plaintiff's contention that the charges against the two directors do not constitute "cause" as a matter of law. It would take too much space to narrate in detail the contents of the president's letter.

I must therefore give my summary of its charges. First of all, it charges that the two directors (Tomlinson and Meyer) failed to cooperate with Vogel in his announced program for rebuilding the company; that their purpose has been to put themselves in control; that they made baseless accusations against him and other management personnel and attempted to divert him from his normal duties as president by bombarding him with correspondence containing unfounded charges and other similar acts; that they moved into the company's building, accompanied by lawyers and accountants, and immediately proceeded upon a planned scheme of harassment. They called for many records, some going back twenty years, and were rude to the personnel. Tomlinson sent daily letters to the directors making serious charges directly and by means of innuendos and misinterpretations.

Are the foregoing charges, if proved, legally sufficient to justify the ouster of the two directors by the stockholders? I am satisfied that a charge that the directors desired to take over control of the corporation is not a reason for their ouster. Standing alone, it is a perfectly legitimate objective which is a part of the very fabric of corporate existence. Nor is a charge of lack of cooperation a legally sufficient basis for removal for cause.

The next charge is that these directors, in effect, engaged in a calculated plan of harassment to the detriment of the corporation. Certainly a director may examine books, ask questions, etc., in the discharge of his duty, but a point can be reached when his actions exceed the call of duty and become deliberately obstructive. In such a situation, if his actions constitute a real burden on the corporation then the stockholders are entitled to relief. The charges in this area made by the Vogel letter are legally sufficient to justify the stockholders in voting to remove such directors. In so concluding I of course express no opinion as to the truth of the charges.

I therefore conclude that the charge of "a planned scheme of harassment" as detailed in the letter constitutes a justifiable legal basis for removing a director.

I next consider whether the directors sought to be removed have been given a reasonable opportunity to be heard by the stockholders on the charges made. * * *

There seems to be an absence of cases detailing the appropriate procedure for submitting a question of director removal for cause for stockholder consideration. I am satisfied, however, that to the extent the matter is to be voted upon by the use of proxies, such proxies may be solicited only after the accused directors are afforded an opportunity to present their case to the stockholders. This means, in my opinion, that an opportunity must be provided such directors to present their defense to the stockholders by a statement which must accompany or precede the initial solicitation of proxies seeking authority to vote for the removal of such director for cause. If not provided then such proxies may not be voted for removal. And the corporation has a duty to see that this opportunity is given the directors at its expense. Admittedly, no such opportunity was given the two directors involved. * * *

I therefore conclude that the procedural sequence here adopted for soliciting proxies seeking authority to vote on the removal of the two directors is contrary to law. The result is that the proxy solicited by the Vogel group, which is based upon unilateral presentation of the facts by those in control of the corporate facilities, must be declared invalid insofar as they purport to give authority to vote for the removal of the directors for cause.

A preliminary injunction will issue restraining the corporation from recognizing or counting any proxies held by the Vogel group and others insofar as such proxies purport to grant authority to vote for the removal of Tomlinson and Meyer as directors of the corporation. * * *

[Chancellor Seitz went on to deal with a number of other questions relating to the use by the Vogel faction of corporate funds and facilities in the solicitation of proxies. He ruled, among other things, that the Vogel faction, which stood for existing policy, was justified in using corporate funds for the solicitation of proxies. He did not rule on whether the Tomlinson faction would also have access to the corporate treasury for that purpose. Finally, the Chancellor declined to issue an injunction ordering the four Vogel directors to attend board meetings so as to constitute a quorum. He held that, under the circumstances, at least, it was not a breach of their fiduciary duty to engage in a concerted plan to prevent the board from acting by refusing to attend meetings.]

---

Chancellor Seitz' ruling that the Vogel faction could use corporate funds to solicit proxies to remove directors who opposed its business policies had substantial precedential support. In *Hall v. Trans-Lux Daylight Picture Screen Corp.*, 20 Del.Ch. 78, 171 A. 226 (1934), the court reasoned that because directors properly can use corporate funds to inform shareholders about transactions for which their approval is sought, directors also should be able to use corporate funds in a contest for control "in the interest of an intelligent exercise of judgment on the part of the stockholders upon policies to be pursued * * *." However, where no question of policy is involved, "where the expenditures [to solicit proxies] are solely in the personal interest of the directors to maintain themselves in office, [they] are not proper." *Id.* at 228. *See, also, Empire Southern Gas Co. v. Gray*, 29 Del.Ch. 95, 102, 46 A.2d 741, 744 (1946).

Of course, as the court pointed out in *Steinberg v. Adams*, 90 F.Supp. 604, 608 (S.D.N.Y.1950), "generally policy and personnel do not exist in separate compartments. A change in personnel is sometimes indispensible to a change in policy. A new board may be the symbol of the shift in policy, as well as the means of obtaining it." Consequently, almost every time a proxy contest arises, incumbent directors will be able to justify use of corporate funds on the grounds that the insurgents' challenge, in essence, is motivated by disagreement about policies the incumbents have pursued.

Incumbents thus have a tremendous advantage in a proxy contest. They have access to the corporate treasury. Insurgents must use their own funds to finance a proxy solicitations, and can recover their costs only if they prevail. *See Steinberg v. Adams, supra*; *Rosenfeld v. Fairchild Engine & Airplane Corp.*, 309 N.Y. 168, 128 N.E.2d 291 (1955).

Incumbent directors, however, may want more than a financial advantage. They may attempt to use their control over the corporation's business and affairs to impede the insurgents' efforts. *Schnell v. Chris–Craft Industries* (Chapter 3) makes clear that such tactics are subject to equitable limitations. More recent cases elaborate that principle.

## 5.  BOARD RESPONSES TO SHAREHOLDER INITIATIVES

## BLASIUS INDUSTRIES, INC. v. ATLAS CORP.

564 A.2d 651 (Del.Ch.1988).

[Blasius began to accumulate Atlas shares for the first time in July, 1987. On October 29, 1987, Blasius disclosed that it owned 9.1% of Atlas' common stock and stated in that it intended to encourage Atlas' management to consider a restructuring of the company. Blasius also disclosed that it was exploring the feasibility of obtaining control of Atlas.

Atlas' management did not welcome the prospect of Blasius' controlling shareholders involving themselves in Atlas' affairs. Atlas' new CEO, Weaver, had overseen a business restructuring of a sort and thought it should be given a chance to produce benefit before another restructuring was attempted.

Early in December, 1987, Blasius suggested that Atlas engage in a leveraged restructuring and distribute to its shareholders a one-time dividend of $35 million in cash and $125 million in subordinated debentures. Atlas's management responded coolly to this proposal. Mr. Weaver expressed surprise that Blasius would suggest using debt to accomplish a substantial liquidation of Atlas at a time when Atlas' future prospects were promising.

On December 30, 1987, Blasius delivered to Atlas a signed written consent (1) adopting a precatory resolution recommending that the board develop and implement a restructuring proposal, (2) amending the Atlas bylaws to, among other things, expand the size of the board from seven to fifteen members—the maximum number under Atlas' charter, and (3) electing eight named persons to fill the new directorships. Blasius also informed Atlas of its intent to solicit consents from other Atlas shareholders pursuant to DGCL § 228.

Mr. Weaver immediately conferred with Mr. Masinter, Atlas' outside counsel and a director, who viewed the consent as an attempt to take control of Atlas. They decided to call an emergency meeting of the board, even though a regularly scheduled meeting was to occur only one week hence, on January 6, 1988. In a telephone meeting held the next day, the board voted to amend Atlas' bylaws to increase the size of the board from seven to nine and then appointed John M. Devaney and Harry J. Winters, Jr. to fill the two newly created positions.]

ALLEN, CHANCELLOR.

Plaintiff attacks the December 31 board action as a selfishly motivated effort to protect the incumbent board from a perceived threat to its control of Atlas. * * *

Defendants, of course, contest every aspect of plaintiffs' claims. They claim the formidable protections of the business judgment rule. * * *

### III.

* * *

While I am satisfied that the evidence is powerful, indeed compelling, that the board was chiefly motivated on December 31 to forestall or preclude the possibility that a majority of shareholders might place on the Atlas board eight new members sympathetic to the Blasius proposal, it is less clear with respect to the more subtle motivational question: whether the existing members of the board did so because they held a good faith belief that such shareholder action would be self-injurious and shareholders needed to be protected from their own judgment.

On balance, I cannot conclude that the board was acting out of a self-interested motive in any important respect on December 31. I conclude rather that the board saw the "threat" of the Blasius recapitalization proposal as posing vital policy differences between itself and Blasius. It acted, I conclude, in a good faith effort to protect its incumbency, not selfishly, but in order to thwart implementation of the recapitalization that it feared, reasonably, would cause great injury to the Company.

The real question the case presents, to my mind, is whether, in these circumstances, the board, even if it *is* acting with subjective good faith * * *, may validly act for the principal purpose of preventing the shareholders from electing a majority of new directors. The question thus posed is not one of intentional wrong (or even negligence), but one of authority *as between the fiduciary and the beneficiary* * * *.

### IV.

The shareholder franchise is the ideological underpinning upon which the legitimacy of directorial power rests. Generally, shareholders have only two protections against perceived inadequate business performance. They may sell their stock (which, if done in sufficient numbers, may so affect security prices as to create an incentive for altered managerial performance), or they may vote to replace incumbent board members.

It has, for a long time, been conventional to dismiss the stockholder vote as a vestige or ritual of little practical importance. It may be that we are now witnessing the emergence of new institutional voices and arrangements that will make the stockholder vote a less predictable affair than it has been. Be that as it may, however, whether the vote is seen functionally as an unimportant formalism, or as an important tool of discipline, it is clear that it is critical to the theory that legitimates the exercise of power by some (directors and officers) over vast aggregations of property that they do not own. Thus, when viewed from a broad, institutional perspective, it can be seen that matters involving the integrity of the shareholder voting process involve consideration not present in any other context in which directors exercise delegated power. * * *

The distinctive nature of the shareholder franchise context also appears when the matter is viewed from a less generalized, doctrinal point of view. From this point of view, as well, it appears that the ordinary considerations to which the business judgment rule originally responded are simply not present in the shareholder voting context. That is, a decision by the board to act for the primary purpose of preventing the effectiveness of a shareholder vote inevitably involves the question who, as between the principal and the agent, has authority with respect to a matter of internal corporate governance. That, of course, is true in a very specific way in this case which deals with the question who should constitute the board of directors of the corporation, but it will be true in every instance in which an incumbent board seeks to thwart a shareholder majority. A board's decision to act to prevent the shareholders from creating a majority of new board positions and filling them does not involve the exercise of *the corporation's power* over its property, or with respect to *its* rights or obligations; rather, it involves allocation, between shareholders as a class and the board, of effective power with respect to governance of the corporation. * * * Action designed principally to interfere with the effectiveness of a vote inevitably involves a conflict between the board and a shareholder majority. Judicial review of such action involves a determination of the legal and equitable obligations of an agent towards his principal. This is not, in my opinion, a question that a court may leave to the agent finally to decide so long as he does so honestly and competently; that is, it may not be left to the agent's business judgment. * * *

Plaintiff argues for a rule of *per se* invalidity once a plaintiff has established that a board has acted for the primary purpose of thwarting the exercise of a shareholder vote. * * *

A *per se* rule that would strike down, in equity, any board action taken for the primary purpose of interfering with the effectiveness of a corporate vote would have the advantage of relative clarity and predictability. It also has the advantage of most vigorously enforcing the concept of corporate democracy. The disadvantage it brings along is, of course, the disadvantage a *per se* rule always has: it may sweep too broadly.

In two recent cases dealing with shareholder votes, this court struck down board acts done for the primary purpose of impeding the exercise of stockholder voting power. In doing so, a *per se* rule was not applied. Rather, it was said that, in such a case, the board bears the heavy burden of demonstrating a compelling justification for such action. * * *

In my view, our inability to foresee now all of the future settings in which a board might, in good faith, paternalistically seek to thwart a shareholder vote, counsels against the adoption of a *per se* rule invalidating, in equity, every board action taken for the sole or primary purpose of thwarting a shareholder vote, even though I recognize the transcending significance of the franchise to the claims to legitimacy of our scheme of corporate governance. It may be that some set of facts would justify such extreme action. This, however, is not such a case. * * *

[In this case], [t]he board was not faced with a coercive action taken by a powerful shareholder against the interests of a distinct shareholder constituency (such as a public minority). It was presented with a consent solicitation by a 9% shareholder. Moreover, here it had time (and understood that it had time) to inform the shareholders of its views on the merits of the proposal subject to stockholder vote. The only justification that can, in such a situation, be offered for the action taken is that the board knows better than do the shareholders what is in the corporation's best interest. While that premise is no doubt true for any number of matters, it is irrelevant (except insofar as the shareholders wish to be guided by the board's recommendation) when the question is who should comprise the board of directors. The theory of our corporation law confers power upon directors as the agents of the shareholders; it does not create Platonic masters. It may be that the Blasius restructuring proposal was or is unrealistic and would lead to injury to the corporation and its shareholders if pursued. * * * The board certainly viewed it that way, and that view, held in good faith, entitled the board to take certain steps to evade the risk it perceived. It could, for example, expend corporate funds to inform shareholders and seek to bring them to a similar point of view. But there is a vast difference between expending corporate funds to inform the electorate and exercising power for the primary purpose of foreclosing effective shareholder action. A majority of the shareholders, who were not dominated in any respect, could view the matter differently than did the board. If they do, or did, they are entitled to employ the mechanisms provided by the corporation law and the Atlas certificate of incorporation to advance that view. They are also entitled, in my opinion, to restrain their agents, the board, from acting for the principal purpose of thwarting that action.

I therefore conclude that, even finding the action taken was taken in good faith, it constituted an unintended violation of the duty of loyalty that the board owed to the shareholders. I note parenthetically that the concept of an unintended breach of the duty of loyalty is unusual but not novel. That action will, therefore, be set aside by order of this court. * * *

*Blasius* applied the principle, announced in *Schnell*, that "inequitable action does not become permissible simply because it is legally possible." But while *Blasius* discussed at greater length than did *Schnell* why an otherwise legal action relating to the corporate electoral process was deemed inequitable, it left unresolved, as did *Schnell*, *what* makes such an action inequitable. In *Stahl v. Apple Bancorp, Inc.*, 579 A.2d 1115 (Del.Ch.1990), Chancellor Allen attempted to place in context *Schnell*, *Blasius* and several other Delaware decisions that have involved this issue.

Apple Bancorp's board had chosen a record date for its annual meeting, but had not formally announced that date. Stahl, who owned 30 percent of Apple's stock, informed the board he intended to conduct a proxy contest to gain control, and subsequently made a cash tender offer for all the bank's stock. The board deferred the record date and the annual meeting. Stahl, relying on *Schnell* and *Blasius*, sued to require the board to set a record date and a date for the annual meeting.

Chancellor Allen denied Stahl's request for relief and offered the following explanation of how his decision related to *Schnell* and its progeny:

> [I]t is well established * * * that where corporate directors exercise their legal powers for an inequitable purpose their action may be rescinded or nullified by a court at the instance of an aggrieved shareholder. The leading Delaware case of *Schnell v. Chris–Craft Industries, Inc.* announced this principle and applied it in a setting in which directors advanced the date of an annual meeting in order to impede an announced proxy contest.

> Under this test the court asks the question whether the directors' purpose is "inequitable." An inequitable purpose is not necessarily synonymous with a dishonest motive. Fiduciaries who are subjectively operating selflessly might be pursuing a purpose that a court will rule is inequitable. Thus, for example, there was no inquiry concerning the board's subjective good faith in *Condec Corporation v. Lunkenheimer Company*, where this court held that the issuance of stock for the principal purpose of eliminating the ability of a large stockholder to determine the outcome of a vote was invalid as a breach of loyalty. * * *

> *Lerman v. Diagnostic Data, Inc.* * * * explicitly expresses the view that inequitable conduct does not necessarily require an evil or selfish motive. There the court held a bylaw invalid in the situation before it where that bylaw would have precluded a shareholder from mounting a proxy contest. The court referred to the fact that the bylaw "whether designedly inequitable or not, has had a terminal effect on the aspirations of Lerman and his group."

> Each of these cases dealt with board action with a principal purpose of impeding the exercise of stockholder power through the vote. They could be read as approximating a *per se* rule that board

action taken for the principal purpose of impeding the effective exercise of the stockholder franchise is inequitable and will be restrained or set aside in proper circumstances.

Consistent with these authorities, in *Blasius* and in *Aprahamian* [*v.* HBO *& Co*]., 531 A.2d 1204 (Del.Ch.1987)], this court held that action designed primarily to impede the effective exercise of the franchise is not evaluated under the business judgment form of review * * *. These statements are simply restatements of the principle applied in *Schnell*. *Blasius* did, however, go on to reject the notion of *per se* invalidity of action taken to interfere with the effective exercise of the corporate franchise; it admitted the possibility that in some circumstances such action might be consistent with the directors equitable obligations. It was suggested, however, that such circumstances would have to constitute "compelling justification," given the central role of the stockholder franchise.

Thus, *Blasius'* reference to "compelling justification" reflects only the high value that the prior cases had placed upon the exercise of voting rights and the inherently particularized and contextual nature of any inquiry concerning fiduciary duties. Neither it nor *Aprahamian* represent new law. * * *

In no sense can the decision not to call a meeting be likened to kinds of board action found to have constituted inequitable conduct relating to the vote. In each of these franchise cases the effect of the board action—to advance (*Schnell*) or defer (*Aprahamian*) a meeting; to adopt a bylaw (*Lerman*); or to fill board vacancies (*Blasius*)— was practically to preclude effective stockholder action (*Schnell, Blasius, Lerman*) or to snatch victory from an insurgent slate on the eve of the noticed meeting (*Aprahamian*). Here the election process will go forward at a time consistent with the company's bylaws and with Section 211 of our corporation law. Defendant's decision does not preclude plaintiff or any other Bancorp shareholder from effectively exercising his vote, nor have proxies been collected that only await imminent counting. Plaintiff has no legal right to compel the holding of the company's annual meeting under Section 211(c) of the Delaware General Corporation Law, nor does he, in my opinion, have a right in equity to require the board to call a meeting now.

579 A.2d at 1121–23.

## 6. SHAREHOLDERS' RIGHT OF INSPECTION

To exercise fully their right to vote, and especially their right to initiate action, shareholders may need access to a corporation's books and records. At common law, a shareholder was deemed to have a right to inspect corporate books and records deriving from her equitable ownership of the corporation's assets. The right extended beyond the formal minutes of official actions "to include the documents, contracts, and papers of the corporation." *Otis–Hidden Co. v. Scheirich*, 187 Ky. 423, 429, 219 S.W. 191, 194 (1920). But, to avoid disruption of the corporation's business, a shareholder was restricted to exercising the right to inspection at reasonable times and places and, more importantly, only when inspection was for a "proper purpose." See, e.g., *In re Steinway*, 159 N.Y. 250, 53 N.E. 1103 (1899); *State ex rel. Rogers v. Sherman Oil Co.*, 31 Del. 570, 117 A. 122 (Del.Super.1922).

Every state corporate statute now provides for a right of inspection, but statutory provisions vary considerably. Some have been construed simply to codify the common law right. *See, e.g., State ex rel. O'Hara v. National Biscuit Co.*, 69 N.J.L. 198, 54 A. 241 (1903); *Dines v. Harris,* 88 Colo. 22, 291 P. 1024 (1930). Others impose limits on which shareholders are eligible to assert the right and which records are subject to inspection. DGCL § 220 (a) limits inspection to stockholders of record, thus making it difficult for investors who hold their shares in nominee accounts to exercise the right. Many states limit inspection rights to shareholders who own a certain percentage of a corporation's shares or who have held their shares for some minimum period. N.Y.B.C.L. § 624(b), which is typical, allows inspection by a shareholder who owns 5 percent of any class of stock or who has held her stock for at least six months. RMBCA § 16.02 grants inspection rights to beneficial owners as well as shareholders of record, but divides corporate records into two categories. Shareholders can readily inspect the articles of incorporation, by-laws, minutes of shareholder meetings and like documents. RMBCA §§ 16.01(e), 16.02(a). But to inspect minutes of board meetings, accounting records, or the shareholder list, a shareholder must have a proper purpose and describe "with reasonable particularity" that purpose and the records to be inspected, which records must be "directly connected" with that purpose. RMBCA § 16.02(b).

The traditional remedy of a shareholder seeking inspection is a writ of mandamus. To prevent obstruction of a shareholder's right to inspect, many statutes make a corporation that refuses to grant inspection liable for the shareholder's costs, including reasonable attorney's fees, on the corporation, unless the corporation can establish that it acted reasonably. RMBCA § 16.04(c).

## A. PROPER PURPOSE

Probably the most difficult hurdle faced by a shareholder seeking inspection of corporate books and records is the establishment of a proper purpose. Statutes usually do not define proper purpose or define it using vague terms such as "a purpose reasonably related to such person's interest as a stockholder." DGCL § 220(b); *see also* Official Comment to RMBCA § 16.02. A shareholder has no right to inspection "if his purpose be to satisfy his curiosity, to annoy or harass the corporation, or to accomplish some object hostile to the corporation or detrimental to its interests." *Albee v. Lamson & Hubbard Corp.*, 320 Mass. 421, 424, 69 N.E.2d 811, 813 (1946). Inspection will be denied where the object is to sell information for personal profit, *State ex rel.*

*Theile v. Cities Service Co.*, 31 Del. 514, 115 A. 773 (1922), or to aid a competing business, *Slay v. Polonia Publishing Co.*, 249 Mich. 609, 229 N.W. 434 (1930). Conversely, determination of the value of shares, *Bankers Trust Co. v. H. Rosenhirsch Co.*, 20 Misc.2d 792, 190 N.Y.S.2d 957 (1959), communication with other shareholders (including solicitation of proxies, solicitation of shareholders to join in a derivative suit and offers to purchase stock), *Weber v. Continental Motors Corp.*, 305 F.Supp. 404 (S.D.N.Y.1969), and ascertainment of possible corporate mismanagement, *Briskin v. Briskin Manufacturing Co.*, 6 Ill.App.3d 740, 286 N.E.2d 571 (1972) have been held to constitute proper purposes. Once a proper purpose has been established, the fact that a shareholder may have other, improper purposes for seeking inspection generally does not constitute a valid reason to refuse inspection. *General Time Corp. v. Talley Industries, Inc.*, 43 Del.Ch. 531, 240 A.2d 755 (Del.1968).

In determining whether the shareholder has alleged or proved a proper purpose for inspection, courts usually have focused on whether the asserted purpose is germane to the shareholder's economic interest in the corporation. Some courts, however, also have had occasion to consider whether inspection is available to a shareholder primarily concerned with a corporation's social or political policies.

## STATE EX REL. PILLSBURY v. HONEYWELL, INC.

291 Minn. 322, 191 N.W.2d 406 (1971).

[Petitioner, a member of a prominent and wealthy Minneapolis family, wanted to stop production by Honeywell Inc. (Honeywell) of antipersonnel fragmentation bombs used in Vietnam. He purchased 100 shares for the "sole purpose" of gaining a voice in Honeywell's affairs and then requested a shareholders list in order to solicit proxies for the election of new directors. When Honeywell refused his request, he filed for a writ of mandamus. After discovery, the court denied relief, holding that the same result would pertain whether it applied Minnesota law or the law of Delaware, Honeywell's state of incorporation.]

KELLY, JUSTICE.

\* \* \*

The trial court ordered judgment for Honeywell, ruling that petitioner had not demonstrated a proper purpose germane to his interest as a stockholder. Petitioner contends that a stockholder who disagrees with management has an absolute right to inspect corporate records for purposes of soliciting proxies. He would have this court rule that such solicitation is per se a "proper purpose." Honeywell argues that a "proper purpose" contemplates concern with investment return. We agree with Honeywell.

This court has had several occasions to rule on the propriety of shareholders' demands for inspection of corporate books and records.

Minn.St. 300.32, not applicable here, has been held to be declaratory of the common-law principle that a stockholder is entitled to inspection for a proper purpose germane to his business interests. While inspection will not be permitted for purposes of curiosity, speculation, or vexation, adverseness to management and a desire to gain control of the corporation for economic benefit does not indicate an improper purpose.

Several courts agree with petitioner's contention that a mere desire to communicate with other shareholders is, per se, a proper purpose. This would seem to confer an almost absolute right to inspection. We believe that a better rule would allow inspections only if the shareholder has a proper purpose for such communication. * * *

The act of inspecting a corporation's shareholder ledger and business records must be viewed in its proper perspective. In terms of the corporate norm, inspection is merely the act of the concerned owner checking on what is in part his property. In the context of the large firm, inspection can be more akin to a weapon in corporate warfare. * * * Because the power to inspect may be the power to destroy, it is important that only those with a bona fide interest in the corporation enjoy that power.

That one must have proper standing to demand inspection has been recognized by statutes in several jurisdictions. Courts have also balked at compelling inspection by a shareholder holding an insignificant amount of stock in the corporation.

Petitioner's standing as a shareholder is quite tenuous. He only owns one share in his own name, bought for the purposes of this suit. He had previously ordered his agent to buy 100 shares, but there is no showing of investment intent. While his agent had a cash balance in the $400,000 portfolio, petitioner made no attempt to determine whether Honeywell was a good investment or whether more profitable shares would have to be sold to finance the Honeywell purchase. Furthermore, petitioner's agent had the power to sell the Honeywell shares without his consent. Petitioner also had a contingent beneficial interest in 242 shares. Courts are split on the question of whether an equitable interest entitles one to inspection. See 5 Fletcher, PRIVATE CORPORATIONS, § 2230 at 862 (Perm. ed. rev. vol. 1967). Indicative of petitioner's concern regarding his equitable holdings is the fact that he was unaware of them until he had decided to bring this suit.

Petitioner had utterly no interest in the affairs of Honeywell before he learned of Honeywell's production of fragmentation bombs. Immediately after obtaining this knowledge, he purchased stock in Honeywell for the sole purpose of asserting ownership privileges in an effort to force Honeywell to cease such production. * * * But for his opposition to Honeywell's policy, petitioner probably would not have bought Honeywell stock, would not be interested in Honeywell's profits and would not desire to communicate with Honeywell's shareholders. His avowed purpose in buying Honeywell stock was to place himself in a position to try to impress his opinions favoring a reordering of priorities upon Honeywell management and its other shareholders. Such a motivation can hardly be deemed a proper purpose germane to his economic interest as a shareholder.[5]

* * * From the deposition, the trial court concluded that petitioner had already formed strong opinions on the immorality and the social and economic wastefulness of war long before he bought stock in Honeywell. His sole motivation was to change Honeywell's course of business because that course was incompatible with his political views. If unsuccessful, petitioner indicated that he would sell the Honeywell stock.

We do not mean to imply that a shareholder with a bona fide investment interest could not bring this suit if motivated by concern with the long-or short-term economic effects on Honeywell resulting from the production of war munitions. Similarly, this suit might be appropriate when a shareholder has a bona fide concern about the adverse effects of abstention from profitable war contracts on his investment in Honeywell.

In the instant case, however, the trial court, in effect, has found from all the facts that petitioner was not interested in even the long-term well-being of Honeywell or the enhancement of the value of his shares. His sole purpose was to persuade the company to adopt his social and political concerns, irrespective of any economic benefit to himself or Honeywell. This purpose on the part of one buying into the corporation does not entitle the petitioner to inspect Honeywell's books and records.

Petitioner argues that he wishes to inspect the stockholder ledger in order that he may correspond with other shareholders with the hope of electing to the board one or more directors who represent his particular viewpoint. * * * While a plan to elect one or more directors is specific and the election of directors normally would be a proper purpose, here the purpose was not germane to petitioner's or Honeywell's economic interest. Instead, the plan was designed to further petitioner's political and social beliefs. Since the requisite propriety of purpose germane to his or Honeywell's economic interest is not present, the allegation that petitioner seeks to elect a new board of directors is insufficient to compel inspection. * * *

The order of the trial court denying the writ of mandamus is affirmed.

---

**5.** We do not question petitioner's good faith incident to his political and social philosophy; nor did the trial court. In a well-prepared memorandum, the lower court stated: "By enumerating the foregoing this Court does not mean to belittle or to be derisive of Petitioner's motivation and intentions because this Court cannot but draw the conclusion that the Petitioner is sincere in his political and social philosophy, but this Court does not feel that this is a proper forum for the advancement of these political-social views by way of direct contact with the stockholders of Honeywell Company or any other company. If the courts were to grant these rights on the basis of the foregoing, anyone who has a political-social philosophy which differs with that of a company in which he becomes a shareholder can secure a writ and any company can be faced with a rash and multitude of these types of actions which are not bona fide efforts to engage in a proxy fight for the purpose of taking over the company or electing directors, which the courts have recognized as being perfectly legitimate and acceptable."

*Pillsbury* probably marks the low tide in the stockholder's right to inspect. The tenor of the times may explain both the result and the court's remark that "the power to inspect may be the power to destroy." While Mr. Pillsbury was launching his campaign against Honeywell, other protestors against the Vietnam war were engaged in more violent activities, including pouring blood on draft board files and even bombing government-supported research facilities.

*Pillsbury* has not been followed by the Delaware courts. *Credit Bureau of St. Paul, Inc. v. Credit Bureau Reports, Inc.*, 290 A.2d 689 (Del.Ch.1972), aff'd 290 A.2d 691 (Del.1972), criticized the decision. In *Conservative Caucus v. Chevron Corp.*, 525 A.2d 569 (Del.Ch.1987), the court upheld a request for a stockholder list by a shareholder seeking to solicit the support of fellow shareholders for a resolution directed at discouraging the corporation from doing business with Angola. The court stated:

> [The *Pillsbury*] holding is, of course, not binding on this court and it was criticized by the Delaware Supreme Court in *Credit Bureau Reports, Inc. v. Credit Bureau of St. Paul, Inc.*
>
> The facts are also different here. Plaintiff has testified that it seeks the stock list to warn the stockholders about the allegedly dire economic consequences which will fall upon Chevron if it continues to do business in Angola. Some of these possible economic consequences, according to plaintiff, are: sanctions by the U.S. Government; adverse consequences imposed by the Export–Import Bank; an embargo by the U.S. Defense Department on purchases of oil which has its source in Angola; a denial of certain federal tax credits; the risk to personnel and facilities of an unstable government; and, the risk of war in Angola. These are surely matters which might have an adverse affect on the value of the stock of Chevron. I, therefore, find that the holding in *Pillsbury* is not persuasive.

*Id.* at 572.

## B.  WHAT COMPRISES A "STOCKHOLDER LIST?"

New issues have arisen as a consequence of changes in corporations' record-keeping practices and investors' patterns of stock ownership. A corporation's records must list only the names of *"stockholders of record"*—persons holding legal title to outstanding shares of stock. See, e.g. RMBCA § 16.01(c). Today, however, most investors hold stock in public corporations in nominee accounts in *"street name."* Consequently, one cannot determine from those corporations' stockholder lists who beneficially owns most of their stock. In fact, one cannot even determine much about the nominee owners of record.

Most stock brokerage firms and financial institutions—which might be called "first tier" nominees—are members of Depositary Trust Company, an entity formed to hold their and their customers' stock. Depositary Trust registers all of its members' stock in one name, "CEDE & Co.," which allows it to simplify stock transfers among its members. But this practice results in many corporations' stockholder lists showing only that CEDE & Co. owns a large portion of their stock. The lists contain no indication either of which brokerage houses and institutions hold that stock or who the beneficial owners are.

Depositary Trust has eliminated the first of these problems. At the request of any corporation, it will prepare in minutes a "CEDE breakdown"—a list of all firms holding stock in the name of CEDE & Co. The corporation then can contact those firms to determine the number of beneficial owners each represents, so as to facilitate distribution through those firms of annual reports, notices of shareholder meetings, and other data. The brokerage firms and institutions generally will not volunteer the names of the customers for whom they hold stock, though; they consider that information confidential.

Brokerage firms, however, must comply with a Securities and Exchange Commission requirement that they ask each customer who holds stock in street name whether she objects to disclosure to her name to corporations in which she has invested. Exchange Act Release. No. 34–22533, 50 Fed.Reg. 42, 672 (1985). Brokerage firms also must deliver within seven business days a list of non-objecting beneficial owners (a "*NOBO list*") to any corporation that requests such a list.

Delaware courts require corporations to deliver to shareholders entitled to inspect stockholder lists both CEDE breakdowns and NOBO lists already within those corporations' possession. *Hatleigh Corp. v. Lane Bryant, Inc.* 428 A.2d 350 (Del.Ch.1981) (CEDE breakdown); *Shamrock Assoc. v. Texas Am. Energy Corp.*, 517 A.2d 658 (Del.Ch.1986) (NOBO list).* They also require a corporation to have a CEDE breakdown produced if it has not already done so. *Tactron, Inc. v. KDI Corp.*, 1985 WL 44699 (Del.Ch.1985). However, in *RB Assoc. of N.J., L.P. v. Gillette Co.*, 1988 WL 27731 (Del.Ch. 1988), the court declined to compel Gillette, which had not requested and had no intention of requesting production of a NOBO list, to request that such a list be produced. After explaining that a CEDE breakdown can be obtained almost instantaneously, which makes production of one necessary in order to put "contesting parties * * * on substantially the same footing, the court continued:

> A NOBO list is different in two material respects. First, the evidence demonstrates that such a list takes approximately ten days to produce. It is not immediately available to the issuer. Second, a modern proxy solicitation can hardly be conducted at all without the

---

* Delaware courts also require production of stock transfer sheets and computer tapes listing a corporation's stockholders. *See* *Tannetics, Inc. v. A.J. Indus., Inc.*, 1974 WL 2038 (Del.Ch.1974).

benefit of a breakdown of the persons for whom a depository company holds its shares. * * *

A NOBO list plays no central role in a proxy contest. While the information it discloses (i.e., the identity of the ultimate owners) may, of course, be of use in telephone solicitations, that information is not necessary for the effective working of the written proxy solicitation process. * * *

* * * Neither broad concepts of fairness, nor the words of Section 220, in my opinion, require that a corporation be forced * * * to exercise the option created by the applicable SEC Rules at the behest of a shareholder. What fairness does require [is that Gillette be ordered to produce a NOBO list if it chooses to request that one be prepared].

*Id.* at * 6–* 7.

## SADLER v. NCR CORPORATION

928 F.2d 48 (2d Cir.1991).

[NCR, a Maryland corporation, was resisting a takeover bid by AT&T, in part by refusing to redeem a "poison pill" that presented a substantial obstacle to AT&T. AT&T sought to eliminate that obstacle by soliciting proxies to remove NCR's incumbent directors and to elect new directors prepared to redeem the poison pill. NCR's articles of incorporation provided that directors could be removed only by the affirmative vote of 80 percent of all outstanding shares.

In connection with its proxy solicitation, AT&T arranged for the Sadlers, New York resident shareholders of NCR, to seek to inspect NCR's shareholder list pursuant to N.Y. BCL § 1315 and compel NCR to request and provide a NOBO list. § 1315 grants inspection rights to New York residents who have held stock in a foreign corporation for more than six months.

The district court held that the Sadlers were qualified to seek inspection pursuant to § 1315, even though they were acting on behalf of AT&T, and also ordered NCR to provide a NOBO list.]

Jon O. Newman, Circuit Judge.

[The court affirmed that the Sadlers were eligible to request inspection, and then turned to their attempt to compel production of a NOBO list.]

The matter was given extended consideration by Chancellor Allen in *RB Associates*. In declining to order compilation of a NOBO list, he distinguished it in two respects from CEDE lists, which Delaware and New York require a corporation to compile upon request of a qualified shareholder. * * *

We do not find either distinction compelling. Since compilation of a NOBO list is a relatively simple mechanical task, the fact that compilation takes longer than for a CEDE list is an insubstantial basis for distinction. As to both sets of information, the underlying data exist in discrete records readily available to be compiled into an aggregate list. Nor are the functions of the lists significantly dissimilar. Both facilitate direct communication with stockholders, in the case of a NOBO list, at least with those beneficial owners who have indicated no objection to disclosure of their names and addresses.

Though Delaware chooses to construe the reach of its requirements on stockholder list disclosure narrowly in this respect, * * * we think New York would apply section 1315 to permit a qualifying shareholder to require the compilation and production of such a list.

Even if the statute might not require compilation of NOBO lists routinely, we agree * * * that compilation was properly ordered in this case. The effect of NCR's 80 percent rule is to count as a "no" vote on the replacement of directors every share that is not voted at the special meeting. Thus, the shares of non-voting beneficial owners who might oppose management if solicited by management opponents armed with a NOBO list are counted in favor of management. Denying such opponents an opportunity to contact the NOBOs is inconsistent with the statute's objective of seeking "to the extent possible, to place shareholders on an equal footing with management in obtaining access to shareholders." *Bohrer* [*v. International Banknote Co.*], 150 A.D.2d [196,] 196–97, 540 N.Y.S.2d [445,] 446 [(1st Dept. 1989)]. In effect, NCR already has the votes of those NOBOs who, for lack of solicitation, decline to vote. As to them, NCR has all the access it needs.

The order of the District Court is affirmed.

# Chapter 13

## CONTROL PROBLEMS IN THE CLOSELY HELD CORPORATION

## A. INTRODUCTION

### 1. OVERVIEW

One of the difficulties of the American law of corporations is that on its face, it attempts to fit small, closely held, or "close," corporations, which characteristically have few shareholders, into the same legal structure as large publicly held corporations such as General Motors and AT&T. The principal difficulty with the failure to differentiate between close and public corporations grows out of the fact that, as we saw in Chapter 6, the shareholders of a close corporation are likely to think of themselves as partners who have elected to incorporate their business for tax reasons or to take advantage of limited liability. They may want the flexibility to design their own control arrangements, but they often will find that such arrangements conflict with the legal norms that govern corporations, such as the principle that the board of directors is responsible for managing the corporation's business. Shareholders in a close corporation may well think it strange that they should be required to act as "directors," especially since they own the business and have the power to elect the directors. What is wrong with their simply agreeing among themselves how the business should be managed?

The tension between the legally-sanctioned model and the needs and desires of the participants in the business venture creates a challenge for the attorney. It is a challenge, however, that an attorney usually can meet by careful planning and drafting. In this chapter we will examine the devices, some within the corporate framework and some extrinsic to it, that are available to the corporate planner.

It is possible to organize a corporation without giving much thought at all to governance arrangements. Commercial services offer to do so for less than $50, plus filing fees. Many people no doubt create corporations in this fashion and agree informally on whatever financial and control arrangements they believe are necessary.

However, working out these arrangements more formally prior to incorporation and memorializing them in a preincorporation agreement has a number of advantages.* It may be desirable to bind the promoters in advance of securing financial commitments from investors. Moreover, as we shall see, some of the more useful control devices must be set forth in the articles (*see, e.g.,* RMBCA § 8.01(b)), while others may be included in a separate agreement. If such an agreement is needed, it often makes sense to write it before any money changes hands. Moreover, from a practical point of view, the discipline of spelling out the details of financial and control arrangements can prove useful. All the parties' arrangements can be taken into account. Misunderstandings can be identified and resolved. Gaps in the structure are more likely to be noticed than if the parties give just casual attention to such matters.

However, limits exist on the utility of contracting as a means of avoiding future disputes. Contracting can be expensive and time consuming. Even when shareholders are prepared to incur the expense, anticipating the problems that actually will arise often is difficult. There is also a danger that dissension will develop relating to hypothetical problems that may well not arise. Some amount of planning usually is better than none, but judgment must be exercised as to how detailed the parties' contractual arrangements should be.

For many years the major hurdle that the planner of the close corporation faced was the reluctance of the courts to give effect to arrangements—whether embodied in the articles, by-laws, or a separate instrument—that departed too far from the traditional statutory model. Two parallel developments, starting primarily in the 1960's, have substantially loosened the bonds of this judicial straitjacket. First, the courts have taken a more realistic view of the practical demands of operating a business as a close corporation and have become far more tolerant of departures from the norm. Second, and perhaps more important, legislatures have recognized the unnecessary rigidity of the traditional structure and the problems that frequently arose out of the strict application of this structure to close corporations. As a corollary, both courts and legislatures have begun to give greater emphasis to a wider range of dispute resolution techniques that do not necessarily require judicial involvement.

A growing number of states have amended their corporation statutes to allow more flexibility to close corporation planners. The most common statutory approach is to presume all corporations are alike but expressly to authorize close corporations to adopt governance structures that vary from the traditional model. *See e.g.,* RMBCA §§ 7.32, 8.01(b). A second approach is the "comprehensive" close corporation statute, which allows

---

* Professor O'Neal distinguishes between a "promoters' contract," which merely binds the parties to proceeding with the organization of a corporation with a defined configuration, and a "shareholders' agreement," which consists of arrangements intended to bind the shareholders in various ways (to be discussed below) that will survive long after the corporation has been formally organized. He suggests that where both ends are sought, it may be best to use two different documents. F. Hodge O'Neal & Robert E. Thompson, O'NEAL'S CLOSE CORP. § 2.29 (3rd ed.).

the corporation to elect treatment under a special statutory regime. DGCL §§ 341–356 provides a good example of such a statute. Only a corporation that meets certain tests and elects close corporation status can make use of those sections of the Delaware statute.

Some jurisdictions, however, have not adopted a more modern statute and the relevant case law may cast doubts on the validity of a governance structure that deviates too much from the statutory norm. In such circumstances, the wisest course of action may be to incorporate in a jurisdiction whose law is more congenial to the needs of the parties even though the resulting corporation may have to register as a foreign corporation where it is actually doing most of its business.

Notwithstanding modern trends, it is still necessary to understand the older rules, not only because they may be operative but because they illuminate the significance of the more modern approach. Consequently, we have included in the following materials some cases that reflect traditional modes of judicial thinking, even though some of the rules they enunciate no longer have much operational significance. In addition, the policy questions these cases raise retain much of their importance.

We note at the outset that there is no generally agreed-upon definition of a "close corporation." In *Donahue v. Rodd Electrotype Co. of New England, Inc.*, 367 Mass. 578, 585, 328 N.E.2d 505, 511 (1975), the court analyzed the characteristics of a close corporation as follows:

> * * * There is no single, generally accepted definition. Some commentators emphasize an "integration of ownership and management," in which the stockholders occupy most management positions. Others focus on the number of stockholders and the nature of the market for the stock. In this view, close corporations have few stockholders; there is little market for corporate stock. The Supreme Court of Illinois adopted this latter view in *Galler v. Galler*, 32 Ill.2d 16, 203 N.E.2d 577 (1964): "For our purposes, a close corporation is one in which the stock is held in a few hands, or in a few families, and wherein it is not at all, or only rarely, dealt in by buying or selling." We accept aspects of both definitions. We deem a close corporation to be typified by: (1) a small number of stockholders; (2) no ready market for the corporate stock; and (3) substantial majority stockholder participation in the management, direction and operations of the corporation.
>
> As thus defined, the close corporation bears striking resemblance to a partnership. Commentators and courts have noted that the close corporation is often little more than an "incorporated" or "chartered" partnership. The stockholders "clothe" their partnership "with the benefits peculiar to a corporation, limited liability, perpetuity and the like." *In the Matter of Surchin (Approved Business Machine Co., Inc.)*, 155 Misc.2d 888, 889, 286 N.Y.S.2d 580, 581 (1967). In essence, though, the enterprise remains one in which ownership is limited to the original parties or transferees of their

stock to whom the other stockholders have agreed, in which ownership and management are in the same hands, and in which the owners are quite dependent on one another for the success of the enterprise. Many close corporations are "really partnerships, between two or three people who contribute their capital, skills, experience and labor." *Kruger v. Gerth*, 16 N.Y.2d 802, 805, 263 N.Y.S.2d 1, 3, 210 N.E.2d 355, 356 (1965) (Desmond, C.J., dissenting). * * *

Frank Easterbrook and Daniel Fischel question the court's analogy and suggest that participants in a close corporation may not want to be governed by partnership law. As discussed in Chapter 6, corporate "default" rules differ from partnership "default" provisions in many respects. The tax consequences of operating as a corporation rather than a partnership also are strikingly different. Noting these differences, Easterbrook and Fischel conclude:

> * * * Proponents of the partnership analogy assume that participants in closely held corporations are knowledgeable enough to incorporate to obtain the benefits of favorable tax treatment but ignorant of all other differences between corporate and partnership law. There is no support for this assumption once you recognize that people have to jump through a lot of formal hoops (assisted by counsel) to incorporate but can become partners by accident. * * *

> * * * A claim that people alert to the tax effects of incorporation were unaware of other effects is hard to take seriously, and when such people do not contract for the use of partnership-like rules, it is appropriate to apply corporate rules.

Frank Easterbrook & Daniel Fischel, THE ECONOMIC STRUCTURE OF CORPORATE LAW 250–251 (1991).

## 2. LAW AND ECONOMICS PERSPECTIVE ON CLOSE CORPORATIONS

In THE ECONOMIC STRUCTURE OF CORPORATE LAW, Easterbrook and Fischel address the problems associated with closely held corporations from a law and economics perspective. *Id.* at 228–232. They focus on the fact that in closely held corporations, risk-bearing and management often are in the same hands.

This feature of closely held corporations has both advantages and disadvantages. Because managers also bear the cost of their actions, there is no specialization of functions. In addition, if managers also must invest in the firm, there are a limited number of qualified managers among whom to choose. Investors are less efficient risk bearers because they commit a greater percentage of their wealth to the firm. In public corporations, investors have greater latitude to diversify their investment portfolios.

In most closely held corporations, fewer conflicts of interest exist between management and the firm because what is good for the manager is good for the firm. Because many closely held corporations are based on familial or other personal relationships, agency costs and conflicts of interest are even further limited. Accordingly, there is less need for monitoring because managers are less likely to engage in self-dealing.

The lack of a public market for corporate shares is a significant detriment to the investors in a closely held corporation. Without a market for shares, investors encounter difficulty in valuing their share holdings. Simply put, there is no market price and shares are difficult to transfer. Moreover, investors do not have the protection offered by a market determined price. The illiquidity of the shares raises the possibility of conflicts over dividend policy. In a public corporation, investors can easily sell their shares if the corporate dividend policy is unacceptable. However, if a closely held corporation does not declare dividends, an investor who needs money is not able to sell her shares.

Easterbrook and Fischel identify another problem which stems from the lack of a public market: close corporation shareholders cannot rely on the market for corporate control to monitor managers' performance. In publicly held corporations, the market for corporate control constrains managers' conduct and facilitates the transfer of assets to higher valued uses. Because restrictions exist on an outsider's ability to acquire shares in a closely-held enterprise, the constraint on the conduct of management provided by the market for corporate control generally does not exist. Due to these potential problems, closely held firms "must promise to outsiders, and on average deliver, at least the competitive risk-adjusted rate of return available from other sorts of ventures." *Id.* at 232.

## B. CONTROL DEVICES RELATING TO SHAREHOLDER VOTING

The most basic control devices are those designed to assure that all or certain shareholders are represented on a corporation's board. Three basic choices are available: An arrangement that simply ensures representation on the board; one that gives some or all shareholders the ability to veto board decisions with which they disagree; or one that contains some dispute resolution device. We begin with cumulative voting, a device designed to assure board representation for minority shareholders.

### 1. CUMULATIVE VOTING

#### PROBLEM

#### PRODUCTION CORPORATION

Production Corporation has an 8 member board of directors and 1500 shares of voting stock issued and outstanding. Assume that George, a Production shareholder, wants to evaluate the possibility of i) getting himself elected to the board, or ii) winning control of a majority of the board (5 positions). At the upcoming shareholders' meeting, George expects that 900 shares will be voted.

1.   How many shares must George assemble to elect himself or a majority of the board under a straight voting system? How many shares are necessary under a cumulative voting system?

2.   Assume cumulative voting is mandated by statute and that you represent the management of Production Corporation, which wishes to frustrate cumulative voting. What actions would you recommend?

———

There are two principal methods for conducting an election of directors. In straight voting each share is entitled to one vote for each director to be elected, but a shareholder is limited in the number of votes she may cast for any given director to the number of shares she owns. This means that any shareholder or group of shareholders controlling 51% of the shares may elect all of the members of the board.

Cumulative voting, the alternative method, is designed to allow shareholder groups to elect directors in rough proportion to the shares held by each group and thus to guarantee minority representation on the board. Under cumulative voting, each share again carries a number of votes equal to the number of directors to be elected, but a shareholder may "cumulate" her votes. Cumulating simply means multiplying the number of votes a shareholder is entitled to cast by the number of directors for whom she is entitled to vote. If there is cumulative voting, the shareholder may cast them all for one candidate or allocate them in any manner among a number of candidates.

The number of shares required to elect a given number of directors under a cumulative voting regime may be calculated by the following formula:

$$x = \frac{s \times d}{D + 1} + 1$$

Where:
x   =   Number of shares required to elect directors;
s   =   Number of shares represented at the meeting;
d   =   Number of directors it is desired to elect; and
D   =   Total number of directors to be elected.

To understand this formula, it is helpful to work through a simple example. Suppose that four directors are to be elected at a meeting at which 1000 shares are represented and will vote. In order to elect one director a minority group would have to control 201 shares. With that number, the minority group would have 804 votes (201 $\times$ 4), which would all be cast for one candidate. The majority would have 799 $\times$ 4 or 3196 votes. If the majority distributed these equally among four candidates, each would receive 799 votes, and the one candidate receiving the minority's 804 votes would be guaranteed a seat. In other words, just over 20% of the shares guarantees the election of one of four directors. If only three directors were to be elected, it would require just over 25% to elect one director. What percentage is necessary to elect one member to a five member board? (Note that the reason for the "+ 1" at the end of the formula is the avoidance of the tie that would occur if, in this example, the minority controlled only 200 votes. Then it would be possible for five candidates each to receive 800 votes.) A little further consideration will easily show how the formula would work if it were desired to elect more than one director.

Statutory treatment of cumulative voting varies greatly. Some jurisdictions provide for mandatory cumulative voting by statute. Missouri provides for mandatory cumulative voting in its state constitution. Most states do not require that cumulative voting be mandatory. In "opt out" states, such as Illinois, Minnesota, Pennsylvania, and Texas, cumulative voting exists unless there is a provision in the corporation's articles to the contrary. In "opt in" states, such as Delaware (DGCL § 214) and New York (N.Y.B.C.L. § 618), cumulative voting only exists to the extent it is provided for in the corporation's articles of incorporation. *See also* RMBCA § 7.28(d).

If the planner has a choice, the issue is most difficult when there is a minority block of shares large enough to make board representation a realistic possibility. If the factions are badly split, minority representation may lessen board participation in critical decisions, leaving such decisions to management who often also will be the majority directors. Critics of cumulative voting insist that to serve its intended function the board must function as a team, and that injecting factionalism into its operations merely reduces its effectiveness. On the other hand, cumulative voting does allow a voice to stockholders with large, but not controlling interests. It also promotes the representation of divergent points of view, which will often result in superior decision-making. Finally, it may discourage self-dealing and other improper conduct by a dominant faction because of the increased flow of information to and monitoring by representatives of minority interests.

A corporation's management occasionally seeks to undermine the effectiveness of cumulative voting to prevent or inhibit the election of minority directors. The easiest method is to classify the board of directors, and stagger the election of directors so each class will be elected in different years. By staggering the elections, there will be fewer vacancies to be filled each year, thereby lowering the total number of votes for each shareholder. As the total number of votes is lowered, the majority has the advantage, as the process moves back toward straight voting. However, statutory limitations exist on how a corporation can classify its board. *Compare,* RMBCA § 8.06 and DGCL § 141(d).

Another method of diluting the effect of cumulative voting is to decrease the size of the board. By so doing, the corporation is again frustrating the intent of cumulative voting by decreasing the total number of votes a shareholder may cast and thereby increasing the percentage of stock necessary for a minority shareholder to elect one director. The courts have generally upheld this technique, even though it undermines cumulative voting. A planner may guard against the implementation of this technique by inserting provisions in the corporation's articles requiring a supermajority of votes in order to reduce the number of directors.

## 2.  OTHER DEVICES WITHIN THE CORPORATE MACHINERY

Parts I–IX of Precision Tools in Chapters 6–11 were designed to introduce you to some of the basic concepts of corporate law and corporate finance. Although each section built on previous units, each was designed to be self-contained, with the answers to the questions often not being dependent on the answers to questions in other parts of the problem. This chapter is intended to integrate the previous materials and to deal with governance arrangements that are peculiar to the closely-held corporation.

The study of such arrangements focuses on the bargaining and contracting which will permit the parties to determine an appropriate structure for their own venture. The challenge a lawyer faces is how best to take advantage of the flexibility the law now allows, to anticipate the future needs and potential problems of the parties, and to create solutions at the outset which will either reduce the likelihood of problems occurring or provide acceptable dispute resolution mechanisms should problems arise. Such planning requires the lawyer to view the transaction as a whole rather than as a series of disconnected parts. In so doing, the parties can determine better their true *interests* rather than their bargaining *positions* (see Roger Fisher & William Ury, GETTING TO YES (1981)) and thus better negotiate workable compromises. These planning skills are among the most important for a business lawyer to possess, regardless of the size of the transaction. They are particularly necessary when, as in Precision Tools, there are relatively few parties and the legal questions are comparatively simple. The emphasis in this chapter, then, is as much on planning and dispute resolution mechanisms as it is on legal doctrine.

## PROBLEM
### PRECISION TOOLS REVISITED—PART I

Review Parts I and V of Precision Tools (Chapters 6 and 9, respectively) and assume that the facts in those parts were developed in a series of meetings in your office. Assume further that during those meetings, Bernie made clear that by "having some voice" in the business, he means the ability to elect one-half of the directors. The parties have tentatively agreed on a four-member board of directors consisting of the three of them and an additional director chosen by Bernie.

1) What advice would you give to the parties as to the desirability of a four-person board?*

---

* Recall the materials in Chapter 7, Sec-     tion A, dealing with the lawyer's profession-

2) How can the capital structure be used to achieve the board representation which the parties desire? Would it matter if Bernie received 40 percent of the common stock of Precision Tools rather than any senior securities and Jessica and Michael each received 30 percent of the common stock?

3) If the parties decided not to use the capital structure as a vehicle for achieving their goal, what other alternatives do they have? Specifically:

a) What types of voting agreements might they enter into? What should be the basic provisions of each of them?

b) What enforcement mechanisms, if any, should each contain?

c) What legal restrictions affect the validity of each?

d) What are the advantages and disadvantages of each?

In answering Question 3, assume that the applicable law is:

a) non-statutory law;

b) RMBCA §§ 2.02, 7.22, 7.30, 7.31, 7.32;

c) DGCL § 218;

d) N.Y.B.C.L. §§ 609(f), (g), 620(a);

e) Calif. Corp. Code § 706.

———

One simple technique for ensuring shareholder representation on the board, which is somewhat more flexible than cumulative voting, is class voting for directors. Class voting entails dividing the voting stock into two or more classes, each of which is entitled to elect one or more directors. RMBCA § 6.01(c); DGCL § 102(a)(4). In the simple case of a corporation with three shareholders, each of whom wishes to be assured of electing one director, three classes of shares would be created (usually denominated, somewhat prosaically, classes "A", "B", and "C"). Each class would have the right to elect one director. Since it is not necessary to issue (or authorize) the same number of shares for each class, class voting can be used to guarantee board representation to a shareholder who owns too few shares to be able to elect a director through cumulative voting. The rights of the different classes may be adjusted in other ways as well. For example, each class might be required to approve all or certain actions that require shareholder approval. In fact, the number and variety of changes that can be built on this basic device are limited only by the imagination of the drafter. Classes can be created that have differing numbers of shares, different rights in the event of liquidation, or different dividend or preemptive rights.

Class voting has its pitfalls. The principal problem is who fills the vacancy in a class when the director dies and is the sole holder of the stock. There are a number of possible answers to that question, but they

al responsibility. The conflict issue has now become more pointed and troublesome.

all affect the future political balance within the company and introduce the possibility of an unwanted person being introduced into the corporate structure. The planner therefore must focus on the future implications of what appears to be a simple present situation.

## 3. DEVICES OUTSIDE THE CORPORATE MACHINERY

Shareholders typically use one of three classes of devices to limit or control the manner in which stock will be voted: (1) voting trusts, (2) irrevocable proxies, and (3) vote pooling agreements.

Shareholders create a *voting trust* by conveying legal title to their stock to a voting trustee or a group of trustees pursuant to the terms of a trust agreement. This transfer is normally registered on the corporation's stock transfer ledger, which shows the trustees as legal owners of the shares. The former shareholders—now beneficiaries of the trust— receive voting trust certificates in exchange for their shares; these evidence their equitable ownership of their stock. Voting trust certificates usually are transferable and entitle the owner to receive whatever dividends are paid on the underlying stock. They are, in effect, shares of stock shorn of their voting power and, in some jurisdictions, certain other rights normally appurtenant to the ownership of stock, such as the right to inspect the corporate books or to institute a derivative suit. See James D. Cox et. al., CORPORATIONS § 13.34 (1995). *But see*, RMBCA § 16.02 and N.Y.B.C.L. § 624(b) which give inspection rights to voting trust certificate holders. Since the terms of the trust agreement are a matter of contract, the trustees may be given full discretion to vote the shares in the trust for the election of directors and for any other matter to come before the shareholders, or may be limited to voting on only certain matters.

At an earlier stage in the development of corporation law, courts tended to view voting trusts with suspicion, in many cases holding them void as against public policy because they separated shareholders' voting power and economic ownership. State legislatures responded by passing statutes permitting voting trusts but subjecting them to certain regulations, usually a limitation on their effective life and a requirement that their terms be made a matter of public record so that other shareholders would know, or could learn, that a voting trust exists. RMBCA § 7.30. *But see* DGCL § 218 which recently was amended to eliminate the 10–year limit on the duration of a voting trust and extensions thereof. Today virtually all jurisdictions have legislation dealing with voting trusts.

Some of the judicial dislike for the voting trust has survived, however, in the doctrine that an arrangement that amounts to a voting trust in operation but does not comply with the terms of a voting trust statute is invalid. The attempted application of this doctrine is illustrated in the *Ringling Brothers* litigation summarized below and in the *Lehrman* case set out following the discussion of *Ringling*.

Many of the same concerns that led to judicial invalidation of voting trusts are equally applicable to the *irrevocable proxy*. It is quite common for a shareholder to give a proxy to vote her shares to someone else, and even to give that person entire discretion to decide how they should be voted. But the ordinary proxy, like any agency power, may be revoked at the will of the principal, and the proxy holder remains subject to the control of the principal. RESTATEMENT (SECOND) OF AGENCY (1958) § 118.

Sometimes, however, the parties want to make the grant of the proxy irrevocable, subject perhaps to some contingency or to the passage of a specified time. In such a case, the shareholder loses control of the exercise of the franchise for the period of the proxy, and it can be said that "the vote is separated from the stock," the very problem that lay at the heart of courts' objections to voting trusts. Thus, whether because they find them to violate basic principles of agency law, or to be against public policy, courts previously evidenced reluctance to enforce an irrevocable proxy.

Agency law does recognize as valid an agency power "coupled with an interest." RESTATEMENT (SECOND) OF AGENCY (1958) §§ 138–139. The modern trend is to recognize this principle in the corporate context and to uphold irrevocable proxies that are "coupled with an interest." The difficulty is to determine what sort of "interest" will support an irrevocable proxy. The more conservative view is that the interest must be in (or pertain to) the stock itself, such as that created by a pledge of the equitable interest by one who has contracted or who has an option to purchase the shares. *In re Chilson*, 19 Del.Ch. 398, 168 A. 82 (1933). Other courts have rejected a formalistic application of agency principles and approached the problem with a greater appreciation of the practical realities of arranging the affairs of a close corporation. Irrevocable proxies have been upheld, for example, where the proxy has been given as an inducement to the holder to furnish money to the corporation. *Hey v. Dolphin*, 92 Hun. 230, 36 N.Y.S. 627 (1895); *Chapman v. Bates*, 61 N.J.Eq. 658, 47 A. 638 (1900).

As the problem presents itself most often to the close corporation planner, the putative proxy holder seldom has a direct interest in the stock. Commonly, two or more shareholders seek to enter into a contractual arrangement involving the grant of irrevocable proxies, the consideration for which is merely the mutual promises of the parties to the agreement. In this situation it is hard to find an "interest" sufficient to support the proxy. Faced with this problem some courts have found that where the proxy holder was induced to purchase stock in reliance on the agreement, her interest in the corporation as shareholder is enough. A few other courts have been willing to go even farther than this already strained interpretation and, though nominally adhering to the doctrine, have broadened it "to such an extent that it is hardly recognizable." F. Hodge O'Neal & Robert B. Thompson, O'NEAL'S CLOSE CORPORATIONS. § 5.13 (3rd ed. 1986). Although not always admitting it, these courts have enforced irrevocable proxies supported by only the mutual promises contained in a shareholders' agreement simply because the business realities of the close corporation seemed to demand it. As one court put it, "The power to vote the stock was necessary in order to make * * * control of the corporation secure." *State ex rel. Everett Trust & Savings Bank v. Pacific Waxed Paper Co.*, 22 Wash.2d 844, 852, 157 P.2d 707, 711 (1945).

Recognizing that the artificial requirement that a proxy must be coupled with an interest in order to be irrevocable makes little sense in the close corporation context, some state legislatures have effectively eliminated it by statute. *See, e.g.* N.Y.B.C.L. §§ 609(f), (g), 620(a). Absent such a statute or a clear holding by the state courts upholding irrevocable proxies in shareholder agreements, the planner is probably well-advised not to rely too heavily on an irrevocable proxy, simpliciter. See William H. Painter, PAINTER ON CLOSE CORPORATIONS § 3.3.7 (3d ed. 1991); L. Proctor Thomas, Comment, *Irrevocable Proxies*, 43 TEX.L.REV. 733 (1965).

The third technique often found in close corporation control arrangements is the so-called *vote pooling agreement*. As is the case with voting trusts and irrevocable proxies, the basic purpose of such an agreement is to bind some (or occasionally all) of the shareholders to vote together—either in a particular way or pursuant to some specified procedure—on designated questions or on all questions that come before the shareholders. It is generally accepted that such agreements are valid. RMBCA § 7.32; N.Y.B.C.L. § 620(a). The difficulty they pose is the manner in which they are to be enforced. The Official Comment to RMBCA § 7.31 states:

> Section 7.31(b) provides that voting agreements may be specifically enforceable. A voting agreement may provide its own enforcement mechanism, as by the appointment of a proxy to vote all shares subject to the agreement; the appointment may be made irrevocable under section 7.22. If no enforcement mechanism is provided, a court may order specific enforcement of the agreement and order the votes cast as the agreement contemplates. This section recognizes that damages are not likely to be an appropriate remedy for breach of a voting agreement, and also avoids the result reached in *Ringling Bros.-Barnum & Bailey Combined Shows v. Ringling*, 29 Del.Ch. 610, 53 A.2d 441 (1947) * * *.

### Note: Ringling Brothers Litigation

*Ringling Bros.–Barnum & Bailey Combined Shows, Inc. v. Ringling*, 29 Del.Ch. 610, 53 A.2d 441 (1947), involved a corporation that had seven directors and 1000 shares of common stock issued and outstanding. Edith Ringling and Aubrey Haley each owned 315 shares and John Ringling North owned 370. The corporation had cumulative voting. If all shares were represented at a meeting, 126 were needed to elect one director, 251 to elect two directors, and 376 to elect three directors. Acting alone, Ringling, Haley, and North each could be sure of electing two directors. The seventh director would be determined by whether

Ringling and Haley pooled their votes. If they did, they could select the seventh director. If they acted alone, North could elect that director.

Ringling and Haley, who were sisters, executed a ten year "Memorandum of Agreement" in 1941. The Agreement was intended to allow them to use their majority shareholdings, and the corporation's cumulative voting structure, to control the corporation. After providing that if either party wished to sell any shares in the corporation she would offer them for sale to the other party on the same terms as those at which she proposed to sell to the outsider, the Agreement provided:

> 2. In exercising any voting rights to which either party may be entitled by virtue of ownership of stock or voting trust certificates held by them in either of said corporations each party will consult and confer with the other and the parties will act jointly in exercising such voting rights in accordance with such agreement as they may reach with respect to any matter calling for the exercise of such voting rights.

> 3. In the event the parties fail to agree with respect to any matter covered by paragraph 2 above, the question in disagreement shall be submitted for arbitration to Karl D. Loos, of Washington, D.C., as arbitrator and his decision thereon shall be binding upon the parties thereto. Such arbitration shall be exercised to the end of assuring for the respective corporations good management and such participation therein by the members of the Ringling family as the experience, capacity and ability of each may warrant. The parties may at any time by written agreement designate any other individual to act as arbitrator in lieu of said Loos.

At the annual shareholders' meeting in 1946, Haley was ill and her husband refused to coordinate his votes with Ringling. Loos, the arbitrator, determined that Ringling and Haley should vote their stock so as to elect five directors. Mr. Haley refused to abide by Loos's decision and cast all his wife's votes for his wife and himself. As a consequence, a third candidate favored by North was elected to the board. Ringling then brought suit to enforce the voting agreement. Haley argued that the arbitration procedure operated as a voting trust, separated voting from ownership, and was void because it did not comply with Delaware's voting trust provisions.

The Court of Chancery, 29 Del.Ch. 318, 49 A.2d 603 (1946) noted: "The stockholders under the present Agreement vote their own stock at all times which is the antithesis of a voting trust because the latter has for its chief characteristic the severance of the voting rights from the other attributes of ownership." 29 Del.Ch. at 329, 49 A.2d at 608. It held the agreement to be a valid shareholder voting agreement, not an illegal voting trust.

Turning to how the agreement should be enforced, the court concluded that "the stock held under the Agreement should have been voted pursuant to the direction of the arbitrator Loos to the parties or their representatives. When a party or her representative refuses to comply with the direction of the arbitrator, while he is properly acting under its provisions (as did Aubrey B. Haley's proxy here), then I believe the Agreement constitutes the willing party to the Agreement an implied agent possessing the irrevocable proxy of the recalcitrant party for the purpose of casting the particular vote. Here an implied agency based on an irrevocable proxy is fully justified to implement the Agreement without doing violence to its terms. Moreover, the provisions of the Agreement make it clear that the proxy may be treated as one coupled with an interest so as to render it irrevocable under the circumstances." 49 A.2d at 611.

On appeal, the Delaware Supreme Court upheld the voting agreement but rejected the Court of Chancery's decision as to how the agreement should be enforced. *Ringling Bros.-Barnum & Bailey Combined Shows, Inc. v. Ringling*, 29 Del.Ch. 610, 53 A.2d 441 (1947). The appellate court sidestepped the noncomplying shareholder's argument that the arbitration procedure operated as a voting trust by holding that the agreement had not transferred any voting rights to the arbitrator, because he lacked formal power to vote the stock.

> Should the agreement be interpreted as attempting to empower the arbitrator to carry his directions into effect? Certainly there is no express delegation or grant of power to do so, either by authorizing him to vote the shares or to compel either party to vote them in accordance with his directions. The agreement expresses no other function of the arbitrator than that of deciding questions in disagreement which prevent the effectuation of the purpose "to act jointly." The power to enforce a decision does not seem a necessary or usual incident of such a function. Mr. Loos is not a party to the agreement. It does not contemplate the transfer of any shares or interest in shares to him, or that he should undertake any duties which the parties might compel him to perform. They provided that they might designate any other individual to act instead of Mr. Loos. The agreement does not attempt to make the arbitrator a trustee of an express trust. What the arbitrator is to do is for the benefit of the parties, not for his own benefit. Whether the parties accept or reject his decision is no concern of his, so far as the agreement or the surrounding circumstances reveal. We think the parties sought to bind each other, but to be bound only to each other, and not to empower the arbitrator to enforce decisions he might make.

> From this conclusion, it follows necessarily that no decision of the arbitrator could ever be enforced if both parties to the agreement were unwilling that it be enforced, for the obvious reason that there would be no one to enforce it. Under the agreement, something more is required after the arbitrator has given his decision in order that it should become compulsory: at least one of the parties must determine that such decision shall be carried into effect. Thus, any "control" of the voting of the shares, which is reposed in the arbitrator, is substantially limited in action under the agreement in that it is subject to the overriding power of the parties themselves.

53 A.2d at 445.

As concerned the appropriate remedy, the court held that since Haley had voted her stock in breach of the agreement, her votes should not be counted. The only effective votes were those cast by Ringling and North.

### Question

What would be the result in *Ringling* under RMBCA § 7.31(b)?

———

*State ex rel. Babione v. Martin*, 97 Ohio App.3d 539, 647 N.E.2d 169 (1994), held that a shareholder agreement did not create a valid voting trust because it failed to comply with statutory requirements relating to voting trusts. Similarly, the court held the shareholders' agreement to "stick together until we get control of the company" was too ambiguous to create a common law vote-pooling agreement.

## LEHRMAN v. COHEN

43 Del.Ch. 222, 222 A.2d 800 (1966).

HERRMANN, JUSTICE.

The primary problem presented on this appeal involves the applicability of the Delaware Voting Trust Statute. Other questions involve the legality of stock having voting power but no dividend or liquidation rights except repayment of par value, and an alleged unlawful delegation of directorial duties and powers.

[Giant Food, Inc., a Delaware corporation that runs a chain of supermarkets, was organized in 1935 by N.M. Cohen and Samuel Lehrman. Initially its voting stock consisted of Class AC shares, all of which were owned by members of the Cohen family, and Class AL shares, all of which were owned by members of the Lehrman family. Each class was entitled to elect two members of a four member board. A settlement of a family dispute that arose after Samuel Lehrman's death in 1949 left his son, Jacob, owning all of the AL shares. The number of AL shares owned by Jacob Lehrman equalled the number of AC shares held by the Cohen family. In order to prevent a deadlock, one share of a third class of stock, AD, was created, which was entitled to elect a fifth director. The AD stock had no right to dividends or distributions in liquidation beyond its $10 value. The one AD share was immediately issued to Joseph B. Danzansky, who had served as the company's counsel since 1944. Danzansky voted to elect himself the fifth director, and remained in that post until the events that gave rise to the suit.]

From the outset and until October 1, 1964, the defendant N.M. Cohen was president of the Company. On that date, a resolution was adopted at the Company's annual stockholders' meeting to give Danzansky a fifteen year executive employment contract at an annual salary of $67,600, and options for 25,000 shares of the non-voting common stock of the Company. The AC and AD stock were voted in favor and the AL stock was voted against the resolution. At a directors meeting held the same day, Danzansky was elected president of the Company by a 3–2 vote, the two AL directors voting in opposition. On December 11, 1964, Danzansky resigned as director and voted his share of AD stock to elect as the fifth director, Millard F. West, Jr., a former AL director and investment banker whose firm was one of the underwriters of the public issue of the Company's stock. The newly constituted board ratified the election of Danzansky as president; and, on January 27, 1965, after the commencement of this action and after a review and report by a committee consisting of the new AD director and one AL director, Danzansky's employment contract was approved and adopted with certain modifications.

The plaintiff brought this action on December 11, 1964, basing it upon two claims: The First Claim charges that the creation, issuance, and voting of the one share of Class AD stock resulted in an arrangement illegal under the law of this State for the reasons hereinafter set forth. The Second Claim, addressed to the events of October 1, 1964, charges that the election of Danzansky as president of the Company and his employment contract violated the terms of the [1949] deadlock-breaking arrangement, as made between the holders of the AC and AL stock, and constituted breaches of contract and fiduciary duty. The plaintiff and the defendants filed cross-motions for summary judgment as to the First Claim. The Court of Chancery, after considering the contentions now before us and discussed *infra,* granted summary judgment in favor of the defendants and denied the plaintiff's motion for summary judgment. The plaintiff appeals.

I.

The plaintiff's primary contention is that the Class AD stock arrangement is, in substance and effect, a voting trust; that, as such, it is illegal because not limited to a ten year period as required by the Voting Trust Statute. The defendants deny that the AD stock arrangement constitutes a disguised voting trust; but they concede that if it is, the arrangement is illegal for violation of the Statute. Thus, issue is clearly joined on the point.

The criteria of a voting trust under our decisions have been summarized by this Court in *Abercrombie v. Davies,* 36 Del.Ch. 371, 130 A.2d 338 (1957). The tests there set forth, accepted by both sides of this cause as being applicable, are as follows: (1) the voting rights of the stock are separated from the other attributes of ownership; (2) the voting rights granted are intended to be irrevocable for a definite period of time; and (3) the principal purpose of the grant of voting rights is to acquire voting control of the corporation.

Adopting and applying these tests, the plaintiff says, as to the first element, that the AD arrangement provides for a divorcement of voting rights from beneficial ownership of the AC and AL stock; that the creation and issuance of the share of AD stock is tantamount to a pooling by the AC and AL stockholders of a portion of their voting stock and giving it to a trustee, in the person of the AD stockholder, to vote for the election of the fifth director; that after the creation of the AD stock, the AC and AL stockholders each hold but 40% of the voting power, and the AD stockholder holds the controlling balance of 20%; that the AD stock has no property rights except the right to a return of the $10. paid as the par value; and that, therefore, there has been a transfer of the voting rights devoid of any participating property rights. So runs the argument of the plaintiff in support of his contention that the first of the *Abercrombie* criteria for a voting trust is met.

The contention is unacceptable. The AD arrangement did not separate the voting rights of the AC or the AL stock from the other attributes of ownership of those classes of stock. Each AC and AL stockholder retains complete control over the voting of his stock; each can vote his stock directly; no AL or AC stockholder is divested of his right to vote his stock as he sees fit; no AL or AC stock can be voted against the shareholder's wishes; and the AL and AC stock continue to elect two directors each.

The AD stock arrangement, as we view it, became a part of the capitalization of the Company. The fact that there is but a single share, or that the par value is nominal, is of no legal significance; the one share and the $10. par value might have been multiplied many times over, with the same consequence. It is true that the creation of the separate class of AD stock may have diluted the voting *power* which had previously existed in the AC and AL stock—the usual consequence when additional voting stock is created—but the creation of the new class did not divest and separate the voting *rights* which remain vested in each AC and AL shareholder, together with the other attributes of the ownership of that stock. The fallacy of the plaintiff's position lies in his premise that since the voting power of the AC and AL stock was reduced by the creation of the AD stock, the percentage of reduction became the *res* of a voting trust. In any recapitalization involving the creation of additional voting stock, the voting power of the previously existing stock is diminished; but a voting trust is not necessarily the result.

Since the holders of the Class AC and Class AL stock of the Company did not separate the voting rights from the other attributes of ownership of those classes when they created the Class AD stock, the first *Abercrombie* test of a voting trust is not met.

This conclusion disposes of the second and third *Abercrombie* tests, i.e., that the voting rights granted are irrevocable for a definite period of time, and that the principal object of the grant of voting rights is voting control of the corporation. Having held that the AC and AL stockholders have not divested themselves of their voting rights, although they may have diluted their voting powers, we do not reach the remaining *Abercrombie* tests, both of which assume the divestiture of voting rights.

In the final analysis, the essence of the question raised by the plaintiff in this connection is this: Is the substance and purpose of the

AD stock arrangement sufficiently close to the substance and purpose of § 218 to warrant its being subjected to the restrictions and conditions imposed by that Statute? The answer is negative not only for the reasons above stated, but also because § 218 regulates trusts and pooling agreements amounting to trusts, not other and different types of arrangements and undertakings possible among stockholders. The AD stock arrangement is neither a trust nor a pooling agreement.

We hold, therefore, that the Class AD stock arrangement is not controlled by the Voting Trust Statute.

## II.

The plaintiff's second point is that even if the Class AD stock arrangement is not a voting trust in substance and effect, the AD stock is illegal, nevertheless, because the creation of a class of stock having voting rights only, and lacking any substantial participating proprietary interest in the corporation, violates the public policy of this State as declared in § 218.

The fallacy of this argument is twofold: First, it is more accurate to say that what the law has disfavored, and what the public policy underlying the Voting Trust Statute means to control, is the separation of the vote from the stock—not from the stock ownership. 5 FLETCHER CYCLOPEDIA CORPORATIONS, § 2080, pp. 363–369; compare *Abercrombie v. Davies*, supra. Clearly, the AD stock arrangement is not violative of that public policy. Secondly, there is nothing in § 218, either expressed or implied, which requires that all stock of a Delaware corporation must have both voting rights and proprietary interests. Indeed, public policy to the contrary seems clearly expressed by 8 Del.C. § 151(a) which authorizes, in very broad terms, such voting powers and participating rights as may be stated in the certificate of incorporation. Non-voting stock is specifically authorized by § 151(a); and in the light thereof, consistency does not permit the conclusion, urged by the plaintiff, that the present public policy of this State condemns the separation of voting rights from beneficial stock ownership.

We conclude that the plaintiff's contention in this regard cannot withstand the force and effect of § 151(a). In our view, that Statute permits the creation of stock having voting rights only, as well as stock having property rights only. The voting powers and the participating rights of the Class AD stock being specified in the Company's certificate of incorporation, we are of the opinion that the Class AD stock is legal by virtue of § 151(a).

* * *

We are told that if the AD stock arrangement is allowed thus to stand, our Voting Trust Statute will become a "dead letter" because it will be possible to evade and circumvent its purpose simply by issuing a class of non-participating voting stock, as was done here. We have three negative reactions to this argument:

First, it presupposes a divestiture of the voting rights of the AC and AL stock—an untenable supposition as has been stated. Secondly, it fails to take into account the main purpose of a Voting Trust Statute: to avoid secret, uncontrolled combinations of stockholders formed to acquire voting control of the corporation to the possible detriment of non-participating shareholders. It may not be said that the AD stock arrangement contravenes that purpose. Finally on this point, if we misconceive the legislative intent, and if the AD stock arrangement in this case reveals a loophole in § 218 which should be plugged, it is for the General Assembly to accomplish—not for us to attempt by interstitial judicial legislation.

## III.

The plaintiff advances yet another reason for invalidating the AD stock. The essence of this argument is that the only function of that class of stock is to break directorial deadlocks; that the issuance of the AD stock is merely a technical device to permit that result; that, as such, it is illegal because it permits the AC and AL directors of the Company to delegate their statutory duties to the AD director as an arbitrator.

As to the means adopted for the accomplishment of that purpose, we find the AD stock arrangement valid by virtue of § 141(a) of the Delaware Corporation Law which provides:

> The business of every corporation organized under the provisions of this chapter shall be managed by a board of directors, except as hereinafter or in its certificate of incorporation otherwise provided.

The AD stock arrangement was created by the unanimous action of the stockholders of the Company by amendment to the certificate of incorporation. The stockholders thereby provided how the business of the corporation is to be managed, as is their privilege and right under § 141(a). It was this stockholder action which delegated to the AD director whatever powers and duties he possesses; they were not delegated to him by his fellow directors, either out of their own powers and duties, or otherwise.

It is settled, of course, as a general principle, that directors may not delegate their duty to manage the corporate enterprise. But there is no conflict with that principle where, as here, the delegation of duty, if any, is made not by the directors but by stockholder action under § 141(a), via the certificate of incorporation.

\* \* \*

Finding no error in the judgment below, it is affirmed.

---

*Oceanic Exploration Co. v. Grynberg*, 428 A.2d 1 (Del.1981), upheld a contract labelled a "voting trust agreement" that was extended under circumstances that did not comply with DGCL § 218. The court recognized that the "agreement" did not fit into the situation contemplated by the language of the statute. Even though the agreement gave voting rights to a trustee, the overall agreement was so multifaceted and extensive that the court held it to be antithetical to the type of agreement to which the voting trust statute was directed and beyond the scope of the statute. The court found that the main purpose of § 218 was " 'to avoid secret, uncontrolled combinations formed to acquire control of the corporation to the possible detriment of non-participating shareholders.' "The contract in question was so far divorced from that purpose that it made the contemplated regulation unnecessary. Finally, the "agreement" violated no current public policy. The court stated that the trend is "not to extend the voting trust restrictions beyond the class of trust being regulated and beyond the reasons for statutory regulation."

# C.  RESTRICTIONS ON THE DISCRETION OF THE BOARD

## PROBLEM
## PRECISION TOOLS REVISITED—PART II

The parties have agreed that Michael will be the president and chief executive officer of the new company; Jessica will be vice-president and chief financial officer; and Bernie will be secretary. Michael will have control over the operational part of the business and Jessica will run its financial end. Because both Michael and Jessica will derive most of their income from the business, each will be paid a reasonable salary. At this time, Bernie will not be paid a salary for his more limited participation.

Jessica and Michael would like to guarantee their officerships; without such a guarantee, they are concerned that future events may permit the other directors to remove them. They would also like to ensure the amount of compensation they are to draw from the corporation for the first few years. Bernie understands their concerns and is willing to enter into some arrangement that would fulfill these objectives, provided that, since he will not draw money in the form of a salary, he has some assurance that their salaries will not be increased above the agreed-upon amount, and that he will receive dividends should the corporation show a profit. The three have asked about the validity of an agreement by which they would bind themselves "to use their best efforts" to elect each other to their respective officerships, to have Michael and Jessica each paid salaries of $75,000 per year, and to have the corporation pay a dividend annually equal to one-third of its net profits. They also want to know whether it is possible to fix the amount of money which can be spent on research and development in the next few years.

1.  Advise Michael and Jessica how to implement their understanding. In this connection, consider:

(a) Whether the agreement can be between only Michael and Jessica or whether it must be unanimous.

(b) Whether the provisions of the agreement can or must be put in the corporation's articles of incorporation or by-laws.

In each case, assume that the applicable law is:

(a) non-statutory law;

(b) DGCL §§ 350, 351 and 354.

(c) RMBCA §§ 2.02 and 7.32;

(d) N.Y.B.C.L. §§ 620 and 715(b);

2. What are the advantages and disadvantages of requiring a high vote and/or high quorum (e.g., 80 percent) in order to amend the articles of incorporation and/or the by-laws with respect to the issues of concern to the parties? Which specific issues? If such requirements are desirable, should they relate to actions by the shareholders, the directors, or both?

In each case, assume that the applicable law is:

(a) non-statutory law;

(b) RMBCA §§ 2.02, 7.25, 7.27, 7.32, 8.24 and 10.21;

(c) N.Y.B.C.L. §§ 616 and 709

You may wish to reconsider the Chesapeake Marine Problem, Chapter 3.

3. In addition to using an agreement or provisions in the articles of incorporation should Michael and Jessica execute employment contracts with the corporation? What benefits are there for them and the corporation? Consider RMBCA §§ 8.43 and 8.44.

## 1. RESTRICTIONS IN SHAREHOLDER VOTING AGREEMENTS

*Haenel v. Epstein*, N.Y.L.J., June 10, 1980 (Sup.Ct.) at 13 summarized as follows New York common law governing shareholder voting agreements that purport to restrict the discretion of the board of directors:

> The New York Court of Appeals, prior to the enactment of Business Corporation Law section 620(a) and 620(b) set forth, in four cases, dubbed "the big four" the law with regard to shareholder agreements.

> *Manson v. Curtis* (223 N.Y. 313, 119 N.E. 559 [1918] ) involved an agreement between the holders of a majority, but not all, of the shares of a corporation. The agreement provided that each party was to name three directors, with a seventh director to be elected as mutually agreed upon. One of the parties, the plaintiff, was to be continued in his position of General Manager for a year and, as such, was to manage the business of the corporation and shape its policy. The court, finding, in effect, the provision concerning election of directors, to be, standing alone, innocent and legal, determined that the agreement as a whole was invalid as its fundamental and dominant purpose was to vest management authority solely in

plaintiff. So construed, the latter provisions were found to deprive the directors of their statutory duty to manage the corporation. The agreement was found totally illegal and not capable of "severability."

Stated simply, the Court of Appeals in *Manson* decided that while it was not illegal for two or more stockholders owning the majority of stock to agree upon the directors whom they would elect, the powers delegated to the non-directors were too broad. (See 50 COLUMBIA LAW REVIEW No. 1, January, 1950, "*The Corporate Director: Can his hands be tied in advance,*" Edmund T. Delaney).

*Manson* recited the law as to the interaction of majority stockholders; dominant managers; and the statutory authority of a board of directors. Employing the often used terminology "a sterilized board of directors," the case set forth the law as follows:

> The affairs of every corporation shall be managed by its board of directors * * *.

> The corporation is the owner of the property but the directors in the performance of their duty possess it, and act in every way as if they owned it.

> Directors are the exclusive executive representatives of the corporation and are charged with the administration of its internal affairs and the management and use of its assets * * *. Clearly the law does not permit the stockholders to create a sterilized board of directors * * *. We conclude that the agreement here is illegal and void and its violation is not a basis for a cause of action. (223 N.Y. at pp. 319–324) (Compare Business Corporation Law section 701).

Manson, significant not only for its holding, but for its dictum on the permissible scope of shareholder agreements, stated in that regard as follows:

> An ordinary agreement, among a minority in number, but a majority in shares, for the purpose of obtaining control of the corporation by the election of particular persons as directors is not illegal. Shareholders have the right to combine their interests and voting powers to secure such control of the corporation and the adoption of an adhesion by it to a specific policy and course of business. Agreements upon a sufficient consideration between them, of such intendment and effect, are valid and binding, if they do not contravene any express charter or statutory provision or contemplate any fraud, oppression or wrong against other stockholders or other illegal object.

This concept, expressed in dictum, later formed the basis of the legislature's enactment of Business Corporation Law 620(a).

Finally, the court in *Manson* indicated that if all stockholders agreed, they "may do as they choose with the corporate concerns and assets, provided the interests of creditors are not affected, because they are the complete owners of the corporation."

* * *

In *McQuade v. Stoneham* (263 N.Y. 323, 189 N.E. 234 [1934] ), the agreement was not between all shareholders, but between the holder of the majority of the shares and two other shareholders. By the agreement's terms, the parties were to use their best efforts to keep one another in office as directors and officers; and salaries, amount of capital, number of shares, by-laws and policy were not to be changed except by unanimous consent. Holding the agreement invalid, the court stated:

> Stockholders may, of course, combine to elect directors. That rule is well settled. As Holmes, Ch.J., pointedly said (*Brightman v. Bates*, 175 Mass. 105, 111, 55 N.E. 809): "If stockholders want to make their power felt, they must unite. There is no reason why a majority should not agree to keep together." The power to unite is, however, limited to the election of directors and is not extended to contracts whereby limitations are placed on the power of directors to manage the business of the corporation by the selection of agents at defined salaries.

> The agreement restricted the powers of the board of directors. It did not condition such intrusion by use of such terms as "subject to the discretion of the Board of Directors" or "so long as they remain faithful, efficient and competent." As such, there was an impermissible usurpation of function.

*Clark v. Dodge* (269 N.Y. 410, 199 N.E. 641 [1936] ) followed. It represented an apparent change in the thinking of the court. Here, the agreement was signed by all shareholders. Dodge was to vote for Clark as director and General Manager so long as Clark proved faithful, efficient and competent. The court sustained a cause of action for specific enforcement of the agreement. In distinguishing *McQuade*, the court held that here the impairment of the directors' powers was slight. The court held as follows:

> There was no attempt to sterilize the board of directors, as in the *Manson* and *McQuade* cases. The only restrictions on Dodge were (a) that as a stockholder he should vote for Clark as a director—a perfectly legal contract; (b) that as a director he should continue Clark as general manager, so long as he proved faithful, efficient and competent—an agreement which could harm nobody; (c) that Clark should always receive as salary or dividends one-fourth of the "net income." For the purposes of this motion, it is only just to construe that phrase as meaning whatever was left for distribution after the directors had in good faith set aside whatever they deemed wise; (d) that no salaries to other officers should be

paid, unreasonable in amount or incommensurate with services rendered—a beneficial and not a harmful agreement.

The court's thinking in *Clark* was influenced by the fact that all stockholders signed the agreement. This is evidenced as follows:

> As the parties to the action are the complete owners of the corporation, there is no reason why the exercise of the power and discretion of the directors cannot be controlled by valid agreement between themselves, provided that the interest of creditors is not affected (269 N.Y. at p. 410).

> Thus, following *Clark*, the state of the law was and is that all stockholders can agree to infringe "slightly" upon the statutory authority of the board of directors. So, too, it was and still is the law that a majority, but less than all the stockholders, can agree to vote for certain persons as directors (see also "*Shareholder Agreements and the Statutory Norm*," 43 CORNELL L.Q. 68, 72–73 [1957] ) * * *.

> *Long Park, Inc. v. Trenton–New Brunswick Theatres Co.* (297 N.Y. 174, 77 N.E.2d 633 [1948] ) is the fourth in the line of the "big four." As in Clark, the agreement involved all shareholders. By its terms, one of the shareholders was to be "manager," and was to be given full authority to supervise the operation of the corporation. The court held the agreement sterilized the board of directors, was a complete surrender of the directors' powers, and, therefore, was invalid as a violation of the statute giving management powers to the directors. Apparently, the court determined that the agreement had exceeded the permissible limits of infringement construed in Clark.

## TRIGGS v. TRIGGS

46 N.Y.2d 305, 413 N.Y.S.2d 325, 385 N.E.2d 1254 (1978).

[The following statement of facts is taken from the dissenting opinion of GABRIELLI, J.]

The bone of contention in this case is control of Triggs Color Printing Corporation, a small firm founded by decedent in 1925. The firm appears to have prospered for some years and, with the passage of time, decedent's three sons became involved in the business to varying degrees. As of 1963, the corporation had issued some 254 shares of voting stock. Of these, decedent personally owned 149 shares and the remainder were distributed equally between his three sons, with each son owning 35 shares. At that time, decedent apparently selected his son Ransford, the plaintiff in this action, as the one he deemed best suited to control the business following decedent's death. To that end, decedent transferred 36 of his shares to plaintiff. Thus, out of the 254 voting shares, decedent owned 113 shares, plaintiff owned 71 shares, and each of the other two sons owned 35 shares.

Shortly thereafter, plaintiff and decedent entered into the written agreement at issue in this case. The two agreed to vote their shares together so as not only to elect both of them as directors, but also to elect decedent chairman of the board at a guaranteed annual salary, and to appoint plaintiff president of the corporation at a guaranteed annual salary. Additionally, the agreement contained the following provision: "It is the present contemplation of Frederick Triggs, Sr. to execute an agreement with the Corporation for the Corporation to repurchase his stock in the event of his death. In the event for any reason that such agreement has not been executed between the said Frederick Triggs, Sr. and the Corporation, then, in that event, the remaining Stockholder, to wit: Ransford D. Triggs, shall have the right and option to purchase the said stock of Frederick Triggs, Sr. for a period of sixty (60) days following the death of Frederick Triggs, Sr."

A few months later, decedent did enter into a repurchase agreement with the corporation. One year later, in 1964, the repurchase agreement with the corporation was canceled by consent of both decedent and the corporation. During the next few years, plaintiff gradually assumed an ever greater role in corporate affairs, and decedent's influence waned. Eventually the two had a falling out, and decedent appears to have begun to regret his choice of plaintiff as his successor. The corporation experienced some financial difficulties under plaintiff's management, and the salary paid to decedent was decreased, at first with his consent and later over his objections. Finally, in February, 1970, decedent executed a codicil to his will by which he bequeathed his 113 shares of voting stock to his other two sons, and declared the 1963 agreement with plaintiff to be null and void. In April, 1970, decedent died.

Following decedent's death, plaintiff sought to exercise the option to purchase the 113 shares from the estate, but the estate refused to transfer the stock. Some four years later, in September, 1974, plaintiff commenced this action seeking to compel the estate to honor the option. * * * Following service of an answer, but some time prior to trial, defendant moved to dismiss the complaint for failure to state a cause of action, alleging for the first time that the agreement was illegal.

OPINION OF THE COURT

JONES, JUDGE.

* * *

After a trial without a jury the court granted respondent specific performance of the stock purchase option. A majority at the Appellate Division agreed, and we now affirm. The pertinent facts are recited in the dissenting opinion.

* * *

Appellant contends that because the March 19, 1963 agreement was not executed or approved by all of the corporate shareholders, its provisions requiring the election of respondent and his father as officers and fixing their compensation constituted an impermissible restriction of the rights and obligations of the board of directors to manage the business of the corporation under the doctrine of *Manson v. Curtis*, 223 N.Y. 313, 119 N.E. 559 and related cases (see 3 White, NEW YORK CORPORATIONS [13th ed.], par. 620.03, subd. [2] ). No argument is made that the stock purchase option, standing alone would be invalid; the assertion is that the agreement must be read as a whole and that it must be invalidated in its entirety. The critical issue is whether, because of the initial inclusion of provisions which could have been said to fetter the authority of the board to select corporate officers and to fix their compensation, the stock purchase provision is now unenforceable.

The uncontroverted evidence is that in the years following the signing of the agreement, the assertedly illegal provisions of the agreement were ignored; no attempt was made to observe or enforce them and the management of corporate affairs was in no way restricted in consequence of the 1963 agreement. The evil to which the cited rule of law is addressed was never sought to be achieved nor was it realized. Although Triggs, Sr., and Ransford continued to serve as directors, the record discloses there were also three or four other, independent directors. That Triggs, Sr., continued to be elected chairman of the board (he was also elected corporate treasurer) and Ransford, corporate president and that for several years their salaries were fixed by the board at the figures stated in the March 19, 1963 agreement was in consequence of action freely taken by the entire board of directors and cannot be attributed to the sanction of the March 19, 1963 agreement of which the other directors, constituting a majority of the board, were wholly unaware. Indeed Triggs, Sr., took no exception when, on May 11, 1965, the board reduced his salary from $20,000 (the agreement figure) to $10,800, and when the board later entirely eliminated his salary his complaint in April of 1969 was predicated on the departure from the board's action of May 11, 1965 rather than on any asserted violation of the provisions of the March 19, 1963 agreement.

The legal issue here, too, depends on what is now an affirmed factual determination. The claim of illegality, raised for the first time some 13 years after the agreement had been signed, must fail because, as the trial court concluded, the March 19, 1963 agreement "did not in any way sufficiently stultify the Board of Directors in the operations of this business" within the doctrine on which appellant would rely.

Analytically we are presented with an agreement which in a single document deals with two different sets of obligations. On the one hand, the agreement contains the stock purchase option exercisable on the death of the father as to which, standing alone, there is no claim of illegality. On the other, there are the provisions with respect to the election of corporate officers and the fixation of their salaries, which are of questionable legality. Any illegality exists, however, only to the extent that the agreement operated to restrict the freedom of the board of directors to manage corporate affairs. * * * The fact is that the courts below have enforced only the stock option provisions of the March 19, 1963 agreement.

\* \* \*

Accordingly, the order of the Appellate Division should be affirmed, with costs.

GABRIELLI, JUDGE (dissenting).

I respectfully dissent. Defendant executor appeals from an order of the Appellate Division which affirmed a judgment of Supreme Court, following a nonjury trial, which granted plaintiff specific performance of an option to purchase certain stock from the estate of his deceased father. The order appealed from should be reversed since the underlying agreement is unenforceable in that it improperly sought to limit the powers of the board of directors to manage the corporation. Moreover, even were the agreement itself valid, the option was terminated in accord with its own provisions some time prior to decedent's death.

\* \* \*

It has long been the law in this State that a corporation must be managed by the board of directors (Business Corporation Law, § 701) who serve as trustees for the benefit of the corporation and all its shareholders. To prevent control of the corporation from being diverted into the hands of individuals or groups who in some cases might not be subject to quite the same fiduciary obligations as are imposed upon directors as a matter of course, the courts have always looked unfavorably towards attempts to circumvent the discretionary authority given the board of directors by law. Such matters normally arise in the context of an agreement between shareholders to utilize their shares so as to force the board of directors to take certain actions. Unless in accord with some statutorily approved mechanism for shifting power from the board of directors to other parties (e.g., Business Corporation Law, § 620, subd. [b]), such agreements have been found valid only where the proponent of the agreement can prove that the violation of the statutory mandate is minimal and, more importantly that there is no danger of harm either to the general public or to other shareholders (see *Clark v. Dodge*, 269 N.Y. 410, 199 N.E. 641).

It is, of course, proper for shareholders to combine in order to elect directors whom they believe will manage the corporation in accord with what those shareholders perceive to be the best interests of the corporation. Thus, an agreement between two shareholders to vote for a particular director or directors is not illegal and may be enforceable in an appropriate case (Business Corporation Law, § 620, subd. [a]). If some shareholders seek to go beyond this, however, if they agree to vote their shares so as to impose their decisions upon the board of directors, such an agreement will normally be unenforceable. The agreement sought to be enforced in this case is just such an agreement.

In essence, the agreement between decedent and plaintiff consisted of three fundamental provisions: first, decedent promised to vote his shares so as to ensure the election of plaintiff as a director and his appointment as president for a 10–year period at a given salary; second, plaintiff promised to vote his shares so as to ensure the continuation of decedent as chairman of the board at a given salary for at least 10 years; and, third, decedent gave plaintiff a conditional option to purchase decedent's voting shares after his death. It is beyond dispute that the promises to secure the appointment of each party at a specific position other than director at a guaranteed annual salary are illegal. Plaintiff contends that the agreement is nonetheless enforceable by analogy to our decision in *Clark v. Dodge*, 269 N.Y. 410, 199 N.E. 641, *supra*, in which we sustained an agreement between two shareholders who together owned all of the shares in the corporation. This argument is based on a fundamental misinterpretation of the significance of our decision in that case. Rather than illustrating any divergence from the great body of other cases which have found such agreements to be illegal and unenforceable, the *Clark* decision reflects a reasoned and flexible application of the principles which are in fact common to all such cases.

The dispositive consideration must always be the possibility of harm to either the other shareholders or to the general public either prospectively at the time the agreement was entered into or at the time it is sought to be enforced. In those cases in which the agreement is made by less than all the shareholders, almost any attempt to reduce the authority granted to the board by law will create a significant potential for harm to other shareholders even if the potential for harm to the general public is minimal. This is so because the effect of such an agreement is to deprive the other shareholders of the benefits and protections which the law perceives to exist when the corporation is managed by an independent board of directors, free to use its own business judgment in the best interest of the corporation.

In *Clark*, the possibility of harm to other shareholders was nonexistent, for in fact there were no other shareholders. In the instant case, in contradistinction, there were and are two other shareholders, not privy to the agreement between plaintiff and decedent. Moreover, the instant agreement for the continuation of plaintiff and decedent in their respective positions is in no way dependent on their performances in those positions, whereas the agreement in *Clark* provided that Clark was to be continued as manager "so long as he proved faithful, efficient and competent" (*Clark v. Dodge*, 269 N.Y. 410, 417, 199 N.E. 641, 643, *supra*).

It has been suggested that even if the agreement is indeed illegal on its face, the defendant, in order to successfully assert the defense of illegality, must prove that the other shareholders did not know of and acquiesce in the agreement. This contention is illogical, and is at any rate inapplicable to the instant case. In this as in all actions the burden of proof is in the first instance always on the plaintiff who must prove his cause of action. * * * [E]ven were the burden with respect to this issue to be improperly placed upon defendant, that burden has been met.

It has also been suggested that the option should be severed from the other provisions of the agreement and separately enforced since it alone would not be illegal. The flaw in this argument is that it improperly assumes that decedent would have given plaintiff this option by itself, without the other parts of their agreement. This assumption is one in which we may not indulge. Indeed, it appears that the illegal parts of the agreement were an intrinsic part of the covenant between these parties. * * *

In sum, law and logic both compel the conclusion that the option which plaintiff seeks to enforce was an inseverable part of a basically illegal agreement. As such, it may not be enforced.

* * *

Accordingly, I vote to reverse the order appealed from and to dismiss the complaint.

Fuchsberg, Judge (dissenting).

My vote too is for reversal. However, the decisional path that I would take differs appreciably not only from that of the majority but from that of my fellow dissenters as well.

Specifically, unlike the other dissenters, I am of the opinion that the parties entered into an enforceable agreement. But, for the reasons well stated both in Judge Gabrielli's alternative rationale and in Mr. Justice Lupiano's dissenting memorandum at the Appellate Division (61 A.D.2d 911, 402 N.Y.S.2d 820), I conclude that we are required to find that the agreement was not ambiguous and that, as a matter of law, it terminated in accordance with its terms during the father's lifetime.

I also take issue with the majority's reasoning that the option was enforceable only because it was separable from an otherwise illegal contract. In my view, the entire agreement is lawful qua agreement, and since it is one entered into between the controlling stockholders of a small, nonpublic corporation, it is not to be scrutinized by a rigid, hypertechnical reading of section 27 of the General Corporation Law, now part of section 701 of the Business Corporation Law.

Small, closely held corporations whose operation is dominated, as its stockholders and creditors usually are aware, by a particular individual or small group of individuals, must be distinguished, legally and pragmatically, from large corporations whose stock is traded on a public securities exchange and where the normal stockholders' relationship to those managing the corporation is bound to be impersonal and remote. Obviously, the latter's operations are rarely, if ever, covered by stockholders' agreements, and the Business Corporation Law itself is the sole restriction on their management.

In the close corporation, investors who themselves are not part of the dominant group commonly rely on the identities of the individuals who run the business and on the likelihood of their continuance in power. As a practical matter, these individuals will be expected to exercise a broad discretion and considerable informality in carrying out their management functions; this flexibility may be regarded as one of the strengths of a smaller organization. Indeed, faith in the integrity and ability of the managers is what usually motivates the investment. Looked at realistically, such corporations, often organized solely to obtain the advantage of limited personal liability for their principals, to qualify for a particular tax classification, or for some similar reason, are frequently "little more * * * than charter partnerships" (*Ripin v. United States Woven Label Co.*, 205 N.Y. 442, 447, 98 N.E. 855, 856). Control of such matters as choice of officers and directors, amounts of executive salaries, and options to buy or sell each other's stock—exactly the sort of things with which the agreement before us dealt—is usually mapped out by agreements among stockholders.

In short, so long as an agreement between stockholders relating to the management of the corporation bears no evidence of an intent to defraud other stockholders or creditors, deviations from precise formalities should not automatically call for a slavish enforcement of the statute. For this is the "governing criteri[on]" by which to test "the validity of a stockholders' agreement" (Delaney, *The Corporate Director: Can His Hands Be Tied in Advance*, 50 COLUM.L.REV. 52, 61; see, also, 1 O'Neal, CLOSE CORPORATIONS, § 5.08). This would not leave without remedy those minority stockholders in close corporations whose interests may be abused. Available to them and at least equally effective are the equitable remedies by which officers and directors can be made to respond for violations of their trust obligations (*Meinhard v. Salmon*, 249 N.Y. 458, 164 N.E. 545).

Analysis of the agreement and its surrounding circumstances here illustrates the wisdom of this approach. The corporation had for a long time been a one-man business in every sense, the man being Triggs, the father. Until he gave a minority interest to each of his sons, he was the owner of all the voting stock; afterwards, it was all owned by the father and his sons, who were preparing to succeed him. At the time of the agreement, the father, together with the son who was the other party to the disputed writing, held the majority of this stock. Given their service in the business, their stockholding, and their relationship to each other and to the history of the corporation, it was to be expected—and not at all extraordinary—that an arrangement for their continuance in office and their compensation would be executed. There is not the slightest indication that, had the parties gone through the routine of presenting the contract to duly called stockholders' and directors' meetings, it would not have been rubber-stamped as a matter of course. It is significant that no other stockholder challenged the agreement during the father's lifetime and that the dispute since then has gravitated only around the son's insistence that the option to purchase his father's shares had not expired, a term which in any event, though it found its way into the stockholders' agreement, related to an essentially personal matter distinct from any corporate management obligations as such.

In sum, given that no other shareholder or member of the general public has been harmed, there is no good reason to measure the agreement by the less sophisticated standards of yesteryear. Tellingly, the often conflicting and unpatterned holdings that characterized our varied decisions on this point in the past have been overshadowed by the enactment of subdivision (b) of section 620 of the Business Corporation Law. At that time, the Legislature expressly indicated that it intended to overrule, at least in part, many of those decisions that struck down shareholders' agreements. In doing so, it made clear its purpose to approve and expand the ruling in *Clark v. Dodge*, 269 N.Y. 410, 199 N.E. 641, *supra*, which upheld a controverted stockholders' agreement in a close corporation context.

---

In *Galler v. Galler*, 32 Ill.2d 16, 203 N.E.2d 577 (1964), two brothers, who together owned in equal parts nearly all the shares of a family corporation, entered into an extensive agreement designed to provide financial protection to each of their families and to assure that their families would retain equal control of the corporation following the death of either brother. The matters covered by the agreement included the number of directors, a supermajority quorum requirement, notice of meetings, voting for named persons as directors, declaration of dividends, and salary continuation arrangements. After the death of one brother, the other refused to abide by the agreement. The widow of the brother who had died then sued for specific performance. An intermediate appellate court that the agreement was void as against public policy because it restricted the discretion of the board of directors. The Illinois Supreme Court reversed.

The court acknowledged that shareholders in close corporations have special needs: there is no ready market for their stock, a large minority shareholder may be at the mercy of an oppressive majority, and, because each director has a substantial share interest, it often is not possible to secure "independent board judgment free from personal motivations concerning corporate policy." Id. at 27, 203 N.E.2d at 584. The court found that despite its breadth and duration (the agreement was intended to govern as long as one of the parties to it was alive), the agreement offended no public policy because it inflicted no harm on the corporation or any other person. Rather, the agreement served the legitimate purpose of providing support and maintenance for the shareholders' immediate families. Consequently, specific performance was ordered.

Subsequent cases have moved in the direction foreshadowed by *Galler* and Judge Fuchsberg's dissent in *Triggs*. Legislatures have moved in the same direction. The RMBCA was amended in 1991 to be more hospitable to contractual arrangements governing close corporations. RMBCA § 7.32 expressly validates seven specific categories of shareholder agreements that modify traditional corporate law norms and contains a catchall authorization of other variations not contrary to public policy. See also DGCL § 350, 351, 354, Calif. Corp. Code § 300, and N.Y.B.C.L. § 620(b). RMBCA § 7.32(b) spells out the requisite procedural formalities. RMBCA § 7.32(c) provides an express statutory rescission remedy to a purchaser of shares who did not know of the existence of the shareholder agreement. RMBCA § 7.32(d) ties the applicability of the new provisions to the absence of a public market for the corporation's shares. Compare DGCL § 342 and Calif. Corp. Code § 158.

However, even under modern statutes interpretative problems arise, particularly with respect to compliance with statutory procedures. *Zion v. Kurtz*, 50 N.Y.2d 92, 428 N.Y.S.2d 199, 405 N.E.2d 681 (1980), involved an agreement between the two stockholders of a Delaware corporation which specified that no "business or activities" shall be conducted without the consent of the minority shareholder. The agreement was not incorporated in the articles, of incorporation and thus did not comply fully with DGCL § 351. In a 4 to 3 decision, the court nevertheless held that the agreement was enforceable.

The majority observed that it was "[c]lear from those provisions [of the close corporation statute] that the public policy of Delaware does not proscribe a provision such as that contained in the shareholders' agreement here in issue even though it takes all management functions away from the directors." Moreover, referring to N.Y.B.C.L. § 620(b), the court stated that it was also "clear that no New York public policy stands in the way of our application of the Delaware statute and decisional law above referred to."

Gabrielli, J., dissented, arguing that the effect of the agreement was to "sterilize" the board of directors. He contended that neither Delaware nor new York courts had shown tolerance for arrangements that deviated from the statutory norm to such an extreme. Although he admitted that the agreement might have been enforced in Delaware if it been in the articles of incorporation, he viewed its inclusion there as a mandatory requirement of the statute. He also disagreed with the majority's view that "Since there are no intervening rights of third persons, the agreement requires nothing that is not permitted by statute, and all of the stockholders of the corporation assented to it, the certificate of incorporation may be ordered reformed, by requiring Kurtz to file the appropriate amendments, or more directly he may be held estopped to rely upon the absence of those amendments from the corporate charter." He concluded that the Delaware and New York statutes require that the close corporation "give notice of its unorthodox management structure through its filed certificate of incorporation. The obvious purpose of such a requirement is to prevent harm to the public before it occurs. If, as the majority's holding suggests, this requirement of notice to the public through the certificate of incorporation is without legal effect unless and until a third party's interests have actually been impaired, then the prophylactic purposes of the statutes governing 'close corporations' would effectively be defeated." *Id.* at 107, 428 N.Y.S.2d at 207, 405 N.E.2d at 688.

## 2. HIGH VOTING OR QUORUM REQUIREMENTS

Control devices designed to provide for minority shareholder representation on the board of directors or otherwise to protect minority shareholders' interests may be worth very little if holders of a majority of a corporation's stock retain the power to expand the board or to amend protective provisions in the corporation's articles or bylaws. Consequently, such control devices often are supplemented by provisions designed to allow one or more participants to veto all board decisions or certain significant decisions, such as those to appoint or remove officers, set salaries, fix dividends, or issue new stock.

The most straightforward way to create veto rights is to require that an extraordinary majority of directors or shareholders must approve all or certain specified actions. One approach is to require unanimous approval. However, many lawyers follow the practice of setting the supermajority requirement sufficiently high to make opposition of one shareholder or one director sufficient to block board or shareholder action. A requirement that a board action be approved by 80% of the directors, for example, effectively requires unanimity if the board has four or fewer members.

The reason for the caution in this area is that a few courts have struck down extraordinary majority voting requirements for one reason or another. The New York Court of Appeals, for example, held in *Benintendi v. Kenton Hotel*, 294 N.Y. 112, 60 N.E.2d 829 (1945), that by-law provisions requiring unanimity for any action by either the board or the shareholders were invalid as against public policy because they made it difficult for the corporation to conduct its business and created a substantial risk of deadlock. See also *Kaplan v. Block*, 183 Va. 327, 31 S.E.2d 893 (1944). Although this ruling was subsequently reversed by the legislature (N.Y.B.C.L. §§ 616 and 709), similar cases in other jurisdictions together with a number of decisions invalidating extraordinary majority requirements on statutory grounds created the small, but ever-nagging possibility that the courts might invalidate such provisions. That possibility seems, however, to be fading. Courts have come more and more to accept the fact that departures by close corporations from the traditional corporate model do not inevitably entail untoward results. For example, *Sutton v. Sutton*, 84 N.Y.2d 37, 614 N.Y.S.2d 369, 637 N.E.2d 260 (1994), upheld as valid under N.Y.B.C.L. § 616(b) a provision in a corporation's articles of incorporation requiring unanimous shareholder approval to transact any business, "including amendment to the articles of incorporation." The court further held that a vote of 70% of the corporation's shares was not sufficient to amend the articles. Moreover, a great many legislatures have enacted statutory provisions that authorize, specifically or by implication, high vote requirements in the articles or by-laws. See, e.g., RMBCA §§ 2.02, 7.25(c), and 8.24(c) and N.Y.B.C.L. §§ 616 and 709.

A high quorum requirement for either shareholder meetings or board meetings, see, e.g., RMBCA §§ 7.27 and 8.24(a), can serve many of the same functions as a supermajority voting requirement or can supplement such a requirement by preventing a board or the shareholders from acting in the absence of one director or shareholder. At least one court has held, however, that where directors deliberately stay away from board meetings in order to prevent some action from being taken, they cannot, as shareholders, "complain of an irregularity which they themselves have caused." *Gearing v. Kelly*, 11 N.Y.2d 201, 203, 227 N.Y.S.2d 897, 898, 182 N.E.2d 391 (1962). But see *Campbell v. Loew's, Inc.* (Chapter 12).

*Jones v. Wallace*, 291 Or. 11, 628 P.2d 388 (1981), involved a by-law which provided that a quorum at a shareholders' meeting consisted of all the corporation's outstanding shares entitled to vote. Based on this by-law, two minority shareholders sought to set aside an action at a meeting at which one shareholder was not present. The court held the by-law invalid because the Oregon statute provided that a provision increasing the quorum requirements for a shareholders' meeting must appear in the articles and this, according to the Court, was "not an unimportant technicality."

## 3. EMPLOYMENT CONTRACTS FOR EXECUTIVES

Contracts of employment normally are not specifically enforceable, even if one of the parties to the contract is a corporation. There have been exceptions, however. In *Jones v. Williams*, 139 Mo. 1, 39 S.W. 486 (1897), for example, the court granted specific performance of a contract employing the plaintiff as editor of a newspaper for five years. It relied in part on the fact that editorial control of a newspaper is a unique sort of power whose loss could not easily be compensated in damages and in part on the fact that the plaintiff had been induced by the contract to leave another position and to invest a substantial sum of money in the stock of the paper.

Specific performance may have much to recommend it in the circumstances that often surround internecine disputes in close corporations. See, e.g., *Collins v. Collins Fruit Co.*, 189 So.2d 262 (Fla.App.1966). Nevertheless, most courts seem unwilling to depart from the standard rule, allowing only an action for damages for breach of contract when an officer is fired before the expiration of her contract. See F. Hodge O'Neal and Robert B. Thompson, O'NEAL'S CLOSE CORPORATIONS § 6.05 (3rd ed. 1986).

Where the contract is for the employment of an officer of a corporation, a more troublesome problem exists. On occasion, courts have held such contracts invalid, not merely unenforceable, because the term of the contract extended beyond that of the board of directors. The theory of most of such holdings is that it is against public policy to allow one board to bind its successors in a matter as important as the appointment of officers. In other cases, whose results perhaps are more defensible, courts have held merely that contracts of employment for an unusually long duration, particularly for the lifetime of the person employed, are invalid. See F. Hodge O'Neal and Robert B. Thompson, O'NEAL'S CLOSE CORPORATIONS § 6.06 (3rd ed. 1986).

A partial answer to the difficulties this may pose is to have the agreement provide that the party is to be employed not as an officer but in some non-elected capacity, such as general manager, sales manager, or operations supervisor. As artificial as this distinction may appear, it seems to have overcome the reluctance of some courts to uphold long-term employment contracts. E.g., *Streett v. Laclede–Christy Co.*, 409 S.W.2d 691 (Mo.1966). See F. Hodge O'Neal & Robert B. Thompson, O'NEAL'S CLOSE CORPORATIONS § 6.10 (3rd ed. 1986).

# D.  RESTRICTIONS ON THE TRANSFER OF SHARES

## PROBLEMS
### PRECISION TOOLS REVISITED—PART III

In the course of your discussions with Jessica, Michael and Bernie, they expressed concern about what would happen to their interests in the corporation should one of them die, withdraw, or have their employment involuntarily terminated. You advised them that it is standard practice for shareholders in close corporations to enter into an agreement by which they restrict the transfer of their stock. Bearing in mind the details of their personal situations set out in Parts I and II of Precision Tools, they have asked you draft such an agreement for them.

In any such agreement, the following questions must be answered:

(1) What events trigger the applicability of the restrictions? The death of one of the parties? The termination of employment (should it make a difference if the termination is voluntary or involuntary)? Should the parties be allowed to make a gift of their stock (to family? third parties?)? Pledge the stock as collateral for a loan?

(2) Who should have the option (or be required) to purchase the shares subject to the restrictions? In what circumstances should the transfer of the shares be mandatory, i.e., the agreement require that upon the triggering event, the shareholder is obligated to sell and the prospective purchaser to buy? Alternatively, when should the transfer be subject to the option of one or more of the parties?

(3) Assuming that more than one person has an interest in purchasing the shares, in what order should there be a right of refusal? If no one exercises the right to purchase the shares under the agreement, is the seller free to sell to a third party without restriction?

(4) How is the price at which any transfers take place to be determined? Will it vary depending upon the occasion for the transfer? Will the agreement specify a price or will it set forth a formula pursuant to which the price will be determined? How often will such a determination be made? Whether or not there is a formula, what happens if the parties fail to agree upon the price?

(5) How will any purchase options be funded?

(6) In what instrument(s) should the restrictions be included? Consider RMBCA § 2.02 and DGCL § 202.

Draft an outline of the alternatives that the parties should consider when answering these questions.

## 1.  INTRODUCTION

Were the closely held enterprise operated as a partnership, the partners would have the right of *delectus personae,* the power of each partner to veto the admission into the partnership of a new member. Uniform Partnership Act, § 18(g). The owners of a small business who have chosen to incorporate also want to have this power. It is appropriate, therefore, that in most closely-held corporations the shareholders include some arrangement in their organizational scheme which approximates the right of *delectus personae.* Such arrangements usually take the form of transfer restriction agreements whereby the ability of the shareholders to alienate their stock is limited in some fashion.

In planning the affairs of the close corporation, there is a practical problem that complicates the drafting, as well as the interpretation, of transfer restriction agreements. It is evident that however carefully the owners of a close corporation and their counsel design machinery to insure the desired balance of control, that machinery can run amok or cease functioning altogether should one of the shareholders sell, give, or bequeath his stock. The second aim of a transfer restriction agreement, then, is to provide for the continuation of a workable control scheme when one of the shareholders dies or decides to sell or give away his interest.

Stock transfer agreements are also extremely important in creating a market for otherwise illiquid shares and planning the estates of the shareholders. Any sound estate plan provides some measure of liquidity to the estate in order to pay the decedent's personal debts, the expenses of administering the estate, and federal and state estate taxes. Where the estate consists in significant part of stock in a closely held corporation, for which shares there is by definition no ready market, the desired liquidity can often be furnished by some sort of stock purchase agreement combined with adequate planning for its funding. In addition, the buy-sell agreement at the time of death of a stockholder assists in establishing a value for the stock at that time. This is important for the purpose of determining the amount of estate taxes that are due; it reduces the risk that the taxing authorities will claim that the stock is worth substantially more than its value as established by the agreement.

Finally, a buy-out provision may meet the desire of shareholders to diversify the assets of their estates to be passed on to their heirs. This diversification is particularly desirable in a close corporation whose success may depend in large measure on the abilities and efforts of one or two shareholders, whose deaths may make it imprudent for the estate to continue to hold the stock.

It is well to keep in mind that there are a variety of ways in which a shareholder may dispose of stock. The most common ones are by sale or bequest. But the planner should also consider the prospect of inter vivos transfers by way of gifts, creation of trusts, pledges, or other means by which the right to vote the stock and receive dividends might pass to the hands of someone other than the original, and perhaps key, shareholder.

Given the sound reasons underlying transfer restrictions, it is curious that their validity and enforceability have been the subject of a great deal of controversy and uncertainty.

The general American rule has been that unreasonable restraints on the alienation of personal property are void. Litigation seeking to soften that rule has often foundered on the poor drafting of the restraints in question. The result has been a number of decisions which have questioned the validity of many transfer restrictions. Recently, however, courts have recognized the need for such restrictions and have become more tolerant in their approach. *See, e.g., Allen v. Biltmore Tissue Corp.*, 2 N.Y.2d 534, 161 N.Y.S.2d 418, 141 N.E.2d 812 (1957). In addition, some statutes expressly authorize transfer restrictions (RMBCA § 6.27 and DGCL § 202) or, indeed, require them for close corporations (DGCL § 342(a)(2)). *See, also,* Model Bus. Corp. Act, Statutory Close Corp. Supplement, §§ 10–17 (Supp.1996).

There are two basic approaches to drafting buy-sell agreements. The designated purchaser may be the corporation that issues the stock, a technique known as an "entity purchase" agreement or "redemption agreement." Alternatively, the purchase option (or occasionally obligation) may be given to the other shareholders, in which case the agreement is known as a "cross-purchase" arrangement. Fairly frequently the two approaches are combined.

## 2.  TYPES OF TRANSFER RESTRICTIONS

Transfer restrictions may take three basic forms, two or more of which are often found combined in the same agreement. First, the restriction may impose limitations on the freedom of a shareholder to transfer stock. Second, the corporation or the remaining shareholders may be given an option to purchase the shares of another shareholder upon the occurrence of certain events, such as the death of a shareholder or the termination of his or her employment with the corporation. Third, what is often called a "buy-sell agreement" may require the corporation or the remaining shareholders to purchase the stock of another shareholder upon the occurrence of similar triggering events. This requirement is often coupled with a coordinate obligation of the shareholder or her estate to sell the stock.

Although transfer restriction agreements are generally a matter of contract and may therefore be cast in whatever form is appropriate for the circumstances of the particular corporation and its shareholders, restrictions on the freedom of shareholder to transfer her shares commonly take one of three forms:

(1) Under a "right of first refusal," before a shareholder is free to sell her stock to a third person it first must be offered to the corporation or to the remaining shareholders (or both) at the same price and on the same terms and conditions offered by the outsider. Typically the right, if extended to the other shareholders, is given in proportion to their respective holdings. If any shareholder is unable to purchase or declines to do so, her allocation may be taken up proportionately by the remaining shareholders.

(2) Another common form of restriction is the first option provision. RMBCA § 6.27(d)(1); DGCL § 202(c)(1). The principal distinction between a first option provision and a right of first refusal is that the offer to the corporation or the remaining shareholders is made at a price and on terms fixed by the arrangement rather than by an offer made by an outside purchaser. Even if the basic restriction is cast in the form of a right of first refusal, it may be desirable to include a first option provision to deal with transfers of stock other than by sale to third parties. Obviously, a right of first refusal would not serve to deal with transfers by gift or devise.

(3) Finally, a shareholder's disposition of stock may be conditioned upon the consent of the corporation's board of directors or of the other shareholders. Modern statutes allow the parties to provide for a consent restriction if such "prohibition is not manifestly unreasonable." RMBCA § 6.27(d)(3); DGCL § 202(c)(3). *See also, Colbert v. Hennessey*, 351 Mass. 131, 217 N.E.2d 914 (1966) (shareholders' agreement requiring consent of shareholders held binding on heirs of parties to the agreement).

Since one of the major purposes of transfer restriction agreements is to give shareholders some degree of control over the identity of co-owners of the business, such agreements often entitle the corporation or its remaining shareholders to purchase the stock of any shareholders who withdraw from the business. Such options may be activated upon the death of a shareholder, the termination of his or her employment, the pledging of her shares to another, or any other action that threatens to replace the shareholder by another. These options typically confer an absolute right to purchase the stock even though the shareholder or her estate may wish to retain the shares.

Where a right of first refusal gives the corporation or the remaining shareholders the option to purchase the shares of a deceased or withdrawing stockholder, a "buy-sell agreement" imposes an obligation to purchase. Usually used to provide liquidity to the estate of a deceased stockholder, these agreements are frequently funded by insurance policies taken out on the lives of the principal stockholders.

Transfer restrictions are most commonly adopted at the time a close corporation is formed; the restriction is a matter of negotiation among the initial shareholders. What is the status of a shareholder who purchases stock, either from the corporation or from one of the initial shareholders, after the transfer restriction becomes effective? The applicability of the agreement to a newcomer may depend on the document in which the agreement is inserted in the first instance: the articles of incorporation, a by-law provision, or a separate contract among the shareholders. A purchasing shareholder may not be bound if the restriction is in an agreement among shareholders to which she is not a party. It is customary, therefore, to make transfer restrictions a part of the by-laws or the articles. As between these two instruments, should there be any difference with respect to the enforceability of the restriction? Consider carefully the language of RMBCA § 2.02. *See* F. Hodge O'Neal & Robert B. Thompson, O'NEAL'S CLOSE CORPORATIONS § 7.13 (3rd ed. 1986).

In order to be valid against a purchaser of the stock without notice, a transfer restriction must be "noted conspicuously" on the stock certificate itself. RMBCA § 6.27(b) and Uniform Commercial Code § 8–204. The term "conspicuous" is defined in RMBCA § 1.40(3). For a judicial interpretation of what is "conspicuous" see *Ling & Co. v. Trinity Savings & Loan Ass'n*, 482 S.W.2d 841 (Tex.1972). Even if not conspicuous, a transfer restriction is enforceable against a transferee with knowledge. RMBCA § 6.27(b).

A related question is whether the shareholders of the corporation may adopt a by-law containing transfer restrictions that is valid against a shareholder who does not consent to the by-law. In *Tu–Vu Drive–In Corp. v. Ashkins*, 61 Cal.2d 283, 38 Cal.Rptr. 348, 391 P.2d 828 (1964), the court gave an affirmative answer to that question. Three years after the corporation in *Tu–Vu* was organized, the board of directors adopted a by-law provision giving a right of first refusal to the other shareholders and then to the corporation, before any shareholder could sell to an outsider. The by-law was approved by the plaintiff, who owned 54% of the stock. Subsequently, one of the minority shareholders granted to an outsider an option to purchase her stock, although it was never exercised. The plaintiff brought an action for a declaratory judgment that the by-law was enforceable over the minority stockholder's asserted right to choose to whom she wished to sell her stock. The question, according to the court, was whether the restriction was an unreasonable restraint on alienation. Holding that it was not, the court said, "In the light of the legitimate interests to be furthered by the by-law [the defendant's] asserted right becomes 'innocuous and insubstantial.' The by-law merely proscribes [the defendant's] choice of transferees while insuring to her the price and terms equal to those offered by the outsider."

## 3.   THE VALUATION PROCESS

The valuation provisions of a share transfer restriction agreement are among the most important—and difficult—to draft. There are a variety of techniques available, of which it is only possible here to suggest a few of the more important. *See generally,* F. Hodge O'Neal, *Restrictions on Transfer of Stock in Closely Held Corporations: Planning and Drafting,* 65 HARV.L.REV. 773 (1952). They include:

1.   *Book Value.* This is a popular method but one that may lead to inequitable results. The book value of a company may bear little relationship to its value as an ongoing concern. Moreover, despite its apparent simplicity, book value turns out in application often to be remarkably ambiguous. Does it, for example, include intangible assets, especially "goodwill"? What about income taxes that are accrued but unpaid, and may not appear on the books? If the corporation carries insurance on life of the shareholder whose death is the occasion for the exercise of a buy-sell provision, are the proceeds of the insurance to be included? Should assets that have appreciated substantially be written up before book value is calculated? If this technique is used, it is desirable that these and other questions be anticipated and dealt with in the agreement; and doing so turns what starts out to be a simple approach into one full of complexity.

2.   *Capitalized Earnings.* An agreement may attempt to reach an objective appraisal of the fair value of the stock which is more sophisticated than that provided by book value by establishing a formula according to which the earnings of the business may be capitalized. Like book value, however, this technique presents certain difficulties of drafting. It is especially critical that the earnings of the business be carefully defined.

3.   *Right of First Refusal.* Where the principal concern is that one of the parties may sell his interest to an outsider, providing that a shareholder must, before selling, offer her shares to the corporation (or the other shareholders) at the same price, and on the same terms and conditions offered by the outsider, has great appeal. This approach may, however, substantially increase the already great difficulties a shareholder in a close corporation faces in selling her stock, because a prospective buyer may well be put off by the prospect of spending considerable effort in negotiating a sale only to have the shares bought out from under her pursuant to a right of first refusal. Moreover, this approach is obviously useful only for prospective sales to third parties and is of no utility in providing for the transfer of shares by gift, devise, or inheritance.

4.   *Appraisal.* It is possible to avoid some of the pitfalls of the preceding methods by simply leaving the valuation of the shares to appraisal by a neutral third party according to some predetermined procedure. One of the most convenient techniques of doing so is to provide for arbitration according to the rules of the American Arbitration Association or some other recognized arbitral organization.

5. *Mutual Agreement.* Another relatively popular technique is for the parties to the agreement to set a value for the shares and to revise it at stated intervals, usually annually. While this may lead to a fairer price, it is subject to the significant drawback that for psychological reasons, the parties often neglect to conduct the revaluations; focusing implicitly on the possibility that one of them might soon die or that they may have a falling out is not a particularly pleasant undertaking.

# CONCORD AUTO AUCTION, INC. v. RUSTIN

627 F.Supp. 1526 (D.Mass.1986).

MEMORANDUM AND ORDER

YOUNG, DISTRICT JUDGE.

Close corporations, Concord Auto Auction, Inc. ("Concord") and E.L. Cox Associates, Inc. ("Associates") brought this action for the specific performance of a stock purchase and restriction agreement (the "Agreement"). Concord and Associates allege that Lawrence H. Rustin ("Rustin") as the administrator of E.L. Cox's estate ("Cox") failed to effect the repurchase of Cox's stock holdings as provided by the Agreement. * * *

* * *

## I.  Background

Both Concord and Associates are Massachusetts Corporations. Concord operates a used car auction for car dealers, fleet operators, and manufacturers. Associates operates as an adjunct to Concord's auction business by guaranteeing checks and automobile titles. Both are close corporations with the same shareholders, all siblings: Cox (now his estate), Powell, and Thomas. At all times relevant to this action, each sibling owned one-third of the issued and outstanding stock in both Concord and Associates.

To protect "their best interests" and the best interests of the two corporations, the three shareholders entered into a stock purchase and restriction agreement on February 1, 1983. The Agreement provides that all shares owned by a shareholder at the time of his or her death be acquired by the two corporations, respectively, through life insurance policies specifically established to fund this transaction. This procedure contemplates the "orderly transfer of the stock owned by each deceased Shareholder." At issue in the instant action are the prerequisites for and effect of the repurchase requirements as set forth in the Agreement.

This dispute arises because Rustin failed to tender Cox's shares as required by Paragraph 2, *Death of Shareholder*. Rustin admits this but alleges a condition precedent: that Powell, specifically, and Thomas failed to effect both the annual meeting and the annual review of the stock price set in the Agreement as required by Paragraph 6, *Purchase Price:* "Each price shall be reviewed at least annually no later than the annual meeting of the stockholders * * * (commencing with the annual meetings for the year 1984) * * *," here February 21, 1984. Rustin implies that, had the required meeting been held, revaluation would or should have occurred and that, after Cox's accidental death in a fire on March 14, 1984, Powell in particular as well as Thomas were obligated to revalue the stock prior to tendering the repurchase price.

There is no dispute that the By–Laws call for an annual meeting on the third Tuesday of February, here February 21, 1984. There is no dispute that none took place or that, when Cox died, the stocks of each corporation had not been formally revalued. No one disputes that Paragraph 6 of the Agreement provides for a price of $672.00 per share of Concord and a price of $744.00 per share for Associates. This totals $374,976 which is covered by insurance on Cox's life of $375,000. There is no substantial dispute that the stock is worth a great deal more, perhaps even twice as much. No one seriously disputes that Paragraph 6 further provides that:

> * * * all parties may, as a result of such review, agree to a new price by a written instrument executed by all the parties and appended to an original of this instrument, and that any such new price shall thereupon become the basis for determining the purchase price for all purposes hereof unless subsequently superceded pursuant to the same procedure. The purchase price shall remain in full force and effect and until so changed.

Rustin asserts that the explicit requirement of a yearly price review "clashes" with the provision that the price shall remain in effect until changed. He argues a trial is required to determine the intent of the parties:

> The question then arises, presenting this Court with a material issue of fact not susceptible to determination on a motion for summary judgment: Did the parties intend, either to reset, or at least to monitor, yearly, the correspondence between the Paragraph 6 price and the current value of the companies? If so, who, if anyone, was principally responsible for effecting the yearly review required by the Agreement, and for insuring an informed review?

In answering these questions the Court first outlines its proper role in the interpretation of this contract.

## II.  Discussion

A Court sitting in diversity will apply the substantive law of the forum state, here Massachusetts. In Massachusetts as elsewhere, absent ambiguity, contracts must be interpreted and enforced exactly as written. Where the language is unambiguous, the interpretation of a contract is a question of law for the court. Further, contracts must be construed in accordance with their ordinary and usual sense.

Contrary to Rustin's assertion, the Court in applying these standards holds that there is no ambiguity and certainly no "clash" between the dual requirements of Paragraph 6 that there be an annual review of share price and that, absent such review, the existing price prevails. When, as here, the Court searches for the meaning of a document containing two unconditional provisions, one immediately following the other, the Court favors a reading that reconciles them. The Court rules that the Agreement covers precisely the situation before it: no revaluation occurred, therefore the price remains as set forth in the Agreement. This conclusion is reasonable, for the Agreement is not a casual memorialization but a formal contract carefully drafted by attorneys and signed by all parties.

Moreover, the Court interprets Paragraph 2 to provide, in unambiguous terms:

> "In the event of the death of any Shareholder subject to this agreement, his respective * * * administrator * * * *shall*, within sixty (60) days after the date of death * * * give written notice thereof to each Company which notice *shall* specify a purchase date not later than sixty (60) days thereafter, *offering to each Company for purchase* as hereinafter provided, and *at the purchase price set forth in Paragraph 6*, all of the Shares owned on said date by said deceased Shareholder. * * * " [Emphasis by the Court].

Rustin, therefore, was unambiguously obligated as administrator of Cox's estate to tender Cox's shares for repurchase by Concord and Associates. His failure to do so is inexcusable unless he raises cognizable defenses.

All of Rustin's defenses turn on two allegations: that his performance is excused because the surviving parties failed to review and to adjust upward the $374,976 purchase price. Rustin contends that the parties meant to review the price per share on an annual basis. No affidavit supports this assertion, nor does any exhibit. In fact, absent any evidence for this proposition, Rustin's assertion is no more than speculation and conjecture. While Rustin contends that the failure to review and revalue constitutes "unclean hands" and a breach of fiduciary duty which excuses his nonperformance, he places before the Court only argument not facts.

It simply does not follow that because a meeting was not held and the prices were not reviewed that a trial of the parties' intentions is required. The Agreement is the best evidence of the parties' intent. Although the text of the Agreement provides that share price "shall" be reviewed "at least annually," the Agreement also states that "The purchase price shall remain in full force and effect unless and until so changed."

* * *

Even if competent evidence adduced at trial would support Rustin's allegations, his proposition would of necessity require judicial intervention, a course this Court does not favor. Rustin produces not a shred of evidence that the parties intended that a court should intercede to set the share price in the event the parties failed to do so themselves. Every first year law student learns that although the courts can lead an opera singer to the concert hall, they cannot make her sing. *Lumley v. Guy*, 118 Eng.Rep. 749 (1853). While this Court will specifically enforce a consensual bargain, memorialized in an unambiguous written document, it will not order the revision of the share price. Such intrusion into the private ordering of commercial affairs offends both good judgment and good jurisprudence. Moreover, the record before the Court indicates that the parties fully intended what their competent counsel drafted and they signed.

Moreover, the nucleus of Rustin's premise is that somehow Powell should have guaranteed the review and revision of the share prices. On the contrary, nothing in the record indicates that a reasonable trier of fact could find that Powell's duties and responsibilities included such omnipotence. More to the point, the By–Laws suggest that several individuals shared the responsibility for calling the required annual meeting: "In case the annual meeting for any year shall not be duly called or held, the Board of Directors or the President shall cuase (sic) a special meeting to be held. * * *" Pursuant to the By–Laws, Cox himself had the power, right, and authority to call a meeting of the stockholders of both companies, in order to review the price per share— or for any other purpose for that matter.

Furthermore, nothing in the record indicates that somehow Powell, Thomas, Concord, or Associates was charged with the duty of raising the share price. In fact, this is discretionary and consensual: "all parties *may*, as a result of such review, *agree* to a new price by a written instrument *executed by all parties.* * * *" Nowhere can the Court find any affirmative duty to guarantee either an annual meeting or a share price revision. To fault Powell for not doing by fiat what must be done by consensus credits Powell with powers she simply does not have. The mere fact that, as a shareholder of Concord and Associates, Powell benefits from the enforcement of the Agreement at the $374,976 purchase price does not, as matter of law, create an obligation on her part to effect a review or revision of the purchase price. One cannot breach a duty where no duty exists, and Rustin cannot manufacture by allegation a duty where neither the Agreement nor the By–Laws lends any support.

Applying the above analysis, the Court discounts three of Rustin's defenses as meritless: that specific performance is not warranted because Concord and Associates breached the Agreement they seek to enforce; that they have unclean hands because they failed to effect a review and revaluation of the shares; and that specific performance is conditional upon an annual review of share value to be held no later than the third Tuesday of February. The record demonstrates no evidence that share transfer is conditional, rather it appears absolute and automatic. Absent a duty to "guarantee" the occurrence of the annual meeting or the "review," the Court cannot find that Powell's failure, if any, to upgrade the share price constitutes a fiduciary breach.

Of Rustin's fourth defense, that the value of the stock increased so substantially that specific enforcement would be unfair and unjust to Cox's estate, little need be said. This defense as well as Rustin's counterclaims rest on the allegation that Powell, in particular, and Thomas "knew" that a revaluation would result in a higher price and "failed to effect an annual review." Of Powell, Rustin argues that she had a "special responsibility" to effect a review of the purchase price because her siblings looked to her for financial expertise and to call a meeting. Nowhere is this "special responsibility" supported by the Agreement or the By–Laws. Rustin also implies that the sisters "knew" that failure to revalue would inure to their benefit. This presumes they knew that Cox would die in an accidental fire three weeks after the deadline for the shareholder meeting. To call this preposterous understates it, for nothing immunized the sisters from an equally unforeseeable accident. Rustin's argument withers in the light of objectivity to a heap of conclusory straws.

Rustin goes on to argue that the sisters had a fiduciary duty to revalue the shares *after Cox's death* and *before tender*. Nowhere in the Agreement is there the slightest indication they were so obligated. Nowhere is there evidence of willfulness, intent to deceive, or knowing manipulation. * * *

Agreements, such as those before the Court, "among shareholders of closely held corporations are common and the purpose of such contracts are clear." * * *

Moreover, specific performance of an agreement to convey will not be refused merely because the price is inadequate or excessive. *New England Trust Co. v. Abbott*, 162 Mass. 148, 155, 38 N.E. 432 (1894); see *Lee v. Kirby*, 104 Mass. 420, 430 (1870); *Allen v. Biltmore Tissue Corp.*, 2 N.Y.2d 534, 543, 161 N.Y.S.2d 418, 141 N.E.2d 812 (1957) ("The validity of the restriction on transfer does not rest on any abstract notion of intrinsic fairness of price. To be invalid, more than mere disparity between option price and current value of the stock must be shown"); *Renberg v. Zarrow*, 667 P.2d 465, 470 (Okla.1983) ("In the absence of fraud, overreaching, or bad faith, an agreement between the stockholders that upon the death of any of them, the stock may be acquired by the corporation is binding. Even great disparity between the price specified in a buy-sell agreement and the actual value of the stock is not sufficient to invalidate the agreement.") The fact that surviving shareholders were allowed to purchase Cox' shares on stated terms and conditions which resulted in the purchase for less than actual value of the stock does not subject the agreement to attack as a breach of the relation of trust and confidence, there being no breach of fiduciary duty.

Rather than evidence of any impropriety, the Court rules that the purchase prices were carefully set, fair when established, evidenced by an Agreement binding all parties equally to the same terms without any indication that any one sibling would reap a windfall. The courts may not rewrite a shareholder's agreement under the guise of relieving one of the parties from the hardship of an improvident bargain. *Id.* at 471 (citations omitted). The Court cannot protect the parties from a bad bargain and it will not protect them from bad luck. Cox, the party whose estate is aggrieved, had while alive every opportunity to call the annual meeting and persuade his sisters to revalue their stock. Sad though the situation be, sadness is not the touchstone of contract interpretation.

\* \* \*

### III.  Conclusion

\* \* \* The Agreement shall be specifically enforced. Rustin's counterclaims are dismissed and, for the reasons set forth above, the Court ALLOWS Concord's and Associates' motions for summary judgment on all matters. Rustin must sell the Cox shares for the $374,976 purchase price to which all parties agreed. Rustin is hereby ORDERED to:

(1) Deliver the certificates for the Cox shares fully endorsed for purchases pursuant to paragraphs 2 and 6 of the February 1, 1983 Agreement no later than thirty days after the date of this order.

(2) Accept a purchase price of $672.00 per share of Auction and $744.00 per share of Associates as set forth in paragraph 6 of the Agreement.

SO ORDERED.

---

The extent to which courts will use fiduciary duties as well as other concepts to protect minority shareholders from oppressive conduct by majority shareholders is discussed later in this chapter.

## 4.  ADDITIONAL DRAFTING PROBLEMS

*Vogel v. Melish*, 46 Ill.App.2d 465, 196 N.E.2d 402 (1964) provides a lesson to the drafter. Two equal shareholders entered into an agreement which provided that "if either party desired to sell, transfer, assign or convey or otherwise dispose of any shares, an offer must be transmitted to the other party who then had the right to accept such offer in full or in part in the manner set forth \* \* \* "in the agreement. The agreement contained no specific provisions with respect to the shares in the event of the death of one of the parties. Strictly construing the agreement, the court concluded that the arrangement "terminated the restriction on alienation at the death of one of the parties." Thus, on the death of one of the shareholders, the transfer of his shares to his executor did not give the surviving shareholder the option to purchase the decedent's shares and all shares were free of any restraint. Perhaps because transfer restrictions are restraints on alienation and therefore disfavored at common law, courts may tend to ignore the intent of the parties and limit the scope of such restrictions.

As we have seen, the parties, in formulating transfer restrictions, may be motivated by a variety of considerations, including the desire to exercise something like the right of *delectus personae,* the maintenance of a control balance within the corporate structure so that no one shareholder becomes dominant, and the provision of liquidity for the estate of a deceased stockholder. Unfortunately, these aims may occasionally conflict. *Helmly v. Schultz,* 219 Ga. 201, 131 S.E.2d 924 (1963) provides an interesting illustration. The transfer restriction agreement there was included in a by-law which provided as follows:

> No stockholder shall sell or give away his stock in the corporation without first offering to sell the same to the remaining stockholders substantially in proportion to the stock already owned by them. Such remaining stockholders shall have fifteen (15) days from the date such offer is made to them in which to purchase said stock before the same may be given or sold to any other person. The price to be paid by such remaining stockholders for such stock shall be the book value of the stock on the first day of the month in which said offer is made. A reference to this bylaw shall appear on each stock certificate issued by the corporation.

When Mrs. Schultz decided to sell her shares, to comply with the by-law, she offered them first to the stockholders adding the condition that all her stock be purchased at the same time and paid for in cash. Only one of the shareholders sought to accept the offer. When Mrs. Schultz refused to sell to him alone, he brought an action for specific performance of the contract he alleged had been formed by his acceptance. The court refused to grant relief, holding that the offer, made "according to the by-laws," was "to *all the stockholders*—each in his proportionate share * * *." Thus the court found that the purpose of the by-law was "to keep the stock ownership in equal proportion among the original stockholders." Had their principal intention been to prevent outsiders from acquiring stock, they could have provided in the transfer restriction for a disproportionate purchase by one or more shareholders.

## 5.  FUNDING

A buy-sell arrangement is of little practical utility unless the person or persons who have the option (or obligation) to purchase have the financial ability to do so. Unless some means of funding is provided, both the shareholders and the corporation may find themselves without the wherewithal to purchase the shares, and the corporation may even be prevented by statutory restrictions from making the purchase if it lacks the necessary surplus.

Where the putative purchaser is the corporation, one means of funding the purchase is the establishment of a sinking fund in which the corporation regularly sets aside money to be saved for that purpose. A second, and more common, technique is for the corporation to purchase and maintain life insurance on the lives of the shareholders in an amount adequate to fund all or a substantial part of any repurchase for which the corporation may become obligated on their death. Where this is the case it is important that the effect of the receipt of insurance proceeds on the value of the corporation be taken into account when drafting the valuation section of the agreement. A third method of funding is to defer payment by the use of promissory notes or installment obligations.

# E. DEALING WITH DISSENSION, DEADLOCK, OPPRESSION AND DISSOLUTION

## PROBLEM

### PRECISION TOOLS REVISITED—PART IV

#### A.

When Michael, Jessica and Bernie formed PTC, they entered into a shareholder voting agreement providing that each would vote for a board of directors made up of the three of them and a fourth person to be designated by Bernie. Pursuant to their mutual understanding, which they did not reduce to writing, Michael was elected president and CEO and Jessica was elected vice-president and chief financial officer.

After operating under this agreement for three years, Jessica and Bernie became increasingly dissatisfied with Michael's performance as president. They decided that he was not an effective executive, that he was indecisive, and that he had allowed PTC's overhead expenses to grow excessively. They were particularly distressed that, for the first time, PTC had operated at a loss. They also were upset by what they perceived to be serious personality clashes between Michael and several key employees. All this led Jessica and Bernie to conclude that unless steps were taken to remove Michael, PTC's decline would continue.

At PTC's next board of directors meeting, Michael defended his performance and argued that PTC's losses were due to a difficult business environment. However, Jessica, Bernie and Bernie's designee voted to remove Michael as an officer and employee and to appoint Jessica president and CEO at a salary substantially higher than Michael had been paid. They also voted not to pay dividends for the foreseeable future and to use all available funds for business development.

    1. Is it likely that Michael would succeed in a suit to restore him to his position as president and/or compel the payment of dividends, assuming that a Columbia court would adopt the same approach the Massachusetts Supreme Judicial Court has followed in cases involving close corporations?

    2. In determining whether Michael has a valid claim, should a Columbia court follow the Massachusetts Court? Would it be better advised to follow the approach of the Delaware Supreme Court? Is there some other methodology that might be more appropriate?

B.

Assume that only Bernie and his designee become dissatisfied with Michael. Jessica continues to support him as CEO. Bernie and his designee then begin to vote against most of the resolutions that Michael and Jessica ask the board to approve, including all proposals to expand the scope of PTC's business. One such proposal was to buy one of PTC's principal suppliers from the estate of its founder at a very attractive price. Bernie explained that he intends to continue to block all major new investments because he has no confidence in Michael's ability to manage PTC. Michael and Jessica, concerned that PTC's competitive position is in jeopardy, offer to buy Bernie's stock. Bernie responds by demanding a price that they believe is unreasonably high.

What is the likelihood that Michael and Jessica would succeed in a suit to hold Bernie liable for the losses PTC has incurred as a consequence of his negative votes, assuming that they can prove PTC has in fact been damaged?

C.

1.   If the facts were as stated in "A" above, would Michael be able to convince a court that he had been oppressed by Jessica and Bernie? If he could prove oppression, what relief could he obtain? Would your answer differ if PTC were incorporated in New York (consider N.Y.B.C.L. §§ 1104–a, 1118, and *Matter of Kemp & Beatley, Inc.*); New Jersey (consider *Muellenberg v. Bikon Corp.*); Columbia (consider RMBCA §§ 14.30, 14.32, 14.34); or Delaware (consider DGCL §§ 226, 352, 353, 355).

2.   If the facts were as stated in "B" above, could Michael and Jessica succeed in a suit to compel the dissolution of PTC? Would dissolution or a mandatory buy-out represent a more attractive remedy from their point of view?

Consider how your answers to all the above questions would influence your recommendations concerning the provisions that Michael, Jessica and Bernie should include in a shareholders' agreement, the articles of incorporation and/or the by-laws, before making their initial investments in PTC. For example, should they adopt a contractual buyout arrangement or required the use of a mediator to deal with freeze-outs and deadlocks? How might each of the parties have reacted to suggestions made by the others?

## 1.  INTRODUCTION

All too frequently in the lives of closely held businesses, a day comes when the owners cease to get along with each other. Conflict may manifest itself in a variety of ways. There are recorded cases in which shareholders have ceased speaking to each other, yet have managed to continue their business for years. In at least a few instances intracorporate disputes have ended in violence. *See Nashville Packet Co. v. Neville*, 144 Tenn. 698, 235 S.W. 64 (1922). One principal source of difficulty is that differences over matters of business policy or practice frequently are aggravated by differences of a more personal nature, which may become still more intense because participants are related to each other or have been close friends. *See* Ronald J. Watkins, Birthright: Murder, Greed and Power in the U–Haul Family Dynasty (1993). One can even think of this aspect of close corporation practice as "corporate domestic relations" law.

The possibility that they may one day have a parting of ways is seldom absent from the thoughts of the individuals who embark on a corporate venture. In many firms, the parties want to plan for that eventuality. Counsel will make them aware that, under the traditional norms of corporate law and absent any special control mechanisms, the owners of a majority of a corporation's stock will have the power to elect the directors and, through their control of the board, to take a large number of actions with which the minority may disagree. If the parties wish to avoid that possibility, they (or their planner) must walk a narrow line between providing protection to minority shareholders and avoiding control mechanisms that are so veto prone or cumbersome that they will make it difficult to manage the corporation's business.

In addition, developing appropriate control mechanisms can be expensive. Consequently, the participants in a venture often will decide that it is not economic to incur the costs involved in anticipating possible areas of disagreement and designing control mechanisms to deal with them. As a result, many close corporations are formed without any special dispute resolution mechanisms. And corporations that do have mechanisms that initially appeared desirable to all the participants may find that they prove ill-suited to some of them when disputes actually arise.

Two kinds of problems of oppression and deadlock recur frequently. First, there are cases in which those who control a corporation pursue a course of action that other shareholders find oppressive, such as "freezing out" minority shareholders by cutting them off from both salary and dividends, thus leaving them holding illiquid stock that generates no current income. Second, there are cases in which one shareholder or group of shareholders exercises veto rights to frustrate all actions preferred by some other shareholder or group of shareholders.

How courts respond to these cases often turns on two factors. One is how the courts view close corporations. Courts in many states, building on the approach set forth in *Donahue v. Rodd Electrotype Co. of New England, Inc.*, 367 Mass. 578, 328 N.E.2d 505 (1975), have held that the relationship among participants in close corporations is so similar to that of partners that they must deal with each other more like partners than like shareholders in a public corporation. Courts in other states have rejected the partnership analogy and held that when participants in a business venture adopt the corporate form, they also agree to be bound by the traditional norms of corporation law, including centralized management and majority rule. *See Nixon v. Blackwell, infra.*

The second factor is whether the legislature in any given state has included in its corporation statute provisions similar to RMBCA §§ 14.30–14.34, which are directed at providing special protections for shareholders in close corporations. Many state laws now authorize courts to order dissolution or to take other remedial actions to protect shareholders who prove either (a) that the directors of a corporation are deadlocked and the deadlock is causing irreparable injury to the corporation or (b) that those who control the corporation have oppressed other shareholders.

## 2.  JUDICIAL PROTECTION OF MINORITY INTERESTS

### WILKES v. SPRINGSIDE NURSING HOME, INC.

370 Mass. 842, 353 N.E.2d 657 (1976).

HENNESSEY, CHIEF JUSTICE.

On August 5, 1971, the plaintiff (Wilkes) filed a bill in equity for declaratory judgment in the Probate Court for Berkshire County, naming as defendants T. Edward Quinn (Quinn), Leon L. Riche (Riche), the First Agricultural National Bank of Berkshire County and Frank Sutherland MacShane as executors under the will of Lawrence R. Connor (Connor), and the Springside Nursing Home, Inc. (Springside or the corporation). Wilkes alleged that he, Quinn, Riche and Dr. Hubert A. Pipkin (Pipkin) entered into a partnership agreement in 1951, prior to the incorporation of Springside, which agreement was breached in 1967 when Wilkes's salary was terminated and he was voted out as an officer and director of the corporation. Wilkes sought, among other forms of relief, damages in the amount of the salary he would have received had he continued as a director and officer of Springside subsequent to March, 1967.

* * * A judgment was entered dismissing Wilkes's action on the merits. We granted direct appellate review. On appeal, Wilkes argued in the alternative that (1) he should recover damages for breach of the alleged partnership agreement; and (2) he should recover damages because the defendants, as majority stockholders in Springside, breached their fiduciary duty to him as a minority stockholder by their action in February and March, 1967.

* * * [W]e reverse so much of the judgment as dismisses Wilkes's complaint and order the entry of a judgment substantially granting the relief sought by Wilkes under the second alternative set forth above.

* * *

[In 1951, Wilkes, Riche, Quinn, and Pipkin purchased a building lot to use as a nursing home.]

* * * [O]wnership of the property was vested in Springside, a corporation organized under Massachusetts law.

Each of the four men invested $1,000 and subscribed to ten shares of $100 par value stock in Springside.[6] At the time of incorporation, it was understood by all of the parties that each would be a director of Springside and each would participate actively in the management and decision making involved in operating the corporation.[7] It was, further, the understanding and intention of all the parties that, corporate resources permitting, each would receive money from the corporation in equal amounts as long as each assumed an active and ongoing responsibility for carrying a portion of the burdens necessary to operate the business.

The work involved in establishing and operating a nursing home was roughly apportioned, and each of the four men undertook his respective tasks. * * *

At some time in 1952, it became apparent that the operational income and cash flow from the business were sufficient to permit the four stockholders to draw money from the corporation on a regular basis. Each of the four original parties initially received $35 a week from the corporation. As time went on the weekly return to each was increased until, in 1955, it totalled $100.

In 1959, after a long illness, Pipkin sold his shares in the corporation to Connor, who was known to Wilkes, Riche and Quinn through past transactions with Springside in his capacity as president of the First Agricultural National Bank of Berkshire County. Connor received a weekly stipend from the corporation equal to that received by Wilkes, Riche and Quinn. He was elected a director of the corporation but never held any other office. He was assigned no specific area of responsibility in the operation of the nursing home but did participate in business discussions and decisions as a director and served additionally as financial adviser to the corporation.

* * *

[Beginning in 1965, personal relationships between Wilkes and the other shareholders began to deteriorate.] As a consequence of the strained relations among the parties, Wilkes, in January of 1967, gave notice of his intention to sell his shares for an amount based on an appraisal of their value. In February of 1967 a directors' meeting was held and the board exercised its right to establish the salaries of its officers and employees.[10] A schedule of payments was established where-

---

**6.** On May 2, 1955, and again on December 23, 1958, each of the four original investors paid for and was issued additional shares of $100 par value stock, eventually bringing the total number of shares owned by each to 115.

**7.** Wilkes testified before the master that, when the corporate officers were elected, all four men "were * * * guaranteed directorships." Riche's understanding of the parties' intentions was that they all

wanted to play a part in the management of the corporation and wanted to have some "say" in the risks involved; that, to this end, they all would be directors; and that "unless you [were] a director and officer you could not participate in the decisions of [the] enterprise."

**10.** The by-laws of the corporation provided that the directors, subject to the approval of the stockholders, had the power to fix the salaries of all officers and employees.

by Quinn was to receive a substantial weekly increase and Riche and Connor were to continue receiving $100 a week. Wilkes, however, was left off the list of those to whom a salary was to be paid. The directors also set the annual meeting of the stockholders for March, 1967.

At the annual meeting in March, Wilkes was not reelected as a director, nor was he reelected as an officer of the corporation. He was further informed that neither his services nor his presence at the nursing home was wanted by his associates.

The meetings of the directors and stockholders in early 1967, the master found, were used as a vehicle to force Wilkes out of active participation in the management and operation of the corporation and to cut off all corporate payments to him. Though the board of directors had the power to dismiss any officers or employees for misconduct or neglect of duties, there was no indication in the minutes of the board of directors' meeting of February, 1967, that the failure to establish a salary for Wilkes was based on either ground. The severance of Wilkes from the payroll resulted not from misconduct or neglect of duties, but because of the personal desire of Quinn, Riche and Connor to prevent him from continuing to receive money from the corporation. Despite a continuing deterioration in his personal relationship with his associates, Wilkes had consistently endeavored to carry on his responsibilities to the corporation in the same satisfactory manner and with the same degree of competence he had previously shown. Wilkes was at all times willing to carry on his responsibilities and participation if permitted so to do and provided that he receive his weekly stipend.

1.  We turn to Wilkes's claim for damages based on a breach of the fiduciary duty owed to him by the other participants in this venture. In light of the theory underlying this claim, we do not consider it vital to our approach to this case whether the claim is governed by partnership law or the law applicable to business corporations. This is so because, as all the parties agree, Springside was at all times relevant to this action, a close corporation as we have recently defined such an entity in *Donahue v. Rodd Electrotype Co. of New England, Inc.* [367 Mass. 578], 328 N.E.2d 505 (1975).

In *Donahue,* we held that "stockholders in the close corporation owe one another substantially the same fiduciary duty in the operation of the enterprise that partners owe to one another." [*Id.* at 593 (footnotes omitted) ], 328 N.E.2d at 515. As determined in previous decisions of this court, the standard of duty owed by partners to one another is one of "utmost good faith and loyalty." Cardullo v. Landau, 329 Mass. 5, 8, 105 N.E.2d 843 (1952). Thus, we concluded in *Donahue,* with regard to "their actions relative to the operations of the enterprise and the effects of that operation on the rights and investments of other stockholders," "[s]tockholders in close corporations must discharge their management

This power, however, up until February, 1967, had not been exercised formally; all payments made to the four participants in the venture had resulted from the informal but unanimous approval of all the parties concerned.

and stockholder responsibilities in conformity with this strict good faith standard. They may not act out of avarice, expediency or self-interest in derogation of their duty of loyalty to the other stockholders and to the corporation." [367 Mass. at 593 n. 18], 328 N.E.2d at 515.

In the *Donahue* case we recognized that one peculiar aspect of close corporations was the opportunity afforded to majority stockholders to oppress, disadvantage or "freeze out" minority stockholders. In *Donahue* itself, for example, the majority refused the minority an equal opportunity to sell a ratable number of shares to the corporation at the same price available to the majority. The net result of this refusal, we said, was that the minority could be forced to "sell out at less than fair value," [367 Mass. at 592], 328 N.E.2d at 515, since there is by definition no ready market for minority stock in a close corporation.

"Freeze outs," however, may be accomplished by the use of other devices. One such device which has proved to be particularly effective in accomplishing the purpose of the majority is to deprive minority stockholders of corporate offices and of employment with the corporation. F.H. O'Neal, "SQUEEZE–OUTS" OF MINORITY SHAREHOLDERS 59, 78–79 (1975). *See* [367 Mass. 589], 328 N.E.2d 505. This "freeze-out" technique has been successful because courts fairly consistently have been disinclined to interfere in those facets of internal corporate operations, such as the selection and retention or dismissal of officers, directors and employees, which essentially involve management decisions subject to the principle of majority control. As one authoritative source has said, "[M]any courts apparently feel that there is a legitimate sphere in which the controlling directors or shareholders can act in their own interest even if the minority suffers." F.H. O'Neal, *supra* at 59 (footnote omitted).

The denial of employment to the minority at the hands of the majority is especially pernicious in some instances. A guaranty of employment with the corporation may have been one of the "basic reason[s] why a minority owner has invested capital in the firm." *Symposium— The Close Corporation*, 52 Nw.U.L.REV. 345, 392 (1957). See F.H. O'Neal, *supra* at 78–79. The minority stockholder typically depends on his salary as the principal return on his investment, since the "earnings of a close corporation * * * are distributed in major part in salaries, bonuses and retirement benefits." 1 F.H. O'Neal, CLOSE CORPORATIONS § 1.07 (1971).[13] Other noneconomic interests of the minority stockholder are likewise injuriously affected by barring him from corporate office. See F.H. O'Neal, "Squeeze–Outs" of Minority Shareholders 79 (1975). Such action severely restricts his participation in the management of the enterprise, and he is relegated to enjoying those benefits incident to his status as a stockholder. See Symposium—The Close Corporation, 52 Nw. U.L.Rev. 345, 386 (1957). In sum, by terminating a minority stockhold-

---

**13.** We note here that the master found that Springside never declared or paid a    dividend to its stockholders.

er's employment or by severing him from a position as an officer or director, the majority effectively frustrate the minority stockholder's purposes in entering on the corporate venture and also deny him an equal return on his investment.

* * * The distinction between the majority action in *Donahue* and the majority action in this case is more one of form than of substance. Nevertheless, we are concerned that untempered application of the strict good faith standard enunciated in *Donahue* to cases such as the one before us will result in the imposition of limitations on legitimate action by the controlling group in a close corporation which will unduly hamper its effectiveness in managing the corporation in the best interests of all concerned. The majority, concededly, have certain rights to what has been termed "selfish ownership" in the corporation which should be balanced against the concept of their fiduciary obligation to the minority.

Therefore, when minority stockholders in a close corporation bring suit against the majority alleging a breach of the strict good faith duty owed to them by the majority, we must carefully analyze the action taken by the controlling stockholders in the individual case. It must be asked whether the controlling group can demonstrate a legitimate business purpose for its action. *See Bryan v. Brock & Blevins Co.*, 343 F.Supp. 1062, 1068 (N.D.Ga.1972), aff'd, 490 F.2d 563, 570–571 (5th Cir.1974); *Schwartz v. Marien*, 37 N.Y.2d 487, 492, 373 N.Y.S.2d 122, 335 N.E.2d 334 (1975). In asking this question, we acknowledge the fact that the controlling group in a close corporation must have some room to maneuver in establishing the business policy of the corporation. It must have a large measure of discretion, for example, in declaring or withholding dividends, deciding whether to merge or consolidate, establishing the salaries of corporate officers, dismissing directors with or without cause, and hiring and firing corporate employees.

When an asserted business purpose for their action is advanced by the majority, however, we think it is open to minority stockholders to demonstrate that the same legitimate objective could have been achieved through an alternative course of action less harmful to the minority's interest. *See Schwartz v. Marien, supra.* If called on to settle a dispute, our courts must weigh the legitimate business purpose, if any, against the practicability of a less harmful alternative.

Applying this approach to the instant case it is apparent that the majority stockholders in Springside have not shown a legitimate business purpose for severing Wilkes from the payroll of the corporation or for refusing to reelect him as a salaried officer and director. The master's subsidiary findings relating to the purpose of the meetings of the directors and stockholders in February and March, 1967, are supported by the evidence. There was no showing of misconduct on Wilkes's part as a director, officer or employee of the corporation which would lead us to approve the majority action as a legitimate response to the disruptive nature of an undesirable individual bent on injuring or destroying the corporation. On the contrary, it appears that Wilkes had always accomplished his assigned share of the duties competently, and that he had never indicated an unwillingness to continue to do so.

It is an inescapable conclusion from all the evidence that the action of the majority stockholders here was a designed "freeze out" for which no legitimate business purpose has been suggested. Furthermore, we may infer that a design to pressure Wilkes into selling his shares to the corporation at a price below their value well may have been at the heart of the majority's plan.[14]

In the context of this case, several factors bear directly on the duty owed to Wilkes by his associates. At a minimum, the duty of utmost good faith and loyalty would demand that the majority consider that their action was in disregard of a long-standing policy of the stockholders that each would be a director of the corporation and that employment with the corporation would go hand in hand with stock ownership; that Wilkes was one of the four originators of the nursing home venture; and that Wilkes, like the others, had invested his capital and time for more than fifteen years with the expectation that he would continue to participate in corporate decisions. Most important is the plain fact that the cutting off of Wilkes's salary, together with the fact that the corporation never declared a dividend, assured that Wilkes would receive no return at all from the corporation.

2.   The question of Wilkes's damages at the hands of the majority has not been thoroughly explored on the record before us. Wilkes, in his original complaint, sought damages in the amount of the $100 a week he believed he was entitled to from the time his salary was terminated up until the time this action was commenced. However, the record shows that, after Wilkes was severed from the corporate payroll, the schedule of salaries and payments made to the other stockholders varied from time to time. In addition, the duties assumed by the other stockholders after Wilkes was deprived of his share of the corporate earnings appear to have changed in significant respects. Any resolution of this question must take into account whether the corporation was dissolved during the pendency of this litigation.

Therefore our order is as follows: So much of the judgment as dismisses Wilkes's complaint and awards costs to the defendants is reversed. * * *

———

Courts have demonstrated varying degrees of sensitivity to claims of unequal treatment raised by minority shareholders. Most, like *Wilkes*, have rejected *Donahue*'s "utmost good faith and loyalty" test in favor of approaches that allow majority shareholders more flexibility to manage the corporation's business as they see fit. But *Wilkes'* approach, too, has its critics.

**14.**  This inference arises from the fact that Connor, acting on behalf of the three controlling stockholders, offered to purchase Wilkes's shares for a price Connor admittedly would not have accepted for his own shares.

In close corporations, freezeouts generally arise in the context of a dispute over the disentanglement of what are essentially partnership arrangements among more or less active participants for whose securities there is no market. The parties are visibly at loggerheads over division of the business's prosperity or over the conduct of its business; their disagreements are of a continuing kind, likely both not to be resolved until the business terminates and to plague the parties as they remain unable to disentangle satisfactorily. There is, therefore, reason to facilitate or encourage the departure of one group or the other from the enterprise—both in terms of the personal well-being of the participants, and because of the impact of continuing disagreements on their conduct of the enterprise. It does not follow that corporate law should permit the controlling group to have an advantage in bargaining over the terms of the break-up. Still, the difficulty with flatly forbidding freezeouts is that, if the majority does not have the power to force the minority out, the majority may be forced to accede to the demands of the minority because of the threat of deadlock. Moreover, unlike the investors in a public corporation, the parties in a close corporation can contract in advance about their arrangements; any skew in the corporate law that permits majority power to displace the minority can thus be offset by contract. Modern statutes purport to offer special solutions for the problem of disentangling the essentially personal relationships of parties in conflict in close corporations. *See, e.g.*, Del.Code tit. 8, §§ 352, 355 (1975); N.Y.—McKinney's Bus.Corp.Law § 1104 (1963); id. § 1111(b)(3), (c). If, notwithstanding such legislation, freezeouts are permitted by statute, any judicially imposed solution will require compliance with some conception of "fairness," however crude it may be. But it is hard to see any role for "business purpose" as a doctrine in filtering permissible from impermissible freezeouts in close corporations, even as that conception is rigorously confined in cases like *Schwartz v. Marien* or *Wilkes v. Springside Nursing Home, Inc.*

Victor Brudney & Marvin A. Chirelstein, *A Restatement of Corporate Freezeouts*, 87 Yale L.J. 1354, 1356–57 n. 9 (1977).

As Brudney & Chirelstein suggest, courts following *Wilkes* face difficult line-drawing problems. Consider the Massachusetts Supreme Judicial Court's post-*Wilkes* treatment of situations in which the majority has dismissed an employee who also was a shareholder. When should such an action, which implicates both employment law and corporation law, be considered a breach of some fiduciary duty owed by the majority to the minority? In *King v. Driscoll*, 418 Mass. 576, 638 N.E.2d 488 (1994), the court held that the public policy exception to Massachusetts' at-will employment rule did not bar a corporation from dismissing an shareholder-employee for having filed a derivative suit. However, the court found that the dismissal violated the fiduciary duty of fair dealing that the corporation's majority shareholders owed to the dismissed shareholder-employee. *Blank v. Chelmsford Ob/Gyn, P.C.*, 420 Mass. 404,

649 N.E.2d 1102 (1995), on the other hand, found no breach of fiduciary duty where the majority shareholders dismissed without cause a shareholder-employee who had signed an employment agreement with the corporation allowing it to dismiss him without cause.

## MEROLA v. EXERGEN CORP.

423 Mass. 461, 668 N.E.2d 351 (1996).

LYNCH, JUSTICE

The plaintiff, a former vice president of Exergen Corporation (Exergen) and a former minority stockholder of that corporation, brought suit in the Superior Court against Exergen and the president and majority stockholder, Francesco Pompei, because of his termination as an officer and employee of Exergen. Count * * * III (breach of fiduciary duty) alleged that the corporation was a "close corporation," and that Pompei, as the majority stockholder, violated his fiduciary obligations to the plaintiff as a minority stockholder by terminating his employment without cause.

* * *

We summarize the facts found by the judge. Exergen was formed in May, 1980, as a corporation in the business of developing and selling infrared heat detection devices. From Exergen's inception to the date of trial, Pompei, the founder, was the majority shareholder in the corporation, as well as its president, owning over sixty per cent of the shares issued. At all relevant times, Pompei actively participated in and controlled the management of Exergen and, as the majority shareholder, had power to elect and change Exergen's board of directors.

The plaintiff began working for Exergen on a part-time basis in late 1980 while he was also employed full time by Analogic Corporation. In the course of conversations with Pompei in late 1981, and early 1982, the plaintiff was offered full-time employment with Exergen, and he understood that, if he came to work there and invested in Exergen stock, he would have the opportunity to become a major shareholder of Exergen and for continuing employment with Exergen.

As of March 1, 1982, the plaintiff resigned from Analogic and began working full time for Exergen. He also then began purchasing shares in Exergen when the company made periodic offerings to its employees. From March, 1982, through June, 1982, the plaintiff purchased 4,100 shares at $2.25 per share, for a total of $9,225. Exergen announced at the Exergen shareholders meeting in September, 1982, another option program to purchase shares at $5 per share within one year. By late 1983, the plaintiff had exercised his option to purchase an additional 1,200 shares. The plaintiff was not offered additional stock options after late 1983.

In response to special questions the jury made the following findings which were adopted by the judge: (1) the plaintiff did not receive an opportunity to become a major shareholder of Exergen; (2) there was a legitimate business purpose for not providing the plaintiff an opportunity to become a major shareholder of Exergen; (3) this business purpose could have been accomplished through an alternative course of action less harmful to the plaintiff's interests; and (4) the plaintiff suffered no damages by not being able to become a major shareholder of Exergen.

With regard to the alleged breach of fiduciary duty for terminating the plaintiff's employment with Exergen, the judge adopted the following findings by the jury: (1) the plaintiff was terminated by Pompei on April 16, 1987, and therefore did not receive continuing employment by Exergen; (2) there was no legitimate business purpose for not continuing the plaintiff's employment by Exergen;* and (3) the plaintiff suffered damages in lost wages, reduced by income from other employment, in the total amount of $50,000.

* * * Based on these findings, the judge ruled that, as matter of law, Pompei breached a fiduciary duty to the plaintiff to honor the reasonable expectations that the plaintiff had concerning investments of time and resources in Exergen, and awarded the plaintiff $50,000 in damages.

* * *

We agree with the judge's conclusion that Exergen was a close corporation, and that stockholders in a close corporation owe one another a fiduciary duty of "utmost good faith and loyalty." *Donahue v. Rodd Electrotype Co.*, *supra* at 593, 328 N.E.2d 505. We, therefore, look to see whether the plaintiff has established a breach of that duty under the principles of *Donahue*. Even in close corporations, the majority interest "must have a large measure of discretion, for example, in declaring or withholding dividends, deciding whether to merge or consolidate, establishing the salaries of corporate officers, dismissing directors with or without cause, and hiring and firing corporate employees." *Wilkes v. Springside Nursing Home, Inc.*, 370 Mass. 842, 851, 353 N.E.2d 657 (1976).

Principles of employment law permit the termination of employees at will, with or without cause excepting situations within a narrow public policy exception. *King v. Driscoll*, 418 Mass. 576, 581–582, 638 N.E.2d 488 (1994), and cases cited. However, the termination of a

---

* The Appeals Court described the circumstances of Merola's dismissal as follows:

Pompei [the controlling shareholder] delivered a written message to the employees at a staff meeting. The message describes the "chemistry" that developed between Pompei and a Ms. Ryan. The message continues, in part, "The result is good and it should continue. Our relationship has blossomed into a very strong one in a very brief time, and has all the elements of becoming a complete and permanent one. This announcement is part of the process of working toward that goal.... We have explored the issues thoroughly with both spouses ... who understand and support our actions. It is a credit to both that we can proceed with a clear conscience, and without guilt."

Plaintiff apparently was fired after he reacted to this incident by advising Pompei that his [Pompei's] relationship with Ryan was not good for the company. [*Merola v. Exergen Corp.*, 38 Mass. App. Court. 462, 467, n.6, 648 N.E.2d 1301, 1304, n. 6 (1995).] [Ed.]

minority shareholder's employment may present a situation where the majority interest has breached its fiduciary duty to the minority interest. *Id.* at 586, 638 N.E.2d 488. *Wilkes v. Springside Nursing Home, Inc., supra* at 852–853, 353 N.E.2d 657. * * *

Here, although the plaintiff invested in the stock of Exergen with the reasonable expectation of continued employment, there was no general policy regarding stock ownership and employment, and there was no evidence that any other stockholders had expectations of continuing employment because they purchased stock. The investment in the stock was an investment in the equity of the corporation which was not tied to employment in any formal way. The plaintiff acknowledged that he could have purchased 5,000 shares of stock while he was working part time before resigning from his position at Analogic Corporation and accepting full-time employment at Exergen. He testified that he was induced to work for Exergen with the promise that he could become a major stockholder. There was no testimony that he was ever required to buy stock as a condition of employment.

Unlike the *Wilkes* case, there was no evidence that the corporation distributed all profits to shareholders in the form of salaries. On the contrary, the perceived value of the stock increased during the time that the plaintiff was employed. The plaintiff first purchased his stock at $2.25 per share and, one year later, he purchased more for $5 per share. This indicated that there was some increase in value to the investment independent of the employment expectation. Neither was the plaintiff a founder of the business, his stock purchases were made after the business was established, and there was no suggestion that he had to purchase stock to keep his job.

The plaintiff testified that, when he sold his stock back to the corporation in 1991, he was paid $17 per share. This was a price that had been paid to other shareholders who sold their shares to the corporation at a previous date, and it is a price which, after consulting with his attorney, he concluded was a fair price. With this payment, the plaintiff realized a significant return on his capital investment independent of the salary he received as an employee.

We conclude that this is not a situation where the majority shareholder breached his fiduciary duty to a minority shareholder. "[T]he controlling group in a close corporation must have some room to maneuver in establishing the business policy of the corporation." *Wilkes v. Springside Nursing Home, Inc., supra* at 851, 353 N.E.2d 657. Although there was no legitimate business purpose for the termination of the plaintiff, neither was the termination for the financial gain of Pompei or contrary to established public policy. Not every discharge of an at-will employee of a close corporation who happens to own stock in the corporation gives rise to a successful breach of fiduciary duty claim. The plaintiff was terminated in accordance with his employment contract and fairly compensated for his stock. He failed to establish a sufficient basis for a breach of fiduciary duty claim under the principles of *Donahue v. Rodd Electrotype Co., supra.*

\* \* \*

Judgment reversed.

———

As the following case illustrates, the Delaware Supreme Court has rejected the idea that it should follow other than a "traditional" approach to evaluate claims made by shareholders in close corporations. Professor O'Kelley has suggested that the Delaware court's approach may reflect efficiency concerns, because making available *ex post* judicial relief "will create disincentives for the parties themselves to identify via contract the mix between opportunism and adaptability that they prefer." He concludes: "A court should create this disincentive only if it is likely that the court will be able to determine *ex post* better than the parties themselves could *ex ante* which governance structure is 'ideal.'" Charles O'Kelley, *Filling Gaps in the Close Corporation Contract: A Transaction Cost Analysis*, 87 Nw. L.Rev. 216, 247 (1992). A related possibility is that the Delaware court prefers to avoid the line-drawing problems posed by cases such as *Merola*.

## NIXON v. BLACKWELL
### 626 A.2d 1366 (Del.1993).

[Plaintiffs, descendants of the founder of E.C. Barton & Co. (the "Corporation"), held Class B non-voting stock. Plaintiffs claimed that the directors of the Corporation had treated defendants unfairly by establishing an employee stock ownership plan ("ESOP") and purchasing key man life insurance to enable defendants and other employees to sell their stock while providing no comparable liquidity for Class B shareholders. The Delaware Supreme Court agreed with the Vice Chancellor that the Corporation had not provided substantially equal treatment to employee and non-employee shareholders, but held that this lack of parity was not unfair because the ESOP and key man insurance advanced legitimate corporate objectives.]

VI.   No Special Rules for a "Closely–Held
Corporation" Not Qualified as a

"Close Corporation" Under Subchapter XIV of
the Delaware General Corporation Law

We wish to address one further matter which was raised at oral argument before this Court: Whether there should be any special, judicially-created rules to "protect" minority stockholders of closely-held Delaware corporations.

The case at bar points up the basic dilemma of minority stockholders in receiving fair value for their stock as to which there is no market and no market valuation. It is not difficult to be sympathetic, in the abstract, to a stockholder who finds himself or herself in that position. A stockholder who bargains for stock in a closely-held corporation and who pays for those shares * * * can make a business judgment whether to buy into such a minority position, and if so on what terms. One could bargain for definitive provisions of self-ordering permitted to a Delaware corporation through the certificate of incorporation or by-laws by reason of the provisions in 8 Del.C. §§ 102, 109, and 141(a). Moreover, in addition to such mechanisms, a stockholder intending to buy into a minority position in a Delaware corporation may enter into definitive stockholder agreements, and such agreements may provide for elaborate earnings tests, buy-out provisions, voting trusts, or other voting agreements. *See, e.g.*, 8 Del.C. § 218.

The tools of good corporate practice are designed to give a purchasing minority stockholder the opportunity to bargain for protection before parting with consideration. It would do violence to normal corporate practice and our corporation law to fashion an ad hoc ruling which would result in a court-imposed stockholder buy-out for which the parties had not contracted.

In 1967, when the Delaware General Corporation Law was significantly revised, a new Subchapter XIV entitled "Close Corporations; Special Provisions," became a part of that law for the first time. While these provisions were patterned in theory after close corporation statutes in Florida and Maryland, "the Delaware provisions were unique and influenced the development of similar legislation in a number of other states. * * *" *See* Ernest L. Folk, III, Rodman Ward, Jr., and Edward P. Welch, 2 FOLK ON THE DELAWARE GENERAL CORPORATION LAW 404 (1988). Subchapter XIV is a narrowly constructed statute which applies only to a corporation which is designated as a "close corporation" in its certificate of incorporation, and which fulfills other requirements, including a limitation to 30 on the number of stockholders, that all classes of stock have to have at least one restriction on transfer, and that there be no "public offering." 8 Del.C. § 342. Accordingly, subchapter XIV applies only to "close corporations," as defined in section 342. "Unless a corporation elects to become a close corporation under this subchapter in the manner prescribed in this subchapter, it shall be subject in all respects to this chapter, except this subchapter." 8 Del.C. § 341. The corporation before the Court in this matter, is not a "close corporation." Therefore it is not governed by the provisions of Subchapter XIV.[19]

**19.** We do not intend to imply that, if the Corporation had been a close corporation under Subchapter XIV, the result in this case would have been different. "[S]tatutory close corporations have not found particular favor with practitioners. Practitioners have for the most part viewed the complex statutory provisions underlying the purportedly simplified operational procedures for close corporations as legal quicksand of uncertain depth and have adopted the view that the objectives sought by the subchapter are achievable for their clients with considerably less uncertainty by cloaking a conventionally created corporation with the panoply of charter provisions, transfer restrictions, by-laws, stockholders' agreements, buy-sell arrangements, irrevocable proxies, voting trusts or other contractual mechanisms which were and remain the traditional method for accomplish-

One cannot read into the situation presented in the case at bar any special relief for the minority stockholders in this closely-held, but not statutory "close corporation" because the provisions of Subchapter XIV relating to close corporations and other statutory schemes preempt the field in their respective areas. It would run counter to the spirit of the doctrine of independent legal significance, and would be inappropriate judicial legislation for this Court to fashion a special judicially-created rule for minority investors when the entity does not fall within those statutes, or when there are no negotiated special provisions in the certificate of incorporation, by-laws, or stockholder agreements.

### Note: Contractual Approaches

Frank Easterbrook and Daniel Fischel argue for a contractual approach to close corporation problems that falls somewhere between the fiduciary approach followed by the Massachusetts courts and the traditional approach of *Nixon v. Blackwell*.* More specifically, Easterbrook and Fischel contend that, having chosen the corporate form, participants in a close corporation are bound by the terms of their "corporate contract." However, they further argue that courts should read into that contract "the bargain parties would have reached themselves if transaction costs were zero." Frank H. Easterbrook & Daniel R. Fischel, THE ECONOMIC STRUCTURE OF CORPORATE LAW 247 (1991). The analytic approach employed in *Wilkes*, they conclude, is consistent with that mode of contractual analysis.

*Jordan v. Duff and Phelps, Inc.*, 815 F.2d 429 (7th Cir.1987), illustrates that viewing the relationship among participants in a close corporation as contractual may not clarify what duties those participants owe to each other. Jordan, a securities analyst, was an at-will employee of Duff & Phelps, Inc. in Chicago. Jordan was eligible to purchase 250 shares pursuant to Duff & Phelps' employee stock purchase plan, had purchased 188 shares and was making installment payments on another 62 shares. A "Stock Restriction and Purchase Agreement" required Jordan to sell his stock back to Duff & Phelps, at its adjusted book value as of the end of the preceding year, if his employment terminated for any reason.

To resolve certain family problems, Jordan decided to accept a job with another firm in a different city. On November 16, 1983, Jordan tendered his resignation to the CEO of Duff & Phelps, who advised him that if he resigned effective December 31, 1983, he would receive the

---

ing the goals sought by the close corporation provisions." David A. Drexler, Lewis S. Black, Jr., and A. Gilchrist Sparks, III, Delaware Corporation Law and Practice § 43.01 (1993).

* One also should be careful about drawing too sharp a contrast between the approaches of the Massachusetts and Delaware courts. In *Riblet Products Corp. v. Nagy*, 683 A.2d 37 (Del.1996), the court reiterated the duties owed by stockholders are the same whether they hold stock in public or close corporations. *Id.* at 39, n.2. But the court also held, as did the Massachusetts court in *Merola*, that the duties of majority stockholders, "*qua* stockholders, * * * are not implicated when the issue involves the rights of the minority stockholder *qua* employee." *Id.* at 37.

increase in the book value of his Duff & Phelps shares through the end
of 1983. The CEO, however, did not tell Jordan that he was in the midst
of negotiations to sell Duff & Phelps to a public corporation.

Jordan made his resignation effective December 31, 1983, and, at
the end of 1983, received a check for $23,225 in exchange for his 188
shares and his release of his right to purchase the additional 62 shares.
Then, on January 10, 1984, Duff & Phelps announced that it had agreed
to be acquired at a price which, had Jordan remained an employee and
exercised his right to purchase the additional 62 shares, would have left
him with stock worth about $452,000. Jordan reacted by attempting to
return the check for $23,225 and demanding that Duff & Phelps pay him
what he would have received had he remained an employee. Duff &
Phelps rejected his demand and Jordan sued, alleging that Duff &
Phelps had a duty to disclose the merger negotiations to him before accepting
his resignation.

Judge Frank Easterbrook, writing for the majority, held that Jordan
had a valid claim. He began his analysis by describing the fiduciary
duties owed by a majority shareholder as reflecting "a standby or off-the-
rack guess about what the parties would agree to if they dickered about
the subject explicitly; parties may contract with greater specificity for
other arrangements." *Id*. at 436. Easterbrook then explained his off-the-
rack guess that Duff & Phelps and Jordan, *as a consequence of their
employment* "*contract*," would have agreed that Duff & Phelps owed
Jordan a duty to disclose the merger negotiations:

> * * * [A] person's status as an employee "at will" does not
> imply that the employer may discharge him for every reason. * * *
> We do not disparage the utility of at-will contracts; this very panel
> recently recognized the value of informal (meaning not legally
> binding) employment relations. * * * But employment at will is still
> a contractual relation, one in which a particular duration ("at will")
> is implied in the absence of a contrary expression. The silence of the
> parties may make it necessary to imply other terms—those we are
> confident the parties would have bargained for if they had signed a
> written agreement. One term implied in every written contract and
> therefore, we suppose, every unwritten one, is that neither party
> will try to take opportunistic advantage of the other. "[T]he funda-
> mental function of contract law (and recognized as such at least
> since Hobbes's day) is to deter people from behaving opportunistical-
> ly toward their contracting parties, in order to encourage the opti-
> mal timing of economic activity and to make costly self-protective
> measures unnecessary." Richard A. Posner, Economic Analysis of
> Law 81 (3d ed. 1986).

815 F.2d at 438.

Judge Richard Posner dissented. He argued that Duff & Phelps
owed Jordan no duty other than to repurchase his stock at adjusted book
value. Posner focused on the fact that Jordan's status as a shareholder
was contingent on his remaining an employee. Because Jordan was an

"at will" employee who Duff & Phelps could discharge at any time, Posner reasoned, his status as a shareholder also was entirely contingent. That negated the existence of a right to be informed; hence, Duff & Phelps had no duty to disclose. Posner also disagreed with Easterbrook's conclusion that Duff & Phelps' had been opportunistic. Because shareholders such as Jordan are adequately protected by market constraints, such as the firm's desire to protect its reputation, he claimed, no occasion for opportunism should be deemed to exist.

The issue underlying the debate between Judges Easterbrook and Posner in *Jordan*—how a court should go about filling in the terms of an incomplete or implicit corporate "contract"—has been the subject of considerable academic commentary. In *Jordan*, Easterbrook side-stepped that issue by basing his decision on Jordan's implicit employment contract. Easterbrook's reluctance to impute broader notions of fiduciary duty to the controlling shareholders of Duff & Phelps may have reflected his view that the choice of the corporate form itself is evidence that the parties intend to be governed by the norms generally applicable to corporate managers and shareholders. See Frank H. Easterbrook & Daniel R. Fischel, THE ECONOMIC STRUCTURE OF CORPORATE LAW 228–252 (1991). In *Nixon*, the Delaware Supreme Court more or less espoused the same point of view.

David Charny also uses contractual analysis as his framework for analyzing the duties owed to minority shareholders in close corporations. In contrast to Easterbrook and Fischel, however, he suggests that in filling in the terms of the corporate "contract," courts should consider not only the express terms of the agreements between the parties, but also informal discussions, past practices, and the participants' reasonable income expectations. David Charny, *Hypothetical Bargains: The Normative Structure of Contract Interpretations*, 89 MICH. L. REV. 1815, 1870–72 (1991). More significantly, where Easterbrook and Fischel generally conclude that shareholders would have bargained for a weak set of fiduciary duties, Professor Charny argues that courts should presume that the parties intended to accord considerable protection to minority shareholders' interests and imply a strong set of fiduciary duties. He points out that if that is not the parties' intent, the parties can simply opt out out of these implied obligations. Approaching the issue in this fashion, Charny adds, will allow courts to more efficiently resolve intra-corporate disputes. *Id.* at 1872.

Jason Johnston comes at the issue from a slightly different angle. He contends that Easterbrook and Fischel's contractual arguments disregard the power disparity between minority and majority shareholders. He claims that their error is to assume that the weaker party, the minority shareholder, typically would prefer to rely on market forces, such as a majority shareholder's interest in preserving her reputation, for protection from opportunistic behavior. In contrast, Professor Johnston suggests that most minority shareholders would prefer to rely on an imperfect legal system, even if it tends to interpret fiduciary duties too broadly. Jason S. Johnston, *Opting In and Opting Out: Bargaining for*

*Fiduciary Duties in Cooperative Ventures*, 70 WASH. U. L. Q. 291, 297 (1992). Johnston also questions claims that imposing broad fiduciary duties would be economically inefficient. *Id*. at 295–98. He argues that if courts can enhance efficiency by implying expansive fiduciary duties as part of the corporate "contract," in many circumstances, minority shareholders will be prepared to make larger firm-specific investments. *Id*. at 333–337.

John Hetherington, who also favors a contract-oriented approach, advances still another argument:

> Bargaining is costly, and the parties may be expected to engage in it only when the prospective benefits exceed the costs. In resolving disputes ex post, the efficiency and productivity of exchange transactions would be enhanced if the courts sought the allocation which the parties would have made ex ante had they then considered that the gains of bargaining exceeded the costs.

John A.C. Hetherington, *Defining the Scope of Controlling Shareholders' Fiduciary Responsibilities*, 22 WAKE FOREST L.REV. 9, 20 (1987). Commenting that the traditional law and economics analysis seems compulsively "committed to preserving the prerogatives of majorities and the vulnerability of at-will employees and close corporation minorities as essential to the maintenance and enhancement of the productivity of business enterprises," Professor Hetherington also notes:

> One is struck in this area by what seems to be the obsessive concern of policymakers, commentators, and, on occasion, judges over the perceived risk that persons in relatively disadvantaged positions—employees at will and small minorities in close corporations—will behave strategically when dealing with those who occupy dominant and controlling positions. Preserving the vulnerability of the disadvantaged in these business relationships becomes a policy goal. The point here is not, of course, that there is no risk of such behavior: it is the implicit normative judgment that the allocation of rights (and wealth) produced by past business arrangements is "right" and that any movement toward reallocation is presumptively undesirable.

John A. C. Hetherington, *Bargaining For Fiduciary Duties: Preserving the Vulnerability of the Disadvantaged?*, 70 WASH. U. L. Q. 341, 351 (1992).

### Note: Tort Approach to Oppression

Some courts have gone beyond reliance on the partnership analogy when dealing with claims by minority shareholders in close corps; they have recognized the tort of freeze-out when they have found patterns of oppressive conduct that deprive the minority shareholders of all financial benefits from the corporation. *Sugarman v. Sugarman*, 797 F.2d 3 (1st Cir.1986), involved a family corporation controlled by Leonard Sugarman, the son of one of the founders and the holder of a majority of the corporation's stock. The plaintiffs, grandchildren of another founder, owned the remainder of the firm's shares. The plaintiffs pleaded "the theory of 'freeze-out' of minority shareholders." 797 F.2d at 6. They alleged that Leonard had deprived them of desired corporate employment, drained off the firm's earnings by paying himself "excessive" compensation, and refused to pay dividends. The court held that neither the payment of excessive salaries nor an offer to repurchase shares at an inadequate price alone was oppressive, but that when such activities are tied to a course of conduct that freezes-out a minority interest from all financial benefits provided by the corporation such conduct would be deemed tortious. Leonard's conduct, the court held, involved all the necessary ingredients.

*Clark v. Lubritz*, 944 P.2d 861 (Nev.1997), involved a corporation set up by five doctors who agreed orally that they would operate as partners and share profits and losses equally. After a few years, the doctors began to develop serious differences of opinion regarding the way the corporation should sell its medical benefits plan. Dr. Lubritz, who had devoted more time to the corporation's business than the other doctors in the corporation's first years, resigned from the board to signal the gravity of his disagreement. For four years, the other doctors divided profits equally with Lubritz. Then for two years they reduced the share of profits distributed to Lubritz without informing him that they were receiving higher payments. When Lubritz learned of that fact and filed suit, the other doctors informed him that they did not intend to make any future payments to him.

The Nevada Supreme Court affirmed a jury's award to Lubritz of $195,000 for breach of contract and breach of fiduciary duty and $200,-000 in punitive damages. The court held that the other doctors had violated their fiduciary duty to make full disclosure to Lubritz "of material facts relating to the partnership affairs," *id*. at 865, and that "the breach of a fiduciary duty arising from the partnership agreement is a separate tort upon which punitive damages may be based." *Id*. at 867.

## 3.  JUDICIAL LIMITATIONS ON THE EXERCISE OF VETO RIGHTS

Minority shareholders frequently attempt to protect their interests by conditioning their investments in close corporations on adoption of a governance structure that will allow one or more minority shareholders to veto some or all decisions of the majority. As we have seen, various combinations of governance devices can readily be used to create such a structure. For example, cumulative voting or a shareholder voting agreement can be used to assure minority representation on the board of directors, and when combined with a supermajority voting or quorum requirement may give a minority the power to block board actions to which it objects.

Minority shareholders can use veto powers selectively, or can elect to create a deadlock. A "deadlock" does not exist whenever there are insufficient number votes to take some given action. Where directors are evenly split on an issue, or where they divide 3–1 when an 80% vote is required, there is no "deadlock;"an action simply has not been approved by the required vote. The corporation otherwise continues to function normally. The term "deadlock" applies to those situations in which relations among the shareholders or directors has deteriorated to the point that virtually no action is possible—whenever one faction says something is black, the other says it is white. The corporation may be able to continue to operate in some fashion, but trying to do business in such circumstances usually is not comfortable or convenient and is unlikely to be profitable.

Nonetheless, one of the factions responsible for creating a deadlock usually will be more comfortable with the status quo than the other. Often, the faction feeling the most pain will turn to the courts for relief.

## SMITH v. ATLANTIC PROPERTIES, INC.

12 Mass.App.Ct. 201, 422 N.E.2d 798 (1981).

CUTTER, JUSTICE.

In December, 1951, Dr. Louis E. Wolfson agreed to purchase land in Norwood for $350,000, with an initial cash payment of $50,000 and a mortgage note of $300,000 payable in thirty-three months. Dr. Wolfson offered a quarter interest each in the land to Mr. Paul T. Smith, Mr. Abraham Zimble, and William H. Burke. Each paid to Dr. Wolfson $12,500, one quarter of the initial payment. Mr. Smith, an attorney, organized the defendant corporation (Atlantic) in 1951 to operate the real estate. Each of the four subscribers received twenty-five shares of stock. Mr. Smith included, both in the corporation's articles of organization and in its by-laws, a provision reading, "No election, appointment or resolution by the Stockholders and no election, appointment, resolution, purchase, sale, lease, contract, contribution, compensation, proceeding or act by the Board of Directors or by any officer or officers shall be valid or binding upon the corporation until effected, passed, approved or ratified by an affirmative vote of eighty (80%) per cent of the capital stock issued outstanding and entitled to vote." This provision (hereafter referred to as the 80% provision) was included at Dr. Wolfson's request and had the effect of giving to any one of the four original shareholders a veto in corporate decisions.

Atlantic purchased the Norwood land. Some of the land and other assets were sold for about $220,000. Atlantic retained twenty-eight acres on which stood about twenty old brick or wood mill-type structures, which required expensive and constant repairs. After the first year, Atlantic became profitable and showed a profit every year prior to 1969, ranging from a low of $7,683 in 1953 to a high of $44,358 in 1954. The mortgage was paid by 1958 and Atlantic has incurred no long-term debt thereafter. Salaries of about $25,000 were paid only in 1959 and 1960. Dividends in the total amount of $10,000 each were paid in 1964 and

1970. By 1961, Atlantic had about $172,000 in retained earnings, more than half in cash.

For various reasons, which need not be stated in detail, disagreements and ill will soon arose between Dr. Wolfson, on the one hand, and the other stockholders as a group.[3] Dr. Wolfson wished to see Atlantic's earnings devoted to repairs and possibly some improvements in its existing buildings and adjacent facilities. The other stockholders desired the declaration of dividends. Dr. Wolfson fairly steadily refused to vote for any dividends. Although it was pointed out to him that failure to declare dividends might result in the imposition by the Internal Revenue Service of a penalty under the Internal Revenue Code, I.R.C. § 531 et seq. (relating to unreasonable accumulation of corporate earnings and profits), Dr. Wolfson persisted in his refusal to declare dividends. The other shareholders did agree over the years to making at least the most urgent repairs to Atlantic's buildings, but did not agree to make all repairs and improvements which were recommended in a 1962 report by an engineering firm retained by Atlantic to make a complete estimate of all repairs and improvements which might be beneficial.

The fears of an Internal Revenue Service assessment of a penalty tax were soon realized. Penalty assessments were made in 1962, 1963, and 1964. These were settled by Dr. Wolfson for $11,767.71 in taxes and interest. Despite this settlement, Dr. Wolfson continued his opposition to declaring dividends. The record does not indicate that he developed any specific and definitive schedule or plan for a series of necessary or desirable repairs and improvements to Atlantic's properties. At least none was proposed which would have had a reasonable chance of satisfying the Internal Revenue Service that expenditures for such repairs and improvements constituted "reasonable needs of the business," I.R.C. § 534(c), a term which includes (see I.R.C. § 537) "the reasonably anticipated needs of the business." Predictably, despite further warnings by Dr. Wolfson's shareholder colleagues, the Internal Revenue Service assessed further penalty taxes for the years 1965, 1966, 1967, and 1968. These taxes were upheld by the United States Tax Court in Atlantic Properties, Inc. v. Commissioner of Int. Rev., 62 T.C. 644 (1974), and on appeal in 519 F.2d 1233 (1st Cir.1975). See the discussion of these opinions in Cathcart, Accumulated Earnings Tax: A Trap for the Wary, 62 A.B.A.J. 1197–1199 (1976). An examination of these decisions makes it apparent that Atlantic has incurred substantial penalty taxes and legal expense largely because of Dr. Wolfson's refusal to vote for the declaration of sufficient dividends to avoid the penalty, a refusal which was (in the Tax Court and upon appeal) attributed in some measure to a tax avoidance purpose on Dr. Wolfson's part.

On January 30, 1967, the shareholders, other than Dr. Wolfson, initiated this proceeding in the Superior Court, later supplemented to reflect developments after the original complaint. The plaintiffs sought a

---

**3.** At least one cause of ill will on Dr. Wolfson's part may have been the refusal of the other shareholders to consent to his transferring his shares in Atlantic to the Louis E. Wolfson Foundation, a charitable foundation created by Dr. Wolfson.

court determination of the dividends to be paid by Atlantic, the removal of Dr. Wolfson as a director, and an order that Atlantic be reimbursed by him for the penalty taxes assessed against it and related expenses. The case was tried before a justice of the Superior Court (jury waived) in September and October, 1979.

The trial judge made findings (but in more detail) of essentially the facts outlined above and concluded that Dr. "Wolfson's obstinate refusal to vote in favor of * * * dividends was * * * caused more by his dislike for other stockholders and his desire to avoid additional tax payments than * * * by any genuine desire to undertake a program for improving * * * [Atlantic] property." She also determined that Dr. Wolfson was liable to Atlantic for taxes and interest amounting to "$11,767.11 plus interest from the commencement of this action, plus $35,646.14 plus interest from August 11, 1975," the date of the First Circuit decision affirming the second penalty tax assessment. The latter amount includes an attorney's fee of $7,500 in the Federal tax cases. She also ordered the directors of Atlantic to declare "a reasonable dividend at the earliest practical date and reasonable dividends annually thereafter consistent with good business practice." In addition, the trial judge directed that jurisdiction of the case be retained in the Superior Court "for a period of five years to [e]nsure compliance." Judgment was entered pursuant to the trial judge's order. After the entry of judgment, Dr. Wolfson and Atlantic filed a motion for a new trial and to amend the judge's findings. This motion, after hearing, was denied, and Dr. Wolfson and Atlantic claimed an appeal from the judgment and the former from the denial of the motion. The plaintiffs * * * requested payment of their attorneys' fees in this proceeding and filed supporting affidavits. The motion was denied, and the plaintiffs appealed.

1. The trial judge, in deciding that Dr. Wolfson had committed a breach of his fiduciary duty to other stockholders, relied greatly on broad language in Donahue v. Rodd Electrotype Co., 367 Mass. 578, 586–597, 328 N.E.2d 505 (1975), in which the Supreme Judicial Court afforded to a minority stockholder in a close corporation equality of treatment (with members of a controlling group of shareholders) in the matter of the redemption of shares. The court (at 592–593, 328 N.E.2d 505) relied on the resemblance of a close corporation to a partnership and held that "stockholders in the close corporation owe one another substantially the same fiduciary duty in the operation of the enterprise that partners owe to one another" (footnotes omitted). That standard of duty, the court said, was the "utmost good faith and loyalty." The court went on to say that such stockholders "may not act out of avarice, expediency or self-interest in derogation of their duty of loyalty to the other stockholders and to the corporation." Similar principles were stated in Wilkes v. Springside Nursing Home, Inc., 370 Mass. 842, 848–852, 353 N.E.2d 657 (1976), but with some modifications, mentioned in the margin, of the sweeping language of the *Donahue* case. * * *

In the *Donahue* case, 367 Mass. at 593 n. 17, 328 N.E.2d 505, the court recognized that cases may arise in which, in a close corporation, majority stockholders may ask protection from a minority stockholder. Such an instance arises in the present case because Dr. Wolfson has been able to exercise a veto concerning corporate action on dividends by the 80% provision (in Atlantic's articles [of] organization and by-laws) already quoted. The 80% provision may have substantially the effect of reversing the usual roles of the majority and the minority shareholders. The minority, under that provision, becomes an ad hoc controlling interest.

\* \* \*

Dr. Wolfson testified that he requested the inclusion of the 80% provision "in case the people [the other shareholders] whom I knew, but not very well, ganged up on me." The possibilities of shareholder disagreement on policy made the provision seem a sensible precaution. A question is presented, however, concerning the extent to which such a veto power possessed by a minority stockholder may be exercised as its holder may wish, without a violation of the "fiduciary duty" referred to in the *Donahue* case, 367 Mass. at 593, 328 N.E.2d 505, as modified in the *Wilkes* case. \* \* \*

The decided cases in Massachusetts do little to answer this question. The most pertinent guidance is probably found in the *Wilkes* case, 370 Mass. at 849–852, 353 N.E.2d 657, \* \* \* essentially to the effect that in any judicial intervention in such a situation there must be a weighing of the business interests advanced as reasons for their action (a) by the majority or controlling group and (b) by the rival persons or group. It would obviously be appropriate, before a court-ordered solution is sought or imposed, for both sides to attempt to reach a sensible solution of any incipient impasse in the interest of all concerned after consideration of all relevant circumstances. See Helms v. Duckworth, 249 F.2d 482, 485–488 (D.C.Cir.1957).

2. With respect to the past damage to Atlantic caused by Dr. Wolfson's refusal to vote in favor of any dividends, the trial judge was justified in finding that his conduct went beyond what was reasonable. The other stockholders shared to some extent responsibility for what occurred by failing to accept Dr. Wolfson's proposals with much sympathy, but the inaction on dividends seems the principal cause of the tax penalties. Dr. Wolfson had been warned of the dangers of an assessment under the Internal Revenue Code, I.R.C. § 531 et seq. He had refused to vote dividends in any amount adequate to minimize that danger and had failed to bring forward, within the relevant taxable years, a convincing, definitive program of appropriate improvements which could withstand scrutiny by the Internal Revenue Service. Whatever may have been the reason for Dr. Wolfson's refusal to declare dividends (and even if in any particular year he may have gained slight, if any, tax advantage from withholding dividends) we think that he recklessly ran serious and unjustified risks of precisely the penalty taxes eventually assessed, risks which were inconsistent with any reasonable interpretation of a duty of "utmost good faith and loyalty." The trial judge (despite the fact that

the other shareholders helped to create the voting deadlock and despite the novelty of the situation) was justified in charging Dr. Wolfson with the out-of-pocket expenditure incurred by Atlantic for the penalty taxes and related counsel fees of the tax cases.[10]

3. The trial judge's order to the directors of Atlantic, "to declare a reasonable dividend at the earliest practical date and reasonable dividends annually thereafter," presents difficulties. It may well not be a precise, clear, and unequivocal command which (without further explanation) would justify enforcement by civil contempt proceedings * * *. It also fails to order the directors to exercise similar business judgment with respect to Dr. Wolfson's desire to make all appropriate repairs and improvements to Atlantic's factory properties. See the language of the Supreme Judicial Court in the *Wilkes* case, 370 Mass. at 850–852, 353 N.E.2d 657, see note 5, *supra*.

The somewhat ambiguous injunctive relief is made less significant by the trial judge's reservation of jurisdiction in the Superior Court, a provision which contemplates later judicial supervision. We think that such supervision should be provided now upon an expanded record. The present record does not disclose Atlantic's present financial condition or what, if anything, it has done (since the judgment under review) by way of expenditures for repairs and improvements of its properties and in respect of dividends and salaries. The judgment, of course, necessarily disregards the general judicial reluctance to interfere with a corporation's dividend policy ordinarily based upon the business judgment of its directors. See Crocker v. Waltham Watch Co., 315 Mass. 397, 402, 53 N.E.2d 230 (1944); Donahue v. Rodd Electrotype Co., 367 Mass. at 590, 328 N.E.2d 505, and authorities cited; 1 O'Neal, Close Corporations § 3.63a and 2 O'Neal § 8.08; Forced Dividends, 1 J.Corp.L. 420 (1976).

Although the reservation of jurisdiction is appropriate in this case (see Nassif v. Boston & Maine R.R., 340 Mass. 557, 566–567, 165 N.E.2d 397 [1960]; Department of Pub. Health v. Cumberland Cattle Co., 361 Mass. 817, 834, 282 N.E.2d 895 [1972]), its purpose should be stated more affirmatively. Paragraph 2 of the judgment should be revised to provide: (a) a direction that Atlantic's directors prepare promptly financial statements and copies of State and Federal income and excise tax returns for the five most recent calendar or fiscal years, and a balance sheet as of as current a date as is possible; (b) an instruction that they confer with one another with a view to stipulating a general dividend and capital improvements policy for the next ensuing three fiscal years; (c) an order that, if such a stipulation is not filed with the clerk of the Superior Court within sixty days after the receipt of the rescript in the Superior Court, a further hearing shall be held promptly (either before the court or before a special master with substantial experience in

---

**10.** We do not now suggest that the standard of "utmost good faith and loyalty" may require some relaxation when applied to a minority ad hoc controlling interest, created by some device, similar to the 80% provision, designed in part to protect the selfish interests of a minority shareholder. This seems to us a difficult area of the law best developed on a case by case basis.

business affairs), at which there shall be received in evidence at least the financial statements and tax returns above mentioned, as well as other relevant evidence. Thereafter, the court, after due consideration of the circumstances then existing, may direct the adoption (and carrying out), if it be then deemed appropriate, of a specific dividend and capital improvements policy adequate to minimize the risk of further penalty tax assessments for the then current fiscal year of Atlantic. The court also may reserve jurisdiction to take essentially the same action for each subsequent fiscal year until the parties are able to reach for themselves an agreed program.

### Note: Other Techniques for Resolving Disputes

Adopting a governance structure that gives each significant shareholder veto rights may appear an attractive alternative to more elaborate pre-incorporation planning. Even if the parties subsequently disagree about particular decisions, their shared interest in enhancing the profitability of the corporation provides a substantial incentive for them to accommodate their differences. But deadlock nonetheless remains a possibility.

Rather than run the risk that a deadlock will develop, the parties should consider whether they would be better off relying on some alternative dispute resolution mechanism. If minority interests are protected by equal representation on the board of directors, the solution may be as simple as providing for an uneven number of directors. However, the selection of the "neutral" director itself may pose a problem and shareholders also may wish to consider how they will fill a vacancy if the "neutral" director dies or resigns (perhaps in disgust). In evaluating these possibilities, recall the deadlock-breaking mechanisms employed in *Ringling* and in *Lehrman v. Cohen*.

The arrangements in both *Lehrman* and *Ringling* partook of many of the characteristics of a simple arbitration agreement. But it is significant that in neither case did the parties characterize the arrangement as a conventional arbitration scheme (although Loos was designated as "arbitrator" in *Ringling*). It is apparent from the opinions, moreover, that the Delaware courts were reluctant to say straightforwardly that they were enforcing an arbitration agreement. Underlying this apparent aversion to applying the law of arbitration to the sort of dispute that often arises in close corporations may be a judicial reservation about the practical limitations of the use of arbitration to resolve disputes over the management of corporations.

To begin with, it is obvious that the directors or shareholders cannot run to an arbitrator every time they disagree over some business decision. Moreover, courts tended to be jealous of incursions by arbitration into their jurisdiction and established a variety of obstacles to the enforcement of arbitration agreements. In most jurisdictions, nearly all of those obstacles now have been removed by legislation providing that agreements to arbitrate are to be given specific performance.

As arbitration has become more popular, and has become a more formal tool for dispute resolution, some of its purported advantages are less significant. While arbitration is for the most part still less costly than litigation, the potential savings resulting from the use of arbitration tend to disappear as the formality of the process increases. Furthermore, delays are not foreign to arbitration, and can occur when parties cannot agree on an arbitrator or a hearing date. Finally, like adjudication, arbitration is ultimately an adversarial process, which may solve a particular dispute or deadlock, but may not reach the root of a problem.

Another alternative dispute resolution mechanism, mediation, does not function on the premise that the problem will be solved by the binding decision of some third party after an adversarial proceeding. Rather, mediation envisions the parties working together, with the help of a neutral mediator, to craft a mutually satisfying solution by which each party will agree to abide.

The role of the mediator is very important if the parties are going to resolve a dispute. A good mediator should remain impartial and be skilled in facilitating communication between the parties. It is important for the mediator to be able to get the parties to see the underlying causes for the dispute or deadlock, and for each to understand the basis for the other's position. No rules exist as to who may serve as mediator. Therefore, the parties can choose any respected neutral third party, even the corporation's attorney where appropriate.

Distinct advantages exist in choosing mediation as a method of dispute resolution. First, in using mediation, the parties retain the greatest amount of control over the procedural format for resolving the dispute or deadlock. Second, the process will hopefully leave each party with a genuine understanding of the other's position. This may pave the way to rebuilding a working relationship. Finally, the informality of the process allows for even more savings than arbitration because attorneys are not required.

Mediation, however, also has its disadvantages. As a result of the non-binding nature of the process, the mediator cannot compel the resolution of a dispute or deadlock. If the mediator cannot induce a settlement between the parties, the process may ultimately resolve nothing. When the parties cannot agree, legal proceedings will likely result, and the entire mediation process ironically will be an extra cost, rather than leading to a cost savings. However, on an ex ante basis, the overall benefits outweigh the overall costs.

For an analysis of alternative dispute resolution techniques, see Lewis D. Solomon & Janet S. Solomon, *Using Alternative Dispute Resolution Techniques To Settle Disputes Among Shareholders of Closely Held Corporations*, 22 WAKE FOREST L.REV. 105 (1987).

## 4. STATUTORY REMEDIES FOR OPPRESSION

In recent years, many states have adopted statutes based on RMBCA § 14.30 and RMBCA § 14.34. RMBCA § 14.30(2) grants a court power to dissolve a corporation if a shareholder establishes that (a) the directors are deadlocked, the shareholders cannot break the deadlock, and the deadlock is injuring the corporation or impairing the conduct of its business; (b) the shareholders are deadlocked and have not been able to elect directors for two years; (c) corporate assets are being wasted; *or* (d) those in control of the corporation are acting "in a manner that is illegal, oppressive or fraudulent." The Official Comment to RMBCA § 14.30 advises courts to be "cautious" when considering claims of oppression "so as to limit [such cases] to genuine abuse rather than instances of acceptable tactics in a power struggle for control of a corporation." In addition, RMBCA § 14.34 authorizes a court to allow any close corporation or any shareholder of a close corporation "to purchase all shares owned by the petitioning shareholder at the fair value of the shares", either within 90 days after a petition is filed under § 14.30(2) or at some later date, which can be a date after a court has found that the petitioning shareholder was being oppressed.

These statutes are designed to provide minority shareholders in close corporations with protections comparable to those that courts in some jurisdictions have used their inherent equity authority to provide. They raise two important interpretive questions. First, when should the conduct of those who control a corporation be deemed "oppressive?" Second, where a court finds oppression (or deadlock), what remedy should it make available, dissolution or buy-out?

Corporate statutes usually provide that a corporation can be dissolved with the approval of the board of directors and the shareholders. *See* RMBCA §§ 14.02–14.07. In the case of both voluntary and court-ordered dissolutions, the existence of a corporation is terminated in an orderly fashion: the corporation sells off its assets, pays off its creditors, and distributes whatever remains to its shareholders. However, a dissident shareholder who brings suit seeking dissolution often will be less interested in terminating the corporation's legal existence than in using the threat of dissolution as leverage to bargain for a better price for her stock. *See generally*, John A. C. Hetherington & Michael P. Dooley, *Illiquidity and Exploitation: A Proposed Statutory Solution to the Remaining Close Corporation Problem*, 63 VA.L.REV. 1 (1977).

Whether that threat will be effective may depend on the nature of the corporation's business. If a business derives its value almost entirely from the corporation's tangible assets, shareholders who wish to continue to operate the business probably will have to pay fair value for those assets, since other prospective purchasers will be able to use them to equally good effect. But if a business derives most of its value from its economic good will, dissolution may not serve the dissident shareholder's interests, because the remaining shareholders may be able to purchase the corporation's tangible assets for their fair market value and to capture the associated good will at no additional cost.

In such a situation, a mandatory buy out of her shares at their "fair market value" will better serve the dissident shareholder's interest. That is so because, in determining how the dissident's shares should be valued, a court presumably will take account of the value of the corporation's economic good will.

At first glance, dissolution or a mandatory buy out may appear a sensible solution when a close corporation is paralyzed because of deadlock or when those in control oppress the other shareholders. However, closer examination makes clear that the problem is more complex. First, there is the question of whether dissolution will be in the best interest of the community of interests known as "the corporation." Are the difficulties so severe that attempts at continued operation would lead only to deterioration of the business and a wasting of assets, or could the corporation continue to operate profitably? Second, will dissolution allow one shareholder or group of shareholders to take over the business at a price unfair to the others? Third, will the prospect of dissolution or a compelled buy out put undue financial pressure on the shareholders who wish to remain? Is the shareholder petitioning for relief really trying to do no more than liquidate an investment that the other participants thought she had permanently committed to the venture?

## MATTER OF KEMP & BEATLEY, INC.

64 N.Y.2d 63, 484 N.Y.S.2d 799, 473 N.E.2d 1173 (1984).

COOKE, CHIEF JUDGE.

When the majority shareholders of a close corporation award *de facto* dividends to all shareholders except a class of minority shareholders, such a policy may constitute "oppressive actions" and serve as a basis for an order made pursuant to section 1104-a of the Business Corporation Law dissolving the corporation. In the instant matter, there is sufficient evidence to support the lower courts' conclusion that the majority shareholders had altered a long-standing policy to distribute corporate earnings on the basis of stock ownership, as against petitioners only. Moreover, the courts did not abuse their discretion by concluding that dissolution was the only means by which petitioners could gain a fair return on their investment.

I

The business concern of Kemp & Beatley, incorporated under the laws of New York, designs and manufactures table linens and sundry tabletop items. The company's stock consists of 1,500 outstanding shares held by eight shareholders. Petitioner Dissin had been employed by the company for 42 years when, in June 1979, he resigned. Prior to resignation, Dissin served as vice-president and a director of Kemp & Beatley. Over the course of his employment, Dissin had acquired stock in the company and currently owns 200 shares.

Petitioner Gardstein, like Dissin, had been a long-time employee of the company. Hired in 1944, Gardstein was for the next 35 years involved in various aspects of the business including material procurement, product design, and plant management. His employment was terminated by the company in December 1980. He currently owns 105 shares of Kemp & Beatley stock.

Apparent unhappiness surrounded petitioners' leaving the employ of the company. Of particular concern was that they no longer received any distribution of the company's earnings. Petitioners considered themselves to be "frozen out" of the company; whereas it had been their experience when with the company to receive a distribution of the company's earnings according to their stockholdings, in the form of either dividends or extra compensation, that distribution was no longer forthcoming.

Gardstein and Dissin, together holding 20.33% of the company's outstanding stock, commenced the instant proceeding in June 1981, seeking dissolution of Kemp & Beatley pursuant to section 1104–a of the Business Corporation Law. Their petition alleged "fraudulent and oppressive" conduct by the company's board of directors such as to render petitioners' stock "a virtually worthless asset." Supreme Court referred the matter for a hearing, which was held in March 1982.

Upon considering the testimony of petitioners and the principals of Kemp & Beatley, the referee concluded that "the corporate management has by its policies effectively rendered petitioners' shares worthless, and * * * the only way petitioners can expect any return is by dissolution". Petitioners were found to have invested capital in the company expecting, among other things, to receive dividends or "bonuses" based upon their stock holdings. Also found was the company's "established buyout policy" by which it would purchase the stock of employee shareholders upon their leaving its employ.

The involuntary-dissolution statute (Business Corporation Law, § 1104–a) permits dissolution when a corporation's controlling faction is found guilty of "oppressive action" toward the complaining shareholders. The referee considered oppression to arise when "those in control" of the corporation "have acted in such a manner as to defeat those expectations of the minority stockholders which formed the basis of [their] participation in the venture." The expectations of petitioners that they would not be arbitrarily excluded from gaining a return on their investment and that their stock would be purchased by the corporation upon termination of employment, were deemed defeated by prevailing corporate policies. Dissolution was recommended in the referee's report, subject to giving respondent corporation an opportunity to purchase petitioners' stock.

Supreme Court confirmed the referee's report. It, too, concluded that due to the corporation's new dividend policy petitioners had been prevented from receiving any return on their investments. Liquidation of the corporate assets was found the only means by which petitioners would receive a fair return. The court considered judicial dissolution of a corporation to be "a serious and severe remedy." Consequently, the order of dissolution was conditioned upon the corporation's being permitted to purchase petitioners' stock. The Appellate Division affirmed, without opinion.

At issue in this appeal is the scope of section 1104–a of the Business Corporation Law. Specifically, this court must determine whether the provision for involuntary dissolution when the "directors or those in control of the corporation have been guilty of * * * oppressive actions toward the complaining shareholders" was properly applied in the circumstances of this case. We hold that it was, and therefore affirm.

## II

Judicially ordered dissolution of a corporation at the behest of minority interests is a remedy of relatively recent vintage in New York. * * *

Section 1104–a (subd. [a], par. [1] ) describes three types of proscribed activity: "illegal", "fraudulent", and "oppressive" conduct. The first two terms are familiar words that are commonly understood at law. The last, however, does not enjoy the same certainty gained through long usage. As no definition is provided by the statute, it falls upon the courts to provide guidance.

The statutory concept of "oppressive actions" can, perhaps, best be understood by examining the characteristics of close corporations and the Legislature's general purpose in creating this involuntary-dissolution statute. It is widely understood that, in addition to supplying capital to a contemplated or ongoing enterprise and expecting a fair and equal return, parties comprising the ownership of a close corporation may expect to be actively involved in its management and operation. The small ownership cluster seeks to "contribute their capital, skills, experience and labor" toward the corporate enterprise (*Kruger v. Gerth*, 16 N.Y.2d 802, 805, 263 N.Y.S.2d 1, 210 N.E.2d 355 [Desmond, Ch. J., dissenting].

As a leading commentator in the field has observed: "Unlike the typical shareholder in the publicly held corporation, who may be simply an investor or a speculator and cares nothing for the responsibilities of management, the shareholder in a close corporation is a co-owner of the business and wants the privileges and powers that go with ownership. His participation in that particular corporation is often his principal or sole source of income. As a matter of fact, providing employment for himself may have been the principal reason why he participated in organizing the corporation. He may or may not anticipate an ultimate profit from the sale of his interest, but he normally draws very little from the corporation as dividends. In his capacity as an officer or employee of the corporation, he looks to his salary for the principal return on his capital investment, because earnings of a close corporation, as is well known, are distributed in major part in salaries, bonuses and retirement benefits." (O'Neal, CLOSE CORPORATIONS [2d ed.], § 1.07, at pp. 21–22 [n. omitted].)

Shareholders enjoy flexibility in memorializing these expectations through agreements setting forth each party's rights and obligations in corporate governance. In the absence of such an agreement, however, ultimate decision-making power respecting corporate policy will be reposed in the holders of a majority interest in the corporation (*see, e.g.,* Business Corporation Law, §§ 614, 708). A wielding of this power by any group controlling a corporation may serve to destroy a stockholder's vital interests and expectations.

As the stock of closely held corporations generally is not readily salable, a minority shareholder at odds with management policies may be without either a voice in protecting his or her interests or any reasonable means of withdrawing his or her investment. This predicament may fairly be considered the legislative concern underlying the provision at issue in this case; inclusion of the criteria that the corporation's stock not be traded on securities markets and that the complaining shareholder be subject to oppressive actions supports this conclusion.

Defining oppressive conduct as distinct from illegality in the present context has been considered in other forums. The question has been resolved by considering oppressive actions to refer to conduct that substantially defeats the "reasonable expectations" held by minority shareholders in committing their capital to the particular enterprise (*see, e.g., Exadaktilos v. Cinnaminson Realty Co.*, 167 N.J.Super. 141, 153–156, 400 A.2d 554, *affd.* 173 N.J.Super. 559, 414 A.2d 994). This concept is consistent with the apparent purpose underlying the provision under review. A shareholder who reasonably expected that ownership in the corporation would entitle him or her to a job, a share of corporate earnings, a place in corporate management, or some other form of security, would be oppressed in a very real sense when others in the corporation seek to defeat those expectations and there exists no effective means of salvaging the investment.

Given the nature of close corporations and the remedial purpose of the statute, this court holds that utilizing a complaining shareholder's "reasonable expectations" as a means of identifying and measuring conduct alleged to be oppressive is appropriate. A court considering a petition alleging oppressive conduct must investigate what the majority shareholders knew, or should have known, to be the petitioner's expectations in entering the particular enterprise. Majority conduct should not be deemed oppressive simply because the petitioner's subjective hopes and desires in joining the venture are not fulfilled. Disappointment alone should not necessarily be equated with oppression.

Rather, oppression should be deemed to arise only when the majority conduct substantially defeats expectations that, objectively viewed, were both reasonable under the circumstances and were central to the petitioner's decision to join the venture. It would be inappropriate, however, for us in this case to delineate the contours of the courts' consideration in determining whether directors have been guilty of oppressive conduct. As in other areas of the law, much will depend on the circumstances in the individual case.

The appropriateness of an order of dissolution is in every case vested in the sound discretion of the court considering the application (*see* Business Corporation Law, § 1111, subd. [a] ). Under the terms of this statute, courts are instructed to consider both whether "liquidation of the corporation is the only feasible means" to protect the complaining shareholder's expectation of a fair return on his or her investment and whether dissolution "is reasonably necessary" to protect "the rights or interests of any substantial number of shareholders" not limited to those complaining (Business Corporation Law, § 1104–a, subd. [b], pars. [1], [2] ). Implicit in this direction is that once oppressive conduct is found, consideration must be given to the totality of circumstances surrounding the current state of corporate affairs and relations to determine whether some remedy short of or other than dissolution constitutes a feasible means of satisfying both the petitioner's expectations and the rights and interests of any other substantial group of shareholders (*see, also,* Business Corporation Law, § 1111, subd. [b], par. [1] ).

By invoking the statute, a petitioner has manifested his or her belief that dissolution may be the only appropriate remedy. Assuming the petitioner has set forth a prima facie case of oppressive conduct, it should be incumbent upon the parties seeking to forestall dissolution to demonstrate to the court the existence of an adequate, alternative remedy. A court has broad latitude in fashioning alternative relief, but when fulfillment of the oppressed petitioner's expectations by these means is doubtful, such as when there has been a complete deterioration of relations between the parties, a court should not hesitate to order dissolution. Every order of dissolution, however, must be conditioned upon permitting any shareholder of the corporation to elect to purchase the complaining shareholder's stock at fair value (*see* Business Corporation Law, § 1118).

One further observation is in order. The purpose of this involuntary dissolution statute is to provide protection to the minority shareholder whose reasonable expectations in undertaking the venture have been frustrated and who has no adequate means of recovering his or her investment. It would be contrary to this remedial purpose to permit its use by minority shareholders as merely a coercive tool * * *. Therefore, the minority shareholder whose own acts, made in bad faith and undertaken with a view toward forcing an involuntary dissolution, give rise to the complained-of oppression should be given no quarter in the statutory protection.

### III

There was sufficient evidence presented at the hearing to support the conclusion that Kemp & Beatley had a long-standing policy of awarding *de facto* dividends based on stock ownership in the form of "extra compensation bonuses." Petitioners, both of whom had extensive experience in the management of the company, testified to this effect.

Moreover, both related that receipt of this compensation, whether as true dividends or disguised as "extra compensation", was a known incident to ownership of the company's stock understood by all of the company's principals. Finally, there was uncontroverted proof that this policy was changed either shortly before or shortly after petitioners' employment ended. Extra compensation was still awarded by the company. The only difference was that stock ownership was no longer a basis for the payments; it was asserted that the basis became services rendered to the corporation. It was not unreasonable for the fact finder to have determined that this change in policy amounted to nothing less than an attempt to exclude petitioners from gaining any return on their investment through the mere recharacterization of distributions of corporate income. Under the circumstances of this case, there was no error in determining that this conduct constituted oppressive action within the meaning of section 1104–a of the Business Corporation Law.

Nor may it be said that Supreme Court abused its discretion in ordering Kemp & Beatley's dissolution, subject to an opportunity for a buy-out of petitioners' shares. After the referee had found that the controlling faction of the company was, in effect, attempting to "squeeze-out" petitioners by offering them no return on their investment and increasing other executive compensation, respondents, in opposing the report's confirmation, attempted only to controvert the factual basis of the report. They suggested no feasible, alternative remedy to the forced dissolution. In light of an apparent deterioration in relations between petitioners and the governing shareholders of Kemp & Beatley, it was not unreasonable for the court to have determined that a forced buy-out of petitioners' shares or liquidation of the corporation's assets was the only means by which petitioners could be guaranteed a fair return on their investments.

Accordingly, the order of the Appellate Division should be modified, with costs to petitioners-respondents, by affirming the substantive determination of that court but extending the time for exercising the option to purchase petitioners-respondents' shares to 30 days following this court's determination.

## MUELLENBERG v. BIKON CORP.

143 N.J. 168, 669 A.2d 1382 (1996).

The opinion of the Court was delivered by O'HERN, J.

This appeal concerns a court's authority to order shareholders representing a majority of corporate ownership to sell their shares to a minority shareholder whose rights had been oppressed by the majority. We find that the provisions of the New Jersey Corporation Business Act, *N.J.S.A.* 14A:12–7(1)(c) and 14A:12–7(8), do, in rare circumstances, authorize a buy-out of the majority. Because unfolding events in this case have confirmed the judgment of the Chancery Division that the parties would be unable to cooperate in the joint management of the enterprise, we reinstate its judgment ordering the majority shareholders to sell their interest to a minority shareholder. * * *

## I

Ralph Muellenberg is a mechanical engineer and an inventor. He has held some 80 patents worldwide in the field of locking devices used generally in the building of machines. These are described variously as "shaft to hub connections," "clamping devices" and "locking assemblies." The devices allow component parts of a machine to attach efficiently to a shaft. In 1972, Muellenberg founded Bikon–Technik GmbH (BTG) in Germany to promote products of his invention. BTG owns the trademarks BIKON, DOBIKON, and BIKON–Technik.

Adda Finanziaria, S.R.L. (Adda) is an Italian holding company owned by the defendant Dario Passerini who is also the general manager and a shareholder in another Italian company, Tecnomeccanica S.N.S. di Sacchi & C. (TM).

Kurt Burg is a mechanical engineer who came to the United States in 1976 from Germany and was employed here by a company known as Ringfeder Corp., also in the clamping device business and a competitor of BTG.

Muellenberg's goal was to establish a family of companies related through common ownership and contract to market his products throughout the world. This integrated ownership structure was aimed at assuring quality and sources of supply. By the end of 1992, worldwide sales of Bikon and Dobikon products (collectively "Bikon Products") totaled nearly $5 million. BTG does not manufacture locking devices itself. In 1979 BTG entered an agreement with TM, which was owned equally by Muellenberg and Adda (Passerini's holding company), to manufacture Bikon products. The agreement provided, among other things, that TM would be the exclusive manufacturer of products for BTG in Italy, that BTG would make specified annual minimum purchases and that BTG would have the exclusive right to sell products manufactured by TM in various countries including the United States (the "Cooperation Agreement"). No royalty or license fees were due to BTG or Muellenberg under the Cooperation Agreement with TM.

Sometime in 1980, Muellenberg and Burg began discussions concerning Burg's possible participation in a United States company to be formed by Muellenberg and Passerini for the promotion and sale of Bikon products in the United States and Canada.[1] Muellenberg had met Burg some years earlier when Burg was a German resident.

To that end Bikon Corp. (BNJ) was incorporated in New Jersey on June 25, 1982. A Stockholders' Agreement provided that Muellenberg, Burg and Passerini would be the initial directors and officers and that Muellenberg would be president. The parties also executed a License

---

**1.** For convenience, we sometimes use the name "Passerini" to denote the inter- ests of Adda and TM and "Muellenberg" to denote the interests of BTG.

Agreement and a Distribution Agreement dated April 12, 1982. The License Agreement granted BNJ the right to exploit Bikon products in the United States in consideration of a license fee to Muellenberg, as owner of the patents, of 5 per cent of the gross receipts of BNJ, payable quarterly.

Pursuant to Burg's request, the Distribution Agreement gave BNJ the right to produce and distribute products developed in accordance with Muellenberg's patents. The Distribution Agreement licensed BNJ to use the common law trademarks BIKON, DOBIKON and the trade name BIKON–Technik in exchange for a fee of 2 per cent of BNJ's gross receipts. BTG also obliged itself to offer newly developed products in the field of shaft to hub connections to BNJ for distribution in the United States. To ensure quality and protect valuable patent and trademark rights, Muellenberg included in the Distribution Agreement a provision requiring that production in the United States be in accordance with drawings and blueprints supplied by BTG which could not be altered without BTG's permission.

Muellenberg, Burg and Passerini subscribed for 100 shares of BNJ stock for $30,000 each. Only Muellenberg invested cash. Burg's subscription was provided in exchange for his knowledge of the trade and Passerini's was credited against merchandise to be manufactured by TM for sale by BNJ. Certificates evidencing ownership of 100 shares of BNJ were issued to Muellenberg, Burg and Passerini.

Muellenberg claims that prior to the formation of Bikon Corp., he made it clear to Burg that he, Muellenberg, was to be in control of the company and would be its president, Burg would be general manager and Passerini would be treasurer. Business operations commenced in Burg's River Vale, New Jersey home. * * *

Despite differences that developed between Muellenberg and Burg, the business prospered. As General Manager and the only officer on site on a regular basis, Burg handled the day-to-day business of BNJ. Muellenberg claims that Burg acted as though he had exclusive control over the business. Disputes arose about the introduction of new products into the BNJ line, the patent and trademark royalty fees, the rent that Burg paid to himself, and Muellenberg's desire to see detailed reports of sales and activities.

Muellenberg also complained that when Passerini fell behind in production capacity, Burg went to Italy without notice to Muellenberg and unilaterally engaged other suppliers. Muellenberg regarded some of them as direct competitors and did not want them to threaten his interests. He viewed introduction into the United States of the Bikon products produced by unlicensed manufacturers as a violation of his patent rights. Burg countered that Passerini had encouraged him to engage the other contractors with Muellenberg's tacit approval.

At first Passerini appeared neutral or inactive. * * *

When Passerini resumed his role, notice was given of a meeting of the shareholders and directors to be held on January 20, 1993, to consider dissolution. On Burg's application, the Chancery Division enjoined any action to dissolve, but not the meeting. Muellenberg and Passerini traveled from Europe to attend the meeting. BNJ's secretary attempted to persuade Burg to attend either by telephone or in person. When Burg refused, the meeting proceeded in his absence.

At that meeting, Muellenberg and Passerini voted to declare a dividend of $180,000 ($600 per share), to retain an outside accountant to determine accrued royalties, to require the signatures of Burg and Muellenberg or Muellenberg alone for future bank withdrawals, and to require Board approval for the selection of suppliers and purchases over $1,000. * * *

At trial, * * * the court found that at the January 20, 1993, shareholders' meeting, Muellenberg and Passerini had begun efforts to freeze out Burg. They had declared a $180,000 dividend that they should have known would deprive Bikon of needed cash to operate and thus take away Burg's ability to perform successfully as general manager. In addition, despite the lack of any showing of abuse by Mr. Burg in operating the company, they began to strip Burg of his day-to-day control as general manager by resolving that bank account withdrawals should be made only by plaintiff or by joint signatures of plaintiff and defendant Burg. And, finally, the court found that the majority directors, as "[p]laintiff's counsel acknowledged . . . in summation," intended to vote Burg out as a director and terminate him as general manager and employee of the company.

The trial court determined that this course of conduct amounted to oppression. It held that the only fair and equitable remedy under the circumstances was to have one or more of the parties buy the stock of the others. The court concluded that Burg should buy out the interests of Muellenberg and Passerini. The parties agreed on the value of the stock. * * * Burg tendered $235,000 each to Muellenberg and Passerini and thereafter changed the name of the corporation to B–Loc Corporation.

On appeal, the Appellate Division reversed and remanded the portion of the trial court's judgment ordering the sale of the shares of Muellenberg and Adda to Burg and terminating Muellenberg and Passerini as corporate officers and directors. * * *

* * * We granted Burg's petition for certification and stayed the effect of the Appellate Division's opinion until we had reviewed it. We now reverse and reinstate the judgment of the Chancery Division.

## II

Unlike their counterparts in a publicly held corporation, shareholders in a close corporation are typically involved in the management and operation of the company. * * *

Because majority shareholders have the power to dictate to the minority the manner in which the corporation is run, a minority shareholder in a close corporation becomes vulnerable when dissension develops. The controlling shareholders' voting power enables them to freeze-out minority shareholders by terminating their employment, excluding them from participation in management decision-making, and reducing their salary and other income.

The vulnerability of minority shareholders is exacerbated by the illiquidity of their financial stake in the company. * * *

Historically, state corporation statutes had provided minority shareholders with little protection against exploitation by controlling shareholders. * * *

Thus for years there was little or no protection that a court could afford oppressed minority shareholders. In *Brenner v. Berkowitz*, [134 N.J. 488 (1993),] Justice Garibaldi furnished an historical overview of the New Jersey Legislature's approach to protecting minority shareholders. She noted that it was not until 1973 that the legislature amended section 14A:12–7 of the Corporation Business Act to provide a specific cause of action to protect minority interests. The present language in 14A:12–7(1)(c) was added by L.1973, c. 366, § 67, effective May 1, 1974. It provides:

(1) The Superior Court, in an action under this section, may appoint a custodian, appoint a provisional director, order a sale of the corporation's stock as provided below, or enter a judgment dissolving the corporation, upon proof that

* * *

(c) In the case of a corporation having 25 or less shareholders, the directors or those in control have acted fraudulently or illegally, mismanaged the corporation, or abused their authority as officers or directors or have acted oppressively or unfairly toward one or more minority shareholders in their capacities as shareholders, directors, officers, or employees.

The legislature intended to expand the protection available to minority shareholders "who are powerless within a corporation, as well as powerless to leave." *Brenner, supra*, 134 N.J. at 506 (citing *N.J.S.A.* 14A:12–7 (West 1968) Comment on 1972 Amendments).

* * *

In this Court's most recent application of section 14A:12–7(1)(c), we defined oppressive conduct to include that which frustrates the reasonable expectations of the minority shareholder. *Brenner, supra*, 134 N.J. at 506. This approach takes into account the fact that shareholders in close corporations may have expectations that differ substantially from those of shareholders in public corporations. It also requires courts to be flexible in their treatment of section 14A:12–7(1)(c) cases because of the fact-sensitive nature of their inquiry. *Brenner, supra*, 134 N.J. at 516.

* * * [M]inority shareholders' expectations must, however, be balanced against the corporation's ability to exercise its business judgment and run its business efficiently. *Id.* at 517. Thus, courts should always be wary of interfering in the internal affairs of a corporation. As we stated in *Brenner*:

> The limited bases for statutory relief * * * reflect an awareness that minority shareholders know the limitations of their power at the time they make their investment in a close corporation. Mere disagreement or discord between the shareholders is not sufficient for a violation of the close corporation statutory provision.

[*Id.* at 506.]

With these principles in mind, we turn to the facts of the case to determine whether the conduct of Muellenberg and Passerini reflects more than a disagreement or discord among shareholders, but rather amounted to the oppression of Burg within the meaning of section 14A:12–7(1)(c).

### III

* * * The trial court did not find any fraud or mismanagement on the part of Muellenberg or Passerini. The question is whether their actions were oppressive. Ordinarily, oppression by shareholders is clearly shown when they have awarded themselves excessive compensation, furnished inadequate dividends, or misapplied and wasted corporate funds. This did not occur here.

The remaining measure of oppression in the small corporation is whether the fair expectations of the parties have been met. * * * In this case, it is reasonable to conclude that Burg's fair expectations were that should he give up his prior employment with a competitor company and enter this small corporation, he would enjoy an important position in the management affairs of the corporation.

It is a close question whether the actions taken by Muellenberg and Passerini at the January 20, 1993, meeting amounted to oppression, as Burg contends. Muellenberg and Passerini claim that their declaration of the first dividend in company history was "fair and reasonable" in light of the company's favorable financial position at that time. They dispute the trial court's conclusion that the dividend would deprive Burg of the needed cash to operate BNJ, asserting that sufficient assets were still available to run the company. Muellenberg also maintains that Burg could not have reasonably expected that he would have exclusive authority and control over the business when BNJ's by-laws named Muellenberg president and chief executive officer.

We agree that it cannot be considered oppression when controlling shareholders seek to rein in management and control the affairs of their corporation. But the expectations of Muellenberg and Passerini that they might exercise majority power conflicted with the expectations of Burg, and were confined by their fiduciary duties to their co-venturer. The equities were close. Burg had devoted the most productive years of his life to building up the company. Due in large measure to Burg's efforts, North American sales of Bikon products rose to over $2,000,000 per year. He could not reasonably have expected that after ten years as general manager he would be frozen out of the business. On the other hand, Muellenberg could not reasonably have expected that he, the founder of the enterprise, and Passerini would be ignored in the conduct of the company's affairs.

In other circumstances, * * * Burg could have learned to manage the business more as a partner than as a sole proprietor. But the events that followed the Appellate Division's decision have confirmed that the trial court, which could assess the demeanor and relationship of the witnesses, had a better sense of the internal dynamics among the shareholders and could foreshadow Burg's inevitable ouster from Bikon's picture. That ouster would not have been a fair accommodation of the reasonable expectations of all shareholders.

The remaining issue was whether Burg or Muellenberg and Passerini should survive with BNJ. In 1988, the Legislature amended *N.J.S.A.* 14A:12–7(8) to permit minority shareholders to petition a court to order a buy-out of the majority. As amended, section 14A:12–7(8) provides that if there is a triggering event, * * * the minority [may] seek a court order for the sale of the stock of "any other shareholder." In most situations, oppressed minority shareholders will lack the resources to buy out the interests of controlling shareholders. As a result, claims of oppression are typically remedied by arranging for the corporation or the majority shareholders to buy out the interests of the minority shareholder. In this case, the record contained the following evidence in support of Burg: Burg was willing and able to purchase the shares of Muellenberg and Passerini; Burg, who owns the land on which BNJ's offices are located, was most active in operating the company since its inception; Burg is the only shareholder who works full-time for BNJ and the company has been his only source of income for over ten years; Burg was primarily responsible for developing the company's contacts in the United States and Canada and is best situated to maintain the existing operation; and finally, it was Burg who sought to preserve the corporation at a time when Muellenberg and Passerini attempted to dissolve it.

On the other hand, without Muellenberg there would have been no business to divide since he had furnished all the start-up capital and was the inventor of the special design features that propelled the company's sales. Much of BNJ's good will may have derived from the use of the Bikon name. It is, however, too close a call to say that the Chancery Court erred in finding a slight edge in favor of Burg as the surviving shareholder.

Thus, while a minority buy-out of the majority is an uncommon remedy, it was the appropriate one here. The trial court acted within its discretion in ordering Muellenberg and Adda to sell their shares in BNJ to Burg. * * *

Any doubt as to which shareholder should be permitted to invoke the buy-out remedy has been largely dissipated by circumstances. Without resolving the factual disputes set forth in the motions to supplement the record, it appears that since we stayed the Appellate Division's decision, Muellenberg has demonstrated an ability to market his products in the United States without Burg. Muellenberg, on behalf of his solely owned company BTG, made arrangements with a company called North American, Inc. for it to market products under the "Bikon" name that may compete with B–Loc. North American began soliciting B–Loc's customers, advising them that it had been granted the exclusive license to manufacture and distribute "Bikon" locking devices in the United States, Canada and Mexico. In addition, its sales catalogue is similar to the catalogue BNJ used previously. Oral argument convinces us that there is nothing to stand in the way of Muellenberg and Passerini continuing in the American market without real detriment to their reasonable expectations in forming BNJ. The trial court's solution is thus "fair and equitable to all parties" as required by *N.J.S.A.* 14A:12–7(8).

As it stands, BNJ (now B–Loc) no longer can use the "Bikon" trade name. That license was terminated by BTG prior to the commencement of this litigation. The good will and trade name of Bikon inures to Muellenberg's new venture, which may engage in the sale of Bikon fasteners in the domestic U.S. market. Now that the patent has expired on the only Bikon product to generate significant sales in this country, B–Loc and North American are able to compete freely with each other. Realistically, all that plaintiffs Muellenberg and Passerini might reasonably require to advance their undertaking would be the customer lists generated during the period of their joint enterprise with Burg. If those lists are not available to them now, a customer list as of the date of the buy-out should be furnished by Burg.

Accordingly, we reverse the judgment of the Appellate Division and reinstate the judgment of the Chancery Division. We leave to that court the resolution of any unresolved issues attendant to the buy-out.

### *Questions re Muellenberg v. Bikon Corp.*

The court points out, with regard to the dispute between the majority shareholders of BNJ and Burg, that "the equities were close." On what basis, then, does the court hold that the majority's actions were oppressive? The court seems to equate "oppression" with any resolution of the dispute between the shareholders that does not represent "a fair accommodation of the reasonable expectations of *all* shareholders." If that is its holding, what are its implications?

## BONAVITA v. CORBO

300 N.J.Super. 179, 692 A.2d 119 (Ch.Div.1996).

LESEMANN, J.S.C.

\* \* \*

## A. FACTS

### 1. Evolution of the corporation

Corbo Jewelers, Inc., (Corbo or the corporation) was organized in 1946 by Michael and Dominic Corbo, and Gerald Bonavita.[3] It began with one store in Bloomfield, New Jersey, gradually expanded to twelve stores, but later retrenched to its present seven locations.

Over the years, as the three incorporators aged, the stockholdings evolved as well. * * * From [1984] on, Alan Corbo [who is Michael Corbo's son] and Gerald Bonavita each owned 50% of the outstanding stock of the corporation.

Over the years, Alan's four children also began working in the business.

Stephen began in 1978 and has become the corporation's chief administrative officer, second in command only to his father. Alan, Jr., began in or around 1979 and functions as diamond buyer. Michael has been with the corporation since 1976. He handles jewelry repairs and special orders. Alan's daughter, Cathy Giamboi, works part time in the Corbo store in Yonkers, New York, and his wife, Stephanie, also works part time. Alan earns $57,000 per year; his three sons each earn $52,000; Cathy earns between $20,000 and $30,000 and Stephanie's earnings are apparently in the same range as Cathy's.

Until his death in late 1994, Gerald Bonavita received the same salary as Alan, even after he virtually stopped working in 1991. Upon Gerald's death, however, Alan advised his widow that the Internal Revenue Service would not approve "salary" deductions for any further such payments and thus they could not be continued. They did, in fact, cease very soon after Gerald's death.

Although Gerald Bonavita and Alan Corbo received the same salary while Bonavita was alive, they played distinctly different corporate roles. Alan filled the role of president and chief executive officer, in fact as well as title. With his son, Stephen, he ran the corporation.

Bonavita played a much more retiring role. Essentially, he ran the Bloomfield store, which was characterized at trial as a "Mom and Pop" operation. He took little, if any, role in overall corporate management, and his wife was more active and had greater knowledge about such matters than he did.

In the mid 1980's, as Gerald Bonavita aged and his health deteriorated, he told Alan Corbo that he wanted to retire and wanted to have the corporation (or Alan) purchase his stock. Some discussions ensued, but the parties did not reach agreement on a buy out. Gradually, Bonavita reduced the time he was spending on corporate business, until he completely retired in March 1991. Julia continued working for a short time thereafter, until she too ceased all work in January 1992.

---

**3.** Gerald Bonavita's wife, Julia, is a sis-   ter of Dominic and Michael Corbo.

### 2. Corporate meetings and elections

As is the case with many closed corporations, so long as the shareholders were in harmony, Corbo conducted its corporate affairs informally and on a family-like basis. * * *

### 3. Plaintiff's complaint; the appointment of a provisional director; and the demand for payment of a dividend

Plaintiff's complaint was filed in December 1991. It alleges a deadlock within the meaning of N.J.S.A. 14A:12–7 and also alleges stockholder "oppression" within the meaning of that statute. Plaintiff sought interim relief, and the court, pursuant to Subsection (1) of N.J.S.A. 14A:12–7 appointed Thomas Herten, Esq., as a "provisional director" to function while the litigation proceeded.

In early 1994, Bonavita formally requested the corporation to pay a dividend of approximately $650,000 to each of the two shareholders—a total of $1,300,000. That sum represented a portion of the corporation's retained earnings on which income tax had already been paid—a point discussed further below. The request was denied, with Alan Corbo opposed to the request and the provisional director declining to join Bonavita in what he regarded as a matter of "business judgment." An attempt to have the court overrule that decision while the suit was pending was unsuccessful and thus no dividend was paid. Bonavita thereafter modified his request to propose a smaller dividend, but that, too, was denied, and Alan Corbo has remained, ever since, adamantly opposed to the payment of any substantial dividend.

### B.   The Claim of Deadlock

Although plaintiff claims there is a corporate "deadlock," that charge is not sharply drawn, and it is not clear just what constitutes the alleged deadlock of which plaintiff complains.

* * *

[T]his is not a case where a corporation is unable to act. It can act. And it did act. It acted by denying plaintiff's demands [for a dividend or a buy-out of her stock]. And it is the result of that action—not an inability to act—which is the basis for plaintiff's claim that she has been left in a hopeless, "no-win" situation. Whether those actions, leading to those results, constitute shareholder oppression is the significant issue presented.

### C.   Plaintiff's Claim of Oppression

* * *

### 2. Defendant's refusal to pay dividends; the financial condition of the corporation; and defendant's exercise of "business judgment"

The essence of plaintiff's claim is that the corporation, as operated by defendant Alan Corbo, provides substantial benefits for Alan Corbo and his family but no benefits for Bonavita. That is certainly an accurate statement.

As noted, the six Corbo family members on the corporate payroll realize approximately $400,000 per year in salary and other benefits. And while there is no claim that the salaries are excessive, neither was there a showing that if the "inside" employment were terminated those family members could earn as much elsewhere. In addition, of course, a job in the family business probably provides considerably more security than one might find in other employment.

It is also clear that Alan Corbo recognized that such continued employment was indeed a substantial benefit. When Gerald Bonavita presented what he claimed was a chance to sell the entire business for a handsome price, Alan Corbo responded by insisting that an essential condition of any such sale must be the ability of his three sons and himself to continue their employment with the new corporate owner.

Such employment is, of course, a frequent and perfectly proper benefit of stockholders in a closed corporation. The difficulty here is that the benefit flows in one direction only: to the Corbos, and not to Bonavita, and there is no compensating, alternative benefit for the Bonavita interests.

Mrs. Bonavita testified that she and her husband had no children who could move into the jewelry stores' operation. She also said, as did her husband in his *de bene esse* deposition before trial, that Mr. Bonavita had hoped to receive some benefits from the corporation before he died, and she has a similar hope now for herself. Otherwise, as she put it, her husband's interest, which she now owns, will be locked forever within Corbo Jewelers, Inc., and will be of absolutely no benefit to her, as it was of no benefit to her husband.

Absent employment, and absent any thought of long-term growth (inapplicable to Julia Bonavita as it was to Gerald Bonavita because of age), the normal corporate benefit which one in the position of Mr. or Mrs. Bonavita might expect would be the payment of dividends. This corporation, however, pays no dividends.

Plaintiff's unsuccessful attempt to have the corporation pay a dividend is noted above. * * * Defendants have made clear that *no dividend* of any significant size will be approved. * * *

Plaintiff argues that Alan Corbo's "no dividend" policy is particularly harsh in view of the extraordinary financial condition of the corporation. That argument has considerable merit.

As of June 30, 1993, the corporate balance sheet showed retained earnings of more than $5,000,000 and, after adjustment for treasury stock held as a liability, showed total stockholders' equity of approximately $4,600,000. Within that $4,600,000 was the so-called AAA account, which totaled $1,390,000, and represented funds on which income tax had already been paid.* * * *

In addition, on June 30, 1993, the corporation had cash, or liquid assets easily convertible into cash, of approximately $1,100,000 and current liabilities of only $12,000.[7] It also owned a building in Rutherford with an appraised value of $525,000, free of any mortgage and—plaintiff argues—available as a source of additional funds through mortgage financing.

Defendants' stated reason for the refusal to pay dividends is the corporation's need for cash. Alan Corbo testified that the business is seasonal and that the corporation's continued profitability requires it to have substantial cash available to buy quickly when "bargains" become available. The ability to do that, without the need to borrow money and pay interest, he maintained, is one reason for the corporation's success over the years.

Alan Corbo also pointed to the anticipated need for substantial renovation expenses for two of the corporation's stores which were approaching the end of leaseholds. In each case, he said, the landlord would require such expenditures as a condition to lease renewal.

\* \* \*

While the facts just described strongly indicate that the corporation can well afford to pay dividends, a contrary decision could hardly be called irrational. Indeed, from Alan Corbo's point of view, the "no dividend" policy undoubtedly makes good sense. Since the primary benefit that he receives from the corporation is continued employment for himself and his family, the maintenance of a $5,000,000 earned surplus, large cash balances, and the non-payment of dividends is certainly in his best interest.

If the Corbo's and Bonavita were in essentially the same position, and each was similarly affected by the decision against paying dividends, that policy could hardly be characterized as anything other than a permissible exercise of business judgment. It would, presumably, be unassailable under the principle that a court will not normally overturn the exercise of such judgment. * * *

But that, of course, is not this case. The problem here is that the operation of the corporation benefits only one of its shareholders—Alan Corbo. It provides no benefit of any kind to Julia Bonavita. * * *

What Julia Bonavita has, and what she will continue to have so long as Alan Corbo is able to make the kinds of decisions he has been making,

---

* Corbo was a "Subchapter S" corporation, whose net profits were taxable directly to its shareholders. Each year, Corbo disbursed to its two stockholders, as dividends, enough money to pay the taxes on Corbo's profits for which they were liable. Corbo retained the remainder of its profits and designated those after-tax profits "AAA account."—Ed.

7. These numbers do not include the excess of accounts receivable ($640,000) over accounts payable ($390,000). Nor do they include inventory.

is a block of stock which has absolutely no value. Alan Corbo has made and will continue to make decisions which are in his best interests (and those of his family) and which ignore the wishes, needs, and best interests of his co-shareholder.

Given the effect of those actions on plaintiff, and regardless of whether defendants' actions might otherwise be termed "wrongful" or "illegal," there is no question that defendants' conduct has destroyed any reasonable expectation that plaintiff may have enjoyed respecting her stock interests. As such, it is clear from the decision of our Supreme Court in *Brenner v. Berkowitz*, 134 N.J. 488, 634 A.2d 1019 (1993), from other New Jersey case law, from comments and analyses by leading text writers, and from decisions in other states, that defendants' actions do indeed constitute "oppression" within the meaning of N.J.S.A. 14A:12–7.

\* \* \*

### D. THE APPROPRIATE REMEDY

N.J.S.A. 14A:12–7 sets out four remedies which a court "may" order to remedy "oppression." A court

> may appoint a custodian, appoint a provisional director, order a sale of the corporation's stock as provided below, or enter a judgment dissolving the corporation. . . .

The statutory power to order a stock sale, as described further in Subsection (8), is a power to order an unwilling party to *sell* stock. It does not authorize a mandatory *purchase* by someone otherwise unwilling to buy.

In *Brenner v. Berkowitz, supra*, however, the Court held that the statutory list of remedies was non-exclusive and that the statute "was not intended to supersede the inherent, common law power of the Chancery Division to achieve equity." 134 N.J. 488, 512, 634 A.2d 1019. \* \* \*

One of those equitable remedies, it held, is the power to order an involuntary purchase of stock held by one of the corporation's shareholders \* \* \*.

That power, however, should be exercised sparingly \* \* \*.

Dissolution, of course, is a "last resort" remedy and something which neither defendant nor plaintiff wants here. What plaintiff does want is an order directing the corporation, or Alan Corbo, to purchase the Bonavita stock. That remedy, as noted, is available, but should be imposed only if the court is satisfied that it represents "the only practical alternative" to dissolution and that some lesser remedy will not suffice.

Neither side in this case has focused on any such alternative remedy. The reason for that seems clear: there is no reasonable, practical lesser remedy which will solve the problem inherent in this relationship and provide plaintiff with the long-range relief to which she is entitled. In short, no other remedy will work.

The problems that brought the parties to this suit are inherent in their relationship. That relationship is not something which this court can alter by an order attempting to modify or control their actions while they remain "married" to each other. The conflict will remain, and its symptoms will reappear in what will inevitably be a continuing war between the two.

Thus, the corporation could certainly be ordered to pay the dividend which plaintiff requests—or at least some smaller dividend, as per the list of thirteen possible "equitable remedies" set out in *Brenner*, and particularly Item (10), which refers to the court's "requiring declaration of a dividend." 134 N.J. at 515, 634 A.2d 1019.

But if that were done, what about next year? Or the year after? Alan Corbo will continue to see such payments as antithetical to the best interests of the corporation. And as he defines the best interests of the corporation—consistent with his best interests and those of his family—his viewpoint would hardly be irrational. But it will continue to be inconsistent with the reasonable expectations of the Bonavita interests.

\* \* \*

And, of course, the differences between the two sides would not manifest themselves only on a single annual question of payment of a dividend. Rather, the continuum of business decisions that arise throughout the year—both large issues and seemingly minor ones—would all be affected by the different approaches of the two sides. Everything from merchandising decisions to capital improvements, opening or closing of stores, and countless subsidiary issues would necessarily be affected by the different philosophies (the different expectations) of the two sides.

In sum, there is no rational basis on which this corporation can continue to exist and operate with half its shares owned by the Corbo interests and half by the Bonavita interests. There must be a "divorce." One method of accomplishing that, raised and explored at trial but shown to be unworkable, would be a division of the corporation's stores between the two shareholders. \* \* \*

That brings us back, then, to plaintiff's request for a compulsory buy out of her stock. And since such a mandatory purchase by the corporation or Alan Corbo represents a less drastic measure than dissolution of the corporation, it is clear that the only feasible, rational remedy here is an order that the corporation (or perhaps Alan Corbo) be required to purchase the Bonavita stock interests.

Based on an analysis and evaluation of the extensive evidence submitted at trial as to the value of the Bonavita stock interests, the court has concluded that the price at which that sale should take place is $1,900,000.

What remains to be resolved, however, are the terms and conditions under which a sale at that price should take place.

\* \* \*

To investigate and consider [this issue], and any others that must be resolved in order to effect the purchase of the Bonavita stock, this court will appoint a special fiscal agent. The agent will consult with the attorneys for the parties; make such independent investigation as may be deemed necessary or appropriate; and may consult with banks, other possible lending sources, accountants, and any one else deemed helpful. The agent will then submit a proposal as to the terms and conditions on which the sale will take place. The parties will have an opportunity to be heard concerning the agent's report, and thereafter, the court will enter a final order fixing the terms and conditions of sale.

### Notes and Questions

1. *Kelley v. Axelsson*, 296 N.J.Super. 426, 687 A.2d 268 (App.Div. 1997), also involved a claim that minority shareholders' reasonable expectations had been frustrated. Plaintiffs, the siblings of Eric Axelsson, Jr. ("Eric"), alleged that Eric had engaged in unfair and oppressive conduct by terminating the payment of dividends, paying excessive salaries to himself and his son, causing the corporation to engage in cash transactions that were not recorded on its books, and diverting corporate assets to himself and/or his children. Eric owned a majority of the corporation's stock and for many years had managed the corporation's business. He had purchased most of his stock from the man who co-founded the corporation with his father and had inherited the rest. His siblings all had acquired their stock through inheritance. Most of them also had worked for the corporation from time to time, but none had held a managerial position.

Plaintiffs introduced evidence that the corporation had paid dividends of $225,000 to $280,000 annually in the years 1984–1990, but had paid a dividend of only $20,000 in 1991 and had paid no dividends thereafter. Plaintiffs also showed that the salaries paid to Eric and his son increased from $180,000 in 1990 to $220,000 in 1991 and $340,000 in 1992. Their argument, apparently, was that these facts, standing alone, sufficed to demonstrate that Eric had acted oppressively or unfairly and had frustrated their reasonable expectations as stockholders.

The court disagreed. It held that "since plaintiffs were never active in the management of the business, but are the owners of stock on which dividends were paid regularly, their only reasonable expectations are that dividends would continue to be paid on their stock if funds are reasonably available for the payment of dividends." *Id.* at 429, 687 A.2d at 270. Plaintiffs' evidence that the corporation had stopped paying dividends at the same time it sharply increased the salaries it paid to Eric and his son was "not adequate to enable a trier of fact to find that the salaries paid to defendant Eric Axelsson, Jr. and to his son were so unreasonably high, even considering the plaintiffs' reasonable expectations of dividends, that they were unfair and oppressive to the minority stockholders." *Id.* The court, however, did hold that an accountant's report introduced by plaintiffs, which concluded (1) the corporation did not systematically record its receipts from cash sales and (2) for the one year the accountant sampled, cash receipts not deposited to the corporation's bank accounts totaled at least $638,000, did constitute evidence sufficient to support a finding that Eric had been guilty of a gross failure to maintain an accounting system which properly recorded the corporation's business and financial transactions. The court also held that such a failure would constitute unfair and oppressive conduct within the meaning of N.J.S.A. 14A:12–7.)

Note that *Bonavito* held it was unreasonable for the corporation to terminate payment of dividends to a minority shareholder, who had inherited her stock from her husband, even though the salaries paid to the Alan Corbo and his children were rather modest, while the court in *Kelley* did not appear troubled by the payment to Eric Axelsson, Jr., and his son of much larger salaries. Do the different results in these cases reflect different approaches to defining minority shareholders' "reasonable expectations" or can they be attributed to the different histories of the corporations involved in these cases? Alternatively should the results be viewed as consistent because both courts held plaintiffs were entitled to some relief?

2. Professor Thompson notes: "The increasing use of the reasonable expectations standard reflects a move away from an exclusive search for egregious conduct by those in control of the enterprise and toward greater consideration of the effect of conduct on the complaining shareholder, even if no egregious conduct by controllers can be shown." Robert B. Thompson, *Corporate Dissolution and Shareholders' Reasonable Expectations*, 66 WASH. U. L. Q. 193, 219–220 (1988). *See, also,* Robert W. Hillman, *The Dissatisfied Participant in the Solvent Business Venture: A Consideration of the Relative Permanence of Partnerships and Close Corporations*, 67 MINN.L.REV. 1 (1982). Easterbrook and Fischel, on the other hand, oppose judicial decisions and state statutes that provide for dissolution if the majority shareholders frustrate a minority shareholder's "reasonable expectations." They argue that this vague and open-ended standard provides disgruntled minority shareholders with an opportunity to coerce majority shareholders by threatening in bad faith to initiate lawsuits seeking dissolution. Frank H. Easterbrook & Daniel R. Fischel, *Close Corporations and Agency Costs*, 38 STAN. L. REV. 271, 288 (1986).

3. Courts in other states also have relied on their inherent equity authority to devise other remedies where they have found minority shareholders have been oppressed or a deadlock exists. In *Baker v. Commercial Body Builders, Inc.*, 264 Or. 614, 507 P.2d 387 (1973), the court listed ten possible forms of relief that it could order short of outright dissolution:

(a) The entry of an order requiring dissolution of the corporation at a specified future date, to become effective only in the event that the stockholders fail to resolve their differences prior to that date.

(b) The appointment of a receiver, not for the purposes of dissolution, but to continue the operation of the corporation for the benefit of all of the stockholders, both majority and minority, until differences are resolved or "oppressive" conduct ceases.

(c) The appointment of a "special fiscal agent" to report to the court relating to the continued operation of the corporation, as a protection to its minority stockholders, and the retention of jurisdiction of the case by the court for that purpose.

(d) The retention of jurisdiction of the case by the court for the protection of the minority stockholders without appointment of a receiver or "special fiscal agent."

(e) The ordering of an accounting by the majority in control of the corporation for funds alleged to have been misappropriated.

(f) The issuance of an injunction to prohibit continuing acts of "oppressive" conduct and which may include the reduction of salaries or bonus payments found to be unjustified or excessive.

(g) The ordering of affirmative relief by the required declaration of a dividend or a reduction and distribution of capital.

(h) The ordering of affirmative relief by the entry of an order requiring the corporation or a majority of its stockholders to purchase the stock of the minority stockholders at a price to be determined according to a specified formula or at a price determined by the court to be a fair and reasonable price.

(i) The ordering of affirmative relief by the entry of an order permitting minority stockholders to purchase additional stock under conditions specified by the court.

(j) An award of damages to minority stockholders as compensation for any injury suffered by them as the result of "oppressive" conduct by the majority in control of the corporation.

507 P.2d at 395–6. In *Hendley v. Lee*, 676 F.Supp. 1317 (D.S.C.1987), which involved a petition for dissolution, the court found that a deadlock existed but rejected both dissolution and a division of the assets of the corporation as remedies. It ordered a buyout. When neither party elected to sell, the court determined who should be required to sell by looking at the financial condition of the parties, their ability to engage in other activities and the tax consequences to each party. Both *Schirmer v. Bear*, 271 Ill.App.3d 778, 208 Ill.Dec. 209, 648 N.E.2d 1131 (1995), and *Kalabogias v. Georgou*, 254 Ill.App.3d 740, 193 Ill.Dec. 892, 627 N.E.2d 51 (Ill.App. 1993), ordered majority shareholders to repurchase stock from minority shareholders in lieu of dissolution. In *Thompson's Point, Inc. v. Safe Harbor Development*, 862 F.Supp. 594 (D.Me.1994), the court

found that grounds for dissolution existed but that neither party wanted the corporation dissolved. The court raised the possibility of appointing an independent director to deal with the tension between the subject corporation's shareholders. However, in *Jordon v. Bowman Apple Products Co., Inc.*, 728 F.Supp. 409 (W.D. Va.1990), the court held that Virginia's adoption of a statute authorizing dissolution or the appointment of a custodian in cases where minority shareholders are oppressed supersedes shareholders' common law right of action for oppression and limited plaintiff's remedies to those available under the statute.

One question that arises both under statutes providing for a buy-out and when a court finds oppression and allows a corporation to purchase a minority shareholder's stock in lieu of dissolution, is what weight should be given to a shareholder agreement regulating transfers of stock. *Matter of Pace Photographers, Ltd.*, 71 N.Y.2d 737, 530 N.Y.S.2d 67, 525 N.E.2d 713 (1988), involved a shareholder agreement fixing the price at which stock could be purchased if any shareholder decided to "sell, hypothecate, transfer, encumber or otherwise dispose of" his stock * * *." The court held that the agreement did not control the price at which the stock should be transferred when the corporation elected to buy a petitioning shareholder's stock pursuant to N.Y.B.C.L. § 1118, because the agreement did not include a dissolution proceeding under N.Y.B.C.L. § 1104–a in its list of voluntary transactions that would trigger the pricing provision.

# Chapter 14

# THE ROLE OF THE SHAREHOLDER IN THE GOVERNANCE OF THE PUBLIC CORPORATION

In Chapter 12, we saw that the statutory corporate governance structure is one in which shareholders elect the directors who then supervise the corporation's business and select the officers who run that business on a daily basis. Statutes remove most decisions about the direction of corporate policy and operation of the corporations' business from the shareholders' power. The statutory model thus largely divorces ownership from control. In practice, in most publicly-held corporations, the separation is greater than the theory might suggest. Shareholders, to be sure, always formally *elect* the directors, but rarely do they play a very meaningful role in *selecting* them. The rules governing access to public corporations' proxy statements make it impractical for most shareholders to nominate or solicit support for candidates for election to the board. Incumbent directors, who govern access to the corporation's proxy statement and can tap the corporate treasury to fund proxy solicitations, effectively determine who is nominated and who is elected. The corporation's chief executive officer is far more likely to influence these decisions than is any shareholder or shareholder group. In short, subject to the often important influence of market forces, most public corporations are firmly controlled by self-perpetuating boards of directors or by the senior corporate officers that those boards ostensibly have elected.

Dean Robert Clark notes that because directors and officers can use the powers that the law delegates to them to advance their personal goals "in ways that hurt other persons having claims on the organization," the central major problem in corporate law "is how to keep managers accountable to their other-directed duties while nonetheless allowing them great discretionary power over appropriate matters." Robert Charles Clark, Corporate Law § 1.5 (1986). The chapters that follow deal with issues that arise largely as a consequence of the separation of ownership and control in public corporations and the possibility that directors or officers will use their powers in ways that are inconsistent with shareholders' interests. This chapter begins with a discussion of theories of the firm—of the nature and character of the public corporation—because those theories provide the backdrop against which doctrinal and policy decisions are debated. The chapter then shifts its focus to shareholders and the extent to which, as "owners," they are (or should be) able to influence decision making in public corporations.

Questions as to the proper role of shareholders in a corporate governance system have been complicated by the major shift in share ownership in recent years. Institutional investors (e.g., pension funds, insurance companies, mutual funds, etc.) now own a large portion of the stock of many corporations—in some, more than half the outstanding stock. Consequently, when discussing shareholders' involvement in corporate decision making, it is important to specify with which "shareholders" one is concerned—individuals, who generally hold relatively small amounts of stock, or institutions, which typically hold, and have the resources to acquire, much larger stock positions.

## A.  THEORIES OF THE FIRM

### 1.  THE BERLE–MEANS CORPORATION

The modern debate about the nature of the public corporation dates from the publication in 1932 of Adolf Berle and Gardiner Means, THE MODERN CORPORATION AND PRIVATE PROPERTY, a study of the characteristics of the two hundred largest corporations listed on the New York Stock Exchange that highlighted the development of a separation between ownership and control.

Adolf A. Berle & Gardiner C. Means, **THE MODERN CORPORATION AND PRIVATE PROPERTY**

66, 84, 86–88 (1932).

[A]  large body of security holders has been created who exercise virtually no control over the wealth which they or their predecessors in interest have contributed to the enterprise. In case of management control, the ownership interest held by the controlling group amounts to but a very small fraction of the total ownership.

* * *

* * * [T]he position of ownership has changed from that of an active to that of a passive agent. In place of actual physical properties over which the owner could exercise direction and for which he was responsible, the owner now holds a piece of paper representing a set of rights and expectations with respect to an enterprise. But over the enterprise and over the physical property—the instruments of production—in which he has an interest, the owner has little control. At the same time he bears no responsibility with respect to the enterprise or its physical property.

* * *

[O]wnership is so widely distributed that no individual or small group has even a minority interest large enough to dominate the affairs of the company. When the largest single interest amounts to but a fraction of one per cent—the case in several of the largest American corporations—no stockholder is in the position through his holdings alone to place important pressure upon the management or to use his holdings as a considerable nucleus for the accumulation of the majority of votes necessary to control.

\* \* \*

In such companies where does control lie? To answer this question, it is necessary to examine in greater detail the conditions surrounding the electing of the board of directors. In the election of the board the stockholder ordinarily has three alternatives. He can refrain from voting, he can attend the annual meeting and personally vote his stock, or he can sign a proxy transferring his voting power to certain individuals selected by the management of the corporation, the proxy committee. As his personal vote will count for little or nothing at the meeting unless he has a very large block of stock, the stockholder is practically reduced to the alternative of not voting at all or else of *handing over his vote to individuals over whom he has no control and in whose selection he did not participate.* In neither case will he be able to exercise any measure of control. Rather, control will tend to be in the hands of those who select the proxy committee by whom, in turn, the election of directors for the ensuing period may be made. Since the proxy committee is appointed by the existing management, the latter can virtually dictate their own successors. Where ownership is sufficiently sub-divided, the management can thus become a self-perpetuating body even though its share in the ownership is negligible. This form of control can properly be called "management control." (Emphasis in original.)

## 2. THE CONTRACTUAL THEORY OF THE CORPORATION

In the late 1970s, a number of economists and lawyers began to advance a contractual theory of the corporation. They agreed that ownership was divorced from control in most public corporations, but saw that as a strength of the corporate form. The central thrust of their argument was that investment is a voluntary activity and that, consequently, relationships among shareholders and between shareholders and managers should be viewed as essentially contractual in nature.

In the 1980s, Professor (later Judge) Frank Easterbrook and Professor Daniel Fischel used the contractual theory to address almost every major issue in corporate law in a series of law review articles that they later revised and published in THE ECONOMIC STRUCTURE OF CORPORATE LAW (1991).

The contractarians' arguments touched off a spirited debate that continues to this day. What follows are excerpts from articles that set forth, criticize and defend the contractual theory of the corporation. As you read them, try to identify the basis for the differences in these commentators' points of view.*

### Henry N. Butler, *The Contractual Theory of the Corporation*
11 GEORGE MASON U. L.REV. 99 (Summer 1989).

### INTRODUCTION

The modern corporation is one of the most successful inventions in history, as evidenced by its widespread adoption and survival as a primary vehicle of capitalism over the past century. Economists, however, have only recently begun * * * to view the firm as a "nexus of contracts" among participants in the organization. When applied to the corporate form of organization, the theory of the firm is often referred to as the contractual theory of the corporation.

* * * The contractual theory views the corporation as founded in private contract, where the role of the state is limited to enforcing contracts. In this regard, a state charter merely recognizes the existence of a "nexus of contracts" called a corporation. Each contract in the "nexus of contracts" warrants the same legal and constitutional protections as other legally enforceable contracts. Moreover, freedom of contract requires that parties to the "nexus of contracts" must be allowed to structure their relations as they desire.

* * *

### I. Background: The Berle–Means Approach to Corporate Governance

* * *

Much of the Berle and Means analysis is based on their belief that shareholders should, but do not, play a major, direct role in monitoring corporate managers. * * * [H]owever, the reality of the large corporation is far from democratic because shareholders rarely have the incentive to exercise their legal rights. * * * The so-called "Wall Street Rule" is that "rationally ignorant" shareholders sell their stock rather than become involved in the internal affairs of the corporation. Because of the seeming indifference of shareholders, Berle and Means and their progeny have assumed that directors and managers are free to operate the corporation in a manner not necessarily in the shareholders' best interest.

---

* This summary does not reflect another body of scholarship that sees the corporation as a socio-economic unit with a variety of contributors, participants and claimants—such as employees, suppliers, consumers, the community, etc.—and faults the contractual theory of the corporation because it fails to address the problem of how corporate law should take account of the interests of those "stakeholders." *See generally* PROGRESSIVE CORPORATE LAW (Lawrence E. Mitchell ed. 1995); Symposium, *The Corporate Stakeholder Conference*, 43 U. TORONTO L.J. 297 (1993); Symposium, *New Directions in Corporate Law*, 50 WASH. & LEE L. REV. 1373 (1993); Symposium, *Corporate Malaise—Stakeholder Statutes: Cause or Cure?*, 21 STETSON L. REV. 1 (1991).

The Berle and Means perspective on the corporation has fostered the view among some legal commentators that corporation law is the only meaningful constraint on managerial behavior. This has led to public policy arguments that place great emphasis on the role of laws in governing the relationship between shareholders and managers. In essence, some commentators have assumed that managers, freed from legal constraints, can abuse shareholders' interests without cost. Corporation law, according to this view, plays a pre-eminent role in maintaining balance in the large corporation characterized by a separation of ownership and control. * * *

* * *

## II. The Theory of the Firm and the Nature of the Corporation

* * *

### C. The Corporate Firm: Residual Claimants, Shareholders, and Monitors

* * * The publicly traded corporation allows individuals with no managerial expertise to participate in corporations as owners by purchasing shares of stock. The corporate form also allows specialization, or centralization, of management functions through the hiring of professional managers. Specifically, the corporation allows individuals with little financial capital, but considerable managerial talents, to specialize as professional managers of corporations. * * *

The presence of "rationally ignorant" shareholders, however, presents managers of corporations with opportunities to engage in activities that are not necessarily in the shareholders' best interests. These so-called "agency costs" are discussed below.

### D. Agency Theory and the Corporation

* * *

In general, agency theory suggests that unity of ownership and control is not a necessary condition of efficient performance of a firm. This perspective stresses the voluntary, contractual nature of the corporation. A first step in understanding this market-oriented approach is to recognize that it is based in part on the assumption that the shareholders' primary interest is in the maximization of the value of their investments and that the contractual relations among participants in the firm must convince shareholders that managers will not abuse the shareholders' interests. A corporation's managers, which are defined to include its officers and directors, are agents of the shareholders. In this view, the so-called separation of ownership and control in the large corporation is an agency relationship, which exists because the benefits of the relationship exceed the agency costs associated with it. * * *

* * *

Agency theory and transaction costs economics attempt to explain the development of institutional arrangements that convince shareholders voluntarily to allow managers to control their resources. The resources devoted to controlling agency costs are properly identified as agency costs. Thus, agency costs include not only the direct costs associated with agents acting in their own interest at the expense of shareholders, but also the costs of controlling managerial agents through legal or market governance arrangements. * * *

### III. Corporate Governance Mechanisms and the Contractual Theory of the Corporation

* * * This section offers a summary of the governance mechanisms that are believed to explain the phenomenal success of the modern corporation.

The discussion focuses on powerful market forces that encourage managers to act in shareholders' interests. * * * In order to raise capital at the lowest possible price, managers must offer contract terms—including evidence of the existence of intra-firm incentive structures—that convince investors that agency costs will be minimized. This section identifies and discusses those contractual terms.

### A. The Market for Corporate Control

A potential concern of investors is that intra-firm corporate governance devices such as managerial incentive contracts designed by entrenched managers, although clearly more useful than monitoring by diffuse shareholders, may not always be effective in controlling managerial agency costs. An alternative control mechanism, beyond the direct control of entrenched managers, is found in the stock market. The stock market discipline of managers is manifest in the threat of tender offer, takeovers, or other forms of changes in corporate control whenever entrenched managers adopt strategies and behavior that fail to maximize the value of the corporation's shares. The so-called market for corporate control provides an external monitoring mechanism that forces managers to be concerned about their shareholders. * * *

If a firm is not performing up to its financial potential under current and expected market conditions, regardless of the reason, then it is an attractive target for a change in corporate control. According to the theory, the acquiring firm purchases the stock of the target company, replaces the inefficient managers with efficient managers, and then reaps a large profit as the stock price rises to reflect the increased earning potential under the more efficient managerial team. In basic terms, the firm's assets are worth more in the hands of the new managers. In many instances, the source of the premium for the replacement of managers is the reduction of agency costs. But a more general view of the role of the market for corporate control is that it is the *threat* of takeover, not the actual occurrence of a takeover, which serves to align managers' interests with shareholders' interests.

\* \* \*

Exclusive reliance on the market for corporate control to solve all of the potential conflicts of interest associated with the separation of ownership and control is neither justified nor necessary. Managerial discretion is constrained by other market and legal mechanisms. \* \* \* Nevertheless, the market for corporate control \* \* \* provides the glue that holds together the nexus of contracts.

\* \* \*

## H.   Corporate Law and Fiduciary Duties

Emphasis on the interaction of market forces under the contractual theory of the corporation has led some scholars to argue that markets will lead managers to adopt optimal governance structures and that corporate law is irrelevant. However, the market mechanisms may be inadequate to deal with last-period, or one-time, divergences when the agent rationally concludes that the benefits of the one-time use of discretion is worth whatever penalties may be forthcoming in the employment market for the agent's services. In this regard, corporate law of fiduciary duties serves as a legal constraint on managerial opportunism.

Moreover, because markets do not operate without cost, it appears that corporate law plays a productive role in the contractual theory of the corporation by providing a standard form contract that reduces the transaction and negotiating costs of reaching and adhering to optimal contracts. \* \* \* The terms of corporate law is one of the governance mechanisms that can be selected by the contracting parties to minimize corporate agency costs.

## I.   Evaluation of the Contractual Theory

\* \* \*

The contractual theory of the corporation does not assert that agency costs are reduced to zero, rather it asserts that agency costs are minimized by the contractual terms agreed upon in the face of market and legal constraints. The contractual theory of the corporation provides theoretical and empirical bases for understanding not only the organization and success of the large corporation, but also the appropriate role of privately negotiated contracts and mandatory legal rules.

———

Robert Charles Clark, *Agency Costs Versus Fiduciary
Duties*, in Pratt & Zeckhauser, Principals and
Agents: The Structure of Business
55–64, 66–69 (1985).

### Pitfalls of the Agency Costs Approach

Much of the economic literature talks about "firms" rather than
"corporations," and does not distinguish sharply between closely held
business organizations (whatever their legal form) and publicly held
corporations. For a number of reasons, failure to make this distinction
clearly can be a source of almost fatal confusion. Throughout this paper,
I will be referring only to publicly held (or "public") business corporations, which of course account for the great bulk of business revenues in
the United States. * * *

### Managers Are Not Agents of Stockholders

To an experienced corporate lawyer who has studied primary legal
materials, the assertion that corporate managers are agents of investors,
whether debtholders or stockholders, will seem odd or loose. The lawyer
would make the following points: (1) corporate officers like the president
and treasurer are agents of the corporation itself; (2) the board of
directors is the ultimate decision-making body of the corporation (and in
a sense is the group most appropriately identified with "the corporation"); (3) directors are not agents of the corporation but are sui generis;
(4) neither officers nor directors are agents of the stockholders; but (5)
both officers and directors are "fiduciaries" with respect to the corporation and its stockholders.

These legal characterizations are not just semantic differences from
the usual terminology of the agency costs literature. To see the distinction, let us first contrast the legal conception of the agent with that of
the corporate director and then examine the more general legal concept
of the fiduciary.

Though lawyers use the concept of agency in a variety of senses, the
core legal concept implies a relationship in which the principal retains
the power to control and direct the activities of the agent. * * *

A review of elementary corporate law shows that this power of the
principal to direct the activities of the agent does not apply to the
stockholders as against the directors or officers of their corporation. By
statute in every state, the board of directors of a corporation has the
power and duty to manage or supervise its business. The stockholders do
not. To appreciate the point fully, consider the following activities:
setting the ultimate goal of the corporation—for example, whether its
legal purpose will be to maximize profits; choosing the corporation's
lines of business—hiring and firing the full-time executives who will
actually run the company; and exercising supervisory power with respect
to the day-to-day operations of the business. Stockholders of a large
publicly held corporation *do not* do these things; as a matter of efficient

operation of a large firm with numerous residual claimants they *should not* do them; and under the typical corporate statute and case law they *cannot* do them.

\* \* \*

The legal relationship between the stockholder and the manager is very different from the legal relationship between the ordinary principal and agent. So what? the reader might ask. Do these differences have any bearing on the kinds of problems that have been at the heart of the agency costs literature? To some degree, yes. Ignoring the legal restrictions on stockholders' decision-making power makes it easier to talk as if stockholders and managers "bargain" over and "contract" about the terms of their relationship, or "implicitly" or "virtually" do so—and this is the next, more serious pitfall of the agency costs literature.

\* \* \*

### A Corporation Is Not a Nexus of Actual Contracts

\* \* \*

[I]s it realistic or useful to view the modern public corporation as consisting only, or even principally, of a set of contracts? I think not. This extreme contractualist viewpoint is almost perverse. It is likely to blind us to most of the features of the modern public corporation that are distinctive, puzzling, and worth exploring. To see this, we must first consider the notion of contract, and then note the extent to which the corporation, considered as a multitude of legal relationships, consists of noncontractual legal relationships.

\* \* \* [T]he core notion of contract, and the most relevant for theorizing about the optimality of commercial relationships, is that the rights and duties between the two parties are specified and fixed by their own voluntary and actual agreement. Let me refer to a set of legal relationships determined solely in this way as constituting an "actual contract."

Most of the particular rules that make up the legal relationships among corporate officers, directors, and stockholders—that is, the relationships that constitute corporate law and give operational meaning to the legal concept of the corporation—are not the product of actual contracts made by the persons subject to them. Furthermore, they are often not the product of "implicit" contracts between these people, if by that term we mean that the individuals actually understood the governing rules but simply did not advert to them when entering their roles as officers, directors, or stockholders.

\* \* \*

### Why It Matters Whether Contracts Are Actual Rather Than Implicit or Standardized

\* \* \*

It may be objected that some corporate law rules seem to fit the model of "standard presumptions" adopted because they fit the normal case, and that it is intuitively plausible that the relevant participants would actually agree to them, if the issue were put to them for explicit consideration and bargaining. This group of rules is likely to include the more elementary structural features of the corporate form of organization, such as limited liability of stockholders and free transferability of shares, which are often embodied in statutes. I agree that there are such rules, and they constitute an important class. In my view, they result from (fairly slow, crude) processes of legal evolution that favor rules that reduce transaction costs. But I would note that with many other rules, it is not at all obvious that they can be analyzed this way; the analysis has to be made in detail before it becomes convincing.

Another objection might be that while most rules of corporate law are imposed on the parties subject to it, they are usually free to "bargain around" them. * * * *Failure* to bargain around a rule then amounts to accepting it, and one might even argue that the nonbargainers "contract" to obey the rule. (Similarly, one can argue that failure to reincorporate in another state implies real consent to those rules that could be changed by reincorporation.)

But some important corporate law rules cannot be bargained around (unless, perhaps, one is willing to depart from the manager or stockholder roles or to modify their parameters drastically). Basic fiduciary duties fall in this category, along with insider trading rules and the norm that directors rather than stockholders manage public corporations. * * *

Moreover, bargaining around is costly. If the cost of bargaining is expected to exceed the benefits, the standard legal rule is simply tolerated—but this does not mean that it is the best available rule to govern the behavior in question. An alternative rule might make some people better off and no one worse off. Yet the substitution need not occur. For example, bargaining around a waivable fiduciary duty * * * might require the preparation and distribution of a special proxy statement and the collection of a stockholder vote. The associated expense may deter many such bargains with investors. A different version of the legal doctrine might eliminate the transaction costs and deterrent effects of the need to seek shareholder consent. Thus, at any given time, it is an open question whether the standard legal rule is better than some imagined or proposed one. The interested commentator will have to make an independent assessment of the costs and benefits of the opposing rules, rather than simply assuming that the existing rule must be fit because it has survived (so far) without provoking much bargaining around.

* * *

*Indeterminacy of Results.* The basic pitfall with implicit-contracts reasoning is that it is frequently indeterminate and therefore manipulable. This is true whether the purpose of the reasoning is to advance positive or normative theory. It is especially true of complex, multifaceted relationships, such as those among directors, officers, stockholders, and the large bureaucratic organizations with which they are associated.

In arguments about which rules rational managers and investors would have agreed to, much depends on what one assumes about the characteristics of the bargaining parties, their knowledge, the bargaining process, and the state of the financial and business world. The implicit-contracts form of reasoning is often indeterminate precisely because there is no consensus about which assumptions to use.

———

Professor Victor Brudney, *Corporate Governance, Agency Costs and the Rhetoric of Contract*, 85 Col.L.Rev. 1403 (1985), agreed with much of Dean Clark's analysis and rejected the idea that the markets can effectively constrain managerial discretion. Brudney noted that because there is no pressure to disclose the magnitude of managerial discretion or the uncertainty of the connection between managerial inputs and rewards, investors have difficulty in assessing the quality of management before investing. He also argued that existing studies fail to demonstrate that an efficient market can be said to exist for managers services or managerial arrangements. Further, he questioned whether the market for a corporation's stock can adequately check managers' discretion. * * *

———

Henry N. Butler & Larry E. Ribstein, *Opting Out of Fiduciary Duties: Response to the Anti–Contractarians*

65 Wash. L. Rev. 1, 12–18 (1990).

C.    Adhesion and Freedom of choice: The Formation of the Corporate Contract

* * *

### 1. The "Adhesion" Analysis

According to [Professor] Brudney, shareholders do not freely consent to corporate arrangements as in "conventional" contracts. Rather, dispersed shareholders must accept, without any direct bargaining over details or alternatives, package deals crafted by managers. In this respect, Brudney greatly overstates the shareholders' plight. In fact, investors are offered a formidable array of investment alternatives—including corporations with different capital and ownership structures, and such diverse investments as limited partnerships, mutual funds, money market accounts, real estate, and simple savings accounts. Clearly investors are not *forced* to accept any particular investment. If contractual volition is lacking—if, as Brudney argues, these are "adhesion" contracts—it is only in the sense that investors do not dicker over individual terms, but accept contractual packages. * * *

* * *

For many reasons, a contracting party does not usually want to "have it my way," but is often willing to accept the * * * corporation's package. In fact, because sellers often offer the terms they believe buyers want, it may be impossible to determine who is dictating the terms of a contract by merely identifying the printer of the contract. Although there is always the chance that the terms could be improved through dickering, this is a costly process in terms of time, attorneys' fees, and other transaction costs.

Not only is the extra cost of a customized contract usually not worth the benefit of dickering, but in many situations a standardized contract is a better one: there is more information available concerning a standardized form; important terms have been clarified by interpretation; and error costs and information costs are less than in individually negotiated deals. * * *

### 2. The Information Problem

Professor Brudney's second concern about using the "rhetoric of contract" in the corporate context is that the average investor lacks sufficient information about the package he is buying. * * *

In general, the issue here should not be what is, and what is not, a "contract" in some abstract sense. Concerns about information and adhesion problems in the corporation amount to a conclusion that voluntary arrangements in the corporation are not, like other voluntary arrangements, presumptively efficient. This conclusion depends on the viability of markets in this setting, and is therefore the subject of economic analysis. The issue cannot be resolved by labels.

### D. The Corporation as "Implicit" Contract

Professor Melvin A. Eisenberg argues that the corporation should not be regarded as fundamentally contractual because many of the terms governing the corporate relationship are merely "implicit bargains" and not real contracts. An implicit bargain is a term used by labor economics to refer to terms that, like real bargains, involve an economic quid pro quo. They are not "real" contracts because they are enforced by market, rather than legal, mechanisms. * * *

The fact that many of the parties to a corporation are governed largely by implicit terms *supports* rather than undermines the contract theory of the corporation. The choice of implicit and explicit terms is one of many examples of how the parties, if unhindered by legal rules, choose the combination of legal and extra-legal devices appropriate to their relationship. It is a clear non sequitur to say that because the parties to firms sometimes choose implicit instead of legally enforceable terms they should be forced to submit to mandatory legal rules. More specifically, the parties' choice of market mechanisms to support an implicit promise by managers not to behave opportunistically should not be trumped by mandatory fiduciary duties.

---

## William W. Bratton, *The Economic Structure of the Post–Contractual Corporation*

87 Nw. U. L.Rev. 180, 180–197 (1992).

### I.  INTRODUCTION

The political economics of corporate law changed abruptly during the 1980s. At the decade's start, the prevailing economics counseled that excess management power needed to be curbed for productivity's sake. Law reform was assumed to be an appropriate means to this end. But this antimanagerial paradigm fell from favor, and by the time the takeover market became white-hot in 1984 and 1985, a "contract paradigm" had taken its place. The large American corporations reemerged as a nexus for a set of contracts among individual factors of production. * * *

Easterbrook and Fischel led corporate legal theory up the mountain of contract. They restated every topic of consequence in the terms of financial economics. In so doing, they captured the rhetoric of academic corporate law, rewriting the story of shareholder-management relations to accord with a theme of self-protection through contract. Where once we had shareholder dependence, they substituted cheap opportunities to diversify firm-specific risk. Where once we had unfair wealth transfers, they substituted market pricing that accounted for the risks of misallocated gains. Where we once had excess management power, they substituted market constraints. Where we once had "needs" that called for reform, they substituted "costs" that blocked reform.

Now Easterbrook and Fischel summarize their enterprise with *The Economic Structure of Corporate Law*. * * *

* * *

[In that book,] Easterbrook and Fischel have stepped back from the nexus-of-contracts corporation because developments in both theory and practice made manifest its inadequacy as a foundation for any plausible legal theory. The theoretical development was the "mandatory/enabling" discussion of the late 1980s. This showed that shareholder-manager relationships did not, in the main, lie within the zone of free contract. The practical development was the failure of crucial subject matter—the law addressed to takeovers—to develop in conformity to the model's predictions. This showed emphatically that corporate law does not always instantiate contractual norms. * * *

*(a) Mandatory corporate law affirmed.*—The mandatory/enabling discussion was an extended consideration of the implications of the nexus-of-contract proposition. The proposition on the table was this: If

the firm is contract, then the parties in interest should be able to "opt-out" of the terms provided by state law and substitute their own terms. Discussion of this proposition iterated contract law's "overreaching" analysis. It turned out that process defects make the corporate charter amendment an inappropriate context for complete freedom of contract, even when viewed through the lens of an economic model. Shareholders have a collective action problem when managers propose charter amendments. Small stakes make it irrational for individual holders to invest in information acquisition. Moreover, managers, by virtue of their control of the structure and timing of the amendment process, can easily turn the shareholders' disadvantaged negotiating position to their own advantage. The upshot is a contract failure: the shareholders rationally vote to approve an amendment that decreases value to them.

A consensus of sorts emerged from the discussion. The amendment process is deemed reliable as to amendments such as poison pills or stock option plans that are company-specific and transaction-specific. But, as to general, open-ended proposals such as broad-brush abolition of director and officer fiduciary duties, contract failure is probable. Therefore, according to the consensus, charter amendments sometimes should be subject to mandatory regulation even under a contract paradigm.

* * * The consensus confirmed the legitimacy of legal intervention in corporate affairs from an economic perspective. * * * Although no one mentioned it at the time, this also began a process of disassociation between corporate law and economics and the nexus-of-contracts concept of the corporation. The process continues today.

Easterbrook and Fischel joined the mandatory/enabling consensus, albeit with qualifications. * * * [S]ince contract turns out to be a matter of degree, the issue goes to the dimensions of the zone of contract freedom provided for by a particular model. Easterbrook and Fischel's zone is rhetorically expansive, but more compact as a practical matter of degree. A blank contracting slate occurs only in respect to recent and prospective initial public offerings. Since most Fortune 500 companies went public long ago, the critical questions respecting most corporations remain legitimate subject matter for legal mandates.

(b) *Takeovers reversed.*—Takeovers made a contractual picture of the public corporation plausible in the first place. * * *

Fittingly, developments begun in the late 1980s in response to takeovers are prompting the nexus-of-contracts corporation's subsequent departure. Shark repellant charter amendments and poison pill plans—"contractual" modifications that entrench management and devalue the shareholders' investment—retained the support of the courts even as they became more widespread and effective. In addition, state legislatures came down emphatically on the side of defending managers. Their antitakeover statutes imposed significant costs on hostile control transfers. Viewed cumulatively, these changes open up a rift between the contract paradigm's implicit normative structure, on the one hand, and that of actual corporate contracts and state corporate law, on the other.

To their credit, Easterbrook and Fischel not only admit, but explore the negative implications of these developments for the contractual corporation. They conclude that takeover law has developed in an inefficient direction. Managers exploit the collective action problem in getting shareholders to assent to shark repellant provisions. And, in the "last period," when managers defend their jobs from attack, the ordinary controls of the capital and labor markets do not operate. Judicial intervention become the only available means to the end of inefficient deployment of assets.

Furthermore, Easterbrook and Fischel abandon the "race to the top" story of state corporate law. * * *

Today, Easterbrook and Fischel speak of the performance of state corporate law with less confidence. In their opinion, while survival still is the best measure of success, state corporate law is a process of satisfying rather than optimizing. No one, moreover, knows what the market wants. Easterbrook and Fischel do find a contractual term to describe the proliferation of antitakeover statutes. * * * They ascribe the legislation to management "opportunism." But this is bravado. Their model no longer fuses state law together with contract so as to make economics the sole determinant of the law's evolution.

---

Victor Brudney, *Contract and Fiduciary
Duty in Corporate Law*

38 B.C. L. Rev. 595, 622–639, 663–664 (1997).

The dominant school of contractarians emphasizes maximizing corporate value rather than assuring appropriate distribution of such value between the assertedly contracting parties—i.e. managers or controllers on the one hand and public stockholders on the other.

The classic fiduciary duty of loyalty is considered to be a significant obstacle to that maximizing goal, particularly as it prophylactically precludes transactions that might maximize—or at least make—gains for the enterprise. The classic fiduciary duty is also said to dampen the incentives of decision-makers by denying them the rewards from self-aggrandizing behavior that they think necessary, in addition to the rewards for which they expressly contract. Hence, the policy aspiration of contractarians is to reduce, if not to eliminate, state-imposed fiduciary restrictions on the power of corporate managers and controllers to engage in conflict of interest transactions or otherwise to serve themselves collaterally at the possible expense of public stockholders.

One doctrinal mechanism for fulfilling that aspiration entails characterizing the fiduciary relationship as simply a contractual relationship, and thus transforming fiduciary obligations to "mere" contract obligations. The suggestion is that state-imposed fiduciary strictures are simply background rules which, like "the law" of contracts, (1) are assumed to have been consented to by the parties and incorporated in their relationship, except where they have agreed otherwise, and (2) are to be interpreted by courts as if they were part of a contract that the parties have deliberately drafted. * * *

The concept that thus immunizes the parties from "outside" state-imposed mandates and validates their arrangements as freely chosen is the notion of imputed consent. Consent to be bound by (and knowledge of the meaning of) state-imposed rules is imputed to the parties' arrangement to the extent that they do not reject any or all of those rules, which they are presumed to be free to do. * * *

### A.  *Traditional Fiduciary Loyalty Obligations*

As we have seen, essential to the fiduciary concept is the function of the fiduciary (a function reasonably expected by the beneficiary) to perform services or operate the beneficiary's property for the benefit of the latter. In the case of trusts or principal and agent relationships (and *pro tanto* of corporate management), the fiduciary must act for the beneficiary's exclusive benefit, and, in the case of partnership or corporate controllers for their shared benefit in proportions designated *ex ante*. The fiduciary's entitlement to expressly provided compensation does not open the door to any other mode of reward from dealing with the corporate assets or the stockholders. Correspondingly, the beneficiary is relieved of any concern about specifying or monitoring the fiduciary's appropriative behavior in the course of exercising the broad discretion necessarily delegated.

In contrast, in the classic contract relationship each party acts to benefit himself or herself in carrying out the common enterprise—except as the terms of their arrangement otherwise forbid. Each is expected to act, in the areas of discretion that the contract permits, for his or her own interests and without any regard (in classical contract doctrine) or with some indeterminate regard (in more modern contract rules) to whether the other is benefited or injured by those acts on his or her own behalf. Consistent with that functional difference, the contract relationship does not require or contemplate that either party will substitute "trust" for "wariness" in the relationship.

To be sure, the contract concept, like the fiduciary concept, requires a limit on the benefits that a party may take for himself or herself from the common enterprise at the other's expense. But the traditional fiduciary concept—whether viewed in terms of exclusive benefit or sharing—would, by definition, forbid or substantially curtail opportunistic behavior by management or controllers that the contract notion permits. Moreover, traditional fiduciary doctrine permits "consent" to departure from those principles only in limited transactions, and in any event it imposes stricter conditions than classic contract norms require for effective consent to modify the arrangements. Thus, disclosure requirements for consent under traditional fiduciary doctrine are more demanding than contract doctrine generally requires. In addition, the volition that drives such consent must be more clearly evident in the traditional fiduciary context than in the classic contract context.

Not only do traditional fiduciary loyalty restrictions thus differ from classic contract rules in content, but fiduciary strictures are not designed like contract background rules to fill gaps in, or enforce, explicitly specified preferences or protective provisions that the parties selected. On the contrary, the fiduciary rules that the State prescribes supply the content of the parties' preferences and protections, not mere "neutral" background rules to implement particular preferences or protections selected by the parties. In contrast to the essentially neutral character of the restrictions on opportunistic behavior imposed by the background rules that are part of contract doctrine, fiduciary rules are historically comprehensive and one-sided. They aim to protect the beneficiary but not the fiduciary against contingencies in areas of conduct in which contracting parties can (and generally do) select adequate protective terms, but beneficiaries and stockholders (even if they are otherwise considered contracting parties) can not. The functional role of management, as actor for the stockholders, and the structural bargaining incapacity and passive posture of the public stockholder which result in the state thus imposing broad fiduciary restrictions, preclude a court from "interpreting" the meaning or scope of these so-called background rules as if they were deliberately and freely adopted by contracting parties.

Indeed, even in the contract ambience, the notion of the parties importing into the contract all or some of the externally imposed background rules—that resolve ambiguities in the terms or enforce the contract—is problematic. It is a strong, and not entirely plausible, suggestion that even relatively knowledgeable parties to contracts understandingly include in their choice of provisions any or all of those background rules. It is even less plausible to convert state-imposed fiduciary strictures into parts of a voluntarily assumed contract. The beneficiary's power to waive, or consent ex ante to departing from, those strictures in specified circumstances does not enhance that plausibility. Whatever may be said of the power of contracting parties expressly to trump or alter state-imposed contract rules, different considerations color—and limit—the power of a beneficiary to opt out of fiduciary loyalty entitlements.

### B. *Corporate Law Fiduciary Loyalty Obligations*

Currently imposed corporate fiduciary obligations substantially dilute classic fiduciary restrictions. Indeed, they contemplate that the fiduciary may benefit at the expense of the beneficiary, or at least fail to share all gains from self-dealing, but they offer no theory to justify—or operating guide lines to measure—the limits of opportunistic behavior. Doctrinally, authorization of the power to self-deal may derive either from rejection of the exclusive benefit principle or from the easy imputation of consent by stockholders to departure from the principle by managers or controllers. Statutory prescriptions appear to rely on both.

In either case, existence of the power to obtain collateral benefits, as by self-dealing, raises the question of limits on its exercise.

As a matter of positive law, restrictions on self-dealing imposed by courts in fiduciary terms in the corporate context are increasingly slack. But their terms may be somewhat tighter than the restrictions that are imposed under classic contract doctrine or might be imposed under contract doctrine that either requires "good faith" by parties in performing contracts, particularly contracts infected with touches of duress or adhesion, or prohibits results that are unconscionable.

\* \* \*

Notwithstanding the movement of positive law, if the limits on self-aggrandizing conduct are to be faithful to their proclaimed origins in fiduciary premises, they should be more restrictive than limits derived from contract premises—even those premises underlying the more flexible contract doctrines that protect structurally dependent (often dispersed) parties disadvantaged by bargaining power and information disparities. \* \* \*

\* \* \*

## C.  The Wealth–Maximizing Norm And The Fiduciary Relationship

The effort to assimilate the fiduciary relationship to "contract" generates questions with respect to the relevant contract concept to be tapped to solve problems of delineating restraints on management's or controlling stockholders' self-serving behavior. There is more than one vision of "contract," and contract doctrine offers more than one approach to such problems.

The suggestion that state-imposed fiduciary strictures are simply terms of a contract to which the parties have consented and which they may freely alter is the predicate for the contractarians' special method of interpreting ambiguities or gaps in the "contract," including the fiduciary background rules that the parties are assumed to have adopted. Gaps or ambiguities with respect to a particular contingency that cannot be resolved from the terms should be resolved by asking what hypothetical, rational, wealth-maximizing parties would have provided to be done in the contingency under scrutiny if they had thought of the problem when they entered into the relationship. \* \* \*

Notwithstanding the contractarians' ideological premise that favors fulfilling individuals' freely made choice, their interpretive methodology rejects that premise. Whether the framework of analysis is characterized as "fiduciary" or as "contract," resort to hypothetical bargainers to resolve ambiguities scants choice by individual actors. It drives the decision not by the moral force of actual individuals' consent inferred in the particular case, but by the dictates of the contractarians' general conception of efficiency in the run of cases.

The proffered joint wealth-maximizing justification does not necessarily implicate maximizing the wealth of each party. On the contrary, both in theory and in practice, it entails the distinct possibility of reducing the wealth of some of the parties while augmenting the wealth of others. * * *

No less important, this justification rests on value or policy preferences that are subject to substantial debate in the context of the relationship between management or controllers and dispersed public stockholders. * * *

* * * Indeed, the explosive increases in rewards to management during the past several years—a phenomenon that has attracted more than casual discontent in the press-have occurred in connection with management's express compensation. In that matter, * * * legal doctrine limiting self-aggrandizing behavior is closest to the contract model and furthest from the fiduciary model. * * *

* * *

CONCLUSION

Conventional contract doctrine entails a substantially different analytic framework and normative import than does traditional fiduciary doctrine in defining the loyalty obligations of the participants and their power to authorize departure from them. The former focuses on a party's entitlement to benefit himself, and the limits of that entitlement. The latter addresses the obligation of the fiduciary to serve the beneficiary, and the resulting disability from benefiting himself except as specified expressly. Courts, aided by commentators, have substantially diluted fiduciary obligations of corporate management and of controlling common stockholders in self-serving behavior vis-a-vis other common stockholders—both the conduct proscribed and the quality of the consent required to waive those proscriptions. Nevertheless, the restraints that corporate fiduciary obligations impose retain enough color of traditional fiduciary loyalty restrictions to distinguish them from those imposed by contract doctrine—except possibly as notions in contract doctrine like the requirements of good faith and unconscionability may expand restrictions on opportunism by contracting parties. The wealth-maximizing normative justifications for thus loosening traditional fiduciary restrictions do not offer a convincing case for overturning their teaching—at least in the absence of empirical evidence that has thus far not been shown; and less utilitarian policy considerations suggest retaining their teaching.

---

## 3. BEYOND CONTRACTUAL THEORY

Developments in the late 1980s, including the increased prominence of institutional investors and growing disenchantment with hostile take-overs as a central component of the corporate governance system, led some scholars to reexamine Berle and Means' assumptions as to the causes of the divorce of ownership from control in American corporations. In the following excerpts, Mark Roe suggests that patterns of corporate ownership and control in the United States are the product of both political and economic forces and outlines the reasons those patterns may persist.

### Mark J. Roe, STRONG MANAGERS AND WEAK OWNERS: THE POLITICAL ROOTS OF THE SEPARATION OF OWNERSHIP FROM CONTROL (1994)*

The public corporation—with its fragmented shareholders buying and selling on the stock exchange—is the dominant form of enterprise in the United States. Why? The conventional paradigm accepted by most corporate law academics is economic. * * *

\* \* \*

Separation of ownership and control was functional, allowing skilled managers without capital to run the firm and separating unskilled descendants from control of a firm they could not run well. Dispersed individuals would hold the stock, frequently in 100–share lots. Institutions would neither hold nor vote big blocks of stock. Banks held none for their own account. Insurers rarely held stock for most of the twentieth century. Mutual funds and pensions have only recently become an important economic phenomenon. They hold stock in small parcels, usually too small to have much influence.

\* \* \*

America's path to the large firm with fragmented ownership might not have been the inevitable result of the marketplace, but of the political economy of American financial history. Quite a bit of evidence indicates that American politics deliberately fragmented financial institutions, their portfolios, and their ability to network stock into influential blocks. * * *

Contractarian thought is one key branch of the economic model. * * * But contractarians (and I am not wholly excluding myself here), who tend to look at state corporate law—particularly Delaware corporate law—to find how law governs the relationship between shareholders and managers, may have misidentified the key arenas for corporate contract-making. True, the state law legal framework roughly corresponds with what contractarian thought would prescribe. But what if it turns out that the key relationships between shareholders and managers are found neither in state corporate law, nor in federal securities law, but in the deep historical regulations governing financial institutions? What if the law prohibited key aggregations of stockholding, that which would occur

---

* This material is excerpted from a draft introduction to STRONG MANAGERS AND WEAK OWNERS: THE POLITICAL ROOTS OF THE SEPARA- TION OF OWNERSHIP FROM CONTROL provided to the authors by Professor Roe.

through financial institutions? What if law did this deliberately for political reasons, not primarily to foster financial safety?

\* \* \*

The prevailing paradigm is that the modern corporation survived because it was the fittest means of dealing with large-scale organization. But if politics cut off lines of development, \* \* \* then whether it is the inevitable form for large-scale firms becomes doubtful. Politics and the organization of financial intermediaries cannot be left out of the equation. \* \* \*

\* \* \*

Another paradigm, a political paradigm, better explains the modern American corporation than the prevailing paradigm does alone. \* \* \* The size and technology story fails to fully explain ownership patterns. There are organizational alternatives to fragmented ownership; the most prominent concentrated institutional ownership, a result prevalent in other countries. Enterprises could have obtained economies of scale and investors could have obtained diversification through large financial intermediaries that brought small investors and large firms together. These institutions could have shared power in the enterprise with the new managers. But American law and politics deliberately diminished the power of financial institutions to hold the large equity blocks that would foster serious oversight of managers \* \* \*. The origin of the modern corporation lies in technology, economics, and politics.

Think about it. Fragmented securities markets are not the only way to move savings from households to the large firm. One could move savings from people to firms directly through securities markets, or indirectly through large financial intermediaries, which could then take big blocks of stock, sit in boardrooms, and balance power with the CEO. The increasing institutionalization of American securities markets and the concentrated ownership abroad mean this was economically viable. \* \* \* The institutional alternatives would raise a distinctive set of problems: bad management in the intermediary, instability of the intermediary, and political discomfort with concentrated private accumulations of power. All these are possible, but do not refute the proposition that there is more than one way to organize large scale enterprise, and that the short list of alternatives has at least one clear contender with the securities markets, namely the powerful financial intermediary.

———

Mark J. Roe, *Chaos and Evolution in Law and Economics*

109 Harv. L. Rev. 641 (1996).

In this essay, I refine the classical evolutionary model from law and economics by modifying it to accommodate three related concepts—one from chaos theory, another of path dependence, and a final one from modern evolutionary theory. If I am successful, we will have a richer understanding of what makes legal and business institutions.

\* \* \*

## I.   THE CLASSICAL EVOLUTIONARY PARADIGM

The classical evolutionary paradigm has a strong grip on law and economics scholarship. What survives is presumptively efficient: if it were inefficient, the practice, the law, or the custom would be challenged by its more efficient competitors. The success of the more efficient practice or law allows it to prosper, while its less efficient competitors wither and die. \* \* \*

Here I shall examine this paradigm of a Darwinian survival of the fittest in law and economics. While I cannot shake myself of its grip completely, the classical evolution-to-efficiency paradigm fails to explain some important phenomena. \* \* \* If we want a finer approximation to explain resultant reality, we must add two or three other paradigms.

The first comes from the science of chaos. Some phenomena are extremely sensitive to the initial conditions: small changes in the original position make for very large changes in outcome. \* \* \* Chaos here does not mean disorder, but that accurate predictions about where a system is headed are hard. \* \* \*

The second paradigm comes from modern thought on evolution. The observed evolutionary outcome often may be the most efficient available, but that result does not mean that evolution is inevitably an onward and upward process. A competitor survived because it was best suited for yesterday's environment, an environment that was destructive of others with which the survivor had competed. But the destroyed group may be best suited for today's environment. Nothing in evolution, however, assures that the destroyed group will reappear. \* \* \*

The third paradigm is path dependence. All three paradigms overlap, and it is with the last that I will begin to detail this inquiry.

## II.   PATH DEPENDENCE

Consider the most basic instance of path dependency. We are on a road and wonder why it winds and goes here instead of there, when a straight road would be a much easier drive. Today's road depends on what path was taken before. Decades ago, a fur trader cut a path through the woods, and the trader, bent on avoiding a wolves' den and other dangerous sites, took a winding indirect route. \* \* \* Later travelers dragged wagons along the same winding path the trader chose, deepening the grooves and clearing away some trees. Travelers continued to deepen and broaden the road even after the dangerous sites were gone. Industry came and settled in the road's bends; housing developments went up that fit the road and industry. Local civic promoters widened the path and paved it into a road suitable for today's trucks.

\* \* \* Today's road, dependent on the path taken by the trader decades ago, is not the one that the authorities would lay down if they were choosing their road today. But society, having invested in the path itself and in the resources alongside the path, is better off keeping the winding road on its current path than paying to build another. * * *

This path-dependent history maps, more or less, onto chaos analysis and evolutionary analysis. The fur trader's path—chosen to avoid danger spots—is the original condition for chaos theory * * *. The competitor— the winding road—survived because it was best suited for yesterday's wolf-infested environment. But the missed adaptation—a straight road— would be best suited for today's environment. We did not have an evolutionary competition between straight and winding roads in today's environment. We are stuck in a local equilibrium. Again, survival does not imply present-day superiority to untried alternatives.

* * *

The United States developed corporate structures with strong managers and weak owners (instead of, say, strong owners and weaker managers) partly due to path dependence. * * *

The rules and practices that weakened financial intermediaries arose because the American public historically abhorred private concentrations of economic power—concentrations that more powerful financial institutions would create, concentrations that a more powerful central government would have made politically palatable, concentrations that would probably be regulated, not destroyed, were they first arising today. * * *

As large-scale industry arose at the end of the nineteenth century, it faced two financing problems created by the absence of nationwide financial institutions: big industry needed to gather lots of capital nationally, and certain organizational forms that worked well with strong financial institutions were unavailable. We developed very good substitutes. We developed, for example, high-quality securities markets, which allowed firms to raise capital in a national market, to remedy the absence of truly national financial institutions. We developed antitrust rules that promoted competition and, because competition pushes even firms with substandard internal governance toward efficiency, the costs of internal governance problems were reduced. America's continent-sized economy allowed enough competition to prevent any corporate governance problems from being too costly.

In time, we adopted new legal and economic institutions that are still not as well developed in other advanced nations. Corporate boards now have well defined legal duties that partly constrain managers, and we have an active bar that pursues lawsuits, some of which are legitimate and functional. We have developed a professionalism that motivates some managers. * * * We have had hostile takeovers, which constrained managers.

Whatever tasks strong financial institutions might have done, other institutions developed to do. Although this take sees efficiency driving business evolution, we must still examine the original conditions to explain the institutions we have. We did not have an economic battle between one form of corporate ownership and another—ownership through decentralized securities markets versus ownership through powerful financial institutions—with one winning and the other losing. We barred the second type, allowed only the first type, and the consequential evolution made that which was available work satisfactorily.

\* \* \*

I have described how America's corporate governance arose from politically induced weak intermediaries, which led to strong managers, superb securities markets, and professionalized directors. \* \* \*

When international competition hit business consciousness in the 1980s, American firms for the first time had to compete against firms with different ownership structures. Germany and Japan had stronger financial intermediaries that owned and controlled big blocks of stock in their largest industrial companies. The American system could not be seen as the inevitable end of corporate evolution, but as one of at least two possible results, each reasonably satisfactory.

\* \* \*

Could both models be equally efficient? Or, to pose the question first in a way that is easier to answer, could either model be highly inefficient?

The answer has to be no. Neither could be highly inefficient. First, the economies, which we have assumed to be advanced, could not have thrived under a governance system that shackled their largest firms from operating satisfactorily. \* \* \*

Second, global product competition should reduce or eliminate the most inefficient features of a governance system. Firms that have weak governance systems should, in the long run, decline. \* \* \*

Third, cheap telecommunications and frequent international corporate governance conferences mean few secrets are left. Nations and businesses can consciously copy one another's better features, can understand that domestic variations previously thought to be impossible survive abroad, and can find ways to fix their systems' worst features.

Global competition challenged national corporate governance systems in two dimensions, one intellectual and one real. In the intellectual dimension, efficiency explanations for the forms of American ownership and corporate power had to seem weaker. Other systems were possible and not grossly inferior. The possibility that the American path to the corporate present was heavily influenced by American politics seemed plausible when other systems worked differently.

Yet for each system to survive, it could not have been grossly inefficient. At a minimum, its inefficiencies had to be counterbalanced by efficiencies elsewhere in the system. \* \* \* [W]ith the German, American, and Japanese economies roughly equally successful, each national corporate governance system could not have been grossly debilitating.

\* \* \*

How would one fit rough equivalence in basic tasks into the path-dependent paradigm? In stark form, I believe that although America started with comparatively weak financial intermediaries, it eventually developed comparatively strong boards. In contrast, although Germany and Japan started with relatively strong intermediaries, they developed comparatively weak boards.

\* \* \*

So does refining the evolutionary model matter?

Yes, in three ways. First, we sometimes want to understand why we have the institutions we have, and efficiency alone cannot explain them all. Second, satisfactory resolution does not mean optimal resolution. Some systems would do better by having more organizational techniques available: firms with different organizational forms would then compete for consumers' allegiance. Third, in analyzing legal business institutions, a path dependence search can affect our presumptions: if an institution, legal rule, or dominant practice arose to resolve a problem that is irrelevant today, then it should get less of a presumption of continuing utility.

When systems emerge to compete with one another, what happens? Would competition lead competitors not only to build on their strengths, but also to adopt both constraints on managers, to converge incompletely? I see evidence of such a trend. In the United States, institutional intermediaries are strengthening. True, American institutional investors neither hold many big blocks of stock in the largest firms nor sit often in boardrooms; but in recent years they have pressed the boards of poorly performing companies to act up and have pressed the boards of all companies to strengthen themselves. The American system is thus adopting some of the foreign techniques of financial institutional strength (not too many and not too strongly, to be sure), mediated through America's path-dependent strength—a system with the potential to develop a good board.

Although I know of no confirming Japanese anecdotes yet, the predictions for Germany also fit an adaptive model. As German firms face competition and experience failure, they should seek to strengthen their weak governance link, the boardroom. The past year or two has seen increased attention in Germany to the potential of the supervisory board, with the board meeting said to be moving at some firms from a mere formality to something closer to a real monitoring procedure.

## B.  THE DYNAMICS OF SHAREHOLDER VOTING

### PROBLEM

### UNIVERSAL NETWARE, INC.—PART I

Universal NetWare, Inc. (UNI), a Delaware corporation, creates and installs computer networks and information management systems for corporations, hospitals, government agencies and other large organizations. UNI was organized 12 years ago and made an initial public offering of its common stock three years later, at a price (adjusted for subsequent stock splits) of $1.50 per share. UNI currently has 100 million shares of common stock outstanding. Its stock is traded on the NASDAQ system. Officers and directors of UNI own approximately 15 million shares and institutional investors own another 55 million.

From shortly after UNI was organized until six months ago, UNI's sales and earnings increased very rapidly. So did the price of its common stock. One year ago, UNI stock was selling at $45.00 per share. Over the next six months, it shot up to $60.00 per share.

Then, six months ago, Oxbridge Health Systems Inc. ("Oxbridge"), a health maintenance organization that was one of UNI's larger customers, announced that it had incurred a loss of $275 million that Oxbridge attributed to billing and pricing errors caused by the information management system UNI had installed. Oxbridge also announced that it had terminated all its contracts with UNI and had filed suit against UNI to recover the full amount of its losses. The same day, UNI issued a press release confirming that it had been sued by Oxbridge and stating that UNI was committed to rectifying any errors it might have made in designing Oxbridge's information management system. UNI also disclosed that shortages of qualified personnel were likely to force it to limit the new business it could accept over the next 12 months.

The following day, the price of UNI stock dropped to $40.00 per share. It subsequently declined to just below $30.00 per share, where it is now trading.

Like most other high-tech companies, UNI has used stock options liberally to motivate, reward and retain its managerial and professional employees. Officers and employees currently hold options to purchase roughly 20 million shares of UNI stock. Of those, options to purchase about 16 million shares are "under water"—they can be exercised only at prices in excess of the current price of UNI stock. UNI's three top executives hold 5 million of the "under water" options; about 350 employees hold the remaining 11 million.

At the most recent meeting of the UNI board, Paul Linch, UNI's CEO, said he was concerned that if UNI did not take action to increase the value of the "under water" options, many of UNI's managerial and professional employees were likely to accept employment with other high-tech firms whose prospects for rapid growth were brighter than those of UNI and whose stock was more likely to appreciate rapidly. Given the tight employment market, losing highly qualified staff would further restrict UNI's ability to pursue new business and might even impair its ability to service its existing customers. Linch proposed that UNI reprice all "under water" options to allow employees to exercise them at the current price of UNI stock—just under $30 per share. He also advised the board that Tanya White, UNI's general counsel, had reviewed his proposal and concluded that it was unclear that the resolution authorizing UNI's stock option plan, which UNI's board had submitted to UNI's shareholders for their approval, gave UNI's board the authority to reprice outstanding options. Consequently, White recommended that the board secure shareholders' approval of an amendment to UNI's stock option plan authorizing the board to reprice outstanding options at a price no lower than the market price of UNI stock on the date of the repricing.

After some discussion, all members of UNI's board agreed that UNI should take action along the lines recommended by Linch. Several directors also noted that the proposed repricing plan was likely to be controversial. They pointed out that a number of pension funds recently have taken the position that repricing of stock options almost always is inappropriate because it insulates a corporation's officers and employees from market and business risks borne by all other shareholders. Those funds believe the function of stock options is to align employees' interests with the interests of shareholders, not guarantee employees extra income. Because UNI's next annual meeting was not scheduled to be held for several months, the board decided to defer final action on Linch's recommendation until its next monthly meeting.

## A

Shortly after the board meeting, Linch sought your advice, as UNI's principal outside counsel, about the proposed option repricing plan. He pointed out that management hold far less stock in UNI than do institutional investors. "What are the risks," he asked, "that UNI's shareholders will not approve the option repricing plan, assuming there is no organized opposition to the plan? Where might opposition to the plan come from?"

How do you respond to Linch's questions?

## B

At its next meeting, the UNI board adopted a resolution recommending that UNI's shareholders approve the amendment to UNI's stock option plan authorizing the board to reprice outstanding options. Linch has advised you that both he and the board believe that it would be a good idea for UNI to issue a press release announcing the board's action. Linch is aware that if the press release violates any S.E.C. rules, it could complicate the management's plan to have UNI's shareholders consider the amendment at the upcoming annual meeting. He has asked you whether the release would violate the proxy rules, especially Rules 14a–1 and 14a–3, if it:

a) Contained a brief description of the repricing plan; stated that the board had adopted a resolution recommending that the shareholders adopt an amendment to the stock option plan authorizing the repricing; and said that the amendment would be put to a shareholder vote at UNI's next annual meeting.

b) In addition to the above, explained that management and the board believe that the plan is in the best interests of UNI's shareholders because it rewards UNI's employees for their loyal service, strengthen's UNI's ability to hire new employees in a tight market, and thus enhances management's ability to promote the long-term interests of UNI and its shareholders.

How do you respond to his questions?

## C

Assume that UNI issued an appropriate press release. Herbert Rogers, an investor with a large and diversified stock portfolio that includes 1,000 shares of UNI common stock, read about the plan and reacted indignantly to it as an effort by UNI's management to enrich itself at shareholders' expense. Rogers would like to mobilize other UNI shareholders to vote against the repricing plan, but has no interest in attempting to oust the incumbent board or seek control of UNI.

You are a lawyer experienced in advising participants in proxy contests. Rogers has asked you what procedures he would have to follow, and what costs he is likely to incur if he were to (1) publicize his views against the plan and/or (2) encourage other shareholders to vote against the plan. Rogers is concerned, among other things, about the possibility that UNI will attempt to embroil him in costly litigation. Rogers also is interested in your view as to the likelihood of successfully defeating the adoption of the plan.

How do you respond to Rogers' questions?

## D

The Columbia Employees Retirement Fund (CERF) is one of UNI's largest institutional shareholders, owning approximately 2 million shares of UNI stock. Elaine Meadows, the state treasurer, is in charge of CERF's investment and voting decisions. She also is seriously considering running for governor next year. Like Rogers, Meadows is offended by stock option repricing plans. Based on informal talks at meetings of institutional investors, she is confident that some other institutions could be convinced to vote against UNI's proposal, but she is not sure how widespread such opposition might be.

You are a lawyer in the law firm that advises CERF on issues relating to its investments, including voting decisions. Meadows has asked you the following questions:

1) If CERF seeks to convince other shareholders to vote against the plan, what requirements under the proxy rules would apply to its activities?

2) How likely is it that other institutions can be convinced to vote against the plan? Are all of UNI's institutional shareholders likely to adopt the same position, or is CERF likely to need the support of individual shareholders for the campaign to succeed?

3) Can Meadows carry on a campaign to defeat the plan consistent with her fiduciary responsibilities to CERF's beneficiaries? Alternatively, could such a campaign trigger any other potential liabilities under the federal securities laws?

4) What criticisms might Meadows face if CERF chose to actively oppose the plan? How might she respond to those criticisms?

How do you respond to Meadows' questions?

## 1. INTRODUCTION

We have already seen that most corporation statutes require that a corporation hold an annual meeting of shareholders to elect the board of directors. There is also a requirement that the shareholders approve certain transactions that affect the structure of a corporation, such as amendments to the articles of incorporation, mergers, and sales of assets. Finally, most corporation statutes permit shareholders to amend corporate by-laws.

In the largest corporations, many thousands of shareholders are scattered throughout the country, each holding a relatively small number of shares. It is simply impossible to convene the shareholders at one time and place to consider and act upon the matters that require their approval. The substitute process that permits effective shareholder action is proxy voting.

The authorization for shareholders to vote by proxy is found in state corporation statutes, of which RMBCA § 7.22 is typical. First, the statute permits shareholders to vote in person or by proxy. Second, it limits the validity of the proxy to a period of 11 months from the date of its execution unless the appointment form specifies a longer period. Under certain circumstances, not relevant in the public corporation, the shareholder can make her appointment of a proxy irrevocable.

As we saw in Chapter 12, "proxy" is simply another word for agent. Ordinarily, one thinks of a principal conferring power upon an agent to accomplish the principal's business. The shareholder's appointment of a proxy, or agent, to act on her behalf at the shareholder meeting is quite different. Most striking is the fact that in connection with voting at the meeting, it is the agents (who are usually members of the management) rather than the principal who solicit the agency relationship. The fact that the shareholders who grant the proxy (the principals) are scattered throughout the country provides a jurisdictional basis for federal regulation of the proxy solicitation process.

The body of law that regulates this process marks one of the great intersections of federal and state law. State law validates the process of proxy voting, and federal law prescribes the conditions on which it may proceed. In § 14(a) of the 1934 Act, Congress effectively delegated the specifics of federal proxy regulation to the Securities and Exchange Commission by declaring it unlawful to use the mails or interstate commerce to solicit proxies any proxy "in contravention of such rules and regulations as the Commission may prescribe as necessary or appropriate in the public interest or for the protection of investors." (Those rules and regulations are described later in this section.)

The main emphasis of the federal securities laws is disclosure. The legislative history of SEC proxy regulation indicates that the Congressional concern was to provide "fair corporate suffrage." H.R.Rep. No. 1383, 73d Cong., 2d Sess. 2, 13–14 (1934). The SEC's operating theory is that fairness is achieved by providing sufficient information to investors to allow them to make an informed choice. The SEC also has tried to neutralize, to a limited extent, the effect of management's control of the proxy soliciting process. Its rules prescribe the form of the proxy creating the formal agency power, define the scope of the agent's power, and require management to provide an opportunity to shareholders to vote on matters that other shareholders intend to bring before the meeting.

On closer examination, "fair suffrage" often is closely related to the substantive fairness of the corporate transaction on which the shareholders are voting. Thus, the extent of federal involvement in corporate law through federal regulation of proxies is more substantial than appears at first. For example, a merger requires shareholder approval under state law. State law does not require the solicitation of proxies to obtain that approval, but if, as is customary in large corporations, a solicitation is undertaken, it is largely regulated by federal law. If the terms of the merger are unfair, shareholders may seek their remedies under state law. If the terms of the merger are not correctly or fairly described in the proxy solicitation (a failing that often accompanies unfairness in the deal), that failure creates a federal claim giving rise to federal remedies. A federal court would have to ponder whether certain aspects of the deal were so significant to an investor's decision that disclosure was required. The answer to that question may entail a federal inquiry into whether the terms of the merger were substantively fair—a question one would have thought to be solely one of state law. For reasons which will become clearer, shareholders often prefer to argue over disclosure rather than substantive fairness, but the underlying issues often are the same. Framing the issue as one of full disclosure federalizes the controversy. We consider questions relating to the federalization of state corporation law in greater detail in Chapter 18.

Another important path that crosses the federal-state intersection is the role of self-regulatory organizations (SROs). While state law authorizes voting by proxies, and federal law conditions the solicitation of proxies upon compliance with federal law, nothing in either federal or state law requires management to solicit proxies. Yet the proxy solicitation process both informs investors and allows them a degree of participation in the decision. The New York Stock Exchange (NYSE), the American Stock Exchange (Amex) and the NASD all require the companies whose securities they list to solicit proxies for all shareholders' meetings.

## 2. THE COLLECTIVE ACTION PROBLEM

Most theories of corporate law, as well as the federal system of proxy regulation, assume that shareholder voting plays a central role in the corporate governance system. Yet the fact remains that shareholders use their franchise as an effective monitoring device only infrequently. The following suggests an explanation for this aspect of shareholder behavior.

### Robert Charles Clark, CORPORATE LAW
pp. 389–394 (1986).

From an economic point of view, there is a strong argument that the power to control a business firm's activities should reside in those who have the right to the firm's residual earnings, that is, those earnings that are left over when all fixed and definite obligations of the firm have been provided for. The intuition behind this argument is that giving control to the residual claimants will place the power to monitor the performance of participants in the firm and the power to control shirking, waste, and so forth in the hands of those who have the best incentive to use the power.

To be sure, the nature of the modern firm complicates this argument, since the benefits of managerial expertise and the need to prevent wasteful duplication of decision making have led to a professional class of managers distinct from public shareholders. Managers have control over ordinary business operations, even though they do not have full ownership rights to their firm's residual earnings. (Of course, they usually own substantial residual claims because of stock option programs and similar arrangements.) Yet it can still be argued that ultimate control ought to reside in the ultimate claimants on the residual earnings.

This viewpoint supports the conclusion that common shareholders should possess voting rights that, at a minimum, give them the power to select or remove the directors and, therefore, the indirect power to control the identity of top management. We could argue further that voting rights should be proportional to one's share of the residual interest in the firm. Otherwise, there would be some misalignment between the power and the incentive to monitor and enforce company performance.

\* \* \*

Whenever shareholders of a publicly held company vote upon matters affecting the corporation, they engage in collective action that suffers from many systemic difficulties. Such difficulties include "rational apathy" of shareholders, the temptation of individual shareholders to take a "free ride," and unfairness to certain shareholders even where collective action is successful.

Often the aggregate cost to shareholders of informing themselves of potential corporate actions, independently assessing the wisdom of such actions, and casting their votes will greatly exceed the expected or actual benefits garnered from informed voting. Recognition of this phenomenon accounts for the usual rules that entrust corporate management with all ordinary business decisions. But the same problem still exists with respect to the major subjects of shareholder voting: the election of directors and the approval or rejection of major organic changes such as mergers.

Consider a simplified case. Outta Control Corp., with 1 million voting common shares outstanding, has 10,000 shareholders, each of whom owns 1 block of 100 shares. The directors propose a plan to merge Outta Control into Purchaser Corp., which would result in the acquisition by the former Outta Control shareholders, in exchange for their old shares, of voting common shares in Purchaser with a total market value of $50 million. In fact, Purchaser would have been willing to exchange $60 million worth of its shares if it had not agreed, under prodding by Outta Control's managers and in return for their cooperation in recommending the merger, to give extraordinary salary increases to those officers of Outta Control who would continue their employment after the merger. Payments would also be made to departing officers under so-called consulting and noncompetition agreements. Moreover, a majority of Outta Control's directors are not officers and would seek a new merger agreement at a much higher price if the current proposal were not approved by the shareholders.

Assume that all of this information is contained in a 240 page proxy statements that is sent to Outta Control's shareholders and that any rational shareholder who reads it would decide to vote against the merger. Assume further that if the merger proposal were disapproved, a new one would be adopted that would yield these shareholders the additional $10 million gain which Purchaser Corp. was prepared to pay. Thus, the actual benefit to be derived from collective shareholder action against the merger plan would be $1000 per shareholder.

Shareholders do not expect, however, to discover a reason for concluding that disapproval will avert a corporate harm or open the door to a larger corporate gain every time they read a proxy statement. To make our problem complete, assume that the shareholders in it make a rational assessment of the probabilities of such an occurrence. Because of their assessment, they assign an expected benefit of $50 per shareholder to collective action of the sort described, that is, action based on each shareholder's reading the proxy statement, making up his mind, and voting.

Now suppose the average cost of informed shareholder action is simply the opportunity cost[4] of reading the proxy statement before sending in the proxy card and that this amount is $120 per shareholder (three hours of reading at $40 per hour—a rather low estimate). Thus the total cost of collective action would be $1.2 million. This cost would still be less than the actual benefit to be gained in this case, from collective action by informed voters. But the cost of such collective action greatly exceeds the expected benefit—$120 versus $50 per shareholder—so sensible shareholders will not read the proxy statement. They will be rationally apathetic. At the same time, management will be shielded from shareholder policing of their fiduciary duties, thereby allowing them to receive compensation that is unnecessary to induce their services.

One legal approach toward improving the efficiency of collective action is to make it cheaper for each shareholder to act in an informed way. Suppose that in our example the opportunity cost of reading the proxy statement concerning the proposed merger were only $10 per shareholder, because the SEC had devised a system of proxy rules that produced extremely concise, quickly understandable proxy statements that emphasize crucial data. Suppose that the SEC also monitors the statement and requires that the crucial information appear in bold face type. The expected benefit of collective action by informed voting is still $50 per shareholder, but the cost of such action is now only $10 per shareholder. The net expected benefit is therefore $40 per shareholder.

Yet the desired collective action still may not occur. Any one shareholder may realize that only 50 percent of the shareholders are needed to block the merger. If the shareholder believes that enough other shareholders will respond to the incentive of the $40 net expected benefit and will act accordingly to produce the desirable collective result, he might decide to save himself the cost of reading the streamlined proxy statement. He can still participate in any benefits of collective action that arise through the work of the other shareholders. He will be a free rider on their efforts. The net expected benefit of his action as a free rider would be $50 rather than $40.

Of course, it may also occur to him that if all the other shareholders thought similarly, no collective action would be taken, and everyone would lose the chance of reaping the benefits. He might realize that giving in to the temptation to achieve an individual gain superior to everyone else's would jeopardize the attainment of collective benefits. Conceivably this realization might prompt him to read the proxy statement. But it is doubtful whether this would happen in practice and, as a matter of theory (game theory, that is), a rational, self-interested shareholder would not do so.[5] The situation is like the prisoner's dilemma of

---

**4.** The cost attributable to doing one thing to the exclusion of another stems from opportunity sacrificed to pursue the chosen course. This sacrifice is called "opportunity cost."

**5.** Why not? Because, whether he assumes the other shareholders will read or will not read, he will expect to be better off if he doesn't. Assume the others will read:

game theory and may call for solutions similar in strategy to those that would solve that dilemma.*

\* \* \*

Let us again alter the hypothetical so that the free rider problem, like the rational apathy problem, effectively disappears. Suppose that one shareholder, Ajax, owns 200,000 shares, while every other shareholder owns only one block of 100 shares. The other facts remain the same. The expected benefit to Ajax is now $100,000, which is, let us assume, more than the expected cost of reading the proxy statement and convincing the holders of 300,100 others shares also to vote against the merger. (He would do this by waging a proxy contest—a technique discussed in the next subsection.) Unless it deeply galls Ajax to think that he will be treated unfairly, he will take action to achieve the collective benefit even if he cannot be reimbursed for the costs and risks of such action.[7] Acting strictly for his own benefit, he will nevertheless have created a collective good for all the other shareholders in the company. The smaller shareholders will get the benefit of his concern without bearing a pro rata share of cost. This phenomenon is an example of what one economist calls the systematic exploitation of the large by the small.

The obvious problem here is one of fairness to the guardian shareholder. Less obviously, problems of allocative efficiency may also arise. The prospect of being taken advantage of by the smaller shareholders may deter investors from becoming dominant shareholders in the first place. The problem once again resembles the prisoner's dilemma, but in this situation the players are all investors as they contemplate buying into any publicly held corporation. But in the real world there are many factors that tempt investors to obtain large percentage interests in companies, not the least of which is the chance of acquiring the various special benefits of controlling the corporation on an ongoing basis. Any force toward misallocation created by the phenomenon of exploitation of the large by the small is likely to be more than offset by these factors. Thus, the only remaining problem will be unfair treatment of the large, but not controlling, shareholder who undertakes a proxy contest or similar action for the corporation's benefit.

His own expected benefit is $50 if he doesn't read, and $40 if he does. Assume the others will not read (so the original merger plan goes through): His own expected benefit is $0 if he doesn't read, but minus $10 if he does.

\* Two persons have been arrested for bank robbery and each is interrogated by the police in separate rooms. Each is told that if she alone confesses, she will receive a sentence of two years, but that if her companion confesses while she refuses, then she will receive a ten year sentence.

Each is also told that a confession from both will produce a six year sentence. Of course, each one understands that silence from both will produce no sentence. The six year term is the predicted result, since neither can risk silence and the ten year sentence.—Eds.

7. We can assume that Ajax will not try to be a free rider because his particular expected benefit is so high that he would not risk depending on action by other shareholders.

## 3. AN ILLUSTRATIVE CASE: DUAL CLASS RECAPITALIZATIONS

A series of events in the late 1980s and early 1990s, involving corporations' efforts to implement dual class recapitalization plans and the SEC's efforts to restrict such plans, illustrate the impact of collective action problems, the limits of the SEC's authority to regulate the corporate governance process, and the important, but often overlooked, role of the SROs.

A dual-class recapitalization involves changing a corporation's capital structure from one where each share of common stock is entitled to cast one vote to one with two classes of common stock, one entitled to cast one vote per share and the other entitled to cast multiple votes per share. Two steps are required to implement such a recapitalization. First, shareholders have to approve a charter amendment that authorizes the issuance of high-vote common stock. Then, some arrangement has to be made to distribute the high-vote stock to the control group and, more importantly, to ensure that a potential acquiror can not buy high-vote stock.

Where managers or a family group control a substantial block of a corporation's stock, a dual-class recapitalization can create a virtually impenetrable barrier to uninvited takeover bids. Consider how such a plan might work in a corporation with 1,000,000 shares of common stock outstanding where the high-vote common stock will have 10 votes per share. Assume that the control group owns 100,000 shares, all of which will be converted into high-vote stock after the recapitalization, and that public shareholders own the remaining 900,000 shares, all of which will remain ordinary, one-vote stock. The control group then will control 1,000,000 votes (100,000 shares times 10 votes per share) and the public shareholders will control only 900,000 votes. Thus, though owning only 10% of the stock, the control group will have the power to elect all members of the board of directors.

Corporations commonly employed one of two mechanisms to ensure that a potential acquiror could not buy high-vote stock. Some distributed high-vote stock to all shareholders but provided in the charter amendment authorizing such stock that, should the stock be transferred to anybody other than a family member of a current beneficial owner (or a trust for the benefit of family members), the high-vote stock automatically would be converted into ordinary common stock.

Other corporations sought to make the high-vote stock less attractive to public shareholders by limiting the dividends payable on it to 90 percent of the dividends payable on ordinary common stock. Then, they gave all shareholders a one-time option to convert their ordinary common stock into high-vote common stock, with the expectation that few shareholders outside the control group would decide to convert. Alternatively, they distributed high-vote (but lower dividend) common stock to all shareholders and gave them the option of converting it into ordinary common stock. In many instances, companies also restricted the transferability of the high-vote common stock. *See, generally,* Jeffrey N. Gordon, *Ties That Bond: Dual Class Common Stock and the Problem of Shareholder Choice,* 76 Calif.L.Rev. 1, 39–42 (1988).

The calculation underlying dual-class recapitalizations was that most public shareholders would undervalue what might best be described as the "residual voting power" of their stock. Since contested corporate elections are infrequent, shareholders generally value stock primarily for the claim it gives them (or their successors) against a company's future cash flows. Shareholders often consider voting rights more a nuisance than a benefit, except when some person outside a company's management seeks to purchase a majority of the company's stock, or otherwise to mobilize the support of the owners of a majority of the stock, in order to use the voting rights associated with that stock to replace the incumbent directors with directors of her own choosing.

State law generally allows corporations to implement such plans, so long as they do not use strong-arm tactics to secure shareholder approval. *See Lacos Land Co. v. Arden Group, Inc.,* 517 A.2d 271 (Del.Ch.1986) (enjoining dual-class plan where CEO had threatened to act in violation of his fiduciary duties if shareholders did not approve plan). A New York Stock Exchange (NYSE) rule posed a more severe obstacle. For more than 60 years, the NYSE would only list a company if all its common stock had one vote per share. *See* New York Stock Exchange Listed Company Manual, § 313.00. This requirement made implementing a dual-class common stock plan problematic for listed companies.

In 1984, competitive pressure began to mount on the NYSE to modify this one share, one vote rule. General Motors had issued a new class of common stock, with only one-half vote per share, to finance its acquisition of Electronic Data Systems. The NYSE, reluctant to delist General Motors, declared a moratorium on enforcement of the rule. Within two years, 46 NYSE-listed companies issued stock that violated the rule, most of it in connection with dual-class recapitalizations, and well over 100 non-NYSE companies also had implemented such plans. Consequently, had the NYSE reinstated enforcement of its rule, listed corporations could react by listing their stock on the Amex or having it traded through NASDAQ.

In 1985, the NYSE proposed to amend its rule to allow common stock with disparate voting rights to be listed, provided that shareholders had approved the disparate voting rights plan. The NYSE then sought SEC approval of the proposed amendment, as it was required to do by Section 19(c) of the Securities Exchange Act of 1934. The SEC held public hearings and solicited comments on whether it should (1) require the NYSE to retain its one share, one vote rule; (2) require additional safeguards before allowing listed companies to adopt dual class common stock plans; or (3) adopt a uniform one share, one vote rule applicable to all exchanges and NASDAQ. The last option would effectively impose a one share, one vote rule on all publicly-traded corporations.

Commentators supporting the NYSE proposal emphasized three lines of argument: "(1) sound economic and policy reasons exist for permitting companies to adopt disparate voting rights plans; (2) there is no empirical evidence that the adoption of disparate voting rights plans affects share prices adversely; and (3) corporate governance matters, such as shareholder voting rights, fall within the realm of state rather than federal control." Securities Exchange Act Rel. No. 34–34263 (June 22, 1987).

Other commentators "offered several reasons why they believed disparate voting rights plans should be prohibited. First, they believed that the shareholder vote is an essential element in corporate accountability." *Id.* Second, they questioned whether a shareholder vote to ratify a disparate voting rights plan effectively protects against management abuse or provides a legitimate means to protect shareholders' rights. Some disputed the significance of studies that concluded that disparate voting rights plans did not reduce significantly shareholder wealth. One suggested that the best measure of the diminution of shareholder wealth such plans produce is the premiums that public shareholders typically receive when managers obtain control by purchasing such shareholders' stock in leveraged buy-out transactions.

Following these hearings, the SEC adopted Rule 19c–4, effectively barring trading in the stock of any domestic corporation that implemented corporate actions that had the effect of nullifying, restricting, or disparately reducing the per share voting rights of outstanding common stock. *Id.* To reach this conclusion, the Commission was forced to acknowledge that, as a consequence of collective action problems, the shareholder voting process, as supplemented by the Commission's disclosure requirements, still left shareholders vulnerable to exploitation by corporate managers.

## VOTING RIGHTS LISTING STANDARDS; DISENFRANCHISEMENT RULE

SEC Release No. 34–25891; 53 FR 26376 (July 12, 1988).

### III. DISCUSSION

* * * In proposing Rule 19c–4, the Commission recognized that regulation of shareholder voting rights under the Federal securities laws raises difficult and complex issues. The Commission noted that the initial NYSE proposal to abandon its one share, one vote standard had important ramifications for management accountability, tender offers and changes in corporate control, the rights of majority and minority shareholders, competition among SROs, and the integrity of the nation's securities markets. The Commission continues to believe that the issue of shareholder voting rights has far-reaching implications, and that a rule ensuring a minimum level of shareholder protection from disenfranchising actions is appropriate and consistent with the purposes of the Act. Further, the Rule, which will operate through the listing standards

of SROs, has been crafted to be consistent with federalism objectives by seeking to minimize intrusion into traditional state regulation. * * *

While certain disparate voting rights plans serve to disenfranchise existing shareholders, the Commission * * * agrees that there may be valid business or economic reasons for issuing disparate voting rights stock. * * * The Commission believes, however, that disparate voting rights plans that disenfranchise existing shareholders are inconsistent with the requirements of the Act. Shareholders who purchase voting shares in a company do so with the understanding that the shares will be accompanied by the voting rights attendant to the stock at the time of purchase. The diminution or limitation of these rights is inconsistent with the investor protection and fair corporate suffrage policies embodied in * * * the Act. * * *

The Commission recognizes that under state law, disparate voting rights plans generally are permitted subject to shareholder approval. The Commission also recognizes, however, that collective action problems may make defeating an issuer recapitalization proposal extremely difficult. * * * Frequently, a disparate voting rights plan is presented to shareholders in a form, such as an offer to exchange higher vote stock for lower vote stock with a dividend sweetener, that provides shareholders with an incentive to accept less than full voting rights stock rather than oppose the recapitalization, although, acting collectively, shareholders as a group might prefer to retain their voting rights and reject the sweetener offered by management. The coercive nature of some disparate voting rights plans may also be exacerbated by management's ability to set the proxy agenda and use corporate funds to lobby shareholders in favor of its proposal. The Commission also has heard testimony from institutional investors describing the pressure placed on managers of corporate pension plans during the shareholder voting process.

Although the Commission does not believe that shareholders invariably are powerless to defeat an issuer-sponsored proposal to recapitalize, the Commission does believe that, because of the forces cited above, the shareholder voting process is not fully effective in preventing the adoption of disparate voting rights plans that disenfranchise shareholders. The Commission believes that it is preferable for a company's insiders wishing to gain voting control to do so through a repurchase of shares in which such repurchase is subject to market discipline and judicial review regarding state corporate fiduciary requirements. * * *

The Commission has reviewed the empirical evidence regarding the wealth impact of disparate voting rights plans on common stock price. * * * [T]he measurement of immediate change in securities price is not a complete indicator of the negative effects of disenfranchising actions. As several commentators have suggested, the negative effects of a permanent deprivation of shareholder voting rights may not appear until some time after the disenfranchising action is announced or occurs, and may be impossible to measure precisely at the time of enactment. For example, loss of independent shareholder control in a company may not manifest itself until sometime in the future through a lower takeover premium offered for the company's shares, or through management actions undertaken without the discipline of accountability to shareholders.[81]

\* \* \*

Finally, in adopting Rule 19c–4, \* \* \* the Commission does not seek to prohibit issuers from issuing stock with restricted or no voting rights, as those restrictions are a consideration the investor will take into account when deciding to purchase a security. Rather, the Commission seeks to prevent the deprivation of voting rights that occurs after a security has been purchased. \* \* \* We believe this approach is consistent with the role of the Commission in regulating the public securities markets for the protection of investors. Rule 19c–4 identifies those situations in which shareholders are disenfranchised and prohibits companies from continued access to the national securities marketplace if they take such action. In doing so, Rule 19c–4 is consistent with the federalism objective of minimal intrusion into areas of traditional state regulation.

## BUSINESS ROUNDTABLE v. SECURITIES AND EXCHANGE COMMISSION

905 F.2d 406 (D.C.Cir.1990).

STEPHEN F. WILLIAMS, CIRCUIT JUDGE:

In 1984 General Motors announced a plan to issue a second class of common stock with one-half vote per share. The proposal collided with a longstanding rule of the New York Stock Exchange that required listed companies to provide one vote per share of common stock. The NYSE balked at enforcement, and after two years filed a proposal with the Securities and Exchange Commission to relax its own rule. The SEC did not approve the rule change but responded with one of its own. On July 7, 1988, it adopted Rule 19c–4, barring national securities exchanges and national securities associations, together known as self-regulatory organizations (SROs), from listing stock of a corporation that takes any corporate action "with the effect of nullifying, restricting or disparately reducing the per share voting rights of [existing common stockholders]."

---

**81.** Recent transactions involving Resorts International illustrate this point. In 1986, there were 5.7 million shares of Class A stock outstanding, having one vote each, and 750,000 shares of Class B stock outstanding with 100 votes each. The Class B stock represented less than 12% of the outstanding shares but had 93% of the voting power. In early 1986, the Class B stock generally traded at a 2–3 point premium (5–7.5%) above the Class A stock, within the 50 dollar range. After the death of Resorts' Chairman in April 1986, negotiations for the Class B holdings of the estate, which constituted approximately 72% of the outstanding shares of the class, culminated with the sale of the Class B stock to Donald Trump at $135 per share in July 1987. Although the price of the Class A rose to the $60 range during July and August 1987, following the purchase of the Class B block it declined steadily to the point where it was trading at the $20 level during February 1988 and currently trades in the $30 range.

The rule prohibits such "disenfranchisement" even where approved by a shareholder vote conducted on one share/one vote principles. Because the rule directly controls the substantive allocation of powers among classes of shareholders, we find it in excess of the Commission's authority under § 19 of the Securities Exchange Act of 1934, as amended (the "Exchange Act"). Neither the wisdom of the requirement, nor of its being imposed at the federal level, is here in question.

* * * As we shall develop below, we find that the Exchange Act cannot be understood to include regulation of an issue that is so far beyond matters of disclosure (such as are regulated under § 14 of the Act), and of the management and practices of self-regulatory organizations, and that is concededly a part of corporate governance traditionally left to the states.

* * *

As mentioned above, the Commission does not suggest that it might support Rule 19c–4 by reference to the first two of the possible heads of jurisdiction in § 19(c)—assurance of fair administration of the self-regulatory organization itself and conformity to the requirements of the Exchange Act or rules thereunder applicable to the organization. Thus it is driven to the third—"otherwise in furtherance of the purposes" of the Exchange Act.

What then are the "purposes" of the Exchange Act? The Commission supports Rule 19c–4 as advancing the purposes of a variety of sections, but we first take its strongest—§ 14's grant of power to regulate the proxy process. The Commission finds a purpose "to ensure fair shareholder suffrage." * * * Indeed, it points to the House Report's declarations that "[f]air corporate suffrage is an important right," and that "use of the exchanges should involve a corresponding duty of according to shareholders fair suffrage." The formulation is true in the sense that Congress's decision can be located under that broad umbrella.

But unless the legislative purpose is defined by reference to the means Congress selected, it can be framed at any level of generality—to improve the operation of capital markets, for instance. In fact, although § 14(a) broadly bars use of the mails (and other means) "to solicit * * * any proxy" in contravention of Commission rules and regulations, it is not seriously disputed that Congress's central concern was with disclosure. See *J.I. Case Co. v. Borak,* ("The purpose of § 14(a) is to prevent management or others from obtaining authorization for corporate action by means of deceptive or inadequate disclosure in proxy solicitation."); see also *Santa Fe Industries, Inc. v. Green,* (emphasizing Exchange Act's philosophy of full disclosure and dismissing the fairness of the terms of the transaction as "at most a tangential concern of the statute" once full and fair disclosure has occurred).

While the House Report indeed speaks of fair corporate suffrage, it also plainly identifies Congress's target—the solicitation of proxies by well informed insiders "without fairly informing the stockholders of the purposes for which the proxies are to be used." The Senate Report contains no vague language about "corporate suffrage," but rather explains the purpose of the proxy protections as ensuring that stockholders have "adequate knowledge" about the "financial condition of the corporation * * * [and] the major questions of policy, which are decided at stockholders' meetings." Finally, both reports agree on the power that the proxy sections gave the Commission—"power to control the conditions under which proxies may be solicited."

That proxy regulation bears almost exclusively on disclosure stems as a matter of necessity from the nature of proxies. Proxy solicitations are, after all, only communications with potential absentee voters. The goal of federal proxy regulation was to improve those communications and thereby to enable proxy voters to control the corporation as effectively as they might have by attending a shareholder meeting.

We do not mean to be taken as saying that disclosure is necessarily the sole subject of § 14. For example, the Commission's Rule 14a–4(b)(2) requires a proxy to provide some mechanism for a security holder to withhold authority to vote for each nominee individually. It thus bars a kind of electoral tying arrangement, and may be supportable as a control over management's power to set the voting agenda, or, slightly more broadly, voting procedures. But while Rule 14a–4(b)(2) may lie in a murky area between substance and procedure, Rule 19c–4 much more directly interferes with the substance of what the shareholders may enact. It prohibits certain reallocations of voting power and certain capital structures, even if approved by a shareholder vote subject to full disclosure and the most exacting procedural rules.

The Commission noted in the preamble to the Proposed Rule its conviction that collective action problems could cause even a properly conducted shareholder vote (with ample disclosure and sound procedures) to bring about results injurious to the shareholders. We do not question these findings. But we think the Commission's reliance on them is a clue to its stretch of the congressional purposes. As the Commission itself observed, "[s]ection 14(a) contains an implicit assumption that shareholders will be able to make use of the information provided in proxy solicitations in order to vote in corporate elections." In 1934 Congress acted on the premise that shareholder voting could work, so long as investors secured enough information and, perhaps, the benefit of other procedural protections. It did not seek to regulate the stockholders' choices. If the Commission believes that premise misguided, it must turn to Congress.

With its step beyond control of voting procedure and into the distribution of voting power, the Commission would assume an authority that the Exchange Act's proponents disclaimed any intent to grant. Noting that opponents expressed alarm that the bill would give the Commission "power to interfere in the management of corporations," the Senate Committee on Banking and Currency said it had "no such intention" and that the bill "furnish[ed] no justification for such an interpretation."

There are, of course, shadings within the notion of "management." With the present rule the Commission does not tell any corporation where to locate its next plant. But neither does state corporate law; it regulates the distribution of powers among the various players in the process of corporate governance, and the Commission's present leap beyond disclosure is just that sort of regulation. The potpourri of listing standards previously submitted to the Commission under § 19(b) suggests the sweep of its current claim. These govern requirements for independent directors, independent audit committees, shareholder quorums, shareholder approval for certain major corporate transactions, and other major issues traditionally governed by state law. If Rule 19c–4 is closely enough related to the proxy regulation purpose of § 14, then all these issues appear equally subject to the Commission's discretionary control.

Surprisingly, the Commission does not concede a lack of jurisdiction over such issues. When questioned at oral argument as to what state corporation rules are not related to "fair corporate suffrage," SEC counsel conceded only that further intrusions into state corporate governance "would present more difficult situations." In fact the Commission's apparent perception of its § 19 powers has been immensely broad, unbounded even by any pretense of a connection to § 14. In reviewing the previous SRO rule changes on issues of independent directors and independent audit committees, it grounded its review in a supposed mandate to "protect investors and the public interest." The Commission made no attempt to limit the concept by reference to the concrete purposes of any section. Rather, it reasoned that the rule changes protected investors by "creat[ing] uniformity that helps to assure investors that all the companies traded in those markets have the fundamental safeguards they have come to expect of major companies." If Rule 19c–4 were validated on such broad grounds, the Commission would be able to establish a federal corporate law by using access to national capital markets as its enforcement mechanism. This would resolve a longstanding controversy over the wisdom of such a move[7] in the face of disclaimers from Congress and with no substantive restraints on the power. It would, moreover, overturn or at least impinge severely on the tradition of state regulation of corporate law. * * * We read the Act as reflecting a clear congressional determination not to make any such broad delegation of power to the Commission.

If the Commission's one share/one vote rule is to survive, then, some kind of firebreak is needed to separate it from corporate governance as a whole. But the Commission's sole suggestion of such a firebreak is a

---

**7.** * * * In 1934, ironically, the President of the New York Stock Exchange actually favored federalization of the corporate law in an attempt to derail the momentum for federal regulation of the securities mar- kets * * *. Rule 19c–4 presents the worst of all worlds from that perspective, turning regulation of securities markets into the vehicle for federalizing corporate law.

reference to "the unique historical background of the NYSE's one share, one vote rule." It is true that in the Senate hearings leading to enactment of the Exchange Act there were a few favorable references to that rule. But these few references are culled from 9500 pages of testimony in the Senate hearings. No legislator directly discussed the NYSE's rule and no references were made to it in any of the Committee Reports. The most these references show is that legislators were aware of the rule and that it was an important part of the background. Even if we imputed the statements to a member of Congress, none comes near to saying, "The purposes of this act, although they generally will not involve the Commission in corporate governance, do include preservation of the one share/one vote principle." And even then we doubt that such a statement in the legislative history could support a special and anomalous exception to the Act's otherwise intelligible conceptual line excluding the Commission from corporate governance.

[The court also rejected the Commission's arguments that §§ 6(b), 15A or 11A of the Securities and Exchange Act authorized it to issue Rule 19c–4.]

* * *

We do not decide whether the Commission could invoke other statutory provisions to provide the legal authority for promulgating these or similar regulations. The sections relied on here are insufficient. Even if other statutory provisions could support the Commission's asserted authority, we cannot supply grounds to sustain the regulations that were not invoked by the Commission below. In any case, a change in the jurisdictional basis would almost certainly alter the substantive content of the final regulations.

The petition for review is granted and Rule 19c–4 is vacated.

### Note: Subsequent Action by the SROs

*Business Roundtable* did not prove to be the last word. It held that the authority of the SEC was limited, but did not address the authority of the SROs to contract with companies seeking to list their stock. In 1994, the NYSE, the NASD and the Amex jointly proposed, and the SEC then approved, a minimum voting rights rule that largely mirrored Rule 19c–4. The new rule is applicable to companies that wish to continue listing their shares but does not require delisting of companies with existing dual-class capital structures. The rule states:

> Voting rights of existing shareholders of publicly traded common stock * * * cannot be disparately reduced or restricted through any corporate action or issuance of stock. Examples of such corporate action or issuance include, but are not limited to, the adoption of time-phased voting plans, the adoption of capped voting rights plans, the issuance of super voting stock, or the issuance of stock with voting rights less than the per share voting rights of the common stock through an exchange offer.

SEC Rel. No. 35121 (1994).

## 4.  HOW THE PROXY PROCESS WORKS: LAW AND PRACTICE

### a.  The Annual Meeting

Annual shareholder meetings have become a rite of spring, since most corporations hold their annual meetings shortly after they have distributed their annual financial statements for the previous year. At that time the shareholders are barraged with documents from their companies—the notice of the annual meeting, a proxy statement, a proxy and an annual report. How does the entire process work?

The board of directors selects the date of the annual meeting which usually is fixed in the by-laws. Because the shareholder body changes daily, it is necessary to fix a record date to determine which shareholders are entitled to receive notice and to vote at the meeting. The corporation maintains a record of its shareholders, and when ownership of stock changes, the transfer agent, customarily a bank, records the change. Since the procedure usually requires several days to take effect, a small number of persons who have sold their stock and no longer consider themselves as shareholders actually appear as shareholders of record on the record date and will be entitled to vote.

### b.  Shareholder Voting

The board of directors must select the nominees for election as directors on whose behalf proxies will be solicited. That is, the material sent to the shareholders solicits authorization for the proxy holder to vote in favor of specified persons who will be placed in nomination at the annual meeting. No one is actually nominated until the meeting has convened, but by that time the shareholder voters will have already instructed their proxy for whom to vote. SEC rules require those soliciting a proxy to disclose for whom they intend to vote, and not deviate from that choice except under unusual circumstances. Other candidates may be nominated at the meeting, but in effect, the votes have been cast and the election decided before the candidates have been nominated. The reason for this result is that the proxy on which the shareholders confer the authority to vote is not a formal ballot on which they make choices but rather, as we have seen, is a power of attorney.

The board of directors must also decide what other matters to submit for action at the meeting. Authority and instructions as to how to vote on those matters will have to be solicited, and disclosure must be made in the proxy material. The directors usually recommend how to vote, and the form of proxy generally provides that shares will be voted in accordance with the board's recommendations unless instructions are given to the contrary. Some of the matters on which directions are sought will be initiated by the board or by management, such as ratification of the board's choice of independent auditors who will examine and certify the financial statements, proposed amendments to the articles of incorporation which have been approved by the board of directors, or approval of management compensation plans. Other items might be matters that shareholders have told management they intend to present at the meeting.

### c.  Filing Proxy Material

After these decisions have been made, the proxy materials, consisting of the proxy statement and the form of proxy, must be prepared for filing with the SEC. To some extent the preparation of the proxy materials constitutes a markup of the previous year's materials, but the rules and the matters on the agenda change from year to year and a substantial effort will be required to prepare the filings. Ordinarily the proxy materials are reviewed by the board of directors but most of the work must be performed by management, which has the data, and by counsel who understands the legal requirements.

After the materials have been filed they are reviewed by the staff of the Division of Corporation Finance. It is customary for the company to wait until it has received comments before sending anything to the shareholders. Otherwise, if the staff has strong objections to material already sent to shareholders, it may recommend that the SEC bring a lawsuit to enjoin the meeting until corrective action is taken. Such an action, needless to say, would be embarrassing and costly to the company, and management considers it prudent to allow the Commission staff full opportunity to comment.

A sample proxy statement and form of proxy appears in Edward S. Adams & John H. Matheson, SELECTED CORPORATIONS AND OTHER BUSINESS ASSOCIATIONS STATUTES, RULES AND FORMS (West).

### d.  Identifying the Shareholders: Street Names

Who are the shareholders and how does one discover their identity in order to communicate with them? In Chapter 12, we saw that the corporation's shareholder list shows the shareholders of record but does not identify the beneficial owners. Today, largely for reasons of convenience, many shareholders choose to have their shares registered in the name of their broker where the shares are kept on deposit. When shares are transferred from one brokerage firm to another on behalf of a customer the change may be reflected only on the records of a central clearing house depository, which is used to minimize the danger of losing stock certificates by eliminating their physical movement. In addition, many shares are owned in trust or custodial accounts under the supervision of a bank. As a consequence of these practices, much of the ownership of securities is recorded in what is known as "street name." The corporation is unaware of who are the beneficial owners of the stock; all it knows is the name of the record holder and at least the number of beneficial owners. If an issuer requests, brokers and banks will furnish the names and addresses of non-objecting or consenting beneficial owners with whom the issuer may communicate directly. In many cases, issuers will not request these lists because they will be required to give them to a plaintiff seeking a shareholder list in litigation. Without such lists, the issuer can communicate only with the record holder.

Because of widespread beneficial ownership, it has become necessary to devise a mechanism for corporations to communicate with beneficial owners so they may direct the voting of their shares. SEC Rules 14a–13, 14b–1 and 14b–2 under the Securities Exchange Act of 1934 require corporations to attempt to communicate with the beneficial owners through the record owners, and establish procedures for doing so. In addition, the rules of self-regulatory organizations provide that a broker may either request voting instructions from the beneficial owners or forward signed proxies to them. These rules also permit the broker to vote the proxy in certain uncontested matters if the beneficial owner does not give instructions to the broker in a timely fashion. See New York Stock Exchange Rule 451 and 452; American Stock Exchange Rules 575 and 577; National Association of Securities Dealers Rules of Fair Practice, Article III Section 1 (providing only for forwarding signed proxies).

### e.  Control of the Machinery

From the foregoing description, it should be obvious that the solicitation of proxies, which is necessary if shareholders are to act as a body, requires an elaborate machinery. Detailed records of shareholders must be maintained, material must be prepared, reviewed, filed and mailed, and counsel must play a significant role. All of this is expensive. The expenses are borne by the company since they relate to a necessary function that management must discharge. If a shareholder seeks to oppose management's proposals, or if she wishes to offer a candidate in opposition to those nominated by the board of directors, she must duplicate the entire process and bear the expense on her own, subject to obtaining reimbursement of expenses in limited circumstances. Can the federal law attain its objective of "fair corporate suffrage" if state law gives management effective control over the solicitation process? On the other hand, is there a practical alternative?

### f.  Counting the Proxies

The final aspect of the proxy machinery involves counting the votes. The proxy holders present their proxies at the meeting and then, having established that they are the agent for the number of shares so evidenced, they cast their ballot. In an uncontested election, no one has any interest in challenging their count. However, if a contested election of directors is involved or if there has been opposition to a proposed transaction, or if approval of a transaction requires more than a majority vote, then the count of the proxies becomes crucial. There are several wrinkles that can make the count contentious. For one thing, proxies are revocable and they may be revoked either by notice to the company or by a later designation of someone else as a proxy to vote in a different way. In the latter case, the later dated proxy constitutes the valid designation of an agent and automatically cancels the earlier designation. But which one is the later proxy? How does one tell? Or, suppose one of the contestants argues that the proxy held by the other side is invalid because the proxy was not signed properly or because some other defect appears. Who settles this question?

Ordinarily, the board of directors designates inspectors of election, and, in some cases, state law requires the appointment of inspectors of election. Generally, these people are not members of management, but are professionals hired to do the job. What law applies? Until recently, the practical answer has been found in the practices of corporate lawyers who have developed such rules as those dealing with proper signatures, fiduciary voting, dating of proxies and the like. If there is an election campaign with two sides actively seeking proxies, the lawyers for each side customarily agree on a set of rules in advance of the meeting to serve as the ground rules applicable to that election. These unofficial documents have guided courts in those instances where the issues are litigated.

There has been a recent increase in the number of cases in which the courts have intervened in the practices of those who act as inspectors of election at shareholder meetings. In many of those cases, the courts have not hesitated to set aside some or all of the disputed proxies because they have disagreed with the way in which the inspectors have resolved the disputes. Some of these cases have resulted from modern technology, i.e., the validity of "proxygrams" (proxies sent by telegrams) or proxies sent by fax machines. For the courts, the analytic conflict is between the need for certainty and a quick resolution of an election on the one hand and the need to protect the shareholder franchise on the other. In Delaware, the legislature has acted to remove whatever ambiguities may have been created by the recent cases. DGCL § 231, added in 1990, addresses voting procedures and requires that public corporations (as defined in the statute), in advance of any shareholder meeting, appoint one or more inspectors to act at the meeting and make a written report thereof. The inspectors may be independent third parties or employees of the corporation. Their duties include ascertaining the number of shares outstanding and the voting power of each, determining the shares represented at a meeting and the validity of proxies and ballots cast, counting all votes and ballots and certifying their result. New subsections 212(c) and (d), also added in 1990, authorize the use of datagram and telecopied proxies and deal with their validity.

## C.  FEDERAL REGULATION OF PROXY SOLICITATIONS

The SEC's rules adopted pursuant to § 14(a) of the Securities Exchange Act of 1934 regulate many aspects of the proxy solicitation process. Those rules apply to every company that has a class of securities listed on a stock exchange or has a class of securities owned by 500 or more holders of record and assets of at least $5,000,000, Securities

Exchange Act §§ 12(b),(g), and refer to all such companies as "registrants."

For many years, the proxy rules applied to all solicitations of proxies in much the same fashion, whether conducted by a company's management, a dissident shareholder, or some other person. The SEC and the courts interpreted the term "solicitation" to include every communication, including every public statement, that was likely to influence a shareholder's decision to grant a proxy and the proxy rules provided that every solicitation had to be accompanied or preceded by a full proxy statement that the SEC staff had reviewed. As a consequence, a shareholder seeking to communicate with other shareholders about some matter to be voted on shareholders' meeting had to (1) file a preliminary proxy statement with the SEC, (2) wait for SEC approval, (3) mail a full proxy statement to all shareholders with whom she communicated, and (4) face the possibility of being sued under Rule 14a–9 for proxy fraud. This requirement greatly impeded non-management shareholders' participation in the corporate electoral process; in effect, they stifled "shareholder democracy."

Reacting to criticism of these requirements, the SEC in 1992 revised its proxy rules to deregulate substantially the proxy solicitation process. The focus of the deregulation was on communications by minority shareholders and other persons not affiliated with the management of the company with respect to which proxies were being solicited. One consequence of this revision was that different rules now govern proxy solicitations by a company's management and solicitations by others.

## 1. THE PROXY RULES AS THEY APPLY TO MANAGEMENT

When management plans to solicit proxies, it must first prepare a proxy statement and a form of proxy. Schedule 14A specifies in considerable detail certain information that management must include in its proxy statement, including information about candidates for election as director and about management's compensation arrangements. In addition, Rule 14a–9 prohibits inclusion of materially false or misleading statements in a proxy solicitation—a prohibition that the SEC interprets as requiring disclosure of both the negative and the positive aspects of any proposal for which management is seeking shareholder approval. Thus, for example, if management is seeking shareholder authorization of an amendment to the articles that will divide the board of directors into classes, the SEC will require management to explain in its proxy statement that classifying the board may serve to discourage uninvited takeover bids, as well as setting forth management's reasons for recommending that shareholders authorize a classified board.

Rule 14a–3 requires that every proxy "solicitation" by management be accompanied or preceded by the definitive proxy statement. In addition, if management is soliciting proxies for an annual meeting or a special meeting at which directors are to be elected, each proxy statement must be accompanied or preceded by an annual report containing certain information specified by the Rule (and which generally contains additional information provided by management).

Rule 14a–4 regulates the form of proxy. Management must give shareholders an opportunity to vote either for or against each matter to be acted upon other than elections to office. If directors are to be elected, the proxy form must provide a means by which shareholders may withhold their votes on directors as a group or on individual candidates. A proxy may confer discretionary authority on matters where the shareholder does not specify a choice if the form of proxy states in boldface type how the proxy will be voted on each matter. The proxy must vote the shares represented at the meeting in accordance with the shareholder's instructions.

Rule 14a–6 requires management to file preliminary copies of its proxy statement and form of proxy with the Commission at least 10 days prior to disseminating those materials to shareholders. However, if the solicitation involves nothing more than an unopposed election of directors, ratification of selection of auditors and shareholder proposals, no preliminary material need be filed. The SEC staff endeavors to review and comment on proxy materials within this 10–day period.

The SEC now places preliminary proxy materials in a public file when they are received, unless they relate to a business combination or other extraordinary transaction, in which event the Commission automatically treats the materials as confidential. In addition, the SEC now allows management to begin soliciting proxies using the preliminary proxy materials it has filed, so long as management does not provide a form of proxy to any shareholders it solicits. This rule is designed to permit management to seek shareholders' reactions to proposals or transactions for which management plans to seek shareholder approval, prior to the filing of definitive proxy materials, and to modify those proposals or transactions if shareholders' initial reactions are negative.

Rule 14a–7 provides that a shareholder who wants to solicit proxies may require the company to mail her soliciting material if she agrees to bear the cost of the mailing. Alternatively, the company can furnish the shareholder with a list of names and addresses for such categories of shareholders as she may specify.

As discussed in greater detail in Section E, Rule 14a–8 requires a company to include in its proxy statement certain resolutions submitted by that company's shareholders. The company also must include a supporting statement provided by the sponsoring shareholder, provided that the resolution and the statement do not exceed 500 words.

## 2.  COMMUNICATIONS REASONABLY CALCULATED TO PROCURE A PROXY

Rule 14a–1 defines "solicitation" to include: (1) any request for a proxy whether or not accompanied by or included in a form of proxy; (2) any request to execute or not to execute, or to revoke, a proxy; or (3) the furnishing of a form of proxy *or other communication* to security holders under circumstances reasonably *calculated* to result in the procurement, withholding or revocation of a proxy. In addition to the traditional proxy, the definition of "proxy" includes a consent or authorization. In the definition of "solicitation," the most important interpretive question concerns the meaning of "calculated." Does it mean "intended" or "likely"? How do the different meanings affect the determination of whether there was a solicitation? Which is more consistent with the purposes of the proxy rules?

*Studebaker Corp. v. Gittlin*, 360 F.2d 692 (2d Cir.1966), illustrates the broad interpretation the SEC and the courts have given the term "solicitation." Gittlin, a shareholder in Studebaker, sought inspection of the company's shareholder list in preparation for an effort to gain control of the board of directors. New York law required that, since he had not been a shareholder for six months, he own or have the support of holders of 5% of Studebaker's stock in order to obtain the list. Gittlin met this requirement by obtaining authorization from 42 other shareholders, and a state court ordered Studebaker to allow inspection. The company then asked a federal court to enjoin enforcement of the state court order, charging that Gittlin had obtained the authorizations in violation of the federal proxy rules.

The SEC, appearing *amicus curiae*, argued that soliciting authorization to inspect the shareholder list was subject to the proxy rules even if the request was not part of a planned proxy solicitation. The Second Circuit responded:

> We need not go that far to uphold the order of the district court. In *SEC v. Okin*, 132 F.2d 784 (2d Cir.1943), this court ruled that a letter which did not request the giving of any authorization was subject to the Proxy Rules if it was part of "a continuous plan" intended to end in solicitation and to prepare the way for success. This was the avowed purpose of Gittlin's demand for inspection of the stockholders list and, necessarily, for his soliciting authorizations sufficient to aggregate the 5% of the stock required by § 1315 of New York's Business Corporation Law. Presumably the stockholders who gave authorizations were told something and, as Judge L. Hand said in *Okin*, "one need only spread the misinformation adequately before beginning to solicit, and the Commission would be powerless to protect shareholders." 132 F.2d at 786. Moreover, the very fact that a copy of the stockholders list is a valuable instrument to a person seeking to gain control, * * * is a good reason for insuring that shareholders have full information before they aid its procurement.

360 F.2d at 696.

A controversy relating to a proposed merger of the Rock Island Railroad with the Union Pacific Railroad in 1963 led to two decisions that illustrate the factors courts consider when deciding whether to subject a communication to the requirements of the proxy rules. On May 13, 1963, the Rock Island and Union Pacific announced an agreement to merge. On June 24, 1963, Chicago and Northwestern Railway unveiled a competing offer for the Rock Island. For Northwestern's offer to succeed, the Rock Island's shareholders would have to vote down the merger with Union Pacific, which the boards of the Rock Island and Union Pacific formally approved on June 27, 1963. Northwestern also needed Interstate Commerce Commission approval of its offer, and applied for that approval on July 3, 1963.

On July 26, 1963, Union Pacific published a newspaper advertisement explaining that it opposed Northwestern's offer because it would affect railroad service adversely. The advertisements appeared in cities served by the Rock Island and in Washington and New York, which the Rock Island did not serve.

A Rock Island shareholder filed suit, claiming that the advertisement was a communication reasonably calculated to procure a proxy and thus constituted an unlawful solicitation. The court disagreed, noting that the ad informed the public about an issue pending before a government agency and thus served a public interest independent of the decision the Rock Island's shareholders would have to make. The court also considered it significant that the Rock Island shareholders' meeting had not been called at the time the ad was published. In fact, the meeting, scheduled for November 15, 1963, was not called until October 1. Brown v. Chicago, R.I. & P.R.R. Co., 328 F.2d 122, 124–5 (7th Cir.1964).

In contrast, once the contestants began to formally solicit proxies, a different court held that another communication not specifically directed at the Rock Island's shareholders nonetheless constituted a solicitation. A brokerage firm prepared a report concluding that the Rock Island's shareholders would benefit more from Northwestern's offer than from Union Pacific's and distributed the report to its customers. Northwestern, which had assisted the brokerage firm in preparing the report, distributed additional copies of the report to Rock Island shareholders. The court held that the report was reasonably calculated to influence a Rock Island shareholder's decision on whether to grant a proxy and therefore was a solicitation. Union Pacific R.R. Co. v. Chicago & N.W. Ry. Co., 226 F.Supp. 400 (N.D.Ill.1964).

*Smallwood v. Pearl Brewing Company*, 489 F.2d 579 (5th Cir.1974), illustrates that the breadth of the term is not unlimited. Approximately two months prior to mailing its proxy statement soliciting shareholder approval of a merger, a company advised its shareholders by letter of the proposed merger. The company also indicated that the board believed that the merger would be beneficial to shareholders. *Smallwood* held that the letter was not a communication reasonably calculated to result in the procurement of a proxy. No proxies were actually mentioned and the correspondence "if not totally innocuous was not overwhelmingly prejudicial either." *Id.* at 601. The court also noted that requiring compliance with the proxy rules would impede prompt disclosure to investors of a major, pending corporate transaction.

This last point has great significance. A constant tension exists between the timing requirements of the proxy rules and the SEC's policy urging prompt disclosure of significant corporate information. Both the courts and the SEC recognize that labeling a communication a "solicitation" stifles some communication; it often will be impractical promptly to prepare and circulate material that meets all requirements of the proxy rules. Consequently, the courts strive to maintain a reasonable balance between serving the needs of the marketplace and protecting the integrity of the proxy solicitation process.

## LONG ISLAND LIGHTING COMPANY v. BARBASH

779 F.2d 793 (2d Cir.1985).

[The Long Island Lighting Company (LILCO) was the focus of a local political campaign, in which candidate Matthews urged public ownership of the utility. Matthews acquired sufficient shares to demand a special shareholders' meeting to consider his proposal. A group favorable to Matthews' proposal, Citizens to Replace LILCO, published a newspaper advertisement accusing LILCO of mismanagement and attempting to pass through to ratepayers needless costs relating to construction of the Seabrook nuclear power plant and urging support for a campaign to have the public power authority acquire LILCO.

LILCO complained that the ad was unlawful because it constituted an unfiled proxy solicitation and because it was false and misleading. The district court declined to hold that the ad represented a solicitation because it appeared in a general publication and could only indirectly affect the proxy contest at LILCO.]

CARDAMONE, CIRCUIT JUDGE:

II

In our view the district court erred in holding that the proxy rules cannot cover communications appearing in publications of general circulation and that are indirectly addressed to shareholders.

* * *

These rules apply not only to direct requests to furnish, revoke or withhold proxies, but also to communications which may indirectly accomplish such a result or constitute a step in a chain of communications designed ultimately to accomplish such a result. * * *

The question in every case is whether the challenged communication, seen in the totality of circumstances, is "reasonably calculated" to influence the shareholders' votes. Determination of the purpose of the communication depends upon the nature of the communication and the circumstances under which it was distributed.

* * *

Deciding whether a communication is a proxy solicitation does not depend upon whether it is "targeted directly" at shareholders. See Rule

14a–6(g), (requiring that solicitations in the form of "speeches, press releases, and television scripts" be filed with the SEC). As the SEC correctly notes in its amicus brief, it would "permit easy evasion of the proxy rules" to exempt all general and indirect communications to shareholders, and this is true whether or not the communication purports to address matters of "public interest." The SEC's authority to regulate proxy solicitations has traditionally extended into matters of public interest.

\* \* \*

WINTER, CIRCUIT JUDGE, dissenting:

In order to avoid a serious first amendment issue, I would construe the federal regulations governing the solicitation of proxies as inapplicable to the newspaper advertisement in question. \* \* \*

## II

The content of the Committee's advertisement is of critical importance. First, it is on its face addressed solely to the public. Second, it makes no mention either of proxies or of the shareholders' meeting demanded by Matthews. Third, the issues the ad addresses are quintessentially matters of public political debate, namely, whether a public power authority would provide cheaper electricity than LILCO. Claims of LILCO mismanagement are discussed solely in the context of their effect on its customers. Finally, the ad was published in the middle of an election campaign in which LILCO's future was an issue.

On these facts, therefore, LILCO's claim raises a constitutional issue of the first magnitude. It asks nothing less than that a federal court act as a censor, empowered to determine the truth or falsity of the ad's claims about the merits of public power and to enjoin further advocacy containing false claims. We need not resolve this constitutional issue, however.

Where advertisements are critical of corporate conduct but are facially directed solely to the public, in no way mention the exercise of proxies, and debate only matters of conceded public concern, I would construe federal proxy regulation as inapplicable, whatever the motive of those who purchase them. This position, which is strongly suggested by relevant case law, *see infra,* maximizes public debate, avoids embroiling the federal judiciary in determining the rightness or wrongness of conflicting positions on public policy, and does not significantly impede achievement of Congress' goal that shareholders exercise proxy rights on the basis of accurate information.

It is of course true that LILCO shareholders may be concerned about public allegations of mismanagement on LILCO's part. However, shareholders are most unlikely to be misled into thinking that advertisements of this kind, particularly when purchased in the name of a committee so obviously disinterested in the return on investment to LILCO's shareholders, are either necessarily accurate or authoritative sources of information about LILCO's management. Such advertisements, which in no way suggest internal reforms shareholders might bring about through the exercise of their proxies, are sheer political advocacy and would be so recognized by any reasonable shareholder.

To be sure, the fact that a corporation has become a target of political advocacy might well justify unease among shareholders. No one seriously asserts, however, that the right to criticize corporate behavior as a matter of public concern diminishes as shareholders' meetings become imminent.

## 3. SOLICITATIONS BY SHAREHOLDERS AND OTHERS

At the time *Barbash* was decided, the proxy rules required every person who solicited a proxy to deliver to every solicitee a proxy statement containing detailed information about the solicitor and various other matters. A communication in the mass media, such as the advertisement at issue in *Barbash*, was deemed to be directed at all of a company's shareholders. Consequently, it was unlawful to publish such an advertisement unless the solicitor had first filed a proxy statement with the SEC, received staff clearance, and circulated copies of that statement to all of the company's shareholders—*i.e.*, all of the persons who would be "solicited" by the newspaper ad. In addition, the ad itself would have to be filed in advance with the SEC and cleared by the staff. Only non-management solicitations directed to not more than 10 persons were exempt from these requirements. Concern that these requirements discouraged shareholder participation in the corporate electoral process led the Commission to review and modify the proxy rules.

### REGULATION OF COMMUNICATIONS AMONG SHAREHOLDERS

SEC Rel. No. 34–31326, pp. 7–17 (Oct. 22, 1992).

The amendments to the proxy rules and other disclosure provisions adopted today follow upon an extensive three-year examination by the Commission of the effectiveness of the proxy voting process and its effect on the corporate governance system in this country. * * *

Within the overall scope of this broad examination, the Commission has focused particularly on the role of its proxy and disclosure rules in impeding shareholder communication and participation in the corporate governance process. This demonstrated effect of the current rules is contrary to Congress's intent that the rules assure fair and effective shareholder suffrage. Apart from attempts to obtain proxy voting authority, to the degree the current rules inhibit the ability of shareholders not seeking proxy authority to analyze and discuss issues pertaining to the operation of a company and its performance, these rules may in fact run exactly contrary to the best interests of shareholders.

The amendments adopted today reflect a Commission determination that the federal proxy rules have created unnecessary regulatory impediments to communication among shareholders and others and to the effective use of shareholder voting rights. The Commission has also determined that modifications in the current rules are desirable to reduce these burdens and to achieve the purposes set forth in the Exchange Act.

\* \* \*

In 1956, the Commission significantly expanded the definition of "solicitation" of a proxy to embrace "any communication" which could be viewed as being "reasonably calculated" to influence a shareholder to give, deny or revoke a proxy. In adopting the sweeping 1956 definition, the Commission sought to address abuses by persons who were actually engaging in solicitations of proxy authority in connection with election contests. The Commission does not seem to have been aware, or to have intended, that the new definition might also sweep within all the regulatory requirements persons who did not "request" a shareholder to grant or to revoke or deny a proxy, but whose expressed opinions might be found to have been reasonably calculated to affect the views of other shareholders positively or negatively toward a particular company and its management or directors. Since any such persuasion—even if unintended—could affect the decision of shareholders even many months later to give or withhold a proxy, such communications at least literally could fall within the new definition.

The literal breadth of the new definition of solicitation was so great as potentially to turn almost every expression of opinion concerning a publicly-traded corporation into a regulated proxy solicitation. \* \* \*

If the current proxy rules apply to a communication, the effect can be very costly. \* \* \*

While voting rights are valuable assets and an uninformed exercise of those rights could represent a wasted opportunity for the voting shareholder, that concern does not justify the government's requiring that all private conversations on matters subject to a shareholder vote be reported to the government. In the Commission's view, the antifraud provisions provide adequate protection against fraudulent and deceptive communications to shareholders on matters presented for a vote by persons not seeking proxy authority and not in the classes of persons ineligible for the exemption.

A regulatory scheme that inserted the Commission staff and corporate management into every exchange and conversation among shareholders, their advisors and other parties on matters subject to a vote certainly would raise serious questions under the free speech clause of the First Amendment, particularly where no proxy authority is being solicited by such persons. This is especially true where such intrusion is not necessary to achieve the goals of the federal securities laws.

The purposes of the proxy rules themselves are better served by promoting free discussion, debate and learning among shareholders and interested persons, than by placing restraints on that process to ensure that management has the ability to address every point raised in the exchange of views. Indeed, the Commission has not perceived, and the comments have not demonstrated, shareholder abuses where proxy authority is not being sought by the person engaged in the communications. However, there have been situations in which discontented shareholders have been subjected to legal threats based on the possibility the shareholder might have triggered proxy filing requirements by expressing disagreement to other shareholders.

---

### a. Exempt Solicitations

The Commission concluded that "the best protection for shareholders and the marketplace is to identify those classes of solicitations that warrant application of the proxy statement disclosure requirement, and to foster the free and unrestrained expression of views by all other parties by the removal of any regulatory cost, burden or uncertainty that could have the effect of deterring the free expression of views by disinterested shareholders who do not seek authority for themselves." *Id.* at 23–24. Consequently, it amended Rule 14a–2 to exempt from the filing requirement of Rule 14a–6 and the proxy statement delivery requirement of Rule 14a–3 any solicitation by a person, whether or not a shareholder, who does not seek proxy voting authority and does not furnish shareholders with a form of proxy. Thus a person soliciting in support of a shareholder proposal can rely on the exemption, so long as she is not seeking proxy voting authority and is not otherwise ineligible. Moreover, if a solicitation is oral or is by a person who owns securities of the registrant worth less than $5 million, no notice relating to the solicitation need be filed with the SEC. A solicitor who owns more than $5 million in securities and conducts a written solicitation must file a notice, within three days *following* the first dissemination of those materials, listing only her name and address and attaching the soliciting materials.

This exemption is not available to (i) the registrant, (ii) a person acting on behalf of or financed by the registrant, (iii) a person soliciting in opposition to a merger or other extraordinary transaction where that person has proposed or plans to propose an alternative transaction to which it will be a party, (iv) certain large shareholders interested in seeking control of the registrant, or (v) a person who would receive a benefit from a successful solicitation that she would not share *pro rata* with other shareholders.

As a result of these amendments, the SEC staff will no longer review proxy soliciting material disseminated by persons not seeking authority to vote other shareholders' stock. The only significant regulatory constraint on such solicitations is Rule 14a–9's prohibition of materially false and misleading statements in a proxy solicitation.

### b. Shareholder Announcements of Voting Decisions

The SEC also amended Rule 14a–1 to exclude from the definition of solicitation an announcement by a shareholder of how she intends to vote and her explanation of her decision. Such an announcement can, without limitation, be published, broadcast, or disseminated to the media. Because it is deemed not to constitute a solicitation, none of the proxy rules apply.

### c.   Regulated Solicitations

The SEC also substantially eliminated staff review of soliciting materials other than management's initial proxy statement. Most such materials now can be filed with the Commission in definitive form at the time they are disseminated. The Commission explained that it "believes that the most cost-effective means to address hyperbole and other claims and opinions viewed as objectionable is not government screening of the contentions or resort to the courts. Rather, the parties should be free to reply to the statements in a timely and cost-effective manner, challenging the basis for the claims and countering with their own views on the subject matter through the dissemination of additional soliciting material." *Id.* at 43.

### d.   The Impact of the Revised Proxy Rules

According to the Investor Responsibility Research Center, an organization that monitors the activities of institutional investors and shareholder activists, the SEC's new rules "energized long-time activists and brought some investors, such as labor unions and money managers, into the process for the first time" during the 1993 proxy season, the first in which the rules were in effect. Patrick S. McGurn, *Shareholder Activism Continues to Thrive*, IRRC CORPORATE GOVERNANCE BULLETIN 7 (May–June 1993). A number of shareholder proponents took advantage of the new rules to actively solicit support for their proposals from institutional investors. Shareholder proposals on governance issues garnered record support, including a majority of the votes cast in several instances. But, in the view of some analysts, the most significant development was corporate managers' increased willingness to meet with activist shareholders and discuss their concerns. This receptivity was stimulated by managers' awareness that shareholders otherwise would find it easier to mobilize support for shareholder proposals or opposition to proposals or candidates that management was supporting.

Stephen Choi conducted a study of proxy voting during the period 1991–1995 on 362 resolutions sponsored by institutional investors to assess the the impact of the new proxy rules. Stephen Choi, *Proxy Issue Contests: Impact of the 1992 Proxy Reforms* (Working Paper 4/25/97). He found that overall support for such resolutions declined from a pre-reform average of 27.4% to a post-reform average of 22.8%. This decline, he hypothesized, was due to changes in the mix of proposals, sponsors, and targeted companies. More specifically, he found that post-reform, unions, charitable organizations and other "new sponsors more interested in using the proxy device as a communication or bargaining tool rather than to maximize shareholder welfare made use of the proxy mechanism." *Id.* at 36. Overall, though, Choi concluded that "the proxy reforms increased the effectiveness of proxy issue contests."

> More specifically, [he] found that proposals with similar characteristics pre-and post-reform that determine the for-vote percentage—including institutional ownership, sponsor identity, proposal type, management ownership, and past company financial performance—received a greater for-vote percentage post-reform. The increase was greatest for those proposals targeting companies with worse corporate governance structures and where institutional investors with sizable holdings at stake are a strong presence. Proxy reform, therefore, provided more benefit to proposals with a higher likelihood of increasing shareholder welfare.

*Id.* at 35.

### e.  *Disclosure of Plans and Proposals by Significant Shareholders*

In rejecting claims that the new rules went too far in deregulating the proxy solicitation process, the SEC observed that the circumstances under which a large shareholder, or a group of shareholders acting together, must disclose to the SEC, the company, other shareholders and the market its plans regarding a given company are adequately addressed by Section 13(d) of the 1934 Act and the rules adopted thereunder. Section 13(d) requires any "person" who becomes the owner of 5 percent of the stock of a registrant to file a Schedule 13D within 10 business days of the acquisition. "Person" is defined to include a "group" and Rule 13(d)–5(b)(1) states that a "group" will be deemed to have "acquired" the shares of its members when two or more persons "agree to act together for the purpose of acquiring, holding, voting or disposing of equity securities."

Schedule 13D requires detailed information about the person filing the Schedule (or each member of the filing group), how that person financed the acquisition of the corporation's securities, the purpose of acquiring those securities, and all "contracts, arrangements, understandings or relationships (legal or otherwise)" relating to the corporation among the members of a group or between the person (or group members) filing the form and any other persons.

*GAF Corp. v. Milstein*, 453 F.2d 709 (2d Cir.1971), upheld a claim that a group made up of four members of the Milstein family, who together owned in excess of 10 percent of a class of GAF stock, "acquired" the stock that those family members owned at the moment they agreed to work together to seek control of GAF and violated § 13(d) by failing to timely file a Schedule 13D. The court noted that § 13(d) was adopted to alert the marketplace to rapid accumulations of stock that might signal a pending shift in control, and stated that the alleged conspiracy among the Milsteins represented the kind of conduct at which the section was directed.

Bernard Black has argued that, with the amendment of the proxy rules, § 13(d), the SEC's expansive interpretation of that section and the rules issued thereunder constitute a very substantial regulatory impediment to increased activism by institutional investors. Bernard S. Black, *Next Steps in Corporate Governance Reform: 13(d) Rules and Control Person Liability*, in Kenneth Lehn & Robert Kamphuis, eds., MODERNIZING SECURITIES REGULATION: ECONOMIC AND LEGAL PERSPECTIVES 197–209 (1992). Black observed that "[t]he 13D filing isn't complex, but it involves substantial litigation risk, which means heavy legal bills, win or lose. Proponents are commonly sued by the SEC or the company's managers for various real or imagined misdisclosures." Black suggested that the SEC act to reduce the obstacles caused by § 13(d) by redefining "group" to exclude agreements to vote a company's stock and by revising the "expansive and litigation-prone disclosure requirements of Schedule 13D." Other commentators made similar suggestions.

*Azurite Corp. Ltd. v. Amster & Co.*, 52 F.3d 15 (2d Cir.1995), suggests the problems posed by § 13(d) may be less severe than Professor Black anticipated.* The plaintiffs, shareholders of Graphic Scanning Corp., contended that defendants, who eventually filed a Schedule 13D announcing that they planned to wage a proxy contest to gain control of Graphic Scanning, had violated § 13(d) by not announcing their plans at an earlier date. Defendants responded that, until the time they announced their plan, a proxy contest was only one of several alternatives they were considering.

The court held that under § 13(d), " 'there is no requirement to make predictions, for example, of future behavior; or to disclose tentative plans; or inchoate plans. It is sufficient to merely identify those matters not fully determined.' " *Id.* at 18 (quoting *Todd Shipyards Corp. v. Madison Fund, Inc.*, 547 F.Supp. 1383, 1387 (S.D.N.Y.1982). In other words, "unless a course of action is decided upon or intended, it need not be disclosed as a plan or proposal under Item 4 [of Schedule 13D]." *Id.* In the absence of any evidence that defendants' thinking about a proxy contest had become sufficiently "fixed" to constitute a "plan or proposal," the court held, plaintiffs' complaint was properly dismissed.

# D.  INSTITUTIONAL INVESTORS AND CORPORATE GOVERNANCE

The portion of corporate stock held by institutional investors—private and public pension funds, mutual funds, insurance companies, bank non-pension trusts, foundations and endowments—has increased rapidly in recent years. Institutional investors held 6.1% of public corporations' outstanding stock in 1950. That percentage increased to 12.6% in 1960, 19.4% in 1970, 33.9% in 1980, and 47.2% in 1990. In the

---

* In addition, the SEC amended its rules, effective February 18,1998, to provide that a passive investor—i.e., one who does not seek to change or influence control of an issuer—that owns up to 20% of an issuer's stock is eligible to file a short-form Schedule 13G rather than the more detailed Schedule 13D.

next six years, the market value of institutions' equity holdings increased dramatically, from $1.7 trillion in 1990 to $4.4 trillion in 1996, but the portion of public corporations' stock held by institutions remained essentially unchanged—47.4%. The Conference Board, INSTITUTIONAL INVESTOR REPORT: FINANCIAL ASSETS & EQUITY HOLDINGS 38 (1997).

Virtually all institutional investors hold very diversified portfolios. Within that framework though, they follow a variety of different investment strategies. In 1996, 17.6% of the equity holdings of all institutional investors were devoted to indexed portfolios, but this figure included 59.2% of the equity holdings of public pension funds, 36.4% of banks' holdings, and 21.3% of the holdings of corporate pension funds. The Conference Board, INSTITUTIONAL INVESTOR REPORT: TURNOVER, INVESTMENT STRATEGIES AND OWNERSHIP PATTERNS 20 (1997).

Institutional investors tended to concentrate their investments in larger companies, but not the largest companies. In 1996, institutions held 58.7% of the stock of the 1,000 largest U.S. corporations (ranked in terms of market value), but only 50.8% of the stock of the 25 largest U.S. corporations. *Id.* at 26, 33. Institutions' holdings included more than 90% of the stock of 5.5% of the 1,000 largest corporations, more than 70% of the stock of 35.5% of those corporations, and more than 50% of the stock of 67.3% of those corporations. In only 12.5% of the 1,000 largest U.S. corporations did institutions hold less than 30% of the stock. *Id.* at 29. On the other hand, in only one of the 25 largest corporations— Gillette—did institutions hold more than 70% of the stock. *Id.* at 34. Among the ten largest U.S. corporations, institutional ownership was most concentrated in Phillip Morris, with the top five institutions holding 17.9% of the stock and the top ten holding 24.7%. *Id.* at 42. It was least concentrated in Microsoft and Exxon, in both of which the top five institutions held 7.6% and the top ten held 11.2%. *Id.* at 40, 41. These data suggest both that corporate ownership now is less fragmented than was the case when Berle and Means first highlighted the divorce of ownership from control and that ownership still is divorced from control.

Two British professors' description of the U.S. corporate governance system remains accurate. It is "characterized by: [a] large number of listed companies; [a] liquid capital market where ownership and control rights are frequently traded; [and] [f]ew intercorporate equity holdings." Julian Franks & Colin Mayer, *Corporate Control: A Synthesis of the International Evidence* 2 (Mimeo. 1992). They also point out that, in contrast, "Continental European and Japanese corporate systems typically have: [f]ew listed companies; [a]n illiquid capital market where ownership and control is infrequently traded; [and] [c]omplex systems of intercorporate holdings." *Id.* at 2–3.

## 1. CONSTRAINTS ON ACTIVISM BY INSTITUTIONAL INVESTORS

Institutional investors, acting collectively, clearly have the potential to exert considerable influence on most publicly-held American corporations. What influence they actually exert is limited, though, by collective action problems and legal constraints.

Recall that the first part of Dean Clark's analysis of collective action problems, in Section B of this chapter, assumes that the shareholder is an individual investor for whom "rational apathy" may be the most efficient course of action. Does that analysis hold if the shareholder is an institutional investor? Professor Bernard Black, who believes institutional investors have the potential to play a constructive role as monitors of corporate management, suggests it does not:

> A shareholder who owns a large percentage stake is more likely to engage in monitoring than a shareholder who owns a smaller stake. Thus legal rules that prevent shareholders from owning large stakes or acting jointly increase incentives to remain passive. Moreover, the higher the cost of making a shareholder proposal, the greater the incentive to remain silent. Thus, rules that increase the cost of a proxy campaign or prevent cost-sharing among shareholders discourage shareholder action. Conversely, rules that shift costs to the company encourage shareholder action.

> Moreover, the standard model overstates the case for passivity. When the voting outcome is in doubt, apathy becomes much less rational as shareholdings grow. Both a shareholder's gains from the voting outcome she favors and the likelihood that her vote will be decisive increase with the number of shares owned. A shareholder who owns 1,000 shares is 1,000 times more likely to cast a decisive vote than a shareholder who owns a single share, and realizes 1,000 times the net gain if her vote is decisive. Thus, the incentive to cast an informed vote increases *exponentially* as shareholdings grow. A 1,000 share holder has 1,000,000 times more incentive to become informed than someone who owns a single share!

> Diversification also enhances incentives to monitor by creating the potential for economies of scale in monitoring. Many process and structural issues arise in similar form at many companies. A shareholder who offers the same proposal at a number of companies can reduce her per-company solicitation cost, while preserving the per-company benefit from success. Similarly, a shareholder who votes on the same proposal many times has reason to invest more time and attention in casting an informed vote.

Bernard Black, *Agents Watching Agents: The Promise Of Institutional Investor Voice*, 39 UCLA L. REV. 811, 821–822 (1992).

On the other hand, Professor Black argues, numerous government regulations, although not directed at constraining institutional activism, have that effect.

> A broad array of state and federal rules makes it hard for a single shareholder to own a large percentage stake in a single company. Other rules encumber joint action by a number of shareholders and increase the cost of a proxy campaign. * * *

For an active shareholder or a shareholder group, owning a 5% stake triggers filing requirements under section 13(d) of the Securities Exchange Act and related S.E.C. rules. Owning a 10% stake can trigger short-swing profit forfeiture under Exchange Act section 16(b) and related S.E.C. rules. * * * Banks, insurers, and mutual funds face additional legal limits on their ability to hold large stakes. Corporate crossholdings are discouraged by an extra layer of taxation, and by unfavorable accounting treatment for stakes under 20%.

The obstacles to owning a large stake are greater for an active shareholder than for a passive shareholder. For example, an active shareholder must report its holdings and plans on Schedule 13D; a passive shareholder can file a shorter Schedule 13G. An active shareholder may have to make a costly filing under the Hart–Scott–Rodino premerger notification rules; a passive shareholder is exempt. Depending on the company's takeover defenses and state of incorporation, a successful proponent could lose voting power under a control share antitakeover statute; incur an obligation to buy everyone else's stock at a premium to market under a cashout law; trigger change-of-control provisions in various debt instruments, employment agreements or employee benefit plans; or even trigger a poison pill. Catch–22 indeed!

Legal obstacles are especially great if shareholders want to choose some directors instead of rubberstamping the incumbents' choices. The S.E.C.'s proxy rules help shareholders on some matters, but mostly create obstacles for director elections. The sponsoring institution(s) risk being deemed to be a control person, or to have "deputized" the director (which would create short-swing profit forfeiture liability under section 16(b)). Choosing directors also creates a risk of insider trading liability under Exchange Act section 10(b), because the director will have access to insider information.

* * *

Often the law is uncertain. This creates legal risk, which is especially troublesome for institutional fiduciaries. They face personal risk on the downside, while their beneficiaries get most of the upside. * * * Legal uncertainty also encourages company managers to sue shareholders, because the managers can impose costs on shareholders even if they lose the suit.

* * *

No single legal rule forecloses shareholder action. But the obstacles are many, and their cumulative effect is large. A shareholder who remains quiet is safe. A shareholder who buys a large stake, especially a shareholder who becomes active on governance issues, pays a price. That price, for a shareholder whose stake is kept small by legal rules, is often enough to make passivity the preferred choice.

*Id.* at 822–824.

Obstacles in addition to those listed by Black also constrain institutional activism. Shares owned by private pension funds often are voted by employees of the sponsoring corporation, who often share with what might be called the "management point of view." However, the Employee Retirement Income Security Act of 1974 (ERISA) imposes fiduciary duties on those employees and thus requires that they act solely in the interest of plan beneficiaries. However, where plan fiduciaries do not face an actual conflict of interest, their voting decisions are unlikely to be challenged successfully.

Fiduciaries of public pension plans (the most active institutions in the corporate governance movement), while not subject to ERISA, are nevertheless governed by state fiduciary law and state statutory law constraining their discretion. They must also comply with the requirements of the Internal Revenue Code, which seem to impose obligations similar to those of ERISA.

The same analysis applies to other types of institutions. Investment companies and investment advisers, while subject to state fiduciary requirements as well as obligations under the Investment Company Act of 1940 and the Investment Advisers Act of 1940, are subject to pressure to produce superior investment performance. Insurance companies, depending on whether they are stock or mutual companies and the nature of the plans they administer, may be subject to ERISA and are, in any event, subject to the traditional corporate duties of care and loyalty. With respect to these latter duties, though, the same difficulties faced by any shareholder in a derivative suit against a corporate manager would obtain in an action challenging a voting decision as a breach of fiduciary duty.

## 2.  INSTITUTIONAL INVESTORS AND MONITORING

Professor Black and others have vigorously debated whether institutional investors have the potential to effectively monitor corporate managers and, to the extent that they do, whether they are likely to achieve their potential.

Bernard Black, *Agents Watching Agents: The
Promise of Institutional Investor Voice*

39 UCLA L. REV. 811, 815–819 (1992).

The case for institutional oversight, broadly speaking, is that product, capital, labor, and corporate control market constraints on managerial discretion are imperfect, corporate managers need to be watched by someone, and the institutions are the only watchers available. The concerns about institutional oversight arise for two main reasons. First, controlling shareholders may divert funds to themselves at the expense of noncontrolling shareholders. Second, the institutions are themselves managed by money managers who need (and often don't get) watching and appropriate incentives. Mutual fund investors, for example, have little information about the corporate governance actions of mutual funds managers, little reason to care, and no power to do anything except sell their shares and invest in another fund. Public pension fund managers are watched as much by state politicians and the press as by fund beneficiaries.

Pure theory can't tell us whether we'd be better off if imperfectly watched money managers did more watching of corporate managers. Institutional detail matters. A complicating factor is that there are many different types of institutions: corporate pension plans; public pension plans; mutual funds; commercial banks; insurers; investment banks; foundations and endowments. Each has its own incentives, conflicts of interests, culture, history, and regulatory scheme. Some can take the lead in corporate governance initiatives. Conflicts of interest make others likely to be only followers.

Regulation is pervasive. It governs what the institutions, as currently constituted, can do. But it also determines, in substantial part, what the institutions are. Banks, mutual funds, insurers, and pension funds are in significant part defined by a web of regulation. Each could be defined differently, if we so choose. Regulatory detail matters.

The benefits and costs of institutional oversight defy easy summary. Taking them as a whole, I believe that there is a strong case for measured reform that will facilitate joint shareholder action not directed at control, and reduce obstacles to particular institutions owning stakes not large enough to confer working control. Such reform will let six or ten institutions collectively have a significant say in corporate affairs, while limiting the power of any one institution to act on its own. I will call this limited role institutional voice. Institutional voice means a world in which particular institutions can easily own a 5–10% stake in particular companies, but can't easily own much more than 10%; in which institutions can readily talk to each other and select a minority of a company's board of directors, but can't easily exercise day-to-day control or select a majority of the board.

Institutional voice should be distinguished from institutional control, from a world where Citibank or Prudential could control General Motors in the way that Deutsche Bank controls Daimler–Benz. The far-reaching reform needed for concentrated control has large potential benefits, because with control can come strong oversight. But strong oversight is inevitably accompanied by strong potential for abuse of control. * * * It's hard to predict how the newly recreated institutions would behave. Thus, the relative costs and benefits of institutional control are unclear.

The line that divides voice from control is admittedly fuzzy. We can see institutional power as lying along a rough continuum, with passivity at one end, voice in the middle, and control at the other end. Today, legal rules, agenda control, conflicts of interests, cultural factors, and historical accident combine to keep financial institutions far over toward the passivity end of the continuum. I believe that legal reform should allow—and where necessary encourage—the institutions to move toward the middle of the continuum. Such reform has little downside risk and holds substantial promise of improved corporate performance. We can't know today how much of that promise will be realized. But as long as the costs are small, institutional voice is worth a try. In economic terms, the expected benefit outweighs the expected cost.

The necessary reform will be partly deregulatory. We need to reduce the legal barriers that discourage institutions from offering shareholder voting proposals, * * * owning large stakes in particular companies, and exercising the influence that stakes could convey. But deregulation is not enough. We also need rules that encourage monitoring. We could, for example, spread some monitoring costs over all shareholders by expanding the range of proposals that shareholders can include in company proxy statements. We may also need new conflict-of-interest rules, plus more aggressive enforcement of the existing rules, to ensure that money managers act in their beneficiaries' interest; agenda rules that increase shareholder influence over the shareholder voting agenda; and rules that limit manager ability to manipulate election outcomes.

The central theme of this Article—Agents Watching Agents—affects institutional monitoring in several ways. First, and most obviously, institutional voice means asking one set of agents (money managers) to watch another set of agents (corporate managers). Money managers have limited incentives to monitor because they keep only a fraction of the portfolio gains. But money managers also won't take the legal chances that an individual shareholder might because they face personal risk if they breach their fiduciary duty or break other legal rules. The institution, however, realizes most of the gains from such misdeeds. That limits the downside risk from institutional voice.

Second, institutional voice requires a number of institutions, including different types of institutions, to join forces to exercise influence. That furthers limits the downside risk from institutional power, because money managers can monitor each others' actions to some extent. Reputation is a central element in this second form of watching. Diversified institutions interact over and over, at many different companies, over a span of years. Institutions that earn good reputations will elicit cooperation from other institutions; institutions that cheat will invite retaliation.

Third, corporate managers can watch their watchers. Corporate managers indirectly control the largest category of institutional investor, the corporate pension fund. Also, if other institutions abuse their power, corporate managers can complain—loudly and often—to state and federal lawmakers. If the costs to other shareholders, including smaller institutions, of abuse of power by the largest institutions exceed the other shareholders' gains from better monitoring, those shareholders will support corporate managers' efforts to clip the large institutions' wings. Political outcomes are hard to predict, but financial institutions have lost political battles before. Money managers know that, which limits their incentive to misbehave in the first place.

Moreover, much of the promise of shareholder monitoring lies in informal shareholder efforts to monitor corporate managers or to express a desire for change in a company's management or policies. That enhances corporate managers' ability to police money manager behavior. Corporate managers can cooperate only with those money managers who earn a reputation for promoting long-term company value.

A second central theme of this Article is diversification. Diversification creates the opportunity for economies of scale in monitoring. Scale economies, in turn, affect the issues that the institutions will care about. Institutions are likely to devote more attention to process and structure issues, which promise scale economies, than to company-specific concerns. Process and structure issues include the value of confidential voting, the desirability of poison pills and other antitakeover devices, the composition and structure of the board of directors, the process by which directors are nominated, whether a company should have a nonexecutive chairman, and the form of management compensation.

Diversification also means that money managers interact repeatedly at different companies. That makes it easier for money managers to watch each other and makes reputation an important constraint on money manager behavior. Diversification also limits the risk that money managers will divert funds to themselves. Insider trading, for example, won't materially affect portfolio performance if done only occasionally, and a money manager who frequently trades on inside information runs a high risk of being caught.

Partly because institutional incentives push against direct, company-specific monitoring, a central reform goal should be to facilitate indirect monitoring through the board of directors. If the institutions can more easily select directors, at least for a minority of board seats, they can hire directors to watch companies on their behalf.* Currently, directors are often more loyal to corporate officers than to the shareholders whom the directors nominally serve. Shareholder-nominated directors will owe more loyalty to shareholders and may be more willing to ask tough questions when a company's performance lags, or when its CEO has dreams of grandeur.

Reform should focus on the process of voting, rather than substantive governance rules. For example, corporate boards may perform better if they include some directors who are nominated by large institutions. But we shouldn't legislate that result. Instead, we should empower the institutions to make their own decisions about optimal governance structures. They have incentives to make good choices—or at least better choices than lawmakers would make. Moreover, procedural reform won't

---

\* A colleague of Professor Black has suggested institutions support cumulative voting as a means of securing representation on corporate boards of directors . *See* Jef-frey N. Gordon, *Institutions as Relational Investors: A New Look at Cumulative Voting*, 94 COLUM.L.REV.124 (1994) [Eds.]

force oversight or impose large regulatory costs on companies or shareholders. Oversight will take place only where the institutions conclude that the benefits of monitoring outweigh the cost.

Critics worry that the institutions will botch the job of monitoring corporate managers. There will undoubtedly be mistakes and false starts. Institutional shareholders won't develop monitoring skills overnight. But we should let them learn from their mistakes, like other actors in our market economy. In practice, legal change will occur gradually. That will make the inevitable mistakes less costly, and allow time to adjust the reforms if the initial efforts have unforeseen consequences. Given the level of congressional inertia, reform should, where possible rely on federal agency action rather than legislative command.

The promise of institutional voice is substantial. In a companion article, I collect evidence of a number of systematic shortfalls in corporate performance. * * * Unshackled institutions could take steps to remedy these shortfalls. There is also limited direct evidence that some institutions already do valuable monitoring. The direct evidence isn't conclusive, but that isn't surprising, since the institutions don't currently do much monitoring. Importantly, there is little evidence that greater shareholder oversight will be harmful.

---

### Melvin Eisenberg, THE STRUCTURE OF THE CORPORATION: A LEGAL ANALYSIS

56–58 (1976).

The appropriate relation between institutional shareholders and their portfolio corporations has prompted considerable debate. Managers and their allies seek to constrain the discretion of such shareholders; shareholder democrats seek to expand it. One issue in the debate has been whether, considering their power and sophistication, institutional investors owe an obligation to their fellow shareholders to oversee corporate managers and to effect management changes when necessary. Generally speaking, the institutional investors have taken the position that their primary obligation is to their own beneficiaries, not to their fellow shareholders in portfolio companies; that they have neither the time nor the skills to exercise an oversight function; and that a company whose management should be changed is normally an unsound investment, so that an investor which does not like incumbent management should switch out of the investment as quickly as possible, rather than stay in and try to accomplish a change. Some of these arguments appear overstated. There are undoubtedly many cases in which a corporation's assets outshine its management and an institution's position is too large to be liquidated except at a substantial loss, so that it would do better to try to change management than to sell the stock. It seems likely that there have been additional, unstated, reasons for the institutions' pro-management position, including obedience to the mores of the financial community, a desire to stay on good terms with management in order to promote a free flow of inside information, and in the case of certain institutions, particularly banks, a desire to obtain or retain business in their noninvestor capacities. Nevertheless, the position that the primary duty of a financial institution is to protect the interests of its own beneficiaries, and that such institutions are in any event not equipped to oversee management, seems essentially sound.

John C. Coffee, Jr., *Liquidity Versus Control: The Institutional Investor as Corporate Monitor*
91 Col. L. Rev. 1277, 1281–1289 (1991).

* * * Put simply, the agents controlling institutional investors have considerable reason to remain "rationally apathetic" about corporate governance and little reason to become active participants. Why? Various reasons will be advanced, but one stands out: * * * a trade-off exists and must be recognized between liquidity and control. Investors that want liquidity may hesitate to accept control.

This assertion—that a preference for liquidity chills the willingness of institutional investors to participate in the control of major corporations—may sound heretical. With only a few exceptions, both practitioners and academics have shared the assumption that institutions are on the verge of becoming active monitors. * * *

* * * [T]wo polar views of the institutional investor compete for supremacy today: (1) the academic view of financial institutions as Prometheus chained to the rock by outmoded regulations that serve only to entrench and insulate incumbent managements, and (2) corporate management's image of these same institutions as frenzied gamblers in a financial casino, each competing to outdo the other in short-term performance. Both sides in this debate share the common assumption that, for better or worse, institutional investors would soon dominate corporate managements in the absence of political constraints.

This Article disagrees with that assumption. It will argue that the primary explanation for institutional passivity is not overregulation, but the insufficiency of existing incentives to motivate institutional money managers to monitor. Although proponents of institutional activism have analyzed at length the potential ability of institutional investors to hold corporate managers accountable, they have largely ignored the question of who holds institutional money managers accountable. The problem of who will guard the guardian is a timeless one, but it is particularly complicated when the proposed guardian is the institutional investor. Not only do the same problems of agency cost arise at the institutional investor level, but there are persuasive reasons for believing that some institutional investors are less accountable to their "owners" than are corporate managements to their shareholders. Put simply, the usual mechanisms of corporate accountability are either unavailable or largely compromised at the institutional level. This conclusion does not deny that there has been overregulation of institutional investors, but it suggests its impact may have been overstated by the new critics. More importantly, this perspective implies that deregulation alone is an inadequate policy response. If the diagnosis that rational apathy will continue to prevail at the institutional level is accurate, then the law must intervene to correct the market's failure by creating adequate incentives for institutional managers to monitor.

\* \* \* [I]s such a union of liquidity and control desirable? Do we want the institutional monitor to have the same ability to exit the firm costlessly as does the individual shareholder? Would the institutional monitor who possessed such liquidity undertake the often costly burden of monitoring? These are difficult questions, but the choices are not limited to a simple yes or no. Rather, public policy could choose any of a number of possible positions along a continuum that runs from allowing investors to combine liquidity and control to requiring an election between them. \* \* \*

At present, any attempt by institutional investors in the United States to exercise control over corporate managements will entail a probable sacrifice of this liquidity, which may be an unacceptable cost to them. Put more generally, when faced with the choice, U.S. institutional investors have traditionally preferred liquidity to control. This empirical observation leads in turn to a broader, normative contention; liquidity and control are antithetical. American law has said clearly and consistently since at least the 1930's that those who exercise control should not enjoy liquidity and vice versa. Ultimately, this Article will defend the proposition that the separation of liquidity and control is not only a cause of institutional passivity, but to some degree should be. In short, those institutions that most desire liquidity would make poor monitors.

Nor should this contention seem surprising: most other industrial societies seems to have reached a similar resolution (either by legal rule or by business adaptation). From a comparative perspective, advanced industrial economies can be classified along a continuum ranging from those, such as Japan and Germany, that permit financial institutions to control corporate managements, but effectively deny them liquidity, to those that inhibit institutional control, but maximize their liquidity. On such a continuum, the dominant American organizational form—the Berle/Means public corporation—represents the latter pole: investors have only limited ability to control management, but near-perfect liquidity in deep and relatively stable financial markets. The oft-repeated "Wall Street Rule" expressed the basic equilibrium that until recently prevailed: dissatisfied investors could sell, but they could not effectively challenge management.

The tension between liquidity and control can also explain why the historic passivity of the institutional investor is declining. \* \* \* Clearly, some institutions—most typically, public pension funds—sponsor shareholder proposals, lobby state legislatures, and, in a few cases, support insurgents in proxy contests. What explains this new activism? On a theoretical level, the trade-off between liquidity and control is simply a context-specific application of Albert O. Hirschman's famous generalization that the members of any organization face a choice between "exit" and "voice." If an easy, low-cost "exit" is possible (such as that provided by securities markets), the members will rationally have little interest in exercising a more costly "voice." But if "exit" is blocked, the members will become more interested in exercising a "voice" in governance decisions. From this perspective, the new activism of American institutional investors can be explained as the product of "voice" becoming less costly, because of the growth in institutional ownership of securities and the resulting increased capacity for collective action, while "exit" has become more difficult, because institutional investors, who increasingly own large unmarketable blocks, must accept substantial price discounts in order to liquidate theses blocks. These trends toward greater "voice" and lesser "exit" seem likely to continue for institutional investors. As a result, greater institutional activism is predictable, even in the face of a static legal environment.

### Thomas A. Smith, *Institutions and Entrepreneurs in American Corporate Finance*

85 Calif. L. Rev. 1, 76–78 (1997).

There is no doubt that the complex tapestry of American corporate finance is partly the result of the unique political history of this country. The same is doubtless the case for the financial and corporate institutions of Germany and Japan, which have histories of their own.

Nonetheless, we do not need to view the traditional passivity of large American financial institutions as an anomaly requiring a special historical explanation. * * * [S]hareholder passivity makes sense in light of the fundamental function financial intermediary institutions perform. Institutions such as banks, pension funds, and insurance companies gather vast amounts of capital from millions of mostly far-from-wealthy people who have, in a sense, fairly simple financial needs. * * * [T]he core function of financial intermediation [is] the provision of guarantees to risk-averse customers who cannot manage risk effectively on their own. This function creates an apparent paradox: institutions accumulate enormous amounts of capital which, perhaps frustratingly to some, must be managed with the extreme sensitivity of financial customers to the soundness of financial intermediaries foremost in mind.

It is natural to think that the vast reserves of capital in a leading insurance company or pension fund represent a reservoir of shareholder power that could, and therefore should, be used to reform corporations for the better. But this alluring promise is mostly illusory. The reason why pools of institutional capital are so big is that small risk-averse financial customers are so many. Unless they can be well insulated from the resulting risk, these customers would not do business with an institution which engaged in large scale political-model-style activism. Instead, they would take their business to more passive institutions.

From this perspective, the diversification and passivity of financial intermediary institutions does not look like the product of politics. Rather, it looks like many other products of economic evolution. It is a system whose implicit and elegant logic emerges as we realize the costs of doing things any other way.

If this account is true, passive institutions will have a distinct competitive advantage over more activist institutions. In increasingly global financial markets, competition of this kind may be inevitable. If so, as world financial markets become more open and competitive, it may be not American financial intermediaries that will come to look more and more like their German and Japanese counterparts, but rather the other way around. It is also possible that German and Japanese institutions, to the extent that they really are fundamentally different from American institutions, might be the product of more, not less, political intervention than are their American counterparts. Given the comparative political histories of Japan, Germany, and the United States since the 1930s, this suggestion is hardly implausible. * * *

By arguing that institutions are inherently passive, I do not mean to endorse current American managerial practices. I merely contend that reforms of corporate managements are best left to entrepreneurs, who are willing to bear the substantial firm-specific risks implicit in managerial reform. Over time, passive institutions will benefit from successful entrepreneurial innovations and reforms as they pass market tests and become standard practice. Finally, some of the reforms political model adherents propose should probably be enacted, not because they would lure institutions into the fray of corporate governance, but because they would help entrepreneurial investors to reform corporations controlled by sub-optimal managers. Institutions and entrepreneurs perform distinct but complementary functions in American corporate finance.

### Edward B. Rock, *The Logic and (Uncertain) Significance of Institutional Shareholder Activism*
79 GEORGETOWN L.J. 445, 469–476 (1991).

Optimists assume that an institutional investor with a two percent stake in a company will behave like an individual investor with a comparable stake. But one cannot assume that agents will act like principals.

#### 1. CONFLICTS OF INTERESTS

Institutional investors are intermediaries: the investment and voting decisions are made by someone other than the beneficiaries. The central problem is whether those managing the assets, whether in-house or outside managers, can be relied upon to act to maximize the value of the assets under their management.

A number of factors may interfere, including widely recognized conflicts of interest. The in-house plan administrator, an executive of the plan sponsor charged with the responsibility of managing the corporation's pension plan, will inevitably face a conflict, implicit or explicit, between managing the pension plan "for the exclusive purpose of providing benefits to participants and their beneficiaries," as required by the Employee Retirement Income Security Act (ERISA), and managing the fund for the benefit of the corporation or management.

Outside money managers likewise face severe conflicts of interest. Corporate managers can and do pressure outside money managers to vote for management's proposals and to help further management's interests. For example, management may threaten to change banks unless the bank votes the shares it holds in a fiduciary capacity for management. Management may similarly threaten the corporation's insurance company. The pressure may be very crude or more subtle.

Structurally, the choice facing any money manager, public or private, in house or outside, is the same as the choice facing the entrepreneurs discussed earlier: the money manager must consider the benefits of acting in the interests of the beneficiaries and the costs of doing so. These costs include both the direct costs of providing the collective good (the cost of monitoring and organizing other shareholders) and the indirect costs of alienating corporate management, the people who allocate funds among outside managers. Whether it is rational for the money manager to provide the collective good will depend on the relative costs and benefits, including the benefits from alternative courses of action. Given the pressures from corporate managers, the question becomes whether money managers have sufficient positive incentives to act in shareholder's interest.

### 2.   The Collective Action Problem Repeated?

#### a.   Economic Incentives

In addition to conflicts of interests, other factors interfere with alignment of the interest of money managers and beneficiaries. The easiest problem to solve may be the collective action problem. If one assumes that money managers or a subset of money managers are collectively better off when corporate management is disciplined, but that, because of the costs and alternatives outlined above, it is not rational for any individual money manager to assume the burden of disciplining, then the collective action problem reemerges and surmounting the problem will become easier as concentration of shareholding increases.

But this assumes that discipline will be in the collective interest of money managers. Under what circumstance will that be true? When does rational apathy among money managers lead to a collective action problem, that is, a situation where, although it is irrational for any individual money manager to provide the collective good, the money managers as a group would be better off if the good were provided?

The short answer is that there are precious few incentives for money managers to act in the interests of their principals. Because of this divergence between the interests of money managers and the interest of their principals, one cannot assume that because improving corporate governance may increase the value of the managed portfolios, improving corporate governance will be in the interests of the money managers. Consider widely diversified and passive (indexed) money managers as paradigm cases. Such money managers are critically important for several reasons. First, most institutional investors are widely diversified. Second, the enormous and increasing evidence that portfolio managers rarely outperform the market has driven more and more assets into passive (indexed) portfolios. Finally, the large public funds that have been particularly prominent in corporate governance matters are largely indexed.

While an increase in discipline may increase the value of the widely diversified and indexed portfolio, and thus benefit the money managers' principals, it is not at all clear that discipline is a collective good for the managers of such a portfolio. To the extent that money managers are evaluated in comparison to other managers and to market indices, such money managers will have no selective incentives to engage in actions that improve the performance of widely diversified funds across the board. A change that benefits all will benefit none.

The potential divergence of the interests of money managers and their principles—a new version of the classic agency problem—is crucial to understanding the potential for institutional shareholder activism. In a provocative article advocating that institutional investors identify and elect professional directors [discussed in Chapter 15], Ronald Gilson and Reinier Kraakman argue that it is in the interest of the passive (indexed) portfolio manager to adopt an active corporate governance strategy. The premise of their argument is that diversified institutional shareholders will benefit from an across the board improvement in the quality of corporate governance because it will increase the value of their portfolios as a whole. But in making that assertion, Gilson and Kraakman ignore the potential divergence of interest between passive portfolio managers and the beneficiaries of the funds they manage. Although adopting a corporate governance strategy may be in the interest of the beneficiaries, Gilson and Kraakman provide no argument for concluding that adopting such a policy will be in the interests of the money managers themselves (on whom they depend). In fact, such a strategy seems unlikely to help passive (indexed) portfolio managers improve their standing in comparison to peers.

Indeed, passive portfolio managers have significant incentives *not* to adopt such a strategy. Not only do they face the conflicts of interest discussed above, they also confront a second, less obvious disincentive. In the competition among passive (indexed) portfolio managers, the principal way to improve performance is to cut costs. The key to competition among indexed fund managers is to be the lowest cost producer because, by hypothesis, everyone produces the same gross gain or loss. But corporate governance activities, to be effective, are costly.

Discipline will be a collective good for money managers when there are selective incentives. For managers who are not widely diversified, typically outside money managers, improved discipline and performance of the firms in their portfolios may selectively improve their performance, relative to competitors who do not hold the stock. This account would suggest that such money managers may face a collective action problem analogous to that faced by shareholders, a problem that might be surmounted if the concentration of shareholdings increases. But several problems confront this account of shareholder activism. First, such money managers are subject to the greatest amount of pressure from client corporations and prospective clients to vote with management. Second, the selective incentive for money widely held by money managers, namely in the large, publicly traded firms in which institutional activism has been greatest. Finally, the leading institutional activists are largely indexed. For these reasons, this account cannot provide the full story.

If the collective benefit from improved corporate performance is unlikely to explain the distribution of shareholder activism across firms, then what does? It may be that the private benefits from shareholder activism, benefits that may be unrelated to improved corporate performance but that may increase as the prominence of the target increases, better explain the focus of shareholder activism. That is, the actual pattern of shareholder activism may be more consistent with the political entrepreneur account.

In addition, certain forms of discipline may be considered tests of a money manager's loyalty, and therefore passing such tests will be in the manager's individual interests. Certain choices may be so clearly in the interests of beneficiaries that a failure to act by money managers would be viewed as shirking, incompetence, or betrayal. But note that in this situation discipline is not in the collective interests of money managers, but is simply a result of competition among money managers. Indeed, not disciplining is the collective good that cannot always be achieved.

### Roberta Romano, *Public Pension Fund Activism in Corporate Governance Reconsidered*
93 Col. L. Rev. 795, 796–852 (1993).

This Article seeks to add a dose of realism to the debate over shareholder activism in corporate governance by underscoring what was once widely recognized in the literature but of late has been overlooked: public pension funds face distinctive investment conflicts that limit the benefits of their activism. Public fund managers must navigate carefully around the shoals of considerable political pressure to temper investment policies with local considerations, such as fostering in-state employment, which are not aimed at maximizing the value of their portfolios' assets. This tension is not an isolated phenomenon. Much of the activity of states in what is referred to as economic development—

providing tax concessions or direct payments to in-state businesses—is in response to similar concerns. * * *

The hypothesized conflict that prevents private funds from opposing incumbent management is consequently not unique to that sector: corporate managers who threaten private fund managers or their employers with loss of business as the price of opposition can just as effectively threaten public funds with economic loss through, for example, local plant closings. Such pressure is, however, likely to be geographically constrained compared to that created by private sector financial relationships, because state officials are most concerned with effects on local labor markets. * * *

Public funds have, in fact, been more active than other institutional investors in corporate governance over the past few years. * * * But as public funds increase their activism and that activism affects the interests of politically organized groups, such as unions and corporate managers, political pressure on these funds will increase significantly. * * *

* * * [S]tate statutes fix the composition of public pension fund boards. Designated board members typically fall into one of three categories: gubernatorial appointees; representatives elected by fund beneficiaries; and individuals named by virtue of their office. The designation of employer executives (state officials) as fund trustees is not unique to public pension plans—trustees of private plans are typically officers of the employer-sponsor. It does, however, raise potentially serious conflict of interest problems, as trustees have dual roles, representing employers as well as employees. The political affiliation of a significant number of fund trustees render public pension funds especially vulnerable to pressure by other state officials. This vulnerability is exacerbated by the magnitude of fund holdings. Particularly in times of fiscal difficulty, fund assets are an inviting target for state officials seeking new sources of financing for local projects. There are numerous examples of governors pressuring public pension funds to use their assets to assist distressed local entities, both public and private.

* * *

[C]ontroversies over the organization of the California and New York pension fund board suggest that board composition makes a difference for fund investment and voting policies. Given that many public fund board members are politicians or political appointees, investment and voting decisions may well be imbued with non-portfolio value-maximizing considerations even when there is no observable political pressure from other state officials. In order to determine whether this is so one must examine whether fund performance varies significantly with board composition. In particular, do funds with a higher proportion of appointed and ex officio board members perform more poorly than those with less politicized board structures?

Board members who are elected by plan participants and are themselves fund beneficiaries are likely to be less susceptible to political influence or pressure because their personal retirement funds are at stake and their positions do not depend on the good graces of state officials. This hypothesis draws support from research on the incentive alignment problems caused by the separation of ownership and control in the modern corporation. Studies have found that corporate performance is positively correlated with the proportion of equity owned by management. Elected board members, as participants in a fund's retirement plan, have a strong interest in plan performance, as do corporate managers who hold stock in their firms. In addition, in some states, pension fund earnings in excess of actuarial requirements can be used to provide cost-of-living adjustments to retirees. The incentives of elected members to ensure that the board follows value-maximizing investment strategies are even greater in such states.

Appointed and ex officio members do not have similar financial incentives, and, although their reputations will be harmed if a plan experiences financial difficulty on their watch, the effect of social investments on plan performance may not be observed until several years later, when board membership has turned over. Unlike publicly traded corporations, for which low stock prices signal poor management decisions, there is no capital market monitoring public pension plan boards' decisions that could inform fund beneficiaries of poor investments and thereby mitigate the intertemporal mismatching of board members' incentives.

There is an important caveat to applying the corporate manager-owner analogy to public pension fund board members. Public employee pensions are government liabilities set by employment contract, and are independent of plan assets. If a plan's assets are insufficient to meet retiree claims, the state's annual contributions will be used entirely to pay current expenses rather than to increase plan assets through investment. Accordingly, even the more political board members have some interest in the growth of fund assets through investments because increased portfolio earnings will reduce required annual contributions. But again, the mismatching of the timing of investment returns and board tenure weakens these members' incentives.

The composition of public fund boards may also explain why public funds are more active in corporate governance than private funds even if private fund managers lack conflicts of interest involving other business relations with issuers. Public funds are frequently managed by individuals with aspirations to higher political office whose reputations can be enhanced by populist crusading against corporate management. * * * Private fund managers do not obtain such personal professional benefits from corporate governance activism. In addition, on-the-job consumption benefits figure more importantly for financial managers in the public sector, where financial compensation is lower than in the private sector. The prototypical free rider problem of corporate governance activities— that only the activist bears the costs of activism while all of the firm's investors receive the benefits—could therefore be mitigated for public funds more readily than for private funds because public funds are more likely to be managed by political entrepreneurs, who benefit personally from such visible activity.

\* \* \*

There is little evidence that public and private fund managers differentially support corporate management in proxy voting. In the vast majority of cases, especially matters touching upon corporate control, both groups of investors appear to follow the same voting strategy. Of course, these data do not address recent gubernatorial efforts to interfere in the internal organization of the New York and California state pension funds. These events indicate that, as public funds become increasingly active in corporate governance, they will experience increased political pressure on both voting and investment decisions. This pressure will produce non-value-maximizing decisions at odds with the interest of other investors. This tendency suggests that shareholder activism by public pension funds will not be able to replace an active market in corporate control as the most potent disciplining force for aligning managers' incentives with shareholders' interests.

———

During the late 1980s and early 1990s, a number of public pension funds and TIAA–CREF, the largest private pension fund, attempted to pressure the managers of many leading corporations to improve corporate performance, reorganize their boards, and remove anti-takeover devices. Some econometric studies of such "public" monitoring found it had no significant effect on shareholder wealth. *See* Stuart L. Gillian & Laura T. Starks, *Relationship Investing and Shareholder Activism by Institutional Investors* (Mimeo. 1995); Jonathan Karpoff, Paul Malatesta & Ralph Walkling, *Corporate governance and shareholder initiatives: Empirical evidence*, 42 J. Fin Econ. 365 (1996); S. Wahal, *Public pension fund activism and firm performance*, 31 J. Fin & Quant. Anal. 1 (1996). Others found abnormal positive returns. *See* M. Smith, *Shareholder Activism by Institutional Investors: Evidence From CalPERS*, 51 J. Fin. Econ. 227 (1996); *cf.* D.Strickland, K. Wiles & M. Zenner, *A requiem for the USA: Is small shareholder monitoring effective?*, 40 J. Fin. Econ. 319 (1996).

Two other econometric studies found positive payoffs associated with "private" monitoring by institutional investors. One focused on efforts by members of the Council of Institutional Investors to bring about improvements in the performance and governance structure of firms that had been performing poorly. It found "substantial evidence that firms on Council of Institutional Investors focus lists outperformed the market and reasonable comparison group firms in the 1991–94 period" and that this was "consistent with the view that coordinated institutional shareholder activism is effective." Tim C. Opler & Jonathan Sokobin, *Does Coordinated Institutional Shareholder Activism Work? An Analysis of the Activities of the Council of Institutional Investors* (Working paper 1997).

The second analyzed correspondence concerning governance issues between TIAA–CREF and 45 portfolio companies. It found that TIAA–CREF was able to reach agreement with targeted companies on issues it raised more than 95% of the time, that in more than 70% of the cases agreement was reached without shareholders ever being asked to vote on the issue, and that target companies acted to comply with these more than 85% agreements of these agreements. The study also found statistically significant abnormal negative returns associated with governance agreements directed at increasing the diversity of the targets' board of directors, statistically significant abnormal positive returns associated with agreements directed at limiting the use of blank check preferred stock as an antitakeover device, and no statistically significant abnormal returns associated at agreements directed at instituting confidential voting by shareholders. Willard T. Carleton, James M. Nelson & Michael S. Weisbach, *The Influence of Institutions on Corporate Governance Through Private Negotiations: Evidence from TIAA–CREF* (___ J. Fin. ___ (forthcoming 1998).

Qualitative social scientists also have investigated institutional investors' relationships with corporate managers. William M. O'Barr & John Conley, Fortune and Folly: the Wealth and Power of Institutional Investing (1992), found that managers of both public and private pension funds were extremely reluctant to become involved in the governance of portfolio companies. In contrast, Michael Useem, Investor Capitalism: How Money managers are Changing the Face of Corporate America (1996), concluded that corporate managers are effectively constrained by institutional investors. Both studies have been criticized by other scholars suspicious of their methodology. One such review also considers the future of institutional investor activism.

John C. Coffee, Jr., *The Folklore of Investor Capitalism*
95 Mich. L. Rev. 1970, 1986–88 (1997).

What will be the future course of investor-manager relations? * * *

The future is undoubtedly contingent, but it is contingent on factors that can to a considerable extent be specified. Among these factors are the following:

1. *Will New Institutional Catalysts Emerge?* More than on any other single factor, the future of institutional activism hinges on coalition formation. Lone Rangers must learn to join the team. Yet, it is also clear that institutions are distrustful of long-term political alliances (probably for good reason) and will not delegate power outside their organization, except on a very short-term, specific basis. Thus, potential bridging organizations, such as the Council of Institutional Investors, have remained weak by design. But can other institutions evolve to fill such a specific, coalition-building role on a case-by-case basis? Some logical candidates for this brokering role already exist. For example, Institutional Shareholder Services Inc. ("ISS") and the Investor Respon-

sibility Research Center ("IRRC") are advisory firms that provide voting advice. * * * But proxy advisory firms do not themselves start proxy contests or put issues on the corporation's agenda. Here, the more significant prototype may be a firm like LENS, an investment advisor that specifically targets underperforming firms and then seeks to improve their management through activist interventions. This approach has promise, but encounters cultural resistance within the institutional investor community. Their success (or lack thereof) may thus prove to be the best measure of the maturity of institutional activism as an economic movement.

2. *Will the Institutionalization of the Market Increase or Wane?* The growth of institutional investors has been fueled by demographics: retirement savings have flooded into pension and mutual funds, expanding them like accordions, as the baby boom generation of the 1950s has begun to near retirement age. Predictably, this dynamic will reverse itself in due course, as the smaller population in the next generation pumps less funds into these same financial institutions. This factor could be offset if small investors learn to prefer mutual funds to self-investing, but the net balance is cloudy.

3. *Will New Types of Institutional Investors or Retirement Savings Vehicles Appear?* The future of the pension fund is not assured. Corporations may shift to 401(k) savings plans, thereby avoiding risks and costs to themselves (including potential liability for underfunding), while shifting risk to the individual employee. A by-product of this transition could be shrinkage of the traditional pension plan and a resurgence in individual shareholdings through 401(k) plans. Again, the net impact on institutionalization is uncertain, because many of these assets may move to the effective control of the major mutual fund families that manage 401(k) plans.

Overshadowing even this uncertainty is the possible privatization of Social Security. If the assets of Social Security are even partially invested in the stock market, a new type of institutional investor could emerge; possibly, even the federal government could emerge to assume a role and stance equivalent to that of a state public pension fund.

4. *Can Coordination Costs be Reduced?* The logic of collective action suggests that the development of more formalized networks among institutional investors represents the most efficient way to economize on the transaction costs of corporate governance. But the slow progress to date on this score suggests that the different categories of institutional investors do not really want to agree on much. Little wonder. Union pension plans, corporate pension plans, and day-trading mutual funds share little in common. Nonetheless, the most logical scenario is for the development of umbrella groups that do not attempt to be so comprehensive or inclusive as to wind-up being stalemated.

5. *Will a Stock Price "Correction" Change Institutional Behavior?* Since the more aggressive confrontations of 1992 and 1993, there has been a recent relative honeymoon between institutions and manage-

ments. Again, this is no surprise, because the stock market has soared to record, stratospheric levels. If what went up comes down, however, institutions may themselves face unprecedented pressures, particularly in the case of mutual funds where shareholders can exit quickly (if not costlessly).

## E.　SHAREHOLDER PROPOSALS

### PROBLEM

### UNIVERSAL NETWARE, INC.—PART II

### A

UNI maintains three manufacturing plants. One, near Lima, Ohio, employs 1,000 people and accounts for a significant portion of that community's payroll. The output of that plant accounts for less than 2% of UNI's revenues and profits. Press reports suggest that, as a cost-saving measure, UNI is likely to close at least that plant, and perhaps all three, in the near future and contract to purchase the components they produce from suppliers in Korea or the Philippines.

Prior to last year's annual shareholder meeting, Students For Social Justice (SFSJ), a student organization at nearby State University, purchased 100 shares of UNI stock that now is trading at $32 per share. SFSJ wants to submit a shareholder proposal for inclusion in UNI's proxy statement for this year's annual meeting. It has prepared a draft resolution reading as follows:

> RESOLVED, that the bylaws be amended to add the following provision: The corporation shall not substantially discontinue the use of any significant business or plant facility unless (1) the company gives one year's notice in writing to the affected employees and community representatives of the extent of the proposed closing or reduction, (2) a hearing is conducted at which an opportunity is provided to employees and citizens of the affected communities to express their views on any aspect of the proposed closing or reduction and (3) the Board of Directors is furnished with a written report of a detailed study on the economic, environmental and social consequences of the proposed action upon the affected community. Such report shall become a record of the Corporation and copies shall be made available to shareholders upon payment of reasonable costs.

SFSJ also has prepared the following draft supporting statement:

> The power to discontinue a plant or other facility carries with it the power to visit major economic, environmental and social consequences upon a particular community—consequences that may be calamitous. The proposed new bylaw simply requires the Board of Directors to be aware of these consequences before the Corporation acts on such matters, which are neither routine nor trivial, and enables the owners of the Corporation to acquire, in addition to

already available financial information, some knowledge concerning the social impact of their company's activities. The Company's disregard for the welfare of its workers necessitates revised procedures in making these far-reaching decisions.

The bylaw would impose requirements upon the Corporation that are similar to but far less extensive than those calling upon federal agencies to furnish environmental impact statements before undertaking certain projects, and for much the same reasons. Application of the bylaw is limited to actions upon "significant" facilities so as to avoid harassment of the company. Implementation and interpretation will devolve upon the Board, which must decide the issue in good faith.

SFSJ has asked your advice as to whether the SEC is likely to require UNI management to include the proposal in its proxy statement. SFSJ also has asked you if there are any changes it should make in its proposal or supporting statement to improve the prospects that UNI will be required to include the proposal in its proxy statement.

How do you respond to these questions?

B

The Columbia Employees Retirement Fund has decided not to solicit proxies in opposition to the UNI stock option repricing plan (see Part I). Instead, CERF is considering submitting the following proposal to UNI for inclusion in the UNI proxy statement for the meeting at which the voting plan will be considered:

RESOLVED, that the shareholders of Universal NetWare, Inc. hereby amend the bylaws of Universal NetWare, Inc., in accordance with the laws of the State of Delaware and the Certificate of Incorporation of Universal NetWare, Inc., by adding the following:

§ ____.____ *Stock Option Plans*. (a) The board of directors shall not authorize the issuance of any option to purchase stock of the corporation to any officer or employee of the corporation or any of its subsidiary corporations, whether pursuant to a stock option plan or otherwise, unless (1) the board of directors has informed the corporation's shareholders of all material facts relating to such stock option or stock option plan and (2) the holders of a majority of the corporation's stock have approved such stock option or stock option plan.

(b) The board of directors shall not reduce the price at which any officer or employee of the corporation or any of its subsidiary corporations may purchase stock of the corporation, pursuant to any outstanding stock option, unless (1) the board of directors has informed the corporation's shareholders of all material facts relating to such proposed repricing and (2) the holders of a majority of the corporation's stock have approved the repricing of such stock option or options.

[Supporting statement omitted]

May UNI management exclude the proposal from the proxy statement?

## 1. EVOLUTION OF THE SHAREHOLDER PROPOSAL RULE

The power that shareholders of a publicly-held corporation theoretically possess to secure corporate action by adopting a resolution at the annual meeting of shareholders is, by itself, illusory. A tiny fraction of the shareholders actually attend the meeting. Practically all the shares are represented by proxy, and state law and the SEC proxy rules either bind the proxy holders to vote in a prescribed way or give the proxy holders complete discretion.

What has happened, as we have already noted, is that the proxy soliciting process has become the surrogate for the meeting. As a result, a shareholder who wants to have a resolution adopted at a shareholders' meeting would, absent Rule 14a–8, be required to solicit proxies in advance and comply with the other requirements described in Section C. If the shareholder wants to take control of the company, this effort might be cost justified. But suppose she simply wants to amend the by-laws to require that the board of directors consist of a majority of independent directors or wants the company to cease doing business with a country that she believes oppresses human rights. In the latter case, in particular, her principal goal may be to focus public attention on an issue, spark some debate and thereby force the corporation to reconsider how and where it is doing business. She will derive no financial benefit from passage of the resolution, and the expense of her own solicitation of proxies cannot be cost justified. Nevertheless, as we saw in Chapter 12, if the matter is appropriate for shareholder action, the shareholder has a right to present the proposal at the meeting. She also may have the right to have the resolution appear in the proxy statement.

In 1938, the SEC took the position that the shareholder had such a right under Section 14(a) of the Securities Exchange Act of 1934, and in 1942 it formalized its views by adopting the first version of the shareholder proposal rule that is now Rule 14a–8. As originally adopted, the rule required management to include in its proxy statement a shareholder proposal that was going to be introduced at the meeting, so long as the proposal was a "proper subject for action by security holders." The SEC considered proposals that dealt with general political, social or economic matters not to be proper subjects for action by shareholders.

The legal basis for the SEC's position is Rule 14a–9, the anti-fraud provision of the proxy rules, which the SEC has interpreted to ensure that the proxy statement accurately reflects all the issues that will properly arise at the meeting. As one court stated:

[S]ince a shareholder may present a proposal at the annual meeting regardless of whether the proposal is included in a proxy solicitation, the corporate circulation of proxy materials which fail to make reference to a shareholder's intention to present a proper proposal at the annual meeting renders the solicitation inherently misleading.

*New York City Employees' Retirement System v. American Brands, Inc.*, 634 F.Supp. 1382, 1386 (S.D.N.Y.1986).

An early case, *S.E.C. v. Transamerica Corp.*, 163 F.2d 511 (3d Cir.1947), provided the standard by which the propriety of the subject matter is to be determined. In *Transamerica*, a shareholder submitted several proposals for inclusion in the company's proxy statement. One proposal would have resulted in shareholder election of the independent public auditors of the company's financial statements; another would have amended the bylaws with respect to the procedure for bylaw amendment. A third resolution would have required the corporation to send a report of the annual meeting to the shareholders. The company excluded all the proposals on the ground that the rule did not require their inclusion; the SEC then sought to enjoin the company's proxy solicitation.

The court agreed with the SEC that a "proper subject" is one that a shareholder may properly bring to a vote under the law of a company's state of incorporation and ruled that all three proposals were properly includible in Transamerica's proxy materials. The election of auditors was clearly within the shareholders' concern since the corporation is run for their benefit, and the financial condition (as shown in the financial statements) is critical to the corporation. The amendment to the bylaws was proper because Delaware law specifically allows shareholders to amend the bylaws. The only basis for exclusion was a provision in the company's own bylaws that required notice of the proposed amendment be contained in the notice of the annual meeting; the court held this self-imposed restriction could not diminish the shareholders' power under state law. The report of the meeting was proper because, the court said, "we can perceive no logical basis for concluding that it is not a proper subject for action by the security holders." *Id.* at 517. In the view of both the court and the SEC, the shareholder proposal rule is a federal mechanism to enhance a state created shareholder right.

The shareholder movement began in the 1930s with an emphasis on shareholder democracy. Proposals often requested that corporations institute cumulative voting or send post-meeting reports to all shareholders. In 1970, the focus of shareholder activism changed dramatically. The new proponents were shareholders more concerned with issues of corporate social responsibility than with shareholder democracy. These shareholders offered proposals relating to the environmental impact of corporate activity, race and sex discrimination, and the conduct of business in parts of the world where human rights were not being respected. The first major effort in this respect was by a group called the Project on Corporate Responsibility, which created Campaign GM in 1970.

Campaign GM sought approval by General Motors (GM) shareholders of several resolutions, the most important of which would have created a Shareholder Committee for Corporate Responsibility to examine GM's social performance and its impact in several designated areas of conduct. The Project also urged GM to elect its first black and first woman to the board of directors. The proposal for a shareholder committee was supported by 2.73% of the votes cast at the meeting. Despite the low vote, within months after the annual meeting, GM's board of directors created a Public Policy Committee and elected its first black member, Rev. Leon Sullivan. About a year later, it elected its first woman member. *See* Donald E. Schwartz, *The Public–Interest Proxy Contest: Reflections on Campaign GM*, 69 Mich.L.Rev. 419 (1971).

Shareholder activists viewed Campaign GM as a success because it demonstrated that a skillful use of publicity could lead to substantive changes in the corporate system even though the proposals themselves were defeated. As a result, many other groups began using shareholder proposals to advance their programs. Church groups, for example, became the most active shareholder proponents and launched a campaign to eliminate or alter corporate presence in South Africa. The so-called Sullivan Principles, developed by Rev. Leon Sullivan, received considerable impetus from shareholder resolutions offered at scores of meetings. Other proponents raised numerous public policy issues, including opposition to the Arab boycott of Israel, national defense, foreign policy, religious discrimination in Northern Ireland and nuclear power. *See* Donald E. Schwartz, *Toward New Corporate Goals: Co–Existence with Society*, 60 Geo.L.J. 57 (1971). Other commentators attacked the use of shareholder proposals to advance social causes, beginning with Henry G. Manne, *Shareholder Social Proposals Viewed by an Opponent*, 24 Stan. L.Rev. 481 (1972).

In the 1980s, a new group of proponents emerged—institutional investors interested in issues of corporate governance. Institutions (as well as individuals and "shareholder rights organizations") began to submit proposals on a variety of governance issues, ranging from promoting diversity on corporate boards of directors to limiting corporations' defenses to uninvited takeover bids. Perhaps more significantly, substantial numbers of takeover-related resolutions began to win the support of a majority of the votes cast a corporations' annual meetings. The number of resolutions that won majority votes increased from 22 in 1995 to 23 in 1996 and to 34 in the first nine months of 1997. *See Record Number of Resolutions Win Majority Votes*, 8 IRRC Corporate Governance Highlights 129 (10/24/97). Most of the resolutions that won majority support asked companies to redeem poison pills, requested that they make poison pills subject to shareholder approval, or suggested that charter provisions establishing classified boards of directors be repealed. Most of the companies whose shareholders adopted these resolutions refused to take the actions requested. *Id.*

## 2. THE RULE IN OPERATION

Paragraph 14a–8(c) contains 13 grounds for excluding a shareholder proposal. These may be classified into eight reasons for omission based upon the proposal itself and five reasons designed to prevent abuse of the shareholder proposal process. *See* Donald E. Schwartz & Elliott J. Weiss, *An Assessment of the SEC Shareholder Proposal Rule*, 65 GEO.L.J. 635, 658 (1977). The most important grounds for exclusion are those in subparagraphs (c)(1), (5) and (7), relating to the propriety of the proposal under state law and the economic significance of the proposal. The SEC has amended the rule on several occasions, and the SEC releases in connection with these amendments constitute their principal legislative history. *See e.g.*, Securities Exchange Act Rel. No. 12999 (Nov. 22, 1976), Securities Exchange Act Rel. No. 19135 (Oct. 14, 1982) (proposing amendments) and Securities Exchange Act Rel. No. 20091 (Aug. 16, 1983). As this book goes to press, the SEC is considering another revision that would restate the Rule in a "plain English" question-and-answer format and revise several of the grounds on which a proposal can be omitted. *See* Securities Exchange Act Rel. No. 34–39093 (Sept. 19, 1997).

### a.  *The Interpretative Process*

The flesh on the bones of Rule 14a–8 is provided primarily through interpretations by the staff of the Division of Corporation Finance of the SEC. The staff furnishes these interpretations in response to company inquiries asking whether it will recommend that the Commission take any enforcement action if the company omits a shareholder proposal from its proxy statement. Because the inquiries deal with possible Commission enforcement action, the staff responses are known as "no-action" letters.

Each year, the staff issues more than 300 no-action letters relating to Rule 14a–8. On rare occasions, the Commission itself makes the substantive interpretation, but the vast majority of interpretations are issued by the staff with no formal Commission review. The letters are available at the SEC's offices in Washington or through computer or other research services. Selected letters are also identified or printed in looseleaf services. The entire body of no-action letters has become the common law of Rule 14a–8.

The process by which a no-action letter is issued most closely resembles a ritual dance in which each party's steps can be clearly predicted. The shareholder sends a letter to the company which may be anything from a simple request that a proposal be included to an elaborate presentation with a legal opinion in support of inclusion, depending upon the sophistication and experience of the proponent. The company then sends a letter to the SEC advising of its intent to omit the proposal, accompanied either by an opinion of counsel stating the grounds on which the proposal can be excluded. This opinion often includes a detailed analysis of past staff no-action letters on the same or related issues; it strongly resembles a traditional brief in litigation in which counsel analyzes and distinguishes existing case law. In some cases, the proponent will submit a reply which may or may not include a contrary legal opinion. When all the papers have been submitted, the staff responds. If the staff concludes that the proposal can be omitted, it advises the company that "[T]here appears to be some basis for your view that the proposal may be excluded pursuant to Rule 14a–8(c) [appropriate subparagraph number]," but does not state what that basis is. If the staff concludes that the proposal cannot be omitted, it states that "the Division is unable to concur in your view that the proposal may be excluded." In such a case, the staff briefly explains the basis for its position.

Sometimes the staff finds a middle ground, which has the effect of helping shareholders who may not be skilled in the arcane art of drafting proposals. This middle ground arises most often when the substance of the proposal may be proper but the form of the proposal renders it excludable. For example, where a proposal framed as a mandate would be a proper subject for shareholder action under state law if it was framed as a recommendation, the staff will concur that there is "some basis" for exclusion because of the form of the proposal but will note that the defect can be cured. The staff also will advise that if the proponent submits an appropriately revised proposal, the staff will not concur in the omission of the proposal from the company's proxy statement.

The SEC has taken the position that these letters do not constitute " 'rulings' or 'decisions' on shareholder proposals management indicates it intends to omit, and [that] they do not adjudicate the merits of management's posture concerning such a proposal." Securities Exchange Act Rel. No. 12599 (July 7, 1976). Courts have agreed. They have held that a SEC no action letter does not fix any legal relationship or constitute final order for purposes of the Administrative Procedure Act. As a consequence, a shareholder aggrieved by a staff or Commission decision to take no action against a company that omits a proposal cannot sue the SEC. *See Amalgamated Clothing & Textile Workers Union v. SEC*, 15 F.3d 254, 257 (2d Cir.1994). She must, instead, sue the company in federal district court. *Id*.

Private enforcement of Rule 14a–8 is available to shareholders who wish to challenge the omission of a proposal. *Roosevelt v. E.I. Du Pont de Nemours & Co.*, 958 F.2d 416 (D.C.Cir.1992), held that a shareholder had an implied private right of action under Rule 14a–8 to maintain a suit against the company for injunctive relief. The court reasoned that Section 14(a) supports such a right of action no less than it supports an action for damages (*see J.I. Case Co. v. Borak*, Chapter 18). Moreover, the court found that it would be demonstrably inequitable to deny the right to sue, and that such a denial "would upset longstanding administrative arrangements and shareholder expectations." *Id*. at 421.

The SEC, of course, has the power to seek an injunction to compel a company to include a shareholder proposal in its proxy statement. See *Transamerica*, supra. However, since the time of *Transamerica*, companies uniformly have followed the practice of acquiescing to the SEC staff's rulings that a proposal cannot be omitted, rather than risking the potential cost and delay involved in litigating that issue.

### b.  *Substantive Grounds for Omission*

Most controversy about shareholder proposals relates to three subsections of Rule 14a–8(c): subsection (c)(1), which allows a corporation to omit a proposal that is not a "proper subject for action by security holders"; subsection (c)(7), which allows a corporation to omit a proposal that involves "ordinary business operations"; and subsection (c)(5), which allows a corporation to omit a proposal that relates to operations that do not meet a minimum economic test *and* are "not otherwise significantly related" to the company's business.

Interpretation of (c)(1) and (c)(7) involves application of the law of the issuer's state of incorporation and the governance concepts we studied in Chapter 12. As we saw there, state law provides that the business and affairs of a corporation are to be managed by, or under the direction of, the board of directors. State law limits shareholders' role to matters for which the statute requires a shareholder vote, issues on which management solicits shareholders' vote, or matters that shareholders properly can raise at a shareholders' meeting.

When analyzed in relation to Rule 14a–8, these governance concepts are easy to state and difficult to apply. The question of what is a "proper subject" is to be decided under state law but there is very little state law on which to base a decision. The principal case on this subject is *Auer v. Dressel*, in which the issue was whether the president of a company was required to call a shareholders' meeting that had been demanded by a shareholder who held sufficient stock to satisfy the statutory requirement. The corporation claimed that it was not obligated to call the meeting because the resolution to be considered made a recommendation to the board concerning a matter within its authority—rehiring the president. The court held that the meeting had to be called, even if the shareholders' vote did not bind the board of directors to act, because the matter to be voted on were sufficiently significant. Even a recommendation would put the directors on notice that they might be removed if they did not act in accordance with the shareholders' wishes.

*Auer* provides the conceptual underpinning for determinations under both (c)(1) and (c)(7). Under (c)(1), as it has been interpreted in recent years, the form of the resolution is significant. If a resolution is mandatory and addresses a matter concerning which shareholders do not have authority to bind the directors or the corporation, it can be omitted as inconsistent with state law. If the resolution is cast as a recommendation, the Note to (c)(1) makes clear that it may be a "proper subject" under state law. In such a case, the question of excludability will turn on the subject matter of the proposal. State law contemplates that "ordinary business" decisions will be made by the company's management. Thus a resolution that deals with "ordinary business" can be excluded under subsection (c)(7) and, inferentially, under the broader rubric of (c)(1). If, on the other hand, a precatory resolution does not deal with "ordinary business," a shareholder has the right to present it at the meeting and the company cannot omit it under either subsection. The antithesis of "ordinary business" appears to be "public policy;" if a proposal that otherwise might be considered to involve "ordinary business" *also* implicates questions of public policy, it cannot be excluded under (c)(7).

A similar methodology is used in determining whether a proposal can be omitted under (c)(5). The principal purpose of (c)(5) is to exclude proposals whose economic significance to the corporation would be *de minimis*; the measuring rod is 5% of sales, assets or earnings. Some proposals, however, may be significant even though they do not meet the statistical test, either because they relate to corporate structure (e.g., cumulative voting) or because they raise public policy issues that relate directly to the corporation's business. Such proposals cannot be excluded under (c)(5). In this sense, the "significantly related" standard set forth in (c)(5) is analytically very similar to the "ordinary business" standard of (c)(7).

As the following materials illustrate, despite the SEC's contention that its no action letters do not constitute "rulings," the law interpreting subsections (c)(1), (c)(5) and (c)(7) is an amalgam of such letters and judicial decisions.

## AMALGAMATED CLOTHING AND TEXTILE WORKERS UNION v. WAL–MART STORES, INC.

821 F.Supp. 877 (S.D.N.Y.1993).

WOOD, DISTRICT JUDGE.

Plaintiffs, Wal–Mart shareholders, sought to enjoin the company from omitting their Proposal from proxy solicitation material the company plans to distribute in advance of Wal–Mart's June 4, 1993 annual meeting. Plaintiffs seek to submit to a shareholder vote a request for Wal–Mart's directors to prepare and distribute reports about Wal–Mart's equal employment opportunity ("EEO") and affirmative action policies, programs and data, along with a description of Wal–Mart's efforts to 1) publicize its EEO policies to suppliers, and 2) purchase goods and services from minority-and female-owned suppliers. Plaintiffs allege that Wal–Mart's omission of their proposal violates Securities and Exchange Commission ("SEC" or "Commission") Rule 14a–8.

Wal–Mart moves to dismiss the Amended Complaint. Wal–Mart asserts that it may exclude the proposal because it "deals with a matter relating to the conduct of [Wal–Mart's] ordinary business operations," an excludable category under Rule 14a–8(c)(7). * * *.

### I. BACKGROUND

Plaintiffs Amalgamated Clothing and Textile Workers Union ("ACTWU") is a labor union representing approximately 250,000 workers internationally. Plaintiffs National Council of Churches of Christ in the U.S.A., Unitarian Universalist Association and Literary Society of Saint

Catherine of Sienna are religious organizations, which invest in socially responsible corporations as part of their religious missions. Each plaintiff believes that "issues concerning equal employment opportunity and affirmative action are important to shareholder value." Plaintiffs' stated ultimate goal is to improve Wal–Mart's EEO record and that of the discount retail store industry; to that end, they submit proposals, such as this one, to foster dialogue between plaintiffs and Wal–Mart and between plaintiffs and other shareholders. * * *

Wal–Mart operates a chain of retail stores throughout the Untied States. * * * As a Delaware corporation, Wal–Mart is subject to Delaware corporate law pertaining to the use of shareholder proxies at annual meetings and is concurrently subject to the rules adopted by the SEC, which regulate the content and solicitation of proxies.

* * * [Plaintiffs'] Proposal requests Wal–Mart's board of directors to prepare the following reports by September 1993:

> 1. A chart identifying employees according to their sex and race in each of the nine major EEOC defined job categories for 1990, 1991, 1992 listing either numbers or percentages in each category.

> 2. A summary description of Affirmative Action Programs to improve performance especially in job categories where women and minorities are under utilized and a description of major problems in meeting the company's goals and objectives in this area.

> 3. A description of steps taken to increase the number of managers who are qualified females and ethnic minorities.

> 4. A description of ways in which Wal–Mart publicizes our company's policies to merchandise suppliers and service providers to encourage forward action on their part as well.

> 5. A description of Wal–Mart's efforts to purchase goods and services from minority and female owned business enterprises.

Plaintiffs envision a brief report, that could, in their view, range from the one page analysis produced by J.C. Penney as part of its annual report to a five page internal memorandum made available to shareholders of CIGNA Corporation.

## II. DISCUSSION

### A. *Regulatory Framework*

* * *

### 3. *Proxy Solicitations*

* * *

Rule 14a–8(a) requires a company to include a shareholder's proposal in the company's proxy statement and provide shareholders with the opportunity to vote on the proposal by executing the proxy card. This ostensibly broad directive is limited by thirteen content-based exceptions. Most relevant to this case is Rule 14–8(c)(7), which permits a company to omit a shareholder proposal if "the proposal deals with a matter relating to the conduct of the ordinary business operations of the registrant." A shareholder proposal pertaining to "ordinary business operations" would be improper if raised at an annual meeting, because the law of most states (including Delaware) leaves the conduct of ordinary business operations to corporate directors and officers rather than the shareholders. See e.g., Del. Code Ann. tit. 8 § 141(a). As one court explained, "management cannot exercise its specialized talents effectively if corporate investors assert the power to dictate the minutiae of daily business decisions." *Medical Committee for Human Rights v. SEC*, 432 F.2d 659, 679 (D.C.Cir.1970), *vacated as moot*, 404 U.S. 403, 92 S.Ct. 577, 30 L.Ed.2d 560 (1972). The SEC adopted this exception to save management the cost and burden of including a proposal in proxy material that would be improper if raised by a shareholder at the annual meeting.

\* \* \*

## B. Standard for Court's Determination Whether a Proposal May Be Excluded as Pertaining to "Ordinary Business Operations"

Determining whether Wal–Mart may exclude plaintiffs' Proposal under the "ordinary business operations" exception requires the court to construe the meaning of the SEC's own rules. When a court interprets an administrative regulation, "the ultimate criterion" is the agency's interpretation of the regulation, which becomes of controlling weight unless that interpretation is "plainly erroneous or inconsistent with the regulations." Thus before deciding whether Wal–Mart may omit the Proposal on the basis of the "ordinary business operations" exception, I must first examine how the SEC interprets Rule 14a–8(c)(7).

### 1. The SEC's Interpretive Release Standard

Both the present form of Rule 14a–8, which contains the phrase "ordinary business operations," and the SEC Interpretive Release that accompanied it, were adopted after a formal notice and comment rule-making period in 1976. The 1976 Release "established the principles by which [the Commission] intended the 'ordinary business' provision of Rule 14a–8 to be interpreted." \* \* \*

The SEC issued the 1976 Interpretive Release to resolve previous interpretive difficulties over Rule 14a–8(c)(7)'s intended meaning. The Release states in pertinent part that

the term "ordinary business operations" has been deemed on occasion to include certain matters which have significant policy, economic or other implications inherent in them. For instance, a proposal that a utility company not construct a proposed nuclear power plant has in the past been considered excludable \* \* \*. In retrospect, however, it seems apparent that the economic and safety considerations attendant to nuclear power plants are of such magnitude that a determination whether to construct one is not an "ordinary" business matter. Accordingly, proposals of that nature as well as others having major implications be considered beyond the realm of an issuer's ordinary business operations, and future interpretive letters of the Commission's staff will reflect that view.

* * * Thus, *where proposals involve business matters that are mundane in nature and do not involve any substantial policy or other considerations, the subparagraph may be relied upon to omit them.*

Adoption of Amendments Relating to Proposals by Security Holders, Exchange Act Release No. 12999, (Dec. 3, 1976) ("1976 Interpretive Release") (emphasis added).[7]

### 2. Development of SEC Interpretation Through No–Action Letter Review Process

The general guidance provided to parties and the court by the 1976 Interpretive Release and state corporate law has been supplemented by the no-action letters issued by the SEC staff and the rare discretionary review of no-action letters provided by the full Commission. No-action letters can provide insight into the meaning of the term "ordinary business operations," because, unlike general interpretive releases, no-action letters address specific issues and build upon the SEC's "vast experience of daily contact with the practical workings of this rule." *Peck v. Greyhound Corp.*, 97 F.Supp. 679, 681 (S.D.N.Y.1951). However, as the SEC itself maintains, the ad hoc nature of these letters means that courts cannot place them on a precedential par with formal rulemaking or adjudication. Before turning to how the SEC has applied Rule 14a–8(c)(7) to similar proposals through numerous no-action letters, the court will, therefore, address the extent to which it must defer to positions taken in no-action letters.

### a. Deference Owed to No–Action Position

An individual no-action letter by itself is not an expression of agency interpretation to which the court must defer. *See Roosevelt* [958 F.2d] at 427 n. 19. * * *

However, although the court need not defer to an individual no-action position, courts have relied on the consistency of the SEC staff's position and reasoning on a given issue, or the lack of consistency, in determining whether a proposal that was deemed excludable by the SEC staff can in fact be omitted under Rule 14a–8(c)(7). * * *

In determining whether to defer to a position drawn from a series of no-action letters, courts must recognize that a change in SEC position

---

**7.** The law of the company's state of incorporation is also a source of authority as to which proposals relate to "ordinary business operations" under Rule 14a–8(c)(7) and which proposals are "proper subject for action by shareholders" under rule 14a–8(c)(1). However,, most states, including Delaware, have not developed the law on this issue beyond the statement that the directors and officers shall mange the business affairs of the corporation. In practice over the last half century the SEC rather than state courts have been determining whether proposals may be excluded on these bases. See Louis Loss & Joel Seligman, 4 Securities Regulation 2012 (3rd ed. 1990) (SEC staff develops a "common law" of includable proposals).

does not necessarily reveal capricious action by the agency; changes in conditions and public perceptions justify changes in the SEC's construction of the "ordinary business operations" exception. The nature of the exceptions permits, if not requires, the SEC to reevaluate earlier positions "in light of new considerations, or changing conditions which indicate that its earlier views are no longer in keeping with the objectives of Rule 14a–8." The SEC has revised its position with respect to the inclusion of proposals on a number of issues formerly excludable under Rule 14a–8(c)(7) such as plant closings, tobacco production, cigarette advertising and all forms of senior executive and director compensation. * * * Thus, an SEC departure from a prior position must be considered in light of changing public and shareholder concerns.* * *

b.  *SEC's No–Action Letter Position on Ordinary Business Operations*

Although the SEC has been dealing with proposals like plaintiffs' since the mid–1970s, its treatment of these proposals has changed over time. Prior to 1983, the SEC took the position that proposals requesting reports on EEO data and policies could not be excluded, because the determination whether a report should be issued was a matter of policy rather than ordinary business operations. In 1983, the SEC changed its interpretation of the exception and determined that the subject of the report requested, rather than the fact that the information requested was in the form of a report, would determine the proposal's excludability under the "ordinary business operations" exception.

Since 1983, the SEC has determined whether employment policy proposals must be included in proxy materials by examining whether the proposals relate to "day-to-day" employment matters and, therefore, are excludable as relating to "ordinary business operations," or whether the proposals relate to significant policy considerations and, therefore are not excludable. Day-to-day employment matters have been interpreted as including matters concerning: employee health benefits, general compensation issues not focused on senior executives, management of the workplace, employee supervision, labor-management relations, employee hiring and firing, conditions of employment and employee training and motivation. The SEC has also viewed a proposal requesting a company to hire contractors from within its service area as excludable under Rule 14a–8(c)(7).

Despite the SEC's general view that employee hiring and firing and supplier decisions are related to a company's ordinary business operations, the SEC has until recently recognized that the issues of EEO and affirmative action raise policy considerations elevating them above the excludable day-to-day issues. Thus, in 1988, the SEC staff stated, and the full Commission affirmed, that AT & T may not exclude a shareholder proposal to phase out those aspects of AT & T's affirmative action program directed toward recruiting, employing or promoting individuals from any particular racial or ethnic group. The staff stated that AT & T could not rely on the exception for "ordinary business operations" because the proposal involved "policy issues," described by the SEC staff as "the Company's affirmative action program, designed to assure equal employment opportunities for minority group members * * *."

Similarly, on February 14, 1991, the SEC took the position that a proposal requesting the publication of EEO data and the adoption of an affirmative action program and a program for purchasing from vendors controlled by women and minorities was not excludable, because it related to "general policy decisions which are beyond the conduct of the Company's day-to-day operations."

In the same vein, on March 8, 1991 the SEC reviewed a proposal that was identical to a proposal plaintiff ACTWU submitted to Wal–Mart in 1991, and contained four of the five requests included in the 1993 Proposal at issue here. The SEC took the position that although the proposal "concerns employment and other matters that involve the Company's ordinary business operations, * * * questions with respect to equal employment opportunity and affirmative action involve policy decisions beyond those personnel matters that constitute the Company's ordinary course of business."

Thus, through March 1991, the SEC's no-action letters determined that companies could not exclude proposals requesting the information requested in plaintiffs' Proposal here. On April 4, 1991, however, the full Commission appeared to shift position, and voted 3–2 to reverse the staff position stated in a no-action letter issued to Capital Cities/ABC. The proposal there requested information quite similar to that requested here in plaintiffs' 1993 Proposal, although a notable difference is that Capital Cities/ABC, the proposal requested a summary of timetables to implement affirmative action programs. The divided Commission determined that the proposal was excludable because it "involves a request for detailed information on the composition of the company's work force, employment practices and policies, and the selection of program content."

* * *

On April 10, 1992, the staff issued Wal–Mart a no-action letter with respect to plaintiffs' 1992 proposal, also relying on the rationale of *Capital Cities/ABC* * * *. Wal–Mart, thereafter, omitted plaintiffs' proposal from its 1992 proxy materials.

In October 1992 the SEC staff expressed in more sweeping terms the view that companies could exclude EEO proposals, reversing the position it took in *AT & T* in 1988 and *Dayton Hudson* in 1991. *See Cracker Barrel Old Country Stores, Inc., No–Action Letter*, 1992 WL 289095, 1992 SEC No–Act. LEXIS 984 * 43 (Oct. 13, 1992). The articulated reason for that decision was that the SEC found distinctions between policies implicating broad social issues and the conduct of day-to-day business simply too hard to draw as regards the employment of the general workforce. The shareholder proposal in *Cracker Barrel* was prompted by that company's announcement of a policy to discriminate against gay men and lesbians. The proposal asked the corporation (1) to include sexual orientation in its anti-discriminatory policy, and (2) to enforce its amended policy. The SEC staff and later the Commission characterized the proposal as requesting that the directors "Implement hiring policies relating to sexual orientation and incorporate such policies into the corporate employment policy statement." Based on this characterization of the proposal, the SEC staff explained:

> Notwithstanding the general view that employment matters concerning the workforce of the company are excludable as matters involving the conduct of day-to-day business, exceptions have been made in some cases where a proponent based an employment-related proposal on "social policy" concerns. In recent years, however, *the line between includable and excludable employment-related proposals based on social policy considerations has become increasingly difficult to draw.* The distinctions recognized by the staff are characterized by many as tenuous, without substance and effectively nullifying the application of the ordinary business exclusion to employment-related proposals.

> The Division has reconsidered the application of Rule 14a–8(c)(7) to employment-related proposals in light of these concerns and the staff's experience with these proposals in recent years. As a result, the Division has determined that *the fact that a shareholder proposal concerning a company's employment policies and practices for the general workforce is tied to a social issue will no longer be viewed as removing the proposal from the realm of ordinary business operations* of the registrant. Rather, determinations with respect to any such proposals are properly governed by the employment-based nature of the proposal.

Id. at * 2–* 3 (emphasis added). On January 15, 1993, the Commission affirmed the Division's position that the proposal was excludable from the Company's proxy material, relying on Rule 14a–8(c)(7), without any further elaboration on the staff's rationale for its determination.

During 1993 the SEC staff issued several no-action letters on shareholder proposals involving employment-related matters. In each case, including those raising EEO issues, the staff decided that the proposal was excludable based on its view that the proposal was "principally directed at the Company's employment policies and practices which are matters relating to the conduct of ordinary business operations."

Thus, the SEC's current no-action position is that it can no longer continue to draw the lines between includable and excludable proposals * * * As a result, shareholder proposals involving EEO and affirmative action policies are now deemed excludable by the SEC because they relate to employment policies, and employment policies are viewed as ordinary business matters.

### C. Whether Wal–Mart May Exclude Plaintiffs' Proposal

Having considered the SEC's formal interpretive guidelines for Rule 14a–8 and the SEC's application of those guidelines through the no-action letter process, the court turns to whether Wal–Mart carries its burden of showing that the Proposal may be excluded from management's proxy material because it falls within the "ordinary business operations" exception. Wal–Mart first contends that the court should defer to *Cracker Barrel* and the 1993 *Wal–Mart* no-action letter, which categorically reject the SEC's prior position on EEO and affirmative action proposals. It alternatively contends that the Proposal's request for "detailed" information about Wal–Mart's employee and supplier relations involves shareholders in the details of implementing rather than adopting corporate policy, and that the Proposal is thus excludable because the choice between ways to implement corporate policy is mundane in nature and does not involve substantial policy considerations.

### 1. Whether the Court Should Defer to the SEC's Cracker Barrel Position

The court does not defer to the SEC's position in *Cracker Barrel* and is not persuaded by its reasoning, because the reasoning in *Cracker Barrel* sharply deviates from the standard articulated in the 1976 Interpretive Release. The parties, the SEC and courts all agree that courts must defer to the 1976 Interpretive Release. As discussed above, that Release interpreted Rule 14a–8(c) (7) as permitting the exclusion of "proposals that are mundane in nature and do not involve any substantial policy or other considerations."

*Cracker Barrel* fails to apply both parts of the Release's conjunctive standard. In *Cracker Barrel*, the Commission explicitly acknowledged that proposals in favor of or against the adoption of an EEO program continue to raise "social policy" issues, and it did not suggest any diminished public or shareholder interest in these social issues. It nonetheless took the position that the SEC's inability to continue to draw lines warranted an across the board rule that any proposal relating to employment matters is excludable because it relates to day-to-day business affairs, regardless of whether the proposal also involves a substantial policy consideration. This interpretation contravenes the 1976 Interpretive Release's explicit recognition that all proposals could be seen as involving some aspect of day-to-day business operations. That recognition underlay the Release's statement that the SEC's determination of whether a company may exclude a proposal should not depend on whether the proposal could be characterized as involving some day-to-day business matter. Rather, the proposal may be excluded only after the proposal is also found to raise no substantial policy consideration. The SEC did not follow the 1976 Interpretive Release standard in *Cracker Barrel* or in the 1993 no-action letter issued to Wal–Mart, in that the

SEC focused only on whether employment policies generally involve day-to-day business matters.[13]

2. *Whether Application of the 1976 Interpretive Release Standard Independently Permits Wal–Mart to Exclude the Proposal*

Having concluded that deference is not owed to *Cracker Barrel* and the 1993 *Wal–Mart* no action letter, the court considers whether Wal–Mart has carried its burden for excluding the Proposal under the standard articulated by the 1976 Interpretive Release and the corpus of SEC no-action letters that properly applied that standard. * * *

Wal–Mart itself does not deny that equality and diversity in the workplace involve substantial policy considerations. Indeed, it would be difficult to sustain such a position in light of, among other things, the continued interest of Congress in employment discrimination since 1964, which was most recently underscored in the Civil Rights and Glass Ceiling Acts of 1991.

Rather, Wal–Mart argues that the Proposal would involve shareholders in dictating the implementation of a policy, albeit one of social import. Plaintiffs challenge that characterization of their Proposal. Regardless of whether the court characterizes the Proposal as seeking to adopt a policy or as seeking to implement a policy, the same inquiry guides the court: Does the proposal involve shareholders in dictating mundane matters that involve no substantial policy considerations?

The Proposal seeks to identify general corporate policy regarding equal employment opportunities and efforts, if any, to promote those policies among its suppliers, on whom Wal–Mart may have some influence. As plaintiffs argue the Proposal does not involve shareholders in demanding, or monitoring compliances with, a specific timetable to accomplish plaintiff's ultimate goal of improving Wal–Mart's EEO record. This aspect of the Proposal notably distinguishes it from the proposal considered in *Capital Cities/ABC* that the Commission found excludable. Plaintiff's Proposal does not require Wal–Mart to gather any employee-related information that it does not already gather for the purpose of complying with government regulations. The Proposal states that the report should be prepared "at reasonable cost, omitting confidential information," and may be comparable to the one or two page reports produced by other companies in Wal–Mart's industry. * * * The Proposal thus generally involves a significant policy consideration and does not otherwise fall within the exception for proposals relating to the conduct of Wal–Mart's "ordinary business operations."

**13.** This is not say that the SEC cannot change its views with regard to what issues involve substantial policy considerations. If the SEC finds that the issues of EEO and affirmative action programs no longer implicate significant policy considerations, the 1976 Interpretive Release permits exclusion of proposals relating to them. No such change of view exists at *Cracker Barrel*.

Nor does the court suggest that the SEC may not abandon the 1976 Interpretive Release altogether, so long as, in doing so, it complies with appropriate procedures, which procedures need not be addressed here. The court's holding today is limited to the proposition that a court should not defer to a position taken by the SEC in a no-action letter that is inconsistent with an SEC interpretation offered in the context of formal notice and comment rulemaking.

However, the court finds that a literal reading of the Proposal suggests that the requested report must contain every "step" Wal–Mart management has taken to increase the number of female and minority managers and state all the "ways" Wal–Mart publicizes its EEO and affirmative action policies. Such "steps" could range from formal policies announced by the board of directors and officers, to the individual acts of each supervisor who implements these policies, and to other personnel and purchasing actions that occur hundreds of times each business day. A request for this latter information is excludable because it involves the mundane matters of Wal–Mart's day-to-day business affairs that involve no substantial policy consideration. The court, therefore, finds that the Proposal may be omitted from Wal–Mart's 1993 proxy material to the extent that plaintiffs agree[14] to the inclusion of the following proposal as an alternative to paragraphs 1–5 of the Proposal they submitted to Wal–Mart:

1. A chart identifying employees according to their sex and race in each of the nine major EEOC defined job categories for 1990, 1991, and 1992, listing either numbers or percentages in each category.

2. A summary description of any Affirmative Action policies and programs to improve performances, including job categories where women and minorities are underutilized.

3. A description of any policies and programs oriented specifically toward increasing the number of managers who are qualified and/or females and/or belong to ethnic minorities.

4. A general description of how Wal–Mart publicizes our company's Affirmative Action policies and programs to merchandise suppliers and service providers.

5. A description of any policies and programs favoring the purchase of goods and services from minority-and/or female owned business enterprises.

In modifying the Proposal, the court notes the practice of the SEC staff to revise a proposal submitted to it to correct minor defects. These changes to the Proposal reflect a balance of the rights of shareholders to obtain information on an issue raising significant policy considerations and the right of management to run the day-to-day affairs of the corporation free from shareholder supervision.

---

## LOVENHEIM v. IROQUOIS BRANDS, LTD.
618 F.Supp. 554 (D.D.C.1985).

Gasch, District Judge.

### I. Background

This matter is now before the Court on plaintiff's motion for preliminary injunction.

---

**14.** Plaintiffs consented to this change in language in an April 19, 1993 telephone conference with the court.

Plaintiff Peter C. Lovenheim, owner of two hundred shares of common stock in Iroquois Brands, Ltd. (hereinafter "Iroquois/Delaware"), seeks to bar Iroquois/Delaware from excluding from the proxy materials being sent to all shareholders in preparation for an upcoming shareholder meeting information concerning a proposed resolution he intends to offer at the meeting. Mr. Lovenheim's proposed resolution relates to the procedure used to force-feed geese for production of paté de foie gras in France,[2] a type of paté imported by Iroquois/Delaware. Specifically, his resolution calls upon the Directors of Iroquois/Delaware to:

> [F]orm a committee to study the methods by which its French supplier produces paté de foie gras, and report to the shareholders its findings and opinions, based on expert consultation, on whether this production method causes undue distress, pain or suffering to the animals involved and, if so, whether further distribution of this product should be discontinued until a more humane production method is developed.

\* \* \*

Iroquois/Delaware has refused to allow information concerning Mr. Lovenheim's proposal to be included in proxy materials being sent in connection with the next annual shareholders meeting. In doing so, Iroquois/Delaware relies on an exception to the general requirement of Rule 14a–8, Rule 14a–8(c)(5). \* \* \*

### C. APPLICABILITY OF RULE 14A–8(C)(5) EXCEPTION

\* \* \*

Iroquois/Delaware's reliance on the argument that this exception applies is based on the following information contained in the affidavit of its president: Iroquois/Delaware has annual revenues of $141 million

---

**2.** Paté de foie gras is made from the liver of geese. According to Mr. Lovenheim's affidavit, force-feeding is frequently used in order to expand the liver and thereby produce a larger quantity of paté. Mr. Lovenheim's affidavit also contains a description of the force-feeding process:

> Force-feeding usually begins when the geese are four months old. On some farms where feeding is mechanized, the bird's body and wings are placed in a metal brace and its neck is stretched. Through a funnel inserted 10–12 inches down the throat of the goose, a machine pumps up to 400 grams of corn-based

mash into its stomach. An elastic band around the goose's throat prevents regurgitation. When feeding is manual, a handler uses a funnel and stick to force the mash down.

Affidavit of Peter C. Lovenheim at ¶ 7. Plaintiff contends that such force-feeding is a form of cruelty to animals. *Id.*

Plaintiff has offered no evidence that force-feeding is used by Iroquois/Delaware's supplier in producing the paté imported by Iroquois/Delaware. However his proposal calls upon the committee he seeks to create to investigate this question.

with $6 million in annual profits and $78 million in assets. In contrast, its paté de foie gras sales were just $79,000 last year, representing a net loss on paté sales of $3,121. Iroquois/Delaware has only $34,000 in assets related to paté. Thus none of the company's net earnings and less than .05 percent of its assets are implicated by plaintiff's proposal. These levels are obviously far below the five percent threshold set forth in the first portion of the exception claimed by Iroquois/Delaware.

Plaintiff does not contest that his proposed resolution relates to a matter of little economic significance to Iroquois/Delaware. Nevertheless he contends that the Rule 14a–8(c)(5) exception is not applicable as it cannot be said that his proposal "is not otherwise significantly related to the issuer's business" as is required by the final portion of that exception. In other words, plaintiff's argument that Rule 14a–8 does not permit omission of his proposal rests on the assertion that the rule and statute on which it is based do not permit omission merely because a proposal is not economically significant where a proposal has "ethical or social significance."[8]

Iroquois/Delaware challenges plaintiff's view that ethical and social proposals cannot be excluded even if they do meet the economic or five percent test. Instead, Iroquois/Delaware views the exception solely in economic terms as permitting omission for any proposals relating to a de minimis share of assets and profits. Iroquois/Delaware asserts that since corporations are economic entities, only an economic test is appropriate.

The Court would note that the applicability of the Rule 14a–8(c)(5) exception to Mr. Lovenheim's proposal represents a close question given the lack of clarity in the exception itself. In effect, plaintiff relies on the word "otherwise," suggesting that it indicates the drafters of the rule intended that other noneconomic tests of significance be used. Iroquois/Delaware relies on the fact that the rule examines other significance in relation to the issuer's business. Because of the apparent ambiguity of the rule, the Court considers the history of the shareholder proposal rule in determining the proper interpretation of the most recent version of that rule.

Prior to 1983, paragraph 14a–8(c)(5) excluded proposals "not significantly related to the issuer's business" but did not contain an objective economic significance test such as the five percent of sales, assets, and earnings specified in the first part of the current version. Although a

---

**8.** The assertion that the proposal is significant in an ethical and social sense relies on plaintiff's argument that "the very availability of a market for products that may be obtained through the inhumane force-feeding of geese cannot help but contribute to the continuation of such treatment." Plaintiff's brief characterizes the humane treatment of animals as among the foundations of western culture and cites in support of this view the Seven Laws of Noah, an animal protection statute enacted by the Massachusetts Bay Colony in 1641, numerous federal statutes enacted since 1877, and animal protection laws existing in all fifty states and the District of Columbia. An additional indication of the significance of plaintiff's proposal is the support of such leading organizations in the field of animal care as the American Society for the Prevention of Cruelty to Animals and The Humane Society of the United States for measures aimed at discontinuing use of force-feeding.

series of SEC decisions through 1976 allowing issuers to exclude proposals challenging compliance with the Arab economic boycott of Israel
allowed exclusion if the issuer did less than one percent of their business
with Arab countries or Israel, the Commission stated later in 1976 that
it did "not believe that subparagraph (c)(5) should be hinged solely on
the economic relativity of a proposal." Securities Exchange Act Release
No. 12,999 (1976). Thus the Commission required inclusion "in many
situations in which the related business comprised less than one percent" of the company's revenues, profits or assets "where the proposal
has raised *policy questions* important enough to be considered "significantly related' to the issuer's business."

As indicated above, the 1983 revision adopted the five percent test of
economic significance in an effort to create a more objective standard.
Nevertheless, in adopting this standard, the Commission stated that
proposals will be includable notwithstanding their "failure to reach the
specified economic thresholds if a significant relationship to the issuer's
business is demonstrated on the face of the resolution or supporting
statement." Securities Exchange Act Release No. 19,135 (1982). Thus it
seems clear based on the history of the rule that "the meaning of "significantly related' is not *limited* to economic significance."

[The court granted plaintiff's motion for a preliminary injunction.]

### Note: Ordinary Business, Public Policy and Management Accountability

It appears that the question of whether a proposal constitutes
ordinary business or is a matter of public policy relates directly to the
issues of management accountability raised in Chapters 4 and 5. The
reason is that if a proposal relates to ordinary business, management can
deprive the shareholders of their "voice" by excluding the proposal from
the proxy statement.

Almost from the outset, both the courts and the SEC have recognized (implicitly or explicitly) the significance of these issues. They
addressed them issues most directly in *Medical Committee for Human
Rights v. SEC*, 432 F.2d 659 (D.C.Cir.1970), *vacated as moot* 404 U.S.
403, 92 S.Ct. 577, 30 L.Ed.2d 560 (1972). The Medical Committee, a
public interest group, opposed the Vietnam War and, particularly, the
manufacture by Dow Chemical Company (Dow) of napalm for use in the
war. Although napalm constituted a small and not very profitable part of
Dow's business, napalm was important to the government's war effort
and Dow strongly defended its manufacture on patriotic grounds.

The Medical Committee submitted a proposal requesting that the
Dow board adopt an amendment to Dow's certificate of incorporation
that would bar the sale of napalm to any buyer unless the buyer gave
reasonable assurance that the napalm would not be used on or against
human beings. Dow refused to include the proposal on the grounds that
it was submitted to promote a general political cause (which was then,

*but is no longer*, a ground for exclusion under Rule 14a–8) and that it related to Dow's ordinary business.

In a strongly-worded opinion, the Court of Appeals for the District of Columbia Circuit held that the proposal could not be omitted. The core of the court's analysis is as follows:

> As our earlier discussion indicates, the clear import of the language, legislative history, and record of administration of section 14(a) is that its overriding purpose is to assure to corporate shareholders the ability to exercise their right—some would say their duty—to control the important decisions which affect them in their capacity as stockholders and owners of the corporation. * * * Here * * * the proposal relates solely to a matter that is completely within the accepted sphere of corporate activity and control. No reason has been advanced in the present proceedings which leads to the conclusion that management may properly place obstacles in the path of shareholders who wish to present to their co-owners, in accord with applicable state law, the question of whether they wish to have their assets used in a manner which they believe to be more socially responsible but possibly less profitable than that which is dictated by present company policy. Thus, even accepting Dow's characterization of the purpose and intent of the Medical Committee's proposal, there is a strong argument that permitting the company to exclude it would contravene the purpose of section 14(a).

> However, the record in this case contains indications that we are confronted with quite a different situation. The management of Dow Chemical Company is repeatedly quoted in sources which include the company's own publications as proclaiming that the decision to continue manufacturing and marketing napalm was made not *because* of business considerations, but *in spite of* them; that management in essence decided to pursue a course of activity which generated little profit for the shareholders and actively impaired the company's public relations and recruitment activities because management considered this action morally and politically desirable. The proper political and social role of modern corporations is, of course, a matter of philosophical argument extending far beyond the scope of our present concern; the substantive wisdom or propriety of particular corporate political decisions is also completely irrelevant to the resolution of the present controversy. What *is* of immediate concern, however, is the question of whether the corporate proxy rules can be employed as a shield to isolate such managerial decisions from shareholder control. * * * We think that there is a clear and compelling distinction between management's legitimate need for freedom to apply its expertise in matters of day-to-day business judgment, and management's patently illegitimate claim of power to treat modern corporations with their vast resources as personal satrapies implementing personal political or moral predilections. It could scarcely be argued that management is more qualified or more entitled to make these kinds of decisions than the share-

holders who are the true beneficial owners of the corporation; and it seems equally implausible that an application of the proxy rules which permitted such a result could be harmonized with the philosophy of corporate democracy which Congress embodied in section 14(a) of the Securities Exchange Act of 1934.

432 F.2d at 681.

*Carter v. Portland General Electric Co.*, 227 Or. 401, 362 P.2d 766 (1961), reflects a narrower view of shareholders' rights. The court, applying Oregon law, affirmed management's refusal to include in the proxy statement a shareholder statement in opposition to management plans for the construction of a dam. A motion on the floor of the meeting was also ruled out of order, and the court refused to overturn any of management's actions. In holding that the shareholder request was not a "proper subject" for shareholder consideration, the court observed:

> * * * Granted, that the proposed dam project would commit a large part of the corporate defendant's assets and credit. By the same token, it also involved extensive engineering, economic, financial and even political considerations. It is impossible to believe that the obviously voluminous character of such data could have been abbreviated to the point that any communication with the stockholders or debate at the annual meeting could have resulted in any knowing or sensible vote by the stockholders.

362 P.2d at 769.

What, then, is "ordinary business"? As the court noted in *Wal–Mart*, the SEC stated in its 1976 amendments to the proxy rules that ordinary business matters are those "that are mundane in nature and do not involve any substantial policy considerations." At first blush, such matters would seem to be relatively simple to identify: the selection of products to be manufactured; the location of a factory; the terms of a labor contract; the compensation package for employees. The problem is that some issues which seem to fall within these examples also raise public policy questions. In *Medical Committee*, the decision to manufacture napalm could be viewed as ordinary business because it is simply the choice of product mix. But because of the context in which the question arose——the Vietnam War——the decision clearly had broad public policy implications which made it proper for shareholders to express their views. The fact that Dow's own management chose to manufacture napalm in spite of, rather than because of, business reasons reinforced the court's decision. In other cases, the SEC staff and the courts base their conclusions on whether a proposal raises what they consider to be a sufficiently important issue of public policy to take it outside the realm of "ordinary business." *See, e.g., Grimes v. Ohio Edison Co.*, 992 F.2d 455 (2d Cir.1993); *Grimes v. Centerior Energy Corp.*, 909 F.2d 529 (D.C.Cir.1990); *New York City Employees' Retirement System v. Brunswick Corp.*, 789 F.Supp. 144 (S.D.N.Y.1992); *New York City Employees' Retirement System v. Dole Food Co.*, 795 F.Supp. 95 (S.D.N.Y.1992), *appeal dismissed* 969 F.2d 1430 (2d Cir.1992).

Following *Wal-Mart,* the SEC continued to opine that proposals relating to employment matters involved "ordinary business." The New York City Employees' Retirement System sought to enjoin the SEC from issuing additional no action letters taking that position. However, in *New York City Employees' Retirement System v. SEC* , 45 F.3d 7 (2d Cir.1995), the Second Circuit held that it did not have the authority to second guess the SEC's advisory interpretations of Rule 14a–8.

The revision of Rule 14a–8 that the SEC proposed in 1997 was designed to make the standards for applying (c)(5) and (c)(7) more objective. The Commission proposed to amend (c)(5) to allow a company to omit a proposal that relates to a matter involving the purchase or sale of services or products that represent $10 million or less in gross revenues or total costs—a substantial reduction from the 5% threshold that had pertained. But the Commission also proposed to delete the exception for proposals that are "otherwise significantly related" to a company's business on the grounds that it was inherently subjective and had made the (c)(5) exclusion meaningless.

As concerned (c)(7), the SEC proposed to drop the term "ordinary business" and to allow exclusion of any proposal that "relates to specific business decisions normally left to the discretion of management." As an independent matter, the SEC also indicated that it intended to reverse the position it took in *Cracker Barrel* on resolutions involving EEO issues.

These proposals provoked considerable opposition from shareholder activists. SEC Chairman Arthur Levitt responded by asking two corporate governance experts to attempt to moderate a compromise. The two experts, after meeting with interested issuers and proponents, recommended that the SEC substantially retain its existing rules but implement its proposed reversal of *Cracker Barrel.* *Letter From Harvey J. Goldschmid and Ira M. Millstein to U.S. Securities and Exchange Commission* (Dec. 23, 1997). That appears to be the position the SEC will adopt.

### *Note: Proposed Bylaws*

In recent years, shareholders have sponsored a number of resolutions proposing to amend bylaws. Most states' corporate statutes allow shareholders to amend the bylaws, so long as the proposed amendment does not conflict with the articles of incorporation or the statute. Thus, under Rule 14a–8, whether a proposed bylaw amendment can be omitted usually turns on whether the proposed bylaw impinges on the authority of the board of directors to manage the corporation's business.

In 1992, the SEC took apparently inconsistent positions on proposals by shareholders of Exxon and Pennzoil to adopt bylaws that would have established shareholder advisory committees (SACs) charged with reviewing and evaluating the performance of those companies' boards of directors and advising the respective boards on matters relating to the "enhancement of shareholder value." Exxon argued that the proposed bylaw was not a proper subject for shareholder action under (c)(1) and that it constituted ordinary business under (c)(7). The SEC staff disagreed. It concluded that New Jersey law did not prohibit a bylaw creating such a committee and stated that "although the purpose of the shareholders' committee is to provide a means of communication with management, the nature and scope of that communication would appear as not involving matters concerning the conduct of the Company's ordinary business operations."

However, the staff subsequently allowed Pennzoil, a Delaware corporation, to omit a similar proposal. Whether it did so because Pennzoil's lawyers articulated more specifically than had Exxon's the manner in which the bylaw would abrogate the power of the board of directors, because the staff perceived differences between Delaware and New Jersey law, or because the proposed bylaw provided that it could only be amended by shareholders remains unclear.

This issue has taken on added importance, though, because in recent years institutional and other investors have reacted to boards of directors' failure to comply with precatory resolutions, urging them to modify or abandon various antitakeover defenses, even though those resolutions have secured majority votes. One obvious alternative is for a shareholder to sponsor a resolution to amend a company's bylaws to prohibit, or restrict use of, some antitakeover defense. In *International Brotherhood of Teamsters General Fund v. Fleming Cos., Inc.*, 1997 U.S. Dist. LEXIS 2980 (W.D. Okla. 1/24/97), the court enjoined Fleming from refusing to include in its proxy statement for its 1997 annual meeting a union-sponsored proposal to amend the bylaws to prohibit Fleming's board from adopting a poison pill without first securing shareholder approval. The court noted that § 1013A of the Oklahoma General Corporation Act allows shareholders to amend bylaws and held that while § 1038 of the Act "vests initiative in the Board of Directors, [it does] does not foreclose shareholder action in this matter." *Id.* at *2. At the time this book went to press, an appeal of the district court's decision was pending in the Tenth Circuit, which had certified the question of whether the Oklahoma Act allows shareholders to adopt such a bylaw to the Oklahoma Supreme Court. It should be noted that the language of the relevant sections of the Oklahoma Act is similar to that of comparable provisions of Delaware law and the corporate laws of other states.

For a good overview of the issues raised by shareholder bylaw proposals, *see* John C. Coffee, Jr., *The Bylaw Battlefield: Can Institutions Change the Outcome of Corporate Control Contests?*, 51 U. MIAMI L. REV. 605 (1997).

# Chapter 15

## THE ROLE OF OUTSIDE DIRECTORS IN THE GOVERNANCE OF THE PUBLIC CORPORATION

### PROBLEM
### WHAT CAN OUTSIDE DIRECTORS CONTRIBUTE?

You are the principal outside counsel to the Columbia Employees Retirement Fund (CERF), which manages an $8 billion investment portfolio, about 40% of which is invested in corporate equities. Several of CERF's trustees have been intrigued by the observation that "all arguments about corporate governance ultimately converge on the role of outside directors." As a consequence, CERF's board of trustees has asked CERF's general manager to prepare an assessment of the impact that outside directors are likely to have on the financial performance of portfolio companies and whether, in light of recent changes in the SEC proxy rules, CERF should become more active in trying to influence the make up of the boards of directors of those companies. The general manager, in turn, has asked you to prepare a memorandum addressing the following questions.

1. Should CERF become more active in trying to influence the make up of the boards of directors of its portfolio companies?

2. What potential roles can outside directors play in the corporate governance system?

3. What are the strengths and weaknesses of a system that relies on outside directors as a principal governance device? Consider:

    a. What duties or tasks can outside directors reasonably be expected to perform?

    b. What kinds of people typically serve as outside directors? How are they selected?

    c. What input do shareholders and other corporate constituencies have in the selection process?

4.   What are the principal weaknesses of boards of directors as they currently operate? Are there changes that are likely to remedy those weaknesses? Are they changes that shareholders should encourage corporations to make?

## A.   INTRODUCTION

Apart from specifying a few decisions that a board of directors cannot delegate, such as the declaration of a dividend, corporate statutes describe directors' duties in very general terms. RMBCA § 8.01, for example, states only that "All corporate powers shall be exercised by or under the authority of, and the business and affairs of the corporation managed under the direction of, its board of directors." DGCL § 141(a) provides simply that "The business and affairs of every corporation * * * shall be managed by or under the direction of a board of directors."

A board of directors consisting of all of a company's senior officers could comply with these statutory mandates, in that it would possess the capability to manage the company's business. But such a board would constitute no more than a committee of senior officers, all wearing hats labeled "Director." It presumably would make the same decisions that its members otherwise would make when wearing their "Officer" hats. As a consequence, such a board would not add value as part of a corporation's governance structure.

Much discussion in recent years has focused on how boards of directors can improve the performance of public corporations. An apparent consensus developed that a majority of the members of the boards of public corporations should be "outside" directors—people who are not part of, and have no strong ties to, the management of the company on whose board they serve. Such directors have the potential to reduce agency costs associated with the separation of ownership from control by "monitoring" managers' performance. *See, e.g.*, Statement of the Business Roundtable, *Corporate Governance and American Competitiveness*, 46 Bus. Law. 241 (1990); Statement of the Business Roundtable, *The Role and Composition of the Board of Directors of the Large Publicly–Owned Corporation*, 33 Bus. Law. 2083 (1978); American Bar Association Committee on Corporate Laws, *Corporate Director's Guidebook*, 33 Bus. Law. 1595 (1978).

However, when one inquires into what is meant by "monitoring," the appearance of consensus evaporates. Some commentators define monitoring narrowly, suggesting that boards should limit themselves to establishing financial goals for the corporation and evaluating senior executives' success in meeting those goals. In this view, a board's principal functions are to discharge top managers whose performance is unsatisfactory and to ensure that management succession arrangements are in place.

Other commentators take a more expansive approach. They would have boards of directors review and approve major corporate actions and become more involved in establishing corporate priorities and long-term objectives. Still other commentators would have the board assume major responsibility for fixing the annual budget and allocating funds among a corporation's operating divisions, as well as reviewing regularly the extent to which the corporation was meeting the goals the board had set. Such a board might be pro-active, initiating some proposals on its own, rather than simply reacting to management's proposals. It also would be more inclined to openly question the latter.

The American Law Institute, after devoting more than ten years to a study of corporate governance issues, suggested that directors' functions and powers be defined as follows.

## ALI, PRINCIPLES OF CORPORATE GOVERNANCE (1994)

§ 3.02. Functions and Powers of the Board of Directors

Except as otherwise provided by statute:

(a) The board of directors of a publicly held corporation should perform the following functions:

(1) Select, regularly evaluate, fix the compensation of, and, where appropriate, replace the principal senior executives.

(2) Oversee the conduct of the corporation's business to evaluate whether the business is being properly managed.

(3) Review and, where appropriate, approve the corporation's financial objectives and major corporate plans and actions.

(4) Review and, where appropriate, approve major changes in, and determinations of other major questions of choice respecting, the appropriate auditing and accounting principles and practices to be used in the preparation of the corporation's financial statements.

(5) Perform such other functions as are prescribed by law, or assigned to the board under a standard of the corporation.

(b) A board of directors also has power to:

(1) Initiate and adopt corporate plans, commitments, and actions.

(2) Initiate and adopt changes in accounting principles and practices.

(3) Provide advice and counsel to the principal senior executives.

(4) Instruct any committee, principal senior executive, or other officer and review the actions of any committee, principal senior executive, or other officer.

(5) Make recommendations to shareholders.

(6) Manage the business of the corporation.

(7) Act as to all other corporate matters not requiring share-holder approval.

(c) Subject to the board's ultimate responsibility for oversight under Subsection (a)(2), the board may delegate to its committees authority to perform any of its functions and exercise any of its powers.

The ALI also recommended that the boards of large public corporations should have a majority of outsiders—directors who have no significant relationships with the corporation's senior executives. ALI, PRINCIPLES OF CORPORATE GOVERNANCE, (1994), § 3A.01. It concluded that for large corporations, a board having a majority of independent directors "is conducive to objective analysis of managerial performance [while] [p]ermitting senior executives to serve on the board ensures knowledgeable and detailed board discussion about the business, and encourages management to take important issues to the board." *Id.*, § 3A.01, Comment *c*. It also suggested that the boards of other public corporations should have at least three independent directors, "in the belief that [three] is the number of directors necessary to attain a critical mass on the board." *Id. See also* American Bar Association Committee on Corporate Laws, *The Corporate Director's Guidebook*, 33 BUS. LAW. 1591, 1625 (1978); NEW YORK STOCK EXCHANGE COMPANY MANUAL § 303.

# B.  HOW BOARDS OF DIRECTORS OPERATE

The first major empirical study of corporate boards concluded that they largely failed to fulfill their primary functions. Myles Mace, DIRECTORS: MYTH AND REALITY (1971). Mace found that directors rarely challenged a CEO or initiated debate on an issue. Directors also generally did not effectively monitor management's performance because CEOs typically provided them with limited information; they devoted little time to reviewing and discussing that information; and boardroom culture emphasized collegiality and the avoidance of controversy. Sometimes, however, directors brought useful expertise to bear on boardroom discussions.

Mace concluded that most outside directors were reluctant to replace an incumbent CEO, no matter how poor the corporation's performance, and that directors usually relied on the CEO to nominate her successor. Only when a vacancy developed suddenly—for example, if a CEO died unexpectedly—did boards generally take the initiative to select a CEO. Finally, Mace found that most boards in fact did not establish basic corporate objectives, strategies and policies. All too often, directors served as little more than "attractive ornaments on the corporate Christmas tree." *Id.* at 107. In a subsequent study, Mace reaffirmed these conclusions. Myles L. Mace, *Directors: Myth and Reality—Ten Years Later*, 32 RUTG. L.REV. 293 (1979).

Mace's work was a powerful indictment of most corporate boards. A more recent study suggested directors had become increasingly involved in corporate affairs. Jay W. Lorsch & Elizabeth MacIver, PAWNS OR POTENTATES: THE REALITY OF AMERICA'S CORPORATE BOARDS (1989). Scandals involving bribery of foreign officials in the 1970's, economic challenges and the fear of personal liability combined to make directors take their duties more seriously and to expect the same from their colleagues. Lorsch and MacIver found that most directors still viewed their primary duties to be selecting a good CEO and replacing a bad one. Most also believed that boards had become—and should be—more active in planning corporate strategy. However, nearly all directors still believed that management should remain firmly in the hands of the CEO and other senior executives, even as they were more willing to question and even challenge decisions and policies they thought were are unwise. Their inclination, though, was to express their concerns privately to the CEO rather than "publicly" in a board meeting. Lorsch and MacIver also found that boards usually did not respond effectively to what they termed "gradual crises"—those that reflected a steady decline in a corporation's long-term competitive position.

Lorsch and MacIver completed their study before the outside directors of General Motors, American Express, Westinghouse, Kodak, and IBM, to name but a few, ousted the CEOs of those companies in 1992 and 1993. Causation is always difficult to identify, but those changes appeared to reflect the confluence of rising pressure from institutional investors and the culmination of a long series of bad business decisions by the ousted CEOs. Whether they also augured a paradigm shift in corporate governance was less clear.

Elliott J. Weiss, *The Board of Directors, Management, and Corporate Takeovers: Opportunities and Pitfalls*, in Arnold W. Sametz (ed.), THE BATTLE FOR CORPORATE CONTROL: SHAREHOLDER RIGHTS, STAKEHOLDER INTERESTS AND MANAGERIAL RESPONSIBILITIES

36–38 (1991).

When we speak of boards of directors, we have in mind the nonmanagement, or outside, members of corporate boards. To be sure, virtually all boards include some of the company's senior executives and some boards include a majority of these inside directors. But nobody takes very seriously the notion that inside directors behave very differently when they are functioning as directors than they do when they are functioning as managers. * * * Thus, when we speak about the relationship between corporate boards and management, we are referring to the relationship between outside directors and senior executives.

* * * The universally held, modern view is that a company's senior executives, not its directors, have primary responsibility for the success or failure of the company's business. The board, in general, is expected only to oversee senior executives and to evaluate their performance.

Most commentators agree that four factors constrain outside directors' ability to perform effectively even these oversight and evaluation functions. First, most directors hold very demanding, full-time jobs as senior officials of other organizations. Consequently, they have limited time available to devote to their secondary jobs as directors of other organizations. * * *

Second, outside directors usually lack expertise in the business of the companies on whose boards they sit. Antitrust laws effectively prohibit companies from having on their boards directors employed by their competitors and, even absent legal prohibitions, few companies would want to invite into their boardrooms people whose primary loyalties ran to one of their competitors. But directors' awareness that they lack relevant expertise is an intimidating factor, making directors understandably reluctant to speak out at board meetings for fear that they will be perceived as naive or uninformed.

Third, directors depend upon a company's executives to supply them with information about the issues the board is to consider and about corporate performance in general; rarely do directors have access to reliable, independent sources of information about corporate activities or management's performance. Executives, of course, generally want the board to approve the proposals they make and to think well of their performance. Consequently, executives rarely are inclined to provide the board with information likely to lead it to reject their proposals or to focus on the negative aspects of their performance. But without such information—or sources from which it might readily be obtained—directors find it difficult to question meaningfully what executives propose to do or how well they have performed.

Finally, directors have little in the way of financial incentives and face little in the way of legal pressures to perform effectively. The fees most directors receive, while substantial if viewed in relation to average workers' salaries, usually represent only a minor portion of directors' income. Few directors own large enough stock positions in the firms on whose boards they sit to motivate them to work hard to ensure that those firms prosper.

* * *

Many commentators believe these constraints limit the contribution directors can make, or can be expected to make, to a company's business success. They also are skeptical about whether directors can deal effectively with situations where managers' and shareholders' interests conflict. They point out that directors' concern about the former, promoting business success, often further impedes their inclination to deal with the latter, since directors, with considerable justification, believe that any effort on their part to limit managers' self-dealing is likely to jeopardize their ability to work effectively with those same managers on solving a company's business problems. * * *

Bayless Manning, *The Business Judgment Rule and the Director's Duty of Attention: Time for Reality*

39 Bus.Law. 1477, 1481–1492 (1984).

### Real-World Conduct of Directors

\* \* \* In the real world, what do such directors—"good" directors—actually do in the discharge of their responsibilities? What is generally expected of them in the market place.[6]

#### *Time Devoted*

The outside directors of a corporation are part-time people with respect to the amount of working time that is allocated to the affairs of the company. The most recent survey (1982) shows that the average director of a publicly held company devotes a total of about 123 hours per year to his board and committee work, including travel. That averages less than 3 hours a week, or about 1.5 working days a month.

Directors of companies in crisis conditions often find themselves compelled to devote much greater amounts of time. Also, in some companies, special agreements (with or without special compensation) between the company and a particular director may obligate him to devote more time to his directorship than the rest of the members of the board.

#### *Complexity of Enterprise*

Many of today's corporations are not only large, they have usually become highly diversified in their business operations—even those that are not conglomerates. They often operate on a worldwide basis, and their products and services have in many cases become highly technical. This diversification and complexity of operations have been overlaid upon the ordinary problems of all businesses: accounting control, personnel succession, labor relations, financial vitality, competition, governmental regulations, profitability, product development, marketing, and the like.

No human being can stay on top of all this in a major company on a one-and-a-half-day-a-month basis.

#### *Pace and Deliberation*

Much of the routine housekeeping work of a board of directors does not demand or warrant significant deliberation. Some important matters that come to the board can be and are dealt with in a deliberate manner over several meetings. A few matters, like the choice of a new CEO from among several in-house candidates, can often be pondered and observed carefully over a period of years, but most significant matters cannot be

---

**6.** While an effort will be made here to keep in mind the great diversity of the nation's tens of thousands of corporations, most of our available data relates to larger companies, and the descriptions offered here may be correspondingly skewed.

dealt with in that way by a board. The pace of commercial events often demands quick response or even, as in takeover situations, almost instant response. Even issues that are fully recognized to be vitally important can often not be considered extensively by a board because its agenda is at the time crammed with other exigent items or with matters which, though less significant, are mandated as compulsory agenda items under applicable laws or regulations.

### Uncertainty and Risk–Taking

Businessmen make business decisions. They are not courts, able and willing to pursue a matter to the last argument in the search of the "right" answer. They are not researchers meticulously seeking truth. They are not scientists striving for ever more refined solutions in a field of narrow specialization. And when an issue comes to a board of directors, the process of discussion and decision is nothing like the lawyer's world of briefs and adversary argumentation. The decisions the businessman must make are fraught with risk, and he is quite accustomed to making these decisions in a hurry on the basis of hunch and manifestly sparse data. The businessman and the board of directors thrive or die in a sea of uncertainty. The chairman of a major bank recently made the point well when he said, "If I'm right three times out of ten, I am doing very well, and if I'm right four times out of ten, I'll do better than anybody else."

\* \* \*

### Decisional Process

To judge by their statements, many lawyers without personal boardroom experience have a total misconception of the decisional process as it actually functions in the boardroom. The lawyer's professional experience in courts, legislatures, and semi-political bodies tends to lead him to assume that all decisional process is inevitably made up of a series of discrete, separate issues presented one at a time, debated by both or all sides, and voted on. In fact boards of directors typically do not operate that way at all, except, perhaps, in conditions of internal warfare or mortal crisis. Actions are usually by consensus. If a significant sentiment of disagreement is sensed by the chairman, the matter is usually put over for later action, and sources of compromise and persuasion are pursued in the interim. Advice from individual directors is most often volunteered to, or solicited by, the CEO informally on a one-on-one basis, rather than pursued in group debate at a board meeting.

### Character of the Agenda

A transcript of a typical board meeting will reflect four kinds of items on the agenda. Fully three quarters of the board's time will be devoted to reports by the management and board committees, routine housekeeping resolutions passed unanimously with little or no discussion, and information responding to specific questions that had earlier been put to the management by directors about a wide range of topics sometimes accompanied by suggestions from the board members, usually procedural in character. Perhaps the remaining one quarter of the meeting time will be addressed to a decision, typically unanimous, on one or two specific different business items, such as the sale of a subsidiary or the establishment of a compensation plan. If, as is the average, a board meets eight times a year, the arithmetic would indicate that a full year of the board's work would contain only ten or fifteen discrete transactional decisions of the type that are generally assumed to make up the main work of the board; and of those discrete transactional matters, many will be neither very important nor controversial, such as a decision to terminate a long-standing banking relationship in favor of a new one that provides better service.

Contrariwise, some issues that have little economic significance may, because of their delicacy, consume great amounts of the board's time— such as the awkward matter of imposing mandatory retirement on the aging founder, builder, and principal owner of the company.

### Agenda-Setting—Initiatives by the Board

Agenda-setting and the scope of board initiative together comprise the single most important, and least understood, aspect of the board's work life.

With the two very important exceptions noted below, the question of what the board will discuss and act on is typically determined by the management or by the corporation's automatic built-in secular equivalent of an ecclesiastical calendar, that is, shareholders' meeting date, fiscal year, cycle of audit committee meetings, and similar matters. The board can, and a good board will, from time to time suggest topics for exploration or discussion, or request the management to report in the near future on this or that matter of interest to the board. The board can press management to get on with a necessary undertaking or desired program, such as the establishment of a job classification system, and to report back to the board about the action taken. But the board itself has little capacity to generate significant proposals, other than generalized suggestions looking toward the establishment of procedures or systems. Almost all of what a board does is made up of matters that are brought to it; matters generated by the board itself are very rare. Typically, boards cannot take, and are not expected to take, initiatives.

There are two major exceptions to this generalization about agenda-setting. Both are of extreme importance, and both are fully understood by normal, healthily functioning boards and managements.

First, no board can deny the existence of a built-in paramount responsibility with regard to what may be called the organic or structural integrity of the company. This organic integrity is essentially made up of two elements. A company must have a *functioning management* in place and operating at all times. A board can itself see that this is done. And a company must have an *internal information system* in place that is generally suitable for an enterprise of the company's character to keep the management informed about what is going on and particularly to provide the accounting data on which to base financial statements. The board cannot design, install, operate, or monitor the operation of such systems; but the board can press for the installation and call for periodic assurances that they are in place. As to these two organic elements of the enterprise, the directors may not wait for the management to bring issues to their attention. The responsibility of the board in these two key regards is inherent and ongoing; it is up to the board to take the initiative to keep itself informed about them and to take such periodic action as its business judgment dictates.

Second, no director or group of directors may choose to ignore credible signals of serious trouble in the company. If a director is informed through a credible source that there is reason to believe that the chief financial officer is a compulsive gambler, the director must take an initiative; he may not sit back and wait for the management to bring the matter to the board's attention. There will usually be a wide range of possible actions which a director could reasonably take to pursue such a matter and thereby fulfill his obligation as a director; but he cannot simply do nothing. Execution of this responsibility of a director will be episodic and, typically, infrequent, but the responsibility itself is ongoing and present every day.

## *Actions Not Taken*

All these realities of directional life add up to a deeper one. From among an infinite number of useful things that a board of directors *might* reasonably have done or looked into in a given time period, the number that will *not* have been done by the most qualified, best-run, and most diligent board in the world will always be far greater than the number that *were* done. If a corporate transaction goes sour, or a company fails, any plaintiff's lawyer of even the most modest talent and imagination will always be able to find a subject matter X as to which he can denounce its directors, declaiming: "Surely any reasonable prudent person in these circumstances would have explored subject X, but this board sat back, did nothing, and did not even inquire into it." That argument in hindsight will always sound plausible. It may appeal to some juries, or even some courts, inexperienced in the reality of business life. But it is most often just hokum and rhetoric.

No court confronted with this retrospective argument about directional delinquency should ever allow itself to forget the reality that at any given time the roster of possible candidates for a place on the agenda of the board is infinite and that agenda items are mutually exclusive, that is, hours spent on one agenda item are hours not spent on an infinity of other possible agenda items. The number of items considered will always be vastly exceeded by the number not considered. And the plaintiff's retrospective indictment, though apparently plausible, is in fact hollow, because it can be as easily designed to hurl against the best-performing board as against the worst.

\* \* \*

### Homework and Scope of Inquiry

Assume that a particular item has in ordinary course come onto the board's agenda and that it is one of that limited number that specifically calls for affirmative decisional action. No one disputes that the board should look into the matter before acting, but in a particular situation, what does that mean? How much time should be devoted to the item (to the exclusion of others)? Is it enough for the directors to read the papers sent by the management? The appendices? A summary cover letter? With what degree of concentration? And what degree of comprehension by the individual director? Regardless of the topic's technical character, what of the director's specialized experience or absence of qualification in the subject? In what degree, if any, should the director carry out research going beyond the documentation provided to him by the company or draw on recollection of data (or rumors) acquired elsewhere? Should the director insist that he be provided an opinion of outside consultants in support of the information and recommendations made by the management?

One does not have to reflect very long about such questions to come to two realizations. The first is that there is no conceivable way to lay down *a priori* answers to such questions. The second is that the point made earlier about agenda-setting in general context has even greater application in the specific. At all times and in all circumstances, the scope of investigation actually undertaken on a matter, whatever it is, will always be less than the possible scope and depth of investigation that could have been undertaken. In every instance of corporate misfortune, it will therefore be an easy cheap shot to fling at the director on the witness stand, "You mean you voted to proceed with this birdcage transaction without even consulting the definitive manual on birdcages put out by the U.S. Department of Commerce?"

No one believes that a director should be able with impunity simply to ignore the work of the board, never doing his homework; but the director's judgment as to the scope of inquiry called for in the circumstances is itself a business judgment of the most basic character.

### Attendance

Apparently the simplest aspect of the topic of directional attention relates to his attending meetings of the board. But consider four instances. Able director W, whose technical experience on one topic is critically valuable to the board, is always well prepared, but he is heavily committed in many activities and able to attend only half the board meetings; X, also a director of broadly experienced competence and helpful when present, is senior and semiretired and he misses half the meetings because he lives abroad half of the year; Y, a director of no special competence, attends all the meetings to no visible good effect; Z, a director of average capacity is lazy and seldom shows up, but he owns sixty percent of the stock of the company. How should the law react to such circumstances?

What of the director who missed the meeting where particular action was taken; as a nonactor, should he be more exposed or less exposed to later attack?

How important is attendance, taken alone? In the real world, the answer will depend on the decisional process actually utilized by the CEO and his board. If the CEO is in continuous consultation with his directors, and if decisions of substance are worked out through prior soundings so that the meeting is only a formality (a very common pattern), or if the CEO arranges the agenda so that big issues do not come up unless his key qualified directors are present to participate, then the whole issue of frequency of attendance may be peripheral at best. A judge who does not regularly show up in his courtroom can be safely concluded not to be doing his job and to be either ill or delinquent, but that image cannot be automatically transferred to the wholly different processes of boards of directors. In most circumstances it will be very hard for a plaintiff to demonstrate that a director's sporadic attendance was causally linked to later difficulties of the company.

*Reliance*

\* \* \*

[D]irectors may safely rely upon officers and employees of the corporation, accountants, engineers, lawyers, and other expert consultants who they have reason to believe are competent. Expert consultation inspired by a perceived need to know on the part of the board is obviously constructive and indispensable. An inoculation of expert outside opinion is also of help in preventing an epidemic of liability in the board room. The law has also become more realistic in recognizing that much of a board's work is, and must be, done in committee, and in according to the board the privilege of reliance upon the work product of its committees.

It is less widely understood, and not explicitly recognized in the law, that the dynamics of the boardroom are also deeply dependent upon a matrix of other reliances among individual officers and directors. Director X, at a meeting asks in respect of particular transaction A, "Will we have any trouble with our auditors if we do A?" Director Y, who is recognized by his colleagues to be the board's most knowledgeable member in matters of accounting (who may, or may not, be a member of the audit committee) says, "Don't worry, X, I don't think we'll have any problem there." Thereupon the conversation moves on to another topic, the group deferring in an informal way to the expertise and judgment of one of its members in whom it has confidence. (The same interchange could, of course, have involved the company's chief financial officer rather than Y.) Does this kind of interchange among businessmen comply with legally articulated standards like "duty to inquire," or "duty to inform itself"? If the answer is "no" (as at least some commentators would undoubtedly say), then the tension between the law and reality is in a crisis condition. To operate at all, any group decisional process must be built on a substrate of such interconnected informal delegation and deference. A board is free to ask any question, but a board that does not have confidence in and rejects the answer it receives is at a point of pathological collapse as a decisional apparatus.

A correlative of the board's reliance must be a special informal obligation on the part of the person or committee relied upon to do his or its homework well or to be willing to answer to a board member's question, "I do not know." The expectations of the rest of the board are that they will receive a specially informed opinion, and they are entitled to get it.

So, once again, the normal decisional process in the boardroom is quite different from the piece-by-piece, person-by-person, issue-by-issue, question-by-question, adversary interrogational and debate process which a lawyer or judge tends to perceive as the normal way to arrive at professional conclusions. (That is one of the major reasons why businessmen think lawyers make poor directors until they learn, if they learn, that corporate decision-making requires other ways of doing.)

### Depth of Inquiry

The point about deference and reliance as an element of "inquiry" has another aspect with which the lawyer will more readily empathize because it matches part of his own working experience. Assuming that the director specifically undertakes to "inquire" into a matter, how deeply should he go? Wherever the questioning stops, it would always be possible to question still further, as every lawyer knows.

In the boardroom context, there is no inherent limit to the possible circumstances and conditions that are relevant to a business decision. When and where to stop is always a matter of sophisticated judgment in the immediate circumstances involving the importance of the decision (as then perceived), the costs of further pursuit, the board's confidence in the answers so far received, the confidence in the persons who purport to have explored the matter and are reporting to the board, the special intensity of the directors' concern about the particular matter, competing demands for attention to other important matters, the rate at which, and the matter on which, the inquirer decides to ration out his always-finite supply of political capital within the board, and so forth. The *gestalt* at the instant that a director decides not to pursue his questions further cannot be faithfully recaptured later in a courtroom setting.

On this topic, it is always easy for a courtroom advocate, a judge, a law review commentator, a journalist, or a politician to write sentences like, "The director cannot just be dumb. He cannot just accept any answer, however preposterous, to his question." But that is only an old rhetorical trick that can be called argument by negative hyperbole.

Negative hyperbole may sometimes be good advocacy, but it is never good law-making. The egregious behavior which the advocate conjures up in such sentences is indeed egregious and is condemnable as such; but such bizarre behavior virtually never occurs in real life, and the tub-thumping sentence stated in the negative provides no future affirmative guidance whatever to counsel, judges, or directors concerning what a well-intentioned director should do.

Setting aside outlandish situations in which the negative hyperbole is not hyperbole but a description of what actually happened, ultimately the law must allow the director to exercise his judgment about the scope and depth of his inquiry, exactly as it must realistically allow the board to exercise its judgment about its agenda.

### Judgment

Finally, we come to the matter of judgment itself. Assume, again, that a board is going through one of those episodes of discrete transactional decision which lawyers' discourse assumes to be normal but is in fact rare. Assume that questions have been asked and inquiry made to a satisfactory extent, whatever that may mean. Now, as perceived by the legal writing, the board weighs the matter and makes a judgment, and it is that judgment that is protected by the business judgment rule.

Boardroom reality is far different from this lawyer-oriented model, not only in the respects discussed earlier but usually in the character of "judgment" itself. The differences are fundamental and warrant comment.

\* \* \*

\* \* \* [O]ne can observe that the work of corporate management and directors has the same general characteristics as that of the high political official or general. Actions are most often multiple. The company's course of conduct is a resultant of countless tradeoffs. Resources are never sufficient. Competitors and others are devoted to obstruction. Occasionally one can discern a clean go or no-go issue that will be decided by a board of directors—whether to shut down all foreign operations and take a big current write-off, for example—but such instances are not frequent, and even when they appear to arise they are nearly always linked to other decisional implications, as when, for example, a board decides not to fire the chief executive today but at the same time takes other moves to pre-position possible successors for tomorrow. As a result, seeking in retrospect to revisit and evaluate a single "judgment on an issue" by a board of directors will almost always be a distortion of reality, because no such free-standing single judgment ever happened.

\* \* \* [J]udgments of boards of directors are mainly in the nature of decisions whether to hurl a veto. A chief executive who generally enjoys the confidence of his board will usually be able to carry any proposal he makes if he does his homework, prepares his supporting arguments, is backed up by his other officers, and—of key importance—personally throws his full weight behind the proposal. Courts and the public must understand that quite commonly a director will go along with a business proposal that he does not really like. He may well think, and will sometimes say aloud in the board meeting, "I do not like this proposal. It seems risky and I believe other uses for the same resources would be more promising. But I may be wrong; I respect the contrary views of my colleagues; and I have to accord great weight to the CEO's strong support for this project. *After all, he is the one who will have the primary responsibility for seeing to it that it works out successfully.* So I will not vote no." When that happens, everyone in the corporate world knows the meaning of the italicized words. The director is saying that he will go along this time, but the CEO is on notice that if he proves to be wrong and the project fails, he may well have lost that director's confidence.

To cite another illustration. Even if a director is strongly opposed to a project, he may still go along because the CEO is determined to proceed and, in the director's best judgment, the disruption that would be caused by firing the CEO at this time would be more injurious to the interests of the company and its shareholders than the negative risks of the project proposed. In such a case, the real business judgment the director makes is not to throw his javelin today. That kind of aggregative judgment is not, in the lawyer's sense, "on the merits" of the narrow particular issue at hand, but it is very much on the issue of the director's perception of the best interests of the company. How can a court later evaluate such a nonjudgment judgment?

Thus, the decisional process of a board of directors only occasionally involves a go or no-go issue at all; often involves a cost-benefit mix of tradeoffs on multiple issues, in search of the least bad result; and is continuously obscured by the weight given by directors to the injury that will likely be visited upon the interests of the company and shareholders if the board splinters or if it suddenly dumps its CEO.

\* \* \*

*Diversity of Enterprise and Style*

\* \* \*

At any one moment in time each company occupies some position on a spectrum that ranges from the wholly owned, one-man business, through the enterprise that is predominantly owned and wholly controlled by one man or one family, through the enterprise that is similarly controlled but has hundreds of shareholders who have no personal interaction with the company's management, and so on up to a great, faceless, meritocratic corporate bureaucracy.

Companies also differ from each other markedly in personality and in operating style. Contemporary literature has hit upon the term "corporate culture" to refer to the evident fact that each company is a distinctive social organization with its own viewpoints, management style, attitudes, self-image, and ways of doing. Every board of directors also has its own personality and manner of working with the management.

\* \* \*

### Spasmodic Intensity of Attention

Not only is company A different from company B. An additional clearly observable phenomenon in the sociology of boardroom life is that the board of company A behaves differently at different times. The intensity and quantity of all forms of the board's attention rises and falls as the company passes through calm or stormy seas. When matters are going well, the board tends to settle into watchful but quiet routine, confident in the management's performance and willing to be led. If the wind begins to rise, the board will stir and come to life, ask many questions, occasionally exercise its veto, and perhaps oust the CEO. If the hurricane comes, the board members will typically respond energetically out of their sense of responsibility, pouring time, energy, study, attention, and initiative into the company's affairs, sometimes to the point of temporarily assuming full executive control. When the storm is weathered, perhaps with a new captain installed, the board will resume a less active but watchful mode. Thus, a degree of attention that would be normal in usual circumstances could be considered as insufficient when the going gets rough.

------

### Note: The Increasing Importance of Board Committees

One change in board structure that has been widely accepted, both in theory and in practice, is the division of the board into committees with different areas of responsibility. By operating through, and dividing the work of the board among, committees, outside directors can more easily increase their oversight of and involvement in corporate affairs.

Reliance on board committees, particularly the audit committee, has increased dramatically, in part as a consequence of SEC proxy disclosure and stock exchange requirements. See Item 6(d)(1) of Schedule 14A; NEW YORK STOCK EXCHANGE COMPANY MANUAL § 303.00. A survey of 878 large industrial and service corporations found that in 1996, all reported they had an audit committee, 99% reported they had a compensation committee and 74% reported they had a nominating committee. Korn/Ferry International, *Board Meeting in Session: 24th Annual Board of Directors Study* 13 (1997). In addition, 35% reported they had a committee concerned with board organization and 31% had a committee devoted to succession planning. *Id.* The average number of directors on all of these committees except the succession planning committee was four, all of whom, on average, were outside directors; the average succession planning committee was made up of five outside directors. *Id.*

An audit committee monitors and investigates a corporation's financial transactions and financial reports. One of its functions is to prevent financial improprieties. The audit committee also is a direct link between the corporation's independent accounting firm and the board of directors. It can perform a wide range of tasks: recommending independent auditors to the full board; conferring with the auditors before, during, and after their audit about its scope, procedures, problems, and results; and discussing with the corporation's internal auditors the nature and effectiveness of their work. Audit committees have also frequently investigated suspect payments and other financial irregularities.

Through its independent access to financial information and its contact with the independent auditors, the audit committee can better inform the board of the company's financial activities and improve the board's monitoring of management. The committee offers management an opportunity to review the company's financial reporting and controls. It also can give a company's internal auditors direct access to the board. Finally, it can shield the external auditors from undue management influence by providing a forum in which the auditors can confer directly with board members about accounting practices, the quality of internal controls, and other potentially troublesome issues.

The ALI proposes that every public corporation with at least 2,000 shareholders and $100 million in assets have an audit committee. *See* ALI, PRINCIPLES OF CORPORATE GOVERNANCE (1994), § 3A.05 (Comment *c* ). As a matter of corporate practice, the ALI recommends that smaller public corporations have audit committees as well. *Id.*, § 3A.02. No audit committee member should be an executive or an employee of the corporation or a relatively recent employee, and at least a majority of the committee members should have no significant relationship to the senior executives whose performance is covered by the financial statements the auditors are charged with reviewing.

The ALI also recommends that large public corporations also have two other committees with members who are independent. A nominating committee should be given primary responsibility for identifying candidates for election to the board (although, the ALI notes, the CEO and senior executives also should be allowed to play a role in proposing nominees). *Id.*, § 3A.04. A compensation committee should be charged with overseeing the manner in which senior executives are paid. *Id.*, § 3A.05. It should avoid overly generous compensation arrangements but should try to ensure that compensation arrangements provide managers with appropriate incentives.

## C.  DO INDEPENDENT BOARDS MATTER?

### 1.  WHO THE OUTSIDE DIRECTORS ARE

Who the directors are clearly influences how a board performs. Most public corporations have boards with a majority of outside directors. A survey of proxy statements filed in 1996 by the 878 largest industrial and service corporations found that they reported an average of two inside directors and nine outside directors. Korn/Ferry International, *supra*, at 10. A second study found that half of the 100 largest U.S. corporations had only one or two inside directors in 1996. SpencerStuart, *1996 Board Index*.

Lorsch and MacIver found that on the boards they studied in the late 1980s, 63% of outside directors of large corporations were CEOs of other companies, almost all of whom were white males more than 55 years old. Lorsch & MacIver, *supra*, at 18. These numbers have shifted somewhat in recent years, but the pool from which outside directors are drawn remains both small and rather homogenous. The 1996 Korn/Ferry survey found that 89% of the corporations surveyed had at least one retired executive from another company on its board, 87% had a CEO or Chief Operating Officer from another company, 73% had an outside investor, 51% had a former government official, 50% had an academician, and only 27% had a commercial banker. Korn/Ferry International, *supra*, at 12.

From 1988 to 1996, the proportion of corporations with female directors increased from 58% to 71%. Moreover, in 1996, 18% of the surveyed corporations had two female directors and 7% had three or more. Fifty-one percent of the surveyed corporations had ethnic minority directors, a sharp increase from 33% in 1988. *Id*. Thirty-five percent of the directors surveyed said they planned to add a woman to the board in the next year, 27% said they expect to add an African–American, 11% said they expect to add a Latino, and 10% said they expect to add an Asian. *Id*.

## 2. THE MEANING OF "INDEPENDENT"

The monitoring model discussed in Section A is premised on the assumption that directors who are independent of management can act to reduce agency costs within the large corporation by checking management overreaching and vetoing unwise management proposals. But what is meant by "independent" and how much is reliance on independent directors is justified? Board members must develop a working relationship among themselves; the board must also work with management. These two goals may be in conflict and a balance must be struck between them. Directors also must be willing to offer constructive criticism of corporate management. A danger exists, however, that outside directors will hesitate to rock the boat, even if they feel strongly that management is wrong in its strategy or decisions. Mace, Lorsch and MacIver, and Manning all point out that even conscientious outside directors usually defer to a CEO who stands behind her proposals and prefer to resign quietly rather than challenge the CEO publicly.

Definitions of who qualifies as an "independent" director vary with context and vary in content. When considering questions relating to directors' fiduciary duties, the ALI uses the term "interested" and counts as interested a director who has a significant financial interest in a particular transaction and a director whose judgment may be influenced by a relationship she has with someone who has such a financial interest. ALI, PRINCIPLES OF CORPORATE GOVERNANCE (1994), § 1.23. We consider this definition further in Chapter 17.

On the other hand, when considering a director's qualification to serve on committees of the board, such as the audit committee, the ALI looks at whether the director has a "significant relationship" with a senior executive. Such a relationship includes employment with the firm within the past two years; being an immediate family member of a senior executive; engaging in transactions with the corporation, directly or indirectly, in an amount exceeding $200,000; or working for a law firm or investment bank that the corporation employs. *Id.*, § 1.34.

The National Association of Corporate Directors considers a director independent if she "[1] has never been an employee of the corporation or any of its subsidiaries; [2] is not a relative of any employee of the company; [3] provides no services to the company; [4] is not employed by any firm providing major services to the company; [and 5] receives no compensation from the company, other than director fees." *See* Report of the NACD Blue Ribbon Commission, DIRECTOR PROFESSIONALISM, Appendix C (1997). The Council of Institutional Investors has adopted a similar definition, but also does not consider independent a director who (1) is employed by a foundation or university that receives significant support from the corporation or one of its affiliates or (2) is part of an interlocking directorate in which the CEO or other executive officer of the corporation serves on the board of another corporation that employs the director. *Id.*

The Business Roundtable, an organization of CEOs of major corporations, abjures any precise definition of independence and favors a more subjective approach.

> The degree of independence of an outside director may be affected by many factors, including the personal stature of the director and any business relationship of the director with the corporation or any business or personal relationship of the director with management. Directors, or firms in which they have an interest, are sometimes engaged to provide legal, consulting, accounting or other services to the corporation, or a director may have an interest in a customer, supplier or business partner of the corporation, or may at an earlier point in his or her career have been an employee or officer of the company. Depending on their significance to the director and to the corporation, such relationships may affect a director's actual or perceived independence. The Business Roundtable believes that, where such relationships exist, boards should be mindful of them and make a judgment about a director's independence based on his or her individual circumstances rather than through the mechanical application of rigid criteria.

The Business Roundtable, STATEMENT ON CORPORATE GOVERNANCE 10–11 (1997).

## 3. CONCERNS ABOUT "STRUCTURAL BIAS"

Some commentators question whether outside directors, even if they satisfy one or another of the above criteria of "independence," will safeguard the interest of shareholders and others. They suggest that outside directors—especially those who are executives of other corporations—have a "structural bias" against taking actions that conflict with the interests or preferences of a corporation's managers—a "mind set" that prevents them from acting independently. One commentator suggests such directors are governed by "The Golden Rule of The Boardroom"—to wit, "Do unto the managers of a company on whose board you sit only what you would have the directors of your company do unto you." Weiss, *supra*, at 40.

Two other commentators conclude:

The process by which board members are selected, the criteria by which their candidacy and continued service are evaluated, and the motives and rewards that impel nominees and directors to serve on the board all interact to form a highly cohesive group of mutually attractive individuals. All available evidence suggests that the strength of this attraction among the directors and the value they each place upon their membership in the group are extremely high. For example, the selection criteria generate boards of directors who have highly similar backgrounds, goals, talents, and work experience: a highly cohesive, cooperative set of directors who share corporate attitudes and loyalties. In addition, the shared perception of mutual agreeableness enhances the interpersonal attraction among ingroup members and this enhanced mutual attraction creates even more conformity. The very high nonmonetary personal value that directors place on continued membership on these highly prestigious boards tend to multiply the overall cohesion of the group even more. Finally, enhanced self-esteem derived from being singled out for membership in the select group and the increased attention associated with continued group membership contribute importantly to ingroup cohesion within the boardroom.

James D. Cox & Harry L. Munsinger, *Bias in the Boardroom: Psychological Foundations and Legal Implications of Corporate Cohesion*, LAW & CONTEMP. PROBS., Summer 1985, at 83, 98–99.

On the other hand, a former SEC Commissioner, corporate executive and experienced practitioner, while noting concern about structural bias, states:

Is the system malfunctioning to the extent that we must look to alternative sources for corporate monitoring? The system of independent directors works reasonably well and has improved considerably over time. Moreover, we may be expecting too much from directors, both because of a failure to understand the nature of the board's relationship to the management and because of a failure to define clearly the board's responsibility in some crucial areas. While the board's basic function is to monitor the management and to hire and fire the CEO, that function cannot be successfully performed in an adversarial environment. Success in business requires risk-taking and risk-taking requires a united team of board and management. Thus, whether the directors are chosen by management, by an independent nominating committee or by an independent chairman, in most companies they will inevitably be identified with the management's strategic policies, which they have approved. The board's identification with the management's goals is a major element in creating the "slowness to act" that some observers find to be a defect in the current system. In my view, it is simply the natural consequence of a strength—the unity of the board and management on strategic corporate issues. Of course, some boards are shamelessly derelict, but there is not a systemic problem unless there is a wide pattern of dereliction; unsatisfactory individual conduct calls for policing, either through the courts or through shareholder action, not a structural solution.

Stephen J. Friedman, *Corporate Governance in the Nineties—Institutional Investors and the Evolution of the Law*, THE BUSINESS LAWYER UPDATE 6 (Jan./Feb. 1992).

## 4. CONSTITUENCY DIRECTORS

In searching for "independent" directors, some commentators have suggested that some directors should represent the interests of constituencies other than shareholders, such as employees., while others have argued that directors should be drawn from groups that are not part of the traditional corporate establishment, such as women and racial and ethnic minorities. Those who support these suggestions argue that directors drawn from these groups will not share the club mentality of current outside directors and will be less likely to be co-opted into deferring automatically to the CEO. Moreover, such directors could improve the board's decision-making by broadening its perspective. *See* Donald E. Schwartz, *The Public–Interest Proxy Contest: Reflections on Campaign GM*, 69 MICH. L.REV. 419 (1971) (discussing an early attempt to broaden the composition of the General Motors board).

One recent survey found "several signs indicate that corporate America is becoming more open to diversifying boards and that it will tap more women minorities as [directors]." IRRC Social Issues Service, 1998 BACKGROUND REPORT D: BOARD DIVERSITY 8 (1998). These include evidence that a substantial majority of corporate CEOs are giving priority to recruiting more female and minority directors.

Others in the corporate community, however, question the value of diversity on corporate boards. In 1996, T. J. Rodgers, the CEO of Cypress Semiconductor Corp., responded to a letter from Sister Doris Gormley, a Catholic nun, explaining that her order had withheld its votes for Cypress's slate of directors because the company's board included no minorities or women, as follows:

The semiconductor business is a tough one * * *. There have been more corporate casualties than survivors. For that reason, our Board of Directors is not a ceremonial watchdog, but a critical management function. The essential criteria for Cypress board membership are as follows:

- Experience as a CEO of an important technology company.
- Direct expertise in the semiconductor business based on education and management experience.
- Direct experience in the management of a company that buys from the semiconductor industry.

A search based on these criteria usually yields a male who is 50-plus years old, has a Masters degree in an engineering science, and has moved up the managerial ladder to the top spot in one or more corporations. Unfortunately, there are currently few minorities and almost no women who chose to be engineering graduate students 30 years ago. (That picture will be dramatically different in 10 years, due to the greater diversification of graduate students in the '80s.) Bluntly stated, a 'woman's view' on how to run our semiconductor company does not help us, unless that woman has an advanced technical degree and experience as a CEO. I do realize there are other industries in which the last statement does not hold true. We would quickly embrace the opportunity to include any woman or minority person who could help us director, because we pursue talent—and we don't care in what package that talent comes.

I believe that placing arbitrary racial or gender quotas on corporate boards is fundamentally wrong. Therefore, not only does Cypress not meet your requirements for boardroom diversification, but we are unlikely to, because it is very difficult to find qualified directors, let alone that also meet investors' racial and gender preferences.

* * *

Choosing a board of directors based on race and gender is a lousy way to run a company. Cypress will never do it. Furthermore, we will never be pressured into it, because bowing to well-meaning, special-interest groups is an immoral way to run a company. * * *

*Letter from T. J. Rodgers to Doris Gormley* (May 23, 1996)(full text avail. at http://www.cypress.com:80/cypress/cyp_news/gormley.htm).

According to IRRC Social Issues Service, *supra* Sister Gormley responded to Rodgers as follows:

Surely, you understand that expanding markets require expanding perspective to meet the demands from diverse cultures in society. * * * Unless this diversity of perspective is well represented among the board and management of the corporation, the very leadership that is expected to set the tone and direction of the company can stifle and frustrate diversity and creativity within the ranks, by sending mixed messages about the organizational culture.

*Id.* at 11.

In any event, suggestions that boards include representatives of non shareholder constituencies also pose serious practical problems. What groups should be represented? How many representatives should each constituency have and how should each constituency select its representative(s)? Will directors responsible to (or representing) different constituencies create a divisive, adversary atmosphere? Will the board become a political organ working out conflicts through shifting alliances among directors representing different interests?

Well-meaning individuals also may lack the expertise and experience requisite to making board decisions. They may offer little constructive input or may be co-opted into the existing corporate apparatus, its goals and functions. There is, in addition, the question of whether privately owned corporations should be asked to perform quasi-governmental functions; reformers might look instead to the political process. *See* Daniel R. Fischel, *The Corporate Governance Movement*, 35 VAND. L.REV. 1259 (1982).

### Bayless Manning, *A Taxonomy of Corporate Law Reform*, in COMMENTARIES ON CORPORATE STRUCTURE AND GOVERNANCE

120–22 (Donald E. Schwartz, ed., 1979).

\* \* \* Must special-interest participationism be accepted as a universal axiom to be applied unthinkingly to every form of organized human behavior? Aside from the question of its wide application to other institutions (armies, churches, schools, ship crews, courts, etc.), the core of the question as addressed to commercial enterprises is whether one recognizes and accepts that the commercial corporation—whether small or large—should be first and foremost an organization designed to operate efficiently to produce goods and services for the society, rather than a political organization designed to maximize political expression. To the degree that the managerial and decisionmaking structure of the incorporated enterprise is altered to resemble a New England town meeting, a Quaker consensus session, an Italian Parliament, or a two-party power negotiation, the capacity of the enterprise to carry out its basic economic function cannot fail to be impeded.

\* \* \*

Seen from [the perspective of economic efficiency], the role of common shareholders as the ultimate constituency of the corporation makes a great deal of sense. Unlike any of the other constituents who tap the income stream of the enterprise-workers, creditors, tax collectors, suppliers, etc., the common shareholder is playing for the entrepreneurial margin and only the entrepreneurial margin. Nothing so clears the mind and sharpens his taste for efficiency as the recognition that everyone else gets paid ahead of him and that he gets nothing unless there is something left over. No other constituency of the enterprise has the same incentive to achieve a high level of efficiency for the enterprise as a whole, since the economic interest of each other constituency is narrower or has a limiting cap on it or runs directly counter to the interest of the aggregate enterprise's cost control. Shareholders—particularly the professional sharp-eyed investors with a nervous focus on the bottom line—perform a vital function for the enterprise and for the efficiency of the economy as a whole.

It is the responsibility of the board of directors and management of an enterprise, and it is to the special economic interest of the common shareholders, to attend to the operating efficiency of the enterprise as a whole. No other group has that perspective of the aggregate. To lodge within the board of directors a cell whose commitment is to a single constituency of the enterprise—whether to employees, lenders, consumers, or any other group—rather than to the interest of the aggregate enterprise is a certain way to dilute and in time to destroy the feature of the corporate form that, more than any other, has accounted for its extraordinary economic success.

———

Not all commentators are as negative toward constituency directors. Alfred F. Conard professes some skepticism but suggests that customers and employees could practicably be represented on boards. However, he questions whether environmentalists would make positive contributions and more generally argues that the interests of corporate constituencies can be served more efficiently by means other than board membership. Alfred F. Conard, *Reflections on Public Interest Directors*, 75 Mich. L.Rev. 941 (1977). Lawrence Mitchell, though, strongly endorses the inclusion of constituency representatives on boards and in board decision making. Lawrence E. Mitchell, *A Critical Look at Corporate Governance*, 45 Vand. L.Rev. 1263 (1992).

Victor Brudney, on the other hand, argues: "[N]either theory nor practice permits the conclusion that the independent director can be as successful a monitor of social responsibility as it is claimed he is, or even as he may be, as a monitor of integrity. And in the context of social responsibility, even more than self-dealing, there is reason to believe that the losses from using him as a substitute for regulation will exceed the gains." Victor Brudney, *The Independent Director–Heavenly City or Potemkin Village?*, 95 Harv. L.Rev. 597, 658 (1981). For a view endorsing

## 5. PROPOSALS TO ENHANCE BOARD PERFORMANCE

In 1997, the National Association of Corporate Directors organized a "Blue Ribbon Commission" made up of corporate executives and directors, representatives of institutional investors, attorneys and academics and chaired by Ira Millstein, an attorney who has served as an advisor to the boards of several major corporations. The Commission considered contemporary developments in the field of corporate governance and issued a report directed at enhancing the performance of corporate boards. Its recommendations follow:

### Report of the NACD Blue Ribbon Commission, DIRECTOR PROFESSIONALISM

1–20 (1997).

### Introduction

The accepted governance paradigm is simple: management is accountable to the board, and the board is accountable to shareholders. * * *

In the view of the Commission, the board does more than mechanically link those who manage the corporation and those who own it. Rather, as a surrogate for dispersed ownership, the board is at the very center of corporate governance itself, ever changing, ever improving.

After careful consideration and debate, this Commission has embraced the term *professionalism* to connote a culture that appears to be evolving in boardrooms not only in the United States but also gradually elsewhere. In this Report, the Commission endeavors to describe and endorse the key elements of this emerging culture of professionalism for board members and for boards.

Professionalism places principal reliance on the actions and attitudes of individual board members. Only if each member of the board understands—and all members agree upon—their joint responsibilities as directors, can the entire board truly fulfill its role.

A professional boardroom culture requires that the governance process be collectively determined by individual board members who:

- are independent of management

- are persons of integrity and diligence who make the necessary commitment of time and energy

- recognize that the board has a function independent of management and explicitly agree on that function, and

- are capable of performing that function as a group, combining diverse skills, perspectives, and experiences.

\* \* \*

### Responsibilities: What Boards Should Do

Director professionalism is found in legal imperatives, but it is by no means limited to them. Beyond its duties of loyalty and care on behalf of shareholders, each board has the freedom—and, the Commission believes, the obligation—to define its role and duties in detail. How a board does this will help to determine the kind of board it will be and the kind of directors it will attract and retain.

\* \* \*

More specifically, as defined by the American Law Institute, The Business Roundtable, the NACD, and other relevant bodies, board responsibilities include:

- approving a corporate philosophy and mission

- selecting, monitoring, evaluating, compensating, and—if necessary—replacing the CEO and other senior executives, and ensuring management succession

- reviewing and approving management's strategic and business plans, including developing a depth of knowledge of the business being served, understanding and questioning the assumptions upon which such plans are based, and reaching an independent judgment as to the probability that the plans can be realized

- reviewing and approving the corporation's financial objectives, plans, and actions, including significant capital allocations and expenditures

- reviewing and approving material transactions not in the ordinary course of business

- monitoring corporate performance against the strategic and business plans, including overseeing the operating results on a regular basis to evaluate whether the business is being properly managed

- ensuring ethical behavior and compliance with laws and regulations, auditing and accounting principles, and the corporation's own governing documents

- assessing its own effectiveness in fulfilling these and other board responsibilities, and

- performing such other functions as are prescribed by law, or assigned to the board in the corporation's governing documents.

\* \* \*

### Processes: How Boards Should Fulfill Their Responsibilities

The board's responsibilities can be executed in a variety of ways depending on the individual board, the individual organization, and the unique environment in which the board and organization functions. There are several common elements, however, that can be identified and promoted ubiquitously to ensure that boards effectively carry out their role and responsibilities.

The Commission believes that eight primary process elements form the cornerstone for establishing the independence and effectiveness of directors and boards, and for creating a culture of director professionalism that will facilitate directors' ability to fulfill their role and discharge their responsibilities. These elements include: establishing a governance committee, creating independent leadership roles, influencing board and committee agendas, determining effective independent selection and compensation methods, requiring stock ownership, establishing an evaluation process, holding "executive sessions" of the independent directors, and accessing independent advice.

***Establishing a Governance Committee.*** * * *

■ Boards should establish a wholly independent committee that is responsible for the governance of the board, and should define the accompanying functions and responsibilities of that committee, including nominating directors for board membership, and setting and monitoring board performance goals. * * *

***Creating Independent Leadership Roles.*** The roles of a non-executive chairman or board leader have been under consideration for some years. * * * The purpose of creating these positions is not to add another layer of power but instead to ensure organization of, and accountability for, the thoughtful execution of certain critical independent director functions. * * *

■ Boards should consider formally designating a non-executive chairman or other independent board leader. If they do not make such a designation, they should designate, regardless of title, independent members to lead the board in its most critical functions, including: agenda-setting with the CEO; CEO and board evaluation; executive sessions; and anticipating or responding to crises.

***Influencing the Agenda.*** * * *

■ Boards should ensure that members are actively involved with their CEO in setting the agendas for full board meetings. A designated director or directors should work with the CEO * * * to ensure that all relevant materials are provided in a timely manner prior to each meeting.

■ For committee meetings, committee chairs should work with the CEO and committee members to create agendas (incorporating other board members' input as provided and to ensure that all relevant materials are provided in a timely manner prior to each meeting.

***Determining Effective, Independent Selection and Compensation Methods.*** * * *

■ Boards should involve all directors in all stages of the CEO and board member selection and compensation processes.

■ Boards should determine the appropriate board size, and periodically assess overall board composition to ensure the most appropriate and effective board membership mix.

■ Boards should institute as a matter of course an independent director succession plan and selection process, through a committee or overseen by a designated director or directors.

■ Boards should require that key committees—compensation, audit, and nominating or governance—include *only* independent directors, and are free to hire independent advisors as necessary. * * *

■ Boards should establish guidelines for, and discuss with some predefined frequency, the number of committees, the size and structure of committees, and the selection and rotation of committee members.

■ Boards should institute a CEO succession plan and selection process, through an independent committee or overseen by a designated director or directors.

*Requiring Stock Ownership.* A significant ownership stake leads to a stronger alignment of interests between directors and shareholders, and between executives and shareholders. * * *

■ Boards should establish a process by which directors can determine the compensation program in a deliberative and objective way.

■ Boards should set a substantial target for stock ownership by each director and a time period during which this target is to be met. * * *

■ Boards should pay directors solely in the form of equity and cash—with equity representing a substantial portion of the total up to 100 percent; boards should dismantle existing benefit programs and avoid creating new ones. * * *

*Establishing an Evaluation Process.* There are three separate aspects to effective evaluation at the board level * * *: CEO evaluation, board evaluation, and individual director evaluation. * * *

■ Boards should regularly and formally evaluate the CEO, the board as a whole, and individual directors.

■ Boards should ensure that independent directors create and control the methods and criteria for evaluating the CEO, the board, and individual directors.

* * *

*Holding Executive Sessions.* * * *

■ Boards should adopt a policy of holding periodic executive sessions at both the full board and committee levels on a preset schedule.

*Accessing Independent Advice.* * * *

■ Board members and senior management, as necessary, should concurrently participate in the selection of outside professionals who give advice both to the board and to management,.

■ Under special circumstances, the board and board committees may wish to hire their own outside counsel, consultants, and other professionals to advise the board.

### Selection: Who Directors Should Be

On an effective board, every member counts. Therefore, each board should identify, select, and retain only directors who will best enable it to fulfill its role and discharge its responsibilities.

\* \* \*

### Personal Characteristics of Directors

■ Boards should seek only candidates who have demonstrated high ethical standards and integrity in their personal and professional dealings, and who are willing to act on—and remain accountable for—their boardroom decisions.

■ Boards should seek only candidates who possess high intelligence and wisdom, and who apply it in decision-making.

■ Boards should seek only candidates who are financially literate. Directors should know how to read a balance sheet, an income statement, and a cash flow statement, and they should understand the use of financial ratios and other indices for evaluating company performance.

■ Boards should seek only candidates who approach others assertively, responsibly, and supportively, and who are willing to raise tough questions in a manner that encourages open discussion.

■ Boards should seek only candidates who have a history of achievements that reflect high standards for themselves and others.

### Core Competencies of the Board

\* \* \* The Commission recommends that *the board as a whole* should possess all of the following *core competencies,* with each candidate contributing knowledge, experience, and skills in at least one domain:

■ Boards should seek candidates with expertise in financial accounting and corporate finance, especially with respect to trends in debt and equity markets.

■ Boards should seek candidates who have a record of making good business decisions.

■ Boards should seek candidates who understand and stay current on general management "best practices" and their application in complex, rapidly evolving business environments.

■ Boards should seek candidates who have the ability and time to perform during periods of both short-term and prolonged crises.

■ Each company's board should have one or more members with appropriate and relevant industry-specific knowledge.

■ Boards of companies that operate or plan to operate in international markets should seek candidates who have business experience in those markets.

■ Boards should seek candidates who understand and possess empowerment skills and who have a history of motivating high-performing talent.

■ Boards should seek candidates with the skills and capacity to provide strategic insight and direction by encouraging innovation, conceptualizing key trends, evaluating strategic decision, and continuously challenging the organization to sharpen its vision.

## Maintaining Board Independence

Board independence is crucial to ensure that the board effectively carries out its mission and responsibilities, and fairly holds management accountable to shareholders.

■ Boards should require that independent directors fill the substantial majority of board seats.

■ Boards should ensure that any director candidate under consideration, with the exception of their own CEO or senior managers, is independent.

* * * [T]o ensure board independence:

■ Boards should define and disclose to shareholders a definition of "independent director."

■ Boards should require that director candidates disclose all existing business relationships between them or their employer and the board's company.

■ Boards should then evaluate the extent to which, if any, a candidate's other activities may impinge on his or her independence as a board member, and determine when relationships are such that a candidate can no longer be considered independent.

## Director Commitment

■ Boards should seek candidates who demonstrate a willingness to rigorously prepare for, attend, and participate in, all board and committee meetings.

■ Boards should select candidates who possess or are willing to develop broad, current knowledge of both critical issues affecting the company (including industry-, technology-, and market-specific information), and directorship roles and responsibilities (including the general legal principles that guide board members).

■ Boards should carefully assess candidates' other commitments.
* * *

■ Boards representatives should have a detailed discussion with the candidate concerning the board's expectations and the candidate's willingness and ability to make the necessary commitment to be an outstanding director.

The Commission recognizes that CEOs may benefit from service on the board of another company and boards may benefit from having directors who serve on other boards. On the other hand, the Commission also is aware that CEOs and directors themselves may have concerns about director over-commitment. Outstanding persons often receive a number of offers for board service; there are substantial psychic and monetary rewards associated with joining corporate boards, and for many individual directors there is only a relatively short period of time during which such rewards are available. * * *

Most companies at present have no governance standards on this issue. The Commission believes that guidelines, however tentative, would be helpful. In recommending guidelines, the Commission realizes that many directors are capable of outstanding service beyond the numerical guidelines.

With these caveats in mind, the Commission recommends that boards in general consider the following guidelines for different categories of candidates:

■ CEOs and other senior executives of public corporations: Boards should prefer individuals who hold no more than one or two public-company directorships[7] (including the position to be offered) in addition to membership on their own company board.

■ Other individuals with full-time positions: Boards should prefer individuals who hold no more than three or four public-company directorships (including the position to be offered) in addition to membership on their own organization's board.

■ Other individuals: Boards should prefer individuals who hold no more than five or six public-company directorships (including the position to be offered).

* * *

■ Boards should require that the CEO and other inside directors submit a resignation as a matter of course upon retirement, resignation, or other significant change in their professional roles and responsibilities.

■ Boards should require that all directors submit a resignation as a matter of course upon retirement, a change in employer, or other significant change in their professional roles and responsibilities.

■ Unless boards have a process to evaluate the performance of individual directors, they should establish tenure conditions under which, as a matter of course, directors should submit a resignation for consideration or offer to withdraw from consideration for renomination.

**7.** Significant time commitments to not-for-profit and private-company director-ships should also be considered in evaluating director availability.

- Boards should identify the skills and experience that the board needs as a team to supplement existing resources and provide talent for future needs.

- Boards should seriously consider, but not choose based solely on, the distinctive skills, perspectives, and experiences that candidates diverse in gender, ethnic background, geographic origin, and professional experience (public, private, and non-profit sectors) can bring to the boardroom.

- Boards should continuously consider a company's status and corporate strategy to determine what director attributes can best contribute to enhance board, and therefore organizational, success under existing and future circumstances, and to ensure that the most appropriate and effective resources are brought to bear at various stages.

\* \* \*

### Evaluation: How Boards and Directors Should Be Judged

Board effectiveness depends not only on director selection but also on the corresponding process of evaluation. Obviously, no one can evaluate directors better than directors themselves—but how should they do this? Fortunately, models abound. An increasing number of companies are establishing processes through which directors can evaluate the boards on which they serve. Some companies are developing tools for director self-evaluation and peer evaluation as well.

\* \* \*

- Boards should designate or establish a committee (governance or other) charged with designing and implementing a board and director evaluation process.

- The board's independent directors should originate and control the assessment methods and criteria, taking into consideration the views of the CEO, and independent directors should control the key committees (nominating, governance, and/or executive) involved in setting and monitoring board performance goals.

- Boards should establish clear goals for the board and director evaluation process, and ensure that all directors have input into developing this process.

- Boards should have broad and flexible authority to establish a process, including procedures and performance criteria, for board and director evaluation and removal that suits the individuals and the company.

- Boards should keep in mind that the very qualities of collegiality and cooperation that enhance the constructiveness of board debate can inhibit the frankness essential for self-evaluation.

- Boards should encourage candor, openness, fairness, and discretion in the evaluation process.

- Boards should ensure that their evaluation process maintains strict confidentiality with respect to each participant's input and feedback.

- Boards should periodically review assessment practices and criteria to measure their effectiveness and responsiveness against changing needs, and to ensure their continued efficacy and appropriateness.

- Boards should disclose evaluation procedures to shareholders in the proxy statement or other shareholder communication. Board disclosure of procedures is distinct from sharing the substance of such deliberations, which should be confidential.

- Boards should periodically review the allocation of powers between management and the board as delineated in the articles of incorporation and corporate bylaws, and determine whether or not these grants of authority are consistent with the changing needs of the business.

- Boards should determine the delegation of responsibilities to specific committees and directors, and communicate the allocation of decision-making powers to affected managers and shareholders.

- Boards should assess how individual members function as a team, and whether structures and processes have been implemented that reinforce this functioning.

- Boards should conduct "post mortems" on how effectively the board responded to a specific crisis to derive useful lessons for handling future emergencies.

- Boards should assess whether they are effectively taking advantage of technological advances such as electronic mail (e-mail) and intranets, which provide opportunities to share information and informal commentary between meetings.

\* \* \*

One of the greatest—and most sensitive—challenges a board faces is deciding whether to replace a director. Because decisions not to renominate, to accept a tendered resignation, or—in the most serious situations—to ask for a director's resignation are difficult for all involved, clarity as to expectations about board service is critical.

\* \* \*

- Boards should emphasize, when a director is invited to join the board, that renomination is not a given, and that all directors are regularly evaluated and receive a *de novo* review at the end of each term. \* \* \*

- Boards should require that all directors submit for consideration a resignation as a matter of course if evaluation indicates that they are not meeting standards established by the board, if their actions reflect poorly upon the board and the company (*e.g.*, scandal, indictment), or if poor health or new and pressing commitments prevent effective functioning.

### Note: Other Proposals for Reform

1.  Shortly after the Blue Ribbon Commission issued its report, The Business Roundtable issued a STATEMENT ON CORPORATE GOVERNANCE that its counsel described as "following a different, more subjective approach to corporate governance standards." John F. Olson & Polly A. Nyquist, *The Business Roundtable's Approach to Corporate Governance*, INSIGHTS 27 (Dec. 1997). As noted above, the Roundtable rejected "bright line" rules for defining who is an independent director in favor of a more subjective standard. The Roundtable also acknowledged that equity compensation of directors should be encouraged, but noted that certain directors, such as those whose principal occupations are in public service or academic settings, may require cash compensation. The Business Roundtable, STATEMENT ON CORPORATE GOVERNANCE 17 (1997).

Like many other organizations, the Roundtable recommended that a substantial majority of corporate boards be independent and that all members of a board's audit, compensation/personnel and nominating/governance committees be outside directors. *Id.* at 10, 17. The Roundtable also agreed that the board's central function is oversight and emphasized that a board should consider the long-term ramifications of corporate strategy. *Id.* at 6, As a corollary, the Roundtable noted that in certain circumstances, a board may conclude that a CEO is doing a good job "even though financial results fall short of plans." *Id.*

On the question of board leadership, the Roundtable neither endorsed or condemned proposals that a board should either separate the roles of CEO and Chairman of the Board or elect an outside director as a "lead director" responsible for overseeing the independent functioning of the board. *Id.* at 13. The Roundtable observed that having one person serve as chairman and CEO can provide a corporation with unity of vision and can provide a useful channel of communication between management and the board. *Id.* In most other respects, the Roundtable's recommendations were similar to those of the Blue Ribbon Commission.

2.  In an earlier work, Martin Lipton and Jay Lorsch agreed that a board's ability to perform is limited by many factors, including lack of time, the amount and complexity of information to be processed in decision-making, a lack of cohesion among board members, deference to the CEO or chairman, and uncertainty regarding their role as directors. They argued that these obstacles can be reduced in several ways. First, boards should be limited to ten directors, with a ratio of at least two independent directors for each inside director. This composition will allow directors to know each other better and work more closely as a team, while allowing greater discussion among those with differing views.

To avoid potential entrenchment of incompetent directors, service on a board should be limited to ten or twelve years and a mandatory retirement age imposed. To ensure that directors are able to spend enough time on their duties, no person should serve on more than three boards. Additionally, both the frequency and length of board meetings should be increased, and all meetings should have specific agendas established in advance to address the corporation's most pressing concerns. Directors should elect their own leader, a person who will coordinate discussions with and, if necessary, challenge the CEO. Boards should also become more involved in establishing and reviewing long-term corporate performance, as well as regularly evaluating the CEO. The directors should meet regularly with the corporation's largest shareholders to hear the latter group's concerns and to reduce tension between those shareholders and the board. Martin Lipton & Jay W. Lorsch, *A Modest Proposal for Improved Corporate Governance*, 48 Bus. Law. 59 (1992).

3.   Ronald Gilson and Reinier Kraakman proposed a different alternative: the creation of a class of professional directors. Ronald J. Gilson & Reinier Kraakman, *Reinventing the Outside Director: An Agenda for Institutional Investors*, 43 Stan. L. Rev. 863 (1991). Gilson and Kraakman argue that part-time outside directors do not adequately protect shareholders' interests. They asserted that even if traditional outside directors, drawn from top management of other corporations, are technically independent, they are tied too closely to the management of the corporations on whose boards they serve.

Gilson and Kraakman did not believe professional directors will supplant the traditional board. Rather, they will form a group within the board large enough to demand information otherwise not forthcoming from management and to have its voice heard in boardroom discussions. The lure of high compensation, professional interest and prestige will be enough to attract highly skilled people, such as professors at graduate business schools and partners from major accounting firms. These directors will possess both the skills and, most important, the time to become familiar with the corporations on whose boards they sit. They will serve on the boards of no more than six corporations. They will be able to conduct independent research if needed, and focus on a particular corporation if a crisis arises. The problem of managerial accountability will not arise because these professional directors will depend on their positions for their livelihoods. If their performance is inadequate, the shareholders will replace them. Moreover, if these directors fail they will have forsaken both their earlier successful careers and their reputations. (Recall Professor Weiss' (Chapter 5) proposal for a National Directors Corps.)

Gilson and Kraakman suggested that institutional investors provide the impetus for this reform. They noted that only those shareholders have the voting power to elect professional directors, but argued that all shareholders would benefit from their efforts. *But see* Martin Lipton & Steven A. Rosenblum, *A New System of Corporate Governance: The*

*Quinquennial Election of Directors*, 58 U. Chi. L.Rev. 187 (1991) (arguing that Gilson and Kraakman's proposal will increase confrontation between directors and institutional shareholders and suggesting that directors be elected every five years, instead of annually, to encourage them to focus on the corporation's long-term health rather than on immediate profits).

## 6. STUDIES OF THE EFFICACY OF OUTSIDER–DOMINATED BOARDS

In recent years, many financial economists have conducted studies directed at determining the impact of outside directors on corporate performance. Two recent surveys conclude that the results of those studies are indeterminate, and that their implications may be indeterminate as well.

Laura Lin, *The Effectiveness of Outside Directors as a Corporate Governance Mechanism: Theories and Evidence*
90 Nw. U. L. Rev. 898, 961–962, 966 (1996).

\* \* \* Although currently available empirical results do not conclusively resolve the debate about effectiveness of outside directors as monitors of management, and much work remains to be done in this area, these studies do cast doubt on the two extreme positions on board effectiveness. More specifically, the empirical data do not support either of the following propositions: (1) that regardless of its composition, the board is ineffective because it is co-opted by management, or (2) that a board composed of a majority of outside directors, who are independent from management, can always be relied on as an effective monitor of managerial decisions.

The following summarizes five major points: First, studies are mixed regarding whether the proportion of outside directors has a positive effect on overall firm performance. Second, there is some support for the proposition that outside directors make a difference in specific transactions involving potential conflicts of interest between management and shareholders—for example, turnover due to poor firm performance, the level and structure of executive compensation, corporate acquisitions, adoption of poison pills, and management buy-outs. Third, certain types of outside directors appear to have better incentives to monitor management than others. For example, there is some evidence that directors with more additional outside directorships seem to act in shareholders' interests. The data are more mixed about how outside directors' equity ownership and business ties affect their incentives to monitor. Fourth, certain factors appear to affect outside directors' ability to monitor management—for example, the length of outside directors' tenure on the board, outside directors' professional qualifications, and the length of the CEO's tenure in office. The data are less clear about the effect of the size and leadership structure of the board. Fifth, there is some evidence suggesting that alternative control mechanisms, such as the market for corporate control and concentration of ownership, may substitute or complement monitoring by directors.

\* \* \*

As noted earlier, some reformers have urged that boards of large, publicly held corporations should contain at least a majority of independent outside directors. The empirical studies suggest that such a reform may not produce as many benefits as the reformers hope. For one thing, the studies suggest that outside directors do not always make a difference in overall firm performance and specific events. Also, there is some support for the proposition that outside directors are not always needed as monitors of management when other control mechanisms are effective. Finally, unless the law can specify the type of outside directors that have the incentives and the abilities to monitor management, management may simply comply with the reform by electing the "wrong" type of outside directors.

By contrast, the studies do suggest that the presence of a majority of outside directors can improve shareholder wealth in some instances. Mandating a majority of outside directors might therefore be defended on the ground that it could *sometimes* produce positive results, even if it did not do so in every case. After all, even if outside directors do not improve shareholder wealth, what negative impact can requiring more outside directors have on the firm's value?

Against this, two possible harms could result from mandating a particular board composition and would therefore have to be considered in evaluating any proposed reform. First, some firms may want to maintain the current number of inside directors serving on their board, in order to take advantage of the insiders' special expertise. \* \* \*

Second, if the firm tries to avoid potential size problems by reducing the number of inside directors serving on its board, this may deprive the board of valuable expertise. Many observers believe that inside directors are valuable to the firm and can contribute to the firm's financial success. For example, insiders can provide the board with direct working knowledge of the company and serve as a communication link between the board and other members of the company. In addition, non-CEO insiders are often placed on the board to be trained as potential successors of the incumbent CEO. As a result, it is conceivable that a firm could have too many independent outside directors under a mandatory board composition regime. \* \* \*

Moreover, the optimal mix of inside and outside directors seems likely to differ from industry to industry and from firm to firm. \* \* \*

To be sure, the case for mandating a particular board composition does not necessarily require that it be a good thing in every possible case. As with any other mandatory rule, the case for mandatory board composition depends heavily on the relative costs of over-and under-inclusiveness, as well as on one's beliefs about the efficiency of the market for corporate structure. * * * Given the uncertainty based on currently available data, the law should proceed with caution before imposing a mandatory board composition.

---

Sanjai Bhagat and Bernard Black conducted a similar survey of other scholars' research and also reexamined data concerning the boards of 957 large public corporations. They also concluded that there is "no convincing evidence that the composition of the board of directors affects overall firm performance." Sanjai Bhagat & Bernard Black, *The Relationship Between Board Composition and Firm Performance*, in Klaus Hopt, Mark Roe & Eddy Wymeersch, eds. CORPORATE GOVERNANCE: THE STATE OF THE ART AND EMERGING RESEARCH ___, ___ (forthcoming 1998). As a consequence, they suggested, "pending the results of additional tests, * * * the burden of proof should perhaps shift to those who support the conventional wisdom that ever-greater board independence is an important element in improved corporate performance." *Id.*

Bhagat and Black advance a number of possible interpretations for the absence of data demonstrating definitively that independent directors have value:

First, it could reflect the limited power of the tests. Stock price and accounting data are noisy, especially over long time horizons.

Second, perhaps today's 'independent' directors are not independent enough. Perhaps, as Gilson & Kraakman argue [in *Reinventing the Outside Director: An Agenda for Institutional Investors, supra*], "corporate boards need directors who are not merely independent [of management], but who are *accountable* [to shareholders] as well." * * *

Perhaps, too, some directors who are classified as independent are not truly independent of management, because they are beholden to the company or its current CEO in ways too subtle to be captured in customary definitions of 'independence.' for example, some nominally independent directors may serve as paid advisors to a company, may be employed by a university or foundation that receives financial support from the company, or may have a personal relationship with the CEO that compromises their independence. * * *

A fourth possibility is that different firms benefit from different board structures. * * * For example, slowly growing firms may need a high proportion of independent directors to control managers' incentives to reinvest the firm's cash flow rather than pay dividends, even when the firm lack profitable reinvestment opportunities. * * *

A fifth explanation * * * is that an optimal board contains a mix of inside, independent, and perhaps also affiliated outside directors, who bring different skills and knowledge to the board. * * *

But if a mixed board is optimal, then many large companies may have too few inside directors to perform this role.

Sixth, maybe some types of independent directors are valuable, while others are not. Maybe CEOs of companies in other industries (who are, by number, the majority of independent directors) are too busy with their own business, know too little about a different business, and are overly generous in compensating another CEO. Maybe 'visibility' directors—well-known persons with limited business experience, often holding multiple directorships and adding gender or racial diversity to a board, are not effective on average. * * * But this explanation, too, suggests that the current push for greater board independence may be fruitless or even counterproductive, unless independent directors have particular attributes, such as close knowledge of the company's industry.

*Id.* at ___-___.

# Chapter 16

# THE DUTY OF CARE OF CORPORATE DIRECTORS

Fiduciary duty is perhaps the most important concept in the Anglo–American law of corporations. The word "fiduciary" comes from the Latin *fides,* meaning faith or confidence, and was originally used in the common law to describe the nature of the duties imposed on a trustee. Perhaps because many of the earliest corporations cases involved charitable corporations, courts began to analogize the duties of a director in managing corporate property to the duties of a trustee in managing trust property.

The original analogy between a trustee and those who control a corporation was a close one. But as corporations began to play a more important role in an increasingly complex commercial world, the strictures based on trust law gradually eroded. Today, the basic notion survives that officers, directors and controlling shareholders owe some sort of enforceable duties to the corporation, and, through the corporation, to the shareholders. Directors' fiduciary duties historically were the duty of care and the duty of loyalty, each discreet and separate from the other. Recently, however, courts have begun to blur the distinction between the two so that it is sometimes difficult to tell when one duty ends and another duty begins. Courts also have begun to recognize a duty of disclosure, sometimes as an independent duty and sometimes linked to the duties of care and loyalty. Using that framework (and necessarily oversimplifying), directors have a duty to exercise reasonable care in their oversight of the corporation's affairs and when making discrete decisions; they have a duty to place the best interests of the corporation above their own personal interests; and they have a duty in some circumstances to disclose information to other directors or to the shareholders.

## A.  INTRODUCTION

Directors are not insurers. Business is inherently risky. Directors, particularly when first elected to a board, may be concerned about the possibility that they will be held liable for losses the corporation suffers as a consequence of the board's decisions. They often ask what they must do to avoid such liability.

The answer to that question often begins with the duty of care. The premises underlying the duty of care are deceptively easy to state but have proved unusually difficult to translate into workable normative or positive statements. No one seriously disagrees with the proposition that directors should perform their duties with reasonable care. And no one seriously disagrees with the proposition that directors who do not benefit from a particular decision should not be held personally liable for good faith errors of judgments if that decision results in losses to the corporation. Yet, as we will see in this chapter, translating those beliefs into legal principles has created many extremely difficult issues.

One can begin analyzing these issues by considering the context in which they arise. Lawyers often are trained to think in a litigation context: what are the liability consequences of specific conduct after the conduct has occurred? But corporate lawyers much more frequently advise clients in a counselling or preventive context: what should (or must) the client do when faced with the responsibility of exercising oversight over the corporation's business? The contextual difference is particularly significant when the director does not benefit from her decision *and* there is a large differential between her compensation and the amount of the corporation's assets. In this context, the question of what should (or must) be done may be viewed as having an aspirational element in addition to providing a possible basis for personal liability. Additionally, as a normative matter, how do we want directors to behave, even in a world in which there is no danger of personal liability?

RMBCA § 8.30(a), which is representative of most state statutes that prescribe a standard of care, answers the aspirational question by stating that "[a] director shall discharge his duties * * * in good faith, with the care an ordinarily prudent person in a like position would exercise under similar circumstances and in a manner he reasonably believes to be in the best interest of the corporation." This standard, as the Official Comment explains, focuses on "the manner in which the director performs his duties, not the correctness of his decision." Moreover, " 'skill,' in the sense of technical competence in a particular field, should not be a qualification for the office of director." Official Comment to Section 8.30(a).

The question of a director's duty of care is closely related to what, precisely, directors do in their capacity as directors. Although the cases and commentary (with the notable exception of Dean Manning's article) do not always recognize it, directors' conduct may be viewed along a continuum. At one end, directors perform a monitoring function; they exercise oversight of the firm's on-going business operations which are under the direct control and supervision of the management. When monitoring, directors may or may not be making discrete decisions; their focus is generally on the continuing operation of the business. At the other end of the spectrum, directors clearly engage in specific decision-making: to build a new plant, raise capital for a new project, acquire another corporation.

At the monitoring end of the continuum, directors' conduct is subject to the test of reasonableness. When specific decision-making is involved, however, the business judgment rule generally protects directors against liability for unwise substantive decisions; if liability is threatened, it is because the directors' decision-making process was faulty. However, there is no clear line between process and substance. When called into question in a particular case, how should the directors' conduct be judged? Should it be by the "reasonable care" standard of RMBCA § 8.30 or by the less stringent business judgment rule? And, in turn, what is the relationship between the duty of care and the business judgment rule? This chapter provides an initial exploration into these issues.

## PROBLEM
### FASHION, INC.—PART I

Loren Peters, age 55, is a wealthy retired businesswoman. She began her career as a model, moved into fashion design, and built a very successful women's clothing company. Because her talents were primarily as a designer, she left most of the details of the business and finance operations to the vice-president of the company, Amy Fine. When her company recently needed to raise substantial additional capital, Loren elected to sell the company to Fashion, Inc. (Fashion), a Columbia corporation primarily engaged in the manufacture and sale of women and children's clothing. Loren received $25 million in Fashion stock in exchange for the stock of her company; Amy, who had also been a stockholder, received $5 million in Fashion stock and chose to retire from the fashion business. At the time of the sale, Lane Brown, the chairman of the board and CEO of Fashion invited Loren to join Fashion's board of directors. He said that the company would value her input and advice, and particularly her expertise in women's fashions.

Fashion has annual sales of more than $2 billion. Its stock is traded on the New York Stock Exchange and has a total market value of about $800 million. No single shareholder owns more than 5% of Fashion's stock.

The Fashion board of directors now has eleven members. In addition to Brown, there are two inside directors: the chief financial officer and the senior vice-president for marketing. The other directors are a partner in Fashion's investment banking firm, a partner in Fashion's regular outside law firm, the retired former CEO of Fashion, the dean of Columbia State University business school, the president of an international children's rights organization, and three CEO's of large publicly-held corporations.

Loren is very interested in becoming a director of Fashion and has come to you to discuss the legal ramifications of doing so. She is concerned about her potential liability for failing to meet her fiduciary duties. She is not concerned about her knowledge of the fashion industry or her basic understanding of finance. She does want to know, however, in how much depth she needs to understand the company's financial statements. She is also aware that, like most large public corporations, Fashion is subject to a wide range of regulatory statutes, both federal and state, with which, in her own company, she had little experience. Accordingly, she wants to know what, if anything, she must do as a director in connection with the company's compliance with these statutes. She also is curious about what protection the company can give her if she should be sued for breach of fiduciary duties. Finally, as she put it, "what are my duties as a director and how am I supposed to fulfill them?"

# B.  THE GENERAL STANDARD OF CARE

## FRANCIS v. UNITED JERSEY BANK

87 N.J. 15, 432 A.2d 814 (1981).

POLLOCK, J.

[Pritchard & Baird, Inc., was a reinsurance broker, a firm that arranged contracts between insurance companies by means of which companies that wrote large policies sold participations in those policies to other companies in order to share the risks. According to the custom in the industry, the selling company pays the applicable portion of the premium to the broker, which deducts its commission and forwards the balance to the reinsuring company. The broker thus handles large amounts of money as a fiduciary for its clients.

As of 1964, all the stock of Pritchard & Baird was owned by Charles Pritchard, Sr., one of the firm's founders, and his wife and two sons, Charles, Jr. and William. They were also the four directors. Charles, Sr., dominated the corporation until 1971, when he became ill and the two sons took over management of the business. Charles, Sr. died in 1973, leaving Mrs. Pritchard and the sons the only remaining directors.

Contrary to the industry practice, Pritchard & Baird did not segregate its operating funds from those of its clients; instead, it deposited all funds in the same account. From this account Charles, Sr. had drawn "loans," that correlated with corporate profits and were repaid at the end of each year. After his death, Charles, Jr. and William began to draw ever larger sums (still characterizing them as "loans") that greatly exceeded profits. They were able to do so by taking advantage of the "float" available to them during the period between the time they received a premium and the time they had to forward it (less commission) to the reinsurer.

By 1975 the corporation was bankrupt. This action was brought by the trustees in bankruptcy against Mrs. Pritchard and the bank as administrator of her husband's estate. Mrs. Pritchard died during the pendency of the proceedings, and her executrix was substituted as defendant. As to Mrs. Pritchard, the principal claim was that she had been negligent in the conduct of her duties as a director of the corporation.]

The "loans" were reflected on financial statements that were prepared annually as of January 31, the end of the corporate fiscal year. Although an outside certified public accountant prepared the 1970 financial statement, the corporation prepared only internal financial statements from 1971–1975. In all instances, the statements were simple documents, consisting of three or four 8 1/2 x 11 inch sheets.

The statements of financial condition from 1970 forward demonstrated:

|      | WORKING CAPITAL DEFICIT | SHAREHOLDERS' LOANS | NET BROKERAGE INCOME |
|------|-------------------------|---------------------|----------------------|
| 1970 | $   389,022             | $   509,941         | $  807,229           |
| 1971 | not available           | not available       | not available        |
| 1972 | $ 1,684,289             | $ 1,825,911         | $1,546,263           |
| 1973 | $ 3,506,460             | $ 3,700,542         | $1,736,349           |
| 1974 | $ 6,939,007             | $ 7,080,629         | $  876,182           |
| 1975 | $10,176,419             | $10,298,039         | $  551,598           |

Mrs. Pritchard was not active in the business of Pritchard & Baird and knew virtually nothing of its corporate affairs. She briefly visited the corporate offices in Morristown on only one occasion, and she never read or obtained the annual financial statements. She was unfamiliar with the rudiments of reinsurance and made no effort to assure that the policies and practices of the corporation, particularly pertaining to the withdrawal of funds, complied with industry custom or relevant law. Although her husband had warned her that Charles, Jr. would "take the shirt off my back," Mrs. Pritchard did not pay any attention to her duties as a director or to the affairs of the corporation. 162 N.J.Super. at 370, 392 A.2d 1233.

After her husband died in December 1973, Mrs. Pritchard became incapacitated and was bedridden for a six-month period. She became listless at this time and started to drink rather heavily. Her physical condition deteriorated, and in 1978 she died. The trial court rejected testimony seeking to exonerate her because she "was old, was grief-stricken at the loss of her husband, sometimes consumed too much alcohol and was psychologically overborne by her sons." 162 N.J.Super. at 371, 392 A.2d 1233. That court found that she was competent to act and that the reason Mrs. Pritchard never knew what her sons "were doing was because she never made the slightest effort to discharge any of her responsibilities as a director of Pritchard & Baird." 162 N.J.Super. at 372, 392 A.2d 1233.

### III.

Individual liability of a corporate director for acts of the corporation is a prickly problem. Generally directors are accorded broad immunity and are not insurers of corporate activities. The problem is particularly nettlesome when a third party asserts that a director, because of nonfeasance, is liable for losses caused by acts of insiders, who in this case were officers, directors and shareholders. Determination of the liability of Mrs. Pritchard requires findings that she had a duty to the clients of Pritchard & Baird, that she breached that duty and that her breach was a proximate cause of their losses.

As a general rule, a director should acquire at least a rudimentary understanding of the business of the corporation. Accordingly, a director should become familiar with the fundamentals of the business in which the corporation is engaged. [*Campbell v. Watson*, 62 N.J.Eq. 395, 416, 50 A. 120, 128 (Ch.1901)] Because directors are bound to exercise ordinary care, they cannot set up as a defense lack of the knowledge needed to exercise the requisite degree of care. If one "feels that he has not had sufficient business experience to qualify him to perform the duties of a director, he should either acquire the knowledge by inquiry, or refuse to act." *Ibid.*

Directors are under a continuing obligation to keep informed about the activities of the corporation. Otherwise, they may not be able to participate in the overall management of corporate affairs. * * * Directors may not shut their eyes to corporate misconduct and then claim that because they did not see the misconduct, they did not have a duty to look. The sentinel asleep at his post contributes nothing to the enterprise he is charged to protect.

Directorial management does not require a detailed inspection of day-to-day activities, but rather a general monitoring of corporate affairs and policies. Accordingly, a director is well advised to attend board meetings regularly. * * * Regular attendance does not mean that directors must attend every meeting, but that directors should attend meetings as a matter of practice. A director of a publicly held corporation might be expected to attend regular monthly meetings, but a director of a small, family corporation might be asked to attend only an annual meeting. The point is that one of the responsibilities of a director is to attend meetings of the board of which he or she is a member. * * *

While directors are not required to audit corporate books, they should maintain familiarity with the financial status of the corporation by a regular review of financial statements. In some circumstances, directors may be charged with assuring that bookkeeping methods conform to industry custom and usage. The extent of review, as well as the nature and frequency of financial statements, depends not only on the customs of the industry, but also on the nature of the corporation and the business in which it is engaged. Financial statements of some small corporations may be prepared internally and only on an annual basis; in a large publicly held corporation, the statements may be produced monthly or at some other regular interval. Adequate financial review normally would be more informal in a private corporation than in a publicly held corporation. * * *

The review of financial statements, however, may give rise to a duty to inquire further into matters revealed by those statements. Upon discovery of an illegal course of action, a director has a duty to object and, if the corporation does not correct the conduct, to resign.

In certain circumstances, the fulfillment of the duty of a director may call for more than mere objection and resignation. Sometimes a director may be required to seek the advice of counsel * * * concerning the propriety of his or her own conduct, the conduct of other officers and directors or the conduct of the corporation. * * * Sometimes the duty of a director may require more than consulting with outside counsel. A director may have a duty to take reasonable means to prevent illegal conduct by co-directors; in any appropriate case, this may include threat of suit. * * *

A director is not an ornament, but an essential component of corporate governance. Consequently, a director cannot protect himself behind a paper shield bearing the motto, "dummy director." * * * The New Jersey Business Corporation Act, in imposing a standard of ordinary care on all directors, confirms that dummy, figurehead and accommodation directors are anachronisms with no place in New Jersey law. * * *

The factors that impel expanded responsibility in the large, publicly held corporation may not be present in a small, close corporation. Nonetheless, a close corporation may, because of the nature of its business, be affected with a public interest. For example, the stock of a bank may be closely held, but because of the nature of banking the directors would be subject to greater liability than those of another close corporation. Even in a small corporation, a director is held to the standard of that degree of care that an ordinarily prudent director would use under the circumstances.

A director's duty of care does not exist in the abstract, but must be considered in relation to specific obligees. In general, the relationship of a corporate director to the corporation and its stockholders is that of a fiduciary. Shareholders have a right to expect that directors will exercise reasonable supervision and control over the policies and practices of a corporation. The institutional integrity of a corporation depends upon the proper discharge by directors of those duties.

While directors may owe a fiduciary duty to creditors also, that obligation generally has not been recognized in the absence of insolvency. With certain corporations, however, directors are deemed to owe a duty to creditors and other third parties even when the corporation is solvent. Although depositors of a bank are considered in some respects to be creditors, courts have recognized that directors may owe them a fiduciary duty. Directors of nonbanking corporations may owe a similar duty when the corporation holds funds of others in trust. * * *

As a reinsurance broker, Pritchard & Baird received annually as a fiduciary millions of dollars of clients' money which it was under a duty to segregate. To this extent, it resembled a bank rather than a small family business. Accordingly, Mrs. Pritchard's relationship to the clientele of Pritchard & Baird was akin to that of a director of a bank to its depositors. * * *

As a director of a substantial reinsurance brokerage corporation, she should have known that it received annually millions of dollars of loss and premium funds which it held in trust for ceding and reinsurance companies. Mrs. Pritchard should have obtained and read the annual statements of financial condition of Pritchard & Baird. Although she had a right to rely upon financial statements prepared in accordance with N.J.S.A. 14A:6–14, such reliance would not excuse her conduct. * * *

From those statements, she should have realized that, as of January 31, 1970, her sons were withdrawing substantial trust funds under the guise of "Shareholders' Loans." The financial statements for each fiscal year commencing with that of January 31, 1970, disclosed that the working capital deficits and the "loans" were escalating in tandem. Detecting a misappropriation of funds would not have required special expertise or extraordinary diligence; a cursory reading of the financial statements would have revealed the pillage.

The judgment of the Appellate Division is affirmed.

### Note: A Unitary Standard?

RMBCA § 8.30(a) refers to the care "an ordinarily prudent person in a like position would exercise." Is that a unitary standard, or is the director's background and experience relevant in determining the appropriate standard of care? Should it matter, for example, if the director is the chief financial officer? A representative of a labor union who has been elected because of a collective bargaining agreement? A person without a general business background who has been elected to express the interests of a minority group? An investment banker whose only contribution at board meetings is in connection with proposed financings? Because of the relative scarcity of cases, the issue has not arisen often and, as in *Francis*, where it has, the director's conduct has verged on total nonfeasance. *See e.g.Barnes v. Andrews*, 298 F. 614 (S.D.N.Y. 1924) (an inactive director must "inform himself of what was going on with some particularity"); *Gamble v. Brown*, 29 F.2d 366 (4th Cir.1928) (aged and infirm director held liable); *McDonnell v. American Leduc Petroleums, Limited*, 491 F.2d 380 (2d Cir.1974) (president and director who "had little business experience" and maintained "passive role" held liable to the extent that the corporation was damaged by conduct of others about which he knew or should have known by examining the corporation's books). *Compare Anderson v. Akers*, 7 F.Supp. 924 (W.D.Ky.1934) (director of "unsound mind" held not liable) *aff'd in part and rev'd in part* 86 F.2d 518 (6th Cir.1936), *rev'd in part per curiam* 302 U.S. 643, 58 S.Ct. 53, 82 L.Ed. 500 (1937); *Harman v. Willbern*, 374 F.Supp. 1149 (D.Kan.1974) (director, who sold his shares and remained on the board "in name only" and who relied on the corporation's officers while the corporation was looted, held not liable).

The trial court's opinion in *Francis v. United Jersey Bank*, 392 A.2d 1233 (N.J.Sup.Ct.1978) contains the following passage:

> It has been urged in this case that Mrs. Pritchard should not be held responsible for what happened while she was a director of Pritchard & Baird because she was a simple housewife who served as a director as an accommodation to her husband and sons. Let me start by saying that I reject the sexism which is unintended but which is implicit in such an argument. There is no reason why the average housewife could not adequately discharge the functions of a director of a corporation such as Pritchard & Baird, despite a lack of business career experience, if she gave some reasonable attention to what she was supposed to be doing. The problem is not that Mrs. Pritchard was a simple housewife. The problem is that she was a person who took a job which necessarily entailed certain responsibilities and she then failed to make any effort whatever to discharge those responsibilities. The ultimate insult to the fundamental dignity and equality of women would be to treat a grown woman as though she were a child not responsible for her acts and omissions.

> It has been argued that allowance should be made for the fact that during the last years in question Mrs. Pritchard was old, was grief-stricken at the loss of her husband, sometimes consumed too much alcohol and was psychologically overborne by her sons. I was not impressed by the testimony supporting that argument. There is no proof whatever that Mrs. Pritchard ever ceased to be fully competent. There is no proof that she ever made any effort as a director to question or stop the unlawful activities of Charles, Jr. and William. The actions of the sons were so blatantly wrongful that it is hard to see how they could have resisted any moderately firm objection to what they were doing. The fact is that Mrs. Pritchard never knew what they were doing because she never made the slightest effort to discharge any of her responsibilities as a director of Pritchard & Baird.

*Id.* at 1241.

At the very least, there appears to be some minimum standard to which all directors will be held. The Official Comment to RMBCA § 8.30(a) states that "[t]he combined phrase 'in a like position * * * under similar circumstances' is intended to recognize that (a) the nature and extent of responsibilities will vary, depending upon such factors as the size, complexity, urgency, and location of activities carried on by the particular corporation, (b) decisions must be made on the basis of the information known to the directors without the benefit of hindsight, and (c) the special background, qualifications, and management responsibilities of a particular director may be relevant in evaluating his compliance with the standard of care. Even though the quoted phrase takes into account the special background, qualifications and management responsibilities of a particular director, it does not excuse a director lacking business experience or particular expertise from exercising the common sense, practical wisdom, and informed judgment of an 'ordinarily prudent person.' "Clear?

## 1. DUTY OF INQUIRY

In a large corporation where directors delegate the on-going operation of the business to management, part of the directors' monitoring function involves the subsequent oversight of those to whom the delegation has been made. How much, and under what circumstances, such oversight is required is a question which directors confront on a continuing basis. To what extent, for example, must the directors inquire into the details of the corporation's financial statements which have been reviewed and certified by the corporation's independent public accountants? Absent some reason to be suspicious, can directors rely on management to bring problems to them? The issue arises most frequently today in the area of law compliance as corporations become subject to an increasing amount of regulation, both statutory and administrative. Many commentators believe that directors *should* institute law compliance programs to avoid future problems. But are directors *legally required* to do so, particularly when there is no evidence that the corporation may not be in compliance? Must there be a "triggering event" before such a requirement arises, or is the establishment of such programs now an established part of a director's legal duty of care?

As you read the following materials, think about the following questions: Should directors be held personally liable for damages suffered by a corporation due to legal violations by subordinates? How closely related to the essential nature of the corporation's business must the violations be? What if the director did not know the illegal conduct was taking place? Is it possible that a corporate officer would not know that the corporation's employees were engaging in illegal activities during the course of their employment? Given that directors have the ability to delegate many of their managerial duties to others, should they be held liable for conduct which was hidden from them? What if the director should have known about the illegal activities but purposefully did not investigate? Finally, what if the director knew of prior violations and implemented a compliance program designed to stop the conduct, but the conduct nevertheless continued?

## GRAHAM v. ALLIS–CHALMERS MANUFACTURING CO.

188 A.2d 125 (Del.Ch.1963).

WOLCOTT, JUSTICE.

This is a derivative action on behalf of Allis–Chalmers against its directors and four of its non-director employees. The complaint is based upon indictments of Allis–Chalmers and the four non-director employees named as defendants herein who, with the corporation, entered pleas of guilty to the indictments. The indictments, eight in number, charged violations of the Federal anti-trust laws. The suit seeks to recover damages which Allis–Chalmers is claimed to have suffered by reason of these violations.

The directors of Allis–Chalmers appeared in the cause voluntarily. The non-director defendants have neither appeared in the cause nor been served with process. Three of the non-director defendants are still employed by Allis–Chalmers. The fourth is under contract with it as a consultant.

The complaint alleges actual knowledge on the part of the director defendants of the anti-trust conduct upon which the indictments were based or, in the alternative, knowledge of facts which should have put them on notice of such conduct.

However, the hearing and depositions produced no evidence that any director had any actual knowledge of the anti-trust activity, or had actual knowledge of any facts which should have put them on notice that anti-trust activity was being carried on by some of their company's employees. The plaintiffs, appellants here, thereupon shifted the theory of the case to the proposition that the directors are liable as a matter of law by reason of their failure to take action designed to learn of and prevent anti-trust activity on the part of any employees of Allis–Chalmers.

By this appeal the plaintiffs seek to have us reverse the Vice Chancellor's ruling of non-liability of the defendant directors upon this theory, and also seek reversal of certain interlocutory rulings of the Vice Chancellor refusing to compel pre-trial production of documents, and refusing to compel the four non-director defendants to testify on oral depositions. We will in this opinion pass upon all the questions raised, but, as a preliminary, a summarized statement of the facts of the cause is required in order to fully understand the issues.

Allis–Chalmers is a manufacturer of a variety of electrical equipment. It employs in excess of 31,000 people, has a total of 24 plants, 145 sales offices, 5000 dealers and distributors, and its sales volume is in excess of $500,000,000 annually. The operations of the company are conducted by two groups, each of which is under the direction of a senior vice president. One of these groups is the Industries Group under the direction of Singleton, director defendant. This group is divided into five divisions. One of these, the Power Equipment Division, produced the products, the sale of which involved the anti-trust activities referred to in the indictments. The Power Equipment Division, presided over by McMullen, non-director defendant, contains ten departments, each of which is presided over by a manager or general manager.

The operating policy of Allis–Chalmers is to decentralize by the delegation of authority to the lowest possible management level capable of fulfilling the delegated responsibility. Thus, prices of products are ordinarily set by the particular department manager, except that if the product being priced is large and special, the department manager might confer with the general manager of the division. Products of a standard character involving repetitive manufacturing processes are sold out of a price list which is established by a price leader for the electrical equipment industry as a whole.

Annually, the Board of Directors reviews group and departmental profit goal budgets. On occasion, the Board considers general questions concerning price levels, but because of the complexity of the company's operations the Board does not participate in decisions fixing the prices of specific products.

The Board of Directors of fourteen members, four of whom are officers, meets once a month, October excepted, and considers a previously prepared agenda for the meeting. Supplied to the Directors at the meetings are financial and operating data relating to all phases of the company's activities. The Board meetings are customarily of several hours duration in which all the Directors participate actively. Apparently, the Board considers and decides matters concerning the general business policy of the company. By reason of the extent and complexity of the company's operations, it is not practicable for the Board to consider in detail specific problems of the various divisions.

The indictments to which Allis–Chalmers and the four non-director defendants pled guilty charge that the company and individual non-director defendants, commencing in 1956, conspired with other manufacturers and their employees to fix prices and to rig bids to private electric utilities and governmental agencies in violation of the anti-trust laws of the United States. None of the director defendants in this cause were named as defendants in the indictments. Indeed, the Federal Government acknowledged that it had uncovered no probative evidence which could lead to the conviction of the defendant directors.

The first actual knowledge the directors had of anti-trust violations by some of the company's employees was in the summer of 1959 from newspaper stories that TVA proposed an investigation of identical bids. Singleton, in charge of the Industries Group of the company, investigated but unearthed nothing. Thereafter, in November of 1959, some of the company's employees were subpoenaed before the Grand Jury. Further investigation by the company's Legal Division gave reason to suspect the illegal activity and all of the subpoenaed employees were instructed to tell the whole truth.

Thereafter, on February 8, 1960, at the direction of the Board, a policy statement relating to anti-trust problems was issued, and the Legal Division commenced a series of meetings with all employees of the company in possible areas of anti-trust activity. The purpose and effect of these steps was to eliminate any possibility of further and future violations of the anti-trust laws.

As we have pointed out, there is no evidence in the record that the defendant directors had actual knowledge of the illegal anti-trust actions of the company's employees. Plaintiffs, however, point to two FTC decrees of 1937 as warning to the directors that anti-trust activity by the company's employees had taken place in the past. It is argued that they were thus put on notice of their duty to ferret out such activity and to take active steps to insure that it would not be repeated.

The decrees in question were consent decrees entered in 1937 against Allis–Chalmers and nine others enjoining agreements to fix uniform prices on condensors and turbine generators. The decrees recited that they were consented to for the sole purpose of avoiding the trouble and expense of the proceeding.

None of the director defendants were directors or officers of Allis–Chalmers in 1937. The director defendants and now officers of the company either were employed in very subordinate capacities or had no connection with the company in 1937. At the time, copies of the decrees were circulated to the heads of concerned departments and were explained to the Managers Committee.

In 1943, Singleton, officer and director defendant, first learned of the decrees upon becoming Assistant Manager of the Steam Turbine Department, and consulted the company's General Counsel as to them. He investigated his department and learned the decrees were being complied with and, in any event, he concluded that the company had not in the first place been guilty of the practice enjoined.

Stevenson, officer and director defendant, first learned of the decrees in 1951 in a conversation with Singleton about their respective areas of the company's operations. He satisfied himself that the company was not then and in fact had not been guilty of quoting uniform prices and had consented to the decrees in order to avoid the expense and vexation of the proceeding.

Scholl, officer and director defendant, learned of the decrees in 1956 in a discussion with Singleton on matters affecting the Industries Group. He was informed that no similar problem was then in existence in the company.

Plaintiffs argue that because of the 1937 consent decrees, the directors were put on notice that they should take steps to ensure that no employee of Allis–Chalmers would violate the anti-trust laws. The difficulty the argument has is that only three of the present directors knew of the decrees, and all three of them satisfied themselves that Allis–Chalmers had not engaged in the practice enjoined and had consented to the decrees merely to avoid expense and the necessity of defending the company's position. Under the circumstances, we think knowledge by three of the directors that in 1937 the company had consented to the entry of decrees enjoining it from doing something they had satisfied themselves it had never done, did not put the Board on notice of the possibility of future illegal price fixing.

Plaintiffs have wholly failed to establish either actual notice or imputed notice to the Board of Directors of facts which should have put them on guard, and have caused them to take steps to prevent the future possibility of illegal price fixing and bid rigging. Plaintiffs say that as a minimum in this respect the Board should have taken the steps it took in 1960 when knowledge of the facts first actually came to their attention as a result of the Grand Jury investigation. Whatever duty, however, there was upon the Board to take such steps, the fact of the 1937 decrees has no bearing upon the question, for under the circumstances they were [put on] notice of nothing.

Plaintiffs are thus forced to rely solely upon the legal proposition advanced by them that directors of a corporation, as a matter of law, are liable for losses suffered by their corporations by reason of their gross inattention to the common law duty of actively supervising and managing the corporate affairs. Plaintiffs rely mainly upon *Briggs v. Spaulding*, 141 U.S. 132, 11 S.Ct. 924, 35 L.Ed. 662.

From the Briggs case and others * * * it appears that directors of a corporation in managing the corporate affairs are bound to use that amount of care which ordinarily careful and prudent men would use in similar circumstances. Their duties are those of control, and whether or not by neglect they have made themselves liable for failure to exercise proper control depends on the circumstances and facts of the particular case.

The precise charge made against these director defendants is that, even though they had no knowledge of any suspicion of wrongdoing on the part of the company's employees, they still should have put into effect a system of watchfulness which would have brought such misconduct to their attention in ample time to have brought it to an end. However, the Briggs case expressly rejects such an idea. On the contrary, it appears that directors are entitled to rely on the honesty and integrity of their subordinates until something occurs to put them on suspicion that something is wrong. If such occurs and goes unheeded, then liability of the directors might well follow, but absent cause for suspicion there is no duty upon the directors to install and operate a corporate system of espionage to ferret out wrongdoing which they have no reason to suspect exists.

The duties of the Allis–Chalmers Directors were fixed by the nature of the enterprise which employed in excess of 30,000 persons, and extended over a large geographical area. By force of necessity, the company's Directors could not know personally all the company's employees. The very magnitude of the enterprise required them to confine their control to the broad policy decisions. That they did this is clear from the record. At the meetings of the Board in which all Directors participated, these questions were considered and decided on the basis of summaries, reports and corporate records. These they were entitled to rely on, not only, we think, under general principles of the common law, but by reason of 8 Del.C. § 141(f) as well, which in terms fully protects a director who relies on such in the performance of his duties.

In the last analysis, the question of whether a corporate director has become liable for losses to the corporation through neglect of duty is determined by the circumstances. If he has recklessly reposed confidence in an obviously untrustworthy employee, has refused or neglected cavalierly to perform his duty as a director, or has ignored either willfully or through inattention obvious danger signs of employee wrongdoing, the law will cast the burden of liability upon him. This is not the case at bar, however, for as soon as it became evident that there were grounds for suspicion, the Board acted promptly to end it and prevent its recurrence.

Plaintiffs say these steps should have been taken long before, even in the absence of suspicion, but we think not, for we know of no rule of law which requires a corporate director to assume, with no justification whatsoever, that all corporate employees are incipient law violators who, but for a tight checkrein, will give free vent to their unlawful propensities.

We therefore affirm the Vice Chancellor's ruling that the individual director defendants are not liable as a matter of law merely because, unknown to them, some employees of Allis–Chalmers violated the antitrust laws thus subjecting the corporation to loss.

The judgment of the court below is affirmed.

———

*Graham* grew out of the heavy electrical equipment price fixing conspiracy, one of the first instances in which executives of major corporations received jail terms for violations of the antitrust laws. For a discussion of those events see John Brooks, BUSINESS ADVENTURES, ch. 7 (1969). Notwithstanding the evidence in the criminal cases and similar evidence in *Graham* that subordinate employees had concealed their illegal behavior from their supervisors, there was skepticism in the press and in Congress that senior executives were, in fact, innocent of all knowledge of what was going on.

There was some indication that the decentralization of Allis–Chalmers discussed by the courts was accompanied by severe pressures on the heads of the various organizational units to show steadily increasing profits for the segment of the organization for which they were responsible. These pressures were apparently independent of the conditions in the particular markets in which the organizational unit operated; it is obviously quite difficult to increase profits at a time of stagnant or declining demand. If this description of the mode of management in use at Allis–Chalmers is correct, was the court too quick to say that it is not necessary for a board of directors to establish "a corporate system of espionage"?

## IN RE CAREMARK INTERNATIONAL
## INC. DERIVATIVE LITIGATION

698 A.2d 959 (Del.Ch.1996).

ALLEN, CHANCELLOR.

Pending is a motion pursuant to Chancery Rule 23.1 to approve as fair and reasonable a proposed settlement of a consolidated derivative action on behalf of Caremark International, Inc. ("Caremark"). The suit involves claims that the members of Caremark's board of directors (the "Board") breached their fiduciary duty of care to Caremark in connection with alleged violations by Caremark employees of federal and state laws and regulations applicable to health care providers. As a result of the alleged violations, Caremark was subject to an extensive four year investigation by the United States Department of Health and Human Services and the Department of Justice. In 1994 Caremark was charged in an indictment with multiple felonies. It thereafter entered into a number of agreements with the Department of Justice and others. Those agreements included a plea agreement in which Caremark pleaded guilty to a single felony of mail fraud and agreed to pay civil and criminal fines. Subsequently, Caremark agreed to make reimbursements to various private and public parties. In all, the payments that Caremark has been required to make total approximately $250 million.

This suit was filed in 1994, purporting to seek on behalf of the company recovery of these losses from the individual defendants who constitute the board of directors of Caremark. The parties now propose that it be settled and, after notice to Caremark shareholders, a hearing on the fairness of the proposal was held on August 16, 1996.

* * *

Legally, evaluation of the central claim made entails consideration of the legal standard governing a board of directors' obligation to supervise or monitor corporate performance. For the reasons set forth below I conclude, in light of the discovery record, that there is a very low probability that it would be determined that the directors of Caremark breached any duty to appropriately monitor and supervise the enterprise. Indeed the record tends to show an active consideration by Caremark management and its Board of the Caremark structures and programs that ultimately led to the company's indictment and to the large financial losses incurred in the settlement of those claims. It does not tend to show knowing or intentional violation of law. Neither the fact that the Board, although advised by lawyers and accountants, did not accurately predict the severe consequences to the company that would ultimately follow from the deployment by the company of the strategies and practices that ultimately led to this liability, nor the scale of the liability, gives rise to an inference of breach of any duty imposed by corporation law upon the directors of Caremark.

* * *

## II.   LEGAL PRINCIPLES
* * *

### B.   *Directors' Duties To Monitor Corporate Operations*

The complaint charges the director defendants with breach of their duty of attention or care in connection with the on-going operation of the corporation's business. The claim is that the directors allowed a situation to develop and continue which exposed the corporation to enormous legal liability and that in so doing they violated a duty to be active monitors of corporate performance. The complaint thus does not charge either director self-dealing or the more difficult loyalty-type problems arising from cases of suspect director motivation, such as entrenchment or sale of control contexts. The theory here advanced is possibly the most difficult theory in corporation law upon which a plaintiff might hope to win a judgment. The good policy reasons why it is so difficult to charge directors with responsibility for corporate losses for an alleged breach of care, where there is no conflict of interest or no facts suggesting suspect motivation involved, were recently described in *Gagliardi v. TriFoods Int'l Inc.*, Del.Ch., 1996 WL 422330 at *7 (July 19, 1996).

1. Potential liability for directorial decisions: Director liability for a breach of the duty to exercise appropriate attention may, in theory, arise in two distinct contexts. First, such liability may be said to follow from a board decision that results in a loss because that decision was ill advised or "negligent". Second, liability to the corporation for a loss may be said to arise from an unconsidered failure of the board to act in circumstances in which due attention would, arguably, have prevented the loss. The first class of cases will typically be subject to review under the director-protective business judgment rule, assuming the decision made was the product of a process that was either deliberately considered in good faith or was otherwise rational. What should be understood, but may not widely be understood by courts or commentators who are not often required to face such questions, is that compliance with a director's duty of care can never appropriately be judicially determined by reference to the content of the board decision that leads to a corporate loss, apart from consideration of the good faith or rationality of the process employed. That is, whether a judge or jury considering the matter after the fact, believes a decision substantively wrong, or degrees of wrong extending through "stupid" to "egregious" or "irrational", provides no ground for director liability, so long as the court determines that the process employed was either rational or employed in a good faith effort to advance corporate interests. To employ a different rule—one that permitted an "objective" evaluation of the decision—would expose directors to substantive second guessing by ill-equipped judges or juries, which would, in the long-run, be injurious to investor inteests. Thus, the business judgment rule is process oriented and informed by a deep respect for all good faith board decisions.

Indeed, one wonders on what moral basis might shareholders attack a good faith business decision of a director as "unreasonable" or "irrational". Where a director in fact exercises a good faith effort to be informed and to exercise appropriate judgment, he or she should be deemed to satisfy fully the duty of attention. If the shareholders thought themselves entitled to some other quality of judgment than such a director produces in the good faith exercise of the powers of office, then the shareholders should have elected other directors. Judge Learned Hand made the point rather better than can I. In speaking of the passive director defendant Mr. Andrews in *Barnes v. Andrews*, Judge Hand said:

> True, he was not very suited by experience for the job he had undertaken, but I cannot hold him on that account. After all it is the same corporation that chose him that now seeks to charge him.... Directors are not specialists like lawyers or doctors.... They are the general advisors of the business and if they faithfully give such ability as they have to their charge, it would not be lawful to hold them liable. Must a director guarantee that his judgment is good? Can a shareholder call him to account for deficiencies that their votes assured him did not disqualify him for his office? While he may not have been the Cromwell for that Civil War, Andrews did not engage to play any such role.

In this formulation Learned Hand correctly identifies, in my opinion, the core element of any corporate law duty of care inquiry: whether there a good faith effort to be informed and exercise judgment.

2.   Liability for failure to monitor: The second class of cases in which director liability for inattention is theoretically possible entail circumstances in which a loss eventuates not from a decision but, from unconsidered inaction. Most of the decisions that a corporation, acting through its human agents, makes are, of course, not the subject of director attention. Legally, the board itself will be required only to authorize the most significant corporate acts or transactions: mergers, changes in capital structure, fundamental changes in business, appointment and compensation of the CEO, etc. As the facts of this case graphically demonstrate, ordinary business decisions that are made by officers and employees deeper in the interior of the organization can, however, vitally affect the welfare of the corporation and its ability to achieve its various strategic and financial goals. If this case did not prove the point itself, recent business history would. Recall for example the displacement of senior management and much of the board of Salomon, Inc.; the replacement of senior management of Kidder, Peabody following the discovery of large trading losses resulting from phantom trades by a highly compensated trader; or the extensive financial loss and reputational injury suffered by Prudential Insurance as a result its junior officers misrepresentations in connection with the distribution of limited partnership interests. Financial and organizational disasters such as these raise the question, what is the board's responsibility with respect to the organization and monitoring of the enterprise to assure that the corporation functions within the law to achieve its purposes?

Modernly this question has been given special importance by an increasing tendency, especially under federal law, to employ the criminal law to assure corporate compliance with external legal requirements, including environmental, financial, employee and product safety as well as assorted other health and safety regulations. In 1991, pursuant to the Sentencing Reform Act of 1984, the United States Sentencing Commission adopted Organizational Sentencing Guidelines which impact importantly on the prospective effect these criminal sanctions might have on business corporations. The Guidelines set forth a uniform sentencing structure for organizations to be sentenced for violation of federal criminal statutes and provide for penalties that equal or often massively exceed those previously imposed on corporations. The Guidelines offer powerful incentives for corporations today to have in place compliance programs to detect violations of law, promptly to report violations to appropriate public officials when discovered, and to take prompt, voluntary remedial efforts.

In 1963, the Delaware Supreme Court in *Graham v. Allis–Chalmers Mfg. Co.* addressed the question of potential liability of board members for losses experienced by the corporation as a result of the corporation having violated the anti-trust laws of the United States. There was no claim in that case that the directors knew about the behavior of subordinate employees of the corporation that had resulted in the liability. Rather, as in this case, the claim asserted was that the directors ought to have known of it and if they had known they would have been under a duty to bring the corporation into compliance with the law and thus save the corporation from the loss. The Delaware Supreme Court concluded that, under the facts as they appeared, there was no basis to find that the directors had breached a duty to be informed of the ongoing operations of the firm. In notably colorful terms, the court stated that "absent cause for suspicion there is no duty upon the directors to install and operate a corporate system of espionage to ferret out wrongdoing which they have no reason to suspect exists." The Court found that there were no grounds for suspicion in that case and, thus, concluded that the directors were blamelessly unaware of the conduct leading to the corporate liability.

How does one generalize this holding today? Can it be said today that, absent some ground giving rise to suspicion of violation of law, that corporate directors have no duty to assure that a corporate information gathering and reporting systems exists which represents a good faith attempt to provide senior management and the Board with information respecting material acts, events or conditions within the corporation, including compliance with applicable statutes and regulations? I certainly do not believe so. I doubt that such a broad generalization of the Graham holding would have been accepted by the Supreme Court in 1963. The case can be more narrowly interpreted as standing for the proposition that, absent grounds to suspect deception, neither corporate boards nor senior officers can be charged with wrongdoing simply for assuming the integrity of employees and the honesty of their dealings on the company's behalf.

A broader interpretation of *Graham v. Allis Chalmers*—that it means that a corporate board has no responsibility to assure that appropriate information and reporting systems are established by management—would not, in any event, be accepted by the Delaware Supreme Court in 1996, in my opinion. In stating the basis for this view, I start with the recognition that in recent years the Delaware Supreme Court has made it clear—especially in its jurisprudence concerning takeovers, from *Smith v. Van Gorkom* through *QVC v. Paramount Communications*—the seriousness with which the corporation law views the role of the corporate board. Secondly, I note the elementary fact that relevant and timely information is an essential predicate for satisfaction of the board's supervisory and monitoring role under Section 141 of the Delaware General Corporation Law. Thirdly, I note the potential impact of the federal organizational sentencing guidelines on any business organization. Any rational person attempting in good faith to meet an organizational governance responsibility would be bound to take into account this development and the enhanced penalties and the opportunities for reduced sanctions that it offers.

In light of these developments, it would, in my opinion, be a mistake to conclude that our Supreme Court's statement in *Graham* concerning "espionage" means that corporate boards may satisfy their obligation to be reasonably informed concerning the corporation, without assuring themselves that information and reporting systems exist in the organization that are reasonably designed to provide to senior management and to the board itself timely, accurate information sufficient to allow management and the board, each within its scope, to reach informed judgments concerning both the corporation's compliance with law and its business performance.

Obviously the level of detail that is appropriate for such an information system is a question of business judgment. And obviously too, no rationally designed information and reporting system will remove the possibility that the corporation will violate laws or regulations, or that senior officers or directors may nevertheless sometimes be misled or otherwise fail reasonably to detect acts material to the corporation's compliance with the law. But it is important that the board exercise a good faith judgment that the corporation's information and reporting system is in concept and design adequate to assure the board that appropriate information will come to its attention in a timely manner as a matter of ordinary operations, so that it may satisfy its responsibility.

Thus, I am of the view that a director's obligation includes a duty to attempt in good faith to assure that a corporate information and reporting system, which the board concludes is adequate, exists, and that failure to do so under some circumstances may, in theory at least, render a director liable for losses caused by non-compliance with applicable legal standards. I now turn to an analysis of the claims asserted with this concept of the directors duty of care, as a duty satisfied in part by assurance of adequate information flows to the board, in mind.

III. ANALYSIS OF THIRD AMENDED COMPLAINT AND SETTLEMENT

\* \* \*

In order to show that the Caremark directors breached their duty of care by failing adequately to control Caremark's employees, plaintiffs would have to show either (1) that the directors knew or (2) should have known that violations of law were occurring and, in either event, (3) that the directors took no steps in a good faith effort to prevent or remedy that situation, and (4) that such failure proximately resulted in the losses complained of, although under *Cede & Co. v. Technicolor, Inc.*, Del.Supr., 636 A.2d 956 (1994) this last element may be thought to constitute an affirmative defense.

1. Knowing violation for statute: Concerning the possibility that the Caremark directors knew of violations of law, none of the documents submitted for review, nor any of the deposition transcripts appear to provide evidence of it. Certainly the Board understood that the company had entered into a variety of contracts with physicians, researchers, and health care providers and it was understood that some of these contracts were with persons who had prescribed treatments that Caremark participated in providing. The board was informed that the company's reimbursement for patient care was frequently from government funded sources and that such services were subject to the ARPL. But the Board appears to have been informed by experts that the company's practices while contestable, were lawful. There is no evidence that reliance on such reports was not reasonable. Thus, this case presents no occasion to apply a principle to the effect that knowingly causing the corporation to violate a criminal statute constitutes a breach of a director's fiduciary duty. *See Roth v. Robertson*, N.Y.Sup.Ct., 118 N.Y.S. 351 (1909); *Miller v. American Tel. & Tel. Co.*, 507 F.2d 759 (3d Cir.1974). It is not clear that the Board knew the detail found, for example, in the indictments arising from the Company's payments. But, of course, the duty to act in good faith to be informed cannot be thought to require directors to possess detailed information about all aspects of the operation of the enterprise. Such a requirement would simple be inconsistent with the scale and scope of efficient organization size in this technological age.

2. Failure to monitor: Since it does appears that the Board was to some extent unaware of the activities that led to liability, I turn to a consideration of the other potential avenue to director liability that the pleadings take: director inattention or "negligence". Generally where a claim of directorial liability for corporate loss is predicated upon ignorance of liability creating activities within the corporation, as in *Graham* or in this case, in my opinion only a sustained or systematic failure of the board to exercise oversight—such as an utter failure to attempt to assure a reasonable information and reporting system exits—will establish the lack of good faith that is a necessary condition to liability. Such a test of liability—lack of good faith as evidenced by sustained or systematic failure of a director to exercise reasonable oversight—is quite high. But, a demanding test of liability in the oversight context is probably beneficial to corporate shareholders as a class, as it is in the board decision context, since it makes board service by qualified persons more likely, while continuing to act as a stimulus to good faith performance of duty by such directors.

Here the record supplies essentially no evidence that the director defendants were guilty of a sustained failure to exercise their oversight function. To the contrary, insofar as I am able to tell on this record, the corporation's information systems appear to have represented a good faith attempt to be informed of relevant facts. If the directors did not know the specifics of the activities that lead to the indictments, they cannot be faulted.

The liability that eventuated in this instance was huge. But the fact that it resulted from a violation of criminal law alone does not create a breach of fiduciary duty by directors. The record at this stage does not support the conclusion that the defendants either lacked good faith in the exercise of their monitoring responsibilities or conscientiously permitted a known violation of law by the corporation to occur. The claims asserted against them must be viewed at this stage as extremely weak.

### B. *The Consideration For Release of Claim*

The proposed settlement provides very modest benefits. Under the settlement agreement, plaintiffs have been given express assurances that Caremark will have a more centralized, active supervisory system in the future. Specifically, the settlement mandates duties to be performed by the newly named Compliance and Ethics Committee on an ongoing basis and increases the responsibility for monitoring compliance with the law at the lower levels of management. In adopting the resolutions required under the settlement, Caremark has further clarified its policies concerning the prohibition of providing remuneration for referrals. These appear to be positive consequences of the settlement of the claims brought by the plaintiffs, even if they are not highly significant. Nonetheless, given the weakness of the plaintiffs' claims the proposed settlement appears to be an adequate, reasonable, and beneficial outcome for all of the parties. Thus, the proposed settlement will be approved.

### *Note: Graham, Caremark and the Duty of Inquiry*

1.   *Caremark* is the first Delaware case that directly suggests that *Graham* might be decided differently today and, as an opinion from the Chancellor, is entitled to considerable weight. At the same time, it is interesting to note the context in which the Chancellor is writing. Consider the procedural posture of the case and contrast it with *Kahn v. Sullivan* in Chapter 5. *Caremark* involves a hearing on the fairness of a settlement to which there were no objectors. Because appeal was unlikely, the court's evaluation of the merits of plaintiff's allegations, probably would not be reviewed by the Delaware Supreme Court. Nevertheless, as George Orwell might say, some dicta is more equal than others, and *Caremark* is viewed as a major statement on the duty of inquiry.

2.   If *Caremark* accurately describes the standard for the duty of inquiry in Delaware, does it provide more or less protection to directors than the standard set out in *Graham*? *Graham* imposes a duty of inquiry only when there are "obvious signs" of employee wrongdoing. The red flag test, however, still requires directors to heed red flags when they are

raised. But to what extent are they responsible for noticing the flags in the first place? *Graham* uses a "reasonable person" or negligence standard, focusing on the director's ability to notice the red flags. To be sure of satisfying this standard, of course, prudent directors should set up fairly elaborate monitoring systems of law compliance.

*Caremark*, by contrast, seems to require some sort of monitoring system even absent a red flag. The directors' decisions with respect to the extent of those systems, however, will receive the protection of the business judgment rule (a gross negligence standard, as we will see) and will lead to liability only in the absence of good faith. Therefore, as long as the directors establish some sort of monitoring system, they generally will not be held liable even if those systems fail. We will consider the relationship between the duty of care and the business judgment rule later in this chapter.

3. Some courts and commentators disagree that Graham would or should be decided differently today. In *In re Baxter International, Inc. Shareholders Litigation*, 654 A.2d 1268, 1270 (Del.Ch.1995), Vice-Chancellor Balick applied the *Graham* red flag test and held that directors could not be held liable for their failure to implement monitoring procedures absent "obvious danger signs." And one writer has argued that *"Allis–Chalmers*, rather than being one of the weaker legs in our law, is one of the stronger and one of the more practical applications of reality to the management of corporations and criticism can be seen as largely, or to a large degree, ivory tower." Rodman Ward, *Fiduciary Standards Applicable to Officers and Directors and the Business Judgment Rule Under Delaware Law*, 3 DEL. J. CORP. L., 244, 247 (1978). For the contrary view, *see* E. Norman Veasey & Bayless Manning, *Codified Standard—Safe Harbor or Uncharted Reef?*, 35 BUS. LAW. 919, 930 (1980). For a discussion of the ALI's change of position on the duty of inquiry and the considerable criticism and pressure from the business community and segments of the organized bar, *see* Joel Seligman, *A Sheep in Wolf's Clothing: The American Law Institute Principles of Corporate Governance Project*, 55 GEO. WASH. L. REV. 325, 360–366 (1987).

4. Although the Delaware Supreme Court has not explicitly overruled *Graham*, it has indicated that there are problems with applying its logic in the contemporary corporate world. Thus in *Aronson v. Lewis*, 473 A.2d 805, 813 n. 7 (Del.1984), the court noted that "[a]lthough questions of director liability in * * * cases [such as *Graham* ] have been adjudicated upon concepts of business judgment, they do not actually present issues of business judgment." And in *Mills Acquisition Co. v. Macmillan, Inc.*, 559 A.2d 1261, 1284 n. 32 (Del.1989), when considering a lack of board oversight in connection with a tender offer, the court observed that "a board can take little comfort in what was said under far different circumstances in [*Graham* ]. Nor can decisions reached under such circumstances be sustained."

5. The ALI provides that a director's duty of care "includes the obligation to make, or cause to be made, an inquiry when, but only

when, the circumstances would alert a reasonable director or officer to the need therefor. The extent of such inquiry shall be such as the director or officer reasonably believes to be necessary." ALI, PRINCIPLES OF CORPORATE GOVERNANCE (1994),§ 4.01 (a)(1). Although seeming to adopt the "triggering event" standard, the comment to § 4.01 strongly suggests that, at least with respect to law compliance programs, Graham should be decided differently today.

Although the comment to ALI § 4.01(a)(1)-(a)(2) states that the Subsection specifically is not intended to expand directors' existing obligations, the ALI cites only four states that have specific statutory provisions requiring inquiry, and it is not clear that these statutes support the ALI's position. One of the states, Washington, has subsequently amended its statute to eliminate the duty to inquire. *See* Wash. Bus. Corp. Act § 23B.08.300 (effective July 1, 1990). The language of the three remaining statutes (Alaska, Pennsylvania and California) parallel the language in California, which provides:

A director shall perform the duties of a director, including duties as a member of any committee of the board upon which the director may serve, in good faith, in a manner such director believes to be in the best interests of the corporation and its shareholders and with such care, *including reasonable inquiry,* as an ordinarily prudent person in a like position would use under similar circumstances.

Calif. Corp. Code § 309 (a) (emphasis added).

The commentary to this section explains the scope of "reasonable inquiry" as follows:

* * * reasonable care under some circumstances could include a duty of inquiry. In other words, a director may not close his eyes to what is going on about him in the conduct of the corporate business and, *if he is put on notice by the presence of suspicious circumstances,* he may be required to make such "reasonable inquiry" as an ordinarily prudent person in his position would make under similar circumstances. There was no intention of imposing upon any director a duty to make an inquiry regardless of the circumstances * * * or to add a separate requirement of inquiry apart from a director's general duty of care. * * *

Calif. Corp. Code Ann. § 309(a) (emphasis added).

6.  Professor Michael P. Dooley disagrees with the ALI's conclusion that corporate directors should know that they will be held personally liable for their failure to implement law compliance programs. He argues that directors should be held secondarily liable for another person's violation of regulatory statutes only if Congress specifically imposes such liability. Dooley also believes that law compliance programs present implementation problems different from those associated with implementation of other corporate programs, such as accounting systems. "Determining which corporate assets need to be secured is relatively easy, but deciding which laws directors should be most concerned about

is not." Michael P. Dooley, *Two Models of Corporate Governance*, 47 Bus. Law. 461, 486 (1992).

## 2. DUE CARE AND CRIMINAL LIABILITY

What should be the relationship between the duty of care under state corporate law and the standard for a director's individual criminal liability that results from a failure to supervise subordinates' activities? This question has arisen most often in areas which have an impact on public health and welfare, such as food and drug contamination and hazardous dumping into the environment.

As early as 1943 the United States Supreme Court held corporate managers liable for criminal acts committed by their subordinates. In *United States v. Dotterweich*, 320 U.S. 277, 64 S.Ct. 134, 88 L.Ed. 48 (1943), the Court found that the corporation's president was subject to criminal prosecution for "introducing or delivering adulterated or mis-branded drugs into interstate commerce" in violation of the Food and Drug Act. 320 U.S. at 278, 64 S.Ct. at 135. The court held that because the Food and Drug Act contained no criminal mens rea, or guilty mind, requirement, the prosecution did not have to prove criminal knowledge on the part of the corporate officer. This lack of criminal mens rea "puts the burden of acting at hazard upon a person otherwise innocent but standing in a responsible relation to a public danger." 320 U.S. at 281, 64 S.Ct. at 136.

In *United States v. Park*, 421 U.S. 658, 95 S.Ct. 1903, 44 L.Ed.2d 489 (1975), the president of Acme Markets, Inc. was charged, along with his company, with five violations of the Federal Food, Drug, and Cosmet-ics Act in allowing food to be held in a company warehouse where it was exposed to contamination by rodents. The company pleaded guilty, but Park pleaded innocent and was tried before a jury which convicted him. He was fined $50 on each of the five counts.

Park's conviction was ultimately affirmed by the Supreme Court in an opinion by Chief Justice Burger, who observed:

> [In] providing sanctions which reach and touch the individuals who execute the corporate mission—and this is by no means necessarily confined to a single corporate agent or employee—the Act imposes not only a positive duty to seek out and remedy violations when they occur but also, and primarily, a duty to implement measures that will insure that violations will not occur. The requirements of foresight and vigilance imposed on responsible corporate agents are beyond question demanding, and perhaps onerous, but they are no more stringent than the public has a right to expect of those who voluntarily assume positions of authority in business enterprises whose services and products affect the health and wellbeing of the public that supports them.

421 U.S at 672, 95 S.Ct. at 1911, 44 L.Ed.2d at 501.

The Court defined "responsible corporate agent" so as to preclude the jury from convicting an officer on the basis of his corporate position alone. Rather, liability attached only if the jury could find that Park "had a responsible relation to the situation, and by virtue of his position * * * had * * * authority and responsibility to deal with the situation." *Id*. at 674, 95 S.Ct. at 1912. The Court found significant Park's awareness that Acme's internal system for ensuring its Philadelphia and Baltimore warehouses' sanitary conditions was not working, and his failure to restructure that system once notified that similar sanitary problems had arisen at two of Acme's warehouses. However, the Court recognized that even the implementation of a new internal system might fail to prevent all violations. The Court indicated that Park could have raised an affirmative defense that he was powerless to prevent the violation, and sought a jury instruction requiring the government to prove beyond a reasonable doubt that he was capable of preventing the violation. *See* Joseph G. Block and Nancy A. Voisin, *Criminal Enforcement of Environmental Laws: The Responsible Corporate Officer Doctrine—Can You Go to Jail for What You Don't Know?*, 22 ENVTL. L. 1347, 1354–55 (1992).

Personal liability of directors for actions of subordinates has also been strenuously debated in the area of environmental violations. Criminal liability is most easily found where the director was aware of the environmental violation, whether she actually instructed her subordinates to perform the illegal acts or simply acquiesced in the performance of such acts by others. Where the director charged with environmental liability did not participate in the illegal acts, imposition of liability is more difficult. It is important to note that the Food and Drug Act, at issue in *Dotterweich* and *Park*, imposes strict criminal liability. Thus, an individual can be found liable under the statute even if she did not participate in, or have actual knowledge of, the criminal acts. Conversely, most modern environmental laws do not impose strict criminal liability, but require the government to prove the violator's criminal knowledge. *See e.g.*, Clean Water Act, 33 U.S.C. § 1319(c)(2)(A), (B)(1994) (CWA); Clean Air Act, 42 U.S.C. § 7413(c)(1), (2), (3), (5) (CAA); Resource Conservation and Recovery Act, 42 U.S.C. § 6928(d) (RCRA). One court struck the inclusion of the responsible corporate officer doctrine in a charge under RCRA against a supervisor who did not participate in the alleged violation because it "would allow a conviction without the requisite specific intent." *United States v. White*, 766 F.Supp. 873, 895 (E.D.Wash.1991).

In contrast to RCRA, which does not mention responsible corporate actors, CWA and CAA expressly include the term "responsible corporate officer" in their definition of who can be found liable. One court has construed this inclusion to show that Congress intended the preservation of water and air resources to outweigh:

> * * * [H]ardships suffered by "responsible corporate officers" who are held criminally liable in spite of their lack of "consciousness of wrongdoing." * * * Under this interpretation a "responsible cor-

porate officer," to be held criminally liable, would not have to "willfully or negligently" cause a permit violation. Instead, the willfulness or negligence of the actor would be imputed to him by virtue of his position of responsibility.

*United States v. Brittain*, 931 F.2d 1413, 1419 (10th Cir.1991).

Thus, it seems that where a criminal statute either calls for strict liability for corporate defendants or includes "responsible corporate officers" in its definition of who can be held liable, a corporate director who fails to supervise subordinates adequately is likely to be held liable for corporate criminal violations.

The question of whether directors are required to institute law compliance programs has been made more complex by the adoption in 1991 of the Federal Sentencing Guidelines for Organizations which make the adoption of such programs extremely beneficial to a corporation. The Guidelines, which provide substantial fines for any corporation convicted of a federal crime, are designed to provide "incentives for organizations to maintain internal mechanisms for deterring, detecting, and reporting criminal conduct." 18 U.S.C.A.App., § 8 (West Supp. 1997). Under the Guidelines, a corporation's culpability, and therefore its sanction, can be reduced by the existence of an "effective program to prevent and detect violations of law." 18 U.S.C. § 8C.25 (West Supp. 1997). Federal criminal laws which are likely to be violated by corporations include those relating to foods and drugs, the environment, employment practices, antitrust and worker safety.

The Guidelines do not address the question of the personal liability for directors where the corporation has committed a crime. The presumption behind the Guidelines is that corporate sanctions will be sufficient to motivate directors and officers to implement law compliance programs because such programs are in the best interests of the corporation. The practical effect of the Guidelines is that law compliance programs which are insufficient to mitigate a corporation's criminal liability are likely to be used as evidence in a derivative suit to show that a director did not act reasonably in carrying out her oversight duties.

It is important to note that a compliance program will not reduce culpability if "high-level personnel" of the organization or anyone in charge of the compliance program participated in, condoned, or was willfully ignorant of the offense. Thus, in order to take advantage of the reduction in culpability offered by the Guidelines' "safe harbor," the corporation's program must be detailed and must comply with all industry standards and government regulations, and any offense charged to the corporation must be committed by low-level, non-supervisory personnel. And, apparently, ineffective law compliance programs will be no more helpful in mitigating corporate liability than the failure to implement any program at all.

# C.  THE BUSINESS JUDGMENT RULE

## PROBLEM

### FASHION, INC.—PART II

You have again heard from Loren Peters, who has been a director of Fashion for the past three years, during which time Fashion's business has continued to thrive. She has just received notice of an emergency meeting of Fashion's board of directors, to be held tomorrow. She telephoned Lane Brown to ask what the meeting was about. He responded that the meeting was to consider a potential acquisition of United Stores, Inc. (United), a large department store chain that is one of Fashion's major customers. From recent newspaper stories, Loren is aware that United is in serious financial difficulty and will require a capital infusion of more than $500 million to avoid bankruptcy. In addition, some major reorganization of United's business probably will be required to enable it to reverse the series of losses that have created the current crisis.

Lane told Loren that he would present the board with a complete report at the meeting, including financial statements prepared by United's accountants, a detailed study of United and the benefits of the acquisition prepared by Linda Jordan, Fashion's chief financial officer, and Lane's own recommendation. He also said that a vote at the meeting was essential because the agreement he had negotiated with United would expire before the transaction could receive shareholder approval unless the steps necessary for such approval were commenced immediately.

Loren knows that Lane is a close personal friend of United's CEO. She is apprehensive about whether Fashion's management has the skills and experience necessary to turn around United's business, especially because neither Lane nor the other top management in Fashion have any substantial experience managing retail operations. She also suspects that, if the terms of the deal seem reasonable, most, if not all, of the other directors will be inclined to go along with Lane's proposal because of the success he has achieved in managing Fashion's business. As before, Loren has asked for your advice as to how to proceed at the upcoming board meeting.

## 1.  THE SCOPE OF THE BUSINESS JUDGMENT RULE

The business judgment rule traditionally protects directors from liability for specific business decisions that result in losses to the corporation. In *Gries Sports Enterprises, Inc. v. Cleveland Browns Football Co., Inc.*, 496 N.E.2d 959 (Ohio 1986), the court observed:

> The business judgment rule is a principle of corporate governance that has been part of the common law for at least one hundred fifty years. It has traditionally operated as a shield to protect directors from liability for their decisions. If the directors are

entitled to the protection of the rule, then the courts should not interfere with or second-guess their decisions. If the directors are not entitled to the protection of the rule, then the courts scrutinize the decision as to its intrinsic fairness to the corporation and the corporation's minority shareholders. The rule is a rebuttable presumption that directors are better equipped than the courts to make business judgments and that the directors acted without self-dealing or personal interest and exercised reasonable diligence and acted with good faith. A party challenging a board of directors' decision bears the burden of rebutting the presumption that the decision was a proper exercise of the business judgment of the board.

\* \* \*

While the business judgment rule protects directors from personal liability in damages, it also applies to cases of "transactional justification," where an injunction is sought against board action, or against a decision itself, in which case the focus is on the decision as contrasted with the liability of the decision maker. There is a distinction between a "transactional justification" case involving or affecting the decision itself and the protection from personal liability of the decision maker. The former is sometimes referred to as involving the business judgment "doctrine," and the latter the business judgment "rule."

*Id.* at 963–964.

Similarly, in *Aronson v. Lewis*, 473 A.2d 805, 812 (Del.1984), the Delaware Supreme Court stated:

\* \* \* The business judgment rule is an acknowledgment of the managerial prerogatives of Delaware directors under Section 141(a). \* \* \* It is a presumption that in making a business decision the directors of a corporation acted on an informed basis, in good faith and in the honest belief that the action taken was in the best interests of the company. \* \* \* Absent an abuse of discretion, that judgment will be respected by the courts. The burden is on the party challenging the decision to establish facts rebutting the presumption. \* \* \*

The Delaware Supreme Court has suggested that the business judgment rule involves both procedural and substantive due care. *Grobow v. Perot*, 539 A.2d 180, 189 (Del.1988). Procedural due care implicates the process used in reaching a decision. Substantive due care raises the question of "whether the complaints state a claim of waste of assets, i.e., whether 'what the corporation has received is so inadequate in value that no person of ordinary, sound business judgment would deem it worth that which the corporation has paid. [*Saxe v. Brady*, 184 A.2d 602, 610 (Del.Ch.1962) ].' "*Grobow*, supra at 184. *See also*, *Litwin v. Allen*, 25 N.Y.S.2d 667 (N.Y.Sup.Ct.1940).

The business judgment rule is essentially a creature of the courts, and statutory treatment is ambiguous at best. DGCL § 141 contains no statement of the required standard of care or of the business judgment rule. RMBCA § 8.30(d), although it relieves directors of liability if they have complied with the balance of the section, does not codify the business judgment rule, and the Official Comment is equally unhelpful. As the Reporter to the ABA Committee on Corporate Laws for the RMBCA has explained, the:

> [s]omewhat ambiguous formulation [in the Official Comment] of very basic concepts about directorial liability was a compromise position taken by the Committee on Corporate Laws only after extended and extremely time-consuming efforts to codify the business judgment rule within the context of § 8.30; these efforts did not lead to anything nearly approaching consensus. The compromise * * * was informally capsulated by one committee member who commented in effect, "we are saying that there is a business judgment rule, that we know what it is and when it should be applied, but we can't define it."

Robert W. Hamilton, CASES AND MATERIALS ON CORPORATIONS—INCLUDING PARTNERSHIPS AND LIMITED PARTNERSHIPS (6th ed. 1998), 682.

For the ALI's formulation of the business judgment rule, see ALI, PRINCIPLES OF CORPORATE GOVERNANCE, § 4.01(c) (1994) .

## JOY v. NORTH

692 F.2d 880 (2d Cir.1982).

WINTER, JUDGE:

While it is often stated that corporate directors and officers will be liable for negligence in carrying out their corporate duties, all seem agreed that such a statement is misleading. Whereas an automobile driver who makes a mistake in judgement as to speed or distance injuring a pedestrian will likely be called upon to respond in damages, a corporate officer who makes a mistake in judgment as to economic conditions, consumer tastes or production line efficiency will rarely, if ever, be found liable for damages suffered by the corporation. Whatever the terminology, the fact is that liability is rarely imposed upon corporate directors or officers simply for bad judgment and this reluctance to impose liability for unsuccessful business decisions has been doctrinally labelled the business judgment rule. Although the rule has suffered under academic criticism, see, e.g., Cary, *Standards of Conduct Under Common Law, Present Day Statutes and the Model Act*, 27 BUS.LAWYER 61 (1972), it is not without rational basis.

First, shareholders to a very real degree voluntarily undertake the risk of bad business judgment. Investors need not buy stock, for investment markets offer an array of opportunities less vulnerable to mistakes in judgment by corporate officers. Nor need investors buy stock in particular corporations. In the exercise of what is genuinely a free choice, the quality of a firm's management is often decisive and information is available from professional advisors. Since shareholders can and do select among investments partly on the basis of management, the business judgment rule merely recognizes a certain voluntariness in undertaking the risk of bad business decisions.

Second, courts recognize that after-the-fact litigation is a most imperfect device to evaluate corporate business decisions. The circumstances surrounding a corporate decision are not easily reconstructed in a courtroom years later, since business imperatives often call for quick decisions, inevitably based on less than perfect information. The entrepreneur's function is to encounter risks and to confront uncertainty, and a reasoned decision at the time made may seem a wild hunch viewed years later against a background of perfect knowledge.

Third, because potential profit often corresponds to the potential risk, it is very much in the interest of shareholders that the law not create incentives for overly cautious corporate decisions. Some opportunities offer great profits at the risk of very substantial losses, while the alternatives offer less risk of loss but also less potential profit. Shareholders can reduce the volatility of risk by diversifying their holdings. In the case of the diversified shareholder, the seemingly more risky alternatives may well be the best choice since great losses in some stocks will over time be offset by even greater gains in others. Given mutual funds and similar forms of diversified investment, courts need not bend over backwards to give special protection to shareholders who refuse to reduce the volatility of risk by not diversifying. A rule which penalizes the choice of seemingly riskier alternatives thus may not be in the interest of shareholders generally.

Whatever its merit, however, the business judgment rule extends only as far as the reasons which justify its existence. Thus, it does not apply in cases, e.g., in which the corporate decision lacks a business purpose, is tainted by a conflict of interest, is so egregious as to amount to a no-win decision, *Litwin v. Allen*, 25 N.Y.S.2d 667 (N.Y.Co.Sup.Ct. 1940), or results from an obvious and prolonged failure to exercise oversight or supervision. * * *

# SMITH v. VAN GORKOM

488 A.2d 858 (Del.1985).

[Trans Union Corporation was a publicly traded, diversified holding company. Its chairman and chief executive officer was Jerome W. Van Gorkom who was then nearing retirement age. Its Board of Directors consisted of five company officers and five outside directors. Four of the latter were chief executive officers of large public corporations; the fifth was the former Dean of the University of Chicago Business School.

At the time of the events in the case, Trans Union faced a major business problem relating to investment tax credits (ITCs). Its competitors generated sufficient taxable income to allow them to make use of all ITCs they generated and took these tax benefits into account in setting the terms of lease notes. Trans Union did not have sufficient income to take advantage of all of its ITCs, but nevertheless had to match its competitors' prices. In July 1980, Trans Union management submitted its annual revision of the company's five year forecast to the board. That report discussed alternative solutions to the ITC problem and concluded that the company had sufficient time to develop its course of action. The report did not mention the possible sale of the company.

On August 27, Van Gorkom met with senior management to consider the ITC problem. Among the ideas mentioned were the sale of Trans Union to a company with a large amount of taxable income, or a leveraged buyout.* This latter alternative was discussed again at a meeting on September 5. At that meeting, the chief financial officer, Donald Romans, presented preliminary calculations based on a price between $50 and $60 per share but did not state that these calculations established a fair price for the company. While Van Gorkom rejected the leveraged buy out idea, he stated that he would be willing to sell his own shares at $55 per share.

Without consulting the board of directors or any officers, Van Gorkom decided to meet with Jay A. Pritzker, a corporate takeover specialist whom he knew socially. Prior to that meeting, Van Gorkom instructed Trans Union's controller, Carl Peterson, to prepare a confidential calculation of the feasibility of a leveraged buy out at $55 per share. On September 13, Van Gorkom proposed a sale of Trans Union to Pritzker at $55 per share. Two days later, Pritzker advised Van Gorkom that he was interested in a purchase at that price. By September 18, after two more meetings that included two Trans Union officers and an outside consultant, Van Gorkom knew that Pritzker was ready to propose a cash-out merger** at $55 per share if Pritzker could also have the option to buy one million shares of Trans Union treasury stock at $38 per share (a price which was 75 cents above the current market price). Pritzker also insisted that the Trans Union board act on his proposal within three days, *i.e.,* by Sunday, September 21 and instructed his attorney to draft the merger documents.

On September 19, without consulting Trans Union's legal department, Van Gorkom engaged outside counsel as merger specialists. He called for meetings of senior management and the board of directors for the next day, but only those officers who had met with Pritzker knew the subject of the meetings.

Senior management's reaction to Pritzker's proposal was completely negative. Romans objected both to the price and to the sale of treasury

---

* A leveraged buyout is a purchase of the shares owned by the public shareholders of a company whereby the buyers, often the company's management, borrow the money from financial institutions that rely on the assets of the company for their security. Thus, the company, in effect, finances its own purchase. In Trans Union's case, a leveraged buyout would have increased the company's interest expense, thus reducing taxable income and exacerbating the ITC problem.—Eds.

** A cash-out merger is a merger in which the shareholders of the acquired company receive cash for their shares. Thus they have no continuing economic interest either in the old company or the new company that succeeds it.—Eds.

shares as a "lock-up". Immediately after this meeting, Van Gorkom met with the board. He made an oral presentation outlining the Pritzker offer but did not furnish copies of the proposed merger agreement. Neither did he tell the board that he had approached Pritzker. He stated that Pritzker would purchase all outstanding Trans Union shares for $55 each and Trans Union would be merged into a wholly owned entity Pritzker formed for this purpose; for 90 days Trans Union would be free to receive but not to solicit competing offers; only published, rather than proprietary information could be furnished to other bidders; the Trans Union board had to act by Sunday evening, September 21; the offer was subject to Pritzker obtaining financing by October 10, 1980; and that if Pritzker met or waived the financing contingency, Trans Union was obliged to sell him one million newly issued shares at $38 per share. According to Van Gorkom, the issue for the board was whether $55 was a fair price rather than the best price. He said that putting Trans Union "up for auction" through a 90 day "market test" would allow the free market an opportunity to judge whether $55 was fair. Outside counsel advised the board that they might be sued if they did not accept the offer, and that a fairness opinion from an investment banker was not legally required.

At the board meeting, Romans stated that his prior studies in connection with a possible leveraged buy out did not indicate a fair price for the stock. However, it was his opinion that $55 was "at the beginning of the range" of a fair price.

The board meeting lasted two hours, at the end of which the board approved the merger, with two conditions:

(1) Trans Union reserved the right to accept any better offer during the 90 day market test period.

(2) Trans Union could share its proprietary information with other potential bidders.

At that time, however, the board did not reserve the right actively to solicit other bids.

Van Gorkom signed the as yet unamended merger agreement, still unread either by himself or the other board members, that evening "in the midst of a formal party which he hosted for the opening of the Chicago Lyric Opera."

On September 22, Trans Union issued a press release announcing a "definitive" merger agreement with Marmon Group, Inc., an affiliate of a Pritzker holding company. Within ten days, rebellious key officers threatened to resign. Van Gorkom met with Pritzker who agreed to modify the agreement provided that the "dissident" officers agreed to stay with Trans Union for at least six months following the merger.

The board reconvened on October 8 and, without seeing their text, approved the proposed amendments regarding the 90 day market test and solicitation of other bids. The board also authorized the company to employ its investment banker to solicit other offers.

Although the amendments had not yet been prepared, Trans Union issued a press release on the following day stating that it could actively seek other offers and had retained an investment banker for that purpose. The release also said that Pritzker had obtained the necessary financing commitments and had acquired one million shares of Trans Union at $38 per share and that if Trans Union had not received a more favorable offer by February 1, 1981, its shareholders would meet to vote on the Pritzker bid. Van Gorkom executed the amendments to the merger agreement on October 10, without consulting the board and apparently without fully understanding that the amendments significantly constrained Trans Union's ability to negotiate a better deal.

Trans Union received only two serious offers during the market test period. One, from General Electric Credit Corporation, fell through when Trans Union would not rescind its agreement with Pritzker to give GE Credit extra time. The other offer, a leveraged buyout by management (except Van Gorkom) arranged through Kohlberg, Kravis, Roberts & Co. ("KKR") was made in early December at $60 per share. It was contingent upon completing equity and bank financing, which KKR said was 80% complete, with terms and conditions substantially the same as the Pritzker deal. Van Gorkom, however, did not view the KKR deal as "firm" because of the financing contingency (even though the Pritzker offer had been similarly conditioned) and he refused to issue a press release about it. KKR planned to present its offer to the Trans Union board, but withdrew shortly before the scheduled meeting, noting that a senior Trans Union officer had withdrawn from the purchasing KKR group after Van Gorkom spoke to him. Van Gorkom denied influencing the officer's decision, and he made no mention of it to the board at the meeting later that day.

The shareholders commenced their lawsuit on December 19, 1980. Management's proxy statement was mailed on January 21 for a meeting scheduled for February 10, 1981. The Trans Union board met on January 26 and gave final approval to both the Pritzker merger and a supplement to its proxy statement which was mailed the next day. On February 10, 1981, the shareholders approved the Pritzker merger by a large majority.]

HORSEY, JUSTICE (for the majority):

II.

We turn to the issue of the application of the business judgment rule to the September 20 meeting of the Board.

The Court of Chancery concluded from the evidence that the Board of Directors' approval of the Pritzker merger proposal fell within the protection of the business judgment rule. The Court found that the Board had given sufficient time and attention to the transaction, since the directors had considered the Pritzker proposal on three different occasions, on September 20, and on October 8, 1980 and finally on January 26, 1981. On that basis, the Court reasoned that the Board had acquired, over the four-month period, sufficient information to reach an informed business judgment on the cash-out merger proposal. The Court ruled:

> * * * that given the market value of Trans Union's stock, the business acumen of the members of the board of Trans Union, the substantial premium over market offered by the Pritzkers and the ultimate effect on the merger price provided by the prospect of other bids for the stock in question, that the board of directors of Trans Union did not act recklessly or improvidently in determining on a course of action which they believed to be in the best interest of the stockholders of Trans Union.

The Court of Chancery made but one finding; *i.e.*, that the Board's conduct over the entire period from September 20 through January 26, 1981 was not reckless or improvident, but informed. This ultimate conclusion was premised upon three subordinate findings, one explicit and two implied. The Court's explicit finding was that Trans Union's Board was "free to turn down the Pritzker proposal" not only on September 20 but also on October 8, 1980 and on January 26, 1981. The Court's implied, subordinate findings were: (1) that no legally binding agreement was reached by the parties until January 26; and (2) that if a higher offer were to be forthcoming, the market test would have produced it, and Trans Union would have been contractually free to accept such higher offer. However, the Court offered no factual basis or legal support for any of these findings; and the record compels contrary conclusions.

Under Delaware law, the business judgment rule is the offspring of the fundamental principle, codified in 8 Del.C. § 141(a), that the business and affairs of a Delaware corporation are managed by or under its board of directors. In carrying out their managerial roles, directors are charged with an unyielding fiduciary duty to the corporation and its shareholders. The business judgment rule exists to protect and promote the full and free exercise of the managerial power granted to Delaware directors. The rule itself "is a presumption that in making a business decision, the directors of a corporation acted on an informed basis, in good faith and in the honest belief that the action taken was in the best interests of the company." [*Aronson v. Lewis*, 473 A.2d 805, 812 (Del. 1984) ] Thus, the party attacking a board decision as uninformed must rebut the presumption that its business judgment was an informed one. *Id.*

The determination of whether a business judgment is an informed one turns on whether the directors have informed themselves "prior to making a business decision, of all material information reasonably available to them." *Id.*

Under the business judgment rule there is no protection for directors who have made "an unintelligent or unadvised judgment." *Mitchell v. Highland–Western Glass*, Del.Ch., 167 A. 831, 833 (1933). A director's duty to inform himself in preparation for a decision derives from the fiduciary capacity in which he serves the corporation and its stockholders. Since a director is vested with the responsibility for the management of the affairs of the corporation, he must execute that duty with the recognition that he acts on behalf of others. Such obligation does not tolerate faithlessness or self-dealing. But fulfillment of the fiduciary function requires more than the mere absence of bad faith or fraud. Representation of the financial interests of others imposes on a director an affirmative duty to protect those interests and to proceed with a critical eye in assessing information of the type and under the circumstances present here.

Thus, a director's duty to exercise an informed business judgment is in the nature of a duty of care, as distinguished from a duty of loyalty. Here, there were no allegations of fraud, bad faith, or self-dealing, or proof thereof. Hence, it is presumed that the directors reached their business judgment in good faith, and considerations of motive are irrelevant to the issue before us.

The standard of care applicable to a director's duty of care has also been recently restated by this Court. In *Aronson*, *supra*, we stated:

> While the Delaware cases use a variety of terms to describe the applicable standard of care, our analysis satisfies us that under the business judgment rule director liability is predicated upon concepts of gross negligence. (footnote omitted)

473 A.2d at 812.

We again confirm that view. We think the concept of gross negligence is also the proper standard for determining whether a business judgment reached by a board of directors was an informed one.

In the specific context of a proposed merger of domestic corporations, a director has a duty under 8 Del.C. § 251(b), along with his fellow directors, to act in an informed and deliberate manner in determining whether to approve an agreement of merger before submitting the proposal to the stockholders. Certainly in the merger context, a director may not abdicate that duty by leaving to the shareholders alone the decision to approve or disapprove the agreement. Only an agreement of merger satisfying the requirements of 8 Del.C. § 251(b) may be submitted to the shareholders under § 251(c).

It is against those standards that the conduct of the directors of Trans Union must be tested, as a matter of law and as a matter of fact, regarding their exercise of an informed business judgment in voting to approve the Pritzker merger proposal.

### III.

The issue of whether the directors reached an informed decision to "sell" the Company on September 20, 1980 must be determined only upon the basis of the information then reasonably available to the directors and relevant to their decision to accept the Pritzker merger proposal. This is not to say that the directors were precluded from altering their original plan of action, had they done so in an informed manner. What we do say is that the question of whether the directors reached an informed business judgment in agreeing to sell the Company, pursuant to the terms of the September 20 Agreement presents, in reality, two questions: (A) whether the directors reached an informed business judgment on September 20, 1980; and (B) if they did not, whether the directors' actions taken subsequent to September 20 were adequate to cure any infirmity in their action taken on September 20. We first consider the directors' September 20 action in terms of their reaching an informed business judgment.

–A–

On the record before us, we must conclude that the Board of Directors did not reach an informed business judgment on September 20, 1980 in voting to "sell" the Company for $55 per share pursuant to the Pritzker cash-out merger proposal. Our reasons, in summary, are as follows:

The directors (1) did not adequately inform themselves as to Van Gorkom's role in forcing the "sale" of the Company and in establishing the per share purchase price; (2) were uninformed as to the intrinsic value of the Company; and (3) given these circumstances, at a minimum, were grossly negligent in approving the "sale" of the Company upon two hours' consideration, without prior notice, and without the exigency of a crisis or emergency.

As has been noted, the Board based its September 20 decision to approve the cash-out merger primarily on Van Gorkom's representations. None of the directors, other than Van Gorkom and Chelberg, had any prior knowledge that the purpose of the meeting was to propose a cash-out merger of Trans Union. No members of Senior Management were present, other than Chelberg, Romans and Peterson; and the latter two had only learned of the proposed sale an hour earlier. Both general counsel Moore and former general counsel Browder attended the meeting, but were equally uninformed as to the purpose of the meeting and the documents to be acted upon.

Without any documents before them concerning the proposed transaction, the members of the Board were required to rely entirely upon Van Gorkom's 20–minute oral presentation of the proposal. No written summary of the terms of the merger was presented; the directors were given no documentation to support the adequacy of $55 price per share for sale of the Company; and the Board had before it nothing more than Van Gorkom's statement of his understanding of the substance of an agreement which he admittedly had never read, nor which any member of the Board had ever seen.

Under 8 Del.C. § 141(e) "directors are fully protected in relying in good faith on reports made by officers." The term "report" has been liberally construed to include reports of informal personal investigations by corporate officers. However, there is no evidence that any "report," as defined under § 141(e), concerning the Pritzker proposal, was presented to the Board on September 20. Van Gorkom's oral presentation of his understanding of the terms of the proposed Merger Agreement,

which he had not seen, and Romans' brief oral statement of his preliminary study regarding the feasibility of a leveraged buy-out of Trans
Union do not qualify as § 141(e) "reports" for these reasons: The former
lacked substance because Van Gorkom was basically uninformed as to
the essential provisions of the very document about which he was
talking. Romans' statement was irrelevant to the issues before the Board
since it did not purport to be a valuation study. At a minimum for a
report to enjoy the status conferred by § 141(e), it must be pertinent to
the subject matter upon which a board is called to act, and otherwise be
entitled to good faith, not blind, reliance. Considering all of the surrounding circumstances—hastily calling the meeting without prior notice
of its subject matter, the proposed sale of the Company without any
prior consideration of the issue or necessity therefor, the urgent time
constraints imposed by Pritzker, and the total absence of any documentation whatsoever—the directors were duty bound to make reasonable
inquiry of Van Gorkom and Romans, and if they had done so, the
inadequacy of that upon which they now claim to have relied would have
been apparent.

The defendants rely on the following factors to sustain the Trial
Court's finding that the Board's decision was an informed one: (1) the
magnitude of the premium or spread between the $55 Pritzker offering
price and Trans Union's current market price of $38 per share; (2) the
amendment of the Agreement as submitted on September 20 to permit
the Board to accept any better offer during the "market test" period; (3)
the collective experience and expertise of the Board's "inside" and
"outside" directors; and (4) their reliance on Brennan's legal advice that
the directors might be sued if they rejected the Pritzker proposal. We
discuss each of these grounds *seriatim:*

(1)

A substantial premium may provide one reason to recommend a
merger, but in the absence of other sound valuation information, the fact
of a premium alone does not provide an adequate basis upon which to
assess the fairness of an offering price. Here, the judgment reached as to
the adequacy of the premium was based on a comparison between the
historically depressed Trans Union market price and the amount of the
Pritzker offer. Using market price as a basis for concluding that the
premium adequately reflected the true value of the Company was a
clearly faulty, indeed fallacious, premise, as the defendants' own evidence demonstrates.

The record is clear that before September 20, Van Gorkom and
other members of Trans Union's Board knew that the market had
consistently undervalued the worth of Trans Union's stock, despite
steady increases in the Company's operating income in the seven years
preceding the merger. The Board related this occurrence in large part to
Trans Union's inability to use its ITCs as previously noted. Van Gorkom
testified that he did not believe the market price accurately reflected
Trans Union's true worth; and several of the directors testified that, as a

general rule, most chief executives think that the market undervalues their companies' stock. Yet, on September 20, Trans Union's Board apparently believed that the market stock price accurately reflected the value of the Company for the purpose of determining the adequacy of the premium for its sale.

\* \* \*

The parties do not dispute that a publicly-traded stock price is solely a measure of the value of a minority position and, thus, market price represents only the value of a single share. Nevertheless, on September 20, the Board assessed the adequacy of the premium over market, offered by Pritzker, solely by comparing it with Trans Union's current and historical stock price.

Indeed, as of September 20, the Board had no other information on which to base a determination of the intrinsic value of Trans Union as a going concern. As of September 20, the Board had made no evaluation of the Company designed to value the entire enterprise, nor had the Board ever previously considered selling the Company or consenting to a buy-out merger. Thus, the adequacy of a premium is indeterminate unless it is assessed in terms of other competent and sound valuation information that reflects the value of the particular business.

Despite the foregoing facts and circumstances, there was no call by the Board, either on September 20 or thereafter, for any valuation study or documentation of the $55 price per share as a measure of the fair value of the Company in a cash-out context. It is undisputed that the major asset of Trans Union was its cash flow. Yet, at no time did the Board call for a valuation study taking into account that highly significant element of the Company's assets.

We do not imply that an outside valuation study is essential to support an informed business judgment; nor do we state that fairness opinions by independent investment bankers are required as a matter of law. Often insiders familiar with the business of a going concern are in a better position than are outsiders to gather relevant information; and under appropriate circumstances, such directors may be fully protected in relying in good faith upon the valuation reports of their management.

Here, the record establishes that the Board did not request its Chief Financial Officer, Romans, to make any valuation study or review of the proposal to determine the adequacy of $55 per share for sale of the Company. The Board rested on Romans' elicited response that the $55 figure was within a "fair price range" within the context of a leveraged buy-out. No director sought any further information from Romans. No director asked him why he put $55 at the bottom of his range. No director asked Romans for any details as to his study, the reason why it had been undertaken or its depth. No director asked to see the study; and no director asked Romans whether Trans Union's finance department could do a fairness study within the remaining 36–hour period available under the Pritzker offer.

Had the Board, or any member, made an inquiry of Romans, he presumably would have responded as he testified: that his calculations were rough and preliminary; and, that the study was not designed to determine the fair value of the Company, but rather to assess the feasibility of a leveraged buy-out financed by the Company's projected cash flow, making certain assumptions as to the purchaser's borrowing needs. Romans would have presumably also informed the Board of his view, and the widespread view of Senior Management, that the timing of the offer was wrong and the offer inadequate.

The record also establishes that the Board accepted without scrutiny Van Gorkom's representation as to the fairness of the $55 price per share for sale of the Company—a subject that the Board had never previously considered. The Board thereby failed to discover that Van Gorkom had suggested the $55 price to Pritzker and, most crucially, that Van Gorkom had arrived at the $55 figure based on calculations designed solely to determine the feasibility of a leveraged buy-out.[19] No questions were raised either as to the tax implications of a cash-out merger or how the price for the one million share option granted Pritzker was calculated.

We do not say that the Board of Directors was not entitled to give some credence to Van Gorkom's representation that $55 was an adequate or fair price. Under § 141(e), the directors were entitled to rely upon their chairman's opinion of value and adequacy, provided that such opinion was reached on a sound basis. Here, the issue is whether the directors informed themselves as to all information that was reasonably available to them. Had they done so, they would have learned of the source and derivation of the $55 price and could not reasonably have relied thereupon in good faith.

None of the directors, Management or outside, were investment bankers or financial analysts. Yet the Board did not consider recessing the meeting until a later hour that day (or requesting an extension of Pritzker's Sunday evening deadline) to give it time to elicit more information as to the sufficiency of the offer, either from inside Management (in particular Romans) or from Trans Union's own investment banker, Salomon Brothers, whose Chicago specialist in merger and acquisitions was known to the Board and familiar with Trans Union's affairs.

**19.** As of September 20 the directors did not know: that Van Gorkom had arrived at the $55 figure alone, and subjectively, as the figure to be used by Controller Peterson in creating a feasible structure for a leveraged buy-out by a prospective purchaser; that Van Gorkom had not sought advice, information or assistance from either inside or outside Trans Union directors as to the value of the Company as an entity or the fair price per share for 100% of its stock; that Van Gorkom had not consulted with the Company's investment bankers or other financial analysts; that Van Gorkom had not consulted with or confided in any officer or director of the Company except Chelberg; and that Van Gorkom had deliberately chosen to ignore the advice and opinion of the members of his Senior Management group regarding the adequacy of the $55 price.

Thus, the record compels the conclusion that on September 20 the Board lacked valuation information adequate to reach an informed business judgment as to the fairness of $55 per share for sale of the Company.

(2)

This brings us to the post-September 20 "market test" upon which the defendants ultimately rely to confirm the reasonableness of their September 20 decision to accept the Pritzker proposal. In this connection, the directors present a two-part argument: (a) that by making a "market test" of Pritzker's $55 per share offer a condition of their September 20 decision to accept his offer, they cannot be found to have acted impulsively or in an uninformed manner on September 20; and (b) that the adequacy of the $17 premium for sale of the Company was conclusively established over the following 90 to 120 days by the most reliable evidence available—the marketplace. Thus, the defendants impliedly contend that the "market test" eliminated the need for the Board to perform any other form of fairness test either on September 20, or thereafter.

Again, the facts of record do not support the defendants' argument. There is no evidence: (a) that the Merger Agreement was effectively amended to give the Board freedom to put Trans Union up for auction sale to the highest bidder; or (b) that a public auction was in fact permitted to occur.

\* \* \*

(3)

The directors' unfounded reliance on both the premium and the market test as the basis for accepting the Pritzker proposal undermines the defendants' remaining contention that the Board's collective experience and sophistication was a sufficient basis for finding that it reached its September 20 decision with informed, reasonable deliberation.[21] *Compare Gimbel v. Signal Companies, Inc.*, Del.Ch., 316 A.2d 599 (1974), *aff'd per curiam*, Del.Supr., 316 A.2d 619 (1974). There, the Court of Chancery [preliminarily] enjoined a board's sale of stock of its wholly-owned subsidiary for an alleged grossly inadequate price. It did so based on a finding that the business judgment rule had been pierced for failure of management to give its board "the opportunity to make a reasonable

---

**21.** Trans Union's five "inside" directors had backgrounds in law and accounting, 116 years of collective employment by the Company and 68 years of combined experience on its Board. Trans Union's five "outside" directors included four chief executives of major corporations and an economist who was a former dean of a major school of business and chancellor of a university. The "outside" directors had 78 years of combined experience as chief executive officers of major corporations and 50 years of cumulative experience as directors of Trans Union. Thus, defendants argue that the Board was eminently qualified to reach an informed judgment on the proposed "sale" of Trans Union notwithstanding their lack of any advance notice of the proposal, the shortness of their deliberation, and their determination not to consult with their investment banker or to obtain a fairness opinion.

and reasoned decision." 316 A.2d at 615. The Court there reached this result notwithstanding the board's sophistication and experience; the company's need of immediate cash; and the board's need to act promptly due to the impact of an energy crisis on the value of the underlying assets being sold—all of its subsidiary's oil and gas interests. The Court found those factors denoting competence to be outweighed by evidence of gross negligence; that management in effect sprang the deal on the board by negotiating the asset sale without informing the board; that the buyer intended to "force a quick decision" by the board; that the board meeting was called on only one-and-a-half days' notice; that its outside directors were not notified of the meeting's purpose; that during a meeting spanning "a couple of hours" a sale of assets worth $480 million was approved; and that the Board failed to obtain a *current* appraisal of its oil and gas interests. The analogy of *Signal* to the case at bar is significant.

(4)

Part of the defense is based on a claim that the directors relied on legal advice rendered at the September 20 meeting by James Brennan, Esquire, who was present at Van Gorkom's request. Unfortunately, Brennan did not appear and testify at trial even though his firm participated in the defense of this action.

Several defendants testified that Brennan advised them that Delaware law did not require a fairness opinion or an outside valuation of the Company before the Board could act on the Pritzker proposal. If given, the advice was correct. However, that did not end the matter. Unless the directors had before them adequate information regarding the intrinsic value of the Company, upon which a proper exercise of business judgment could be made, mere advice of this type is meaningless; and, given this record of the defendants' failures, it constitutes no defense here.[22]

A second claim is that counsel advised the Board it would be subject to lawsuits if it rejected the $55 per share offer. It is, of course, a fact of corporate life that today when faced with difficult or sensitive issues, directors often are subject to suit, irrespective of the decisions they make. However, counsel's mere acknowledgement of this circumstance cannot be rationally translated into a justification for a board permitting itself to be stampeded into a patently unadvised act. While suit might result from the rejection of a merger or tender offer, Delaware law makes clear that a board acting within the ambit of the business judgment rule faces no ultimate liability. Thus, we cannot conclude that the mere threat of litigation, acknowledged by counsel, constitutes either legal advice or any valid basis upon which to pursue an uninformed course.

---

**22.** Nonetheless, we are satisfied that in an appropriate factual context a proper exercise of business judgment may include, as one of its aspects, reasonable reliance upon the advice of counsel. This is wholly outside the statutory protections of 8 Del.C. § 141(e) involving reliance upon reports of officers, certain experts and books and records of the company.

–B–

[The court examined the board's post-September 20 conduct and determined that the board had been grossly negligent and that its conduct did not cure the deficiencies in its September 20 actions.]

## IV.

[As to] questions which were not originally addressed by the parties in their briefing of this case * * * [t]he parties' response, including reargument, has led the majority of the Court to conclude: (1) that since all of the defendant directors, outside as well as inside, take a unified position, we are required to treat all of the directors as one as to whether they are entitled to the protection of the business judgment rule; and (2) that considerations of good faith, including the presumption that the directors acted in good faith, are irrelevant in determining the threshold issue of whether the directors as a Board exercised an informed business judgment. For the same reason, we must reject defense counsel's *ad hominem* argument for affirmance: that reversal may result in a multi-million dollar class award against the defendants for having made an allegedly uninformed business judgment in a transaction not involving any personal gain, self-dealing or claim of bad faith. * * *

[P]laintiffs have not claimed, nor did the Trial Court decide, that $55 was a grossly inadequate price per share for sale of the Company. That being so, the presumption that a board's judgment as to adequacy of price represents an honest exercise of business judgment (absent proof that the sale price was grossly inadequate) is irrelevant to the threshold question of whether an informed judgment was reached.

## V.

The defendants ultimately rely on the stockholder vote of February 10 for exoneration. The defendants contend that the stockholders' "overwhelming" vote approving the Pritzker Merger Agreement had the legal effect of curing any failure of the Board to reach an informed business judgment in its approval of the merger.

The parties tacitly agree that a discovered failure of the Board to reach an informed business judgment in approving the merger constitutes a voidable, rather than a void, act. Hence, the merger can be sustained, notwithstanding the infirmity of the Board's action, if its approval by majority vote of the shareholders is found to have been based on an informed electorate. *Cf. Michelson v. Duncan*, Del.Supr., 407 A.2d 211 (1979), *aff'g in part and rev'g in part*, Del.Ch. 386 A.2d 1144 (1978). The disagreement between the parties arises over: (1) the Board's burden of disclosing to the shareholders all relevant and material information; and (2) the sufficiency of the evidence as to whether the Board satisfied that burden.

The burden must fall on defendants who claim ratification based on shareholder vote to establish that the shareholder approval resulted from a fully informed electorate. On the record before us, it is clear that the Board failed to meet that burden.

\* \* \*

## VI.

To summarize: we hold that the directors of Trans Union breached their fiduciary duty to their stockholders (1) by their failure to inform themselves of all information reasonably available to them and relevant to their decision to recommend the Pritzker merger; and (2) by their failure to disclose all material information such as a reasonable stockholder would consider important in deciding whether to approve the Pritzker offer.

We hold, therefore, that the Trial Court committed reversible error in applying the business judgment rule in favor of the director defendants in this case.

On remand, the Court of Chancery shall conduct an evidentiary hearing to determine the fair value of the shares represented by the plaintiffs' class, based on the intrinsic value of Trans Union on September 20, 1980. \* \* \* Thereafter, an award of damages may be entered to the extent that the fair value of Trans Union exceeds $55 per share.

\* \* \*

Reversed and Remanded for proceedings consistent herewith.

McNEILLY, JUSTICE, dissenting:

The majority opinion reads like an advocate's closing address to a hostile jury. And I say that not lightly. Throughout the opinion great emphasis is directed only to the negative, with nothing more than lip service granted the positive aspects of this case. In my opinion Chancellor Marvel (retired) should have been affirmed. The Chancellor's opinion was the product of well reasoned conclusions, based upon a sound deductive process, clearly supported by the evidence and entitled to deference in this appeal. Because of my diametrical opposition to all evidentiary conclusions of the majority, I respectfully dissent.

It would serve no useful purpose, particularly at this late date, for me to dissent at great length. I restrain myself from doing so, but feel compelled to at least point out what I consider to be the most glaring deficiencies in the majority opinion. The majority has spoken and has effectively said that Trans Union's Directors have been the victims of a "fast shuffle" by Van Gorkom and Pritzker. That is the beginning of the majority's comedy of errors. The first and most important error made is the majority's assessment of the directors' knowledge of the affairs of Trans Union and their combined ability to act in this situation under the protection of the business judgment rule.

Trans Union's Board of Directors consisted of ten men, five of whom were "inside" directors and five of whom were "outside" directors. The "inside" directors were Van Gorkom, Chelberg, Bonser, William B.

Browder, Senior Vice–President–Law, and Thomas P. O'Boyle, Senior Vice–President–Administration. At the time the merger was proposed the inside five directors had collectively been employed by the Company for 116 years and had 68 years of combined experience as directors. The "outside" directors were A.W. Wallis, William B. Johnson, Joseph B. Lanterman, Graham J. Morgan and Robert W. Reneker. With the exception of Wallis, these were all chief executive officers of Chicago based corporations that were at least as large as Trans Union. The five "outside" directors had 78 years of combined experience as chief executive officers, and 53 years cumulative service as Trans Union directors.

The inside directors wear their badge of expertise in the corporate affairs of Trans Union on their sleeves. But what about the outsiders? Dr. Wallis is or was an economist and math statistician, a professor of economics at Yale University, dean of the graduate school of business at the University of Chicago, and Chancellor of the University of Rochester. Dr. Wallis had been on the Board of Trans Union since 1962. He also was on the Board of Bausch & Lomb, Kodak, Metropolitan Life Insurance Company, Standard Oil and others.

William B. Johnson is a University of Pennsylvania law graduate, President of Railway Express until 1966, Chairman and Chief Executive of I.C. Industries Holding Company, and member of Trans Union's Board since 1968.

Joseph Lanterman, a Certified Public Accountant, is or was President and Chief Executive of American Steel, on the Board of International Harvester, Peoples Energy, Illinois Bell Telephone, Harris Bank and Trust Company, Kemper Insurance Company and a director of Trans Union for four years.

Graham Morgan is a chemist, was Chairman and Chief Executive Officer of U.S. Gypsum, and in the 17 and 18 years prior to the Trans Union transaction had been involved in 31 or 32 corporate takeovers.

Robert Reneker attended University of Chicago and Harvard Business Schools. He was President and Chief Executive of Swift and Company, director of Trans Union since 1971, and member of the Boards of seven other corporations including U.S. Gypsum and the Chicago Tribune.

Directors of this caliber are not ordinarily taken in by a "fast shuffle". I submit they were not taken into this multi-million dollar corporate transaction without being fully informed and aware of the state of the art as it pertained to the entire corporate panorama of Trans Union. True, even directors such as these, with their business acumen, interest and expertise, can go astray. I do not believe that to be the case here. These men knew Trans Union like the back of their hands and were more than well qualified to make on the spot informed business judgments concerning the affairs of Trans Union including a 100% sale of the corporation. Lest we forget, the corporate world of then and now operates on what is so aptly referred to as "the fast track". These men were at the time an integral part of that world, all professional business men, not intellectual figureheads.

The majority of this Court holds that the Board's decision, reached on September 20, 1980, to approve the merger was not the product of an *informed* business judgment, that the Board's subsequent efforts to amend the Merger Agreement and take other curative action were *legally and factually* ineffectual, and that the Board did *not deal with complete candor* with the stockholders by failing to disclose all material facts, which they knew or should have known, before securing the stockholders' approval of the merger. I disagree.

## ON MOTIONS FOR REARGUMENT

Following this Court's decision, Thomas P. O'Boyle, one of the director defendants, sought, and was granted, leave for change of counsel. Thereafter, the individual director defendants, other than O'Boyle, filed a motion for reargument and director O'Boyle, through newly-appearing counsel, then filed a separate motion for reargument. Plaintiffs have responded to the several motions and this matter has now been duly considered.

* * * Although O'Boyle continues to adopt his fellow directors' arguments, O'Boyle now asserts in the alternative that he has standing to take a position different from that of his fellow directors and that legal grounds exist for finding him not liable for the acts or omissions of his fellow directors. * * *

We reject defendant O'Boyle's new argument as to standing because not timely asserted. Our reasons are several. *One,* in connection with the supplemental briefing of this case in March, 1984, a special opportunity was afforded the individual defendants, including O'Boyle, to present any factual or legal reasons why each or any of them should be individually treated. Thereafter, at argument before the Court on June 11, 1984, the following colloquy took place between this Court and counsel for the individual defendants at the outset of counsel's argument:

> Counsel: I'll make the argument on behalf of the nine individual defendants against whom the plaintiffs seek more than $100,000,000 in damages. That is the ultimate issue in this case, whether or not nine honest, experienced businessmen should be subject to damages in a case where—
>
> Justice Moore: Is there a distinction between Chelberg and Van Gorkom vis-a-vis the other defendants?
>
> Counsel: No, sir.
>
> Justice Moore: None whatsoever?
>
> Counsel: I think not.

*Two,* in this Court's Opinion dated January 29, 1985, the Court relied on the individual defendants as having presented a unified defense. We stated:

The parties' response, including reargument, has led the majority of the Court to conclude: (1) that since all of the defendant directors, outside as well as inside, take a unified position, we are required to treat all of the directors as one as to whether they are entitled to the protection of the business judgment rule. * * *

### Note: Van Gorkom and its Aftermath

1.  The defendant directors of Trans Union settled *Van Gorkom* by paying $23.5 million to the plaintiff class. The payments were made to approximately 12,000 former shareholders of Trans Union who held stock between September 19, 1980 and February 10, 1981. Of that amount, the directors' liability insurance carrier paid about $10 million. *Wall Street Journal*, Aug. 2, 1985, at 18 col. 3. Nearly all of the balance was paid by the Pritzker group on behalf of Trans Union defendant directors, although the Pritzker group was not a defendant. Bayless A. Manning, *Reflections and Practical Tips on Life in the Boardroom After Van Gorkom*, 41 Bus.Law. 1 (1985).

2.  Justice Moore has written of *Van Gorkom* that there was "one aspect of the case that the Court found especially troublesome. Trans Union's directors were stalwart in their unified defense of what occurred. This position was taken even though it was obvious that certain directors were more culpable than others, and in the face of the Court's invitation that they take separate positions with a clear hint of exoneration for all but the most culpable insiders. Indeed, one of the directors was ill and did not even attend the meeting at which the merger was approved. In a way, they were "daring" us to find them all liable in a strategic maneuver to save certain insiders. In light of our decision finding all the directors liable, the strategic maneuver to cast down the gauntlet before the Delaware Supreme Court hardly appears to have been among the wisest decisions in the annals of corporate America." Andrew G.T. Moore II, *The 1980s—Did We Save the Stockholders While the Corporation Burned?* 70 Wash. Univ. L.Q. 277, 281–282 (1992).

Suppose that defendants had accepted the court's invitation. What legal theory would the court have used to exonerate directors whom they subsequently found to be grossly negligent in not being fully informed about the fair value of the Trans Union stock? Are there varying degrees of gross negligence for different purposes?

3.  *Van Gorkom* created a firestorm in much of the corporate community. Few had believed that the Delaware Supreme Court would hold experienced directors liable in a case in which the shareholders received a 50% premium over the existing market price for their stock, notwithstanding Justice Moore's colloquy with counsel in the final reargument. One commentator called the decision "one of the worst decisions in the history of corporate law." Daniel R. Fischel, *The Business Judgment Rule and the Trans Union Case*, 40 Bus.Law. 1437, 1455 (1985). Two prominent practitioners called the decision "misguided" and argued that it rested both on "a simple misunderstanding of how the

world works: how business decisions are made, how bargains are struck" and on a "widespread fallacy" that courts can evaluate and discipline directors' decisions better than the market. Leo Herzel & Leo Katz, *Smith v. Van Gorkom: The Business of Judging Business Judgment*, 41 Bus. Law. 1187, 1188–1191 (1986). *But see* Diedre A. Burgman & Paul N. Cox, *Corporate Directors, Corporate Realities and Deliberative Process: an Analysis of the Trans Union Case*, 11 J.Corp.L. 311 (1986).

As we will see in Section D, the legislative response to *Van Gorkom* in Delaware and elsewhere was the almost immediate adoption of statutory provisions allowing the exculpation of directors from personal liability for the breach of the duty of care. With the passage of time, the firestorm subsided and the landscape looks very different from the way it appeared to the decision's initial critics. The "greater randomness and unpredictability on the part of future courts passing on future board decisions" that Herzel and Katz predicted does not seem to have occurred. More important, *Van Gorkom* has been reinterpreted by subsequent courts and scholars. As Justice Moore has noted, "[i]t is said that the case pushed aside the business judgment rule and a court substituted its own business judgment. That is incorrect. *Van Gorkom* was much more a case about the process in the takeover environment than anything else." 70 Wash U. L.Q. at 281. And recall that in *Caremark*, Chancellor Allen cited *Van Gorkom* as the first case involving the "jurisprudence concerning takeovers" in which the Delaware Supreme Court indicated its "seriousness" about the role of the corporate board. 698 A.2d at 969.

## 2. DUE CARE AND THE BUSINESS JUDGMENT RULE

Although the business judgment rule can be stated without much difficulty, its meaning is much harder to express. One scholar defined the problem as follows:

> In the eyes of most commentators, [the statutory standard of due care] is aspirational and does not provide the test for directorial liability. Rather, the liability standard is the so-called business judgment rule, which shields even negligent directors from liability in many circumstances * * *. Other interpretations of the relationship between the duty of care and the business judgment rule are possible. Section 4.01 of the Principles of Corporate Governance views the business judgment rule as a 'safe harbor': A director who fails to meet the standards of the business judgment rule may nevertheless avoid liability by establishing that he or she met the due care standards of good faith and the ordinary prudence of persons in a like situation. Yet a third interpretation of the relationship between the principle of due care and the business judgment rule is that the latter is simply an articulation of what the basic due care standard means. Despite these different approaches to what appears to be a fundamental issue relating to directorial liability, it appears unlikely that in practical application these formulations will bring different results.

Robert W. Hamilton, *Reliance and Liability Standards for Outside Directors*, 24 WAKE FOREST L. REV. 5, 22–23 (1989).

### Bayless Manning, *The Business Judgment Rule and the Director's Duty of Attention: Time for Reality.*
### 39 BUS.LAW. 1477, 1492–1495 (1984).

The center of the analytic difficulty is this. In the general field of negligence law we are all able to talk of the "reasonable man" and of the prudent standard of performance because we have from our daily experience a clear conception of what the actor is doing and a fairly clear conception of the way in which people normally do it. We know what an automobile driver is doing; he is driving a car. We all know from general experience how one would normally do that in the circumstances—and therefore how he should do it.

The situation with regard to the directors of corporations is totally different. There is no agreed upon roster of functions of a director, analogous to driving the car. We do not have any common standard or experience as to what directors do; and what they do varies from company to company, from situation to situation, and from time to time.

Abandoning all effort to state what directors do, the present law simply announces that they must do it "carefully," like a prudent person. But, once again, we have no external measuring rod for assessing how the directors should do it (whatever "it" is). There is no common experience among courts or juries as to how "it" is normally done, and therefore should be done.

However abstract these statements may sound, the point is not abstract at all. A negligent transgression presupposes a departure from normal behavior. The whole concept of negligence and of "reasonable man" presupposes as a predicate a clear conception of *what* the person is doing, and a community understanding of a standard of normalcy about *how* he should do it. *Both those pieces are missing in the case of the work of corporate directors.*

Next, the cases that have been litigated have concerned discrete judgments by boards, and the courts' responses drawing on standard tort language have been addressed to individual discrete events. But the heart of the director's true responsibility is attention to his ongoing multiple functions: a process, a flow of events, a continuum of the company's current history. Analogies to driving automobiles just do not fit, because the law of negligence tort is aimed not at a flow of generalized performances, but at a discrete incident in which someone was hurt. To use technical language, the referent of the automobile driver's legal duty is the isolated event of the accident, not his general performance as a driver. In the case of a director, the proper referent for his legal duty should be the *flow* of his performance of his directorial functions, not the individual incident.

The analytic legal problem is still more acute. Most negligence torts are acts of commission as where the driver negligently runs over the pedestrian. The legal articulations of the business judgment rule have, on this analogy, always presupposed that the directors took a particular action; the law then addressed the question whether they had exercised due care in doing so. The traditional formulation of the business judgment rule explicitly assumes that it is available to protect the director if, but only if, some specific transactional act was taken. As has been stated here in several forms, however, in major part the life and activity of the boardroom does not consist of taking affirmative action on individual matters; it is instead a continuing flow of supervisory process, punctuated only occasionally by a discrete transactional decision. In corporate litigation tomorrow, arising out of the debris of a company that has failed, the charge that will be leveled at the directors is that they were "negligent" in the they passively stood by without taking affirmative action about this or that. If that is the charge, then by existing definitions the business judgment rule would not be available to protect the director. That would mean, astonishingly, that, given the realities of the way boards operate, the business judgment rule would not operate at all in respect of fully ninety percent of what directors are actually engaged in.

---

The relationship between the duty of care and the business judgment rule is complex; as Professor Hamilton indicates, both courts and commentators have struggled to arrive at a coherent formulation that links the two. A part of the problem is that although both the duty of care and the business judgment rule require the director to be informed, the standard for measuring a director's conduct may differ, depending on whether the court is invoking the duty of care or the business judgment rule. On the one hand, the tort-like standard applicable to the duty of care suggests that directors will be held to an ordinary negligence standard. On the other hand, as the Delaware Supreme Court stated in *Aronson*, "[U]nder the business judgment rule director liability is predicated upon concepts of gross negligence." 473 A.2d 805, 812 (Del.1984). Whether that statement also means that, under Delaware law, the standard for the duty of care outside the business judgment rule is also gross negligence is not clear.

Another part of the problem is that courts often confuse the decision-making process with the substantive outcome when determining director liability. The business judgment rule, of course, is intended to remove courts from scrutinizing the substance of specific decisions, but both the business judgment rule and the duty of care can involve judicial examination of the director's process. This confusion is what is troubling Manning in the foregoing excerpt. But, as one commentator has noted:

> * * * [T]he argument that courts should not try to improve upon the performance of managers addresses a false issue. The issue in duty of care litigation is the process, not the merits, of decision-

making. Courts do not make business decisions. They evaluate board procedure, a matter well within judicial competence. * * * Only two elements appear fundamental to a realistic standard of care, and these two elements alone ought to define the limits of due care. The first is an alertness to potentially significant corporate problems. The second is an obligation of deliberative decisionmaking on issues of fundamental corporate concern.

Stuart R. Cohn, *Demise of the Director's Duty of Care: Judicial Avoidance of Standards and Sanctions Through the Business Judgment Rule*, 62 TEX. L. REV. 591, 607, 613 (1983).

Several recent cases illustrate the difficulty which courts sometimes have in distinguishing between the duty of care and the business judgment rule. In *Brane v. Roth*, 590 N.E.2d 587 (Ind.Ct.App.1992), the directors of a rural grain elevator cooperative authorized the co-op's manager to engage in hedging transactions for the co-op to protect against losses from changes in grain prices. The manager did not hedge sufficiently and the co-op suffered substantial losses. In a derivative suit by the stockholders against the directors, the trial court found that "the directors breached their duties by retaining a manager inexperienced in hedging; failing to maintain reasonable supervision over him; and failing to attain knowledge of the basic fundamentals of hedging to be able to direct the hedging activities and supervise the manager properly." *Id.* at 589–90.

The Indiana Court of Appeals affirmed the trial court's judgment for the plaintiffs. On appeal the directors argued that they should have been protected by the business judgment rule because they had relied appropriately on the manager. In rejecting this argument, the court noted that the business judgment rule does not protect directors who "failed to inform themselves of all material information reasonably available to make their decision." That conclusion, of course, is consistent with the business judgment rule: as we have seen, "judgment" implies an informed judgment.

But at this point, the court switched analytic gears, finding that the directors' "failure to provide adequate supervision of the manager's actions was a *breach of their duty of care* to protect Co-op's interests in a reasonable manner." (emphasis added). *Id.* at 592. Then, returning to its earlier analysis, the court found that the business judgment rule did not shield the directors from liability. Thereafter, the court rejected a gross negligence standard for the directors' conduct (which arguably would have been required in a business judgment rule case) and held, instead, that ordinary negligence (the standard under the then-existing Indiana statute) was all that was required.

The implications of *Caremark* and *Brane* are substantial. Both cases suggest that directors may lose the protection of the business judgment rule with respect to activities that are *both* part of on-going monitoring and a specific business decision if, after the decision, the directors do not exercise reasonable care in supervising the effects of the decision. Although these cases can be read as consistent with the ALI's formulation in § 4.01(a)(1)—the circumstances should have alerted a reasonable director to make inquiry—an equally persuasive reading is that the decisions impose a greater duty than would the ALI, which allows such inquiry "as the director * * * reasonably believes to be necessary." And, of course, unlike Mrs. Pritchard in *Francis*, the directors in these cases did not totally abdicate their duties as directors. Rather, they failed to exercise reasonable care in one specific area.

*Hoye v. Meek*, 795 F.2d 893 (10th Cir.1986) also illustrates the difficulty that courts have in distinguishing between the duty of care and the business judgment rule. In *Hoye*, the Guaranty Trust Company, of which Meek was a director and president, suffered large losses from some of its investments. In a suit by the trustee in bankruptcy, the trial court held that Meek had breached his duty of care by failing to curb the extent of the investment and to monitor the company's investment decisions and results, and by delegating excessive authority to his son. On appeal, the Tenth Circuit rejected Meek's argument that he was entitled to the protection of the business judgment rule and stated:

> * * * We are not persuaded by appellant's argument that, because Maxwell had operated the company at a profit for seven years, the directors' and president's duty to monitor activities was dissipated. * * * [D]irectors and officers are charged with knowledge of those things which it is their duty to know and ignorance is not a basis for escaping liability. Where suspicions are aroused, or should be aroused, it is the directors' duty to make necessary inquiries. We hold that appellant failed to make the necessary inquiries. He had a duty to keep abreast of Guaranty's investments, particularly investments that posed a double risk of decrease in market price and an increase in transactional costs.

> Appellant of course would not be required to have the ability to predict increasing interest rates during the two-year period here involved. A decision made in good faith, based on sound business judgment, would not alone subject appellant to liability. * * * But in order to come within the ambit of the business judgment rule, a director must be diligent and careful in performing the duties he has undertaken. In the instant case, appellant's breach of duty resulted from both his delegation of authority to Maxwell without adequate supervision and his failure to avert Guaranty's continued exposure to increasing indebtedness. At each monthly board meeting during this two-year period, the directors could have decided to halt this increasing exposure to risk.

> Assuming appellant's good faith, that alone was not sufficient to shield him from liability. It is undisputed that, as Guaranty was on the verge of filing for bankruptcy, appellant attempted to find other sources of capital for the company. This eleventh hour effort, however, was not sufficient to fulfill his duty of care as a director

and president. The Oklahoma statute requires good faith *and* the diligence, care and skill of a prudent man.

795 F.2d at 896 (emphasis in original).

### 3. RELIANCE

In *Van Gorkom*, the court rejected the directors' argument that they were protected from liability because they relied on the information that Van Gorkom presented to them. Such reliance is not unusual. Indeed, directors—especially outside directors, who are necessarily less involved in the everyday affairs of a corporation—routinely rely on the chief executive officer and other top management for information and recommendations in connection with their decision-making. Such reliance is clearly efficient, and it is sound policy that directors generally should be entitled to rely on that information when the care with which they have acted is challenged. *See Bates v. Dresser*, 251 U.S. 524, 40 S.Ct. 247, 64 L.Ed. 388 (1920). There may be limits, however, on the extent to which reliance may be justified. Reports to the board may contain on their face sufficient warning of their own inadequacy to put a reasonable director on notice that better information should be demanded. And reports prepared by or under the supervision of corporate employees who have a personal interest in the outcome of the decision on which they bear may require closer than usual scrutiny. *See Gallin v. National City Bank*, 155 Misc. 880, 281 N.Y.S. 795 (1935) (directors liable for excess payments made pursuant to bonus plan after relying on false figures prepared under supervision of beneficiaries of plan).

Directors also frequently rely on opinions provided by attorneys, accountants, engineers, financial specialists, and other expert professional advisors. Here again the general rule is that such reliance is justified and protects directors who relied in good faith on such advice against liability if the advice turns out to be poor. In *Gilbert v. Burnside*, 13 A.D.2d 982, 216 N.Y.S.2d 430 (1961), *aff'd* 11 N.Y.2d 960, 229 N.Y.S.2d 10, 183 N.E.2d 325 (1962), a shareholder brought a derivative suit seeking reimbursement from the directors for money expended by the corporation preparatory to an acquisition that was ultimately declared illegal. Significantly, the directors had relied upon the advice of counsel that the proposed acquisition was legal. The trial court held for the plaintiff. In reversing that decision the Appellate Division said, "The judgment below determines, in effect, that these financiers (the Glen Alden directors) knew, or should have known, more Pennsylvania law than eminent Pennsylvania counsel." 13 A.D.2d at 983, 216 N.Y.S.2d at 432. The case law pertaining to reliance on counsel in duty of care cases is summarized in Douglas W. Hawes & Thomas J. Sherrard, *Reliance on Advice of Counsel As Defense in Corporate and Securities Cases*, 62 U.Va.L.Rev. 1, 42–49 (1976).

Reliance imposes certain duties on directors. Under RMBCA § 8.30(b), a director must make "a judgment as to the reliability and competence of the source of information upon which he proposes to rely." Official Comment to RMBCA § 8.30(b). Furthermore, "[i]nherent in the concept of good faith is the requirement that, in order to rely on a report, statement, opinion, or other matter, the director must have read the report or statement in question, or have been present at a meeting at which it was orally presented, or have taken other steps to become generally familiar with its contents." *Id.*

If the purpose of permitting reliance is to facilitate efficient decision-making, what does that last statement mean? Does it literally mean that a director who does not read a lengthy and highly technical report that she would not understand if she did read it cannot rely on its contents and conclusions? Or does it mean that such a report, in order to be the basis for reliance, must contain at least a summary which *is* understandable to a lay reader, even if the body of the report is not? What "other steps" might a director take?

As discussed in Chapter 15, in recent years, committees have assumed much greater significance in the operation of the board. RMBCA § 8.30 (b)(3) permits directors to rely on a committee if the director "reasonably believes the committee merits confidence." The section recognizes the difference between reliance on an expert and reliance on a committee. Thus "in Section 8.30(b)(3), the concept of 'confidence' is substituted for 'competence' in order to avoid any inference that technical skills are a prerequisite." Official Comment to Section 8.30(b). *See* Arthur W. Hahn & Carol B. Manzoni, *The Monitoring Committee and Outside Directors' Evolving Duty of Care*, 9 Loy. U. chi.L.J. 585 (1978).

## 4. CAUSATION

Claims that directors failed to exercise reasonable care or that directors' decisions are not protected by the business judgment rule generally fall into one of two categories. In nonfeasance cases, such as *Francis* and *Graham*, the plaintiff's charge is that if directors had carried out their responsibilities with more diligence, they would have prevented some series of events that caused the corporation a loss. In transactional cases, such as *Van Gorkom*, the plaintiff's charge is that if the directors had not approved of some specific, identifiable transaction, a loss that the corporation or its shareholders incurred as a consequence of that transaction would have been avoided.

It would seem to follow that an essential element of plaintiffs' case, in both nonfeasance and transactional situations is proof that the defendant directors' negligence, and not some other factor, caused the loss in question. Moreover, in *Francis, Van Gorkom,* and numerous other cases, courts have held that plaintiffs who establish that directors breached their duty of care also must prove that the directors' breach was the proximate cause of their loss.

This principle traces to Judge Learned Hand's decision in *Barnes v. Andrews*, 298 F. 614 (S.D.N.Y.1924). There Judge Hand found that Andrews, a director of a corporation that had become bankrupt, had been inexcusably inattentive in carrying out his directorial responsibilities. Nonetheless, Judge Hand declined to hold Andrews liable because plaintiff had not proven that Andrews' negligence had caused the corporation to fail:

> * * * This cause of action rests upon a tort, as much though it be a tort of omission as though it had rested upon a positive act. The plaintiff must accept the burden of showing that the performance of the defendant's duties would have avoided loss, and what loss it would have avoided. * * *
>
> When the corporate funds have been illegally lent, it is a fair inference that a protest would have stopped the loan, and that the director's neglect caused the loss, but when a business fails from general mismanagement, business incapacity, or bad judgment, how is it possible to say that a single director could have made the company successful, or how much in dollars he could have saved? Before this cause can go to a master, the plaintiff must show that, had Andrews done his full duty, he could have made the company prosper, or at least could have broken its fall. He must show what sum he could have saved the company. Neither of these has he made any effort to do.
>
> The defendant is not subject to the burden of proving that the loss would have happened, whether he had done his duty or not. If he were, it would come to this: That, if a director were once shown slack in his duties, he would stand charged prima facie with the difference between the corporate treasury as it was, and as it would be, judged by a hypothetical standard of success. How could such a standard be determined? How could any one guess how far a director's skill and judgment would have prevailed upon his fellows, and what would have been the ultimate fate of the business, if they had? How is it possible to set any measure of liability, or to tell what he would have contributed to the event? Men's fortunes may not be subjected to such uncertain and speculative conjectures. It is hard to see how there can be any remedy, except one can put one's finger on a definite loss and say with reasonable assurance that protest would have deterred, or counsel persuaded, the managers who caused it. No men of sense would take the office, if the law imposed upon them a guaranty of the general success of their companies as a penalty for any negligence.

*Id.* at 616–617.

As is evidenced by *Barnes,* requiring proof that a director caused a given loss reduces considerably the likelihood that inattentive directors will be held liable in cases of general business failure. Even with the benefit of 20/20 hindsight, plaintiffs often will find it impossible to prove that had the directors been more diligent, the business would have flourished. However, as *Francis* demonstrates, that burden is not insurmountable. The court there defined Mrs. Pritchard's duties in a fashion that allowed it to conclude her failure to perform was in fact the proximate cause of the corporation's losses:

In this case, the scope of Mrs. Pritchard's duties was determined by the precarious financial condition of Pritchard & Baird, its fiduciary relationship to its clients and the implied trust in which it held their funds. Thus viewed, the scope of her duties encompassed all reasonable action to stop the continuing conversion. Her duties extended beyond mere objection and resignation to reasonable attempts to prevent the misappropriation of the trust funds. * * *

Within Pritchard & Baird, several factors contributed to the loss of the funds: commingling of corporate and client monies, conversion of funds by Charles, Jr. and William and dereliction of her duties by Mrs. Pritchard. The wrongdoing of her sons, although the immediate cause of the loss, should not excuse Mrs. Pritchard from her negligence which also was a substantial factor contributing to the loss. Her sons knew that she, the only other director, was not reviewing their conduct; they spawned their fraud in the backwater of her neglect. Her neglect of duty contributed to the climate of corruption; her failure to act contributed to the continuation of that corruption. Consequently, her conduct was a substantial factor contributing to the loss.

Analysis of proximate cause is especially difficult in a corporate context where the allegation is that nonfeasance of a director is a proximate cause of damage to a third party. * * * Nonetheless, where it is reasonable to conclude that the failure to act would produce a particular result and that result has followed, causation may be inferred. We conclude that even if Mrs. Pritchard's mere objection had not stopped the depredations of her sons, her consultation with an attorney and the threat of suit would have deterred them. That conclusion flows as a matter of common sense and logic from the record. Whether in other situations a director has a duty to do more than protest and resign is best left to case-by-case determinations. In this case, we are satisfied that there was a duty to do more than object and resign. Consequently, we find that Mrs. Pritchard's negligence was a proximate cause of the misappropriations.

To conclude, by virtue of her office, Mrs. Pritchard had the power to prevent the losses sustained by the clients of Pritchard & Baird. With power comes responsibility. She had a duty to deter the depredation of the other insiders, her sons. She breached that duty and caused plaintiffs to sustain damages.

432 A.2d at 827–829.

Nonetheless, proof that directors' breach of their duty of care caused a given loss is much easier in a transactional setting. Where directors have been shown to have wrongfully approved some given transaction, a plaintiff usually can plausibly contend that had the directors been more diligent, the transaction would not have occurred and the resulting loss would have been avoided. In *Van Gorkom,* for example, plaintiffs established that Trans Union's directors had been grossly negligent in agreeing to sell the company for $55 per share. That, however, did not necessarily mean the directors were liable. Indeed, the Delaware Supreme Court remanded the case with instructions that the Court of Chancery "conduct an evidentiary hearing to determine the fair value of [Trans Union's stock as of the date of the board's decision. * * * Thereafter, an award of damages *may be entered* to the extent that the fair value of Trans Union exceeds $55 per share." 488 A.2d at 893 (emphasis added). The implication of the court's instructions, consistent with *Barnes'* causation requirement, appeared to be that if the Court of Chancery determined Trans Union had not been worth more than $55 per share, no damages would be awarded.

The litigation involving the sale of Technicolor, Inc. caused the Delaware courts to revisit the causation question. A former shareholder claimed that Technicolor's directors had negligently agreed to sell the company for the inadequate price of $23 per share. After a trial on the merits, the Chancellor, relying on *Barnes,* dismissed the shareholder's claim on the ground that even if the directors had been negligent, the shareholder had suffered no loss because Technicolor's fair value at the time it was sold was only $21.60 per share. *Cinerama, Inc. v. Technicolor, Inc.,* 1991 WL 111134 (Del.Ch.1991) ("*Cede I*").

The Delaware Supreme Court reversed. *Cede & Co. v. Technicolor, Inc.,* 634 A.2d 345 (Del.1993) ("*Cede II*"). Reviewing the Chancellor's factual findings, the court found that Technicolor's directors had improperly approved the sale because they had failed to inform themselves "of all material information that [was] reasonably available to them." *Id.* at 367. The court then characterized the Chancellor's reliance on *Barnes* as "misguided," reasoning that "*Barnes,* a tort action, does not control a claim for breach of fiduciary duty." *Id.* at 371. Continuing, the court held that: "A breach of either the duty of loyalty or the duty of care rebuts the presumption that the directors have acted in the best interests of the shareholders, and requires the directors to prove that the transaction was entirely fair." *Id.*

On remand, the Chancellor again found that $23 was a fair price and that the transaction satisfied the entire fairness standard. *Cinerama, Inc. v. Technicolor, Inc.,* 663 A.2d 1134 (Del.Ch.1994)("*Cede III*") The Delaware Supreme Court affirmed this finding and, in so doing, both addressed the causation issue and seemingly mischaracterized the nature of the remand in *Van Gorkom.*

> This Court's instructions on remand in *Cede II* were not identical to those in Smith v. Van Gorkom. In *Cede II*, this Court held that the directors' breach of the duty of care had rebutted the presumption of the business judgment rule. However, in *Cede II*, this Court did not decide unresolved issues concerning Cinerama's allegations that the directors had violated the duty of loyalty. As to Cinerama's disclosure claims, this Court affirmed the Court of Chancery's rejection of Cinerama's contentions. Nevertheless, this

Court raised additional questions, sua sponte, for the Court of Chancery to address on remand * * *

In *Van Gorkom*, this Court concluded that the board of directors' failure to inform itself before recommending a merger to the stockholders constituted a breach of the fiduciary duty of care and rebutted the presumptive protection of the business judgment rule. In *Van Gorkom*, this Court also concluded that the directors had violated the duty of disclosure. This Court then held that the directors were liable for damages, since the record after trial reflected that the compound breaches of the duties of care and disclosure could not withstand an entire fairness analysis. Consequently, because this Court had decided the substantive entire fairness issue adversely to the board in *Van Gorkom*, the only issue to remand was the amount of damages the Court of Chancery should assess in accordance with [*Weinberger v. UOP, Inc.*, Chapter 23].

Whereas in *Van Gorkom* liability was decided before remand, in this case, a condition precedent to a finding of liability was an adverse determination regarding entire fairness after remand. This explains this Court's discussion in *Cede II* of *Barnes v. Andrews*. This Court rejected the proof of injury requirement in *Barnes* because:

> To inject a requirement of proof of injury into the [business judgment] rule's formulation for burden shifting purposes is to lose sight of the underlying purpose of the rule. Burden shifting does not create per se liability on the part of the directors; rather, it is a procedure by which Delaware courts of equity determine under what standard of review director liability is to be judged. To require proof of injury as a component of the proof necessary to rebut the business judgment presumption would be to convert the burden shifting process from a threshold determination of the appropriate standard of review to a dispositive adjudication on the merits. *Id.* at 371.

> Consequently, in *Cede II* this Court held that injury or damages becomes a proper focus only after a transaction is determined not to be entirely fair. At that point, the measure of damages for any breach of fiduciary duty, under an entire fairness standard of review, is "not necessarily limited to the difference between the price offered and the 'true' value as determined under the appraisal proceedings. Under *Weinberger*, the [Court of Chancery] 'may fashion any form of equitable and monetary relief as may be appropriate, including rescissory damages.' " Thus, this Court concluded that "the tort principles of *Barnes* have no place in a business judgment rule standard of review."

*Cinerama, Inc. v. Technicolor, Inc.*, 663 A.2d 1156, 1165–66 (Del.1995) ("*Cede IV*").

For the more traditional view of the need to prove causation in an action for breach of fiduciary duty, *see F.D.I.C. v. Bierman*, 2 F.3d 1424, 1434 (7th Cir.1993) ("It is well established that a director will not be liable for losses to the corporation absent a showing that his act or omission proximately caused the subsequent losses").

## 5. REBUTTING THE PRESUMPTION OF THE BUSINESS JUDGMENT RULE

Recall that the business judgment rule is often stated as a rebuttable presumption. The difficulty of rebutting the presumption has acted as a virtually impregnable shield for directors when the wisdom of their business decisions are challenged. But suppose that the plaintiff is able to rebut the presumption, either because the director was not independent and thus not acting in good faith or was not fully informed. Is rebuttal enough to establish the defendants liability? If not, what happens in the next stage of the litigation?

Answering these questions involves the concept of fairness that will be developed more fully in the next chapter. In *Cede II*, the Delaware Supreme Court held that "a breach of either the duty of loyalty or the duty of care rebuts the presumption that the directors have acted in the best interests of the shareholders, and requires the directors to prove that the transaction was entirely fair." 634 A.2d at 371. Chancellor Allen interpreted this language to mean that "under the Delaware version of the 'business judgment rule,' if a shareholder establishes director negligence, thus overcoming the presumption, he or she has established a prima facie case of liability. *Cede III*, 663 A.2d 1134, 1137 (Del.Ch. 1994).

On appeal, the Delaware Supreme Court stated:

> The business judgment rule "operates as both a procedural guide for litigants and a substantive rule of law." *Cede II*, 634 A.2d at 360. As a procedural guide the business judgment presumption is a rule of evidence that places the initial burden of proof on the plaintiff. In *Cede II*, this Court described the rule's evidentiary, or procedural, operation as follows:
>
> > If a shareholder plaintiff fails to meet this evidentiary burden, the business judgment rule attaches to protect corporate officers and directors and the decisions they make, and our courts will not second-guess these business judgments. If the rule is rebutted, the burden shifts to the defendant directors, the proponents of the challenged transaction, to prove to the trier of fact the "entire fairness" of the transaction to the shareholder plaintiff.

Burden shifting does not create per se liability on the part of the directors. Rather, it "is a procedure by which Delaware courts of equity determine under what standard of review director liability is to be judged." In remanding this case for review under the entire fairness standard, this Court expressly acknowledged that its holding in *Cede II* did not establish liability.

Where, as in this case, the presumption of the business judgment rule has been rebutted, the board of directors' action is examined under the entire fairness standard. This Court has described the dual aspects of entire fairness, as follows:

> The concept of fairness has two basic aspects: fair dealing and fair price. The former embraces questions of when the transaction was timed, how it was initiated, structured, negotiated, disclosed to the directors, and how the approvals of the directors and the stockholders were obtained. The latter aspect of fairness relates to the economic and financial considerations of the proposed merger, including all relevant factors: assets, market value, earnings, future prospects, and any other elements that affect the intrinsic or inherent value of a company's stock.... However, the test for fairness is not a bifurcated one as between fair dealing and price. All aspects of the issue must be examined as a whole since the question is one of entire fairness.

*Weinberger v. UOP, Inc.*, 457 A.2d at 711. Thus, the entire fairness standard requires the board of directors to establish "to the court's satisfaction that the transaction was the product of both fair dealing and fair price." * * *

Because the decision that the procedural presumption of the business judgment rule has been rebutted does not establish substantive liability under the entire fairness standard, such a ruling does not necessarily present an insurmountable obstacle for a board of directors to overcome. Thus, an initial judicial determination that a given breach of a board's fiduciary duties has rebutted the presumption of the business judgment rule does not preclude a subsequent judicial determination that the board action was entirely fair, and is, therefore, not outcome-determinative per se. To avoid substantive liability, notwithstanding the quantum of adverse evidence that has defeated the business judgment rule's protective procedural presumption, the board will have to demonstrate entire fairness by presenting evidence of the cumulative manner by which it otherwise discharged all of its fiduciary duties.

*Cede IV*, 663 A.2d at 1162–63.

As you will see in the next chapter, the traditional concept of "fairness" is the range of values that two independent parties might agree to in an arms-length transaction. Where a director is financially interested in the transaction, fairness can be a useful measuring rod for determining its validity, although many questions arise in that determination. Under *Weinberger*, if the test is "entire fairness," the traditional concept of fairness is expanded to include review of the way in which the transaction was negotiated ("fair dealing") as well as the fairness of the price. When a director is financially interested in the transaction, there may not be a great deal of difference between traditional fairness and "entire fairness."

But suppose, as was true in *Van Gorkom*, there is an arms-length transaction and the presumption of the business judgment rule is rebutted because the directors were not fully informed. Is fairness an appropriate standard for determining liability and, if so, how would it be determined? Does the failure to be informed constitute a *per se* breach of the fair dealing requirement so that a plaintiff would only have to prove an unfair price? Or can the directors successfully argue that their failure is evaluated differently when rebutting the presumption of the business judgment rule than when determining whether they have satisfied their duty of fair dealing? Consider the Delaware Supreme Court's discussion of *Van Gorkom* in *Cede IV*. Does it answer these questions satisfactorily?

## 6. THE BUSINESS JUDGMENT RULE AND ILLEGAL CONDUCT

Although the business judgment rule will act as a shield from liability for the director who makes business decisions which he believes in good faith are in the best interests of the company, the presumption will be lost if it can be shown that the director acted fraudulently, illegally or with a conflict of interest. The latter will be treated in the next chapter. The following case shows how a court deals with directors who involve the corporation in illegal acts.

### MILLER v. AMERICAN TELEPHONE & TELEGRAPH CO.
507 F.2d 759 (3d Cir.1974).

SEITZ, CHIEF JUDGE.

Plaintiffs, stockholders in American Telephone and Telegraph Company ("AT & T"), brought a stockholders' derivative action in the Eastern District of Pennsylvania against AT & T and all but one of its directors. The suit centered upon the failure of AT & T to collect an outstanding debt of some $1.5 million owed to the company by the Democratic National Committee ("DNC") for communications services provided by AT & T during the 1968 Democratic national convention. Federal diversity jurisdiction was invoked under 28 U.S.C.A. § 1332.

Plaintiffs' complaint alleged that "neither the officers or directors of AT & T have taken any action to recover the amount owed" from on or about August 20, 1968, when the debt was incurred, until May 31, 1972, the date plaintiffs' amended complaint was filed. The failure to collect was alleged to have involved a breach of the defendant directors' duty to exercise diligence in handling the affairs of the corporation, to have resulted in affording a preference to the DNC in collection procedures in violation of § 202(a) of the Communications Act of 1934, 47 U.S.C.A. § 202(a) (1970), and to have amounted to AT & T's making a "contribution" to the DNC in violation of a federal prohibition on corporate campaign spending, 18 U.S.C.A. § 610 (1970).

On motion of the defendants, the district court dismissed the complaint for failure to state a claim upon which relief could be granted. 364 F.Supp. 648 (E.D.Pa.1973). The court stated that collection procedures were properly within the discretion of the directors whose determination would not be overturned by the court in the absence of an allegation that the conduct of the directors was "plainly illegal, unreasonable, or in breach of a fiduciary duty * * *." *Id.* at 651. Plaintiffs appeal from dismissal of their complaint.

## I.

The pertinent law on the question of the defendant directors' fiduciary duties in this diversity action is that of New York, the state of AT & T's incorporation. The sound business judgment rule, the basis of the district court's dismissal of plaintiffs' complaint, expresses the unanimous decision of American courts to eschew intervention in corporate decision-making if the judgment of directors and officers is uninfluenced by personal considerations and is exercised in good faith. Underlying the rule is the assumption that reasonable diligence has been used in reaching the decision which the rule is invoked to justify. *Casey v. Woodruff*, 49 N.Y.S.2d 625, 643 (Sup.Ct.1944).

Had plaintiffs' complaint alleged only failure to pursue a corporate claim, application of the sound business judgment rule would support the district court's ruling that a shareholder could not attack the directors' decision. Where, however, the decision not to collect a debt owed the corporation is itself alleged to have been an illegal act, different rules apply. When New York law regarding such acts by directors is considered in conjunction with the underlying purposes of the particular statute involved here, we are convinced that the business judgment rule cannot insulate the defendant directors from liability if they did in fact breach 18 U.S.C.A. § 610, as plaintiffs have charged.

*Roth v. Robertson*, 64 Misc. 343, 118 N.Y.S. 351 (Sup.Ct.1909), illustrates the proposition that even though committed to benefit the corporation, illegal acts may amount to a breach of fiduciary duty in New York. In *Roth,* the managing director of an amusement park company had allegedly used corporate funds to purchase the silence of persons who threatened to complain about unlawful Sunday operation of the park. Recovery from the defendant director was sustained on the ground that the money was an illegal payment:

> * * * For reasons of public policy, we are clearly of the opinion that payments of corporate funds for such purposes as those disclosed in this case must be condemned, and officers of a corporation making them held to a strict accountability, and be compelled to refund the amounts so wasted for the benefit of stockholders. * * * To hold any other rule would be establishing a dangerous precedent, tacitly countenancing the wasting of corporate funds for purposes of corrupting public morals. *Id.* at 346, 118 N.Y.S. at 353.

The plaintiffs' complaint in the instant case alleges a similar "waste" of $1.5 million through an illegal campaign contribution.

*Abrams v. Allen,* 297 N.Y. 52, 74 N.E.2d 305 (1947), reflects an affirmation by the New York Court of Appeals of the principle of *Roth* that directors must be restrained from engaging in activities which are against public policy. In *Abrams* the court held that a cause of action was stated by an allegation in a derivative complaint that the directors of Remington Rand, Inc., had relocated corporate plants and curtailed production solely for the purpose of intimidating and punishing employees for their involvement in a labor dispute. The Court of Appeals acknowledged that, "depending on the circumstances," proof of the allegations in the complaint might sustain recovery, *inter alia,* under the rule that directors are liable for corporate loss caused by the commission of an "unlawful or immoral act." *Id.* at 55, 74 N.E.2d at 306. In support of its holding, the court noted that the closing of factories for the purpose alleged was opposed to the public policy of the state and nation as embodied in the New York Labor Law and the National Labor Relations Act. *Id.* at 56, 74 N.E.2d at 307.

The alleged violation of the federal prohibition against corporate political contributions not only involves the corporation in criminal activity but similarly contravenes a policy of Congress clearly enunciated in 18 U.S.C.A. § 610. That statute and its predecessor reflect congressional efforts: (1) to destroy the influence of corporations over elections through financial contributions and (2) to check the practice of using corporate funds to benefit political parties without the consent of the stockholders. *United States v. CIO,* 335 U.S. 106, 113, 68 S.Ct. 1349, 92 L.Ed. 1849 (1948).

The fact that shareholders are within the class for whose protection the statute was enacted gives force to the argument that the alleged breach of that statute should give rise to a cause of action in those shareholders to force the return to the corporation of illegally contributed funds. Since political contributions by corporations can be checked and shareholder control over the political use of general corporate funds effectuated only if directors are restrained from causing the corporation to violate the statute, such a violation seems a particularly appropriate basis for finding breach of the defendant directors' fiduciary duty to the corporation. Under such circumstances, the directors cannot be insulated from liability on the ground that the contribution was made in the exercise of sound business judgment.

Since plaintiffs have alleged actual damage to the corporation from the transaction in the form of the loss of a $1.5 million increment to AT & T's treasury, we conclude that the complaint does state a claim upon which relief can be granted sufficient to withstand a motion to dismiss.

## II.

We have accepted plaintiffs' allegation of a violation of 18 U.S.C.A. § 610 as a shorthand designation of the elements necessary to establish a breach of that statute. This is consonant with the federal practice of notice pleading. That such a designation is sufficient for pleading purposes does not, however, relieve plaintiffs of their ultimate obligation to prove the elements of the statutory violation as part of their proof of breach of fiduciary duty. At the appropriate time, plaintiffs will be required to produce evidence sufficient to establish three distinct elements comprising a violation of 18 U.S.C.A. § 610: that AT & T (1) made a contribution of money or anything of value to the DNC (2) in connection with a federal election (3) for the purpose of influencing the outcome of that election. The first two of these elements are obvious from the face of the statute; the third was supplied by legislative history prior to being made explicit by 1972 amendments to definitions applicable to § 610.

The order of the district court will be reversed and the case remanded for further proceedings consistent with this opinion.

## D.  LIMITATION OF DIRECTORS' LIABILITY

### PROBLEM

### FASHION, INC.—PART III

Two years have passed since the events in Part II. At the board meeting to approve the merger with United, Wendy Andrews, one of the outside directors, raised a number of questions about United and complained that, notwithstanding the reports at the meeting, she had not had sufficient time to study the transaction. The final vote on the merger was 10 in favor and none against. Andrews abstained and Donald Coleman, another outside director, was absent. Thereafter, the merger received shareholder approval.

Subsequent events have proved disastrous to Fashion. The acquisition necessitated additional capital of $750 million, adversely affecting Fashion's financial position and causing it to incur substantial losses. In the past two years, the price of Fashion's stock has declined more than 50%. Last year, a shareholder of Fashion brought a derivative suit against the entire Fashion board, alleging gross negligence in connection with the merger.

1.  After the complaint was filed, the defendants requested the corporation to advance $100,000 to them in order to pay a retainer to their counsel in the lawsuit. May the board authorize this payment? If not, what procedures must the defendants follow to obtain the advance? Must any conditions be imposed on this payment?

2.  In the course of the litigation, defendants incurred expenses of $1,000,000, consisting of legal, accounting and experts' fees, court costs, and other administrative costs. Assume that the case was settled with the directors agreeing to pay $15 million to the corporation. Of that amount, $10 million was to be paid under Fashion's D & O liability policy. Thereafter, defendants requested the corporation to indemnify them for all their expenses.

(a) May the corporation make the requested payment?

(b) What procedures must be followed?

(c) Are there any limits on the payment?

(d) If the corporation refuses to indemnify, do the defendants have any other means to recover their expenses?

## 1. INTRODUCTION

In the 1980s, corporate directors' fear of liability increased dramatically. Indeed, some outside directors withdrew from board membership altogether or declined to stand for re-election. To allay these fears, many states enacted legislation to reduce the risk of directors' personal liability for monetary damages. The statutory responses took three different forms: the adoption of a charter provision eliminating or reducing the personal liability of directors for monetary damages, primarily in due care cases; a change in the standard of liability to require a higher degree of fault than ordinary negligence; and a limit on the monetary amount for which a director could be held personally liable.

These statutes are designed to shield officers and directors of large, publicly-held corporations from the wide variety of potential liabilities and expenses that they face. Corporate executives may be actual or potential defendants in derivative suits or direct actions by shareholders, or in civil actions brought by third parties. They may also be the subject of civil actions, criminal actions or administrative proceedings instituted by the government. They are occasionally required to pay substantial damages, penalties or fines, and, more frequently, must incur large expenses for legal counsel in the defense of actual or threatened actions.

In addition to statutory exculpation provisions, most directors and officers are protected against some of those costs by indemnification and insurance. These are contractual arrangements between directors and corporations that shift all or a part of the risk of liability for wrongdoing from the individual to the corporate entity. The fear of being subject to personal liability is a real barrier to corporations' ability to attract and retain competent executives. This fear especially affects less wealthy officers and directors. Until recently, corporate law itself gave added protection to executives in the performance of their duties through application of the business judgment rule, which acted as an almost impenetrable shield. In recent years, however, that shield has shown some signs of erosion. As *Van Gorkom* illustrates, the amount of potential damages can be very great.

Statutory exculpation and indemnification are closely related. As the ABA Committee on Corporate Laws has noted:

> * * * Liability limitation insulates the director from personal liability for acts or omissions that have not yet occurred but that might otherwise give rise to personal liability. Indemnification protects the director from personal liability for acts or omissions that occurred in the past. Both liability limitation and indemnification shift from the director to the corporation the ultimate economic cost

for the director's acts and omissions. Both liability limitation and indemnification, therefore, are addressed to the issue of allocation, between the directors and the corporation, of the economic cost of certain actual or alleged wrongful conduct by a director.

American Bar Association Committee on Corporate Laws, *Changes in the Model Business Corporation Act—Amendments Pertaining to Indemnification and Advance for Expenses*, 49 Bus. Law. 741, 742 (1994).

Some critics recognize the need to reduce the risks and costs of frivolous litigation but argue that the risk shifting created by indemnification and insurance reduces management's incentive to act responsibly and thus impedes an effective system of management accountability. *See* Joseph W. Bishop, *Sitting Ducks and Decoy Ducks: New Trends in the Indemnification of Corporate Directors and Officers*, 77 Yale L.J. 1078 (1968).

Other scholars defend the efficiency of the existing system. Professor Reinier Kraakman argues that while it would appear that imposing personal liability would lead to the maximum control over organizational conduct, risk shifting is generally a more efficient way of achieving the desired behavior. He notes that stockholders are efficient risk-bearers because of their ability to diversify their investments. By contrast, corporate managers are undiversified risk bearers who are not able to work for more than one firm at a time. Hence, unless they are paid to do otherwise, they will tend to evaluate business decisions with a risk-averse bias that may be detrimental to the best interests of the stockholders. Reinier Kraakman, *Corporate Liability Strategies and the Cost of Legal Controls*, 93 Yale L.J. 857 (1984).

Kraakman contends that the inefficiency of managers as risk-bearers extends to their inability to bear the inevitable legal risks which any business must face, no matter how well it is managed. If personal liability attaches to those risks, then "competent corporate decisionmakers will either demand insulation from them or require compensation for bearing them." *Id*. at 865. He concludes that because enterprise liability works with little personal risk to the managers, it should be the norm, with managerial liability being imposed only when enterprise liability is likely to fail.

## 2.  STATUTORY EXCULPATION OF DIRECTORS

DGCL § 102(b)(7) and RMBCA § 2.02(b)(4) exemplify statutes that permit a charter provision to reduce directors' personal liability for violations of the duty of due care. These sections are not self-executing; they require the stockholders affirmatively to adopt any exculpatory provision in the articles of incorporation. The Delaware statute limits exculpation by excluding from its coverage a breach of the director's duty of loyalty to the corporation or its shareholders, acts or omissions not in good faith, intentional misconduct, knowing violations of law, and transactions in which the director has obtained an improper personal benefit, such as from insider trading.

Similarly, the RMBCA excludes from its coverage liability for improperly received financial benefits, intentional infliction of harm on the corporation or the shareholders, and intentional violations of criminal law. In addition, RMBCA § 2.02(b)(4) does not exculpate a director for making unlawful distributions. Both statutes apply only to liability for monetary damages and have no effect on the availability of equitable relief for a breach of fiduciary duty. Like DGCL § 102(b)(7), RMBCA § 2.02(b)(4) requires shareholder approval of exculpatory provisions. Unlike Delaware, however, the RMBCA contains no exceptions for the duty of loyalty or for "acts or omissions not in good faith." In rejecting these exclusions, the ABA Committee on Corporate Laws noted that the phrase "duty of loyalty" appeared nowhere else in the Delaware statute and that the "acts or omissions" standard was potentially too vague. Committee on Corporate Laws, *Changes in the Revised Model Business Corporation Act—Amendment Pertaining to the Liability of Directors*, 45 BUS. LAW. 695, 697 (1990).

Over two-thirds of state corporate laws now allow some form of charter provision to limit director liability. The exceptions provided by other states that differ from those allowed by DGCL § 102(b)(7) and RMBCA § 2.02(b)(4) include actions that create liability to a third party and improper appropriations of business opportunities of the corporation. At least eleven states have followed RMBCA § 2.02(b)(4) in omitting a "duty of loyalty" exception.

A few states have changed statutorily the standard of conduct giving rise to personal liability. For example, under Indiana law, a director who has breached or failed to perform her duties in accordance with the statutory standard of care will not be liable for the breach or failure unless her conduct constituted "willful misconduct or recklessness." Ind.Code Ann. § 23–1–35(1)(e)(2). This limitation applies to actions for equitable relief as well as damages, and includes suits by both third parties and stockholders. Unlike the charter option provisions, these statutes are self-executing. They do not require shareholder approval to become effective nor do they permit the corporation to opt out of the liability limitation provisions, even if the stockholders wish to do so.

Virginia is the only state whose statute allows a limit to be placed on the amount of damages for which a director or officer can be held liable. Except where the director or officer has engaged in willful misconduct or a knowing violation of criminal law or federal or state securities law, Va.Code Ann. § 13.1–692.1 limits personal liability to the amount that is the lesser of: 1) the monetary limit specified in the corporation's articles of incorporation or, if approved by the shareholders, the by-laws; or 2) the greater of $100,000 or the compensation received from the corporation during the preceding twelve months. Like the statutes that change the standard of conduct, the Virginia provision does not require shareholder approval to become effective. Thus, absent a contrary provision in the articles of incorporation or by-laws, the liability of a director or officer will be limited to the greater of $100,000 or her cash compensation for the past year. In the decision on the remand of *Sandberg v.*

*Virginia Bankshares, Inc.* (discussed in Chapter 18), 979 F.2d 332 (4th Cir.1992), the Court of Appeals concluded that a jury's finding that directors had acted in conscious disregard of whether a proxy statement contained material misrepresentations was sufficient to satisfy the "knowing violation" provision of the Virginia statute. Accordingly, the court held that the liability cap was inapplicable. *Id.* at 343.

The Virginia statute has the seeming virtue of certainty; directors will know *ex ante* the maximum extent of their liability for a breach of the duty of due care. At the same time, as one commentator has pointed out, perhaps the reason why no other state has adopted such a cap is that "no specific dollar limit can ever be appropriate for the thousands of corporations typically chartered under the law of any state. While $100,000 may be the right limit for some corporations, it will be too high or too low for others." James J. Hanks, Jr., *Evaluating Recent State Legislation on Director and Officer Liability Limitation and Indemnification*, 43 Bus. Law. 1207, 1236 (1988).

The ALI takes a still different and unique approach. Its goal is to adopt "a concept of mitigation of disproportionate liability, not abrogation of the duty of care." Thus the ALI goes beyond the existing statutory scheme to recommend that, even absent an enabling statute, courts uphold a corporate charter provision limiting directors' and officers' liability for certain breaches of their duty of care. ALI, PRINCIPLES OF CORPORATE GOVERNANCE, (1994) § 7.19. The ALI does not permit complete exculpation of directors; the corporation can never reduce the amount for which directors can be held liable to less than the director's annual compensation. If damages are less than the compensation, the director is responsible for the full amount. If damages exceed the director's annual salary, the director is liable for an amount at least equal to the compensation. The board retains the right to set the exculpation level at any amount higher than the director's annual salary. The ALI explicitly rejects exculpation for breaches of directors' duty of loyalty, partly because investors would not be able to estimate the cost to them of such a provision.

The ALI explains that:

> The rationale for such a limitation rests on a variety of considerations, of which five stand out: First and most fundamentally, it is justified on grounds of fairness, because the potential liability in cases where it applies would otherwise be excessive in relation to the nature of the defendant's culpability and the economic benefits expected from serving the corporation. Second, such a limitation should reduce the pressures on directors to act in an unduly risk-averse manner. Realistically, the risk of liability for due care violations tends to be one-sided: directors can be held liable for excessively risky acts or decisions, but not, as practical matter, for excessively cautious ones. Given the frequently nominal investment of directors in their corporation's stock, a substantial risk of liability for negligence might lead risk-averse directors to opt for more hesitant

policies than shareholders desire (particularly to the extent that shareholders hold reasonably diversified portfolios and so are substantially protected against any firm-specific risk). Third, it is likely that the duty of care will be implemented by courts more evenly and appropriately when the potential penalties that may result are not perceived as Draconian. Fourth, such a limitation may serve to reduce the cost of insurance (often borne by the corporation) because the likely exposure of the insurer is reduced. Although the threat of derivative litigation is only one of the determinants of the cost of D & O insurance, a limitation on due care liability at least contributes to cost reduction and also protects defendants from the danger that their insurance coverage may be inadequate or that an exception to their coverage may be applicable to this case.

Finally, a limitation on liability also reduces the economic incentives for the plaintiff's attorney to sue, at least in those circumstances where the ceiling would be applicable, because under § 7.17 a plaintiff's attorney's fees are limited to a reasonable percentage of the total recovery.

*Id.* Comment *c.*

Perhaps the most extreme position is that of Professor Kenneth Scott who has argued that "very little of any value would be lost by outright abolition of the legal duty of care and its accompanying threat of a lawsuit." He contends that "[O]ther pressures and incentives bear on management's performance—competition in the product and capital markets, the managerial labor market, and executive incentive compensation arrangements. And, even without any threat of negligence liability, the board members, to protect their own reputation as directors, managers, or professionals and to maximize the value of their own stock holdings or those they represent, have reason to monitor and, if necessary, oust top management." Furthermore, "[t]he objective of promoting careful decisions by the board is also not much enhanced by the duty of care action. * * * If subsequently-determined personal liability ever became a significant factor, the board members would be biased towards taking fewer business risks and following more costly and time-consuming decisionmaking procedures. It is most doubtful whether that would be in the best interest of shareholders." Kenneth E. Scott, *Corporation Law and the American Law Institute Corporate Governance Project*, 35 Stan.L.Rev. 927, 935–37 (1983).

Any attempt to exculpate directors from liability raises serious public policy questions. Should there ever be a limit on a director's liability for a breach of the duty of due care? If so, is not the issue so fundamental that shareholders should always decide whether, and to what extent, to exculpate directors? However, in a large, publicly-held corporation, where the role of the shareholder is likely to be limited to approving management's proposals as set forth in the proxy material, can a shareholder vote on this question ever be meaningful?

James J. Hanks, Jr., *Evaluating Recent State Legislation on Director and Officer Liability Limitation and Indemnification*

43 Bus. Law. 1207, 1231–1236 (1988).

The principal public policy issue in director and officer liability legislation is the allocation of the economic cost of the directors' exculpated conduct. * * *

Charter option statutes simply permit the stockholders to decide for themselves whether to assume this risk or to leave it with the directors. By contrast, the other director liability statutes enacted to date are direct or indirect determinations by the legislatures to shift the risk from the directors to the stockholders. Self-executing statutes are a direct legislative determination that this risk should be borne by the stockholders. * * *

In considering this type of legislation from a policy viewpoint, it is not only appropriate but necessary to consider the role of the director in corporate governance and in the larger society. Supporters of legislatively shifting the costs of directors' misconduct from the directors to the stockholders argue that the role of directors is different from that of other purveyors of personal services. * * * Directors * * * act for the owners, [and] they make the decisions that the owners would otherwise have to make. Unless they engage in conduct in which no reasonable owner would be likely to engaged, directors should not expect to be monetarily liable. * * * Except for * * * egregious situations, it is difficult to justify imposing monetary liability on a director for the result of his decisions.

Nothing in the history of the development of corporations or corporation law suggests that the personal assets of directors were intended to constitute a financial safety net for stockholders or others willing to second-guess directors' decisions. In any event, the damage claims in stockholder derivative suits against directors and officers typically far exceed the aggregate net worth of the individual defendants. As a practical matter, dollar-for-dollar recovery by the corporation from its directors of officers for their wrongful conduct is (and probably always has been) a myth. In addition, this type of exposure for directors and officers may be viewed as inconsistent with the principle of limited liability for investors that has been the foundation of corporation law and finance for generations. * * *

In the end, sounder policy reasons permit the stockholders to decide whether to limit the liability of their directors, at least as to suits by the corporation or the stockholders. After all, it is the stockholders' money at stake. As long as the right of the stockholders to exculpate their directors is limited to liability to the corporation or to the stockholders themselves (in either derivative or direct suits), the state's regulatory interests should be minimal.

## 3.  INDEMNIFICATION

The right of a corporate officer or director to be indemnified and the power of the corporation to indemnify her voluntarily against damages, fines, or penalties growing out of the performance of corporate duties are governed by both corporate statutes and the articles of incorporation, by-laws or private contracts of the corporation.

The common law concerning the *right* of a corporate officer or director to indemnification was long confused. Little precedent guided corporations as to the limitations on their *power* to indemnify directors and officers. Dissatisfaction with the judicial handling of indemnification eventually led New York to enact the first indemnification statute in 1941. Today every jurisdiction has adopted legislation dealing with the matter, and most have enacted comprehensive indemnification statutes.

Indemnification provisions are of two types, permissive and mandatory; comprehensive statutes include both. A permissive, or enabling, provision gives a corporation the power to indemnify its corporate managers under certain circumstances. Mandatory statutes accord a director or officer who meets the statutory standards a right to indemnification.

**American Bar Association Committee on Corporate Laws,** *Changes in the Model Business Corporation Act—Amendments Pertaining to Indemnification and Advance for Expenses*

49 Bus.Law. 741, 749–50 (1994).

The provisions for indemnification and advance for expenses of the Model Act are among the most complex and important in the entire Act. Subchapter E of chapter 8 is an integrated treatment of this subject and strikes a balance among important social policies. Its substance is based almost entirely on an amendment to the 1969 Model Act adopted in 1980 and substantially revised in 1994.

1.  Policy Issues Raised by Indemnification and Advance for Expenses

Indemnification (including advance for expenses) provides financial protection by the corporation for its directors against exposure to expenses and liabilities that may be incurred by them in connection with legal proceedings based on an alleged breach of duty in their service to or on behalf of the corporation. Today, when both the volume and the cost of litigation have increased dramatically, it would be difficult to persuade responsible persons to serve as directors if they were compelled to bear personally the cost of vindicating the propriety of their conduct in every instance in which it might be challenged. While reasonable people may differ as to what constitutes a meritorious case, almost all would agree that corporate directors should have appropriate protection against personal risk and that the rule of *New York Dock Co. v. McCollom,* 16 N.Y.S.2d 844 (N.Y.Sup.Ct.1939), which denied reimbursement to directors who successfully defended their case on the merits, should as a matter of policy be overruled by statute.

The concept of indemnification recognizes that there will be situations in which the director does not satisfy all of the elements of the standard of conduct set forth in section 8.30(a) or the requirements of some other applicable law but where the corporation should nevertheless be permitted (or required) to absorb the economic costs of any ensuing litigation. A carefully constructed indemnification statute should identify these situations.

If permitted too broadly, however, indemnification may violate equally basic tenets of public policy. It is inappropriate to permit management to use corporate funds to avoid the consequences of certain conduct. For example, a director who intentionally inflicts harm on the corporation should not expect to receive assistance from the corporation for legal or other expenses and should be required to satisfy from his personal assets not only any adverse judgment but also expenses incurred in connection with the proceeding. Any other rule would tend to encourage socially undesirable conduct.

A further policy issue is raised in connection with indemnification against liabilities or sanctions imposed under state or federal civil or criminal statutes. A shift of the economic cost of these liabilities from the individual director to the corporation by way of indemnification may in some instances frustrate the public policy of those statutes.

The fundamental issue that must be addressed by an indemnification statute is the establishment of policies consistent with these broad principles: to ensure that indemnification is permitted only where it will further sound corporate policies and to prohibit indemnification where it might protect or encourage wrongful or improper conduct. As phrased by one commentator, the goal of indemnification is to "seek the middle ground between encouraging fiduciaries to violate their trust, and discouraging them from serving at all." Joseph F. Johnston, *Corporate Indemnification and Liability Insurance for Directors and Officers*, 33 Bus.Law. 1993, 1994 (1978). The increasing number of suits against directors, the increasing cost of defense, and the increasing emphasis on diversifying the membership of boards of directors all militate in favor of workable arrangements to protect directors against liability to the extent consistent with established principles.

\* \* \*

E. Norman Veasey, Jesse A. Finkelstein & C. Stephen Bigler, *Delaware Supports Directors With a Three–Legged Stool of Limited Liability, Indemnification and Insurance*
42 Bus.Law. 401, 404–412 (1987).

Section 145 of the Delaware General Corporation Law is the statutory authority for indemnification. It combines specific statutory rights and limitations on indemnification. It applies to any person involved (as a plaintiff or defendant) in actual or threatened litigation or an investigation by reason of the status of such person as an officer, director, employee, or agent of the corporation or of another corporation, trust, partnership, joint venture, or other enterprise he served at the request of the indemnifying corporation.

\* \* \*

The general statutory framework of the entitlement to ultimate indemnification is found in subsections (a) and (b) of section 145. Section 145(a) permits indemnification of officers, directors, employees, and agents for attorneys' fees and other expenses as well as judgments or amounts paid in settlement in civil cases. This subsection applies only to third-party actions, not to actions brought by or in the right of the corporation. The person seeking indemnification must have acted in good faith and in a manner he reasonably believed to be in or not opposed to the best interests of the corporation in respect of the claim made against him. In criminal cases the indemnitee may be indemnified for fines and costs provided that, in addition to the foregoing standard of conduct, he did not have reasonable cause to believe his conduct was unlawful.

Section 145(b) pertains to actions brought by or in the right of the corporation. Most frequently, of course, it applies to derivative suits. This subsection permits indemnification only for attorneys' fees and other expenses. It does not permit indemnification of judgments or amounts paid in settlement. The principal difference between section 145(a) and section 145(b), aside from the fact that the latter permits indemnification only for expenses and attorneys' fees, is that section 145(b) does not permit any indemnification "in respect of any claim, issue or matter as to which such person shall have been adjudged to be liable to the corporation," although it does permit some limited court relief "to the extent that the Court of Chancery or the court in which such action or suit was brought shall determine upon application that, despite the adjudication of liability but in view of all the circumstances of the case, such person is fairly and reasonably entitled to indemnity for such expenses [as the] court shall deem proper." There are no definitive criteria in the statute or the case law articulating the showing that must be made to satisfy the court that indemnification is proper.

\* \* \* [Under section 145(b)] it seems that indemnification may not be made (absent court relief provided in the statute) if the director has been adjudged liable to the corporation on any recognized basis of personal liability such as self-dealing, statutory violations, or gross negligence. This provision must be harmonized with the contemporaneously adopted section 102(b)(7) authorizing the limitation on or elimination of liability of directors in certain cases.

It is important to keep in mind the distinctions between indemnification in respect of third-party actions and that applicable to derivative actions. Section 145(b) permits indemnification only of expenses in derivative suits and does not authorize indemnification of judgments or amounts paid in settlement in derivative suits. On the other hand, such broader indemnification power is expressly authorized for third-party actions by section 145(a). It can be argued that since section 145(b) does not expressly prohibit indemnification of judgments or amounts paid in settlement in derivative suits, such indemnification may be provided under the "nonexclusive" provision of section 145(f). It would seem that since subsections (a) and (b) should be read in *pari materia,* the express inclusion of the broader indemnification power in (a) and its exclusion in (b) demonstrates a legislative intent to prohibit indemnification of judgments or amounts paid in settlement in derivative suits. The policy behind this distinction is based on the fact that in a derivative action the ultimate plaintiff is the corporation on whose behalf the suit is brought. Consequently, any resulting money judgment against, or settlement funds provided by, the defendant is paid to the corporation in order to make it whole. The corporation would not receive that benefit if it were to reimburse a defendant for the amount of the judgment or settlement funds that the defendant is required to pay the corporation.

As mentioned above, section 145(a) authorizes indemnification for various classes of indemnitees in third-party actions, while section 145(b) does so for actions brought by or in the right of the corporation. Although the scope of the permitted indemnification differs, these statutes are permissive. Implementation of the authority granted requires action by the corporation. Indemnification may, therefore, be denied unless it is made mandatory by statute or otherwise.

Mandatory indemnification by statute is provided in section 145(c).

* * *

The phrase found in section 145(c), "on the merits or otherwise," permits the indemnitee to be indemnified as a matter of right in the event he wins a judgment on the merits in his favor or if he successfully asserts a "technical" defense, such as a defense based upon a statute of limitations. The same statutory language contemplates the dismissal of the suit in conjunction with a negotiated settlement where the dismissal is with prejudice and without any payment or assumption of liability. A dismissal without prejudice, however, is insufficient to invoke mandatory indemnification under the statute.

––––––––––

Until 1984, the indemnification provisions of the Model Business Corporation Act (now the RMBCA) were "substantially identical" to those of Delaware because the drafting committees for the two statutes worked together to produce a joint document. Unhappiness with certain features of the indemnification statutes and the construction given them by Delaware courts in particular led the drafters of the Model Act to amend it in 1980 and to revise it substantially in 1994. The current version significantly expands a director's right to indemnification and an advance of litigation expenses as well as a court's power to order indemnification on its own initiative. It also contains a new section

2.02(b)(5) which permits a corporation to adopt a provision in its articles of incorporation indemnifying a director to the same extent that the director's liability can be limited under section 2.02(b)(4). For a detailed explanation of the indemnification provisions of the RMBCA, *see* American Bar Association Committee on Corporate Laws, *Changes in the Model Business Corporation Act—Amendments Pertaining to Indemnification and Advance for Expenses*, 49 Bus. Law. 741 (1994).

## WALTUCH v. CONTICOMMODITY SERVICES, INC.

88 F.3d 87 (2d Cir.1996).

JACOBS, CIRCUIT JUDGE:

Famed silver trader Norton Waltuch spent $2.2 million in unreimbursed legal fees to defend himself against numerous civil lawsuits and an enforcement proceeding brought by the Commodity Futures Trading Commission (CFTC). In this action under Delaware law, Waltuch seeks indemnification of his legal expenses from his former employer. The district court denied any indemnity, and Waltuch appeals.

As vice-president and chief metals trader for Conticommodity Services, Inc., Waltuch traded silver for the firm's clients, as well as for his own account. In late 1979 and early 1980, the silver price spiked upward as the then-billionaire Hunt brothers and several of Waltuch's foreign clients bought huge quantities of silver futures contracts. Just as rapidly, the price fell until (on a day remembered in trading circles as "Silver Thursday") the silver market crashed. Between 1981 and 1985, angry silver speculators filed numerous lawsuits against Waltuch and Conticommodity, alleging fraud, market manipulation, and antitrust violations. All of the suits eventually settled and were dismissed with prejudice, pursuant to settlements in which Conticommodity paid over $35 million to the various suitors. Waltuch himself was dismissed from the suits with no settlement contribution. His unreimbursed legal expenses in these actions total approximately $1.2 million.

Waltuch was also the subject of an enforcement proceeding brought by the CFTC, charging him with fraud and market manipulation. The proceeding was settled, with Waltuch agreeing to a penalty that included a $100,000 fine and a six-month ban on buying or selling futures contracts from any exchange floor. Waltuch spent $1 million in unreimbursed legal fees in the CFTC proceeding.

Waltuch brought suit in the United States District Court for the Southern District of New York against Conticommodity and its parent company, Continental Grain Co. (together "Conti"), for indemnification of his unreimbursed expenses. Only two of Waltuch's claims reach us on appeal.

Waltuch first claims that Article Ninth of Conticommodity's articles of incorporation requires Conti to indemnify him for his expenses in both the private and CFTC actions. Conti responds that this claim is barred by subsection (a) of § 145 of Delaware's General Corporation Law, which permits indemnification only if the corporate officer acted "in good faith," something that Waltuch has not established. Waltuch counters that subsection (f) of the same statute permits a corporation to grant indemnification rights outside the limits of subsection (a), and that Conticommodity did so with Article Ninth (which has no stated good-faith limitation). The district court held that, notwithstanding § 145(f), Waltuch could recover under Article Ninth only if Waltuch met the "good faith" requirement of § 145(a). On the factual issue of whether Waltuch had acted "in good faith," the court denied Conti's summary judgment motion and cleared the way for trial. The parties then stipulated that they would forgo trial on the issue of Waltuch's "good faith," agree to an entry of final judgment against Waltuch on his claim under Article Ninth and § 145(f), and allow Waltuch to take an immediate appeal of the judgment to this Court. Thus, as to Waltuch's first claim, the only question left is how to interpret §§ 145(a) and 145(f), assuming Waltuch acted with less than "good faith." As we explain in part I below, we affirm the district court's judgment as to this claim and hold that § 145(f) does not permit a corporation to bypass the "good faith" requirement of § 145(a).

Waltuch's second claim is that subsection (c) of § 145 requires Conti to indemnify him because he was "successful on the merits or otherwise" in the private lawsuits. The district court ruled for Conti on this claim as well. The court explained that, even though all the suits against Waltuch were dismissed without his making any payment, he was not "successful on the merits or otherwise," because Conti's settlement payments to the plaintiffs were partially on Waltuch's behalf. Id. at 311. For the reasons stated in part II below, we reverse this portion of the district court's ruling, and hold that Conti must indemnify Waltuch under § 145(c) for the $1.2 million in unreimbursed legal fees he spent in defending the private lawsuits.

## I

Article Ninth, on which Waltuch bases his first claim, is categorical and contains no requirement of "good faith":

> The Corporation shall indemnify and hold harmless each of its incumbent or former directors, officers, employees and agents ... against expenses actually and necessarily incurred by him in connection with the defense of any action, suit or proceeding threatened, pending or completed, in which he is made a party, by reason of his serving in or having held such position or capacity, except in relation to matters as to which he shall be adjudged in such action, suit or proceeding to be liable for negligence or misconduct in the performance of duty.

Conti argues that § 145(a) of Delaware's General Corporation Law, which does contain a "good faith" requirement, fixes the outer limits of a corporation's power to indemnify; Article Ninth is thus invalid under Delaware law, says Conti, to the extent that it requires indemnification of officers who have acted in bad faith.

In order to escape the "good faith" clause of § 145(a), Waltuch argues that § 145(a) is not an exclusive grant of indemnification power, because § 145(f) expressly allows corporations to indemnify officers in a manner broader than that set out in § 145(a). Waltuch contends that the "nonexclusivity" language in § 145(f) is a separate grant of indemnification power, not limited by the good faith clause that governs the power granted in § 145(a). Conti on the other hand contends that § 145(f) must be limited by "public policies," one of which is that a corporation may indemnify its officers only if they act in "good faith."

In a thorough and scholarly opinion, Judge Lasker agreed with Conti's reading of § 145(f), writing that "it has been generally agreed that there are public policy limits on indemnification under Section 145(f)," although it was "difficult ... to define precisely what limitations on indemnification public policy imposes." 833 F.Supp. at 307, 308. * * * As will be evident from the discussion below, we adopt much of Judge Lasker's analysis.

### A.    DELAWARE CASES

No Delaware court has decided the very issue presented here; but the applicable cases tend to support the proposition that a corporation's grant of indemnification rights cannot be inconsistent with the substantive statutory provisions of § 145, notwithstanding § 145(f). We draw this rule of "consistency" primarily from our reading of the Delaware Supreme Court's opinion in *Hibbert v. Hollywood Park, Inc.*, 457 A.2d 339 (Del.1983). In that case, Hibbert and certain other directors sued the corporation and the remaining directors, and then demanded indemnification for their expenses and fees related to the litigation. The company refused indemnification on the ground that directors were entitled to indemnification only as defendants in legal proceedings. The court reversed the trial court and held that Hibbert was entitled to indemnification under the plain terms of a company bylaw that did not draw an express distinction between plaintiff directors and defendant directors. Id. at 343. The court then proceeded to test the bylaw for consistency with § 145(a):

> Furthermore, *indemnification here is consistent with current Delaware law*. Under 8 Del.C. § 145(a) ..., "a corporation may indemnify any person who was or is a party or is threatened to be made a party to any threatened, pending or completed" derivative or third-party action. By this language, indemnity is not limited to only those who stand as a defendant in the main action. The corporation can also grant indemnification rights beyond those provided by statute. 8 Del.C. § 145(f).

*Id*. at 344 (emphasis added and citations omitted). This passage contains two complementary propositions. Under § 145(f), a corporation may provide indemnification rights that go "beyond" the rights provided by § 145(a) and the other substantive subsections of § 145. At the same time, any such indemnification rights provided by a corporation must be "consistent with" the substantive provisions of § 145, including

§ 145(a). In *Hibbert*, the corporate bylaw was "consistent with" § 145(a), because this subsection was "not limited to" suits in which directors were defendants. Hibbert's holding may support an inverse corollary that illuminates our case: if § 145(a) had been expressly limited to directors who were named as defendants, the bylaw could not have stood, regardless of § 145(f), because the bylaw would not have been "consistent with" the substantive statutory provision.

A more recent opinion of the Delaware Supreme Court, analyzing a different provision of § 145, also supports the view that the express limits in § 145's substantive provisions are not subordinated to § 145(f). In *Citadel Holding Corp. v. Roven*, 603 A.2d 818, 823 (Del.1992), a corporation's bylaws provided indemnification "to the full extent permitted by the General Corporation Law of Delaware." The corporation entered into an indemnification agreement with one of its directors, reciting the parties' intent to afford enhanced protection in some unspecified way. The director contended that the agreement was intended to afford mandatory advancement of expenses, and that this feature (when compared with the merely permissive advancement provision of § 145(e)) was the enhancement intended by the parties. The corporation, seeking to avoid advancement of expenses, argued instead that the agreement enhanced the director's protection only in the sense that the pre-contract indemnification rights were subject to statute, whereas his rights under the contract could not be diminished without his consent. *Id.*

In rejecting that argument, the court explained that indemnification rights provided by contract could not exceed the "scope" of a corporation's indemnification powers as set out by the statute.* * * *Citadel* thus confirms the dual propositions stated in *Hibbert*: indemnification rights may be broader than those set out in the statute, but they cannot be inconsistent with the "scope" of the corporation's power to indemnify, as delineated in the statute's substantive provisions.

### B.  STATUTORY READING

The "consistency" rule suggested by these Delaware cases is reinforced by our reading of § 145 as a whole. Subsections (a) (indemnification for third-party actions) and (b) (similar indemnification for derivative suits) expressly grant a corporation the power to indemnify directors, officers, and others, if they "acted in good faith and in a manner reasonably believed to be in or not opposed to the best interest of the corporation." These provisions thus limit the scope of the power that they confer. They are permissive in the sense that a corporation may exercise less than its full power to grant the indemnification rights set out in these provisions. By the same token, subsection (f) permits the corporation to grant additional rights: the rights provided in the rest of § 145 "shall not be deemed exclusive of any other rights to which those seeking indemnification may be entitled." But crucially, subsection (f) merely acknowledges that one seeking indemnification may be entitled to "other rights" (of indemnification or otherwise); it does not speak in terms of corporate power, and therefore cannot be read to free a corporation from the "good faith" limit explicitly imposed in subsections (a) and (b).

An alternative construction of these provisions would effectively force us to ignore certain explicit terms of the statute. Section 145(a) gives Conti the power to indemnify Waltuch "if he acted in good faith and in a manner reasonably believed to be in or not opposed to the best interest of the corporation." This statutory limit must mean that there is no power to indemnify Waltuch if he did not act in good faith. Otherwise, as Judge Lasker pointed out, § 145(a)—and its good faith clause—would have no meaning: a corporation could indemnify whomever and however it wished regardless of the good faith clause or anything else the Delaware Legislature wrote into § 145(a).

When the Legislature intended a subsection of § 145 to augment the powers limited in subsection (a), it set out the additional powers expressly. Thus subsection (g) explicitly allows a corporation to circumvent the "good faith" clause of subsection (a) by purchasing a directors and officers liability insurance policy. Significantly, that subsection is framed as a grant of corporate power:

> A corporation shall have power to purchase and maintain insurance on behalf of any person who is or was a director, officer, employee or agent of the corporation ... against any liability asserted against him and incurred by him in any such capacity, or arising out of his status as such, *whether or not the corporation would have the power to indemnify him against such liability under this section.*

The italicized passage reflects the principle that corporations have the power under § 145 to indemnify in some situations and not in others. Since § 145(f) is neither a grant of corporate power nor a limitation on such power, subsection (g) must be referring to the limitations set out in § 145(a) and the other provisions of § 145 that describe corporate power. If § 145 (through subsection (f) or another part of the statute) gave corporations unlimited power to indemnify directors and officers, then the final clause of subsection (g) would be unnecessary: that is, its grant of "power to purchase and maintain insurance" (exercisable regardless of whether the corporation itself would have the power to indemnify the loss directly) is meaningful only because, in some insurable situations, the corporation simply lacks the power to indemnify its directors and officers directly.

A contemporaneous account from the principal drafter of Delaware's General Corporation Law confirms what an integral reading of § 145 demonstrates: the statute's affirmative grants of power also impose limitations on the corporation's power to indemnify. Specifically, the good faith clause (unchanged since the Law's original enactment in 1967) was included in subsections (a) and (b) as a carefully calculated improvement on the prior indemnification provision and as an explicit limit on a corporation's power to indemnify * * *

Waltuch argues at length that reading § 145(a) to bar the indemnification of officers who acted in bad faith would render § 145(f) meaningless. This argument misreads § 145(f). That subsection refers to "any other rights to which those seeking indemnification or advancement of expenses may be entitled." Delaware commentators have identified various indemnification rights that are "beyond those provided by statute," *Hibbert*, 457 A.2d at 344, and that are at the same time consistent with the statute:

> [S]ubsection (f) provides general authorization for the adoption of various procedures and presumptions making the process of indemnification more favorable to the indemnitee. For example, indemnification agreements or by-laws could provide for: (i) mandatory indemnification unless prohibited by statute; (ii) mandatory advancement of expenses, which the indemnitee can, in many instances, obtain on demand; (iii) accelerated procedures for the "determination" required by section 145(d) to be made in the "specific case"; (iv) litigation "appeal" rights of the indemnitee in the event of an unfavorable determination; (v) procedures under which a favorable determination will be deemed to have been made under circumstances where the board fails or refuses to act; [and] (vi) reasonable funding mechanisms.

E. Norman Veasey, et al., *Delaware Supports Directors With a Three-Legged Stool of Limited Liability, Indemnification, and Insurance*, 42 BUS. LAW. 399, 415 (1987). Moreover, subsection (f) may reference non-indemnification rights, such as advancement rights or rights to other payments from the corporation that do not qualify as indemnification.

We need not decide in this case the precise scope of those "other rights" adverted to in § 145(f). We simply conclude that § 145(f) is not rendered meaningless or inoperative by the conclusion that a Delaware corporation lacks power to indemnify an officer or director "unless [he] 'acted in good faith and in a manner reasonably believed to be in or not opposed to the best interest of the corporation.'" As a result, we hold that Conti's Article Ninth, which would require indemnification of Waltuch even if he acted in bad faith, is inconsistent with § 145(a) and thus exceeds the scope of a Delaware corporation's power to indemnify. Since Waltuch has agreed to forgo his opportunity to prove at trial that he acted in good faith, he is not entitled to indemnification under Article Ninth for the $2.2 million he spent in connection with the private lawsuits and the CFTC proceeding. We therefore affirm the district court on this issue.

## II

Unlike § 145(a), which grants a discretionary indemnification power, § 145(c) affirmatively requires corporations to indemnify its officers and directors for the "successful" defense of certain claims:

Waltuch argues that he was "successful on the merits or otherwise" in the private lawsuits, because they were dismissed with prejudice without any payment or assumption of liability by him. Conti argues that the claims against Waltuch were dismissed only because of Conti's $35 million settlement payments, and that this payment was contributed, in part, "on behalf of Waltuch."]

The district court agreed with Conti that "the successful settlements cannot be credited to Waltuch but are attributable solely to Conti's settlement payments. It was not Waltuch who was successful, but Conti who was successful for him." 833 F.Supp. at 311. The district court held that § 145(c) mandates indemnification when the director or officer "is vindicated," but that there was no vindication here:

> Vindication is also ordinarily associated with a dismissal with prejudice without any payment. However, a director or officer is not vindicated when the reason he did not have to make a settlement payment is because someone else assumed that liability. Being bailed out is not the same thing as being vindicated.

*Id.* We believe that this understanding and application of the "vindication" concept is overly broad and is inconsistent with a proper interpretation of § 145(c).

No Delaware court has applied § 145(c) in the context of indemnification stemming from the settlement of civil litigation. One lower court, however, has applied that subsection to an analogous case in the criminal context, and has illuminated the link between "vindication" and the statutory phrase, "successful on the merits or otherwise." In *Merritt-Chapman & Scott Corp. v. Wolfson*, 321 A.2d 138 (Del.Super.Ct.1974), the corporation's agents were charged with several counts of criminal conduct. A jury found them guilty on some counts, but deadlocked on the others. The agents entered into a "settlement" with the prosecutor's office by pleading nolo contendere to one of the counts in exchange for the dropping of the rest. *Id.* at 140. The agents claimed entitlement to mandatory indemnification under § 145(c) as to the counts that were dismissed. In opposition, the corporation raised an argument similar to the argument raised by Conti:

> [The corporation] argues that the statute and sound public policy require indemnification only where there has been vindication by a finding or concession of innocence. *It contends that the charges against [the agents] were dropped for practical reasons*, not because of their innocence....

> The statute requires indemnification to the extent that the claimant "has been successful on the merits or otherwise." *Success is vindication*. In a criminal action, any result other than conviction must be considered success. *Going behind the result*, as [the corporation] attempts, is neither authorized by subsection (c) nor consistent with the presumption of innocence.

*Id.* at 141 (emphasis added).

Although the underlying proceeding in *Merritt* was criminal, the court's analysis is instructive here. The agents in *Merritt* rendered consideration—their guilty plea on one count—to achieve the dismissal of the other counts. The court considered these dismissals both "success" and (therefore) "vindication," and refused to "go[ ] behind the result" or to appraise the reason for the success. In equating "success" with "vindication," the court thus rejected the more expansive view of vindication urged by the corporation. Under *Merritt's* holding, then, vindication, when used as a synonym for "success" under § 145(c), does not mean moral exoneration. Escape from an adverse judgment or other detriment, for whatever reason, is determinative. According to *Merritt*, the only question a court may ask is what the result was, not why it was.[12]

Conti's contention that, because of its $35 million settlement payments, Waltuch's settlement without payment should not really count as settlement without payment, is inconsistent with the rule in *Merritt*. Here, Waltuch was sued, and the suit was dismissed without his having paid a settlement. Under the approach taken in *Merritt*, it is not our business to ask why this result was reached. Once Waltuch achieved his settlement gratis, he achieved success "on the merits or otherwise." And, as we know from *Merritt*, success is sufficient to constitute vindication (at least for the purposes of § 145(c)). Waltuch's settlement thus vindicated him.

The concept of "vindication" pressed by Conti is also inconsistent with the fact that a director or officer who is able to defeat an adversary's claim by asserting a technical defense is entitled to indemnification under § 145(c). In such cases, the indemnitee has been "successful" in the palpable sense that he has won, and the suit has been dismissed, whether or not the victory is deserved in merits terms. If a technical defense is deemed "vindication" under Delaware law, it cannot matter why Waltuch emerged unscathed, or whether Conti "bailed [him] out", or whether his success was deserved. Under § 145(c), mere success is vindication enough.

This conclusion comports with the reality that civil judgments and settlements are ordinarily expressed in terms of cash rather than moral victory. No doubt, it would make sense for Conti to buy the dismissal of the claims against Waltuch along with its own discharge from the case, perhaps to avoid further expense or participation as a non-party, poten-

---

**12.**  Our adoption of *Merritt's* interpretation of the statutory term "successful" does not necessarily signal our endorsement of the result in that case. The *Merritt* court sliced the case into individual counts, with indemnification pegged to each count independently of the others. We are not faced with a case in which the corporate officer claims to have been "successful" on some parts of the case but was clearly "unsuccessful" on others, and therefore take no position on this feature of the *Merritt* holding.

We also do not mean our discussion of *Merritt* to suggest that the line between success and failure in a criminal case may be drawn in the same way in the civil context. In a criminal case, conviction on a particular count is obvious failure, and dismissal of the charge is obvious success. In a civil suit for damages, however, there is a monetary continuum between complete success (dismissal of the suit without any payment) and complete failure (payment of the full amount of damages requested by the plaintiff). Because Waltuch made no payment in connection with the dismissal of the suits against him, we need not decide whether a defendant's settlement payment automatically renders that defendant "unsuccessful" under § 145(c).

tial cross-claims, or negative publicity. But Waltuch apparently did not accede to that arrangement, and Delaware law cannot allow an indemnifying corporation to escape the mandatory indemnification of subsection (c) by paying a sum in settlement on behalf of an unwilling indemnitee.

\* \* \*

For all of these reasons, we agree with Waltuch that he is entitled to indemnification under § 145(c) for his expenses pertaining to the private lawsuits.

### Note: Interpreting Indemnification Statutes

1. One of the biggest problems facing a potential indemnitee is that she will be required to incur immediate expenses such as legal fees long before a final determination is made as to the propriety of her conduct. Can the corporation make advance payments to her to meet these ongoing costs? If so, must someone make a determination as to the probable outcome of the litigation and whether she is likely to satisfy the standard of conduct after the dust settles? Must an advance for litigation expenses be secured? If so, then a dichotomy is created between rich directors who can afford to pay litigation expenses, regardless of whether the corporation advances these expenses, and poorer directors, who might be unable to afford either litigation or the security for any bond that might be required to secure the advances.

Recent statutes have eliminated the statutory requirement for such a bond and have permitted advances upon the giving of an undertaking to repay and the satisfaction of other conditions. *See* DGCL § 145(e). In *Swenson v. Thibaut*, 39 N.C.App. 77, 250 S.E.2d 279 (1978), the court took a similar approach. The plaintiff-shareholder in a derivative suit sought to enjoin the advancing of legal fees to the defendant directors. The court construed a section of the North Carolina statute that was similar to former RMBCA § 8.53 in requiring the director to give an ''undertaking'' to repay the advances if she was unsuccessful in her defense. The court rejected the argument that the term ''undertaking'' meant the posting of full security for all advances and defined it to be a written promise not made under seal given as security for the performance of an act. The court also rejected the argument that the advance was prohibited by the North Carolina equivalent of former RMBCA § 8.31, noting that, in any event, the advances had been approved by disinterested directors.

In *Citadel Holding Corporation v. Roven*, 603 A.2d 818 (Del.1992), the Delaware Supreme Court interpreted the terms of an indemnity agreement that promised to indemnify a director for claims arising ''by reason of his service as a director.'' *Id.* at 820. Despite a specific provision in the agreement that excluded any obligation on the corporation to indemnify the director for liability under Section 16(b) of the Securities Exchange Act of 1934 (relating to short-swing profits) the court held that the only limit on advancement of litigation expenses was ''reasonableness.'' Reasonable expenses included the defendant's attorneys' fees, although these expenses were limited to actions related to the corporation's business.

In *Advanced Mining Systems, Inc. v. Fricke*, 623 A.2d 82 (Del.Ch. 1992), the Delaware Court of Chancery interpreted DGCL § 145(e) to hold that the advancement of legal expenses and ultimate indemnification are two distinct acts. If a board approves advancing expenses, it is making "essentially * * * a decision to advance credit." *Id.* at 84 Although the board may decide that it is in the best interests of the corporation to advance these expenses, the statute does not require it to do so. Only a specific provision in the articles of incorporation, by-laws or private agreement between the director and corporation can mandate an advance. *See also, Heffernan v. Pacific Dunlop GNB Corp.*, 965 F.2d 369 (7th Cir.1992); *See* Lewis S. Black, Jr. and Frederick H. Alexander, *Advancing Litigation Expenses Under Mandatory Indemnification Provisions*, 26 REV. SEC. & COMMODITIES REG. 65 (1993).

RMBCA § 8.58(a) takes the opposite approach and does not distinguish between indemnification and the right to receive an advance for expenses. As the Official Comment notes, "a provision requiring indemnification to the fullest extent permitted by law shall be deemed, absent an express statement to the contrary, to include an obligation to advance expenses under section 8.53. This provision of the statute is intended to avoid a decision such as that of the Delaware Supreme Court in *Advanced Mining Systems v. Fricke*."

2. Litigation creates a number of different expenses, including court costs, attorneys' fees, fines, judgments and amounts paid in settlement. Clear public policy reasons require differentiating among them, and the statutes do so. For example, if a corporation could indemnify a director for amounts paid in settlement of a derivative suit, it would be taking from the director with one hand while giving the same amount with the other, a situation that would not be true in a third-party action.

DGCL § 145(b) expressly excludes amounts paid in settlement from expenses that can be indemnified in a derivative suit. By contrast, RMBCA § 8.54(a)(3) gives the court the power to order indemnification of the amounts paid in settlement in a derivative suit if, as the Official Comment states, "there are facts peculiar to [the director's] situation that make it fair and reasonable to both the corporation and to the director to override an intra-corporate declination or any otherwise applicable statutory prohibition against indemnification." The presumption in the RMBCA is that such situations will be extremely rare.

3. As *Waltuch* suggests, among the hardest questions are those connected with the required standard of conduct for indemnification. If after trial, a court determines that an indemnitee is innocent of the charges leveled against her, that determination is sufficient to warrant indemnification. But suppose the indemnitee wins on a technical defense such as the statute of limitations? What about a nolo contendere plea? And suppose the case is settled rather than going to trial so that the court never passes on the merits of the plaintiff's claim concerning the

indemnitee's conduct? In *B & B Investment Club v. Kleinert's, Inc.*, 472 F.Supp. 787 (E.D.Pa.1979), a securities fraud action, the defendant treasurer negotiated a settlement that involved a dismissal with prejudice but no monetary payment; the defendant president settled by paying $35,000. The court held that the treasurer's settlement constituted success on the merits even though the plaintiffs contended that they had settled for no money from the treasurer only because of the president's payment. In *Dornan v. Humphrey*, 278 App.Div. 1010, 106 N.Y.S.2d 142 (1951), the directors were determined to have been successful "on the merits or otherwise" when a derivative suit was dismissed because of the statute of limitations. In *Galdi v. Berg*, 359 F.Supp. 698 (D.Del.1973), however, the defendant-director was unable to obtain mandatory indemnification when a derivative suit alleging negligence was dismissed without prejudice because the same issue was being litigated in another pending case. The court concluded that the dismissal did not constitute "success on the merits or otherwise" under the Delaware statute.

The standard of conduct required to indemnify a director should be related to the standard of care required of her in performing her duties, but should they be the same? RMBCA § 8.51 varies the standard from that found in § 8.30 by permitting indemnification if the director acts in a manner which she reasonably believed was "not opposed to" the best interests of the corporation. What does that phrase mean? Is it a device for lowering the standard of care in the indemnification context? Or is it designed to deal with specific types of cases in which there are valid policy reasons to permit indemnification even if the standard of care has not been satisfied? *See* the Official Comment to RMBCA § 8.51(a) for an explanation of why the two standards should *not* be the same.

4.    Closely related to the standard of conduct is the question of who determines whether it has been met. The statutes suggest four possibilities: the board of directors, the stockholders, independent legal counsel, or a court. Consider the pros and cons of each. In connection with a determination by the board, be aware of a potential trap. Suppose that the board is hostile to the indemnitee and refuses to indemnify her, notwithstanding the statute. Should she have an alternate route to secure the indemnification which the statute contemplates?

The 1994 amendments to the RMBCA permit the determinations made under the statute to be made by the board through a majority of its disinterested directors. § 8.50 defines a "disinterested director" as one who, at the time of the vote, "is not (i) a party to the proceeding, or (ii) an individual having a familial, financial, professional, or employment relationship with the director whose indemnification or advance for expenses is the subject of the decision being made, which relationship would, in the circumstances, reasonably be expected to exert an influence on the director's judgment when voting on the decision being made." Keep this definition in mind when you read the next chapter which focuses, among other things, on the significance of decisions made by disinterested directors.

As lawyers, you should be concerned whether there can be such an animal as an "independent" legal counsel when the issue is whether management is entitled to indemnification. The by-laws of some corporations contain a definition of independent legal counsel similar to the following: "A law firm, or a member of a law firm that is experienced in matters of corporation law and neither presently is, nor in the past five years has been, retained to represent: (1) the company or indemnitee in any matter material to either such party, or (2) any other party to the proceeding giving rise to a claim for indemnification hereunder." The by-law also includes any person who would be considered to have a conflict of interest under the applicable standards of professional conduct. *See* Ohio Gen.Corp.L. § 1701.13(E)(4)(b).

5. What about the expenses which a director incurs in enforcing her statutory rights? In *Mayer v. Executive TeleCard, Ltd.*, 1997 WL 225756 (Del.Ch.1997), the Delaware Court of Chancery held that an indemnitee who successfully establishes her right to indemnification is not entitled to the fees and expenses she incurs in establishing that right.

6. Critics argue that the problems of indemnification are exacerbated because no state or federal law requires the corporation to disclose indemnification payments to the stockholders. They contend that a corporation which must disclose such payments will be more careful in making them; presumably, the payments themselves might be the subject of a further derivative suit by a stockholder alleging a waste of corporate assets. Because such payments are not considered to be compensation, they do not come within the SEC's proxy rules. RMBCA, § 16.21(a) requires disclosure in the corporation's annual report to stockholders but most state statutes, including Delaware, do not have a similar requirement.

### Note: Charter, By-Law and Contract Provisions

Whether because of uncertainty as to the scope of indemnification allowed or required under the applicable statutory and case law or because of a desire to amplify or clarify the various rights and obligations of the corporation and its executives, many corporations include in their articles of incorporation or by-laws some provision relating to indemnification. In addition, in recent years, directors' increasing fear of liability and the higher cost or actual unavailability of liability insurance has led many corporations to enter into indemnification agreements with their management that are separate from the indemnification provided for in corporate articles of incorporation and by-laws.

In many cases, the corporate by-law will do nothing more than track the statute while the indemnification agreement will contain provisions that go beyond the express indemnification sections of the statute. Are such provisions valid simply because they are in a contract rather than in a by-law? RMBCA § 8.59 limits these provisions to those consistent with the statute but, as previously noted, the statutory provisions are extremely broad. DGCL § 145(f) provides specifically that statutory rights and procedures concerning indemnification are not exclusive. Thus, a corporation may indemnify a director through its own policies under circumstances not prescribed in the statute. It is doubtful, however, that a corporation could agree to indemnify a director for *any* action undertaken. As one article noted:

> * * * Some commentators have criticized section 145(f) as too liberal and have expressed concern that public policy could be subverted if, for instance, a director is indemnified according to a by-law in spite of a finding in a derivative suit that he had breached his fiduciary duty to the corporation. Although there is no case law on point, it is probable that a Delaware court would not allow indemnification under a by-law or pursuant to a contract when the proposed indemnification is prohibited by law or public policy. To the extent the statute can be read to embody the public policy limitations of indemnification, a by-law or agreement purporting to expand these limits would likely be void as violative of public policy.

E. Norman Veasey et al., *Delaware Supports Directors With a Three-Legged Stool of Limited Liability, Indemnification and Insurance*, 42 Bus.Law. 401, 414 (1987).

## 4. INSURANCE

Directors' and officers' liability insurance ("D & O insurance") is a relatively recent development. It was not until the mid–1960s, when an increasing number of lawsuits began to generate fears of liability, that these policies began to find favor among large numbers of corporations. Various factors, both legal and social, combined in the 1980s to lead insurance companies to increase their premiums and either reduce the coverage of, or cancel completely, liability insurance. These factors included greater numbers of initial stock offerings, bankruptcies, and corporate mergers and acquisitions, all of which increased the number of claims against directors. *See* Roberta Romano, *What Went Wrong With Directors' and Officers' Liability Insurance?*, 14 Del.J.Corp.L. 1 (1989). Additionally, the size of claims paid increased dramatically, especially to shareholders bringing derivative suits. Courts tended to place the risk burden on the insurers by interpreting policies in favor of the insured even when the claim would appear to not be covered by the policy. Romano discounts the impact that *Van Gorkom* had in causing the insurance crisis, noting that it was already underway when that case was decided. By the end of the decade, the insurance crisis seems to have peaked. Romano suggests that the crisis perhaps reflected partly the apex of a normal business cycle and that corrections made in the insurance market structure itself relieved the pressure on D & O insurance policies. Nevertheless, the concerns that initially gave rise to D & O insurance remain valid today, and the policy issues that liability insurance raises are particularly significant in creating an adequate system of management accountability.

Most state statutes contain express authorization for corporations to purchase D & O insurance. RMBCA § 8.57; DGCL § 145(g). New York's statute, which differs slightly from the RMBCA and Delaware provisions, states that "it is the public policy of this state to spread the risk of corporate management, notwithstanding any other general or special law of this state or of any other jurisdiction including the federal government." N.Y. B.C.L. § 726(e).

A D & O policy consists of two separate but integral parts. *See* Joseph Hinsey IV, *The New Lloyd's Policy Form for Directors and Officers Liability Insurance—An Analysis*, 33 Bus.Law. 1961 (1978); Joseph F. Johnston, Jr., *Corporate Indemnification and Liability Insurance for Directors and Officers*, 33 Bus.Law. 1993 (1978). The first part is designed to reimburse the corporation for its lawful expenses in connection with indemnifying its directors and officers. This part of a D & O policy reduces the amounts that corporate directors or officers would otherwise be required to pay in those instances where the corporation is unable or, less likely, unwilling to indemnify. It thus encourages and facilitates corporate indemnification of directors and officers. The second part insures individuals, acting in their capacity as officers or directors of the insured corporation, against losses, including judgments and settlements. Their coverage under D & O policies is limited in a number of ways. A deductible amount for each director and officer and for the corporation serves as a deterrent to carelessness or misconduct. Directors and officers also usually bear a certain percentage, typically 5%, of the loss above the deductible amount. The payment of fines and penalties imposed in a criminal suit or action are excluded from the definition of "loss," as are other fines, penalties, and punitive damages imposed by a final adjudication that are uninsurable under the law pursuant to which the policy is construed. D & O policies generally do not provide coverage for costs that may be protected against through other types of insurance. Additionally, many policies contain "laser" exclusions, tailored to eliminate coverage for risks inherent in a specific corporation.

The premiums for a D & O policy are costly and are set on a case-by-case basis taking into account the size of the corporation, its type of business, financial condition and merger and acquisition history, the number of directors and officers, the corporation's past litigation history, and special circumstances, such as governmental investigations, adverse publicity potential and political activity. Small corporations have experienced difficulty in obtaining D & O policies because fewer checks and balances are built into their corporate structures. The premiums for a D & O policy are generally split between the corporation and the individual on a ninety-ten basis, with the corporation bearing the larger share.

D & O insurance provides protection beyond that which indemnification can afford in several important areas. First, amounts paid in judgment or settlement in a derivative suit can be recovered under the standard D & O policy, assuming that none of the limitations described above are applicable. Second, such insurance covers conduct that does not satisfy the statutory standard but which does not constitute "active and deliberate dishonesty." For example, in *Van Gorkom*, given the finding that the directors were grossly negligent in not informing themselves sufficiently prior to approving the merger, statutory indemnification would have been unlikely. However, the corporation's insurance carrier paid $10,000,000—the full policy limit—as part of the $23,000,-000 settlement of the case. Thus, even a finding of gross negligence will not necessarily preclude payment under a D & O policy where the wrongs committed were not wilful or dishonest. Finally, a D & O policy provides protection if the corporation becomes insolvent or is otherwise unable to pay indemnification or if the corporation refuses to do so, assuming that the other requirements of the policy are satisfied.

To some, there is something troubling about a statute that allows a corporation to insure its executives for conduct sufficiently egregious to be outside the scope of indemnification. For such critics, this trouble is exacerbated by the fact that insurance is expensive and is paid for almost entirely by the corporation. As one group of writers has argued, "the question is * * * whether wrongful acts should be indemnified at all. Why should an executive of a drug company be indemnified for the costs of a criminal fine if he is convicted of allowing a harmful drug to injure several thousand people when the same act as a private individual would send him to jail? An untenable double standard has been created. The more powerful an executive becomes, the less likely he is to pay for an abuse of power." Ralph Nader et al., TAMING THE GIANT CORPORATION, 108 (1976).

Those who defend the existing statutory scheme do so with a very simple argument: the public policy question of the scope of insurance coverage is a question of insurance law rather than corporate law. The statute only authorizes the purchase of insurance and leaves the determination of the limits on that insurance to insurance companies and state insurance commissioners. *See* S. Samuel Arsht, *The Business Judgment Rule Revisited*, 8 HOFSTRA L.REV. 93 (1979).

The question of the scope of insurance has another aspect which we have seen before in other contexts: who should bear the risks of malfeasance? Those who support the present system would argue that this is a question to be decided by the insurance companies through their exclusions and pricing policies. If those companies reach conclusions that are harmful from a corporate perspective, stockholders are free to change their investment to a company which does not insure or whose management is less likely to engage in litigation-provoking activities. To be valid, this argument must assume that stockholders have information about the existence and coverage of D & O insurance and the payments under the policy, an assumption that is not generally true. Thus, if we are talking about the market setting the limits on corporate behavior, it is a market with limited information.

# Chapter 17

# DUTY OF LOYALTY

## A. INTRODUCTION: ON CONFLICTS OF INTEREST AND THE DUTY OF LOYALTY

In Chapter 16, we saw how the duty of care attempts to solve the problems that arise when a director does not act in the best interests of the shareholders in her decision-making, even if she does not benefit personally from her decision. In this chapter, we will examine how the duty of loyalty (or fair dealing, as some commentators call it) deals with agency costs in situations in which a director's decision may not be in the best interests of the shareholders precisely because she *does* benefit from that decision. Simply put, the duty of loyalty requires a manager to place the corporation's best interests (and thus those of the stockholders) above her own.

Consider a transaction in which a director proposes to sell property to her corporation. As a director, she has a duty to maximize the value of the transaction to the corporation by having the corporation pay the lowest possible price. As the owner of the property, her own best interest is to receive the highest possible price. The economic imperatives of the two positions are in clear conflict. The transaction involves "self-dealing;" the director has a "conflict of interest" when she votes on the transaction.

Even though the director is subject to competing demands because of her financial stake in the transaction, the existence of a conflict does not mean that the consummated transaction will be unfair to the corporation.

\* \* \* [I]t is important to keep firmly in mind that it is a contingent risk we are dealing with—that an interest conflict is not in itself a crime or a tort or necessarily injurious to others. Contrary to much popular usage, having a "conflict of interest" is not something one is "guilty of"; it is simply a state of affairs. Indeed, in many situations, the corporation and the shareholders may secure major benefits from a transaction despite the presence of a director's conflicting interest. Further, while history is replete with selfish acts, it is also oddly counterpointed by numberless acts taken contrary to self interest.

RMBCA Subchapter F, Introductory Comment.

Self-dealing transactions can be both fair and beneficial to a corporation. Were it not so, it would be very easy to formulate a rule proscribing directors from engaging in transactions with their corporations. An "interested" director, however, will frequently be uniquely situated to help the corporation. She may have knowledge about how the corporation will benefit from the transaction and the ability to effectuate the transaction at minimal cost. It has long been recognized that a prohibition against directors engaging in transactions with their corporations,

> * * * [W]hile it would afford little protection to the corporation against actual fraud or oppression, would deprive it of the aid of those most interested in giving aid judiciously, and best qualified to judge of the necessity of that aid, and of the extent to which it may safely be given.

*Twin–Lick Oil v. Marbury*, 91 U.S. (1 Otto) 587, 589, 23 L.Ed. 328 (1875).

Some self-dealing transactions *are* unfair to the corporation; the interested director is appropriating the difference between the fair market value of the transaction to the corporation and the payment actually made. Thus, the effect of an unfair self-dealing transaction is no different from the direct diversion of corporate funds or assets. However, self-dealing is apt to be more common than flagrant diversion because the interested director:

> * * * [m]ay more easily rationalize an inflated purchase price than outright stealing. It is frequently possible to identify and exaggerate some reasons why [a corporation] should pay dearly for some particular piece of land or property. That having been done, [the director] may continue to think of himself as a just and honorable man.

Robert Charles Clark, CORPORATE LAW 143 (1986).

The principal difficulty in this area of the law is establishing appropriate criteria for measuring the validity of the transaction. The business judgment rule, which is premised on the director's independent judgment, does not provide an appropriate standard because in a conflict transaction, by definition, the director's judgment cannot be independent. A substitute test, however, has proved difficult to articulate. A director who engages in a transaction with the corporation may well be acting in good faith, but how is that to be tested? The law requires that the transaction be "fair" to the corporation, but fairness itself can be difficult to determine. Should a court focus on the terms of the transaction or the process by which it was authorized?

The issue of divided loyalty is not limited to situations in which a director engages, directly or indirectly, in a transaction with the corporation, although that is the focus of this chapter. Subsequent chapters will consider conflicting loyalties in different contexts: insider trading (Chapter 19), sale of control (Chapter 21), protection of control (Chapter 22), and parent-subsidiary mergers (Chapter 23). The methodology may differ with the context, but the question remains the same: how should a court evaluate the conduct of a director who is faced with what, put broadly, is a conflict of interest?

## Victor Brudney, *Contract Law and Fiduciary Duty in Corporate Law*

38 B.C. L.Rev. 595, 611–616, 622–635 (1997).

### B. MANAGEMENT'S AND CONTROLLER'S FIDUCIARY OBLIGATIONS TO STOCKHOLDERS OF PUBLIC CORPORATIONS

#### 1. Management

When the fiduciary notion is examined in the context of the relationship of management of a public investor-owned corporation to the enterprise and the holders of its common stock, a still different configuration of interests and needs must be addressed. Management's fiduciary obligations of loyalty, although perhaps not formally attributable to the agency concept, are substantially the same as those of agents. Those duties are sometimes said to run to the corporation, sometimes to the stockholders (generally the common stockholders) and sometimes to both. In any event, management's duty of loyalty requires the same self-denying behavior on its part, whether its duty is owed to the corporation or to the common stockholders. Traditional fiduciary loyalty obligations would forbid management from benefiting itself (except for specified compensation) in dealing with corporate assets, the corporation or the stockholders, and require it to direct its energies to benefiting solely the corporation and pro tanto the stockholders.

The public stockholder, like the commercial principal and the partner, seeks increase in the value of his or her investment. The virtues of centralized management in effecting that goal preclude both officers and directors from being subject to the daily control of stockholders, as a commercial agent in such matters might be. Moreover, the wealth-enhancing function of management implicates taking risks with the assets that are not permitted to a trustee. But neither the reasons for centralized management nor for the risk-taking function of management preclude binding both officers and directors with the fiduciary's traditional obligation of loyalty. If management's temptation to self-aggrandize is strong, the restraints imposed by reputation considerations do not seem equally strong—or at least any stronger than in the case of trustees or commercial agents or partners.

The public stockholder is considerably more in need of the exclusive benefit principle and its prophylactic implementation to protect against self-serving behavior by management than a partner (at least an active partner) or an individual principal in the typical commercial context is likely to be. The stockholder, like the settlor of a trust, is unable to specify the opportunistic behavior against which he or she needs protection and is not much more able than the trust beneficiary to monitor the decisions being made under such restrictions or enforce compliance with those terms. Nor does the public stockholder have the capacity of a commercial principal to specify limits, monitor management, select officers or threaten, much less terminate, their tenure. And while in theory stockholders elect "independent" directors to perform those functions, the latter are likely to owe their selection more to managers than to stockholders and are not easily removable by stockholders.

No less significant, in the context of investor-owned public corporations, the notion of "consent" by the stockholders to departure from the exclusive benefit principle is a problematic construct, whether given ex ante in general terms or ex post by way of voting approval of a specific transaction. If not entirely a fiction, it is a far cry from the actual consent that may be given by a settlor of a trust, a commercial principal or a participating partner.

American corporate law has addressed both the matter of the rigor of the fiduciary strictures and the problem of stockholder consent to departure from them. Over the course of the last century, although the conditions underlying the historic application of the exclusive benefit principle and its prophylactic implementation in the corporate context have not changed materially, the principle has been abandoned, notwithstanding the continued characterization of management's relationship and obligations to the enterprise and its stockholders as fiduciary. As the legal doctrine has evolved, the restrictions on managerial conduct no longer prophylactically forbid self-aggrandizing behavior. Although the exclusive benefit principle is not formally rejected, the governing doctrine effects its rejection in part by the ease with which it finds stockholder consent to its avoidance by "disinterested" directors or dispersed stockholders, and in part, by its concept of "fairness." To the extent that the formally required consent need not be adequately informed or volitional, and the test of fairness permits the fiduciary to obtain some or all of the gain from self-dealing for itself, the restrictions on self-aggrandizement are not simply looser than required by traditional fiduciary notions, but they tend to become invisible.

Moreover, the role of the court in reviewing challenges to a particular claim of consent or fairness contemplates (and embodies) little critical assessment of the actuality of the consent and little more check on managerial determination of such "fairness." Notwithstanding occasional pious allusions to the exclusive benefit principle in opinions, the surviving body of corporate fiduciary doctrine has lost that principle's normative underpinning. Apart from occasional references to the "market" as benchmark, it offers murky and permeable limits on management's self-aggrandizing behavior and serves more as an admonitory ghost that hovers than a substantive proscription.

Possibly the dilution of fiduciary loyalty strictures in the context of corporate management responds to perceptions of lesser need (because of the restraining influence of market pressures and reputational concerns) and of larger net costs of over-prohibiting than in the cases of agency and trusts or partnership. But the perceptions of lesser need or greater cost are hard to justify. Moreover, the benefits to stockholders of self-aggrandizing conduct by managers, if real, can be obtained by consent; and because the consent required from stockholders or their "agents" (disinterested directors) is largely fictitious and readily obtained, the reluctance to continue background prophylactic restrictions on self-aggrandizing behavior by officers and directors of public corporations is something of a puzzle. So too is the movement of doctrine in the direction of looser (or indeed abandonment of) restrictions of fairness if such consent is obtained.

\* \* \*

[In the portion of this article excerpted in Chapter 14, Section A, Professor Brudney argues that fiduciary norms, not contractual principles, should govern self-dealing transactions involving corporate managers and controlling shareholders. He also observes that "[c]urrently imposed corporate fiduciary obligations substantially dilute classic fiduciary restrictions" and criticizes this trend in corporation law. He continues:]

\* \* \* Analytically, the function of the fiduciary requires courts to approach gray areas in the interpretive process with a sense that the center of gravity of the fiduciary obligation is in the beneficiary's interests. In contrast, the center of gravity of the obligation of an arm's-length contracting party is in its own, rather than the other party's, interests. Even if contract doctrines—such as good faith or unconscionability—locate the center somewhere in between, neither contract theory nor contract doctrine requires one party to focus solely on the interests of the other or permits the courts to interpret the contract through a lens with such a focus.

Diluted corporate fiduciary obligations start from the exclusive benefit principle, and the question is how far from that starting point the fiduciary may be permitted to go in appropriating benefits for itself. Claims of bad faith or unconscionability start from the premise that the party charged was entitled to seek all the advantage the contract might permit, and the question is how to limit the benefits he or she may appropriate at the expense of the other party. The concept of "fairness" should not carry the same substantive import in the fiduciary context that it may in the contract context. "Fairness" in corporate law fiduciary terms is said to embody limits on the consensual allocation of gains to management or controllers from self-aggrandizing conduct by reference to arm's-length bargains or "the market" restriction that is said to limit managers' or controllers' gains more rigorously than does the freedom of the parties to deal under contract rules, particularly classic contract rules. It is not self-evident that the market or the hypothetical arm's-length bargain is a sufficiently restrictive standard of fairness for a fiduciary.

To depart from the exclusive benefit rule as has corporate law, and substitute a "fairness" test, does not require shifting the fiduciary relationship to the arm's-length relationship contemplated by the market for an exchange transaction. On the contrary, although the departure may contemplate the possibility of some gain for the fiduciary, the weakness of the stockholders' consent argues for a deterrent sanction that the market standard simply cannot supply. The information asymmetry and uneven bargaining relationship between the parties coupled with the "trust" that colors their dealings require the fiduciary to end up with less gain than the market might give, and the beneficiary to receive a better "deal" than a stranger might give. Delineating the limits of that "deal" is difficult. But that does not justify the otherwise questionable use of the contract-derived market test simply because "the market is there."

In any event, in the cases likely to present challenges, a market is generally not available to measure fairness. Instead, fairness is sought as the product of a bargain that the parties would have struck if they were dealing at arm's length. It may be achieved anywhere within a range, generally a wide range, of possible results by the opinions of experts hired by the parties, who generally rely on the terms of actual transactions that they deem comparable to the transaction at hand. The fiduciary relationship, even as diluted for corporate managers or controllers, suggests a location of fairness within that range that is considerably less favorable to management or controllers than do contract premises, including good faith requirements. The fiduciary concept of "fairness" thus invoked implies, and appears in many cases (even if not in all) to produce, tighter restraints on management's and controllers' conduct than contract doctrine would require. It has similarly more restrictive implications for controllers' conduct, particularly in control transactions.

The only restrictions on self-dealing in corporate law that are systematically colored more by the contract notion than by the diluted fiduciary concept appear in the limits on management's express compensation. To measure the limits of management's substantively, if not formally, self-appropriated compensation by reference to "waste" suggests analogy to the contract notion of "unconscionability." Judicial review of the board's decision in terms of "business judgment" further supports the idea of the discretion available to parties in a "mere" contractual relationship. While the phenomenon can be explained, it is hard to see how it can be justified.

In sum, traditional fiduciary loyalty strictures more rigorously protect common stockholders against opportunistic behavior by managers or controllers than does classic contract doctrine. Even the diluted corporate law fiduciary obligations should—and often do—offer more protection than does classic contract doctrine.

## PROBLEM
### STARCREST CORPORATION—PART I

Starcrest Corporation constructs, owns and operates hotels and restaurants throughout the United States. It has built, many of these hotels and restaurants after acquiring the raw land on which they sit. Starcrest is a public company, founded by the Adams family in 1935, whose common stock is listed on the New York Stock Exchange.

In 1955, Starcrest sold 60% of its stock to public investors. Members of the Adams family continue to own the remaining 40%. Elizabeth Adams, the president and chief executive officer, owns 25% and other family members who are not active in the business own the remaining 15%. The board of directors consists of Elizabeth Adams; Paul Baker, the chief financial officer; Robert Crown, the vice-president for sales; Linda Diamond, the general counsel; and Michael Brown, Ruth Grey and Robert White, each of whom is a prominent business executive having no other connections with Starcrest. Baker and Crown have been officers for more than ten years. Diamond joined Starcrest two years ago. Prior to that, she was a senior associate in its principal outside law firm in which she devoted most of her time to Starcrest's work.

Many years ago, Adams inherited a large tract of raw land from a distant uncle. Until recently, she had paid little attention to this land. Now, however, Starcrest is considering building another hotel in this area. Although she knew very little about real estate in the area, conversations with her uncle's lawyer (who specialized in probate work) convinced her that the land was worth $10 million. For the next 30 days, she sought to sell the land privately to sophisticated buyers in the area, none of whom offered more than $5 million. Somewhat daunted, she next listed the land with a real estate broker for a thirty-day period at price of $7.5 million, but received no offers.

In early March, at Adams' request, Patricia Jones, the head of the Corporation's real estate department, appraised the land as a possible site for a new hotel. After examining other sites in the area, none of which seemed as suitable for a new hotel, Jones concluded that the land was worth the $7.5 million Elizabeth was asking. On March 15, Adams offered to sell the land to Starcrest for $7.5 million. She accompanied her offer with a copy of Jones' appraisal. She did not disclose that she had unsuccessfully tried to sell the land before offering it to the Corporation because she did not believe that this information was material to the board of directors in making its decision.

In response to the offer, the board of directors established a committee consisting of Brown, Grey and Diamond to evaluate the offer. Because none of the committee members were experts in real estate, they hired an outside consultant who opined that the land might conceivably be worth $7.5 million but that he wouldn't pay that price. The committee also obtained a formal appraisal from an outside appraiser which valued the land at $5 million.

In June, relying primarily on Jones' appraisal and that of its outside appraiser, the committee recommended that the Corporation offer to purchase the land for $6.5 million, a price that Elizabeth had indicated she was willing to accept. The committee's report set out in detail the procedures it had followed and the basis for the recommendation. Grey dissented from the recommendation on the grounds that there was insufficient evidence to justify paying more than $5 million. The board accepted the committee's recommendation by a vote of 5-1. Grey again dissented and White did not attend the meeting at which the decision was made. Elizabeth did not participate in any of the deliberations of either the committee or the board of directors and did not vote on the transaction.

On Diamond's advice, the Corporation submitted the transaction to the shareholders for ratification at the annual meeting in October. The proxy statement disclosed all the information available to the board of directors and process by which the board reached its decision. At the meeting, the shareholders ratified the transaction with Elizabeth and other Adams family members voting. 54% of the outstanding stock voted in favor; 22% opposed.

It is now one week after the meeting and two days before the parties are scheduled to close the transaction. Grant, a shareholder of the Corporation, learned of the transaction through reading the proxy statement. She believes that the transaction constitutes a windfall to Adams and has consulted you to see what liabilities, if any, Adams and the board of directors may have in connection with the transaction and what remedies, if any, may be available. In advising Grant, answer the following questions, assuming that the applicable law is:

    a) DGCL § 144.

    b) A statute based on former RMBCA § 8.31.

    c) RMBCA Subchapter F.

1.a) Will a court use the business judgment rule or a fairness test to determine whether to enjoin the transaction or impose personal liability on Adams? The board of directors?

    b) Who will have the burden of proof in litigation?

    c) Will the party with the burden of proof be able to establish the fairness or unfairness of the transaction if the court determines that is the applicable standard?

2. Can the shares of the Adams family be counted in determining whether the transaction has been effectively ratified? What effect does shareholder ratification have on any claim for liability?

3. What role does the duty of loyalty play in monitoring directors' performances? To the extent that market mechanisms may be available to reduce the likelihood that directors will engage in self-dealing to the

detriment of the corporation, are those mechanisms likely to be effective?

# B.  THE COMMON LAW STANDARD

## 1.  ORIGINS AND EVOLUTION

In an extremely influential article, Harold Marsh traces the evolution of the judicial treatment of conflict of interest transactions from the mid-nineteenth century to modern times. Harold Marsh, *Are Directors Trustees?, Conflict of Interest and Corporate Morality*, 22 BUS.LAW. 35 (1966). Marsh argues that in 1880, the general rule was that such a transaction was voidable by the corporation or its shareholders whether or not a majority of disinterested directors had approved it or that the transaction was fair. This absolute voidability stemmed from the courts' belief "that the corporation was entitled to the unprejudiced judgment and advice of all its directors and therefore it did no good to say that the interested director did not participate in the making of the contract on behalf of the corporation." *Id*. at 37.

By 1910, the general rule had changed such that "a contract between a director and his corporation was valid if it was approved by a disinterested majority of his fellow directors and was not found to be unfair or fraudulent by the court if challenged; but that a contract in which a majority of the board was interested was voidable at the instance of the corporation or its shareholders without regard to any question of fairness." *Id*. at 39–40. Marsh cannot find a "reasoned defense of this change in legal philosophy, or the slightest attempt to refute the powerful arguments which had been made in support of the previous rule." *Id*. at 40. He attributes the change either to a judicial recognition of the courts' impotence to check the rapid growth of interested director transactions or to the more technical doctrine of trust law which permitted a trustee to deal with his cestui que trust if she made full disclosure and did not take unfair advantage of the cestui.

Marsh suggests that by 1960, the evolution to the contemporary standard was complete. The general rule now is that "no transaction of a corporation with any or all of its directors was automatically voidable at the suit of a shareholder, whether there was a disinterested majority of the board or not; but that the courts would review such a contract and subject it to rigid and careful scrutiny, and would invalidate the contract if it was found to be unfair to the corporation." *Id*. at 43. He notes that it is difficult to point to the exact time the rule changed or, indeed, that it has changed in a particular state. He contends that courts basically ignored earlier decision but that, through their opinions, they have, explicitly or implicitly, adopted the modern rule. *Id*. at 43–44.

Marsh's analysis went unchallenged until a recent article by Norwood P. Beveridge, Jr., The *Corporate Director's Fiduciary Duty of Loyalty: Understanding the Self-interested Director Transaction*, 41 DE-PAUL L.REV. 655 (1992). Beveridge notes that "[a]ll current thinking on the corporate director's duty of loyalty appears to start with the proposition, which seems now to be universally accepted, that transactions between a director and his corporation at common law were generally voidable without regard to fairness." *Id.* at 659. Beveridge's thesis is simple: "[T]his proposition is completely erroneous." *Id.* at 662.

Beveridge argues that in 1880, the general rule was exactly opposite from what Marsh had contended. Citing contemporary treatises, he claims that interested director transactions were not always voidable. Thus it is unnecessary to determine why there had been a change in legal philosophy from 1880 to 1910 because, in fact, there had been none. He also contends that neither agency nor trust law categorically prohibited transactions between a fiduciary and her beneficiary. Rather, the law barred the fiduciary from standing on both sides of the transaction. He concludes that "[i]f we examine the cases cited by Professor Marsh in support of his assertion that interested director contracts were voidable in spite of fairness, we will see that the cases were actually concerned with transactions in which the interested director was active in representing both sides of the deal." *Id.* at 662.

## 2. THE MODERN STANDARD

The requirements for the validity of an interested director transaction are now governed by statutes in most states. Common law jurisprudence on the duty of loyalty is of continuing vitality, however, because many of these statutes have been held to have codified common law standards.

## SHLENSKY v. SOUTH PARKWAY BUILDING CORP.

19 Ill.2d 268, 166 N.E.2d 793 (1960).

[The plaintiffs, minority shareholders of South Parkway Building Corporation (Building Corporation), sued to require defendant directors to personally account for damages suffered by the corporation in the various transactions. The trial court held that defendants breached their fiduciary duties in all of the challenged transactions and ordered an accounting for the benefit of the shareholders. The appellate court reversed on the ground that, under Illinois law, the plaintiffs had failed to sustain the burden of establishing that the transactions were fraudulent.

The main operating asset of the Building Corporation was a 3–story commercial building on a city lot in Chicago. Since the inception of Building Corporation, defendant Englestein was a director and majority shareholder of the corporation. In each of the challenged transactions the second party was a corporation owned by Englestein in which he acted as either an officer or director or both. In each case, the court found that the transactions were approved by an interested majority of the Building Corporation's board of directors.]

BRISTOW, J.

In [*Dixmoor Golf Club, Inc. v. Evans*, 325 Ill. 612, 156 N.E. 785 (1927)] this court stated at page 616 of 325 Ill., at page 787 of 156 N.E.:

"The directors of a corporation are trustees of its business and property for the collective body of stockholders in respect to such business. They are subject to the general rule, in regard to trusts and trustees, that they cannot, in their dealings with the business or property of the trust, use their relation to it for their own personal gain. It is their duty to administer the corporate affairs for the common benefit of all the stockholders, and exercise their best care, skill, and judgment in the management of the corporate business *solely in the interest of the corporation.* * * * It is a breach of duty for the directors to place themselves in a position where their personal interests would prevent them from acting for the best interests of those they represent." (Italics ours.)

The court expounded that while a director is not disqualified from dealing with the corporation and buying its property, or selling property to it, the transaction will be subject to the closest scrutiny, and if not conducted with the utmost fairness, "to the end that the corporation shall have received full value," it will be set aside. The court then held that since the board of directors therein was dominated by one member, and had purchased land from him for the corporation at a price that was 2½ times more than required by his option, the transaction would be set aside, even though the corporation had use for the land, and had received some benefit from the transaction.

The same year, this court in *White v. Stevens*, 326 Ill. 528, 158 N.E. 101, 103, without referring to the *Dixmoor* case, reiterated that a director may deal with the corporation of which he is a member, provided he acts fairly and for the interest of the company. The court also recognized that corporations having directors in common may contract with each other "if the contracts are fair and reasonable," but emphasized that such transactions would be carefully scrutinized by equity. In the case before it, where the allegedly offending corporation had "procured the furniture for the hotel company at prices charged by manufacturers and wholesalers and furnished it to the hotel company at the same price," the court found that "the most careful scrutiny fails to disclose any unfairness to or overreaching of the hotel company in the entire transaction."

* * * [I]n *Winger v. Chicago City Bank & Trust Co.*, 394 Ill. 94, 67 N.E.2d 265, * * * [a]fter reviewing the English and American authorities on the fiduciary status of corporate directors, the court * * * reaffirmed the rule in the *Dixmoor* case, and noted further that the fact that directors do not deal directly with themselves, but deal with another corporation which they own or control, will not change the effect of the transaction. In fact, the court pointed out that it is practically the unanimous opinion of courts that, even if only one of the directors voting for the transaction profited thereby, and his vote was necessary, the transaction would be tainted with the same illegality and fraud as though they were all interested. Under those circumstances, the directors have the burden of overcoming the presumption against the validity of the transaction, by showing its fairness and propriety.

* * * [W]e find that the *Winger* case, construed in its entirety, holds that transactions between corporations with common directors may be avoided only *if unfair,* and that the directors who would sustain the challenged transaction have the burden of overcoming the presumption against the validity of the transaction by showing its fairness.

While the acts of the directors in the *Winger* case may have been a more flagrant breach of fiduciary duty, as defendants contend, than those involved in the instant case—depending upon one's view point— those circumstances do not change the rule of law applied by the court. Moreover, we agree with the court that no distinction should be made, as defendants suggest, between transactions of a director with his corporation and those in which he hides behind the corporate veil and deals through another corporation which he owns or controls.

* * *

In the leading case of *Geddes v. Anaconda Copper Mining Co.,* 254 U.S. 590, 41 S.Ct. 209, 65 L.Ed. 425, followed by an imposing body of authority, the operative facts were somewhat analogous to those in the case at bar in that they involved transactions between corporations with common directors and allegedly inadequate consideration. The challenged transaction there, however, involved a sale of all the corporate property, whereas the transactions in the instant case involve agreements allegedly siphoning a substantial portion of the corporate assets. The United States Supreme Court, after noting that the record showed beyond controversy that Ryan was an officer and director and dominated the affairs of the buying and selling companies, as well as their boards of directors, set aside the transaction. In so doing, the court promulgated the oft quoted rule at page 599 of 254 U.S., at page 212 of 41 S.Ct.: "The relation of directors to corporations is of such a fiduciary nature that transactions between boards having common members are regarded as jealously by the law as are personal dealings between a director and his corporation, and where the fairness of such transactions is challenged the burden is upon those who would maintain them to show their entire fairness and where a sale is involved the full adequacy of the consideration. Especially is this true where a common director is dominating in influence or in character. This court has been consistently emphatic in the application of this rule, which, it has declared, is founded in soundest morality, and we now add in the soundest business policy."

In our judgment, the *Geddes* rule, which is essentially the same as that applied in the *Winger* case, is not only legally cogent, but is consistent with the entire concept of the fiduciary relation in the fabric of our commercial law. The contrary rule, urged by defendants, whereby those attacking the transactions of fiduciaries would have the burden of establishing its unfairness or fraudulency is not only without substantial support in the case law, but would put a premium on sharp practices by directors by putting the onus of proof on their victims, and would also tend to further separate corporate management from ownership.

In contrast, the rule of the *Geddes* and *Winger* cases, insofar as it provides that the directors shall have the burden of establishing the fairness and propriety of the transactions, not only protects shareholders from exploitation, but permits flexibility in corporate dealings. While the concept of "fairness" is incapable of precise definition, courts have stressed such factors as whether the corporation received in the transaction full value in all the commodities purchased; the corporation's need for the property; its ability to finance the purchase; whether the transaction was at the market price, or below, or constituted a better bargain than the corporation could have otherwise obtained in dealings with others; whether there was a detriment to the corporation as a result of the transaction; whether there was a possibility of corporate gain siphoned off by the directors directly or through corporations they controlled; and whether there was full disclosure—although neither disclosure nor shareholder assent can convert a dishonest transaction into a fair one.

Moreover, where the corporate directors fail to establish the fairness of the challenged transaction, it may either be set aside, or affirmed and damages recovered for the losses sustained by the corporation.

In the light of this analysis of the appropriate rules and guiding considerations, we shall determine the propriety of the five challenged transactions of the board of the Building Corporation herein.

Inasmuch as the authorization of the payment of $100,000 to the Store [one of the three tenants in the building owned by the Building Corporation] for its fixtures was conditioned on the subsequent modification of its lease, we shall consider these transactions together. It is undisputed that at the time of these transactions the board of the Building Corporation consisted of seven members, and that director Sturm resigned in protest of the payment of $100,000 to the Store. The remaining six directors present and voting for that purchase included Englestein, the owner and president of the Store; Mackie, a Store director; and Bernstein, who was the lawyer for Englestein and for the Store, as well as for Englestein's other business enterprises. We cannot, under the circumstances, perceive just how defendants can seriously characterize Bernstein as an independent and disinterested director representing only the Building Corporation.

It is therefore apparent that the fixture purchase authorized on March 18, 1948, could not conceivably be deemed to have been approved by an independent and disinterested majority of directors of the Building Corporation. Furthermore, as pointed out in the *Geddes* case, it is not the mere number of common directors which determines whether approval has been given by an independent and disinterested majority of directors, but rather whether a majority of the directors are dominated by an individual or a group.

Nor was the modification of the Store lease on May 4, 1948, effected by an independent and disinterested majority. At that time only five members of the board were present, Townsend being out of town and apparently informed by telephone, and the votes of approval included Englestein, Mackie and Bernstein, along with Teter, and Peyla, who thought that the Store rent was being increased. Therefore, in view of the lack of approval by a disinterested majority, it was incumbent upon defendants to sustain the burden of establishing the fairness of these transactions.

It is uncontroverted that the Building Corporation had no commercial use for the fixtures, which even included the asphalt tile and built-in partitions, all of which were continued to be used by the Store. Moreover, since the used fixtures had limited intrinsic value, as compared with their cost of $100,000, the only consideration which the corporation could realize from this substantial outlay would be through its rental charges. While the directors on May 4, 1948, increased the minimum rent payable by the Store by some $5,000, they eliminated practically all of the percentage rents, except the 1½ per cent on sales over $1,100,000, which was tantamount to a 40% reduction in future rents, and also waived some $24,316 of accrued rent owed by the Store.

In defense of this transaction, defendants and the Appellate Court stress that the economic health of the Store was of great value to the Building Corporation, since it meant the retention of a tenant and benefited all the other tenants, which were economically interdependent, and therefore justified pouring money into the Store. In our judgment, however, the economic interdependence of the tenancies (Neisner's, Walgreen's, and the Store) hardly justifies giving one of them—the Store owned by Englestein—all of the financial benefits, and requiring the other tenants to pay rents which were 10 to 20 times higher per square foot than the rent paid by Englestein's Store. In this connection, the evidence showed that the rent paid by the Store, even in 1948, was $20,737, or $.24 per square foot, as compared with rentals of $42,875 or $2.00 per square foot paid by Neisner's for similar space, and $30,708 or $5.44 per square foot paid by Walgreen's. It is also difficult for us to comprehend just why the Store was such a valuable tenant when other tenants paid much higher rentals, and when the record shows that the subsequent tenant of the premises willingly paid a rental over 2½ times as much as that paid by the Store.

It is therefore patent from the evidence that defendants not merely failed to establish the fairness of this $100,000 used fixture purchase and rent reduction scheme, but that it was tantamount to a deliberate depletion of corporate assets, for the benefit of another corporation in which 3 of the 6 directors had adverse interests. Under those circumstances, the findings and orders of the master and chancellor that defendants' conduct constituted a breach of their fiduciary duty, for which they must account to the Building Corporation, were neither contrary to the manifest weight of the evidence, nor predicated on a conclusive presumption, as defendants argue. It was therefore error for the Appellate Court to have set aside those findings.

# C.  THE STATUTORY APPROACH

## REMILLARD BRICK CO. v. REMILLARD–DANDINI CO.

109 Cal.App.2d 405, 241 P.2d 66, 73–77 (1952).

[Stanley and Sturgis controlled a majority of the shares of Remillard–Dandini Co. Remillard–Dandini Co. owned all the shares of San Jose Brick & Tile, Ltd. Stanley and Sturgis controlled the boards of directors of Remillard–Dandini Co. and San Jose Brick & Tile, Ltd. and were executive officers of both corporations and drew salaries from them. The court refers to Remillard–Dandini Co. and San Jose Brick & Tile, Ltd. as the "manufacturing companies." Stanley and Sturgis owned, controlled and operated Remillard–Dandini Sales Corp. which the court refers to as the "sales corporation."

Plaintiff, a minority shareholder of Remillard–Dandini Co., alleged that the majority directors of the manufacturing companies used their power to have the manufacturing companies enter into contracts with the sales corporation, so that the manufacturing companies were stripped of their sales function, and that through the sales corporation, Stanley and Sturgis realized profits which would have gone to the manufacturing companies. Stanley and Sturgis maintained that the minority shareholder and the minority directors of the manufacturing companies were informed of their interests in the contracts. The court invalidated the contracts.]

PETERS, PRESIDING JUSTICE.

It is argued that, since the fact of common directorship was fully known to the boards of the contracting corporations, and because the * * * majority stockholders consented to the transaction, the minority stockholder and directors of the manufacturing companies have no legal cause to complain. In other words, it is argued that if the majority directors and stockholders inform the minority that they are going to mulct the corporation, section 820 of the Corporations Code* constitutes

---

* Section 820 of the Corporations Code, enacted in 1947 and based on former section 311 of the Civil Code, provided:

Directors and officers shall exercise their powers in good faith, and with a view to the interests of the corporation. No contract or other transaction between a corporation and one or more of its directors, or between a corporation and any corporation, firm, or association in which one or more of its directors are directors or are financially interested, is either void or voidable because such director or directors are present at the meeting of the board of directors or a committee thereof which authorizes or approves the contract or transaction, or because his or their votes are counted for such purpose, if the circumstances specified in any of the following subdivisions exist:

(a) The fact of the common directorship or financial interest is disclosed or known to the board of directors or committee and noted in the minutes, and the board or committee authorizes, approves, or ratifies the contract or transaction in good faith by a vote sufficient for the purpose without counting the vote or votes of such director or directors.

an impervious armor against any attack on the transaction short of actual fraud. If this interpretation of the section were sound, it would be a shocking reflection on the law of California. It would completely disregard the first sentence of section 820 setting forth the elementary rule that "Directors and officers shall exercise their powers in good faith, and with a view to the interests of the corporation", and would mean that if conniving directors simply disclose their dereliction to the powerless minority, any transaction by which the majority desire to mulct the minority is immune from attack. That is not and cannot be the law.

Section 820 of the Corporations Code is based on former section 311 of the Civil Code, first added to our law in 1931. Stats. of 1931, Chap. 862, p. 1777. Before the adoption of that section it was the law that the mere existence of a common directorate, at least where the vote of the common director was essential to consummate the transaction, invalidated the contract. That rule was changed in 1931 when section 311 was added to the Civil Code, and limited to a greater extent by the adoption of section 820 of the Corporations Code. If the conditions provided for in the section appear, the transaction cannot be set aside simply because there is a common directorate. Here, undoubtedly, there was a literal compliance with subdivision b of the section. The fact of the common directorship was disclosed to the stockholders, and the * * * majority stockholders, did approve the contracts.

But neither section 820 of the Corporations Code nor any other provision of the law automatically validates such transactions simply because there has been a disclosure and approval by the majority of the stockholders. That section does not operate to limit the fiduciary duties owed by a director to all the stockholders, nor does it operate to condone acts which, without the existence of a common directorate, would not be countenanced. That section does not permit an officer or director, by an abuse of his power, to obtain an unfair advantage or profit for himself at the expense of the corporation. The director cannot, by reason of his position, drive a harsh and unfair bargain with the corporation he is supposed to represent. If he does so, he may be compelled to account for unfair profits made in disregard of his duty. Even though the requirements of section 820 are technically met, transactions that are unfair and unreasonable to the corporation may be avoided. CALIFORNIA CORPORATION LAWS by Ballantine and Sterling (1949 ed.), p. 102, § 84. It would be a shocking concept of corporate morality to hold that because the majority directors or stockholders disclose their purpose and interest,

(b) The fact of the common directorship or financial interest is disclosed or known to the shareholders, and they approve or ratify the contract or transaction in good faith by a majority vote or written consent of shareholders entitled to vote.

(c) The contract or transaction is just and reasonable as to the corporation at the time it is authorized or approved.

Common or interested directors may be counted in determining the presence of a quorum at a meeting of the board of directors or a committee thereof which authorizes, approves, or ratifies a contract or transaction.—Eds.

they may strip a corporation of its assets to their own financial advantage, and that the minority is without legal redress. Here the unchallenged findings demonstrate that Stanley and Sturgis used their majority power for their own personal advantage and to the detriment of the minority stockholder. They used it to strip the manufacturing companies of their sales functions—functions which it was their duty to carry out as officers and directors of those companies. There was not one thing done by them acting as the sales corporation that they could not and should not have done as officers and directors and in control of the stock of the manufacturing companies. It is no answer to say that the manufacturing companies made a profit on the deal, or that Stanley and Sturgis did a good job. The point is that those large profits that should have gone to the manufacturing companies were diverted to the sales corporation. The good job done by Stanley and Sturgis should and could have been done for the manufacturing companies. If Stanley and Sturgis, with control of the board of directors and the majority stock of the manufacturing companies, could thus lawfully, to their own advantage, strip the manufacturing companies of their sales functions, they could just as well strip them of their other functions. If the sales functions could be stripped from the companies in this fashion to the personal advantage of Stanley and Sturgis, there would be nothing to prevent them from next organizing a manufacturing company, and transferring to it the manufacturing functions of these companies, thus leaving the manufacturing companies but hollow shells. This should not, is not, and cannot be the law.

It is hornbook law that directors, while not strictly trustees, are fiduciaries, and bear a fiduciary relationship to the corporation, and to all the stockholders. They owe a duty to all stockholders, including the minority stockholders, and must administer their duties for the common benefit. The concept that a corporation is an entity cannot operate so as to lessen the duties owed to all of the stockholders. Directors owe a duty of highest good faith to the corporation and its stockholders. It is a cardinal principle of corporate law that a director cannot, at the expense of the corporation, make an unfair profit from his position. He is precluded from receiving any personal advantage without fullest disclosure to and consent of *all* those affected. The law zealously regards contracts between corporations with interlocking directorates, will carefully scrutinize all such transactions, and in case of unfair dealing to the detriment of minority stockholders, will grant appropriate relief. Where the transaction greatly benefits one corporation at the expense of another, and especially if it personally benefits the majority directors, it will and should be set aside. In other words, while the transaction is not voidable simply because an interested director participated, it will not be upheld if it is unfair to the minority stockholders. These principles are the law in practically all jurisdictions.

### Note: Compliance with an Interested Director Statute

One of the most difficult problems under the interested director statutes is determining the consequences of compliance with one of the two approval mechanisms that the statutes contain. The statute in *Remillard* is representative of most contemporary statutes which provide that an interested director transaction will not automatically be void or voidable *either* because there has been disclosure to, and approval by, a disinterested decision-maker (directors or shareholders) *or* because the transaction is fair to the corporation. Under such a provision, what role does a court have in determining the fairness of the transaction to the corporation? Because the statute is written in the disjunctive, one possible answer is that there will be judicial consideration of fairness only if there has been no prior approval by a disinterested decision-maker. If this interpretation is correct, it would represent a major reduction in judicial scrutiny (and, hence, potentially less protection for minority shareholders), particularly from the early days of the common law. See, Ahmed Bulbulia & Arthur R. Pinto, *Statutory Responses to Interested Directors' Transactions: A Watering Down of Fiduciary Standards?*, 53 NOTRE DAME L.REV.. 201 (1977). It could, however, be viewed as economically efficient and less costly because it would give prospective certainty to a transaction in which the decisional process has been good, presumably on the theory that good process will lead to substantively fair decisions in most instances.

Alternatively, the statute can be read as removing the absolute bar against interested director transactions but leaving no clear standard in its stead. Support for this reading comes from the language in many statutes that a transaction that satisfies one or more of the tests will not be void or voidable *solely* because of the director's interest. *See, e.g.*, DGCL § 144. Under this construction, the statute relates primarily to the burden of proof in litigation challenging a conflict of interest transaction rather than to the validity of the transaction itself. Thus, the burden of establishing validity initially would be on the interested director but would shift to the shareholder challenging the transaction if there had been approval by a disinterested decision-maker. This interpretation always leaves the question of the transaction's fairness for the court to determine; approval by a disinterested decision-maker only shifts the burden of who must establish fairness or unfairness. While this interpretation can be supported as a means of deterring management self-dealing, it can be read to be inconsistent with the statute's literal language.

The problem of interpretation stems from the differing stages of development of the case law at the time the statutes were enacted. Many jurisdictions had adopted a general rule that contracts between interested directors would not automatically be invalidated, but had not expressly overruled earlier cases applying an automatic voidability rule. Some jurisdictions retained vestiges of the automatic voidability rule in specific situations, e.g., where the interested director represented both parties to the transaction in the bargaining process, where the interested director was counted for purposes of determining the presence of a quorum, or where the interested director's vote was necessary for approval of the transaction. Thus, if the statute was designed to reverse the case law, the question remains: what case law?

Unfortunately legislative history and official commentaries (where they are available) are of little help. *See, e.g.,* the discussion of the legislative history of the New York statute in Note, *The Status of the Fairness Test Under Section 713 of the New York Business Corporation Law*, 76 COLUM.L.REV. 1156, 1166–74, 1179–82 (1976). Given the long-standing disfavor with which director conflict of interest transactions have been viewed, however, it might be thought that a legislative enactment purporting to shield them completely from judicial scrutiny would have done so explicitly. Indeed, one court, in interpreting the New Jersey statute, stated that "notwithstanding the use of 'or' to connect the subdivisions of the statute, the preferable construction is to require that a particular transaction pass muster under each subdivision." *Scott v. Multi–Amp Corp.*, 386 F.Supp. 44, 67 (D.N.J.1974).

The Delaware courts' interpretations of D.G.C.L. § 144 illustrates these difficulties. In *Fliegler v. Lawrence*, 361 A.2d 218 (Del.Supr.1976), a shareholder brought a derivative suit on behalf of Agau Mines against its officers and directors (including the named defendant Lawrence), and another corporation, United States Antimony Corp. (USAC), which was owned primarily by Lawrence and the other defendants. Lawrence had acquired, in his individual capacity, certain mining properties which he transferred to USAC. Agau later acquired USAC in exchange for 800,000 shares of Agau stock. Fliegler, a minority shareholder of Agau, challenged Agau's acquisition of USAC, claiming it was unfair. The defendants contended that they had been relieved of the burden of proving fairness because the transaction had been ratified by Agau's shareholders pursuant to § 144(a)(2). The court, however, held that the purported ratification did not affect the burden of proof because the majority of shares voted in favor of the acquisition were cast by the defendants in their capacity as Agau stockholders. Only one-third of the disinterested shareholders cast votes. Thus, the *Fliegler* court determined that despite the absence of any provision in § 144(a)(2) requiring *disinterested* shareholder approval of an interested director transaction, it would impose such a requirement before shifting the burden of proof from the interested director to the challenging shareholder.

Having decided the burden of proof question, the court then addressed the proper interpretation of the disjunctive language of § 144. The court rejected the argument that compliance with § 144(a)(2) automatically validated the transaction and concluded that the statute "merely removes an 'interested director' cloud when its terms are met and provides against invalidation of an agreement 'solely' because such a director or officer is involved. Nothing in the statute sanctions unfairness to Agau or removes the transaction from judicial scrutiny." *Id.* at 222.

In *Marciano v. Nakash*, 535 A.2d 400 (Del.1987), the Delaware Supreme Court found a transaction to be fair that, because of a deadlock at both the shareholder and director level, had not been approved by either disinterested shareholders or directors. The court characterized *Fliegler* as having "refused to view section 144 as either completely preemptive of the common law duty of director fidelity of as constituting a grant of broad immunity" and cited with approval *Fliegler*'s "merely removes an 'interested director' cloud" language. *Id.* at 404.

In a footnote, however, the court observed:

> Although in this case none of the curative steps afforded under section 144(a) were available because of the director-shareholder deadlock, a non-disclosing director seeking to remove the cloud of interestedness would appear to have the same burden under section 144(a)(3), as under prior case law, of proving the intrinsic fairness of a questioned transaction which had been approved or ratified by the directors or shareholders. Folk, THE DELAWARE GENERAL CORP. LAW: A COMMENTARY AND ANALYSIS, 86 (1972). On the other hand, approval by fully-informed disinterested directors under section 144(a)(1), or disinterested stockholders under section 144(a)(2), permits invocation of the business judgment rule and limits judicial review to issues of gift or waste with the burden of proof upon the party attacking the transaction.

*Id.* at 405, n.3. *See also Oberly v. Kirby*, 592 A.2d 445, 467 (Del.1991) ("The key to upholding an interested transaction is the approval of some neutral decision-making body. Under § 144, a transaction will be sheltered from shareholder challenge if approved by either a committee of independent directors, the shareholders, or the courts * * * "). The disjunctive reading in footnote 3 is also consistent with other decisions of the Delaware Supreme Court. *See, e.g., Puma v. Marriott*, 283 A.2d 693 (Del.Ch.1971) (not decided under § 144 but applying business judgment standard of review where disinterested directors approved purchase of corporations owned by family group including inside directors, according to terms not dictated by inside directors).

More recent Delaware cases appear to have rejected the view that § 144 imposes disjunctive requirements. In *Kahn v. Lynch Communication Systems, Inc.*, 638 A.2d 1110 (Del.1994), discussing the duties of a controlling shareholder in a transaction not governed by § 144, the court held that fairness was always the standard of review and that approval by a disinterested decision-maker, rather than permitting the application of the business judgment rule, simply shifted the burden of proof from the controlling shareholder to the shareholder-plaintiff. In the *Cinerama* litigation (discussed in Chapter 16), in a different transactional context, Chancellor Allen, cited *Kahn* to support his observation that "as construed by our Supreme Court recently, compliance with the terms of Section 144 does not restore to the board the presumption of the business judgment rule; it simply shifts the burden to plaintiff to prove unfairness." *Cinerama, Inc. v. Technicolor, Inc.*, 663 A.2d 1134, 1154 (Del.Ch.1994). Most recently, Vice–Chancellor Chandler, citing both *Cinerama* and *Kahn*, noted:

* * * [T]he Delaware Supreme Court has, since *Marciano* * * * was decided, more fully developed the standard by which this Court should judge a board's actions when it engages in a transaction with one or more of its own directors * * *. It is now clear that even if a board's action falls within the safe harbor of section 144, the board is not entitled to receive the protection of the business judgment rule. Compliance with section 144 merely shifts the burden to the plaintiffs to demonstrate that the transaction was unfair.

*Cooke v. Oolie*, 1997 WL 367034, *9 (Del.Ch.1997).

Commentators similarly have offered competing views as to the proper interpretation of *Fliegler* and *Marciano*. *See* Melvin A. Eisenberg, *Self–Interested Transactions in Corporate Law*, 13 J. Corp. L. 997 (1988), and E. Norman Veasey, et al., *Counseling Directors on the Business Judgment Rule and the Duty of Loyalty*, 731 PLI/Corp. 475 (Westlaw 1991) and Charles Hansen, John F. Johnson & Frederick H. Alexander, *The Role of Disinterested Directors in "Conflict" Transactions: The ALI Corporate Governance Project and Existing Law*, 45 Bus.Law. 2083 (1990).

If all this appears confusing, the reason is simple: it is confusing. The courts have done little to make the analysis clear. No Delaware Supreme Court decision squarely decides the issue. *Marciano* contains two different readings of § 144. Later cases either ignore the ambiguity in *Marciano* (*see Citron v. E.I. DuPont de Nemours & Co.*, 584 A.2d 490, 500–01 (Del.Ch.1990) or cite cases that do not directly involve § 144, such as *Kahn*, to support different constructions of § 144 without seeming to consider whether the fact they involve different transactional contexts should lead to different results. Of such difficulties are lawyers' practices made.

The RMBCA regime is no simpler. As discussed in greater detail in Section E, in 1989, the Corporate Laws Committee of the American Bar Association amended the RMBCA to replace the then existing § 8.31 (similar to DGCL § 144) with Subchapter F. The purpose of the amendment was to substitute a bright line test for the uncertainty of the existing statutory regime and to reduce judicial intervention in self-dealing transactions. In many cases, Subchapter F will not change the result, but the analytic methodology will change substantially. As of the writing of this book, thirteen states have adopted Subchapter F. For the moment, former § 8.31 remains representative of most statutes and will be considered as such in this Section.

## D. ENTIRE FAIRNESS: SUBSTANTIVE AND PROCEDURAL

As we have seen, although the validity of an interested director transaction may be subject to review under the business judgment rule in some circumstances, that is not the general rule. Rather, at both common law and under existing statutes, the test is whether the transaction was "fair" to the corporation at the time it was entered into. *Shlensky* and the cases it cites refer to the test as one of "entire fairness," a concept which *Weinberger* developed more fully. We examined this concept briefly in Chapter 16 in connection with the consequences of rebutting the presumption of the business judgment rule. Entire fairness has substantive and procedural elements (*Weinberger*'s "fair dealing" and "fair price"), both of which must be satisfied in order for the transaction to be considered "fair."

## 1. Substantive Fairness

The elements of substantive fairness set out in *Shlensky* stress a comparison of the fair market value of the transaction to the price the corporation actually paid, as well as the corporation's need for and ability to consummate the transaction. The test often has been articulated as "whether the proposition submitted would have commended itself to an independent corporation." *International Radio Telegraph Co. v. Atlantic Communication Co.*, 290 Fed. 698 (2d Cir.1923). To the extent that this formulation contemplates independent arms-length negotiation as providing the basis for fair market value, fairness is not limited to a single number; a range of potential values could satisfy the test of substantive fairness. But this concept becomes problematic in situations where it is difficult or impossible to determine a reliable fair market value such as raw land, undeveloped mines or an intangible asset like undeveloped patent rights. Because of the difficulties in defining substantive fairness precisely, courts often appear to be influenced in their determination of whether a transaction was substantively fair by whether there were procedural irregularities in the interested director's efforts to validate the transaction. In such a case, the presence or absence of procedural safeguards may lead to the inference of substantive fairness or unfairness in the transaction.

## 2. Procedural Fairness

### A. *Disinterested Director Approval*

One test for procedural fairness is whether the transaction was approved by disinterested directors. Under this test, a director is "disinterested" if neither she nor her family nor any entity in which she has a financial interest have a financial interest in the transaction, and if her judgment is not adversely affected by her relationship with the interested director. At common law, many cases held that a transaction between an interested director and her corporation was voidable without regard to its substantive fairness if the director's vote was needed to make up the majority to approve it or if the director's presence was necessary to constitute a quorum to bring the matter to a vote.

## ALI, PRINCIPLES OF CORPORATE
## GOVERNANCE (1994)

### § 1.23.  INTERESTED

(a) A director or officer is "interested" in a transaction if:

(1) The director or officer, or an associate of the director or officer, is a party to the transaction or conduct;

(2) The director or officer has a business, financial, or familial relationship with a party to the transaction or conduct, and that relationship would reasonably be expected to affect the director's or officer's judgment with respect to the transaction or conduct in a manner adverse to the corporation;

(3) The director or officer, an associate of the director or officer, or a person with whom the director or officer has a business, financial, or familial relationship, has a material pecuniary interest in the transaction (other than usual and customary directors' fees and benefits) and that interest and (if present) that relationship would reasonably be expected to affect the directors's or officer's judgment in a manner adverse to the corporation; or

(4) The director or officer is subject to a controlling influence by a party to the transaction or conduct or a person who has a material pecuniary interest in the transaction or conduct, and that controlling influence could reasonably be expected to affect the director's or officer's judgment with respect to the transaction or conduct in a manner adverse to the corporation.

\* \* \*

**Comment**

\* \* \*

A person who neither is an associate of, nor has a pecuniary interest in, or financial relationship to, a party to the transaction or conduct will normally not be interested within the meaning of § 1.23. However, § 1.23 permits a court to conclude that a "familial relationship" may cause a person to be considered an interested director or officer even if the person is not an associate \* \* \*. On the facts of a given case, and particularly where a corporation is not a publicly held corporation, a court may conclude that a familial relationship that is more remote than one that would constitute the person an associate, but which involves the same degree of intimacy as a relationship with a family member who is an associate, may be sufficiently significant as to cause the person to be an interested director or officer. Furthermore, a court may determine that parties to a relationship who share a common home have a "familial relationship" for purposes of § 1.23 even though the relationship is not a legally established matrimonial relationship. * * *

What appears to be disinterested board approval may be disregarded by a court where the board is in fact subject to a controlling influence by a director who is interested in the transaction or conduct. Such an influence is most likely to occur in the case of a board that is dominated by a controlling shareholder.

It is not intended that a person would be treated as subject to a controlling influence, and therefore interested, because of a long-time friendship or other social relationship, or solely because of a long-time business association through service on the same board of directors or other relationship not involving direct pecuniary dealing. However, where senior executives of two corporations sit on each other's board of directors, and each senior executive is in a position to review the other's compensation or other transactions or conduct in which the senior executive is pecuniarily interested, a court could consider that fact in determining whether in the circumstances of a particular case each of the senior executives is interested when reviewing each other's conflict-of-interest transactions or conduct.

A director is not interested under § 1.23 solely because the director receives or has an expectation of continuing to receive usual and customary director's fees, or because the director wants to continue the directorship for nonpecuniary reasons, or because a particular transaction in control threatens the loss of the position as a director and therefore of usual and customary directors' fees. Although a usual and customary directors' fee may constitute a significant portion of the annual income of a particular director, that fact alone will not cause the director to be considered interested for purposes of § 1.23 when, as a member of a group of non-management directors, the director considers a transaction in control that could result in the termination of his or her directorship.

––––––––––

Under RMBCA § 8.31(c), a majority of the disinterested directors on the board of directors or a committee of the board can constitute a quorum to authorize, approve, or ratify a conflict of interest transaction, but more than one director must approve a transaction. The presence of an interested director at the meeting does not affect the validity of action taken by disinterested directors. § 8.31 does not define "interested" or a "direct" interest, although § 8.31(b) does define the concept of "indirect" interest to include an entity in which the director has a financial or managerial interest.

N.Y.B.C.L. § 713(a)(1) provides that if there are insufficient disinterested directors to approve the transaction under normal quorum requirements, the transaction may be authorized by unanimous vote of the disinterested directors. DGCL § 144(a) requires only that the transaction be authorized "by the affirmative votes of a majority of the disinterested directors, even though the disinterested directors be less than a quorum." It could be argued that under either of these provisions a "unanimous" or "majority" vote of one director would suffice to meet the requirements for disinterested director approval. Would you counsel reliance on such an interpretation?

### B.  Domination

Even if a director is "disinterested" in the transaction, board approval will not validate the transaction if the otherwise disinterested directors were "dominated" by a party interested in the transaction. "Domination" is largely defined by judicial decisions.

In *Shlensky*, the court stated, "[I]t is not the mere number of common directors which determines whether approval has been given by an independent and disinterested majority of directors, but rather whether a majority of the directors are dominated by an individual or group." 19 Ill.2d 268, 284, 166 N.E.2d 793, 802 (1960). The question of domination is especially acute where the interested director is also a major or controlling shareholder.

*Globe Woolen Co. v. Utica Gas & Electric Co.*, 224 N.Y. 483, 121 N.E. 378 (1918) involved a contract between Globe Woolen and Utica Gas, a utility company. Maynard, the president of Globe Woolen also was a controlling shareholder of, and the dominant figure on the Utica Gas board. He had negotiated the challenged contract which had proved to be disastrously disadvantageous to Utica Gas. The court found that Maynard dominated the Utica Gas board and that he was "interested" in the transaction. Although his refusal to vote gave the transaction the form and presumption of propriety, the court held that the transaction unfair and voidable by Utica Gas. Judge Cardozo wrote:

> * * * [As a result of the contract, Utica Gas has] supplied the plaintiff with electric current for nothing, and owes, if the contract stands, about $11,000 for the privilege. These elements of unfairness, Mr. Maynard must have known, if indeed his knowledge be material. He may not have known how great the loss would be. He may have trusted to the superior technical skill of Mr. Greenidge [an employee of Utica Gas] to compute with approximate accuracy the comparative cost of steam and electricity. But he cannot have failed to know that he held a one-sided contract, which left the defendant at his mercy. He was not blind to the likelihood that in a term of ten years there would be changes in the business. The swiftness with which some of the changes followed permits the inference that they were premeditated. * * * But whether these and other changes were premeditated or not, at least they were recognized as possible. With that recognition, no word of warning was uttered to Greenidge or to any of the defendant's officers. There slumbered within these contracts a potency of profit which the plaintiff neither ignored in their making nor forgot in their enforcement.

> It is no answer to say that this potency, if obvious to Maynard, ought also to have been obvious to other members of the committee.

They did not know, as he did, the likelihood or the significance of changes in the business. There was need, too, of reflection and analysis before the dangers stood revealed. For the man who framed the contracts there was opportunity to consider and to judge. His fellow members, hearing them for the first time, and trustful of his loyalty, would have no thought of latent peril. That they had none is sufficiently attested by the fact that the contracts were approved. There was inequality, therefore, both in knowledge and in the opportunity for knowledge. It is not important in such circumstances whether the trustee foresaw the precise evils that developed. The inference that he did, might not be unsupported by the evidence. But the indefinite possibilities of hardship, the opportunity in changing circumstances to wrest unlooked-for profits and impose unlooked-for losses, these must have been foreseen. Foreseen or not, they were there, and their presence permeates the contracts with oppression and inequity.

We hold, therefore, that the refusal to vote does not nullify as of course an influence and predominance exerted without a vote. We hold that the constant duty rests on a trustee to seek no harsh advantage to the detriment of his trust, but rather to protest and renounce if through the blindness of those who treat with him he gains what is unfair. And because there is evidence that in the making of these contracts, that duty was ignored, the power of equity was fittingly exercised to bring them to an end.

*Id.* at 380–8.

————

Closely related to the *Globe Woolen* case are transactions in which the interested director represents both the corporation and himself in the bargaining process. One court has suggested that "[i]ndispensable to liability for violation of his fiduciary obligation as to any personal transaction with the corporation is the demonstration that a director has acted in a dual capacity—for himself as well as the corporation." *Borden v. Guthrie*, 23 A.D.2d 313, 260 N.Y.S.2d 769, 774 (1965), *aff'd* 17 N.Y.2d 571, 268 N.Y.S.2d 330, 215 N.E.2d 511 (1966). *Cf. David J. Greene & Co. v. Dunhill International, Inc.*, 249 A.2d 427, 430–31 (Del.Ch.1968), in which the court indicated that:

* * * [I]n the absence of divided interests, the judgment of the majority stockholders and/or the board of directors * * * is presumed made in good faith and inspired by a bona fides of purpose. But when the persons * * * who control the making of a transaction and the fixing of its terms, are on both sides, then the presumption and deference to sound business judgment are no longer present.

### Note: The Cleveland Browns Case

*Gries Sports Enterprises, Inc. v. Cleveland Browns Football Co., Inc.*, 26 Ohio St.3d 15, 496 N.E.2d 959 (1986) held that the directors of the corporation that owned the Cleveland Browns football team who approved the purchase of all of the stock of the Cleveland Stadium Corp. (CSC) were neither disinterested nor independent and that the acquisition was unfair to the Browns' minority shareholders. The Browns' board consisted of Gries (who owned 43 percent of the outstanding stock of the Browns), Modell (who owned 53 percent of the stock of the Browns and who was president and chief executive officer of the Browns), Modell's wife, Bailey (general counsel and a full-time employee of the Browns), Berick (outside legal counsel for the Browns and owner of less than 1 percent of the stock of the Browns), Cole and Wallack (full-time employees of the Browns). Modell owned 80 percent of the stock of CSC; the remaining 20 percent was owned by various individuals including Berick, Bailey, Cole and Wallack. Modell was president and Bailey was secretary and general counsel of CSC. In connection with the issues of interested directors and domination, the court concluded that the Browns' directors, Bailey, Berick, Cole and Wallack, were "interested" "because they had received a personal financial benefit from the challenged transaction" which was not equally shared by the stockholders. It also held that under Delaware case law, Berick was dominated because it was his job to do what Modell requested.

In analyzing the position of Berick and Bailey, one dissenting justice questioned what he called "the majority's simplistic analysis that merely because Berick was an officer in the Browns, and functioned accordingly, that he was not an independent director."

Berick's disinterest is * * * attacked by asserting that he, as outside legal counsel through his law firm, planned and prepared both transactions. As a matter of law, the presence of outside directors enhances the presumption of validity attributable to a director's actions. *See, e.g., Puma v. Marriott*, 283 A.2d 693 (Del.Ch. 1971). In this case, the fee ultimately paid to Berick's firm for legal services was approximately twenty to twenty-five thousand dollars, which is asserted by appellants to be a financial interest in the outcome of the transaction. It is also asserted that because Modell offered to buy Berick's shares of Browns stock, that Berick was dominated by Modell.

However, the fee for services paid to Berick's firm was not at all dependent on the transactions at issue. Payment was owed and would have been made, despite the outcome of the board's vote. Nor was the law firm dependent on the Browns, since the Browns constituted less than one percent of that firm's business. Also, Berick refused to sell his shares of stock to Modell. Although Berick was enthusiastic concerning the acquisition of CSC, nothing about his opinion indicates anything other than a personal viewpoint. The fact that Berick sits as a director on the boards of a number of corporations, public and private, indicates a professional attitude. Thus, there was no dominance or tainting self-interest in his vote.

The majority fully misstates the law of Delaware by its statement that "Bailey's dual positions as an officer and general counsel for both corporations make him an 'interested' director." There are no Delaware cases which support this view. In fact, the cases utilized by the majority would agree that an interested director is one who is on both sides of the transaction, and who somehow wrongfully receives a benefit.

Bailey, who is in-house counsel to the Browns, is said to be an interested director because he helped to structure the two transactions. It was also alleged that Modell dominated him because he was presented to the board by Modell for the position of director and, at times, Modell sent Bailey to negotiate for him.

The law of Delaware makes it clear that positional relationships, without more, do not rise to disqualification of the director's vote. In the view of the Delaware Supreme Court, "it is not enough to charge that a director was nominated by or elected at the behest of those controlling the outcome of a corporate election. That is the usual way a person becomes a corporate director. It is the care, attention and sense of individual responsibility to the performance of one's duties, not the method of election, that generally touches on independence." [*Aronson v. Lewis*, 473 A.2d 805 (Del.1984).] "Such contentions do not support any claim under Delaware law that * * * directors lack independence." *Id.* at 815. Instead, it must be demonstrated that the directors "through personal or other relationships * * * are beholden to the controlling person." *Id.*

Because of Bailey's position, he would naturally have negotiated for the Browns and, consequently, Modell. He was approved as a director by the entire board, including Gries. At no time was there proof of any self-dealing by Bailey. He personally believed the Browns should acquire CSC so as to control the team's playing facilities. Mere like-mindedness on issues hardly rises to the level of domination or self-interest.

*Id.* at 977–78.

———

It is important to note that courts have generally refused to find that "structural bias," alone, resulting from long-term non-financial relations of trust among directors, amounts to domination. Domination always appears to require an element of financial dependence on the "dominating" director, for example, in the form of employment or future business.

### C. Shareholder Approval

An interested director transaction can also be found to be procedurally fair if it has been approved or subsequently ratified by shareholder vote provided that the material facts as to the transaction and the director's interest were disclosed to the shareholders. At common law, many cases held that if the terms of the transaction were substantively fair, the shares of the interested director could be voted in favor of ratification. Other decisions held that such shares could not be voted because interested directors could not ratify their own contracts with the corporation. Courts were divided as to whether a majority of informed shareholders could ratify a fraudulent transaction, or whether such ratification required unanimous approval. Where those issues did not arise, shareholder ratification created a presumption that the transaction was fair. Thus, some courts indicated that shareholder ratification has the effect of shifting the burden of proof to the party challenging the transaction to show that the terms were so unequal as to amount to waste. *See Gottlieb v. Heyden Chemical Corp.*, 33 Del.Ch. 177, 91 A.2d 57 (1952); *Eliasberg v. Standard Oil Co.*, 23 N.J.Super. 431, 92 A.2d 862 (Ch.Div.1952), *aff'd* 12 N.J. 467, 97 A.2d 437 (1953). Where, however, the interested directors own a majority of the shares, shareholder ratification generally does not shift the burden of proving unfairness to the challenging party. *See Brundage v. New Jersey Zinc Co.*, 226 A.2d 585 (1967); *Pappas v. Moss*, 393 F.2d 865 (3d Cir.1968); *David J. Greene & Co. v. Dunhill International, Inc.*, 249 A.2d 427 (Del.Ch.1968).

It appears that the shareholder approval provision of the interested director statutes, at least as interpreted by *Remillard Brick* and other decisions, codify the common law. Thus an interested director transaction is not void or voidable if the director's interest is disclosed to the shareholders and the shareholders approve the transaction. However, technical compliance with the statutory procedures will not immunize a transaction from scrutiny for fairness where the interested directors are also majority shareholders who vote in favor of the transaction. Would the rationale of *Remillard Brick* apply where the interested directors own a controlling but less than majority interest in the corporation? Where they own less than a controlling interest, but their votes are necessary for majority approval of a transaction?

To avoid the uncertainty of whether shareholder approval is valid if the interested directors vote their shares, it is now common to obtain "majority of the minority" shareholder approval as a condition of the transaction, particularly in controlled mergers. See *Weinberger, infra* Chapter 23. Calif. Corp.Code § 310(a)(1)) adopts the "majority of the minority" approach in transactions in which the directors have a material financial interest.

The ALI's definition of an "interested" shareholder is narrower than its definition of an "interested" director. Thus, § 1.23(b) defines a shareholder as "interested" in a transaction "if either the shareholder or, to the shareholder's knowledge, an associate of the shareholder is a party to the transaction or the shareholder is also an interested director with respect to the same transaction." The ALI explains the difference by stating that "due to the practical difficulties that may arise in seeking to determine whether shareholders in a publicly owned corporation have an interest in a transaction, the test whether a shareholder is interested has been framed more narrowly than in the case of a director." ALI, Principles of Corporate Governance (1994), Comment to § 1.23. Is this explanation persuasive, or does the difference arise from the different roles that shareholders and directors generally play in a corporate governance system?

In that connection, consider the views of Harold Marsh:

> The rule [permitting shareholder approval of an interested director transaction after full disclosure] has been justified on the basis that where there is shareholder ratification the case is precisely analogous to that of a trustee dealing with his cestui que trust after full disclosure, and is not at all a case of a trustee dealing with himself. However, the validity of this analogy may be seriously questioned. When a trustee deals with his cestui que trust who is an individual that is sui juris, after full disclosure, then the cestui que trust is able to negotiate for himself and there is no more danger of fraud or over-reaching than in any other business transaction. However, when the shareholders of a Publicly-held company are asked to ratify a transaction with interested directors they cannot as a practical matter *negotiate* for the corporation. They are, they must be, limited to rejecting or accepting the deal formulated by the interested directors. Even if it be assumed that the deal is fair, that is not what the shareholders are entitled to. They are entitled to have someone negotiate the best deal obtainable for their corporation, fair or unfair. This the interested directors cannot do. As the New Hampshire court said, it is "impossible for common directors to procure the lowest rates for one party and the highest rates for the other. * * * They were not arbitrators, called in to adjust conflicting claims. * * *"

Harold Marsh, *Are Directors Trustees? Conflict of Interest and Corporate Morality*, 22 BUS.LAW. 35, 48–49 (1966).

Consider the following recent attempt by the Delaware Court of Chancery to explicate the effect of shareholder ratification on interested director transactions. As you read it, keep in mind the previous discussion of the effect of director approval of such transactions.

### LEWIS v. VOGELSTEIN
699 A.2d 327 (Del.Ch.1997).

ALLEN, CHANCELLOR.

This shareholders' suit challenges a stock option compensation plan for the directors of Mattel, Inc., which was approved or ratified by the shareholders of the company at its 1996 Annual Meeting of Shareholders ["1996 Plan" or "Plan"]

\* \* \*

I.

The facts as they appear in the pleading are as follows. The Plan was adopted in 1996 and ratified by the company's shareholders at the

1996 annual meeting. It contemplates two forms of stock option grants to the company's directors: a one-time grant of options on a block of stock and subsequent, smaller annual grants of further options.

With respect to the one-time grant, the Plan provides that each outside director will qualify for a grant of options on 15,000 shares of Mattel common stock at the market price on the day such options are granted (the "one-time options"). The one-time options are alleged to be exercisable immediately upon being granted although they will achieve economic value, if ever, only with the passage of time. It is alleged that if not exercised, they remain valid for ten years.

With respect to the second type of option grant, the Plan qualifies each director for a grant of options upon his or her re-election to the board each year (the "Annual Options"). The maximum number of options grantable to a director pursuant to the annual options provision depends on the number of years the director has served on the Mattel board. Those outside directors with five or fewer years of service will qualify to receive options on no more than 5,000 shares, while those with more than five years service will qualify for options to purchase up to 10,000 shares. Once granted, these options vest over a four year period, at a rate of 25% per year. When exercisable, they entitle the holder to buy stock at the market price on the day of the grant. According to the complaint, options granted pursuant to the annual options provision also expire ten years from their grant date, whether or not the holder has remained on the board.

When the shareholders were asked to ratify the adoption of the Plan, as is typically true, no estimated present value of options that were authorized to be granted under the Plan was stated in the proxy solicitation materials.

## II.

As the presence of valid shareholder ratification of executive or director compensation plans importantly affects the form of judicial review of such grants, it is logical to begin an analysis of the legal sufficiency of the complaint by analyzing the sufficiency of the attack on the disclosures made in connection with the ratification vote.

### A. DISCLOSURE OBLIGATION:

[The court rejected plaintiff's claim that defendants had a duty to disclose the estimated present value of the stock option grants to which directors might become entitled under the 1996 Plan.]

## III.

* * * I turn to the motion to dismiss the complaint's allegation to the effect that the Plan, or grants under it, constitute a breach of the directors' fiduciary duty of loyalty. As the Plan contemplates grants to the directors that approved the Plan and who recommended it to the shareholders, we start by observing that it constitutes self-dealing that would ordinarily require that the directors prove that the grants involved were, in the circumstances, entirely fair to the corporation.

However, it is the case that the shareholders have ratified the directors' action. That ratification is attacked only on the ground just treated. Thus, for these purposes I assume that the ratification was effective. The question then becomes what is the effect of informed shareholder ratification on a transaction of this type (i.e., officer or director pay).

### A. SHAREHOLDER RATIFICATION UNDER DELAWARE LAW:

What is the effect under Delaware corporation law of shareholder ratification of an interested transaction? The answer to this apparently simple question appears less clear than one would hope or indeed expect. Four possible effects of shareholder ratification appear logically available: **First**, one might conclude that an effective shareholder ratification acts as a complete defense to any charge of breach of duty. **Second**, one might conclude that the effect of such ratification is to shift the substantive test on judicial review of the act from one of fairness that would otherwise be obtained (because the transaction is an interested one) to one of waste. **Third**, one might conclude that the ratification shifts the burden of proof of unfairness to plaintiff, but leaves that shareholder-protective test in place. **Fourth**, one might conclude (perhaps because of great respect for the collective action disabilities that attend shareholder action in public corporations) that shareholder ratification offers no assurance of assent of a character that deserves judicial recognition. Thus, under this approach, ratification on full information would be afforded no effect. Excepting the fourth of these effects, there are cases in this jurisdiction that reflect each of these approaches to the effect of shareholder voting to approve a transaction.[10]

In order to state my own understanding I first note that by shareholder ratification I do not refer to every instance in which shareholders vote affirmatively with respect to a question placed before them. I exclude from the question those instances in which shareholder votes are a necessary step in authorizing a transaction. Thus the law of ratification as here discussed has no direct bearing on shareholder action to amend a certificate of incorporation or bylaws. * * * [N]or does that law bear on shareholder votes necessary to authorize a merger, a sale of substantially all the corporation's assets, or to dissolve the enterprise. For analytical purposes one can set such cases aside.

1. *Ratification generally*: I start with principles broader than those of corporation law. Ratification is a concept deriving from the law of agency which contemplates the ex post conferring upon or confirming of the legal authority of an agent in circumstances in which the agent had no authority or arguably had no authority. To be effective, of course, the

---

**10.** *See, e.g., In re Wheelabrator Technologies, Inc., Shareholders Litig.*, Del.Ch., 663 A.2d 1194 (1995) (effect one: effective ratification eliminates any claim for breach of duty of care but only breach of care); *Michelson v. Duncan*, Del.Supr., 407 A.2d 211, 224 (1979) (effect two: effective ratification of director interested transaction triggers waste standard); *Citron v. E.I. Du-Pont de Nemours & Co.*, Del.Ch., 584 A.2d 490, 500–502 (1990), quoted with approval in *Kahn v. Lynch Communication Systems, Inc.*, Del.Supr. 638 A.2d 1110 (1994) (effect three: effective ratification shifts burden of fairness to plaintiff).

agent must fully disclose all relevant circumstances with respect to the transaction to the principal prior to the ratification. Beyond that, since the relationship between a principal and agent is fiduciary in character, the agent in seeking ratification must act not only with candor, but with loyalty. Thus an attempt to coerce the principal's consent improperly will invalidate the effectiveness of the ratification.

Assuming that a ratification by an agent is validly obtained, what is its effect? One way of conceptualizing that effect is that it provides, after the fact, the grant of authority that may have been wanting at the time of the agent's act. Another might be to view the ratification as consent or as an estoppel by the principal to deny a lack of authority. In either event the effect of informed ratification is to validate or affirm the act of the agent as the act of the principal.

Application of these general ratification principles to shareholder ratification is complicated by three other factors. **First**, most generally, in the case of shareholder ratification there is of course no single individual acting as principal, but rather a class or group of divergent individuals—the class of shareholders. This aggregate quality of the principal means that decisions to affirm or ratify an act will be subject to collective action disabilities; that some portion of the body doing the ratifying may in fact have conflicting interests in the transaction; and some dissenting members of the class may be able to assert more or less convincingly that the "will" of the principal is wrong, or even corrupt and ought not to be binding on the class. In the case of individual ratification these issues won't arise, assuming that the principal does not suffer from multiple personality disorder. Thus the collective nature of shareholder ratification makes it more likely that following a claimed shareholder ratification, nevertheless, there is a litigated claim on behalf of the principal that the agent lacked authority or breached its duty. The **second**, mildly complicating factor present in shareholder ratification is the fact that in corporation law the "ratification" that shareholders provide will often not be directed to lack of legal authority of an agent but will relate to the consistency of some authorized director action with the equitable duty of loyalty. Thus shareholder ratification sometimes acts not to confer legal authority—but as in this case—to affirm that action taken is consistent with shareholder interests. **Third**, when what is "ratified" is a director conflict transaction, the statutory law—in Delaware Section 144 of the Delaware General Corporation Law—may bear on the effect.[12]

---

**12.** Most jurisdictions have enacted statutes that appear to offer a procedural technique for removing courts from a fairness evaluation of the terms of director conflict transactions. Generally courts have given them a very narrow interpretation, however. In Delaware that statute enacted in 1967—Act of July 3, 1967, Ch. 50, 56 Del.Laws 151, 170 (1967) amended in 1969—is Section 144 of the DGCL. Early on it was narrowly held that compliance with that section simply removed the automatic taint of a director conflict transaction, but nevertheless left the transaction subject to substantive judicial review for fairness. *See* Fliegler v. Lawrence, Del.Supr., 361 A.2d 218, 222 (1976) (involving claimed independent board action, not ratification by shareholders). This interpretation tended to be the general judicial response to these "safe-harbor" statutes. *See Cookies Food Prod.,*

2. Shareholder ratification: These differences between shareholder ratification of director action and classic ratification by a single principal, do lead to a difference in the effect of a valid ratification in the shareholder context. The principal novelty added to ratification law generally by the shareholder context, is the idea—no doubt analogously present in other contexts in which common interests are held—that, in addition to a claim that ratification was defective because of incomplete information or coercion, shareholder ratification is subject to a claim by a member of the class that the ratification is ineffectual (1) because a majority of those affirming the transaction had a conflicting interest with respect to it or (2) because the transaction that is ratified constituted a corporate waste. As to the second of these, it has long been held that shareholders may not ratify a waste except by a unanimous vote. The idea behind this rule is apparently that a transaction that satisfies the high standard of waste constitutes a gift of corporate property and no one should be forced against their will to make a gift of their property. In all events, informed, uncoerced, disinterested shareholder ratification of a transaction in which corporate directors have a material conflict of interest has the effect of protecting the transaction from judicial review except on the basis of waste.[13]

## B. The Waste Standard:

The judicial standard for determination of corporate waste is well developed. Roughly, a waste entails an exchange of corporate assets for consideration so disproportionately small as to lie beyond the range at which any reasonable person might be willing to trade. Most often the claim is associated with a transfer of corporate assets that serves no corporate purpose; or for which no consideration at all is received. Such a transfer is in effect a gift. If, however, there is *any substantial* consideration received by the corporation, and if there is a *good faith judgment* that in the circumstances the transaction is worthwhile, there should be no finding of waste, even if the fact finder would conclude *ex post* that the transaction was unreasonably risky. Any other rule would deter corporate boards from the optimal rational acceptance of risk. * * * Courts are ill-fitted to attempt to weigh the "adequacy" of consideration under the waste standard or, ex post, to judge appropriate degrees of business risk.

---

*Inc. v. Lakes Warehouse Distrib., Inc.*, 430 N.W.2d 447, 452–453 (Iowa 1988) (requiring directors who engage in self-dealing to prove that they have acted in good faith). *See also Cohen v. Ayers*, 596 F.2d 733, 740 (7th Cir.1979) (stating that under New York statutory law, in an unratified transaction involving interested directors the burden is on the directors to establish the fairness of the transaction, but where shareholder or disinterested-director ratification has occurred, the burden shifts to the challenger).

**13.** Claims of breach of a duty of care seem difficult to relate to analysis under the waste standard. Duty of care analysis in this or other settings relate to deviations from ordinary care in the circumstances. Probably for this reason, it has been held, on authority, that ratification of a transaction that is thereafter made the subject of a breach of care claim is effective to defeat such a claim completely. *See In re Wheelabrator Tech., Inc. Shareholders Litig.*, Del. Ch., 663 A.2d 1194, 1200 (1995).

[The court concluded that plaintiff's complaint should not be dismissed because the one time option grants to the directors were sufficiently unusual as to require further inquiry into whether they constituted waste. This portion of the court's opinion is set forth in Section F, below.]

## D. Disclosure

Procedural fairness requires full disclosure of the existence of a conflict, and of other "material" information concerning the substance of the transaction, to the disinterested directors or to the shareholders from whom approval of the transaction is sought. Indeed, some cases have suggested that the failure to make full disclosure constitutes per se unfairness. Although that is not the general rule, as we will see more fully in Chapter 18, the duty of disclosure has taken on increasingly greater significance in evaluating a transaction. Recall the Delaware Supreme Court's analysis of the role of disclosure in determining "fair dealing" in *Cede* in Chapter 16.

In *State ex rel. Hayes Oyster Co. v. Keypoint Oyster Co.*, 391 P.2d 979 (1964), the president, a director and substantial shareholder, arranged for the sale of corporate properties to another corporation in which he was to have an interest. The transaction was submitted to the shareholders for their approval, but without disclosure of the director's interest. The director voted a majority of the stock, including his own, in favor of the sale. In invalidating the transaction, the court stated:

\* \* \* [T]his court has abolished the mechanical rule whereby any transaction involving corporate property in which a director has an interest is voidable at the option of the corporation. Such a contract cannot be voided if the director or officer can show that the transaction was fair to the corporation. However, non-disclosure by an interested director or officer is, in itself, unfair. This wholesome rule can be applied automatically without any of the unsatisfactory results which flowed from a rigid bar against any self-dealing.

\* \* \*

\* \* \* [The] shareholders and directors had the right to know of Hayes' interest in [the properties] in order to intelligently determine the advisability of retaining Hayes as president and manager under the circumstances, and to determine whether or not it was wise to enter into the contract at all, in view of Hayes' conduct. In all fairness, they were entitled to know that their president and director might be placed in a position where he must choose between the interest[s of the two corporations in conducting their business with one another.]

*Id.* at 984.

Although this language suggests that only the existence of the director's interest in the transaction need be disclosed, the court also said that the director was obligated to disclose fully all relevant or material information concerning the transaction to the directors and shareholders. This statement reflects the views of most common law courts. The question of what is "material information" will be considered more closely in Chapter 18.

## E.  CONTEMPORARY STATUTORY REFORM: SUBCHAPTER F AND THE ALI PRINCIPLES OF CORPORATE GOVERNANCE

As we have seen, case law interpreting statutes similar to RMBCA § 8.31 is less clear than a mountain lake. Two major efforts have attempted to clarify the law relating to conflict of interest transactions. In 1989, the Committee on Corporate Laws of the American Bar Association adopted a new Subchapter F to replace the existing § 8.31. The basic provisions of the new sections do not differ materially from existing law in many respects, but they try are designed to preserve the disjunctive force of the word "or" and to provide specific "bright line" definitions of who is an "interested" director and what constitutes a "transaction" to which Subchapter F is applicable. If directors follow the prescribed procedures, the transaction will be subject only to the business judgment rule and not to a fairness standard. The ALI, by contrast, continues to provide a more pro-active role for courts in reviewing the fairness of the transaction. The ALI modifies existing statutes; Subchapter F revamps them.

## ALI, PRINCIPLES OF CORPORATE GOVERNANCE (1994)

### § 5.02.  Transactions With the Corporation

(a) *General Rule.* A director or senior executive who enters into a transaction with the corporation (other than a transaction involving the payment of compensation) fulfills the duty of fair dealing with respect to the transaction if:

(1) disclosure concerning the conflict of interest and the transaction is made to the corporate decisionmaker who authorizes in advance or ratifies the transaction; and

(2) Either (A) the transaction is fair to the corporation when entered into;

(B) the transaction is authorized in advance, following disclosure concerning the conflict of interest and the transaction, by disinterested directors or, in the case of a senior executive who is not a director, authorized in advance by a disinterested superior, who could reasonably have concluded that the transaction was fair to the corporation at the time of such authorization;

(C) the transaction is ratified, following such disclosure, by disinterested directors who could reasonably have concluded that the transaction was fair to the corporation at the time it was entered into, provided (i) a corporate decisionmaker who is not interested in the transaction acted for the corporation in the transaction and could have reasonably concluded the transaction to be fair to the corporation; (ii) the interested director or senior executive made disclosure to such decisionmaker pursuant to Subsection (a)(1) to the extent he or she then knew of the material facts; (iii) the interested director or senior executive did not act unreasonably in failing to seek advance authorization of the transaction by disinterested directors or a disinterested superior; and (iv) the failure to obtain advance authorization of the transaction from disinterested directors or a disinterested superior did not adversely affect the interests of the corporation in a significant way; or

  (D) the transaction is authorized in advance or ratified, following such disclosure, by disinterested shareholders and does not constitute a waste of corporate assets at the time of the shareholder action.

  (b) *Burden of Proof.* A party who challenges a transaction between a director or senior executive and the corporation has the burden of proof, except that if such party establishes that none of the requirements of Subsections (a)(2)(B), (a)(2)(C), or (a)(2)(D) is satisfied, the director or the senior executive has the burden of proving that the transaction was fair to the corporation.

  (c) *Ratification of Disclosure or Nondisclosure.* The disclosure requirements of § 5.02(a)(1) will be deemed to be satisfied if at any time (but no later than a reasonable time after suit is filed challenging the transaction) the transaction is ratified, following such disclosure, by the directors, the shareholders, or the corporate decisionmaker who initially approved the transaction or such decisionmaker's successor.

---

## 1. "INTERESTED" DIRECTORS AND "CONFLICT OF INTEREST" TRANSACTIONS

  Sections 8.60 and 8.61 of Subchapter F attempt to frame the definition of who is "interested" in a transaction, and what constitutes a "conflict of interest transaction" much more tightly than does § 8.31. The Official Comment to § 8.31 states:

  For purposes of section 8.31 a director should normally be viewed as interested in a transaction if he or the immediate members of his family have a financial interest in the transaction *or a relationship with the other parties to the transaction such that the relationship might reasonably be expected to affect his judgment in the particular matter in a manner adverse to the corporation.* (emphasis added).

The Official Comment to Subchapter F describes the italicized language as overly broad and leading to uncertainty by corporate directors at best, and vague and destabilizing at worst. Subchapter F takes a markedly different approach.

> Section 8.61(a) is a key component in the design of subchapter F. It draws a bright-line circle, declaring that the definitions of section 8.60 wholly occupy and preempt the field of directors' conflicting interest transactions. Of course, outside this circle there is a penumbra of director interests, desires, goals, loyalties, and prejudices that may, in a particular context, run at odds with the best interests of the corporation, but section 8.61(a) forbids a court to ground remedial action on any of them. If a plaintiff charges that a director had a conflict of interest with respect to a transaction of the corporation because the other party was his cousin, the answer of the court should be: "No. A cousin as such and without more, is not included in section 8.60(3) as a related person—and under section 8.61(a), I have no authority to reach out farther." If a plaintiff contends that the director had a conflict of interest in a corporate transaction because the other party is president of the golf club the director wants desperately to join, the court should respond: "No. The only director's conflicting interest on the basis of which I can set aside a corporate transaction or impose other sanctions is a financial interest as defined by section 8.60."

Official Comment to Section 8.61.

The ALI differs philosophically with this approach. The ALI acknowledges that the definition of "related person" in RMBCA § 8.60 is narrower than is provided in its Principles but argues:

> * * * The Model Act bases its bright-line test approach on the need for certainty in the area of conflict of interest transactions. The Reporters believe that in the area of avoidable conflict of interest transactions the desirability of affording certainty to a person with a potentially conflicting interest is outweighed by the desirability of encouraging oversight by disinterested directors in cases where a director has a relationship with a person transacting business with the corporation that is sufficiently substantial that it would reasonably be expected to affect the director's judgment with respect to the transaction in a manner adverse to the corporation. * * *

ALI, Principles of Corporate Governance (1994), § 5.02, Reporter's Note 13.

Section 8.60's narrowly circumscribed definition of "related person" clearly is intended to leave a number of questionable situations immune from judicial scrutiny on the ground that "the legislative draftsman who chooses to suppress marginal anomalies by resorting to generalized statements of principle will pay a cost in terms of predictability." Recall the debate between Professor Cary and Judge Winter in Chapter 7. What factors should be considered in a cost-benefit analysis? Should such an analysis be the basis for the normative judgments found in a statute? If not, on what should such a normative judgment be based?

## 2.  FAIRNESS

In many ways, Subchapter F takes the same approach as modern interested director statutes in evaluating substantive fairness. "[A] 'fair' price is any price in that broad range which an unrelated party might have been willing to pay or willing to accept * * * following a normal arm's-length business negotiation, in the light of the knowledge that would have been reasonably acquired in the course of such negotiations. * * * " Official Comment to § 8.61.

This range of fairness is narrower than the range of discretion to which directors' decisions are entitled under the business judgment standard of Section 8.30. The Official Comment to § 8.61 also points out that courts must consider "whether the transaction was one reasonably likely to yield favorable results * * * from the perspective of furthering the corporation's business activities" in addition to scrutinizing the price and terms of the transaction.

The most important element of fairness in Subchapter F is that Section 8.61(b)(3) appears to provide that a transaction which is "fair" should be upheld, whether or not it was approved by directors or shareholders in compliance with §§ 8.62 and 8.63. However, the Official Comment states:

> * * * [I]n some circumstances, the behavior of the director having the conflicting interest can itself affect the finding and content of "fairness." The most obvious illustration of unfair dealing arises out of the director's failure to disclose fully his interest or hidden defects known to him regarding the transaction. Another illustration could be the exertion of improper pressure by the director upon the other directors. When the facts of such unfair dealing become known, the court should offer the corporation its option as to whether to rescind the transaction on grounds of "unfairness" even if it appears that the terms were "fair" by market standards and the corporation profited from it. * * * Thus, the course of dealing—or process—is a key component to a "fairness" determination under subsection (b)(3).

Official Comment to Section 8.61.

Another part of the Official Comment also suggests that the protection of the business judgment rule may not be as absolute under Subchapter F as it is in other contexts:

> * * * Consider, for example, a situation in which it is established that the board of a manufacturing corporation approved a cash loan to a director where the duration, security and interest terms of the loan were at prevailing commercial rates, but (i) the loan was not made in the course of the corporation's business activities and (ii) the loan required a commitment of limited working capital that would otherwise have been used in furtherance of the corporation's business activities. Such a loan transaction would not be afforded safe-harbor protection by section 8.62(b)(1) since the

board did not comply with the requirement in section 8.30(a) that the board's action be, in its reasonable judgment, in the best interests of the corporation—that is, that the action will, as the board judges the circumstances at hand, yield favorable results (or reduce detrimental results) as judged from the perspective of furthering the corporation's business activities.

If a determination is made that the terms of a director's conflicting interest transaction, judged according to the circumstances at the time of commitment, were manifestly unfavorable to the the corporation, that determination would be relevant to an allegation that the directors' action was not taken in good faith and therefore did not comply with section 8.30(a).

Official Comment to Section 8.61.

Does this comment thrust the courts back into determining fairness, notwithstanding Subchapter F's attempt to limit judicial intervention? Or should Subchapter F be read to shield a conflict of interest transaction whose terms are fair by market standards and from which the corporation benefits, even if the interested director failed to disclose material facts about the transaction? This result would overrule decisions such as *Hayes Oyster*, which held that disclosure is an indispensable element of fairness. Is this a desirable result?

The ALI clearly thinks not. It squarely takes the position that "fairness" is impossible without full disclosure of material facts. It acknowledges that fairness is often a range, but it argues that "[i]f an undisclosed material fact had been disclosed. * * * the corporation might have declined to transact at that high price, or might have bargained the price down lower in the range." ALI, Principles of Corporate Governance (1994), Part V Introductory Note.

## 3. JUDICIAL REVIEW

Subchapter F attempts to extend the business judgment rule to conflict of interest transactions that have been approved after full disclosure by disinterested directors or shareholders. It is here that the ALI approach differs most profoundly from Subchapter F. The Comment to § 5.02(a)(2)(B) states:

> * * * There are several reasons why a self-interested transaction should be subject to a closer scrutiny than is required by the business judgment rule even if the transaction has been [approved by disinterested directors].

> First, transactions of the types covered by § 5.02 are as a matter of accepted business practice normally regarded as deserving of closer scrutiny than in the case of transactions with unrelated third parties. In fact, corporate codes of conduct adopted by many public companies prohibit transactions between the corporation and its officers and employees. The New York Stock Exchange, which no longer seeks to prohibit such transactions and leaves their evalua-

tion to company management, nevertheless states in its Listed Company Manual [§ 307.00] that: "The Exchange continues to believe that a publicly owned company of the size and character appropriate for listing on the Exchange should be able to operate on its own merit and credit standing free from the suspicions that may arise when business transactions are consummated with insiders."

Second, the presence of close relationships among colleagues on the board or in management, particularly in smaller corporations, may sometimes interfere with the ability of directors or superiors to deal with a colleague with the degree of wariness that is employed in arm's length transactions.

Third, a court may under appropriate facts have cause to inquire whether the process of approval produced an unfair result—because, for example, the approval was obtained by improper pressure exerted on the decisionmakers by the interested director or senior executive.

Fourth, for the reasons set forth above, courts are likely to consider the fairness of self-interested transactions no matter what the test is said to be, where the circumstances suggest that the transaction is unfair to the corporation. If the test were framed in terms of the business judgment rule, there is a substantial risk that courts would unduly enlarge the scope of review under that rule in order to provide a fairness review with the potential for a similar result in settings where the business judgment rule is applied outside Part V.

While a greater degree of scrutiny of transactions subject to § 5.02 is appropriate than that afforded by the business judgment rule, § 5.02(a)(2)(B) accords two very significant effects to approval of such transactions by disinterested directors or a disinterested superior.

First, advance approval by disinterested directors * * * shifts the burden of proof to the party attacking the transaction. Where a self-interested transaction has not been approved by disinterested directors * * * the burden of proof is on the self-interested director * * * to show that the transaction was fair.

Second, advance approval by disinterested directors * * * changes the standard by which the self-interested transaction is measured. Under § 5.02(a)(2)(B) * * * a person attacking the transaction has the burden of proving not simply that the transaction is unfair, but that the terms of the transaction are so clearly outside the range of reasonableness that the directors * * * who authorized the transaction could not reasonably have concluded at the time of such authorization that the transaction was fair to the corporation. This test is intended to be substantially easier for the interested director * * * to satisfy than a pure fairness test, although not as easy to satisfy as the rationality test of the business judgment standard.

Professor Michael Dooley suggests that the ALI approach and that of Subchapter F reflect two fundamentally different approaches to corporate law. Michael P. Dooley, *Two Models of Corporate Governance*, 47 Bus. Law. 461 (1992). To date, thirteen states have adopted Subchapter F.

## F. EXECUTIVE COMPENSATION

There are four basic forms of executive compensation: salaries; bonuses; stock options and other plans based on stock value; and deferred compensation (pension) plans. To this might be added fringe benefits (or "perks"). Depending on which commentators you believe (and which companies you observe), some of these forms of compensation—especially bonuses and incentive compensation plans based on stock value—are either outrageous wastes of corporate funds or moderate and useful devices that align executives' interests with those of shareholders. From the point of view of the executive, there are a number of factors that enter into the structuring of the ideal compensation package, including income and estate tax considerations, the executive's age and retirement plans, outside income, and preference as to balance between risk and potential gain.

From the point of view of the corporation, the principal considerations should be whether an incentive compensation plan does in fact align executives interests with those of shareholders and how large the incentives need to be to motivate executives to perform effectively. Corporations also are concerned with maximizing the deductibility of the total compensation paid for the purposes of computing the corporation's income tax and limiting the dilution of capital resulting from the issuance of options that allow executives (and employees) to purchase stock at below-market prices.

### Note: The American Tobacco Litigation

Litigation involving bonuses paid to the officers of the American Tobacco Co. represents a landmark in the development of the law of executive compensation. In 1912, American Tobacco's shareholders adopted a by-law providing for payment of annual bonus payments to the corporation's officers in amounts equal to a percentage of net profits in excess of a stated threshold. The soaring fortunes of American Tobacco led to a dramatic increase in the amount of those bonuses. By 1930, the bonus paid to George W. Hill, the president of American Tobacco, reached $842,507. A shareholder brought a derivative suit to recover allegedly excessive compensation paid to Hill and five American Tobacco vice presidents. In *Rogers v. Hill*, 289 U.S. 582, 53 S.Ct. 731, 77 L.Ed. 1385 (1933), the Supreme Court, reversing a Second Circuit decision dismissing plaintiff's complaint, stated:

> It follows from what has been shown that when adopted the by-law was valid. But plaintiff alleges that the measure of compensation fixed by it is not now equitable or fair. And he prays that the

court fix and determine the fair and reasonable compensation of the individual defendants, respectively, for each of the years in question. The allegations of the complaint are not sufficient to permit consideration by the court of the validity or reasonableness of any of the payments of account of fixed salaries, or of special credits, or of the allotments of stock therein mentioned. Indeed, plaintiff alleges that other proceedings have been instituted for the restoration of special credits, and his suits to invalidate the stock allotments were recently considered here. *Rogers v. Guaranty Trust Co.*, 288 U.S. 123, 53 S.Ct. 295, 77 L.Ed. 652. The only payments that plaintiff by this suit seeks to have restored to the company are the payments made to the individual defendants under the by-law.

We come to consider whether these amounts are subject to examination and revision in the District Court. As the amounts payable depend upon the gains of the business, the specified percentages are not per se unreasonable. The by-law was adopted in 1912 by an almost unanimous vote of the shares represented at the annual meeting and presumably the stockholders supporting the measure acted in good faith and according to their best judgment. * * * Plaintiff does not complain of any [payments] made prior to 1921. Regard is to be had to the enormous increase of the company's profits in recent years. The 2½ per cent yielded President Hill $447,870.30 in 1929 and $842,507.72 in 1930. The 1½ per cent yielded to each of the vice-presidents, Neiley and Riggio, $115,141.86 in 1929 and $409,495.25 in 1930 and for these years payments under the by-law were in addition to the cash credits and fixed salaries shown in the statement.

While the amounts produced by the application of the prescribed percentages give rise to no inference of actual or constructive fraud, the payments under the by-law have by reason of increase of profits become so large as to warrant investigation in equity in the interest of the company. Much weight is to be given to the action of the stockholders, and the by-law is supported by the presumption of regularity and continuity. But the rule prescribed by it cannot, against the protest of a shareholder, be used to justify payments of sums as salaries so large as in substance and effect to amount to spoliation or waste of corporate property. The dissenting opinion of Judge Swan indicates the applicable rule: "If a bonus payment has no relation to the value of services for which it is given, it is in reality a gift in part and the majority stockholders have no power to give away corporate property against the protest of the minority." 60 F.2d 109, 113. The facts alleged by plaintiff are sufficient to require that the District Court, upon a consideration of all the relevant facts brought forward by the parties, determine whether and to what extent payments to the individual defendants under the by-law constitute misuse and waste of the money of the corporation. * * *

*Id.* at 590–92.

Other shareholders subsequently sued to recover bonus payments made in later years. In *Heller v. Boylan*, 29 N.Y.S.2d 653 (Sup.Ct.1941), *aff'd mem.* 263 App.Div. 815, 32 N.Y.S.2d 131 (1st Dept.1941), the court rejected their attack, stating:

> Yes, the Court possesses the *power* to prune these payments, but openness forces the confession that the pruning would be synthetic and artificial rather than analytic or scientific. Whether or not it would be fair and just, is highly dubious. Yet, merely because the problem is perplexing is no reason for eschewing it. It is not timidity, however, which perturbs me. It is finding a rational or just gauge for revising these figures were I inclined to do so. No blueprints are furnished. The elements to be weighed are incalculable; the imponderables, manifold. To act out of whimsy or caprice or arbitrariness would be more than inexact—it would be the precise antithesis of justice; it would be a farce.

> If comparisons are to be made, with whose compensation are they to be made—executives? Those connected with the motion picture industry? Radio artists? Justices of the Supreme Court of the United States? The President of the United States? Manifestly, the material at hand is not of adequate plasticity for fashioning into a pattern or standard. Many instances of positive underpayment will come to mind, just as instances of apparent rank overpayment abound. Haplessly, intrinsic worth is not always the criterion. A classic might perhaps produce trifling compensation for its author, whereas a popular novel might yield a titanic fortune. Merit is not always commensurately rewarded, whilst mediocrity sometimes unjustly brings incredibly lavish returns. Nothing is so divergent and contentious and inexplicable as values.

> Courts are ill-equipped to solve or even to grapple with these entangled economic problems. Indeed, their solution is not within the juridical province. Courts are concerned that corporations be honestly and fairly operated by its directors, with the observance of the formal requirements of the law; but what is reasonable compensation for its officers is primarily for the stockholders. This does not mean that fiduciaries are to commit waste, or misuse or abuse trust property, with impunity. A just cause will find the Courts at guard and implemented to grant redress. But the stockholder must project a less amorphous plaint than is here presented.

> On this branch of the case, I find for the defendants. Yet it does not follow that I affirmatively approve these huge payments. It means that I cannot by any reliable standard find them to be waste or spoliation; it means that I find no valid ground for disapproving what the great majority of stockholders have approved. In the circumstances, if a ceiling for these bonuses is to be erected, the stockholders who built and are responsible for the present structure must be the architects. Finally, it is not amiss to accent the antiseptic policy stressed by Judge Liebell in *Winkelman et al. v.*

*General Motors Corporation,* D.C.S.D.N.Y. decided August 14, 1940, 39 F.Supp. 826, that: "The duty of the director executives participating in the bonus seems plain—they should be the first to consider unselfishly whether under all the circumstances their bonus allowances are fair and reasonable".

*Id.* at 679–80.

### Note: Recent Developments

In the years following the American Tobacco litigation, most publicly-held corporations followed the practice of seeking approval of executive compensation plans from disinterested directors, disinterested shareholders, or both, so as to minimize the possibility of successful legal challenges. By securing such approval, corporations placed on shareholders who wished to challenge such a plan the burden of proving that it involved waste. *See* Section D. Courts rarely allowed complaints challenging such plans as wasteful to survive motions to dismiss. The courts' attitude is perhaps best exemplified by Chancellor Allen's decision holding that a grant of immediately exercisable stock options is not corporate waste if "there is some rational basis for directors to conclude that the amount and form of compensation is appropriate." *Steiner v. Meyerson,* 1995 WL 441999 (Del.Ch.1995). Chancellor Allen observed:

> Absent an allegation of fraud or conflict of interest courts will not review the substance of corporate contracts; the waste theory represents a theoretical exception to the statement very rarely encountered in the world of real transactions. There surely are cases of fraud; of unfair self-dealing and, much more rarely negligence. But rarest of all—and indeed, like Nessie, possibly non-existent— would be the case of disinterested business people making non-fraudulent deals (non-negligently) that meet the legal standard of waste!

*Id.* at *5.

The courts' *laissez faire* attitude no doubt encouraged many executives to seek additional compensation. At the same time, commentators and consultants were urging corporations to attempt to align executives' interests with the interests of shareholders by offering executives highly contingent, long-term incentive compensation tied to the price of their corporation's stock. Boards of directors responded by authorizing, or urging shareholders to authorize, generous stock option plans. These plans, plus the rapid rise stock prices in the mid–1990s, led to sharp increases in the compensation paid to corporate executives, and, in particular, to CEOs. *Business Week* reported that CEOs' average total compensation increased 30% in 1995 and "an astounding 54% [in 1996]; to $5,781.300." *Executive Pay: It's Out of Control,* Business Week 58, 59 (Apr. 21, 1997.) Reflecting growing criticism of executive compensation, the front cover of the same issue of *Business Week* trumpeted: "By relying heavily on stock options, many companies make exorbitant payouts for so-so performance, dilute real shareholder return, and glorify CEOs at the expense of other employees." *Id.*, front cover.

Similarly, Graef Crystal, a former executive compensation consultant turned critic, reported that in the roughly 1,000 publicly-held companies he analyzed, 60 CEOs were paid more than $10 million in 1996 and 17 were paid more than $20 million. Crystal further observed:

> * * * [T]he variability of pay from one company to another is amazing. For 1996, 42 percent of the variation in CEO pay levels could be accounted for by company size and performance. Bigger companies pay a lot more than smaller companies, while better performing companies pay a tiny bit more than worse-performing companies. But that leaves 58 percent of the variation in pay unexplained. *It seems completely random.*

Graef Crystal, *Maximum Wage*, Slate (<http://www.slate.com.>) (July 17, 1997) (emphasis added).

Two other scholars observe that "high powered incentive contracts * * * create enormous opportunities for self dealing for the managers, especially if these contracts are negotiated with poorly motivated boards of directors * * *." Andrei Shleifer & Robert W. Vishny, *A Survey of Corporate Governance* 14 (NBER Working Paper 5554, April 1996). They note a recent research paper that found managers often receive stock option grants shortly before good news is announced and delay such grants until after bad news is announced. They suggest "that options are often not so much an incentive device as a somewhat covert mechanism of self-dealing." *Id.*

It is difficult to assess what impact this cascade of criticism is having, or should have, on courts' attitude toward shareholder suits challenging executive compensation plans. *Cf.* Detlev Vagts, *Challenges to Executive Compensation: For the Markets or the Courts*?, 8 J. Corp.L. 231 (1983). In *Zupnick v. Goizueta*, 698 A.2d 384 (Del.Ch.1997), Vice Chancellor Chandler, relying on *Steiner v. Meyerson*, *supra*, held that a complaint alleging that Coca Cola's grant to Robert Goizueta, its CEO, of options to purchase one million shares of Coca Cola stock did not state a cause of action for waste, even though the grant was largely designed to compensate Mr. Goizueta for his past performance. The court noted that during the period Mr. Goizueta had served as CEO, the market value of Coke's outstanding stock had increased by nearly $69 billion.

On the other hand, the following may suggest a shift in the attitude of Chancellor Allen, who wrote *Steiner*, and may augur a shift in the attitude of other judges as well.

# LEWIS v. VOGELSTEIN

699 A.2d 327, 336–339 (Del.Ch.1997).*

## III.

### C.  Ratification of Officer or Director Option Grants

Let me turn now to the history of the Delaware law treating shareholder ratification of corporate plans that authorize the granting of stock options to corporate officers and directors. What is interesting about this law is that while it is consistent with the foregoing general treatment of shareholder ratification—*i.e.*, it appears to hold that informed, non-coerced ratification validates any such plan or grant, unless the plan is wasteful—in its earlier expressions, the waste standard used by the courts in fact was not a waste standard at all, but was a form of "reasonableness" or proportionality review.

1. *Development of Delaware law of option compensation*: It is fair to say I think that Delaware law took a skeptical or suspicious stance towards the innovation of stock option compensation as it developed in a major way following World War II. *See, e.g., Kerbs, et al. v. California Eastern Airways, Inc.*, Del.Supr., 90 A.2d 652 (1952); *Gottlieb v. Heyden Chem. Corp.*, Del.Supr., 91 A.2d 57 (1952); *Id.*, 90 A.2d 660 (1952); *Id.*, Del.Ch., 99 A.2d 507 (1953). Such skepticism is a fairly natural consequence of the common law of director compensation and of the experience that corporate law judges had over the decades with schemes to water stock or to divert investors funds into the hands of promoters or management.

The early Delaware cases on option compensation established that, even in the presence of informed ratification, in order for stock option grants to be valid a two part test had to be satisfied. First it was seen as necessary that the court conclude that the grant contemplates that the corporation will receive "sufficient consideration." *E.g., Kerbs*, at 90 A.2d 652, 656 (1952). "Sufficient consideration" as employed in the early cases does not seem like a waste standard: "Sufficient consideration to the corporation may be, inter alia, the retention of the services of an employee, or the gaining of the services of a new employee, *provided there is a reasonable relationship between the value of the services … and the value of the options …*". *Kerbs* at 656 (emphasis added).

Secondly it was held early on that, in addition, the plan or the circumstances of the grant must include "conditions or the existence of circumstances which may be expected to insure that the contemplated consideration will in fact pass to the corporation." *Kerbs* at 656 (emphasis added). Elsewhere the Supreme Court spoke of "circumstances which may reasonably be regarded as *sufficient to insure* that the corporation will receive that which it desires …". *Id.* at 657 (emphasis added).

---

* The portion of Chancellor Allen's decision describing the stock option plan at issue and holding that it should be reviewed under the waste standard is reproduced in Section D.2.c, above.—Ed.

This (1) weighing of the reasonableness of the relationship between the value of the consideration flowing both ways and (2) evaluating the sufficiency of the circumstances to insure receipt of the benefit sought, seem rather distant from the substance of a waste standard of judicial review. Indeed these tests seem to be a form of heightened scrutiny that is now sometimes referred to as an intermediate or proportionality review. *Cf. Unocal Corp. v. Mesa Petroleum, Co.*, [(Chapter 22)]: *Paramount Communications v. QVC Network*, [(Chapter 22)].

In all events, these tests were in fact operationally very problematic. Valuing an option grant (as part of a reasonable relationship test) is quite difficult, even under today's more highly developed techniques of financial analysis. This would be especially true where, as this case exemplifies, the options are tied to and conditioned upon a continued status as an officer or director. Even more problematic is valuing—or judicially reviewing a judgment of equivalency of value of—the future benefits that the corporation hopes to obtain from the option grant. There is no objective metric to gauge *ex ante* incentive effects of owning options by officers or directors. Beyond this operational problem, the approach of these early option cases may be thought to raise the question, why was it necessary for the court reviewing a stock option grant to conclude that the circumstances "insure" that the corporation will receive the benefits it seeks to achieve. In other contexts, even where interested transactions are involved, a fair (*i.e.*, valid and enforceable) contract might contemplate payment in exchange for a probability of corporation benefit. A corporation, for example, certainly could acquire from an officer or director at a fair price a property interest that had only prospective commercial value.

In *Beard v. Elster*, Del.Supr., 160 A.2d 731 (1960), the Delaware Supreme Court relaxed slightly the general formulation of *Kerbs*, et al., and rejected the reading of *Kerbs* to the effect that the corporation had to have (or insure receipt of) *legally cognizable* consideration in order to make an option grant valid. The court also emphasized the effect that approval by an independent board or committee might have. It held that what was necessary to validate an officer or director stock option grant was a finding that a reasonable board could conclude from the circumstances that the corporation may reasonably expect to receive a proportionate benefit. A good faith determination by a disinterested board or committee to that effect, at least when ratified by a disinterested shareholder vote, entitled such a grant to business judgment protection (i.e., classic waste standard). After *Beard*, judicial review of officer and director option grants sensibly focused in practice less on attempting independently to assess whether the corporation in fact would receive proportionate value, and more on the procedures used to authorize and ratify such grants. But *Beard* addressed only a situation in which an independent committee of the board functioned on the question.

2. *Current law on ratification effect on option grants*: A substantive question that remains however is whether in practice the waste standard that is utilized where informed shareholders ratify a grant of options

adopted and recommended by a self-interested board is the classical waste test (i.e., no consideration; gift; no person of ordinary prudence could possibly agree, etc.) or whether, in fact, it *is a species of intermediate review* in which the court assesses reasonableness in relationship to perceived benefits.

The Supreme Court has not expressly deviated from the "proportionality" approach to waste of its earlier decision, although in recent decades it has had few occasions to address the subject. In *Michelson v. Duncan*, Del.Supr., 407 A.2d 211 (1979), a stock option case in which ratification had occurred, however, the court repeatedly referred to the relevant test where ratification had occurred as that of "gift or waste" and plainly meant by waste, the absence of *any consideration* (" . . . when there are issues of fact as to the *existence of consideration*, a full hearing is required regardless of shareholder ratification." 407 A.2d at 223). Issues of "sufficiency" of consideration or adequacy of assurance that a benefit or proportionate benefit would be achieved were not referenced.

The Court of Chancery has interpreted the waste standard in the ratified option context as invoking not a proportionality or reasonableness test a la *Kerbs* but the traditional waste standard referred to in *Michelson. See, e.g., Steiner v. Meyerson*, Del.Ch., C.A. No. 13139, 1995 WL 441999, Allen, C. (July 18, 1995); *Zupnick v. Goizueta*, Del.Ch., 698 A.2d 384, Jacobs, V.C. (1997) (both granting motions to dismiss shareholder claims that options grants constituted actionable waste).

In according substantial effect to shareholder ratification these more recent cases are not unmindful of the collective action problem faced by shareholders in public corporations. These problems do render the assent that ratification can afford very different in character from the assent that a single individual may give. In this age in which institutional shareholders have grown strong and can more easily communicate, however, that assent, is, I think, a more rational means to monitor compensation than judicial determinations of the "fairness," or sufficiency of consideration, which seems a useful technique principally, I suppose, to those unfamiliar with the limitations of courts and their litigation processes. In all events, the classic waste standard does afford some protection against egregious cases or "constructive fraud."

\* \* \*

Before ruling on the pending motion to dismiss the substantive claim of breach of fiduciary duty, under a waste standard, I should make one other observation. The standard for determination of motions to dismiss is of course well established and understood. Where under any state of facts consistent with the factual allegations of the complaint the plaintiff would be entitled to a judgment, the complaint may not be dismissed as legally defective. It is also the case that in some instances "mere conclusions" may be held to be insufficient to withstand an otherwise well made motion. Since what is a "well pleaded" fact and what is a "mere conclusion" is not always clear, there is often and inevitably some small room for the exercise of informed judgment by courts in determining motions to dismiss under the appropriate test. Consider for example allegations that an arm's-length corporate transaction constitutes a waste of assets. Such an allegation is inherently factual and not easily amenable to determination on a motion to dismiss and indeed often not on a motion for summary judgment. Yet it cannot be the case that allegations of the facts of any (or every) transaction coupled with a statement that the transaction constitutes a waste of assets, necessarily states a claim upon which discovery may be had; such a rule would, in this area, constitute an undue encouragement to strike suits. Certainly some set of facts, if true, may be said as a matter of law not to constitute waste. For example, a claim that the grant of options on stock with a market price of say $5,000 to a corporate director, exercisable at a future time, if the optionee is still an officer or director of the issuer, constitutes a corporate waste, would in my opinion be subject to dismissal on motion, despite the contextual nature of judgments concerning waste. *See Steiner v. Meyerson, supra; Zupnick v. Goizueta, supra.* In some instances the facts alleged, if true, will be so far from satisfying the waste standard that dismissal is appropriate.

This is not such a case in my opinion. Giving the pleader the presumptions to which he is entitled on this motion, I cannot conclude that no set of facts could be shown that would permit the court to conclude that the grant of these options, particularly focusing upon the one-time options, constituted an exchange to which no reasonable person not acting under compulsion and in good faith could agree. In so concluding, I do not mean to suggest a view that these grants are suspect, only that one time option grants to directors of this size seem at this point sufficiently unusual to require the court to refer to evidence before making an adjudication of their validity and consistency with fiduciary duty. Thus, for that reason the motion to dismiss will be denied. It is so Ordered.

# G. CORPORATE OPPORTUNITY

The corporate opportunity doctrine is a branch of the duty of loyalty. The doctrine forbids a director, officer, or managerial employee from diverting to herself a business opportunity that "belongs" to the corporation. As one of the leading cases, *Guth v. Loft,* 5 A.2d 503, 511 (Del.1939), noted, a corporate fiduciary cannot take a business opportunity for herself if it is one that the corporation can financially undertake; is within the line of the corporation's business and is advantageous to the corporation; and is one in which the corporation has an interest or a reasonable expectancy.

As with so much else in the duty of loyalty, the proposition is relatively simple to state and difficult to apply. The problem is to separate "opportunities" that should be turned over to the corporation from those that can properly be exploited by the individual. The issue arises because a corporation can only act through its agents, some of whom may have interests outside the corporation. When a business opportunity is presented to such a person (usually a director or officer), is she free to accept it for herself, or must she first offer it to the corporation? And which opportunities that belong to the corporation may she nevertheless take because the corporation, for some reason, is unable to do so?

To answer these questions, one must balance a number of interests. First, the corporation must ensure that its managers and its resources are directed to furthering its own legitimate business interests. Those in positions of trust and confidence cannot be permitted to abuse their positions to further their own economic interests at the expense of their employers. On the other hand, by cordoning off a class of business opportunities as belonging to the corporation, the doctrine effectively prohibits managers from competing with the corporation by using those opportunities, even in the absence of an explicit non-competition agreement. Larger social interests therefore, are implicated as well. Society benefits when the party best able to take advantage of an opportunity is permitted to pursue it. If the definition of a corporate opportunity is too broad, society suffers because competition is chilled. Those with specialized abilities to recognize entrepreneurial opportunities will be forced by artificial pressures to forego exploiting them.

The corporate opportunity doctrine differs from other types of fiduciary duties with respect to the harm that the corporation suffers. In every other breach of fiduciary duty, actual harm to the corporation must be shown. With a corporate opportunity, however, the harm to the corporation is not actual; the breach arises because the corporate manager took the opportunity for herself and failed to present it to the corporation. Had she presented it, the corporation might have rejected it; had the corporation accepted it, the opportunity might not have been profitable. This last aspect of the doctrine is most relevant in determining the appropriate remedy for the unlawful taking of a corporate opportunity.

## PROBLEM
### STARCREST CORPORATION—PART II

A little over a year ago, Starcrest Corporation, which constructs, owns and operates hotels and restaurants throughout the United States, began to discuss the possibility of buying or building a gambling casino. After a management presentation to the directors on the advantages and disadvantages of such a step, the board authorized the officers to begin an active search for specific prospects. Management's initial investigations in the United States turned up nothing that seemed appropriate.

Robert White, a director of Starcrest, has extensive personal investments in a variety of fields, including substantial real estate holdings. He is also the president and chairman of the board of Petro Investments, Inc., a holding company whose assets are invested primarily in real estate. Shortly after the board meeting at which the directors of Starcrest were informed of management's initial investigations, White met an old business acquaintance while on a trip to the Bahamas. White's friend told him that a casino there had just come on the market at what the friend said was a very attractive price. The friend further advised White that if he acted quickly the seller would take $10 million in cash for the casino. White immediately called the real estate broker who was handling the casino, and within two days signed a contract on behalf of Petro to purchase it. Twelve months later, Petro resold the casino at a $6 million profit.

Beatrice Parker, a Starcrest shareholder, who has recounted essentially these facts and has asked you about the possibility of success of a derivative suit against White. How should you advise her under the traditional corporate opportunity doctrine? The ALI's version of the corporate opportunity doctrine? What additional information would you need to know?

## 1. TRADITIONAL CORPORATE OPPORTUNITY DOCTRINE

### FARBER v. SERVAN LAND COMPANY, INC.

662 F.2d 371 (5th Cir.1981).

[In 1959, Charles Serianni and other investors formed Servan Land Company,(Servan) to build and operate a golf course and country club near Fort Lauderdale, Florida. Serianni and A.I. Savin owned a majority of the stock and were Servan's principal officers. There were eight other stockholders, including Jack Farber, the plaintiff in this action. Servan acquired 160 acres of land on which to build the course and, shortly thereafter acquired an additional twenty acres abutting the course.

At the 1968 annual stockholders' meeting, a Servan director and stockholder said that James Farquhar, the vendor of the twenty acre tract, was willing to sell another 160 acres of abutting land to the corporation that was suitable for use as an additional golf course. After some discussion, the stockholders took no action to authorize the purchase of the land. In March 1969, Serianni and Savin, in their individual capacities, bought the 160 acres that had been discussed at the stockholders' meeting.

There was no discussion of the purchase at the 1969 annual stockholders' meeting, held in April 1969. In 1970, Farber learned of the purchase from a third party, and at the annual stockholders' meeting, he inquired about it. Savin and Serianni acknowledged the purchase, but there is conflicting evidence as to whether the stockholders ratified the purchase.

In 1973, Serianni, Savin and the corporation entered into an agreement with a purchaser to sell as a package the corporation's assets and the 160 acres of adjoining land Serianni and Savin had bought; each contract of sale was conditioned upon execution of the other. Of the aggregate sales price, the defendants allocated $5,000,000 to the corporation and $3,353,700 to Savin and Serianni, though this division was not based on any appraisal of the respective properties.

At a special directors' and stockholders' meeting, all the stockholders except Farber approved the sale and voted to liquidate Servan. After the sale was completed Farber brought a derivative suit alleging that Savin and Serianni's purchase constituted the taking of a corporate opportunity. Farber also sought appointment of an appraiser to determine the proper allocation of the purchase price.

The district court found that Serianni had been the "driving force" of Servan from its inception. The court also found that, although there was a possibility of real estate development, such development was not one of the purposes for which Servan had been formed. After reviewing the events of the 1968 stockholders' meeting, the court said that Serianni and Savin should have called a special stockholders' meeting to give the stockholders the opportunity to have the corporation purchase the land before Serianni and Savin did so individually. The court noted, however, that the corporation benefitted from their purchase because the entire package was worth more when the assets and real estate were sold in 1973. Finally, the court found that Farber was entitled to an appraisal to determine whether the corporation should have received a larger portion of the total sale price of the properties than the $5 million allocated by Serianni and Savin.

The appraiser subsequently valued the corporation's properties at $4,065,915, and the Serianni–Savin property at $3,950,925. Thus Serianni and Savin had allotted to the corporation a greater percentage of the proceeds of the sale than would have been allocated using the appraiser's figures.

After the appraisal, the district court issued a memorandum opinion which set forth its earlier findings and incorporated the results of the appraisal. The court again noted that Servan had profited from the purchase by Serianni and Savin. It also found that the acreage did not constitute a corporate opportunity because the property bore no substantial relationship to Servan's primary purpose of operating a golf course. Thus the purchase was not "antagonistic to any significant corporate purpose."]

TJOFLAT, CIRCUIT JUDGE:

I

* * *

Farber appealed the district court's decision, and this court vacated and remanded it for clarification, stating: "if, as seems to be clearly expressed, there was no corporate opportunity, why should, as is three times stated, Serianni and Savin have offered the 160 adjacent acres to the corporation? The holdings are inconsistent." *Farber v. Servan Land Co., Inc.*, 541 F.2d 1086, 1088 (5th Cir.1976). * * * We stated:

If the corporate opportunity doctrine is otherwise applicable it is not made inapplicable by the realization of a substantial gain from a fortuitous sale of its assets at the same time as the sale of the property asserted to be a corporate opportunity to a lone buyer who would not have bought either property without the other. If a corporate opportunity existed the corporation and its stockholders would have been entitled to the profits from the sale of both parcels.

*Id.*

On remand, the district court failed to explain why it found that Serianni and Savin had a duty to offer the opportunity to purchase the 160 acres to the corporation, but it reaffirmed its finding that "Seriani (sic) and Savin had satisfactorily sustained the burden of establishing the propriety of the transaction." * * *

Farber appeals once again.

## II

In reviewing the district court's decision we must evaluate its resolution of four key issues: whether a corporate opportunity existed; whether the stockholders declined the opportunity by failing to act; whether the stockholders ratified Serianni and Savin's purchase; and whether the subsequent benefit the corporation received in selling its assets in conjunction with Serianni and Savin's 160 acres rectifies any wrong it might have suffered through the defendants' initial purchase of the land.

### A. THE EXISTENCE OF A CORPORATE OPPORTUNITY

In Florida, a corporate director or officer "occupies a quasi-fiduciary relation to the corporation and the existing stockholders. He is bound to act with fidelity and the utmost good faith." *Flight Equipment & Engineering Corp. v. Shelton*, 103 So.2d 615, 626 (Fla.1958). Because he "occupies a fiduciary relationship to the corporation, (he) will not be allowed to act in hostility to it by acquiring for his own benefit any intangible assets of the corporation * * *. He cannot make a private profit from his position or, while acting in that capacity, acquire an interest adverse to that of the corporation * * *." *Pruyser v. Johnson*, 185 So.2d 516, 521 (Fla.App.1966).

If one occupying a fiduciary relationship to a corporation acquires, "in opposition to the corporation, property in which the corporation has an interest or tangible expectancy or which is essential to its existence," he violates what has come to be known as the "doctrine of 'corporate opportunity'." * * * Florida has long recognized the doctrine of corporate opportunity, and has described a corporate opportunity as a business opportunity in which the corporation has an interest for a "valid and significant corporate purpose." *Pan American Trading & Trapping v. Crown Paint, Inc.*, 99 So.2d 705, 706 (Fla.1957). The opportunity need not be "of the utmost importance to the welfare of the corporation," *Pan American*, 99 So.2d at 706, to be protected from preemption by the corporation's directors and officers. As we elaborated in the first appeal of this case, however, the opportunity must "fit into the present activities of the corporation or fit into an established corporate policy which the acquisition of the opportunity would forward." *Farber*, 541 F.2d at 1088.

In its initial opinion the district court found that no corporate opportunity existed:

> The court finds the possibility of real estate development was contemplated by the stockholders. For example, Mr. Forman testified, via deposition, that scarcely a meeting of the stockholders occurred without discussing the acquiring of additional property from Mr. Farquhar. However, the possibility of real estate development would always be in the minds of a group of affluent businessmen. This does not mean that real estate development was actually part of the corporate purpose and the court specifically finds that real estate development was not a purpose for which the corporation was formed * * *.

> The mere fact that the land was adjacent to the corporate land in itself does not support a conclusion that therefore the acreage was a corporate opportunity. The property had no substantial relation to the corporation's primary purpose of operating a golf course and the individual purpose was not antagonistic to any significant corporate purpose and thus the facts do not fall within the general proposition that an officer of a corporation cannot acquire title to or an interest in property prejudicial to the corporation.

*Farber v. Servan Land Co., Inc.*, 393 F.Supp. at 635, 638. We find that the district court's findings of fact do not support its legal conclusion that the opportunity to buy Farquhar's 160 acres was not a corporate opportunity.

It should be noted that the district court not only found that the stockholders frequently discussed acquisition of Mr. Farquhar's land at their meetings; it also found that the stockholders had discussed this matter at the last meeting, just shortly before Serianni and Savin made their purchase, and that they had "indicated a sense of approval to the idea of acquiring abutting land from Mr. Farquhar." Further, the court heard testimony that the corporation needed the land on the perimeter of the golf course, and evidence that the corporation had bought additional land from Mr. Farquhar in the past and that it had bought and operated a lodge located on part of that land. These facts make it clear that the opportunity to acquire the Farquhar land was an advantageous one that fit into a present, significant corporate purpose, as well as an ongoing corporate policy, and that the corporation had an active interest in it. Accordingly, the opportunity to buy the land constituted a corporate opportunity.

B. WHETHER THE STOCKHOLDERS DECLINED THE OPPORTUNITY

In addition to finding that no corporate opportunity existed, the district court found that if one did exist, "it was rejected by the corporation." The court apparently reached this conclusion because after deciding at their annual meeting that the opportunity to purchase the land should be investigated, the stockholders did not vote, at that meeting, to commit the funds available from the refinancing to purchase the Farquhar property. We find that this failure does not indicate a decision to refrain from pursuing the opportunity to purchase. Indeed, since the stockholders apparently lacked specific information about Mr. Farquhar's terms of sale, it would have been illogical to make a commitment of funds at that time. It is true that there is no evidence to indicate that the stockholders undertook formal investigation of the potential purchase between the time of the meeting and the time of Serianni and Savin's purchase. It should be noted, however, that Serianni was the president of the corporation and the only active director. The other stockholders customarily relied upon him to exercise the executive powers of the corporation, since most of them resided in other states. Because the other stockholders relied upon Serianni to initiate the investigation on the corporation's behalf, he may not now translate his own inaction into a corporate rejection of the opportunity, thus allowing him to buy the land personally. The district court's finding that the corporation rejected the opportunity is clearly erroneous.

### C. Ratification of the Purchase

As another ground for its decision, the district court held that the stockholders ratified Serianni and Savin's purchase at their May 9, 1970 meeting. Farber attacks this finding on two grounds. First, he argues that it was clearly erroneous to rely on the corporate minutes, which indicated a vote to ratify, rather than on his court reporter's transcript of the meeting, which indicates no ratification attempt.

The district court received adequate evidence that the corporate minutes were valid and reliable. This left it with an issue of credibility, and this court, on appeal, cannot say that the district judge's decision to rely on the corporate minutes was clearly erroneous. This is especially so since official minutes of corporate meetings are generally considered the best evidence of corporate business transacted.

Farber also argues that even if the ratification vote did take place, it cannot be used to prohibit his derivative action. We agree. When ratification is possible and the proceedings are proper, stockholders may sanction the act of a corporate officer or director and thus abolish any cause of action that the corporation might have against that individual. Not all acts may be ratified, and the Florida courts have not indicated whether stockholders are capable of ratifying a director or officer's breach of fiduciary duty. We do not need to decide whether ratification was possible here, however, because even if it was, the manner of ratification in this case renders the ratification a nullity.

According to the corporate minutes, all of the directors present at the annual meeting, except the plaintiff, voted to ratify the land purchase. Both of the purchasing directors were present, and between the two of them, they held four-sevenths of the stock. While it is true that directors ordinarily may vote their stock on measures in which they have a personal interest, most authorities agree that " '(t)he violation of their duty by corporate directors cannot be ratified by the action of those who were guilty of participation in the wrongful acts, even though they constitute a majority of the directors or of the stockholders.' "*Chesapeake Construction Corp. v. Rodman*, 256 Md. 531, 537, 261 A.2d 156, 159 (Md.App.1970) (quoting 19 C.J.S. CORPORATIONS § 763(b) at p. 112). Thus, Serianni and Savin may not bind Farber by ratifying their own inappropriate acts. Farber is entitled to bring a derivative action.

### D. THE EFFECT OF BENEFIT TO THE CORPORATION

Finally, in finding in favor of the defendants, the district court relied heavily on the notion that by valuing the two properties favorably for the corporation when they were sold jointly, and by selling the properties together, thus raising the value of each, Serianni and Savin benefitted the corporation. This benefit, according to the court, precluded any recovery for breach of fiduciary duty in obtaining the Farquhar acres in the first place.

As we stated in the first appeal, however:

> If the corporate opportunity doctrine is otherwise applicable it is not made inapplicable by the realization of a substantial gain from a fortuitous sale of its assets at the same time as the sale of the property asserted to be a corporate opportunity to a lone buyer who would not have bought either property without the other. *If a corporate opportunity existed the corporation and its stockholders would have been entitled to the profits from the sale of both parcels.*

*Farber*, 541 F.2d at 1088 (emphasis added).

Further, it has already been established that Serianni and Savin apportioned the proceeds of the joint sale without the benefit of an appraisal of the individual properties. While it may be to their credit that they overvalued the corporate property in the apportionment, they have not contended, nor has the district court found, that this overvaluation constituted a deliberate settlement between the parties for damages incurred in the defendants' acquisition of the Farquhar property. Despite the undervaluation of their own property relative to the corporation's assets, Serianni and Savin made a handsome profit on the sale. The two directors must hold those profits in trust for the corporation.

### III

We find that the opportunity to buy Mr. Farquhar's 160 acres constituted a corporate opportunity and that the defendants, Serianni and Savin, breached their fiduciary duties to the corporation by preempting that opportunity. We also find that the attempted ratification of the preemption does not preclude Farber from bringing a derivative suit on behalf of the corporation.

The corporation is entitled to the profits of the directors' subsequent sale of the 160 acres. We remand the case to the district court to determine the proper amount of damages and the appropriate method for distributing those damages.

REVERSED AND REMANDED.

## 2. WHAT IS A CORPORATE OPPORTUNITY?

Courts have traditionally used one or more tests to determine whether a corporate opportunity exists: (1) interest or expectancy; (2) line of business; (3) fairness; and (4) a combination of these tests.

### A. INTEREST OR EXPECTANCY

The interest or expectancy analysis is the earliest to have developed. See, e.g., *Lagarde v. Anniston Lime & Stone Co.*, 126 Ala. 496, 28 So. 199 (1900). This is the test applied in *Farber*. In *Litwin v. Allen*, 25 N.Y.S.2d 667, 686 (Sup.Ct.1940) the court suggested how to discern whether the corporation has an interest or expectancy:

> This corporate right or expectancy, this mandate upon directors to act for the corporation, may arise from various circumstances, such as, for example, the fact that directors had undertaken to negotiate in the field on behalf of the corporation, or that the corporation was in need of the particular business opportunity to the knowledge of the directors, or that the business opportunity was seized and developed at the expense, and with the facilities of the corporation. It is noteworthy that in cases which have imposed this type of liability upon fiduciaries, the thing determined by the court to be the subject of the trust was a thing of special and unique value to the [beneficiary]; for example, real estate, a proprietary formula valuable to the corporation's business, patents indispensable or valuable to its business, a competing enterprise or one required for the growth and expansion of the corporation's business or the like.

Because of its indeterminacy, the "interest or expectancy" standard has proved difficult to apply. The concept appears to be "something much less tenable than ownership—less than a legal right to exclude independent third parties from acquiring the project; and less even contingent contractual claims." Victor Brudney & Robert Charles Clark, *A New Look at Corporate Opportunities*, 94 HARV.L.REV. 997, 1013–14 (1981) ("Brudney & Clark").

### B. LINE OF BUSINESS

Under the line of business test, a corporation has a prior claim to a business opportunity presented to an officer or director that falls within the firm's line of business. The test is closely related to the "interest or expectancy" standard; indeed, some courts use both terms in determining the existence of a corporate opportunity. In *Guth v. Loft*, 23 Del.Ch. 255, 5 A.2d 503, 514 (1939), the court explained the concept as follows:

> * * * The phrase is not within the field of precise definition, nor is it one that can be bounded by a set formula. It has a flexible meaning, which is to be applied reasonably and sensibly to the facts

and circumstances of the particular case. Where a corporation is engaged in a certain business, and an opportunity is presented to it embracing an activity as to which it has fundamental knowledge, practical experience and ability to pursue, which, logically and naturally is adaptable to its business having regard for its financial position, and is one that is consonant with its reasonable needs and aspirations for expansion, it may be properly said that the opportunity is in the line of the corporation's business.

Courts typically apply the test to extend beyond a corporation's existing operations. The rationale for such an application is simple. Courts recognize that corporations are dynamic entities. Furthermore, shareholders reasonably expect that a corporation will go beyond the status quo and take advantage of highly profitable, but safe, opportunities. Note, *When Opportunity Knocks: An Analysis of the Brudney and Clark and ALI Principles of Corporate Governance Proposals for Deciding Corporate Opportunity Claims*, 11 J.Corp.L. 255, 258 (1986).

The line of business test also is problematic in many situations. It often may be difficult to determine whether the corporation's shareholders reasonably expected that every opportunity within the corporation's line of business would first be offered to the corporation.

## C.  FAIRNESS: ALONE OR IN COMBINATION WITH OTHER STANDARDS

Some courts prefer a fairness test. In *Durfee v. Durfee & Canning, Inc.*, 80 N.E.2d 522, 529 (Mass.1948), the court stated:

> * * * [T]he true basis of the governing doctrine [of corporate opportunity] rests fundamentally on the unfairness in the particular circumstances of a director, whose relation to the corporation is fiduciary, taking advantage of an opportunity * * * when the interests of the corporation justly call for protection. This calls for the application of ethical standards of what is fair and equitable * * * [in] particular sets of facts.

The fairness test is premised on removing the temptation for officers and directors to breach their fiduciary duty by making such breaches profitless. *Id.* at 528–29. However, an amorphous fairness test produces uncertainty in application and unpredictability in result. Thus, the test does not provide a reliable guide to an officer or director concerning the scope of her duty to offer a specific opportunity to the corporation.

As a consequence of this uncertainty, some courts have attempted to combine the line of business doctrine with the fairness test. In *Miller v. Miller*, 222 N.W.2d 71, 81 (Minn.1974), the court first determined when an opportunity was a corporate opportunity under the line of business test. If this test was satisfied, then under the second test, the officer or director would be liable unless she could sustain the burden of showing she did not violate her duties of good faith, loyalty, and fair dealing. The court stated that the following factors would be relevant in determining whether the taking of an opportunity was fair to the corporation:

* * * [T]he nature of the officer's relationship to the management and control of the corporation; whether the opportunity was presented to him in his official or individual capacity; his prior disclosure of the opportunity to the board of directors or shareholders and their response; whether or not he used or exploited corporate facilities, assets, or personnel in acquiring the opportunity; whether his acquisition harmed or benefited the corporation; and all other facts and circumstances bearing on an officer's good faith and whether he exercised the diligence, devotion, care and fairness toward the corporation which ordinarily prudent men would exercise under similar circumstances in like position.

*Id.* at 81–82.

The *Miller* approach appears to give an officer or director who may have usurped a corporate opportunity another line of defense under the fairness rubric. Commentators have criticized the *Miller* approach as "add[ing] only a new layer of confusion to an already murky area of the law, without forwarding the analysis in any significant fashion." Brudney & Clark, 94 HARV.L.REV. at 999 n.2. Because of the multitude of factors a trier of fact considers in determining "fairness", particularly whether an individual's usurpation of the opportunity harmed the corporation, the *Miller* test is not useful as a planning vehicle or litigation predictor. *Cf. Southeast Consultants, Inc. v. McCrary Engineering Corp.,* 273 S.E.2d 112 (Ga.1980) (substituting interest or expectancy test for line of business test in first step of the *Miller* analysis).

## D. MULTIPLE CORPORATIONS: TO WHOM IS THE DUTY OWED?

The difficulties involved in applying the line of business test are exacerbated when a director or officer holds positions in two or more corporations or is a corporate manager in one corporation and a substantial shareholder in another and dominates the latter through her ability to select its officers and directors. See Comment, *Corporate Opportunity,* 74 HARV.L.REV. 765, 770–771 (1961). In *Johnston v. Greene,* 121 A.2d 919 (Del.1956), Odlum, a financier, who was an officer and director of numerous corporations, was offered, in his individual capacity, the chance to acquire the stock of Nutt–Shel, a corporation 100% owned by Hutson, and several patents pertaining to its business. The business of Nutt–Shel had no close relation to the business of Airfleets, Inc., of which Odlum was president. Odlum turned over to Airfleets the opportunity to buy the stock of Nutt–Shel, but purchased the patents for his friends and associates and, to a limited extent, for himself. Airfleets, a corporation with a large amount of cash, possessed the financial capability to buy the patents. The board of Airfleets, dominated by Odlum, voted to buy only the stock. In a shareholders' derivative action against Odlum and the directors. the Delaware Supreme Court found that Odlum had not breached his duty in the sale of the patents. In discussing the problem of multiple conflicting loyalties, the court stated:

* * * At the time when the Nutt–Shel business was offered to Odlum, his position was this: He was the part-time president of Airfleets. He was also president of Atlas—an investment company. He was a director of other corporations and a trustee of foundations interested in making investments. If it was his fiduciary duty, upon being offered any investment opportunity, to submit it to a corporation of which he was a director, the question arises, Which corporation? Why Airfleets instead of Atlas? Why Airfleets instead of one of the foundations? So far as appears, there was no specific tie between the Nutt–Shel business and any of these corporations or foundations. Odlum testified that many of his companies had money to invest, and this appears entirely reasonable. How, then, can it be said that Odlum was under any obligation to offer the opportunity to one particular corporation? And if he was not under such an obligation, why could he not keep it for himself?

Plaintiff suggests that if Odlum elects to assume fiduciary relationships to competing corporations he must assume the obligations that are entailed by such relationships. So he must, but what are the obligations? The mere fact of having funds to invest does not ordinarily put the corporations "in competition" with each other, as that phrase is used in the law of corporate opportunity. There is nothing inherently wrong in a man of large business and financial interests serving as a director of two or more investment companies, and both Airfleets and Atlas (to mention only two companies) must reasonably have expected that Odlum would be free either to offer to any of his companies any business opportunity that came to him personally, or to retain it for himself—provided always that there was no tie between any of such companies and the new venture or any specific duty resting upon him with respect to it.

It is clear to us that the reason why the Nutt–Shel business was offered to Airfleets was because Odlum, having determined that he did not want it for himself, chose to place the investment in that one of his companies whose tax situation was best adapted to receive it. He chose to do so, although he could probably have sold the stock to an outside company at a profit to himself. If he had done so, who could have complained? If a stockholder of Airfleets could have done so, why not a stockholder of Atlas as well?

*Id.* at 924–25.

## 3. WHEN MAY A CORPORATE MANAGER TAKE AN OPPORTUNITY FOR HERSELF?

### BURG v. HORN
380 F.2d 897 (2d Cir.1967).

LUMBARD, CHIEF JUSTICE:

Darand was incorporated in September 1953 with a capital of $5500, subscribed equally by the three stockholders, Mrs. Burg and George and

Max Horn, all of whom became directors, and immediately purchased a low-rent building in Brooklyn. The Horns, who were engaged in the produce business and had already acquired three similar buildings in Brooklyn through wholly-owned corporations, urged the Burgs, who were close friends then also residing in Brooklyn, to 'get their feet wet' in real estate, and the result was the formation of Darand. The Burgs testified that they expected the Horns to offer any low-rent properties they found in Brooklyn to Darand, but that there was not discussion or agreement to that effect. The Horns carried on the active management of Darand's properties. * * *

Darand sold its first property and acquired another in 1956, and purchased two more buildings in 1959. From 1953 to 1963, nine similar properties were purchased by the Horns, individually or through wholly-owned corporations. * * *

In 1962 the Burgs moved to California, and disagreements thereafter arose between them and the Horns concerning the accounting for rent receipts and expenditures of Darand. This action seeking an accounting for receipts and expenditures and the imposition of a constructive trust on the alleged corporate opportunities was brought in 1964. After a six-day trial, [the trial judge] held that the Horns had failed to account for $7,893.36 of rent receipts for 1961–1964. This holding has not been appealed. He found, however, that there was no agreement that all low-rent buildings found by the Horns should be offered to Darand, and that the Burgs were aware of the purposes of the loans from Darand and Louis Burg and of at least some of the Horns' post-1953 acquisitions. He therefore declined to hold that those acquisitions were corporate opportunities of Darand. * * *

[There is no evidence that the properties in question were sought by or offered to Darand, or necessary to its success.] Plaintiff apparently contends that defendants were as a matter of law under a duty to acquire for Darand further properties like those it was operating. She is seemingly supported by several commentators, who have stated that any opportunity within a corporation's 'line of business' is a corporate opportunity. *E.g.*, Note, *Corporate Opportunity*, 74 HARV.L.REV. 765, 768–69 (1961); Note, *A Survey of Corporate Opportunity*, 45 GEO.L.J. 99, 100–01 (1956). This statement seems to us too broad a generalization. We think that under New York law a court must determine in each case, by considering the relationship between the director and the corporation, whether a duty to offer the corporation all opportunities within its 'line of business' is fairly to be implied. Had the Horns been full-time employees of Darand with no prior real estate ventures of their own, New York law might well uphold a finding that they were subject to such an implied duty. But as they spent most of their time in unrelated produce and real estate enterprises and already owned corporations holding similar properties when Darand was formed, as plaintiff knew, we agree with [the trial judge] that a duty to offer Darand all such properties coming to their attention cannot be implied absent some further evidence of an agreement or understanding to that effect.

\* \* \*

HAYS, CIRCUIT JUDGE (dissenting):

I dissent.

My brothers hold that the scope of a director's duty to his corporation must be measured by the facts of each case. However, although they are unable to find any New York case presenting the same facts as those before us, they conclude that New York law does not support the imposition of liability in the circumstances of this case. I do not agree.

In an often quoted passage, the New York Court of Appeals laid down the principles of fiduciary conduct:

> Many forms of conduct permissible in a workaday world for those acting at arm's length, are forbidden to those bound by fiduciary ties. A trustee is held to something stricter than the morals of the market place. Not honest alone, but the punctilio of an honor the most sensitive, is then the standard of behavior. As to this there has developed a tradition that is unbending an inveterate. Uncompromising rigidity has been the attitude of courts of equity when petitioned to undermine the rule of undivided loyalty by the "disintegrating erosion" of particular exceptions. Only thus has the level of conduct for fiduciaries been kept at a level higher than that trodden by the crowd. *Meinhard v. Salmon*, 249 N.Y. 458, 464, 164 N.E. 545, 546, 62 A.L.R.1 (1928).

Applying these standards to the instant case it seems clear that in the absence of a contrary agreement or understanding between the parties, the Horns, who were majority stockholders and managing officers of the Darand Corporation and whose primary function was to locate suitable properties for the company were under a fiduciary obligation to offer such properties to Darand before buying the properties for themselves. That the Horns used Darand's funds to effectuate certain of these purchases reinforces the conclusion that their conduct was improper and failed to comport with the standards established by law.

Since the Horns were under a fiduciary duty imposed by law not to take advantage for themselves of corporate opportunities, it is irrelevant that, as the district court found, there was no agreement under which "the Horns would contract their real estate activities or offer every property they located to Darand." *A fortiori* the Horns were not free to select the best properties for themselves.

———

## ALI, PRINCIPLES OF CORPORATE GOVERNANCE (1994)

### § 5.05   TAKING OF CORPORATE OPPORTUNITIES BY DIRECTORS OR SENIOR EXECUTIVES

(a) General Rule. A director or senior executive may not take advantage of a corporate opportunity unless:

(1) The director or senior executive first offers the corporate opportunity to the corporation and makes disclosure concerning the conflict of interest and the corporate opportunity;

(2) The corporate opportunity is rejected by the corporation; and

(3) Either:

    (A) The rejection of the opportunity is fair to the corporation;

    (B) The opportunity is rejected in advance, following such disclosure, by disinterested directors or, in the case of a senior executive who is not a director, by a disinterested superior, in a manner that satisfies the standards of the business judgment rule; or

    (C) The rejection is authorized in advance or ratified, following such disclosure, by disinterested shareholders and the rejection is not equivalent to a waste of corporate assets

(b) Definition of a Corporate Opportunity. For purposes of this Section, a corporate opportunity means:

(1) Any opportunity to engage in a business activity of which a director or senior executive becomes aware, either:

    (A) In connection with the performance of functions as a director or senior executive, or under circumstances that should reasonably lead the director or senior executive to believe that the person offering the opportunity expects it to be offered to the corporation; or

    (B) Through the use of corporate information or property, if the resulting opportunity is one that the director or senior executive should reasonably be expected to believe would be of interest to the corporation; or

(2) Any opportunity to engage in a business activity of which a senior executive becomes aware and knows is closely related to a business in which the corporation is engaged or expects to engage.

(c) Burden of Proof. A party who challenges the taking of a corporate opportunity has the burden of proof, except that if such party establishes that the requirements of Subsection (a)(3)(B) or (C) are not met, the director or the senior executive has the burden of proving that the rejection and the taking of the opportunity were fair to the corporation.

(d) Ratification of Defective Disclosure. A good faith but defective disclosure of the facts concerning the corporate opportunity may be cured if at any time (but no later than a reasonable time after suit is filed challenging the taking of the corporate opportunity) the original rejection of the corporate opportunity is ratified, following the required disclosure, by the board, the shareholders, or the corporate decisionmaker who initially approved the rejection of the corporate opportunity, or such decisionmaker's successor.

(e) Special Rule Concerning Delayed Offering of Corporate Opportunities. Relief based solely on failure to first offer an opportunity to the corporation under Subsection (a)(1) is not available if: (1) such failure resulted from a good faith belief that the business activity did not constitute a corporate opportunity, and (2) not later than a reasonable time after suit is filed challenging the taking of the corporate opportunity, the corporate opportunity is to the extent possible offered to the corporation and rejected in a manner that satisfies the standards of Subsection (a).

### Note: ALI § 5.05 and Other Approaches

Even if a manager has taken a corporate opportunity, her conduct may not constitute a breach of duty to the corporation if she can demonstrate that the corporation was precluded from taking advantage of the opportunity; that the offer came to her in her personal capacity rather than as a manager of the corporation; or that the corporation rejected the opportunity.

1. Courts differ in their willingness to consider whether the corporation is financially unable to take advantage of the opportunity either because of financial difficulty or a lack of liquid assets. In *Irving Trust Co. v. Deutsch*, 73 F.2d 121, 124 (2d Cir.1934), *rev'g in part* 2 F.Supp. 971 (S.D.N.Y.1932), *cert. denied* 294 U.S. 708, 55 S.Ct. 405, 79 L.Ed. 1243 (1935), the court stated:

> * * * Nevertheless, [these facts which raise some question whether the corporation actually lacked the funds or credit necessary for carrying out a contract] tend to show the wisdom of a rigid rule forbidding directors of a solvent corporation to take over for their own profit a corporate contract on the plea of the corporation's financial inability to perform. If the directors are uncertain whether the corporation can make the necessary outlays, they need not embark it upon the venture; if they do, they may not substitute themselves for the corporation any place along the line and divert possible benefits into their own pockets.

*Id.* at 124.

Other courts are less rigid. Some allow corporate managers to retain an opportunity if the corporation did not then "have the liquid funds available" to take advantage of it. Corporate managers must use their best efforts to uncover the financing needed by their corporation to acquire an opportunity. A director or officer, however, need not advance funds to enable a corporation to take advantage of a business opportunity. *See, A.C. Petters Co. v. St. Cloud Enterprises, Inc.*, 222 N.W.2d 83 (1974). See also *Gauger v. Hintz*, 55 N.W.2d 426 (1952).

With respect to the relevance of corporate inability to undertake an opportunity, Brudney and Clark conclude:

There is no reason to allow the diverters to exploit opportunities that they claim the corporation is unable to exploit, if the claimed inability may be feasibly eliminated. To permit claims of disability to become the subject of judicial controversy when they can only be disproved by outsiders with great difficulty and at considerable expense is to tempt participants to actions whose impropriety is visible but rarely subject to effective challenge. Availability of the defense of corporate incapacity reduces the incentive to solve corporate financing and other problems.

The argument against the defense of incapacity or disability may be less forceful for close corporations than for public corporations because of the greater familiarity of the participants with the affairs of the firm, their better access to relevant information, and the relative manageability of the problems. But the arguments against the defense are not without power in the close corporation context as well, as several courts have noted. Moreover, the possibility of obtaining consent to non-pro rata participation in a venture that the corporation appears unable to exploit should remove the seeming harshness of a rule that does not allow the defense of corporate incapacity. Indeed, rejection by the other participants of a request to assist in curing the incapacity might occur in circumstances that imply consent to the requesting person's taking the opportunity.

Brudney & Clark, 94 HARV.L.REV. at 1022. Is it possible that if the corporation is simply in serious financial difficulty or lacks liquid assets but is still a going concern, "the very existence of a prospective profit-making venture may generate additional financial backing and may convince creditors to be less importunate in their demands." Comment, *Corporate Opportunity*, 74 HARV.L.REV. 765, 772–73 (1961).

2. More important is whether the opportunity has been offered to and rejected by an independent board of directors after full disclosure. *Gaynor v. Buckley*, 203 F.Supp. 620 (D.Or.1962), *aff'd on other grounds* 318 F.2d 432 (9th Cir.1963). As a prerequisite to developing an opportunity personally, an officer or director must generally tender the opportunity to the corporation. *See, e.g., Kerrigan v. Unity Savings Ass'n*, 317 N.E.2d 39, 43–44 (1974). After an officer or director has tendered an opportunity to the corporation, it may accept or reject the opportunity.

By accepting the opportunity, the corporation precludes an officer or director from developing it individually. Rejection of an opportunity by a disinterested board usually is dispositive of a subsequent claim that the officer or director usurped a corporate opportunity.

The taking of an opportunity which has been rejected by a controlled board may be validated if the rejection is otherwise fair to the corporation. See, e.g., *Turner v. American Metal Co.*, 50 N.Y.S.2d 800, 812 (1944). See also *Johnston v.* Greene, *supra*. However, should an officer or director be allowed to prevail on a showing of fairness? One commentator has stated:

> Allowing the fiduciary to attempt to show the fairness of the diversion in these circumstances gives undeserved weight to board action that bears no resemblance to a rejection based on unfettered business judgment. Moreover, an inability to establish board domination which in fact existed would cloak the rejection with the protection of the business judgment rule. * * * Given the difficulty of proving that the board is dominated, the rejection of an opportunity by a dominated board may give the diverting party the protection of the business judgment rule. If the board is shown to be interested or dominated, the director still has the opportunity to prove the fairness of the diversion. Because of the amorphous nature of the fairness test, the diverting fiduciary may prevail even when the corporation's interests cry out for protection.

Note, *When Opportunity Knocks: An Analysis of the Brudney & Clark and ALI Principles of Corporate Governance for Deciding Corporate Opportunity Claims*, 11 J.Corp.L. 255, 272–73 (1986).

3.  Building on this analysis, the central feature of ALI § 5.05 is the strict requirement of full disclosure prior to taking advantage of any corporate opportunity. § 5.05(a)(1). "If the opportunity is not offered to the corporation, the director or senior executive will not have satisfied § 5.05(a)." *Id.* at comment to § 5.05(a). The corporation must then formally reject the opportunity. § 5.05(a)(2). To date, two courts have explicitly adopted the ALI approach. The Maine Supreme Judicial Court noted:

> * * * The disclosure-oriented approach provides a clear procedure whereby a corporate officer may insulate herself through prompt and complete disclosure from the possibility of a legal challenge. The requirement of disclosure recognizes the paramount importance of the corporate fiduciary's duty of loyalty. At the same time it protects the fiduciary's ability pursuant to the proper procedure to pursue her own business ventures free from the possibility of a lawsuit.

*Northeast Harbor Golf Club, Inc. v. Harris*, 661 A.2d 1146, 1152 (Me. 1995). *See also, Klinicki v.Lundgren*, 298 Or. 662, 695 P.2d 906 (Or. 1985) (adopting an earlier version of § 5.05 which remained unchanged).

Other courts have not been willing to make disclosure an absolute pre-requisite to the validity of the taking. In *Broz v. Cellular Information Systems, Inc.*, 673 A.2d 148 (Del.1996), the Delaware Supreme Court held that Broz, a director of Cellular Information Systems (CIS), did not usurp a corporate opportunity by acquiring a cellular telephone license for a corporation of which he was the sole shareholder. CIS itself lacked an interest in the license and did not have the financial ability to make the acquisition. It was, however, the subject of a potential acquisition by a corporation that would have wanted to acquire the license. The court found that the acquisition had come to Broz individually rather than in his capacity as a director of CIS and that he had ascertained from CIS' top management and some of its directors that CIS did not wish to acquire the license for itself. The court noted that although a director might be be shielded from liability had the director formally offered the opportunity to the corporation, there was no legal requirement that the director do so. The court recognized that the manner in which Broz had discussed the issue with the other directors did not constitute formal board assent. Nevertheless, given Broz' attempts to determine whether CIS might be interested, the court concluded that his failure to present the opportunity formally did not result in the improper usurpation of a corporate opportunity. The court declined to impose "a new requirement onto the law of corporate opportunity, *viz.*, the requirement of formal presentation under circumstances where the corporation does not have an interest, expectancy or financial ability." *Id.* at 157.

*Ostrowski v. Avery*, 703 A.2d 117 (Conn.1997) involved an alleged usurpation of a corporate opportunity by the son of the majority share-holder who consented to the development of a business venture at a time when the corporation's board had exhibited some interest in the same type of venture. The Connecticut Supreme Court found that because of the familial relationship, the consenting director could not have been considered "disinterested" and thus could not have authorized the son's pursuit of the opportunity. The court thus concluded that there had not been appropriate disclosure sufficient to justify the son's conduct.

In addressing the consequences of the failure to make adequate disclosure, the court recognized the appeal of the ALI approach and the importance of disclosure but declined to adopt § 5.05 because it offered "no opportunity to differentiate among the variety of financial circumstances in which an alleged usurpation of a corporate opportunity may arise." *Id.* at 126. Rather, the court adopted:

> * * * [T]wo major propositions of law decided by *Broz*. We agree with the principle that adequate disclosure of a corporate opportunity is an absolute defense to fiduciary liability for alleged usurpation of such a corporate opportunity. A corporate fiduciary who avails himself or herself of such a safe harbor should not be held accountable subsequently for opportunities embraced or forgone. * * * We also agree that, without prior adequate disclosure, a corporate fiduciary still may prove bona fides by clear and convincing evidence, by establishing that his or her conduct has not harmed

the corporation. We add, however, that, in assessing such harm, the trier of fact must give special weight to the effect of nondisclosure on the corporation's entrepreneurial opportunities.

*Id.* at 128.

4. It also may be significant if the opportunity has been presented to and rejected by the shareholders after full disclosure. In the context of the publicly held corporation, Brudney and Clark argue that the proxy process usually will not result in truly informed consent. They maintain that "consent to the officer's taking a corporate opportunity approaches the kind of waste for which unanimous stockholder approval is traditionally required." Brudney & Clark, 94 HARV.L.REV. at 1033. Thus, they conclude that all officers and directors, except outside directors, of public corporations should be precluded from taking any active, outside business opportunities. Several justifications are advanced for this rule. A strict rule would protect the usually powerless shareholders in public corporations from diversions of corporate assets. The scope of opportunities of public corporations suitable for exploitation is greater than in close corporations. The pursuit of active, outside business interests would distract full-time officers from corporate affairs. However, as to outside directors, a corporate opportunity would exist only when such a director has used corporate resources in acquiring or developing an opportunity. The narrower duty rests on the basis of the more limited responsibilities and remuneration of outside directors. *Id.* at 1023–25, 1042–1044. Alternatively, if "lawmakers decide that a safety valve is needed for the rare case in which genuine corporate consent [to a diversion] is available in the public corporation context, after the board rejects an opportunity, the shareholders would be required to approve the rejection before an officer or director could exploit the opportunity." *Id.* at 1035.

However, Brudney and Clark urge a more flexible approach for close corporations in light of the basically contractual nature of the venture. They reason:

> * * * Investors in public corporations are usually passive and widely scattered contributors of money to be managed by preselected officers to whom they effectively delegate full decision making power over operating matters. In contrast, investors in private ventures are fairly small in number and tend to know one another. They make more conscious choices when selecting managers from among themselves. They are likely to be active participants rather than merely passive contributors of funds. And they can consent in a more meaningful way to diversions of corporate assets by fellow participants, either when they form or join enterprises, or on the occasion of the diversion. Accordingly, such investors have less need of categorical strictures on such diversions.

*Id.* at 1003.

In proposing guidelines for shareholders in close corporations to take opportunities, Brudney and Clark would permit the participants to consent, subject to certain limitations, in advance or contemporaneously to the diversion of a new project. They suggest that "[a] requirement of contemporaneous consent [to a diversion] could be cast in terms either of board consent or of stockholder consent by vote, either unanimously or by a simple majority." *Id.* at 1011 n. 43.

It is important to recall, however, that not all close corporations fit Brudney and Clark's active participant model. Many contain passive participants in need of protections similar to those provided the shareholders of large, publicly held corporations. *See, e.g., Farber,* supra.

5. For an interesting critique of both the traditional and ALI formulations of the corporate opportunity doctrine, see Pat K. Chew, *Competing Interests in the Corporate Opportunity Doctrine,* 67 N.C. L. REV. 435 (1989). Chew asserts that courts focus too narrowly on the corporation's interest in most decisions. This focus has led corporations to use the corporate opportunity doctrine in lieu of negotiating consensual non-competition agreements with their managers. As a consequence, courts have failed to recognize the individual manager's rights to pursue her own line of expertise once she has left her corporation. Such a failure, in turn, unnecessarily chills competition and the creation of experimental ventures and small businesses. Professor Chew notes:

> * * * In generations of cases, courts applying the corporate opportunity doctrine have focused on the protection of the corporation's interest. The cases cast the corporation as the surprised, vulnerable, and righteous victim of unscrupulous directors and officers who succumb to their personal greed in derogation of their proper corporate duties. A closer and more thoughtful analysis of actual corporate opportunity disputes and their consequences reveals that this picture is simplistic and unrealistic. * * *
>
> [T]he practical consequences for corporate fiduciaries are drastic. In many instances fiduciaries who lose corporate opportunity lawsuits are effectively prohibited from competing with their former corporations. This results even though the fiduciaries have not signed noncompetition agreements. Such de facto restraints are contrary to individuals' rights to pursue freely their interests and talents and to society's long-standing goal of promoting competition. This consequence is especially worrisome because the categories of individuals subject to the doctrine, and hence subject to a prohibition against competition, are expanding.

*Id.* at 436–38.

Chew expresses particular concern that the corporate opportunity doctrine has been expanded to cover "key employees," who are not on notice that they are subject to the fiduciary duties the doctrine is designed to enforce. For a case that Chew contends appropriately balanced the competing corporate, individual, and social interests were, *see Science Accessories Corp. v. Summagraphics Corp.,* 425 A.2d 957, 963 (Del.1980) (opportunity in line of business of electronics manufacturer held not corporate when developed off-hours by corporation's chief engineer, head of R & D, and supervisor of manufacturing who made only de minimis use of corporate facilities and resources).

## 4. REMEDIES FOR USURPING A CORPORATE OPPORTUNITY

In general, the remedy for any completed breach of fiduciary duty is the award of damages in the amount of the harm the corporation suffered from the breach. When dealing with the taking of a corporate opportunity, however, the problem of the appropriate remedy is somewhat more complex. Recall that the original harm in such a case is that the corporate manager took the opportunity for herself and failed to present it to the corporation. Had she presented it, the corporation might have rejected it; had the corporation accepted it, there is no evidence as to how successful the corporation would have been in developing and using it. Thus the gain realized by the offending manager is not necessarily co-extensive with the actual harm suffered by the corporation. Indeed, to establish a breach of duty for taking a corporate opportunity, unlike any other breach of fiduciary duty, it is not necessary to show that the corporation suffered *actual* harm from the taking. The harm is that the corporation was deprived of the right to take the opportunity for itself.

One possible remedy is to assess damages in the amount of the profits realized by the usurping manager on the theory of unjust enrichment. Profit is generally easy to measure if the manager has already sold the opportunity, although as *Farber* illustrates, valuation problems may arise. This is all the more true if the manager's profit results from reselling the opportunity to the corporation from which she took it.

The traditional remedy is the imposition of a constructive trust upon the manager's new business. This approach eliminates messy valuation problems and effectively permits the corporation to recover any lost profits which it might otherwise have realized. The offending manager, however, is entitled to expenditures she have made in pursuing the opportunity, including her reasonable compensation. *See generally Phoenix Airline Services, Inc. v. Metro Airlines, Inc.*, 194 Ga.App. 120, 390 S.E.2d 219, 227 (1989) (Pope, J. concurring), *rev'd on other grounds* 397 S.E.2d 699 (1990).

## H.   THE RESPONSIBILITIES OF CONTROLLING STOCKHOLDERS

Thus far, our discussion of fiduciary duties has focused exclusively on directors and officers. But no analysis of fiduciary duties, and particularly the duty of loyalty, would be complete without examining the position of controlling stockholders. As we have seen, directors and officers generally manage the corporation's business, but they owe their position to the stockholders who have selected them. Thus, a stockholder who has the power to select a majority of the board of directors in effect controls the corporation even if she herself is not an officer or director.

One obvious example of a controlling stockholder is a parent corporation that owns all or a majority of the stock of a subsidiary. Similarly, an individual who owns more than 50% of of a corporation's voting stock will be considered to be its controlling stockholder.

A long line of cases supports the proposition that a stockholder may vote her stock as she pleases and has no fiduciary obligation to her fellow stockholders. Nevertheless, courts also treat the actions of controlling stockholders as similar to those of directors and officers, at least when those stockholders engage in transactions with the corporations they control. This approach makes sense because the directors of the controlled corporations, who must approve or authorize such transactions, may be viewed as agents of the controlling shareholders. Thus the Supreme Court has said of dominant and controlling stockholders:

> * * * Their powers are powers in trust. * * * Their dealings with the corporation are subjected to rigorous scrutiny and where any of their contracts or engagements with the corporation is challenged the burden is on the director or stockholder not only to prove the good faith of the transaction but also to show its inherent fairness from the view point of the corporation and those interested therein.

*Pepper v. Litton*, 308 U.S. 295, 306, 60 S.Ct. 238, 245, 84 L.Ed. 281 (1939).

Corporate statutes generally do not address transactions between corporations and their controlling stockholders. Thus there is no provision analogous to DGCL § 144. The ALI would impose a duty of loyalty on controlling stockholders that will be satisfied if: "(1) the transaction is fair to the corporation when entered into; or (2) the transaction is authorized in advance or ratified by disinterested shareholders following disclosure concerning the conflict of interest and the transaction does not constitute a waste of corporate assets at the time of the shareholder action." ALI, PRINCIPLES OF CORPORATE GOVERNANCE, § 5.10(a)(1)-(2) (1994). Unlike interested director transactions, approval by a majority of disinterested directors will not affect the standard by which the transaction is reviewed, but it will shift the burden of proof to a shareholder challenging the transaction if there has been such approval.

Notwithstanding the foregoing analysis, it is important to keep in mind that the relationship between a controlling stockholder and her corporation is not precisely the same as that between a director or officer and the corporation. Directors and officers have voluntarily assumed the role of fiduciary that is inherent in a corporate office; controlling stockholders have never formally contracted with the minority stockholders to whom they may be held to owe a fiduciary duty. What, then, are the reasonable expectations of a stockholder who invests in a corporation that already has a controlling stockholder or who becomes a minority stockholder through no volitional act of her own? And how do those expectations affect the nature of the duty owed to the minority stockholder? For example, does a minority stockholder in a subsidiary expect that the parent will refrain from transactions with the subsidiary? If not, what should be the terms of such transactions? Does she expect that the parent is permanently locked into the existing relationship and cannot later decide to eliminate the minority interests? Does "self-dealing," as we have used the term earlier in this chapter, mean the same thing when we are talking about parent-subsidiary transactions? This section addresses some of these questions; others are considered in Chapters 21 and 23.

PROBLEM
STARCREST CORPORATION—PART III

Review facts of Part I of the problem.

Many years ago, members of the Adams family purchased all the stock of Universal Produce Company, a leading supplier of fresh fruits and vegetables to hotels and restaurants. Harold Adams, the chief executive officer of Universal and Elizabeth's brother, owns 25% of Universal stock (and also owns 3% of Starcrest stock). Elizabeth owns 20% of Universal. Initially, Starcrest hotels purchased fruit and vegetables from Universal at then-current market prices but have not done so in recent years.

Because of recent weather conditions, Starcrest has had increasing difficulty in obtaining a regular supply of several kinds of gourmet vegetables at reasonable prices. Starcrest uses these vegetables to prepare "signature" dishes that it serves at most of its restaurants. These dishes account for a large portion of those restaurants' volume and substantially increase their profitability.

Elizabeth recently mentioned this vegetable supply problem to Harold. Harold responded by proposing that Universal enter into a long-term supply contract with Starcrest pursuant to which Universal would supply Starcrest with the vegetables it needs. Because performing the contract would force Universal to give up some of its existing customers and devote more of its facilities to Starcrest's needs, and because of unpredictable future weather and market prices, Harold has suggested that the average price for the vegetables that Universal supplies be 110% of the average price Starcrest has paid for those vegetables for the past two years.

Elizabeth has asked you, as counsel to the Adams family, to advise her of the legal risks to her, the Adams family, Universal and Starcrest if Starcrest were to enter into such a contract. She also has asked you to advise her of what steps, if any, she or Starcrest could take to minimize those risks.

**SINCLAIR OIL CORP. v. LEVIEN**

280 A.2d 717 (Del.1971).

Wolcott, Chief Justice:

This is an appeal by the defendant, Sinclair Oil Corporation (hereafter Sinclair), from an order of the Court of Chancery, in a derivative action requiring Sinclair to account for damages sustained by its subsidiary, Sinclair Venezuelan Oil Company (hereafter Sinven), organized by Sinclair for the purpose of operating in Venezuela, as a result of dividends paid by Sinven, the denial to Sinven of industrial development, and a breach of contract between Sinclair's wholly-owned subsidiary, Sinclair International Oil Company, and Sinven.

Sinclair, operating primarily as a holding company, is in the business of exploring for oil and of producing and marketing crude oil and oil products. At all times relevant to this litigation, it owned about 97% of Sinven's stock. The plaintiff owns about 3000 of 120,000 publicly held shares of Sinven. Sinven, incorporated in 1922, has been engaged in petroleum operations primarily in Venezuela and since 1959 has operated exclusively in Venezuela.

Sinclair nominates all members of Sinven's board of directors. The Chancellor found as a fact that the directors were not independent of Sinclair. Almost without exception, they were officers, directors, or employees of corporations in the Sinclair complex. By reason of Sinclair's domination, it is clear that Sinclair owed Sinven a fiduciary duty. Sinclair concedes this.

The Chancellor held that because of Sinclair's fiduciary duty and its control over Sinven, its relationship with Sinven must meet the test of intrinsic fairness. The standard of intrinsic fairness involves both a high degree of fairness and a shift in the burden of proof. Under this standard the burden is on Sinclair to prove, subject to careful judicial scrutiny, that its transactions with Sinven were objectively fair.

Sinclair argues that the transactions between it and Sinven should be tested, not by the test of intrinsic fairness with the accompanying shift of the burden of proof, but by the business judgment rule under which a court will not interfere with the judgment of a board of directors unless there is a showing of gross and palpable overreaching. *Meyerson v. El Paso Natural Gas Co.*, 246 A.2d 789 (Del.Ch.1967). A board of directors enjoys a presumption of sound business judgment, and its decisions will not be disturbed if they can be attributed to any rational business purpose. A court under such circumstances will not substitute its own notions of what is or is not sound business judgment.

We think, however, that Sinclair's argument in this respect is misconceived. When the situation involves a parent and a subsidiary, with the parent controlling the transaction and fixing the terms, the test of intrinsic fairness, with its resulting shifting of the burden of proof, is applied. The basic situation for the application of the rule is the one in which the parent has received a benefit to the exclusion and at the expense of the subsidiary.

Recently, this court dealt with the question of fairness in parent-subsidiary dealings in *Getty Oil Co. v. Skelly Oil Co.* [267 A.2d 883 (Del.1970)]. In that case, both parent and subsidiary were in the business of refining and marketing crude oil and crude oil products. The Oil Import Board ruled that the subsidiary, because it was controlled by the parent, was no longer entitled to a separate allocation of imported crude oil. The subsidiary then contended that it had a right to share the quota of crude oil allotted to the parent. We ruled that the business judgment standard should be applied to determine this contention. Although the subsidiary suffered a loss through the administration of the oil import quotas, the parent gained nothing. The parent's quota was derived solely from its own past use. The past use of the subsidiary did not cause an increase in the parent's quota. Nor did the parent usurp a quota of the subsidiary. Since the parent received nothing from the subsidiary to the exclusion of the minority stockholders of the subsidiary, there was no self-dealing. Therefore, the business judgment standard was properly applied.

A parent does indeed owe a fiduciary duty to its subsidiary when there are parent-subsidiary dealings. However, this alone will not evoke the intrinsic fairness standard. This standard will be applied only when the fiduciary duty is accompanied by self-dealing—the situation when a parent is on both sides of a transaction with its subsidiary. Self-dealing occurs when the parent, by virtue of its domination of the subsidiary, causes the subsidiary to act in such a way that the parent receives something from the subsidiary to the exclusion of, and detriment to, the minority stockholders of the subsidiary.

We turn now to the facts. The plaintiff argues that, from 1960 through 1966, Sinclair caused Sinven to pay out such excessive dividends that the industrial development of Sinven was effectively prevented, and it became in reality a corporation in dissolution.

From 1960 through 1966, Sinven paid out $108,000,000 in dividends ($38,000,000 in excess of Sinven's earnings during the same period). The Chancellor held that Sinclair caused these dividends to be paid during a period when it had a need for large amounts of cash. Although the dividends paid exceeded earnings, the plaintiff concedes that the payments were made in compliance with 8 Del.C. § 170, authorizing payment of dividends out of surplus or net profits. However, the plaintiff attacks these dividends on the ground that they resulted from an improper motive—Sinclair's need for cash. The Chancellor, applying the intrinsic fairness standard, held that Sinclair did not sustain its burden of proving that these dividends were intrinsically fair to the minority stockholders of Sinven.

Since it is admitted that the dividends were paid in strict compliance with 8 Del.C. § 170, the alleged excessiveness of the payments alone would not state a cause of action. Nevertheless, compliance with the applicable statute may not, under all circumstances, justify all dividend payments. If a plaintiff can meet his burden of proving that a dividend cannot be grounded on any reasonable business objective, then the courts can and will interfere with the board's decision to pay the dividend.

Sinclair contends that it is improper to apply the intrinsic fairness standard to dividend payments even when the board which voted for the dividends is completely dominated. In support of this contention, Sinclair relies heavily on *American District Telegraph Co. [ADT] v. Grinnell Corp.*, (N.Y.Sup.Ct.1969) aff'd. 33 A.D.2d 769, 306 N.Y.S.2d 209 (1969). Plaintiffs were minority stockholders of ADT, a subsidiary of Grinnell. The plaintiffs alleged that Grinnell, realizing that it would soon have to sell its ADT stock because of a pending anti-trust action, caused ADT to pay excessive dividends. Because the dividend payments conformed with applicable statutory law, and the plaintiffs could not prove an abuse of discretion, the court ruled that the complaint did not state a cause of action. Other decisions seem to support Sinclair's contention.

We do not accept the argument that the intrinsic fairness test can never be applied to a dividend declaration by a dominated board, although a dividend declaration by a dominated board will not inevitably demand the application of the intrinsic fairness standard. If such a dividend is in essence self-dealing by the parent, then the intrinsic fairness standard is the proper standard. For example, suppose a parent dominates a subsidiary and its board of directors. The subsidiary has outstanding two classes of stock, X and Y. Class X is owned by the parent and Class Y is owned by minority stockholders of the subsidiary. If the subsidiary, at the direction of the parent, declares a dividend on its Class X stock only, this might well be self-dealing by the parent. It would be receiving something from the subsidiary to the exclusion of and detrimental to its minority stockholders. This self-dealing, coupled with the parent's fiduciary duty, would make intrinsic fairness the proper standard by which to evaluate the dividend payments.

Consequently it must be determined whether the dividend payments by Sinven were, in essence, self-dealing by Sinclair. The dividends resulted in great sums of money being transferred from Sinven to Sinclair. However, a proportionate share of this money was received by the minority shareholders of Sinven. Sinclair received nothing from Sinven to the exclusion of its minority stockholders. As such, these dividends were not self-dealing. We hold therefore that the Chancellor erred in applying the intrinsic fairness test as to these dividend payments. The business judgment standard should have been applied.

We conclude that the facts demonstrate that the dividend payments complied with the business judgment standard and with 8 Del.C. § 170. The motives for causing the declaration of dividends are immaterial unless the plaintiff can show that the dividend payments resulted from improper motives and amounted to waste. The plaintiff contends only that the dividend payments drained Sinven of cash to such an extent that it was prevented from expanding.

The plaintiff proved no business opportunities which came to Sinven independently and which Sinclair either took to itself or denied to Sinven. As a matter of fact, with two minor exceptions which resulted in losses, all of Sinven's operations have been conducted in Venezuela, and Sinclair had a policy of exploiting its oil properties located in different countries by subsidiaries located in the particular countries.

From 1960 to 1966 Sinclair purchased or developed oil fields in Alaska, Canada, Paraguay, and other places around the world. The plaintiff contends that these were all opportunities which could have been taken by Sinven. The Chancellor concluded that Sinclair had not proved that its denial of expansion opportunities to Sinven was intrinsically fair. He based this conclusion on the following findings of fact. Sinclair made no real effort to expand Sinven. The excessive dividends paid by Sinven resulted in so great a cash drain as to effectively deny to Sinven any ability to expand. During this same period Sinclair actively pursued a company-wide policy of developing through its subsidiaries new sources of revenue, but Sinven was not permitted to participate and was confined in its activities to Venezuela.

However, the plaintiff could point to no opportunities which came to Sinven. Therefore, Sinclair usurped no business opportunity belonging to Sinven. Since Sinclair received nothing from Sinven to the exclusion of and detriment to Sinven's minority stockholders, there was no self-dealing. Therefore, business judgment is the proper standard by which to evaluate Sinclair's expansion policies.

Since there is no proof of self-dealing on the part of Sinclair, it follows that the expansion policy of Sinclair and the methods used to achieve the desired result must, as far as Sinclair's treatment of Sinven is concerned, be tested by the standards of the business judgment rule. Accordingly, Sinclair's decision, absent fraud or gross overreaching, to achieve expansion through the medium of its subsidiaries, other than Sinven, must be upheld.

Even if Sinclair was wrong in developing these opportunities as it did, the question arises, with which subsidiaries should these opportunities have been shared? No evidence indicates a unique need or ability of Sinven to develop these opportunities. The decision of which subsidiaries would be used to implement Sinclair's expansion policy was one of business judgment with which a court will not interfere absent a showing of gross and palpable overreaching. *Meyerson v. El Paso Natural Gas Co.*, 246 A.2d 789 (Del.Ch.1967). No such showing has been made here.

Next, Sinclair argues that the Chancellor committed error when he held it liable to Sinven for breach of contract.

In 1961 Sinclair created Sinclair International Oil Company (hereafter International), a wholly owned subsidiary used for the purpose of coordinating all of Sinclair's foreign operations. All crude purchases by Sinclair were made thereafter through International.

On September 28, 1961, Sinclair caused Sinven to contract with International whereby Sinven agreed to sell all of its crude oil and refined products to International at specified prices. The contract provided for minimum and maximum quantities and prices. The plaintiff contends that Sinclair caused this contract to be breached in two respects. Although the contract called for payment on receipt, International's payments lagged as much as 30 days after receipt. Also, the contract required International to purchase at least a fixed minimum amount of crude and refined products from Sinven. International did not comply with this requirement.

Clearly, Sinclair's act of contracting with its dominated subsidiary was self-dealing. Under the contract Sinclair received the products produced by Sinven, and of course the minority shareholders of Sinven were not able to share in the receipt of these products. If the contract was breached, then Sinclair received these products to the detriment of Sinven's minority shareholders. We agree with the Chancellor's finding that the contract was breached by Sinclair, both as to the time of payments and the amounts purchased.

Although a parent need not bind itself by a contract with its dominated subsidiary, Sinclair chose to operate in this manner. As Sinclair has received the benefits of this contract, so must it comply with the contractual duties.

Under the intrinsic fairness standard, Sinclair must prove that its causing Sinven not to enforce the contract was intrinsically fair to the minority shareholders of Sinven. Sinclair has failed to meet this burden. Late payments were clearly breaches for which Sinven should have sought and received adequate damages. As to the quantities purchased, Sinclair argues that it purchased all the products produced by Sinven. This, however, does not satisfy the standard of intrinsic fairness. Sinclair has failed to prove that Sinven could not possibly have produced or someway have obtained the contract minimums. As such, Sinclair must account on this claim.

Finally, Sinclair argues that the Chancellor committed error in refusing to allow it a credit or setoff of all benefits provided by it to Sinven with respect to all the alleged damages. The Chancellor held that setoff should be allowed on specific transactions, e.g., benefits to Sinven under the contract with International, but denied an over all setoff against all damages claimed. We agree with the Chancellor, although the point may well be moot in view of our holding that Sinclair is not required to account for the alleged excessiveness of the dividend payments.

We will therefore reverse that part of the Chancellor's order that requires Sinclair to account to Sinven for damages sustained as a result of dividends paid between 1960 and 1966, and by reason of the denial to Sinven of expansion during that period. We will affirm the remaining portion of that order and remand the cause for further proceedings.

————

The *Meyerson* case referred to in *Sinclair* concerned the fairness of a parent corporation's filing a consolidated tax return with its subsidiary and using the losses of the subsidiary to offset the parent's income and reduce the parent's tax. The court rejected a minority shareholder's contention that this practice was unfair. Does the ruling of the court leaving that decision to the judgment of the board reflect a view that there is no self-dealing involved, or is the court saying that there are no established legal standards to invoke?

## TRANS WORLD AIRLINES, INC. v. SUMMA CORP.
### 374 A.2d 5 (Del.Ch.1977).

[Howard Hughes owned all the stock of Hughes Tool Company ("Toolco") which owned 78% of the stock of TWA. While competitive airlines were acquiring jet aircraft from Boeing and Douglas in the late 1950's, TWA was not allowed to negotiate for the purchase of planes by itself but instead was forced to rely on Toolco which was unable to arrange financing for a long while. TWA sought an accounting and damages for the delay it suffered from Toolco's refusal to allow TWA to bargain for itself, which it charged was motivated by Toolco's desire to secure a tax advantage from the transaction. Toolco said that this was not a self-dealing transaction because the parent derived no benefit to the detriment of the minority.]

MARVEL, CHANCELLOR:

\* \* \*

First of all, I am satisfied that the mere fact that Toolco engaged in the acquisition, financing, leasing, and ultimately in the sale of jet aircraft is not, in itself, of significance in this case because a parent company may concern itself with the purchase and sale of equipment to be used by a subsidiary, the basic question being rather whether or not TWA suffered injury by reason of being barred from dealing in such area on its own.

I conclude that the basic prerequisites to the application of the intrinsic fairness rule are found in the instant case. First of all, it is conceded that Toolco and Hughes exercised control over the affairs of TWA during the period in question, particularly in the area of the financing and acquisition of jet aircraft, the policy for which over a substantial period was dictated by the defendants, jet aircraft having been leased by Toolco to TWA on a day to day basis prior to agreement on a satisfactory financing arrangement. Furthermore, while Toolco ultimately turned over to TWA the jet aircraft in question once a financing plan was agreed upon, there is no doubt but that the defendants bargained on both sides of such transactions, causing TWA to act in such a way as to cause defendants to derive advantages at the expense of TWA to the exclusion of and to the detriment of the latter's minority shareholders. Accordingly, by refusing to allow TWA to select and finance the purchase of its own jet aircraft, the defendants were in a position to mete out to TWA such jet aircraft as they chose. In other words, by preventing TWA from making its own arrangements for the acquisition of jet planes, the defendants retained the capability of arranging the terms of such acquisitions so as to benefit themselves. In addition, in the event of the development of problems in connection with such acquisitions, as ultimately came to pass, in the task of obtaining long term financing for TWA, the defendants remained free to dispose of such aircraft to other air carriers.

Thus, it is clear on the present record that the minority shareholders of TWA received nothing in exchange for the strictures imposed by defendants on plaintiff's operations and that such stockholders may have suffered injury as a result of the loss of TWA's freedom to compete. As charged in the complaint, TWA might well have been able to earn substantially more income for its minority as well as majority stockholders through increased business activity during the period of its being dominated had it not been subject to the strictures imposed by the defendants.

––––––––

The saga of Howard Hughes and TWA appears to have come to an end, *Summa Corp. v. Trans World Airlines, Inc.*, 540 A.2d 403 (Del. 1988), and as Justice Moore noted in that opinion, the case in length of time, if in no other respect, is most reminiscent of *Jarndyce* and *Jarndyce* in Charles Dickens, BLEAK HOUSE. The Delaware Supreme Court affirmed the Court of Chancery's finding that Toolco had breached its fiduciary duties to TWA. The court cited *Weinberger v. UOP, Inc.* (Chapter 23) and *Sinclair v. Levien* as providing the appropriate analytic framework and concluded that Toolco's conduct "hardly comports with basic concepts of fair dealing under the fiduciary standards of Delaware corporation law." The court rejected Toolco's argument that TWA did not need certain aircraft and that it should not be held liable for TWA's lost profits arising from Toolco's failure to order such aircraft. As the court noted, "this argument, like Toolco's others, ignores the fact that the intrinsic fairness test placed the burden upon Toolco to prove that it was not the cause of TWA's lost profits. * * * The trial court found, and we agree, that Toolco failed to meet that burden." *Id*. at 407. Thus the court affirmed the Court of Chancery's award of $48,349,022.48 in damages and interest.

# Chapter 18

# DUTY OF DISCLOSURE TO SHAREHOLDERS

If fiduciary duties are one of the critical elements in the relationship between shareholders and management, it fairly may be said that disclosure lies at the heart of much of the law of fiduciary duties. We have already seen the importance of disclosure to the corporate decision-maker in a number of contexts. A director must be fully informed in order to gain the protection of the business judgment rule; disinterested shareholders or directors must be fully informed in a conflict of interest transaction in order to validate the transaction or to shift the burden of proof in litigation challenging the transaction; a director may be guilty of appropriating a corporate opportunity if she does not disclose the opportunity to the board before taking it for herself. And, clearly, full disclosure is paramount in the shareholder voting process.

In this latter connection, we have also seen that the proxy solicitation has become the substitute for the shareholders meeting in public corporations even though, as a formal matter, the meeting is actually held. The proxy process, in turn, reflects the intersection of state and federal law. Thus, when considering the duty of disclosure owed to the shareholder as decision-maker, it is necessary to examine how that duty has developed under both federal and state law and how those two bodies of law interrelate.

## PROBLEM
## NATIONAL METAL PRODUCTS

### I

National Metal Products, Inc. ("National") is a Delaware corporation whose common stock is traded on the New York Stock Exchange. The company manufactures specialized metal products. Its sales for the most recent year were $500 million.

In February, the board of directors approved a merger with International Petroleum Corporation ("IPC") whereby National would issue additional shares of its common stock equal to 25% of the outstanding shares. The transaction required shareholder approval by both companies under state law. The proxy material sought approval of the merger and the election of directors. The candidates for election were the incumbent directors of National and Sanford, the CEO of IPC. At the meeting in May, the shareholders voted overwhelmingly to approve the merger and management's slate of directors.

The proxy statement contained all the information required by SEC rules concerning the merger and the candidates for election to the board. Among the statements made about the merger was the following: "The board of directors recommends approval of the merger. The board's recommendation is based upon its review of management's report and recommendations and the financial statements of IPC. It is the board's judgment, premised on this information, that the merger is in the best interests of the company and its shareholders."

Several months later, the following facts became known:

A.   The merger was negotiated between Meacham, the CEO of National, and Sanford, the CEO of IPC. It was taken up by National's board at a regular meeting where Meacham and other members of management made a brief presentation and answered questions. Financial statements of IPC had been given to each member of the board two days before the meeting. After about 30 minutes of discussion, the board voted unanimously in favor of the merger. This was the same procedure that National had followed with three other acquisitions during the past two years.

B.   The acquisition has proven costly to National, largely because of a price-fixing scheme that has recently come to light. Several years before the merger, management of IPC learned that its field managers had engaged in the scheme with several other independent oil producers. Senior management ordered the practice halted. Sanford informed Meacham of these past practices during the negotiations, and explained that it was common in the industry, but Meacham made no mention of these facts and his conversation with Sanford to the National board, nor was he asked any questions relating to possible price fixing.

Several months after the merger, it was revealed that the price-fixing practices had continued even after the merger with National. As a result, substantial contracts between National (through IPC) and some refineries were cancelled, and there was a likelihood both of large private suits under the anti-trust laws and criminal prosecutions. National has decided to dismiss some key managers who were engaged in this activity.

No mention of the past activity was made in the proxy statement.

C.   National entered into a settlement of a claim by two local environmental protection agencies that the company violated their rules on emission controls. The violations were caused by furnaces in two older smelting plants of National, where management had decided to attempt compliance by patching up old emission control systems rather than replacing them with new and expensive electronic equipment. The company was fined $500,000. At the time the proxy statement was issued, the board was aware of management's decision on the furnaces and the risks but decided, on advice of counsel, that no disclosure was necessary in the proxy statement.

Rogers, the owner of 1,000 shares of National common stock believes that the proxy statement for the meeting was materially false and misleading in violation of Rule 14a–9 of the SEC proxy rules.

### *Questions*

1. Assuming there were violations of rule 14a–9, can Rogers, after learning of the facts, bring suit based on federal law to obtain relief for those violations? What type of relief may be available?

2. Are there any material misstatements or omissions in the proxy statement in violation of Rule 14a–9?

3. Assuming that there are material misstatements or omissions, what causal connection can Rogers show between the violations he can establish and the injury of which he complains?

4. Suppose that Rogers believes that even if there were no material misstatements or omissions in the proxy statement, the merger was unfair because National paid too much to acquire IPC. Does Rogers have a valid claim under either the proxy rules or Rule 10b–5, either before or after the shareholder vote, based on a showing that the terms of the merger were unfair and that the unfairness was not directly disclosed?

5. Does Rogers have a claim under state law in connection with the proxy solicitation? If so, against whom? What must Rogers prove to prevail on his claim?

## A.   IMPLIED PRIVATE RIGHTS OF ACTION UNDER THE PROXY RULES

### *Note: A Student Guide to J.I. Case Co. v. Borak*

The case that follows this note, the *Borak* case, is one of the most significant decisions in the interpretation of the federal securities laws and one of the most important landmarks at the intersection of corporate and securities law. Understanding its full significance, however, requires some background in the business and procedural aspects of the case.

Plaintiff Carl Borak was a stockholder in J.I. Case Co., a company that proposed to merge with American Tractor Corp. Borak contended that the merger involved improper self-dealing by the managers of his corporation and that the minority shareholders were treated unfairly.

Borak brought suit in federal district court to enjoin the merger. Jurisdiction was based on diversity of citizenship. The court denied the injunction, the merger was consummated and Borak's old corporation ceased to exist. A threshold issue was the capacity in which Borak was suing. Was the suit a class action, brought directly on behalf of the stockholders, or a derivative suit on behalf of the corporation? As we saw in Chapter 3, a derivative suit is one to enforce a right on behalf of the corporation that the corporation itself has not asserted. With rare exceptions, any damages that are awarded or amounts paid in settlement go to the corporation. A direct action, by contrast, alleges that the shareholders suffered direct injury in their capacity as shareholders.

The proxy solicitation used in approving the merger affects a corporate transaction (the merger between two corporations); thus any harm in the solicitation is arguably to the corporation. But the solicitation is also used to enable a shareholder to exercise her individual right to vote. Thus there are both direct and derivative elements in an action challenging the validity of the proxy solicitation

A key question in *Borak* involved the applicability of state substantive law. If the suit were brought only as a derivative suit, Borak would have had to comply with the state procedural requirements in derivative suits, including posting security for litigation expenses borne by defendant. These expenses include court costs and, in the court's discretion, the defendant's attorneys' fees. This requirement applies to diversity cases if it is required by the law of the forum state, which, in turn, may refer to the law of the state of incorporation. The purpose of this requirement is to protect the corporation and the individual defendants from the expense of defending frivolous suits. Although the bond itself may be expensive, the principal risk is that a plaintiff may have to make good on the bond and pay the underlying expenses if the litigation is unsuccessful.

Wisconsin had a security-for-expenses provision that would have been applicable to the common law suit, if it were derivative but not if the suit were a direct action. The district court characterized the suit as derivative and, because Borak refused to post security, dismissed the complaint. Thereafter, Borak amended his complaint to seek relief under § 14(a) of the Securities Exchange Act of 1934 and Rule 14a–9 of the SEC proxy rules. He also claimed that the state procedural requirements did not apply to his federal claim; thus he could not be required to post a bond.

In ruling on the amended complaint, the district court held that Borak's federal claim entitled him only to prospective or declaratory relief, i.e., an injunction or a ruling on the law. The court dismissed the other pleas for relief because Borak refused to post security. The district court reasoned that insofar as Borak requested the kind of relief under federal law that could be obtained only from his common law claim, such as damages, rescission or an order undoing or amending the terms of the merger, his request converted his federal claim into a state law claim. Borak appealed from all these rulings.

The Seventh Circuit reversed the district court. It held that the common law claim was both derivative and direct and thus was not subject to the security for expenses requirements. More important, the court held that the relief available under the federal count, as to which no security could be demanded, could be either prospective or retrospective, whichever was necessary to make the federal substantive requirements effective. Consequently, plaintiff could obtain the relief he sought even if the state claim were dropped. The decision created a conflict with the Sixth Circuit which had earlier ruled that only prospective relief could be granted for violation of the proxy rules. *Dann v. Studebaker–Packard Corp.*, 288 F.2d 201 (6th Cir.1961).

If the action is held to be a class or direct action, the issue of security for expenses vanishes, but the question as to the scope of available relief remains. The district court's view as to the narrow scope of relief available under federal law is important if the available state law remedies are narrow. As a class claimant, however, Borak would be able to press both the common law and federal claim, and whatever relief could *not* be granted under federal law might still be granted under common law.

Under the district court's interpretation of federal remedies, it is not clear whether a court could dispense all the relief Borak requested, even if it had the powers of both federal and state courts. The reason for that is that Borak would be made to rely, very largely, on state remedies, and hope that state law would grant a full sweep of remedies in this context. The result might vary from state to state; some states might not allow damages or post-merger equitable relief. Other differences might exist between the relief that could be obtained from a federal court with full remedial powers and a state court. The statute of limitations might not be the same. The burden of proof might differ. Therefore, Borak sought to have the suit construed as a class action, so that he could press both federal and state claims. He also hoped to have the court rule that under both federal and state law, he would be entitled to both prospective relief and retrospective relief (damages).

## J.I. CASE CO. v. BORAK

377 U.S. 426, 84 S.Ct. 1555, 12 L.Ed.2d 423 (1964).

MR. JUSTICE CLARK delivered the opinion of the Court.

This is a civil action brought by respondent, a stockholder of petitioner J.I. Case Company, charging deprivation of the pre-emptive rights of respondent and other shareholders by reason of a merger between Case and the American Tractor Corporation. It is alleged that the merger was effected through the circulation of a false and misleading proxy statement by those proposing the merger. The complaint was in two counts, the first based on diversity and claiming a breach of the directors' fiduciary duty to the stockholders. The second count alleged a violation of § 14(a) of the Securities Exchange Act of 1934 with reference to the proxy solicitation material. The trial court held that as to this count it had no power to redress the alleged violations of the Act but was limited solely to the granting of declaratory relief thereon under

§ 27 of the Act.[2] * * * On interlocutory appeal the Court of Appeals reversed. * * * We granted certiorari. We consider only the question of whether § 27 of the Act authorizes a federal cause of action for rescission or damages to a corporate stockholder with respect to a consummated merger which was authorized pursuant to the use of a proxy statement alleged to contain false and misleading statements violative of § 14(a) of the Act. * * *

## I.

Respondent, the owner of 2,000 shares of common stock of Case acquired prior to the merger, brought this suit based on diversity jurisdiction seeking to enjoin a proposed merger between Case and the American Tractor Corporation (ATC) on various grounds, including breach of the fiduciary duties of the Case directors, self-dealing among the management of Case and ATC and misrepresentations contained in the material circulated to obtain proxies. The injunction was denied and the merger was thereafter consummated. * * * The claims pertinent to the asserted violation of the Securities Exchange Act were predicated on diversity jurisdiction as well as on § 27 of the Act. They alleged: that petitioners, or their predecessors, solicited or permitted their names to be used in the solicitation of proxies of Case stockholders for use at a special stockholders' meeting at which the proposed merger with ATC was to be voted upon; that the proxy solicitation material so circulated was false and misleading in violation of § 14(a) of the Act and Rule 14a–9 which the Commission had promulgated thereunder; that the merger was approved at the meeting by a small margin of votes and was thereafter consummated; that the merger would not have been approved but for the false and misleading statements in the proxy solicitation material; and that Case stockholders were damaged thereby. The respondent sought judgment holding the merger void and damages for himself and all other stockholders similarly situated, as well as such further relief "as equity shall require." The District Court ruled that the Wisconsin security for expenses statute did not apply to Count 2 since it arose under federal law. However, the court found that its jurisdiction was limited to declaratory relief in a private, as opposed to a government, suit alleging violation of § 14(a) of the Act. * * *

## II.

It appears clear that private parties have a right under § 27 to bring suit for violation of § 14(a) of the Act. Indeed, this section specifically

---

**2.** Section 27 of the Act, 48 Stat. 902–903, 15 U.S.C.A. § 78aa, provides in part: "The district courts of the United States, the Supreme Court of the District of Columbia, and the United States courts of any Territory or other place subject to the jurisdiction of the United States shall have exclusive jurisdiction of violations of this title or the rules and regulations thereunder, and of all suits in equity and actions at law brought to enforce any liability or duty created by this title or the rules and regulations thereunder. Any criminal proceeding may be brought in the district wherein any act or transaction constituting the violation occurred. Any suit or action to enforce any liability or duty created by this title or rules and regulations thereunder, or to enjoin any violation of such title or rules and regulations, may be brought in any such district or in the district wherein the defendant is found or is an inhabitant or transacts business, and process in such cases may be served in any other district of which the defendant is an inhabitant or wherever the defendant may be found."

grants the appropriate District Courts jurisdiction over "all suits in equity and actions at law brought to enforce any liability or duty created" under the Act. The petitioners make no concessions, however, emphasizing that Congress made no specific reference to a private right of action in § 14(a); that, in any event, the right would not extend to derivative suits and should be limited to prospective relief only. In addition, some of the petitioners argue that the merger can be dissolved only if it was fraudulent or non-beneficial, issues upon which the proxy material would not bear. But the causal relationship of the proxy material and the merger are questions of fact to be resolved at trial, not here. We therefore do not discuss this point further.

## III.

While the respondent contends that his Count 2 claim is not a derivative one, we need not embrace that view, for we believe that a right of action exists as to both derivative and direct causes.

The purpose of § 14(a) is to prevent management or others from obtaining authorization for corporate action by means of deceptive or inadequate disclosure in proxy solicitation. The section stemmed from the congressional belief that "[f]air corporate suffrage is an important right that should attach to every equity security bought on a public exchange." H.R.Rep. No. 1383, 73d Cong., 2d Sess., 13. It was intended to "control the conditions under which proxies may be solicited with a view to preventing the recurrence of abuses which * * * [had] frustrated the free exercise of the voting rights of stockholders." *Id.*, at 14. "Too often proxies are solicited without explanation to the stockholder of the real nature of the questions for which authority to cast his vote is sought." S.Rep. No. 792, 73d Cong., 2d Sess., 12. These broad remedial purposes are evidenced in the language of the section which makes it "unlawful for any person * * * to solicit or to permit the use of his name to solicit any proxy or consent or authorization in respect of any security * * * registered on any national securities exchange in contravention of such rules and regulations as the Commission may prescribe as necessary or appropriate in the public interest *or for the protection of investors*." (Italics supplied.) While this language makes no specific reference to a private right of action, among its chief purposes is "the protection of investors," which certainly implies the availability of judicial relief where necessary to achieve that result.

The injury which a stockholder suffers from corporate action pursuant to a deceptive proxy solicitation ordinarily flows from the damage done the corporation, rather than from the damage inflicted directly upon the stockholder. The damage suffered results not from the deceit practiced on him alone but rather from the deceit practiced on the stockholders as a group. To hold that derivative actions are not within the sweep of the section would therefore be tantamount to a denial of private relief. Private enforcement of the proxy rules provides a necessary supplement to Commission action. As in anti-trust treble damage litigation, the possibility of civil damages or injunctive relief serves as a most effective weapon in the enforcement of the proxy requirements. The Commission advises that it examines over 2,000 proxy statements annually and each of them must necessarily be expedited. Time does not permit an independent examination of the facts set out in the proxy material and this results in the Commission's acceptance of the representations contained therein at their face value, unless contrary to other material on file with it. Indeed, on the allegations of respondent's complaint, the proxy material failed to disclose alleged unlawful market manipulation of the stock of ATC, and this unlawful manipulation would not have been apparent to the Commission until after the merger.

We, therefore, believe that under the circumstances here it is the duty of the courts to be alert to provide such remedies as are necessary to make effective the congressional purpose. As was said in *Sola Electric Co. v. Jefferson Electric Co.*, 317 U.S. 173, 176, 63 S.Ct. 172, 174, 87 L.Ed. 165 (1942):

> When a federal statute condemns an act as unlawful, the extent and nature of the legal consequences of the condemnation, though left by the statute to judicial determination, are nevertheless federal questions, the answers to which are to be derived from the statute and the federal policy which it has adopted.

It is for the federal courts "to adjust their remedies so as to grant the necessary relief" where federally secured rights are invaded. "And it is also well settled that where legal rights have been invaded, and a federal statute provides for a general right to sue for such invasion, federal courts may use any available remedy to make good the wrong done." *Bell v. Hood*, 327 U.S. 678, 684, 66 S.Ct. 773, 777, 90 L.Ed. 939 (1946). Section 27 grants the District Courts jurisdiction "of all suits in equity and actions at law brought to enforce any liability or duty created by this title * * *." In passing on almost identical language found in the Securities Act of 1933, the Court found the words entirely sufficient to fashion a remedy to rescind a fraudulent sale, secure restitution and even to enforce the right to restitution against a third party holding assets of the vendor. *Deckert v. Independence Shares Corp.*, 311 U.S. 282, 61 S.Ct. 229, 85 L.Ed. 189 (1940). This significant language was used:

> The power *to enforce* implies the power to make effective the right of recovery afforded by the Act. And the power to make the right of recovery effective implies the power to utilize any of the procedures or actions normally available to the litigant according to the exigencies of the particular case. At 288 of 311 U.S., at 233 of 61 S.Ct.

Nor do we find merit in the contention that such remedies are limited to prospective relief. This was the position taken in *Dann v. Studebaker–Packard Corp.*, 6 Cir., 288 F.2d 201, where it was held that the "preponderance of questions of state law which would have to be interpreted and applied in order to grant the relief sought * * * is so great that the federal question involved * * * is really negligible in comparison." But we believe that the overriding federal law applicable here would, where the facts required, control the appropriateness of redress despite the provisions of state corporation law, for it "is not uncommon for federal courts to fashion federal law where federal rights are concerned." *Textile Workers Union of America v. Lincoln Mills*, 353 U.S. 448, 457, 77 S.Ct. 912, 918, 1 L.Ed.2d 972 (1957). In addition, the fact that questions of state law must be decided does not change the character of the right; it remains federal. * * *

Moreover, if federal jurisdiction were limited to the granting of declaratory relief, victims of deceptive proxy statements would be obliged to go into state courts for remedial relief. And if the law of the State happened to attach no responsibility to the use of misleading proxy statements, the whole purpose of the section might be frustrated. Furthermore, the hurdles that the victim might face (such as separate suits, as contemplated by *Dann v. Studebaker–Packard Corp.*, *supra*, security for expenses statutes, bringing in all parties necessary for complete relief, etc.) might well prove insuperable to effective relief.

IV.

Our finding that federal courts have the power to grant all necessary remedial relief is not to be construed as any indication of what we believe to be the necessary and appropriate relief in this case. We are concerned here only with a determination that federal jurisdiction for this purpose does exist. Whatever remedy is necessary must await the trial on the merits.

The other contentions of the petitioners are denied.

Affirmed.

### Note: Implied Private Rights of Action

Although seemingly straightforward, the Court's opinion in *Borak* is curious in several ways. Note that Section 14(a) provides no express cause of action for those injured by a violation of the section; if one exists, it must be judicially implied. Because the action is one "arising under the laws of the United States," and therefore is predicated on legislative authority, it is curious that the Court did not analyze Congressional intent in the enactment of § 14(a). In fact, the legislative history is sparse and does not indicate whether Congress contemplated that private suits could or could not be brought under § 14(a), an omission which subsequent courts have found significant in deciding whether to imply a private right of action under other statutory provisions.

The Court also does not discuss the carefully detailed pattern of express remedies provided in the Securities Exchange Act of 1934 and its companion statute, the Securities Act of 1933, or the effect that implied remedies would have on those provisions. The 1934 Act authorizes the SEC to seek injunctive relief for a violation of any provision of the Act. It also provides express remedies for investors who are injured by manipulation (§ 9), for corporations whose insiders engage in buying and selling the company's stock (§ 16) and, most important, for investors who are injured as a result of any false or misleading information contained in a document filed with the SEC (§ 18). These remedies were carefully constructed and balanced; they extended relief beyond common law protections, but the tradeoff was the imposition of tight procedural restrictions and a short statute of limitations. Implied remedies, of course, were not the subject of that bargain. Because the proxy statement which was the basis of the suit was a document filed with the SEC and subject to liability under § 18, the Court might have found that a private right should not be implied where an express remedy was already available, even though the plaintiff could not avail himself of the remedy in this particular case.

Rather than using either of these approaches, the Court chose to base its decision on § 27, which confers exclusive jurisdiction on the federal courts for violations of the statute and provides for service of process and venue. Section 27 is necessary, whether or not private rights of action are implied, because jurisdiction and venue must be provided for both SEC enforcement actions and the express remedies in the statute. Had there been no express remedies, of course, § 27 could be read as indicating either that Congress intended that remedies be implied or that the SEC have exclusive enforcement power.

The Court could have adopted a still different methodology—the statutory tort theory—in deciding whether to imply a private right of action. The statutory tort theory can be traced back to Dean Ezra Ripley Thayer's seminal article, *Public Wrong and Private Action*, 27 HARV. L.REV. 317 (1914), which argued that it was unreasonable conduct for a defendant to violate a statute. Since a statutory violation was negligence per se, the courts upheld private recovery based upon such violation. Not every violation would lead to an implied private cause of action under this theory, however. As the American Law Institute emphasized in the RESTATEMENT (SECOND) OF TORTS (1997) § 286, the plaintiff must also be part of the class the statute was intended to protect. To use the theory would have forced the Court to decide whether Borak was such a person and thus to answer the question it so carefully avoided in the actual opinion: the capacity in which Borak was suing.

The Supreme Court and lower federal courts used a statutory tort analysis both before and after *Borak*. See *Texas & Pacific Railway v. Rigsby*, 241 U.S. 33, 36 S.Ct. 482, 60 L.Ed. 874 (1916); *Wyandotte Transportation Co. v. United States*, 389 U.S. 191, 88 S.Ct. 379, 19 L.Ed.2d 407 (1967). In the securities laws, a federal district court implied a private right of action under Rule 10b–5 under the 1934 Act, which prohibits false or misleading statements, or deceptive or manipulative acts or practices in connection with the purchase or sale of securities. *Kardon v. National Gypsum Co.*, 69 F.Supp. 512 (E.D.Pa.1946). The court found that the violation of the statute was a tort and granted relief for the plaintiff who was a member of the protected class.

*Borak* also raises the question of the proper role of federal courts in determining the substantive standard of conduct to which persons governed by a statute are subject. That role, of course, was altered by *Erie Railroad Co. v. Tompkins*, 304 U.S. 64, 58 S.Ct. 817, 82 L.Ed. 1188 (1938), which held that there was no general federal common law. Thereafter, federal courts develop their own body of federal law only when there is a federal statute that does not spell out the rights of private parties. In so doing, the courts analyze Congressional intent.

How is Congressional intent determined? Does a court ask whether Congress specifically intended that the federal courts would create federal common law, including private rights of action, under a particular statute, or should the court determine whether there is a private right of action on the basis of Congress' policy or purpose in a particular federal program and the need for a private remedy? *See Wheeldin v. Wheeler*, 373 U.S. 647, 83 S.Ct. 1441, 10 L.Ed.2d 605 (1963). Some commentators have urged that Congressional intent be examined in light of the traditional tort theory. Professor Louis Loss, the leading scholar of securities law, argued that Congressional silence about implied private rights of action in the face of "accepted" doctrine was best understood as justifying the conclusion that Congress intended the courts to follow this doctrine, thereby creating private rights of action. 9 Louis Loss and Joel Seligman, SECURITIES REGULATION 4333–4334 (3d ed. 1992). Virtually none of this analysis is found in the *Borak* opinion.

The Supreme Court continued to support implied private rights of action under the federal securities laws in the years immediately following the *Borak* decision. In *Mills v. Electric Auto–Lite Co.*, 396 U.S. 375, 90 S.Ct. 616, 24 L.Ed.2d 593 (1970), private stockholder actions to enforce the substantive provisions of the securities laws were hailed as "corporate therapeutics," 396 U.S. at 396, 90 S.Ct. at 627. In *Superintendent of Insurance v. Bankers Life & Casualty Co.*, 404 U.S. 6, 13 n. 9, 92 S.Ct. 165, 169 n. 9, 30 L.Ed.2d 128 (1971), the Court acknowledged the existence of an implied right of action under Rule 10b–5 without any discussion in the main body of the opinion.

In the mid–1970's, the Supreme Court began to curtail the availability of implied private rights of action under federal law. Most important was *Cort v. Ash*, 422 U.S. 66, 95 S.Ct. 2080, 45 L.Ed.2d 26 (1975), where a unanimous Court refused to imply a private right of action under the Federal Election Campaign Law. A stockholder of Bethlehem Steel Corporation asserted that the corporation had illegally expended funds in the 1972 Presidential election, and brought a derivative suit to recover the expenditures. In rejecting the stockholder's claim, the Court laid down four factors for determining whether an implied private right of action exists:

1. Is the plaintiff one of the class for whose *especial* benefit the statute was enacted?

2. Is there any indication of legislative intent, explicit or implicit, either to create or deny the private remedy?

3. Is it consistent with the underlying purposes of the legislative scheme to imply such a remedy?

4.  Is the cause of action one traditionally relegated to state law in an area basically the concern of the states, so that it would be inappropriate to infer a cause of action based solely on federal law?

*Id.* at 78.

*Cort* moves away from the *Borak* analysis and attempts to incorporate the Court's various concerns about the growing role of, and burden on, federal courts. Further, by instructing the courts to look at state law in interpreting a federal statute, the Court was advocating an approach antithetical to the approach followed by the Court from *Rigsby* to *Borak*. Since *Cort,* the Supreme Court has struggled to find an appropriate analysis for when to imply a private right of action under a federal statute, and generally has been reluctant to imply such rights. *See* Robert H.A. Ashford, *Implied Causes of Action Under Federal Laws: Calling the Court Back to Borak*, 79 Nw.U.L.Rev. 227 (1984).

# B.  MATERIALITY

## TSC INDUSTRIES, INC. v. NORTHWAY, INC.

426 U.S. 438, 96 S.Ct. 2126, 48 L.Ed.2d 757 (1976).

[National Industries acquired 34% of TSC Industries stock by purchase from the founding family, and then placed five of its nominees on TSC's board of directors. The two companies agreed to a sale of TSC's assets to National in exchange for stock and warrants of National. A joint proxy statement was issued by the two companies. A shareholder of TSC sued for violation of Section 14(a) of the Securities Exchange Act of 1934 and Rule 14a–9. The shareholder claimed, among other things, that the proxy statement failed to state that purchase of the 34% block of stock, which was disclosed, gave it control of TSC. The District Court found no material omissions from the proxy statement, but the Court of Appeals reversed.]

MR. JUSTICE MARSHALL delivered the opinion of the Court.

The question of materiality, it is universally agreed, is an objective one, involving the significance of an omitted or misrepresented fact to a reasonable investor. Variations in the formulation of a general test of materiality occur in the articulation of just how significant a fact must be or, put another way, how certain it must be that the fact would affect a reasonable investor's judgment.

The Court of Appeals in this case concluded that material facts include "all facts which a reasonable shareholder *might* consider important." 512 F.2d at 330 (emphasis added). This formulation of the test of materiality has been explicitly rejected by at least two courts as setting too low a threshold for the imposition of liability under Rule 14a–9. *Gerstle v. Gamble–Skogmo, Inc.*, 478 F.2d 1281, 1301–1302 (C.A.2 1973); *Smallwood v. Pearl Brewing Co.*, 489 F.2d 579, 603–604 (C.A.5 1974). In these cases, panels of the Second and Fifth Circuits opted for the conventional tort test of materiality—whether a reasonable man *would* attach importance to the fact misrepresented or omitted in determining his course of action. * * *

In arriving at its broad definition of a material fact as one that a reasonable shareholder *might* consider important, the Court of Appeals in this case relied heavily upon language of this Court in *Mills v. Electric Auto–Lite Co., supra.* That reliance was misplaced. The *Mills* Court did characterize a determination of materiality as at least "embod[ying] a conclusion that the defect was of such a character that it might have been considered important by a reasonable shareholder who was in the process of deciding how to vote." But if any language in *Mills* is to be read as suggesting a general notion of materiality, it can only be the opinion's subsequent reference to materiality as a "requirement that the defect have a significant *propensity* to affect the voting process." For it was that requirement that the Court said "adequately serves the purpose of ensuring that a cause of action cannot be established by proof of a defect so trivial, or so unrelated to the transaction for which approval is sought, that correction of the defect or imposition of liability would not further the interests protected by § 14(a)." Even this language must be read, however, with appreciation that the Court specifically declined to consider the materiality of the omissions in *Mills*. The references to materiality were simply preliminary to our consideration of the sole question in the case—whether proof of the materiality of an omission from a proxy statement must be supplemented by a showing that the defect actually caused the outcome of the vote. It is clear, then, that *Mills* did not intend to foreclose further inquiry into the meaning of materiality under Rule 14a–9.

## C

In formulating a standard of materiality under Rule 14a–9, we are guided, of course, by the recognition in *Borak* and *Mills* of the Rule's broad remedial purpose. That purpose is not merely to ensure by judicial means that the transaction, when judged by its real terms, is fair and otherwise adequate, but to ensure disclosures by corporate management in order to enable the shareholders to make an informed choice. As an abstract proposition, the most desirable role for a court in a suit of this sort, coming after the consummation of the proposed transaction, would perhaps be to determine whether in fact the proposal would have been favored by the shareholders and consummated in the absence of any misstatement or omission. But as we recognized in *Mills,* such matters are not subject to determination with certainty. Doubts as to the critical nature of information misstated or omitted will be commonplace. And particularly in view of the prophylactic purpose of the Rule and the fact that the content of the proxy statement is within management's control, it is appropriate that these doubts be resolved in favor of those the statute is designed to protect.

We are aware, however, that the disclosure policy embodied in the proxy regulations is not without limit. Some information is of such dubious significance that insistence on its disclosure may accomplish more harm than good. The potential liability for Rule 14a–9 violation can be great indeed, and if the standard of materiality is unnecessarily low, not only may the corporation and its management be subjected to liability for insignificant omissions or misstatements, but also management's fear of exposing itself to substantial liability may cause it simply to bury the shareholders in an avalanche of trivial information—a result that is hardly conducive to informed decisionmaking. Precisely these dangers are presented, we think, by the definition of a material fact adopted by the Court of Appeals in this case—a fact which a reasonable shareholder *might* consider important. We agree with Judge Friendly, speaking for the Court of Appeals in *Gerstle,* that the "might" formulation is "too suggestive of mere possibility, however unlikely."

The general standard of materiality that we think best comports with the policies of Rule 14a–9 is as follows: An omitted fact is material if there is a substantial likelihood that a reasonable shareholder would consider it important in deciding how to vote. This standard is fully consistent with *Mills* general description of materiality as a requirement that "the defect have a significant *propensity* to affect the voting process." It does not require proof of a substantial likelihood that disclosure of the omitted fact would have caused the reasonable investor to change his vote. What the standard does contemplate is a showing of a substantial likelihood that, under all the circumstances, the omitted fact would have assumed actual significance in the deliberations of the reasonable shareholder. Put another way, there must be a substantial likelihood that the disclosure of the omitted fact would have been viewed by the reasonable investor as having significantly altered the "total mix" of information made available.

* * * In considering whether summary judgment on the issue is appropriate, we must bear in mind that the underlying objective facts, which will often be free from dispute, are merely the starting point for the ultimate determination of materiality. The determination requires delicate assessments of the inferences a "reasonable shareholder" would draw from a given set of facts and the significance of those inferences to him, and these assessments are peculiarly ones for the trier of fact. Only if the established omissions are "so obviously important to an investor, that reasonable minds cannot differ on the question of materiality" is the ultimate issue of materiality appropriately resolved "as a matter of law" by summary judgment.

### III

The omissions found by the Court of Appeals to have been materially misleading as a matter of law involved two general issues—the degree of National's control over TSC at the time of the proxy solicitation, and the favorability of the terms of the proposed transaction to TSC shareholders.

## A. NATIONAL'S CONTROL OF TSC

The Court of Appeals concluded that two omitted facts relating to National's potential influence, or control, over the management of TSC were material as a matter of law. First, the proxy statement failed to state that at the time the statement was issued, the chairman of the TSC board of directors was Stanley Yarmuth, National's president and chief executive officer, and the chairman of the TSC executive committee was Charles Simonelli, National's executive vice president. Second the statement did not disclose that in filing reports required by the SEC, both TSC and National had indicated that National "may be deemed to be a 'parent' of TSC as that term is defined in the Rules and Regulations under the Securities Act of 1933." The Court of Appeals noted that TSC shareholders were relying on the TSC board of directors to negotiate on their behalf for the best possible rate of exchange with National. It then concluded that the omitted facts were material because they were "persuasive indicators that the TSC board was in fact under the control of National, and that National thus 'sat on both sides of the table' in setting the terms of the exchange."

We do not agree that the omission of these facts, when viewed against the disclosures contained in the proxy statement, warrants the entry of summary judgment against TSC and National on this record. Our conclusion is the same whether the omissions are considered separately or together.

The proxy statement prominently displayed the facts that National owned 34% of the outstanding shares in TSC, and that no other person owned more than 10%. It also prominently revealed that 5 out of 10 TSC directors were National nominees, and it recited the positions of those National nominees with National—indicating, among other things, that Stanley Yarmuth was president and a director of National, and that Charles Simonelli was executive vice president and a director of National. These disclosures clearly revealed the nature of National's relationship with TSC and alerted the reasonable shareholder to the fact that National exercised a degree of influence over TSC. In view of these disclosures, we certainly cannot say that the additional facts that Yarmuth was chairman of the TSC board of directors and Simonelli chairman of its executive committee were, on this record, so obviously important that reasonable minds could not differ on their materiality.

[The Court also found that the other omissions were not material as a matter of law. It reversed the entry of summary judgment for the plaintiff and remanded to allow a fact-finder to determine the materiality of the omissions discussed above.]

### *Note: Materiality Under Federal Law*

As the Court makes clear in *TSC*, not every misstatement or omission is material. Must the omission or false or misleading statement have played a significant role in bringing about the matter submitted to a vote? Do only those errors which bear upon the financial soundness of the investment have bearing on a shareholder's decision to grant a proxy? Do other factors, not easily quantifiable, have anything to do with a shareholder's decision? Do the proxy rules have any aim other than the protection of the shareholder's interest?

These questions have jurisdictional significance. To the extent that a company may be held liable for failing to disclose information that is material in relation to some goal other than investor protection, great sweep is given to the federal securities laws and to the SEC's power to govern corporate conduct. Section 14(a) of the Securities Exchange Act of 1934 gives the Commission power to prescribe rules and regulations it deems "necessary or appropriate in the public interest or for the protection of investors." Presumably the words "in the public interest" have some meaning that, according to one writer, "would seem at least to permit the Commission to take into account the broader public interest when acting in areas near the margins of investor protection * * *." Russell B. Stevenson, Jr., *The SEC and Foreign Bribery*, 32 Bus.Law. 53 (1976). However, the Supreme Court in *NAACP v. Federal Power Commission*, 425 U.S. 662, 96 S.Ct. 1806, 48 L.Ed.2d 284 (1976) held that similar language in another statute should be read to confine the agency's power close to its main purposes, which in the case of the SEC means the protection of investors. And, as we saw in Chapter 14, the Court of Appeals in *Business Roundtable* strongly suggested that there were limits to the SEC's authority under Section 14(a) in areas of traditional state corporate governance.

To what extent is the failure to disclose violations of the law a material omission? One answer might be that the violation of law is material if the penalty imposed on the corporation is financially significant so as to be relevant to a traditional investment analysis. But suppose the violation results in relatively insignificant penalties or, even better from the company's standpoint, was incurred in the course of obtaining substantial benefits for the company. For example, a company might have violated some environmental law which enabled it to dispose of waste products at a great saving. Or it might have bribed a public official in return for which it received substantial economic benefits which it retains. Are investors interested in requiring disclosure of that information especially where the disclosure might deter the company from securing the economic advantage? Should there be liability under the proxy rules for omitting these facts? Or would it constitute a compounding of the original violation, brought within the scope of securities laws because of a failure to disclose that violation?

The cases that deal with these questions do not always arise under Section 14(a), but they are relevant to interpreting that section. Thus, the SEC found that United States Steel Corporation had violated the reporting requirements of Section 13(a) of the Securities Exchange Act of 1934 when it failed to disclose the company's frequent violations of environmental requirements, which resulted in fines to the company. *In the Matter of United States Steel Corporation*, Rel. No. 34–16223 (Sept. 27, 1979). It was the *pattern* of the company's behavior combined with its intransigent attitude toward the environmental violations rather than the isolated violation, that probably caused the SEC to charge disclosure violations.

In *Levine v. NL Industries, Inc.*, 926 F.2d 199 (2d Cir.1991), plaintiffs argued that the failure to disclose the costs of failing to comply with environmental regulations constituted a violation of Rule 10b–5. Noting both SEC rules and the decision in *United States Steel*, the court acknowledged that such information would normally be material and thus required to be disclosed. In this case, however, the court found that there had been no breach of the duty to disclose because the United States government had indemnified the company against such costs.

For an expression of the SEC's concern about the adequacy of disclosure of environmental liability, *see* SEC Staff Accounting Bulletin 92 (June 8, 1993).

In the REPORT OF THE SECURITIES AND EXCHANGE COMMISSION ON QUESTIONABLE AND ILLEGAL CORPORATE PAYMENTS AND PRACTICES, submitted to the Senate Banking, Housing and Urban Affairs Committee in 1976, the SEC contended that questionable or illegal payments were material facts regardless of the size of the payments or their impact on the corporations' business. The Commission argued that the disclosure requirements are intended to facilitate the stockholders' evaluation of management's stewardship, and that "investors should be vitally interested in the quality and integrity of management." Several courts have endorsed this approach, albeit in particular contexts. In *SEC v. Kalvex, Inc.*, 425 F.Supp. 310 (S.D.N.Y.1975), the court held that the proxy statement's failure to disclose that a candidate for director had arranged for illegal kick-backs of a small amount was a material omission because of the bearing that the information had on the candidate's integrity. Similarly, in *Cooke v. Teleprompter Corp.*, 334 F.Supp. 467 (S.D.N.Y.1971), the court found that it was a material omission to fail to disclose that a candidate for the board had been convicted of bribing public officials. Teleprompter's operations depended upon receiving an FCC license, heightening the importance of information the FCC might deem important. In *SEC v. Jos. Schlitz Brewing Co.*, 452 F.Supp. 824 (E.D.Wis.1978) the court found that the failure to disclose illegal or improper payments made to induce the sale of the company's products was material because of the bearing it had on the integrity of management.

The SEC and the courts now limit disclosure about management integrity to those situations where the rules specifically mandate disclosure or where the conduct has had a materially adverse *economic* impact on the corporation. A former SEC Commissioner has written that self-dealing by directors and officers is a material fact, particularly in the context of proxy statements where directors are standing for office. Bevis Longstreth, *SEC Disclosure Policy Regarding Management Integrity*, 38 BUS.LAW. 1413 (1983). But both the Commission and the courts have moved away from an earlier position that it was material to disclose whether directors or officers had engaged in illegal conduct even if they did not receive any personal benefit. *Gaines v. Haughton*, 645 F.2d 761 (9th Cir.1981). Disclosure of "material" facts does not require directors and officers to accuse themselves of antisocial or illegal policies in the proxy statement. Alleged violations of banking laws or labor laws, for example, supposedly revealing questionable moral or ethical conduct, are not "material" for purposes of the proxy rules. The emphasis of the disclosure requirements is on quantitatively significant information, not qualitative information except for self-dealing conduct.

In addition to providing a sufficient basis for a voting decision, disclosure may deter wrongful conduct. That is, disclosure can have a therapeutic effect. The Advisory Committee on Corporate Disclosure to the SEC recommended (with one of the authors of this book dissenting) that "the Commission should not adopt disclosure requirements which have as their principal objective the regulation of corporate conduct." In commenting upon that report the Commission said "it does not believe, however, that the benefits to be derived from such a statement would, on balance outweigh the difficulties which it might create * * *. Decisions as to whether to require disclosure frequently do affect conduct and Congress was well aware of this consequence and thought it would often be beneficial." PRELIMINARY RESPONSES OF THE COMMISSION TO THE RECOMMEN-DATIONS OF THE ADVISORY COMMITTEE ON CORPORATE DISCLOSURE, *Securities Act Release No. 5906*, Fed.Sec.L.Rep. (CCH) ¶ 81,505 (Feb. 15, 1978).

In some cases, the real focus of the shareholder's attack is management's conduct; the claim of inadequate disclosure in violation of the proxy rules becomes the vehicle for plaintiffs' obtaining federal jurisdiction rather than attempting to establish a breach of fiduciary duty under state law. For example, if the proxy statement for a patently unfair merger contained materially false and misleading statements, but the shareholders rejected the merger, no suit under Section 14(a) could be maintained. In such a case, the shareholder could not show how any loss was caused by the violation. The more likely scenario, however, is the converse: the facts establishing the unfairness of the merger were fully and painfully disclosed, but the shareholders approved. The loss is plain enough—the transaction was unfair—but has there been a violation of the proxy rules? Must the unfairness be identified and the merger characterized as unfair? In other words, do the rules require more than disclosure of facts from which the decision maker can draw her own conclusions? If so, the result would appear to be the federalization of state law fiduciary duties in the guise of implementing the full disclosure policy of the federal securities laws. Keep these questions in mind in reading the materials in Section E.

In *Golub v. PPD Corp.*, 576 F.2d 759 (8th Cir.1978), plaintiffs alleged that a corporation's sale of assets to a related person was unfair, and that the proxy statement did not disclose management's improper motives. The court upheld dismissal of the complaint, stating:

> * * * [The] plaintiffs are not complaining about any absence of facts in the proxy statement. Their complaint is that those who

prepared the statement did not "disclose" what the plaintiffs say was the true motivation of * * * management in selling the assets of the company, and did not characterize the bonus aspects of the transaction as plaintiffs would have it characterized. Under the ['34] Act and regulations plaintiffs were not entitled to have such a "disclosure" or such a characterization.

It is quite possible that plaintiffs may have a claim against the defendants or some of them under applicable state law. If so, plaintiffs are free to pursue that claim in an appropriate forum.
* * *

*Id.* at 764–65.

Similarly, in *Wallerstein v. Primerica Corp.*, 701 F.Supp. 393 (E.D.N.Y.1988), the court rejected plaintiff's claim that the company's proxy statement was materially false and misleading because it stated that the board of directors had "carefully reviewed" the terms of a proposed merger when the board had not. The court noted that, absent anything more, a breach of fiduciary duty did not give rise to a claim under the federal securities laws. The court also found that the plaintiffs had suggested that the directors had not exercised reasonable diligence in connection with the transaction. Accordingly, the court concluded that plaintiffs' assertion "advanced as a 14a–9 claim * * * is a thinly but unsuccessfully disguised breach of fiduciary duty claim." *Id.* at 397.

Although the test for materiality is keyed to the "reasonable shareholder," the context in which the question of materiality arises often will influence the answer. In *Justin Industries, Inc. v. Choctaw Securities, L.P.*, 920 F.2d 262 (5th Cir.1990), the target of a takeover bid, as a defensive tactic, amended its bylaws to include a supermajority provision for the removal of directors. The company failed to disclose the amendments in various SEC filings in violation of the 1934 Act. The amendments were subsequently rescinded. While the bylaws were in force, the directors were re-elected in an unopposed election. The bidder sued to set aside the election and to have a new election ordered in which it could run its own candidates. The district court denied the motion for an injunction, holding that the failure to disclose the amendments was not material because a "typical investor" would not have found them significant.

Although affirming the denial of the preliminary injunction, the Fifth Circuit reversed on the question of materiality and questioned the use of the "typical investor" standard. Noting that changes in the relative power of shareholders and directors were fundamental to the corporate governance system, the court suggested that "striking changes" in that relationship strongly suggested materiality. Here, the context mattered. Although not every change in the bylaws would be material, where the company had recently signaled its opposition to any hostile takeover, "the average investor mulling the future value of his or her stake and considering for whom to vote in the director elections could well consider the bylaw changes material." *Id.* at 267.

## C. CAUSATION

### MILLS v. ELECTRIC AUTO–LITE CO.
396 U.S. 375, 90 S.Ct. 616, 24 L.Ed.2d 593 (1970).

Mr. Justice Harlan delivered the opinion of the Court.

This case requires us to consider a basic aspect of the implied private right of action for violation of § 14(a) of the Securities Exchange Act of 1934, recognized by this Court in J.I. Case Co. v. Borak, 377 U.S. 426 (1964). As in *Borak* the asserted wrong is that a corporate merger was accomplished through the use of a proxy statement that was materially false or misleading. The question with which we deal is what causal relationship must be shown between such a statement and the merger to establish a cause of action based on the violation of the Act.

I

Petitioners were shareholders of the Electric Auto–Lite Company until 1963, when it was merged into Mergenthaler Linotype Company. They brought suit on the day before the shareholders' meeting at which the vote was to take place on the merger against Auto–Lite, Mergenthaler, and a third company, American Manufacturing Company, Inc. The complaint sought an injunction against the voting by Auto–Lite's management of all proxies obtained by means of an allegedly misleading proxy solicitation; however, it did not seek a temporary restraining order, and the voting went ahead as scheduled the following day. Several months later petitioners filed an amended complaint, seeking to have the merger set aside and to obtain such other relief as might be proper.

In Count II of the amended complaint, which is the only count before us, petitioners predicated jurisdiction on § 27 of the 1934 Act. They alleged that the proxy statement sent out by the Auto–Lite management to solicit shareholders' votes in favor of the merger was misleading, in violation of § 14(a) of the Act and SEC Rule 14a–9 thereunder. Petitioners recited that before the merger Mergenthaler owned over 50% of the outstanding shares of Auto–Lite common stock, and had been in control of Auto–Lite for two years. American Manufacturing in turn owned about one-third of the outstanding shares of Mergenthaler, and for two years had been in voting control of Mergenthaler and, through it, of Auto–Lite. Petitioners charged that in light of these circumstances the proxy statement was misleading in that it told Auto–Lite shareholders that their board of directors recommended approval of the merger without also informing them that all 11 of Auto–Lite's directors were nominees of Mergenthaler and were under the "control and domination of Mergenthaler." Petitioners asserted the right to complain of this alleged violation both derivatively on behalf of Auto–Lite and as representatives of the class of all its minority shareholders.

On petitioners' motion for summary judgment with respect to Count II, the District Court for the Northern District of Illinois ruled as a matter of law that the claimed defect in the proxy statement was, in light of the circumstances in which the statement was made, a material omission. The District Court concluded, from its reading of the *Borak* opinion, that it had to hold a hearing on the issue whether there was "a causal connection between the finding that there has been a violation of the disclosure requirements of § 14(a) and the alleged injury to the plaintiffs" before it could consider what remedies would be appropriate.

After holding such a hearing, the court found that under the terms of the merger agreement, an affirmative vote of two-thirds of the Auto–Lite shares was required for approval of the merger, and that the respondent companies owned and controlled about 54% of the outstanding shares. Therefore, to obtain authorization of the merger, respondents had to secure the approval of a substantial number of the minority shareholders. At the stockholders' meeting, approximately, 950,000 shares, out of 1,160,000 shares outstanding were voted in favor of the merger. This included 317,000 votes obtained by proxy from the minority shareholders, votes that were "necessary and indispensable to the approval of the merger." The District Court concluded that a causal relationship had thus been shown, and it granted an interlocutory judgment in favor of petitioners on the issue of liability, referring the case to a master for consideration of appropriate relief.

The District Court made the certification required by 28 U.S.C. § 1292(b), and respondents took an interlocutory appeal to the Court of Appeals for the Seventh Circuit. That court affirmed the District Court's conclusion that the proxy statement was materially deficient, but reversed on the question of causation. The court acknowledged that, if an injunction had been sought a sufficient time before the stockholders' meeting, "corrective measures would have been appropriate." 403 F.2d 429, 435 (1968). However, since this suit was brought too late for preventive action, the courts had to determine "whether the misleading statement and omission caused the submission of sufficient proxies," as a prerequisite to a determination of liability under the Act. If the respondents could show, "by a preponderance of probabilities, that the merger would have received a sufficient vote even if the proxy statement had not been misleading in the respect found," petitioners would be entitled to no relief of any kind. *Id.,* at 436.

The Court of Appeals acknowledged that this test corresponds to the common law fraud test of whether the injured party relied on the misrepresentation. However, rightly concluding that "[r]eliance by thousands of individuals, as here, can scarcely be inquired into" (*id.,* at 436 n. 10), the court ruled that the issue was to be determined by proof of the fairness of the terms of the merger. If respondents could show that the merger had merit and was fair to the minority shareholders, the trial court would be justified in concluding that a sufficient number of shareholders would have approved the merger had there been no deficiency in the proxy statement. In that case respondents would be entitled to a judgment in their favor.

Claiming that the Court of Appeals has construed this Court's decision in *Borak* in a manner that frustrates the statute's policy of enforcement through private litigation, the petitioners then sought review in this Court. We granted certiorari, believing that resolution of this basic issue should be made at this stage of the litigation and not postponed until after a trial under the Court of Appeals' decision.

## II

As we stressed in *Borak,* § 14(a) stemmed from a congressional belief that "[f]air corporate suffrage is an important right that should attach to every equity security bought on a public exchange." * * * The decision below, by permitting all liability to be foreclosed on the basis of a finding that the merger was fair, would allow the stockholders to be bypassed, at least where the only legal challenge to the merger is a suit for retrospective relief after the meeting has been held. A judicial appraisal of the merger's merits could be substituted for the actual and informed vote of the stockholders.

The result would be to insulate from private redress an entire category of proxy violations—those relating to matters other than the terms of the merger. Even outrageous misrepresentations in a proxy solicitation, if they did not relate to the terms of the transaction, would give rise to no cause of action under § 14(a). Particularly if carried over to enforcement actions by the Securities and Exchange Commission itself, such a result would subvert the congressional purpose of ensuring full and fair disclosure to shareholders.

Further, recognition of the fairness of the merger as a complete defense would confront small shareholders with an additional obstacle to making a successful challenge to a proposal recommended through a defective proxy statement. The risk that they would be unable to rebut the corporation's evidence of the fairness of the proposal, and thus to establish their cause of action, would be bound to discourage such shareholders from the private enforcement of the proxy rules that "provides a necessary supplement to Commission action." *J.I. Case Co. v. Borak*, 377 U.S., at 432, 84 S.Ct. at 1560.[5]

---

**5.** The Court of Appeals' ruling that "causation" may be negated by proof of the fairness of the merger also rests on a dubious behavioral assumption. There is no justification for presuming that the shareholders of every corporation are willing to accept any and every fair merger offer put before them; yet such a presumption is implicit in the opinion of the Court of Appeals. That court gave no indication of what evidence petitioners might adduce, once respondents had established that the merger proposal was equitable, in order to show that the shareholders would nevertheless have rejected it if the solicitation had not been misleading. Proof of actual reliance by thousands of individuals would, as the court acknowledged, not be feasible, see R. JENNINGS & H. MARSH, SECURITIES REGULATION, CASES AND MATERIALS 1001 (2d ed. 1968) * * *. In practice, therefore, the objective fairness of the proposal would seemingly be determinative of liability. But in view of the many other factors that might lead shareholders to prefer their current position to that of owners of a larger, combined enterprise, it is pure conjecture to assume that the fairness of the proposal will always be determinative of their vote.

Such a frustration of the congressional policy is not required by anything in the wording of the statute or in our opinion in the *Borak* case. Section 14(a) declares it "unlawful" to solicit proxies in contravention of Commission rules, and SEC Rule 14a–9 prohibits solicitations "containing any statement which * * * is false or misleading with respect to any material fact, or which omits to state any material fact necessary in order to make the statements therein not false or misleading * * *." Use of a solicitation that is materially misleading is itself a violation of law, as the Court of Appeals recognized in stating that injunctive relief would be available to remedy such a defect if sought prior to the stockholders' meeting. In *Borak,* which came to this Court on a dismissal of the complaint, the Court limited its inquiry to whether a violation of § 14(a) gives rise to "a federal cause of action for rescission or damages," 377 U.S., at 428, 84 S.Ct. at 1558. Referring to the argument made by petitioners there "that the merger can be dissolved only if it was fraudulent or non-beneficial, issues upon which the proxy material would not bear," the Court stated: "But the causal relationship of the proxy material and the merger are questions of fact to be resolved at trial, not here. We therefore do not discuss this point further." *Id.,* at 431, 84 S.Ct. at 1559. In the present case there has been a hearing specifically directed to the causation problem. The question before the Court is whether the facts found on the basis of that hearing are sufficient in law to establish petitioners' cause of action, and we conclude that they are.

Where the misstatement or omission in a proxy statement has been shown to be "material," as it was found to be here, that determination itself indubitably embodies a conclusion that the defect was of such a character that it might have been considered important by a reasonable shareholder who was in the process of deciding how to vote.[6] This requirement that the defect have a significant *propensity* to affect the voting process is found in the express terms of Rule 14a–9, and it adequately serves the purpose of ensuring that a cause of action cannot be established by proof of a defect so trivial, or so unrelated to the transaction for which approval is sought, that correction of the defect or imposition of liability would not further the interests protected by § 14(a).

There is no need to supplement this requirement, as did the Court of Appeals, with a requirement of proof of whether the defect actually

---

**6.** In this case, where the misleading aspect of the solicitation involved failure to reveal a serious conflict of interest on the part of the directors, the Court of Appeals concluded that the crucial question in determining materiality was "whether the minority shareholders were sufficiently alerted to the board's relationship to their adversary to be on their guard." 403 F.2d, at 434. An adequate disclosure of this relationship would have warned the stockholders to give more careful scrutiny to the terms of the merger than they might to one recommended by an entirely disinterested board. Thus, the failure to make such a disclosure was found to be a material defect "as a matter of law," thwarting the informed decision at which the statute aims, regardless of whether the terms of the merger were such that a reasonable stockholder would have approved the transaction after more careful analysis. See also *Swanson v. American Consumer Industries, Inc.,* 415 F.2d 1326 (C.A.7th Cir.1969).

had a decisive effect on the voting. Where there has been a finding of materiality, a shareholder has made a sufficient showing of causal relationship between the violation and the injury for which he seeks redress, if, as here, he proves that the proxy solicitation itself, rather than the particular defect in the solicitation materials, was an essential link in the accomplishment of the transaction. This objective test will avoid the impracticalities of determining how many votes were affected, and, by resolving doubts in favor of those the statute is designed to protect, will effectuate the congressional policy of ensuring that the shareholders are able to make an informed choice when they are consulted on corporate transactions.[7] * * *

## III

Our conclusion that petitioners have established their case by showing that proxies necessary to approval of the merger were obtained by means of a materially misleading solicitation implies nothing about the form of relief to which they may be entitled. We held in *Borak* that upon finding a violation the courts were "to be alert to provide such remedies as are necessary to make effective the congressional purpose," noting specifically that such remedies are not to be limited to prospective relief. 377 U.S., at 433, 434. In devising retrospective relief for violation of the proxy rules, the federal courts should consider the same factors that would govern the relief granted for any similar illegality or fraud. One important factor may be the fairness of the terms of the merger. Possible forms of relief will include setting aside the merger or granting other equitable relief, but, as the Court of Appeals below noted, nothing in the statutory policy "requires the court to unscramble a corporate transaction merely because a violation occurred." 403 F.2d, at 436. In selecting a remedy the lower courts should exercise " 'the sound discretion which guides the determinations of courts of equity,' "keeping in mind the role of equity as "the instrument for nice adjustment and reconciliation between the public interest and private needs as well as between competing private claims." *Hecht Co. v. Bowles*, 321 U.S. 321, 329–330 (1944), quoting from *Meredith v. Winter Haven*, 320 U.S. 228, 235 (1943). * * *

Monetary relief will, of course, also be a possibility. Where the defect in the proxy solicitation relates to the specific terms of the merger, the district court might appropriately order an accounting to ensure that the shareholders receive the value that was represented as coming to them. On the other hand, where, as here, the misleading aspect of the solicitation did not relate to terms of the merger, monetary relief might be afforded to the shareholders only if the merger resulted in a reduction of

---

**7.** We need not decide in this case whether causation could be shown where the management controls a sufficient number of shares to approve the transaction without any votes from the minority. Even in that situation, if the management finds it necessary for legal or practical reasons to solicit proxies from minority shareholders, at least one court has held that the proxy solicitation might be sufficiently related to the merger to satisfy the causation requirement, *see Laurenzano v. Einbender*, 264 F.Supp. 356 (D.C.E.D.N.Y.1966).

the earnings or earnings potential of their holdings. In short, damages should be recoverable only to the extent that they can be shown. If commingling of the assets and operations of the merged companies makes it impossible to establish direct injury from the merger, relief might be predicated on a determination of the fairness of the terms of the merger at the time it was approved. These questions, of course, are for decision in the first instance by the District Court on remand, and our singling out of some of the possibilities is not intended to exclude others. * * *

## IV

Although the question of relief must await further proceedings in the District Court, our conclusion that petitioners have established their cause of action indicates that the Court of Appeals should have affirmed the partial summary judgment on the issue of liability. The result would have been not only that respondents, rather than petitioners, would have borne the costs of the appeal, but also, we think, that petitioners would have been entitled to an interim award of litigation expenses and reasonable attorneys' fees. We agree with the position taken by petitioners, and by the United States as *amicus,* that petitioners, who have established a violation of the securities laws by their corporation and its officials, should be reimbursed by the corporation or its survivor for the costs of establishing the violation. * * *

While the general American rule is that attorneys' fees are not ordinarily recoverable as costs, both the courts and Congress have developed exceptions to this rule for situations in which overriding considerations indicate the need for such a recovery. A primary judge-created exception has been to award expenses where a plaintiff has successfully maintained a suit, usually on behalf of a class, that benefits a group of others in the same manner as himself. To allow the others to obtain from the plaintiff's efforts without contributing equally to the litigation expenses would be to enrich the others unjustly at the plaintiff's expense. This suit presents such a situation. The dissemination of misleading proxy solicitations was a "deceit practiced on the stockholders as a group," *J.I. Case Co. v. Borak*, 377 U.S. at 482, 84 S.Ct. at 1560, and the expenses of petitioners' lawsuit have been incurred for the benefit of the corporation and the other shareholders.

The fact that this suit has not yet produced, and may never produce, a monetary recovery from which the fees could be paid does not preclude an award based on this rationale. * * *

In many suits under § 14(a), particularly where the violation does not relate to the terms of the transaction for which proxies are solicited, it may be impossible to assign monetary value to the benefit. Nevertheless, the stress placed by Congress on the importance of fair and informed corporate suffrage leads to the conclusion that, in vindicating the statutory policy, petitioners have rendered a substantial service to the corporation and its shareholders. Whether petitioners are successful in showing a need for significant relief may be a factor in determining whether a further award should later be made. But regardless of the relief granted, private stockholders' actions of this sort "involve corporate therapeutics," and furnish a benefit to all shareholders by providing an important means of enforcement of the proxy statute. To award attorneys' fees in such a suit to a plaintiff who has succeeded in establishing a cause of action is not to saddle the unsuccessful party with the expenses but to impose them on the class that has benefited from them and that would have had to pay them had it brought the suit.

For the foregoing reasons we conclude that the judgment of the Court of Appeals should be vacated and the case remanded to that court for further proceedings consistent with this opinion.

It is so ordered.

### Note: Mills and Afterward

On remand, the fairness of the transaction became relevant to the question of relief. The District Court found that the merger was unfair to the minority shareholders and awarded damages of $1,233,918. The Court of Appeals reversed, again holding that the merger was fair to Auto–Lite's minority shareholders. 552 F.2d 1239 (7th Cir.1977), *cert. denied* 434 U.S. 922, 98 S.Ct. 398, 54 L.Ed.2d 279 (1977). The court also held that plaintiff's attorneys would be entitled to fees from the corporation only for the period up to the Supreme Court decision. Lead counsel was awarded a fee of $250,000, not an overly generous amount considering the time devoted to the case.

In an interesting aftermath to the decision in the *Wal-Mart* shareholder proposal case in Chapter 14, the Second Circuit affirmed Judge Wood's award of $54,100 in attorneys fees to plaintiffs. *Amalgamated Clothing and Textile Workers v. Wal–Mart Stores, Inc.*, 54 F.3d 69 (2d Cir. 1995). The court relied on Part IV of the Supreme Court's opinion in *Mills* and held "that the promotion of corporate suffrage regarding a significant policy issue confers a substantial benefit regardless of the percentage of votes cast for or against the proposal at issue." 54 F.3d at 71–72. The court noted that the result of the suit to compel inclusion of the shareholder proposal in the proxy statement was to "facilitate communications among the shareholders as well as between shareholders and management * * *. Thus the communication * * * conferred a substantial benefit on the company's shareholders. The benefit is similar to the benefit resulting from a successful claim under Rule 14a–9, prohibiting omission of material facts from proxy statements, and fees are regularly allowed for successful 14a–9 lawsuits." *Id.*

## D.   DISCLOSURE AND FIDUCIARY STANDARDS UNDER FEDERAL LAW

Thus far, we have examined situations where shareholders have acted as decision-makers. In such cases, if there is a material misstatement or omission, the shareholder may be deceived when voting. Put differently, accurate information is necessary in order to preserve the integrity of the voting process. More difficult questions arise when a transaction does not require shareholder decision-making. Can a shareholder be deceived in such a situation? If so, how does the "deception" occur? Moreover, if the shareholder is not a decision-maker, how can there be causation, even if a material misstatement is made? Or, indeed, if there is *no* disclosure at all?

These question often arise in connection with transactions that, at least arguably, involve some financial unfairness. As we have seen, proof of financial unfairness may not be sufficient to establish a breach of fiduciary duty. State law principles, at times, insulate arguably unfair transactions from judicial scrutiny, especially if those transactions have been approved by independent directors or independent shareholders. In addition, state law often makes it difficult to maintain class actions or to sue defendants domiciled in different states.

In order to avoid litigating their claims under state law, or to obtain procedural advantages available to plaintiffs in actions brought under the federal securities laws, aggrieved shareholders often used the latter to challenge transactions they believed were unfair. When proxies had been solicited and the proxy solicitation constituted an "essential link" in effectuating the transaction, their task was simple—they sued under § 14(a) and Rule 14a–9. Where no proxy solicitation occurred, their task became more complex. The most attractive alternative often was a suit under § 10(b) of the 1934 Act and SEC Rule 10b–5.

Rule 10b–5 is concerned with decisions to purchase or sell stock, rather than with decisions about how to vote. It prohibits both false and misleading statements and fraudulent acts and practices in connection with the purchase or sale of any security. The earliest cases brought under Rule 10b–5 all involved traditional informational fraud. When plaintiffs attempted to expand Rule 10b–5 to challenge unfair or "constructively fraudulent," transactions, the courts rebuffed their initial efforts. *See Birnbaum v. Newport Steel Corp.*, 193 F.2d 461 (2d Cir.1952), *cert. denied* 343 U.S. 956, 72 S.Ct. 1051, 96 L.Ed. 1356 (1952); *Pappas v. Moss*, 393 F.2d 865 (3d Cir.1968).

Then came *Schoenbaum v. Firstbrook*, 405 F.2d 215 (2d Cir.1968). A shareholder of Banff brought suit under Rule 10b–5, alleging that Banff had sold some of its stock to Aquitaine, its majority shareholder, at an unfair price in a transaction approved unanimously by Banff's non-Aquitaine directors. No shareholder vote was required in the transaction. The Second Circuit, *en banc*, reversed the dismissal of the shareholder's complaint, reasoning:

> In the present case it is alleged that Aquitaine exercised a controlling influence over the issuance to it of treasury stock of Banff for a wholly inadequate consideration. If it is established that the transaction took place as alleged, it constituted a violation of Rule 10b–5, Subdivision (3) because Aquitaine engaged in an "act, practice or

course of business which operates or would operate as a fraud or deceit upon any person, in connection with the purchase or sale of any security." Moreover, Aquitaine and the directors of Banff were guilty of deceiving the stockholders of Banff (other than Aquitaine).

*Id.* at 219–20.

This passage, and particularly the word "moreover," engendered considerable debate. Had the court ruled that it was sufficient, to state a claim under Rule 10b–5, to allege that a controlling shareholder had breached its fiduciary duty by purchasing stock from its majority-owned subsidiary at an unfair price? Or had the court upheld the complaint on the ground that Banff's shareholders (other than Aquitaine) were deceived? And, if the latter was the case, how had the deception occurred, since the stock sale did not require shareholder approval? The theory for finding deception apparently was based on the view that the non-Aquitaine directors of Banff were the surrogates for the Banff shareholders in the transaction. Thus, if the directors were deceived, so were the shareholders, even though the latter did not participate in the transaction.

*Superintendent of Insurance v. Bankers Life & Casualty Co.*, 404 U.S. 6, 92 S.Ct. 165, 30 L.Ed.2d 128 (1971), deepened the confusion. Through a complex series of transactions, the principal defendant Begole stole $5 million that Manhattan Casualty Co. should have received for selling certain Treasury bonds and used that money to finance his purchase of all Manhattan's stock. When Begole thereafter looted Manhattan, New York's Superintendent of Insurance brought suit under Rule 10b–5 against several parties who allegedly had aided and abetted Begole's scheme. The Court upheld the Superintendent's complaint, stating "Manhattan was injured as an investor through a deceptive device" because it received nothing for its Treasury bonds. But, in the view of most observers, the case really involved not informational fraud but simple theft by a corporate insider—a classic breach of fiduciary duty.

The high-water mark for the expanded view of Rule 10b–5 was *Green v. Santa Fe Industries, Inc.*, 533 F.2d 1283 (2d Cir.1976), involving a transaction in which a majority shareholder cashed out the minority interest in a short-form merger at a price far below the asset value of the corporation's stock. No vote by minority shareholders was required under Delaware law, and no advance notice of the merger was provided to the minority shareholders. As in *Schoenbaum*, it was difficult to argue that the minority shareholders had been deceived. Moreover, under Delaware law at that time, it appeared that appraisal was the exclusive remedy for minority shareholders in such a transaction, and they were advised of their ability to exercise their appraisal rights. Nevertheless, the Second Circuit interpreted *Schoenbaum* and *Superintendent of Insurance* to hold that Rule 10b–5 provided a remedy for constructive fraud and reversed dismissal of a claim that the majority shareholder had violated Rule 10b–5, stating: "Lest there be any lingering doubt on this point, we now hold that [in cases involving a breach of fiduciary duty], including the one now before us, no allegation or proof of misrepresentation or non-disclosure is necessary." *Id.* at 1287.

## 1. INFORMATIONAL VS. CONSTRUCTIVE FRAUD

### SANTA FE INDUSTRIES, INC. v. GREEN

430 U.S. 462, 97 S.Ct. 1292, 51 L.Ed.2d 480 (1977).

MR. JUSTICE WHITE delivered the opinion of the Court.

The issue in this case involves the reach and coverage of § 10(b) of the Securities Exchange Act of 1934 and Rule 10b–5 thereunder in the context of a Delaware short-form merger transaction used by the majority stockholder of a corporation to eliminate the minority interest.

I

In 1936, petitioner Santa Fe Industries, Inc. (Santa Fe), acquired control of 60% of the stock of Kirby Lumber Corp. (Kirby), a Delaware corporation. Through a series of purchases over the succeeding years, Santa Fe increased its control of Kirby's stock to 95%; the purchase prices during the period 1968–1973 ranged from $65 to $92.50 per share. In 1974, wishing to acquire 100% ownership of Kirby, Santa Fe availed itself of § 253 of the Delaware Corporation Law, known as the "short-form merger" statute. Section 253 permits a parent corporation owning at least 90% of the stock of a subsidiary to merge with that subsidiary, upon approval by the parent's board of directors, and to make payment in cash for the shares of the minority stockholders. The statute does not require the consent of, or advance notice to, the minority stockholders. However, notice of the merger must be given within 10 days after its effective date, and any stockholder who is dissatisfied with the terms of the merger may petition the Delaware Court of Chancery for a decree ordering the surviving corporation to pay him the fair value of his shares, as determined by a court-appointed appraiser subject to review by the court.

Santa Fe obtained independent appraisals of the physical assets of Kirby—land, timber, buildings, and machinery—and of Kirby's oil, gas, and mineral interests. These appraisals, together with other financial information, were submitted to Morgan Stanley & Co. (Morgan Stanley), an investment banking firm retained to appraise the fair market value of Kirby stock. Kirby's physical assets were appraised at $320 million (amounting to $640 for each of the 500,000 shares); Kirby's stock was valued by Morgan Stanley at $125 per share. Under the terms of the merger, minority stockholders were offered $150 per share.

The provisions of the short-form merger statute were fully complied with. The minority stockholders of Kirby were notified the day after the merger became effective and were advised of their right to obtain an appraisal in Delaware court if dissatisfied with the offer of $150 per share. They also received an information statement containing, in addition to the relevant financial data about Kirby, the appraisals of the value of Kirby's assets and the Morgan Stanley appraisal concluding that the fair market value of the stock was $125 per share.

Respondents, minority stockholders of Kirby, objected to the terms of the merger, but did not pursue their appraisal remedy in the Delaware Court of Chancery. Instead, they brought this action in federal court on behalf of the corporation and other minority stockholders, seeking to set aside the merger or to recover what they claimed to be the fair value of their shares. The amended complaint asserted that, based on the fair market value of Kirby's physical assets as revealed by the appraisal included in the information statement sent to minority shareholders, Kirby's stock was worth at least $772 per share. The complaint alleged further that the merger took place without prior notice to minority stockholders; that the purpose of the merger was to appropriate the difference between the "conceded pro rata value of the physical assets," and the offer of $150 per share—to "freez[e] out the minority stockholders at a wholly inadequate price," and that Santa Fe, knowing the appraised value of the physical assets, obtained a "fraudulent appraisal" of the stock from Morgan Stanley and offered $25 above that appraisal "in order to lull the minority stockholders into erroneously believing that [Santa Fe was] generous." This course of conduct was alleged to be "a violation of Rule 10b–5 because defendants employed a 'device, scheme, or artifice to defraud' and engaged in an 'act, practice or course of business which operates or would operate as a fraud or deceit upon any person, in connection with the purchase or sale of any security.' "Morgan Stanley assertedly participated in the fraud as an accessory by submitting its appraisal of $125 per share although knowing the appraised value of the physical assets.

The District Court dismissed the complaint for failure to state a claim upon which relief could be granted. 391 F.Supp. 849 (S.D.N.Y. 1975). * * *

A divided Court of Appeals for the Second Circuit reversed. 533 F.2d 1283 (1976). It first agreed that there was a double aspect to the case; first, the claim that gross undervaluation of the minority stock itself violated Rule 10b–5; and second, that "without any misrepresentation or failure to disclose relevant facts, the merger itself constitutes a violation of Rule 10b–5" because it was accomplished without any corporate purpose and without prior notice to the minority stockholders. *Id.*, at 1285. As to the first aspect of the case, the Court of Appeals did not disturb the District Court's conclusion that the complaint did not allege a material misrepresentation or nondisclosure with respect to the value of the stock; and the court declined to rule that a claim of gross undervaluation itself would suffice to make out a Rule 10b–5 case. With respect to the second aspect of the case, however, the court fundamentally disagreed with the District Court as to the reach and coverage of Rule 10b–5. The Court of Appeals' view was that, although the Rule plainly reached material misrepresentations and nondisclosures in connection with the purchase or sale of securities, neither misrepresentation nor nondisclosure was a necessary element of a Rule 10b–5 action; the Rule reached "breaches of fiduciary duty by a majority against minority shareholders without any charge of misrepresentation or lack of disclosure." * * *

### III

[The Court held that § 10(b) of the Act and, consequently, Rule 10b–5 prohibits only conduct involving manipulation or deception.]

As we have indicated, the case comes to us on the premise that the complaint failed to allege a material misrepresentation or material failure to disclose. The finding of the District Court, undisturbed by the Court of Appeals, was that there was no "omission" or "misstatement" in the information statement accompanying the notice of merger. On the basis of the information provided, minority shareholders could either accept the price offered or reject it and seek an appraisal in the Delaware Court of Chancery. Their choice was fairly presented, and they were furnished with all relevant information on which to base their decision.[14]

We therefore find inapposite the cases relied upon by respondents and the court below, in which the breaches of fiduciary duty held violative of Rule 10b–5 included some element of deception. * * * [Those] cases do not support the proposition, adopted by the Court of Appeals below and urged by respondents here, that a breach of fiduciary duty by majority stockholders, without any deception, misrepresentation, or nondisclosure, violates the statute and the Rule.

It is also readily apparent that the conduct alleged in the complaint was not "manipulative" within the meaning of the statute. "Manipulation" is "virtually a term of art when used in connection with securities markets." *Ernst & Ernst*, 425 U.S., at 199, 96 S.Ct., at 1384. * * * No doubt Congress meant to prohibit the full range of ingenious devices that might be used to manipulate securities prices. But we do not think it would have chosen this "term of art" if it had meant to bring within the scope of § 10(b) instances of corporate mismanagement such as this, in which the essence of the complaint is that shareholders were treated unfairly by a fiduciary.

### IV

The language of the statute is, we think, "sufficiently clear in its context" to be dispositive here, but even if it were not, there are

---

**14.** In addition to their principal argument that the complaint alleges a fraud under clauses (a) and (c) of Rule 10b–5, respondents also argue that the complaint alleges nondisclosure and misrepresentation in violation of clause (b) of the Rule. Their major contention in this respect is that the majority stockholder's failure to give the minority advance notice of the merger was a material nondisclosure, even though the Delaware short-form merger statute does not require such notice. But respondents do not indicate how they might have acted differently had they had prior notice of the merger. Indeed, they accept the conclusion of both courts below that under Delaware law they could not have enjoined the merger because an appraisal proceeding is their sole remedy in the Delaware courts for any alleged unfairness in the terms of the merger. Thus, the failure to give advance notice was not a material nondisclosure within the meaning of the statute or the Rule. *Cf. TSC Industries, Inc. v. Northway, Inc.*, 426 U.S. 438, 96 S.Ct. 2126, 48 L.Ed.2d 757 (1976).

additional considerations that weigh heavily against permitting a cause of action under Rule 10b–5 for the breach of corporate fiduciary duty alleged in this complaint. Congress did not expressly provide a private cause of action for violations of § 10(b). Although we have recognized an implied cause of action under that section in some circumstances, *Superintendent of Insurance v. Bankers Life & Cas. Co., supra,* 404 U.S., at 13 n. 9, 92 S.Ct., at 169, we have also recognized that a private cause of action under the antifraud provisions of the Securities Exchange Act should not be implied where it is "unnecessary to ensure the fulfillment of Congress' purposes" in adopting the Act. *Piper v. Chris–Craft Industries,* 430 U.S., at 41, 97 S.Ct., at 949. *Cf. J.I. Case Co. v. Borak,* 377 U.S. 426, 431–433, 84 S.Ct. 1555, 12 L.Ed.2d 423 (1964). As we noted earlier, the Court repeatedly has described the "fundamental purpose" of the Act as implementing a "philosophy of full disclosure"; once full and fair disclosure has occurred, the fairness of the terms of the transaction is at most a tangential concern of the statute. As in *Cort v. Ash,* 422 U.S. 66, 78, 80, 95 S.Ct. 2080, 2087, 2090, 45 L.Ed.2d 26 (1975), we are reluctant to recognize a cause of action here to serve what is "at best a subsidiary purpose" of the federal legislation.

A second factor in determining whether Congress intended to create a federal cause of action in these circumstances is "whether 'the cause of action [is] one traditionally relegated to state law * * *.'" *Piper v. Chris–Craft Industries, Inc.,* 430 U.S., at 40, 97 S.Ct., at 949, quoting Cort v. Ash, *supra,* at 78, 95 S.Ct., at 2087. The Delaware Legislature has supplied minority shareholders with a cause of action in the Delaware Court of Chancery to recover the fair value of shares allegedly undervalued in a short-form merger. Of course, the existence of a particular state-law remedy is not dispositive of the question whether Congress meant to provide a similar federal remedy, but as in *Cort* and *Piper,* we conclude that "it is entirely appropriate in this instance to relegate respondent and others in his situation to whatever remedy is created by state law." 422 U.S., at 84, 95 S.Ct., at 2091; 430 U.S., at 41, 97 S.Ct., at 949.

The reasoning behind a holding that the complaint in this case alleged fraud under Rule 10b–5 could not be easily contained. It is difficult to imagine how a court could distinguish, for purposes of Rule 10b–5 fraud, between a majority stockholder's use of a short-form merger to eliminate the minority at an unfair price and the use of some other device, such as a long-form merger, tender offer, or liquidation, to achieve the same result; or indeed how a court could distinguish the alleged abuses in these going private transactions from other types of fiduciary self-dealing involving transactions in securities. The result would be to bring within the Rule a wide variety of corporate conduct traditionally left to state regulation. In addition to posing a "danger of vexatious litigation which could result from a widely expanded class of plaintiffs under Rule 10b–5," *Blue Chip Stamps v. Manor Drug Stores,* 421 U.S., at 740, 95 S.Ct., at 1927, this extension of the federal securities laws would overlap and quite possibly interfere with state corporate law.

Federal courts applying a "federal fiduciary principle" under Rule 10b–5 could be expected to depart from state fiduciary standards at least to the extent necessary to ensure uniformity within the federal system. Absent a clear indication of congressional intent, we are reluctant to federalize the substantial portion of the law of corporations that deals with transactions in securities, particularly where established state policies of corporate regulation would be overridden. As the Court stated in *Cort v. Ash, supra:* "Corporations are creatures of state law, and investors commit their funds to corporate directors on the understanding that, except where federal law *expressly* requires certain responsibilities of directors with respect to stockholders, state law will govern the internal affairs of the corporation." 422 U.S., at 84, 95 S.Ct., at 2091 (emphasis added).

We thus adhere to the position that "Congress by § 10(b) did not seek to regulate transactions which constitute no more than internal corporate mismanagement." *Superintendent of Insurance v. Bankers Life & Cas. Co.*, 404 U.S., at 12, 92 S.Ct., at 169. There may well be a need for uniform federal fiduciary standards to govern mergers such as that challenged in this complaint. But those standards should not be supplied by judicial extension of § 10(b) and Rule 10b–5 to "cover the corporate universe."

The judgment of the Court of Appeals is reversed, and the case is remanded for further proceedings consistent with this opinion.

So ordered.

Mr. Justice Brennan dissents and would affirm for substantially the reasons stated in the majority and concurring opinions in the Court of Appeals, 533 F.2d 1283 (C.A.2 1976).

### Note: From Santa Fe to Virginia Bankshares

In *Santa Fe* the plaintiffs conceded that disclosure to shareholders would have served no function, not only because they had no vote but because their only remedy was appraisal. Hence, there could be no "material" omission in the failure to disclose. Under this approach, therefore, the availability of a federal cause of action under Rule 10b–5 seems to turn on whether there may also be a state cause of action, presumably for breach of fiduciary duty.

*Goldberg v. Meridor*, 567 F.2d 209 (2d Cir.1977), *cert. denied* 434 U.S. 1069, 98 S.Ct. 1249, 55 L.Ed.2d 771 (1978), involved such a situation. Goldberg, a stockholder of Universal Gas & Oil Company, Inc. (UGO), brought suit against UGO's controlling parent, Maritimecor, S.A. and a number of other parties, challenging Maritimecor's sale of essentially all of its assets to UGO in exchange for up to 4,200,000 shares of UGO stock and the assumption by UGO of Maritimecor's debts. Goldberg alleged that this transaction, for which shareholder approval was neither required or solicited, violated Rule 10b–5.

The essence of the amended complaint was that the exchange was unfair to UGO because Maritimecor had huge current liabilities and few liquid assets. Thus, UGO was likely to be rendered insolvent by the challenged transaction. The defendants moved to dismiss, on the ground that the amended complaint failed to allege the deception or non-disclosure needed to state a claim under rule 10b–5. In response, plaintiff's counsel submitted an affidavit which asserted that "insofar as plaintiff Goldberg, a minority shareholder, is concerned, there has been no disclosure to him of the fraudulent nature of the transfer of Maritimecor assets and liabilities for stock of UGO." Annexed to the affidavit were two press releases describing the agreement. It was asserted that these two press releases failed to disclose certain conflicts of interest; that current liabilities of Maritimecor exceeded the shareholder's net equity; and that Maritimecor had, in fact, overstated its assets since they showed a higher value than appropriate for UGO shares.

The Second Circuit held that the complaint should be treated as if it had alleged that the press releases were materially misleading and that one of UGO's directors was deceived or not fully informed as to the effects of the transaction. Judge Friendly stated:

> Here the complaint alleged "deceit * * * upon UGO's minority shareholders" and, if amendment had been allowed as it should have been, would have alleged misrepresentation as to the UGO–Maritimecor transaction at least in the sense of failure to state material facts "necessary in order to make the statements made, in the light of the circumstances under which they were made, not misleading," Rule 10b–5(b). The nub of the matter is that the conduct attacked in [*Santa Fe* ] did not violate the "fundamental purpose" of the Act as implementing a "philosophy of full disclosure", 430 U.S. at 478, 97 S.Ct. at 1303; the conduct here attacked does.

> Defendants contend that even if all this is true, the failure to make a public disclosure or even the making of a misleading disclosure would have no effect, since no action by stockholders to approve the UGO–Maritimecor transaction was required. * * *

> * * * Here there is surely a significant likelihood that if a reasonable director of UGO had known the facts alleged by plaintiff rather than the barebones of the press releases, he would not have voted for the transaction with Maritimecor.

> Beyond this Goldberg and other minority shareholders would not have been without remedy if the alleged facts had been disclosed. The doubts entertained by our brother as to the existence of injunctive remedies in New York, * * * are unfounded. * * * [There have been a number of New York cases involving] suits by stockholders acting in their own behalf to enjoin the sale of all corporate assets or a merger transaction as to which New York afforded dissenters the remedy of an appraisal. Where an appraisal remedy is not available, the courts of New York have displayed no hesitancy in granting injunctive relief. * * *

The availability of injunctive relief if the defendants had not lulled the minority stockholders of UGO into security by a deceptive disclosure, as they allegedly did, is in sharp contrast to [*Santa Fe,*] where the disclosure following the merger transaction was full and fair, and, as to the premerger period, respondents accepted "the conclusion of both courts below that under Delaware law they could not have enjoined the merger because an appraisal proceeding is their sole remedy in the Delaware courts for any alleged unfairness in the terms of the merger."

*Id.* at 218–220.

――――――

*Goldberg* left open the question of precisely what plaintiffs must show concerning the availability of a state law remedy. Subsequent courts have divided on this issue. The Third Circuit, in *Healey v. Catalyst Recovery of Pennsylvania,* 616 F.2d 641 (3d Cir.1980), held that there must be a reasonable probability that the shareholder could have used the information to obtain an injunction. The Fifth Circuit, in *Alabama Farm Bureau Mutual Casualty Co., Inc. v. American Fidelity Life Insurance Co.,* 606 F.2d 602 (5th Cir.1979), *cert. denied* 449 U.S. 820, 101 S.Ct. 77, 66 L.Ed.2d 22 (1980), held that "all that is required to establish 10b–5 liability is a showing that state law remedies are available, and that the facts shown make out a prima facie case for relief; it is not necessary to go further and prove that the state action would have been successful." 606 F.2d at 614.

However, both the Seventh and Ninth Circuits have demanded a higher threshold, insisting that the plaintiff show both the availability of a claim under state law, and that the state court would have granted the requested relief. *Wright v. Heizer Corp.,* 560 F.2d 236 (7th Cir.1977), *cert. denied* 434 U.S. 1066, 98 S.Ct. 1243, 55 L.Ed.2d 767 (1978); *Kidwell ex rel. Penfold v. Meikle,* 597 F.2d 1273 (9th Cir.1979).

The latter approach has been criticized as unsound. One commentator observed that because the state law claim ultimately turns on the fairness of the transaction, a federal court ruling on the availability of a Rule 10b–5 cause of action would be required to make its own determination of fairness—precisely what *Santa Fe* sought to avoid. *See* Note, *Suits for Breach of Fiduciary Duty Under Rule 10b–5 after Santa Fe Industries Inc. v. Green,* 91 HARV.L.REV. 1874 (1978). See Ralph C. Ferrara & Marc I. Steinberg, *A Reappraisal of Santa Fe: Rule 10b–5 and the New Federalism,* 129 U.PA.L.REV. 263 (1980). On the other hand, under the approach of the Third and Fifth Circuits, plaintiff may have a remedy under Rule 10b–5 even if no relief would be available under state law—a result that also seems at odds with *Santa Fe.*

*Goldberg* can also be viewed as an effort by the Second Circuit (whose decision in *Santa Fe* the Supreme Court had reversed) to bring back into federal court issues that the Court had indicated were more properly left to state law. In *Field v. Trump,* 850 F.2d 938 (2d Cir.1988), *cert. denied* 489 U.S. 1012, 109 S.Ct. 1122, 103 L.Ed.2d 185 (1989), the Second Circuit limited its holding in *Goldberg* in a manner that address- es the federalism concerns of *Santa Fe*. The court reaffirmed *Goldberg*'s holding that a misstatement would be material if shareholders were lulled into foregoing an injunction that was available under state law and necessary to prevent irreparable injury to the corporation. However, the court limited application of this theory to cases involving "willful misconduct of a self-serving nature" and not simple mismanagement or breaches of fiduciary duty. The court justified this limitation by noting that *Goldberg* "involved out-and-out 'looting' and 'stealing,' "under facts that did not require it "to distinguish between conduct that is 'reason- able' and 'unreasonable,' or 'informed' and 'uninformed,' distinctions that are the hallmarks of state fiduciary law." *Id.* at 948–49.

## VIRGINIA BANKSHARES, INC. v. SANDBERG

501 U.S. 1083, 111 S.Ct. 2749, 115 L.Ed.2d 929 (1991).

JUSTICE SOUTER delivered the opinion of the Court.

Section 14(a) of the Securities Exchange Act of 1934, authorizes the Securities and Exchange Commission to adopt rules for the solicitation of proxies, and prohibits their violation. In *J.I. Case Co. v. Borak,* we first recognized an implied private right of action for the breach of § 14(a) as implemented by SEC Rule 14a–9, which prohibits the solicita- tion of proxies by means of materially false or misleading statements.

The questions before us are whether a statement couched in conclu- sory or qualitative terms purporting to explain directors' reasons for recommending certain corporate action can be materially misleading within the meaning of Rule 14a–9, and whether causation of damages compensable under § 14(a) can be shown by a member of a class of minority shareholders whose votes are not required by law or corporate bylaw to authorize the corporate action subject to the proxy solicitation. We hold that knowingly false statements of reasons may be actionable even though conclusory in form, but that respondents have failed to demonstrate the equitable basis required to extend the § 14(a) private action to such shareholders when any indication of congressional intent to do so is lacking.

I

In December 1986, First American Bankshares, Inc., (FABI), a bank holding company, began a "freeze-out" merger, in which the First American Bank of Virginia (Bank) eventually merged into Virginia Bankshares, Inc., (VBI), a wholly owned subsidiary of FABI. VBI owned 85% of the Bank's shares, the remaining 15% being in the hands of some 2,000 minority shareholders. FABI hired the investment banking firm of Keefe, Bruyette & Woods (KBW) to give an opinion on the appropriate price for shares of the minority holders, who would lose their interests in the Bank as a result of the merger. Based on market quotations and unverified information from FABI, KBW gave the Bank's executive committee an opinion that $42 a share would be a fair price for the minority stock. The executive committee approved the merger proposal at that price, and the full board followed suit.

Although Virginia law required only that such a merger proposal be submitted to a vote at a shareholders' meeting, and that the meeting be preceded by circulation of a statement of information to the shareholders, the directors nevertheless solicited proxies for voting on the proposal at the annual meeting set for April 21, 1987. In their solicitation, the directors urged the proposal's adoption and stated they had approved the plan because of its opportunity for the minority shareholders to achieve a "high" value, which they elsewhere described as a "fair" price, for their stock.

Although most minority shareholders gave the proxies requested, respondent Sandberg did not, and after approval of the merger she sought damages in the United States District Court for the Eastern District of Virginia from VBI, FABI, and the directors of the Bank. She pleaded two counts, one for soliciting proxies in violation of § 14(a) and Rule 14a–9, and the other for breaching fiduciary duties owed to the minority shareholders under state law. Under the first count, Sandberg alleged, among other things, that the directors had not believed that the price offered was high or that the terms of the merger were fair, but had recommended the merger only because they believed they had no alternative if they wished to remain on the board. At trial, Sandberg invoked language from this Court's opinion in *Mills v. Electric Auto–Lite Co.,* to obtain an instruction that the jury could find for her without a showing of her own reliance on the alleged misstatements, so long as they were material and the proxy solicitation was an "essential link" in the merger process.

The jury's verdicts were for Sandberg on both counts, after finding violations of Rule 14a–9 by all defendants and a breach of fiduciary duties by the Bank's directors. The jury awarded Sandberg $18 a share, having found that she would have received $60 if her stock had been valued adequately. * * *

On appeal, the United States Court of Appeals for the Fourth Circuit affirmed the judgments, holding that certain statements in the proxy solicitation were materially misleading for purposes of the Rule, and that respondents could maintain their action even though their votes had not been needed to effectuate the merger. 891 F.2d 1112 (1989). We granted certiorari because of the importance of the issues presented. 495 U.S. __ (1990).

* * *

A

We consider first the actionability per se of statements of reasons, opinion or belief. Because such a statement by definition purports to express what is consciously on the speaker's mind, we interpret the jury verdict as finding that the directors' statements of belief and opinion were made with knowledge that the directors did not hold the beliefs or opinions expressed, and we confine our discussion to statements so made.[5] That such statements may be materially significant raises no serious question. The meaning of the materiality requirement for liability under § 14(a) was discussed at some length in *TSC Industries, Inc. v. Northway, Inc.*, where we held a fact to be material "if there is a substantial likelihood that a reasonable shareholder would consider it important in deciding how to vote." We think there is no room to deny that a statement of belief by corporate directors about a recommended course of action, or an explanation of their reasons for recommending it, can take on just that importance. Shareholders know that directors usually have knowledge and expertness far exceeding the normal investor's resources, and the directors' perceived superiority is magnified even further by the common knowledge that state law customarily obliges them to exercise their judgment in the shareholders' interest. * * * Naturally, then, the share owner faced with a proxy request will think it important to know the directors' beliefs about the course they recommend, and their specific reasons for urging the stockholders to embrace it.

1

But, assuming materiality, the question remains whether statements of reasons, opinions, or beliefs are statements "with respect to * * * material fact[s]" so as to fall within the strictures of the Rule. Petitioners argue that we would invite wasteful litigation of amorphous issues outside the readily provable realm of fact if we were to recognize liability here on proof that the directors did not recommend the merger for the stated reason. * * *

Attacks on the truth of directors' statements of reasons or belief, however, need carry no such threats. Such statements are factual in two senses: as statements that the directors do act for the reasons given or hold the belief stated and as statements about the subject matter of the reason or belief expressed. In neither sense does the proof or disproof of such statements implicate the concerns expressed in *Blue Chip Stamps*.* The root of those concerns was a plaintiff's capacity to manufacture claims of hypothetical action, unconstrained by independent evidence. Reasons for directors' recommendations or statements of belief are, in contrast, characteristically matters of corporate record subject to documentation, to be supported or attacked by evidence of historical fact outside a plaintiff's control. Such evidence would include not only corporate minutes and other statements of the directors themselves, but

---

**5.** In *TSC Industries, Inc. v. Northway, Inc.*, we reserved the question whether scienter was necessary for liability generally under § 14(a). We reserve it still.

* In *Blue Chip Stamps v. Manor Drug Stores*, 421 U.S. 723 (1975), discussed in Chapter 19, the Court held that a private action for damages under Rule 10b–5 can only be maintained by a person who actual-

ly purchased or sold securities. The Court justified its holding in large part by pointing to the speculative nature of a claim brought by a person who can only allege that, had she known the truth, she would have purchased or sold securities, and to the vexatious potential of litigation based on such a claim.—Eds.

circumstantial evidence bearing on the facts that would reasonably underlie the reasons claimed and the honesty of any statement that those reasons are the basis for a recommendation or other action, a point that becomes especially clear when the reasons or beliefs go to valuations in dollars and cents.

It is no answer to argue, as petitioners do, that the quoted statement on which liability was predicated did not express a reason in dollars and cents, but focused instead on the "indefinite and unverifiable" term, "high" value, much like the similar claim that the merger's terms were "fair" to shareholders.[7] The objection ignores the fact that such conclusory terms in a commercial context are reasonably understood to rest on a factual basis that justifies them as accurate, the absence of which renders them misleading. Provable facts either furnish good reasons to make a conclusory commercial judgment, or they count against it, and expressions of such judgments can be uttered with knowledge of truth or falsity just like more definite statements, and defended or attacked through the orthodox evidentiary process that either substantiates their underlying justifications or tends to disprove their existence. * * * In this case, whether $42 was "high," and the proposal "fair" to the minority shareholders depended on whether provable facts about the Bank's assets, and about actual and potential levels of operation, substantiated a value that was above, below, or more or less at the $42 figure, when assessed in accordance with recognized methods of valuation.

Respondents adduced evidence for just such facts in proving that the statement was misleading about its subject matter and a false expression of the directors' reasons. Whereas the proxy statement described the $42 price as offering a premium above both book value and market price, the evidence indicated that a calculation of the book figure based on the appreciated value of the Bank's real estate holdings eliminated any such premium. The evidence on the significance of market price showed that KBW had conceded that the market was closed, thin and dominated by FABI, facts omitted from the statement. There was, indeed, evidence of a "going concern" value for the Bank in excess of $60 per share of common stock, another fact never disclosed. However conclusory the directors' statement may have been, then, it was open to attack by garden-variety evidence, subject neither to a plaintiff's control nor ready

---

**7.** Petitioners are also wrong to argue that construing the statute to allow recovery for a misleading statement that the merger was "fair" to the minority shareholders is tantamount to assuming federal authority to bar corporate transactions thought to be unfair to some group of shareholders. It is, of course, true that we said in *Santa Fe Industries, Inc. v. Green*, 430 U.S. 462, 479 (1977), that " '[c]orporations are creatures of state law, and investors commit their funds to corporate directors on the understanding that, except where federal law expressly requires certain responsibilities of directors with respect to stockholders, state law will govern the internal affairs of the corporation,' " quoting *Cort v. Ash*, 422 U.S. 66, 84 (1975). But § 14(a) does impose responsibility for false and misleading proxy statements. Although a corporate transaction's "fairness" is not, as such, a federal concern, a proxy statement's claim of fairness presupposes a factual integrity that federal law is expressly concerned to preserve. * * *

manufacture, and there was no undue risk of open-ended liability or uncontrollable litigation in allowing respondents the opportunity for recovery on the allegation that it was misleading to call $42 "high."

2

Under § 14(a), then, a plaintiff is permitted to prove a specific statement of reason knowingly false or misleadingly incomplete, even when stated in conclusory terms. In reaching this conclusion, we have considered statements of reasons of the sort exemplified here, which misstate the speaker's reasons and also mislead about the stated subject matter (e.g., the value of the shares). A statement of belief may be open to objection only in the former respect, however, solely as a misstatement of the psychological fact of the speaker's belief in what he says. * * *

The question arises, then, whether disbelief, or undisclosed belief or motivation, standing alone, should be a sufficient basis to sustain an action under § 14(a), absent proof by the sort of objective evidence described above that the statement also expressly or impliedly asserted something false or misleading about its subject matter. We think that proof of mere disbelief or belief undisclosed should not suffice for liability under § 14(a), and if nothing more had been required or proven in this case we would reverse for that reason. * * *

* * * [T]o recognize liability on mere disbelief or undisclosed motive without any demonstration that the proxy statement was false or misleading about its subject would authorize § 14(a) litigation confined solely to what one skeptical court spoke of as the "impurities" of a director's "unclean heart." This, we think, would cross the line that *Blue Chip Stamps* sought to draw. * * * We, therefore, hold disbelief or undisclosed motivation, standing alone, insufficient to satisfy the element of fact that must be established under § 14(a).

C

Petitioners' fall-back position assumes the same relationship between a conclusory judgment and its underlying facts that we described in Part II–B–1, *supra*. Thus, petitioners argue that even if conclusory statements of reason or belief can be actionable under § 14(a), we should confine liability to instances where the proxy material fails to disclose the offending statement's factual basis. There would be no justification for holding the shareholders entitled to judicial relief, that is, when they were given evidence that a stated reason for a proxy recommendation was misleading, and an opportunity to draw that conclusion themselves.

The answer to this argument rests on the difference between a merely misleading statement and one that is materially so. While a misleading statement will not always lose its deceptive edge simply by joinder with others that are true, the true statements may discredit the other one so obviously that the risk of real deception drops to nil. Since liability under § 14(a) must rest not only on deceptiveness but materiality as well (i.e., it has to be significant enough to be important to a reasonable investor deciding how to vote), petitioners are on perfectly firm ground insofar as they argue that publishing accurate facts in a proxy statement can render a mislead·˜ ʒ proposition too unimportant to ground liability.

But not every mixture with the true will neutralize the deceptive. If it would take a financial analyst to spot the tension between the one and the other, whatever is misleading will remain materially so, and liability should follow. The point of a proxy statement, after all, should be to inform, not to challenge the reader's critical wits. Only when the inconsistency would exhaust the misleading conclusion's capacity to influence the reasonable shareholder would a § 14(a) action fail on the element of materiality.

### III

The second issue before us, left open in *Mills v. Electric Auto–Lite Co.*, 396 U.S. at 385, n. 7, is whether causation of damages compensable through the implied private right of action under § 14(a) can be demonstrated by a member of a class of minority shareholders whose votes are not required by law or corporate bylaw to authorize the transaction giving rise to the claim. * * *

Although a majority stockholder in *Mills* controlled just over half the corporation's shares, a two-thirds vote was needed to approve the merger proposal. * * * [The] Court found the solicitation essential, as contrasted with one addressed to a class of minority shareholders without votes required by law or by-law to authorize the action proposed, and left it for another day to decide whether such a minority shareholder could demonstrate causation.

In this case, respondents address *Mills'* open question by proffering two theories that the proxy solicitation addressed to them was an "essential link" under the *Mills* causation test. They argue, first, that a link existed and was essential simply because VBI and FABI would have been unwilling to proceed with the merger without the approval manifested by the minority shareholders' proxies, which would not have been obtained without the solicitation's express misstatements and misleading omissions. On this reasoning, the causal connection would depend on a desire to avoid bad shareholder or public relations, and the essential character of the causal link would stem not from the enforceable terms of the parties' corporate relationship, but from one party's apprehension of the ill will of the other.

In the alternative, respondents argue that the proxy statement was an essential link between the directors' proposal and the merger because it was the means to satisfy a state statutory requirement of minority shareholder approval, as a condition for saving the merger from voidability resulting from a conflict of interest on the part of one of the Bank's directors, Jack Beddow, who voted in favor of the merger while also serving as a director of FABI. * * * On this theory, causation would depend on the use of the proxy statement for the purpose of obtaining votes sufficient to bar a minority shareholder from commencing proceedings to declare the merger void.

Although respondents have proffered each of these theories as establishing a chain of causal connection in which the proxy statement is claimed to have been an "essential link," neither theory presents the proxy solicitation as essential in the sense of *Mills'* causal sequence, in which the solicitation links a directors' proposal with the votes legally required to authorize the action proposed. As a consequence, each theory would, if adopted, extend the scope of *Borak* actions beyond the ambit of *Mills,* and expand the class of plaintiffs entitled to bring *Borak* actions to include shareholders whose initial authorization of the transaction prompting the proxy solicitation is unnecessary.

* * * The rule that has emerged in the years since *Borak* and *Mills* came down is that recognition of any private right of action for violating a federal statute must ultimately rest on congressional intent to provide a private remedy. From this the corollary follows that the breadth of the right once recognized should not, as a general matter, grow beyond the scope congressionally intended.

[Justice Souter reviewed the text and legislative history of the Securities Exchange Act of 1934 and concluded that they provide no guidance with respect to the intended scope of a private right of action.]

The congressional silence that is thus a serious obstacle to the expansion of cognizable *Borak* causation is not, however, a necessarily insurmountable barrier. [In *Blue Chip Stamps* ], we looked to policy reasons for deciding where the outer limits of the right should lie. We may do no less here, in the face of respondents' pleas for a private remedy to place them on the same footing as shareholders with votes necessary for initial corporate action.

### A

The same threats of speculative claims and procedural intractability [that were present in *Blue Chip Stamps* ] are inherent in respondents' theory of causation linked through the directors' desire for a cosmetic vote. Causation would turn on inferences about what the corporate directors would have thought and done without the minority shareholder approval unneeded to authorize action. * * * The issues would be hazy, their litigation protracted, and their resolution unreliable. Given a choice, we would reject any theory of causation that promised such prospects, and we reject this one.

### B

The theory of causal necessity derived from the requirements of Virginia law dealing with postmerger ratification seeks to identify the essential character of the proxy solicitation from its function in obtaining the minority approval that would preclude a minority suit attacking the merger. Since the link is said to be a step in the process of barring a class of shareholders from resort to a state remedy otherwise available, this theory of causation rests upon the proposition of policy that § 14(a) should provide a federal remedy whenever a false or misleading proxy statement results in the loss under state law of a shareholder plaintiff's state remedy for the enforcement of a state right. * * *

This case does not, however, require us to decide whether § 14(a) provides a cause of action for lost state remedies, since there is no indication in the law or facts before us that the proxy solicitation resulted in any such loss. The contrary appears to be the case. Assuming the soundness of respondents' characterization of the proxy statement as materially misleading, the very terms of the Virginia statute indicate that a favorable minority vote induced by the solicitation would not suffice to render the merger invulnerable to later attack on the ground of the conflict. The statute bars a shareholder from seeking to avoid a transaction tainted by a director's conflict if, inter alia, the minority shareholders ratified the transaction following disclosure of the material facts of the transaction and the conflict. Va.Code § 13.1–691(A)(2) (1989). Assuming that the material facts about the merger and Beddow's interests were not accurately disclosed, the minority votes were inadequate to ratify the merger under state law, and there was no loss of state remedy to connect the proxy solicitation with harm to minority shareholders irredressable under state law. Nor is there a claim here that the statement misled respondents into entertaining a false belief that they had no chance to upset the merger, until the time for bringing suit had run out.[14]

IV

The judgment of the Court of Appeals is reversed.

Justice Scalia, concurring in part and concurring in the judgment.

As I understand the Court's opinion, the statement "In the opinion of the Directors, this is a high value for the shares" would produce liability if in fact it was not a high value and the Directors knew that. It would not produce liability if in fact it was not a high value but the Directors honestly believed otherwise. The statement "The Directors voted to accept the proposal because they believe it offers a high value" would not produce liability if in fact the Directors' genuine motive was quite different—except that it would produce liability if the proposal in fact did not offer a high value and the Directors knew that.

I agree with all of this. However, not every sentence that has the word "opinion" in it, or that refers to motivation for Directors' actions, leads us into this psychic thicket. Sometimes such a sentence actually

---

**14.** Respondents do not claim that any other application of a theory of lost state remedies would avail them here. It is clear, for example, that no state appraisal remedy was lost through a § 14(a) violation in this case. Respondent Weinstein and others did seek appraisal under Virginia law in the Virginia courts; their claims were rejected on the explicit grounds that although "[s]tatutory appraisal is now considered the exclusive remedy for stockholders opposing a merger," "dissenting stockholders in bank mergers do not even have this solitary remedy available to them," because "Va. Code § 6.1–43 specifically excludes bank mergers from application of § 13.1–730 [the Virginia appraisal statute]." Weinstein does not claim that the Virginia court was wrong and does not rely on this claim in any way. Thus, the § 14(a) violation could have had no effect on the availability of an appraisal remedy, for there never was one.

represents facts as facts rather than opinions—and in that event no more need be done than apply the normal rules for § 14(a) liability. I think that is the situation here. In my view, the statement at issue in this case is most fairly read as affirming separately both the fact of the Directors' opinion and the accuracy of the facts upon which the opinion was assertedly based. It reads as follows:

> "The Plan of Merger has been approved by the Board of Directors because it provides an opportunity for the Bank's public shareholders to achieve a high value for their shares." * * *

Had it read "because in their estimation it provides an opportunity, etc." it would have set forth nothing but an opinion. As written, however, it asserts both that the Board of Directors acted for a particular reason and that that reason is correct. This interpretation is made clear by what immediately follows: "The price to be paid is about 30% higher than the [last traded price immediately before announcement of the proposal]. * * * [T]he $42 per share that will be paid to public holders of the common stock represents a premium of approximately 26% over the book value. * * * [T]he bank earned $24,767,000 in the year ended December 31, 1986. * * * " These are all facts that support—and that are obviously introduced for the purpose of supporting—the factual truth of the "because" clause, i.e., that the proposal gives shareholders a "high value."

If the present case were to proceed, therefore, I think the normal § 14(a) principles governing misrepresentation of fact would apply.

Justice Stevens, with whom Justice Marshall joins, concurring in part and dissenting in part.

* * * The case before us today involves a merger that has been found by a jury to be unfair, not fair. The interest in providing a remedy to the injured minority shareholders therefore is stronger, not weaker, than in *Mills*. The interest in avoiding speculative controversy about the actual importance of the proxy solicitation is the same as in *Mills*. Moreover, as in *Mills,* these matters can be taken into account at the remedy stage in appropriate cases. Accordingly, I do not believe that it constitutes an unwarranted extension of the rationale of *Mills* to conclude that because management found it necessary—whether for "legal or practical reasons"—to solicit proxies from minority shareholders to obtain their approval of the merger, that solicitation "was an essential link in the accomplishment of the transaction." In my opinion, shareholders may bring an action for damages under § 14(a) of the Securities Exchange Act of 1934 whenever materially false or misleading statements are made in proxy statements. That the solicitation of proxies is not required by law or by the bylaws of a corporation does not authorize corporate officers, once they have decided for whatever reason to solicit proxies, to avoid the constraints of the statute. I would therefore affirm the judgment of the Court of Appeals.

Justice Kennedy, with whom Justice Marshall, Justice Blackmun, and Justice Stevens join, concurring in part and dissenting in part.

I am in general agreement with Parts I and II of the majority opinion, but do not agree with the views expressed in Part III regarding the proof of causation required to establish a violation of § 14(a). With respect, I dissent from Part III of the Court's opinion. * * *

## II

### A

The severe limits the Court places upon possible proof of nonvoting causation in a § 14(a) private action are justified neither by our precedents nor any case in the courts of appeals. These limits are said to flow from a shift in our approach to implied causes of action that has occurred since we recognized the § 14(a) implied private action in *J.I. Case Co. v. Borak.*

* * * According to the Court, acceptance of non-voting causation theories would "extend the scope of *Borak* actions beyond the ambit of *Mills.*" But *Mills* did not purport to limit the scope of *Borak* actions, and as footnote 7 of *Mills* indicates, some courts have applied nonvoting causation theories to *Borak* actions for at least the past 25 years.

To the extent the Court's analysis considers the purposes underlying § 14(a), it does so with the avowed aim to limit the cause of action and with undue emphasis upon fears of "speculative claims and procedural intractability." The result is a sort of guerrilla warfare to restrict a well established implied right of action. If the analysis adopted by the Court today is any guide, Congress and those charged with enforcement of the securities laws stand forewarned that unresolved questions concerning the scope of those causes of action are likely to be answered by the Court in favor of defendants.

### B

The Court seems to assume, based upon the footnote in *Mills* reserving the question, that Sandberg bears a special burden to demonstrate causation because the public shareholders held only 15 percent of the Bank's stock. Here, First American Bankshares, Inc. (FABI) and Virginia Bankshares, Inc. (VBI) retained the option to back out of the transaction if dissatisfied with the reaction of the minority shareholders, or if concerned that the merger would result in liability for violation of duties to the minority shareholders. The merger agreement was conditioned upon approval by two-thirds of the shareholders and VBI could have voted its shares against the merger if it so decided. To this extent, the Court's distinction between cases where the "minority" shareholders could have voted down the transaction and those where causation must be proved by nonvoting theories is suspect. Minority shareholders are identified only by a post hoc inquiry. The real question ought to be whether an injury was shown by the effect the nondisclosure had on the entire merger process, including the period before votes are cast.

The Court's distinction presumes that a majority shareholder will vote in favor of management's proposal even if proxy disclosure suggests that the transaction is unfair to minority shareholders or that the board of directors or majority shareholder are in breach of fiduciary duties to the minority. If the majority shareholder votes against the transaction in order to comply with its state law duties, or out of fear of liability, or upon concluding that the transaction will injure the reputation of the business, this ought not to be characterized as nonvoting causation. Of course, when the majority shareholder dominates the voting process, as was the case here, it may prefer to avoid the embarrassment of voting against its own proposal and so may cancel the meeting of shareholders at which the vote was to have been taken. For practical purposes, the result is the same: because of full disclosure the transaction does not go forward and the resulting injury to minority shareholders is avoided. The Court's distinction between voting and nonvoting causation does not create clear legal categories.

## III

Our decision in *Mills* rested upon the impracticality of attempting to determine the extent of reliance by thousands of shareholders on alleged misrepresentations or omissions. If minority shareholders hold sufficient votes to defeat a management proposal and if the misstatement or omission is likely to be considered important in deciding how to vote, then there exists a likely causal link between the proxy violation and the enactment of the proposal; and one can justify recovery by minority shareholders for damages resulting from enactment of management's proposal.

If, for sake of argument, we accept a distinction between voting and nonvoting causation, we must determine whether the *Mills* essential link theory applies where a majority shareholder holds sufficient votes to force adoption of a proposal. The merit of the essential link formulation is that it rests upon the likelihood of causation and eliminates the difficulty of proof. Even where a minority lacks votes to defeat a proposal, both these factors weigh in favor of finding causation so long as the solicitation of proxies is an essential link in the transaction. * * *

## B

There is no authority whatsoever for limiting § 14(a) to protecting those minority shareholders whose numerical strength could permit them to vote down a proposal. One of Section 14(a)'s "chief purposes is 'the protection of investors.' "Those who lack the strength to vote down a proposal have all the more need of disclosure. The voting process involves not only casting ballots but also the formulation and withdrawal of proposals, the minority's right to block a vote through court action or the threat of adverse consequences, or the negotiation of an increase in price. The proxy rules support this deliberative process. These practicalities can result in causation sufficient to support recovery.

The facts in the case before us prove this point. Sandberg argues that had all the material facts been disclosed, FABI or the Bank likely would have withdrawn or revised the merger proposal. The evidence in the record, and more that might be available upon remand meets any reasonable requirement of specific and nonspeculative proof.

* * * I conclude that causation is more than plausible; it is likely, even where the public shareholders cannot vote down management's proposal. Causation is established where the proxy statement is an essential link in completing the transaction, even if the minority lacks sufficient votes to defeat a proposal of management.

### IV

The majority avoids the question whether a plaintiff may prove causation by demonstrating that the misrepresentation or omission deprived her of a state law remedy. * * * The majority asserts that respondents show no loss of a state law remedy, because if "the material facts of the transaction and Beddow's interest were not accurately disclosed, then the minority votes were inadequate to ratify the merger under Virginia law." This theory requires us to conclude that the Virginia statute governing director conflicts of interest, incorporates the same definition of materiality as the federal proxy rules. I find no support for that proposition. If the definitions are not the same, then Sandberg may have lost her state law remedy. For all we know, disclosure to the minority shareholders that the price is $42 per share may satisfy Virginia's requirement. If that is the case, then approval by the minority without full disclosure may have deprived Sandberg of the ability to void the merger.

* * * I would affirm the judgment of the Court of Appeals.

### Note: Virginia Bankshares, Inc. v. Sandberg

1.  Justice Scalia suggests that directors can reduce their exposure to liability if they make clear they are expressing opinions, not facts. This would seem to follow from his observation that with the addition of the bracketed words, the following sentence would "set forth nothing but an opinion."

> The Plan of Merger has been approved by the Board of Directors because [in their estimation] it provides an opportunity for the Bank's public shareholders to achieve a high value for their shares.

Is this reading of the Court's opinion accurate, or would the Court hold that the quoted sentence constituted a misstatement of material fact so long as documentary or circumstantial evidence demonstrated the merger did not provide "a high value" to the Bank's public shareholders?

2.  In *Shapiro v. UJB Financial Corp.*, 964 F.2d 272 (3d Cir.1992), the Third Circuit addressed some of the federalism concerns raised in *Virginia Bankshares* and *Santa Fe*. Shareholders in a financially troubled bank holding company brought a class action suit against the company and its officers and directors alleging that they suffered economic losses as a result of public statements that portrayed UJB in a "falsely optimistic manner." The shareholders alleged that defendants had stated that UJB's "loan loss reserves were adequate, loan review procedures and policies were stringently and continuously applied, lend-

ing opportunities were balanced appropriately against risks, and financial results were positive" when, in fact, none of these things were true. The district court held that the alleged misrepresentations or omissions involved simple mismanagement and not fraud, and consequently were not actionable under the federal securities laws.

The Third Circuit reversed. It first stated that "a reasonable investor would be influenced significantly by knowledge that a bank has knowingly or recklessly hidden its true financial status by deliberately misstating its level of non-performing loans, failing to provide adequate reserves, and indulging its problem loan customers." *Id.* at 281. It then agreed with the district court that the failure to provide adequate reserves by itself is not actionable under the federal securities laws. The court also stated that if a defendant has not commented on the nature and quality of its management practices, there is no violation of the federal securities laws for failing to characterize them as poor. Nevertheless, in this case, plaintiffs alleged that the defendants did in fact address the quality of its management practices, thereby declaring the subjects of their representations to be material to reasonable shareholders. Once the defendants put the subjects "in play," they were bound to speak truthfully about them. The court went on to hold that *Virginia Bankshares* permitted plaintiffs to prove that the defendants' conclusory statements about the soundness of UJB's management practices were knowingly false or misleading. The court, however, directed plaintiffs to refile their complaint because the language of their complaint, as filed, failed adequately to distinguish the securities law violations from the mismanagement. "It is difficult to discern whether plaintiffs are alleging that defendants made material statements that the reserves were adequate when in fact they were not, or whether plaintiffs are merely alleging that the reserves were inadequate." *Id.* at 284.

Assuming that the plaintiffs in *Shapiro* are able to reformulate their complaint in a satisfactory manner, will the evidence they present in the federal securities law case differ substantially from the evidence they would have to present in a state trial alleging that the defendants violated their duty of care? Recall the concerns voiced by some commentators at the close of the discussion of *Goldberg v. Meridor*. Are these criticisms not equally relevant to Note 7 of *Virginia Bankshares*?

3. In *Virginia Bankshares*, the Court suggests that "corporate minutes or other statements of the directors themselves" may support claims that directors' recommendations or statements of opinion were false. Rarely, however, will minutes of board meetings or other formal corporate records contain evidence that explicitly conflicts with or undermines directors' recommendations. Consequently, shareholders generally will have to rely on circumstantial evidence to prove such claims. *Mendell v. Greenberg*, 938 F.2d 1528 (2d Cir.1990), interpreted *Virginia Bankshares* to require that a hearing be held on the fair value of the stock of a corporation involved in a merger as the first step in determining whether the directors' recommendation that shareholders approve the merger consideration was false or misleading. If this interpretation is

correct, claims relating to directors' recommendations ultimately may be decided on the basis of judgments relating to a transaction's "fairness." Does Note 7 of the Court's opinion deal adequately with this possibility?

4. In *Mills*, the Court held that plaintiffs could maintain their action under Rule 14a–9 and recover reasonable attorney fees, even if the trial court ultimately determined the merger they had voted to approve was fair. In *Virginia Bankshares,* the Court upheld a finding that the proxy statement was materially misleading, tacitly accepting the trial court's finding that the Bank's shareholders had received $42 for stock worth $60 per share, but nonetheless held plaintiffs could not maintain an action under Rule 14a–9. The Court seems to justify this holding by pointing out that, assuming plaintiffs could prove these elements of their case in a state court, "there was no loss of state remedy to connect the proxy solicitation with harm to shareholders irredressable under state law," i.e., the plaintiffs could recover their losses under Virginia law.

Justice Kennedy questions the Court's assumption that Virginia law incorporates the same definition of materiality as the federal proxy rules. This question appears to have some validity, especially given the uncertainty that existed prior to *Virginia Bankshares* as to when, if ever, directors' recommendations constituted statements of material fact. In addition, the Court's approach is difficult to reconcile with the statement in *Borak* that "if the law of the State happened to attach no responsibility to the use of misleading proxy statements, the whole purpose of the section might be frustrated." On the other hand, in the years since *Borak,* state courts have tended to impose on corporate managers a duty of disclosure similar to the duty imposed by Section 14(a) and Rule 14a–9. If that aspect of the policy considerations supporting the decision in *Borak* no longer has much force, to what extent does the Court's holding on the causation issue in *Sandberg* foreshadow further attrition of the private right of action under § 14(a)? The nature of the state law duty of disclosure will be considered in the last section of this chapter.

### *Note: Causation*

In *Virginia Bankshares*, the Court's holding that the Bank's proxy solicitation was not an "essential link" in effectuating the merger appears to be grounded in its finding that the minority shareholders' votes were "not required by law or corporate bylaw to authorize the transaction giving rise to the claim." In many other settings, corporations solicit shareholder approval of transactions although such approval is "not required by law or corporate bylaw." These include transactions that directors have the authority to approve, but nonetheless submit to shareholders for approval or ratification; transactions involving the issuance of substantial amounts of stock, where New York Stock Exchange rules require shareholder approval if the new stock is to be listed; and agreements between parent companies and controlled subsidiaries that are made subject to the approval of a majority of the subsidiary's minority shareholders. Are proxy solicitations in connection with such transactions "essential," for purposes of demonstrating that some violation of Rule 14a–9 caused some cognizable injury to shareholders who were solicited?

"Causation" is one of the law's most central, yet most troublesome concepts. Indeed, philosophy students will recall that it has been a problematic concept in that discipline at least since the work of David Hume. In the more prosaic discipline of law, however, problems with the concept arise primarily not because of epistemological quandaries, but because its meaning may differ in different contexts. As applied to the tort of misrepresentation (or deceit), the RESTATEMENT (SECOND) OF TORTS (1977) speaks of Causation in Fact (Section 546) and Legal Causation (Section 548A). Causation in Fact occurs when one's actual reliance was a substantial factor in determining the course of conduct resulting in loss, while Legal Causation, and consequently liability, arises only if the loss might reasonably be expected to result from the reliance.

There is a "but for" element to causation under this widely accepted formulation. Although that element is needed to establish causation in fact, it is not sufficient to establish liability. The missing element is referred to as "legal" cause or "proximate" cause. For instance, "but for" a misrepresentation, plaintiff might not have bought the property sold by defendant; her loss, nevertheless, might have resulted from a general economic decline. *See* ALI FEDERAL SECURITIES CODE § 202(19), Comment 3(c) (1980).

The Court in *Mills* refused to make reliance an element of the test of causation, finding that a showing of materiality was sufficient to show that there was a relationship between violation and injury, so long as the solicitation of proxies was "an essential link in the accomplishment of the transaction." This is a policy choice, and its consequence is to facilitate private enforcement of violations of the proxy rules. *See* Note, *Causation and Liability in Private Actions for Proxy Violations,* 81 YALE L.J. 107 (1970).

As applied to liability under the main anti-fraud provisions of the federal securities laws, the concept of causation increasingly has been separated into two tests: *transaction* causation and *loss* causation. Loss causation is relatively easy to demonstrate—the transaction caused harm to the plaintiff. In *Borak,* the shareholders of the disappearing company received less for their shares than the shares were worth. Transaction causation, which is harder to prove, requires the plaintiff to show that the defendant's violation caused the company to engage in the transaction in question. Thus, in *Mills,* the loss was occasioned by the merger and the merger was caused by the solicitation of proxies to secure sufficient votes for its approval.

Where is the causal relationship between allegedly improper transactions such as illegal payments by the corporation or a breach of fiduciary duty by corporate managers, and any false or misleading statements in the proxy material? The harm can be shown in the form of the illegal or wasteful payments and their side effects. These payments, or their excessive nature were not disclosed in the proxy material sent to share-holders. Because the shareholders did not vote to approve the transactions that caused the loss, transaction causation was lacking in these circumstances. *Abbey v. Control Data Corp.*, 603 F.2d 724 (8th Cir.1979).

On the other hand, where shareholders challenged the election of directors alleging that the proxy material failed to disclose their cover up of illegal payments, transaction causation was established because the issue of the election of directors had been submitted to the shareholders. Of course, plaintiff still must show that the omission was material. *Weisberg v. Coastal States Gas Corp.*, 609 F.2d 650 (2d Cir.1979). In contrast with *Abbey,* the plaintiff in *Weisberg* did not challenge the illegal payments, but only the election of directors.

The Ninth Circuit carried the foregoing analysis further in *Gaines v. Haughton*, 645 F.2d 761 (9th Cir.1981). Agreeing that when the plaintiff attacks the election, not the improper payments, the analysis shifts from causation to materiality, the court drew a distinction between non-disclosure of self-dealing conduct, which is presumptively material, and "allegations of simple breach of fiduciary duty/waste of corporate assets—the non-disclosure of which is never material for § 14(a) purposes."

The court elaborated on this latter point:

Many corporate actions taken by directors in the interest of the corporation might offend and engender controversy among some stockholders. Investors share the same diversity of social and political views that characterize the polity as a whole. The tenor of a company's labor relations policies, economic decisions to relocate or close established plants, commercial dealings with foreign countries which are disdained in certain circles, decisions to develop (or not to develop) particular natural resources or forms of energy technology, and the promulgation of corporate personnel policies that reject (or embrace) the principle of affirmative action, are just a few examples of business judgments, soundly entrusted to the broad discretion of the directors, which may nonetheless cause shareholder dissent and provoke claims of "wasteful," "unethical," or even "immoral" business dealings. Should corporate directors have a duty under § 14(a) to disclose all such corporate decisions in proxy solicitations for their re-election? We decline to extend the duty of disclosure under § 14(a) to these situations. While we neither condone nor condemn these and similar types of corporate conduct (including the now illegal practice of questionable foreign payments), we believe the aggrieved shareholders have sufficient recourse to state law claims against the responsible directors and, if all else fails, can sell or trade their stock in the offending corporation in favor of an enterprise more compatible with their own personal goals and values.

*Id.* at 778–79.

The question of causation also arises when the alleged wrongdoer owns sufficient stock to assure approval of the transaction in question.

The Court left this issue open in Note 7 in *Mills* and subsequently resolved it in *Virginia Bankshares*.

## 2. LOST STATE REMEDIES

Recall that *Goldberg* and its progeny raised questions about the relationship between a cause of action under Rule 10b–5 and the availability of state law remedies in an allegedly unfair transaction. In that connection, *Virginia Bankshares* raises several new problems. It seems to render uncertain the holding in *Goldberg* that minority shareholders state a cause of action under Rule 10b–5 when claiming that they were lulled into not seeking to enjoin a merger because of the board's deceptive disclosures. First, the Court rejected the minority shareholders' theory of causation on the grounds that the theory "would turn on inferences about what the corporate directors might have done without the minority shareholder approval unneeded to authorize action." A major criticism of *Goldberg* has been its implicit presumption that but for the omission of material information, the plaintiffs would have rushed to state court to seek, and could have obtained, an injunction to prevent the merger. Is the Court's refusal in *Virginia Bankshares* to speculate about 'what might have been' equally pertinent to a *Goldberg* claim?

Second, *Virginia Bankshares* implicitly raises the question of what constitutes the "loss" of a state law remedy. Does being lulled by a deceptive disclosure into not seeking an injunction until it is too late constitute such a loss? Note that *Virginia Bankshares* closes with the caveat that there was no "claim here that the statement misled respondents into entertaining a false belief that they had no chance to upset the merger, until the time for bringing suit had run out." Does this statement save *Goldberg* or does it introduce a completely new methodology which focuses on whether the time has passed to seek a state law remedy rather than on whether such remedy was available at the time of the omission or misstatement?

## WILSON v. GREAT AMERICAN INDUSTRIES, INC.

### 979 F.2d 924 (2d Cir.1992).

[Following the merger of Chenango Industries into Great American Industries, minority shareholders of Chenango sued Great American, Chenango, and various officers and directors connected with those corporations. The shareholders alleged that defendants violated, *inter alia*, Rule 14a–9 because of omissions and material misrepresentations in a joint proxy statement/prospectus issued in 1979 in connection with the merger. After a protracted series of court decisions, it was held that these proxy materials did contain material misrepresentations in violation of Rule 14a–9, and plaintiffs were awarded damages for the losses they claimed to have suffered. Defendants and plaintiffs appealed the district court decisions awarding damages. After these appeals were filed, the Supreme Court handed down its decision in *Virginia Bankshares*,

*Inc. v. Sandberg.* The defendants then requested that the district court reconsider its prior decisions awarding damages. Defendants claimed that the plaintiffs' suit should have been dismissed on the ground that, as minority shareholders without power to influence the proposed merger, they suffered no compensable damages under Section 14(a) of the Securities Exchange Act of 1934, notwithstanding that their votes were solicited by proxies containing material misrepresentations. The district court granted reconsideration, but declined to depart from its prior holdings that because the fact that the plaintiffs in this case may have been deprived of appraisal rights and other forms of equitable relief under state law, *Virginia Bankshares* was not controlling and did not clearly indicate that the plaintiffs had no cause of action.]

CARDAMONE, CIRCUIT JUDGE:

\* \* \* Under rules set forth in that case, defendants continue, minority shareholders situated as are plaintiffs can prove no damages from proxy misrepresentations under § 14(a). In addition, § 14(a) does not provide a private cause of action for lost state remedies—such as appraisal rights—and, even if a federal private cause of action is available, it does not provide greater relief than that provided under state law. As to that, defendants declare, plaintiffs cannot prove the defective proxy caused them to lose any state remedies. In the discussion that follows that leads us to affirm the district court in part, reverse it in part, and remand this case once again, we readily acknowledge our share of responsibility for its necessity.

DISCUSSION

I

A. *Intervening Supreme Court Decision*

The Supreme Court in *Virginia Bankshares* did not hold that minority shareholders whose votes number too few to affect the outcome of a shareholder vote may never recover damages under § 14(a) or that no implied private cause of action for such shareholders is provided under that section of the Act. And, it expressly declined to decide whether § 14(a) provides an implied federal remedy for minority shareholders deprived of certain state remedies as a result of deceptive proxy solicitations. ___ U.S. at ___ & n. 14, 111 S.Ct. at 2766 & n. 14. To the extent that this Circuit recognizes such a remedy, defendants incorrectly contend therefore that *Virginia Bankshares* precludes plaintiffs from seeking such relief. \* \* \*

One theory of causation advanced by the plaintiffs in *Virginia Bankshares* was that, but for the defective proxies, the minority shareholders would not have voted in favor of the merger. In that event, dissenting votes would have preserved their right to pursue under Virginia law avoidance of the merger based on an alleged conflict of interest on the part of one the Bank's directors. Recognizing the possibility that a sufficient causal relationship might be established between a materially deceptive proxy and lost state remedies to support an implied right of recovery, the Court reasoned that causation under this theory could not be established because plaintiffs had not proved any loss.

Virginia law barred suits seeking to avoid a merger tainted by a director's conflict of interest only if the ratifying vote was procured pursuant to full disclosure of the material facts of the transaction, including the conflict of interest. Plaintiffs' contention that the proxy contained material misrepresentations necessarily prevented their loss of relief under this state law. Plaintiffs failed to allege any other lost state remedy. Hence, since plaintiffs failed to establish the necessary injury required under a theory of causation alleging lost state remedies, they could not succeed under such theory. The Supreme Court therefore found it unnecessary to decide whether § 14(a) provided such implied relief.

### B.   Plaintiff's Theories of Recovery

Plaintiffs in the present action seek recovery under four separate federal securities law provisions. In reversing the trial court's dismissal, we imposed liability only under § 14(a), without commenting on plaintiffs' other three causes of action. The necessary implication of our imposing liability under § 14(a) is the recognition of an implied private cause of action for minority shareholders who cannot affect the outcome of a corporate vote. In doing so, we did not comment on what theory of causation defendants' liability rested. Perhaps we presumed that plaintiffs had suffered an injury causally related to the defective proxy because defendants in Wilson I had not contested—and the district court found—causation.

Plaintiffs set forth two theories of causation to support their claims. They assert first that an implied action under any of the four securities law provisions pleaded should be recognized because 85 percent of the voting shares, or 12 percent of the minority shareholders in addition to the controlling majority shareholders, had to approve the merger in order for the exchange of stock to take place without tax consequences. * * * [W]e reject this theory of causation.

Plaintiffs' second theory of causation—one with more merit and upon which § 14(a) causes of action have been sustained in the past—is that their deceptively procured vote in favor of the merger deprived them of their state appraisal rights under N.Y.Bus.Corp.Law §§ 623 (a)(b) (McKinney 1986); § 910(a)(1) (McKinney Supp.1992). We and other courts have recognized that plaintiffs might prevail on such a § 14(a) theory. *See Cole v. Schenley Indus., Inc.*, 563 F.2d 35, 39–40 (2d Cir.1977) (on a motion to dismiss complaint, implied right recognized when insignificant minority shareholders had state law alternatives to accepting merger); *Schlick v. Penn–Dixie Cement Corp.*, 507 F.2d 374, 381–84 (2d Cir.1974) (though insignificant minority shareholders had no appraisal rights under state law, deprivation of measures other than casting proxies may support implied right to recovery under § 14(a)). *See also Swanson v. American Consumers Indus., Inc.*, 475 F.2d 516, 520–21

(7th Cir.1973) (insignificant minority shareholders entitled to recovery for lost state appraisal rights under § 10(b)). *Cf. Scattergood v. Perelman*, 945 F.2d 618, 626 n. 4 (3d Cir.1991) (noting possibility that implied right of recovery might exist for lost state remedies).

As noted, *Virginia Bankshares* left open the possibility that § 14(a) might include this type of implied right to recover and did not address whether the causal relationship between a deceptive proxy and lost state remedies was sufficient to support a federal remedy. Defendants, having failed to contest causation prior to the present appeal * * * should hardly be allowed to argue the point now, especially when to permit such puts them in a better position than if they had made this objection earlier and lost.

We continue to believe that a minority shareholder, who has lost his right to a state appraisal because of a materially deceptive proxy, may make "a sufficient showing of causal relationship between the violation and the injury for which he seeks redress." *Mills*, 396 U.S. at 385, 90 S.Ct. at 622. The transaction effected by a proxy involves not only the merger of the corporate entities, and the attendant exchange of stock, but also the forfeiture of shareholders' appraisal rights. The injury sustained by a minority shareholder powerless to affect the outcome of the merger vote is not the merger but the loss of his appraisal right. The deceptive proxy plainly constitutes an "essential link" in accomplishing the forfeiture of this state right.

That the causal nexus between the merger and the proxy is absent when the minority stockholder's vote cannot affect the merger decision does not necessarily mean a causal link between the proxy and some other injury may not exist. We recognize that loss causation or economic harm to plaintiffs must be shown, as well as proof that the misrepresentations induced plaintiffs to engage in the subject transaction, that is, transaction causation. Here loss causation may be established when a proxy statement prompts a shareholder to accept an unfair exchange ratio for his shares rather than recoup a greater value through a state appraisal. And transaction causation may be shown when a proxy statement, because of material misrepresentations, causes a shareholder to forfeit his appraisal rights by voting in favor of the proposed corporate merger.

Even though the proxy was not legally required in this case, when defendants choose to issue a proxy plaintiffs have a right to a truthful one. With the Securities Exchange Act of 1934, Congress sought to promote fair corporate suffrage with respect to " 'every equity security' "by requiring an " 'explanation to the stockholder of the real nature of the questions for which authority to cast his vote is sought.' "*Mills*, 396 U.S. at 381, 90 S.Ct. at 620 (quoting H.R.Rep. No. 1383, 73d Cong., 2d Sess. 13–14 (1934)); *see also J.I. Case Co. v. Borak*, 377 U.S. 426, 431–32, 84 S.Ct. 1555, 1559–60, 12 L.Ed.2d 423 (1964). Congress' interest in the protection of investors and the " 'free exercise of [their] voting rights,' "*Borak*, 377 U.S. at 431, 84 S.Ct. at 1559 (quoting H.R.Rep. No.

1383, 73d Cong., 2d Sess. 14 (1934)), should not vary in degree according to the ability of the shareholder to affect the merger, if the vote nevertheless may result in a different sort of injury which full disclosure might have avoided.

The statute does not suggest that the prohibition of material misrepresentation in a proxy extends only to necessary proxies that are mailed to shareholders the solicitation of whose votes may affect the outcome of the proposed corporate action. That a controlling group of shareholders may accomplish any corporate change they want does not insulate them from liability for injury occasioned when they commit the sort of fraud that § 14(a) seeks to prevent. *See Swanson v. American Consumer Indus., Inc.*, 415 F.2d 1326, 1331–32 (7th Cir.1969). To decline to extend the protection of § 14(a) to plaintiffs, we think, might sanction overreaching by controlling shareholders when the minority shareholders most need § 14(a)'s protection. At the same time, allowing the action does not pose a threat of "speculative claims and procedural intractability," *Virginia Bankshares*, ___ U.S. at ___, 111 S.Ct. at 2765, because the forfeiture of state appraisal rights is a question separate from the effectuation of the merger and does not require courts to guess how or whether the majority shareholders would have proceeded in the face of minority dissent.

Although a finding of materiality in a proxy solicitation may satisfy the elements of loss and transaction causation for forfeited state appraisal rights, plaintiffs must also prove that they in fact lost state appraisal rights. *See Virginia Bankshares*, ___ U.S. at ___ & n. 14, 111 S.Ct. at 2766 & n. 14. * * * Accordingly, we must remand this matter for the limited purpose of determining whether the proxy solicitation actually resulted in the loss of any remedies available to plaintiffs under New York law.

―――――

In *Mills*, the Court assumed without discussion that the "transaction" to which the "essential link" related was the allegedly unfair merger. And in *Santa Fe*, the Court found that there could be no deception (and, therefore, no causation) where appraisal was the only remedy available to a dissatisfied shareholder. In *Wilson*, however, the Second Circuit found that there could be causation if there were a link between "the proxy and *some other injury*" rather than between the proxy and the merger (emphasis added). Moreover, there can be transaction causation where a materially misleading proxy statement "causes a shareholder to forfeit his appraisal rights by voting in favor of the proposed corporate merger." Is *Wilson* consistent with either *Mills* or *Santa Fe*, or does it create a new definition of "transaction" in determining whether there is causation?

For an extensive discussion of *Virginia Bankshares* in a case involving Rule 13–3 under the 1934 Act, *see Howing Co. v. Nationwide Corp.*, 972 F.2d 700 (6th Cir.1992), *cert. denied* 507 U.S. 1004, 113 S.Ct. 1645, 123 L.Ed.2d 266 (1993).

# E.  FAULT

In Note 5 of *Virginia Bankshares*, the Court left open the question of whether the standard of culpability to which the directors will be held in a Section 14(a) action is negligence or scienter (the traditional fraud standard). The language of Section 14(a), which simply prohibits the solicitation of proxies in violation of the SEC's rules, provides no guidance nor does the legislative history. The two principal liability provisions of the federal securities laws, Section 11 of the Securities Act of 1933 and Rule 10b–5 provide different answers: Section 11 contains an explicit negligence standard, while Rule 10b–5 requires the more exacting test of scienter. *See Ernst & Ernst v. Hochfelder*, 425 U.S. 185, 96 S.Ct. 1375, 47 L.Ed.2d 668 (1976).

Lower federal courts are also divided. In *Gould v. American–Hawaiian Steamship Co.*, 535 F.2d 761 (3d Cir.1976), the court held that an outside director "was responsible with his fellow directors for the action of the board in which he participated as well as for his acts or failure to act * * *. The [lower] court held that in any event [the outside director would have known that the proxy statement in its final form was false if he had read it, which it was his duty to do as a member of the board of directors which was issuing the document to solicit the shareholders' proxies. The [lower] court concluded that under these circumstances the [outside director] was liable for the materially false and misleading proxy statement * * *. As we have seen, the District Court held negligence to be the appropriate standard under § 14(a) and we agree." *Id.* at 776–77.

By contrast, in *Adams v. Standard Knitting Mills*, 623 F.2d 422 (6th Cir.1980) the court held that scienter was the appropriate standard, at least with respect to the corporation's outside accountants. The court stated that "[a]lthough we are not called on in this case to decide the standard of liability of the corporate issuer of proxy material, we are influenced by the fact that the accountant here, unlike the corporate issuer, does not directly benefit from the proxy vote and is not in privity with the stockholder. Unlike the corporate issuer, the preparation of financial statements to be appended to proxies and other reports is the daily fare of accountants, and the accountant's potential liability for relatively minor mistakes would be enormous under a negligence standard. * * * [I]n the instant case there was no proof of investor reliance on the notes to the financial statements which erroneously described the restriction on payment of dividends. We can see no reason for a different standard of liability for accountants under the proxy provisions than under 10(b). *Id.* at 429. Perhaps the high threshold for the accountant's liability can be explained by the firm's lack of financial involvement in the transaction, but what justifies the relatively low standard for the outside directors' liability? See *Fradkin v. Ernst*, 571 F.Supp. 829 (N.D.Ohio 1983).

In *Herskowitz v. Nutri/System, Inc.*, 857 F.2d 179 (3d Cir.1988) the court extended the *Gould* negligence standard for directors to outside advisers to the corporation such as accountants and investment bankers. The court rejected the scienter standard in *Adams* because it was bound by *Gould*. However, as the court noted, "since an investment banker rendering a fairness opinion in connection with a leveraged buyout knows full well that it will be used to solicit shareholder approval, and is well paid for the service it performs, we see no convincing reason for not holding it to the same standard of liability as the management it is assisting." *Id.* at 190.

# F.  STATE LAW DUTY OF DISCLOSURE

## 1.  STATE LAW REGULATION OF PROXY SOLICITATIONS

State regulation of proxy solicitations is a logical outgrowth of state statutes governing notice to shareholders of shareholder meetings. States have regulated proxy solicitations longer than has the federal government, yet far fewer cases have arisen under state law because of "judicial reluctance squarely to meet the problem of adequate disclosure in proxy solicitation." Note, *Standards of Disclosure in Proxy Solicitation of Unlisted Securities*, 1960 Duke L.J. 623, 628 (1960). State courts have been reluctant to embroil themselves in the "internal affairs" of corporations and have viewed any judicial intervention in the proxy process as an extraordinary measure. It was this reluctance that the Court noted in *Borak* when it observed that some states might attach no responsibility to misleading proxy statements.

The common law standards for the validity of a proxy solicitation evolved slowly. At the turn of the century, it appears that the principal test for validity was whether the shareholder had given the proxy voluntarily. Unless an individual shareholder could prove "that he gave [his proxy] under any constraint or misapprehension or otherwise than as a matter of his own free will and personal preference," a suit objecting to the use of a proxy given in response to a request for it was certain to fail. *State ex rel. Pugh v. Meredith*, 183 Iowa 783, 167 N.W. 626 (Iowa 1918). The proxy solicitor, over time, came to be held to owe a fiduciary duty to the shareholder from whom she solicits proxies not to make false or misleading communications in doing so.

Prior to *Borak*, voluntariness gave way in state courts to concepts of fairness and common law fraud and misrepresentation. The following excerpt from the dissenting opinion in *Brown v. Ward*, 593 P.2d 247 (Alaska 1979) summarizes the evolution of state law principles.

Ward contends that since Congress intended state law to control, in the absence of a statute, the elements of common law fraud and misrepresentation should control. However, the few courts which have addressed this issue have not so held. Rather, they have taken a compromise position between the federal standard and the common law tort of misrepresentation. See "*Standards of Disclosure in Proxy Solicitation of Unlisted Securities*," [1960 Duke L.J. 623

(1960)] n. 6, at 623; Aranow and Einhorn, "*State Court Review of Corporate Elections*," 56 COL.L.REV. 155 (1956).

New York has had the most case law in this area. *In Re Scheuer*, 59 N.Y.S.2d 500 (Sup.1942), was an action by an aggrieved shareholder to have proxies invalidated because the solicitation material reported that certain new equipment expenditures had been deducted from gross earnings when, in fact, they were charged to capital. The court found that the actions of those engaged in securing the proxies had deviated from "the exacting standards of fairness" required in proxy solicitation and were misleading, whether done "carelessly, recklessly, or deliberately." 59 N.Y.S.2d at 501. Unfortunately, these standards were not further described. *Continental Bank & Trust Co. v. 200 Madison Ave. Corp.*, 43 N.Y.S.2d 402 (Sup.1943), added that the alleged misrepresentation must be material such as to "influence any layman to give a proxy where he would not otherwise have done so." 43 N.Y.S.2d at 407–8. *Wyatt v. Armstrong*, 186 Misc. 216, 59 N.Y.S.2d 502 (1945), reasserted the *Scheuer* test. It held that proxies solicited without notification that the nominees, if elected, intended to resign was a concealment tantamount to fraud and misrepresentation. The test was whether the solicitation was "so clouded with doubt or tainted with questionable circumstances that the standards of fair dealing" were abused, depriving shareholders of the knowing freedom to vote. 59 N.Y.S.2d at 505, 508.

The last in this line of cases was *In Re R. Hoe & Co.*, 14 Misc.2d 500, 137 N.Y.S.2d 142 (1954), aff'd, 309 N.Y. 719, 128 N.E.2d 420 (1955). After an election of directors, the displaced management sought to have the election set aside because the winning shareholder insurgents had made misrepresentations about management in their proxy solicitation material. The court found that there was a factual basis for the shareholders allegations against management. Management had fully availed itself of the opportunity to present its view to the shareholders. And, though the fight was bitter, the solicitation was not so tainted with fraud as to require judicial intervention to avoid an inequitable result. The court noted that "a certain amount of innuendo, misstatement, exaggeration and puffing must be allowed as a natural by-product of a bitter campaign." 137 N.Y.S.2d at 147–48. *See also, Bresnick v. Home Title Guaranty Company*, 175 F.Supp. 723 (S.D.N.Y.1959).

The view that shareholders would be better protected if the standard of proof for misleading proxy solicitation material were less rigorous than common law misrepresentation was best stated in *Willoughby v. Port*, 182 F.Supp. 496 (S.D.N.Y.1960). There, two directors sought a preliminary injunction against another director's use of proxies he had solicited, claiming that the director had misstated the attitude of the corporate counsel. The court said:

"Those who seek the proxies of their fellow corporate shareholders assume a fiduciary obligation. Even if the publicity here was defective only in that it did not tell the whole truth, the failure to make a full disclosure would have been a breach of fiduciary obligation. As things stand, I cannot find that any stockholder who sends defendants his proxy is doing so uninfluenced by the false impression. * * * Defendants are responsible for any such false impression and consequently cannot have the advantage of the proxies obtained thereby." (citations omitted) 182 F.Supp. at 499.

593 P.2d at 255–256.

––––––––

Only three states, Alaska, Illinois and South Carolina, have enacted statutes regulating proxy solicitations. No cases directly construing these statutes have arisen, and many of the same questions that arose in connection with *Borak* remain.

Alaska enacted a statute in 1977 which prohibits false and misleading proxy solicitations. Alaska Stat. § 45.55.160 (1992). The statute establishes an agency to prosecute violations. *Id.* at § 45.55.200. Section 139 specifically requires those corporations organized under the Alaska Native Claims Settlement Act to file their proxy solicitation materials with the agency. Although the statute does not provide an express private right of action, the majority in *Brown v. Ward, supra,* implicitly recognized such an action under the statute so long as the corporation was required to file with the enforcing agency. 593 P.2d at 249 (Alaska 1979).

The Illinois and South Carolina statutes also prohibit the use of false and misleading statements when soliciting proxies, using language which closely resembles Rule 14a–9 of the federal proxy rules. Unlike Alaska, Illinois and South Carolina do not set up an agency to enforce the statute or provide explicit penalties for violators. Like the Alaska statute, these statutes do not establish a private cause of action, and there are no cases construing them.

Delaware and other states, to a lesser degree, have not limited their regulation of corporate communications to proxy solicitations. A growing body of state law mandates that all communications between corporate fiduciaries and shareholders fully disclose all material information on the subject of the communication. The principal difference between regulation of disclosure and regulation of proxy solicitation is that only corporate fiduciaries owe the broader duty of disclosure, while the duties owed in connection with a proxy solicitation attach to anyone soliciting proxies, whether or not a corporate fiduciary.

## 2. ORIGINS AND EVOLUTION OF THE DUTY OF DISCLOSURE

The Delaware duty of disclosure can be traced ultimately to a now repealed state statute: 8 Del.C. § 144 (1953). That section held directors and officers jointly and severally liable for damages resulting from their knowing distribution or publication of materially false written statements about the condition of the corporation. While the statute on its face mandated no affirmative duty to disclose, a court held that it required a director making a written statement to shareholders concerning the condition of the corporation to "disclose all material facts." *Hall v. John S. Isaacs & Sons Farms*, 146 A.2d 602, 609–10 (Del.Ch.1958). Nine years after the decision in *Hall*, Section 144 was repealed without explanation; however, *Kelly v. Bell*, 254 A.2d 62, 71 (Del.Ch.1969), *aff'd* 266 A.2d 878 (Del.1970) decided after the repeal, reaffirmed the principle of *Hall* regarding disclosure.

The principal evolution of the state law duty of disclosure began in 1977 with the Delaware Supreme Court's decision in *Lynch v. Vickers Energy Corp.*, 383 A.2d 278 (Del.1977). Among other things, *Lynch* expanded the class of those owing the duty to include majority shareholders and further defined the affirmative aspects of the duty. In *Lynch*, the majority shareholder, Vickers, made a tender offer at $12 per share for the remaining shares of Transocean that Vickers did not own. The offer included a circular made jointly by Vickers and the directors of Transocean which did not disclose that: (1) a "highly qualified" petroleum engineer who was a member of Transocean's management appraised the company to be worth more than Vickers' offer and (2) Vickers' management had authorized open market purchases of Transocean's shares during the period immediately preceding the offer for bids of up to $15 a share. The court held that Vickers in this context owed a duty of "complete candor" to disclose all "germane facts" to the minority shareholders. The court feared that majority shareholders, as insiders, could use their special knowledge to the detriment of those on the outside. Thus, the duty of disclosure seemed to emanate from the duty of loyalty owed by controlling shareholders.

### 3.  UNDER WHAT CIRCUMSTANCES DOES THE DUTY ARISE?

Those who are in a fiduciary relationship to the shareholders, including at least directors and controlling shareholders, owe shareholders a duty of disclosure. *Lacos Land Co. v. Arden Group*, 517 A.2d 271, 279 (Del.Ch.1986) states: "[I]t is, of course, well-established in our law that an element of the fiduciary duty that directors owe to shareholders is the duty, arising when the board is required or elects to seek shareholder action, to disclose fully and fairly pertinent information within the board's control." In *Lacos Land*, the board solicited proxies to obtain shareholder approval of a dual-class recapitalization that would effectively place voting control in the hands of the controlling shareholder. The court found that the board had violated its disclosure duty because the proxy statement led one to think that the controlling shareholder was a "restricted person" when in reality she was not.

*Kahn v. Household Acquisition Corp.*, 591 A.2d 166 (Del.1991), applied the duty of disclosure to controlling shareholders. Household Acquisition Corporation ("HAC"), the controlling shareholder of Wien, attempted to merge with Wien by having the minority either approve the merger or tender their shares. The proxy statement HAC sent to the minority shareholders did not disclose that Wien had moved forward in its negotiations with the Civil Aeronautics Board regarding the subsidies Wien would receive for the coming year. The court found that the controlling shareholder had a duty of disclosure that information, a duty emanating from the duty of fair dealing HAC, as Wien's controlling shareholder, owed to the minority shareholders.

As a general rule, those not in a fiduciary relationship with shareholders do not owe them a duty of disclosure. *Zirn v. VLI Corp.*, 1992 WL 136450 (Del.Ch.1992) *rev'd on other grounds* 621 A.2d 773 (Del. 1993), held that a third party tender offeror, here AHP, was not responsible under the state law duty of disclosure for a misleading proxy statement it sent to shareholders of a corporation it was attempting to purchase. The court noted, however, that once AHP became the controlling shareholder as a result of its tender offer, the state law duty of disclosure applied to all subsequent communications by AHP.

Additionally, corporate fiduciaries are not responsible for the failures of non-fiduciaries to disclose. In *Citron v. Fairchild Camera & Instrument Corp.*, 569 A.2d 53 (Del.1989), a third party did not disclose allegedly "material" information in his tender offer to Fairchild. The Delaware Supreme Court upheld the Court of Chancery's finding that the Fairchild board was not legally responsible for the third party's alleged violations "absent some proof that the two * * * engaged in joint conduct to mislead the shareholders." *Id.* at 70.

When shareholders bring suit charging breach of the duty of disclosure, the corporation itself is frequently named as a defendant. Does such an action make sense conceptually? Can the corporation *per se*, as opposed to its directors or controlling shareholder, owe a duty to its shareholders? Delaware courts have indicated that because a corporation *qua* corporate entity cannot stand in a fiduciary relationship to its stockholders, it cannot be liable for breach of a fiduciary duty of disclosure. *See In re Dataproducts Corp. Shareholders Litig.*, 1991 WL 165301 (Del.Ch.1991). The court went on to explain, however, that it:

> * * *[I]s not to say that a corporation owes no duty or can never be held liable under Delaware law if it promulgates false and misleading disclosures to its shareholders. Rather, it means that under Delaware law any disclosure duty owed by the corporation to its shareholders must be predicated upon a theory of legal or equitable fraud. * * * Legal (i.e., common law) fraud requires (1) a false representation (usually of fact) by the defendant, (2) the defendant's knowledge or belief that the representation was false or made with reckless indifference to the truth, (3) an intent to induce the plaintiff to act or refrain from acting, (4) the plaintiff's action or inaction taken in justifiable reliance upon the representation, and (5) damage to the plaintiff as a result of such reliance. Equitable fraud requires a showing of those same elements, except for element

(2). That is, in equity the defendant does not have to know or believe that his statement was false or have acted in reckless disregard of the truth. Rather, equitable fraud can be founded upon a negligent or an innocent misrepresentation.

*Id.* at *6–*7. *See also, Gaffin v. Teledyne, Inc.*, 611 A.2d 467 (Del.1992). How do the theories of legal or equitable fraud differ from the fiduciary duty to disclose material information to shareholders?

The duty of disclosure arises when a fiduciary asks the shareholders to act as corporate decision-maker. *Stroud v. Grace*, 606 A.2d 75 (Del. 1992) clearly affirms that principle but slightly limits its scope. In *Stroud* the board of directors of a closely held corporation approved controversial by-law amendments that established new qualifications for board membership. The board then sought shareholder ratification at the annual meeting. The notice of the meeting which was sent to the shareholders included a copy of the amended by-laws but did not explain the purpose of these amendments. The board, however, did explain their purpose at the meeting. In upholding the actions of the board, the court reaffirmed the principle that "directors of Delaware corporations are under a fiduciary duty to disclose fully and fairly all material information within the board's control when it seeks shareholder action." *Id.* at 84.

Under most circumstances, application of this principle would have meant that the board's failure to explain the purpose of the proposed amendments constituted a material omission in breach of its fiduciary duty. Here, however, the court limited the principle, holding that the common law duty of disclosure did not override the specific disclosure requirements for the notice of meeting that were specifically set out in the statute, *i.e.*, the time and place of the meeting and a copy or summary of any amendment to the corporation's certificate of incorporation. The effect of this limitation is likely to be slight; few statutory provisions contain explicit disclosures that would override the general duty of disclosure.

*Stroud* might be thought to allow a board to bypass the duty of disclosure by foregoing a proxy solicitation in the hope of passing a controversial measure at a lightly attended annual meeting. The court suggested, however, that *Schnell* (Chapter 3) would forbid such conduct if it was intended to manipulate the shareholder vote inequitably.

Courts have held that both directors and controlling shareholders have a duty of disclosure when they place the shareholder in a position in which she has to decide whether to sell her stock or seek appraisal, whether in a traditional merger, a tender offer by a controlling shareholder or a tender offer by the corporation for its own shares (a self-tender). *See Lynch*, supra; *Glassman v. Wometco Cable Television*, 1989 WL 1160 (Del.Ch.1989); *Eisenberg v. Chicago Milwaukee Corp.*, 537 A.2d 1051 (Del.Ch.1987). Courts also have extended the duty of disclosure to short-form mergers, even though no shareholder vote is required. *Shell Petroleum, Inc. v. Smith*, 606 A.2d 112 (Del.1992).

It is not clear whether there is a duty of disclosure when no shareholder action is required. Delaware Court of Chancery decisions are divided and the Delaware Supreme Court recently declined to resolve the conflict. *Kahn v. Roberts*, 679 A.2d 460, 467 (1996). *Compare Bragger v. Budacz*, 1994 WL 698609 (Del.Ch.1994) (dismissing claims that information statement issued in connection with a spin-off was misleading because no shareholder action was solicited) *with Kahn v. Roberts*, 1994 WL 70118 (Del.Ch.1994) (no dismissal of disclosure claim when directors provide information when no shareholder action needed or sought).

For excellent analyses of the duty of disclosure under Delaware law, see Lawrence A. Hamermesh, *Calling Off the Lynch Mob: The Corporate Director's Fiduciary Disclosure Duty*, 49 VAND. L.REV. 1087 (1996); David C. McBride & Martin S. Lessner, *General Comparison of Delaware Fiduciary Duty of Disclosure Obligations Under the Securities Exchange Act of 1934 (Including the Private Securities Litigation Reform Act of 1995)*, 18 BANK & CORP. GOVERNANCE L.REP. 563 (1997).

## 4. MATERIALITY UNDER STATE LAW

Fiduciaries must disclose "all material information." In *Rosenblatt v. Getty Oil Co.*, 493 A.2d 929, 944 (Del.1985), the Delaware Supreme Court expressly adopted the Supreme Court's definition of materiality set forth in in *TSC, supra*. Because of language in *Lynch v. Vickers* and subsequent decisions to the effect that a "duty of candor" required the disclosure of all "germane" information, there was some initial confusion as to the extent to which the federal and Delaware standards were coextensive The Delaware Supreme Court resolved this confusion in *Stroud* when it stated:

> [T]he term "duty of candor" does not import a unique or special rule of disclosure. It represents nothing more than the well-recognized proposition that directors of Delaware corporations are under a fiduciary duty to disclose fully and fairly all material information within the board's control when it seeks shareholder action. * * * Thus, the term "duty of candor" has no well accepted meaning in the disclosure context. Its use is both confusing and imprecise given the well-established principles and duties of disclosure that otherwise exist. Thus, it is more appropriate for our courts to speak of a duty of disclosure based on a materiality standard rather than the unhelpful language that has crept into Delaware court decisions as a "duty of candor." This is entirely consistent with our prior statements of Delaware law regarding the duty and standard of disclosure.

606 A.2d at 84.

*Arnold v. Society for Savings Bancorp*, 650 A.2d 1270 (Del. Supr.1994) involved the materiality of certain disclosures in a merger proxy statement. The principal misstatement concerned Bancorp's efforts to sell its most profitable subsidiary, Fidelity Acceptance Corporation (FAC) prior to the merger. These efforts resulted in a contingent bid, but the sale was never consummated. The ultimate merger proxy statement described the failed proposal but did not disclose the amount of the bid or the qualified estimates as to the value of the Bancorp shares that had been generated in connection with the proposal. In granting summary judgment for the defendants, the Court of Chancery held that the contingent FAC bid was immaterial as a matter of law under the circumstances. The Delaware Supreme Court reversed and held that the Bancorp directors had violated their duty of disclosure to the Bancorp shareholders. It remanded the question of whether, in light of DGCL § 102(b)(7), there was a remedy available against the corporate defendants

The Delaware Supreme Court emphasized that it was "not deciding that the FAC bid was material as a matter of law." *Id.* at 1282. Rather, it held only that "once defendants traveled down the road of partial disclosure of the history leading up to the Merger and used the vague language described, they had an obligation to provide the stockholders with an accurate, full and fair characterization of those historic events." *Id.* at 1280.

This latter statement could be viewed as inconsistent with the United States Supreme Court's decision in *Basic, Inc. v. Levinson* (Chapter 19), which rejected the argument that "once a statement is made denying the existence of any [merger] discussions, even discussions that might not have been material in absence of the denial are material because they make the statement made untrue." This inconsistency, however, may be more apparent than real and illustrates the difficulty of distinguishing between materiality as a matter of fact and as a matter of law. Because *Arnold* arose on a motion for summary judgment, the court had to accept the facts in the light most favorable to the defendants rather than having had factual findings made after an evidentiary hearing. Thus the Delaware Supreme Court may be viewed as having held that for purposes of summary judgment, the half-truths about the FAC offer could be viewed as material as a matter of fact so that summary judgment would be inappropriate. At the same time, the court was not prepared to say that the same half truths would be immaterial as a matter of law.

Recall that the federal cases under Rule 14a–9 do not require directors to characterize their conduct as unlawful or constituting a breach of fiduciary duty. Delaware law is consistent with those cases. *See, e.g., Brody v. Zaucha*, 697 A.2d 749, 754 (Del.1997) in which the court noted that "[i]t is settled Delaware law that a director need not make self-accusatory statements nor engage in 'self-flagellation' by confessing to wrongdoing that has not been formally adjudicated by a court of law."

In determining whether a fiduciary's omission of information or false statement in a disclosure is material, whether the directors acted in good faith appears to be irrelevant. In *Shell Petroleum, Inc. v. Smith*, 606 A.2d 112 (Del.1992), the controlling shareholder released erroneous information to the shareholders concerning the value of the corporation. Although the error was inadvertent, the court nonetheless held the controlling shareholder liable for the omission because it controlled the preparation of the materials and thus had constructive knowledge of the error. "It is only logical that a majority shareholder who directs a subsidiary to prepare certain disclosure materials and then distributes those materials to minority shareholders should be held accountable for any errors contained therein." *Id.* at 116.

In effect, fiduciaries are held to a standard of strict liability for violations of the duty of disclosure: they are liable for its breach whether or not they are acting in good faith. How is the business judgment rule for director decisions affected by what approaches a strict liability disclosure standard? In *In re Anderson, Clayton Shareholders' Litig.*, 519 A.2d 669 (Del.Ch.1986), the court held:

> * * * [T]he question whether shareholders have, under the circumstances, been provided with appropriate information upon which an informed choice on a matter of fundamental corporate importance may be made, is not a decision concerning the management of business and affairs of the enterprise (8 Del.C. § 141(a)) of the kind the business judgement rule is intended to protect; it is rather a matter relating to the directors' duty to shareholders who are technically outside the corporation.

*Id.* at 675.

Although the Delaware and federal definitions of materiality are the same, it is not clear that the different courts would apply them identically. *See* J. Robert Brown, Jr., THE REGULATION OF CORPORATE DISCLOSURE, § 9.03[3] (Supp. 1996).

## 5. "VOLUNTARY" DISCLOSURES AND LOST STATE REMEDIES

What duty does a fiduciary owe to shareholders when a vote is sought but not required or needed to accomplish a contemplated transaction? Recall *Virginia Bankshares,* in which proxies were solicited even though management had sufficient votes to approve the transaction without the vote of the minority shareholders. Although *Virginia Bankshares* found causation lacking under Section 14(a) of the 1934 Act in such a situation, Delaware has not yet directly addressed the question as a matter of state law. The Delaware Supreme Court has indicated, however, that a duty of full and fair disclosure arises whenever directors are either required to seek a shareholder vote or elect to do so. *Stroud v. Milliken Enterprises, Inc.*, 552 A.2d 476, 480 (Del.1989).

In light of Delaware's seeming willingness to impose the duty of disclosure when a board "voluntarily" seeks approval of a transaction by a majority of the minority shareholders, how much insulation does *Virginia Bankshares* give the board, even if no action can be brought under federal law? Have developments under state law overtaken the Court's concern in *Borak* that if a victim of a deceptive proxy statement were "obliged to go into state courts for remedial relief * * * [and] the law of the State happened to attach no responsibility to the use of misleading proxy statements, the whole purpose of [federal proxy regulation] might be frustrated?" Alternatively, does the reasoning the Court used in *Virginia Bankshares* suggest that, if state law provides a plaintiff with a remedy for an alleged violation of the duty of disclosure, that plaintiff cannot assert a federal claim based on the theory that defendant's misrepresentation caused her to lose a remedy she otherwise would have had under state law? For further discussion of the interrelationship between federal and state law on disclosure after *Virginia Bankshares*, *see* Jesse A. Finkelstein, Mark J. Gentile and J. Michael Christopher, *The Potential Implications of Virginia Bankshares for Delaware Law*, INSIGHTS, May 1992, at 26.

# Chapter 19

## REGULATION OF SECURITIES TRADING

We study the regulation of securities trading in a corporations course for at least two reasons. Securities trading often involves corporate management and thus necessarily involves the fiduciary duties we have studied previously; securities trading also affects the market for a corporation's stock and thus implicates the market's role in the corporate governance system. In this chapter we will consider some of the legal problems associated with securities transactions in the public securities markets. Before turning to legal issues, however, it is useful to review how securities markets operate, the significance of information to those markets and how the two are linked.

## A. INTRODUCTION TO SECURITIES TRADING

There are two types of public securities markets: stock exchanges and the NASDAQ (National Association of Securities Dealers Automated Quotation System) market*. A stock exchange has a physical central marketplace, the "floor" of the exchange, where broker-dealers who are members of the exchange buy and sell securities that are listed on the exchange ("listed securities") for customers and for their own accounts. The principal stock exchanges are the New York Stock Exchange and the American Stock Exchange.

An investor who wishes to buy or sell a listed security places an order with a broker, whose firm will handle the transaction itself if it is a member of an exchange on which the security is traded and will forward the order to a member firm if it is not. The order is sent to a floor trader who is physically present on the floor of the exchange. The floor trader goes to the place where the security is traded (the "post"). A number of other floor traders (the "crowd") and a "specialist," who is required to maintain a continuous market in the security, are always at the post. The specialist trades both for her own account (in which case she is

---

* The NASDAQ market was formerly known as the over-the-counter market. That market still exists in stocks in which there is limited trading.

acting as a "dealer") and for the accounts of others who have given her orders to execute (in which case she is acting as a "broker"). The specialist's role is an important one; her market-making furnishes liquidity in the trading of the security, permitting easier matching of buy and sell orders and causing the price of the stock to move more smoothly. Orders for relatively small amounts of stock are handled through an automated execution system.

There are two principal types of customers' orders: "limit orders" and "market orders." The former direct the broker to buy or sell at a particular price. The latter call for a trade at the prevailing price. A market order brought to the post is executed immediately at the prevailing market price. Another broker in the crowd may match it with a countervailing order or, if no broker holds such an order, the specialist will accept the order either for her own account or carrying out a limit order. The specialist maintains a "book" in which she keeps track of limit orders left with her by brokers who are not present continuously at her post.

An "over-the-counter" market like NASDAQ differs in important respects from the more familiar auction markets, like the New York and American Stock Exchanges. The NYSE and AMEX markets are distinguished by a physical exchange floor where buy and sell orders actually "meet," with prices set by the interaction of those orders under the supervision of a market "specialist." In a dealer market like NASDAQ, the market exists electronically, in the form of a communications system which constantly receives and reports the prices at which geographically dispersed market makers are willing to buy and sell different securities. These market makers compete with one another to buy and sell the same securities using the electronic system; NASDAQ is, then, an electronic inter-dealer quotation system.

In a dealer market, market makers create liquidity by being continuously willing to buy and sell the security in which they are making a market. In this way, an individual who wishes to buy or sell a security does not have to wait until someone is found who wishes to take the opposite side in the desired transaction. To account for the effort and risk required to maintain liquidity, market makers are allowed to set the prices at which they are prepared to buy and sell a particular security; the difference between the listed "ask" and "bid" prices is the "spread" that market makers capture as compensation.

The electronic quotation system ties together the numerous market makers for all over-the-counter securities available on NASDAQ. All NASDAQ market makers are required to input their bid and offer prices to the NASD computer, which collects the information and transmits, for each security, the highest bid price and lowest ask price currently available. These prices are called the "National Best Bid and Offer," or NBBO. The NASD computer, publicly available to all NASDAQ market makers, brokers and dealers, displays and continuously updates the NBBO for each offered security.

*Newton v. Merrill, Lynch, Pierce, Fenner & Smith,* 135 F.3d 266, 268 (3d Cir.1998).

## B. ECONOMIC THEORY, SECURITIES MARKETS AND SECURITIES TRANSACTIONS

### 1. INFORMATION AND SECURITIES MARKETS

If a security's market price (1) reflected *all* information, *both public and private*, about the cash flows that investors holding that security would receive, and (2) represented the *best possible estimate* of the present value of those future cash flows, three consequences would follow. First, inside trading would not be profitable, because whatever information an insider possessed would already be reflected in a security's price. Second, publication of false or misleading information about a public company would cause no harm, because the market price would reflect the (private) information that what had been published was false or misleading. Third, attempting to out-perform the market would be futile, because under-priced and over-priced securities would not exist.

It seems clear, however, that the first specified condition is not satisfied in the real world. Several studies have found that corporate insiders, who have access to private information that allows them to anticipate significant changes in their companies' businesses, earn abnormal returns—*i.e.*, returns in excess of market averages, adjusted for risk—when they trade their companies' securities. On the other hand, there is substantial evidence that securities markets incorporate public information into securities prices almost instantaneously. Consequently, persons other than insiders cannot expect to earn abnormal returns by by buying or selling securities on the basis of information that has been public for more than a few minutes (or seconds). However, an investor who purchases or sells a security on the basis of materially false or misleading information almost certainly will realize a lower than normal return on that investment. The market, not knowing the information in question was false or misleading, will have incorporated it into the price the investor paid. Then, when the truth is revealed, the market will re-price the security to reflect that information.

Whether a security's market prices represents the *best possible estimate* of the present value of the future cash flows an investor will realize by holding that security—what one might call the *true* or *inherent* value of that security—presents a more complicated question. The fact that millions of investors attempt to outperform the market makes clear that they, at least, believe some securities are underpriced and others are overpriced. The fact that a few investors, such as Warren Buffet, have earned abnormal returns over extended periods of time provides more concrete evidence that not all securities trade at their inherent value.

On the other hand, a study of the performance of 115 mutual funds for the period from 1955 through 1964, Michael Jensen, *The Performance of Mutual Funds in the Period 1955–64*, 23 J. FIN. 389 (1968), found that, before expenses, about half the funds performed better and about half performed worse than a randomly selected portfolio of equal riskiness. After expenses, only 43 of the funds outperformed the randomly selected portfolio. Moreover, the funds that outperformed the randomly selected portfolio in one period outperformed that portfolio in a subsequent period only about half the time, further suggesting that any given fund's superior performance in one period more likely was due to luck than to the skill of its managers. (As one can imagine, these findings did not produce a sense of euphoria in the mutual fund industry.)

Several subsequent studies of the institutional investors' performance have produced similar results. This has led many pension funds and many individual investors to conclude that they should give up on, or greatly limit, efforts to outperform the market. As a consequence, a great deal of money (probably more than $1 trillion) now is invested in *index funds* that seek to do no more than mirror the return on some stock market index, most often the S & P 500.

The fact that so much money is invested in index funds does not necessarily mean that most investors—or even most investors in index funds—believe that the market prices of most securities accurately reflects those securities' inherent values. Many investors may simply have concluded that, given the talent and resources other people are devoting to attempting to "beat the market," they are better off minimizing their transaction costs (by investing in index funds) and devoting their talents and resources to other ends.

No evidence suggests that stock markets do not respond to new information promptly and with relative efficiency. But a substantial literature suggests that the prices of securities often vary from their inherent value and that stock markets therefore often are not "efficient." What position one takes in this debate turns, to some considerable degree, on what one means by "efficient." Consider, in this regard, the following statement by one eminent economist:

> All estimates of value are noisy, so we can never know how far away price is from value. However, we might define an efficient market as one in within a factor of 2 of value, *i.e.*, the price is more than half of value and less than twice value. The factor of 2 is arbitrary, of course. Intuitively, though, it seems reasonable to me, in light of sources of uncertainty about value and the strength of the forces tending to cause price to return to value. By this definition, I think almost all markets are efficient almost all of the time. "Almost all" means at least 90%.

Fischer Black, *Noise*, 46 J. FIN. 529, 533 (1986).

But the debate over market efficiency also encompasses issues relating to whether investors consistently act rationally or frequently are driven by emotion, whether investors' decisions reflect cognitive biases, and whether investors can earn abnormal returns by basing their decisions not on what they believe securities are worth but on what they believe other investors will believe those securities are worth.** For a good summary of the principal elements of this debate, *see* Ronald J. Gilson & Bernard S. Black, (SOME OF) THE ESSENTIALS OF FINANCE AND INVESTMENT 159–181 (1993).

## 2.  AN OVERVIEW OF THE ISSUES

Much of this chapter deals with insider trading and its impact on securities markets. The paradigm case of insider trading is simple: the president of a high-technology company whose stock is traded on NASDAQ learns that the first prototypes of a new product in which the company has invested substantial resources is not performing as anticipated. As a consequence, the company will not be able to bring the product to market on schedule and may have to abandon it entirely. Either event will jeopardize the company's competitive position. Before the company discloses this information, the president sells a large portion of the stock he owns through NASDAQ. Immediately after the information is disclosed, the company's stock price drops sharply and remains at the lower price. You will read a great deal about the law regulating the president's conduct (and variations on that conduct which implicate other actors). Before assessing the judicial and legislative responses to this conduct and without regard to what the law is or should be, consider the following questions and the readings which shed light on them.

1.  Who is hurt by the president's sales?

    a.  The person who bought the stock from the president.

    b.  All the stockholders in the corporation.

    c.  The corporation itself.

    d.  The "market."

2.  If there was harm, how did it occur?

    a.  Through the president's sale.

    b.  Through the corporation's non-disclosure.

---

** *See* John Maynard Keynes, THE GENERAL THEORY OF EMPLOYMENT, INTEREST AND MONEY 156 (1936):

[P]rofessional investment may be likened to those newspaper competitions in which the competitors have to pick the six prettiest faces from a hundred photographs, the prize being awarded to the competitor whose choice most nearly corresponds to the average preference of the competitors as a whole; so that each competitor has to pick, not those faces which he himself finds prettiest, but those which he thinks likeliest to catch the fancy of the other competitors, all of whom are looking at the problem from the same point of view.

For a more contemporary and more sophisticated exposition of essentially the same theory, *see* Andrei Shleifer & Lawrence Summers, *The Noise Trader Approach to Finance*, 4 J. ECON. PERSP. 19 (1990).

    c.  Through the combination of these.

  3.  If the president must pay damages, who should recover?

    a.  The person who bought the stock from the president.

    b.  All those who bought stock at or about the same time the president sold.

    c.  All those who bought stock from the time the president sold to the time the corporation disclosed the problem.

    d.  The corporation.

  4.  How much should the president pay in damages?

    a.  The amount of the loss he avoided.

    b.  The amount of the losses suffered by those who are allowed to recover (how are those losses to be measured?).

    c.  An amount sufficient to deter others from engaging in the same kind of conduct.

## 3. ECONOMIC THEORY AND INSIDER TRADING

For many years, there was little debate over the foregoing questions; courts, the S.E.C. and commentators all generally condemned insider trading. Although Henry Manne's defense of the practice in his book, INSIDER TRADING AND THE STOCK MARKET (1966) ("Manne"), sparked some discussion in the late 1960's, little scholarly analysis explored the phenomenon in depth.* To many people, insider trading resembled playing cards with a marked deck; little attention was paid to the precise nature of the cheating. Although most writers still oppose insider trading, some recent scholars, particularly those who bring the "law and economics" perspective to the question, have argued that insider trading is beneficial to investors and to the market and should not be prohibited. Their arguments, while not generally accepted, have led to a scholarly reexamination of many conclusions which had previously seemed axiomatic and a questioning of premises which had appeared to be self-evident. Although the wave of insider trading scandals of the late 1980s changed the atmosphere in which this debate occurred, the theoretical underpinnings of the debate are still significant in assessing the regulatory structure of insider trading.

*Harm to Investors from Insider Trading.* At first blush, it seems simple to identify what is wrong with insider trading and who is hurt by it. It is unfair to permit insiders who have an informational advantage which other investors cannot overcome to benefit personally from that advantage, particularly when the information has been generated for a corporate purpose rather than for their own individual gain. Thus, when an investor enters the market, it would seem axiomatic that he would be harmed by a trade with someone who had inside information. The

---

* *See* Roy A. Schotland, *Unsafe at any Price: A Reply to Manne, Insider Trading and the Stock Market*, 53 VA.L.REV. 1425 (1966), Henry G. Manne, *Insider Trading and the Law Professors*, 23 VAND.L.REV. 547 (1970).

insider knows the real value of the stock, and can exploit this information when trading with an outsider. *See* Victor Brudney, *Insiders, Outsiders, and Informational Advantages Under the Federal Securities Laws*, 93 HARV.L.REV. 322, 356–57 (1979).

Closer analysis reveals certain problems with this intuitive argument. Trading in the securities of publicly-held companies does not occur in face-to-face transactions. Rather, it occurs in anonymous markets where buyers and sellers are randomly matched with each other. Moreover, as Professor Cox has noted: "Insider trading is at most a fortuity for the investor because the investor is no worse off when the insider trades than when the insider does not trade. The investor's decision to sell or purchase is unaffected by whether the insider is also secretly buying or selling shares in the open market. If the insider neither trades nor discloses his confidential material information, one can nevertheless expect the investor to pursue his trading plan. Sellers naturally are disadvantaged by the nondisclosure of good news, just as buyers are disadvantaged by the nondisclosure of bad news. These considerations, however, cast no light on why the insider's decision to trade should prompt disclosure." James D. Cox, *Insider Trading and Contracting: A Critical Response to the "Chicago School,"* 1986 DUKE L.J. 628, 635 (1986) ("Cox"). Notwithstanding this criticism, the intuitive argument remains popular. *See* James Brooks, THE TAKEOVER GAME, 316–17 (1987).

Among the more innovative theories of the harm from insider trading is that of Professor Wang, whose analysis is based on a phenomenon that he calls "The Law of Conservation of Securities." William K. S. Wang, *Trading on Material, Non Public Information on Impersonal Markets: Who is Harmed, and Who Can Sue Whom Under SEC Rule 10b–5?*, 54 S.CAL.L.REV. 1217 (1981). Wang argues that insider trading harms specific individuals, although the investors who trade with insiders are not necessarily the people who are harmed. He maintains that the insider's trades preempt (and thereby injure) those who would otherwise have been able to trade the shares acquired or sold by the insider. He further contends that an insider may also cause injury by inducing trades that otherwise would not have occurred without his participation in the market. Under Wang's analysis, investors who are induced to sell are harmed because they fail to realize the price increase that results from the subsequent announcement of good news. Similarly, investors who are induced to buy, suffer a price decrease when bad news is ultimately disclosed. *Id*. at 1234–35.

Under Wang's theory, disclosure will not always prevent potential victims from being harmed. Wang argues that disclosure prevents harm to induced traders but does not protect the preempted trader because the latter's transaction might otherwise have been precluded by new transactions at prices reflecting the disclosure. In short, public disclosure improves the position of one type of potential victim but not the other. *Id*. at 1252.

Like other theories, Wang's argument is valid only if the insider's trading significantly increases the trading activity in the stock. And, as Professor Cox has noted, even in such a case, "the harm in the preempted price situation is likely to be small; in the increased trading situation, the insider's trading causes the parallel trader to dispose of a dog or acquire a pearl." Cox, *supra*, at 635, n. 33.

*Delayed Disclosure.* Many writers argue that one consequence of legalizing insider trading is that it will interfere with the market's allocational efficiency because insiders will delay disclosure of material information so that they can benefit from it prior to public disclosure. Professor Haft also notes that because information flows up the corporate ladder through many stages, the possibility of delay is magnified as those at each stage take advantage of it before passing it along. Robert J. Haft, *The Effect of Insider Trading Rules on the Internal Efficiency of the Large Corporation*, 80 MICH.L.REV. 1051 (1982).

The extent to which disclosure will be delayed may turn on whether the undisclosed information is good news or bad news. Professor Scott argues that insiders who can profit from delayed disclosure have more incentive to cause the corporation to disclose information when the information is positive than when it is negative. Positive news about the firm benefits all stockholders, including the insiders, so that insiders will be anxious to profit from it, whereas they can delay the impact of negative news by simply not trading. Scott believes that the price movements which ordinarily signal the market that undisclosed information is present and which are said to dampen price shocks when that information is ultimately released do not occur in the case of bad news. He therefore concludes that a regime which allows insider trading encourages prompt disclosure of good news and, in the case of bad news, permits at least some information to reach the market sooner than it would have if such trading were banned. Kenneth E. Scott, *Insider Trading: Rule 10b–5, Disclosure and Corporate Privacy*, 9 J. LEGAL STUD. 801, 810–11 (1980).

Judge (formerly Professor) Easterbrook agrees in principle that insider trading allows some types of information to reach the market but disagrees with Scott's argument that a firm's incentive to disclose depends on whether the news is positive or negative. Instead, he contends that firms need to be credible in communicating to investors and that this credibility is furthered only if the firm promptly releases bad news along with the good. Frank H. Easterbrook, *Insider Trading, Secret Agents, Evidentiary Privileges, and the Production of Information*, 1981 SUP.CT.REV. 309, 327 (1981) ("Easterbrook").

One response to Easterbrook's argument might be that because prohibiting insider trading reduces the ability of insiders to profit on favorable developments, the prohibition may also diminish incentives to communicate all information to investors. Scott, *supra*, at 813. This diminished incentive would bring a concomitant reduction in the likelihood that the corporation would release any information to securities analysts, whose livelihood depends on assembling and organizing information for their clients. Because the analysts' information-gathering process enhances the efficiency of the market, prohibiting insider trading would reduce that efficiency. Michael P. Dooley, *Enforcement of Insider Trading Restrictions*, 66 Va.L.Rev. 1 (1980).

*Portfolio Theory and the Cost of Capital.* Another series of arguments against insider trading is based on portfolio theory. Because insider trading occurs randomly, investors do not know *ex ante* which firms will have material inside information or which firm's insiders will trade on that information. Because investors cannot make such distinctions accurately, and because they believe that insider trading is harmful, they must assume that every investment presents the same risk of insider trading as does the market as a whole. Accordingly, while some investors will refrain completely from investing, most will discount the value of any individual firm by the average agency costs of all firms. The consequence of such discounting is that the risk of insider trading, while seemingly non-systemic (i.e., related to a specific company or industry and thus capable of being protected against through portfolio diversification) is in fact systemic (i.e., inherent in every security). Because the risk is systematic, diversification cannot reduce it; indeed, increased diversification will simply guarantee that the investor's risk is that of the entire market. *See* Mark Klock, *Mainstream Economics and the Case For Prohibiting Inside Trading*, 10 Ga. St. U. L.Rev. 297, 335 (1994); Lawrence M. Ausubel, *Insider Trading in a Rational Expectations Economy*, 80 Am. Econ. Rev. 1022 (1990).

If this theory is correct, an investor is not harmed by insider trading because he can self-insure against such behavior by discounting all stocks by the risk of such trading for all firms. This discounting protects him in his inability to distinguish firms in which insider trading occurs from those in which it does not. And if his portfolio is efficiently diversified, his losses from insider trading will be offset by increased returns in corporations where such trading does not occur, even though the investor could not have known in advance which firms would fall into each category.

The consequence of the foregoing argument is that insider trading will harm firms rather than investors because it will increase their cost of capital by the amount that investors discount the price of their securities. To reduce this discount, firms may seek to incur bonding and monitoring costs (see Chapter 2) which will enable them to signal investors that they have a lower likelihood of insider trading. However, as we have previously seen, despite such efforts, it is impossible to eliminate insider trading completely because it will not be economical for a firm to do so at any cost. Thus, if firms cannot engage in meaningful signaling, investors will not distinguish among firms on the basis of whether insider trading occurs and will continue discounting the price they pay for their investments.

Professors Carlton and Fischel reject the argument that investors prefer to invest in companies that forbid insider trading. They argue that if investors had such a preference, a competitive market for capital would lead firms to ban such trading so that they could signal investors that they had reduced their agency costs. Carlton and Fischel conclude that the absence of widespread efforts by firms to prohibit insider trading through employment contracts or corporate charters suggests either that investors are indifferent to such trading or, in some circumstances, they may believe it is beneficial. Dennis W. Carlton & Daniel R. Fischel, *The Regulation of Insider Trading*, 35 STAN.L.REV. 857, 858 (1983) ("Carlton & Fischel").

Judge Posner is doubtful. He notes the high costs of enforcing any prohibition and the many opportunities to evade such a ban and concludes that these, as well as "the more fundamental one that insider trading is inherently easy to conceal may explain why corporations have made little effort on their own to ban the practice, leaving this function to public regulation instead * * * [i]f the probability of detection is so low that heavy penalties * * * would be necessary to curtail the practice, it might not pay companies to try to curtail it." Richard A. Posner, ECONOMIC ANALYSIS OF THE LAW, 418 (4th Ed. 1992) ("Posner"). *See, also,* Easterbrook, *supra* at 333–34.

*Effect of Insider Trading on Stock Prices.* Perhaps the most strongly held view in support of insider trading is that it will permit smoother changes in stock prices until the stock reaches its equilibrium price after the inside information has been publicly disclosed. Manne, *supra*, at 78–104. To the extent that insider trading affects stock prices, those who trade with the insider will sell at higher prices on good news or purchase at a lower price on bad news than if the insider had not traded. Moreover, not all information is in a form which is immediately communicable to the market; in those situations, increased trading volume attributable to insider trading signals the market that there is undisclosed information which is not being reflected in the share price. In some cases, this information may be confidential information that a firm would otherwise not wish to disclose to its competitors; insider trading conveys at least some of this information to the market. Carlton & Fischel, *supra*, at 879. Similarly, where other market participants are able to determine that insider trading is occurring, additional information may be conveyed to the market. Frank H. Easterbrook & Daniel R. Fischel, THE ECONOMIC STRUCTURE OF CORPORATE LAW 256–57 (1991) ("Easterbrook & Fischel").

In light of the pervasiveness of this argument, it is surprising that there has been relatively little attempt to challenge its premises and conclusions. Professor Cox has argued vigorously that the argument is seriously flawed. He points out that for the investor who trades with the insider, smoother prices are a poor second choice to having the information being disclosed prior to the trade. As he notes, "[t]he insider's opposite is far better off with the price established by the insider's disclosure of the information than he is with a price that has been modestly nudged by the insider's secret trading. In the case of the insider's non-disclosure of bad news, the opposite trader emerges owning a stock that has a lower price after disclosure than its purchase price; and in the case of good news, the insider's opposite emerges having sold the security for an amount substantially below its price following disclosure." Moreover, he argues that price changes occur much more quickly and efficiently through public disclosure than through trading because there are too many other factors affecting a stock price to permit an investor to discern clearly that there is undisclosed inside information reflected in that price. Cox, *supra*, at 646.

Cox also contends that the stock price argument proves too much. "If accepted, this position justifies massive trading and tipping to ensure that sufficient trading occurs to propel the stock to the equilibrium price appropriate for the nondisclosed information. Such widespread trading, however, compromises the corporate interest that justified nondisclosure in the first place." *Id.* at 648.

It should also be noted that some trades are time-induced and would benefit from smoother price movements. Other trades, however, are induced by changes in volume or price; these latter would more likely be harmed by the price movements caused by the insider's trading.

*Insider Trading as Management Compensation.* Some scholars argue that insider trading should not be regulated because it compensates managers and provides them with an additional incentive to take risks that will benefit investors. Originally propounded by Manne, *supra*, at 138–143, this argument had been generally rejected because it appeared to permit managers to benefit from bad news which could have the product of their own mistakes. However, Carlton and Fischel have revived it. They contend that because managements are inherently risk-averse, it is necessary to provide them with incentives to make business decisions which have the potential to increase the value of the firm substantially. If the firm's value does increase, all investors—insiders and outsiders—will share in the growth. Thus Carlton and Fischel argue that the insiders do not secure their gains at the expense of outsiders because the total wealth of the firm has increased. Put differently, they maintain that insider trading does not cause outsiders to get a smaller piece of the pie; rather, all investors benefit from a substantially larger pie. Carlton & Fischel, *supra* at 870–873.

Easterbrook and Fischel expand upon the argument that insider trading should be permitted as a means of managerial compensation. Allowing insider trading in effect permits the manager to renegotiate his compensation package with his every stock transaction. Thus, a "manager who observes an investment for the firm * * * will be more inclined to pursue this opportunity if rewarded on success. * * * Basing compensation in part on trading is one method for distinguishing superior from inferior managers." Easterbrook & Fischel, *supra* at 258.

For Carlton and Fischel, permitting managers to profit from bad news is consistent with the theory of insider trading as a compensation device; a manager will be more willing to take risks if he knows that he can profit by selling short prior to public disclosure of the failure. Insider trading, whether on good or bad news, is thus a means of rewarding entrepreneurial risk-taking, whether or not those risks succeed.

There are serious problems with this latter argument. If a manager can profit from either success or failure, why should he care which occurs? He is far more likely to be concerned with his own interests than with maximizing the value of the firm for the shareholders, and he will end by being risk-neutral rather than risk-preferring. Cox, *supra* at 651. *See, also,* Posner, *supra* at 417.

Professor Cox uses the foregoing response to Carlton and Fischel as the basis for maintaining that continuing external regulation of insider trading is warranted. He contends that there is no reason to believe that permitting such trading is in the shareholders' interest. He points out that managers control the amount of such trading and can thus distort the costs and benefits to investors. Consequently, shareholders have little to gain and much to lose by permitting insider trading; a ban would be consistent with what the parties would have negotiated were negotiations feasible.

Cox offers three other reasons to support his conclusion. First, he argues that knowledge of a manager's sources of compensation is essential to understand his discretionary behavior and that investors will be better protected when compensation is tied to performance rather than to the ability to profit from external events. Second, he maintains that an assessment of a manager's performance is possible only when an investor has knowledge of the manager's costs and the firm's productivity. Finally, he notes that shareholders expect managers to concentrate on the shareholders' best interests rather than their own private investments; the prohibition against insider trading "stems from the shareholders' expectation that a manager is paid to look after the shareholders' welfare, not his own." Cox, *supra* at 657–58.

For a comprehensive review of the theoretical debate about insider trading, *see* William K.S. Wang & Marc I. Steinberg, INSIDER TRADING 13–117 (1996). Louis Loss & Joel Seligman, SECURITIES REGULATION 3448–3466 (3rd ed.) and Frank H. Easterbrook & Daniel R. Fischel, THE ECONOMIC STRUCTURE OF CORPORATE LAW 256–262 (1991), provide contrasting views on these issues.

## PROBLEM
## STANDARD ELECTRONICS CORPORATION

Standard Electronics Corporation (Standard) is a Delaware corporation. It manufactures a wide variety of products which are used in high technology communications industries. It has assets of $500 million and, in its most recent fiscal year, had sales of $550 million and earnings of $30 million. The company went public six years ago and its common stock is now listed on the New York Stock Exchange. In the last year, Standard's stock has traded between $19 and $28 per share and has recently been trading at about $25 per share. In order to provide incentives for its staff, it introduced an employee stock option plan almost immediately after going public and, to provide stock for that plan, Standard has been purchasing its own stock on the New York Stock Exchange on alternate Fridays pursuant to a prearranged schedule. The three trustees of the plan are the company's president, Herbert Jones, its treasurer, and one of its outside directors.

The industry is highly capital intensive and intensely competitive; Standard has succeeded because of its ability to develop new products. In March of this year, its laser division discovered a process which would enable it to produce laser discs on which both graphics and large amounts of text could be stored. This process would also permit the company to produce the discs in far greater quantity and at far lower prices than at present. On April 1, the division's research team advised Jones that to develop the product to its full potential, heavy capital investments would be required. They indicated that with adequate financing, the company could gain a significant head start over its competitors.

On April 2, Jones met with the company's general counsel, Abigail Benedict, to discuss the stock market implications of the new process. The two decided that the information was to be kept highly confidential within the company and was to be referred to only by the code name "Nirvana." Benedict reminded Jones that the company had a code of conduct requiring senior officers to obtain advance clearance from her office for their securities transactions. She recommended that clearance be denied to all senior management and that an embargo be placed on all transactions by those working on the Nirvana project until the project had been made public. Jones accepted this recommendation and, on the same day, circulated a confidential memorandum to all Nirvana project employees notifying them of the embargo.

Three days after this memorandum was issued, Steve Davis, a marketing vice-president, asked Benedict's office for permission to buy some stock. He was told that senior management was temporarily barred from trading but was not told why. Nevertheless, he bought 3,000 shares at about $26 per share on the same day. In addition, on April 7, without asking anyone, Amy Stevens, the research director of the Nirvana project, bought 5,000 shares at $24 per share.

On April 5, Jones met with the board of directors to discuss how best to finance the development of the new product. Jones again stressed the need for secrecy and the use of Nirvana as a code name. In addition to the full board, the meeting was attended by Ted Long, a partner of Goldwin & Co., a well-established investment banking firm which had underwritten the company's public offering and which continued to give it financial advice. Long proposed several alternative means of financing the project, including, among others, a merger with a company with substantial capital or the sale of a large block of stock. The Board reached no decision and retained Goldwin to advise how best to finance the development. Long advised the Board that it would be necessary for the company, even at the preliminary stage, to prepare a disclosure document which might be shown to potential investors. The board instructed Benedict to work with Potter & Moore, Goldwin's counsel, in preparing such a document.

On May 5, one week before the company's annual meeting of stockholders, Long reported to the board that Goldwin was engaged in confidential discussions with several possible investors but that it was not prepared to present a formal recommendation. At the annual meeting, a stockholder asked Jones about new developments or products. Jones replied that "there is nothing I can report on now, although we are always hopeful that something exciting will emerge from the company's on-going research." His statement was accurately quoted on the Dow Jones News Service and in the Wall Street Journal.

On June 7, Long presented Goldwin's formal report to the full board. In that report, Goldwin stated that if the new product could be fully developed commercially, Goldwin projected Standard's value at between $40 and $45 per share. Long also told the board that because of the project's degree of risk, a sale of a large block of stock could not be made at prices reflecting fair value, but that Goldwin had approached Universal Products, Inc. (Universal), a diversified high technology company whose shares are listed on the New York Stock Exchange, concerning a merger between the two companies at a price of $45–50 per share. After discussing Goldwin's report, the board authorized Jones to enter into formal negotiations with Universal and to furnish any necessary confidential information to Universal.

From June 15–30, representatives of Standard and Universal met to review and discuss confidential and public financial data concerning Standard. At the end of the June 30 meeting, Universal's president said that he would seek authorization from his board to acquire Standard at a price of slightly more than $50 per share for each share of Standard stock. Later that day, both companies received calls from the New York Stock Exchange, asking them to comment on the large number of rumors that were circulating concerning a possible merger. On advice of counsel, the companies advised the Exchange that they were not in a position to comment because they had not reached a definitive agreement as to the price to be paid or the form the acquisition might take.

On July 7 both boards approved a merger in which Universal would issue stock having a value of $51 per share for 100% of the stock of Standard. The final agreement was signed on July 10 and, at the request of both companies, the New York Stock Exchange halted trading in both companies' stock until the companies issued a joint press release disclosing the terms of the merger. When trading resumed the following day, Standard stock traded at $43 per share.

You are an associate in a prominent law firm which specializes in corporate and securities law matters and which has represented Standard for a number of years. The senior partner has just sent you a memorandum detailing the above facts which he has developed from a series of meetings with Jones. He has concluded his memo as follows:

"I certainly hope we don't have another *Texas Gulf Sulphur* on our hands. Certainly we have advised the company on how best to deal with the whole problem of 10b–5 and insider trading. The merger with Universal hasn't closed yet and I need to know how serious the problems are. By the way, even though we probably won't represent everyone, I would like to know about personal as well as corporate liability. In your memo, I would like you to cover the following issues:

"1) Let's begin at the beginning. Before there was a Rule 10b–5 (difficult as that may to be imagine), there was some common law dealing with insider trading and, as I recall, there have been some common law decisions recently, although some of the cases may have been brought in federal court. Is there any common law liability on these facts and, if so, who could recover? How serious is the possibility that someone might be liable for damages under both common and federal law?

"2) I understand that materiality is an essential element of a Rule 10b–5 violation, but the facts here confuse me. Depending on whose conduct we are looking at, there are several possible material facts—the embargo, the discovery or the merger (or some combination of these). At what point, if ever, was the information about the new product or the merger material? It seems to me that if everyone was just speculating about future profits, there may be no problem with any of what transpired. What additional information do we need to know?

"3) I am concerned about Davis and Stevens. Neither of them are directors of Standard, but might they be considered insiders for purposes of 10b–5 liability? Look at Darke in the *Texas Gulf Sulphur* case. What is the requisite culpable state of mind?

"4) Long has told me that after a squash game with Bill Baker, one of his partners, in response to a casual question about Standard, Long said that it looks like they've hit the jackpot in a deal with Universal. Long says it was inadvertent, and I am inclined to believe him. You know that Goldwin has a large number of institutional clients, many of whom are handled by Baker. Who knows whether and what they may have been told or what they may have done with the information? I once thought that everyone in this chain would be liable, but now, frankly, I'm not so sure.

"a) Look at footnote 14 in *Dirks*. Are Goldwin, Long and Baker insiders for purposes of this deal?

"b) Baker surely was fortunate to have stumbled into this information and some internal antenna should have cautioned him against doing anything with it. But, in fact, he had nothing to do with the deal. Does the misappropriation theory apply to him? If so, who can recover from him?

"c) On any theory, analyze the potential liability of any of Goldwin's clients who traded after talking to Baker.

"d) We don't know what Baker told his clients. Could he or Goldwin be liable for the clients' trades if Baker recommended the purchase of Standard stock but did not specifically disclose material non-public information?

"5) It now appears that Pamela Hobbes, one of the lawyers at Potter and Moore who was working on the disclosure document, upon learning of the discovery, bought 1,000 shares of Standard stock for herself and told various members of her family who bought an additional 5,000 shares.

"a) Could Hobbes be considered an insider in these circumstances even though she was not directly retained by Standard?

"b) Does the misappropriation theory apply to Hobbes and, if so, who could bring suit against her? What damages or other relief might be granted?

"c) How does the tipper-tippee analysis apply to Hobbes and her family?

"6) I'm unclear about the corporate obligation to disclose. Did Standard have any legal duty to do so? After all, they weren't buying or selling stock on the basis of that information, unless you count that stock option plan. Don't we get some comfort from the fact that there was a regular stock buying program unrelated to the discovery? I'm not delighted with what Jones said at the annual meeting, but what else could he have done, given the need to keep the information confidential? Has the law evolved to a point where such confidence is illegal? What ever happened to the old doctrines of reliance and causation to say nothing of a culpable state of mind? I'm sure that Universal's counsel will want our views on the response to the New York Stock Exchange. I understand that the SEC may disagree with us; how much danger does that pose?

"7) Four months before purchasing Standard stock, Davis had sold 1,000 shares which he then owned. Is he liable under Section 16(b) of the 1934 Act and, if so, what are the consequences?"

# C. THE COMMON LAW

## 1. INTRODUCTION

The law governing the trading of securities is today largely federal law and, more specifically, law developed under § 10(b) of the Securities Exchange Act of 1934 and SEC Rule 10b–5. Federal law has largely supplanted state law in this area for several reasons. Most investigations of possible insider trading are conducted by the Securities and Exchange Commission and federal prosecutors, whose authority is limited to enforcing federal law. Due to a combination of procedural and substantive advantages not available in state courts, most private suits alleging either insider trading or disclosure fraud also are brought in federal court.

However, state law, particularly as it relates to insider trading, remains relevant for at least two reasons. First, federal law regulating insider trading builds on common law concepts. As a consequence, one needs to understand state law in order to appreciate the doctrinal issues federal courts have faced and the doctrinal choices they have made. Second, shareholders in close corporations, in particular, continue to seek remedies under state law against insiders who they believe have used deceit to induce them to sell stock at an inadequate price. *See Van Schaack Holdings, Ltd. v. Van Schaack*, 867 P.2d 892 (Colo.1994).

The contours of the common law tort of deceit vary from one state to another. A review of the elements of that tort, however, can help one understand why the common law proved an inadequate tool for dealing with securities fraud, especially when it involved transactions on impersonal securities markets, such as the New York Stock Exchange.

The traditional action for deceit required the plaintiff to prove five elements: (1) The defendant misrepresented a material fact (2) with knowledge of its falsity or with reckless disregard for the truth and (3) with the intention that the plaintiff rely and (4) plaintiff justifiably relied on defendant's misrepresentation (5) to her detriment.

That action suffered from several serious drawbacks when applied to securities transactions. The most important may have been that the defendant often had *omitted* material information when dealing with the plaintiff, rather than affirmatively misrepresenting some material fact. In order to demonstrate that the defendant's silence was fraudulent, the plaintiff then was required to prove that the defendant had a duty to disclose the omitted information prior to trading. In addition, if a plaintiff had purchased or sold securities in an impersonal market, she often found it difficult to prove reliance. The defendant would argue that because the plaintiff did not know with whom she was trading, she could not establish that she had relied on defendant's silence.

## 2.  DUTY TO SHAREHOLDERS AND INVESTORS

### GOODWIN v. AGASSIZ
283 Mass. 358, 186 N.E. 659 (1933).

Rugg, Chief Justice.

[A stockholder of the Cliff Mining Company, the stock of which was listed on the Boston Stock Exchange, sought relief for losses suffered in the sale through the exchange of 700 shares of the company's stock to the defendants, who were officers and directors of the corporation. The court accepted the trial judge's findings that Cliff had started exploration for copper on its land in 1925, acting on certain geological surveys. The exploration was not successful, however, and the company removed its equipment in May, 1926.

Meanwhile, in March, 1926, an experienced geologist wrote a report theorizing as to the existence of copper deposits in the region of the company's holdings. The defendants, believing there was merit to the theory, secured options to land adjacent to the copper belt. Also, anticipating an increase in the value of the stock if the theory proved correct, the defendants purchased shares of the company's stock through an agent.

When the plaintiff learned of the termination of the original exploratory operations from a newspaper article—for which defendants were in no way responsible—he immediately sold his stock.]

The contention of the plaintiff is that the purchase of his stock in the company by the defendants without disclosing to him as a stockholder their knowledge of the geologist's theory, their belief that the theory was true, had value, the keeping secret the existence of the theory, discontinuance by the defendants of exploratory operations begun in 1925 on property of the Cliff Mining Company and their plan ultimately to test the value of the theory, constitute actionable wrong for which he as stockholder can recover.

The trial judge ruled that conditions may exist which would make it the duty of an officer of a corporation purchasing its stock from a stockholder to inform him as to knowledge possessed by the buyer and not by the seller, but found, on all the circumstances developed by the trial and set out at some length by him in his decision, that there was no fiduciary relation requiring such disclosure by the defendants to the plaintiff before buying his stock in the manner in which they did.

The question presented is whether the decree dismissing the bill rightly was entered on the facts found.

The directors of a commercial corporation stand in a relation of trust to the corporation and are bound to exercise the strictest good faith in respect to its property and business. The contention that directors also occupy the position of trustee toward individual stockholders in the corporation is plainly contrary to repeated decisions of this court and cannot be supported. In *Smith v. Hurd*, 12 Metc. 371, 384, 46 Am.Dec. 690, it was said by Chief Justice Shaw: "There is no legal privity, relation, or immediate connexion, between the holders of shares in a bank, in their individual capacity, on the one side, and the directors of the bank on the other. The directors are not the bailees, the factors, agents or trustees of such individual stockholders." * * *

The principle thus established is supported by an imposing weight of authority in other jurisdictions. A rule holding that directors are trustees for individual stockholders with respect to their stock prevails in comparatively few states; but in view of our own adjudications it is not necessary to review decisions to that effect.

While the general principle is as stated, circumstances may exist requiring that transactions between a director and a stockholder as to stock in the corporation be set aside. The knowledge naturally in the possession of a director as to the condition of a corporation places upon him a peculiar obligation to observe every requirement of fair dealing when directly buying or selling its stock. Mere silence does not usually amount to a breach of duty, but parties may stand in such relation to each other that an equitable responsibility arises to communicate facts. Purchases and sales of stock dealt in on the stock exchange are commonly impersonal affairs. An honest director would be in a difficult situation if he could neither buy nor sell on the stock exchange shares of stock in his corporation without first seeking out the other actual ultimate party to the transaction and disclosing to him everything which a court or jury might later find that he then knew affecting the real or speculative value of such shares. Business of that nature is a matter to be governed by practical rules. Fiduciary obligations of directors ought not to be made so onerous that men of experience and ability will be deterred from accepting such office. Law in its sanctions is not coextensive with morality. It cannot undertake to put all parties to every contract on an equality as to knowledge, experience, skill and shrewdness. It cannot undertake to relieve against hard bargains made between competent parties without fraud. On the other hand, directors cannot rightly be allowed to indulge with impunity in practices which do violence to prevailing standards of upright businessmen. Therefore, where a director personally seeks a stockholder for the purpose of buying his shares without making disclosure of material facts within his peculiar knowledge and not within reach of the stockholder, the transaction will be closely scrutinized and relief may be granted in appropriate instances. *Strong v. Repide*, 213 U.S. 419, 29 S.Ct. 521, 53 L.Ed. 853 * * *.

The precise question to be decided in the case at bar is whether on the facts found the defendants as directors had a right to buy stock of the plaintiff, a stockholder. Every element of actual fraud or misdoing by the defendants is negatived by the findings. Fraud cannot be presumed; it must be proved. *Brown v. Little, Brown & Co., Inc.*, 269 Mass. 102, 117, 168 N.E. 521. The facts found afford no ground for inferring fraud or conspiracy. The only knowledge possessed by the defendants not open to the plaintiff was the existence of a theory formulated in a thesis by a geologist as to the possible existence of copper deposits where certain geological conditions existed common to the property of the Cliff Mining Company and that of other mining companies in its neighborhood. This thesis did not express an opinion that copper deposits would be found at any particular spot or on property of any specified owner. Whether that theory was sound or fallacious, no one knew, and so far as appears has never been demonstrated. The defendants made no representations to anybody about the theory. No facts found placed upon them any obligation to disclose the theory. A few days after the thesis expounding the theory was brought to the attention of the defendants, the annual report by the directors of the Cliff Mining Company for the calendar year 1925, signed by Agassiz for the directors, was issued. It did not cover the time when the theory was formulated. The report described the status of the operations under the exploration which had been begun in 1925. At the annual meeting of the stockholders of the company held early in April, 1926, no reference was made to the theory. It was then at most a hope, possibly an expectation. It had not passed the nebulous stage. No disclosure was made of it. The Cliff Mining Company was not harmed by the nondisclosure. There would have been no advantage to it, so far as appears, from a disclosure.

The disclosure would have been detrimental to the interests of another mining corporation in which the defendants were directors. In the circumstances there was no duty on the part of the defendants to set forth to the stockholders at the annual meeting their faith, aspirations and plans for the future. Events as they developed might render advisable radical changes in such views. Disclosure of the theory, if it ultimately was proved to be erroneous or without foundation in fact, might involve the defendants in litigation with those who might act on the hypothesis that it was correct. The stock of the Cliff Mining Company was bought and sold on the stock exchange. The identity of buyers and sellers of the stock in question in fact was not known to the parties and perhaps could not readily have been ascertained. The defendants caused the shares to be bought through brokers on the stock exchange. They said nothing to anybody as to the reasons actuating them. The plaintiff was no novice. He was a member of the Boston stock exchange and had kept a record of sales of Cliff Mining Company stock. He acted upon his own judgment in selling his stock. He made no inquiries of the defendants or of other officers of the company. The result is that the plaintiff cannot prevail.

Decree dismissing bill affirmed with costs.

### Note: Common Law Rules

*Goodwin* sets out what is generally described as the "majority rule": directors and officers owe a fiduciary duty only to the corporation and, accordingly, are under no affirmative obligation to disclose material non-public information when purchasing or selling securities in an impersonal market.

However, *Goodwin* also recognized that a different rule might apply to when insiders purchase stock in face-to-face transactions—the "special facts doctrine" enunciated in *Strong v. Repide*, 213 U.S. 419, 29 S.Ct. 521, 53 L.Ed. 853 (1909). Under this doctrine, although an insider normally owes no fiduciary duty to individual shareholders, a plaintiff may be afforded a remedy when, in particular circumstances, non-disclosure amounts to unconscionable behavior by the insider.

The defendant in *Strong* was a director, the majority stockholder, and general manager of the corporation. He was authorized by the board of directors to conduct negotiations leading to the sale to the United States government of otherwise worthless land that was one of the corporation's principal assets. At the time of the transaction in question, he alone knew that the government was prepared to pay a substantial price for that land. To keep secret his identity, the defendant used an agent to purchase shares owned by plaintiff, in a face-to-face transaction, at a price that did not reflect the price the government was prepared to pay for the land. The Supreme Court granted rescission of the sale of stock, saying, "That the defendant was a director of the corporation is but one of the facts upon which the liability is asserted, the existence of all the others in addition making such a combination as rendered it the plain duty of the defendant to speak." 213 U.S. at 431, 29 S.Ct. at 525.

A third "rule" that has steadily attracted more adherents among state courts, is that officers and directors have a fiduciary duty to to disclose material nonpublic information in any face-to-face stock transaction with a shareholder, regardless of whether there are special circumstances. This duty "exists because the stockholders have placed the directors in a strategic position where they can secure firsthand knowledge of important developments. * * * [T]he detailed information a director has of corporate affairs is in a very real sense property of the corporation, and * * * no director should be permitted to use such information for his own benefit at the expense of his stockholders." *Taylor v. Wright*, 69 Cal.App.2d 371, 159 P.2d 980, 984–85 (1945).

This "strict" or "Kansas" rule had its origin in *Hotchkiss v. Fischer*, 136 Kan. 530, 16 P.2d 531 (1932). The plaintiff, an impoverished widow from Burr Oak, Kansas, came to Topeka shortly before a board meeting to inquire of the defendant, who was president and a director of the corporation, whether she could expect a dividend. If not, she believed she would have to sell her stock. The president replied that he could not say whether a dividend would be declared until the board met. He showed her the corporation's financial statements, explained them, but maintained a rather pessimistic stance. The widow sold her stock to him for $1.25 per share. Three days later, the corporation declared a dividend of $1 per share. The court held that in such a transaction, the officer or director "acts in a relation of scrupulous trust and confidence," and his behavior is therefore subject to the closest scrutiny.

Courts applied the "special facts" doctrine and the "Kansas rule" only to transactions between insiders and existing shareholders. If an insider sold stock to someone who was not a shareholder, common law courts held, there was no breach of fiduciary duty because the purchaser did not become a shareholder until after the transaction was completed. They also held that where an insider purchased stock in in impersonal market, the fact she had not made any representation directly to her counterparty relieved her from liability.

## 3.  DUTY TO THE CORPORATION

### DIAMOND v. OREAMUNO
24 N.Y.2d 494, 301 N.Y.S.2d 78, 248 N.E.2d 910 (1969).

FULD, CHIEF JUDGE.

Upon this appeal from an order denying a motion to dismiss the complaint as insufficient on its face, the question presented—one of first impression in this court—is whether officers and directors may be held accountable to their corporation for gains realized by them from transactions in the company's stock as a result of their use of material inside information.

The complaint was filed by a shareholder of Management Assistance, Inc. (MAI) asserting a derivative action against a number of its officers and directors to compel an accounting for profits allegedly acquired as a result of a breach of fiduciary duty. It charges that two of the defendants—Oreamuno, chairman of the board of directors, and Gonzalez, its president—had used inside information, acquired by them solely by virtue of their positions, in order to reap large personal profits from the sale of MAI shares and that these profits rightfully belong to the corporation. Other officers and directors were joined as defendants on the ground that they acquiesced in or ratified the assertedly wrongful transactions.

MAI is in the business of financing computer installations through sale and lease back arrangements with various commercial and industrial users. Under its lease provisions, MAI was required to maintain and repair the computers but, at the time of this suit, it lacked the capacity to perform this function itself and was forced to engage the manufacturer of the computers, International Business Machines (IBM), to service the machines. As a result of a sharp increase by IBM of its charges for such service, MAI's expenses for August of 1966 rose considerably and its net earnings declined from $262,253 in July to $66,233 in August, a decrease of about 75%. This information, although earlier known to the defendants, was not made public until October of 1966. Prior to the release of the information, however, Oreamuno and Gonzalez sold off a total of 56,500 shares of their MAI stock at the then current market price of $28 a share.

After the information concerning the drop in earnings was made available to the public, the value of a share of MAI stock immediately fell from the $28 realized by the defendants to $11. Thus, the plaintiff alleges, by taking advantage of their privileged position and their access to confidential information, Oreamuno and Gonzalez were able to realize $800,000 more for their securities than they would have had this inside information not been available to them. * * * A motion by the defendants to dismiss the complaint * * * for failure to state a cause of action was granted by the court at Special Term. * * *

It is well established, as a general proposition, that a person who acquires special knowledge or information by virtue of a confidential or fiduciary relationship with another is not free to exploit that knowledge or information for his own personal benefit but must account to his principal for any profits derived therefrom. This, in turn, is merely a corollary of the broader principle, inherent in the nature of the fiduciary relationship, that prohibits a trustee or agent from extracting secret profits from his position of trust.

In support of their claim that the complaint fails to state a cause of action, the defendants take the position that, although it is admittedly wrong for an officer or director to use his position to obtain trading profits for himself in the stock of his corporation, the action ascribed to them did not injure or damage MAI in any way. Accordingly, the defendants continue, the corporation should not be permitted to recover the proceeds. They acknowledge that, by virtue of the exclusive access which officers and directors have to inside information, they possess an unfair advantage over other shareholders and, particularly, the persons who had purchased the stock from them but, they contend, the corporation itself was unaffected and, for that reason, a derivative action is an inappropriate remedy.

It is true that the complaint before us does not contain any allegation of damages to the corporation but this has never been considered to be an essential requirement for a cause of action founded on a breach of fiduciary duty. This is because the function of such an action, unlike an ordinary tort or contract case, is not merely to compensate the plaintiff for wrongs committed by the defendant but, as this court declared many years ago (*Dutton v. Willner*, 52 N.Y. 312, 319) "to *prevent* them, by removing from agents and trustees all inducement to attempt dealing for their own benefit in matters which they have undertaken for others, or to which their agency or trust relates." (Emphasis supplied.)

Just as a trustee has no right to retain for himself the profits yielded by property placed in his possession but must account to his beneficiaries, a corporate fiduciary, who is entrusted with potentially valuable information, may not appropriate that asset for his own use even though, in so doing, he causes no injury to the corporation. The primary concern, in a case such as this, is not to determine whether the corporation has been damaged but to decide, as between the corporation and the defendants, who has a higher claim to the proceeds derived from the exploitation of the information. In our opinion, there can be no justification for permitting officers and directors, such as the defendants, to retain for themselves profits which, it is alleged, they derived solely from exploiting information gained by virtue of their inside position as corporate officials.

In addition, it is pertinent to observe that, despite the lack of any specific allegation of damage, it may well be inferred that the defendants' actions might have caused some harm to the enterprise. Although the corporation may have little concern with the day-to-day transactions in its shares, it has a great interest in maintaining a reputation of integrity, an image of probity, for its management and in insuring the continued public acceptance and marketability of its stock. When officers and directors abuse their position in order to gain personal profits, the effect may be to cast a cloud on the corporation's name, injure stockholder relations and undermine public regard for the corporation's securities. As Presiding Justice Botein aptly put it, in the course of his opinion for the Appellate Division, "[t]he prestige and good will of a corporation, so vital to its prosperity, may be undermined by the revelation that its chief officers had been making personal profits out of corporate events which they had not disclosed to the community of stockholders." (29 A.D.2d at p. 287, 287 N.Y.S.2d at p. 303.)

The defendants maintain that extending the prohibition against personal exploitation of a fiduciary relationship to officers and directors of a corporation will discourage such officials from maintaining a stake in the success of the corporate venture through share ownership, which, they urge, is an important incentive to proper performance of their duties. There is, however, a considerable difference between corporate officers who assume the same risks and obtain the same benefits as other shareholders and those who use their privileged position to gain special advantages not available to others. The sale of shares by the defendants for the reasons charged was not merely a wise investment decision which any prudent investor might have made. Rather, they were assertedly able in this case to profit solely because they had information which was not available to any one else—including the other shareholders whose interests they, as corporate fiduciaries, were bound to protect.

Although no appellate court in this State has had occasion to pass upon the precise question before us, the concept underlying the present cause of action is hardly a new one. (See, e.g., Securities Exchange Act of 1934 [48 U.S.Stat. 881], § 16[b]; U.S.Code, tit. 15, § 78p, subd. [b]; *Brophy v. Cities Serv. Co.*, 31 Del.Ch. 241; RESTATEMENT, 2D, AGENCY, § 388, comment c.) Under Federal law (Securities Exchange Act of 1934, § 16[b] ), for example, it is conclusively presumed that, when a director, officer or 10% shareholder buys and sells securities of his corporation within a six-month period, he is trading on inside information. The remedy which the Federal statute provides in that situation is precisely the same as that sought in the present case under State law, namely, an action brought by the corporation or on its behalf to recover all profits derived from the transactions.

In providing this remedy, Congress accomplished a dual purpose. It not only provided for an efficient and effective method of accomplishing its primary goal—the protection of the investing public from unfair treatment at the hands of corporate insiders—but extended to the corporation the right to secure for itself benefits derived by those insiders from their exploitation of their privileged position. * * *

Although the provisions of section 16(b) may not apply to all cases of trading on inside information, it demonstrates that a derivative action can be an effective method for dealing with such abuses which may be used to accomplish a similar purpose in cases not specifically covered by the statute. In *Brophy v. Cities Serv. Co.*, *supra*, for example, the Chancery Court of Delaware allowed a similar remedy in a situation not covered by the Federal legislation. One of the defendants in that case was an employee who had acquired inside information that the corporate plaintiff was about to enter the market and purchase its own shares. On the basis of this confidential information, the employee, who was not an officer and, hence, not liable under Federal law, bought a large block of shares and, after the corporation's purchases had caused the price to rise, resold them at a profit. The court sustained the complaint in a derivative action brought for an accounting, stating that "[p]ublic policy will not permit an employee occupying a position of trust and confidence toward his employer to abuse that relation to his own profit, regardless of whether his employer suffers a loss" (31 Del.Ch., at p. 246, 70 A.2d, at p. 8). And a similar view has been expressed in the Restatement, 2d Agency (§ 388, comment c):

> c. *Use of confidential information.* An agent who acquires confidential information in the course of his employment or in violation of his duties has a duty * * * to account for any profits made by the use of such information, although this does not harm the principal. * * * So, if [a corporate officer] has "inside" information that the corporation is about to purchase or sell securities, or to declare or to pass a dividend, profits made by him in stock transactions undertaken because of his knowledge are held in constructive trust for the principal.

In the present case, the defendants may be able to avoid liability to the corporation under section 16(b) of the Federal law since they had held the MAI shares for more than six months prior to the sales. Nevertheless, the alleged use of the inside information to dispose of their stock at a price considerably higher than its known value constituted the same sort of "abuse of a fiduciary relationship" as is condemned by the Federal law. Sitting as we are in this case as a court of equity, we should not hesitate to permit an action to prevent any unjust enrichment realized by the defendants from their allegedly wrongful act.

The defendants recognize that the conduct charged against them directly contravened the policy embodied in the Securities Exchange Act but, they maintain, the Federal legislation constitutes a comprehensive and carefully wrought plan for dealing with the abuse of inside information and that allowing a derivative action to be maintained under State law would interfere with the Federal scheme. Moreover, they urge, the existence of dual Federal and State remedies for the same act would create the possibility of double liability.

An examination of the Federal regulatory scheme refutes the contention that it was designed to establish any particular remedy as exclusive. In addition to the specific provisions of section 16(b), the Securities and Exchange Act contains a general anti-fraud provision in section 10(b) (U.S.Code, tit. 15, § 78j, subd. [b] ) which, as implemented by rule 10b–5 (Code of Fed.Reg., tit. 17, § 240.10b–5) under that section, renders it unlawful to engage in a variety of acts considered to be fraudulent. In interpreting this rule, the Securities and Exchange Commission and the Federal courts have extended the common-law definition of fraud to include not only affirmative misrepresentations, relied upon by the purchaser or seller, but also a failure to disclose material information which might have affected the transaction.

Accepting the truth of the complainant's allegations, there is no question but that the defendants were guilty of withholding material information from the purchasers of the shares and, indeed, the defendants acknowledge that the facts asserted constitute a violation of rule 10b–5. The remedies which the Federal law provides for such violation, however, are rather limited. An action could be brought, in an exceptional case, by the SEC for injunctive relief. This, in fact, is what happened in the *Texas Gulf Sulphur* case (401 F.2d 833). The purpose of such an action, however, would appear to be more to establish a principle than to provide a regular method of enforcement. A class action under the Federal rule might be a more effective remedy but the mechanics of such an action have, as far as we have been able to ascertain, not yet been worked out by the Federal courts and several questions relating thereto have never been resolved. These include the definition of the class entitled to bring such an action, the measure of damages, the administration of the fund which would be recovered and its distribution to the members of the class. Of course, any individual purchaser, who could prove an injury as a result of a rule 10b–5 violation can bring his own action for rescission but we have not been referred to a single case in which such an action has been successfully prosecuted where the public sale of securities is involved. The reason for this is that sales of securities, whether through a stock exchange or over-the-counter, are characteristically anonymous transactions, usually handled through brokers, and the matching of the ultimate buyer with the ultimate seller presents virtually insurmountable obstacles. Thus, unless a section 16(b) violation is also present, the Federal law does not yet provide a really effective remedy.

In view of the practical difficulties inherent in an action under the Federal law, the desirability of creating an effective common-law remedy is manifest. "Dishonest directors should not find absolution from retributive justice", Ballantine observed in his work on CORPORATIONS ( [rev.ed., 1946], p. 216), "by concealing their identity from their victims under the mask of the stock exchange." There is ample room in a situation such as is here presented for a "private Attorney General" to come forward and enforce proper behavior on the part of corporate officials through the medium of the derivative action brought in the name of the corporation. Only by sanctioning such a cause of action will there be any effective method to prevent the type of abuse of corporate office complained of in this case.

There is nothing in the Federal law which indicates that it was intended to limit the power of the States to fashion additional remedies to effectuate similar purposes. Although the impact of Federal securities regulation has on occasion been said to have created a "Federal corporation law," in fact, its effect on the duties and obligations of directors and officers and their relation to the corporation and its shareholders is only occasional and peripheral. The primary source of the law in this area ever remains that of the State which created the corporation. Indeed, Congress expressly provided against any implication that it intended to pre-empt the field by declaring, in section 28(a) of the Securities Exchange Act of 1934 (48 U.S.Stat. 903), that "[t]he rights and remedies provided by this title shall be in addition to any and all other rights and remedies that may exist at law or in equity".

Nor should we be deterred, in formulating a State remedy, by the defendants' claim of possible double liability. Certainly, as already indicated, if the sales in question were publicly made, the likelihood that a suit will be brought by purchasers of the shares is quite remote. But, even if it were not, the mere possibility of such a suit is not a defense nor does it render the complaint insufficient. It is not unusual for an action to be brought to recover a fund which may be subject to a superior claim by a third party. If that be the situation, a defendant should not be permitted to retain the fund for his own use on the chance that such a party may eventually appear. A defendant's course, if he wishes to protect himself against double liability, is to interplead any and all possible claimants and bind them to the judgment.

In any event, though, no suggestion has been made either in brief or on oral argument that any purchaser has come forward with a claim against the defendants or even that anyone is in a position to advance such a claim. As we have stated, the defendants' assertion that such a party may come forward at some future date is not a basis for permitting them to retain for their own benefit the fruits of their allegedly wrongful acts. For all that appears, the present derivative action is the only effective remedy now available against the abuse by these defendants of their privileged position.

\* \* \*

The order appealed from should be affirmed, with costs, and the question certified answered in the affirmative.

## FREEMAN v. DECIO
### 584 F.2d 186 (7th Cir.1978).

WOOD, JR., CIRCUIT JUDGE.

\* \* \*

### I.

#### DIAMOND V. OREAMUNO AND INDIANA LAW

Both parties agree that there is no Indiana precedent directly dealing with the question of whether a corporation may recover the profits of corporate officials who trade in the corporation's securities on the basis of inside information. However, the plaintiff suggests that were the question to be presented to the Indiana courts, they would adopt the holding of the New York Court of Appeals in *Diamond v. Oreamuno*. There, building on the Delaware case of *Brophy v. Cities Service Co.*, the court held that the officers and directors of a corporation breached their fiduciary duties owed to the corporation by trading in its stock on the basis of material non-public information acquired by virtue of their official positions and that they should account to the corporation for their profits from those transactions. Since *Diamond* was decided, few courts have had an opportunity to consider the problem there presented. In fact, only one case has been brought to our attention which raised the question of whether *Diamond* would be followed in another jurisdiction. In *Schein v. Chasen*, [313 So.2d 739 (Fla.1975)], the * * * court not only stated that it would not "give the unprecedented expansive reading to *Diamond* sought by appellants" but that, furthermore, it did not "choose to adopt the innovative ruling of the New York Court of Appeals in *Diamond* [itself]." 313 So.2d 739, 746 (Fla.1975). Thus, the question here is whether the Indiana courts are more likely to follow the New York Court of Appeals or to join the Florida Supreme Court in refusing to undertake such a change from existing law.

It appears that from a policy point of view it is widely accepted that insider trading should be deterred because it is unfair to other investors who do not enjoy the benefits of access to inside information. The goal is not one of equality of possession of information—since some traders will always be better "informed" than others by dint of greater expenditures of time and resources, greater experience, or greater analytical abilities—but rather equality of access to information. * * * Yet, a growing body of commentary suggests that pursuit of this goal of "market egalitarianism" may be costly. In addition to the costs associated with enforcement of the laws prohibiting insider trading, there may be a loss in the efficiency of the securities markets in their capital allocation function. The basic insight of economic analysis here is that securities prices act as signals helping to route capital to its most productive uses and that insider trading helps assure that those prices will reflect the best information available (i.e., inside information) as to where the best opportunities lie.[13] However, even when confronted with the possibility of a trade-off between fairness and economic efficiency, most authorities appear to find that the balance tips in favor of discouraging insider trading.

Over 40 years ago Congress was stirred by examples of flagrant abuse of inside information unearthed during the hearings preceding the 1933 and 1934 Securities Acts to include in the latter a section aimed at insider trading. Section 16(b) provides for the automatic recovery by corporations of profits made by insiders in short-swing transactions within a six-month period. This automatic accountability makes the rule one of relatively easy application and avoids very difficult problems concerning the measurement of damages, yet upon occasion leads to harsh results. The section has been characterized as a "crude rule of thumb." It is too narrow in that only short-swing trading and short

---

**13.** However, it has been suggested that insider trading may harm the securities markets in indirect ways. For one thing, outsiders might be less willing to invest in securities markets marked by the preva-lence of a practice which they consider unfair. In addition an equal, if not greater degree of allocative efficiency can normally be achieved if the inside information is made public.

selling are covered, leaving untouched other ways of profiting from inside information in the securities market. It is too broad in that short-swing trades not actually made on the basis of inside information are also caught in the Section's web of liability.

The SEC has also used its full panoply of powers to police insider trading through enforcement actions and civil actions. The agency has relied, *inter alia,* on Section 17(a) of the 1933 Act, Section 15(c)(1) of the 1934 Act, and Rule 10b–5. The relief obtained has included not only injunctions and suspension orders, but also disgorgement of profits earned in insider trading.

Lastly, the "victims" of insider trading may recover damages from the insiders in many instances. Absent fraud, the traditional common law approach has been to permit officers and directors of corporations to trade in their corporation's securities free from liability to other traders for failing to disclose inside information. However, there has been a movement towards the imposition of a common law duty to disclose in a number of jurisdictions, at least where the insider is dealing with an existing stockholder. A few jurisdictions now require disclosure where certain "special facts" exist, and some even impose a strict fiduciary duty on the insider *vis-à-vis* the selling shareholder. But the most important remedies available to those injured by insider trading are found in the federal securities laws and in particular Rule 10b–5. Judicial development of a private right of action under that rule has led to significant relaxation of many of the elements of common law fraud, including privity, reliance, and the distinction between misrepresentation and non-disclosure. The rule has proven a favorite vehicle for damage suits against insiders for failing to disclose material information while trading in their corporation's stock. * * * Lastly, persons injured by insider trading may be able to take advantage of the liability sections of state securities laws. A number of states, including Indiana, have enacted laws containing antifraud provisions modeled on Rule 10b–5. *See* Burns Ind.Stat.Ann. § 23–2–1–12.

Yet, the New York Court of Appeals in *Diamond* found the existing remedies for controlling insider trading to be inadequate. Although the court felt that the device of a class action under the federal securities laws held out hope of a more effective remedy in the future, it concluded that "the desirability of creating an effective common-law remedy is manifest." 301 N.Y.S.2d at 85, 248 N.E.2d at 915. It went on to do so by engineering an innovative extension of the law governing the relation between a corporation and its officers and directors. The court held that corporate officials who deal in their corporation's securities on the basis of non-public information gained by virtue of their inside position commit a breach of their fiduciary duties to the corporation. This holding represents a departure from the traditional common law approach, which was that a corporate insider did not ordinarily violate his fiduciary duty to the corporation by dealing in the corporation's stock, unless the corporation was thereby harmed.

\* \* \*

There are a number of difficulties with the *Diamond* court's ruling. Perhaps the thorniest problem was posed by the defendants' objection that whatever the ethical status of insider trading, there is no injury to the corporation which can serve as a basis for recognizing a right of recovery in favor of the latter. The Court of Appeals' response to this argument was two-fold, suggesting first that no harm to the corporation need be shown and second that it might well be inferred that the insiders' activities did in fact cause some harm to the corporation. \* \* \* Some might see the *Diamond* court's decision as resting on a broad, strict-trust notion of the fiduciary duty owed to the corporation: no director is to receive any profit, beyond what he receives from the corporation, solely because of his position. Although once accepted, this basis for the *Diamond* rule would obviate the need for finding a potential for injury to the corporation, it is not at all clear that current corporation law contemplates such an extensive notion of fiduciary duty. It is customary to view the *Diamond* result as resting on a characterization of inside information as a corporate asset. The lack of necessity for looking for an injury to the corporation is then justified by the traditional "no inquiry" rule with respect to profits made by trustees from assets belonging to the trust *res*. However, to start from the premise that all inside information should be considered a corporate asset may presuppose an answer to the inquiry at hand. It might be better to ask whether there is any potential loss to the corporation from the use of such information in insider trading before deciding to characterize the inside information as an asset with respect to which the insider owes the corporation a duty of loyalty (as opposed to a duty of care). This approach would be in keeping with the modern view of another area of application of the duty of loyalty—the corporate opportunity doctrine. Thus, while courts will require a director or officer to automatically account to the corporation for diversion of a corporate opportunity to personal use, they will first inquire to see whether there was a possibility of a loss to the corporation—i.e., whether the corporation was in a position to potentially avail itself of the opportunity—before deciding that a corporate opportunity in fact existed. Similarly, when scrutinizing transactions between a director or officer and the corporation under the light of the duty of loyalty, most courts now inquire as to whether there was any injury to the corporation, i.e., whether the transaction was fair and in good faith, before permitting the latter to avoid the transaction. An analogous question might be posed with respect to the *Diamond* court's unjust enrichment analysis: is it proper to conclude that an insider has been unjustly enriched *vis-à-vis* the corporation (as compared to other traders in the market) when there is no way that the corporation could have used the information to its own profit, just because the insider's trading was made possible by virtue of his corporate position?

Not all information generated in the course of carrying on a business fits snugly into the corporate asset mold. Information in the form of trade secrets, customer lists, etc., can easily be categorized as a valuable or potentially valuable corporate "possession," in that it can be directly used by the corporation to its own economic advantage. However, most information involved in insider trading is not of this ilk, e.g., knowledge of an impending merger, a decline in earnings, etc. If the corporation were to attempt to exploit such non-public information by dealing in its own securities, it would open itself up to potential liability under federal and state securities laws, just as do the insiders when they engage in insider trading. This is not to say that the corporation does not have any interests with regard to such information. It may have an interest in either preventing the information from becoming public or in regulating the timing of disclosure. However, insider trading does not entail the disclosure of inside information, but rather its use in a manner in which the corporation itself is prohibited from exploiting it.

Yet, the *Diamond* court concluded that it might well be inferred that insider trading causes some harm to the corporation * * *. It must be conceded that the unfairness that is the basis of the wide-spread disapproval of insider trading is borne primarily by participants in the securities markets, rather than by the corporation itself. By comparison, the harm to corporate goodwill posited by the *Diamond* court pales in significance. At this point, the existence of such an indirect injury must be considered speculative, as there is no actual evidence of such a reaction. Furthermore, it is less than clear to us that the nature of this harm would form an adequate basis for an action for an accounting based on a breach of the insiders' duty of loyalty, as opposed to an action for damages based on a breach of the duty of care. The injury hypothesized by the *Diamond* court seems little different from the harm to the corporation that might be inferred whenever a responsible corporate official commits an illegal or unethical act using a corporate asset. Absent is the element of loss of opportunity or potential susceptibility to outside influence that generally is present when a corporate fiduciary is required to account to the corporation.

The *Brophy* case is capable of being distinguished on this basis. Although the court there did not openly rely on the existence of a potential harm to the corporation, such a harm was possible. Since the corporation was about to begin buying its own shares in the market, by purchasing stock for his own account the insider placed himself in direct competition with the corporation. To the degree that his purchases might have caused the stock price to rise, the corporation was directly injured in that it had to pay more for its purchases. The other cases cited by the *Diamond* court also tended to involve an agent's competition with his principal, harm to it, disregard for its instructions, or the like. * * *

A second problem presented by the recognition of a cause of action in favor of the corporation is that of potential double liability. The *Diamond* court thought that this problem would seldom arise, since it thought it unlikely that a damage suit would be brought by investors where the insiders traded on impersonal exchanges. * * *. The Second Circuit also gave consideration to the possibility of double liability in *Schein v. Chasen*, 478 F.2d at 824–25, but concluded that double liability could be avoided by methods such as that employed in *SEC v. Texas Gulf Sulphur Co.*, 312 F.Supp. 77, 93 (S.D.N.Y.1970), where the defendants' disgorged profits were placed in a fund subject first to the claims of injured investors, with the residue payable to the corporation. The efficacy of the *Diamond* court's suggestion of resort to an interpleader action is open to question. The creation of a fund subject to the superior claims of injured investors also poses some difficulties. Although some observers have suggested that double liability be imposed so as to more effectively deter insider trading and that it is analytically justifiable since the two causes of action involved are based on separate legal wrongs, the *Diamond* and *Schein* courts' concern for avoiding double liability may implicitly reflect the view that a right of recovery in favor of the corporation was being created because of the perceived likelihood that the investors who are the true victims of insider trading would not be able to bring suit. When the latter in fact bring an action seeking damages from the insiders, thereby creating the possibility of double liability, the need for a surrogate plaintiff disappears and the corporation's claim is implicitly relegated to the back seat.

Since the *Diamond* court's action was motivated in large part by its perception of the inadequacy of existing remedies for insider trading, it is noteworthy that over the decade since *Diamond* was decided, the 10b–5 class action has made substantial advances toward becoming the kind of effective remedy for insider trading that the court of appeals hoped that it might become. Most importantly, recovery of damages from insiders has been allowed by, or on the behalf of, market investors even when the insiders dealt only through impersonal stock exchanges, although this is not yet a well-settled area of the law. In spite of other recent developments indicating that such class actions will not become as easy to maintain as some plaintiffs had perhaps hoped, it is clear the remedies for insider trading under the federal securities laws now constitute a more effective deterrent than they did when *Diamond* was decided.

* * * [H]aving carefully examined the decision of the New York Court of Appeals in *Diamond,* we are of the opinion that although the court sought to ground its ruling in accepted principles of corporate common law, that decision can best be understood as an example of judicial securities regulation. Although the question is a close one, we believe that were the issue to be presented to the Indiana courts at the present time, they would most likely join the Florida Supreme Court in refusing to adopt the New York court's innovative ruling.

* * *

The judgment of the district court is affirmed.

American Law Institute, PRINCIPLES OF CORPORATE GOVERNANCE § 5.04 provides that, in general, "a director or senior executive may not use * * * material non-public information * * * to secure a pecuniary benefit." Comment d(2)(a) explains:

> A director or senior executive may sometimes secure a pecuniary benefit by using undisclosed corporate information to buy or sell the corporation's securities in the open market or in a privately negotiated transaction with a third party or the corporation. In certain of these situations there are conflicting judicial decisions whether the director or senior executive has breached a duty of fair dealing to the corporation. * * * Section 5.04(a) provides that such use of inside information is a breach of the duty of fair dealing, on the theory that the director or senior executive has used corporate information to secure a pecuniary benefit. Section 5.04 would also be violated if the director's or senior executive's use of corporate information causes harm to the corporation.
>
> Some cases have denied recovery to the corporation based on the use of inside information in the purchase or sale of securities when the corporation itself has suffered no harm. *See Freeman v. Decio.* Section 5.04 rejects this approach and in so doing follows the result reached by the New York Court of Appeals in *Diamond v. Oreamuno*, by permitting the corporation to recover for unjust enrichment based on a violation of § 5.04. Section 5.04(a) would also permit the corporation to seek damages for any actual harm it suffers as a result of the unauthorized use of material inside information. However, § 5.04(a) does not authorize the corporation to seek damages on behalf of shareholders who may have a claim based on harm suffered by them. Furthermore, to the extent that shareholders assert harm to themselves in violation of § 5.04(a) as a result of insider trading, the primary right to recovery would be in the shareholders, and under § 5.04(c) the corporation would not also be entitled to obtain recovery on the same facts for a violation of § 5.04(a) on a theory of unjust enrichment. * * *
>
> The cases uniformly reject the conclusion that unrelated third parties who have been given information by the corporation or who have received information as a tippee are subject to a duty of loyalty to the corporation. Such persons may nevertheless be liable to the corporation or its shareholders on a theory of participation in a breach of the duty of fair dealing owed by a director or senior executive who wrongfully supplies the inside information, or on a theory of breach of duty owed by an agent to a principal, or under a theory of breach of an agreement to hold the information received confidential, or for violation of federal or state securities laws. *See Dirks v. Securities and Exchange Commission*, 463 U.S. 646, 77 L.Ed.2d 911 (1983).

\* \* \* Section 5.04 is not intended to detract from federal or state securities laws, and its limitation on the use of material non-public information is no more extensive than the limitation already imposed by those laws, although the remedial consequences may differ in a given case. \* \* \*

A person who becomes a shareholder as a result of a purchase of securities from a director or senior executive will be deemed a shareholder for purposes of asserting a right under § 5.04, if the director or senior executive failed to disclose material inside information in making the sale.

Because § 5.04 is not intended to detract from federal or state securities laws and may conceivably give rise to claims by both the corporation and aggrieved shareholders, the court should take appropriate steps to limit the possibility of multiple recovery against the director or senior executive on varying theories of liability under state and federal law, unless specific separate damages can be shown. \* \* \*

# D.   FEDERAL REGULATION—RULE 10b–5

## 1.  INTRODUCTION

The SEC's Rule 10b–5 is "a judicial oak which has grown from little more than a legislative acorn." *Blue Chip Stamps v. Manor Drug Stores*, 421 U.S. 723, 95 S.Ct. 1917, 44 L.Ed.2d 539 (1975). It is responsible for a large portion of a body of law that often is referred to as "federal corporation law"—almost always in quotation marks because of the implications of such a phrase in a post-Erie legal system.

The authority for the adoption of the rule is § 10(b) of the Securities Exchange Act of 1934, itself no more than a brief statement of a broad anti-fraud principle. The legislative history of § 10(b) is described in *SEC v. Texas Gulf Sulphur Co.*, 401 F.2d 833, 859 (2d Cir.1968):

Section 10(b) of the Act \* \* \* was taken by the Conference Committee from Section 10(b) of the proposed Senate bill, S. 3420, and taken from it verbatim insofar as here pertinent. The only alteration made by the Conference Committee was to substitute the present closing language of Section 10(b), " \* \* \* in contravention of such rules and regulations as the Commission may prescribe as necessary or appropriate in the public interest or for the protection of investors" for the closing language of the original Section 10(b) of S. 3420, " \* \* \* which the Commission may declare to be detrimental to the interests of investors." 78 CONG.REC. 10261 (1934).

The Report of the Senate Committee which presented S. 3420 to the Senate summarized Section 10(b) as follows:

Subsection (b) authorizes the Commission by rules and regulations to prohibit or regulate the use of *any other manipulative or deceptive practices which it finds detrimental to the interests of the investor.* (Emphasis supplied.)

S.REP. No. 792, 73rd Cong., 2d Sess. 18 (1934).

Indeed, from its very inception, Section 10(b), and the proposed sections in H.R. 1383 and S. 3420 from which it was derived, have always been acknowledged as catchalls. *See* Bromberg, *Securities Law: SEC Rule 10b–5*, p. 19 (1967). In the House Committee hearings on the proposed House bill, Thomas G. Corcoran, Counsel with the Reconstruction Finance Corporation and a spokesman for the Roosevelt Administration, described the broad prohibitions contained in § 9(c), the section which corresponded to Section 10(b) of S. 3420 and eventually to Section 10(b) of the Act, as follows: "Subsection (c) says, 'Thou shalt not devise any other cunning devices' * * * Of course subsection (c) is a catchall clause to prevent manipulative devices. I do not think there is any objection to that kind of a clause. The Commission should have the authority to deal with new manipulative devices." *Stock Exchange Regulation, Hearings before the House Committee on Interstate and Foreign Commerce*, 73rd Cong., 2d Sess. 115 (1934). Although several other witnesses objected to the breadth of the proposed prohibition that Corcoran was supporting, the section as enacted did not in any way limit the broad scope of the "in connection with" phrase. See 3 Loss, SECURITIES REGULATION, 1424 n. 7 (2d ed. 1961).

The SEC probably had no idea when it adopted Rule 10b–5 in 1942 what the courts would make of its briefly worded prohibition against fraud and deceit. The rule was first held to support an implied private action for damages in *Kardon v. National Gypsum Co.*, 69 F.Supp. 512 (E.D.Pa.1946). The principal parties in the suit were two family groups, each of which owned 50 percent of the stock of a corporation. The defendants learned that National Gypsum was interested in purchasing the corporation and bought the shares of the plaintiffs without telling them of that fact. The defendants then conveyed the corporation's assets to National Gypsum, reaping a substantial profit. Plaintiffs asserted that the defendants were guilty of fraud and deceit in connection with the purchase of their stock. The court held that, although neither § 10(b) nor Rule 10b–5 explicitly provided a private remedy for a violation of their prohibitions, it was appropriate for the court to create one, citing the tort law principle that the violation of a statute resulting in an injury to another is a tort. The lower courts generally followed *Kardon* in implying a private right of action for damages under Rule 10b–5, and the Supreme Court finally confirmed it in *Superintendent of Insurance v. Bankers Life & Casualty Co.*, 404 U.S. 6, 13 n. 9, 92 S.Ct. 165, 169 n. 9, 30 L.Ed.2d 128 (1971).

*In re Cady, Roberts & Co.*, 40 S.E.C. 907 (1961), ushered in the modern era of insider trading analysis. The S.E.C. brought an action under Rule section 10(b)–5 against the brokerage firm of Cady, Roberts & Co. and Gintel, one of its partners. On November 25, 1959, the directors of Curtiss–Wright Corp. met to consider the declaration of a dividend. The stock price had recently moved up and Gintel had purchased a substantial number of shares for his clients. He had also begun to dispose of some of those shares on the day before the meeting. The directors voted to cut the dividend and Cowdin, a director of Curtiss–Wright and an associate at Cady, Roberts, left the meeting after this decision but prior to its public disclosure, which was inadvertently delayed. Cowdin informed Gintel of Curtiss–Wright's decision; Gintel immediately sold his customers' shares and those in a trust for his children and sold short for his own account.

In concluding that Gintel had violated Rule 10b–5, the Commission announced the principle that a corporate insider who possessed material, nonpublic corporate information had an obligation to disclose the information or abstain from trading in the corporation's securities. Chairman Cary explained:

> Analytically, the obligation rests on two principal elements; first, the existence of a relationship giving access, directly or indirectly, to information intended to be available only for a corporate purpose and not for the personal benefit of anyone, and second, the inherent unfairness involved where a party takes advantage of such information knowing it is unavailable to those with whom he is dealing.

40 S.E.C. at 912.

The SEC also responded to Gintel's claims that he owed no duties to those to whom he had sold Curtis–Wright stock if the purchasers were not already Curtis–Wright shareholders and that, because he had made no representations to the purchasers and had sold on the New York Stock Exchange, he had not deceived anyone, either actually or constructively. The Commission tacitly acknowledged that Gintel's conduct would not have been deemed deceptive at common law. But, it maintained:

> There is no valid reason why persons who purchase stock from an officer, director or other person having the responsibilities of an 'insider' should not have the same protection afforded by disclosure of special information as persons who sell stock to them. * * * [I]t is clearly not appropriate to introduce these [common law distinctions] into the broader anti-fraud concepts embodied in the securities acts. [Moreover, i]t would be anomalous indeed if the protection afforded by the antifraud provisions were withdrawn from transactions effected on exchanges, primary markets for securities transactions.

*Id.* at 914.

In short, the Commission based its conclusion that corporate insiders have an obligation to disclose or abstain in large part on its view that insider trading was exactly the kind of conduct Congress intended to make unlawful when it passed the 1934 Act.

## 2. THE SCOPE OF THE RULE

Rule 10b–5 gives rise to two distinct sets of duties: (1) a duty not to trade on inside information and (2) duties relating to the disclosure of material information. The following case frames both sets of issues and serves as a point of reference for the materials that follow.

## SECURITIES AND EXCHANGE COMMISSION v. TEXAS GULF SULPHUR CO.

401 F.2d 833 (2d Cir.1968), cert. denied 394 U.S. 976, 89 S.Ct. 1454, 22 L.Ed.2d 756 (1969).

Before LUMBARD, CHIEF JUDGE, and WATERMAN, MOORE, FRIENDLY, SMITH, KAUFMAN, HAYS, ANDERSON and FEINBERG, CIRCUIT JUDGES.

WATERMAN, CIRCUIT JUDGE:

This action was commenced in the United States District Court for the Southern District of New York by the Securities and Exchange Commission (the SEC) pursuant to Sec. 21(e) of the Securities Exchange Act of 1934 (the Act), 15 U.S.C. § 78u(e), against Texas Gulf Sulphur Company (TGS) and several of its officers, directors and employees*, to enjoin certain conduct by TGS and the individual defendants said to violate Section 10(b) of the Act, 15 U.S.C. Section 78j(b), and Rule 10b–5 (17 CFR 240.10b–5) (the Rule), promulgated thereunder, and to compel the rescission by the individual defendants of securities transactions assertedly conducted contrary to law. The complaint alleged (1) that defendants Fogarty, Mollison, Darke, Murray, Huntington, O'Neill, Clayton, Crawford, and Coates had either personally or through agents purchased TGS stock or calls thereon from November 12, 1963 through April 16, 1964 on the basis of material inside information concerning the results of TGS drilling in Timmins, Ontario, while such information remained undisclosed to the investing public generally or to the particular sellers**; (2) that defendants Darke and Coates had divulged such information to others for use in purchasing TGS stock or calls[3] or recommended its purchase while the information was undisclosed to the public or to the sellers; [3] that defendants Stephens, Fogarty, Mollison, Holyk, and Kline had accepted options to purchase TGS stock on Feb. 20, 1964 without disclosing the material information as to the drilling progress to either the Stock Option Committee or the TGS Board of

---

* The positions in TGS held by each of the defendants were: Claude O. Stephens, President and Director; Charles F. Fogarty, Executive Vice President and Director; Thomas S. Lamont, Director; Francis G. Coates, Director; Harold B. Kline, Vice President and General Counsel; Richard D. Mollison, Vice President; David M. Crawford, Secretary; Richard H. Clayton, Engineer; Walter Holyk, Chief Geologist; Kenneth H. Darke, Geologist; Earl L. Huntington, Attorney; John A. Murray, Office Manager. [Eds.]

** TGS stock was purchased by insiders at prices between $17–5/8 and $18–1/8 in November. The price rose steadily to about $33 on April 12, 1964, the date of the first press release issued by TGS. It then dipped to about $30 per share. [Eds.]

3. A "call is a negotiable option contract by which the bearer has the right to buy from the writer of the contract a certain number of shares of a particular stock at a fixed price on or before a certain agreed-upon date.

Directors * * *. The case was tried at length before Judge Bonsal of the Southern District of New York, sitting without a jury. Judge Bonsal in a detailed opinion decided, *inter alia,* that the insider activity prior to April 9, 1964 was not illegal because the drilling results were not "material" until then; that Clayton and Crawford had traded in violation of law because they traded after that date; that Coates had committed no violation as he did not trade before disclosure was made * * *. 258 F.Supp. 262, at 292–296 (S.D.N.Y.1966). Defendants Clayton and Crawford appeal from that part of the decision below which held that they had violated Sec. 10(b) and Rule 10b–5 and the SEC appeals from the remainder of the decision which dismissed the complaint against defendants TGS, Fogarty, Mollison, Holyk, Darke, Stephens, Kline, Murray, and Coates.

* * *

### The Factual Setting

This action derives from the exploratory activities of TGS begun in 1957 on the Canadian Shield in eastern Canada. In March of 1959, aerial geophysical surveys were conducted over more than 15,000 square miles of this area by a group led by defendant Mollison, a mining engineer and a Vice President of TGS. The group included defendant Holyk, TGS's chief geologist, defendant Clayton, an electrical engineer and geophysicist, and defendant Darke, a geologist. These operations resulted in the detection of numerous anomalies, i.e., extraordinary variations in the conductivity of rocks, one of which was on the Kidd 55 segment of land located near Timmins, Ontario.

On October 29 and 30, 1963, Clayton conducted a ground geophysical survey on the northeast portion of the Kidd 55 segment which confirmed the presence of an anomaly and indicated the necessity of diamond core drilling for further evaluation. Drilling of the initial hole, K–55–1, at the strongest part of the anomaly was commenced on November 8 and terminated on November 12 at a depth of 655 feet. Visual estimates by Holyk of the core of K–55–1 indicated an average copper content of 1.15% and an average zinc content of 8.64% over a length of 599 feet. This visual estimate convinced TGS that it was desirable to acquire the remainder of the Kidd 55 segment, and in order to facilitate this acquisition TGS President Stephens instructed the exploration group to keep the results of K–55–1 confidential and undisclosed even as to other officers, directors, and employees of TGS. The hole was concealed and a barren core was intentionally drilled off the anomaly. Meanwhile, the core of K–55–1 had been shipped to Utah for chemical assay which, when received in early December, revealed an average mineral content of 1.18% copper, 8.26% zinc, and 3.94% ounces of silver per ton over a length of 602 feet. These results were so remarkable that neither Clayton, an experienced geophysicist, nor four other TGS expert witnesses, had ever seen or heard of a comparable initial exploratory drill hole in a base metal deposit. So, the trial court concluded, "There is no doubt that the drill core of K–55–1 was unusually good and that it excited the interest and speculation of those who knew about it." Id. at 282. By March 27, 1964, TGS decided that the land acquisition program had advanced to such a point that the company might well resume drilling, and drilling was resumed on March 31.

During this period, from November 12, 1963 when K–55–1 was completed, to March 31, 1964 when drilling was resumed, certain of the individual defendants listed in fn. 2, supra, and persons listed in fn. 4, supra, said to have received "tips" from them, purchased TGS stock or calls thereon. Prior to these transactions these persons had owned 1135 shares of TGS stock and possessed no calls; thereafter they owned a total of 8235 shares and possessed 12,300 calls.

On February 20, 1964, also during this period, TGS issued stock options to 26 of its officers and employees whose salaries exceeded a specified amount, five of whom were the individual defendants Stephens, Fogarty, Mollison, Holyk, and Kline. Of these, only Kline was unaware of the detailed results of K–55–1, but he, too, knew that a hole containing favorable bodies of copper and zinc ore had been drilled in Timmins. At this time, neither the TGS Stock Option Committee nor its Board of Directors had been informed of the results of K–55–1, presumably because of the pending land acquisition program which required confidentiality. All of the foregoing defendants accepted the options granted them.

When drilling was resumed on March 31, hole K–55–3 was commenced 510 feet west of K–55–1 and was drilled easterly at a 45° angle so as to cross K–55–1 in a vertical plane. Daily progress reports of the drilling of this hole K–55–3 and of all subsequently drilled holes were sent to defendants Stephens and Fogarty (President and Executive Vice President of TGS) by Holyk and Mollison. Visual estimates of K–55–3 revealed an average mineral content of 1.12% copper and 7.93% zinc over 641 of the hole's 876–foot length. On April 7, drilling of a third hole, K–55–4, 200 feet south of and parallel to K–55–1 and westerly at a 45° angle, was commenced and mineralization was encountered over 366 of its 579–foot length. Visual estimates indicated an average content of 1.14% copper and 8.24% zinc. Like K–55–1, both K–55–3 and K–55–4 established substantial copper mineralization on the eastern edge of the anomaly. On the basis of these findings relative to the foregoing drilling results, the trial court concluded that the vertical plane created by the intersection of K–55–1 and K–55–3, which measured at least 350 feet wide by 500 feet deep extended southward 200 feet to its intersection with K–55–4, and that "There was real evidence that a body of commercially minable ore might exist." Id. at 281–82.

On April 8 TGS began with a second drill rig to drill another hole, K–55–6, 300 feet easterly of K–55–1. This hole was drilled westerly at an angle of 60° and was intended to explore mineralization beneath K–55–1. While no visual estimates of its core were immediately available, it was readily apparent by the evening of April 10 that substantial copper mineralization had been encountered over the last 127 feet of the hole's

569–foot length. On April 10, a third drill rig commenced drilling yet another hole, K–55–5, 200 feet north of K–55–1, parallel to the prior holes, and slanted westerly at a 45° angle. By the evening of April 10 in this hole, too, substantial copper mineralization had been encountered over the last 42 feet of its 97–foot length.

Meanwhile, rumors that a major ore strike was in the making had been circulating throughout Canada. On the morning of Saturday, April 11, Stephens at his home in Greenwich, Conn. read in the New York Herald Tribune and in the New York Times unauthorized reports of the TGS drilling which seemed to infer a rich strike from the fact that the drill cores had been flown to the United States for chemical assay. Stephens immediately contacted Fogarty at his home in Rye, N.Y., who in turn telephoned and later that day visited Mollison at Mollison's home in Greenwich to obtain a current report and evaluation of the drilling progress. The following morning, Sunday, Fogarty again telephoned Mollison, inquiring whether Mollison had any further information and told him to return to Timmins with Holyk, the TGS Chief Geologist, as soon as possible "to move things along." With the aid of one Carroll, a public relations consultant, Fogarty drafted a press release designed to quell the rumors, which release, after having been channeled through Stephens and Huntington, a TGS attorney, was issued at 3:00 P.M. on Sunday, April 12, and which appeared in the morning newspapers of general circulation on Monday, April 13. It read in pertinent part as follows:

NEW YORK, April 12—The following statement was made today by Dr. Charles F. Fogarty, executive vice president of Texas Gulf Sulphur Company, in regard to the company's drilling operations near Timmins, Ontario, Canada. Dr. Fogarty said:

"During the past few days, the exploration activities of Texas Gulf Sulphur in the area of Timmins, Ontario, have been widely reported in the press, coupled with rumors of a substantial copper discovery there. These reports exaggerate the scale of operations, and mention plans and statistics of size and grade of ore that are without factual basis and have evidently originated by speculation of people not connected with TGS.

"The facts are as follows. TGS has been exploring in the Timmins area for six years as part of its overall search in Canada and elsewhere for various minerals—lead, copper, zinc, etc. During the course of this work, in Timmins as well as in Eastern Canada, TGS has conducted exploration entirely on its own, without the participation by others. Numerous prospects have been investigated by geophysical means and a large number of selected ones have been core-drilled. These cores are sent to the United States for assay and detailed examination as a matter of routine and on advice of expert Canadian legal counsel. No inferences as to grade can be drawn from this procedure.

"Most of the areas drilled in Eastern Canada have revealed either barren pyrite or graphite without value; a few have resulted in discoveries of small or marginal sulphide ore bodies.

"Recent drilling on one property near Timmins has led to preliminary indications that more drilling would be required for proper evaluation of this prospect. The drilling done to date has not been conclusive, but the statements made by many outside quarters are unreliable and include information and figures that are not available to TGS.

"The work done to date has not been sufficient to reach definite conclusions and any statement as to size and grade of ore would be premature and possibly misleading. When we have progressed to the point where reasonable and logical conclusions can be made, TGS will issue a definite statement to its stockholders and to the public in order to clarify the Timmins project."

* * *

The release purported to give the Timmins drilling results as of the release date, April 12. From Mollison, Fogarty had been told of the developments through 7:00 P.M. on April 10, and of the remarkable discoveries made up to that time, detailed supra, which discoveries, according to the calculations of the experts who testified for the SEC at the hearing, demonstrated that TGS had already discovered 6.2 to 8.3 million tons of proven ore having gross assay values from $26 to $29 per ton. TGS experts, on the other hand, denied at the hearing that proven or probable ore could have been calculated on April 11 or 12 because there was then no assurance of continuity in the mineralized zone.

The evidence as to the effect of this release on the investing public was equivocal and less than abundant. On April 13 the New York Herald Tribune in an article head-noted "Copper Rumor Deflated" quoted from the TGS release of April 12 and backtracked from its original April 11 report of a major strike but nevertheless inferred from the TGS release that "recent mineral exploratory activity near Timmins, Ontario, has provided preliminary favorable results, sufficient at least to require a step-up in drilling operations." Some witnesses who testified at the hearing stated that they found the release encouraging. On the other hand, a Canadian mining security specialist, Roche, stated that "earlier in the week [before April 16] we had a Dow Jones saying that they [TGS] didn't have anything basically" and a TGS stock specialist for the Midwest Stock Exchange became concerned about his long position in the stock after reading the release. The trial court stated only that "While, in retrospect, the press release may appear gloomy or incomplete, this does not make it misleading or deceptive on the basis of the facts then known." Id. at 296.

Meanwhile, drilling operations continued. By morning of April 13, in K–55–5, the fifth drill hole, substantial copper mineralization had been encountered to the 580 foot mark, and the hole was subsequently drilled to a length of 757 feet without further results. Visual estimates revealed an average content of 0.82% copper and 4.2% zinc over a 525–foot section. Also by 7:00 A.M. on April 13, K–55–6 had found mineralization to the 946–foot mark. On April 12 a fourth drill rig began to drill K–55–7, which was drilled westerly at a 45° angle, at the eastern edge of the anomaly. The next morning the 137 foot mark had been reached, fifty feet of which showed mineralization. By 7:00 P.M. on April 15, the hole had been completed to a length of 707 feet but had only encountered additional mineralization during a 26–foot length between the 425 and 451–foot marks. A mill test hole, K–55–8, had been drilled and was complete by the evening of April 13 but its mineralization had not been reported upon prior to April 16. K–55–10 was drilled westerly at a 45° angle commencing April 14 and had encountered mineralization over 231 of its 249–foot length by the evening of April 15. It, too, was drilled at the anomaly's eastern edge.

While drilling activity ensued to completion, TGS officials were taking steps toward ultimate disclosure of the discovery. On April 13, a previously-invited reporter for The Northern Miner, a Canadian mining industry journal, visited the drillsite, interviewed Mollison, Holyk and Darke, and prepared an article which confirmed a 10 million ton ore strike. This report, after having been submitted to Mollison and returned to the reporter unamended on April 15, was published in the April 16 issue. A statement relative to the extent of the discovery, in substantial part drafted by Mollison, was given to the Ontario Minister of Mines for release to the Canadian media. Mollison and Holyk expected it to be released over the airways at 11 P.M. on April 15th, but, for undisclosed reasons, it was not released until 9:40 A.M. on the 16th. An official detailed statement, announcing a strike of at least 25 million tons of ore, based on the drilling data set forth above, was read to representatives of American financial media from 10:00 A.M. to 10:10 or 10:15 A.M. on April 16, and appeared over Merrill Lynch's private wire at 10:29 A.M. and, somewhat later than expected, over the Dow Jones ticker tape at 10:54 A.M.

Between the time the first press release was issued on April 12 and the dissemination of the TGS official announcement on the morning of April 16, the only defendants before us on appeal who engaged in market activity were Clayton and Crawford and TGS director Coates. Clayton ordered 200 shares of TGS stock through his Canadian broker on April 15 and the order was executed that day over the Midwest Stock Exchange. Crawford ordered 300 shares at midnight on the 15th and another 300 shares at 8:30 A.M. the next day, and these orders were executed over the Midwest Exchange in Chicago at its opening on April 16. Coates left the TGS press conference and called his broker son-in-law Haemisegger shortly before 10:20 A.M. on the 16th and ordered 2,000 shares of TGS for family trust accounts of which Coates was a trustee but not a beneficiary; Haemisegger executed this order over the New

York and Midwest Exchanges, and he and his customers purchased 1500 additional shares.

During the period of drilling in Timmins, the market price of TGS stock fluctuated but steadily gained overall. On Friday, November 8, when the drilling began the stock closed at 17 3/8; on Friday, November 15, after K–55–1 had been completed, it closed at 18. After a slight decline to 16 3/8 by Friday, November 22, the price rose to 20 7/8 by December 13, when the chemical assay results of K–55–1 were received, and closed at a high of 24 1/8 on February 21, the day after the stock options had been issued. It had reached a price of 26 by March 31, after the land acquisition program had been completed and drilling had been resumed, and continued to ascend to 30 1/8 by the close of trading on April 10, at which time the drilling progress up to then was evaluated for the April 12th press release. On April 13, the day on which the April 12 release was disseminated, TGS opened at 30 1/8, rose immediately to a high of 32 and gradually tapered off to close at 30 7/8. It closed at 30 1/4 the next day, and at 29 3/8 on April 15. On April 16, the day of the official announcement of the Timmins discovery, the price climbed to a high of 37 and closed at 36 3/8. By May 15, TGS stock was selling at 58 1/4.

## I. The Individual Defendants

### A. Introductory

\* \* \*

Rule 10b–5 was promulgated pursuant to the grant of authority given the SEC by Congress in Section 10(b) of the Securities Exchange Act of 1934 (15 U.S.C. § 78j(b)). By that Act Congress proposed to prevent inequitable and unfair practices and to insure fairness in securities transactions generally, whether conducted face-to-face, over the counter, or on exchanges, see 3 Loss, SECURITIES REGULATION 1455–56 (2d ed. 1961). The Act and the Rule apply to the transactions here, all of which were consummated on exchanges. Whether predicated on traditional fiduciary concepts, *see, e.g., Hotchkiss v. Fischer*, 136 Kan. 530, 16 P.2d 531 (Kan.1932), or on the "special facts" doctrine, *see, e.g., Strong v. Repide*, 213 U.S. 419, 29 S.Ct. 521, 53 L.Ed. 853 (1909), the Rule is based in policy on the justifiable expectation of the securities marketplace that all investors trading on impersonal exchanges have relatively equal access to material information, *see* Cary, *Insider Trading in Stocks*, 21 BUS.LAW. 1009, 1010 (1966), Fleischer, *Securities Trading and Corporation Information Practices: The Implications of the Texas Gulf Sulphur Proceeding*, 51 VA.L.REV. 1271, 1278–80 (1965). The essence of the Rule is that anyone who, trading for his own account in the securities of a corporation has "access, directly or indirectly, to information intended to be available only for a corporate purpose and not for the personal benefit of anyone" may not take "advantage of such information knowing it is unavailable to those with whom he is dealing," i.e., the investing public. *Matter of Cady, Roberts & Co.*, 40 SEC 907, 912 (1961).

Insiders, as directors or management officers are, of course, by this Rule, precluded from so unfairly dealing, but the Rule is also applicable to one possessing the information who may not be strictly termed an "insider" within the meaning of Sec. 16(b) of the Act. *Cady, Roberts, supra.* Thus, anyone in possession of material inside information must either disclose it to the investing public, or, if he is disabled from disclosing it in order to protect a corporate confidence, or he chooses not to do so, must abstain from trading in or recommending the securities concerned while such inside information remains undisclosed. So, it is here no justification for insider activity that disclosure was forbidden by the legitimate corporate objective of acquiring options to purchase the land surrounding the exploration site; if the information was, as the SEC contends, material, its possessors should have kept out of the market until disclosure was accomplished. *Cady, Roberts, supra* at 911.

### B.  Material Inside Information

An insider is not, of course, always foreclosed from investing in his own company merely because he may be more familiar with company operations than are outside investors. An insider's duty to disclose information or his duty to abstain from dealing in his company's securities arises only in "those situations which are essentially extraordinary in nature and which are reasonably certain to have a substantial effect on the market price of the security if [the extraordinary situation is] disclosed." Fleischer, [*supra*, at] 1289.

Nor is an insider obligated to confer upon outside investors the benefit of his superior financial or other expert analysis by disclosing his educated guesses or predictions. The only regulatory objective is that access to material information be enjoyed equally, but this objective requires nothing more than the disclosure of basic facts so that outsiders may draw upon their own evaluative expertise in reaching their own investment decisions with knowledge equal to that of the insiders.

This is not to suggest, however, as did the trial court, that "the test of materiality must necessarily be a conservative one, particularly since many actions under Section 10(b) are brought on the basis of hindsight," 258 F.Supp. 262 at 280, in the sense that the materiality of facts is to be assessed solely by measuring the effect the knowledge of the facts would have upon prudent or conservative investors. As we stated in *List v. Fashion Park, Inc.*, 340 F.2d 457, 462, "The basic test of materiality * * * is whether a *reasonable* man would attach importance * * * in determining his choice of action in the transaction in question. Restatement, Torts § 538(2)(a); *accord* Prosser, TORTS 554–55; I. Harper & James, TORTS 565–66." (Emphasis supplied.) This, of course, encompasses any fact "* * * which in reasonable and objective contemplation *might* affect the value of the corporation's stock or securities * * *." *List v. Fashion Park, Inc., supra* at 462, quoting from *Kohler v. Kohler Co.*, 319 F.2d 634, 642 (7 Cir.1963). (Emphasis supplied.) Such a fact is a material fact and must be effectively disclosed to the investing public prior to the commencement of insider trading in the corporation's securities. The speculators and chartists of Wall and Bay Streets are also "reasonable" investors entitled to the same legal protection afforded conservative traders. Thus, material facts include not only information disclosing the earnings and distributions of a company but also those facts which affect the probable future of the company and those which may affect the desire of investors to buy, sell, or hold the company's securities.

In each case, then, whether facts are material within Rule 10b–5 when the facts relate to a particular event and are undisclosed by those persons who are knowledgeable thereof will depend at any given time upon a balancing of both the indicated probability that the event will occur and the anticipated magnitude of the event in light of the totality of the company activity. Here, notwithstanding the trial court's conclusion that the results of the first drill core, K–55–1, were "too 'remote' * * * to have had any significant impact on the market, i.e., to be deemed material," 258 F.Supp. at 283, knowledge of the possibility, which surely was more than marginal, of the existence of a mine of the vast magnitude indicated by the remarkably rich drill core located rather close to the surface (suggesting minability by the less expensive open-pit method) within the confines of a large anomaly (suggesting an extensive region of mineralization) might well have affected the price of TGS stock and would certainly have been an important fact to a reasonable, if speculative, investor in deciding whether he should buy, sell, or hold. After all, this first drill core was "unusually good and * * * excited the interest and speculation of those who knew about it." 258 F.Supp. at 282.

Our disagreement with the district judge on the issue does not, then, go to his findings of basic fact, as to which the "clearly erroneous" rule would apply, but to his understanding of the legal standard applicable to them. Our survey of the facts found below conclusively establishes that knowledge of the results of the discovery hole, K–55–1, would have been important to a reasonable investor and might have affected the price of the stock.[12] On April 16, The Northern Miner, a trade publication in wide circulation among mining stock specialists, called K–55–1, the discovery hole, "one of the most impressive drill holes completed in modern times." Roche, a Canadian broker whose firm specialized in mining securities, characterized the importance to investors of the results of K–55–1. He stated that the completion of "the first drill hole" with "a 600 foot drill core is very very significant * * * anything over 200 feet is considered very significant and 600 feet is just beyond your wildest

---

**12.** We do not suggest that material facts must be disclosed immediately; the timing of disclosure is a matter for the business judgment of the corporate officers entrusted with the management of the corporation within the affirmative disclosure requirements promulgated by the exchanges and by the SEC. Here, a valuable corporate purpose was served by delaying the publication of the K–55–1 discovery. We do intend to convey, however, that where a corporate purpose is thus served by withholding the news of a material fact, those persons who are thus quite properly true to their corporate trust must not during the period of nondisclosure deal personally in the corporation's securities or give to outsiders confidential information not generally available to all the corporations' stockholders and to the public at large.

imagination." He added, however, that it "is a natural thing to buy more stock once they give you the first drill hole." Additional testimony revealed that the prices of stocks of other companies, albeit less diversified, smaller firms, had increased substantially solely on the basis of the discovery of good anomalies or even because of the proximity of their lands to the situs of a potentially major strike.

Finally, a major factor in determining whether the K–55–1 discovery was a material fact is the importance attached to the drilling results by those who knew about it. In view of other unrelated recent developments favorably affecting TGS, participation by an informed person in a regular stock-purchase program, or even sporadic trading by an informed person, might lend only nominal support to the inference of the materiality of the K–55–1 discovery; nevertheless, the timing by those who knew of it, of their stock purchases and their purchases of *short-term* calls—purchases in some cases by individuals who had never before purchased calls or even TGS stock—virtually compels the inference that the insiders were influenced by the drilling results. This insider trading activity, which surely constitutes highly pertinent evidence and the only truly objective evidence of the materiality of the K–55–1 discovery, was apparently disregarded by the court below in favor of the testimony of defendants' expert witnesses, all of whom "agreed that one drill core does not establish an ore body, much less a mine," 258 F.Supp. at 282–283. Significantly, however, the court below, while relying upon what these defense experts said the defendant insiders *ought* to have thought about the worth to TGS of the K–55–1 discovery, and finding that from November 12, 1963 to April 6, 1964 Fogarty, Murray, Holyk and Darke spent more than $100,000 in purchasing TGS stock and calls on that stock, made no finding that the insiders were motivated by any factor other than the extraordinary K–55–1 discovery when they bought their stock and their calls. No reason appears why outside investors, perhaps better acquainted with speculative modes of investment and with, in many cases, perhaps more capital at their disposal for intelligent speculation, would have been less influenced, and would not have been similarly motivated to invest if they had known what the insider investors knew about the K–55–1 discovery.

Our decision to expand the limited protection afforded outside investors by the trial court's narrow definition of materiality is not at all shaken by fears that the elimination of insider trading benefits will deplete the ranks of capable corporate managers by taking away an incentive to accept such employment. Such benefits, in essence, are forms of secret corporate compensation, *see* Cary, CORPORATE STANDARDS AND LEGAL RULES, 50 CALIF.L.REV. 408, 409–10 (1962), derived at the expense of the uninformed investing public and not at the expense of the corporation which receives the sole benefit from insider incentives. Moreover, adequate incentives for corporate officers may be provided by properly administered stock options and employee purchase plans of which there are many in existence. In any event, the normal motivation induced by stock ownership, i.e., the identification of an individual with corporate progress, is ill-promoted by condoning the sort of speculative insider activity which occurred here; for example, some of the corporation's stock was sold at market in order to purchase short-term calls upon that stock, calls which would never be exercised to increase a stockholder equity in TGS unless the market price of that stock rose sharply.

The core of Rule 10b–5 is the implementation of the Congressional purpose that all investors should have equal access to the rewards of participation in securities transactions. It was the intent of Congress that all members of the investing public should be subject to identical market risks,—which market risks include, of course, the risk that one's evaluative capacity or one's capital available to put at risk may exceed another's capacity or capital. The insiders here were not trading on an equal footing with the outside investors. They alone were in a position to evaluate the probability and magnitude of what seemed from the outset to be a major ore strike; they alone could invest safely, secure in the expectation that the price of TGS stock would rise substantially in the event such a major strike should materialize, but would decline little, if at all, in the event of failure, for the public, ignorant at the outset of the favorable probabilities would likewise be unaware of the unproductive exploration, and the additional exploration costs would not significantly affect TGS market prices. Such inequities based upon unequal access to knowledge should not be shrugged off as inevitable in our way of life, or, in view of the congressional concern in the area, remain uncorrected.

We hold, therefore, that all transactions in TGS stock or calls by individuals apprised of the drilling results of K–55–1 were made in violation of Rule 10b–5. Inasmuch as the visual evaluation of that drill core (a generally reliable estimate though less accurate than a chemical assay) constituted material information, those advised of the results of the visual evaluation as well as those informed of the chemical assay traded in violation of law. The geologist Darke possessed undisclosed material information and traded in TGS securities. Therefore we reverse the dismissal of the action as to him and his personal transactions. The trial court also found, 258 F.Supp. at 284, that Darke, after the drilling of K–55–1 had been completed and with detailed knowledge of the results thereof, told certain outside individuals that TGS "was a good buy." These individuals thereafter acquired TGS stock and calls. The trial court also found that later, as of March 30, 1964, Darke not only used his material knowledge for his own purchases but that the substantial amounts of TGS stock and calls purchased by these outside individuals on that day, was "strong circumstantial evidence that Darke must have passed the word to one or more of his 'tippees' that drilling on the Kidd 55 segment was about to be resumed." 258 F.Supp. at 284. Obviously if such a resumption were to have any meaning to such "tippees," they must have previously been told of K–55–1.

Unfortunately, however, there was no definitive resolution below of Darke's liability in these premises for the trial court held as to him, as it held as to all the other individual defendants, that this "undisclosed information" never became material until April 9. As it is our holding that the information acquired after the drilling of K–55–1 was material, we, on the basis of the findings of direct and circumstantial evidence on the issue that the trial court has already expressed, hold that Darke violated Rule 10b–5(3) and Section 10(b) by "tipping" and we remand, pursuant to the agreement of the parties, for a determination of the appropriate remedy. As Darke's "tippees" are not defendants in this action, we need not decide whether, if they acted with actual or constructive knowledge that the material information was undisclosed, their conduct is as equally violative of the Rule as the conduct of their insider source, though we note that it certainly could be equally reprehensible.

With reference to Huntington, the trial court found that he "had no detailed knowledge as to the work" on the Kidd–55 segment, 258 F.Supp. 281. Nevertheless, the evidence shows that he knew about and participated in TGS's land acquisition program which followed the receipt of the K–55–1 drilling results, and that on February 26, 1964 he purchased 50 shares of TGS stock. Later, on March 16, he helped prepare a letter for Dr. Holyk's signature in which TGS made a substantial offer for lands near K–55–1, and on the same day he, who had never before purchased calls on any stock, purchased a call on 100 shares of TGS stock. We are satisfied that these purchases in February and March, coupled with his readily inferable and probably reliable, understanding of the highly favorable nature of preliminary operations on the Kidd segment, demonstrate that Huntington possessed material inside information such as to make his purchase violative of the Rule and the Act.

### C.  When May Insiders Act?

Appellant Crawford, who ordered the purchase of TGS stock shortly before the TGS April 16 official announcement, and defendant Coates, who placed orders with and communicated the news to his broker immediately after the official announcement was read at the TGS-called press conference, concede that they were in possession of material information. They contend, however, that their purchases were not proscribed purchases for the news had already been effectively disclosed. We disagree.

Crawford telephoned his orders to his Chicago broker about midnight on April 15 and again at 8:30 in the morning of the 16th, with instructions to buy at the opening of the Midwest Stock Exchange that morning. The trial court's finding that "he sought to, and did, 'beat the news,'" 258 F.Supp. at 287, is well documented by the record. The rumors of a major ore strike which had been circulated in Canada and, to a lesser extent, in New York, had been disclaimed by the TGS press release of April 12, which significantly promised the public an official detailed announcement when possibilities had ripened into actualities. The abbreviated announcement to the Canadian press at 9:40 A.M. on the 16th by the Ontario Minister of Mines and the report carried by The Northern Miner, parts of which had sporadically reached New York on the morning of the 16th through reports from Canadian affiliates to a few New York investment firms, are assuredly not the equivalent of the official 10–15 minute announcement which was not released to the American financial press until after 10:00 A.M. Crawford's orders had been placed before that. Before insiders may act upon material information, such information must have been effectively disclosed in a manner sufficient to insure its availability to the investing public. Particularly here, where a formal announcement to the entire financial news media had been promised in a prior official release known to the media, all insider activity must await dissemination of the promised official announcement.

Coates was absolved by the court below because his telephone order was placed shortly before 10:20 A.M. on April 16, which was after the announcement had been made even though the news could not be considered already a matter of public information. 258 F.Supp. at 288. This result seems to have been predicated upon a misinterpretation of dicta in *Cady, Roberts,* where the SEC instructed insiders to "keep out of the market until the established procedures for public release of the information are *carried out* instead of hastening to execute transactions in advance of, and in frustration of, the objectives of the release," 40 S.E.C. at 915 (emphasis supplied). The reading of a news release, which prompted Coates into action, is merely the first step in the process of dissemination required for compliance with the regulatory objective of providing all investors with an equal opportunity to make informed investment judgments. Assuming that the contents of the official release could instantaneously be acted upon,[18] at the minimum Coates should have waited until the news could reasonably have been expected to appear over the media of widest circulation, the Dow Jones broad tape, rather than hastening to insure an advantage to himself and his broker son-in-law.

\* \* \*

## II.  *The Corporate Defendant*

*Introductory*

At 3:00 P.M. on April 12, 1964, evidently believing it desirable to comment upon the rumors concerning the Timmins project, TGS issued the press release quoted in pertinent part in the text. \* \* \* The SEC argued below and maintains on this appeal that this release painted a misleading and deceptive picture of the drilling progress at the time of

---

**18.**  Although the only insider who acted after the news appeared over the Dow Jones broad tape is not an appellant and therefore we need not discuss the necessity of considering the advisability of a "reasonable waiting period" during which outsiders may absorb and evaluate disclosures, we note in passing that, where the news is of a sort which is not readily translatable into investment action, insiders may not take advantage of their advance opportunity to evaluate the information by acting immediately upon dissemination. In any event, the permissible timing of insider transactions after disclosures of various sorts is one of the many areas of expertise for appropriate exercise of the SEC's rule-making power, which we hope will be utilized in the future to provide some predictability of certainty for the business community.

its issuance, and hence violated Rule 10b–5(2). TGS relies on the holding of the court below that "The issuance of the release produced no unusual market action" and "In the absence of a showing that the purpose of the April 12 press release was to affect the market price of TGS stock to the advantage of TGS or its insiders, the issuance of the press release did not constitute a violation of Section 10(b) or Rule 10b–5 since it was not issued 'in connection with the purchase or sale of any security' "and, alternatively, "even if it had been established that the April 12 release was issued in connection with the purchase or sale of any security, the Commission has failed to demonstrate that it was false, misleading or deceptive." 258 F.Supp. at 294.

Before further discussing this matter it seems desirable to state exactly what the SEC claimed in its complaint and what it seeks. The specific SEC allegation in its complaint is that this April 12 press release " * * * was materially false and misleading and was known by certain of defendant Texas Gulf's officers and employees, including defendants Fogarty, Mollison, Holyk, Darke and Clayton, to be materially false and misleading."

The specific relief the SEC seeks is, pursuant to Section 21(e) of Securities Exchange Act of 1934, 15 U.S.C.A. § 78u(e), a permanent injunction restraining the issuance of any further materially false and misleading publicly distributed informative items.

B.   The "In Connection With * * * " Requirement.

In adjudicating upon the relationship of this phrase to the case before us it would appear that the court below used a standard that does not reflect the congressional purpose that prompted the passage of the Securities Exchange Act of 1934.

The dominant congressional purposes underlying the Securities Exchange Act of 1934 were to promote free and open public securities markets and to protect the investing public from suffering inequities in trading, including, specifically, inequities that follow from trading that has been stimulated by the publication of false or misleading corporate information releases. * * *

Therefore it seems clear from the legislative purpose Congress expressed in the Act, and the legislative history of Section 10(b) that Congress when it used the phrase "in connection with the purchase or sale of any security" intended only that the device employed, whatever it might be, be of a sort that would cause reasonable investors to rely thereon, and, in connection therewith, so relying, cause them to purchase or sell a corporation's securities. There is no indication that Congress intended that the corporations or persons responsible for the issuance of a misleading statement would not violate the section unless they engaged in related securities transactions or otherwise acted with wrongful motives; indeed, the obvious purposes of the Act to protect the investing public and to secure fair dealing in the securities markets would be seriously undermined by applying such a gloss onto the legislative language. Absent a securities transaction by an insider it is almost impossible to prove that a wrongful purpose motivated the issuance of the misleading statement. The mere fact that an insider did not engage in securities transactions does not negate the possibility of wrongful purpose; perhaps the market did not react to the misleading statement as much as was anticipated or perhaps the wrongful purpose was something other than the desire to buy at a low price or sell at a high price. Of even greater relevance to the Congressional purpose of investor protection is the fact that the investing public may be injured as much by one's misleading statement containing inaccuracies caused by negligence as by a misleading statement published intentionally to further a wrongful purpose. We do not believe that Congress intended that the proscriptions of the Act would not be violated unless the makers of a misleading statement also participated in pertinent securities transactions in connection therewith, or unless it could be shown that the issuance of the statement was motivated by a plan to benefit the corporation or themselves at the expense of a duped investing public.

\* \* \*

\* \* \* Accordingly, we hold that Rule 10b–5 is violated whenever assertions are made, as here, in a manner reasonably calculated to influence the investing public, e.g., by means of the financial media, if such assertions are false or misleading or are so incomplete as to mislead irrespective of whether the issuance of the release was motivated by corporate officials for ulterior purposes. It seems clear, however, that if corporate management demonstrates that it was diligent in ascertaining that the information it published was the whole truth and that such diligently obtained information was disseminated in good faith, Rule 10b–5 would not have been violated.

### C.   Did the Issuance of the April 12 Release Violate Rule 10b–5?

Turning first to the question of whether the release was misleading, i.e., whether it conveyed to the public a false impression of the drilling situation at the time of its issuance, we note initially that the trial court did not actually decide this question. Its conclusion that "the Commission has failed to demonstrate that it was false, misleading or deceptive," 258 F.Supp. at 294, seems to have derived from its views that "The defendants are to be judged *on the facts known to them* when the April 12 release was issued," 258 F.Supp. at 295 (emphasis supplied), that the draftsmen "exercised reasonable business judgment under the circumstances," 258 F.Supp. at 296, and that the release was not "misleading or deceptive *on the basis of the facts then known*," 258 F.Supp. at 296 (emphasis supplied) rather than from an appropriate primary inquiry into the meaning of the statement to the reasonable investor and its relationship to truth. While we certainly agree with the trial court that "in retrospect, the press release may appear gloomy or incomplete," 258 F.Supp. at 296, we cannot, from the present record, by applying the standard Congress intended, definitively conclude that it was deceptive or misleading to the reasonable investor, or that he would have been misled by it. Certain newspaper accounts of the release viewed the release as confirming the existence of preliminary favorable developments, and this optimistic view was held by some brokers, so it could be that the reasonable investor would have read between the lines of what appears to us to be an inconclusive and negative statement and would have envisioned the actual situation at the Kidd segment on April 12. On the other hand, in view of the decline of the market price of TGS stock from a high of 32 on the morning of April 13 when the release was disseminated to 29-3/8 by the close of trading on April 15, and the reaction to the release by other brokers, it is far from certain that the release was generally interpreted as a highly encouraging report or even encouraging at all. Accordingly, we remand this issue to the district court that took testimony and heard and saw the witnesses for a determination of the character of the release in the light of the facts existing at the time of the release, by applying the standard of whether the reasonable investor, in the exercise of due care, would have been misled by it.

In the event that it is found that the statement was misleading to the reasonable investor it will then become necessary to determine whether its issuance resulted from a lack of due diligence. The only remedy the Commission seeks against the corporation is an injunction, and therefore we do not find it necessary to decide whether just a lack of due diligence on the part of TGS, absent a showing of bad faith, would subject the corporation to any liability for damages. We have recently stated in a case involving a private suit under Rule 10b-5 in which damages and an injunction were sought, " 'It is not necessary in a suit for equitable or prophylactic relief to establish all the elements required in a suit for monetary damages.' " *Mutual Shares Corp. v. Genesco, Inc.*, 384 F.2d 540, 547, quoting from *SEC v. Capital Gains Research Bureau, Inc.*, 375 U.S. 180, 193, 84 S.Ct. 275, 11 L.Ed.2d 237 (1963).

We hold only that, in an action for injunctive relief, the district court has the discretionary power under Rule 10b-5 and Section 10(b) to issue an injunction, if the misleading statement resulted from a lack of due diligence on the part of TGS. The trial court did not find it necessary to decide whether TGS exercised such diligence and has not yet attempted to resolve this issue. While the trial court concluded that TGS had exercised "reasonable *business* judgment under the circumstances," 258 F.Supp. at 296 (emphasis supplied) it applied an incorrect *legal* standard in appraising whether TGS should have issued its April 12 release on the basis of the facts known to its draftsmen at the time of its preparation, 258 F.Supp. at 295, and in assuming that disclosure of the full underlying facts of the Timmins situation was not a viable alternative to the vague generalities which were asserted. 258 F.Supp. at 296.

It is not altogether certain from the present record that the draftsmen could, as the SEC suggests, have readily obtained current reports of the drilling progress over the weekend of April 10-12, but they certainly should have obtained them if at all possible for them to do so. However, even if it were not possible to evaluate and transmit current data in time to prepare the release on April 12, it would seem that TGS could have delayed the preparation a bit until an accurate report of a rapidly changing situation was possible. See 258 F.Supp. at 296. At the very least, if TGS felt compelled to respond to the spreading rumors of a spectacular discovery, it would have been more accurate to have stated that the situation was in flux and that the release was prepared as of April 10 information rather than purporting to report the progress "to date." Moreover, it would have obviously been better to have specifically described the known drilling progress as of April 10 by stating the basic facts. Such an explicit disclosure would have permitted the investing public to evaluate the "prospect" of a mine at Timmins without having to read between the lines to understand that preliminary indications were favorable—in itself an understatement.

The choice of an ambiguous general statement rather than a summary of the specific facts cannot reasonably be justified by any claimed urgency. The avoidance of liability for misrepresentation in the event that the Timmins project failed, a highly unlikely event as of April 12 or April 13, did not forbid the accurate and truthful divulgence of detailed results which need not, of course, have been accompanied by conclusory assertions of success. Nor is it any justification that such an explicit disclosure of the truth might have "encouraged the rumor mill which they were seeking to allay." 258 F.Supp. at 296.

We conclude, then, that, having established that the release was issued in a manner reasonably calculated to affect the market price of TGS stock and to influence the investing public, we must remand to the district court to decide whether the release was misleading to the reasonable investor and if found to be misleading, whether the court in its discretion should issue the injunction the SEC seeks.

\* \* \*

CONCLUSION

In summary, therefore, we affirm the finding of the court below that appellants Richard H. Clayton and David M. Crawford have violated 15 U.S.C.A. § 78j(b) and Rule 10b–5; we reverse the judgment order entered below dismissing the complaint against appellees Charles F. Fogarty, Richard H. Clayton, Richard D. Mollison, Walter Holyk, Kenneth H. Darke, Earl L. Huntington, and Francis G. Coates, as we find that they have violated 15 U.S.C.A. § 78j(b) and Rule 10b–5. As to these eight individuals we remand so that in accordance with the agreement between the parties the Commission may notice a hearing before the court below to determine the remedies to be applied against them. We reverse the judgment order dismissing the complaint against Claude O. Stephens, Charles F. Fogarty, and Harold B. Kline as recipients of stock options, direct the district court to consider in its discretion whether to issue injunction orders against Stephens and Fogarty, and direct that an order issue rescinding the option granted Kline and that such further remedy be applied against him as may be proper by way of an order of restitution \* \* \*.

* * * [W]e reverse the judgment dismissing the complaint against Texas Gulf Sulphur Company, remand the cause as to it for further determination below, in light of the approach explicated by us in the foregoing opinion, as to whether, in the exercise of its discretion the injunction against it which the Commission seeks should be ordered.

---

On remand, the district court ordered those TGS insiders who had, prior to April 16, purchased TGS stock or recommended its purchase to others to disgorge their profits and those of their tippees to the corporation. The profits were held to be "the difference between the mean average price of TGS common stock on the New York Stock Exchange on April 17, 1964, which has been stipulated by the parties to be 40 3/8, and the purchase price of their shares." *SEC v. Texas Gulf Sulphur Co.*, 312 F.Supp. 77 (S.D.N.Y.1970), *aff'd* 446 F.2d 1301 (2d Cir.1971). The decree made no provision for attempting to contact the defrauded sellers from whom the defendants or their tippees had bought. The damages paid by the defendants were, however, to be held in an escrow account, subject to court order, for five years after which any amount that had not been paid out to private claimants would become the property of the corporation. The settlement of some of the private actions arising from the insider trading aspects of the case is set forth in *Cannon v. Texas Gulf Sulphur Co.*, 55 F.R.D. 308 (S.D.N.Y.1972).

## 3. REGULATION OF TRADING ON NON–PUBLIC INFORMATION

### CHIARELLA v. UNITED STATES

445 U.S. 222, 100 S.Ct. 1108, 63 L.Ed.2d 348 (1980).

Mr. Justice Powell delivered the opinion of the Court.

The question in this case is whether a person who learns from the confidential documents of one corporation that it is planning an attempt to secure control of a second corporation violates § 10(b) of the Securities Exchange Act of 1934 if he fails to disclose the impending takeover before trading in the target company's securities.

I

Petitioner is a printer by trade. In 1975 and 1976, he worked as a "markup man" in the New York composing room of Pandick Press, a financial printer. Among documents that petitioner handled were five announcements of corporate takeover bids. When these documents were delivered to the printer, the identities of the acquiring and target corporations were concealed by blank spaces or false names. The true names were sent to the printer on the night of the final printing.

The petitioner, however, was able to deduce the names of the target companies before the final printing from other information contained in the documents. Without disclosing his knowledge, petitioner purchased stock in the target companies and sold the shares immediately after the takeover attempts were made public. By this method, petitioner realized a gain of slightly more than $30,000 in the course of 14 months. Subsequently, the Securities and Exchange Commission (Commission or SEC) began an investigation of his trading activities. In May 1977, petitioner entered into a consent decree with the Commission in which he agreed to return his profits to the sellers of the shares. On the same day, he was discharged by Pandick Press.

In January 1978, petitioner was indicted on 17 counts of violating § 10(b) of the Securities Exchange Act of 1934 (1934 Act) and SEC Rule 10b–5. After petitioner unsuccessfully moved to dismiss the indictment, he was brought to trial and convicted on all counts.

The Court of Appeals for the Second Circuit affirmed petitioner's conviction. 588 F.2d 1358 (1978). We granted certiorari, 441 U.S. 942, 99 S.Ct. 2158, 60 L.Ed.2d 1043 (1979), and we now reverse.

II

* * *

This case concerns the legal effect of the petitioner's silence. The District Court's charge permitted the jury to convict the petitioner if it found that he willfully failed to inform sellers of target company securities that he knew of a forthcoming takeover bid that would make their shares more valuable. In order to decide whether silence in such circumstances violates § 10(b), it is necessary to review the language and legislative history of that statute as well as its interpretation by the Commission and the federal courts.

Although the starting point of our inquiry is the language of the statute, *Ernst & Ernst v. Hochfelder*, 425 U.S. 185, 197, 96 S.Ct. 1375, 1382, 47 L.Ed.2d 668 (1976), § 10(b) does not state whether silence may constitute a manipulative or deceptive device. Section 10(b) was designed as a catchall clause to prevent fraudulent practices. *Id.*, at 202, 206. But neither the legislative history nor the statute itself affords specific guidance for the resolution of this case. When Rule 10b–5 was promulgated in 1942, the SEC did not discuss the possibility that failure to provide information might run afoul of § 10(b).

The SEC took an important step in the development of § 10(b) when it held that a broker-dealer and his firm violated that section by selling securities on the basis of undisclosed information obtained from a director of the issuer corporation who was also a registered representative of the brokerage firm. In *Cady, Roberts & Co.*, 40 S.E.C. 907 (1961), the Commission decided that a corporate insider must abstain from trading in the shares of his corporation unless he has first disclosed all material inside information known to him. The obligation to disclose or abstain derives from

> [a]n affirmative duty to disclose material information[,] [which] has been traditionally imposed on corporate "insiders," particular officers, directors, or controlling stockholders. We, and the courts have

consistently held that insiders must disclose material facts which are known to them by virtue of their position but which are not known to persons with whom they deal and which, if known, would affect their investment judgment. *Id.,* at 911.

The Commission emphasized that the duty arose from (i) The existence of a relationship affording access to inside information intended to be available only for a corporate purpose, and (ii) the unfairness of allowing a corporate insider to take advantage of that information by trading without disclosure. *Id.,* at 912, and n. 15.

That the relationship between a corporate insider and the stockholders of his corporation gives rise to a disclosure obligation is not a novel twist of the law. At common law, misrepresentation made for the purpose of inducing reliance upon the false statement is fraudulent. But one who fails to disclose material information prior to the consummation of a transaction commits fraud only when he is under a duty to do so. And the duty to disclose arises when one party has information "that the other [party] is entitled to know because of a fiduciary or similar relation of trust and confidence between them." In its *Cady, Roberts* decision, the Commission recognized a relationship of trust and confidence between the shareholders of a corporation and those insiders who have obtained confidential information by reason of their position with that corporation. This relationship gives rise to a duty to disclose because of the "necessity of preventing a corporate insider from [taking] * * * unfair advantage of the uninformed minority stockholders." *Speed v. Transamerica Corp.,* 99 F.Supp. 808, 829 (D.Del.1951).

The Federal courts have found violations of § 10(b) where corporate insiders used undisclosed information for their own benefit. *E.g., SEC v. Texas Gulf Sulphur Co.,* 401 F.2d 833 (C.A.2 1968), *cert. denied,* 404 U.S. 1005, 92 S.Ct. 561, 30 L.Ed.2d 558 (1971). The cases also have emphasized, in accordance with the common-law rule, that "[t]he party charged with failing to disclose market information must be under a duty to disclose it." *Frigitemp Corp. v. Financial Dynamics Fund, Inc.,* 524 F.2d 275, 282 (C.A.2 1975). Accordingly, a purchaser of stock who has no duty to a prospective seller because he is neither an insider nor a fiduciary has been held to have no obligation to reveal material facts.

This Court followed the same approach in *Affiliated Ute Citizens v. United States,* 406 U.S. 128, 92 S.Ct. 1456, 31 L.Ed.2d 741 (1972). A group of American Indians formed a corporation to manage joint assets derived from tribal holdings. The corporation issued stock to its Indian shareholders and designated a local bank as its transfer agent. Because of the speculative nature of the corporate assets and the difficulty of ascertaining the true value of a share, the corporation requested the bank to stress to its stockholders the importance of retaining the stock. *Id.,* at 146, 92 S.Ct., at 1468. Two of the bank's assistant managers aided the shareholders in disposing of stock which the managers knew was traded in two separate markets—a primary market of Indians selling to non-Indians through the bank and a resale market consisting entirely of non-Indians. Indian sellers charged that the assistant managers had violated § 10(b) and Rule 10b–5 by failing to inform them of the higher prices prevailing in the resale market. The Court recognized that no duty of disclosure would exist if the bank merely had acted as a transfer agent. But the bank also had assumed a duty to act on behalf of the shareholders, and the Indian sellers had relied upon its personnel when they sold their stock. *Id.,* at 152, 92 S.Ct., at 1471. Because these officers of the bank were charged with a responsibility to the shareholders, they could not act as market makers inducing the Indians to sell their stock without disclosing the existence of the more favorable non-Indian market. *Id.,* at 152–153, 92 S.Ct., at 1471–1472.

Thus, administrative and judicial interpretations have established that silence in connection with the purchase or sale of securities may operate as a fraud actionable under § 10(b) despite the absence of statutory language or legislative history specifically addressing the legality of nondisclosure. But such liability is premised upon a duty to disclose arising from a relationship of trust and confidence between parties to a transaction. Application of a duty to disclose prior to trading guarantees that corporate insiders, who have an obligation to place the shareholder's welfare before their own, will not benefit personally through fraudulent use of material nonpublic information.[12]

### III

In this case, the petitioner was convicted of violating § 10(b) although he was not a corporate insider and he received no confidential information from the target company. Moreover, the "market information" upon which he relied did not concern the earning power or operations of the target company, but only the plans of the acquiring company. Petitioner's use of that information was not a fraud under § 10(b) unless he was subject to an affirmative duty to disclose it before trading. In this case, the jury instructions failed to specify any such duty. In effect, the trial court instructed the jury that petitioner owed a duty to everyone; to all sellers, indeed, to the market as a whole. The jury simply was told to decide whether petitioner used material, nonpublic information at a time when "he knew other people trading in the securities market did not have access to the same information." Record, at 677.

The Court of Appeals affirmed the conviction by holding that "*[a]nyone*—corporate insider or not—who regularly receives material nonpublic information may not use that information to trade in securities without incurring an affirmative duty to disclose." 588 F.2d 1358,

---

**12.** "Tippees" of corporate insiders have been held liable under § 10(b) because they have a duty not to profit from the use of inside information that they know is confidential and know or should know came from a corporate insider, *Shapiro v. Merrill Lynch, Pierce, Fenner & Smith,* 495 F.2d 228, 237–238 (C.A.2 1974). The tippee's obligation has been viewed as arising from his role as a participant after the fact in the insider's breach of a fiduciary duty. Subcommittees of American Bar Association Section of Corporation, Banking, and Business Law, Comment Letter on Material, Non–Public Information (Oct. 15, 1973) reprinted in BNA, Securities Regulation & Law Report No. 233, at D–1, D–2 (Jan. 2, 1974).

1365 (C.A.2 1978) (emphasis in original). Although the court said that its test would include only persons who regularly receive material nonpublic information, *id.,* at 1366, its rationale for that limitation is unrelated to the existence of a duty to disclose.[14] The Court of Appeals, like the trial court, failed to identify a relationship between petitioner and the sellers that could give rise to a duty. Its decision thus rested solely upon its belief that the federal securities laws have "created a system providing equal access to information necessary for reasoned and intelligent investment decisions." 588 F.2d, at 1362. The use by anyone of material information not generally available is fraudulent, this theory suggests, because such information gives certain buyers or sellers an unfair advantage over less informed buyers and sellers.

This reasoning suffers from two defects. First not every instance of financial unfairness constitutes fraudulent activity under § 10(b). *See Santa Fe Industries Inc. v. Green,* 430 U.S. 462, 474–477, 97 S.Ct. 1292, 1301–1303, 51 L.Ed.2d 480 (1977). Second, the element required to make silence fraudulent—a duty to disclose—is absent in this case. No duty could arise from petitioner's relationship with the sellers of the target company's securities, for petitioner had no prior dealings with them. He was not their agent, he was not a fiduciary, he was not a person in whom the sellers had placed their trust and confidence. He was, in fact, a complete stranger who dealt with the sellers only through impersonal market transactions.

We cannot affirm petitioner's conviction without recognizing a general duty between all participants in market transactions to forgo actions based on material, nonpublic information. Formulation of such a broad duty, which departs radically from the established doctrine that duty arises from a specific relationship between two parties, should not be undertaken absent some explicit evidence of congressional intent.

As we have seen, no such evidence emerges from the language or legislative history of § 10(b). Moreover, neither the Congress nor the Commission ever has adopted a parity-of-information rule. Instead the

---

**14.** The Court of Appeals said that its "regular access to market information" test would create a workable rule embracing "those who occupy * * * strategic places in the market mechanism." *United States v. Chiarella,* 588 F.2d 1358, 1365 (C.A.2 1978). These considerations are insufficient to support a duty to disclose. A duty arises from the relationship between parties, see n. 9, *supra,* and accompanying text, and not merely from one's ability to acquire information because of his position in the market.

The Court of Appeals also suggested that the acquiring corporation itself would not be a "market insider" because a tender offeror creates, rather than receives, information and takes a substantial economic risk that its offer will be unsuccessful. *Id.,* at 1366–1367. Again, the Court of Appeals departed from the analysis appropriate to recognition of a duty. The Court of Appeals for the Second Circuit previously held, in a manner consistent with our analysis here, that a tender offeror does not violate § 10(b) when it makes preannouncement purchases precisely because there is no relationship between the offeror and the seller. "We know of no rule of law * * * that a purchaser of stock, who was not an 'insider' and had no fiduciary relation to a prospective seller, had any obligation to reveal circumstances that might raise a seller's demands and thus abort the sale." *General Time Corp. v. Talley Industries,* 403 F.2d 159, 164 (C.A.2 1968), *cert. denied,* 393 U.S. 1026, 89 S.Ct. 631, 21 L.Ed.2d 570 (1969).

problems caused by misuse of market information have been addressed by detailed and sophisticated regulation that recognizes when use of market information may not harm operation of the securities markets. For example, the Williams Act limits but does not completely prohibit a tender offeror's purchases of target corporation stock before public announcement of the offer. Congress' careful action in this and other areas contrasts, and is in some tension, with the broad rule of liability we are asked to adopt in this case.

Indeed, the theory upon which the petitioner was convicted is at odds with the Commission's view of § 10(b) as applied to activity that has the same effect on sellers as the petitioner's purchases. "Warehousing" takes place when a corporation gives advance notice of its intention to launch a tender offer to institutional investors who then are able to purchase stock in the target company before the tender offer is made public and the price of shares rises. In this case, as in warehousing, a buyer of securities purchases stock in a target corporation on the basis of market information which is unknown to the seller. In both of these situations, the seller's behavior presumably would be altered if he had the nonpublic information. Significantly, however, the Commission has acted to bar warehousing under its authority to regulate tender offers after recognizing that action under § 10(b) would rest on a "somewhat different theory" than that previously used to regulate insider trading as fraudulent activity.

We see no basis for applying such a new and different theory of liability in this case. As we have emphasized before, the 1934 Act cannot be read " 'more broadly than its language and the statutory scheme reasonably permit.' " *Touche Ross & Co. v. Redington*, 442 U.S. 560, 578, 99 S.Ct. 2479, 2490, 61 L.Ed.2d 82 (June 18, 1979), quoting *SEC v. Sloan*, 436 U.S. 103, 116, 98 S.Ct. 1702, 1711, 56 L.Ed.2d 148 (1978). Section 10(b) is aptly described as a catch-all provision, but what it catches must be fraud. When an allegation of fraud is based upon nondisclosure, there can be no fraud absent a duty to speak. We hold that a duty to disclose under § 10(b) does not arise from the mere possession of nonpublic market information. The contrary result is without support in the legislative history of § 10(b) and would be inconsistent with the careful plan that Congress has enacted for regulation of the securities markets. *Cf. Santa Fe Industries Inc. v. Green*, 430 U.S., at 479, 97 S.Ct., at 1304.

\* \* \*

## IV

In its brief to this Court, the United States offers an alternative theory to support petitioner's conviction. It argues that petitioner breached a duty to the acquiring corporation when he acted upon information that he obtained by virtue of his position as an employee of a printer employed by the corporation. The breach of this duty is said to support a conviction under § 10(b) for fraud perpetrated upon both the acquiring corporation and the sellers.

We need not decide whether this theory has merit for it was not submitted to the jury. * * *

The jury instructions demonstrate that petitioner was convicted merely because of his failure to disclose material, nonpublic information to sellers from whom he bought the stock of target corporations. The jury was not instructed on the nature or elements of a duty owed by petitioner to anyone other than the sellers. Because we cannot affirm a criminal conviction on the basis of a theory not presented to the jury, Rewis v. United States, 401 U.S. 808, 814 (1971), see Dunn v. United States, 442 U.S. 100, 106 (1979), we will not speculate upon whether such a duty exists, whether it has been breached, or whether such a breach constitutes a violation of § 10(b).

The judgment of the Court of Appeals is reversed.

MR. CHIEF JUSTICE BURGER, dissenting.

I believe that the jury instructions in this case properly charged a violation of § 10(b) and Rule 10b-5, and I would affirm the conviction.

I

As a general rule, neither party to an arm's-length business transaction has an obligation to disclose information to the other unless the parties stand in some confidential or fiduciary relation. See W. Prosser, Law of Torts § 106 (2d ed. 1955). This rule permits a businessman to capitalize on his experience and skill in securing and evaluating relevant information; it provides incentive for hard work, careful analysis, and astute forecasting. But the policies that underlie the rule also should limit its scope. In particular, the rule should give way when an informational advantage is obtained, not by superior experience, foresight, or industry, but by some unlawful means. * * * I would read § 10(b) and Rule 10b-5 to encompass and build on this principle: to mean that a person who has misappropriated nonpublic information has an absolute duty to disclose that information or to refrain from trading.

The language of § 10(b) and of Rule 10b-5 plainly support such a reading. By their terms, these provisions reach *any* person engaged in *any* fraudulent scheme. This broad language negates the suggestion that congressional concern was limited to trading by "corporate insiders" or to deceptive practices related to "corporate information." Just as surely Congress cannot have intended one standard of fair dealing for "white collar" insiders and another for the "blue collar" level. The very language of § 10(b) and Rule 10b-5 "by repeated use of the word 'any' [was] obviously meant to be inclusive." *Affiliated Ute Citizens v. United States*, 406 U.S. 128, 151, 92 S.Ct. 1456, 1471, 31 L.Ed.2d 741 (1972).

The history of the statute and of the Rule also supports this reading. The antifraud provisions were designed in large measure "to assure that dealing in securities is fair and without undue preferences or advantages among investors." H.R.Conf.Rep. No. 94-229, p. 91 (1975). These provisions prohibit "those manipulative and deceptive practices which have been demonstrated to fulfill no useful function." S.Rep. No. 792, 73d

Cong., 2d Sess., 6 (1934). An investor who purchases securities on the basis of misappropriated nonpublic information possesses just such an "undue" trading advantage; his conduct quite clearly serves no useful function except his own enrichment at the expense of others.

This interpretation of § 10(b) and Rule 10b–5 is in no sense novel. It follows naturally from legal principles enunciated by the Securities and Exchange Commission in its seminal *Cady, Roberts* decision. * * *

Finally, it bears emphasis that this reading of § 10b and Rule 10b–5 would not threaten legitimate business practices. So read, the antifraud provisions would not impose a duty on a tender offeror to disclose its acquisition plans during the period in which it "tests the water" prior to purchasing a full 5% of the target company's stock. * * * Likewise, market specialists would not be subject to a disclose-or-refrain requirement in the performance of their everyday market functions. In each of these instances, trading is accomplished on the basis of material, nonpublic information, but the information has not been unlawfully converted for personal gain.

## II

The Court's opinion, as I read it, leaves open the question whether § 10(b) and Rule 10b–5 prohibit trading on misappropriated nonpublic information. Instead, the Court apparently concludes that this theory of the case was not submitted to the jury. In the Court's view, the instructions given the jury were premised on the erroneous notion that the mere failure to disclose nonpublic information, however acquired, is a deceptive practice. And because of this premise, the jury was not instructed that the means by which Chiarella acquired his informational advantage—by violating a duty owed to the acquiring companies—was an element of the offense. See *ante*, at 1118.

The Court's reading of the District Court's charge is unduly restrictive. Fairly read as a whole and in the context of the trial, the instructions required the jury to find that Chiarella obtained his trading advantage by misappropriating the property of his employer's customers. * * *

[T]he evidence shows beyond all doubt that Chiarella, working literally in the shadows of the warning signs in the printshop, misappropriated—stole to put it bluntly—valuable nonpublic information entrusted to him in the utmost confidence. He then exploited his ill-gotten informational advantage by purchasing securities in the market. In my view, such conduct plainly violates § 10(b) and Rule 10b–5. Accordingly, I would affirm the judgment of the Court of Appeals.

### Note: A Guide to Tipping (or When 15% Is Not Enough)

*Texas Gulf Sulphur* and *Chiarella* made it clear that section 10(b) and Rule 10b–5 make it unlawful for a director, senior executive or other employee of a public corporation to use material nonpublic information to purchase or sell that corporation's stock. They did not make it clear whether the same prohibition applies to a person who has obtained material nonpublic information but who is not an insider of the corporation whose stock she is trading. The following outline is designed to help you understand the some of the permutations of the situations in which such trading occurs.

A.   Terminology

    1.   Tipper. A tipper is a person who discloses material nonpublic information.

    2.   Tippee. A tippee is a person who receives material nonpublic information from a tipper. If the tippee subsequently discloses the information, he becomes a tipper as well as a tippee and the person to whom he discloses becomes a:

    3.   Sub-tippee.

B.   Categories of People Involved

    1.   The tipper is an insider or employee of the corporation.

    2.   The tipper is not an employee but has a confidential relationship with the corporation.

    3.   The tippee is a complete outsider.

    4.   The tippee has an intermediate position arising from the nature of her profession and its relationship to the corporation, i.e., securities analyst.

C.   Situations Covered

    1.   The tipper tips but does not trade; the tippee trades.

    2.   The tipper trades and tips; the tippee trades.

    3.   Neither the tipper nor the tippee trade; the tippee tips; the sub-tippee trades.

    4.   The chain in situations 1–3 is extended to more remote sub-tippees with the same conduct.

D.   Possible Theories of Tipper and/or Tippee Liability

    1.   Parity of Information

    2.   Equal Access to Information

    3.   Fairness

    4.   Breach of Fiduciary Duty to Disclose or Abstain

    5.   Misappropriation

As you read the following materials, keep in mind that the market's ability to price securities accurately depends on market participants' securing access to new information on a timely basis. The courts have struggled with the problem of how to permit such access without creating unfair disparities in the information available to market participants.

## DIRKS v. SECURITIES AND EXCHANGE COMMISSION

463 U.S. 646, 103 S.Ct. 3255, 77 L.Ed.2d 911 (1983).

JUSTICE POWELL delivered the opinion of the Court.

Petitioner Raymond Dirks received material nonpublic information from "insiders" of a corporation with which he had no connection. He disclosed this information to investors who relied on it in trading in the shares of the corporation. The question is whether Dirks violated the antifraud provisions of the federal securities laws by this disclosure.

I

In 1973, Dirks was an officer of a New York broker-dealer firm who specialized in providing investment analysis of insurance company securities to institutional investors. On March 6, Dirks received information from Ronald Secrist, a former officer of Equity Funding of America. Secrist alleged that the assets of Equity Funding, a diversified corporation primarily engaged in selling life insurance and mutual funds, were vastly overstated as the result of fraudulent corporate practices. Secrist also stated that various regulatory agencies had failed to act on similar charges made by Equity Funding employees. He urged Dirks to verify the fraud and disclose it publicly.

Dirks decided to investigate the allegations. He visited Equity Funding's headquarters in Los Angeles and interviewed several officers and employees of the corporation. The senior management denied any wrongdoing, but certain corporation employees corroborated the charges of fraud. Neither Dirks nor his firm owned or traded any Equity Funding stock, but throughout his investigation he openly discussed the information he had obtained with a number of clients and investors. Some of these persons sold their holdings of Equity Funding securities, including five investment advisers who liquidated holdings of more than $16 million.[2]

While Dirks was in Los Angeles, he was in touch regularly with William Blundell, the *Wall Street Journal*'s Los Angeles bureau chief. Dirks urged Blundell to write a story on the fraud allegations. Blundell did not believe, however, that such a massive fraud could go undetected and declined to write the story. He feared that publishing such damaging hearsay might be libelous.

During the two-week period in which Dirks pursued his investigation and spread word of Secrist's charges, the price of Equity Funding

---

**2.** Dirks received from his firm a salary plus a commission for securities transactions above a certain amount that his clients directed through his firm. See 21 S.E.C. Docket, at 1402, n. 3. But "[i]t is not clear how many of those with whom Dirks spoke promised to direct some brokerage business through [Dirks' firm] to compensate Dirks, or how many actually did so." 220 U.S.App.D.C., at 316, 681 F.2d, at 831. The Boston Company Institutional Investors, Inc., promised Dirks about $25,000 in commissions, but it is unclear whether Boston actually generated any brokerage business for his firm. * * *

stock fell from $26 per share to less than $15 per share. This led the New York Stock Exchange to halt trading on March 27. Shortly thereafter California insurance authorities impounded Equity Funding's records and uncovered evidence of the fraud. Only then did the Securities and Exchange Commission (SEC) file a complaint against Equity Funding[3] and only then, on April 2, did the *Wall Street Journal* publish a front-page story based largely on information assembled by Dirks. Equity Funding immediately went into receivership.

The SEC began an investigation into Dirks' role in the exposure of the fraud. After a hearing by an administrative law judge, the SEC found that Dirks had aided and abetted violations of § 17(a) of the Securities Act of 1933, 15 U.S.C. § 77q(a), § 10(b) of the Securities Exchange Act of 1934, 15 U.S.C. § 78j(b), and SEC Rule 10b–5, 17 CFR § 240.10b–5 (1982), by repeating the allegations of fraud to members of the investment community who later sold their Equity Funding stock. The SEC concluded: "Where 'tippees'—regardless of their motivation or occupation—come into possession of material 'information that they know is confidential and know or should know came from a corporate insider,' they must either publicly disclose that information or refrain from trading." 21 S.E.C. Docket 1401, 1407 (1981) (footnote omitted) (quoting *Chiarella v. United States*, 445 U.S. 222, 230 n. 12, 100 S.Ct. 1108, 1116 n. 12, 63 L.Ed.2d 348 (1980)). Recognizing, however, that Dirks "played an important role in bringing [Equity Funding's] massive fraud to light," 21 S.E.C. Docket, at 1412, the SEC only censured him.

Dirks sought review in the Court of Appeals for the District of Columbia Circuit. The court entered judgment against Dirks "for the reasons stated by the Commission in its opinion." App. to Pet. for Cert. C–2. Judge Wright, a member of the panel, subsequently issued an opinion. Judge Robb concurred in the result and Judge Tamm dissented; neither filed a separate opinion. Judge Wright believed that "the obligations of corporate fiduciaries pass to all those to whom they disclose their information before it has been disseminated to the public at large." 220 U.S.App.D.C. 309, 324, 681 F.2d 824, 839 (1982). Alternatively, Judge Wright concluded that, as an employee of a broker-dealer, Dirks had violated "obligations to the SEC and to the public completely independent of any obligations he acquired" as a result of receiving the information. *Id.*, at 325, 681 F.2d, at 840.

In view of the importance to the SEC and to the securities industry of the question presented by this case, we granted a writ of certiorari. 459 U.S. 1014, 103 S.Ct. 371, 74 L.Ed.2d 506 (1982). We now reverse.

## II

In the seminal case of *In re Cady, Roberts & Co.*, 40 S.E.C. 907 (1961), the SEC recognized that the common law in some jurisdictions

---

**3.** As early as 1971, the SEC had received allegations of fraudulent accounting practices at Equity Funding. Moreover, on March 9, 1973, an official of the California Insurance Department informed the SEC's regional office in Los Angeles of Secrist's charges of fraud. Dirks himself voluntarily presented his information at the SEC's regional office beginning on March 27.

imposes on "corporate 'insiders,' particularly officers, directors, or controlling stockholders" an "affirmative duty of disclosure * * * when dealing in securities." *Id.,* at 911, and n. 13. The SEC found that not only did breach of this common-law duty also establish the elements of a Rule 10b–5 violation, but that individuals other than corporate insiders could be obligated either to disclose material nonpublic information before trading or to abstain from trading altogether. *Id.,* at 912. In *Chiarella,* we accepted the two elements set out in *Cady, Roberts* for establishing a Rule 10b–5 violation: "(i) the existence of a relationship affording access to inside information intended to be available only for a corporate purpose, and (ii) the unfairness of allowing a corporate insider to take advantage of that information by trading without disclosure." 445 U.S., at 227, 100 S.Ct., at 1114. In examining whether Chiarella had an obligation to disclose or abstain, the Court found that there is no general duty to disclose before trading on material nonpublic information, and held that "a duty to disclose under § 10(b) does not arise from the mere possession of nonpublic market information." *Id.,* at 235, 100 S.Ct., at 1118. Such a duty arises rather from the existence of a fiduciary relationship. *See id.,* at 227–235, 100 S.Ct. at 1114–1118.

Not "all breaches of fiduciary duty in connection with a securities transaction," however, come within the ambit of Rule 10b–5. *Santa Fe Industries, Inc. v. Green,* 430 U.S. 462, 472, 97 S.Ct. 1292, 1300, 51 L.Ed.2d 480 (1977). There must also be "manipulation or deception." *Id.,* at 473, 97 S.Ct., at 1300. In an inside-trading case this fraud derives from the "inherent unfairness involved where one takes advantage" of "information intended to be available only for a corporate purpose and not for the personal benefit of anyone." *In re Merrill Lynch, Pierce, Fenner & Smith, Inc.,* 43 S.E.C. 933, 936 (1968). Thus, an insider will be liable under Rule 10b–5 for inside trading only where he fails to disclose material nonpublic information before trading on it and thus makes "secret profits." *Cady, Roberts,* 40 S.E.C., at 916, n. 31.

### III

We were explicit in *Chiarella* in saying that there can be no duty to disclose where the person who has traded on inside information "was not [the corporation's] agent, * * * was not a fiduciary, [or] was not a person in whom the sellers [of the securities] had placed their trust and confidence." 445 U.S., at 232, 100 S.Ct., at 1116. Not to require such a fiduciary relationship, we recognized, would "depar[t] radically from the established doctrine that duty arises from a specific relationship between two parties" and would amount to "recognizing a general duty between all participants in market transactions to forego actions based on material, nonpublic information." *Id.,* at 232, 233, 100 S.Ct., at 1116, 1117. This requirement of a specific relationship between the shareholders and the individual trading on inside information has created analytical difficulties for the SEC and courts in policing tippees who trade on inside information. Unlike insiders who have independent fiduciary duties to both the corporation and its shareholders, the typical tippee has no such relationships.[14] In view of this absence, it has been unclear how a tippee acquires the *Cady, Roberts* duty to refrain from trading on inside information.

## A

The SEC's position, as stated in its opinion in this case, is that a tippee "inherits" the *Cady, Roberts* obligation to shareholders whenever he receives inside information from an insider:

> "In tipping potential traders, Dirks breached a duty which he had assumed as a result of knowingly receiving confidential information from [Equity Funding] insiders. Tippees such as Dirks who received non-public material information from insiders become 'subject to the same duty as [the] insiders.' *Shapiro v. Merrill Lynch, Pierce, Fenner & Smith, Inc.* [495 F.2d 228, 237 (C.A.2 1974) (quoting *Ross v. Licht*, 263 F.Supp. 395, 410 (S.D.N.Y.1967)) ]. Such a tippee breaches the fiduciary duty which he assumes from the insider when the tippee knowingly transmits the information to someone who will probably trade on the basis thereof. * * * Presumably, Dirks' informants were entitled to disclose the [Equity Funding] fraud in order to bring it to light and its perpetrators to justice. However, Dirks— standing in their shoes—committed a breach of the fiduciary duty which he had assumed in dealing with them, when he passed the information on to traders." 21 S.E.C. Docket, at 1410, n. 42.

This view differs little from the view that we rejected as inconsistent with congressional intent in *Chiarella*. In that case, the Court of Appeals agreed with the SEC and affirmed Chiarella's conviction, holding that " '[a]nyone—corporate insider or not—who regularly receives material nonpublic information may not use that information to trade in securities without incurring an affirmative duty to disclose.' " *United States v. Chiarella*, 588 F.2d 1358, 1365 (C.A.2 1978) (emphasis in original). Here, the SEC maintains that anyone who knowingly receives nonpublic material information from an insider has a fiduciary duty to disclose before trading.

---

**14.** Under certain circumstances, such as where corporate information is revealed legitimately to an underwriter, accountant, lawyer, or consultant working for the corporation, these outsiders may become fiduciaries of the shareholders. The basis for recognizing this fiduciary duty is not simply that such persons acquired nonpublic corporate information, but rather that they have entered into a special confidential relationship in the conduct of the business of the enterprise and are given access to information solely for corporate purposes. *See SEC v. Monarch Fund*, 608 F.2d 938, 942 (C.A.2 1979); *In re Investors Management Co.*, 44 S.E.C. 633, 645 (1971); *In re Van Alystne, Noel & Co.*, 43 S.E.C. 1080, 1084– 1085 (1969); *In re Merrill Lynch, Pierce, Fenner & Smith, Inc.*, 43 S.E.C. 933, 937 (1968); *Cady, Roberts*, 40 S.E.C., at 912. When such a person breaches his fiduciary relationship, he may be treated more properly as a tipper than a tippee. *See Shapiro v. Merrill Lynch, Pierce, Fenner & Smith, Inc.*, 495 F.2d 228, 237 (C.A.2 1974) (investment banker had access to material information when working on a proposed public offering for the corporation). For such a duty to be imposed, however, the corporation must expect the outsider to keep the disclosed nonpublic information confidential, and the relationship at least must imply such a duty.

In effect, the SEC's theory of tippee liability in both cases appears rooted in the idea that the antifraud provisions require equal information among all traders. This conflicts with the principle set forth in *Chiarella* that only some persons, under some circumstances, will be barred from trading while in possession of material nonpublic information. Judge Wright correctly read our opinion in *Chiarella* as repudiating any notion that all traders must enjoy equal information before trading: "[T]he 'information' theory is rejected. Because the disclose-or-refrain duty is extraordinary, it attaches only when a party has legal obligations other than a mere duty to comply with the general antifraud proscriptions in the federal securities laws." 220 U.S.App.D.C., at 322, 681 F.2d, at 837. *See Chiarella,* 445 U.S., at 235, n. 20, 100 S.Ct., at 1118, n. 20. We reaffirm today that "[a] duty [to disclose] arises from the relationship between parties * * * and not merely from one's ability to acquire information because of his position in the market." 445 U.S., at 232–233, n. 14, 100 S.Ct., at 1116, n. 14.

Imposing a duty to disclose or abstain solely because a person knowingly receives material nonpublic information from an insider and trades on it could have an inhibiting influence on the role of market analysts, which the SEC itself recognizes is necessary to the preservation of a healthy market.[17] It is commonplace for analysts to "ferret out and analyze information," 21 S.E.C., at 1406, and this often is done by meeting with and questioning corporate officers and others who are insiders. And information that the analysts obtain normally may be the basis for judgments as to the market worth of a corporation's securities. The analyst's judgment in this respect is made available in market letters or otherwise to clients of the firm. It is the nature of this type of information, and indeed of the markets themselves, that such information cannot be made simultaneously available to all of the corporation's stockholders or the public generally.

### B

The conclusion that recipients of inside information do not invariably acquire a duty to disclose or abstain does not mean that such tippees always are free to trade on the information. The need for a ban on some tippee trading is clear. Not only are insiders forbidden by their fiduciary relationship from personally using undisclosed corporate information to their advantage, but they may not give such information to an outsider for the same improper purpose of exploiting the information for

---

**17.** The SEC expressly recognized that "[t]he value to the entire market of [analysts'] efforts cannot be gainsaid; market efficiency in pricing is significantly enhanced by [their] initiatives to ferret out and analyze information, and thus the analyst's work redounds to the benefit of all investors." 21 S.E.C., at 1406. The SEC asserts that analysts remain free to obtain from management corporate information for purposes of "filling in the 'interstices in analysis' * * *." Brief for Respondent 42 (quoting *Investors Management Co.,* 44 S.E.C., at 646). But this rule is inherently imprecise, and imprecision prevents parties from ordering their actions in accord with legal requirements. Unless the parties have some guidance as to where the line is between permissible and impermissible disclosures and uses, neither corporate insiders nor analysts can be sure when the line is crossed. *Cf. Adler v. Klawans,* 267 F.2d 840, 845 (C.A.2 1959) (Burger, J., sitting by designation).

their personal gain. See 15 U.S.C. § 78t(b) (making it unlawful to go indirectly "by means of any other person" any act made unlawful by the federal securities laws). Similarly, the transactions of those who knowingly participate with the fiduciary in such a breach are "as forbidden" as transactions "on behalf of the trustee himself." *Mosser v. Darrow,* 341 U.S. 267, 272, 71 S.Ct. 680, 682, 95 L.Ed. 927 (1951). As the Court explained in *Mosser,* a contrary rule "would open up opportunities for devious dealings in the name of the others that the trustee could not conduct in his own." 341 U.S., at 271, 71 S.Ct., at 682. *See SEC v. Texas Gulf Sulphur, Co.,* 446 F.2d 1301, 1308 (CA2), *cert. denied,* 404 U.S. 1005, 92 S.Ct. 561, 30 L.Ed.2d 558 (1971). Thus, the tippee's duty to disclose or abstain is derivative from that of the insider's duty. *See* Tr. of Oral Ar. 38. *Cf. Chiarella,* 445 U.S., at 246, n. 1, 100 S.Ct., at 1124, n. 1 (Blackmun, J., dissenting). As we noted in *Chiarella,* "[t]he tippee's obligation has been viewed as arising from his role as a participant after the fact in the insider's breach of a fiduciary duty." 445 U.S., at 230, n. 12, 100 S.Ct., at 1116, n. 12.

Thus, some tippees must assume an insider's duty to the shareholders not because they receive inside information, but rather because it has been made available to them *improperly.* And for Rule 10b–5 purposes, the insider's disclosure is improper only where it would violate his *Cady, Roberts* duty. Thus, a tippee assumes a fiduciary duty to the shareholders of a corporation not to trade on material nonpublic information only when the insider has breached his fiduciary duty to the shareholders by disclosing the information to the tippee and the tippee knows or should know that there has been a breach. As Commissioner Smith perceptively observed in *Investors Management Co.:* "[T]ippee responsibility must be related back to insider responsibility by a necessary finding that the tippee knew the information was given to him in breach of a duty by a person having a special relationship to the issuer not to disclose the information * * *." 44 S.E.C., at 651 (concurring in the result). Tipping thus properly is viewed only as a means of indirectly violating the *Cady, Roberts* disclose-or-abstain rule.

## C

In determining whether a tippee is under an obligation to disclose or abstain, it thus is necessary to determine whether the insider's "tip" constituted a breach of the insider's fiduciary duty. All disclosures of confidential corporate information are not inconsistent with the duty insiders owe to shareholders. In contrast to the extraordinary facts of this case, the more typical situation in which there will be a question whether disclosure violates the insider's *Cady, Roberts* duty is when insiders disclose information to analysts. In some situations, the insider will act consistently with his fiduciary duty to shareholders, and yet release of the information may affect the market. For example, it may not be clear—either to the corporate insider or to the recipient analyst— whether the information will be viewed as material nonpublic information. Corporate officials may mistakenly think the information already has been disclosed or that it is not material enough to affect the market.

Whether disclosure is a breach of duty therefore depends in large part on the purpose of the disclosure. This standard was identified by the SEC itself in *Cady, Roberts:* a purpose of the securities laws was to eliminate "use of inside information for personal advantage." 40 S.E.C., at 912, n. 15. Thus, the test is whether the insider personally will benefit, directly or indirectly, from his disclosure. Absent some personal gain, there has been no breach of duty to stockholders. And absent a breach by the insider, there is no derivative breach. As Commissioner Smith stated in *Investors Management Co.:* "It is important in this type of case to focus on policing insiders and what they do * * * rather than on policing information *per se* and its possession * * *." 44 S.E.C., at 648 (concurring in the result).

The SEC argues that, if inside-trading liability does not exist when the information is transmitted for a proper purpose but is used for trading, it would be a rare situation when the parties could not fabricate some ostensibly legitimate business justification for transmitting the information. We think the SEC is unduly concerned. In determining whether the insider's purpose in making a particular disclosure is fraudulent, the SEC and the courts are not required to read the parties' minds. Scienter in some cases is relevant in determining whether the tipper has violated his *Cady, Roberts* duty. But to determine whether the disclosure itself "deceive[s], manipulate[s], or defraud[s]" shareholders, *Aaron v. SEC*, 446 U.S. 680, 686, 100 S.Ct. 1945, 1950, 64 L.Ed.2d 611 (1980), the initial inquiry is whether there has been a breach of duty by the insider. This requires courts to focus on objective criteria, *i.e.*, whether the insider receives a direct or indirect personal benefit from the disclosure, such as a pecuniary gain or a reputational benefit that will translate into future earnings. *Cf.* 40 S.E.C., at 912, n. 15; Brudney, *Insiders, Outsiders, and Informational Advantages Under the Federal Securities Laws*, 93 HARV.L.REV. 324, 348 (1979) ("The theory * * * is that the insider, by giving the information out selectively, is in effect selling the information to its recipient for cash, reciprocal information or other things of value for himself * * * "). There are objective facts and circumstances that often justify such an inference. For example, there may be a relationship between the insider and the recipient that suggests a *quid pro quo* from the latter, or an intention to benefit the particular recipient. The elements of fiduciary duty and exploitation of nonpublic information also exist when an insider makes a gift of confidential information to a trading relative or friend. The tip and trade resemble trading by the insider himself followed by a gift of the profits to the recipient.

Determining whether an insider personally benefits from a particular disclosure, a question of fact, will not always be easy for courts. But it is essential, we think, to have a guiding principle for those whose daily activities must be limited and instructed by the SEC's inside-trading rules, and we believe that there must be a breach of the insider's fiduciary duty before the tippee inherits the duty to disclose or abstain.

In contrast, the rule adopted by the SEC in this case would have no limiting principle.

### IV

Under the inside-trading and tipping rules set forth above, we find that there was no actionable violation by Dirks. It is undisputed that Dirks himself was a stranger to Equity Funding, with no pre-existing fiduciary duty to its shareholders. He took no action, directly or indirectly, that induced the shareholders or officers of Equity Funding to repose trust or confidence in him. There was no expectation by Dirks' sources that he would keep their information in confidence. Nor did Dirks misappropriate or illegally obtain the information about Equity Funding. Unless the insiders breached their *Cady, Roberts* duty to shareholders in disclosing the nonpublic information to Dirks, he breached no duty when he passed it on to investors as well as to the *Wall Street Journal*.

It is clear that neither Secrist nor the other Equity Funding employees violated their *Cady, Roberts* duty to the corporation's shareholders by providing information to Dirks.[18] The tippers received no monetary or personal benefit for revealing Equity Funding's secrets, nor was their purpose to make a gift of valuable information to Dirks. As the facts of this case clearly indicate, the tippers were motivated by a desire to

---

18. In this Court, the SEC appears to contend that an insider invariably violates a fiduciary duty to the corporation's shareholders by transmitting nonpublic corporate information to an outsider when he has reason to believe that the outsider may use it to the disadvantage of the shareholders. * * *

The dissent argues that "Secrist violated his duty to Equity Funding shareholders by transmitting material nonpublic information to Dirks with the intention that Dirks would cause his clients to trade on that information." *Post,* at 12. By perceiving a breach of fiduciary duty whenever inside information is intentionally disclosed to securities traders, the dissenting opinion effectively would achieve the same result as the SEC's theory below, *i.e.,* mere possession of inside information while trading would be viewed as a Rule 10b–5 violation. But *Chiarella* made it explicitly clear there is no general duty to forego market transactions "based on material, nonpublic information." 445 U.S., at 233, 100 S.Ct., at 1117. Such a duty would "depar[t] radically from the established doctrine that duty arises from a specific relationship between two parties." *Ibid.*

Moreover, to constitute a violation of Rule 10b–5, there must be fraud. *See Ernst & Ernst v. Hochfelder,* 425 U.S. 185, 199, 96 S.Ct. 1375, 1383, 47 L.Ed.2d 668 (1976) (statutory words "manipulative," "device," and "contrivance * * * connot[e] intention-

al or willful conduct designed to *deceive or defraud* investors by controlling or artificially affecting the price of securities") (emphasis added). There is no evidence that Secrist's disclosure was intended to or did in fact "deceive or defraud" anyone. Secrist certainly intended to convey relevant information that management was unlawfully concealing, and—so far as the record shows—he believed that persuading Dirks to investigate was the best way to disclose the fraud. Other efforts had proved fruitless. Under any objective standard, Secrist received no direct or indirect personal benefit from the disclosure.

The dissenting opinion focuses on shareholder "losses," "injury," and "damages," but in many cases there may be no clear causal connection between inside trading and outsiders' losses. In one sense, as market values fluctuate and investors act on inevitably incomplete or incorrect information, there always are winners and losers; but those who have "lost" have not necessarily been defrauded. On the other hand, inside trading for personal gain is fraudulent, and is a violation of the federal securities laws. * * *. Thus, there is little legal significance to the dissent's argument that Secrist and Dirks created new "victims" by disclosing the information to persons who traded. In fact, they prevented the fraud from continuing and victimizing many more investors.

expose the fraud. See *supra*, at 1–2. In the absence of a breach of duty to shareholders by the insiders, there was no derivative breach by Dirks. See n. 20, *supra*. Dirks therefore could not have been "a participant after the fact in [an] insider's breach of a fiduciary duty." *Chiarella*, 445 U.S., at 230, n. 12, 100 S.Ct., at 1116, n. 12.

### V

We conclude that Dirks, in the circumstances of this case, had no duty to abstain from use of the inside information that he obtained. The judgment of the Court of Appeals therefore is

Reversed.

JUSTICE BLACKMUN, with whom JUSTICE BRENNAN and JUSTICE MARSHALL join, dissenting.

The Court today takes still another step to limit the protections provided investors by § 10(b) of the Securities Exchange Act of 1934. *See Chiarella v. United States*, 445 U.S. 222, 246, 100 S.Ct. 1108, 1123, 63 L.Ed.2d 348 (1980) (dissenting opinion). The device employed in this case engrafts a special motivational requirement on the fiduciary duty doctrine. This innovation excuses a knowing and intentional violation of an insider's duty to shareholders if the insider does not act from a motive of personal gain. Even on the extraordinary facts of this case, such an innovation is not justified.

\* \* \*

### II

### A.

No one questions that Secrist himself could not trade on his inside information to the disadvantage of uninformed shareholders and purchasers of Equity Funding securities. *See* Brief for United States as *Amicus Curiae* 19, n. 12. Unlike the printer in *Chiarella*, Secrist stood in a fiduciary relationship with these shareholders. As the Court states, *ante*, at 5, corporate insiders have an affirmative duty of disclosure when trading with shareholders of the corporation. *See Chiarella*, 445 U.S., at 227, 100 S.Ct., at 1114. This duty extends as well to purchasers of the corporation's securities. *Id.*, at 227, n. 8, 100 S.Ct., at 1114, n. 8 citing *Gratz v. Claughton*, 187 F.2d 46, 49 (CA2), *cert. denied*, 341 U.S. 920, 71 S.Ct. 741, 95 L.Ed. 1353 (1951).

The Court also acknowledges that Secrist could not do by proxy what he was prohibited from doing personally. *Mosser v. Darrow*, 341 U.S. 267, 272, 71 S.Ct. 680, 682, 95 L.Ed. 927 (1951). But this is precisely what Secrist did. Secrist used Dirks to disseminate information to Dirks' clients, who in turn dumped stock on unknowing purchasers. Secrist thus intended Dirks to injure the purchasers of Equity Funding securities to whom Secrist had a duty to disclose. Accepting the Court's view of tippee liability, it appears that Dirks' knowledge of this breach makes him liable as a participant in the breach after the fact.

## B

The Court holds, however, that Dirks is not liable because Secrist did not violate his duty; according to the Court, this is so because Secrist did not have the improper purpose of personal gain. In so doing, the Court imposes a new, subjective limitation on the scope of the duty owed by insiders to shareholders. The novelty of this limitation is reflected in the Court's lack of support for it.

The insider's duty is owed directly to the corporation's shareholders. *See* Langevoort, *Insider Trading and the Fiduciary Principle: A Post-Chiarella Restatement,* 70 CALIF.L.REV. 1, 5 (1982); 3A W. Fletcher, PRIVATE CORPORATIONS § 1168.2, pp. 288–289 (1975). As *Chiarella* recognized, it is based on the relationship of trust and confidence between the insider and the shareholder. 445 U.S., at 228, 100 S.Ct., at 1114. That relationship assures the shareholder that the insider may not take actions that will harm him unfairly. The affirmative duty of disclosure protects against this injury.

## C

The fact that the insider himself does not benefit from the breach does not eradicate the shareholder's injury. *Cf.* RESTATEMENT (SECOND) OF TRUSTS § 205, Comments c and d (1959) (trustee liable for acts causing diminution of value of trust); 3 A. SCOTT ON TRUSTS § 205, p. 1665 (1967) (trustee liable for any losses to trust caused by his breach). It makes no difference to the shareholder whether the corporate insider gained or intended to gain personally from the transaction; the shareholder still has lost because of the insider's misuse of nonpublic information. The duty is addressed not to the insider's motives, but to his actions and their consequences on the shareholder. Personal gain is not an element of the breach of this duty.[11]

\* \* \*

**11.** The Court seems concerned that this case bears on insiders' contacts with analysts for valid corporate reasons. It also fears that insiders may not be able to determine whether the information transmitted is material or nonpublic. When the disclosure is to an investment banker or some other adviser, however, there is normally no breach because the insider does not have scienter: he does not intend that the inside information be used for trading purposes to the disadvantage of shareholders. Moreover, if the insider in good faith does not believe that the information is material or nonpublic, he also lacks the necessary scienter. *Ernst & Ernst v. Hochfelder,* 425 U.S. 185, 197 (1976). In fact, the scienter requirement functions in part to protect good faith errors of this type.

Should the adviser receiving the information use it to trade, it may breach a separate contractual or other duty to the corporation not to misuse the information. Absent such an arrangement, however, the adviser is not barred by Rule 10b–5 from trading on that information if it believes that the insider has not breached any duty to his shareholders. *See Walton v. Morgan Stanley & Co.,* 623 F.2d 796, 798–799 (C.A.2 1980).

The situation here, of course, is radically different. *Ante,* at 11, n. 17 (Dirks received information requiring no analysis "as to its market relevance"). Secrist divulged the information for the precise purpose of causing Dirks' clients to trade on it. I fail to understand how imposing liability on Dirks will affect legitimate insider-analyst contacts.

### III

The improper purpose requirement not only has no basis in law, but it rests implicitly on a policy that I cannot accept. The Court justifies Secrist's and Dirks' action because the general benefit derived from the violation of Secrist's duty to shareholders outweighed the harm caused to those shareholders, *see* Heller, Chiarella, *SEC Rule 14e–3 and Dirks: "Fairness" versus Economic Theory*, 37 Bus.Lawyer 517, 550 (1982); Easterbrook, *Insider Trading, Secret Agents, Evidentiary Privileges, and the Production of Information*, 1981 S.Ct.Rev. 309, 338—in other words, because the end justified the means. Under this view, the benefit conferred on society by Secrist's and Dirks' activities may be paid for with the losses caused to shareholders trading with Dirks' clients.[14]

Although Secrist's general motive to expose the Equity Funding fraud was laudable, the means he chose were not. Moreover, even assuming that Dirks played a substantial role in exposing the fraud, he and his clients should not profit from the information they obtained from Secrist. Misprision of a felony long has been against public policy. * * * As a citizen, Dirks had at least an ethical obligation to report the information to the proper authorities. The Court's holding is deficient in policy terms not because it fails to create a legal norm out of that ethical norm, but because it actually rewards Dirks for his aiding and abetting.

Dirks and Secrist were under a duty to disclose the information or to refrain from trading on it. I agree that disclosure in this case would have been difficult. I also recognize that the SEC seemingly has been less than helpful in its view of the nature of disclosure necessary to satisfy the disclose-or-refrain duty. The Commission tells persons with inside information that they cannot trade on that information unless they disclose; it refuses, however, to tell them how to disclose. *See In re Faberge, Inc.,* 45 S.E.C. 249, 256 (1973) (disclosure requires public release through public media designed to reach investing public generally). This seems to be a less than sensible policy, which it is incumbent on the Commission to correct. The Court, however, has no authority to remedy the problem by opening a hole in the congressionally mandated prohibition on insider trading, thus rewarding such trading.

### IV

In my view, Secrist violated his duty to Equity Funding shareholders by transmitting material nonpublic information to Dirks with the intention that Dirks would cause his clients to trade on that information. Dirks, therefore, was under a duty to make the information publicly

---

**14.** This position seems little different from the theory that insider trading should be permitted because it brings relevant information to the market. *See* H. Manne, Insider Trading and the Stock Market 59–76, 111–146 (1966); Manne, *Insider Trading and the Law Professors*, 23 Vand.L.Rev. 547, 565–576 (1970). The Court also seems to embrace a variant of that extreme theory, which postulates that insider trading causes no harm at all to those who purchase from the insider. Both the theory and its variant sit at the opposite end of the theoretical spectrum from the much maligned equality-of-information theory, and never have been adopted by Congress or ratified by this Court. *See* Langevoort, 70 Calif.L.Rev., at 1 and n. 1. The theory rejects the existence of any enforceable principle of fairness between market participants.

available or to refrain from actions that he knew would lead to trading. Because Dirks caused his clients to trade, he violated § 10(b) and Rule 10b–5. Any other result is a disservice to this country's attempt to provide fair and efficient capital markets. I dissent.

### Note: The Misappropriation Theory

*Chiarella* and *Dirks* resolved three major issues. Most importantly, they confirmed lower court rulings that section 10(b) and Rule 10b–5 make it unlawful for an insider or temporary insider of a corporation to trade that corporation's stock on the basis of material, nonpublic information. They also confirmed that it is unlawful for an insider or temporary insider, acting in breach of a fiduciary duty owed to a corporation, to disclose to another—*i.e.*, to "tip"—material, nonpublic information about that corporation. Finally, they made clear that section 10(b) and Rule 10b–5 do not embody the equal access principle on which the *Texas Gulf Sulfur* court relied—section 10(b) and Rule 10b–5 do not bar a person who is not an insider, temporary insider or one of their tippees from trading a corporation's stock simply because she possesses material information not available to other traders.

*Chiarella* and *Dirks* did not address, and therefore did not resolve, whether section 10(b) and Rule 10b–5 make it unlawful for a person who has no connection to a corporation to trade that corporation's securities on the basis of material, nonpublic information that she misappropriated from some third party. Subsequent to *Chiarella*, circuit courts of appeal divided on the question of whether such trading is unlawful. Three circuits, all of which ruled prior to the Supreme Court's decision in *Central Bank of Denver, N.A. v. First Interstate Bank of Denver, N.A.*, 511 U.S. 164, 114 S.Ct. 1439, 128 L.Ed.2d 119 (1994), concluded that it is unlawful for someone outside a corporation to trade on the basis of misappropriated information. *See United States v. Newman*, 664 F.2d 12 (2d Cir.1981), *cert. denied*, 464 U.S. 863, 104 S.Ct. 193, 78 L.Ed.2d 170 (1983); *SEC v. Clark*, 915 F.2d 439 (9th Cir.1990); *SEC v. Cherif*, 933 F.2d 403 (7th Cir.1991), *cert. denied*, 502 U.S. 1071, 112 S.Ct. 966, 117 L.Ed.2d 131 (1992). Two circuits, both of which ruled after *Central Bank,* rejected the misappropriation theory. *See United States v. Bryan*, 58 F.3d 933 (4th Cir.1995); *United States v. O'Hagan*, 92 F.3d 612 (8th Cir.1996), *rev'd,* ___ U.S. ___, 117 S.Ct. 2199, 138 L.Ed.2d 724 (1997).

*Carpenter v. United States*, 484 U.S. 19, 108 S.Ct. 316, 98 L.Ed.2d 275 (1987), which was decided prior to *Central Bank*, compounded the uncertainty as to the validity of the misappropriation theory. *Carpenter* dealt with the conduct of R. Foster Winans, the author of the influential "Heard on the Street" column in *The Wall Street Journal*. Winans provided information about soon-to-be-published columns to a group of brokers, who purchased or sold short stocks that the columns would discuss, then sold or repurchased those stocks shortly after the columns were published.* *Carpenter* differed from most other misappropriation

* Even though the columns discussed information already in circulation within the

cases in that the *Journal*—the source of Winans' information—neither traded the securities involved nor received information from corporate clients who intended to do so. A divided panel of the Second Circuit held Winans' had violated Rule 10b–5 by trading on information he had misappropriated from the *Journal* and also affirmed Winans' conviction for mail and wire fraud. An equally divided (4–4) Supreme Court affirmed Winans' 10b–5 conviction without opinion. The Court also unanimously affirmed Winans' conviction for mail and wire fraud, reasoning that Winans had deprived the Journal of its exclusive property right to control information about material it planned to publish.

The division among the circuits concerning the validity of the misappropriation theory revolved around two issues. One concerned the distinction between constructive and informational fraud. A fiduciary commits "constructive fraud" when she engages in conduct that is financially unfair to her beneficiary; she engages in "informational fraud"—or "deception"—when she misrepresents a material fact or fails to disclose such a fact in violation of her duty to disclose. *See* Robert C. Clark, Corporate Law 151–157 (1986). Many breaches of fiduciary duty involve both kinds of fraud and shareholders have a state law remedy against a fiduciary who engages in either kind of fraud.

However, as we saw in Chapter 18, *Santa Fe Industries, Inc. v. Green* held that Rule 10b–5 provides a remedy only for deception—*i.e.,* informational fraud—because section 10(b) speaks only of deception (and manipulation). *Chiarella* and *Dirks* paid lip service to this holding but appeared to conflate the concepts of informational and constructive fraud. The Second Circuit followed much the same path in its decisions endorsing the misappropriation theory. *See Newman,* 664 F.2d at 16; *SEC v. Materia,* 745 F.2d 197, 201 (2d Cir.1984); *Carpenter,* 791 F.2d at 1027; *United States v. Chestman,* 947 F.2d 551 (2d Cir.1991); *but see id.* at 575 (Winter, J., dissenting in part).

*Central Bank* reaffirmed *Santa Fe*'s holding that section 10(b) requires proof of "the making of a material misstatement (or omission) or the commission of a manipulative act" and thus appeared to call into question the validity of the misappropriation theory. The Fourth and Eighth Circuits relied on this aspect of *Central Bank* to support their conclusion that the misappropriation theory could not be reconciled with the language of section 10(b). They reasoned that it premised liability on a finding of breach of the fiduciary duty that the misappropriator owed to the source of her information.

The Fourth and Eighth Circuits also concluded that the misappropriation theory was invalid because the person injured by the misappropriator's breach of fiduciary duty was not a participant in any relevant securities transaction. Thus, in their view, even if misappropriation somehow could be viewed as "deceptive," the deception did not have the

investment community—*i.e.,* "heard on the Street"—stocks mentioned in the column regularly increased in price if that information was positive and declined in price if that information was negative.

necessary connection to a purchase or sale of securities. The Second, Seventh and Ninth Circuits, in contrast, reasoned that where a fiduciary had misappropriated information for the purpose of buying or selling securities, the nexus between the misappropriation and the misappropriator's trading satisfied the "in connection with" requirement of section 10(b).

## UNITED STATES v. O'HAGAN

___ U.S. ___, 117 S.Ct. 2199, 138 L.Ed.2d 724 (1997).

JUSTICE GINSBURG delivered the opinion of the Court.

\* \* \*

### I

Respondent James Herman O'Hagan was a partner in the law firm of Dorsey & Whitney in Minneapolis, Minnesota. In July 1988, Grand Metropolitan PLC (Grand Met), a company based in London, England, retained Dorsey & Whitney as local counsel to represent Grand Met regarding a potential tender offer for the common stock of the Pillsbury Company, headquartered in Minneapolis. Both Grand Met and Dorsey & Whitney took precautions to protect the confidentiality of Grand Met's tender offer plans. O'Hagan did no work on the Grand Met representation. Dorsey & Whitney withdrew from representing Grand Met on September 9, 1988. Less than a month later, on October 4, 1988, Grand Met publicly announced its tender offer for Pillsbury stock.

On August 18, 1988, while Dorsey & Whitney was still representing Grand Met, O'Hagan began purchasing call options for Pillsbury stock. Each option gave him the right to purchase 100 shares of Pillsbury stock. \* \* \* By the end of September, he owned 2,500 unexpired Pillsbury options, apparently more than any other individual investor. O'Hagan also purchased, in September 1988, some 5,000 shares of Pillsbury common stock, at a price just under $39 per share. When Grand Met announced its tender offer in October, the price of Pillsbury stock rose to nearly $60 per share. O'Hagan then sold his Pillsbury call options and common stock, making a profit of more than $4.3 million.

The Securities and Exchange Commission (SEC or Commission) initiated an investigation into O'Hagan's transactions, culminating in a 57–count indictment. The indictment alleged that O'Hagan defrauded his law firm and its client, Grand Met, by using for his own trading purposes material, nonpublic information regarding Grand Met's planned tender offer. According to the indictment, O'Hagan used the profits he gained through this trading to conceal his previous embezzlement and conversion of unrelated client trust funds. A jury convicted O'Hagan on all \* \* \* counts, and he was sentenced to a 41–month term of imprisonment.

A divided panel of the Court of Appeals for the Eighth Circuit reversed \* \* \*. Liability under § 10(b) and Rule 10b–5, the Eighth

Circuit held, may not be grounded on the "misappropriation theory" of securities fraud on which the prosecution relied. * * *

Decisions of the Courts of Appeals are in conflict on the propriety of the misappropriation theory under § 10(b) and Rule section 10(b)–5. * * * We granted certiorari and now reverse the Eighth Circuit's judgment.

## II

We address first the Court of Appeals' reversal of O'Hagan's convictions under § 10(b) and Rule 10b–5. Following the Fourth Circuit's lead, *see United States v. Bryan*, the Eighth Circuit rejected the misappropriation theory as a basis for § 10(b) liability. We hold, in accord with several other Courts of Appeals,[3] that criminal liability under § 10(b) may be predicated on the misappropriation theory.

## A

* * *

[Section 10(b)] proscribes (1) using any deceptive device (2) in connection with the purchase or sale of securities, in contravention of rules prescribed by the Commission. The provision, as written, does not confine its coverage to deception of a purchaser or seller of securities, *see United States v. Newman*; rather, the statute reaches any deceptive device used "in connection with the purchase or sale of any security."

* * *

Liability under Rule 10b–5, our precedent indicates, does not extend beyond conduct encompassed by § 10(b)'s prohibition. *See Ernst & Ernst v. Hochfelder*, (scope of Rule 10b–5 cannot exceed power Congress granted Commission under § 10(b)); *see also Central Bank of Denver, N.A. v. First Interstate Bank of Denver, N. A.*, ("We have refused to allow [private] 10b–5 challenges to conduct not prohibited by the text of the statute.").

Under the "traditional" or "classical theory" of insider trading liability, § 10(b) and Rule 10b–5 are violated when a corporate insider trades in the securities of his corporation on the basis of material, nonpublic information. Trading on such information qualifies as a "deceptive device" under § 10(b), we have affirmed, because "a relationship of trust and confidence [exists] between the shareholders of a corporation and those insiders who have obtained confidential information by reason of their position with that corporation." *Chiarella*. That relationship, we recognized, "gives rise to a duty to disclose [or to abstain from trading] because of the 'necessity of preventing a corporate insider from ... tak[ing] unfair advantage of ... uninformed ... stockholders.'" The classical theory applies not only to officers, directors, and other permanent insiders of a corporation, but also to attorneys, accountants, consul-

---

**3.** *See, e.g., United States v. Chestman*, 947 F. 2d 551, 566 (C.A.2 1991) (*en banc*), *cert. denied,* 503 U.S. 1004 (1992); *SEC v. Cherif*, 933 F. 2d 403, 410 (C.A.7 1991), *cert. denied,* 502 U.S. 1071 (1992); *SEC v. Clark*, 915 F. 2d 439, 453 (C.A.9 1990).

tants, and others who temporarily become fiduciaries of a corporation. *See Dirks v. SEC*, 463 U.S. at 655, n. 14.

The "misappropriation theory" holds that a person commits fraud "in connection with" a securities transaction, and thereby violates § 10(b) and Rule 10b-5, when he misappropriates confidential information for securities trading purposes, in breach of a duty owed to the source of the information. *See* Brief for United States 14. Under this theory, a fiduciary's undisclosed, self-serving use of a principal's information to purchase or sell securities, in breach of a duty of loyalty and confidentiality, defrauds the principal of the exclusive use of that information. In lieu of premising liability on a fiduciary relationship between company insider and purchaser or seller of the company's stock, the misappropriation theory premises liability on a fiduciary-turned-trader's deception of those who entrusted him with access to confidential information.

The two theories are complementary, each addressing efforts to capitalize on nonpublic information through the purchase or sale of securities. The classical theory targets a corporate insider's breach of duty to shareholders with whom the insider transacts; the misappropriation theory outlaws trading on the basis of nonpublic information by a corporate "outsider" in breach of a duty owed not to a trading party, but to the source of the information. The misappropriation theory is thus designed to "protec[t] the integrity of the securities markets against abuses by 'outsiders' to a corporation who have access to confidential information that will affect th[e] corporation's security price when revealed, but who owe no fiduciary or other duty to that corporation's shareholders." *Ibid.*

In this case, the indictment alleged that O'Hagan, in breach of a duty of trust and confidence he owed to his law firm, Dorsey & Whitney, and to its client, Grand Met, traded on the basis of nonpublic information regarding Grand Met's planned tender offer for Pillsbury common stock. App. 16. This conduct, the Government charged, constituted a fraudulent device in connection with the purchase and sale of securities.[5]

## B

We agree with the Government that misappropriation, as just defined, satisfies § 10(b)'s requirement that chargeable conduct involve a "deceptive device or contrivance" used "in connection with" the purchase or sale of securities. We observe, first, that misappropriators, as the Government describes them, deal in deception. A fiduciary who "[pretends] loyalty to the principal while secretly converting the princi-

---

**5.** The Government could not have prosecuted O'Hagan under the classical theory, for O'Hagan was not an "insider" of Pillsbury, the corporation in whose stock he traded. Although an "outsider" with respect to Pillsbury, O'Hagan had an intimate association with, and was found to have traded on confidential information from,

Dorsey & Whitney, counsel to tender offeror Grand Met. Under the misappropriation theory, O'Hagan's securities trading does not escape Exchange Act sanction, as it would under the dissent's reasoning, simply because he was associated with, and gained nonpublic information from, the bidder, rather than the target.

pal's information for personal gain," Brief for United States 17, "dupes" or defrauds the principal.

We addressed fraud of the same species in *Carpenter v. United States*, which involved the mail fraud statute's proscription of "any scheme or artifice to defraud." Affirming convictions under that statute, we said in *Carpenter* that an employee's undertaking not to reveal his employer's confidential information "became a sham" when the employee provided the information to his co-conspirators in a scheme to obtain trading profits. A company's confidential information, we recognized in *Carpenter*, qualifies as property to which the company has a right of exclusive use. The undisclosed misappropriation of such information, in violation of a fiduciary duty, the Court said in *Carpenter*, constitutes fraud akin to embezzlement—" 'the fraudulent appropriation to one's own use of the money or goods entrusted to one's care by another.' " *Carpenter*'s discussion of the fraudulent misuse of confidential information, the Government notes, "is a particularly apt source of guidance here, because [the mail fraud statute] (like Section 10(b)) has long been held to require deception, not merely the breach of a fiduciary duty." Brief for United States 18, n. 9 (citation omitted).

Deception through nondisclosure is central to the theory of liability for which the Government seeks recognition. As counsel for the Government stated in explanation of the theory at oral argument: "To satisfy the common law rule that a trustee may not use the property that [has] been entrusted [to] him, there would have to be consent. To satisfy the requirement of the Securities Act that there be no deception, there would only have to be disclosure." Tr. of Oral Arg. 12; *see generally* RESTATEMENT (SECOND) OF AGENCY §§ 390, 395 (1958) (agent's disclosure obligation regarding use of confidential information).[6]

The misappropriation theory advanced by the Government is consistent with *Santa Fe Industries, Inc. v. Green*, 430 U.S. 462 (1977), a decision underscoring that § 10(b) is not an all-purpose breach of fiduciary duty ban; rather, it trains on conduct involving manipulation or deception. *See id.*, at 473–476. In contrast to the Government's allegations in this case, in *Santa Fe Industries*, all pertinent facts were disclosed by the persons charged with violating § 10(b) and Rule 10b–5, *see id.*, at 474; therefore, there was no deception through nondisclosure to which liability under those provisions could attach, *see id.*, at 476. Similarly, full disclosure forecloses liability under the misappropriation theory: Because the deception essential to the misappropriation theory involves feigning fidelity to the source of information, if the fiduciary discloses to the source that he plans to trade on the nonpublic informa-

---

**6.** Under the misappropriation theory urged in this case, the disclosure obligation runs to the source of the information, here, Dorsey & Whitney and Grand Met. Chief Justice Burger, dissenting in Chiarella, advanced a broader reading of § 10(b) and Rule 10b–5; the disclosure obligation, as he envisioned it, ran to those with whom the misappropriator trades. 445 U. S., at 240 ("a person who has misappropriated nonpublic information has an absolute duty to disclose that information or to refrain from trading"); *see also id.*, at 243, n. 4. The Government does not propose that we adopt a misappropriation theory of that breadth.

tion, there is no "deceptive device" and thus no § 10(b) violation-although the fiduciary-turned-trader may remain liable under state law for breach of a duty of loyalty.[7]

We turn next to the § 10(b) requirement that the misappropriator's deceptive use of information be "in connection with the purchase or sale of [a] security." This element is satisfied because the fiduciary's fraud is consummated, not when the fiduciary gains the confidential information, but when, without disclosure to his principal, he uses the information to purchase or sell securities. The securities transaction and the breach of duty thus coincide. This is so even though the person or entity defrauded is not the other party to the trade, but is, instead, the source of the nonpublic information. A misappropriator who trades on the basis of material, nonpublic information, in short, gains his advantageous market position through deception; he deceives the source of the information and simultaneously harms members of the investing public.

The misappropriation theory targets information of a sort that misappropriators ordinarily capitalize upon to gain no-risk profits through the purchase or sale of securities. Should a misappropriator put such information to other use, the statute's prohibition would not be implicated. The theory does not catch all conceivable forms of fraud involving confidential information; rather, it catches fraudulent means of capitalizing on such information through securities transactions.

The Government notes another limitation on the forms of fraud § 10(b) reaches: "The misappropriation theory would not ... apply to a case in which a person defrauded a bank into giving him a loan or embezzled cash from another, and then used the proceeds of the misdeed to purchase securities." Brief for United States 24, n. 13. In such a case, the Government states, "the proceeds would have value to the malefactor apart from their use in a securities transaction, and the fraud would be complete as soon as the money was obtained." *Ibid.* In other words, money can buy, if not anything, then at least many things; its misappropriation may thus be viewed as sufficiently detached from a subsequent securities transaction that § 10(b)'s "in connection with" requirement would not be met. *Ibid.*

The dissent's charge that the misappropriation theory is incoherent because information, like funds, can be put to multiple uses, *see post*, at 4–8, misses the point. The Exchange Act was enacted in part "to insure the maintenance of fair and honest markets," 15 U.S.C. § 78b, and there is no question that fraudulent uses of confidential information fall within § 10(b)'s prohibition if the fraud is "in connection with" a securities transaction. It is hardly remarkable that a rule suitably

---

**7.** Where, however, a person trading on the basis of material, nonpublic information owes a duty of loyalty and confidentiality to two entities or persons-for example, a law firm and its client-but makes disclosure to only one, the trader may still be liable under the misappropriation theory.

applied to the fraudulent uses of certain kinds of information would be stretched beyond reason were it applied to the fraudulent use of money.

\* \* \*

The misappropriation theory comports with § 10(b)'s language, which requires deception "in connection with the purchase or sale of any security," not deception of an identifiable purchaser or seller. The theory is also well-tuned to an animating purpose of the Exchange Act: to insure honest securities markets and thereby promote investor confidence. *See* 45 Fed. Reg. 60412 (1980) (trading on misappropriated information "undermines the integrity of, and investor confidence in, the securities markets"). Although informational disparity is inevitable in the securities markets, investors likely would hesitate to venture their capital in a market where trading based on misappropriated nonpublic information is unchecked by law. An investor's informational disadvantage vis-a-vis a misappropriator with material, nonpublic information stems from contrivance, not luck; it is a disadvantage that cannot be overcome with research or skill. *See* Brudney, *Insiders, Outsiders, and Informational Advantages Under the Federal Securities Laws,* 93 HARV. L. REV. 322, 356 (1979) ("If the market is thought to be systematically populated with ... transactors [trading on the basis of misappropriated information] some investors will refrain from dealing altogether, and others will incur costs to avoid dealing with such transactors or corruptly to overcome their unerodable informational advantages.").

In sum, considering the inhibiting impact on market participation of trading on misappropriated information, and the congressional purposes underlying § 10(b), it makes scant sense to hold a lawyer like O'Hagan a § 10(b) violator if he works for a law firm representing the target of a tender offer, but not if he works for a law firm representing the bidder. The text of the statute requires no such result.[9] The misappropriation at issue here was properly made the subject of a § 10(b) charge because it meets the statutory requirement that there be "deceptive" conduct "in connection with" securities transactions.

C

Court of Appeals rejected the misappropriation theory primarily on two grounds. First, as the Eighth Circuit comprehended the theory, it requires neither misrepresentation nor nondisclosure. *See* 92 F. 3d, at 618. As we just explained, however, *see supra,* at 8–10, deceptive nondis-

---

**9.** As noted earlier, however, *see supra,* at 9–10, the textual requirement of deception precludes § 10(b) liability when a person trading on the basis of nonpublic information has disclosed his trading plans to, or obtained authorization from, the principal- even though such conduct may affect the securities markets in the same manner as the conduct reached by the misappropriation theory. Contrary to the dissent's suggestion, *see post,* at 11–13, the fact that § 10(b) is only a partial antidote to the problems it was designed to alleviate does not call into question its prohibition of conduct that falls within its textual proscription. Moreover, once a disloyal agent discloses his imminent breach of duty, his principal may seek appropriate equitable relief under state law. Furthermore, in the context of a tender offer, the principal who authorizes an agent's trading on confidential information may, in the Commission's view, incur liability for an Exchange Act violation under Rule 14e–3(a).

closure is essential to the § 10(b) liability at issue. Concretely, in this case, "it [was O'Hagan's] failure to disclose his personal trading to Grand Met and Dorsey, in breach of his duty to do so, that ma[de] his conduct 'deceptive' within the meaning of [§ ]10(b)." Reply Brief 7.

Second and "more obvious," the Court of Appeals said, the misappropriation theory is not moored to § 10(b)'s requirement that "the fraud be 'in connection with the purchase or sale of any security.' " *See* 92 F. 3d, at 618 (quoting 15 U.S.C. § 78j(b)). According to the Eighth Circuit, three of our decisions reveal that § 10(b) liability cannot be predicated on a duty owed to the source of nonpublic information: *Chiarella; Dirks;* and *Central Bank.* "[O]nly a breach of a duty to parties to the securities transaction," the Court of Appeals concluded, "or, at the most, to other market participants such as investors, will be sufficient to give rise to § 10(b) liability." We read the statute and our precedent differently, and note again that § 10(b) refers to "the purchase or sale of any security," not to identifiable purchasers or sellers of securities.

\* \* \*

The Court did not hold in *Chiarella* that the only relationship prompting liability for trading on undisclosed information is the relationship between a corporation's insiders and shareholders. That is evident from our response to the Government's argument before this Court that the printer's misappropriation of information from his employer for purposes of securities trading-in violation of a duty of confidentiality owed to the acquiring companies-constituted fraud in connection with the purchase or sale of a security, and thereby satisfied the terms of § 10(b). The Court declined to reach that potential basis for the printer's liability, because the theory had not been submitted to the jury. But four Justices found merit in it. And a fifth Justice stated that the Court "wisely le[ft] the resolution of this issue for another day." *Id.*, at 238 (STEVENS, J., concurring).

*Chiarella* thus expressly left open the misappropriation theory before us today. Certain statements in *Chiarella*, however, led the Eighth Circuit in the instant case to conclude that § 10(b) liability hinges exclusively on a breach of duty owed to a purchaser or seller of securities. The Court said in *Chiarella* that § 10(b) liability "is premised upon a duty to disclose arising from a relationship of trust and confidence between parties to a transaction," 445 U. S., at 230 (emphasis added), and observed that the printshop employee defendant in that case "was not a person in whom the sellers had placed their trust and confidence," see *id.*, at 232. These statements rejected the notion that § 10(b) stretches so far as to impose "a general duty between all participants in market transactions to forgo actions based on material, nonpublic information," *id.*, at 233, and we confine them to that context. The statements highlighted by the Eighth Circuit, in short, appear in an opinion carefully leaving for future resolution the validity of the misappropriation theory, and therefore cannot be read to foreclose that theory.

*Dirks*, too, left room for application of the misappropriation theory in cases like the one we confront. * * *

* * *

No showing had been made in *Dirks* that the "tippers" had violated any duty by disclosing to the analyst nonpublic information about their former employer. The insiders had acted not for personal profit, but to expose a massive fraud within the corporation. Absent any violation by the tippers, there could be no derivative liability for the tippee. Most important for purposes of the instant case, the Court observed in *Dirks*: "There was no expectation by [the analyst's] sources that he would keep their information in confidence. Nor did [the analyst] misappropriate or illegally obtain the information. . . ." *Id.*, at 665. *Dirks* thus presents no suggestion that a person who gains nonpublic information through misappropriation in breach of a fiduciary duty escapes § 10(b) liability when, without alerting the source, he trades on the information.

Last of the three cases the Eighth Circuit regarded as warranting disapproval of the misappropriation theory, *Central Bank* held that "a private plaintiff may not maintain an aiding and abetting suit under § 10(b)." 511 U. S., at 191. * * *

Furthermore, *Central Bank*'s discussion concerned only private civil litigation under § 10(b) and Rule 10b–5, not criminal liability. *Central Bank*'s reference to purchasers or sellers of securities must be read in light of a longstanding limitation on private § 10(b) suits. In *Blue Chip Stamps v. Manor Drug Stores*, we held that only actual purchasers or sellers of securities may maintain a private civil action under § 10(b) and Rule 10b–5. We so confined the § 10(b) private right of action because of "policy considerations." Criminal prosecutions do not present the dangers the Court addressed in *Blue Chip Stamps*, so that decision is "inapplicable" to indictments for violations of § 10(b) and Rule 10b–5.

In sum, the misappropriation theory, as we have examined and explained it in this opinion, is both consistent with the statute and with our precedent. Vital to our decision that criminal liability may be sustained under the misappropriation theory, we emphasize, are two sturdy safeguards Congress has provided regarding scienter. To establish a criminal violation of Rule 10b–5, the Government must prove that a person "willfully" violated the provision. *See* 15 U.S.C. § 78ff(a). Furthermore, a defendant may not be imprisoned for violating Rule 10b–5 if he proves that he had no knowledge of the rule. O'Hagan's charge that the misappropriation theory is too indefinite to permit the imposition of criminal liability, thus fails not only because the theory is limited to those who breach a recognized duty. In addition, the statute's "requirement of the presence of culpable intent as a necessary element of the offense does much to destroy any force in the argument that application of the [statute]" in circumstances such as O'Hagan's is unjust.

The Eighth Circuit erred in holding that the misappropriation theory is inconsistent with § 10(b).

[The Court also reversed the Eight Circuit's rulings that the SEC had exceeded its authority by adopting Rule 14e–3(a), which proscribes trading on undisclosed information in the tender offer setting, even in the absence of a duty to disclose, and that O'Hagan could not be convicted for mail fraud.]

[The opinion of JUSTICE SCALIA, concurring in part and dissenting in part, is omitted.]

JUSTICE THOMAS, with whom THE CHIEF JUSTICE joins, concurring in the judgment in part and dissenting in part.

Today the majority upholds respondent's convictions for violating § 10(b) of the Securities Exchange Act of 1934, and Rule 10b–5 promulgated thereunder, based upon the Securities and Exchange Commission's "misappropriation theory." Central to the majority's holding is the need to interpret § 10(b)'s requirement that a deceptive device be "use[d] or employ[ed], in connection with the purchase or sale of any security." 15 U.S.C. § 78j(b). Because the Commission's misappropriation theory fails to provide a coherent and consistent interpretation of this essential requirement for liability under § 10(b), I dissent.

* * *

I

I do not take issue with the majority's determination that the undisclosed misappropriation of confidential information by a fiduciary can constitute a "deceptive device" within the meaning of § 10(b). Nondisclosure where there is a pre-existing duty to disclose satisfies our definitions of fraud and deceit for purposes of the securities laws. *See Chiarella v. United States*, 445 U.S. 222, 230 (1980).

Unlike the majority, however, I cannot accept the Commission's interpretation of when a deceptive device is "use[d] ... in connection with" a securities transaction. Although the Commission and the majority at points seem to suggest that *any* relation to a securities transaction satisfies the "in connection with" requirement of § 10(b), both ultimately reject such an overly expansive construction and require a more integral connection between the fraud and the securities transaction. The majority states, for example, that the misappropriation theory applies to undisclosed misappropriation of confidential information "for securities trading purposes," *ante*, at 2207, thus seeming to require a particular intent by the misappropriator in order to satisfy the "in connection with" language. *See also ante*, at 2209 (the "misappropriation theory targets information of a sort that misappropriators ordinarily capitalize upon to gain no-risk profits through the purchase or sale of securities") (emphasis added); *ante*, at 2209–2210 (distinguishing embezzlement of money used to buy securities as lacking the requisite connection). The Commission goes further, and argues that the misappropriation theory satisfies the "in connection with" requirement because it "depends on an *inherent* connection between the deceptive conduct and the purchase or sale of a security." Brief for United States 21 (emphasis added); *see also ibid.* (the "misappropriated information had personal value to respondent *only* because of its utility in securities trading") (emphasis added).

\* \* \*

In upholding respondent's convictions \* \* \*, the majority \* \* \* points to various policy considerations underlying the securities laws, such as maintaining fair and honest markets, promoting investor confidence, and protecting the integrity of the securities markets. *Ante*, at 2209, 2210. But the repeated reliance on such broad-sweeping legislative purposes reaches too far and is misleading in the context of the misappropriation theory. It reaches too far in that, regardless of the overarching purpose of the securities laws, it is not illegal to run afoul of the "purpose" of a statute, only its letter. The majority's approach is misleading in this case because it glosses over the fact that the supposed threat to fair and honest markets, investor confidence, and market integrity comes not from the supposed fraud in this case, but from the mere fact that the information used by O'Hagan was nonpublic.

As the majority concedes, because "the deception essential to the misappropriation theory involves feigning fidelity to the source of information, if the fiduciary discloses *to the source* that he plans to trade on the nonpublic information, there is no 'deceptive device' and thus no § 10(b) violation." *ante*, at 2209 (emphasis added). Indeed, were the source expressly to authorize its agents to trade on the confidential information-as a perk or bonus, perhaps—there would likewise be no § 10(b) violation. Yet in either case—disclosed misuse or authorized use—the hypothesized "inhibiting impact on market participation," *ante*, at 2210, would be identical to that from behavior violating the misappropriation theory: "Outsiders" would still be trading based on nonpublic information that the average investor has no hope of obtaining through his own diligence.[6]

The majority's statement that a "misappropriator who trades on the basis of material, nonpublic information, in short, *gains his advantageous market position through deception; he deceives the source of the information and simultaneously harms members of the investing public,*" *ante*, at 2209 (emphasis added), thus focuses on the wrong point. Even if it is true that trading on nonpublic information hurts the public, it is true whether or not there is any deception of the source of the information. Moreover, as we have repeatedly held, use of nonpublic information to trade is not itself a violation of § 10(b). *E.g., Chiarella*, 445 U. S., at 232–233. Rather, it is the use of fraud "in connection with" a securities

---

**6.** That the dishonesty aspect of misappropriation might be eliminated via disclosure or authorization is wholly besides the point. The dishonesty in misappropriation is in the relationship between the fiduciary and the principal, not in any relationship between the misappropriator and the market. No market transaction is made more or less honest by disclosure to a third-party principal, rather than to the market as a whole. As far as the market is concerned, a trade based on confidential information is no more "honest" because some third party may know of it so long as those on the other side of the trade remain in the dark.

transaction that is forbidden. Where the relevant element of fraud has no impact on the integrity of the subsequent transactions as distinct from the nonfraudulent element of using nonpublic information, one can reasonably question whether the fraud was used in connection with a securities transaction. And one can likewise question whether removing that aspect of fraud, though perhaps laudable, has anything to do with the confidence or integrity of the market.

\* \* \*

### Note: Life After *Chiarella*, *Dirks* and *O'Hagan*

*Chiarella*, *Dirks* and *O'Hagan* provide broad guidelines for determining when a person violates Section 10(b) and Rule 10b–5 by trading on the basis of material, nonpublic information. *Chiarella* held that such a violation occurs when there is a duty to disclose arising from a fiduciary duty or relationship of trust and confidence between the parties to the transaction. *Dirks* indicated, in footnote 14, that an outsider, such as an underwriter, accountant, attorney or consultant who receives nonpublic corporate information with the expectation that it will be kept confidential must abstain from trading on the basis of that information. *O'Hagan* established that trading on the basis of material nonpublic information obtained in any position of trust and confidence can constitute a violation of Rule 10b–5, even though the misappropriator owes no duty to the person with whom she trades.

*Dirks* also held that tipping constitutes a breach of fiduciary duty if "the insider will benefit, directly or indirectly, from his disclosure" and that a "tippee" violates Rule 10b–5 if she "knows or should know that there has been a breach." Comparable prohibitions would appear to apply to one who tips misappropriated information and to one who trades on the basis of such a tip.

This note will examine cases in which lower courts have interpreted and applied these guidelines. It deals with the following questions:

(a) What constitutes a benefit to the tipper such that the tip would constitute a breach of fiduciary duty requiring a tippee who knew or should have known of the breach to abstain or disclose?;

(b) Under what circumstances can an outsider be held to have a duty to the corporation's shareholders under the *Dirks* footnote 14 test?;

(c) Under what circumstances can outsiders, including family members, be held to have violated Rule 10b–5 based on a misappropriation theory?; and

(d) To establish liability on the part of tippees, is it sufficient they trade while they knowingly possessed material inside information, or must the trading be causally connected with the misappropriated information?

*1.  Benefit to Tipper*

In *S.E.C. v. Switzer*, 590 F.Supp. 756 (W.D.Okl.1984), Switzer, then the football coach of the University of Oklahoma, was sitting in the bleachers at a track meet. He overheard Platt, the chief executive officer of Phoenix Resources Company ("Phoenix"), tell his wife that he might be out of town the following week because there was a possibility that Phoenix would be liquidated. The court found that Platt's purpose in telling his wife of the trip was so that child care arrangements could be made. The court also found that the Platts did not know that Switzer was on a bench behind them during this conversation.

Switzer, who knew of Platt's position with Phoenix, and several of Switzer's friends, made substantial investments in Phoenix based on the information regarding Phoenix's possible liquidation. The SEC argued that Switzer and his friends were liable under Rule 10b–5 as tippees.

The court held, however, that Platt did not breach a fiduciary duty to Phoenix's shareholders by disclosing this information since he did not personally benefit, directly or indirectly, from the disclosure. Accordingly, under the *Dirks* test, Switzer and his friends were held to have breached no duty to Phoenix's stockholders and thus were not liable as tippees.

It can be argued that the combination of Platt's imprudent disclosure (arguably a breach of his duty of care) and Switzer's knowledge of the nonpublic nature of that information should be enough to constitute a 10b–5 violation. But *Dirks* requires more. It requires the tipper, or corporate insider, also to have benefitted from the breach. Moreover, *Dirks* also appears to require that the tipper's benefit to be connected in some way with the tippee's trading.

*United States v. Libera*, 989 F.2d 596 (2d Cir.1993), was one of numerous insider trading cases based on access to advance copies of *Business Week* magazine. The tippees received their copies of the magazine from employees of the company that printed it. That company had a policy prohibiting its employees from disclosing the magazine's contents before it was published. The Second Circuit concluded that, as a matter of law, the employer-employee relationship was sufficient to establish a duty not to disclose which the printer's employees breached by providing advance copies of the magazine to others.

The court also held that a tipper could be found liable even if the tipper did not know that the tippee would trade on the basis of the misappropriated information. The fact that a tipper knows she is breaching a duty to the owner of the information "suffices to establish the tipper's expectation that the breach will lead to some kind of misuse of the information." "This is so," the court reasoned, "because it may be presumed that the tippee's interest in the information is, in contemporary jargon, not for nothing." "To allow a tippee to escape liability because the government cannot prove to a jury's satisfaction that the tipper knew exactly what misuse would result from the tipper's wrongdoing would not fulfill the purpose of the misappropriation theory, which is to protect property rights to information * * *. Indeed," the court indicated, "such a requirement would serve no purpose other than to create a loophole for such misuse." *Id.* at 600.

*S.E.C. v. Maio,* 51 F.3d 623 (7th Cir.1995), involved the application of *Dirks* to a situation involving misappropriated information. Ferrero, the CEO of Anacomp, Inc., told Maio, a personal friend who he had helped with investments, that Anacomp was planning to make a tender offer for Xidex Corp. Maio then purchased Xidex stock. The court held that Maio had violated Rule 10b–5 because he knew or should have known that Ferrero violated a fiduciary duty he owed to Anacomp by telling Maio about the planned tender offer. Because Ferrero had misappropriated the information, Maio's duty was derivative of Ferrero's breach.

### 2. Constructive Insiders

In *S.E.C. v. Lund,* 570 F.Supp. 1397 (C.D.Cal.1983), Lund, the chief executive officer, president and Chairman of the Board of Directors of Verit Industries was asked by Horowitz, a member of Verit's board, and the chief executive officer, president and chairman of P & F Industries, ("P & F"), if Verit would be interested in providing $600,000 capital for a joint venture involving a gambling casino between P & F and Jockey Club Casino Corporation. Soon after, but apparently prior to any public disclosure regarding the venture, Lund purchased 10,000 shares of P & F stock, which he subsequently sold at a profit. The court concluded that under *Dirks,* Lund could not be liable as a tippee because Horowitz had not breached a fiduciary duty to P & F's shareholders by disclosing information concerning the venture to Lund. The court did hold, however, that Lund was liable as a "temporary insider," since the "information was made available to Lund solely for corporate purposes." Consider whether the latter conclusion is correct. *Dirks* footnote 14 states that to qualify as a constructive insider, an outsider must know the corporation expects her to keep the information confidential. Was that the situation in *Lund?*

### 3. Family Relationships

In *United States v. Chestman,* 947 F.2d 551 (2d Cir.1991) (*en banc*), *cert. denied* 503 U.S. 1004, 112 S.Ct. 1759, 118 L.Ed.2d 422 (1992), Robert Chestman, a stockbroker, learned from a client, Keith Loeb, that the Great Atlantic & Pacific Tea Co. (A & P) planned to acquire the Waldbaum supermarket chain. Ira Waldbaum, the CEO of Waldbaum, had told his sister that he had agreed to sell the Waldbaum chain and cautioned her that the information was confidential. His sister passed the news on to her daughter, Keith Loeb's wife, who then conveyed the information to Keith but told him to treat it as confidential. Keith proceeded to place an order to purchase Waldbaum stock with Chestman and told him that he had received "definite * * * accurate" information regarding the sale of Waldbaum for a substantial premium. Chestman also bought Waldbaum stock for his own account.

Chestman was convicted of trading as a "tippee" on the basis of material nonpublic information that Loeb had misappropriated in breach of a duty he owed to the Waldbaum family and his wife. The Second Circuit reversed.* The majority had "little trouble finding the evidence insufficient to establish a fiduciary relationship or its functional equivalent between Keith Loeb and the Waldbaum family." It held that "[k]inship alone does not create the necessary relationship," *id.* at 570, and that Keith's wife could make him a fiduciary simply by asking him to keep the information confidential. Consequently, the court concluded, "because Keith owed neither [his wife] nor the Waldbaum family a fiduciary duty or its functional equivalent, he did not defraud them by disclosing news of the pending tender offer to Chestman. Absent a predicate act of fraud by Keith Loeb, the alleged misappropriator, Chestman could not be derivatively liable as Loeb's tippee * * *." *Id.* at 571.

Judge Ralph Winter, joined by five other judges, dissented. He argued: "When members of a family have benefitted from the family's control of a corporation and are in a position to acquire such information in the ordinary course of family interactions, that position comes with it a duty not to trade. * * * Such a duty is of course based on mutual understandings among family members * * * and owed to the family. However, the duty originates in the corporation and is ultimately intended to protect the corporation and its public shareholders." *Id.* at 579 (Winter, J., dissenting). The dissent also saw "no room for argument over whether there was sufficient evidence for the jury to find that Chestman knew Keith Loeb was violating an obligation. The record fairly brims with Chestman's consciousness that Keith Loeb was behaving improperly." *Id.* at 580–81 (Winter, J., dissenting).

### 4. *Tippee's State of Mind*

*United States v. Teicher*, 987 F.2d 112 (2d Cir.1993), involved the question of whether proof a tippee traded while in possession of material, nonpublic information is sufficient to establish causation in an insider trading case, or whether the government must prove defendants traded on the basis of that information. A young attorney had provided defendants with information about ongoing or contemplated transactions involving clients of the law firm that employed him. The defendants were arbitrageurs whose business involved gathering information ranging from rumors to public reports about publicly traded companies.

The Second Circuit held that a violation of Rule 10b–5 occurs "when a trade is conducted in 'knowing possession' of material nonpublic information obtained in breach of a fiduciary or similar duty." *Id.* at 120. In addition to relying on the fact that the SEC has consistently endorsed the interpretation that Rule 10b–5 only requires "knowing possession,"

---

* However, the court affirmed Chestman's conviction under SEC Rule 14e–3(a), which prohibits trading on the basis of material, non-public information about a pending tender offer.

the court set forth three factors which favor a "knowing possession" standard.

First, both Section 10(b) and Rule 10b–5 require that a deceptive practice be conducted in connection with the purchase or sale of a security. The "in connection with" clause has been construed flexibly, the court asserted, to include deceptive practices "touching" the sale of securities, a very tenuous relationship.

Second, the "knowing possession" standard "comports with the oft-quoted maxim that one with a fiduciary or similar duty to hold material nonpublic information in confidence must either disclose or abstain with regard to trading." Thus, an insider who has a fiduciary obligation not to disclose material nonpublic information must abstain from trading. It "would be consistent with the disclose or abstain rule that a tippee acquire the same duty as his fiduciary tipper." *Id.*

Third, a "knowing possession" test has the "attribute of simplicity." The test "recognizes that one who trades while knowingly possessing material inside information has an information advantage over other traders." *Id.* This advantage may manifest itself in a variety of forms, including trading on the information, rescinding a previously decided transaction, or proceeding with a previously planned transaction. In contrast, "a requirement of causal connection between the information and the trade could frustrate attempts to distinguish between legitimate trades and those conducted in connection with inside information." *Id.*

### Note: Remedies for Insider Trading Violations

Section 20A of the 1934 Act creates a private right of action on behalf of contemporaneous traders against insiders, constructive insiders, tippers, and tippees (as well as their controlling persons) who trade while in possession of material nonpublic information. The liability of defendants in actions by contemporaneous traders is limited to the actual profits realized or losses avoided, reduced by the amount of any disgorgement obtained by the SEC under its broad authority to seek injunctive relief. Courts have generally required the same disgorgement of insiders' gains. *See Elkind v. Liggett & Myers, Inc.*, 635 F.2d 156 (2d Cir.1980). The liability of controlling persons is governed by section 20(a) of the 1934 Act, which permits such persons to defend by showing that they acted in good faith and did not know of the violation of their controlled person.

Pursuant to section 21A of the 1934 Act, the SEC is authorized to seek judicially imposed civil penalties against insiders, constructive insiders, tippers, and tippees of up to three times the profits gained or the losses avoided in unlawful insider trading. These civil penalties are *in addition* to other remedies. Thus, an insider, tipper, or tippee may be required to disgorged her profits, whether in an SEC or private action, and pay a treble damage penalty. The civil penalty can be imposed only at the instance of the SEC.

Section 21A(b) also permits the imposition of civil penalties on controlling persons, such as employers, of up to $1 million or three times the insider's profits (whichever is greater) if the controlling person knowingly or recklessly disregards the insider trading by persons under its control. Section 21A(e) of the 1934 Act also encourages private watchdogs by providing for the payment of bounties to people who provide information concerning insider trading.

The penalties for criminal securities violations include sentences of up to a maximum of ten years and maximum fines of $1 million for individuals and $2 million for nonnatural persons. Section 32(a) of the 1934 Act.

The Securities Enforcement and Penny Stock Act of 1990, which amended Section 8 of the 1933 Act and Section 21 of the 1934 Act, gives the SEC administrative "cease and desist" authority, and authorizes the SEC to impose civil penalties under Section 21B of the 1934 Act.

## 4. DISCLOSURE DUTIES OF CORPORATIONS

### SECURITIES EXCHANGE ACT RELEASE
No 34–8995 (1970).

The Securities and Exchange Commission today reiterated the need for publicly held companies to make prompt and accurate disclosure of information, both favorable and unfavorable, to security holders and the investing public. Companies subject to the reporting requirements of the Securities Exchange Act of 1934 are, at the present time, generally required to file annual reports within 120 days after the end of their fiscal years, semi-annual reports within 45 days after the end of the 6–month period and current reports within 10 days after the end of the month in which a reportable event has occurred * * *.

Notwithstanding the fact a company complies with such reporting requirements, it still has an obligation to make full and prompt announcements of material facts regarding the company's financial condition. The responsibility for making such announcement rests, and properly so, with the management of the company. They are intimately aware of the factors affecting the operations of the business. Management of noninvestment companies are cognizant of factors affecting profits and losses, such as curtailment of operations, decline of orders, or costs overruns on major contracts. They are also cognizant of liquidity problems such as a decreased inflow of collections from sales to customers, the availability or lack of availability of credit from suppliers, banks, and other financial institutions, and the inability to meet maturing obligations when they fall due * * *.

The policy of prompt corporate disclosure of material business events is embodied in the rules and directives of the major exchanges. It should be noted that unless adequate and accurate information is available, a company may not be able to purchase its own securities or make acquisitions using its securities, and its insiders may not be able to trade its securities without running a serious risk of violating Section 10(b) of the Securities Exchange Act of 1934 and Rule 10b–5 thereunder.

Corporate managements are urged to review their policies with respect to corporate disclosure and endeavor to set up procedures which will insure that prompt disclosure be made of material corporate developments, both favorable and unfavorable, so that investor confidence can be maintained in an orderly and effective securities market.

NEW YORK STOCK EXCHANGE LISTED COMPANY MANUAL, *Section 2: Disclosure and Reporting Material Information*

### 202.01   Internal Handling of Confidential Corporate Matters

Unusual market activity or a substantial price change has on occasion occurred in a company's securities shortly before the announcement of an important corporate action or development. Such incidents are extremely embarrassing and damaging to both the company and the Exchange since the public may quickly conclude that someone acted on the basis of inside information.

Negotiations leading to mergers and acquisitions, stock splits, the making of arrangements preparatory to an exchange or tender offer, changes in dividend rates or earnings, calls for redemption, and new contracts, products, or discoveries are the type of developments where the risk of untimely and inadvertent disclosure of corporate plans are most likely to occur. Frequently, these matters require extensive discussion and study by corporate officials before final decisions can be made. Accordingly, extreme care must be used in order to keep the information on a confidential basis.

Where it is possible to confine formal or informal discussions to a small group of the top management of the company or companies involved, and their individual confidential advisors where adequate security can be maintained, premature public announcement may properly be avoided. In this regard, the market action of a company's securities should be closely watched at a time when consideration is being given to important corporate matters. If unusual market activity should arise, the company should be prepared to make an immediate public announcement of the matter.

At some point it usually becomes necessary to involve other persons to conduct preliminary studies or assist in other preparations for contemplated transactions, e.g., business appraisals, tentative financing arrangements, attitude of large outside holders, availability of major blocks of stock, engineering studies and market analyses and surveys. Experience has shown that maintaining security at this point is virtually impossible. Accordingly, fairness requires that the company make an immediate public announcement as soon as disclosures relating to such important matters are made to outsiders.

The extent of the disclosures will depend upon the stage of discussions, studies, or negotiations. So far as possible, public statements should be definite as to price, ratio, timing and/or any other pertinent information necessary to permit a reasonable evaluation of the matter. As a minimum, they should include those disclosures made to outsiders. Where an initial announcement cannot be specific or complete, it will need to be supplemented from time to time as more definitive or different terms are discussed or determined.

Corporate employees, as well as directors and officers, should be regularly reminded as a matter of policy that they must not disclose confidential information they may receive in the course of their duties and must not attempt to take advantage of such information themselves.

In view of the importance of this matter and the potential difficulties involved, the Exchange suggests that a periodic review be made by each company of the manner in which confidential information is being handled within its own organization. A reminder notice of the company's policy to those in sensitive areas might also be helpful.

A sound corporate disclosure policy is essential to the maintenance of a fair and orderly securities market. It should minimize the occasions where the Exchange finds it necessary to temporarily halt trading in a security due to information leaks or rumors in connection with significant corporate transactions.

While the procedures are directed primarily at situations involving two or more companies, they are equally applicable to major corporate developments involving a single company.

### 202.03  Dealing With Rumors or Unusual Market Activity

The market activity of a company's securities should be closely watched at a time when consideration is being given to significant corporate matters. If rumors or unusual market activity indicate that information on impending developments has leaked out, a frank and explicit announcement is clearly required. If rumors are in fact false or inaccurate, they should be promptly denied or clarified. A statement to the effect that the company knows of no corporate developments to account for the unusual market activity can have a salutary effect. It is obvious that if such a public statement is contemplated, management should be checked prior to any public comment so as to avoid any embarrassment or potential criticism. If rumors are correct or there are developments, an immediate candid statement to the public as to the state of negotiations or of development of corporate plans in the rumored area must be made directly and openly. Such statements are essential despite the business inconvenience which may be caused and even though the matter may not as yet have been presented to the company's Board of Directors for consideration.

### 202.05   Timely Disclosure of Material News Developments

A listed company is expected to release quickly to the public any news or information which might reasonably be expected to materially affect the market for its securities. This is one of the most important and fundamental purposes of the listing agreement which the company enters into with the Exchange.

A listed company should also act promptly to dispel unfounded rumors which result in unusual market activity or price variations.

## STATE TEACHERS RETIREMENT
## BOARD v. FLUOR CORP.

654 F.2d 843 (2d Cir.1981).

[The plaintiff, a public pension fund, sued Fluor Corporation, a large engineering and construction firm, for alleged violations of Rule 10b–5 and of the New York Stock Exchange Listing Agreement and Company Manual. On February 28, 1975 Fluor signed a $1 billion contract to build a large coal gasification plant in South Africa known as SASOL II. The agreement provided for an "embargo" on all publicity about the contract until March 10, 1975, apparently to allow the South African party to complete delicate negotiations with the French government for financing.

During the week of March 3, the volume of trading in Fluor stock grew and the price moved up slightly. Rumors began to circulate that Fluor had received a large contract, and several securities professionals called the company to inquire about them. On March 6 a representative of the New York Stock Exchange contacted Fluor and suggested that it might be advisable to suspend trading. Fluor agreed, and trading was suspended on March 7. However, between March 3 and March 6, State Teachers had sold some $6.4 million worth of Fluor stock.

The Court of Appeals held, among other things, that Fluor had not breached a duty to disclose its contract or to halt trading in its stock pending an announcement.]

1.   Duty to Disclose or Halt Trading

State Teachers asserts that Fluor had a duty to disclose the signing of the SASOL II contract during the week of March 3 when rumors became rampant and the price and volume of its stock shot upward. We disagree. Under all the circumstances, and particularly in light of its agreement with SASOL to make no announcement until March 10, Fluor was under no obligation to disclose the contract. A company has no duty to correct or verify rumors in the marketplace unless those rumors can be attributed to the company. *Elkind v. Liggett & Myers, Inc.*, 635 F.2d 156 (2d Cir.1980). There is no evidence that the rumors affecting the volume and price of Fluor stock can be attributed to Fluor. Fluor responded to inquiries from analysts between March 4 and March 6 without comment on the veracity of the rumors and without making any material misrepresentation.

Moreover, even if the facts here give rise to a duty to disclose, there is no showing of any intent to defraud investors or any conduct which was reckless in any degree. Fluor's actions between March 3 and March 6 were made in a good faith effort to comply with the publicity embargo. The record completely lacks any evidence of *scienter*—a prerequisite to liability under section 10(b). *Ernst & Ernst v. Hochfelder, supra.* Indeed, at oral argument, counsel for State Teachers conceded that Fluor may not have had a duty to disclose the SASOL II contract under the circumstances.

State Teachers argues that, in any event, Fluor was under a duty to do what it could to halt trading in its stock once it learned that rumors regarding the SASOL II contract were affecting the price of the stock. This issue was not specifically addressed by the district court. State Teachers now argues that once an issuer decides as a matter of business judgment to withhold material information, it then assumes a duty to protect that news from selective disclosure which may disrupt the public market in its stock. In such a circumstance, the issuer must notify the Exchange and request a trading suspension until the news may be made public. State Teachers argues that this duty arises where, as here, the issuer becomes aware that the precise details of the material information are circulating in the market. It submits that this duty (i) is assumed by any issuer who has its stock traded on a public stock exchange and (ii) is consonant with the purpose of the Securities Exchange Act of 1934 to insure the integrity of the marketplace.

\* \* \* State Teachers further argues that an issuer who fails to fulfill this duty to request a halt in trading, knowing that a selling stockholder may suffer a loss, is reckless; therefore, the *scienter* requirement for liability to attach in a section 10(b) private action is satisfied.

Under the circumstances presented in this case, we find that Fluor had no duty under section 10(b) to notify the Exchange and request that trading in its shares be suspended. Fluor first heard of rumors in the marketplace regarding the SASOL II contract on March 4. At that point, the volume of trading in Fluor stock had increased over previous weeks but there was no significant change in price. It was not until March 6 that the volume of trading in the stock and its price increased dramatically. The record indicates that no one at Fluor knew the reason for these market developments. That day, Fluor told the New York Stock Exchange that the signing of the SASOL II contract might be an explanation for the activity, and it agreed to the suggestion of the Exchange that trading be suspended. There was no trading on March 7. These facts obviate any suggestion that Fluor acted recklessly, much less with the fraudulent intent necessary for liability under section 10(b). *See, e.g., Chiarella v. United States*, 445 U.S. 222, 100 S.Ct. 1108, 63 L.Ed.2d 348 (1980); *Ernst & Ernst v. Hochfelder, supra.* Fluor acted scrupulously when it revealed to the Exchange that the signing of the

SASOL II contract might be an explanation for what the Exchange perceived as unusual market activity in Fluor stock. Fluor's good faith is further evidenced by its endorsement of the Exchange's decision to halt trading. For us to say that Fluor should have notified the Exchange at some earlier time would be to create a standard of liability under section 10(b) which gives undue weight to hindsight.

\* \* \*

### Note: Business Judgment and the Duty to Disclose

*Financial Industrial Fund, Inc. v. McDonnell Douglas Corp.*, 474 F.2d 514 (10th Cir.1973), involved a mutual fund that bought shares of Douglas Aircraft (which later merged to become McDonnell Douglas) a week before the company issued a press release that revealed its profits would be substantially below previously published forecasts. The decline was due to shortages of materials and skilled workers and incorrect costing estimates. Plaintiff argued that management knew about, and should have disclosed, the shortfall well before it issued the press release. McDonnell Douglas responded that the timing of the disclosure of negative performance was, under the facts, within management's discretion.

The court held that material information must be "available and ripe for publication" before a duty to disclose arises. In the instant case, while management had an inkling of the situation prior to disclosure, it did not have reliable specific figures. The court further held that the defendant exercised "good faith and due diligence" in ascertaining and verifying the information. In essence, the court suggested that a company would not be held liable so long as its management had exercised reasonable business judgment in deciding on the timing of disclosure.

## BASIC INCORPORATED v. LEVINSON

485 U.S. 224, 108 S.Ct. 978, 99 L.Ed.2d 194 (1988).

JUSTICE BLACKMUN delivered the opinion of the Court.

This case requires us to apply the materiality requirement of § 10(b) of the Securities Exchange Act of 1934, and the Securities and Exchange Commission's Rule 10b–5, promulgated thereunder, in the context of preliminary corporate merger discussions. \* \* \*

I

Prior to December 20, 1978, Basic Incorporated was a publicly traded company primarily engaged in the business of manufacturing chemical refractories for the steel industry. As early as 1965 or 1966, Combustion Engineering, Inc., a company producing mostly alumina-based refractories, expressed some interest in acquiring Basic, but was deterred from pursuing this inclination seriously because of antitrust concerns it then entertained. In 1976, however, regulatory action opened the way to a renewal of Combustion's interest. The "Strategic Plan," dated October 25, 1976, for Combustion's Industrial Products Group included the objective: "Acquire Basic Inc. $30 million."

Beginning in September 1976, Combustion representatives had meetings and telephone conversations with Basic officers and directors, including petitioners here, concerning the possibility of a merger. During 1977 and 1978, Basic made three public statements denying that it was engaged in merger negotiations.[4] On December 18, 1978, Basic asked the New York Stock Exchange to suspend trading in its shares and issued a release stating that it had been "approached" by another company concerning a merger. On December 19, Basic's board endorsed Combustion's offer of $46 per share for its common stock, and on the following day publicly announced its approval of Combustion's tender offer for all outstanding shares.

Respondents are former Basic shareholders who sold their stock after Basic's first public statement of October 21, 1977, and before the suspension of trading in December 1978. Respondents brought a class action against Basic and its directors, asserting that the defendants issued three false or misleading public statements and thereby were in violation of § 10(b) of the 1934 Act and of Rule 10b–5. Respondents alleged that they were injured by selling Basic shares at artificially depressed prices in a market affected by petitioners' misleading statements and in reliance thereon.

The District Court adopted a presumption of reliance by members of the plaintiff class upon petitioners' public statements that enabled the court to conclude that common questions of fact or law predominated over particular questions pertaining to individual plaintiffs. The District Court therefore certified respondents' class. On the merits, however, the District Court granted summary judgment for the defendants. It held that, as a matter of law, any misstatements were immaterial: there were no negotiations ongoing at the time of the first statement, and although negotiations were taking place when the second and third statements were issued, those negotiations were not "destined, with reasonable certainty, to become a merger agreement in principle."

**4.** On October 21, 1977, after heavy trading and a new high in Basic stock, the following news item appeared in the Cleveland Plain Dealer:

"[Basic] President Max Muller said the company knew no reason for the stock's activity and that no negotiations were under way with any company for a merger. He said Flintkote recently denied Wall Street rumors that it would make a tender offer of $25 a share for control of the Cleveland-based maker of refractories for the steel industry." App. 363.

On September 25, 1978, in reply to an inquiry from the New York Stock Exchange, Basic issued a release concerning increased activity in its stock and stated that

"management is unaware of any present or pending company development that would result in the abnormally heavy trading activity and price fluctuation in company shares that have been experienced in the past few days." Id., at 401.

On November 6, 1978, Basic issued to its shareholders a "Nine Months Report 1978." This Report stated:

"With regard to the stock market activity in the Company's shares we remain unaware of any present or pending developments which would account for the high volume of trading and price fluctuations in recent months." Id., at 403.

The United States Court of Appeals for the Sixth Circuit affirmed the class certification, but reversed the District Court's summary judgment, and remanded the case. 786 F.2d 741 (1986). The court reasoned that while petitioners were under no general duty to disclose their discussions with Combustion, any statement the company voluntarily released could not be " 'so incomplete as to mislead.' " *Id.*, at 746, quoting *SEC v. Texas Gulf Sulphur Co.*, 401 F.2d 833, 862 (C.A.2 1968) (*en banc*), *cert. denied sub nom. Coates v. SEC*, 394 U.S. 976 (1969). In the Court of Appeals' view, Basic's statements that no negotiations were taking place, and that it knew of no corporate developments to account for the heavy trading activity, were misleading. With respect to materiality, the court rejected the argument that preliminary merger discussions are immaterial as a matter of law, and held that "once a statement is made denying the existence of any discussions, even discussions that might not have been material in absence of the denial are material because they make the statement made untrue." 786 F.2d, at 749.

The Court of Appeals joined a number of other circuits in accepting the "fraud-on-the-market theory" to create a rebuttable presumption that respondents relied on petitioners' material misrepresentations, noting that without the presumption it would be impractical to certify a class. * * * *See* 786 F.2d, at 750–751.

We granted certiorari, to resolve the split, see Part III, *infra,* among the Courts of Appeals as to the standard of materiality applicable to preliminary merger discussions, and to determine whether the courts below properly applied a presumption of reliance in certifying the class, rather than requiring each class member to show direct reliance on Basic's statements.*

## II

The 1934 Act was designed to protect investors against manipulation of stock prices. *See* S.Rep. No. 792, 73d Cong., 2d Sess., 1–5 (1934). Underlying the adoption of extensive disclosure requirements was a legislative philosophy: "There cannot be honest markets without honest publicity. Manipulation and dishonest practices of the market place thrive upon mystery and secrecy." H.R.Rep. No. 1383, 73d Cong., 2d Sess., 11 (1934). This Court "repeatedly has described the 'fundamental purpose' of the Act as implementing a 'philosophy of full disclosure.' " *Santa Fe Industries, Inc. v. Green*, 430 U.S. 462, 477–478 (1977), quoting *SEC v. Capital Gains Research Bureau, Inc.*, 375 U.S. 180, 186 (1963).

Pursuant to its authority under § 10(b) of the 1934 Act, the Securities and Exchange Commission promulgated Rule 10b–5. Judicial interpretation and application, legislative acquiescence, and the passage of time have removed any doubt that a private cause of action exists for a

---

* The portion of the opinion dealing with the fraud-on-the-market theory is set out in          Section B–1 of this Chapter. [Eds.]

violation of § 10(b) and Rule 10b–5, and constitutes an essential tool for enforcement of the 1934 Act's requirements.

The Court previously has addressed various positive and common-law requirements for a violation of § 10(b) or of Rule 10b–5. * * * The Court also explicitly has defined a standard of materiality under the securities laws, *see TSC Industries, Inc. v. Northway, Inc.*, 426 U.S. 438 (1976), concluding in the proxy-solicitation context that "[a]n omitted fact is material if there is a substantial likelihood that a reasonable shareholder would consider it important in deciding how to vote." *Id.*, at 449. Acknowledging that certain information concerning corporate developments could well be of "dubious significance," *id.*, at 448, the Court was careful not to set too low a standard of materiality; it was concerned that a minimal standard might bring an overabundance of information within its reach, and lead management "simply to bury the shareholders in an avalanche of trivial information—a result that is hardly conducive to informed decisionmaking." *Id.*, at 448–449. It further explained that to fulfill the materiality requirement "there must be a substantial likelihood that the disclosure of the omitted fact would have been viewed by the reasonable investor as having significantly altered the 'total mix' of information made available." *Id.*, at 449. We now expressly adopt the *TSC Industries* standard of materiality for the § 10(b) and Rule 10b–5 context.

### III

The application of this materiality standard to preliminary merger discussions is not self-evident. Where the impact of the corporate development on the target's fortune is certain and clear, the *TSC Industries* materiality definition admits straightforward application. Where, on the other hand, the event is contingent or speculative in nature, it is difficult to ascertain whether the "reasonable investor" would have considered the omitted information significant at the time. Merger negotiations, because of the ever-present possibility that the contemplated transaction will not be effectuated, fall into the latter category.

### A

Petitioners urge upon us a Third Circuit test for resolving this difficulty. Under this approach, preliminary merger discussions do not become material until "agreement-in-principle" as to the price and structure of the transaction has been reached between the would-be merger partners. *See Greenfield v. Heublein, Inc.*, 742 F.2d 751, 757 (C.A.3 1984), *cert. denied*, 469 U.S. 1215 (1985). By definition, then, information concerning any negotiations not yet at the agreement-in-principle stage could be withheld or even misrepresented without a violation of Rule 10b–5.

Three rationales have been offered in support of the "agreement-in-principle" test. The first derives from the concern expressed in *TSC Industries* that an investor not be overwhelmed by excessively detailed and trivial information, and focuses on the substantial risk that preliminary merger discussions may collapse: because such discussions are inherently tentative, disclosure of their existence itself could mislead investors and foster false optimism. *See Greenfield v. Heublein, Inc.*, 742 F.2d, at 756; *Reiss v. Pan American World Airways, Inc.*, 711 F.2d 11, 14 (C.A.2 1983). The other two justifications for the agreement-in-principle standard are based on management concerns: because the requirement of "agreement-in-principle" limits the scope of disclosure obligations, it helps preserve the confidentiality of merger discussions where earlier disclosure might prejudice the negotiations; and the test also provides a usable, bright-line rule for determining when disclosure must be made.

None of these policy-based rationales, however, purports to explain why drawing the line at agreement-in-principle reflects the significance of the information upon the investor's decision. The first rationale, and the only one connected to the concerns expressed in *TSC Industries,* stands soundly rejected, even by a Court of Appeals that otherwise has accepted the wisdom of the agreement-in-principle test. "It assumes that investors are nitwits, unable to appreciate—even when told—that mergers are risky propositions up until the closing." *Flamm v. Eberstadt*, 814 F.2d, at 1175. Disclosure, and not paternalistic withholding of accurate information, is the policy chosen and expressed by Congress. We have recognized time and again, a "fundamental purpose" of the various securities acts, "was to substitute a philosophy of full disclosure for the philosophy of *caveat emptor* and thus to achieve a high standard of business ethics in the securities industry." *SEC v. Capital Gains Research Bureau, Inc.*, 375 U.S. 180, 186 (1963). The role of the materiality requirement is not to "attribute to investors a child-like simplicity, an inability to grasp the probabilistic significance of negotiations," *Flamm v. Eberstadt*, 814 F.2d, at 1175, but to filter out essentially useless information that a reasonable investor would not consider significant, even as part of a larger "mix" of factors to consider in making his investment decision. *TSC Industries, Inc. v. Northway, Inc.*, 426 U.S., at 448–449.

The second rationale, the importance of secrecy during the early stages of merger discussions, also seems irrelevant to an assessment whether their existence is significant to the trading decision of a reasonable investor. To avoid a "bidding war" over its target, an acquiring firm often will insist that negotiations remain confidential, see, *e.g., In re Carnation Co.*, Exchange Act Release No. 22214, 33 SEC Docket 1025 (1985), and at least one Court of Appeals has stated that "silence pending settlement of the price and structure of a deal is beneficial to most investors, most of the time." *Flamm v. Eberstadt*, 814 F.2d, at 1177.

We need not ascertain, however, whether secrecy necessarily maximizes shareholder wealth—although we note that the proposition is at least disputed as a matter of theory and empirical research—for this case does not concern the *timing* of a disclosure; it concerns only its accuracy and completeness. We face here the narrow question whether information concerning the existence and status of preliminary merger discussions is significant to the reasonable investor's trading decision. Arguments based on the premise that some disclosure would be "premature" in a sense are more properly considered under the rubric of an issuer's duty to disclose. The "secrecy" rationale is simply inapposite to the definition of materiality.

The final justification offered in support of the agreement-in-principle test seems to be directed solely at the comfort of corporate managers. A bright-line rule indeed is easier to follow than a standard that requires the exercise of judgment in the light of all the circumstances. But ease of application alone is not an excuse for ignoring the purposes of the securities acts and Congress' policy decisions. Any approach that designates a single fact or occurrence as always determinative of an inherently fact-specific finding such as materiality, must necessarily be over-or underinclusive. In *TSC Industries* this Court explained: "The determination [of materiality] requires delicate assessments of the inferences a 'reasonable shareholder' would draw from a given set of facts and the significance of those inferences to him. * * * *" 426 U.S., at 450. After much study, the Advisory Committee on Corporate Disclosure cautioned the SEC against administratively confining materiality to a rigid formula. Courts also would do well to heed this advice.

We therefore find no valid justification for artificially excluding from the definition of materiality information concerning merger discussions, which would otherwise be considered significant to the trading decision of a reasonable investor, merely because agreement-in-principle as to price and structure has not yet been reached by the parties or their representative.

## B

The Sixth Circuit explicitly rejected the agreement-in-principle test, as we do today, but in its place adopted a rule that, if taken literally, would be equally insensitive, in our view, to the distinction between materiality and the other elements of an action under Rule 10b–5:

"When a company whose stock is publicly traded makes a statement, as Basic did, that 'no negotiations' are underway, and that the corporation knows of 'no reason for the stock's activity,' and that 'management is unaware of any present or pending corporate development that would result in the abnormally heavy trading activity,' information concerning ongoing acquisition discussions becomes material *by virtue of the statement denying their existence.*

\* \* \*

"In analyzing whether information regarding merger discussions is material such that it must be affirmatively disclosed to avoid a violation of Rule 10b–5, the discussions and their progress are the primary considerations. However, once a statement is made denying the existence of any discussions, even discussions that might not have been material in absence of the denial are material because they make the statement made untrue." 786 F.2d, at 748–749 (emphasis in original).

This approach, however, fails to recognize that, in order to prevail on a Rule 10b–5 claim, a plaintiff must show that the statements were *misleading* as to a *material* fact. It is not enough that a statement is false or incomplete, if the misrepresented fact is otherwise insignificant.

### C

Even before this Court's decision in *TSC Industries,* the Second Circuit had explained the role of the materiality requirement of Rule 10b–5, with respect to contingent or speculative information or events, in a manner that gave that term meaning that is independent of the other provisions of the Rule. Under such circumstances, materiality "will depend at any given time upon a balancing of both the indicated probability that the event will occur and the anticipated magnitude of the event in light of the totality of the company activity." Interestingly, neither the Third Circuit decision adopting the agreement-in-principle test nor petitioners here take issue with this general standard. Rather, they suggest that with respect to preliminary merger discussions, there are good reasons to draw a line at agreement on price and structure.

In a subsequent decision, the late Judge Friendly, writing for a Second Circuit panel, applied the *Texas Gulf Sulphur* probability/magnitude approach in the specific context of preliminary merger negotiations. After acknowledging that materiality is something to be determined on the basis of the particular facts of each case, he stated:

> "Since a merger in which it is bought out is the most important event that can occur in a small corporation's life, to wit, its death, we think that inside information, as regards a merger of this sort, can become material at an earlier stage than would be the case as regards lesser transactions—and this even though the mortality rate of mergers in such formative stages is doubtless high."

*SEC v. Geon Industries, Inc.,* 531 F.2d 39, 47–48 (C.A.2 1976). We agree with that analysis.[16]

Whether merger discussions in any particular case are material therefore depends on the facts. Generally, in order to assess the probability that the event will occur, a factfinder will need to look to indicia of interest in the transaction at the highest corporate levels. Without attempting to catalog all such possible factors, we note by way of example that board resolutions, instructions to investment bankers, and actual negotiations between principals or their intermediaries may serve as indicia of interest. To assess the magnitude of the transaction to the issuer of the securities allegedly manipulated, a factfinder will need to consider such facts as the size of the two corporate entities and of the

---

**16.** The SEC in the present case endorses the highly fact-dependent probability/magnitude balancing approach of *Texas Gulf Sulphur.* It explains: "The *possibility* of a merger may have an immediate importance to investors in the company's securities even if no merger ultimately takes place." Brief for SEC as *Amicus Curiae* 10. The SEC's insights are helpful, and we accord them due deference.

potential premiums over market value. No particular event or factor short of closing the transaction need be either necessary or sufficient by itself to render merger discussions material.[17]

As we clarify today, materiality depends on the significance the reasonable investor would place on the withheld or misrepresented information.[18] The fact-specific inquiry we endorse here is consistent with the approach a number of courts have taken in assessing the materiality of merger negotiations. Because the standard of materiality we have adopted differs from that used by both courts below, we remand the case for reconsideration of the question whether a grant of summary judgment is appropriate on this record.

\* \* \*

## V

In summary:

1. We specifically adopt, for the § 10(b) and Rule 10b–5 context, the standard of materiality set forth in TSC Industries, Inc. v. Northway, Inc., 426 U.S., at 449.

2. We reject "agreement-in-principle as to price and structure" as the bright-line rule for materiality.

3. We also reject the proposition that "information becomes material by virtue of a public statement denying it."

---

**17.** To be actionable, of course, a statement must also be misleading. Silence, absent a duty to disclose, is not misleading under Rule 10b–5. "No comment" statements are generally the functional equivalent of silence. *See In re Carnation Co., supra.* See also New York Stock Exchange Listed Company Manual § 202.01 \* \* \* (premature public announcement may properly be delayed for valid business purpose and where adequate security can be maintained); American Stock Exchange Company Guide §§ 401–405 \* \* \* (similar provisions).

It has been suggested that given current market practices, a "no comment" statement is tantamount to an admission that merger discussions are underway. *See Flamm v. Eberstadt,* 814 F.2d, at 1178. That may well hold true to the extent that issuers adopt a policy of truthfully denying merger rumors when no discussions are underway, and of issuing "no comment" statements when they are in the midst of negotiations. There are, of course, other statement policies firms could adopt; we need not now advise issuers as to what kind of practice to follow, within the range permitted by law. Perhaps more importantly, we think that creating an exception to a regulatory scheme founded on a prodisclosure legislative philosophy, because complying with the regulation might be "bad for business," is a role for Congress, not this Court. \* \* \*

**18.** We find no authority in the statute, the legislative history, or our previous decisions, for varying the standard of materiality depending on who brings the action or whether insiders are alleged to have profited.

We recognize that trading (and profit making) by insiders can serve as *an* indication of materiality, see SEC v. Texas Gulf Sulphur Co., 401 F.2d, at 851. We are not prepared to agree, however, that "[i]n cases of the disclosure of inside information to a favored few, determination of materiality has a different aspect than when the issue is, for example, an inaccuracy in a publicly disseminated press release." *SEC v. Geon Industries, Inc.,* 531 F.2d 39, 48 (C.A.2 1976). Devising two different standards of materiality, one for situations where insiders have traded in abrogation of their duty to disclose or abstain (or for that matter when any disclosure duty has been breached), and another covering affirmative misrepresentations by those under no duty to disclose (but under the ever-present duty not to mislead), would effectively collapse the materiality requirement into the analysis of defendant's disclosure duties.

4. Materiality in the merger context depends on the probability that the transaction will be consummated, and its significance to the issuer of the securities. Materiality depends on the facts and thus is to be determined on a case-by-case basis.

\* \* \*

---

*Stransky v. Cummins Engine Co., Inc.*, 51 F.3d 1329 (7th Cir.1995), confirmed that a company has a duty to correct, within a reasonable time, a historical statement that the company believed was true when made but subsequently discovers was false or misleading. On the other hand, *Stransky* held that where subsequent events render inaccurate a forward-looking statement that a company believed was true when made and for which the company had a reasonable basis, the company has no duty to "update" that statement. The court reasoned that liability cannot be based on circumstances that arise *after* a speaker has made a statement; neither can it result from the silence of one who has no duty to speak.

As to when a forward-looking statement is materially false or misleading, seven circuit courts of appeal, relying on the statement in *Virginia Bankshares v. Sandberg*, (Chapter 18) that "publishing accurate facts in a proxy statement can render a misleading proposition too unimportant to ground liability," have adopted the "bespeaks caution" doctrine: "a mechanism by which a court can rule as a matter of law (typically in a motion to dismiss for failure to state a cause of action or a motion for summary judgment) that defendants' forward-looking representations contained enough cautionary language or risk disclosure to protect the defendant against claims of securities fraud." Donald C. Langevoort, *Disclosures that "Bespeak Caution"*, 49 Bus.Law. 481, 482–83 (1994).

Of potentially greater significance is the enactment of § 21E of the Securities Exchange Act of 1934, a "safe harbor for forward-looking statements," as part of the Private Securities Litigation Reform Act of 1995. Congress promulgated this "safe harbor" largely out of concern that the threat of litigation was deterring many companies from issuing "forward-looking statements," and that securities markets thus were less fully informed than they otherwise might be.

Section 21E(i) provides that the term "forward-looking statement" includes

(A) a statement containing a projection of revenues, income (including income loss), earnings (including earnings loss) per share, capital expenditures, dividends, capital structure, or other financial items;

(B) a statement of the plans and objectives of management for future operations, including plans or objectives relating to the products or services of the issuer;

(C) a statement of future economic performance, including any such statement contained in a discussion and analysis of financial condition by the management or in the results of operations included pursuant to the rules and regulations of the Commission; [and]

(D) any statement of the assumptions underlying or relating to any statement described in subparagraph (A), (B), or (C)[.]

Section 21E(c)(1) provides that an issuer, a person acting on behalf of an issuer, and certain other persons

shall not be liable [in any private action arising under the 1934 Act] with respect to any forward-looking statement, whether written or oral, if and to the extent that—

(A) the forward-looking statement is—

(i) identified as a forward-looking statement, and is accompanied by meaningful cautionary statements identifying important factors that could cause actual results to differ materially from those in the forward-looking statement; or

(ii) immaterial; or

(B) the plaintiff fails to prove that the forward-looking statement—

(i) if made by a natural person, was made with actual knowledge by that person that the statement was false or misleading; or

(ii) if made by a business entity; was—

(I) made by or with the approval of an executive officer of that entity; and

(II) made or approved by such officer with actual knowledge by that officer that the statement was false or misleading.*

This section's reference to statements that are "immaterial" effectively codifies the "bespeaks caution" doctrine. The section's reference to "meaningful cautionary statements identifying important factors that could cause actual results to differ materially from those in the forward-looking statement" is the focus of considerable controversy. The Conference Committee stated that it "expects the cautionary statements identify important factors that could cause results to differ materially—but not all factors." It continued:

Failure to include the particular factor that ultimately causes the forward-looking statement not to come true will not mean that the statement is not protected by the safe harbor.

---

* Section 21E(c)(2) contains comparable provisions relating to oral forward-looking statements. Section 21E(b) lists several categories of forward-looking statements to which the safe harbor does not apply. The Private Securities Litigation Reform Act also added a substantially identical "safe harbor" provision to the Securities Act of 1933.

It is unclear what this statement suggests, and how the safe harbor will apply, with regard to a company that deliberately omits from its cautionary statement a factor that the company knows is likely to cause a forward-looking statement not to come true, while listing *other* factors that also might cause the forward-looking statement not to come true.

## 5. ELEMENTS OF A 10B–5 ACTION FOR DISCLOSURE FRAUD

The court's holding in *Texas Gulf Sulphur* that the corporation's press release qualified as a statement made "in connection with" ongoing trading in TGS stock spawned an explosion of private actions under Rule 10b–5 and forced the courts to consider more closely the elements of such an action. In *Mitchell v. Texas Gulf Sulphur Co.*, 446 F.2d 90 (10th Cir.1971), *cert. denied* 404 U.S. 1004, 92 S.Ct. 564, 30 L.Ed.2d 558 (1971), *reh. denied* 404 U.S. 1064, 92 S.Ct. 734, 30 L.Ed.2d 754 (1972), the court noted that in a "civil action instituted on the basis of 10b–5 violations, the keynote of which is fraud, the full panoply of common law fraud elements—misrepresentation or nondisclosure, materiality, scienter, intent to defraud, reliance and causation—have crept in and played varying roles of significance." Neither Section 10(b) nor Rule 10b–5 explicitly contain these requirements and for a time courts, while paying deference to the general analytical structure of the traditional common law action, reshaped them so that, as the court said in *Mitchell*, "a number of these elements have diminished in importance." More recent Supreme Court decisions, however, make clear that these elements have continuing vitality. We now examine the key elements in a private action for damages: (1) standing, (2) scienter, and (3) privity, reliance, and causation.

### a. Standing

*Blue Chip Stamps v. Manor Drug Stores*, 421 U.S. 723, 95 S.Ct. 1917, 44 L.Ed.2d 539 (1975), held that a plaintiff in a private action for damages under Rule 10b–5 had to be an actual purchaser or seller of securities. The Second Circuit first enunciated this rule in *Birnbaum v. Newport Steel Corp.*, 193 F.2d 461 (2d Cir.1952), *cert. denied* 343 U.S. 956, 72 S.Ct. 1051, 96 L.Ed. 1356 (1952), and virtually every lower court to have considered the issue, including the Ninth Circuit in *Blue Chip*, had been adopted

The Court observed that the *Birnbaum* rule barred three classes of potential plaintiffs: (1) Potential purchasers of shares who allege that they did not purchase because of an unduly pessimistic assessment of the corporation's prospects; (2) Actual shareholders who allege that they decided not to sell because of an unduly optimistic assessment of the corporation's prospects; and (3) Shareholders, creditors, and others who suffer a loss in the value of their investment because of corporate or insider activities which violate Rule 10b–5.

The Court observed that while members of the second and third classes could satisfy the *Birnbaum* rule by bringing a derivative action if the corporation was itself a purchaser or seller of securities, the first class (of which the plaintiff in *Blue Chip* was a member) would be precluded from maintaining a 10b–5 action by the *Birnbaum* rule. The Court concluded that this result was justified by the fact that Rule 10b–5 presents a danger of vexatious litigation different in degree and kind from that which accompanies litigation in general.

The Court noted that a 10b–5 complaint which had very little chance of success at trial might nonetheless have substantial settlement value. A plaintiff could use a largely groundless suit to frustrate or delay the normal business activity of defendants through the extensive use of discovery devices, thus representing "an *in terrorem* increment of the settlement value, rather than a reasonably founded hope that the process will reveal relevant evidence." 421 U.S. at 741, 95 S.Ct. at 1928. In particular, the trier of fact would be forced to determine "rather hazy issues of fact the truth of which depended almost entirely on oral testimony." Because there can be no documentation of why a plaintiff failed to purchase stock, proof of those reasons would often rely entirely upon a plaintiff's uncorroborated oral testimony. The Court reasoned that:

> In the absence of the *Birnbaum* doctrine, bystanders to the securities marketing process could await developments on the sidelines without risk, claiming that inaccuracies in disclosure caused non-selling in a falling market and that unduly pessimistic predictions by the issuer followed by a rising market caused them to allow retrospectively golden opportunities to pass. 421 U.S. at 747, 95 S.Ct. at 1931.

By contrast, the *Birnbaum* rule, which requires a plaintiff at least to demonstrate the often objectively verifiable fact of having purchased or sold securities, arguably mitigates the possibility of suits being filed by riskless bystanders.

By itself, the decision in *Blue Chip* was neither surprising nor disturbing. But the tone of Justice Rehnquist's opinion was significant. In just five years, the Court had moved from the "corporate therapeutics" of *Mills v. Electric Auto–Lite* to the "vexatious litigation" of *Blue Chip*. In so doing, the Court also called into question a carefully constructed system of exceptions to *Birnbaum* (including on on which the Ninth Circuti had relied) and foreshadowed a more restrictive interpretation of the federal securities laws.

### b. Scienter

*Ernst & Ernst v. Hochfelder*, 425 U.S. 185, 96 S.Ct. 1375, 47 L.Ed.2d 668 (1976), held that to succeed in a 10b–5 action a plaintiff must prove that defendant acted with scienter—an intent to deceive, manipulate or defraud. Plaintiffs' case rested on a theory of negligent nonfeasance: that defendant Ernst & Ernst, an accounting firm retained as an auditor by First Securities Company of Chicago, had not followed appropriate auditing procedures and thus had failed to discover a scheme by which

First Securities' president had induced plaintiffs to invest in non-existent "escrow" accounts and converted the funds to his own use. Plaintiffs did not accuse Ernst & Ernst of fraud or intentional misconduct.

The Court began its analysis by observing that section 10(b) makes unlawful the use or employment of "any manipulative or deceptive device or contrivance" which violates SEC rules. It then noted:

> The words "manipulative or deceptive," when used in conjunction with "device or contrivance," strongly suggest that § 10(b) was intended to proscribe knowing or intentional misconduct. * * * [T]he use of the words "manipulative," "device" and "contrivance" * * * make unmistakable a congressional intent to proscribe a type of conduct quite different from negligence. Use of the word "manipulative" is especially significant. It is and was virtually a term of art when used in connection with securities markets. It connotes intentional or willful conduct designed to deceive or defraud investors by controlling or artificially affecting the price of securities. 425 U.S. at 197–199, 96 S.Ct. at 1382–83.

The Court next turned to the legislative history and found it

> * * * difficult to believe that any lawyer, legislative draftsman, or legislator would use these words if the intent was to create liability for merely negligent acts or omissions. Neither the legislative history nor the briefs supporting respondents identify any usage or authority for construing "manipulative [or cunning] devices" to include negligence. 425 U.S. at 203, 96 S.Ct. at 1385.

The Court also found "no indication that Congress intended anyone to be liable for [manipulative] practices unless he acted other than in good faith. The catchall provision of § 10(b) should be interpreted no more broadly." 425 U.S. at 206, 96 S.Ct. at 1387.

Finally, the Court addressed the S.E.C.'s argument that subsections (2) and (3) of Rule 10(b)–5 encompass negligent as well as intentional behavior. The Court held that because Rule 10b–5 was adopted pursuant to the authority granted by section 10(b), its scope could not exceed that authority. Having interpreted section 10(b) as limited to the prevention of intentional wrongdoing, the Court could not extend the scope of the statute to validate a rule that barred negligent misconduct.

*Hochfelder* left open two important questions: whether reckless misconduct satisfies the scienter requirement and whether scienter is required in an S.E.C. injunctive action as well as a private damage action. The Court answered the second question affirmatively in *Aaron v. SEC*, 446 U.S. 680, 100 S.Ct. 1945, 64 L.Ed.2d 611 (1980). Relying on *Hochfelder*'s discussion of the use of the terms "manipulative," "device" and "contrivance," the Court held that scienter is a required element of a Rule 10b–5 offense, no matter who the plaintiff is or what remedy is being sought.

The Supreme Court has yet to decide whether proof of recklessness suffices to satisfy Rule 10(b)–5. However, federal courts of appeals uniformly have held that it will. *See Hollinger v. Titan Capital Corp.*, 914 F.2d 1564, 1568 n. 6 (9th Cir.1990), *cert. denied*, 499 U.S. 976, 111 S.Ct. 1621, 113 L.Ed.2d 719 (1991) (citing cases from 11 circuits). The courts of appeals also appear to be reaching a consensus that a standard first adopted at the appellate level by the Seventh Circuit in *Sundstrand Corp. v. Sun Chemical Corp.*, 553 F.2d 1033 (7th Cir.), *cert. denied*, 434 U.S. 875, 98 S.Ct. 224, 54 L.Ed.2d 155 (1977), represents the appropriate definition of recklessness:

> Reckless conduct may be defined as a highly unreasonable omission, involving not merely simple, or even inexcusable negligence, but an extreme departure from the standards of ordinary care, and which presents a danger of misleading buyers and sellers that is either known to the defendant or is so obvious that the actor must have been aware of it.

*Id.* at 1044–45. The *Sundstrand* court observed that while this definition of recklessness "might not be the conceptual equivalent of intent as a matter of general philosophy, it does serve as a proper legally functional equivalent of intent. . . ." *Id.* at 1045.

Issues relating to scienter most frequently have been litigated in the context of motions by defendants to dismiss complaints alleging securities fraud for failure to satisfy the requirement of Fed.R.Civ.P. 9(b) that "the circumstances constituting fraud" must be pled with particularity. The Private Securities Litigation Reform Act of 1995 supplements Rule 9(b) by adding to the Securities Exchange Act of 1934 a new § 21D(b)(2) which requires that, in any private action for damages brought under the Act, the complaint must "state with particularity facts giving rise to a strong inference that the defendant acted with the required state of mind." The language of § 21D(b)(2) is based on a standard that the Second Circuit has applied for several years to complaints alleging securities fraud. *See Beck v. Manufacturers Hanover Trust Co.*, 820 F.2d 46, 50 (2d Cir.1987), *cert. denied*, 484 U.S. 1005, 108 S.Ct. 698, 98 L.Ed.2d 650 (1988). The Second Circuit has held that a plaintiff can satisfy this test by pleading either (a) that defendant had a motive and the opportunity to misrepresent material facts or (b) circumstantial evidence suggesting that defendant consciously or recklessly misrepresented material facts. *Id.* at 50. Where plaintiff is unable to plead facts suggesting motive, "the strength of [her] circumstantial allegations must be correspondingly greater." *Id.* Lower federal courts currently are divided on whether to adopt the Second Circuit standard when interpreting § 21D(b)(2).

### c. *Privity, Reliance and Causation*

As noted above, *Texas Gulf Sulphur* rejected the corporate defendant's argument that because it was not trading TGS stock, its issuance of an allegedly misleading pres release was not "in connection with the purchase or sale of securities." *Heit v. Weitzen*, 402 F.2d 909 (2d Cir.1968), applied TGS' "in connection with" holding to a private suit for damages. It allowed a suit against a corporation to proceed where its statements were reasonably calculated to influence investors.

The Court also has grappled with the issue of how a plaintiff in a 10(b)–5 action can prove reliance and causation. *Affiliated Ute Citizens v. United States*, 406 U.S. 128, 92 S.Ct. 1456, 31 L.Ed.2d 741 (1972), involved claims by members of the Ute tribe that they had sold stock in a tribal corporation to two employees of the bank where their stock was deposited in reliance on the advice of those employees, and that the employees had not disclosed the stock's true value and their position as market makers in the stock. The Court held the defendants were fiduciaries who had violated their duty to disclose all material information:

> Under the circumstances of this case, involving primarily a failure to disclose, positive proof of reliance is not a prerequisite to recovery. All that is necessary is that the facts withheld be material in the sense that a reasonable investor might have considered them important in the making of this decision. * * * This obligation to disclose and this withholding of a material fact establish the requisite element of causation in fact.

406 U.S. at 154, 92 S.Ct. at 1472.

To deal with the problem of proving reliance in open-market transactions, the Supreme Court embraced a version of the "fraud-on-the-market theory."

## BASIC, INCORPORATED v. LEVINSON

485 U.S. 224, 108 S.Ct. 978, 99 L.Ed.2d 194 (1988).*

### IV

### A

We turn to the question of reliance and the fraud-on-the-market theory.

\* \* \*

Our task, of course, is not to assess the general validity of the theory, but to consider whether it was proper for the courts below to apply a rebuttable presumption of reliance, supported in part by the fraud-on-the-market theory.

This case required resolution of several common questions of law and fact concerning the falsity or misleading nature of the three public statements made by Basic, the presence or absence of scienter, and the materiality of the misrepresentations, if any. In their amended complaint, the named plaintiffs alleged that in reliance on Basic's statements

---

* The portion of the Court's opinion dealing with the duty to disclose preliminary merger negotiations was set out earlier in this Section. [Eds.]

they sold their shares of Basic stock in the depressed market created by petitioners. Requiring proof of individualized reliance from each member of the proposed plaintiff class effectively would have prevented respondents from proceeding with a class action, since individual issues then would have overwhelmed the common ones. * * *

Petitioners and their *amici* complain that the fraud-on-the-market theory effectively eliminates the requirement that a plaintiff asserting a claim under Rule 10b–5 prove reliance. They note that reliance is and long has been an element of common-law fraud and argue that because the analogous express right of action includes a reliance requirement, see, *e.g.*, § 18(a) of the 1934 Act, as amended, so too must an action implied under § 10(b).

We agree that reliance is an element of a Rule 10b–5 cause of action. Reliance provides the requisite causal connection between a defendant's misrepresentation and a plaintiff's injury. There is, however, more than one way to demonstrate the causal connection. Indeed, we previously have dispensed with a requirement of positive proof of reliance, where a duty to disclose material information had been breached, concluding that the necessary nexus between the plaintiffs' injury and the defendant's wrongful conduct had been established. See Affiliated Ute Citizens v. United States, 406 U.S., at 153–154. Similarly, we did not require proof that material omissions or misstatements in a proxy statement decisively affected voting, because the proxy solicitation itself, rather than the defect in the solicitation materials, served as an essential link in the transaction. See Mills v. Electric Auto–Lite Co., 396 U.S. 375, 384–385 (1970).

The modern securities markets, literally involving millions of shares changing hands daily, differ from the face-to-face transactions contemplated by early fraud cases, and our understanding of Rule 10b–5's reliance requirement must encompass these differences.[22]

* * *

### B

Presumptions typically serve to assist courts in managing circumstances in which direct proof, for one reason or another, is rendered difficult. The courts below accepted a presumption, created by the fraud-

**22.** Actions under Rule 10b–5 are distinct from common-law deceit and misrepresentation claims, *see Blue Chip Stamps v. Manor Drug Stores*, 421 U.S. 723, 744–745 (1975), and are in part designed to add to the protections provided investors by the common law, *see Herman & MacLean v. Huddleston*, 459 U.S. 375, 388–389 (1983).

"In face-to-face transactions, the inquiry into an investor's reliance upon information is into the subjective pricing of that information by that investor. With the presence of a market, the market is interposed between seller and buyer and, ideally, transmits information to the investor in the processed form of a market price. Thus the market is performing a substantial part of the valuation process performed by the investor in a face-to-face transaction. The market is acting as the unpaid agent of the investor, informing him that given all the information available to it, the value of the stock is worth the market price." *In re LTV Securities Litigation*, 88 F.R.D. 134, 143 (N.D.Tex.1980).

on-the-market theory and subject to rebuttal by petitioners, that persons who had traded Basic shares had done so in reliance on the integrity of the price set by the market, but because of petitioners' material misrepresentations that price had been fraudulently depressed. Requiring a plaintiff to show a speculative state of facts, *i. e.*, how he would have acted if omitted material information had been disclosed or if the misrepresentation had not been made would place an unnecessarily unrealistic evidentiary burden on the Rule 10b-5 plaintiff who has traded on an impersonal market.

Arising out of considerations of fairness, public policy, and probability, as well as judicial economy, presumptions are also useful devices for allocating the burdens of proof between parties. The presumption of reliance employed in this case is consistent with, and, by facilitating Rule 10b-5 litigation, supports, the congressional policy embodied in the 1934 Act. In drafting that Act, Congress expressly relied on the premise that securities markets are affected by information, and enacted legislation to facilitate an investor's reliance on the integrity of those markets:

> "No investor, no speculator, can safely buy and sell securities upon the exchanges without having an intelligent basis for forming his judgment as to the value of the securities he buys or sells. The idea of a free and open public market is built upon the theory that competing judgments of buyers and sellers as to the fair price of a security brings [*sic*] about a situation where the market price reflects as nearly as possible a just price. Just as artificial manipulation tends to upset the true function of an open market, so the hiding and secreting of important information obstructs the operation of the markets as indices of real value." H.R.Rep. No. 1383, *supra*, at 11.

The presumption is also supported by common sense and probability. Recent empirical studies have tended to confirm Congress' premise that the market price of shares traded on well-developed markets reflects all publicly available information, and, hence, any material misrepresentations.[24] It has been noted that "it is hard to imagine that there ever is a buyer or seller who does not rely on market integrity. Who would knowingly roll the dice in a crooked crap game?" *Schlanger v. Four-Phase Systems Inc.*, 555 F.Supp. 535, 538 (S.D.N.Y.1982). Indeed, nearly every court that has considered the proposition has concluded that where materially misleading statements have been disseminated into an impersonal, well-developed market for securities, the reliance of individ-

---

**24.** *See In re LTV Securities Litigation,* 88 F.R.D. 134, 144 (N.D.Tex.1980) (citing studies); Fischel, *Use of Modern Finance Theory in Securities Fraud Cases Involving Actively Traded Securities*, 38 Bus.Law. 1, 4, n. 9 (1982) (citing literature on efficient-capital-market theory); Dennis, *Materiality and the Efficient Capital Market Model: A Recipe for the Total Mix*, 25 Wm. & Mary L.Rev. 373, 374–381, and n. 1 (1984). We need not determine by adjudication what economists and social scientists have debated through the use of sophisticated statistical analysis and the application of economic theory. For purposes of accepting the presumption of reliance in this case, we need only believe that market professionals generally consider most publicly announced material statements about companies, thereby affecting stock market prices.

ual plaintiffs on the integrity of the market price may be presumed. Commentators generally have applauded the adoption of one variation or another of the fraud-on-the-market theory. An investor who buys or sells stock at the price set by the market does so in reliance on the integrity of that price. Because most publicly available information is reflected in market price, an investor's reliance on any public material misrepresentations, therefore, may be presumed for purposes of a Rule 10b–5 action.

C

The Court of Appeals found that petitioners "made public, material misrepresentations and [respondents] sold Basic stock in an impersonal, efficient market. Thus, the class, as defined by the district court, has established the threshold facts for proving their loss." 786 F.2d at 751.[27] The court acknowledged that petitioners may rebut proof of the elements giving rise to the presumption, or show that the misrepresentation in fact did not lead to a distortion of price or that an individual plaintiff traded or would have traded despite his knowing the statement was false. *Id.*, at 750, n. 6.

Any showing that severs the link between the alleged misrepresentation and either the price received (or paid) by the plaintiff, or his decision to trade at a fair market price, will be sufficient to rebut the presumption of reliance. For example, if petitioners could show that the "market makers" were privy to the truth about the merger discussions here with Combustion, and thus that the market price would not have been affected by their misrepresentations, the causal connection could be broken: the basis for finding that the fraud had been transmitted through market price would be gone.[28] Similarly, if, despite petitioners' allegedly fraudulent attempt to manipulate market price, news of the merger discussions credibly entered the market and dissipated the effects of the misstatements, those who traded Basic shares after the corrective statements would have no direct or indirect connection with the fraud.[29] Petitioners also could rebut the presumption of reliance as to plaintiffs who would have divested themselves of their Basic shares without relying on the integrity of the market. For example, a plaintiff

---

**27.** The Court of Appeals held that in order to invoke the presumption, a plaintiff must allege and prove: (1) that the defendant made public misrepresentations; (2) that the misrepresentations were material; (3) that the shares were traded on an efficient market; (4) that the misrepresentations would induce a reasonable, relying investor to misjudge the value of the shares; and (5) that the plaintiff traded the shares between the time the misrepresentations were made and the time the truth was revealed. *See* 786 F.2d at 750.

Given today's decision regarding the definition of materiality as to preliminary merger discussions, elements (2) and (4) may collapse into one.

**28.** By accepting this rebuttable presumption, we do not intend conclusively to adopt any particular theory of how quickly and completely publicly available information is reflected in market price. Furthermore, our decision today is not to be interpreted as addressing the proper measure of damages in litigation of this kind.

**29.** We note there may be a certain incongruity between the assumption that Basic shares are traded on a well-developed, efficient, and information-hungry market, and the allegation that such a market could remain misinformed, and its valuation of Basic shares depressed, for 14 months, on the basis of the three public statements. Proof of that sort is a matter for trial. * * *

who believed that Basic's statements were false and that Basic was indeed engaged in merger discussions, and who consequently believed that Basic stock was artificially underpriced, but sold his shares nevertheless because of other unrelated concerns, *e.g.*, potential antitrust problems, or political pressures to divest from shares of certain businesses, could not be said to have relied on the integrity of a price he knew had been manipulated.

————

Notably, the Court accepted the fraud on the market theory largely to facilitate securities class actions. If each class member had to prove reliance, individual issues would predominate over those common to the class in most fraud on the market situations, precluding maintenance of class actions under Fed.R.Civ.P 23.

In addition to proving reliance (transaction causation), a plaintiff must establish loss causation. To show loss causation, the plaintiff must prove that, if the defendant had not violated Rule 10b–5 by misstating or failing to disclose material facts, the plaintiff would not suffered the injury for which damages are sought. Loss causation is shown if the defendant's misstatements or omissions of material facts touch on the actual reasons why the plaintiff suffered an investment loss. Loss causation is not established if the plaintiff suffered an investment loss for reasons that are unrelated to the defendant's misrepresentations or nondisclosures. *Bastian v. Petren Resources Corp.*, 892 F.2d 680, 684–85 (7th Cir.1990), *cert. denied* 496 U.S. 906, 110 S.Ct. 2590, 110 L.Ed.2d 270 (1990).

# E.   FEDERAL REGULATION—SECTION 16

Insider trading was one of the principal problems Congress addressed in the 1934 Act. The practice was so widespread that, although publicly condemned, it had come to be accepted by many in the financial world as one of the forms of compensation to which corporate officials were entitled. This view was abetted by the common law, which, as we have seen, did little to prevent insider trading. Moreover, even had the common law prohibited it, the prohibition would have been difficult to enforce in the anonymity of the stock exchanges.

Although determined to make a strong statement against insider trading, Congress did not establish a general rule against trading on the basis of material nonpublic information, or an enforcement mechanism for such a rule. Rather, Congress simply attacked one narrow type of stock trading often associated with the misuse of inside information. At the time, it was thought that in many, if not most of the more flagrant cases of insider trading, the insider bought and sold (or, more rarely sold and bought) stock of his company within a relatively short period of time. Since the capital gains period of the tax laws was then six months, there was good reason to suspect that in most cases someone with access to inside information who bought and sold within six months (and therefore forewent the favorable tax treatment available for profits made on trades separated by a longer period) was doing so to take advantage of some special knowledge. It was only a step from this perception to the simple and readily enforceable, if crude, principle of Section 16(b), which provides that any profits realized by an insider (as defined) on a purchase followed by a sale, or a sale followed by a purchase, within a six-month period, "shall inure to and be recoverable by the issuer." Although the section explicitly states that its purpose is "preventing the unfair use of information which may have been obtained by [the insider] by reason of his relationship to the issuer," there is no need to show any such "unfair use." All that is necessary is offsetting trades within six months by someone with the necessary relationship to the corporation.

Section 16 applies to the directors and officers of a corporation and to any person who is the "beneficial owner" of more than ten percent of a class of equity securities of the corporation registered under Section 12 of the 1934 Act. To ensure that potential plaintiffs can learn about violations of Section 16(b), Section 16(a) requires those covered by the statute to file reports with the SEC disclosing the ownership of their equity securities as well as any changes in that ownership. The latter report must be filed within ten days after the end of the month in which the transaction takes place. The Commission publishes a monthly compilation of these reports, and summaries appear regularly in a number of financial publications.

Section 16(b) has a self-contained remedy provision with its own procedures which make it a hybrid form of derivative suit. Thus, the security holder, who need not be a contemporaneous owner, must make a demand on the directors unless demand would be futile. Thereafter, the corporation has sixty days to decide whether to institute suit. If it does not, the action may be maintained by the holder at the time of suit who remains such through the trial. The contemporaneous ownership requirement of F.R.C.P. 23.1 does not apply. *See* Thomas Lee Hazen, THE LAW OF SECURITIES REGULATION 629–630 (2d ed. 1990).

A security holder will have little incentive to bring an action under Section 16(b) when the proceeds will go to the corporation whose gain will normally be of only the remotest benefit to him. And, as with conventional derivative suits, the moving force in Section 16(b) actions is generally plaintiff's counsel who seeks the fees that are awarded in a successful action. Indeed, courts have held that it is no defense to a Section 16(b) action that the suit was motivated primarily by the desire to obtain such fees. *Magida v. Continental Can Co., Inc.*, 231 F.2d 843 (2d Cir.1956).

Notwithstanding the benefits that a Section 16(b) action can confer on a corporation, the stockholder's attorney will not always be able to recover her fees when the corporation has recovered the profits from the insider. In *Portnoy v. Gold Reserve Corp.*, 711 F.Supp. 565 (E.D.Wash. 1989), the company became aware of the Section 16(b) violation when it filed the insider's reporting form and took immediate steps to recover his profits directly. After the report was made public, a number of demands were made upon the company to recover the profits and a derivative suit was instituted to achieve the same end. Upon being advised that the company had already received the profits, plaintiff's attorney applied for counsel fees for the benefit his work had conferred on the company. The court rejected the application, holding that the attorney's efforts "were not a substantial or motivating factor in [the company's] eventual pursuit and recovery of the short-swing profits." In addition, the court noted that there were substantial policy considerations militating against the payment of fees in cases where the corporation itself had been vigilant in enforcing its own rights.

### Note: Interpretative Problems Under Section 16

#### 1.   Who is an "Officer"?

The definition of "officer" includes executive officers and chief financial or accounting officers as well as any person, regardless of title, who performs significant "policy-making functions." Rule 16a–1(f). Or, as an early case stated, whether a person is "a corporate employee performing important executive duties of such character that he would be likely, in discharging these duties, to obtain confidential information about the company's affairs that would aid him if he engaged in personal market transactions." *Colby v. Klune*, 178 F.2d 872, 873 (2d Cir.1949). The definition of "officer" makes it clear that a person's functions determine the applicability of Section 16. An officer includes any person who is engaged in a significant policy-making function for the corporation (Rule 16a–1(f)). In *Merrill Lynch, Pierce, Fenner & Smith, Inc. v. Livingston*, 566 F.2d 1119 (9th Cir.1978), the Ninth Circuit held that where a company had three hundred and fifty "executive vice presidents," the title created an inference that there were opportunities to obtain confidential information; the court found that the defendant vice-president had not violated Section 16(b) because he was able to prove that his title was merely honorary and did not carry with it the executive responsibilities which might be assumed. *Id.* at 1122–1123. At a time when corporate law has increasingly held officers and directors to a high standard of care, does *Livingston* constitute strong precedent for deciding who is an officer?

How far down the corporate structure does Section 16 reach? In *Lee National Corp. v. Segur*, 281 F.Supp. 851 (E.D.Pa.1968), the court held that an officer of a subsidiary of the issuer was not subject to Section 16(b) liability unless he was actually performing the functions of an officer of the parent corporation. Does that analysis give too much weight to the external formalities of corporate organization?

#### 2.   Who is a "Beneficial Owner"?

Beneficial ownership, solely for purposes of determining a person's status as a 10% shareholder, is defined with reference to the framework of Section 13(d) of the 1934 Act. Rule 16a–1(a)(1). For all other purposes under Section 16, beneficial ownership is determined by whether a Section 16 insider has a pecuniary interest (as defined) in the security. Rule 16a–1(a)(2).

In *Whiting v. Dow Chemical Co.*, 523 F.2d 680 (2d Cir.1975), the court stated that the term "beneficial owner" should be read "more expansively than it [is] in the law of trusts." The court went on to say that "[f]or purposes of the family unit, shares to which legal title is held by one spouse may be said to be 'beneficially owned' by the other, the insider, if the ordinary rewards are used for their joint benefit * * * While we cannot earmark the proceeds of Mrs. Whiting's particular sales as going to household and family support, we know from the findings that the larger part of their joint maintenance came from her estate, the bulk of it in Dow stock. We also know that they engaged in joint estate planning. So that while it is true that if they ever separated, Mrs. Whiting would take her Dow shares, it is also true that while they continue to live as a married couple, there is hardly anything Mrs. Whiting gets out of the ownership that appellant does not share." Id. at 688. *See also, Whittaker v. Whittaker Corp.*, 639 F.2d 516 (9th Cir.1981) (corporate insider who exercised virtually complete control over his mother's affairs through a power of attorney held to be "beneficial owner" of her securities since he enjoyed "benefits substantially equivalent to those of ownership.") See Rules 16a–1(a)(2)(i) and (ii)(A) and 16a–1(e).

Not every court stretches the concept of "beneficial ownership" that far. The Seventh Circuit has held that profits accruing to an insider's grown children who were beneficiaries of a trust were not necessarily subject to the short swing recovery provision. In *CBI Industries, Inc. v. Horton*, 682 F.2d 643 (7th Cir.1982), a corporate executive sold 3000 shares of stock, and within six months bought 2000 shares for his sons' trusts. The court limited the concept of "profit" under Section 16(b) by concluding that it meant only direct pecuniary benefit to the insider and not the sense of enhanced well being that comes from the increased pecuniary wealth of his children. The insider, although a co-trustee of his children's trusts, could not use trust assets or income to pay his personal expenses. Today, Section 16(b) would not apply to a person's interest in securities held in trust except if the ownership requirements of Rule 16a–8 are met.

In computing the requisite ten percent ownership, it is necessary to count the beneficial ownership of all equity securities, including those securities which could be acquired through the exercise of conversion rights. Rule 16a–2(b). This computation is based on the assumption that there is a full conversion of all rights by all holders. The term "equity security" includes convertible securities, but convertibles themselves do not constitute a separate class of equity securities for Section 16(b) purposes. *Chemical Fund, Inc. v. Xerox Corp.*, 377 F.2d 107 (2d Cir. 1967). The actual conversion is exempt from the definition of "purchase" and "sale" under Rule 16b–9.

In a complicated case, one court has held that seven corporations, all controlled by the same individual were not joint beneficial owners of stock owned by any of the corporations for purposes of Section 16(b) liability. *Mayer v. Chesapeake Insurance Company Limited*, 877 F.2d 1154 (2d Cir.1989). In that case, Victor Posner controlled APL Corp. and six other related corporations, all of which owned stock in Peabody International Corp. APL had clearly made short-swing profits in Peabody stock. Plaintiff argued that because Posner controlled the other companies, their stock should be aggregated so as to make APL a ten percent owner at an earlier date, thereby increasing its liability for trading within the six-month period. With one dissent, the court rejected this argument, finding that no entity other than APL was able to use the proceeds from APL's sale of its Peabody stock. The court declined to extend the "group" concept of Section 13(d) of the 1934 Act to Section 16(b). What would be the result in this case under Rule 16a–1(a)(1)?

### 3. Who Is a "Director?"

A partnership or corporation may be deemed to be a director if one of its members or officers serves as a director of the corporation whose shares it trades and is found to have been "deputized" to represent the partnership or corporation. Deputization is a question of fact and must be proved by the plaintiff. Where a partner had not been deputized to represent the partnership on a corporate board, liability under Section 16(b) will attach only to his or her share of the partnership's profits from the partnership's trading activities. *Blau v. Lehman*, 368 U.S. 403, 82 S.Ct. 451, 7 L.Ed.2d 403 (1962); *Feder v. Martin Marietta Corp.*, 406 F.2d 260 (2d Cir.1969).

### 4. The Timing of Purchases and Sales: When Does Liability Attach?

An officer or director is subject to the strictures of Section 16(b) even though he may not have been in office at the time of both purchase and sale. *Feder v. Martin Marietta Corp.*, 406 F.2d 260 (2d Cir.1969); *Adler v. Klawans*, 267 F.2d 840 (2d Cir.1959). By contrast, a beneficial owner may be liable only if he owned more than ten percent of the stock at the time of both purchase and sale. Thus where a ten percent shareholder, within six months, sells enough shares to reduce his holdings to a fraction less than ten percent and then in a separate transaction, sells the remaining shares, the profit realized from the first sale is recoverable by the corporation but the profit from the second is not. *Reliance Electric Co. v. Emerson Electric Co.*, 404 U.S. 418, 92 S.Ct. 596, 30 L.Ed.2d 575 (1972). Applying the same principle, one who purchases enough shares to become a ten percent shareholder and then sells some shares within six months is not liable for any profit realized. *Foremost McKesson, Inc. v. Provident Securities Co.*, 423 U.S. 232, 96 S.Ct. 508, 46 L.Ed.2d 464 (1976). Because Section 16(b) refers to transactions in a period of "less than six months," there will be no liability if the transactions are *exactly* six months apart. *Morales v. Reading & Bates Offshore Drilling Co.*, 392 F.Supp. 41 (N.D.Okl.1975).

The reason for treating officers and directors differently from owners of more than ten percent of the stock is that "officers and directors have more ready access to the intimate business secrets of corporations and factors which can affect the market value of stock. * * * Moreover, a director or officer can usually stimulate more directly actions which affect stock values * * *." *Adler v. Klawans, supra* at 845.

### 5. Computation of "Profits Realized."

In order to increase the deterrent effect of the statute, courts compute the "profits" from a series of several purchases and sales within six months so as to produce the maximum damages. In the leading case of *Smolowe v. Delendo Corp.*, 136 F.2d 231 (2d Cir.1943), the defendants argued that their profits should be computed as they would be for income tax purposes, i.e., stock certificate numbers should be used to determine the actual profits earned from the purchase and sale of particular shares; if the certificate numbers are not known, profits should be calculated on a first-in-first-out basis. The court rejected this approach, holding that to give the statute its full effect, the shares with the lowest purchase price should be matched against those with the highest sale price, ignoring any losses this would produce. This method has achieved some bizarre results. In one case the defendant was required to pay $300,000 to the corporation for "profits" earned over several six month periods of trading although he had actually incurred a net loss of $400,000 on the transactions. *Gratz v. Claughton*, 187 F.2d 46 (2d Cir.1951), *cert. denied* 341 U.S. 920, 71 S.Ct. 741, 95 L.Ed. 1353 (1951).

### 6. Definition of "Purchase" and "Sale".

The problems that have generated the greatest amount of litigation under Section 16(b) are those related to the definitions of "purchase" and "sale." Where a transaction involves cash for stock, no questions arise. Where, however, the transaction is "unorthodox," the analysis is more difficult. In a merger transaction, for example, the shareholders of the acquired corporation normally exchange their shares for shares of the surviving corporation. It is not clear under Section 16(b), however, whether this exchange involves a "sale" of the stock of the old corporation and "purchase" of shares of the new. When faced with this question, the courts have generally taken a pragmatic approach, depending on the presence or absence of the potential for speculative abuse in the transaction. *See e.g., Kern County Land Co. v. Occidental Petroleum Corp.*, 411 U.S. 582, 93 S.Ct. 1736, 36 L.Ed.2d 503 (1973). Thus when officers or directors of the acquired corporation become officers or directors of the acquiring corporation after the merger, the exchange is a "purchase" because of their access to inside information. *Gold v. Sloan*, 486 F.2d 340 (4th Cir.1973). *See also Newmark v. RKO General, Inc.*, 425 F.2d 348 (2d Cir.1970). On the other hand, when a successful bidder in a tender offer thereafter causes a merger with the target company, the exchange in the merger by the losing offeror of the target company's stock it had previously acquired is not a "sale." *Kern County Land Co. v. Occidental Petroleum Corp., supra.*

In *Colan v. Mesa Petroleum Co.*, 951 F.2d 1512 (9th Cir.1991), *cert. denied* 504 U.S. 911, 112 S.Ct. 1943, 118 L.Ed.2d 548 (1992), the Ninth Circuit held that a beneficial owner's exchange of its common stock for nonconvertible debt securities in a self-tender is a "sale" triggering short-swing profits liability. Subsequent to the decision in *Unocal Corp. v. Mesa Petroleum Co.* (Chapter 23), Mesa entered into an agreement to exchange the 7.8 million shares of Unocal common stock that it owned for negotiable debt securities which it later sold for about $589 million. A Unocal shareholder filed suit on behalf of Unocal alleging violations of Section 16(b) seeking to recover Mesa's short-swing profits.

The Court of Appeals held that Mesa's exchange constituted a "sale" that triggered short-swing liability under Section 16(b). The court distinguished *Kern County Land* case in which the Supreme Court had held that an exchange of stock did not constitute a Section 16 sale because the exchange had been required pursuant to a merger and thus was involuntary. In *Colan*, the court noted, Mesa "had the choice of participating in the tender offer or holding onto [its] stock."

The court also rejected Mesa's argument that a voluntary exchange may be exempt from the reach of Section 16 if a beneficial owner is coerced economically into participating or suffering a financial loss. The court concluded that this line of reasoning would contravene the "intent of Congress in enacting the bright-line, flat rule set forth in Section 16(b) requiring disgorgement of profits."

Other transactions that have been held not to be purchases or sales include: gifts, *Shaw v. Dreyfus*, 172 F.2d 140 (2d Cir.1949); certain stock reclassifications, *Roberts v. Eaton*, 212 F.2d 82 (2d Cir.1954); and some conversions of securities, *Petteys v. Butler*, 367 F.2d 528 (8th Cir.1966), *cert. denied* 385 U.S. 1006, 87 S.Ct. 712, 17 L.Ed.2d 545 (1967), and *Blau v. Lamb*, 363 F.2d 507 (2d Cir.1966), *cert. denied* 385 U.S. 1002, 87 S.Ct. 707, 17 L.Ed.2d 542 (1967).

### 7. Derivative Securities.

The rules define the application of Section 16 to standardized options (puts and calls) and other derivative securities. Rule 16a–4(a). Under these rules, insiders will not be able to avoid liability for short-swing profits under Section 16(b) by resorting to purchases and sales of derivative securities. Transactions in derivative securities can be matched against transactions in the underlying securities and against each other. Short-swing profits obtained by insiders through the use of derivative securities are, therefore, recoverable under Section 16(b).

# Chapter 20

# SHAREHOLDER LITIGATION

## A.  INTRODUCTION

A derivative suit is an action on behalf of another "person" brought by one who has an interest in that person but is not its normal decision maker. We have already encountered derivative suits as the vehicle through which fiduciary duties are enforced. In the typical derivative suit, a shareholder is allowed to assert the corporation's rights on the theory that the board of directors, which is charged with that responsibility, has failed to do so. Any recovery from a derivative suit belongs to the corporation, the real party in interest, rather than to the plaintiff-shareholder. Plaintiff's counsel, who plays a major role in initiating derivative suit litigation, receives a fee from the corporation on the theory that she is entitled to compensation for conferring a benefit on the corporation.

The modern derivative suit originated from mid–19th century English equity and trust theory, as a means of allowing shareholders to challenge management abuses. Professor Bert Prunty notes that as corporations grew larger, "[t]he resulting concentration of power produced abuses * * *. The evolution of the derivative suit is the record of the efforts of judges and lawyers to enforce * * * [management] responsibility without destroying the right of a majority of the members of a corporate body to govern the affairs of that body and without assuming the burden of all intra-corporate conflict." Bert S. Prunty, *The Shareholders' Derivative Suit: Notes on its Derivation*, 32 N.Y.U. L.Rev. 980, 992–93 (1957). American courts adopted and refined the derivative suit, focusing from the start on the relationship between corporate directors and shareholders.

The stockholder-plaintiff in a derivative suit acts in a representative capacity for all the injured shareholders. Indeed, F.R.C.P. 23.1 requires that the plaintiff must "fairly and adequately represent the interests of the shareholders * * * similarly situated in enforcing the rights of the corporation." Courts stress the obligations that fall on a stockholder when she initiates a derivative suit. The Supreme Court has characterized the stockholder as assuming "a position, not technically as a trustee perhaps, but one of a fiduciary character. He sues, not for himself alone, but as representative of a class comprising all who are similarly situated * * * He is a self-chosen representative and a volunteer champion." *Cohen v. Beneficial Industrial Loan Corp.*, 337 U.S. 541, 549, 69 S.Ct. 1221, 1227, 93 L.Ed. 1528 (1949). Having assumed that role, the plaintiff cannot later abandon it for personal benefit. *Cf. Young v. Higbee Co.*, 324 U.S. 204, 213, 65 S.Ct. 594, 599, 89 L.Ed. 890 (1945). *See also Heckmann v. Ahmanson*, 168 Cal.App.3d 119, 214 Cal.Rptr. 177 (1985) (stockholder-plaintiff's agreement to dismiss individual claim and not oppose dismissal of derivative suit as a condition of sale of stock to defendant-corporation at a substantial premium could constitute stockholder's use of position as class representative for its own financial advantage).

## ALI, PRINCIPLES OF CORPORATE GOVERNANCE (1994)

Part VII, Chapter 1, Introductory Note.

### THE DERIVATIVE ACTION

* * * [It must be recognized] that the derivative action is neither the initial nor the primary protection for shareholders against managerial misconduct. A variety of social and market forces also operate to hold corporate officials accountable: the professional standards of managers, oversight by outside directors, the disciplinary power of the market, and shareholder voting—all these mechanisms plus the regulatory authority of governmental agencies would constitute significant protections in the absence of private litigation. Even if dissatisfied shareholders had no other recourse than to sell their shares, such action, taken collectively, might also inhibit managerial overreaching, to the extent it depressed the value of the corporation's stock, which management typically also holds. Yet, no single technique of accountability (including market and legal remedies) is likely to be optimal under all circumstances. Each has its characteristic and well-known limitations, and, as a result, shareholders are best served by an overlapping system of protections. When properly structured, the derivative action should enhance the capabilities of these other mechanisms of accountability by (1) ensuring a measure of judicial oversight, (2) providing for a remedy that does not depend upon the ability of widely dispersed shareholders to take coordinated action, and (3) protecting the market for corporate control from unreasonable interferences. In addition, the derivative action may offer the only effective remedy in those circumstances where a control group has the ability to engage in self-dealing transactions with the corporation.

The social utility of the derivative action must also be judged in terms of the alternative of greater public regulation, to which society would likely turn if private mechanisms of enforcement proved inadequate. Over the long run, the availability of private enforcement should reduce the need for public enforcement and bureaucratic oversight of corporate conduct. Moreover, private enforcement multiplies society's enforcement resources, and also probably minimizes enforcement costs, because the private enforcer is typically compensated only when he is successful. In this light, [the ALI's] focus on private litigation remedies reflects a preference for private ordering and a desire to minimize the need for governmental regulation.

Nonetheless, private enforcement, as represented by the derivative action, should not be idealized. Experience suggests that the social costs associated with intracorporate litigation can sometimes outweigh the benefits. In overview, two problems stand out: First, the threat of liability for violations of the duty of care may reduce managerial incentives to take business risks, with resulting loss to shareholders and to the economy generally. * * * Second, in both class and derivative litigation, incentives exist for a private enforcer to bring a non-meritorious action for its nuisance or settlement value. * * * Even in meritorious cases, a private enforcer can reach an inadequate or even collusive settlement that exchanges a low corporate recovery for a high award of attorneys' fees that is paid by the corporation. * * *

In light of these problems associated with private enforcement, [the ALI] assigns only a limited role to the derivative action as a mechanism of corporate accountability. * * *

--------

While recognizing the problems that the ALI identifies, Chancellor Allen sees more merit in derivative suits.

* * * I first note in briefest summary the important role of the derivative suit and its stockholder reimbursement component in the efficient operation of the corporate form.

A fundamental condition of the corporate form when stockholders are widely dispersed, as typically occurs in public corporations, is that individual shareholders have little incentive to bear the costs associated with activities that monitor board of director (or management) performance. Of course, a fundamental advantage that the corporate form offers to owners of capital is the utility that an investor gains through centralized management. Centralized management allows passive (low cost) ownership and promotes investor diversification. Limited liability and the entity status of a corporation similarly allow investors to be relatively passive. While the conditions that allow investors to be rationally passive are a primary source of utility, they can also lead to inefficiency to the extent centralized management may have incentives that are not perfectly aligned with those of the residual owners of the firm, which is inevitably the case. This imperfect alignment of incentives will inevitably lead to excess costs associated with centralized management. For that reason *some* expenditures for shareholder monitoring would be efficient. Such monitoring is, of course, more or less costly to the shareholder who engages in it. In a public company with widely distributed shares any particular shareholder has very little incentive to incur those costs himself in pursuit of a collective good, since unless there is some method to force a sharing of costs, he will bear all of the costs and only a (small) pro rata share of any gains that the monitoring yields. Thus, it is likely that in a public corporation there will be less shareholder monitoring expenditures than would be optimum from the point of the shareholders as a collectivity. One way the corporation law deals with this conundrum is through the derivative lawsuit and the recognized practice of awarding to successful shareholder champions and their attorney's risk-adjusted reimbursement payments (i.e., contingency based attorneys fees). The derivative suit offers to risk-accepting shareholders and lawyers a method and incentives to pursue monitoring activities that are wealth increasing for the collectivity (the corporation or the body of its shareholders). Of course that remedy itself suffers from deep agency problems and can lead to a variety of problems that for the most part can be passed over today.

*Bird v. Lida, Inc.,* 681 A.2d 399, 402–03 (Del.Ch.1996)

# B.  POLICY OBJECTIVES

## 1.  THE PARTIES' INCENTIVES

To understand fully the policy issues that derivative suits raise, one must appreciate the economic incentives of the principal players in these suits and the conflicts that these incentives create. Because any recovery in a derivative suit goes to the corporation, the nominal shareholder-plaintiff receives no direct pecuniary benefit from successful litigation; her benefit comes from an increase in the corporation's stock price attributable to the recovery. Thus, the plaintiff wants to maximize the size of that recovery, an interest shared by the corporation itself. The defendant, usually a senior executive or director, seeks to minimize her costs, which consist of monies paid in judgment or settlement and attorneys' fees. As in any contingent fee litigation, plaintiff's counsel will receive a fee if the suit results in a favorable judgment or a settlement; she earns nothing if the plaintiff loses. The size of the fee generally will be based either on the time spent on the litigation or on a percentage of the total recovery.

Unlike most litigation in which the plaintiff's gain comes at the defendant's expense, a derivative suit is not a zero-sum game; in fact, both plaintiff *and* defendant can recover many of their litigation costs from the corporation. The defendant in a derivative suit, particularly if she is a director, is not like a defendant in other actions. As we saw in Chapter 16, under most state corporate laws, a corporation may indemnify a director for her expenses in a derivative suit if she has not been *adjudged* to have breached her duty to the corporation and otherwise meets the standards for indemnification. These expenses include attorneys' fees, which can be substantial, and, in some jurisdictions, even the amounts paid in settlement. Thus, a risk-averse defendant has a strong incentive to agree to a relatively small settlement and be indemnified for substantially all her expenses rather than risk an adverse judicial decision. To the extent that the monetary settlement is reduced through the inclusion of non-pecuniary relief, the defendant's economic risk is lessened still further. Because indemnification usually is paid by insurance which the corporation purchases at its own expense, a settlement may result in the shareholders paying part of the cost of the defense, notwithstanding that the defendant may have breached her duty to the corporation.

Similarly, the plaintiff in a derivative suit is not like most plaintiffs, and her relationship with her lawyer is not like most lawyer-client relationships in contingent fee litigation. In most litigation, counsel must operate within the bounds set by her client. When the client tells counsel to litigate, counsel litigates; when the client prefers to settle, the lawyer settles. By contrast, the shareholder in a derivative suit has only a nominal economic interest and usually gives no directions. Additionally, in most contingent litigation the client knows she has been injured and seeks out a lawyer; in the derivative suit, it is not uncommon for the lawyer to seek out the client and advise her of the wrong that has occurred. Indeed, one commentator has called plaintiff's counsel "the engine that drives the derivative action." John C. Coffee, Jr., *American Law Institute's Corporate Governance Project: Remedies: Litigation and Corporate Governance: An Essay on Steering Between Scylla and Charybdis*, 52 GEO.WASH.L.REV. 789, 800 (1984). Finally, in a derivative suit, the lawyer has far more at stake than the plaintiff shareholder. Thus, plaintiff's counsel has an incentive to agree to settlements that shareholders collectively might view as inadequate, in order to assure that she receives a fee for her work.

Some of the problems described above are present in any form of contingent litigation. They are more troublesome here because of the representative nature of the derivative suit. Nuisance suits are not peculiar to the corporate setting. Nevertheless, in order to discourage abuses by people purporting to act on the corporation's behalf, the law has singled out derivative suits for the imposition of special procedural restrictions and judicial oversight. Among other things, this chapter examines the reasons for these restrictions, how they operate, and how to evaluate their efficacy and desirability. The class action is another tool of shareholder litigation, but it is a device with broader applicability and will not be examined here.

## 2. RATIONALES FOR THE DERIVATIVE SUIT

The original rationale for the derivative suit appears to have been compensatory; the corporation has been harmed by the defendant's acts and can be made whole if the defendant pays the appropriate damages. There are, however, several problems with such a rationale. First, because the recovery goes to the corporation, whose shareholder body is changing constantly, those who were shareholders when the wrong occurred and have subsequently sold their shares at a price which reflects that wrong do not share in the subsequent recovery. Similarly, those who purchased at the depressed price receive a windfall when the recovery ultimately occurs.

A second problem is that the amount of the corporate injury may not be the same as that suffered by the shareholders. As Professors Coffee and Schwartz have noted: "Even assuming an efficient securities market that automatically translates any injury suffered by the corporation into a decline in its share values, it is still plausible that the stockholders' aggregate loss will exceed that of the corporation—basically because the events will be seen by the marketplace as creating a risk of repetition * * * [F]or legal purposes, the corporation's loss is a historical concept, measured by accounting conventions and limited to injuries that have actually occurred; in contrast, the shareholder's loss may be greater, because in a securities market that discounts future possibilities, predictions of future loss are immediately converted into a present decline in share values." John C. Coffee, Jr. & Donald E. Schwartz, *The Survival of the Derivative Suit: An Evaluation and a Proposal for Legislative Reform*, 81 COLUM. L. REV. 261, 304 (1981). Still another problem with the compensatory rationale is that because the corporation pays indemnification and the plaintiff's attorneys fees, the corporation can never be fully compensated for the wrong, particularly when the suit is settled.

Coffee and Schwartz argue that deterrence rather than compensation should be the principal rationale for the derivative suit. However, as they recognize, there are also serious problems with the deterrence rationale. To begin with, the plaintiff is cast in the role of a "bounty hunter," seeking a reward for assuring that the deterrence function has been performed. Indeed, the role of plaintiff in a deterrence system is such that anyone, regardless of the nature of her interest in the corporation, could play it. Moreover, even if it were possible to limit appropriate plaintiffs, the litigation costs that the corporation incurred might exceed its recovery. The excess could be rationalized as necessary to achieve the desired level of deterrence.

Some scholars have used agency cost literature and portfolio theory in analyzing the rationale for the derivative suit. Professor Cox, who basically favors a compensatory approach, notes that these can be used to support a deterrence rationale:

> The important teaching of portfolio theory explains the beneficial effects of holding an efficient portfolio. An efficient portfolio requires investments in a large number of firms in different industries. A fully diversified investor assumes the risk of the market as a whole, generally referred to as systematic risk, and avoids the risk specific to each individual firm. The preceding discussion of agency costs suggested that the average agency cost for all firms constitutes one source of systematic risk reflected in any firm's cost of capital. So viewed, an important contribution of derivative suits is their potential impact upon the level of systematic risk by deterring managerial misbehavior and not simply compensating the specific

firm whose managers have misbehaved. Consequently, management misbehavior that affects a specific firm, arguably, does not harm investors holding an efficient portfolio because the misconduct's impact is offset by the randomness of firm-specific gains and losses, which sum to zero. Therefore, under this view, resources expended to redress a corporation's injury are not efficiently employed because they consume rather than increase wealth. On the other hand, if derivative suits have the collateral effect of widely mitigating agency costs so that the threat of suit effectively reduces systematic risk, they are economically justified. With this reduction, the investor can make sharper comparisons between investments, including risk-free assets and non-managed risky assets.

James D. Cox, *Compensation, Deterrence and the Market*, 52 GEO. WASH. L. REV. 745, 748–49 (1984).

Professor Coffee pursues the implications of this argument in analyzing whether it is appropriate for a corporation to incur more in litigation costs than the maximum possible recovery. Under Professor Cox's analysis, if corporate expenditures reduce average agency costs by deterring potential wrongdoers, the fully diversified shareholder will benefit in a case where $300,000 is expended to recover $200,000. Notwithstanding his sympathy for a deterrence rationale, Coffee is troubled by this result. He notes that, "it is open-ended: one does not know whether expenditures of $400,000, $500,000 or even more would also produce a deterrent benefit in excess of the costs incurred. Nor can one begin to estimate the marginal deterrent benefit, if any, of each additional successful derivative action." John C. Coffee, Jr., *Litigation and Corporate Governance: An Essay on Steering Between Scylla and Charybdis*, 52 GEO. WASH. L. REV. 789, 807–08 (1984). For Coffee, however, the greatest problem with using the average agency cost analysis is that most shareholders are not fully diversified and thus would lose, rather than gain, when corporate expenditures exceeded the corporate recovery, even if a deterrent surplus were created that would benefit all diversified investors.

A more serious question is whether derivative suits, whatever their rationale, actually improve corporate governance through their effects on corporate managers' behavior. *See* Roberta Romano, *The Shareholder Suit: Litigation Without Foundation?*, 7 J. L.ECON. & ORG. 55 (1991). Sampling a number of shareholder suits, including both derivative and class-action proceedings, Romano concluded that "shareholder litigation is a weak, if not ineffective, instrument of corporate governance." *Id.* at 84. Plaintiffs rarely prevail in derivative lawsuits, and any monetary settlement is extremely small on a per share basis (recovery is significantly higher for class actions than derivative suits). Negotiated settlements sometimes include changes in board structure or composition, but Romano argues that these changes usually are cosmetic, so that even indirect benefits from derivative suits are minimal. Shareholder suits do not deter managers from improper actions, because insurance and indemnification provisions normally cover their expenses. Romano suggests that the main beneficiaries of shareholder suits are the attorneys who collect fees for pursuing them.

Questions as to the underlying rationale and incentives of derivative suits are of more than academic interest; they also raise issues of practicality and public policy. How much of a deviation from the normal principles of corporate governance should be allowed in the conduct of a derivative suit? How should the costs of derivative suits be balanced against the burdens? These large questions are subsumed in smaller ones: What are the requirements for standing? What objections can be raised to the right of the particular plaintiff to act for the corporation? What preliminary steps must be taken before the plaintiff can bring suit? Can the directors prevent the suit from proceeding? How can settlement of a suit be achieved? Who pays the counsel fees? What are the special responsibilities of lawyers in this type of litigation? As you read the following materials, consider how the courts and legislatures have grappled with these questions. To what extent is the derivative suit appropriately viewed as an effective weapon in the arsenal of corporate governance or, rather, is the old appellation, "strike suit," still appropriate?

## PROBLEM
### STARCREST CORPORATION—PART IV

Reread the facts of Part I of the Starcrest Corporation problem in Chapter 17.

Two years have passed. Surveys conducted after Starcrest acquired the land from Elizabeth disclosed the existence of a previously undiscovered structural fault that made the land unsuitable for a hotel. After considerable efforts, Starcrest has been unable to sell the land for more than $3.5 million.

In answering the following questions, assume that the applicable law is that of:

a) Delaware

b) Columbia

### A

Herman Patterson is a retired businessman who owns a few shares of stock in many public corporations, including 10 shares of the stock of Starcrest. This stock is held in the name of Herman's brokerage firm. Your firm has represented Herman for many years, and he has been the named plaintiff in many shareholder suits in which your firm has been lead counsel. You have recently talked to Herman and advised him of your belief that the contract between Starcrest and Elizabeth might constitute a breach of fiduciary duty as well as a violation of the federal proxy rules. Specifically, you have told him that Starcrest's board may have known that the land was overvalued when they approved the transaction. At your request, he has agreed to be the plaintiff in a derivative suit challenging the sale and the related proxy disclosure.

Pamela Gilbert, the partner for whom you work, has asked you to analyze several questions:

1.  If the most promising causes of action involve unfair self-dealing and possible proxy violations under state and federal law, should the suit be brought as a derivative suit or a direct suit (probably in the form of a class action)?

2.  Does Herman have standing to bring a derivative suit?

3.  If the action is cast as a derivative suit, must Herman first make a demand on the directors?

## B

Assume that you are an associate at the firm that has done the Corporation's corporate and securities work for some time. Robert Carey, the partner for whom you work, advised Starcrest on the transaction in question. He discussed it with Elizabeth and with other top company officials and reviewed the contract and various other corporate documents.

Herman has filed suit in the federal district court in Columbia, alleging both that the lease transaction violated state law and that its approval violated the federal proxy rules. The complaint further alleged that no demand was made on the Board because it would have been futile to do so. Carey has asked you to research the following questions:

4.  Suppose the Board appointed Brown, Grey and White to serve as a special litigation committee, with Frank Berger, formerly a justice of the state supreme court, as special counsel. The committee's function would be to consider both the merits of the claim and, if the claim was meritorious, whether it would be in the best interest of the corporation to pursue it. If the committee, after investigating Herman's allegations, concluded that it would not be in the best interest of the corporation for the suit to continue, and the corporation moved to dismiss, what would be the likely result?

5.  If Starcrest moves to require the posting of security for expenses, will Herman have to comply if the suit is brought in New York? In Columbia? In Delaware? Does it matter whether the cause of action is based on federal or state law?

6.  Can your firm represent both Starcrest and Elizabeth in the lawsuit? If not, who, if anyone, can it represent?

7.  Will Herman be able to depose Carey concerning his conversations with Elizabeth about the transaction? Will Herman be able to obtain discovery of the opinion of Carey's firm provided to the Board concerning the fairness of the contract?

## C

You are clerk to Judge Beard, to whom the case has been assigned. After preliminary discovery by plaintiff, the parties have submitted a proposed settlement of the suit in which they agree to the following terms:

A.   Elizabeth will repurchase the land for $3.5 million. If she is able to sell the land for more than that amount within one year, she will pay Starcrest 1/3 of the difference between her sale price and 3.5 million. In no event, however, will she pay more than an additional $500,000.

B.   All subsequent contracts between the Corporation and its officers and directors must be approved by a majority of all the unaffiliated directors.

C.   Counsel fees of $500,000 are to be paid by the Corporation to Gilbert.

8.   What procedures must be followed before the settlement is approved?

9.   Would you recommend that the judge approve the settlement?

## C.   WHAT IS A DERIVATIVE SUIT?

Determining whether an action is direct or derivative sometimes can be complicated. It is an important distinction primarily because of the procedural hurdles that the shareholder-plaintiff in a derivative action must overcome. These include limitations on standing, the need for demand on the corporation's board of directors, the ability of the board to seek dismissal of the action before trial, and the posting of a bond as security for expenses. Recall the Student Guide to *J.I.Case Co. v. Borak* in Chapter 18

John W. Welch, *Shareholders Individual and Derivative Actions: Underlying Rationales and the Closely Held Corporation*, 9 J. CORP. L. 147, 157 (1984) points out that:

> [T]he following actions are frequently mentioned as being, by definition, actionable only derivatively: actions for misfeasance or misappropriation of corporate property; actions for the enforcement of corporate contracts with third parties; actions against corporate directors for competing with the corporation; suits alleging that corporate officers received excessive salaries; third party torts against the corporation; and actions to correct false entries by directors in the records of the corporation.

### ALI, PRINCIPLES OF CORPORATE GOVERNANCE (1994)

§ *7.01.   Direct and Derivative Actions Distinguished*

*Comment:*

c.   *Characterization of an action.* * * * [A] wrongful act that depletes corporate assets and thereby injures shareholders only indirectly, by reason of the prior injury to the corporation, should be seen as derivative in character; conversely, a wrongful act that is separate and distinct from any corporate injury, such as one that denies or interferes with the rightful incidents of share ownership, gives rise to a direct action. Sometimes this result has been justified in terms of an "injury" test that looks to whose interests were more directly damaged; at other times, the test has been phrased in terms of the respective rights of the corporation and its shareholders; but regardless of the verbal formula employed, the results have been substantially similar. * * *

Although some discrepancies exist in the case law, most courts have properly considered actions such as the following as direct actions: (1) actions to enforce the right to vote, to protect preemptive rights, to prevent the improper dilution of voting rights, or to enjoin the improper voting of shares; (2) actions to compel dividends or to protect accrued dividend arrearages; (3) actions challenging the use of corporate machinery or the issuance of stock for a wrongful purpose (such as an attempt to perpetuate management in control or to frustrate voting power legitimately acquired by existing shareholders); (4) actions to enjoin an ultra vires or unauthorized act; (5) actions to prevent oppression of, or fraud against, minority shareholders; (6) actions to compel dissolution, appoint a receiver, or obtain similar equitable relief; (7) actions challenging the improper expulsion of shareholders through mergers, redemptions, or other means; (8) actions to inspect corporate books and records; (9) actions to require the holding of a shareholders' meeting or the sending of notice thereof; and (10) actions to hold controlling shareholders liable for acts undertaken in their individual capacities that depress the value of the minority's shares. In some instances, actions that essentially involve the structural relationship of the shareholder to the corporation (which thus should be seen as direct actions) may also give rise to a derivative action when the corporation suffers or is threatened with a loss. * * * In such cases, the plaintiff may opt to plead either a direct or a derivative action, or to bring both actions simultaneously, unless the court finds that the plaintiff is unable to provide fair and adequate representation. * * *

*d. Relevant criteria.* Section 7.01 does not attempt an exhaustive catalogue of direct versus derivative shareholder actions. Commentators have recognized that close questions can arise whether a particular right or claim belongs more to the corporation or to its shareholders. * * * In borderline cases, the following policy considerations deserve to be given close attention by the court:

First, a derivative action distributes the recovery more broadly and evenly than a direct action. Because the recovery in a derivative action goes to the corporation, creditors and others having a stake in the corporation benefit financially from a derivative action and not from a direct one. Similarly, although all shareholders share equally, if indirectly, in the corporate recovery that follows a successful derivative action, the injured shareholders other than the plaintiff will share in the recovery from a direct action only if the action is a class action brought on behalf of all these shareholders.

Second, once finally concluded, a derivative action will have a preclusive effect that spares the corporation and the defendants from being exposed to a multiplicity of suits.

Third, a successful plaintiff is entitled to an award of attorneys' fees in a derivative action directly from the corporation, but in a direct action the plaintiff must generally look to the fund, if any, created by the action.

Finally, characterizing the suit as derivative may entitle the board to take over the action or to seek dismissal of the action (subject to the conditions set forth in § 7.05 and §§ 7.07–7.13). Thus, in some circumstances the characterization of the action will determine the available defenses.

In practice, the most important result of characterizing an action as direct or derivative is the tendency for derivative actions to be more complex procedurally and to impose additional restrictions on the eligibility of the plaintiffs who may maintain them. For these reasons, the plaintiff usually wishes to characterize the action as direct, while the defendant prefers to characterize it as derivative. In general, courts have been more prepared to permit the plaintiff to characterize the action as direct when the plaintiff is seeking only injunctive or prospective relief. In such situations, the policy considerations favoring a derivative action are less persuasive, because typically the requested relief will not involve significant financial damages against corporate officials, the period in which the corporation is exposed to multiple suits will be relatively brief, and the relief will benefit all shareholders proportionately.

### Note: Features of a Derivative Suit

#### 1. Close Corporations.

The policy reasons for imposing the procedural requirements of a derivative suit where a publicly held corporation is concerned may be absent in a suit involving a close corporation where often there is a close identity between shareholders and managers. *See* John W. Welch, *Shareholders, Individual and Derivative Actions: Underlying Rationales and the Closely Held Corporation*, 9 J. Corp. L. 147, 170 (1984). Also, in a close corporation the likelihood of a strike suit is much smaller because the suit is very often a personal dispute between minority and majority stockholders. Nevertheless, there may be other reasons for requiring that the action be maintained as a derivative suit; for example, creditors may need protection by having the damages awarded to the corporation rather than to an individual shareholder.

In recognition of these differences, ALI Principles of Corporate Governance (1994), § 7.01(d) provides that:

> In the case of a closely held corporation, the court in its discretion may treat an action raising derivative claims as a direct

action, exempt it from those restrictions and defenses applicable only to derivative actions, and order an individual recovery, if it finds that to do so will not (i) unfairly expose the corporation or the defendants to a multiplicity of actions, (ii) materially prejudice the interests of creditors of the corporation, or (iii) interfere with a fair distribution of the recovery among all interested persons.

Several courts have recently adopted the ALI's approach, either directly or indirectly. In *Barth v. Barth*, 659 N.E.2d 559 (Ind.1995), the Indiana Supreme Court adopted § 7.01(d), concluding that it "represents a fair and workable approach for balancing the relative interests in closely-held corporation shareholder litigation." *Id.* at 562. *See also, Watson v. Button*, 235 F.2d 235 (9th Cir.1956) on which the ALI approach is based. Some states also have adopted the ALI test in cases involving close corporation freezeouts. *See, e.g., Richards v. Bryan*, 19 Kan.App.2d 950, 879 P.2d 638 (Kan.App. 1994). *But see Bagdon v. Bridgestone/Firestone, Inc.*, 916 F.2d 379 (7th Cir.1990), (although acknowledging that Ohio would do so when dealing with freezeouts, court refused to extend Delaware's "special injury" test into a general exception for close corporations pursuant to which they would be treated as if they were partnerships for purposes of determining whether an action is direct or derivative).

### 2. Individual Recovery.

Because a derivative suit asserts a cause of action belonging to the corporation, any monetary recovery usually goes directly to the corporation. Creditors and shareholders benefit indirectly by the strengthening of the corporation. If recovery were awarded to individual shareholders, it would in effect, be a distribution of corporate assets to the shareholders either as a dividend or in partial liquidation of the corporation, something that courts do not usually order. *Eshleman v. Keenan*, 22 Del.Ch. 82, 194 A. 40 (1937), *aff'd* 23 Del.Ch. 234, 2 A.2d 904 (1938) (where the corporation is a going concern conducting a profitable business, individual recovery in a derivative action is inappropriate because it would interfere with the management responsibilities of the directors).

Occasionally courts have held that special circumstances require that a monetary judgment be awarded directly to the shareholders on a pro rata basis. In *Perlman v. Feldmann*, 219 F.2d 173 (2d Cir.1955), *cert. denied* 349 U.S. 952, 75 S.Ct. 880, 99 L.Ed. 1277 (1955), (Chapter 21) minority shareholders brought a derivative suit against Feldmann, who had sold his 37% controlling interest in a steel manufacturer. The court awarded damages in the amount of the premium paid to Feldmann and ordered that they be be paid pro rata to the injured stockholders. If the corporation had received the award, the syndicate that purchased the shares would have recovered some of the premium it paid for the controlling shares. *See* Note, *Individual Pro Rata Recovery in Stockholders' Derivative Suits*, 69 HARV.L.REV. 1314 (1956).

Courts have awarded individual recovery in other limited circumstances. *See Eaton v. Robinson*, 31 A. 1058 (R.I.1895) (majority shareholders/directors voted themselves excessive salaries in a scheme to deprive derivative action plaintiffs of their share in a judgment if their litigation were successful); *Matthews v. Headley Chocolate Co.*, 100 A. 645 (Md.1917) (successor controlling stockholders purchased their stock with full knowledge of excessive salaries paid by the corporation to their predecessor controlling stockholders); *Di Tomasso v. Loverro*, 293 N.Y.S. 912 (1937), *aff'd* 12 N.E.2d 570 (N.Y.1937) (the wrongdoers were themselves substantial shareholders of the corporation); *Sale v. Ambler*, 6 A.2d 519 (Pa.1939) (the corporation no longer was a going concern and the parties to the suit owned all the shares of the corporation).

*Glenn v. Hoteltron Systems*, 547 N.E.2d 71 (N.Y.1989), involved an action between the only two shareholders in a close corporation. The plaintiff alleged that the defendant had diverted corporate assets and opportunities for his own benefit. The court held that the damages should be awarded to the corporation, rather than to the plaintiff even though the defendant who had caused the injury would benefit from the payment in his capacity as a 50 percent owner of the corporation. The court conceded that it was an "anomaly" that the wrongdoer-shareholder would ultimately share in the damages awarded but concluded that this factor was not sufficiently important to justify a judicial exception to the general rule that the corporation should receive the benefits from a successful derivative action. The court recognized that its holding might not sufficiently deter wrongdoing but noted that other interests also were at stake. Thus, for example, the rights of a corporate creditor whose claims were superior to those of the shareholder might be impaired if the court were to award an asset that had been diverted from the corporation directly to a shareholder.

### 3. Jury Trial.

The derivative suit was originally a remedy available in equity, allowing shareholders to enforce a corporate cause of action against officers, directors or third parties. As with all suits in equity, parties had no right to a jury trial. When the Seventh Amendment, which preserves the right to a jury trial in suits at common law, was adopted, a corporation's suit to enforce a legal right was an action carrying the right to a jury trial. The derivative suit's status under the Seventh Amendment was uncertain until *Ross v. Bernhard*, 396 U.S. 531, 90 S.Ct. 733, 24 L.Ed.2d 729 (1970). In *Ross*, shareholders brought suit against the directors of an investment company, Lehman Corporation and its broker, Lehman Brothers, alleging breach of fiduciary duty, breach of contract, gross negligence and violations of the Investment Company Act. The Supreme Court held that a shareholder-plaintiff was entitled to a jury trial in a derivative action as to those issues on which the corporation would have been entitled to a jury trial had it sued in its own right.

The Court set forth a three part test to determine the legal or equitable nature of an issue. "The 'legal' nature of an issue is determined by considering, first, the pre-merger [of law and equity] custom with reference to such questions; second, the remedy sought; and third, the practical abilities and limitations of juries." 396 U.S. at 538 n.10, 90 S.Ct. at 738 n.10, 24 L.Ed.2d at 736 n.10. The Court found that the breach of contract and gross negligence claims would have entitled the corporation to a jury trial. The Court did not decide if a claim for breach of fiduciary duty, by itself, was properly triable to a jury. However, subsequent courts have found that some actions based solely on a breach of fiduciary duty are wholly equitable and not triable to a jury, because the remedy is restitutionary in nature. *Maldonado v. Flynn*, 477 F.Supp. 1007, (S.D.N.Y.1979). This holding, however, does not reflect judicial consensus, and courts have not used *Ross* to determine whether specific issues are legal or equitable. In most cases, a court's analysis relies most heavily on the type of remedy sought.

Most derivative suits are brought in state court where the Seventh Amendment does not apply. *Minneapolis & St. Louis Railroad Co. v. Bombolis*, 241 U.S. 211, 217, 36 S.Ct. 595, 596, 60 L.Ed. 961, 963 (1916). Thus, the right to a jury trial in state court becomes a question of state constitutional law. Some state courts have specifically adopted *Ross*. Others treat a derivative action as involving an equitable remedy and reject the right to a jury trial, although many states, including Delaware, have not directly addressed the issue. Deborah DeMott, SHAREHOLDER DERIVATIVE ACTIONS: LAW AND PRACTICE, § 4.18 (1987 & Supp. 1997).

# D.  STANDING

## BANGOR PUNTA OPERATIONS, INC. v. BANGOR & AROOSTOOK RAILROAD CO.

417 U.S. 703, 94 S.Ct. 2578, 41 L.Ed.2d 418 (1974).

MR. JUSTICE POWELL delivered the opinion of the Court.

This case involves an action by a Maine railroad corporation seeking damages from its former owners for violations of federal antitrust and securities laws, applicable state statutes, and common-law principles. The complaint alleged that the former owners had engaged in various acts of corporate waste and mismanagement during the period of their control. The shareholder presently in control of the railroad acquired more than 99% of the railroad's shares from the former owners long after the alleged wrongs occurred. We must decide whether equitable principles applicable under federal and state law preclude recovery by the railroad in these circumstances.

I

Respondent Bangor & Aroostook Railroad Co. (BAR), a Maine corporation, operates a railroad in the northern part of the State of Maine. Respondent Bangor Investment Co., also a Maine corporation, is a wholly owned subsidiary of BAR. Petitioner Bangor Punta Corp. (Bangor Punta), a Delaware corporation, is a diversified investment company with business operations in several areas. Petitioner Bangor Punta

Operations, Inc. (BPO), a New York corporation, is a wholly owned subsidiary of Bangor Punta.

On October 13, 1964, Bangor Punta, through its subsidiary BPO, acquired 98.3% of the outstanding stock of BAR. * * * On October 2, 1969, Bangor Punta, again through its subsidiary, sold all of its stock for $5,000,000 to Amoskeag Co., a Delaware investment corporation. Amoskeag assumed responsibility for the management of BAR and later acquired additional shares to give it ownership of more than 99% of all the outstanding stock.

In 1971, BAR and its subsidiary filed the present action against Bangor Punta and its subsidiary in the United States District Court for the District of Maine. The complaint specified 13 counts of alleged mismanagement, misappropriation, and waste of BAR's corporate assets occurring during the period [when] Bangor Punta controlled BAR. Damages were sought in the amount of $7,000,000 for violations of both federal and state laws. * * *

The District Court granted petitioners' motion for summary judgment and dismissed the action. 353 F.Supp. 724 (1972). The court first observed that although the suit purported to be a primary action brought in the name of the corporation, the real party in interest and hence the actual beneficiary of any recovery, was Amoskeag, the present owner of more than 99% of the outstanding stock of BAR. The court then noted that Amoskeag had acquired all of its BAR stock long after the alleged wrongs occurred and that Amoskeag did not contend that it had not received full value for its purchase price, or that the purchase transaction was tainted by fraud or deceit. Thus, any recovery on Amoskeag's part would constitute a windfall because it had sustained no injury. With this in mind, the court then addressed the claims based on federal law and determined that Amoskeag would have been barred from maintaining a shareholder derivative action because of its failure to satisfy the "contemporaneous ownership" requirement of Fed Rule Civ Proc 23.1(1).[3] * * *.

The United States Court of Appeals for the First Circuit reversed. 482 F.2d 865 (1973). * * *

We granted petitioners' application for certiorari. 414 U.S. 1127, 94 S.Ct. 863, 38 L.Ed.2d 752 (1974). We now reverse.

## II

### A

We first turn to the question whether respondent corporations may maintain the present action under § 10 of the Clayton Act, 15 U.S.C. § 20, and § 10(b) of the Securities Exchange Act of 1934, 15 U.S.C.A.

---

**3.** Rule 23.1(1), which specifies the requirements applicable to shareholder derivative actions, states that the complaint shall aver that "the plaintiff was a shareholder or member at the time of the transaction of which he complains * * *." This provision is known as the "contemporaneous ownership" requirement. See 3B J. Moore, Federal Practice ¶ 23.1 et seq. (2d ed 1974).

§ 78j(b), and Rule 10b–5, 17 CFR § 240.10b–5. The resolution of this issue depends upon the applicability of the settled principle of equity that a shareholder may not complain of acts of corporate mismanagement if he acquired his shares from those who participated or acquiesced in the allegedly wrongful transactions. This principle has been invoked with special force where a shareholder purchases all or substantially all the shares of a corporation from a vendor at a fair price, and then seeks to have the corporation recover against that vendor for prior corporate mismanagement. The equitable considerations precluding recovery in such cases were explicated long ago by Dean (then Commissioner) Roscoe Pound in *Home Fire Insurance Co. v. Barber* [67 Neb. 644, 93 N.W. 1024 (1903).] Dean Pound, writing for the Supreme Court of Nebraska, observed that the shareholders of the plaintiff corporation in that case had sustained no injury since they had acquired their shares from the alleged wrongdoers after the disputed transactions occurred and had received full value for their purchase price. Thus, any recovery on their part would constitute a windfall, for it would enable them to obtain funds to which they had no just title or claim. Moreover, it would in effect allow the shareholders to recoup a large part of the price they agreed to pay for their shares, notwithstanding the fact that they received all they had bargained for. Finally, it would permit the shareholders to reap a profit from wrongs done to others, thus encouraging further such speculation. Dean Pound stated that these consequences rendered any recovery highly inequitable and mandated dismissal of the suit.

The considerations supporting the *Home Fire* principle are especially pertinent in the present case. As the District Court pointed out, Amoskeag, the present owner of more than 99% of the BAR shares, would be the principal beneficiary of any recovery obtained by BAR. Amoskeag, however, acquired 98.3% of the outstanding shares of BAR from petitioner Bangor Punta in 1969, well after the alleged wrongs were said to have occurred. Amoskeag does not contend that the purchase transaction was tainted by fraud or deceit, or that it received less than full value for its money. Indeed, it does not assert that it has sustained any injury at all. Nor does it appear that the alleged acts of prior mismanagement have had any continuing effect on the corporations involved or the value of their shares. Nevertheless, by causing the present action to be brought in the name of respondent corporations, Amoskeag seeks to recover indirectly an amount equal to the $5,000,000 it paid for its stock, plus an additional $2,000,000. All this would be in the form of damages for wrongs petitioner Bangor Punta is said to have inflicted, not upon Amoskeag, but upon respondent corporations during the period in which Bangor Punta owned 98.3% of the BAR shares. In other words, Amoskeag seeks to recover for wrongs Bangor Punta did to *itself* as owner of the railroad. At the same time it reaps this windfall, Amoskeag desires to retain all its BAR stock. Under *Home Fire,* it is evident that Amoskeag would have no standing in equity to maintain the present action.[8]

**8.** Conceding the lack of equity in any recovery by Amoskeag, the dissent argues that the present action can nevertheless be maintained because there are 20 minority

We are met with the argument, however, that since the present action is brought in the name of respondent corporations, we may not look behind the corporate entity to the true substance of the claims and the actual beneficiaries. The established law is to the contrary. Although a corporation and its shareholders are deemed separate entities for most purposes, the corporate form may be disregarded in the interests of justice where it is used to defeat an overriding public policy. In such cases, courts of equity, piercing all fictions and disguises, will deal with the substance of the action and not blindly adhere to the corporate form. Thus, where equity would preclude the shareholders from maintaining an action in their own right, the corporation would also be precluded. It follows that Amoskeag, the principal beneficiary of any recovery and itself estopped from complaining of petitioners' alleged wrongs, cannot avoid the command of equity through the guise of proceeding in the name of respondent corporations which it owns and controls. * * *

## III

In reaching the contrary conclusion, the Court of Appeals stated that it could not accept the proposition that Amoskeag would be the "sole beneficiary" of any recovery by BAR. 482 F.2d, at 868. The court noted that in view of the railroad's status as a "quasi-public" corporation and the essential nature of the services it provides, the public had an identifiable interest in BAR's financial health. Thus, any recovery by BAR would accrue to the benefit of the public through the improvement in BAR's economic position and the quality of its services. The court thought that this factor rendered any windfall to Amoskeag irrelevant.

At the outset, we note that the Court of Appeals' assumption that any recovery would necessarily benefit the public is unwarranted. As that court explicitly recognized, any recovery by BAR could be diverted to its shareholders, namely Amoskeag, rather than reinvested in the railroad for the benefit of the public. Nor do we believe this possibility can be avoided by respondents' suggestion that the District Court impose limitations on the use BAR might make of the recovery. There is no support for such a result under either federal or state law. BAR would be entitled to distribute the recovery in any lawful manner it may choose, even if such distribution resulted only in private enrichment. In sum,

shareholders, holding less than 1% of the BAR stock, who owned their shares "during the period from 1960 through 1967 when the transactions underlying the railroad's complaint took place, and who still owned that stock in 1971 when the complaint was filed." Post, at 722, 41 L.Ed.2d, at 432. The dissent would conclude that the existence of these innocent minority shareholders entitles BAR, and hence Amoskeag, to recover the entire $7,000,000 amount of alleged damages.

Aside from the illogic of such an approach, the dissent's position is at war with the precedents, for the *Home Fire* principle has long been applied to preclude full recovery by a corporation even where there are innocent minority shareholders who acquired their shares prior to the alleged wrongs. * * * The dissent also mistakes the factual posture of this case, since the respondent corporations did not institute this action for the benefit of the minority shareholders. See discussion at n.15, infra.

there is no assurance that the public would receive any benefit at all from these funds.

The Court of Appeals' position also appears to overlook the fact that Amoskeag, the actual beneficiary of any recovery through its ownership of more than 99% of the BAR shares, would be unjustly enriched since it has sustained no injury. It acquired substantially all the BAR shares from Bangor Punta subsequent to the alleged wrongs and does not deny that it received full value for its purchase price. No fraud or deceit of any kind is alleged to have been involved in the transaction. The equitable principles of *Home Fire* preclude Amoskeag from reaping a windfall by enhancing the value of its bargain to the extent of the entire purchase price plus an additional $2,000,000. Amoskeag would in effect have acquired a railroad worth $12,000,000 for only $5,000,000. Neither the federal antitrust or securities laws nor the applicable state laws contemplate recovery by Amoskeag in these circumstances.

The Court of Appeals further stated that it was important to insure that petitioners would not be immune from liability for their wrongful conduct and noted that BAR's recovery would provide a needed deterrent to mismanagement of railroads. Our difficulty with this argument is that it proves too much. If deterrence were the only objective, then in logic any plaintiff willing to file a complaint would suffice. No injury or violation of a legal duty to the particular plaintiff would have to be alleged. The only prerequisite would be that the plaintiff agree to accept the recovery, lest the supposed wrongdoer be allowed to escape a reckoning. Suffice it to say that we have been referred to no authority which would support so novel a result, and we decline to adopt it.

We therefore conclude that respondent corporations may not maintain the present action.[15] The judgment of the Court of Appeals is reversed.

So ordered.

MR. JUSTICE MARSHALL, with whom MR. JUSTICE DOUGLAS, MR. JUSTICE BRENNAN, and MR. JUSTICE WHITE join, dissenting.

* * *

I cannot agree. Having read the precedents relied upon by the majority, I respectfully submit that they not only do not support, but indeed directly contradict the result reached today. While purporting to

---

**15.** Our decision rests on the conclusion that equitable principles preclude recovery by Amoskeag, the present owner of more than 99% of the BAR shares. The record does not reveal whether the minority shareholders who hold the remaining fraction of 1% of the BAR shares stand in the same position as Amoskeag. Some courts have adopted the concept of a pro-rata recovery where there are innocent minority shareholders. Under this procedure, damages are distributed to the minority shareholders in-dividually on a proportional basis, even though the action is brought in the name of the corporation to enforce primary rights. See, e.g., *Matthews v. Headley Chocolate Co.*, 130 Md. 523, 536–540, 100 A. 645, 650–652 (1917). In the present case, respondents have expressly disavowed any intent to obtain a pro-rata recovery on behalf of the 1% minority shareholders of BAR. We therefore do not reach the question whether such recovery would be appropriate. * * *

rely on settled principles of equity, the Court sadly mistakes the facts of this case and the established powers of an equity court. In my view, no windfall recovery to Amoskeag is inevitable, or even likely, on the facts of this case. But even if recovery by respondents would in fact be a windfall to Amoskeag, the Court disregards the interests of the railroad's creditors, as well as the substantial public interest in the continued financial viability of the Nation's railroads which have been so heavily plagued by corporate mismanagement, and ignores the powers of the court to impose equitable conditions on a corporation's recovery so as to insure that these interests are protected. The Court's decision is also inconsistent with prior decisions of this Court limiting the application of equitable defenses when they impede the vindication, through private damage actions, of the important policies of the federal antitrust laws. * * *

* * * Although first Bangor Punta and then Amoskeag owned the great majority of the shares of respondent railroad, the record shows that there are many minority shareholders who owned BAR stock during the period from 1960 through 1967 when the transactions underlying the railroad's complaint took place, and who still owned that stock in 1971 when the complaint was filed. Any one of these minority shareholders would have had the right, during the 1960–1967 period, as well as thereafter, to bring a derivative action on behalf of the corporation against the majority shareholder for misappropriation of corporate assets.

* * * To begin with, it is not at all clear from the record that any recovery had by the railroad will in fact be a windfall to Amoskeag, its present majority shareholder.

But let us assume that the majority is correct in finding some windfall recovery to Amoskeag inevitable in this case. This is still but one of several factors which a court of equity should consider in determining whether the public interest would best be served by piercing the corporate veil in order to bar this action. The public interest against windfall recoveries is no doubt a significant factor which a court of equity should consider. But in this case it is clearly outweighed by other considerations, equally deserving the recognition of a court of equity, supporting the maintenance of the railroad's action against those who have defrauded it of its assets. Equity should take into account, for example, the railroad's relationships with its creditors. BAR owes a debt of approximately $23 million, indicating almost 90% debt ownership of the enterprise. If the allegations of the complaint are true, the conversion and misappropriation of corporate assets committed by petitioners placed the railroad close to the brink of bankruptcy, to the certain detriment of its creditors. * * *

Surely the corporation, as an entity independent of its shareholders, has an interest of its own in assuring that it can meet its responsibility to its creditors. And I do not see how it can do so unless it remains free to bring suit against those who have defrauded it of its assets. The

Court's result, I fear, only gives added incentive to abuses of the corporate form which equity has long sought to discourage—allowing a majority shareholder to take advantage of the protections of the corporate form while bleeding the corporation to the detriment of its creditors, and then permitting the majority shareholder to sell the corporation and remain free from any liability for its wrongdoing.

More importantly, equity should take into account the public interest at stake in this litigation. * * *

The significance of the public interest in the financial well-being of railroads should be self-evident in these times, with many of our Nation's railroads in dire financial straits and with some of the most important lines thrown into reorganization proceedings. Indeed, the prospect of large-scale railroad insolvency in the Northeast United States was deemed by Congress to present a national emergency, prompting enactment of the Regional Rail Reorganization Act of 1973, in which the Federal Government, for the first time, committed tax dollars to a long-term commitment to preserve adequate railroad service for the Nation. * * *

The Court gives short shrift, however, to the public interest. While recognizing that respondents' complaint is based primarily on federal antitrust and securities statutes designed to benefit the public, and while conceding that the statutorily designated plaintiffs are respondent corporations, the Court nevertheless holds that these plaintiffs cannot maintain this action because any recovery by Amoskeag would violate established principles of equity. I cannot agree, for the public interest and the legislative purpose should always be heavily weighed by a court of equity. As this Court has frequently recognized, equity should pierce the corporate veil only when necessary to serve some paramount public interest, or "where it otherwise would present an obstacle to the due protection or enforcement of public or private rights." *New Colonial Ice Co. v. Helvering*, 292 U.S. at 442, 54 S.Ct. at 791. Here, however, it is the failure to recognize the railroad's own right to maintain this suit which undercuts the public interest.

### Note: The Standing Requirement

#### 1. General

Because a derivative suit seeks to enforce a right in the name of the corporation, standing generally has been limited to those with an ownership interest in the corporation. The rationale is that it is the owners who have suffered most directly from the harm to the corporation and it is they who should have a right to assert the corporation's right to redress. Simple ownership generally is not sufficient. In almost all jurisdictions, the plaintiff must have been a shareholder at the time of the wrong complained of and at the time of the suit and must remain a shareholder throughout the litigation. Taken together, these requirements are designed to assure that the corporation's rights will be vigorously prosecuted by someone whose harm is actual and who is interested in a successful outcome.

The standing requirements, like the Court's argument in *Bangor Punta*, assume that the principal purpose of the derivative suit is compensation. Were it deterrence, as the Court noted, no need would exist for the contemporaneous ownership requirement; "any plaintiff willing to file a complain would suffice. No injury or violation of a legal duty to the particular plaintiff would have to be alleged." For a thoughtful discussion of the deterrence argument in *Bangor Punta*, see *Damerow Ford Co. v. Bradshaw*, 128 Or.App. 606, 876 P.2d 788 (Or.App. 1994) in which the court declined to adopt a broad rule embodying it. Rather, the court held that "when the purchaser buys shares from one whom the purchaser knows, or has reason to believe, has engaged in, or has acquiesced in, corporate wrongdoing, he or she is not a *bona fide* purchaser without notice of those facts." *Id.* at 794

The standing requirements in most states are generally similar. *See* RMBCA § 7.40; N.Y.B.C.L. § 626. These requirements may be found in the corporate statute, the procedure statute or the applicable court rules. *See* F.R.C.P. 23.1.

### 2. Security Ownership

In most jurisdictions, a derivative suit may be brought by either a holder of record or a beneficial owner of stock; only a few jurisdictions adhere to an earlier requirement that the shareholder be a holder of record or a registered owner. RMBCA § 7.40(e) includes in its definition of "shareholder" a person whose shares are held in a voting trust as well as the more traditional "street name" owner of shares. The meaning of "beneficial owner", however, is not entirely clear. The ALI would give standing to a "holder of an equity security" and defines "holder" as a person with "a substantial beneficial interest" in the stock, leaving the determination of "substantial beneficial interest" to judicial development. ALI, Principles of Corporate Governance (1994), § 7.02.

Suppose the plaintiff is not and never was a shareholder of the corporation that was a party to in the transaction of which she complains, but instead owns stock in a corporation that owns stock of that corporation. The action would then be a double derivative suit, or possibly a triple derivative suit. In *Brown v. Tenney*, 532 N.E.2d 230 (Ill.1988), the court found standing for a stockholder in P Corporation who claimed an injury to S Corporation, a wholly owned subsidiary of P Corporation. There was no doubt that the plaintiff's interest in P Corporation was economically affected by what happened to S Corporation. The justification for allowing a remote derivative suit is that both the corporation that suffered the wrong and its parent corporation which had the right to bring the derivative suit, were controlled by those charged with inflicting the injury. *United States Lines v. United States Lines Co.*, 96 F.2d 148 (2d Cir.1938). The ALI would allow multiple derivative suits but only "where the shareholder's corporation holds at least a *de facto* controlling interest in the injured subsidiary." ALI, PRINCIPLES OF CORPORATE GOVERNANCE (1994) § 7.02 Comment f.

### 3. Creditor Standing

In most jurisdictions, only those holding equity securities may institute a derivative suit. RMBCA § 7.40. Common and preferred stock are clearly equity securities; the difficult problem is in classifying convertible debt securities. As we saw in Chapter 9, a convertible debt security is a hybrid which contains elements of both debt and equity. The holder of a convertible security has the protections of a debt holder, but the interest paid on the security is less because of the holder's right to convert her investment into equity. In *Harff v. Kerkorian*, 324 A.2d 215 (Del.Ch.1974), the court held that a holder of convertible subordinated debentures had no standing to sue because only a person who was a shareholder could maintain a derivative action. Although the court noted that an equitable owner of stock would be considered a shareholder, it held that the owner of convertible debentures was a holder of a debt instrument rather than the equitable owner of the shares into which the debentures were convertible until such time as she actually converted her debentures. By contrast, in *Hoff v. Sprayregan*, 52 F.R.D. 243 (S.D.N.Y.1971), the court held that the holder of convertible debentures satisfied the F.R.C.P. 23.1 "shareholder" requirement in a suit alleging a violation of Rule 10b–5 under the Securities Exchange Act of 1934. In reaching its decision, the court relied on the fact that the 1934 Act defined "equity security" to include convertible debentures. See Note, *Derivative Actions—Harff v. Kerkorian—Standing of Convertible Holders in Delaware*, 1 J.CORP.L. 413 (1976).

The reason that creditors do not have standing to bring derivative suits is that they are not the owners of the corporation. The theory appears to be based on two major premises. First, the perspective of creditors is different from that of stockholders; because creditors are more risk-averse, they are more likely to challenge management decisions which might be properly considered as within an acceptable range of business risks. Second, creditors can negotiate contractual provisions restricting managers' discretion and thus do not need the added protection of the derivative suit. Only when the corporation has become insolvent or if a director has acted with an intent to defraud the creditor have courts been willing to permit a creditor to maintain a derivative suit.

Some commentators have argued for a more relaxed rule. *See* Lawrence E. Mitchell, *The Fairness Rights of Bondholders*, 65 N.Y.U. L. REV. 1165 (1990); Morey McDaniel, *Bondholders and Stockholders*, 14 J. CORP. L. 205 (1988); Morey McDaniel, *Bondholders and Corporate Governance*, 41 BUS.LAW. 413 (1986); Note, *Creditors' Derivative Suits on Behalf of Solvent Corporations*, 88 YALE L.J. 1299 (1979). McDaniel notes that while large creditors may be able to protect themselves contractually against an increased risk of default arising after the loan has been made, smaller creditors often do not have the economic leverage to negotiate such protection. He argues that directors should have fiduciary duties to creditors and that creditors should have standing to bring a derivative suit where stockholder action is unlikely to occur or it is necessary to provide adequate protection to creditors. Whatever the theoretical force of these arguments, courts have almost universally rejected them. *See, e.g., Metropolitan Life Insurance Co. v. RJR Nabisco, Inc.*, 716 F.Supp. 1504 (S.D.N.Y.1989); *Simons v. Cogan*, 542 A.2d 785 (Del.Ch.1987), aff'd 549 A.2d 300 (Del.1988); *Katz v. Oak Industries*, 508 A.2d 873 (Del.Ch.1986). For the argument that these cases misunderstand the nature of the indenture and the contracting process, see Martin Riger, *The Trust Indenture as Bargained Contract: The Persistence of Myth*, 16 J. CORP. L. 211 (1991).

As with other aspects of the standing question, whether creditors should have standing may turn on the purpose of the derivative suit. Some lenders may be well suited to monitor corporate management because of restrictive provisions in the indenture. Moreover, because derivative suits often are motivated by the economic incentives of plaintiff's counsel, there might not be a large risk of an increase in frivolous suits if creditors were permitted to sue. On the other hand, as the ALI has noted in rejecting creditor standing, the interests of creditors generally depart substantially from those of shareholders and the possibility of "creditor suits based on broad concepts of fiduciary duty might chill the board's willingness to accept desirable business risks." ALI, PRINCIPLES OF CORPORATE GOVERNANCE (1994), § 7.02, Reporter's Note 2. For an extensive bibliography on the rights of bondholders, see Victor Brudney and William W. Bratton, BRUDNEY AND CHIRELSTEIN'S CORPORATE FINANCE: CASES AND MATERIALS 225 (4th ed. 1993).

### 4. Contemporaneous Ownership

Many jurisdictions require that the plaintiff have been a shareholder at the time of the wrong complained of or that she acquired her shares by operation of law from such a person. RMBCA § 7.40(a); F.R.C.P. 23.1; N.Y.B.C.L. § 626. This requirement ensures that the plaintiff acting on the corporation's behalf actually have suffered some form of economic harm. Were there no such requirement, a person could purchase her stock at a price which reflected the harm already done to the corporation and, if the suit succeeded, receive a windfall through the corporation's recovery of damages. Thus, in *Bangor Punta* (which the Court analyzed as if it were a derivative suit), the Court found that the plaintiff-shareholder had no standing because it had received what it had bargained for and was not entitled to a windfall recovery of damages, although there were minority shareholders of the railroad who were owners at the time of the wrong. On the other hand, if a qualified shareholder brings a derivative suit, the subsequent purchaser will receive the same windfall. This suggests that the main purpose of the contemporaneous ownership requirement is to prevent persons from "buying lawsuits."

Some jurisdictions have relaxed the strict contemporaneous ownership requirement. California permits a suit if "there is a strong prima facie case in favor of the claim asserted on behalf of the corporation * * * [and] the plaintiff acquired the shares before there was disclosure to the public or to the plaintiff of the wrongdoing of which plaintiff complains" and certain other criteria are satisfied. Calif.Corp.Code § 800(b)(1)(1977). *See also* Pa. Bus. Corp. Law § 1782 and ALI, PRINCIPLES OF CORPORATE GOVERNANCE (1994), § 7.02(a)(1). Where the security is publicly traded, the harm to the corporation has not been reflected in the stock price until there has been public disclosure of the alleged wrongdoing. Hence, permitting a person who purchased after the wrongdoing but before its public disclosure will not do violence to the basic rationale of the contemporaneous ownership requirement.

What happens when the original plaintiff is not a contemporaneous owner and thus lacks standing from the outset but a qualified shareholder subsequently seeks to intervene to maintain the action? At first blush, it might appear that without an appropriate plaintiff, the suit was invalid from the outset. However, courts have generally recognized that the claim belongs to the corporation rather than to the shareholder plaintiff who has brought the action and have permitted such intervention. *See In re MAXXAM, Inc./Federated Development Shareholders Litigation*, 698 A.2d 949, 956–58 (Del.Ch.1996).

Some courts also have permitted suit when the plaintiff could show that the original misconduct had a continuing effect on the corporation and hence on the value of the shares. The cases are not clear, however, on what constitutes a continuing effect or when the so-called "continuing wrong" doctrine should apply. In *Nickson v. Filtrol Corp.*, 262 A.2d 267 (Del.Ch.1970), the corporation's managers caused the corporation to purchase certain bonds before the plaintiff became a shareholder. The court rejected plaintiff's argument that the purchase price was unfair and that the retention of the bonds continued the wrong which had occurred through the purchase. The court held that the only actionable wrong was the purchase of the bonds and reasoned that were the retention also to be actionable, the contemporaneous ownership requirement would be eviscerated.

Not all courts have reached the same result. In *Forbes v. Wells Beach Casino, Inc.*, 307 A.2d 210 (Me.1973), plaintiff was denied a contractual right to purchase property from a corporation, a right which he claimed was improperly diverted to the defendant at a price below plaintiff's bid. As in *Nickson*, the defendant retained the property. Plaintiff then bought stock in the corporation and brought a derivative suit for the loss to the corporation. The court held that under the "continuing wrong" doctrine, a plaintiff who purchased shares after a wrongful taking of property but remained a shareholder while the wrongful holding continued was not barred from bringing suit. Similarly, in *Palmer v. Morris*, 316 F.2d 649 (5th Cir.1963), the "continuing wrong" theory prevented dismissal of a derivative suit which challenged a contract entered into prior to the shareholder's purchase of stock but under which payments were still being made. The attack was not against the initial transaction but against the current payments.

The "continuing wrong" doctrine is difficult to understand conceptually. In order to recover, the plaintiff must attack the original transaction but she is not permitted to recover for any part of that transaction which occurred before she acquired her stock. If she acquired her shares at a price which has discounted the harm of the original transaction, why should she be permitted to challenge that transaction? If not, why should she be able to challenge its subsequent effects? After all, any plaintiff lacking standing to challenge the original misconduct can always argue that it has had some continuing effect.

### 5.  *Continuing Interest*

Either directly or by implication from the applicable statute, many jurisdictions require that the plaintiff maintain an interest in her shares throughout the litigation. Thus, although F.R.C.P. 23.1 does not explicitly require a continuing interest, courts have inferred the requirement from the provision that "a derivative action may not be maintained if it appears that the plaintiff does not fairly and adequately represent the interests of the shareholders * * * similarly situated in enforcing the rights of the corporation." A continuing interest is required to protect against the possibility that a plaintiff (and her attorney) who can no longer benefit from a corporate recovery might have an incentive to accept a low settlement or to prosecute the litigation less vigorously. *See Lewis v. Chiles*, 719 F.2d 1044 (9th Cir.1983).

The issue often arises when shareholders attempt to assert a claim on behalf of a corporation which has been merged out of existence or on behalf of the surviving corporation. The general rule is that a merger deprives a shareholder of the merged corporation of standing to bring a derivative suit for conduct arising before the merger. The theory is that the cause of action is an asset of the merged corporation which passes to the surviving corporation. The two principal exceptions to the rule are where the merger itself is the subject of a claim of fraud or where it is a reorganization which does not affect the plaintiff's ownership of the enterprise. *Lewis v. Anderson*, 477 A.2d 1040 (Del.1984); *Schreiber v. Carney*, 447 A.2d 17 (Del.Ch.1982). Where, however, the transaction was structured as a sale of assets followed by a dissolution, the shareholders were found to have standing under New York law to sue the erstwhile directors of their now dissolved corporation. *Independent Investor Protective League v. Time, Inc.*, 406 N.E.2d 486 (N.Y.1980). The difference in result appears to turn on the statutory provision applicable to the underlying transaction. The New York statute governing dissolution recognizes that shareholders in a dissolved corporation have a continuing interest in securing the full benefits of the dissolution. By contrast, merger statutes provide that the rights of the merged corporation are transferred to the surviving corporation by operation of law. Recall the analysis in Chapter 12. Is the distinction between the two cases sensible if there is no economic significance to the choice of form of the transaction?

Recent cases have begun to loosen the general rule. In *Alford v. Shaw*, 398 S.E.2d 445 (N.C.1990), defendants argued that plaintiffs lost standing to sue because the corporation on whose behalf they had been suing had merged into another corporation. The North Carolina court rejected this argument, noting that nothing in the statute requires that plaintiffs remain shareholders after the suit has been brought. The court also found that the facts of the case, involving a challenge to the conduct surroundings the merger itself, permitted an equitable exception to the continuous ownership principle. Thus the court held that "under these facts, * * * if in the course of a shareholder derivative suit defendants' actions terminate the plaintiffs' shareholder status and these actions are closely related to the grounds for the derivative suit, the plaintiffs would retain standing to continue prosecution of the suit they initiated. To hold otherwise, that is to hold that a merged corporation or its shareholders loses standing to sue in a situation in which the allegedly wrongful activities of the defendants forced the plaintiffs to lose their status would be highly inequitable." *Id.* at 451–52.

In *Blasband v. Rales*, 971 F.2d 1034 (3d Cir.1992), the plaintiff was a stockholder in Easco Hand Tools, Inc. which merged with Danaher Corp., becoming its wholly-owned subsidiary. Easco shareholders, including the plaintiff, received Danaher stock in the merger as consideration for their Easco stock. The plaintiff filed a derivative suit on Easco's behalf, alleging that an investment that Easco had made in junk bonds prior to the merger constituted a breach of the directors' fiduciary duty to the Easco shareholders. The Third Circuit reversed the district court's holding that the plaintiff did not have standing to sue because he no longer owned shares in Easco. The court compared the case to a double derivative suit. It reasoned that if a subsidiary is harmed, its parent company is also harmed and is entitled to seek relief. Easco's cause of action against its directors for the junk bond transaction passed to Danaher with the merger. As a shareholder in the parent company, Danaher, Blasband retained an indirect economic interest in its subsidiary, Easco. This interest gave him standing to sue derivatively on Easco's behalf if both boards failed to pursue the claim. If Blasband had received shares in the post-merger Easco, he would have retained standing to file a derivative suit on its behalf. The fact that he received shares in its parent company instead was deemed irrelevant to his standing.

The ALI would permit a suit to be maintained where the plaintiff's interest has been involuntarily eliminated through a cash-out merger or other similar technique after the suit has been brought or where no shareholder of the surviving corporation can assert the corporate claim. In the latter situation, the ALI would permit a contemporaneous owner of the merged corporation who has been eliminated voluntarily to bring suit rather than have the right be forfeited. ALI, Principles of Corporate Governance (1994), § 7.02(a)(2).

### 6.  Auctioning Derivative Suits

If one accepts the deterrence rationale, a derivative suit should be brought by the party with the greatest incentive to litigate the case fully. One proposal that would expand the class of persons who could bring a derivative suit is to auction the right to pursue such suits to the highest bidder. *See* Jonathan R. Macey and Geoffrey P. Miller, *The Plaintiff's Attorney's Role in Class Action and Derivative Litigation: Economic Analysis and Recommendations for Reform*, 58 U. CHI. L. REV. 1 (1991). An auction is an attractive alternative if the judge finds that: 1) there is a large number of claimants, each with a small amount at stake so that none individually has the incentive to litigate; 2) multiple lawsuits have been filed, so that their consolidation would increase efficiency; 3) the claims are similar enough to be combined into a single lawsuit; and 4) the case does not necessitate active participation by the class members, so that the winning bidder can assume control of the suit completely and litigate it effectively.

After deciding that an auction is appropriate for a particular case, the judge has the task of defining the claim, although this definition remains subject to later amendment. After appropriate notice, the highest sealed bid that meets a preset minimum is awarded the right to pursue the suit. The class members need not be involved after this stage; the winning bidder will simply litigate in the name of a "Jane Doe" or "Richard Roe" plaintiff. The attorney who filed the claim initially will be compensated for her services from this bid amount, even though she surrenders all rights in the suit to the winning bidder. The defendant is allowed to bid; if she wins the auction, the case is essentially over. If another party wins, the case continues much as any other.

The proposal to auction derivative lawsuits is not without drawbacks, as Macey and Miller acknowledge. Prior to bids being made, the claim itself needs to be defined precisely to establish claim preclusion. The trial court overseeing the auction will be allowed to order limited discovery of the defendant, both to define the claim and enable the potential purchasers to ascertain exactly for what they are bidding. Macey and Miller admit that the uncertainty surrounding the claim might discount the value of the suit. An auction is not feasible if the plaintiffs seek injunctive rather than monetary relief; for example, no one will bid to ensure that civil rights are enforced. Additionally, a possibility exists that bidders will collude to manipulate the bidding process and keep the price of the suit artificially low. Ethics and the threat of disbarment, however, should prevent such collusion. Courts will need to develop new procedures for ensuring that all members of the plaintiff class cooperate with the auction winner in the suit and that all potential claims are consolidated in a single case.

Perhaps the largest obstacle to the auction proposal is finding enough bidders who will compete to ensure a sufficiently high price. The potentially huge recoveries will attract bidders with large financial resources to the auctions. As a solution to the limited class of bidders with the financial resources to bid on these claims, Macey and Miller argue that *anyone* should be allowed to bid. including venture capitalists, investors, limited partnerships or even the corporation itself. As the auction system develops, the authors suggest that specialized financial arrangements will be created to provide enough bidders to keep the auction prices sufficiently high to reflect the suits' value. As an alternative, if not enough financing appears, Macey and Miller propose that courts auction the litigation rights to these suits, rather than the claim itself, to the lawyer who will pursue the case for the lowest percentage of the recovery. This alternative, however, reintroduces agency costs; lawyers will once again have an incentive to settle cases prematurely to assure themselves of at least some fees. For an argument that auctions will not necessarily result in the highest possible price for the claim because bidders will recognize the superior position and greater information possessed by the defendant and discount their bids, *see* Randall S. Thomas and Robert G. Hansen, *Auctioning Class Action and Derivative Lawsuits: A Critical Analysis,* 87 Nw. U.L. Rev. 423 (1993); see also Jonathan R. Macey and Geoffrey P. Miller, *Auctioning Class Action and Derivative Suits: A Rejoinder*, 87 Nw. U.L. Rev. 458 (1993).

## E.   INTERNAL CORPORATE PROCEDURES

Directors, not shareholders, manage the corporation. Certainly individual, self-appointed shareholder-plaintiffs do not manage the corporation. Generally, courts will not interfere in a decision by a board of directors that establishes or carries out corporate policy. This doctrine of noninterference stems from the business judgment rule, which carries with it a presumption of reasonableness. Decisions to litigate are managerial judgments, at least as the norm. Derivative suits, which assert the corporation's rights, depart from this norm insofar they allow persons other than the board of directors to act on behalf of corporation in bringing, maintaining and settling such suits. In recognition of this departure, courts and legislatures have sought to maintain some balance between the role of directors and a shareholder's ability to litigate on behalf of the corporation.

The issue arises in two contexts. The first is that a shareholder must exhaust her intra-corporate remedies before bringing a derivative suit by making a demand on the board of directors to take corrective action. Courts relax this requirement only where such demand would be futile because it seems clear the directors would refuse to act. The second is that, in some circumstances, the board of directors can act to cause the corporation to dismiss a derivative suit after it has been brought on the ground that the action is not in the best interest of the corporation. These two issues are closely related but, ultimately, are analytically distinct. Both recognize that given the incentives to initiate derivative suits, there is a risk that frivolous and opportunistic suits will be brought. Each is an attempt to screen out the frivolous suits from the meritorious. The problem is in designing screening devices with the right mesh.

## 1. DEMAND ON DIRECTORS

All jurisdictions require, as a condition to bringing a shareholder derivative suit, that the plaintiff make a demand on directors to take appropriate corrective action to remedy alleged misconduct. Most jurisdictions excuse such demand if it would be "futile." Curiously, the necessity for demand is stated as a pleading requirement; the plaintiff must plead that demand has been made or specifically state why demand would be futile. F.R.C.P. 23.1. In contrast to a "futility" regime, RMBCA § 7.42 requires that demand be made in every case but bars a shareholder from bringing suit for 90 days from the date of demand unless the shareholder has been notified earlier that her demand was rejected, that the statute of limitations would expire within the 90 days, or that irreparable injury to the corporation would result from waiting the full time period. The RMBCA approach is referred to as a "universal demand" requirement.

The demand requirement has become increasingly controversial in the past two decades, largely because of the consequences of the board of directors' rejection of the demand. If the suit can proceed even if the board rejects the demand, there is more reason to have a universal demand requirement. If, however, the board's rejection of the demand effectively bars plaintiff's suit, there is a greater need for judicial scrutiny of the reasons for the rejection and the process by which the decision was reached. It is such scrutiny that has given rise to a large body of case law as to the circumstances under which demand is "futile." In a "futility" regime, plaintiffs view demand as an extraneous procedural hurdle that allows defendant directors to shield their misdeeds behind the business judgment rule. Defendants argue that the process of considering demand amounts to a corporate decision on the merit and wisdom of the litigation. They contend that this process is an important aspect of the board's governance role which should be respected by courts as any other business decision and left undisturbed unless the decision was clearly wrongful.

## ARONSON v. LEWIS

473 A.2d 805 (Del.1984).

MOORE, JUSTICE:

\* \* \* [W]hen is a stockholder's demand upon a board of directors, to redress an alleged wrong to the corporation, excused as futile prior to the filing of a derivative suit? We granted this interlocutory appeal to the defendants, Meyers Parking System, Inc. (Mcycrs), a Delaware corporation, and its directors, to review the Court of Chancery's denial of their motion to dismiss this action, pursuant to Chancery Rule 23.1, for the plaintiff's failure to make such a demand or otherwise demonstrate its futility. The Vice Chancellor ruled that plaintiff's allegations raised a "reasonable inference" that the directors' action was unprotected by the business judgment rule. Thus, the board could not have impartially considered and acted upon the demand. See *Lewis v. Aronson*, Del.Ch., 466 A.2d 375, 381 (1983).

We cannot agree with this formulation of the concept of demand futility. In our view demand can only be excused where facts are alleged with particularity which create a reasonable doubt that the directors' action was entitled to the protections of the business judgment rule. Because the plaintiff failed to make a demand, and to allege facts with particularity indicating that such demand would be futile, we reverse the Court of Chancery and remand with instructions that plaintiff be granted leave to amend the complaint.

## I.

The issues of demand futility rest upon the allegations of the complaint. The plaintiff, Harry Lewis, is a stockholder of Meyers. The defendants are Meyers and its ten directors, some of whom are also company officers.

In 1979, Prudential Building Maintenance Corp. (Prudential) spun off its shares of Meyers to Prudential's stockholders. Prior thereto Meyers was a wholly owned subsidiary of Prudential. Meyers provides parking lot facilities and related services throughout the country. Its stock is actively traded over-the-counter.

This suit challenges certain transactions between Meyers and one of its directors, Leo Fink, who owns 47% of its outstanding stock. Plaintiff claims that these transactions were approved only because Fink personally selected each director and officer of Meyers.

Prior to January 1, 1981, Fink had an employment agreement with Prudential which provided that upon retirement he was to become a consultant to that company for ten years. This provision became operable when Fink retired in April 1980. Thereafter, Meyers agreed with Prudential to share Fink's consulting services and reimburse Prudential for 25% of the fees paid Fink. Under this arrangement Meyers paid Prudential $48,332 in 1980 and $45,832 in 1981.

On January 1, 1981, the defendants approved an employment agreement between Meyers and Fink for a five year term with provision for automatic renewal each year thereafter, indefinitely. Meyers agreed to pay Fink $150,000 per year, plus a bonus of 5% of its pre-tax profits over $2,400,000. Fink could terminate the contract at any time, but Meyers could do so only upon six months' notice. At termination, Fink was to become a consultant to Meyers and be paid $150,000 per year for the first three years, $125,000 for the next three years, and $100,000 thereafter for life. Death benefits were also included. Fink agreed to devote his best efforts and substantially his entire business time to advancing Meyers' interests. The agreement also provided that Fink's compensation was not to be affected by any inability to perform services on Meyers' behalf. Fink was 75 years old when his employment agreement with Meyers was approved by the directors. There is no claim that he was, or is, in poor health.

Additionally, the Meyers board approved and made interest-free loans to Fink totalling $225,000. These loans were unpaid and outstanding as of August 1982 when the complaint was filed. At oral argument defendants' counsel represented that these loans had been repaid in full.

The complaint charges that these transactions had "no valid business purpose", and were a "waste of corporate assets" because the amounts to be paid are "grossly excessive", that Fink performs "no or little services", and because of his "advanced age" cannot be "expected to perform any such services". The plaintiff also charges that the existence of the Prudential consulting agreement with Fink prevents him from providing his "best efforts" on Meyers' behalf. Finally, it is alleged that the loans to Fink were in reality "additional compensation" without any "consideration" or "benefit" to Meyers.

The complaint alleged that no demand had been made on the Meyers board because:

13. * * * such attempt would be futile for the following reasons:

(a) All of the directors in office are named as defendants herein and they have participated in, expressly approved and/or acquiesced in, and are personally liable for, the wrongs complained of herein.

(b) Defendant Fink, having selected each director, controls and dominates every member of the Board and every officer of Meyers.

(c) Institution of this action by present directors would require the defendant-directors to sue themselves, thereby placing the conduct of this action in hostile hands and preventing its effective prosecution.

Complaint, at 13.

The relief sought included the cancellation of the Meyers–Fink employment contract and an accounting by the directors, including Fink, for all damage sustained by Meyers and for all profits derived by the directors and Fink. * * *

* * *

IV

A.

A cardinal precept of the General Corporation Law of the State of Delaware is that directors, rather than shareholders, manage the business and affairs of the corporation. 8 Del.C. § 141(a). Section 141(a) states in pertinent part:

"The *business and affairs* of a corporation organized under this chapter *shall be managed by or under the direction* of a board of directors except as may be otherwise provided in this chapter or in its certificate of incorporation."

8 Del.C. § 141(a) (Emphasis added). The existence and exercise of this power carries with it certain fundamental fiduciary obligations to the corporation and its shareholders. Moreover, a stockholder is not powerless to challenge director action which results in harm to the corporation. The machinery of corporate democracy and the derivative suit are potent tools to redress the conduct of a torpid or unfaithful management. The derivative action developed in equity to enable shareholders to sue in the corporation's name where those in control of the company refused to assert a claim belonging to it. The nature of the action is two-fold. First, it is the equivalent of a suit by the shareholders to compel the corporation to sue. Second, it is a suit by the corporation, asserted by the shareholders on its behalf, against those liable to it.

By its very nature the derivative action impinges on the managerial freedom of directors. Hence, the demand requirement of Chancery Rule 23.1 exists at the threshold, first to insure that a stockholder exhausts his intracorporate remedies, and then to provide a safeguard against strike suits. Thus, by promoting this form of alternate dispute resolution, rather than immediate recourse to litigation, the demand requirement is a recognition of the fundamental precept that directors manage the business and affairs of corporations.

In our view the entire question of demand futility is inextricably bound to issues of business judgment and the standards of that doctrine's applicability. The business judgment rule is an acknowledgment of the managerial prerogatives of Delaware directors under Section 141(a). It is a presumption that in making a business decision the directors of a corporation acted on an informed basis, in good faith and in the honest belief that the action taken was in the best interests of the company. Absent an abuse of discretion, that judgment will be respected by the courts. The burden is on the party challenging the decision to establish facts rebutting the presumption.

The function of the business judgment rule is of paramount significance in the context of a derivative action. It comes into play in several ways—in addressing a demand, in the determination of demand futility, in efforts by independent disinterested directors to dismiss the action as inimical to the corporation's best interests, and generally, as a defense to the merits of the suit. However, in each of these circumstances there are certain common principles governing the application and operation of the rule.

First, its protections can only be claimed by disinterested directors whose conduct otherwise meets the tests of business judgment. From the standpoint of interest, this means that directors can neither appear on both sides of a transaction nor expect to derive any personal financial benefit from it in the sense of self-dealing, as opposed to a benefit which devolves upon the corporation or all stockholders generally. *See also* 8 Del.C. § 144. Thus, if such director interest is present, and the transaction is not approved by a majority consisting of the disinterested directors, then the business judgment rule has no application whatever in determining demand futility. See 8 Del.C. § 144(a)(1).

Second, to invoke the rule's protection directors have a duty to inform themselves, prior to making a business decision, of all material information reasonably available to them. Having become so informed, they must then act with requisite care in the discharge of their duties. While the Delaware cases use a variety of terms to describe the applicable standard of care, our analysis satisfies us that under the business judgment rule director liability is predicated upon concepts of gross negligence.

However, it should be noted that the business judgment rule operates only in the context of director action. Technically speaking, it has no role where directors have either abdicated their functions, or absent a conscious decision, failed to act. But it also follows that under applicable principles, a conscious decision to refrain from acting may nonetheless be a valid exercise of business judgment and enjoy the protections of the rule. * * *

Delaware courts have addressed the issue of demand futility on several earlier occasions. * * * The rule emerging from these decisions is that where officers and directors are under an influence which sterilizes their discretion, they cannot be considered proper persons to conduct litigation on behalf of the corporation. Thus, demand would be futile.

However, those cases cannot be taken to mean that any board approval of a challenged transaction automatically connotes "hostile interest" and "guilty participation" by directors, or some other form of sterilizing influence upon them. Were that so, the demand requirements of our law would be meaningless, leaving the clear mandate of Chancery Rule 23.1 devoid of its purpose and substance.

The trial court correctly recognized that demand futility is inextricably bound to issues of business judgment, but stated the test to be based on allegations of fact, which, if true, "show that there is a reasonable inference" the business judgment rule is not applicable for purposes of a pre-suit demand.

The problem with this formulation is the concept of reasonable inferences to be drawn against a board of directors based on allegations in a complaint. As is clear from this case, and the conclusory allegations upon which the Vice Chancellor relied, demand futility becomes virtually automatic under such a test. Bearing in mind the presumptions with which director action is cloaked, we believe that the matter must be approached in a more balanced way.

Our view is that in determining demand futility the Court of Chancery in the proper exercise of its discretion must decide whether, under the particularized facts alleged, a reasonable doubt is created that:

(1) the directors are disinterested and independent and (2) the challenged transaction was otherwise the product of a valid exercise of business judgment. Hence, the Court of Chancery must make two inquiries, one into the independence and disinterestedness of the directors and the other into the substantive nature of the challenged transaction and the board's approval thereof. As to the latter inquiry the court does not assume that the transaction is a wrong to the corporation requiring corrective steps by the board. Rather, the alleged wrong is substantively reviewed against the factual background alleged in the complaint. As to the former inquiry, directorial independence and disinterestedness, the court reviews the factual allegations to decide whether they raise a reasonable doubt, as a threshold matter, that the protections of the business judgment rule are available to the board. Certainly, if this is an "interested" director transaction, such that the business judgment rule is inapplicable to the board majority approving the transaction, then the inquiry ceases. In that event futility of demand has been established by any objective or subjective standard.[8] * * *

However, the mere threat of personal liability for approving a questioned transaction, standing alone, is insufficient to challenge either the independence or disinterestedness of directors, although in rare cases a transaction may be so egregious on its face that board approval cannot meet the test of business judgment, and a substantial likelihood of director liability therefore exists. In sum the entire review is factual in nature. The Court of Chancery in the exercise of its sound discretion must be satisfied that a plaintiff has alleged facts with particularity which, taken as true, support a reasonable doubt that the challenged transaction was the product of a valid exercise of business judgment. Only in that context is demand excused.

### B.

Having outlined the legal framework within which these issues are to be determined, we consider plaintiff's claims of futility here: Fink's domination and control of the directors, board approval of the Fink–Meyers employment agreement, and board hostility to the plaintiff's derivative action due to the directors' status as defendants.

Plaintiff's claim that Fink dominates and controls the Meyers' board is based on: (1) Fink's 47% ownership of Meyers' outstanding stock, and (2) that he "personally selected" each Meyers director. Plaintiff also alleges that mere approval of the employment agreement illustrates Fink's domination and control of the board. In addition, plaintiff argued on appeal that 47% stock ownership, though less than a majority,

---

**8.** We recognize that drawing the line at a majority of the board may be an arguably arbitrary dividing point. Critics will charge that we are ignoring the structural bias common to corporate boards throughout America, as well as the other unseen socialization processes cutting against independent discussion and decisionmaking in the boardroom. The difficulty with structural bias in a demand futile case is simply one of establishing it in the complaint for purposes of Rule 23.1. We are satisfied that discretionary review by the Court of Chancery of complaints alleging specific facts pointing to bias on a particular board will be sufficient for determining demand futility.

constituted control given the large number of shares outstanding, 1,245,-745.

Such contentions do not support any claim under Delaware law that these directors lack independence. In *Kaplan v. Centex Corp.*, Del.Ch., 284 A.2d 119 (1971), the Court of Chancery stated that "[s]tock ownership alone, at least when it amounts to less than a majority, is not sufficient proof of domination or control". *Id.* at 123. Moreover, in the demand context even proof of majority ownership of a company does not strip the directors of the presumptions of independence, and that their acts have been taken in good faith and in the best interests of the corporation. There must be coupled with the allegation of control such facts as would demonstrate that through personal or other relationships the directors are beholden to the controlling person. To date the principal decisions dealing with the issue of control or domination arose only after a full trial on the merits. Thus, they are distinguishable in the demand context unless similar particularized facts are alleged to meet the test of Chancery Rule 23.1. * * *

The requirement of director independence inheres in the conception and rationale of the business judgment rule. The presumption of propriety that flows from an exercise of business judgment is based in part on this unyielding precept. Independence means that a director's decision is based on the corporate merits of the subject before the board rather than extraneous considerations or influences. While directors may confer, debate, and resolve their differences through compromise, or by reasonable reliance upon the expertise of their colleagues and other qualified persons, the end result, nonetheless, must be that each director has brought his or her own informed business judgment to bear with specificity upon the corporate merits of the issues without regard for or succumbing to influences which convert an otherwise valid business decision into a faithless act.

Thus, it is not enough to charge that a director was nominated by or elected at the behest of those controlling the outcome of a corporate election. That is the usual way a person becomes a corporate director. It is the care, attention and sense of individual responsibility to the performance of one's duties, not the method of election, that generally touches on independence.

We conclude that in the demand-futile context a plaintiff charging domination and control of one or more directors must allege particularized facts manifesting "a direction of corporate conduct in such a way as to comport with the wishes or interests of the corporation (or persons) doing the controlling". *Kaplan*, 284 A.2d at 123. The shorthand shibboleth of "dominated and controlled directors" is insufficient. In recognizing that *Kaplan* was decided after trial and full discovery, we stress that the plaintiff need only allege specific facts; he need not plead evidence. Otherwise, he would be forced to make allegations which may not comport with his duties under Chancery Rule 11.

Here, plaintiff has not alleged any facts sufficient to support a claim of control. The personal-selection-of-directors allegation stands alone, unsupported. At best it is a conclusion devoid of factual support. The causal link between Fink's control and approval of the employment agreement is alluded to, but nowhere specified. The director's approval, alone, does not establish control, even in the face of Fink's 47% stock ownership. The claim that Fink is unlikely to perform any services under the agreement, because of his age, and his conflicting consultant work with Prudential, adds nothing to the control claim. Therefore, we cannot conclude that the complaint factually particularizes any circumstances of control and domination to overcome the presumption of board independence, and thus render the demand futile.

### C.

Turning to the board's approval of the Meyers–Fink employment agreement, plaintiff's argument is simple: all of the Meyers directors are named defendants, because they approved the wasteful agreement; if plaintiff prevails on the merits all the directors will be jointly and severally liable; therefore, the directors' interest in avoiding personal liability automatically and absolutely disqualifies them from passing on a shareholder's demand.

Such allegations are conclusory at best. In Delaware mere directorial approval of a transaction, absent particularized facts supporting a breach of fiduciary duty claim, or otherwise establishing the lack of independence or disinterestedness of a majority of the directors, is insufficient to excuse demand. Here, plaintiff's suit is premised on the notion that the Meyers–Fink employment agreement was a waste of corporate assets. So, the argument goes, by approving such waste the directors now face potential personal liability, thereby rendering futile any demand on them to bring suit. Unfortunately, plaintiff's claim fails in its initial premise. The complaint does not allege particularized facts indicating that the agreement is a waste of corporate assets. Indeed, the complaint as now drafted may not even state a cause of action, given the directors' broad corporate power to fix the compensation of officers.

In essence, the plaintiff alleged a lack of consideration flowing from Fink to Meyers, since the employment agreement provided that compensation was not contingent on Fink's ability to perform any services. The bare assertion that Fink performed "little or no services" was plaintiff's conclusion based solely on Fink's age and the *existence* of the Fink–Prudential employment agreement. As for Meyers' loans to Fink, beyond the bare allegation that they were made, the complaint does not allege facts indicating the wastefulness of such arrangements. Again, the mere existence of such loans, given the broad corporate powers conferred by Delaware law, does not even state a claim.

In sustaining plaintiff's claim of demand futility the trial court relied on *Fidanque v. American Maracaibo Co.*, Del.Ch., 92 A.2d 311, 321 (1952), which held that a contract providing for payment of consulting fees to a retired president/director was a waste of corporate assets. *Id.* In

*Fidanque,* the court found after trial that the contract and payments were in reality compensation for past services. *Id.* at 320. This was based upon facts not present here: the former president/director was a 70 year old stroke victim, neither the agreement nor the record spelled out his consulting duties at all, the consulting salary equalled the individual's salary when he was president and general manager of the corporation, and the contract was silent as to continued employment in the event that the retired president/director again became incapacitated and unable to perform his duties. *Id.* at 320–21. Contrasting the facts of *Fidanque* with the complaint here, it is apparent that plaintiff has not alleged facts sufficient to render demand futile on a charge of corporate waste, and thus create a reasonable doubt that the board's action is protected by the business judgment rule.

### D.

Plaintiff's final argument is the incantation that demand is excused because the directors otherwise would have to sue themselves, thereby placing the conduct of the litigation in hostile hands and preventing its effective prosecution. This bootstrap argument has been made to and dismissed by other courts. Its acceptance would effectively abrogate Rule 23.1 and weaken the managerial power of directors. Unless facts are alleged with particularity to overcome the presumptions of independence and a proper exercise of business judgment, in which case the directors could not be expected to sue themselves, a bare claim of this sort raises no legally cognizable issue under Delaware corporate law.

### VI.

In sum, we conclude that the plaintiff has failed to allege facts with particularity indicating that the Meyers directors were tainted by interest, lacked independence, or took action contrary to Meyers' best interests in order to create a reasonable doubt as to the applicability of the business judgment rule. Only in the presence of such a reasonable doubt may a demand be deemed futile, hence, we reverse the Court of Chancery's denial of the motion to dismiss, and remand with instructions that plaintiff be granted leave to amend his complaint to bring it into compliance with Rule 23.1 based on the principles we have announced today.

Reversed and remanded.

## RALES v. BLASBAND

634 A.2d 927 (Del.1993).

VEASEY, CHIEF JUSTICE:

This certified question of law comes before the Court pursuant to Article IV, Section 11(9) of the Delaware Constitution and Supreme Court Rule 41. The question of law was certified by the United States District Court for the District of Delaware (the "District Court"), and was accepted by this Court on June 16, 1993.

The underlying action pending in the District Court is a stockholder derivative action filed on March 25, 1991, by Alfred Blasband ("Blasband") on behalf of Danaher Corporation, a Delaware corporation ("Danaher"). Following Blasband's filing of an amended complaint (the "amended complaint"), the defendants filed a motion to dismiss and moved to certify the following question of law to this Court:

> In the context of this novel action, which is neither a simple derivative suit nor a double derivative suit, but which the United States Court of Appeals for the Third Circuit describes as a "first cousin to a double derivative suit," has plaintiff Alfred Blasband, in accordance with the substantive law of the State of Delaware, alleged facts to show that demand is excused on the board of directors of Danaher Corporation, a Delaware corporation?

After consideration of the allegations of the amended complaint, the briefs, and the oral argument of the parties in this Court, it is our conclusion that the certified question must be answered in the affirmative. Because the amended complaint does not challenge a decision of the board of directors of Danaher (the "Board"), the test enunciated in *Aronson v. Lewis*, Del.Supr., 473 A.2d 805 (1984) is not implicated. In the unusual context of this case, demand on the Board is excused because the amended complaint alleges particularized facts creating a reasonable doubt that a majority of the Board would be disinterested or independent in making a decision on a demand.

## I. FACTS

Blasband is currently a stockholder of Danaher. Prior to 1990 Blasband owned 1100 shares of Easco Hand Tools, Inc., a Delaware corporation ("Easco"). Easco entered into a merger agreement with Danaher in February 1990 whereby Easco became a wholly-owned subsidiary of Danaher (the "Merger").

Steven M. Rales and Mitchell P. Rales (the "Rales brothers") have been directors, officers, or stockholders of Easco and Danaher at relevant times. Prior to the merger, the Rales brothers were directors of Easco, and together owned approximately 52 percent of Easco's common stock. They continued to serve as directors of Easco after the Merger.

The Rales brothers also own approximately 44 percent of Danaher's common stock. Prior to the Merger, Mitchell Rales was President and Steven Rales was Chief Executive Officer of Danaher. The Rales brothers resigned their positions as officers of Danaher in early 1990, but continued to serve as members of the Board. The Board consists of eight members. The other six members are Danaher's President and Chief Executive Officer, George Sherman ("Sherman"), Donald E. Ehrlich ("Ehrlich"), Mortimer Caplin ("Caplin"), George D. Kellner ("Kellner"), A. Emmett Stephenson, Jr. ("Stephenson"), and Walter Lohr ("Lohr"). A number of these directors have business relationships with the Rales brothers or with entities controlled by them.

The central focus of the amended complaint is the alleged misuse by the Easco board of the proceeds of a sale of that company's 12.875% Senior Subordinated Notes due 1998 (the "Notes"). On or about September 1, 1988, Easco sold $100 million of the Notes in a public offering (the "Offering"). * * * The prospectus [for the Offering] stated that "[p]ending such uses, the Company will invest the balance of the net proceeds from this offering in government and other marketable securities which are expected to yield a lower rate of return than the rate of interest borne by the Notes."

Blasband alleges that the defendants did not invest in "government and other marketable securities," but instead used over $61.9 million of the proceeds to buy highly speculative "junk bonds" offered through Drexel Burnham Lambert Inc. ("Drexel"). Blasband alleges that these junk bonds were bought by Easco because of the Rales brothers' desire to help Drexel at a time when it was under investigation and having trouble selling such bonds. * * *

The amended complaint alleges that these investments have declined substantially in value, resulting in a loss to Easco of at least $14 million. Finally, Blasband complains that the Easco and Danaher boards of directors refused to comply with his request for information regarding the investments.

## II. Scope and Standard of Review

The parties have raised a threshold issue regarding this Court's ability to consider the legal standards which are applicable to the certified question. Blasband contends that the role of this Court in responding to the certified question is limited to a mechanical application of the two-part test set forth in *Aronson*. The defendants disagree, and argue that the Court should apply a test more stringent than the *Aronson* test to protect corporations against strike suits.

* * * The certified question does not limit the issue presented to the mere application of the *Aronson* test, but instead calls upon this Court to decide whether Blasband's amended complaint establishes that demand is excused under the "substantive law of the State of Delaware." It is therefore necessary for this Court to determine what the applicable "substantive law" is before we can decide whether demand on the Board should be excused. Accordingly, the language of the question certified to this Court requires a consideration of the appropriate legal principles, including the applicability of the *Aronson* test in this unusual context, so that we may properly decide the issue presented to us.

## III. The Standards for Determining Whether Demand Is Excused in This Derivative Suit

Because derivative suits challenge the propriety of decisions made by directors pursuant to their managerial authority, we have repeatedly held that the stockholder plaintiffs must overcome the powerful presumptions of the business judgment rule before they will be permitted to pursue the derivative claim. * * *

Although [the *Aronson*] standards are well-established, they cannot be applied in a vacuum. Not all derivative suits fall into the paradigm addressed by *Aronson* and its progeny. The essential predicate for the *Aronson* test is the fact that a *decision* of the board of directors is being challenged in the derivative suit. * * *

Under the unique circumstances of this case, an analysis of the Board's ability to consider a demand requires a departure here from the standards set forth in *Aronson*. The Board did not approve the transaction which is being challenged by Blasband in this action. In fact, the Danaher directors have made no decision relating to the subject of this derivative suit. Where there is no conscious decision by directors to act or refrain from acting, the business judgment rule has no application. The absence of board action, therefore, makes it impossible to perform the essential inquiry contemplated by *Aronson*—whether the directors have acted in conformity with the business judgment rule in approving the challenged transaction.

Consistent with the context and rationale of the *Aronson* decision, a court should not apply the *Aronson* test for demand futility where the board that would be considering the demand did not make a business decision which is being challenged in the derivative suit. This situation would arise in three principal scenarios: (1) where a business decision was made by the board of a company, but a majority of the directors making the decision have been replaced;[8] (2) where the subject of the derivative suit is not a business decision of the board;[9] and (3) where, as here, the decision being challenged was made by the board of a different corporation.

---

**8.** This first scenario was addressed by the Court of Chancery in *Harris v. Carter*, Del.Ch., 582 A.2d 222 (1990):

> In the special case, however, where there is a change in board control between the date of the challenged transaction and the date of suit, it might open the way to error to focus on the board existing at the time of the challenged transaction. What, in the end, is relevant is not whether the board that approved the challenged transaction was or was not interested in that transaction but whether the present board is or is not disabled from exercising its right and duty to control corporate litigation.
>
> I do not consider that *Aronson* intended to determine that demand under Rule 23.1 upon an independent board that has come into existence after the time of the "challenged transaction" would be excused if the board that approved the challenged transaction did not qualify for business judgment protection.

*Id.* at 230 (emphasis added). Because the new board in *Harris* was not yet in place at the time of the original complaint in that case, the Court of Chancery did not need to determine how, or if, *Aronson* would apply where there was a change in the board prior to the derivative suit being filed.

**9.** For example, if a stockholder brings a derivative suit alleging that a third party breached a contract with the corporation, demand should not be excused simply because the subject matter of the suit—the third party's breach of contract—does not implicate the business judgment rule. Similarly, where directors are sued derivatively because they have failed to do something (such as a failure to oversee subordinates), demand should not be excused automatically in the absence of allegations demonstrating why the board is incapable of considering a demand. Indeed, requiring demand in such circumstances is consistent with the board's managerial prerogatives because it permits the board to have the opportunity to take action where it has not previously considered doing so.

Instead, it is appropriate in these situations to examine whether the board that would be addressing the demand can impartially consider its merits without being influenced by improper considerations. Thus, a court must determine whether or not the particularized factual allegations of a derivative stockholder complaint create a reasonable doubt that, as of the time the complaint is filed, the board of directors could have properly exercised its independent and disinterested business judgment in responding to a demand. If the derivative plaintiff satisfies this burden, then demand will be excused as futile.

In so holding, we reject the defendants' proposal that, for purposes of this derivative suit and future similar suits, we adopt either a universal demand requirement or a requirement that a plaintiff must demonstrate a reasonable probability of success on the merits. The defendants seek to justify these stringent tests on the need to discourage "strike suits" in situations like the present one. This concern is unfounded.

A plaintiff in a double derivative suit is still required to satisfy the *Aronson* test in order to establish that demand on the *subsidiary's* board is futile. The *Aronson* test was designed, in part, with the objective of preventing strike suits by requiring derivative plaintiffs to make a threshold showing, through the allegation of particularized facts, that their claims have some merit. Moreover, defendants' proposal of requiring demand on the parent board in all double derivative cases, even where a board of directors is interested, is not the appropriate protection against strike suits. While defendants' alternative suggestion of requiring a plaintiff to demonstrate a reasonable probability of success is more closely related to the prevention of strike suits, it is an extremely onerous burden to meet at the pleading stage without the benefit of discovery.[10] Because a plaintiff must satisfy the *Aronson* test in order to show that demand is excused on the subsidiary board, there is no need to create an unduly onerous test for determining demand futility on the parent board simply to protect against strike suits.

---

**10.** Although derivative plaintiffs may believe it is difficult to meet the particularization requirement of *Aronson* because they are not entitled to discovery to assist their compliance with Rule 23.1, they have many avenues available to obtain information bearing on the subject of their claims. For example, there is a variety of public sources from which the details of a corporate act may be discovered, including the media and governmental agencies such as the Securities and Exchange Commission. In addition, a stockholder who has met the procedural requirements and has shown a specific proper purpose may use the summary procedure embodied in 8 *Del.C.* § 220 to investigate the possibility of corporate wrongdoing. *Compaq Computer Corp. v. Horton*, Del.Supr., 631 A.2d 1 (1993). Surprisingly, little use has been made of section 220 as an information-gathering tool in the derivative context. Perhaps the problem arises in some cases out of an unseemly race to the court house, chiefly generated by the "first to file" custom seemingly permitting the winner of the race to be named lead counsel. The result has been a plethora of superficial complaints that could not be sustained. Nothing requires the Court of Chancery, or any other court having appropriate jurisdiction, to countenance this process by penalizing diligent counsel who has employed these methods, including section 220, in a deliberate and thorough manner in preparing a complaint that meets the demand excused test of *Aronson*.

## IV.  Whether the Board Is Interested or Lacks Independence

In order to determine whether the Board could have impartially considered a demand at the time Blasband's original complaint was filed, it is appropriate to examine the nature of the decision confronting it. A stockholder demand letter would, at a minimum, notify the directors of the nature of the alleged wrongdoing and the identities of the alleged wrongdoers. The subject of the demand in this case would be the alleged breaches of fiduciary duty by the Easco board of directors in connection with Easco's investment in Drexel "junk bonds." The allegations of the amended complaint, which must be accepted as true in this procedural context, claim that the investment was made solely for the benefit of the Rales brothers, who were acting in furtherance of their business relationship with Drexel and not with regard to Easco's best interests. Such conduct, if proven, would constitute a breach of the Easco directors' duty of loyalty.

The task of a board of directors in responding to a stockholder demand letter is a two-step process. First, the directors must determine the best method to inform themselves of the facts relating to the alleged wrongdoing and the considerations, both legal and financial, bearing on a response to the demand. If a factual investigation is required, it must be conducted reasonably and in good faith. Second, the board must weigh the alternatives available to it, including the advisability of implementing internal corrective action and commencing legal proceedings. * * * In carrying out these tasks, the board must be able to act free of personal financial interest and improper extraneous influences. We now consider whether the members of the Board could have met these standards.

### A.  Interest

The members of the Board at the time Blasband filed his original complaint were Steven Rales, Mitchell Rales, Sherman, Ehrlich, Caplin, Kellner, Stephenson, and Lohr. The Rales brothers and Caplin were also members of the Easco board of directors at the time of the alleged wrongdoing. Blasband's amended complaint specifically accuses the Rales brothers of being the motivating force behind the investment in Drexel "junk bonds." The Board would be obligated to determine whether these charges of wrongdoing should be investigated and, if substantiated, become the subject of legal action.

A director is considered interested where he or she will receive a personal financial benefit from a transaction that is not equally shared by the stockholders. Directorial interest also exists where a corporate decision will have a materially detrimental impact on a director, but not on the corporation and the stockholders. In such circumstances, a director cannot be expected to exercise his or her independent business judgment without being influenced by the adverse personal consequences resulting from the decision.

We conclude that the Rales brothers and Caplin must be considered interested in a decision of the Board in response to a demand addressing the alleged wrongdoing described in Blasband's amended complaint. Normally, "the mere threat of personal liability for approving a questioned transaction, standing alone, is insufficient to challenge either the independence or disinterestedness of directors. . . ." *Aronson,* 473 A.2d at 815. Nevertheless, the Third Circuit has already concluded that "Blasband has pleaded facts raising at least a reasonable doubt that the [Easco board's] use of proceeds from the Note Offering was a valid exercise of business judgment." *Blasband* I, 971 F.2d at 1052. This determination is part of the law of the case, *Blasband* II, 979 F.2d at 328, and is therefore binding on this Court. Such determination indicates that the potential for liability is not "a mere threat" but instead may rise to "a substantial likelihood." *See Aronson,* 473 A.2d at 815.

Therefore, a decision by the Board to bring suit against the Easco directors, including the Rales brothers and Caplin, could have potentially significant financial consequences for those directors. Common sense dictates that, in light of these consequences, the Rales brothers and Caplin have a disqualifying financial interest that disables them from impartially considering a response to a demand by Blasband.

## B.  Independence

Having determined that the Rales brothers and Caplin would be interested in a decision on Blasband's demand, we must now examine whether the remaining Danaher directors are sufficiently independent to make an impartial decision despite the fact that they are presumptively disinterested. As explained in *Aronson,* "[i]ndependence means that a director's decision is based on the corporate merits of the subject before the board rather than extraneous considerations or influences." 473 A.2d at 816. To establish lack of independence, Blasband must show that the directors are "beholden" to the Rales brothers or so under their influence that their discretion would be sterilized. *Id.* at 815; * * * *Lewis v. Aronson,* Del.Ch., C.A. No. 6919, Hartnett, V.C. (May 1, 1985) (on remand) (holding that demand was excused because the plaintiff's amended complaint alleged sufficient specific facts to create a reasonable doubt regarding the board's independence because it was beholden to a 47 percent stockholder). We conclude that the amended complaint alleges particularized facts sufficient to create a reasonable doubt that Sherman and Ehrlich, as members of the Board, are capable of acting independently of the Rales brothers.

Sherman is the President and Chief Executive Officer of Danaher. His salary is approximately $1 million per year. Although Sherman's continued employment and substantial remuneration may not hinge solely on his relationship with the Rales brothers, there is little doubt that Steven Rales' position as Chairman of the Board of Danaher and Mitchell Rales' position as Chairman of its Executive Committee place them in a position to exert considerable influence over Sherman. In light of these circumstances, there is a reasonable doubt that Sherman can be expected to act independently considering his substantial financial stake in maintaining his current offices.

Ehrlich is the President of Wabash National Corp. ("Wabash"). His annual compensation is approximately $300,000 per year. Ehrlich also has two brothers who are vice presidents of Wabash. The Rales brothers are directors of Wabash and own a majority of its stock through an investment partnership they control. As a result, there is a reasonable doubt regarding Ehrlich's ability to act independently since it can be inferred that he is beholden to the Rales brothers in light of his employment.

Therefore, the amended complaint pleads particularized facts raising a reasonable doubt as to the independence of Sherman and Ehrlich. Because of their alleged substantial financial interest in maintaining their employment positions, there is a reasonable doubt that these two directors are able to consider impartially an action that is contrary to the interests of the Rales brothers.

## V.  Conclusion

We conclude that, under the "substantive law" of the State of Delaware, the *Aronson* test does not apply in the context of this double derivative suit because the Board was not involved in the challenged transaction. Nevertheless, we do not agree with the defendants' argument that a more stringent test should be applied to deter strike suits. Instead, the appropriate inquiry is whether Blasband's amended complaint raises a reasonable doubt regarding the ability of a majority of the Board to exercise properly its business judgment in a decision on a demand had one been made at the time this action was filed. Based on the existence of a reasonable doubt that the Rales brothers and Caplin would be free of a financial interest in such a decision, and that Sherman and Ehrlich could act independently in light of their employment with entities affiliated with the Rales brothers, we conclude that the allegations of Blasband's amended complaint establish that DEMAND IS EXCUSED on the Board. The certified question is therefore answered in the AFFIRMATIVE.

### Note: The Demand Requirement

A.  *Post–Aronson Delaware Law on Demand Futility*

1.  Until *Rales,* many commentators argued that *Aronson* created serious hurdles for plaintiffs to overcome by requiring them to allege facts that could rebut the presumption of the business judgment rule at the pleading stage without the benefit of discovery. *See* Jack C. Coffee, Jr., *New Myths and Old Realities: The American Law Institute Faces the Derivative Action*, 48 Bus.Law. 1407 (1993); Joel Seligman, *The New Corporate Law*, 59 Brook.L.Rev. 1 (1993). One important line of cases, involving derivative suits by shareholders of General Motors to force the board to rescind a repurchase of stocks and notes from Ross Perot for $742 million, did demonstrate the difficulty of proving futility in Delaware. *Grobow v. Perot*, 526 A.2d 914 (Del.Ch.1987), *aff'd* 539 A.2d 180

(Del.1988); *Levine v. Smith*, 591 A.2d 194 (Del.1991). In *Grobow*, the plaintiffs charged that the price that General Motors paid Perot for his shares was excessive, amounting to a waste of corporate assets. They alleged that demand was futile because the repurchase was essentially an attempt by the board to entrench themselves in office and rid the board of Perot and his public criticism of their management of the company.

The trial court held that the "reasonable doubt" standard required the plaintiffs to plead particularized facts sufficient to sustain a "judicial finding" either that the directors were interested, lacked independence or failed to exercise business judgment. The court also found that the fairness of the challenged transaction was a "pivotal question" in an *Aronson* analysis. On appeal, the Delaware Supreme Court declined:

> [T]o approve the use of a "judicial finding" standard as the minimum criterion below which presuit demand will not be excused. We think it sufficient simply to say that the Court of Chancery must weigh the presumption of the business judgment rule that attaches to a board of directors' decision against the well-pleaded facts alleged in a plaintiff's demand-futility complaint. In that respect, the suggestion in the Trial Court's Opinion that a transaction is first analyzed from the standpoint of fairness is erroneous. Fairness becomes an issue only if the presumption of the business judgment is defeated.

539 A.2d at 186–87. *Grobow* also made clear that the two-part test for determining demand futility set forth in *Aronson* is disjunctive: a plaintiff must allege facts that show that the directors were not disinterested *and* that the transaction was not the product of a valid exercise of business judgment. *Id.* at 186.

*Grobow* was consolidated with another action challenging the same repurchase, *Levine v. Smith*, 591 A.2d 194 (Del.1991). Although the plaintiff in *Levine* had made demand, the Delaware Supreme Court addressed the circumstances leading to the dismissal of demand as futile. The court wrote that the "premise of a shareholder claim of futility of demand is that a majority of the board of directors either has a financial interest in the challenged transaction or lacks independence or otherwise failed to exercise due care. On either showing, it may be inferred that the board is *incapable* of exercising its power and authority to pursue the derivative claims directly." *Id.* at 205

The implications of *Aronson*, *Grobow* and *Levine* for the continued efficacy of the derivative suit were potentially profound. At one level, the decisions vested substantial power in the trial court to determine, solely on the basis of the pleadings, whether the lawsuit could be maintained. In *Grobow* and *Levine*, the court may well have viewed the litigation as an attempt to procure a settlement by keeping alive a well publicized intra-corporate dispute that General Motors had already spent $750 million to resolve. However the rules set forth in these cases had the potential to govern situations in which the potential for opportunism by shareholders or their attorneys was not so obvious.

Of equal significance, under the court's formulation, demand would not be excused, and hence the litigation would not be able to continue, if a self-dealing transaction had been approved by a disinterested board even if the underlying transaction would not be insulated from review by the business judgment rule. In *Aronson*, for example, plaintiffs alleged that the transactions with Fink constituted a breach of *his* fiduciary duty of loyalty and that the rest of the board had, independently, breached *their* fiduciary duties by approving those transactions. Because the plaintiffs were unable to show that the board was not independent, the court viewed the challenged transaction as being within the protection of the business judgment rule. It never considered whether, as to Fink, the challenge should receive a hearing on the merits because *he* would not be protected by the business judgment rule.

*Rales* and its progeny, however, demonstrate the responsiveness of the Delaware Supreme Court to the perception that it had established rules that were unduly harsh to shareholders. Recall Professor Cary's critique in Chapter 7. Thus, in *Grimes v. Donald*, 673 A.2d 1207 ((Del. 1996), the court directly addressed the argument that *Aronson* "erected unfortunate barriers to derivative litigation" and stated simply "We disagree," citing an article by former Justice Moore, the author of *Aronson*. Andrew G.T. Moore II, *Shareholder Rights Still Alive and Well in Delaware: The Derivative Suit: A Death Greatly Exaggerated.* 38 St. Louis U.L.J. 1997 (1994). 673 A.2d at 1217, n.16. The court then cited 33 post-*Aronson* cases in which demand had been excused under the *Aronson* test.

2. In *Kaplan v. Peat, Marwick, Mitchell & Co.*, 540 A.2d 726 (Del.1988), the Delaware Supreme Court addressed the question of whether the corporation can be neutral as to the maintenance of a derivative suit and, if so, whether such neutrality excuses demand. The court stated:

> When a corporation takes a position regarding a derivative action asserted on its behalf, it cannot effectively stand neutral. Because of the inherent nature of the derivative action, a corporation's failure to object to a suit brought on its behalf must be viewed as an approval for the shareholders' capacity to sue derivatively. We hold, therefore, that when a corporation chooses to take a position in regards to a derivative action asserted on its behalf, it must affirmatively object to or support the continuation of the litigation.

*Id.* at 731. Hence, a position of neutrality is viewed as tacit approval of the continuation of the litigation, excusing demand by the plaintiff.

B. *Other Standards for Futility*

1. Courts tend to insist that demand be made unless the plaintiff can show that the elements of the business judgment rule are not present; i.e., that there was self-dealing, a biased decision maker or a transaction that constitutes waste. *See* Note, *The Demand and Standing Requirements in Stockholder Derivative Actions*, 44 U.Chi.L.Rev. 168 (1976). Some jurisdictions are stricter than Delaware in allowing excep-

tions to the demand rule. *In re Kauffman Mutual Fund Actions*, 479 F.2d 257 (1st Cir.1973), *cert. denied* 414 U.S. 857, 94 S.Ct. 161, 38 L.Ed.2d 107 (1973), required a showing that the defendant directors were charged with self-dealing (not established by their having approved the transaction) and that the transaction was "completely undirected to a corporate purpose." 479 F.2d at 265. Most courts rely on standards similar to Delaware's but, as one commentator notes, "Inevitably, under any standard, the question of demand futility is fact-oriented and for this reason some courts appear unwilling to commit themselves to rigid application of an exacting standard." Deborah DeMott, SHAREHOLDER DERIVATIVE ACTIONS: LAW AND PRACTICE § 5:13 (Supp. 1992).

2.    A lawsuit may allege that directors neglected their oversight functions rather than that they engaged in misconduct in connection with a business decision. For example, the complaint may assert breach of the duty of care by reason of a failure to monitor the business adequately, *See Caremark*, *Brane* and *Hoye* in Chapter 16. Given the confusing relationship between the duty of care and the business judgment rule, what must be pleaded to demonstrate demand futility in such a case? What is the relevance of the "reasonable doubt" standard?

In that connection, notwithstanding *Caremark*, *Graham v. Allis– Chalmers* retains continuing viability in the area of demand futility. In *In re Baxter International, Inc. Shareholders Litigation*, 654 A.2d 1268 (Del.Ch.1995), plaintiffs alleged that the directors had failed to exercise reasonable care in the oversight and management of Baxter's affairs in connection with a scheme to defraud the Veterans Administration and that demand would be futile because of the risk of the directors' liability. The defendants argued that there was not a substantial likelihood of liability because Baxter's certificate of incorporation exempted them from liability for the alleged misconduct. The Court of Chancery, after citing *Rales* as establishing the appropriate standard for demand futility, rejected the plaintiffs' argument. The court noted that the plaintiffs had failed to allege bad faith, intentional misconduct, a knowing violation of law or any other conduct for which the directors could be liable. Relying on *Graham*, the court found that the "plaintiff has not pled with particularity that the directors ignored obvious danger signs of employee wrongdoing. Rather plaintiff's claim is premised on a presumption that employee wrongdoing would not occur if directors performed their duty properly. Plaintiffs' position is inconsistent with *Graham*." *Id.* at 1271.

3.    Plaintiffs often plead that demand should be excused because all or a majority of the board of directors approved the challenged transaction or were otherwise involved in the wrongdoing. One of the leading cases in this area, *Lewis v. Graves*, 701 F.2d 245 (2d Cir.1983), applying Delaware law, held that the mere naming of a majority, or even all of the directors, as defendants because they approved the transaction at issue will not excuse demand. Plaintiff alleged that the directors of J. Ray McDermott & Co., Inc., ("McDermott") all of whom were named as defendants, had approved the issuance of stock under an executive compensation plan to a minority of the directors who were officers and,

further, that the board had approved McDermott's acquisition of Babcock & Wilcox to ensure their positions with the company. The complaint offered no facts as to how the acquisition would entrench their positions. No further specific facts of participation were alleged. Plaintiff sued all the directors and asserted that demand would be futile because it would be asking the directors to institute suit against themselves. The court held that "absent specific allegations of self-dealing or bias on the part of a majority of the board, mere approval and acquiescence are insufficient to render demand futile." *Id.* at 248. Further:

> * * * The fact that a corporation's directors have previously approved transactions subsequently challenged in a derivative suit does not inevitably lead to the conclusion that those directors, bound by their fiduciary obligations to the corporation, will refuse to take up the suit. This is particularly true where the directors' prior acquiescence was obtained through fraud or where the dealings in question otherwise went sour for the corporation. Moreover, Rule 23.1 would be substantially diluted if prior board approval standing alone established futility. Derivative suits are almost invariably directed at major, allegedly illegal, corporate transactions. By virtue of their offices, directors ordinarily participate in the decision making involved in such transactions. Excusing demand on the mere basis of prior board acquiescence, therefore, would obviate the need for demand in practically every case.

> * * * If a derivative plaintiff could show self-interest in a transaction by mere conclusory allegations that the defendant directors approved a business acquisition simply to secure their own positions, without providing any logical or factual nexus between the transaction and the asserted entrenchment, the demand requirement of Rule 23.1 would again become virtually meaningless.

*Id.* at 248–50. *See also*, *Elgin v. Alfa Corp.*, 598 So.2d 807, 815 (Ala. 1992), ("our case law clearly indicates, and has so indicated for nearly a century, that where the majority of the directors are themselves the alleged wrongdoers, a derivative action plaintiff can be excused from director-demand because such a demand can be deemed futile.")

4. New York may have taken a different approach in *Barr v. Wackman*, 329 N.E.2d 180 (N.Y.1975). The New York Court of Appeals sustained the excusing of demand under N.Y. B.C.L. § 626(c) in a case charging self-dealing by the officer-directors of Talcott National Corporation ("Talcott") and breaches of the duty of due care (but no self-dealing) against the outside directors, who were a majority of the board. The complaint charged that after the boards of Talcott and Gulf & Western ("G & W") agreed in principle on G & W's acquisition of Talcott, the latter's board approved a number of transactions made for the benefit of Talcott's inside directors and G & W, but not Talcott or its shareholders. These transactions included approval of favorable employment contracts for Talcott officers, approval of an allegedly excessive finder's fee, and the sale of a Talcott subsidiary at a loss. The defendants

claimed that at most the complaint indicated erroneous business judgment.

Judge Fuchsberg explained:

The basic question is whether from the particular circumstances of the liability charged it may be inferred that the making of such a demand will be excused where the alleged wrongdoers control or comprise a majority of the directors. * * * And, while justification for failure to give directors notice prior to the institution of a derivative action is not automatically to be found in bare allegations which merely set forth prima facie personal liability of directors without spelling out some detail, such justification may be found when the claim of liability is based on formal action of the board in which the individual directors were participants.

It is not sufficient, however, merely to name a majority of the directors as parties defendant with conclusory allegations of wrongdoing or control by wrongdoers. This pleading tactic would only beg the question of actual futility and ignore the particularity requirement of the statute. The complaint here does much more than simply name the individual board members as defendants. It sets out, with particularity, a series of transactions allegedly for the benefit of Gulf & Western and the affiliated directors. Though there are no allegations that the unaffiliated directors personally benefited from the transactions, they are claimed to have disregarded Talcott's interests for the sole purpose of accommodating Gulf & Western, which, in turn, would allegedly reciprocate by promoting the self-interest of the affiliated directors. Acting officially, the board, qua board, is claimed to have participated or acquiesced in assertedly wrongful transactions

* * * If true, the allegations of the complaint * * * state a cause of action against the defendants, including the unaffiliated directors, for breach of their duties of due care and diligence to the corporation. Plaintiff may prove that the exercise of reasonable diligence and independent judgment under all the circumstances by the unaffiliated directors, at least to meaningfully check the decisions of the active corporate managers, would have put them on notice of the claimed self-dealing of the affiliated directors and avoided the alleged damage to Talcott. If the unaffiliated directors abdicated their responsibility, they may be liable for their omissions. Taking their potential liability from the face of the complaint, plaintiff's failure to make a demand on the board was warranted.

We reject appellants' proposition that allegations of directorial fraud or self-interest is, in every case, a prerequisite to excusing a derivative shareholder from making a demand on a board. * * * Directors undertake affirmative duties of due care and diligence to a corporation and its shareholders in addition to their obligation merely to avoid self-dealing. That unaffiliated directors may not have personally profited from challenged actions does not necessarily end the question of their potential liability to the corporation and the consequent unlikelihood that they would prosecute the action. * * *

> * * * As a consequence, a derivative shareholder's complaint may, in a particular case, withstand a motion to dismiss for failure to make a demand upon the board, even though a majority of the board are not individually charged with fraud or self-dealing. Particular allegations of formal board participation in and approval of active wrongdoing may, as here, suffice to defeat a motion to dismiss. We believe the better approach in these cases is to rest the determination of the necessity for a demand in the sound discretion of the court to which the issue is first presented, to be determined from the sufficiency of the complaint, liberally construed.

*Id.* at 186–88.

Is the allegation of participation in *Barr* any more particularized in its description of wrongful conduct than the allegation in *Graves*? Are these cases consistent or do they represent different approaches to the demand requirement?

To deal with the possibility that *Barr* could be interpreted to allow a plaintiff to establish demand futility simply by alleging acts for which a majority of the directors might be liable, the New York Court of Appeals recently restated the demand futility standard in *Marx v. Akers*, 644 N.Y.S.2d 121, 666 N.E.2d 1034, 1040–41 (N.Y.1996).

> * * * (1) Demand is excused because of futility when a complaint alleges with particularity that a majority of the board of directors is interested in the challenged transaction. Director interest may either be self-interest in the transaction at issue, or a loss of independence because a director with no direct interest in a transaction is "controlled" by a self-interested director. (2) Demand is excused because of futility when a complaint alleges with particularity that the board of directors did not fully inform themselves about the challenged transaction to the extent reasonably appropriate under the circumstances. The "long-standing rule" is that a director "does not exempt himself from liability by failing to do more than passively rubber-stamp the decisions of the active managers." (3) Demand is excused because of futility when a complaint alleges with particularity that the challenged transaction was so egregious on its fact that it could not have been the product of sound business judgment of the directors.

### C. Successful Pleading of Demand Futility

1. In *Rales*, the Delaware Supreme Court pointed to the use of DGCL § 220 as means of obtaining information necessary to show demand futility on the face of the complaint. The court reiterated this idea in *Grimes*, 673 A.2d at 1216, n.11, and subsequent litigation indicates that the court's suggestion is being followed. *See, e.g., Security First Corp. v. U.S. Die Casting & Devlop. Co.*, 687 A.2d 563 (Del.1997);

*Thomas & Betts Corp. v. Leviton Manufacturing Co., Inc.*, 681 A.2d 1026 (Del.1996). The court has recognized that the inspection rights under DGCL § 220 are not co-extensive with a plaintiff's right to a more comprehensive discovery order. How to strike the appropriate balance between the two is the problem which the courts are now attempting to solve.

2.  The Delaware courts have become increasingly sympathetic to demand futility claims in duty of loyalty cases. They are also paying increased attention to the independence of the outside directors, relying heavily on the analysis that *Rales* suggested.

In *Friedman v. Beningson*, 1995 WL 716762 (Del.Ch.1995), the court held that demand was excused in a case involving alleged insider trading and manipulation of corporate information where the principal defendant, Beningson, was a 36% shareholder and CEO of the company and dominated the board. The court found that the complaint had alleged facts indicating that Beningson could affect consulting fees of $48,000 paid to one director on a three-person board. Relying on *Rales*, the court noted that those fees, "when considered in the context of other facts alleged, represents a substantial interest subject to possible corporate retribution had [the director] exercised judgment in a way displeasing to the financially interested 36% Shareholder/CEO." *Id.* at *15.

*Steiner v. Meyerson*, 1995 WL 441999 (Del.Ch.1995) involved challenges to various contracts in which Meyerson, the CEO of Telxon Corp., had a financial interest. In addition to Meyerson, the board consisted of the president of Telxon, a partner in a law firm which provided services to Telxon, and two directors who had not business dealings with Telxon. The defendants moved to dismiss the complaint for failure to state a claim and for failure to satisfy the demand requirement. Chancellor Allen dismissed the claims insofar as they were based on corporate waste but held that as claims for the breach of the duty of loyalty, they were sufficiently pleaded to survive defendants' motions.

3.  Pleadings are more likely to raise a reasonable doubt that directors are disinterested and independent if the directors are alleged to have engaged in conduct that violates a specific statute rather than simply constituting a breach of fiduciary duty. For example, in *Shields v. Erikson*, 1989 WL 100001 (N.D.Ill.1989), the court applied Delaware law to excuse demand as futile when the plaintiff alleged that the directors received "numerous gifts and goodies" wrongfully charged to the United States government. The plaintiff charged that each director, or at least a majority of them, had participated in these illegal acts, which had resulted in fines and penalties against the corporation. The court held that the allegations were sufficient to create a reasonable doubt that the defendant directors were independent and disinterested.

4.  Another context in which plaintiffs have often been successful in proving futility is when directors may be unable to be reimbursed for their liability to the corporation through insurance or indemnification. In *First American Bank and Trust by Levitt v. Frogel*, 726 F.Supp. 1292

(S.D.Fla.1989), the plaintiff sued a bank and several of its officers and directors for violations of the federal securities laws and breaches of fiduciary duty. Applying Florida law (which uses Delaware law for guidance), the court focused on the plaintiff's allegations "that the officers and directors' liability insurance policy contains a provision which prohibits the board from instituting or authorizing any suit on behalf of the Bank against an officer or a director. Insurance coverage would cease if such a suit were brought or authorized by the Bank or the directors." *Id.* at 1298. Consequently, the court concluded that demand was futile because directors could not be expected to bring a derivative lawsuit when they had no protection against personal liability.

In *Grill v. Hoblitzell*, 771 F.Supp. 709 (D.Md.1991), applying Maryland law, plaintiff argued that demand would be futile because the corporation's director and officer indemnification policy covered damages awarded in a derivative suit brought by a shareholder but not one instituted by the board. The court granted the defendants' motion to dismiss for failure to make demand, but permitted the plaintiff to amend his complaint to plead with greater particularity the specifics of the corporation's insurance policy. The court noted that if the original charges were true, "it may very well be that a demand upon the directors to institute an action seeking monetary relief from any present or past director would be futile. * * * [S]ince a recovery under an insurance policy is self-evidently different from recovery against personal assets,* * * the directors may have deprived themselves of the ability to exercise independent judgment as to the advisability of instituting an action against any officer or director for mismanagement and thereby divested themselves of the power to govern this aspect of the corporation's affairs." *Id.* at 713.

5.  Courts appear to be paying increased attention to lawyers who serve as directors. Thus, in *Steiner v. Meyerson, supra,* the most interesting part of Chancellor Allen's treatment of the demand question related to Goodman, the partner in Telxon's law firm. The defendants argued that he was an outside director who could not be dominated or influenced by Meyerson. In rejecting that argument, the Chancellor noted that the complaint alleged that Goodman's law firm had received nearly $1million in fees from Telxon in the effective year of the challenged agreements. The Chancellor stated:

> Goodman's firm is a small one. Realism of the kind signaled by *Rales* requires one to acknowledge the possibility that a partner at a small law firm bringing in close to $1 million in revenues from a single client in one year may be sufficiently beholden to, or at least significantly influenced by, that client as to affect the independence of his judgment. * * * As Meyerson is Telxon's chief executive officer, he undoubtedly possesses the authority to hire and fire the corporation's legal counsel. For this reason, the pleadings raise a reasonable doubt concerning Goodman's independence in assessing the merits of a demand letter attacking the agreements. * * *

*Id. at \*10*

One court has held that demand may be futile where counsel is conflicted in connection with its investigation of the plaintiff's claim. In *Stepak v. Addison*, 20 F.3d 398 (11th Cir.1994) , the board of directors, after investigating the claim, refused the demand. The law firm that conducted the investigation and advised the board had previously represented some of the defendants in related criminal proceedings. After a thoughtful analysis of the role of counsel in a derivative suit, the court held that demand had been wrongfully refused. The court stated:

> \* \* \* [I]f a shareholder pleads with sufficient particularity facts that, taken as true, show that a board's consideration of his demand was dominated by a law firm that represents or previously represented an alleged wrongdoer in criminal proceedings related to the very subject matter of the demand, then the shareholder raises a reasonable doubt that the board's rejection of his demand was an informed decision protected by the business judgment rule. In such a case, the shareholder's complaint is entitled, on a wrongful refusal theory, to survive a Rule 23.1 motion to dismiss.

*Id*. at 407.

Recall the discussion of the independence of counsel in *Gries Sports Enterprises v. Cleveland Browns Football Co*. in Chapter 17.

### E.    Universal Demand

1.  Most jurisdictions follow Delaware's pattern of requiring demand except when it would be futile. Universal demand, in contrast, eliminates the futility exception; a plaintiff must always make demand prior to filing a derivative suit. The ALI has adopted such a requirement, although it permits a narrow exception where requiring demand would cause "irreparable injury to the corporation." The ALI offers three rationales for universal demand. First, it will reduce threshold litigation to determine whether demand is actually futile and therefore should be excused. Second, universal demand is a form of alternative dispute resolution that allows the board an opportunity to correct any wrong that may have occurred. Moreover, making demand is relatively easy and adds little to the plaintiff's burden in bringing a claim. Third, universal demand provides a single, clear standard of judicial review for demand-excused and demand-refused cases. ALI, PRINCIPLES OF CORPORATE GOVERNANCE (1994), § 7.03, Comment e. *See Zapata Corp. v. Maldonado*, 430 A.2d 779 (Del.1981), *infra*. Additionally, the ALI notes that the entire area of law is confusing because there is no consensus as to what constitutes "futility." The ALI criticizes Delaware particularly for requiring too much judicial subjectivity in interpreting the "reasonable doubt" standard set forth in *Aronson*.

RMBCA § 7.42 also establishes a universal demand requirement. As of the writing of this book, fourteen states have adopted a requirement patterned on § 7.42.

2. *Kamen v. Kemper Financial Services*, 500 U.S. 90, 111 S.Ct. 1711, 114 L.Ed.2d 152 (1991), involved the question of whether demand was required in a derivative suit under Section 20(a) of the Investment Company Act of 1940. Plaintiff had alleged that demand would have been futile. The district court dismissed the complaint on the ground that plaintiff had failed to allege sufficient facts to demonstrate futility. The Seventh Circuit affirmed on different grounds. 908 F.2d 1338 (7th Cir.1990) It adopted, as a rule of federal common law, the ALI's universal demand requirement, noting that the futility exception had produced "gobs" of litigation involving speculation about a board's inchoate action.

The Supreme Court reversed and held that in an action under a federal statute such as the Investment Company Act of 1940, a federal court must apply the demand futility exception as defined by the law of the defendant corporation's state of incorporation. The Court stated:

> Because the contours of the demand requirement—when it is required, and when excused—determine *who* has the power to control corporate litigation, we have little trouble concluding that this aspect of state law relates to the allocation of governing powers within the corporation. * * *

> KFS contends that the scope of a federal common law demand requirement need not be tied to the allocation of power to control corporate litigation. This is so, KFS suggests, because a court adjudicating a derivative action based on federal law could sever the requirement of shareholder demand from the standard used to review the directors' decision to bar initiation of, or to terminate, the litigation. Drawing on the ALI's Principles of Corporate Governance, the Court of Appeals came to this same conclusion. Freed from the question of the directors' power to control the litigation, the universal-demand requirement, KFS maintains, would force would-be derivative suit plaintiffs to exhaust their intracorporate remedies before filing suit and would spare both the courts and the parties the expense associated with the often protracted threshold litigation that attends the collateral issue of demand futility.

> We reject this analysis. Whatever its merits as a matter of legal reform, we believe that KFS' proposal to detach the demand standard from the standard for reviewing board action would require a quantum of federal common lawmaking that exceeds federal courts' interstitial mandate. Under state law, the determination whether a derivative representative can initiate a suit without making demand typically is made at the outset of the litigation and is based on the application of the State's futility doctrine to circumstances as they then exist. Under KFS' proposal, federal courts would be obliged to develop a body of principles that would replicate the substantive effect of the State's demand futility doctrine but that would be applied *after* demand has been made and refused. The ALI, for example, has developed an elaborate set of standards that calibrates

the deference afforded the decision of the directors to the character of the claim being asserted by the derivative plaintiff. *See* ALI, PRINCIPLES OF CORPORATE GOVERNANCE § 7.08 (Tent.Draft No. 8, Apr. 15, 1988); id., § 7.08, Comment *c,* p. 120 (noting that Principles "dra[w] a basic distinction between the standard of review applicable to actions that are founded on a breach of the duty of care and the standard of review applicable to actions that are founded on a breach of the duty of loyalty"). Whether a federal court adopts the ALI's standards wholesale or instead attempts to devise postdemand review standards more finely tuned to the distinctive allocation of managerial decisionmaking power embodied in any given jurisdiction's demand futility doctrine, KFS' suggestion would impose upon federal courts the very duty "to fashion an entire body of federal corporate law" that *Burks* sought to avoid.

*Id.* at 101–05.

3.  Under the ALI's approach, the board will always be required to respond to the demand. If the board refuses the demand, its refusal may increase the plaintiffs' burden in another manner. The ALI would allow the board to include a statement with its demand refusal that asserts that the board was "not interested in the transaction or conduct * * * and that those directors constituted a majority of the entire board and were capable as a group of objective judgment in the circumstances * * * " ALI, PRINCIPLES OF CORPORATE GOVERNANCE (1994), § 7.04(a)(2). If a board includes such a statement and provides specific reasons in support, the plaintiff must plead, with particularity, facts that, if true, raise a "significant prospect" that 1) the board's statement is false; 2) if the business judgment rule applies, the defendants fail to meet its standards; or 3) if a standard other than the business judgment rule applies, the disinterested directors could not have reasonably determined that demand refusal was in the corporation's best interests. *Id.* at § 7.04(a)(2)(A–C). If the plaintiff fails to plead such particularized facts, the defendants are entitled to dismissal of the complaint prior to discovery, and will normally move to dismiss. The ALI's definition of "interested" when applied to derivative suits provides that a director is not necessarily considered "interested" because she is a defendant in the case if the complaint is 1) based only on the director's approval or acquiescence of the transaction at issue, and 2) does not allege particularized facts that, if, true, raise a significant prospect that the director is liable to the corporation or the shareholders. *Id.* § 1.23(c)(2)(A)-(B). The ALI's requirement, drafted in final form after the Institute had formally adopted the entire Project, was highly controversial. *See* Paul H. Dawes and Mark W. Smith, *The Demand Requirement and the Special Litigation Committee in Derivative Actions,* 26 REV. SEC. AND COMM. REG. 77 (1993).

### D.  Consequences of the Board's Refusal to Sue

Suppose demand is made. How long must a plaintiff wait before bringing suit? The prevailing view is that the board must respond within a reasonable time. The board needs an opportunity to study the matter, and a complex transaction may entail a lengthy investigation. The case may be in a state of suspended animation for months. If the board refuses to bring suit after demand, does the shareholder still have a right to sue? Remember, if demand is "accepted," the derivative suit is automatically barred, since the directors will bring suit or negotiate a settlement directly in the name of the corporation.

*Grimes* stated that "a stockholder who makes a demand is entitled to know promptly what action the board has taken in response to the demand." 673 A.2d at 1218. In *Rubin v. Posner*, 701 F.Supp. 1041 (D.Del.1988), suit was filed one month after demand had been received and defendants moved to dismiss partly on the ground that the corporation had not had adequate time to reply to the demand. The court denied the motion, finding that the corporation had not acted reasonably in its response to the demand. The court noted that,the suit did not involve complex technological issues, a large number of defendants, or a difficult factual situation. In addition, the court found that the board had apparently taken no action between receipt of the demand and the filing of the suit.

RMBCA § 7.42 bars suit for 90 days from the date of demand unless irreparable injury would result from waiting the full time period or the shareholder has been notified earlier that her demand was rejected.

*F. Demand on Stockholders*

Although all jurisdictions have some requirement for demand on directors, most have abandoned an earlier requirement that demand also be made on shareholders. Delaware, for example, amended its law in 1967 to eliminate this requirement. *S. Solomont & Sons Trust, Inc. v. New England Theatres Operating Corp.*, 93 N.E.2d 241 (Mass.1950), exemplifies the so-called "Massachusetts" or "strict" rule which always requires demand on shareholders as a precondition to the bringing of a derivative suit; only a few other states follow the Massachusetts rule. Deborah DeMott, *Demand in Derivative Actions: Problems of Interpretation and Function*, 19 U.C.DAVIS L.REV. 461, 476–7 (1986). In cases involving federal claims, such as those arising under the federal securities laws, demand on shareholders is not "necessary." *See* F.R.C.P. 23.1. In fact, the courts see demand on shareholders as presenting an impermissible barrier to a federal remedy. *Levitt v. Johnson*, 334 F.2d 815 (1st Cir.1964), *cert. denied* 379 U.S. 961, 85 S.Ct. 649, 13 L.Ed.2d 556 (1965).

## 2. TERMINATING DERIVATIVE SUITS

One internal procedure that defendants have used after demand has been made or a suit has begun is the creation of a special litigation committee. Appointed by the board and comprised of directors disinterested in the transactions at issue, such a committee has the task of determining whether the litigation should be terminated. Arguably it must address two business decisions: whether the lawsuit has merit and whether the corporation has more to gain or to lose from its prosecution.

Should the court view those decisions as simply another exercise of business judgment or should it examine them more closely?

The legality of special litigation committees is no longer in question. *Burks v. Lasker*, 441 U.S. 471, 99 S.Ct. 1831, 60 L.Ed.2d 404 (1979); *Gall v. Exxon*, 418 F.Supp. 508 (S.D.N.Y.1976). Nevertheless, their use raises important questions of corporate governance. Judicial deference to decisions of these committees has the potential to curtail almost totally the availability of a shareholder's right to use courts for redress of alleged breaches of fiduciary duty, including the duty of loyalty. Those who oppose the use of this mechanism argue that litigation is for courts to resolve, not for committees potentially dominated by defendants or those loyal to those charged with wrongdoing. However, considerable savings may be achieved when independent, diligent directors perform their accustomed role of protecting the corporate interest. They may be able to screen wasteful litigation effectively without shielding managers who may have breached their fiduciary duties. If the use of such committees is a permissible technique, the law must decide in what categories of cases it may be used, what procedures must be followed, what opportunity the plaintiff should be given to discover facts, what role the courts will play when the motion to terminate the litigation is made and whether there should be any limitations as to the types of defendants who may utilize this procedure.

# ZAPATA CORP. v. MALDONADO

### 430 A.2d 779 (Del.1981).

[In 1970, Zapata Corporation granted options to certain of its officers and directors to purchase stock at $12.15 per share. The options could be exercised in installments, with the final installment exercisable not before July 14, 1974. At around that time, when the stock had reached a price of between $18–19, the Company planned to make a tender offer for its own shares at $25.00 per share. The company planned to announce the tender offer just prior to July 14, 1974. The effect of the announcement would be to increase the market value of the shares to approximately $25.00 per share. As a result, there would be an additional federal income tax liability on persons who exercised the option, since the tax liability was measured as the difference between the option price ($12.15) and the market price at the time of exercise (about $25).

It was alleged that in order to reduce their individual income tax liability, the board of directors voted to accelerate the exercise date to a time prior to the announcement of the tender offer. The optionees could then exercise when a lower market price prevailed. However, this had the further effect of reducing the corporation's corresponding tax deduction for officers' compensation because the corporation could deduct only $18.00 per share although the price would appreciate on announcement of the offer to $25.00. In effect, the option holders and the corporation were caught in a zero sum game: one could not win without the other losing. A majority of the directors had a direct interest in the outcome of the game since they were option holders.

In 1975, derivative suits were filed in both state and federal courts, alleging breach of fiduciary duty by directors who voted to accelerate the option exercise date and federal proxy rule violations in connection with the re-election of the directors who had so benefitted at the expense of the Corporation. Both of these suits were styled *Maldonado v. Flynn*.

Four years after the filing of these suits, the Zapata Board appointed two new directors and constituted them as the "Independent Investigation Committee of Zapata Corporation." The committee retained as counsel the law firm of one of the directors. Within three months of their appointment, the Committee filed a "Report and Determination" to the effect that all of the law suits should be dismissed. At their direction, the Corporation's counsel then moved for dismissal of the action.

The Federal District Court in New York concluded that the board of a Delaware corporation had authority to terminate derivative litigation. The court observed, with respect to the exercise of business judgment in this case:

> [T]he Committee labored under no compulsion to conclude that the actions were lacking in merit. Such a finding is not a prerequisite to the exercise of business judgment though of course it is a factor that may well be considered. To the contrary, the essence of the business judgment rule in this context is that directors may freely find that certain *meritorious* actions are not in the corporation's best interests to pursue. Indeed, here liability is not a foregone conclusion as the issue of materiality remains for trial determination.

> The final substantive judgment whether a particular lawsuit should be maintained requires a balance of many factors—ethical, commercial, promotional, public relations, employee relations, fiscal as well as legal. The factors to be taken into account and their evaluation are for the Committee expressly appointed to consider them and are beyond the judicial reach. In the last analysis the decision required to be made and that in fact was made is not a legal but a business judgment. * * *

The court found no conflict with the policy of the federal proxy rules. *Maldonado v. Flynn*, 485 F.Supp. 274 (S.D.N.Y.1980).

The Delaware Chancery Court held otherwise and ruled that the case could not be dismissed. *Maldonado v. Flynn*, 413 A.2d 1251 (Del.Ch. 1980).]

QUILLEN, JUSTICE.

* * * We limit our review in this interlocutory appeal to whether the Committee has the power to cause the present action to be dismissed.

We begin with an examination of the carefully considered opinion of the Vice Chancellor which states, in part, that the "business judgment" rule does not confer power "to a corporate board of directors to terminate a derivative suit", 413 A.2d at 1257. His conclusion is particularly pertinent because several federal courts, applying Delaware law, have held that the business judgment rule enables boards (or their committees) to terminate derivative suits, decisions now in conflict with the holding below.

As the term is most commonly used, and given the disposition below, we can understand the Vice Chancellor's comment that "the business judgment rule is irrelevant to the question of whether the Committee has the authority to compel the dismissal of this suit." 413 A.2d at 1257. Corporations, existing because of legislative grace, possess authority as granted by the legislature. Directors of Delaware corporations derive their managerial decision making power, which encompasses decisions whether to initiate, or refrain from entering, litigation, from 8 Del.C. § 141(a). This statute is the fount of directorial powers. The "business judgment" rule is a judicial creation that presumes propriety, under certain circumstances, in a board's decision. Viewed defensively, it does not create authority. In this sense the "business judgment" rule is not relevant in corporate decision making until after a decision is made. It is generally used as a defense to an attack on the decision's soundness. The board's managerial decision making power, however, comes from § 141(a). The judicial creation and legislative grant are related because the "business judgment" rule evolved to give recognition and deference to directors' business expertise when exercising their managerial power under § 141(a).

In the case before us, although the corporation's decision to move to dismiss or for summary judgment was, literally, a decision resulting from an exercise of the directors' (as delegated to the Committee) business judgment, the question of "business judgment", in a defensive sense, would not become relevant until and unless the decision to seek termination of the derivative lawsuit was attacked as improper. This question was not reached by the Vice Chancellor because he determined that the stockholder had an individual right to maintain this derivative action.

Thus, the focus in this case is on the power to speak for the corporation as to whether the lawsuit should be continued or terminated. As we see it, this issue in the current appellate posture of this case has three aspects: the conclusions of the Court below concerning the continuing right of a stockholder to maintain a derivative action; the corporate power under Delaware law of an authorized board committee to cause dismissal of litigation instituted for the benefit of the corporation; and the role of the Court of Chancery in resolving conflicts between the stockholder and the committee.

Accordingly, we turn first to the Court of Chancery's conclusions concerning the right of a plaintiff stockholder in a derivative action. We find that its determination that a stockholder, once demand is made and refused, possesses an independent, individual right to continue a derivative suit for breaches of fiduciary duty over objection by the corporation, as an absolute rule, is erroneous. * * *

Moreover, *McKee v. Rogers,* Del.Ch., 156 A. 191 (1931), stated "as a general rule" that "a stockholder cannot be permitted * * * to invade the discretionary field committed to the judgment of the directors and sue in the corporation's behalf when the managing body refuses. This rule is a well settled one." 156 A. at 193.

The *McKee* rule, of course, should not be read so broadly that the board's refusal will be determinative in every instance. Board members, owing a well-established fiduciary duty to the corporation, will not be allowed to cause a derivative suit to be dismissed when it would be a breach of their fiduciary duty. Generally disputes pertaining to control of the suit arise in two contexts.

Consistent with the purpose of requiring a demand, a board decision to cause a derivative suit to be dismissed as detrimental to the company, after demand has been made and refused, will be respected unless it was wrongful.[10] A claim of a wrongful decision not to sue is thus the first exception and the first context of dispute. Absent a wrongful refusal, the stockholder in such a situation simply lacks legal managerial power.

But it cannot be implied that, absent a wrongful board refusal, a stockholder can never have an individual right to initiate an action. For, as is stated in *McKee,* a "well settled" exception exists to the general rule.

[A] stockholder may sue in equity in his derivative right to assert a cause of action in behalf of the corporation, *without prior demand* upon the directors to sue, when it is apparent that a demand would be futile, that the officers are under an influence that sterilizes discretion and could not be proper persons to conduct the litigation.

*Id.* at 193 (emphasis added). This exception, the second context for dispute, is consistent with the Court of Chancery's statement below, that "[the stockholder's individual right to bring the action does not ripen, however, * * * unless he can show a demand to be futile." *Maldonado,* 413 A.2d at 1262.

These comments in *McKee* and in the opinion below make obvious sense. A demand, when required and refused (if not wrongful), terminates a stockholder's legal ability to initiate a derivative action. But where demand is properly excused, the stockholder does possess the ability to initiate the action on his corporation's behalf.

---

**10.** In other words, when stockholders, after making demand and having their suit rejected, attack the board's decision as improper, the board's decision falls under the "business judgment" rule and will be respected if the requirements of the rule are met. That situation should be distinguished from the instant case, where demand was not made, and the *power* of the board to seek a dismissal, due to disqualification, presents a threshold issue. We recognize that the two contexts can overlap in practice.

These conclusions, however, do not determine the question before us. Rather, they merely bring us to the question to be decided. It is here that we part company with the Court below. * * * We see no inherent reason why the "two phases" of a derivative suit, the stockholder's suit to compel the corporation to sue and the corporation's suit should automatically result in the placement in the hands of the litigating stockholder sole control of the corporate right throughout the litigation. To the contrary, it seems to us that such an inflexible rule would recognize the interest of one person or group to the exclusion of all others within the corporate entity. Thus, we reject the view of the Vice Chancellor as to the first aspect of the issue on appeal.

The question to be decided becomes: When, if at all, should an authorized board committee be permitted to cause litigation, properly initiated by a derivative stockholder in his own right, to be dismissed? As noted above, a board has the power to choose not to pursue litigation when demand is made upon it, so long as the decision is not wrongful. If the board determines that a suit would be detrimental to the company, the board's determination prevails. Even when demand is excusable, circumstances may arise when continuation of the litigation would not be in the corporation's best interests. Our inquiry is whether, under such circumstances, there is a permissible procedure under § 141(a) by which a corporation can rid itself of detrimental litigation. If there is not, a single stockholder in an extreme case might control the destiny of the entire corporation. This concern was bluntly expressed by the Ninth Circuit in *Lewis v. Anderson*, 9th Cir., 615 F.2d 778, 783 (1979), *cert. denied*, 449 U.S. 869, 101 S.Ct. 206, 66 L.Ed.2d 89 (1980): "To allow one shareholder to incapacitate an entire board of directors merely by leveling charges against them gives too much leverage to dissident shareholders." But, when examining the means, including the committee mechanism examined in this case, potentials for abuse must be recognized. This takes us to the second and third aspects of the issue on appeal.

Before we pass to equitable considerations as to the mechanism at issue here, it must be clear that an independent committee possesses the corporate power to seek the termination of a derivative suit. Section 141(c) allows a board to delegate all of its authority to a committee. Accordingly, a committee with properly delegated authority would have the power to move for dismissal or summary judgment if the entire board did.

Even though demand was not made in this case and the initial decision of whether to litigate was not placed before the board, Zapata's board, it seems to us, retained all of its corporate power concerning litigation decisions. If Maldonado had made demand on the board in this case, it could have refused to bring suit. Maldonado could then have asserted that the decision not to sue was wrongful and, if correct, would have been allowed to maintain the suit. The board, however, never would have lost its statutory managerial authority. The demand requirement itself evidences that the managerial power is retained by the board.

When a derivative plaintiff is allowed to bring suit after a wrongful refusal, the board's authority to choose whether to pursue the litigation is not challenged although its conclusion—reached through the exercise of that authority—is not respected since it is wrongful. Similarly, Rule 23.1, by excusing demand in certain instances, does not strip the board of its corporate power. It merely saves the plaintiff the expense and delay of making a futile demand resulting in a probable tainted exercise of that authority in a refusal by the board or in giving control of litigation to the opposing side. But the board entity remains empowered under § 141(a) to make decisions regarding corporate litigation. The problem is one of member disqualification, not the absence of power in the board.

The corporate power inquiry then focuses on whether the board, tainted by the self-interest of a majority of its members, can legally delegate its authority to a committee of two disinterested directors. We find our statute clearly requires an affirmative answer to this question. As has been noted, under an express provision of the statute, § 141(c), a committee can exercise all of the authority of the board to the extent provided in the resolution of the board. Moreover, at least by analogy to our statutory section on interested directors, 8 Del.C. § 141, it seems clear that the Delaware statute is designed to permit disinterested directors to act for the board.

We do not think that the interest taint of the board majority is per se a legal bar to the delegation of the board's power to an independent committee composed of disinterested board members. The committee can properly act for the corporation to move to dismiss derivative litigation that is believed to be detrimental to the corporation's best interest.

Our focus now switches to the Court of Chancery which is faced with a stockholder assertion that a derivative suit, properly instituted, should continue for the benefit of the corporation and a corporate assertion, properly made by a board committee acting with board authority, that the same derivative suit should be dismissed as inimical to the best interests of the corporation.

At the risk of stating the obvious, the problem is relatively simple. If, on the one hand, corporations can consistently wrest bona fide derivative actions away from well-meaning derivative plaintiffs through the use of the committee mechanism, the derivative suit will lose much, if not all, of its generally-recognized effectiveness as an intra-corporate means of policing boards of directors. If, on the other hand, corporations are unable to rid themselves of meritless or harmful litigation and strike suits, the derivative action, created to benefit the corporation, will produce the opposite, unintended result. It thus appears desirable to us to find a balancing point where bona fide stockholder power to bring corporate causes of action cannot be unfairly trampled on by the board of directors, but the corporation can rid itself of detrimental litigation.

As we noted, the question has been treated by other courts as one of the "business judgment" of the board committee. If a "committee, composed of independent and disinterested directors, conducted a proper review of the matters before it, considered a variety of factors and reached, in good faith, a business judgment that [the] action was not in the best interest of [the corporation", the action must be dismissed. The issues become solely independence, good faith, and reasonable investigation. The ultimate conclusion of the committee, under that view, is not subject to judicial review.

We are not satisfied, however, that acceptance of the "business judgment" rationale at this stage of derivative litigation is a proper balancing point. While we admit an analogy with a normal case respecting board judgment, it seems to us that there is sufficient risk in the realities of a situation like the one presented in this case to justify caution beyond adherence to the theory of business judgment.

The context here is a suit against directors where demand on the board is excused. We think some tribute must be paid to the fact that the lawsuit was properly initiated. It is not a board refusal case. Moreover, this complaint was filed in June of 1975 and, while the parties undoubtedly would take differing views on the degree of litigation activity, we have to be concerned about the creation of an "Independent Investigation Committee" four years later, after the election of two new outside directors. Situations could develop where such motions could be filed after years of vigorous litigation for reasons unconnected with the merits of the lawsuit.

Moreover, notwithstanding our conviction that Delaware law entrusts the corporate power to a properly authorized committee, we must be mindful that directors are passing judgment on fellow directors in the same corporation and fellow directors, in this instance, who designated them to serve both as directors and committee members. The question naturally arises whether a "there but for the grace of God go I" empathy might not play a role. And the further question arises whether inquiry as to independence, good faith and reasonable investigation is sufficient safeguard against abuse, perhaps subconscious abuse. * * *

It seems to us that there are two other procedural analogies that are helpful in addition to reference to Rules 12 and 56. There is some analogy to a settlement in that there is a request to terminate litigation without a judicial determination of the merits. "In determining whether or not to approve a proposed settlement of a derivative stockholders' action [when directors are on both sides of the transaction], the Court of Chancery is called upon to exercise its own business judgment." *Neponsit Investment Co. v. Abramson*, Del.Supr., 405 A.2d 97, 100 (1979). In this case, the litigating stockholder plaintiff facing dismissal of a lawsuit properly commenced ought, in our judgment, to have sufficient status for strict Court review.

Finally, if the committee is in effect given status to speak for the corporation as the plaintiff in interest, then it seems to us there is an analogy to Court of Chancery Rule 41(a)(2) where the plaintiff seeks a dismissal after an answer. Certainly, the position of record of the litigating stockholder is adverse to the position advocated by the corporation in the motion to dismiss. Accordingly, there is perhaps some wisdom to be gained by the direction in Rule 41(a)(2) that "an action shall not be dismissed at the plaintiff's instance save upon order of the Court and upon such terms and conditions as the Court deems proper."

Whether the Court of Chancery will be persuaded by the exercise of a committee power resulting in a summary motion for dismissal of a derivative action, where a demand has not been initially made, should rest, in our judgment, in the independent discretion of the Court of Chancery. We thus steer a middle course between those cases which yield to the independent business judgment of a board committee and this case as determined below which would yield to unbridled plaintiff stockholder control. In pursuit of the course, we recognize that "[t]he final substantive judgment whether a particular lawsuit should be maintained requires a balance of many factors—ethical, commercial, promotional, public relations, employee relations, fiscal as well as legal." *Maldonado v. Flynn, supra,* 485 F.Supp. at 285. But we are content that such factors are not "beyond the judicial reach" of the Court of Chancery which regularly and competently deals with fiduciary relationships, disposition of trust property, approval of settlements and scores of similar problems. We recognize the danger of judicial overreaching but the alternatives seem to us to be outweighed by the fresh view of a judicial outsider. Moreover, if we failed to balance all the interests involved, we would in the name of practicality and judicial economy foreclose a judicial decision on the merits. At this point, we are not convinced that is necessary or desirable.

After an objective and thorough investigation of a derivative suit, an independent committee may cause its corporation to file a pretrial motion to dismiss in the Court of Chancery. The basis of the motion is the best interests of the corporation, as determined by the committee. The motion should include a thorough written record of the investigation and its findings and recommendations. Under appropriate Court supervision, akin to proceedings on summary judgment, each side should have an opportunity to make a record on the motion. As to the limited issues presented by the motion noted below, the moving party should be prepared to meet the normal burden under Rule 56 that there is no genuine issue as to any material fact and that the moving party is entitled to dismiss as a matter of law. The Court should apply a two-step test to the motion.

First, the Court should inquire into the independence and good faith of the committee and the bases supporting its conclusions. Limited discovery may be ordered to facilitate such inquiries. The corporation should have the burden of proving independence, good faith and a reasonable investigation, rather than presuming independence, good faith and reasonableness. If the Court determines either that the committee is not independent or has not shown reasonable bases for its conclusions, or, if the Court is not satisfied for other reasons relating to the process, including but not limited to the good faith of the committee, the Court shall deny the corporation's motion. If, however, the Court is satisfied under Rule 56 standards that the committee was independent and showed reasonable bases for good faith findings and recommendations, the Court may proceed, in its discretion, to the next step.

The second step provides, we believe, the essential key in striking the balance between legitimate corporate claims as expressed in a derivative stockholder suit and a corporation's best interests as expressed by an independent investigating committee. The Court should determine, applying its own independent business judgment, whether the motion should be granted.[18] This means, of course, that instances could arise where a committee can establish its independence and sound bases for its good faith decisions and still have the corporation's motion denied. The second step is intended to thwart instances where corporate actions meet the criteria of step one, but the result does not appear to satisfy its spirit, or where corporate actions would simply prematurely terminate a stockholder grievance deserving of further consideration in the corporation's interest. The Court of Chancery of course must carefully consider and weigh how compelling the corporate interest in dismissal is when faced with a non-frivolous lawsuit. The Court of Chancery should, when appropriate, give special consideration to matters of law and public policy in addition to the corporation's best interests.

If the Court's independent business judgment is satisfied, the Court may proceed to grant the motion, subject, of course, to any equitable terms or conditions the Court finds necessary or desirable.

The interlocutory order of the Court of Chancery is reversed and the cause is remanded for further proceedings consistent with this opinion.

### Note: Terminating Derivative Suits

1. The court in *Zapata* distinguished between a case where demand on directors was required and one where demand was excused. Only in the latter situation did the full force of the opinion apply. No demand was made in *Zapata*, nor did the defendants urge its necessity. Thus the *Zapata* court was not called upon to explore the question of when demand was required. That issue is what *Aronson* and its progeny address. *Zapata* did, however, reserve a role for the courts in reviewing a special committee's motion to terminate a derivative suit and rejected reliance on the business judgment rule as the appropriate standard for such review.

2. *Auerbach v. Bennett*, 393 N.E.2d 994 (N.Y.1979) adopted a different approach. A derivative suit was brought against directors and the independent auditor of General Telephone and Electronics Corporation following disclosure that the company had made illegal payments and bribes, and that some of the individual defendants had been personally involved. The board appointed a special litigation committee consisting of three directors, all of whom had joined the board after the

---

**18.** This step shares some of the same spirit and philosophy of the statement by the Vice Chancellor: "Under our system of law, courts and not litigants should decide the merits of litigation." 413 A.2d at 1263.

incidents in question and one of whom was appointed to the board after the suit was brought. The committee concluded that none of the defendants had breached the duty of due care, that none had profited personally and that it was not in the best interest of the corporation for the derivative suit to proceed.

The New York Court of Appeals affirmed the trial court's grant of the committee's motion for summary judgment. The court viewed the case through the lens of the business judgment rule and found that the rule precluded judicial scrutiny of the merits of the committee's decision concerning the underlying litigation. The court noted that the rule did not "foreclose inquiry * * * into the disinterested independence of those members of the board chosen by it to make the corporate decision on its behalf—here the members of the special litigation committee. Indeed the rule shields the deliberations and conclusions of the chosen representatives of the board only if they possess a disinterested independence and do not stand in a dual relation which prevents an unprejudicial exercise of judgment." *Id.* at 1001.

After finding that plaintiff had failed to produce evidence calling into question the independence of the committee members, the court considered how far its review of the committee's action should extend.

> * * * First, there was the selection of procedures appropriate in the pursuit of its charge, and second there was the ultimate substantive decision, predicated on the procedures chosen and the data produced thereby, not to pursue the claims advanced in the shareholders' derivative actions. The latter, substantive decision falls squarely within the embrace of the business judgment doctrine, involving as it did the weighing and balancing of legal, ethical, commercial, promotional, public relations, fiscal and other factors familiar to the resolution of many if not most corporate problems. To this extent the conclusion reached by the special litigation committee is outside the scope of our review. Thus, the courts cannot inquire as to which factors were considered by that committee or the relative weight accorded them in reaching that substantive decision * * *. Inquiry into such matters would go to the very core of the business judgment made by the committee. To permit judicial probing of such issues would be to emasculate the business judgment doctrine as applied to actions and determinations of the special litigation committee. Its substantive evaluation of the problems posed and its judgment in their resolution are beyond our reach.

*Id.* at 1002.

However, the court added that review of the methodologies and procedures followed by the committee were areas for which the courts are "well equipped by long and continuing experience to make determinations. In fact they are better qualified in this regard than are corporate directors in general * * *. While the court may properly inquire as to the adequacy and appropriateness of the committee's investigative procedures and methodologies, it may not under the guise of consideration of such factors trespass in the domain of business judgment." *Id.*

*Auerbach* does not seem to contemplate *Zapata*'s discretionary second-step, which allows the court to dismiss the committee's recommendation that the suit be terminated even though the committee was independent, disinterested and conducted a thorough investigation with reasonable bases for its conclusions. The decision involved—whether to allow a lawsuit to proceed—is different in analytical process and risk exposure from the ordinary business decision. When considering what to do about the possible suit, the board or committee takes a backward look, much as it does when it considers ratification of a self-dealing act by a director, rather than a risk-laden forward look. For a critique of *Auerbach, see* Charles W. Murdock, *Corporate Governance—The Role of Special Litigation Committees*, 68 Wash. L. Rev. 79 (1993).

Nevertheless, some courts feel the need to install a kind of screening device against excessive, costly and time consuming litigation. If functioning properly (as *Auerbach* conceives it), the special litigation committee can be an alternative dispute resolution mechanism that provides quick and satisfactory common-sense answers to the charges raised in a derivative suit. Critics of the committee process cannot ignore the strong desire to avoid these costly lawsuits particularly in light of studies finding that derivative suits generate relatively few tangible benefits of the shareholders. *See* Section G.

3.  The *Auerbach* court sometimes refers to the business judgment *rule* and at other times speaks of the business judgment *doctrine*. The business judgment rule, as we have seen, is a policy of judicial abstinence that shields directors from liability for their business decisions. It comes into play when a shareholder seeks to impose liability on the directors for having made a costly and allegedly erroneous decision. The *doctrine* fulfills another goal. It functions not as a shield but rather as a sword, recognizing the decisionmaking primacy of the board. It is an expression of corporate governance, not liability. *See* Joseph Hinsey IV, Business Judgment and the American Law Institute's Corporate Governance Project: the Rule, the Doctrine, and the Reality, 52 Geo.Wash.L.Rev. 609, 611 (1984).

Thus in *Auerbach,* two decisions were involved. The first concerned illegal payments and the second concerned a decision to terminate the suit to recover those payments. The plaintiff sued to recover the loss arising from the first decision. He was met by the second decision, which he challenged, but he did not seek to impose liability on those who made the decision. The *rule* would govern the question of whether anyone would be liable for her decision, an issue arising only with respect to the first decision. The *doctrine* applies only to the second decision, where the issue was whether the court should defer to the decision not to sue those who made the first decision and paid the bribes. The conduct involved in the first decision was conceivably protected by the business judgment rule, (although arguably not if an illegal act was involved). Yet if the doctrine applied to the second decision, a shareholder would be precluded from recovering the corporate loss resulting from the first decision.

4. *Zapata*'s two-step approach to demand has not been universally applauded by the lower courts that must apply it. Indeed, the elaborate procedures that flow from the full application of *Zapata* were described in *Kaplan v. Wyatt*, 484 A.2d 501 (Del.Ch.1984), *aff'd* 499 A.2d 1184 (Del.1985), as a "legal mouthful." *Kaplan* involved a derivative suit brought by a shareholder of Coastal Corporation against the chief executive officer, alleging self-dealing and excessive compensation. A special litigation committee consisting of two members was appointed. One member of the committee was a substantial shareholder of other companies that had extensive business dealings with Coastal. Independent counsel and auditors were named to assist the committee. The committee found that the suit had no merit and filed a motion to dismiss the suit.

The Chancellor granted the motion after finding that the committee was independent and that the procedural requirements of *Zapata* had been satisfied. He emphasized that even if a committee was independent and its investigation reasonably supported, a court reviewing a committee's recommendation to dismiss a suit could reject the recommendation if, in its own business judgment, dismissal would not be in the corporation's best interest.

The Chancellor also discussed the problems of a board using a special litigation committee to investigate a derivative suit and the court relying on the committee's recommendation. After a thorough review of what it interpreted as the *Zapata* requirements, the Chancellor wrote:

> * * * I fail to see how the Special Litigation Committee procedure can be taken lightly or stated any less explicitly given that which is at stake. For it must be kept in mind that the entire procedure is designed to provide a means, if warranted, to throw a derivative plaintiff out of Court before he has an opportunity to engage in any discovery whatever in support of the merits of his cause of action purportedly brought on the corporation's behalf. In fact, the *Zapata* procedure takes the case away from the plaintiff, turns his allegations over to special agents appointed on behalf of the corporation for the purpose of making an informal, internal investigation of his charges, and places the plaintiff on the defensive once a motion to dismiss is filed by the Special Litigation Committee, leaving him to snipe away at the bona fides of the Committee and its extra-judicial investigation in a last-ditch effort to salvage a right to present the case on the corporation's behalf as he sees it. The procedure also asks the Court to consider dismissing the case prior to the time that the facts pertaining to the plaintiff's allegations are developed in an adversarial context unlike the procedure that has existed heretofore. As to whether this new departure in derivative litigation is good or bad I offer no judgment. Certainly, it has its justification in legal theory as is ably expressed in *Zapata*.

However, it is fraught with practical complications at the trial court level. It certainly does not speed up the course of derivative litigation and, based upon what I have seen so far, it is doubtful that it reduces the expense or inconvenience of derivative litigation to the corporation.

*Id.* at 509–10.

5.   North Carolina, after initially embracing *Auerbach,* emphatically rejected it in *Alford v. Shaw,* 358 S.E.2d 323 (N.C.1987). After extensive litigation, the Supreme Court refused to apply the business judgment rule to a special litigation committee's recommendation to dismiss the principal portion of the litigation. The court observed a trend away from *Auerbach* and held that North Carolina's "liberal" derivative suit provisions, requiring judicial approval for dismissal or settlement of a derivative suit, compelled judicial examination of the substance of the proposed action. "To rely blindly on the report of a corporation-appointed committee which assembled such materials on behalf of the corporation is to abdicate the judicial duty to consider the interests of shareholders imposed by the statute. This abdication is particularly inappropriate in a case such as this one, where shareholders allege serious breaches of fiduciary duties owed to them by the directors controlling the corporation." *Id.* at 327.

Unlike *Zapata,* the court did not limit inquiry into the merits to cases where demand was futile and therefore excused. "[C]ourt approval is required for disposition of *all* derivative suits, even where the directors are not charged with fraud or self-dealing, or where the plaintiff and the board agree to discontinue, dismiss, compromise, or settle the lawsuit." *Id.*

Moreover, the court observed that the statutory requirement imposing the burden of proving fairness on interested persons in self-dealing cases requires that "the court must make a fair assessment of the report * * *, along with all other facts and circumstances in the case, in order to determine whether the defendants will be able to show that the transaction complained of was just and reasonable to the corporation." *Id.* at 328.

6.   *Cuker v. Mikalauskas,* 547 Pa. 600, 692 A.2d 1042 (1997) held that under Pennsylvania law, the business judgment rule permitted the board of directors to terminate a derivative suit brought by minority shareholders. The court specifically adopted ALI, PRINCIPLES OF CORPORATE GOVERNANCE (1994) §§ 7.02–7.10 and § 7.13 dealing with derivative suits. The court noted:

> * * * In doing so we have weighed many considerations. First, the opinion of the trial court, the questions certified to the Superior Court, and the inability of PECO to obtain a definitive ruling from the lower courts all demonstrate the need for specific guidance from this court on how such litigation should be managed; the ALI principles provide such guidance in specific terms which will simplify this litigation. Second, we have often found ALI guidance helpful

in the past, most frequently in adopting or citing sections of various Restatements; the scholarship reflected in work of the American Law Institute has been consistently reliable and useful. Third, the principles set forth by the ALI are generally consistent with Pennsylvania precedent. Fourth, although the ALI Principles incorporate much of the law of New York and Delaware, other states with extensive corporate jurisprudence, the ALI Principles better serve the needs of Pennsylvania. Although New York law parallels Pennsylvania law in many respects, it does not set forth any procedures to govern the review of corporate decisions relating to derivative litigation, and this omission would fail to satisfy the needs evident in this case. Delaware law permits a court in some cases ("demand excused" cases) to apply its own business judgment in the review process when deciding to honor the directors' decision to terminate derivative litigation. In our view, this is a defect which could eviscerate the business judgment rule and contradict a long line of Pennsylvania precedents. Delaware law also fails to provide a procedural framework for judicial review of corporate decisions under the business judgment rule.

*Id.* at 1049.

7.   Both *Zapata* and *Auerbach,* in perhaps only slightly varying degrees, rely upon the ability of independent directors to make a fair and impartial decision on behalf of the corporation. Other courts have expressed skepticism about whether directors can be truly independent when asked to function in this manner.

In *Joy v. North*, 692 F.2d 880, 888 (2d Cir.1982), *cert. denied* 460 U.S. 1051, 103 S.Ct. 1498, 75 L.Ed.2d 930 (1983), the court held that Connecticut would follow *Zapata,* but noted:

> * * * [T]he reality is * * * that special litigation committees created to evaluate the merits of certain litigation are appointed by defendants to that committee. It is not cynical to expect that such committees will tend to view derivative actions against the other directors with skepticism. Indeed if the involved directors expected any results other than a recommendation of termination, at least as to them, they would probably never establish the committee.

Suspicion about the nature of the special litigation committee caused the Iowa Supreme Court to reject both *Zapata* and *Auerbach.* In *Miller v. Register and Tribune Syndicate, Inc.*, 336 N.W.2d 709, 716 (Iowa 1983), the court commented:

> * * * It is tacitly, if not expressly, conceded by the defendant corporation and the defendant directors, in the present case that the board itself could not seek dismissal of the action against the majority of its own members by invoking the business judgment rule. The question which naturally arises is whether, given this circumstance, the board has the power to delegate to a committee the authority to do that which it may not do itself. * * *

The central theme of these concerns [about special litigation committees] has been focused on the "structural bias' approach, which suggests that it is unrealistic to assume that the members of independent committees are free from personal, financial or moral influences which flow from the directors who appoint them. The argument is made that this is all the more so where, as in the present derivative action, the members of the special committee are fellow directors.

The court denied power to Iowa corporations to create special litigation committees to bind the corporation in its conduct of the litigation. However, the court held that the corporation could apply to the court for appointment of a "special panel" to make an investigation and take binding action on behalf of the corporation. *See also Will v. Engebretson & Co., Inc.*, 213 Cal.App.3d 1033, 261 Cal.Rptr. 868 (1989), (even a special litigation committee made up entirely of outside directors has an "inherent structural bias" that warrants judicial review of the committee's independence and good faith in urging the dismissal of a derivative suit).

8.　Professors James Cox, a law professor, and Harry Munsinger, a psychologist, offer the following analysis in support of suspicions of "structural bias:"

　　* * * The directors called upon to evaluate a derivative suit against their colleagues are not, and generally have not been, isolated from the suit's defendants. As members of the board of directors they continue to interact with the defendants, who usually remain directors or officers of the corporation. Even members of a special litigation committee who were appointed *after* the derivative suit was initiated are legally bound under the organic requirements for committee membership to serve as directors on the full board. The new special litigation committee members and the defendant directors therefore serve as colleagues on the same corporate board in addressing an array of nonderivative suit issues. Consequently, the judges and those to be judged associate on a regular basis in discharging their many tasks as corporate directors during the preliminary derivative suit skirmishes. In doing so, they share a mutual duty to serve the corporate interest, and they often adopt a common view of that corporate interest. Analogous studies suggest that the effect of these shared experiences is not only to bond the directors and the defendants together but also to form a basis upon which the directors can be expected to give greater weight to the defendant's values, attitudes, and perceptions than to those of outgroup members like the plaintiff. Indeed, the greater the interaction between the defendants and directors, in terms of frequency and degree of task complexity, the stronger the favoritism the directors can be expected to express toward the defendants. While this favoritism does not necessarily cause the outgroup member (the plaintiff) to be held at a lower level of esteem, in an absolute sense, than when there was no interaction between ingroup members, on a

relative scale a greater regard results for ingroup members than for outgroup members.

More is involved in the dynamics of intergroup discrimination in the demand or special litigation committee context than the seemingly simple categorization of the nondefendant directors as "directors," a category which also includes the defendants. As seen earlier, individuals place great value on their selection to and membership on a corporation's board: They are attracted to their colleagues and value greatly the associations they reap from the directorship. The relative attractiveness and rewards of board membership to the nondefendant director are important considerations in the director's ability to be an impartial arbitrator of a colleague's behavior.

James D. Cox and Harry Munsinger, *Bias in the Boardroom: Psychological Foundations and Legal Implications of Corporate Cohesion*, 48 LAW & CONTEMP. PROBS., 83, 103–4 (1985).

*Aronson* rejects the structural bias argument, absent a showing of specific facts. In *Kaplan v. Wyatt*, 499 A.2d 1184 (Del.1985), *aff'g* 484 A.2d 501 (Del.Ch.1984), the court held that particularized allegations that a corporate director had investments and affiliations with companies that did substantial business with the defendant corporation was not enough to establish bias because there was no showing of "personal dealings" or other impairment to the director's independence.

A rare example of a Delaware court finding structural bias is the Court of Chancery's decision in *Lewis v. Fuqua*, 502 A.2d 962 (Del.Ch. 1985), *appeal denied* 504 A.2d 571 (Del.1986), where all but one member of the board were sued for appropriating a corporate opportunity. That director (former Governor, then president of Duke University, and later Senator Terry Sanford) was then appointed as a one-person special litigation committee. The court found that he was not independent because:

> He was a member of the Board of Directors of Fuqua Industries at the time the challenged actions took place; he is one of the defendants in this suit; he has had numerous political and financial dealings with J.B. Fuqua who is the chief executive officer of Fuqua Industries and who allegedly controls the Board; he is President of Duke University which is a recent recipient of a $10 million pledge from Fuqua Industries and J.B. Fuqua; and J.B. Fuqua has, in the past, made several contributions to Duke University and is a Trustee of the University.

*Id.* at 966–67.

9. *Zapata* assigns several important roles to the courts. The traffic cop function with respect to discovery is analyzed in *Kaplan*. The court's more important function, however, is to exercise its own business judgment as to the ultimate question—should the lawsuit be terminated?

If the standard of the business judgment rule does not govern the issue, how should the court analyze the question of whether it is in the best interests of the corporation to maintain the lawsuit? In *Joy v. North, supra,* Judge Winter suggested that "the function of the court's review is to determine the balance of probabilities as to likely future benefit to the corporation, not to render a decision on the merits, fashion the appropriate legal principles or resolve issues of credibility. Where the legal rule is unclear and the likely evidence in conflict, the court need only weigh the uncertainties, not resolve them. The court's function is thus not unlike a lawyer's determining what a case is" worth "for purposes of settlement. Where the court determines that the likely recoverable damages discounted by the probability of a finding of liability are less than the costs to the corporation in continuing the action it should dismiss the case". 692 F.2d at 892–93.

10.   As noted above, both the ALI and the RMBCA adopt a universal demand requirement, but they differ substantially in their treatment of judicial review of a subsequent decision by a Special Litigation Committee to dismiss the litigation. The ALI adheres to none of the approaches to special litigation committees described above. It bifurcates the judicial standard of review based on whether the claim charges a breach of the duty of loyalty or the duty of care. If the duty of care is involved, the court should uphold a recommendation to dismiss a claim unless the decision by the board or committee fails the business judgment rule. If the claim alleges a breach of the duty of loyalty, the ALI recommends stricter judicial scrutiny. In such cases, the board or committee must determine that dismissal is in the best interests of the corporation; this determination must be "based on grounds that the court deems to warrant reliance." In deciding whether the findings "warrant reliance," a court should examine the adequacy of the investigation, the level of the board's involvement in the transaction, the plausibility of the reasons presented by the board or committee to support dismissal and, most importantly, the nature of the claim. Scrutiny should be more stringent if the nature of the claim involves charges of "knowing and culpable violations of the law," including those acts that are "morally reprehensible under generally prevailing standards."

The ALI imposes a stiff burden of proof on defendants if they retain a "significant improper benefit" from the challenged transaction. Strict scrutiny of these cases is designed to deter such conduct, although the defendants can overcome their burden even here if the injury to the corporation caused by allowing the case to continue outweighs the harm to the public interest resulting from terminating the lawsuit. ALI, PRINCIPLES OF CORPORATE GOVERNANCE (1994), §§ 7.08, 7.10.

*Houle v. Low,* 556 N.E.2d 51 (Mass.1990) followed the ALI approach. After an extensive review of the case law in other jurisdictions, the court concluded that special litigation committees were permitted under Massachusetts law. The court noted, however, that because of the danger of "structural bias" and the lack of independence, "a great deal of judicial oversight is necessary in each case," and held that the burden of proving independence, a lack of bias and good faith falls on the corporation. In the case, the committee consisted of one director who had a close professional relationship with the defendants and other shareholders and depended on them for her future economic success. Under those circumstances, the court remanded for a further determination of her independence.

Assuming that the committee was independent, the court found that the second step requires a trial judge to determine "whether the committee reached a reasonable and principled decision. Even in those cases where a committee is independent and conducts a thorough investigation, the judge may conclude that the committee's decision is contrary to the great weight of the evidence." *Id.* at 59. Citing the ALI PRINCIPLES OF CORPORATE GOVERNANCE § 7.08 (T.D. No. 8, 1988), the court said that the trial court should look to factors such as "the likelihood of a judgment in the plaintiff's favor, the expected recovery as compared to out-of-pocket costs, whether the corporation itself took corrective action, whether the balance of corporate interests warrants dismissal, and whether dismissal would allow any defendant who has control of the corporation to retain a significant improper benefit." *Id.*

11. In contrast to the ALI, RMBCA § 7.44 requires dismissal of a derivative suit if an appropriate decision-maker concludes, after "reasonable inquiry on which its conclusions are based that the maintenance of the [suit] is not in the best interests of the corporation." The determination must be made by a majority vote of either the independent directors constituting a quorum or a committee consisting of two or more independent directors who have been appointed by a majority of independent directors, regardless of whether the latter constitute a quorum.

As the Official Comment makes clear, § 7.44 is not intended to modify the general standard of conduct of directors; the analysis we examined in Chapter 16 applies to the decision-making process used in determining whether to dismiss a derivative suit under § 7.44. Most important, the court will not review the reasonableness of the determination if the directors who make the decision are independent.

The question of the independence of the directors who are members of the committee and those who appoint them directly implicates the issue of structural bias. The Official Comment states:

> The decisions which have examined the qualifications of directors making the determination have required that they be both "disinterested" in the sense of not having a personal interest in the transaction being challenged as opposed to a benefit which devolves upon the corporation or all shareholders generally, and "independent" in the sense of not being influenced in favor of the defendants by reason of personal or other relationships. Only the word "independent" has been used in section 7.44(b) because it is believed that this word necessarily also includes the requirement that a person have no interest in the transaction. The concept of an independent director is not intended to be limited to non-officer or "outside" directors but may in appropriate circumstances include directors who are also officers.

Many of the special litigation committees involved in the reported cases consisted of directors who were elected after the alleged wrongful acts by the directors who were named as defendants in the action. Subsection (c)(1) makes it clear that the participation of non-independent directors or shareholders in the nomination or election of a new director shall not prevent the new director from being considered independent. This sentence therefore rejects the concept that the mere appointment of new directors by the non-independent directors makes the new directors not independent in making the necessary determination because of an inherent structural bias. Clauses (2) and (3) also confirm the decisions by a number of courts that the mere fact that a director has been named as a defendant or approved the action being challenged does not cause the director to be considered not independent. * * *

The structure of § 7.44 places great weight on who has the burden of proof concerning the independence of the directors recommending dismissal. The Official Comment states:

Since section 7.42 requires demand in all cases, the distinction between demand excused and demand required cases does not apply. Subsections (d) and (e) of section 7.44 carry forward the distinction, however, by establishing pleading rules and allocating the burden of proof depending on whether there is a majority of independent directors. Subsection (d), like Delaware law, assigns the plaintiff the threshold burden of alleging facts establishing that a majority of the board is not independent. If there is an independent majority, the burden remains with the plaintiff to plead and establish that the requirements of section 7.44(a) have not been met. If there is no independent majority, the burden is on the corporation on the issues delineated in section 7.44(a). In this case, the corporation must prove both the independence of the decisionmakers and the propriety of the inquiry and determination.

Subsections (d) and (e) of section 7.44 thus follow the first *Aronson* standard in allocating the burden of proof depending on whether the majority of the board is independent. The Committee decided, however, not to adopt the second *Aronson* standard for excusing demand (and thus shifting the burden to the corporation) based on whether the decision of the board that decided the challenged transaction is protected by the business judgment rule. The Committee believes that the only appropriate concern in the context of derivative litigation is whether the board considering the demand has a disabling conflict.

### Note: Demand, Special Litigation Committees and Conceding Futility or a Lack of Independence

In *Stotland v. GAF Corp.*, 469 A.2d 421 (Del.1983), the court held that plaintiff, by making demand on the board mooted the claim that demand was futile. And in *Abbey v. Computer & Communications Tech-*

*nology*, 457 A.2d 368 (Del.Ch.1983), the court found that the board of directors, by appointing a special litigation committee, had conceded that they were interested in the transaction and not protected by the business judgment rule. Finally, in *Allison v. General Motors Corp.*, 604 F.Supp. 1106 (D.Del.1985), *aff'd mem.* 782 F.2d 1026 (3d Cir.1985), the board successfully avoided the holding in *Abbey* by delegating to a committee only the power to investigate and recommend while retaining final decisionmaking power itself.

In *Spiegel v. Buntrock*, 1988 WL 124324 (Del.Ch.1988), *aff'd* 571 A.2d 767 (Del.1990), the Court of Chancery concluded that a disinterested board that referred a derivative plaintiff's demand to a special litigation committee did not abandon the protection of the "plain vanilla business judgment rule." The court stated that the more elaborate procedures enunciated in *Zapata* in which the court applies its own independent business judgment before terminating the litigation, were inapplicable. The court refused to interpret *Abbey* as requiring that "the act of appointing a special committee itself, in all instances" compels the conclusion that the board was disabled. The court read *Abbey* as merely drawing a "factual inference" and not establishing a legal proposition that the appointment of a special litigation committee to function for the board necessarily triggers application of the *Zapata* test "even if the original complaint did not allege facts excusing the demand." The court noted that *Zapata* is "a narrow exception to the business judgment form of judicial review that ordinarily precludes courts from exercising substantive judgment about the wisdom or fairness of business decisions made advisedly by independent boards in good faith." Thus, the *Zapata* form of review applies only where demand on the board is excused. In *Spiegel*, the plaintiff did not allege facts sufficient to "raise a reasonable doubt" that the board was disabled from determining whether it was in the corporation's interest to pursue the claim at issue.

In *Peller v. Southern Co.*, 911 F.2d 1532 (11th Cir.1990), the court permitted a derivative suit to proceed against the boards of an electric utility and its wholly-owned subsidiary despite the failure to make demand and despite the subsequent recommendation of an independent litigation committee that the case be dismissed. Georgia Power Co., a Georgia corporation, was a wholly-owned subsidiary of Southern Co., a Delaware corporation. Plaintiff, a shareholder of the parent, alleged that the two companies and their directors had acted negligently in connection with the construction of a nuclear power plant and a storage facility. Plaintiff also alleged that demand would have been futile because the defendant directors were insiders who participated in the challenged conduct.

At this point, the timing of events became significant. In July 1986, the court stayed the litigation pending the appointment and report of an independent litigation committee to investigate plaintiff's claims. The committee was chosen in September 1986 and given the sole authority to evaluate the merits of the litigation. Its report was due on November 30, 1987. At the same time, the Georgia Public Service Commission, in connection with a rate case, investigated much of the same evidence that the committee considered. The Commission's report, issued on October 2, 1987, concluded that the two companies had made a number of imprudent management decisions and disallowed $300 million from the rate base. The litigation committee's report, issued one day before the Commission's report, concluded that the challenged decisions were either correct or reasonable business judgments when they were made. Thus, as a matter of business judgment, the committee determined that the derivative suit was not in the best interests of the companies or the shareholders and that it should be dismissed.

On October 13, 1987, the companies moved to dismiss or, alternatively, for summary judgment on the plaintiff's suit on the ground that, because demand was not excused, the business judgment rule required the court to defer to the committee's decision to dismiss the suit. The district court held that demand was excused and that, after subsequent discovery, the motion to dismiss should be denied.

Applying Delaware law, the court considered the interplay between *Abbey* and *Spiegel. Under Abbey,* if a board responds to a derivative suit by appointing a special litigation committee with the sole authority to decide whether to pursue the litigation *before* moving to dismiss for failure to make demand, the board has conceded its disqualification and demand is excused. By contrast, under *Spiegel,* if the committee is established *after* the motion to dismiss, no such concession is made. By appointing the committee before moving to dismiss for failure to make demand, defendants had conceded that demand was excused. The court of appeals noted that the order of events was "completely different from the order in *Spiegel* and virtually identical to the order in *Abbey.*"

*Seminaris v. Landa*, 662 A.2d 1350 (Del.Ch.1995) revisited the relationship between *Abbey* and *Spiegel.* In *Seminaris*, plaintiffs alleged that the defendants had conspired to release inaccurate financial information, resulting in an SEC investigation, securities law class action suits, and the resignation of the principal defendant. The corporation appointed a special committee to investigate the entire matter prior to plaintiffs filing their suit and later authorized the committee to consider plaintiffs' allegations. After receiving the committee's report, defendants moved to dismiss for failure to make demand. The Court of Chancery found that *Spiegel* permitted the appointment of the committee prior to the motion to dismiss without conceding demand futility. Absent a showing of particularized facts to indicate such a concession or that the committee members were interested, the court held that the plaintiff was required to show that demand was excused. The court found that this was "not the rare case * * * where defendants' actions were so egregious that a substantial likelihood of director liability exists." *Id.* at 1354. *See* the discussion of *Baxter International, supra.*

## F. SECURITY FOR EXPENSES

1. Ten states provide that the plaintiff may be required to post security for expenses in a derivative action if her financial stake in the corporation is below a minimum threshold. Such a provision requires the plaintiff to secure a bond to cover anticipated expenses in the litigation. "Expenses" entail far more than the "costs" that the losing party is frequently assessed; the main item is attorney's fees. Costs related to discovery may also be included. While the cost of the bond itself may not be great, the real risk is in having to pay the amount of expenses it secures if the court chooses to impose them, a risk that often will appear too costly for a plaintiff with little to gain personally from the suit. The minimum holding to avoid posting security may be expressed as a percentage of ownership (5 percent in New York) or a dollar amount ($50,000 in New York and $25,000 in New Jersey). California and Texas leave setting the threshold to the discretion of the courts. Neither Delaware nor the RMBCA provide for the posting of security.

Who is served by the elimination of security for expenses requirement? Professors Jonathan Macey and Geoffrey Miller in *Toward an Interest–Group Theory of Delaware Corporate Law*, 65 TEX. L. REV. 469 (1987), argue that the corporate bar benefits most from the elimination of a security for expense provision, at least in Delaware, and that it is in the economic interest of the Delaware bar to encourage derivative litigation to occur in Delaware. The elimination of procedural hurdles, such as security for expenses, is one way of achieving this goal.

2. The policy considerations underlying security for expenses legislation were summarized by Mr. Justice Jackson in *Cohen v. Beneficial Industrial Loan Corp.*, 337 U.S. 541, 69 S.Ct. 1221, 93 L.Ed. 1528 (1949), in which the Supreme Court upheld such statutes against a constitutional attack and furthermore found that the *Erie* doctrine required their application in diversity suits. Mr. Justice Jackson wrote:

> Unfortunately, the remedy [of stockholder derivative suits] itself provided opportunity for abuse, which was not neglected. Suits sometimes were brought not to redress real wrongs, but to realize upon their nuisance value. They were bought off by secret settlements in which any wrongs to the general body of share owners were compounded by the suing stockholder, who was mollified by payments from corporate assets. These litigations were aptly characterized in professional slang as "strike suits." And it was said that these suits were more commonly brought by small and irresponsible than by large stockholders, because the former put less to risk and a small interest was more often within the capacity and readiness of management to compromise than a large one.

3. Derivative suit abuses such as those noted by Mr. Justice Jackson led New York to adopt the first security for expenses statute in 1944. This statute followed the Wood Report, a study of derivative suit

litigation sponsored by the New York State Chamber of Commerce that listed the "common and principal abuses" of derivative suits. The Report found that most such actions were brought by stockholders having so little stake in any possible recovery that it was not credible that they would prosecute the case on their own. Indeed, only attorneys were likely to profit substantially in the event of success. Under the old New York rule, suits were brought by plaintiffs who purchased stock immediately prior to suit to gain standing. A few attorneys controlled the bulk of the litigation, suggesting that they also instigated it. Plaintiffs, defendants, and their attorneys treated derivative suits as their private concern, without regard to the impact on the corporation or its shareholders.

4. The impact of the legislation has been less than expected. One reason is that a plaintiff confronted with a motion for security may request a shareholder list for the purpose of circularizing the stockholder body to enlist co-plaintiffs who will own in the aggregate enough stock to avoid the statute's application. *See Baker v. MacFadden Publications*, 90 N.E.2d 876 (N.Y.1950). Corporate management, when they are defendants, are likely to blanch at the idea of the circulation of a letter to shareholders describing, in forceful terms, their alleged misdeeds. A public corporation would be required to make these disclosures in a proxy statement thereby giving added publicity to the alleged wrongdoing.

5. Finally, it is important to note that state security for expenses statutes are inapplicable in federal courts where the action is founded on a federal question. *Fielding v. Allen*, 181 F.2d 163 (2d Cir.1950), *cert. denied* 340 U.S. 817, 71 S.Ct. 46, 95 L.Ed. 600 (1950). *McClure v. Borne Chemical Co.*, 292 F.2d 824 (3d Cir.1961), *cert. denied* 368 U.S. 939, 82 S.Ct. 382, 7 L.Ed.2d 339 (1961). Where the plaintiff also asserts a claim arising under state law, relying either on pendent jurisdiction or diversity of citizenship to establish jurisdiction, the usual practice is to require the posting of security for only that portion of the costs expected to arise out of the defense of the state law portion of the complaint. *See, e.g., Epstein v. Solitron Devices, Inc.*, 388 F.2d 310 (2d Cir.1968); *Fielding v. Allen, supra.*

# G. SETTLEMENT AND ATTORNEYS' FEES

## 1. INTRODUCTION

The settlement of lawsuits has always played a major role in the American judicial system. Few ever go to trial or reach final judgment; most are dismissed or settled. Because settlement generally saves both time and money and reflects the compromise agreed to by the parties to the suit themselves, courts generally look with favor on the settlement process and are reluctant to interfere with the parties' own arrangements. In addition, settlement prevents ceaseless litigation being brought by shareholders. Judicial approval of a derivative suit settlement acts as res judicata and bars any further adjudication of the issues raised.

Settlements occur no less frequently in derivative suits than in other cases, but the nature of a derivative suit creates problems that do not often arise elsewhere. As noted at the beginning of the chapter, the interests of plaintiffs and their counsel can diverge widely. Shareholders, who do not gain directly from the recovery in a derivative suit, are primarily interested in the impact of the recovery on the value of their shares. In contrast, plaintiff's counsel has at least three incentives: to maximize fees, minimize the amount of time needed to generate those fees, and reduce the risk of the complete loss of any fee. Thus, she may prefer to share in a smaller, speedier but more certain settlement than to risk a trial, where the outcome is necessarily unclear and where she may wind up uncompensated for many years of work. Because of the possibility of opportunism, the fact that the parties to the litigation favor a settlement does not carry the normal assurance that the settlement reflects their discounted best estimate of the likely result if the case went to trial. Consequently, F.R.C.P. 23.1, RMBCA § 7.40 and many state statutes require judicial approval of any settlement, compromise, discontinuance or dismissal of a derivative suit.

As you read the following materials, consider the extent to which the settlement of derivative suits should be driven by the merits of the underlying litigation. Why does it matter if a case reaches trial so that its merits are ultimately determined? Does the judicial system suffer if some defendants pay unwarranted expenses and plaintiffs see little compensation while lawyers reap the benefits? Can a judge protect the plaintiffs' interest in the absence of an advocate for the plaintiffs, if plaintiffs' attorneys appear to be more concerned with their own economic return? Recall Chancellor Allen's observations in *Bird v. Lida*, *supra*. If more cases were actually litigated, there would be at least the benefit of more precedent upon which later litigants could base their determinations of what a case is truly worth. If the merits do not matter in the settlement negotiations, do derivative suits provide enough of a deterrent to management to justify furthering such suits?

## 2. JUDICIAL REVIEW OF SETTLEMENTS

From reading judicial opinions, it is generally difficult to appreciate the manner in which the incentive structure of a derivative suit affects the the settlement process. The following two cases provide an interesting contrast. The first, *Shlensky v. Dorsey*, illustrates the traditional judicial approach to settlements. The second, *Epstein v. MCA, Inc.*, although a class action, gives unusual insight into how the inherent conflicts between the shareholders and their attorneys are not always captured by the printed word.

# SHLENSKY v. DORSEY

574 F.2d 131 (3d Cir.1978).

MARIS, CIRCUIT JUDGE.

The eight actions comprising the consolidated derivative suit now before us were instituted between March and November of 1975 in five separate district courts, including the District Court for the Western District of Pennsylvania to which the suits were eventually transferred and there consolidated. Named as defendants are Gulf, eighteen of its present and former officers and directors, an officer of a former Gulf subsidiary, and Price Waterhouse, Gulf's former independent certified public accountant and auditor. The shareholders seek recovery on behalf of Gulf of allegedly illegally expended corporate funds in excess of $18,800,000, incidental monetary damages and costs incurred by Gulf, equitable relief and the plaintiffs' litigation expenses.

The derivative suits arose out of public revelations in 1973 and 1975 by Gulf officials and the Securities and Exchange Commission of alleged illegal corporate action. Investigation by the Watergate Special Prosecution Force into the activities of the Finance Committee to Re–Elect the President (in 1972) precipitated Gulf's disclosure in 1973 that its vice president in charge of government relations, Claude C. Wild, Jr., had, in 1971 and 1972, donated out of corporate funds $100,000, $15,000 and $10,000 to the 1972 presidential election campaigns of President Nixon, Representative Mills and Senator Jackson, respectively. The contributions amounting to $125,000 were subsequently returned to Gulf. In November 1973 Gulf and Wild pleaded guilty to criminal charges of violations of the Federal Election Campaign Act, 18 U.S.C. § 610. Gulf was fined $5,000 and Wild, $1,000. * * *

Opting to settle the case rather than proceed to trial, the parties, with the exception of Price Waterhouse, entered into a "Stipulation of Compromise and Settlement" and on September 29, 1976, petitioned the district court for its approval. * * *

Gulf agreed to reimburse and indemnify the settling defendants * * * as to their reasonable expenses, including counsel fees, incurred in connection with the consolidated action or any other action, judgment or penalty arising out of the matters * * *. Gulf also agreed to the adoption of and further implementation of already initiated internal auditing and reporting procedures designed to avoid a recurrence of unlawful political contributions.

The North River Insurance Company, the insurance carrier under Gulf's directors' and officers' liability and corporate reimbursement policy, agreed to pay $2,000,000 to Gulf conditioned on the execution of releases by Gulf and the defendants named as insured in the policy.

Certain of the individual defendants agreed not to contest the rescission by Gulf's board of directors on July 13, 1976, of stock option rights and attendant stock appreciation rights previously granted them under the 1974 stock option plan and the board's denial of incentive compensation awards for 1975 amounting to $370,000. Gulf agreed to refuse delivery to other defendants of Gulf stock valued at $250,000 previously awarded them. Other Gulf employees, not defendants, consented to the denial of incentive compensation due them aggregating $23,882.28. A retired employee * * * was denied all future payments to him under a 1964 agreement with Gulf. Gulf admitted reimbursement by recipients of illegal or unauthorized contributions from Gulf funds amounting to $57,261.55.

Lastly, based upon the complexity of the litigation, the competence of the attorneys and accountants involved and the benefits to Gulf and its shareholders from the compromise and settlement of the case, Gulf agreed not to oppose an application, with supporting data, to the district court by the plaintiffs' attorneys and accountants for payment by Gulf of their reasonable fees and reimbursement of their expenses in an amount not to exceed $600,000 for fees and $25,000 for expenses.

A summary of the settlement terms was sent to the more than 300,000 Gulf shareholders of record with directions to file in advance of a settlement hearing to be held November 18, 1976, their written objections, if any, to the settlement and notice of their intention to appear if they desired to do so. * * *

* * * [T]he district court conducted a hearing on the plaintiffs' application for accountants' and attorneys' fees and expenses. The district court found the objective value of the time spent by the persons involved in representing the plaintiffs to be in the aggregate $407,-429.50. That amount was increased by the court by $167,570.50 in consideration of such factors as the contingent nature of success in the litigation, the benefits achieved by the settlement terms and the quality of the services performed. The court accordingly found $575,000 to be representative of fair and reasonable fees. The court also approved reimbursement of the attorneys' and accountants' expenses in the amount of $32,777.95 and directed by order entered November 19, 1976, payment by Gulf of a total of $607,777.95 for fees and reimbursement of expenses of the plaintiffs' accountants and attorneys.

Turning to the district court's determination that the settlement was fair and reasonable, we bear in mind that the scope of our review is very limited. For the district court has wide discretion in making that decision * * *.

The principal factor to be considered in determining the fairness of a settlement concluding a shareholders' derivative action is the extent of the benefit to be derived from the proposed settlement by the corporation, the real party in interest. The adequacy of the recovery provided the corporation by the settlement must be considered in the light of the best possible recovery, of the risks of establishing liability and proving damages in the event the case is not settled, and of the cost of prolonging the litigation.

Given the amount of unlawfully disbursed corporate funds alleged to total $18,800,000 and taking into consideration the risks of establishing liability and damages, set forth at length in the district court's findings of fact and conclusions of law, we cannot say that it was an abuse of the district court's discretion to conclude that $3,500,000 represented a fair and reasonable settlement amount even without taking into consideration the additional nonmonetary benefits to Gulf referred to but not valued by the district court. * * *

One of the factors to be considered in determining the fairness of a settlement disposing of a class action is the reaction of the members of the class. * * * Here the overwhelming majority of Gulf shareholders have not objected to the settlement and Gulf, for the benefit of which the suit was filed, has agreed to its terms.

Bearing in mind all of the factors—the $2,000,000 contribution to Gulf by its insurer under a directors' and officers' liability insurance policy in exchange for its release from further liability under the policy, the agreements of the individual defendants to give up their claims against Gulf for compensation and stock option rights valued by the district court at approximately $1,500,000, the additional cost of protracted litigation, the risk of successful prosecution of the claims given up, the fact that so very few shareholders objected to the settlement, the corporation's approval of the settlement, and the fact that the settlement provides a substantial net benefit to Gulf after payment of plaintiffs' counsel fees and expenses—we cannot say that the district court abused its discretion in approving the settlement as a fair compromise and settlement of the action before it.

## EPSTEIN v. MCA, INC.

126 F.3d 1235 (9th Cir.1997).

[The litigation arose from Matshutsita Electric Industries Co.'s friendly tender offer for MCA at $71 per share. At the time of the offer, Matshusita also entered into separate agreements with Wasserman and Sheinberg, the two principal officers of MCA. Under those agreements, Wasserman was to receive preferred stock in a tax-free transaction in exchange for his shares and Sheinberg was to receive a payment of $21 million if the tender offer succeeded.

The offer gave rise to two class actions: one in Delaware state court alleging only state law claims, and the other in federal district court in California alleging violations of tender offer rules 10b–13 and 14d–10 under the Securities Exchange Act of 1934. See Chapter 22, Section D.2. Both actions alleged that certain payments to Sheinberg and Wasserman, officers of MCA, were illegal. Matshusita won the federal case and while the judgment was on appeal, the parties to the Delaware action agreed to a settlement in which the class members who did not opt out of the class would waive all claims in connection with the tender offer, including the ones in the federal action. The Court of Chancery approved the settlement and the Delaware Supreme Court affirmed.

The Supreme Court, in a 5–4 decision, held that the Delaware settlement judgment was entitled to full faith and credit under the express terms of the Full Faith and Credit Act, notwithstanding that the state court judgment might preclude litigation of exclusively federal claims.

In the federal action, the Ninth Circuit noted that if the $21 million that Sheinberg received was a premium for the 1,179,635 shares he owned, the damages to each tendering shareholder would be $17.80 per share, or a total of about $2 billion. *Epstein v. MCA, Inc.*, 50 F.3d 644, 649 (9th Cir.1995)

On remand, resolving an issue it had not decided in the original litigation, the Ninth Circuit held that it would withhold full faith and credit from the Delaware judgment because it violated the due process rights of the absent class members to adequate representation.]

* * *

## II

We now turn to the merits of the adequacy of representation issue. * * * First, we determine whether there was a disabling conflict of interest between Delaware counsel and the MCA shareholders who tendered their shares. Second, we review the actual conduct of Delaware counsel in discharging their fiduciary duty to protect the interests of those shareholders.

### A

The essence of the Epstein plaintiffs' position on the claimed conflict of interest is that the Delaware settlement was the product of a one-sided bargaining process because their representatives went to the table with no credible bargaining power. Not surprisingly, Matsushita makes no serious attempt to challenge this position, relying almost exclusively on their arguments as to why we cannot reach the merits. It is axiomatic that a plaintiff's power to negotiate a reasonable settlement derives from the threat of going to trial with a credible chance of winning. * * *

The Delaware class plaintiffs and their counsel could not carry out a threat to litigate the federal claims in this case, and Matsushita knew it.

The inability of the class representatives to exercise any leverage on behalf of the Epstein plaintiffs was the result of three basic facts. First, they could not litigate the federal claims because Congress has said that Exchange Act claims may not be litigated in state courts. Thus, the claims that Matsushita violated SEC Rule 14d–10 by paying premiums to Messrs. Wasserman and Sheinberg were not and could not have been pleaded in the Delaware action. Moreover, there was no discovery on those claims; indeed, the Delaware plaintiffs probably were unable to conduct any discovery on the federal claims because the facts relevant to those claims had no apparent relevance to the subject matter of the state law claim that the MCA directors had breached their fiduciary duties in failing to maximize shareholder value upon a change of corporate control. Finally, Matsushita would have had reason to discount the value of any settlement made with the state plaintiffs against the risk that a state court judgment releasing Exchange Act claims would not survive a collateral attack on the ground that the Delaware courts had no jurisdiction to release exclusively federal claims especially in light of the absence of any overlapping issues of fact between the state and federal claims. Matsushita must have recognized that it would subject itself to a substantial risk by settling the federal claims in state court rather than federal court, and would have had to discount its bottom line in the state settlement negotiations accordingly. The denouement was predictable: Matsushita used its infinitely superior bargaining power vis-a-vis the state class representatives to settle the Exchange Act claims at a rock bottom price.

Second, the class representatives not only lacked the bargaining power that comes with a credible threat of going to trial and winning, they also lacked the ability to make a credible threat that they could put Matsushita at risk by going to trial on the state claims and proving facts material to the federal claims that would be binding upon Matsushita through issue preclusion. * * * While the Delaware class representatives lacked the muscle to put Matsushita at risk on the federal claims, the existence of their state class action, however worthless standing alone, served to provide Matsushita with an opportunity to try to get rid of the federal claims at a bargain basement price. If the parties could get court approval of a settlement that released the federal claims, Matsushita would have at least a fair shot of using the judgment to block the federal action with a full faith and credit argument. That is, of course, exactly what Matsushita did as soon as the judgment became final. * * *

Third, Matsushita had a further bargaining advantage, quite apart from its knowledge that the Delaware plaintiffs could not put it at risk on the federal claims. Matsushita also knew that class counsel had an extraordinary incentive to settle and settle quickly because that was the only way they could extract a fee out of the federal claims. Class counsel could not benefit from the federal claims by going to trial for the obvious reason that the federal claims could not be litigated in state court. Moreover, the pendency of a parallel action in federal court—the Epstein case—meant that Delaware class counsel were at risk of being "beaten to the punch" and getting no return on the federal claims at all. Matsushita knew that it was negotiating a release of the federal claims with class counsel who could not litigate those claims and whose self-interest gave them an incentive to settle and settle fast.

What all this demonstrates is that there was a jarring misalignment of interests between class counsel and members of the federal class. It was plainly in the best interest of counsel to settle the federal claims at any price. For them, any settlement was better than no settlement because settlement was the only way they could make any money on the federal claims—indeed, given that the state claims were essentially worthless, it was the only way that Delaware counsel could get any compensation at all. Delaware counsel were not, after all, serving as pro bono counsel to the MCA shareholders who tendered their shares.

It was not, in contrast, in the best interest of the clients—the MCA shareholders—to settle their Exchange Act claims at any price. Their interest lay in settling those claims for a sufficient amount to make it imprudent to take the risk of litigation. That risk, of course, would have to be realistically assessed in terms of the chances of prevailing on either or both of their claims that Matsushita had violated SEC Rules 10b–13 and 14d–10 in paying premiums to Messrs. Wasserman and Sheinberg. Indeed, the misalignment of interests and incentives between class counsel and their clients in these extraordinary circumstances was so great that it is fair to say that counsel's interests were more in line with the interests of Matsushita than those of their clients.

This was not the adequate representation of absent class members that due process requires "at all times." * * * The interests of Delaware counsel in this case were nothing but antagonistic to the interests of the MCA shareholders who tendered their shares. As a result of the three factors described above, which make this case extraordinary on its facts, Delaware counsel's overriding economic interest lay in settling the federal claims at any price and winning the race to judgment. The interests of the MCA shareholders who tendered their shares, in contrast, lay in pursuing those claims vigorously and either obtaining a reasonable settlement or litigating the claims in federal court. Their interests certainly did not lie in agreeing to a settlement that gave the attorneys a $1,000,000 fee but nothing for themselves—the settlement originally proposed by Delaware counsel—nor in agreeing to a settlement of 2 [sic]per share, *inclusive* of attorneys' fees—the settlement Delaware counsel ultimately persuaded the Vice Chancellor to approve. The inability of Delaware counsel to litigate the federal claims, their further inability even to obtain a judgment on the state law claims that could have had issue preclusive effect on the federal claims, and the pendency of a competing parallel class action in federal court caused the economic interests of Delaware counsel to be fundamentally "antagonistic to the interests" of the Epstein plaintiffs. *Id.* * * * Here, there is no question that there was antagonism between the interests of the lawyers and the interests of their clients. That antagonism made their representation of the MCA shareholders who tendered their shares inadequate as a matter of law.

### B

In addition to the argument that Delaware counsel had a disabling conflict of interest, the Epstein plaintiffs contend that the actual conduct of Delaware counsel in settling the federal claims fell far short of the representation that due process requires. Rather, they claim, Delaware counsel completely failed to investigate or develop their federal claims and basically "rolled over" during settlement negotiations, ultimately entering into a settlement that was essentially worthless except for their own fees. This course of conduct, they conclude, falls well below the level of representation that is required to bind absentees. We agree.

Adequate representation requires that counsel "vigorously and tenaciously protect[ ] the interests of the class." *Gonzales* [*v. Cassidy*, 474 F.2d 67 (5th Cir.1973), adopted by the Ninth Circuit] , at 75. "Vigorous" and "tenacious" protection requires, at a minimum, that counsel pursue their clients' claims, make a reasonable effort to assess the fair settlement value of those claims, and pursue a settlement that approximates that value, always taking into account the ever-present risks of litigation. The inadequacy of Delaware counsel's representation is brought into sharp focus by their vigorous disparagement of the federal claims throughout the course of the settlement proceedings. Indeed, Delaware counsel's representation of those claims surpassed inadequacy and sank to the level of subversion. Counsel consistently sought to convince, not only their clients, but their adversaries and the Chancery Court itself that the federal claims had no merit. They repeatedly and summarily dismissed those claims as "frivolous" without ever conducting any discovery or any meaningful analysis of the legal issues, much less presenting the claims in a favorable light. In sharp contrast, the Epstein counsel earnestly pursued those same claims in federal court, recognizing their merit and successfully demonstrating that merit in persuading this court to reverse an adverse summary judgment ruling below. This contrast makes it all the more clear that Delaware counsel's representation of the MCA shareholders who tendered their shares fails even the most minimal standards of adequacy.

1

Barely fifteen days after the Epstein counsel filed a class action in federal court on the exclusively federal claims, Delaware counsel negotiated the release of those claims. This first Delaware settlement proposed to release all claims, state and federal, arising out of the Matsushita–MCA merger, in exchange for $1 million in attorney fees, no monetary compensation for shareholders, and an amended poison pill provision of dubious value. * * * In recommending the settlement of those claims, counsel told their clients that "the substantial benefits the plaintiffs and the other members of the Class can expect to receive by virtue of the Settlement" outweighed "the risks, burdens and costs of continued litigation * * * [and the] uncertainties relating to proof of the allegations contained in the various actions." Counsel put no flesh on this bare-bones analysis. In particular, they never explained why litigation of the state law claims would put the federal claims at "risk." Moreover, the notice for the settlement hearing offered no defense of the proposition that the benefits of the settlement were "substantial" in relation to the value of the federal claims it released. Rather, the notice merely assured class members that counsel had conducted "extensive investigation of the facts and examination of the law involved," and had concluded that the settlement was fair. It is hard to imagine what Delaware counsel meant by an "extensive investigation," since the record shows no discovery at all on the facts underlying the federal claims. Indeed, this lack of discovery is hardly surprising. As discussed above, Delaware counsel were probably disabled from developing the federal claims through traditional discovery, since discovery in state court was limited to matters relevant to the subject matter of the state claims—that the MCA directors had violated their fiduciary duty to attempt to secure a better deal than the one Matsushita offered the shareholders.

Indeed, the record is clear that Delaware counsel had not conducted an extensive investigation into the merits of the federal claims in order to determine their fair settlement value. Delaware counsel admitted to the Chancery Court that they had reviewed the Wasserman claim "relatively quickly" before concluding that the claim was "frivolous" and would be "a waste of our time." In fact, in their cursory review, Delaware counsel simply adopted two of the defenses raised by Matsushita in federal court.* * *

* * *

Despite the best efforts of Delaware counsel to disparage the Exchange Act claims of the absentees they were "representing," the Chancery Court rejected the first settlement because the Wasserman claim had "significant value" while the state law claims had "little or no merit." *In re MCA Shareholders Litig.*, 598 A.2d at 690. On the merits of the federal claim, the Chancery Court was far from convinced that Delaware counsel's [legal arguments] controlled. * * * In addition, the Chancery Court refused to accept Delaware counsel's uncritical account of the value of Wasserman's deal: * * * In light of the "substantial merit" of the Wasserman claim, the court held that it would be unfair to release all federal claims in a settlement that offers "no real monetary benefit to the Class" but awards the attorneys $1 million in fees. *Id.* at 695–96. The court dismissed the value of the revised poison pill provision as "illusionary [sic]." *Id.* at 696.

2

The record of the Delaware action shows no activity for the ten months following April 25, 1991. The case lay dormant until the district court in Los Angeles entered summary judgment on February 10, 1992. During the same interval, Epstein counsel were vigorously pursuing the federal claims, as demonstrated by over ten pages of docket entries in district court. Eight months later, Delaware counsel agreed to settle the exclusively federal claims for the sum of $2 million—a bare 2 (*sic*) a share, inclusive of attorney fees. In advocating the second settlement to the class and the Vice Chancellor, Delaware counsel continued to disparage the federal claims. They rested their disparagement primarily on the position that the district court's entry of summary judgment was "dispositive as to [the federal claim's] lack of substantial merit." They failed to point out, however, that the Ninth Circuit affords no deference to a district court's decision on summary judgment, but reviews such determinations de novo. Nor did Delaware counsel make any effort to assess the likelihood of reversal by the Ninth Circuit. They merely reiterated Matsushita's arguments in an effort to convince the Chancery Court once again that the federal claims were worthless. In fact, Delaware counsel specifically urged the Chancery Court "not [to] delve into the ultimate merits of [the federal] claims upon appeal as if it were reviewing de novo the dismissal," but instead that it treat the district court's decision as "dispositive."

Delaware counsel * * * urged the Chancery Court to give the dismissal of the federal claims "presumptive effect." Counsel claimed to have "reviewed the law and * * * reviewed the briefs and * * * looked at the findings of fact" in the federal action before determining that the federal claims were "so fraught with uncertainty, that those claims are so weak, that the record in that proceedings * * * is so horrendous, that the prospect of anything emerging from that case is so remote, that $2 million more than adequately compensates—much more than adequately compensates for the release of all the federal and state claims." Without citing any caselaw regarding private rights of action under Rule 10b–13 or Rule 14d–10, Delaware counsel reasoned that, as a general matter, the Supreme Court and the Ninth Circuit had drastically narrowed the bases upon which private rights will be implied under any statute. Based on these generalizations and their reading of [the statute and rules], counsel concluded that the "weight of authority" suggested that neither Rule 10b–13 nor Rule 14d–10 authorizes a private right and characterized the federal claims as "lacking in substantial merit."

Counsel's "analysis," however, disregarded two cases, from the Second and Third Circuits, that are square holdings that there is a private right of action under Rule 14d–10. *See Polaroid Corp. v. Disney*, 862 F.2d 987, 991, 997 (3d Cir.1988); *Field v. Trump*, 850 F.2d 938, 946 (2d Cir.1988). Counsel's failure to report these cases to class members and to the Vice Chancellor is even more astonishing given that they actually cited *Field* on the issue of the timing of the Wasserman transaction. For counsel not to cite *Field* on the private right of action issue, or to cite *Polaroid* at all, is inexcusable. * * *

\* \* \*

Finally, to cap off their disparagement of their clients' Exchange Act claims, Delaware counsel asserted generally that the federal claims should not stand in the way of settlement because "damages on the federal claims are highly uncertain." Counsel simply ignored the obvious: that damages on the Sheinberg claim, at least, were both easily calculable and uncontested. * * * Thus, a simple calculation * * * would yield damages of about $1.4 billion on a successful Sheinberg claim. Even so, counsel stuck to its strategy of disparaging the federal claims in their effort to get the Vice Chancellor to approve the settlement that would produce them a fee.

\* \* \*

It is clear, however, that Delaware counsel was aware of the Sheinberg claim. Counsel described that claim, if only briefly, in their notice to the class members as "a payment to defendant Sheinberg, which defendants asserted was * * * incentive compensation," but which plaintiffs alleged was a "covert premium * * * designed to induce Sheinberg to tender his shares." In contrast, Epstein counsel learned about the $21 million payment and investigated it, questioning both Wasserman and Sheinberg about it at their depositions. Their answers revealed that no MCA board documents prior to the date of the tender offer referred to any such payment to Sheinberg. Epstein counsel relied in part on this evidence to argue the existence of a genuine issue of material fact and convince this court to reverse the summary judgment on this claim. Yet, despite the * * * value of the Sheinberg claim if a trier of fact were to find that the $21 million was a premium paid to induce Sheinberg to support the tender offer and not incentive compensation for past services, Delaware counsel stood mute on the claim while urging the Vice Chancellor to approve the settlement of $2 million, or 2 (*sic*) per share, inclusive of attorneys fees. Once again, the conduct of Delaware counsel in the performance of their fiduciary duties was inexcusable.

In sum, the only "vigorous" and "tenacious" work that Delaware counsel performed on behalf of the Epstein plaintiffs was to convince the Chancery Court to adopt their adversary's position and view the federal claims as essentially worthless. This was not merely "inadequate" representation, it was hostile representation that served the interests of counsel in getting a fee, but did not serve the interests of the MCA shareholders in getting a settlement based upon a thorough and fair assessment of their Exchange Act claims. To bind the Epstein plaintiffs to the Delaware judgment under these circumstances would violate their due process right to have their interests adequately represented at all times.

## Note: Judicial Review of Settlements

Because shareholders rarely participate in settlement negotiations in a derivative suit, the court has a potentially large role to play in determining whether to accept the settlement that counsel for both sides has arrived at. As one court has noted, "the law promotes the value of fair settlements by affording a process in which some degree of assurance can be afforded to absent class members or shareholders that the settlement is fair to them at least in the judgment of a disinterested and experienced judge." *Needham v. Cruver*, 1995 WL 510039 (Del.Ch.1995). When a settlement is presented to the court, the burden of proof as to its fairness rests with its proponents. As *Shlensky* indicates, a court will be most concerned with the extent of the net benefit which the settlement confers upon the corporation. In most cases, the court will give greatest weight to the adequacy of the proposed financial settlement when compared to the potential recovery if the plaintiff succeeded at trial. To make such an evaluation, the court must discount the possible recovery at trial by the time value of money over the period during which recovery will be delayed and by the risk factors inherent in any litigation. The court also should, but does not always, consider the amount of plaintiffs' counsel fees and indemnification that may be paid under both alternatives. *See* ALI, PRINCIPLES OF CORPORATE GOVERNANCE (1994), § 7.14(b). The Delaware Supreme Court has enumerated the following factors to be considered in evaluating proposed settlements, factors to which most courts generally adhere:

> * * * (1) the probable validity of the claims, (2) the apparent difficulties in enforcing the claims through the courts, (3) the collectibility of any judgment recovered, (4) the delay, expense and trouble of litigation, (5) the amount of compromise as compared with the amount and collectibility of a judgment, and (6) the views of the parties involved, pro and con.

*Polk v. Good*, 507 A.2d 531, 536 (Del.1986)

Evaluating the fairness of the settlement becomes more difficult when the settlement provides nonpecuniary benefits to the corporation. Often, outside directors will be added to the board or independent audit and nominating committees will be created. Similarly, settlements will include provisions requiring directors to surrender stock options or to sell their shares back to the corporation. Recent empirical studies have shown that such relief has become increasingly common. *See* Roberta Romano, *The Shareholder Suit: Litigation Without Foundation?*, 7 J. L. & ECON. ORG. 55 (1991). Professor Romano found that approximately one-half of the derivative suit settlements included structural relief. In contrast, the corporation appeared to receive monetary relief in about 20 percent of these settlements. While internal corrective measures are useful to the corporation in remedying past misdeeds, they raise a separate problem: in the words of the ALI, "such therapeutic relief can sometimes represent a counterfeit currency by which the parties can increase the apparent value of the settlement and thereby justify higher attorney's fees for plaintiff's counsel, who is often the real party in interest." To deal with this problem, the ALI recommends that the court review the value of non-pecuniary relief both when evaluating the settlement and when computing plaintiff's counsel fees. ALI, PRINCIPLES OF CORPORATE GOVERNANCE (1994), § 7.14, Comment c. *See, Girsh v. Jepson*, 521 F.2d 153 (3d Cir.1975).

Judicial approval of a proposed settlement seems to be necessary to protect stockholders but a number of factors may hinder the court's review. Because the parties to the suit have already agreed to the settlement, they will be reluctant to point out its weaknesses. The court thus may be forced to scrutinize the settlement without the benefit of any adversarial review. The nature of the proceeding may lead the court to place too much weight on the therapeutic non-pecuniary aspects of the settlement, given the materials provided by the parties involved. It is not that the court cannot ask the right questions; rather, the danger is that the court will not know what the right questions are.

Courts have dealt with these problems in a number of ways. In a few cases, they have undertaken their own investigation into the merits or have appointed special masters to do so. On occasion, they have asked for expert advice from governmental agencies such as the SEC. The most common solution, however, is to afford notice and an opportunity for a hearing to stockholders who wish to object to the settlement. In the federal courts and many state courts, judicial approval of the settlement must be preceded by notice to affected stockholders. The nature of the notice provisions and when notice may be excused, however, vary considerably. F.R.C.P. 23.1 only requires notice "in such manner as the court directs," and many states have statutes or court rules that track this language. RMBCA § 7.40 is slightly more specific, requiring notice when the proposed settlement "will substantially affect the interest of the corporation's shareholders or a class of shareholders." The most critical concern to the parties in giving notice is who will bear its cost. Where the case involves a large public corporation with millions of shares and thousands of stockholders, these costs may be prohibitive. In recent years, courts have sought flexible approaches to the problem and have permitted parties to provide notice either through publication or by notifying a random and representative number of shareholders rather than requiring individual written notice to be mailed to all shareholders.

When notice has been given to shareholders, courts may provide for a hearing on the fairness of the settlement at which objecting stockholders may seek to demonstrate why the settlement should be rejected. While the shareholders' failure to object to the settlement should not be construed as implying approval, courts often will approve the settlement if no opposition is presented. A shareholder who does wish to object to the settlement faces substantial hurdles. Generally, she lacks detailed information about the merits of the action and the manner in which the settlement was negotiated. To obtain this information, she may have to challenge plaintiff's counsel who is nominally representing all the shareholders but who has a vested interest in having the settlement approved. The stockholder usually must also act within a fairly limited time period between the notice and the hearing.

In *Saylor v. Lindsley*, 456 F.2d 896 (2d Cir.1972), after hearing evidence introduced from objecting stockholders, the court conducted a mini-trial on the merits of the settlement and found it was unfair to the corporation. The extent to which stockholders can introduce evidence is a matter of judicial discretion. Courts have permitted limited discovery and the introduction of evidence through interrogatories, depositions, affidavits and expert testimony. The mini-trial is also not uncommon, although, as the court in *Saylor* noted, it is intended to focus only on the terms of the settlement and not on the merits of the original claim.

Even when courts express skepticism about the benefits of a proposed settlement, they are reluctant to overturn a settlement. *In re Chicago and North Western Transportation Company Shareholders Litigation*, 1995 WL 389627 (Del.Ch.1995) involved an attempt to enjoin a merger on the grounds that the terms of the merger were not fair, the directors had failed to seek the highest value reasonably available to the shareholders, and there had not been full disclosure of all material facts concerning the merger in the proxy statement. On the eve of the injunction hearing, the parties settled the litigation by having the defendants make additional disclosures to the shareholders in a supplemental proxy statement. In connection with the settlement, plaintiffs counsel sought attorneys' fees and expenses of $525,000. A stockholder objected to the settlement on the ground that the settlement provided no benefit whatsoever to the shareholders and benefitted only plaintiffs' counsel to the tune of the $525,000.

A reluctant Court of Chancery approved the settlement. The court admitted that a lawsuit that caused the directors of a corporation to give the shareholders material facts about a merger prior to the shareholder vote had benefitted the shareholders. The court found, however, that only three facts in the supplemental proxy statement were material and that the other benefits in the settlement were "meager." Those findings led the court to conclude that the attorney fee request was disproportionate to the benefit obtained for the class and to reduce the award to $300,000.

These cases illustrate what Elliott J. Weiss and John S. Beckerman have called the reluctance "to leave plaintiffs' attorneys empty-handed even when they conclude that those attorneys have provided nothing of value to the class." Elliott J. Weiss & John S. Beckerman, *Let the Money Do the Monitoring: How Institutional Investors Can Reduce Agency Costs in Securities Class Actions*, 104 YALE L.J. 2053 (1995). To illustrate their point, Weiss and Beckerman analyze litigation involving Oracle Securities Corp., a consolidated class action and derivative suit. In the class action portion, Judge Walker used a competitive bidding process to determine lead counsel. demonstrating "a sophisticated grasp of agency-cost issues." Weiss and Beckerman then describe what happened in the derivative suit.

> In Oracle * * * a "piggyback" derivative action was filed * * * seeking to hold certain Oracle officers and directors liable for subjecting Oracle to litigation expenses and potential liability in the securities class action and for a minor amount of alleged insider trading. * * * [T]he parties eventually negotiated a linked settlement. Oracle agreed to pay $23.25 million and Arthur Andersen & Co., Oracle's auditor, agreed to pay $1.75 million to a settlement fund in the securities class action. Class counsel's fee, $4.8 million plus expenses, was established by its winning bid. The derivative plaintiffs dismissed their claims that Oracle's management had breached its fiduciary duties and that Oracle should sue Arthur Andersen, receiving in consideration for their dismissal only Oracle's acknowledgment that it had made certain changes in its insider trading and revenue recognition policies. Oracle also agreed to pay derivative plaintiffs' counsel a fee of up to $750,000.
>
> In his first opinion evaluating the settlement [*In re Oracle Securities Litigation*, 829 F.Supp. 1176 (N.D.Cal.1993)] Judge Walker pointed out that "[t]he sole benefit which the derivative settlement confers upon Oracle's current shareholders is a termination of the expenses associated with [the consolidated class and derivative

actions]," in exchange for which derivative plaintiffs' counsel was requesting a fee of $750,000. The judge had no problem with the notion that the derivative claims should be dismissed, agreeing with the parties that they were "virtually meritless," but questioned whether counsel was entitled to the requested fee. He also directed Oracle to retain independent counsel to advise its board as to whether the settlement was in Oracle's best interests.

Oracle dutifully appointed two disinterested directors to a special litigation committee (SLC) and retained Latham & Watkins as independent counsel to the SLC. The SLC conducted an investigation and prepared a sixty-seven-page report (at an undisclosed cost) concluding that the settlement proposed by the parties was in Oracle's best interests.

The SLC considered and rejected the strategy of causing Oracle to move to terminate the derivative action entirely, reasoning that although such a motion was very likely to succeed, Oracle probably would have to spend about as much on litigating the motion as the court was likely to order it to pay to plaintiffs' counsel. The court agreed [*In re Oracle Securities Litigation*, 852 F.Supp. 1437 (N.D.Cal.1994)]. The court also agreed with the SLC's decision to grant a release to Arthur Andersen, finding that there was insufficient evidence to support a claim that Arthur Andersen had been negligent.

The court then turned to the question of what fee should be awarded to derivative plaintiffs' attorneys, noting that they were entitled to a fee only if the claim they had asserted was "meritorious" and they had provided Oracle with a substantial benefit. Despite his earlier endorsement of the SLC's conclusion that there was virtually no evidentiary support for either the derivative claim or a claim by Oracle against Arthur Andersen, Judge Walker characterized the derivative complaint as "meritorious," asserting that plaintiffs had a "reasonable hope" of proving that the defendants in the derivative action had engaged in intentional or reckless mismanagement.

Judge Walker next considered whether derivative plaintiffs had provided Oracle with a substantial benefit. Their agreement to drop their prosecution of an action with no apparent merit-which the court's earlier decision had characterized as the "sole benefit" of the derivative settlement-clearly did not provide the requisite benefit. Nor did Oracle's changes in accounting and insider trading policies, "most or all" of which, Judge Walker found, "appear to have resulted from SEC pressure." That left Arthur Andersen's $1.75 million contribution to the class action settlement fund.

Judge Walker had already taken that payment into account when he calculated the fee payable to plaintiffs' attorneys in the class action. He also observed that it was "at least somewhat doubtful" that any portion of Arthur Andersen's contribution was attributable to the efforts of derivative plaintiffs. Nonetheless, Judge Walker concluded that "it is fair to give derivative counsel the benefit of the doubt and ascribe the [entire] Arthur Andersen contribution to the derivative litigation" and awarded derivative counsel a $525,000 fee and $69,384.76 in expenses. In short, he allowed this aspect of the derivative and class action game to be played as it traditionally has been played.

*Id.* at 2072–74.

Courts often cite their limited review power as justification for not intervening more fully in every aspect of a settlement. As the Delaware Supreme Court noted in *Kahn v. Sullivan* (Chapter 5), "[t]he Court's role in reviewing the proposed Settlement, however, is quite restricted. If the Court was a stockholder of Occidental it might vote for new directors, if it was on the Board it might vote for new management and if it was a member of the Special Committee it might vote against the Museum project. But its options are limited in reviewing a proposed settlement to applying Delaware law to the facts adduced in the record and then determining in its business judgment whether, on balance, the settlement is reasonable." 594 A.2d 48, 58 fn. 23.

A Vice Chancellor of the Delaware Court of Chancery (now a Justice on the Delaware Supreme Court) recently studied judicial approval of shareholder litigation settlements in that court. *See* Carolyn Berger and Darla Pomeroy, *Settlement Fever*, 2 Bus. L. Today 7 (Sept./Oct. 1992). In a 2 1/2 year period, the Court of Chancery approved 96 of 98 proposed class action and derivative settlements, with 95% being approved as submitted. One settlement was rejected because it conferred no benefit on the shareholders; the other case was awaiting notice to the class members. Fee awards to attorneys averaged 92% of the amount requested, with two-thirds granted in full. Subsequent cases are consistent with the article, although courts appear to be somewhat more willing to reduce the amount of requested attorneys fees.

Given the conflicts between plaintiffs and their counsel, should Vice Chancellor Berger's statistics give plaintiffs reason for concern or for thanks when they consider how well the courts protect their interests in the settlement process? How useful is the requirement of judicial approval when courts can express as much doubt about a settlement's value as was done in *Kahn* and yet still grant approval? Do we want or need courts to spend a great deal of time reviewing settlements to which the parties have voluntarily agreed? Will this time spent simply reduce the conservation of judicial resources that is seen as a primary benefit of avoiding litigation?

If, as happens rarely, the corporation assumes control of the litigation, the courts are removed from the settlement process. In *Wolf v. Barkes*, 348 F.2d 994 (2d Cir.1965), the plaintiff in a derivative suit sought to enjoin a settlement of the underlying allegations by the corporation with the defendant-officers. The plaintiff's concern was that the corporate settlement would constitute a presumptively valid defense to the derivative suit, on the basis of which the defendants could move to dismiss it even though the settlement between the corporation and the defendants had been without judicial approval.

The court held that the notice and approval provisions of F.R.C.P. 23.1 did not apply to the settlement because the corporation was not settling a derivative suit. The court recognized the plaintiff's concerns, but pointed out that a corporation always retains the power to settle its own litigation directly. The court noted that the plaintiff still could attack the settlement in a separate action on the ground that it constituted waste or fraud in a self-dealing transaction. Would a court give the same type of review to the settlement in that suit that it would when considering whether to approve a settlement? What are the consequences to plaintiff's counsel from the decision in this case?

### 3.  ATTORNEYS' FEES

Under the "American" rule which generally applies in litigation in the United States, the successful party is not entitled to recover attorneys' fees from the losing party absent statutory authorization. However, the courts, exercising equitable powers, have permitted a plaintiff whose efforts have led to the creation of a fund benefitting others as well as herself to recover some of the costs of the litigation, including attorneys' fees, from that fund. In a derivative suit, although the corporation which receives the fund is not the direct client of plaintiff's counsel, counsel will be awarded a fee if the corporation has derived a benefit, either monetary or nonmonetary, from the successful prosecution or settlement of the suit.

Recent cases have examined the extent of the benefit that must be conferred before fees will be awarded and the relationship between the benefit and the fees. Perhaps the most unusual case was *Tandycrafts, Inc. v. Initio Partners*, 562 A.2d 1162 (Del.1989) where the court sustained the award of counsel fees to an individual shareholder who had voluntarily dismissed an individual action against a corporation and its directors after the corporation had taken corrective action to cure allegedly false and misleading disclosure in a proxy statement. The Court of Chancery determined that the litigation, although moot, had conferred a significant benefit on the corporation and had awarded counsel fees, notwithstanding that the plaintiff had neither sued derivatively nor on behalf of a class.

In affirming, the Delaware Supreme Court noted that a corporate benefit need not be defined solely in economic terms and that changes in corporate policy or, as in this case, greater disclosure, might justify the award of counsel fees. The court then stated that "[O]nce it is determined that action benefitting the corporation chronologically followed the filing of a meritorious suit, the burden is upon the corporation to demonstrate 'that the lawsuit did not in any way cause their action.'" *Id.* at 1165.

The court also addressed the need for a derivative or class suit as a prerequisite to granting attorneys fees and noted:

> \* \* \* If, as here, the shareholder commences an individual action with consequential benefit for all other members of a class, or for the corporation itself, there is no justification for denying recourse to the fee shifting standard which has evolved for the therapeutic purpose of rewarding individual effort which flows to a class. We believe the better reasoned approach to be that there is no class action or derivative suit prerequisite to an award of attorneys' fees under the common benefit exception \* \* \* "The form of suit is not a deciding factor; rather the question to be determined is whether a plaintiff, in bringing a suit either individually or representatively, has conferred a benefit on others." (Citation omitted).

*Id.* at 1166.

Shortly thereafter, in *Zlotnick v. Metex, Inc.*, 1989 WL 150767 (Del.Ch.1989) (Unpublished Case) the Court of Chancery reluctantly followed *Tandycrafts*. Plaintiff had sued to enjoin a proposed merger on the grounds that the merger price was grossly unfair. After suit was filed, an improved offer was accepted by both parties to the merger as a result of actions of a special committee of the board of the target company. In reviewing the request for attorneys' fees, the court noted the holding in *Tandycrafts* that placed the burden on the defendant to show that the lawsuit did not cause the improved offer. The difficulty, as the court correctly pointed out, is that more than one cause may have led to the improved offer. Nevertheless, the defendants failed to meet their burden of proof and thus had to pay a fee of $60,000, an amount that the court noted, "considering the meager services rendered, is generous." *See also, Robert M. Bass Group v. Evans*, 1989 WL 137936 (Del.Ch.1989) (Unpublished Case).

*BTZ, Inc. v. Great Northern Nekoosa* Corp., 47 F.3d 463 (1st Cir. 1995), affirmed a district court's refusal to award any attorneys' fees to plaintiff's counsel in a Maine class action that had been brought in connection with the takeover of Great Northern. The court found that the Maine action had had no effect on the ultimate outcome of the takeover and simply mirrored more significant litigation in Connecticut. Recognizing concerns about excessive litigation costs, the court stated:

> The district court's robust skepticism of the benefits contributed by BTZ's counsel is especially appropriate given the increasing concerns that redundant or peripheral legal services may parasitize the litigation efforts of lead counsel, yet command a substantial fee. Insofar as lead counsel reasonably perceive a consequent dilution of the limited resources available for legal services, allowances for phantom legal services frustrate the adversary process and undermine the congressional policy favoring private enforcement of the securities laws.

*Id.* at 466.

In *Lindy Brothers Builders, Inc. of Philadelphia v. American Radiator & Standard Sanitary Corp.*, 487 F.2d 161 (3d Cir.1973), *appeal following remand* 540 F.2d 102 (3d Cir.1976), the Third Circuit established the so-called "lodestar" test for computing attorneys' fees. This test is favored by the FEDERAL JUDICIAL MANUAL FOR COMPLEX LITIGATION. A Third Circuit Task Force Report has described the "lodestar" method as follows:

> * * * First, the court must determine the hours reasonably expended by counsel that created, protected, or preserved the fund. Second, the number of compensable hours is multiplied by a reasonable hourly rate for the attorney's services. Hourly rates may vary according to the status of the attorney who performed the work (that is, the attorney's experience, reputation, practice, qualifications, and similar factors) or the nature of the services provided. This multiplication of the number of compensable hours by the reasonable hourly rate [constitutes] the "lodestar" of the court's fee determination.

> The "lodestar" then could be increased or decreased based upon the contingent nature or risk in the particular case involved and the quality of the attorney's work. An increase or decrease of the lodestar amount is referred to as a "multiplier." In determining whether to increase the lodestar to reflect the contingent nature of the case, * * * "the district court should consider any information that may help to establish the probability of success." However, "[t]he court may find that the contingency was so slight or the amount found to constitute reasonable compensation for the hours worked was so large a proportion of the total recovery that an increased allowance for the contingent nature of the fee would be minimal." As to the quality multiplier, it was to be employed only for "an unusual degree of skill, superior or inferior, exhibited by counsel in the specific case before the court."

REPORT OF THE THIRD CIRCUIT TASK FORCE, COURT AWARDED ATTORNEY FEES, 3–4 (1985). *See also, Silberman v. Bogle*, 683 F.2d 62 (3d Cir.1982).

The alternative to the "lodestar" method is an approach pursuant to which courts calculate the fee as a percentage of the total recovery. Under this latter method, awards generally range between 20%–35% when the award is below $1 million and 15%–20% when it is more.

Neither approach is entirely successful in resolving the structural conflicts inherent in settlements. If the lodestar formula is used, it is obviously in plaintiff's counsel's interest to prolong the suit and maximize the time spent on the case. Thus, counsel would prefer to reject an early settlement offer or negotiate its terms for a prolonged period of time. Defendants who also have a strong incentive to settle will often tacitly acquiesce in this scenario by extending the time needed to negotiate the settlement. This structural collusion may benefit counsel, but it works against the plaintiff-shareholders and the corporation whose interest is to settle the case as favorably and quickly as possible.

The risk of implicit structural collusion exists even when, prior to the settlement, there have been no negotiations as to plaintiff's counsel fees. *See* John C. Coffee, Jr., *Understanding the Plaintiff's Attorney: The Implications of Economic Theory for Private Enforcement of Law Through Class and Derivative Actions*, 86 COLUM.L.REV. 669 (1986). The very use of the lodestar formula may make it difficult to separate the fees from the rest of the settlement. Because the amount of counsel's fee is not directly linked to the amount of the award, counsel who has expended a substantial amount of time on the case will have an incentive to settle for an amount which is less than the shareholders might want to accept. This incentive is increased at the time when the hours which counsel has spent exceed the gain which she expected from the case *ex ante* based upon her estimate of the odds of success.

While the lodestar test seems to encourage plaintiff's counsel to diverge from the best interests of her client, the percentage of the recovery method is similarly problematic. Often, plaintiff's counsel will seek to settle the case very early so as to avoid expending too much effort and time. Since the marginal value of the settlement decreases as the amount of time invested by plaintiff's counsel rises, counsel will attempt to delay any serious investment of time in discovery, and, instead, negotiate a settlement that may be premature and possibly inadequate. Under the percentage of recovery method, plaintiff's counsel also may be reluctant to include non-pecuniary benefits in a settlement because no value will be attached to those benefits in determining the amount of her fees.

The percentage of recovery value method also tends to increase case splitting and fee splitting among different counsel. By diversifying the risks involved in any one case among a number of different lawyers, the lead counsel can reduce the effort put into the case and, hence, the costs that would be incurred if the case is not settled or litigated successfully. Such case splitting both decreases the incentive for plaintiff's counsel to settle early and reduces the effectiveness of counsel's work, thereby weakening the likelihood of a large recovery for the corporation. *See* John C. Coffee, Jr., *The Unfaithful Champion: The Plaintiff as Monitor of Shareholder Litigation*, 48 LAW & CONTEMP. PROB. 5 (1985); John C. Coffee, Jr., *Rescuing the Private Attorney General: Why the Model of the Lawyer as Bounty Hunter is Not Working*, 42 MD.L.REV. 215 (1983).

The difficulties with both approaches led the Third Circuit, the creator of the lodestar method, to appoint a Task Force to re-examine the problems arising from court awarded attorney fees. The Task Force report notes that when the question of attorneys' fees arises, the role of plaintiff's counsel changes from that of fiduciary for her client to a claimant against the fund created for her client's benefit. In such a situation, the role of the judge also changes; she must now act as a fiduciary for the fund's beneficiaries because there is no one else in the proceedings who is likely to do so.

To obviate the conflicts and problems described above, the Task Force recommended that "at the earliest practicable moment," the court, either on motion or its own initiative, attempt to establish a percentage fee which will be satisfactory to both the court and plaintiff's counsel. In making such an attempt, the court should appoint a representative on behalf of the putative fund beneficiaries to negotiate a fee arrangement with plaintiff's counsel in the same way that any contingent fee would be negotiated. The agreement would then be submitted to the court for its approval; if the parties could not agree on the fee structure, the court would then attempt to work out a solution which would be satisfactory to plaintiff's counsel. The Task Force assumes that in most cases, the fee would be a sliding scale based on the estimated ultimate recovery with the percentage decreasing as the size of the recovery increased. To promote an early settlement, the fee arrangement could provide incentives based on how quickly and efficiently the case was resolved. The Task Force believes that its recommendations may deal effectively with two of the principal problems caused by the lodestar approach. First, by establishing the fee early in the case, counsel has less of an inducement to increase the hours spent on the case as Lindy would have encouraged. Second, there will be a greater incentive for plaintiff's counsel to settle cases more quickly because delay will not increase his compensation. REPORT OF THE THIRD CIRCUIT TASK FORCE, COURT AWARDED ATTORNEY FEES, 21–26 (1985).

The concern of the Third Circuit Task Force is shared by at least one court. *In re Activision Securities Litigation*, 723 F.Supp. 1373, 1378 (N.D.Cal.1989) held that in future cases involving a common fund (whether derivative or class), absent extraordinary circumstances, the percentage of recovery for plaintiffs' counsel will always be set at 30 percent of the fund. The court also noted that its review of recent reported common fund cases disclosed that the fee awards almost always ranged around this amount. Hence the court concluded that the lodestar approach did not achieve "the stated purposes of proportionality, predictability and protection of the class. [They] encourage abuses such as unjustified work and protracting the litigation. [They] add to the work load of already overworked district courts. In short, [they] do not encourage efficiency, but rather * * * add inefficiency to the process."

Interestingly, Delaware courts have avoided choosing between the lodestar and percentage of recovery methods for determining attorneys fees. Rather, as one court has noted, they "have traditionally considered as most important the benefit that the litigation produced in determining the appropriate amount of attorneys fees to award." Thus they "avoid the tendency to make hours expended the essential inquiry." Additionally, Delaware courts do not consider themselves bound by the amount of the attorneys fees that the parties have negotiated. To do so is to "ignore the institutional role of the Court, which is obliged under our law to determine whether a fee award is fair and reasonable. Although it would be much easier for the Court to defer to the fee request that has been negotiated between plaintiffs' counsel and defendants' counsel, it would also be an abdication of the Court's responsibility to the stockholder class." *In re Dr. Pepper/Seven Up Companies, Inc. Shareholders Litigation*, 1996 WL 74214 (Del.Ch.1996).

# H.  ROLE OF COUNSEL

Can the lawyer who has represented the corporation now represent the individual directors—who very often will be the management of the corporation—in a derivative suit? While it is true that counsel represented the corporation, it is also the fact that she rendered advice to the individuals relating to the transaction being challenged. It is natural for those individuals now to turn to that lawyer and ask that she represent them when litigation arises. But is such representation in conflict with the lawyer's responsibility to the corporation—which has been her client? Will representation of the individual defendants necessarily cause the counsel to reveal confidences of the corporation in breach of her professional responsibility?

### *Developments in the Law—Conflicts of Interest in the Legal Profession*
94 HARV.L.REV. 1244, 1339–1342 (1981).

#### SHAREHOLDER DERIVATIVE SUITS

A derivative suit is nominally brought "to enforce a right of the corporation against a third party, and recovery in the suit must generally go to the corporation. But it may nevertheless be in the entity's interest to oppose a derivative suit. The entity's decision to oppose the suit or merely remain a passive bystander is of more than academic interest, because various potentially decisive procedural defenses can be raised only by the entity. The corporate attorney directed by management to resist such a suit, when the real defendant to the suit is a corporate insider, must be concerned that opposing the suit may be in the insider's—but not in the shareholders'—best interest.

The possibility for conflict of interest here is universally recognized. Although early cases found joint representation permissible where no conflict of interest was obvious, the emerging rule is against dual representation in all derivative actions. Outside counsel must thus be retained to represent one of the defendants. The cases and ethics opinions differ on whether there must be separate representation from the outset or merely from the time the corporation seeks to take an active role. Furthermore, this restriction on dual representation should not be waivable by consent in the usual way; the corporation should be presumptively incapable of giving valid consent.

It has been suggested that the outside lawyer should represent the individual defendants, perhaps as an indirect means of ensuring that their legal fees are not borne by the corporation. The better rule is to require that outside counsel represent the corporation, while the corporate attorney represents the insider defendant; the question of expenses would be decided separately. This rule recognizes that while the in-house attorney is nominally the representative of the corporation, his personal loyalties will inevitably be to the individual executives who hired him.

A corollary of the principle that the entity interests do not necessarily coincide with the position taken by the plaintiff in a derivative suit is that a former corporate attorney may not represent a shareholder in a derivative suit against the same corporation. If one looks only to the form of the suit, there would appear to be no conflict here—after all, the derivative suit purportedly seeks to advance the interests of the attorney's former client—but in reality these suits are often opposed to the entity's true interests.

## CANNON v. UNITED STATES ACOUSTICS CORP.

398 F.Supp. 209 (N.D.Ill.1975), *aff'd in relevant part*
*per curiam* 532 F.2d 1118 (7th Cir.1976).

[In this derivative suit, plaintiff alleged that the individual defendants committed numerous violations of the federal securities laws: granting themselves illegal stock options; causing the corporation to issue them additional shares based upon false claims that the stock was paid for rent, services and other expenses; usurpation of corporate opportunities; and the payment of illegal compensation.

Plaintiff sought to disqualify the law firm that represented both the corporation and the individual defendants. The defendants asserted that the conflict was theoretical only, and that if any real conflict did arise, they would withdraw.

The court disqualified counsel from representing the corporation. It found the thrust of the rules to be that "The interest of the corporate client is paramount and should not be influenced by any interest of the individual corporate officials." It summarized the law as follows:]

MARSHALL, DISTRICT JUDGE.

* * * These are serious charges. If they are proved, the corporations stand to gain substantially. The CPR unquestionably prohibits one lawyer from representing multiple clients when their interests are in conflict. The code goes so far as to say that if the clients' interests are potentially differing, the preferable course is for the lawyer to refuse the employment initially. In addition, at least one influential bar association has issued an opinion stating that dual representation is subject to conflicts of interest even when the corporation takes a passive role in the litigation. The case law on the question is not consistent; older cases hold dual representation is not improper, while more recent decisions hold that it is, both in derivative shareholder suits and in suits under 29 U.S.C.A. § 501 (1970).

As previously discussed the court is bound to apply the CPR to lawyers practicing before it. The code is clear that multiple representation is improper when the client's interests are adverse. Nevertheless, defendants' counsel argue there is no present conflict and should one arise they will withdraw their representation of the individual defendants and represent only the corporations. There are a number of problems with this solution. First, the complaint on its face establishes a conflict that cannot be ignored despite counsel's good faith representations. Second, counsel overlooks the hardship on the court and the parties if in the middle of this litigation new counsel must be obtained because a conflict arises. Lastly, although counsel offers to withdraw its representation of the individual defendants and remain counsel for the corporations if a conflict should arise, the appropriate course, as suggested by [*Lewis v. Shaffer Stores Co.*, 218 F.Supp. 238 (S.D.N.Y.1963) ] and [*Murphy v. Washington American League Base Ball Club, Inc.*, 324 F.2d 394 (D.C.Cir.1963) ], is for the corporation to retain independent counsel. Under this procedure, once counsel has examined the evidence, a decision can be made regarding the role the corporation will play in the litigation. This decision will be made without the possibility of any influence emanating from the representation of the individual defendants, and will also eliminate the potential problem of confidences and secrets reposed by the individual defendants being used adverse to their interests by former counsel should new counsel have had to have been selected under the approach suggested by defense counsel. This solution, concededly, is not without its disabilities. The corporations' rights to counsel of their choice are infringed and in a closely held corporation, as here, the financial burden is increased. Nevertheless, on balance, the corporations must obtain independent counsel.

---

Although *Cannon* reflects the prevailing view as to the propriety of joint representation, there has been much litigation dealing with the disqualification of attorneys in a variety of contexts and it is difficult to draw definite conclusions about when joint representation will be permitted in derivative suits. *See* Annotation, *Representation of Conflicting Interests As Disqualifying Attorney From Acting in a Civil Case*, 31 ALR3d 715 (1970); Annotation, *Disqualification of Law Firm From Representing Party in Federal Civil Suit Involving Former Client of That Firm*, 56 ALR Fed. 194 (1982). *See also*, Opinion 842, Committee on Professional Ethics of Association of Bar of the City of New York (1960).

### Note: Attorney–Client Privilege

Perhaps the most difficult operational questions for counsel concern the scope of the attorney-client privilege and the work product doctrine. The attorney-client privilege exists to protect a client's confidential communications to her attorney. Where the client is a natural person, it is easier to identify the situations in which the need for the privilege arises than it is in the corporate setting. In the latter, counsel often has consulted with individual members of management in her role as counsel to the corporation. Were those conversations privileged? Was counsel engaged in a meeting with the "client" when she spoke to the managers?

Is a memorandum from the chief executive officer to field employees concerning business practices privileged if it is designed to elicit information which will be furnished to counsel but lacks the formal trappings of confidentiality? An action brought by a shareholder—either a derivative suit or a class action—makes the analysis of these questions still more complex because such a suit involves a dispute among different parts of the corporate whole. In such a case, what does it mean to say that the "corporation" is the client?

In *Garner v. Wolfinbarger*, 430 F.2d 1093 (5th Cir.1970), counsel asserted that the attorney-client privilege prevented him from testifying as to the advice he gave the "corporation" in a transaction involving the sale of securities. The sale was attacked in a shareholder suit alleging fraud under the federal securities laws. The court stated:

> It is urged that disclosure is injurious to both the corporation and the attorney. Corporate management must manage. It has the duty to do so and requires the tools to do so. Part of the managerial task is to seek legal counsel when desirable, and, obviously, management prefers that it confer with counsel without the risk of having the communications revealed at the instance of one or more dissatisfied stockholders. The managerial preference is a rational one, because it is difficult to envision the management of any sizeable corporation pleasing all of its stockholders all of the time, and management desires protection from those who might second-guess or even harass in matters purely of judgment.

> But in assessing management assertions of injury to the corporation it must be borne in mind that management does not manage for itself and that the beneficiaries of its action are the stockholders. Conceptualistic phrases describing the corporation as an entity separate from its stockholders are not useful tools of analysis. They serve only to obscure the fact that management has duties which run to the benefit ultimately of the stockholders. For example, it is difficult to rationally defend the assertion of the privilege if all, or substantially all, stockholders desire to inquire into the attorney's communications with corporate representatives who have only nominal ownership interests, or even none at all. There may be reasonable differences over the manner of characterizing in legal terminology the duties of management, and over the extent to which corporate management is less of a fiduciary than the common law trustee. There may be many situations in which the corporate entity or its management, or both, have interests adverse to those of some or all stockholders. But when all is said and done management is not managing for itself.

> The representative and the represented have a mutuality of interest in the representative's freely seeking advice when needed and putting it to use when received. This is not to say that management does not have allowable judgment in putting advice to use. But management judgment must stand on its merits, not

behind an ironclad veil of secrecy which under all circumstances preserves it from being questioned by those for whom it is, at least in part, exercised.

\* \* \*

In summary, we say this. The attorney-client privilege still has viability for the corporate client. The corporation is not barred from asserting it merely because those demanding information enjoy the status of stockholders. But where the corporation is in suit against its stockholders on charges of acting inimically to stockholder interests, protection of those interests as well as those of the corporation and of the public require that the availability of the privilege be subject to the right of the stockholders to show cause why it should not be invoked in the particular instance.

\* \* \*

There are many indicia that may contribute to a decision of presence or absence of good cause, among them the number of shareholders and the percentage of stock they represent; the bona fides of the shareholders; the nature of the shareholders' claim and whether it is obviously colorable; the apparent necessity or desirability of the shareholders having the information and the availability of it from other sources; whether, if the shareholders' claim is of wrongful action by the corporation, it is of action criminal, or illegal but not criminal, or of doubtful legality; whether the communication related to past or to prospective actions; whether the communication is of advice concerning the litigation itself; the extent to which the communication is identified versus the extent to which the shareholders are blindly fishing; the risk of revelation of trade secrets or other information in whose confidentiality the corporation has an interest for independent reasons.

*Id.* at 1101–04.

Professor Hazard has said of the court's good cause test that it "circumscribes the problem rather nicely but does not progress much toward comprehending it." Geoffrey Hazard, *Triangular Lawyer Relationships*, 1 Geo. J. Leg. Ethics 15, 31 (1987). *See* Keith W. Johnson, Evidence: *Fausek v. White: The Sixth Circuit Garners Support For A Good Cause Exception To The Attorney–Client Privilege*, 18 U. Dayton L. Rev. 313 (1993); Note, *The Shareholders' Derivative–Claim Exception to the Attorney–Client Privilege*, 48 Law.&Contemp. Prob. 199 (1985).

*Bailey v. Meister Brau, Inc.*, 55 F.R.D. 211 (N.D.Ill.1972) was a class action against the officers and directors of the corporation in which the plaintiff was a shareholder in the acquisition of that corporation by Meister Brau. The officer whose communications with counsel were sought was an officer of both the acquiring and the acquired corporations. In asserting the attorney-client privilege, he argued that he had been wearing his "Meister Brau hat" during the discussions of the purchase of the acquired company. The court rejected this argument, holding that "[a] fiduciary cannot turn his responsibilities on and off like a faucet * * * As long as that [fiduciary duty] existed, so did the concomitant interest of the [acquired company's] shareholders in knowing his legal communications concerning the future of their company." *Id.* at 214.

In *Valente v. Pepsico, Inc.*, 68 F.R.D. 361 (D.Del.1975), the court extended *Garner* to permit minority shareholders of Wilson Sporting Goods Co., the acquired corporation in a merger with Pepsico, to compel the production of certain documents prepared by Pepsico's attorney concerning the possible tax consequences of the merger. The court held that documents prepared by counsel for directors of Pepsico who were also directors of Wilson were not protected by the attorney-client privilege because of the rule that where an attorney serves two clients, otherwise confidential communications are not privileged in a subsequent controversy between the two. The court also held that documents prepared by both house counsel and outside counsel for Pepsico were not protected because of Pepsico's fiduciary obligations as a controlling shareholder to the minority shareholder.

*Garner* rests on the "joint client" exception to the attorney-client privilege. In shareholder actions, that exception is premised upon the fiduciary duties owed by corporate management to the shareholders and the status of the shareholders as beneficiaries of management's operation of corporate affairs. This rationale is clearly well suited to derivative suits in which the plaintiff is seeking to assert the corporation's interest. Should it apply in a class action where the interests of the plaintiff shareholders and the corporation are opposed? Some courts have so held. *See Cohen v. Uniroyal, Inc.*, 80 F.R.D. 480 (E.D.Pa.1978); *In re Transocean Tender Offer Securities Litigation*, 78 F.R.D. 692 (N.D.Ill.1978). One court has applied the *Garner* rule in litigation between a corporation and its debenture holders. *Broad v. Rockwell International Corp.*, [1976–77 Transfer Binder], Fed.Sec.L.Rep. (CCH) ¶ 95,894 (N.D.Tex. 1977). In *Garner* itself, the court indicated that the form of the suit was not relevant to its decision. 430 F.2d at 1097, n. 11.

*Garner* suggests that the interests of a corporation and its shareholders are never inconsistent or adversarial. But suppose that the corporation has more than one class of stock. Are the interests of preferred stockholders, for example, always consistent with those of the common stockholders? Consider the materials in Chapter 9. *See* Note, *The Attorney–Client Privilege and the Corporation in Shareholder Litigation*, 50 S.Cal.L.Rev. 303 (1977).

In re *Bairnco Corp. Securities Litigation*, 148 F.R.D. 91 (S.D.N.Y. 1993) concerned plaintiffs' ability to overcome a corporation's attorney-client privilege under the *Garner* good cause standard. Plaintiffs sued Bairnco under Rule 10b–5 for misleading statements made by its wholly owned subsidiary, Keene, that discounted the potential liability arising from asbestos litigation. After Keene later admitted its uncertainty concerning the impact of the litigation on its profitability, Bairnco's stock fell more than 50 percent. Some of the documents that plaintiffs sought in discovery to prove that the misstatements were designed to inflate the company's stock artificially included advice from counsel to the corporation. The court, relying on *Garner*, ordered the documents to be produced because of "the existence of a fiduciary duty or mutuality of interest between the corporation and its shareholders at the time of the communications sought to be discovered," led the court to order the documents produced. *Id.* at 98.

The extent of the privilege was interpreted in *Upjohn Co. v. United States*, 449 U.S. 383, 101 S.Ct. 677, 66 L.Ed.2d 584 (1981). Counsel undertook an investigation of reports that the company had made questionable payments to foreign officials to secure business. Counsel sent questionnaires to foreign managers and conducted interviews. The government subpoenaed the resulting documents, and counsel resisted the subpoena on the basis of the attorney-client privilege. The Sixth Circuit rejected the claim on grounds that it was limited to discussions with members of the "control group" of the corporation. The Supreme Court stated:

> In the case of the individual client the provider of information and the person who acts on the lawyer's advice are one and the same. In the corporate context, however, it will frequently be employees beyond the control group as defined by the court below— "officers and agents * * * responsible for directing [the company's] actions in response to legal advice"—who will possess the information needed by the corporation's lawyers. Middle-level—and indeed lower-level—employees can, by actions within the scope of their employment, embroil the corporation in serious legal difficulties, and it is only natural that these employees would have the relevant information needed by corporate counsel if he is adequately to advise the client with respect to such actual or potential difficulties.
> * * *

> The control group test adopted by the court below thus frustrates the very purpose of the privilege by discouraging the communication of relevant information by employees of the client to attorneys seeking to render legal advice to the client corporation. The attorney's advice will also frequently be more significant to noncontrol group members than to those who officially sanction the advice, and the control group test makes it more difficult to convey full and frank legal advice to the employees who will put into effect the client corporation's policy. * * *

> The narrow scope given the attorney-client privilege by the court below not only makes it difficult for corporate attorneys to formulate sound advice when their client is faced with a specific legal problem but also threatens to limit the valuable efforts of corporate counsel to ensure their client's compliance with the law. In light of the vast and complicated array of regulatory legislation confronting the modern corporation, corporations, unlike most indi-

viduals, "constantly go to lawyers to find out how to obey the law," Burnham, *The Attorney–Client Privilege in the Corporate Arena*, 24 Bus. Law. 901, 913 (1969), particularly since compliance with the law in this area is hardly an instinctive matter * * *. The test adopted by the court below is difficult to apply in practice, though no abstractly formulated and unvarying "test" will necessarily enable courts to decide questions such as this with mathematical precision. But if the purpose of the attorney-client privilege is to be served, the attorney and client must be able to predict with some degree of certainty whether particular discussions will be protected. An uncertain privilege, or one which purports to be certain but results in widely varying applications by the courts, is little better than no privilege at all. The very terms of the test adopted by the court below suggest the unpredictability of its application. The test restricts the availability of the privilege to those officers who play a "substantial role" in deciding and directing a corporation's legal response.

*Id.* at 391–93.

Despite *Upjohn*'s broad scope, *Garner* and its progeny continue to survive, albeit with some limitations. Thus in *In re LTV Securities Litigation*, 89 F.R.D. 595 (N.D.Tex.1981), the first reported case after *Upjohn* to address the availability of the attorney-client privilege in shareholder actions, the court upheld the attorney-client privilege for various materials relating to counsel's internal investigation and report to the company as well as materials prepared for the litigation at issue. Although supporting the "free interchange" idea of *Upjohn,* the court also sustained the "good cause" standard of *Garner.* The court's decision was based largely on a "temporal distinction"; all the materials had been prepared after the events which were the subject matter of the litigation. *See also, Quintel Corp., N.V. v. Citibank, N.A.*, 567 F.Supp. 1357 (S.D.N.Y.1983) (fiduciary relationship outweighed interests protected by attorney-client privilege).

Notwithstanding *Garner* and *Upjohn,* the availability of the privilege may be difficult to determine when the communications between the lawyer and his corporate client involve questions of both business and law, a situation which is most likely to arise when counsel is also a director or officer of the corporation. *See S.E.C. v. Gulf & Western Industries, Inc.*, 518 F.Supp. 675 (D.D.C.1981) (where counsel was also director and member of pension fund investment committee requiring him to spend considerable time at corporation's offices, "it cannot be assumed that all of his discussions with corporate officials involved legal advice").

The distinction between business and legal advice also may arise where the lawyer is not a director or an officer. *See KLM v. Checchi,* 1997 WL 525861 (Del.Ch.1997). (minority shareholder entitled to discovery of discussions between directors and counsel concerning the adoption of a poison pill that was detrimental to shareholder because shareholder did not seek litigation advice, "any legal advice at the meeting could be segregated from business discussions with little difficulty given the nature of the specific purpose of the meeting" and the lawyer "served as much as a business advisor as a legal advisor and * * * the response to questions were communicated in a business capacity and not in a legal setting").

### *Note: Sanctions*

We have already seen that critics of derivative suits view them as a device for unscrupulous lawyers to threaten or institute frivolous litigation in the hope of obtaining a settlement from which they will personally benefit. *Blue Chip Stamps v. Manor Drug Stores*, 421 U.S. 723, 95 S.Ct. 1917, 44 L.Ed.2d 539 (1975). While such conduct may always have been possible, a number of existing mechanisms now make it more difficult to succeed. First, courts have always had the inherent power to impose monetary sanctions on an attorney whose conduct constitutes an abuse of judicial process. *Roadway Express, Inc. v. Piper*, 447 U.S. 752, 100 S.Ct. 2455, 65 L.Ed.2d 488 (1980). Secondly, Rule 11 of the Federal Rules of Civil Procedure was amended in 1983 to require attorneys to believe, after reasonable inquiry, that every pleading, motion or other paper filed in court be well grounded in fact, be based on a reasonable interpretation of law and not interposed for an improper purpose such as harassment, unnecessary delay or needless increase in the cost of litigation. If the Rule is violated, the court is required to impose sanctions, which may include opposing counsel's fees, on the person who signed the document, his client, or both. There has been an increasing volume of litigation under Rule 11 and courts have shown a willingness to impose sanctions on offending lawyers, including representatives of major law firms. See Note, *The 1983 Amendments to Rule 11: Answering the Critics' Concern with Judicial Self-Restraint*, 61 NOTRE DAME L.REV. 798 (1986); Note, *The Dynamics of Rule 11: Preventing Frivolous Litigation by Demanding Professional Responsibility*, 61 N.Y.U.L.REV. 300 (1986).

## GARR v. U.S. HEALTHCARE, INC.

22 F.3d 1274 (3d Cir. 1994).

GREENBERG, CIRCUIT JUDGE.

### I.  INTRODUCTION

This matter is before the court on an appeal from orders of the district court entered on February 5, 1993, and July 6, 1993, imposing sanctions on appellants Arnold Levin and Harris J. Sklar pursuant to Fed.R.Civ.P. 11. We will set forth the background of this case in detail as the issues should be considered in the context of both this case and the related litigation we will describe. The district court's opinion concluding that there had been Rule 11 violations is published as *Greenfield v. U.S. Healthcare, Inc.*, 146 F.R.D. 118 (E.D.Pa.1993), and its subsequent opinion fixing the amount of the sanctions is dated July 6, 1993.

*Greenfield v. U.S. Healthcare, Inc.,* No. 92–6345, 1993 WL 257315 (E.D.Pa. July 6, 1993).

This action arose in the aftermath of an article in the *Wall Street Journal* published on November 4, 1992, entitled "U.S. Healthcare Insiders Sold Stock Before Last Week's 17% Price Decline." The article recited that U.S. Healthcare, Inc. insiders, including Leonard Abramson, its chairman and president, had been heavy sellers of its stock before a 17% two-day drop in its price in the week before publication of the article. The article indicated the drop had been precipitated by disappointing earnings.

James R. Malone, Jr., a member of the Haverford, Pennsylvania, law firm of Greenfield & Chimicles, who read the article on the morning it was published, was interested in its contents because his firm specialized in securities litigation.[1] Indeed, in an extraordinary allegation, not denied by Malone, U.S. Healthcare in the Rule 11 proceedings charged that Greenfield & Chimicles maintained a list of corporate stockholders available to become plaintiffs in securities litigation. Robert K. Greenfield was on that list.[2] It is undisputed that after Malone read the article he examined a "representative sampling of stories relating to U.S. Healthcare," as well as a report on background information on the company. He also obtained considerable other information about U.S. Healthcare, including filings it had made with the Securities and Exchange Commission.

Malone does not contend that at the time that he was doing this research he had a client who had expressed any interest in the article to him. Rather, Malone was seeking to generate a lawsuit. Thus, in the pithy words of the district court, "[h]aving a case but no client," he called Greenfield who lives in Florida to discuss the U.S. Healthcare situation. Malone described the *Wall Street Journal* article to Greenfield and established that he owned stock in U.S. Healthcare. Malone asked Greenfield whether he would like Greenfield & Chimicles to file a suit on his behalf if the firm believed that there had been actionable wrongdoing, and Greenfield answered affirmatively. Within hours Malone determined that a certain class of U.S. Healthcare stockholders had "a legitimate and cognizable legal claim" stemming in part from the insiders' stock sales.

Events continued to unfold rapidly on November 4, 1992, for on that day Malone prepared and filed a class action complaint on behalf of Greenfield under section 10(b) of the Securities Exchange Act of 1934. The gravamen of the complaint was that U.S. Healthcare and Abramson had issued false and misleading statements which were filed with the Securities and Exchange Commission and which caused Greenfield and the stockholder class to purchase U.S. Healthcare stock at artificially

---

**1.** This arrangement reverses the traditional regime which contemplates that the client start the steps towards formation of an attorney-client relationship by seeking legal representation.

**2.** Robert K. Greenfield is not related to the Richard D. Greenfield of Greenfield & Chimicles.

inflated prices. The complaint asserted controlling person liability against Abramson under section 20 of the Securities Exchange Act. In the complaint, Malone recited that Greenfield fairly and adequately could represent the interest of the class of stockholders on whose behalf the action was being brought. Inasmuch as Malone mailed the complaint to Greenfield on November 4, 1992, Malone filed it before Greenfield received it. Obviously Malone did not think it important for Greenfield to see the complaint before it was filed even though Malone regards Greenfield as a distinguished retired corporate attorney.

On November 5, 1992, Malone on behalf of Allen Strunk filed a second class action against U.S. Healthcare and Abramson. The *Strunk* action repeated the allegations word for word from the *Greenfield* case except that the name of the plaintiff and the number of shares he owned were changed. Malone filed this action after Fred Taylor Isquith, an attorney in New York, contacted him and asked him to represent Strunk.

Malone and Strunk's New York lawyers were not the only attorneys interested in the U.S. Healthcare situation. On November 4, 1992, appellant Arnold Levin of the Philadelphia firm of Levin, Fishbein, Sedran & Berman, also read the *Wall Street Journal* article. Levin and his firm have what he characterized as "a long-standing professional relationship" with Greenfield & Chimicles, and Levin had a high regard for Greenfield & Chimicles' ethical standards and skill in handling federal securities law suits. On November 4, 1992, after Levin had read the article, Malone called him to discuss the merits of bringing a section 10(b) action against U.S. Healthcare and Abramson. Malone mentioned the *Wall Street Journal* article, and said he had done research into whether a section 10(b) action could be brought. Malone also told Levin that he had prepared such a complaint. Levin requested that Malone fax him a copy of the complaint, and Malone promptly did so. Levin then read the Greenfield complaint and reread the Wall Street Journal article and concluded, as he set forth in his affidavit, that "[b]ased upon my experience and understanding from the two documents," and in "reliance on the integrity of the pre-filing investigation of Greenfield & Chimicles," the section 10(b) action had merit.

There was even more interest in the U.S. Healthcare situation for on November 4, 1992, appellant Harris J. Sklar, a Philadelphia attorney in individual practice, also read the article. According to his affidavit, Sklar discussed the possibility of bringing an action against U.S. Healthcare with his client Scott Garr who was a U.S. Healthcare stockholder, and Garr authorized Sklar to bring the case on a class action basis. Sklar, however, saw the need to obtain co-counsel and consequently called Levin, as he had worked with him in the past. Levin then told Sklar of his dealings with Malone, and Levin and Sklar discussed the possibility of a suit. Sklar asked Levin to fax him a copy of the Greenfield complaint and Levin did so. Sklar then reviewed the complaint and, in his words as set forth in his affidavit, "[b]ased on my understanding of the securities laws and the facts as described in the

*Wall Street Journal*," he determined that the complaint had merit. Sklar thus again spoke to Levin and indicated that Levin could file the class action on behalf of Scott Garr and Patricia Garr, his wife. On November 6, 1992, Levin and Sklar filed that complaint which replicated the *Greenfield* and *Strunk* complaints except that the names of the plaintiffs and the number of shares they owned were changed.

There was now an extraordinary development. On November 6, 1992, the same day that Levin and Sklar filed the Garr complaint, U.S. Healthcare and Abramson moved in the district court for the imposition of sanctions pursuant to Rule 11 in the *Greenfield, Strunk,* and *Garr* actions. This motion was a formidable document, as with attachments it exceeded 100 pages. At oral argument we asked U.S. Healthcare's attorney, Alan J. Davis, how it was possible that he filed this motion on the same day the *Garr* complaint was filed. He explained that he had anticipated that following the filing of the Greenfield complaint there would be additional complaints and accordingly his firm had a person waiting in the clerk's office to obtain copies of them when they were filed. He further explained that in class actions additional complaints are generated so that the original attorney will have allies when a vote is taken to determine the lead attorney. The lead attorney position is coveted as it is likely to bring its occupant the largest share of the fees generated by the litigation.

In their brief, U.S. Healthcare and Abramson explained the basis for the motion in detail. They asserted that Malone, Levin, and Sklar failed to conduct "even the most cursory factual and legal investigation" of the case and that if they had done so they would have determined that the complaints had no basis in fact or law. The brief indicated that the three complaints demonstrated the "all too familiar pattern of an instant class action lawsuit based on newspaper reports followed by a covey of cut and paste copycat complaints."

As if what we have described is not remarkable enough, there was yet an additional extraordinary development in the *Greenfield* case. On November 8, 1992, Robert K. Greenfield finally read the complaint, and at that time came to the realization that he had made a mistake in bringing the action because he knew of no basis for it and because his son had substantial business dealings with U.S. Healthcare. Thus, he directed Malone to withdraw the complaint. When U.S. Healthcare and Abramson learned of Robert K. Greenfield's position, they supplemented their motion for Rule 11 sanctions to assert that Malone had failed to make a reasonable inquiry into whether Greenfield fairly and adequately could protect the interests of the plaintiff class.

\* \* \*

Thereafter, the district court filed its reported opinion of February 4, 1993. After setting forth the background of the case at length, the court found that Malone could not be sanctioned under Rule 11 with respect to the accuracy of the information on which he had predicated the *Greenfield* complaint because his inquiry into the underlying facts "was reasonable under the circumstances." However, the court found that Malone had violated Rule 11 with respect to the allegation in the complaint that Greenfield fairly and adequately could protect the interests of the class. But it also found that it could not say that Malone had made an inadequate inquiry into Strunk's ability fairly and adequately to protect the class. Accordingly, as Malone's factual inquiry into the merits of the case against U.S. Healthcare and Abramson had been reasonable, the court did not impose sanctions in the *Strunk* action.

The district court next discussed whether sanctions should be imposed on Levin and Sklar. In this regard the court pointed out that Levin cited our opinion in *Lewis v. Curtis*, 671 F.2d 779 (3d Cir.), *cert. denied*, 459 U.S. 880, 103 S.Ct. 176, 74 L.Ed.2d 144 (1982), in which we indicated that reliance on an article in the *Wall Street Journal* is not based "on an insubstantial or meaningless investigation" and that plaintiffs and their attorneys "need not make further expenditures to prove independently that which may be read with some confidence of truthfulness and accuracy in a respected financial journal." The court observed that Lewis was decided under Fed.R.Civ.P. 23.1 and that we have never applied that case under Rule 11. It then held that Rule 11 imposes a "non-delegable duty upon the signing attorney to conduct his own independent analysis of the facts and law which form the basis of a pleading or motion." The court rejected Levin's argument that he could rely on the integrity of the investigation by Greenfield & Chimicles, and it therefore ruled that Sklar could not rely on that investigation either. Ultimately the court held "that Levin and Sklar sought to act more quickly than fulfilling their duty would have allowed" and that "Levin['s] and Sklar's inquiry, or lack thereof, was unreasonable under the circumstances and a violation of Rule 11."

\* \* \*

## II.  DISCUSSION

\* \* \*

\* \* \* The signer's signature on a pleading, motion, or other paper certifies the signer has done three things: (1) read the pleading, motion, or paper; (2) made a reasonable inquiry into the contents of the pleading, motion, or other paper and concluded that it is well grounded in fact and warranted in law; and (3) has not acted in bad faith in signing the document. The court determines the reasonableness of an inquiry by applying an objective standard. It is clear that the signer has a "personal, nondelegable responsibility" to comply with the requirements of Rule 11 before signing the document.

A signer's obligation personally to comply with the requirements of Rule 11 clearly does not preclude the signer from any reliance on information from other persons. For example, no one could argue fairly that it would be unreasonable for an attorney to rely on witnesses to an accident before bringing a personal injury action. After all, the accident hardly can be reconstructed for the benefit of a plaintiff's attorney.

Similarly, an attorney is not always foreclosed from relying on information from other persons. * * *

It is also important to observe that when the court examines the sufficiency of the inquiry into the facts and law, it must avoid drawing on the wisdom of hindsight and should test the signer's conduct by determining what was reasonable when the document was submitted. Thus, if under an objective standard, the signer made a reasonable inquiry both as to the fact and the law at the time a document was submitted, subsequent developments showing that the signer's position was incorrect will not subject the signer to Rule 11 sanctions for having submitted the document. On the other hand, a signer making an inadequate inquiry into the sufficiency of the facts and law underlying a document will not be saved from a Rule 11 sanction by the stroke of luck that the document happened to be justified. As the court indicated in *Vista Mfg., Inc. v. Trac–4 Inc.*, 131 F.R.D. 134, 138 (N.D.Ind.1990), "A shot in the dark is a sanctionable event, even if it somehow hits the mark." The court in *Vista* correctly stated the law, for if a lucky shot could save the signer from sanctions, the purpose of Rule 11 "to deter baseless filings" would be frustrated.

There is also a temporal element in a determination of whether an inquiry was reasonable. Thus, we have recognized that a factor in ascertaining the reasonableness of the signer's inquiry is the amount of time available to investigate the facts and law involved. * * *

Application of the foregoing principles requires us to affirm. We, of course, are exercising the abuse of discretion standard, for this is not a case in which the historical facts underlying the court's determination are in dispute. As Levin and Sklar explain in their brief: "Here, Levin acquired the knowledge from one whom he knew to be competent securities law counsel, Malone, coupled with the knowledge Levin obtained from the Wall Street Journal, and his experienced understanding of the securities laws. [sic] Levin passed this information on to Sklar so that he too could make the same certification."

We do not doubt that sometimes it is difficult to reconcile the tension between the requirement that a signer personally discharge the Rule 11 obligations and the acknowledgement that a signer may rely on another party's inquiry in some cases. But this appeal presents no difficulties. Malone's declaration described the scope of his inquiry in great detail. He obtained a representative sampling of stories regarding U.S. Healthcare and a "disclo" report giving a great deal of financial information regarding U.S. Healthcare, including five-year figures showing sales, net income, earnings per share, and growth rate. He also considered financial ratios and examined forms filed with the Securities and Exchange Commission showing trading in U.S. Healthcare stock by insiders. In fact, in the district court's view, Malone's inquiry was inadequate only as to Greenfield's status as the class representative.

On the other hand, Levin and Sklar relied only on the *Wall Street Journal* article, the *Greenfield* complaint, and Malone. They made no effort to examine the numerous materials Malone assembled, and they cannot justify their failure to have done so. They do not contend that Malone would not at their request have sent the materials to them. Alternatively, we see no reason why they could not have seen the materials by travelling the short distance from their offices in Philadelphia to Malone's office in Haverford, a Philadelphia suburb. We also point out that the documents on which Malone relied were all accessible to the public so that Levin and Sklar could have obtained them themselves.

Furthermore, there were no time constraints requiring Levin and Sklar to file the Garr complaint on an expedited basis. The *Wall Street Journal* article was published on November 4, 1992, and Levin and Sklar filed the Garr complaint two days later. Levin and Sklar do not contend that they were confronted with a statute of limitations problem compelling immediate action. * * *

We also point out that Levin and Sklar have advanced no other reason why the Garr complaint had to have been filed within two days of the publication of the article. They do not contend, for example, that the Garrs needed emergency relief, nor do they suggest that U.S. Healthcare or Abramson might have evaded process or concealed assets if the suit had not been filed so quickly. While at oral argument the suggestion was made that class actions are brought quickly so that the attorney filing the case may control the litigation, we would not regard that reason as in any way detracting from the reasonable inquiry otherwise required under Rule 11.

At bottom, there is no escape from the conclusion that Levin and Sklar abdicated their own responsibilities and relied excessively on Malone contrary to Rule 11. Furthermore, they did not rely on Malone only as to some small portion of the case. Rather, they relied on his inquiry to justify the entire cause of action. Indeed, they filed the complaint Malone had prepared, changing only the name of the plaintiffs and the number of shares owned. We recognize that it could be argued that it would have been pointless for Levin and Sklar to make an inquiry into the merits of the case sufficient to satisfy Rule 11 as Malone already had done so. Yet Rule 11 requires that an attorney signing a pleading must make a reasonable inquiry personally. The advantage of duplicate personal inquiries is manifest: while one attorney might find a complaint well founded in fact and warranted by the law, another, even after examining the materials available to the first attorney, could come to a contrary conclusion. Overall, we conclude that the Rule 11 violation in this case is so clear that even on a plenary review, we would uphold the sanctions imposed on Levin and Sklar. Accordingly, under the deferential abuse of discretion standard, we certainly must affirm the district court's determination that sanctions were required.

In reaching our result, we have not overlooked Levin's and Sklar's reliance on *Lewis v. Curtis*, 671 F.2d 779. Rather, we determine that the case does not help them. In fact, in *Lewis v. Curtis* we did not discuss or even cite Rule 11. Indeed, insofar as germane here, in *Lewis v. Curtis* we merely indicated that reliance on an article in the *Wall Street Journal* is not based "on an insubstantial or meaningless investigation" for purposes of Rule 23.1. Rule 23.1, however, deals with the requirement in derivative actions that the plaintiff verify certain allegations of the complaint. But Rule 23.1 has no counterpart to the Rule 11 requirement that a pleading, motion or other paper be signed only after "reasonable inquiry." Thus, an attorney cannot rely on *Lewis v. Curtis* in determining whether an inquiry is reasonable under Rule 11.

There is another reason why *Lewis v. Curtis* is inapposite and why Levin's and Sklar's reliance on the *Wall Street Journal* never could have been sufficient in this case. A significant aspect of the Garr complaint was that U.S. Healthcare had been filing false and misleading quarterly reports with the Securities and Exchange Commission to the injury of Garr and the class. Yet inasmuch as the Wall Street Journal article never suggested that U.S. Healthcare had been filing false reports, Levin and Sklar could not reasonably have relied on the article for that information. Indeed, neither Levin nor Sklar even asserts that he ever saw these publicly available reports before they filed the Garr complaint. We are at a total loss to understand how attorneys can urge that they have made a reasonable inquiry into the facts and the law of a case when their complaint is predicated on allegedly false statements in documents which they have not bothered to read.

\* \* \*

### III. CONCLUSION

The orders of February 5, 1993, and July 6, 1993, will be affirmed.

ROTH, CIRCUIT JUDGE, dissenting:

Although I share the majority's view that Levin and Sklar's conduct fell far short of the ideal, I do not share its belief that Rule 11 sanctions are appropriate in this situation. Instead, I believe that, when a court finds that an attorney has filed a meritorious complaint, the court should not go on to inquire whether the attorney conducted an adequate investigation prior to filing the complaint. I therefore respectfully dissent.

Except for changes in the named plaintiffs and the number of shares they owned, the complaint filed by Levin and Sklar on behalf of the Garrs was identical to the complaints filed by Malone on behalf of Greenfield and Strunk. As the majority notes, the district court did not dismiss the Strunk complaint, thereby implicitly finding that on its face it stated a valid claim. Presumably, had the district court not determined that Levin and Sklar violated Rule 11, it would not have dismissed the Garr complaint. Thus it is safe to assume that the district court believed that the Garr complaint on its face was meritorious.

In holding that the imposition of sanctions was appropriate in this case, the majority relies on the following statement in an opinion from a district court in another circuit: "A shot in the dark is a sanctionable event, even if it somehow hits the mark." *Vista* \* \* \*. Though this statement has the virtue of being colorful, as the basis of the majority's reasoning it suffers from three flaws. First, *Vista* does not support the majority's position; despite the quoted statement the court imposed no sanctions. Second, in relying on *Vista* the majority overlooks apparent statements of law to the contrary by the *Vista* court's own circuit, the Seventh, and by the Second Circuit. Finally, the majority's conclusion that the *Vista* rule is necessary to further the purposes of Rule 11 is the product of an incomplete analysis of both the policies animating Rule 11 and the impact of that rule on the effectiveness of Rule 11. \* \* \*

\* \* \*

Indeed, this court has remarked that we "have interpreted [Rule 11's] language to prescribe sanctions, including fees, only in the 'exceptional circumstance' ... where a claim or motion is patently unmeritorious or frivolous." Taken as a whole, these cases support the notion that sanctions are inappropriate where, as here, there was a reasonable basis for a complaint even if the attorney filing it failed adequately to inquire into the existence of that basis. [Citations omitted—Eds.]

\* \* \*

On the whole, the goals of deterring abuses of the system and streamlining litigation would be better served by the standard I advocate. Because the vast majority of "shots in the dark" will not hit their target, almost all of them will be subject to sanction. I find it difficult to believe that this slightly reduced probability of sanction will encourage lawyers to take blind shots. The deterrent function of Rule 11 to prevent baseless filings will not be undermined by not sanctioning when a complaint on its face does have merit. \* \* \*

Moreover, in cases in which the complaint states a meritorious claim, we must consider whether we want to encourage a secondary line of inquiry into the adequacy of the attorney's research. I believe that opening up such a line of attack, which will require courts to engage in pure speculation in the worst case and will lead to a waste of the court's time and resources in the best case, will create a greater clog in the courts' efficient functioning than will the failure to sanction the rare case of the successful shot in the dark.

The majority is eager to sanction counsel in this case because it believes sanctions are necessary to discourage the indiscriminate filing of lawsuits. As I have pointed out above, it is unlikely that the majority's rule would have a greater effect in this regard than my standard. Ironically, however, the majority's approach will encourage the indiscriminate filing of motions for sanctions. This case, in which the motion for sanctions was prepared before defendants had even seen the Garr complaint and was waiting at the courthouse for the complaint to be filed, provides a perfect example of the sort of behavior that the majority's reasoning will encourage. Were the court to hold that facially meritorious but inadequately investigated complaints are not subject to sanction, defendants would have less incentive to file such motions. Indeed, defendants under such a regime would more likely be subject to sanction for filing an unmeritorious motion for sanctions before conducting an adequate investigation into the merit of the complaint.

\* \* \*

[With four of the thirteen judges dissenting, the court denied a petition for rehearing *en banc*. 22 F.3d 1274, 1283.]

# Chapter 21

# SALE OF CONTROL

---

## A. INTRODUCTION

"Control," as used in this and the following chapter, means the power to determine the policies of a corporation's business. Control arises in two ways, First, absent special voting rules applicable to the board of directors or to shareholders, a person who owns more than 50 percent of a corporation's stock controls that corporation because she can select a majority of the board of directors. In addition, as we saw in Chapter 17, a person who owns a large block of stock that is less than 50 percent often has *de facto* control, because she usually is in the best position to mobilize sufficient votes to elect a majority of the board unless another person owns a comparable block. If that is the case, no one may be able to exercise control through stock ownership.

Control also can arise from incumbency. In public corporations where ownership is fragmented among thousands or millions of shareholders, incumbent directors and managers usually possess *de facto* control because of their power to choose management's candidates for election as directors. They also can use corporate resources to support election of those candidates. As you read the following materials, consider which type of control is at issue.

Control is valuable; the power to dictate how corporate resources should be used makes it possible for a controlling person to eliminate many of the agency costs associated with the divorce of ownership from control. Persons who control a company often can command a premium price when they seek to sell their stock, because of the power to exercise control. In addition, a non-controlling person who believes those who currently control a company are not managing it efficiently may find it attractive to purchase control, even at a substantial premium over current market prices, with a view to better employing the company's assets and thereby increasing the company's profits. Similarly, an outsider may pay a premium to acquire control of a company whose operations she believes she can efficiently integrate with the operations of other companies she controls.

Acquiring control also may be attractive for less legitimate reasons. Control can be exploited. A controlling person may find it easy to misappropriate a corporation's assets, to appoint herself and her associates to corporate offices and pay themselves excessive compensation, or to cause the corporation to transact business on unfair terms with other entities that she or her associates own or control. To be sure, the duties of care and loyalty apply to a controlling person's decisions regarding these and similar matters. But breaches of those duties often are difficult to detect, challenge, or remedy. Consequently, when control is sold at a premium price, one must consider whether the transaction serves some legitimate end, or whether the acquiror is paying the premium as a kind of "bribe" to obtain a position in which she can enrich herself at the expense of a corporation's remaining shareholders and, if she bankrupts the corporation, at the expense of creditors as well.

The difficulty comes in distinguishing between legitimate and improper transfers of control. Every sale of stock by a controlling person, if it is accompanied by the departure of the controlling person from the company, necessarily carries with it a change in management and dominion over the company's assets. If more than 50% of the stock is sold, the investment properties and the control properties of that stock are inseparable. It is impossible to sell one without selling the other. It almost defies nature to say that, in such circumstances, one can sell stock but cannot sell control.

Transactions involving a sale of stock accompanied by a sale of control have troubled legal commentators for years. Professor Adolf A. Berle theorized that the control element of a controlling person's stock is an asset belonging to the corporation. He observed that the value of control stemmed from the fact that corporations may act without the consent of all shareholders, so long as the requisite majority approves the action in question. Therefore, he maintained, the corporate mechanism imparts value to some stock, when combined in sufficient numbers, that is not possessed by other stock. This added value, he concluded, should belong to the corporation. *See* Adolf A. Berle, Jr. & Gardiner Means, THE MODERN CORPORATION AND PRIVATE PROPERTY 207–52 (rev. ed. 1968). The implication of Berle's theory is that the premium that the seller of a control block is entitled to keep is limited to the relatively modest cost of assembling the control block. Any excess belongs to the corporation.

Other commentators believe that exploitation of minority shareholders presents the greatest danger. William D. Andrews, *The Stockholder's Right to Equal Opportunity in the Sale of Shares*, 78 HARV. L.REV. 505 (1965), argues that "a controlling shareholder should not be free to sell, at least to an outsider, except pursuant to a purchase offer made equally available to other shareholders." Id. at 506. Other commentators maintain that the law should impose few if any restrictions on transfers of control because most such transfers are beneficial; they move corporate resources into the hands of those who value them most highly and therefore are apt to utilize them most efficiently. Frank E. Easterbrook

& Daniel R. Fischel, *Corporate Control Transactions*, 91 YALE L.J. 698, 698 (1982) assert "that those who produce a gain [through a transfer of control] should be allowed to keep it, subject to the constraint that other parties to the transaction be at least as well off as before the transaction." Consequently, "[a]ny attempt to require sharing simply reduces the likelihood that there will be gains to share." *Id.*

More recently, Einer Elhauge has pointed out that the rules advanced by Andrews and by Easterbrook and Fischel both may serve useful purposes, but that both also have drawbacks. Any rule designed to facilitate transfers of control also is certain to facilitate some potentially exploitative transactions, while any rule designed to discourage all exploitative transfers of control surely will deter some potentially beneficial transactions. Consequently, Professor Elhauge suggests, the debate should focus not on absolutes, but on the trade-offs involved. See Einer Elhauge, *The Triggering Function of Sale of Control Doctrine*, 59 U. CHI. L. REV. 1465 (1992).

Courts also largely have rejected the extreme positions. The basic rule is that control can be sold at a premium price. Only in special circumstances does this rule not apply. The New York Court of Appeals has summarized this rule as follows:

> Recognizing that those who invest the capital necessary to acquire a dominant position in the ownership of a corporation have the right of controlling that corporation, it has long been settled law that, absent looting of corporate assets, conversion of a corporate opportunity, fraud or other acts of bad faith, a controlling stockholder is free to sell, and a purchaser is free to buy, that controlling interest at a premium price.

*Zetlin v. Hanson Holdings, Inc.*, 48 N.Y.2d 684, 685, 421 N.Y.S.2d 877, 878, 397 N.E.2d 387, 388 (1979).

## PROBLEM
### GOTHAM TRIBUNE

Gotham Tribune, Inc. (GTI), publisher of the Gotham Tribune, is a publicly owned Columbia corporation whose stock is traded on the New York Stock Exchange. In recent months the price of the stock has been fairly stable at about $15 per share. Burt and Ernie, sons of the founder of the paper, each owns 15 percent of the stock and holds office as co-chief executive of GTI. GTI has 10 million shares of common stock outstanding.

GTI Timber, Inc., a wholly-owned subsidiary of GTI, owns substantial timber property in Canada and is a large producer of newsprint. Timber supplies all of the Tribune's needs and sells to other users as well. The Tribune pays the same price as Timber's other customers. There is a growing shortage of newsprint and prices are on the rise. For this reason and others, the Tribune has contributed a relatively declining amount to GTI's profits and Timber has contributed increasingly more. GTI earned $15 million, or $1.50 per share last year, of which $5 million was contributed by Timber. Were it not for Timber, GTI stock probably would sell for six or seven times its remaining earnings of $1.00 per share. Timber, as an independent company, probably would sell for $8.00 to $9.00 per share. However, the Tribune is the pride of GTI's management and is generally acclaimed to be one of the region's finest papers.

World Publishers, Inc. publishes more than 50 newspapers. Most of them are highly profitable; all are very different from the Tribune. Some of the differences suggest why those papers are more profitable than the Tribune. The papers are directed at a mass market; they emphasize the sensational; and they rely heavily on wire services, rather than separate and expensive news gathering bureaus, for national and international news.

World recently offered to buy Timber from GTI for $50 million in cash and long-term debentures, subject to a commitment to continue supplying newsprint of the Tribune. GTI's board, composed of Burt, Ernie, GTI's attorney, the president of Timber and five business people who have no other connection with GTI, voted unanimously to reject World's offer as inadequate, since it was only ten times Timber's earnings for the prior year.

World then approached Burt and Ernie and offered to buy their stock for $21 per share, or a total of $63 million. Burt wanted to accept the offer; he is anxious to get out of the newspaper business and enter politics. Ernie, however, initially decided not to sell. That appeared to scuttle the deal, since World's offer was for both their shares.

Ernie subsequently became apprehensive that World might make another offer to Burt or might make a tender offer directly to GTI's public shareholders, which could leave him as a minority stockholder with little influence over GTI. Moreover, World agreed that if Ernie stepped down as co-CEO, it would continue him as a director and as publisher of the Tribune, at a salary higher than his present salary. Under these circumstances, Ernie tentatively agreed with Burt to accept World's $63 million offer.

As part of their contract with World, Burt and Ernie also would have to arrange for GTI's other directors to resign seriatim and for a slate of candidates suggested by World to be elected in their stead.* Burt and Ernie know little about any of World's candidates. They are aware that World's CEO has a reputation as a flamboyant entrepreneur. They also are familiar with the details of an exposé the Tribune published last year linking World's second-in-command to payoffs of labor racketeers tied to newspaper distribution companies.

Before proceeding to sign a contract with World, Ernie has sought the advice of counsel. The partner in charge of this matter has sent you a memorandum setting forth the facts stated above and further noting:

---

* Seriatim replacement of directors works as follows: If the board consists of A, B and C, who agree to elect X, Y and Z in their place, first A resigns and B and C elect X. Then B resigns and C and X elect Y. C then resigns and X and Y elect Z.

This is the kind of situation for which shareholder's suits are made, and I have advised our client of the high probability of litigation. I asked Ernie whether World could be induced to pay the same price for all GTI stock now held by public shareholders; he said World has made clear they are not willing to proceed in that fashion. That eliminates what probably would be the best way to minimize litigation problems.

Assume that Ernie wants to go forward only if we conclude that he is likely to prevail in any lawsuits that may be brought by GTI shareholders. The threshold issue is whether this transaction involves a sale of control. Assuming it does, could shareholders sustain claims of looting, sale of corporate office, or usurpation of corporate opportunity or other breaches of fiduciary duty. Is there anything that Ernie should do prior to closing to protect himself against such claims? Does he have any responsibility for what happens to GTI or its shareholders after World assumes control? Could a shareholder successfully claim that by giving World control of Timber, Ernie has converted a corporate opportunity into a personal profit? Even if we assume that Ernie will take any protective actions that we believe are necessary, can he nonetheless be required to give up some or all of the premium he will receive for his stock? If so, is there some other way to restructure the deal so as to avoid such liability?

Prepare to respond to the partner's questions.

## B.  THE DUTY OF CARE IN THE SALE OF CONTROL

### SWINNEY v. KEEBLER CO.

480 F.2d 573 (4th Cir.1973).

WINTER, CIRCUIT JUDGE.

[Plaintiffs were holders of defaulted debentures of Meadors, Inc. who brought a class action against Meadors and prior owners of its stock to obtain payment of the debentures or recover damages equal to the amounts unpaid. The district court found for plaintiffs.]

Since Keebler is the only defendant who has appealed, we will confine our consideration to the case against it. The district court found that, in connection with the successive sales of Meadors' stock from Keebler to Atlantic to Flora Mir Distributing, Meadors had been looted by Atlantic and its corporate assets dissipated, with the result, among others, that the interest and principal of the debentures were in default. Although the district court made no finding that Keebler had looted Meadors and, indeed, made no finding of any intentional wrongdoing on the part of Keebler, it nevertheless held Keebler liable for violation of its obligation to Meadors and Meadors' debenture holders "[i]n light of all the circumstances known to Keebler * * * to conduct such investigation of the purchaser [Atlantic] as would convince a reasonable man that the sale was legitimate, or to refrain from making the sale." *Swinney v. Keebler Company*, 329 F.Supp. 216, 224 (D.S.C.1971).

We disagree that the circumstances were such as to give rise to an obligation on the part of Keebler to conduct an investigation of Atlantic beyond that which was actually conducted or to refrain from making the sale. Accordingly, we reverse and direct the entry of judgment for Keebler.

## I.

Briefly stated, Keebler bought the stock of Meadors, a candy manufacturer, on August 7, 1963. At the time of the purchase, Meadors was in serious financial trouble and its debentures had a book value of less than one-half of their principal amount. Keebler operated Meadors, manufacturing and distributing candy and causing it to engage in other profitable operations so as to utilize a substantial tax loss carryback. By February, 1968, Meadors had total assets of $581,491, including cash of $321,337, and a net worth of $230,000.

Prior to February, 1968, Keebler decided to withdraw from the manufacture of candy, but not its sale and distribution, and it concluded to sell Meadors. It employed a broker to find a buyer and subsequently began negotiations with Flora Mir Candy.

Negotiations with Flora Mir Candy proceeded to the point where the buyer was preparing to purchase Meadors for $176,000, although not all aspects of the transaction had been agreed upon, when on February 9, 1968, a Keebler officer, Mr. Chester Burchsted, received a telephone call from a broker, Mr. Olen, who indicated that Atlantic might be interested in purchasing Meadors.

Burchsted and Olen met in the Newark airport on the morning of February 14, 1968, and as a result of the meeting an afternoon session was arranged in New York at the offices of Keebler's lawyers between Atlantic's counsel, Ivan Ezrine, Esquire, and several representatives of Keebler, including Edward Vincek, Esquire, Keebler's general counsel. In the meantime, Keebler's negotiations with Flora Mir Candy were suspended.

During the afternoon meeting, Keebler's various representatives questioned Ezrine concerning Atlantic, its financing structure and its corporate and financial history. Ezrine told Keebler that Atlantic was a prospering small holding company which was becoming a conglomerate and wanted to diversify by expanding into the candy business. Ezrine gave Keebler recent unaudited financial statements, prepared by certified public accountants, which showed that Atlantic had a net worth of $997,000 as of December 31, 1967, and net income of $158,588 for that calendar year.

At the February 14 meeting, Keebler and Atlantic negotiated an agreement for the sale of Meadors' stock, and the agreement was executed that day or the next. The contract documents were patterned largely on those which had been prepared while the negotiations with Flora Mir Candy were continuing. Among other things, the following agreements were reached: (1) the sales price was set at $235,000, (2) Atlantic represented its financial statement of December 31, 1967 as true, correct, and prepared in accordance with generally accepted accounting principles, (3) Atlantic promised, as a condition of the sale, that its financial strength on the closing date would be substantially the same or better than shown in its December 31, 1967 statements, (4) Atlantic agreed to guarantee Meadors' accounts payable and accruals, (5) Atlantic agreed to guarantee payment of the interest and principal of the Meadors' seven percent subordinated debentures, and (6) Atlantic agreed to indemnify Keebler from any liability arising out of the sale.

Keebler, for its part, warranted as true and correct its representations including the Meadors' balance sheet, the list of outstanding contracts and the list of Meadors' tangible properties. Keebler promised to use its best efforts to retain Meadors' personnel except officers and directors who were Keebler's nominees, and it agreed to purchase $562,000 worth of candy from Meadors within the ensuing nine-month period.

The closing was held in Greenville, South Carolina, on February 19. Prior thereto, Atlantic sent its certified public accountant to the Meadors' plant twice to inspect it. The accountant found a minor discrepancy in the properties of Meadors and the parties agreed to a $5,000 reduction in the ultimate purchase price paid by Atlantic on that account. Once at the negotiating session and once prior to the closing, Ezrine inquired of Vincek as to the possibility of making some arrangement to avoid Atlantic's bringing the funds for consummation of the transaction from New York. Both times Vincek rejected the suggestion and advised Ezrine that it was Atlantic's responsibility to finance the purchase.

At the closing, various documents were executed and delivered, including a licensing agreement which permitted Meadors to use Keebler's "Kitchen Rich" trademark under which Meadors' candy had been sold, and a detailed bill of sale conveying to Meadors all machinery and equipment theretofore on lease from Keebler. Although there was no evidence to show that Keebler was aware of what had transpired, Atlantic made a one-day borrowing of $235,000 from the People's National Bank, a bank in Greenville where Meadors had its account. Atlantic deposited the loan proceeds in an account in its name, then bought a $230,000 banker's check drawn on a New York bank in favor of Keebler for the adjusted purchase price. After the closing, Atlantic transferred $310,000 from the Meadors' account to its own account and repaid the loan. The transfer of funds was shown on Meadors' books as a loan to Atlantic—an account receivable—and on Atlantic's books as a loan from Meadors—an account payable.

Keebler had nothing further to do with Meadors after the closing except for the purchase of candy pursuant to the candy contract.

Atlantic retained ownership of Meadors for approximately four months and repaid approximately $33,200 of its loan. During this period, Meadors paid its trade accounts and made a profit of approximately $19,000. Atlantic's efforts to build up an independent sales force and find markets for its candy other than Keebler were largely unsuccessful, and Atlantic then sold the stock to Flora Mir Distributing, a subsidiary of Flora Mir Candy, on June 25, 1968, for a purchase price of $352,000. At that closing, Atlantic's accounts payable to Meadors was repaid; but Flora Mir Distributing, perpetuating the pattern established by Atlantic, thereafter withdrew funds from Meadors, reflected on Meadors' books as a loan to Flora Mir Distributing. Flora Mir Distributing acquired other candy companies, and Flora Mir Distributing treated itself and its subsidiaries as a single company, transferring monies and properties from one to the other. Initially, the group experienced success with their combined operations, but ultimately the combination became short of working capital and went into bankruptcy.

## II.

The parties do not seriously dispute the applicable law. The district court correctly, we think, drew upon the leading case of *Insuranshares Corporation v. Northern Fiscal Corporation*, 35 F.Supp. 22 (E.D.Pa. 1940), which held the sellers of a controlling interest in a corporation liable to the corporation when the buyers proceeded to loot it after their acquisition of control. Liability was predicated upon breach of a duty not to transfer control since the circumstances surrounding the transfer were "such as to awaken suspicion and put a prudent man on his guard—unless a reasonably adequate investigation discloses such facts as would convince a reasonable person that no fraud is intended or likely to result." 35 F.Supp. at 25.

In *Insuranshares,* the suspicious circumstances included (1) the defendants' probable knowledge that the purchase was to be financed by a pledge of the corporation's assets, (2) the corporation's president's clear predisposition to allow a sale to be financed by pledging those assets as security, (3) defendants' awareness of the purchasers' plan to have a large part of the corporation's assets converted into cash prior to the sale, (4) the inflated price or premium paid for control, especially given the nature of the business which was an investment trust with no physical assets but only the ready equivalent of cash in the form of marketable securities, (5) warnings from the sellers' attorneys as to their potential liabilities for dealing with little-known purchasers, and (6) the fact that the corporation had been looted five years before by a different group who had gained control by using the same method of financing.

The standard of conduct to which *Insuranshares* holds controlling transferors had been widely accepted. Generally, the owner of corporate stock may dispose of his shares as he sees fit. A dominant or majority stockholder does not become a fiduciary for other stockholders *merely* by owning stock. In selling their stock, the stockholders necessarily act for themselves, and not as trustees for the other stockholders. But majority stockholders who assume the management of the corporation, as Keebler did here, can be said to stand in fiduciary relation to the minority under certain circumstances. Thus, while the majority is not an absolute insurer against any wrongs which may be done to the corporation after the transfer of control or against any decisions by the new owners that may not be in the best interest of the minority, if the sellers of control are in a position to foresee the likelihood of fraud on the corporation, including its creditors, or on the remaining stockholders, at the hands of the transferee, their fiduciary duty imposes a positive duty to investigate the motives and reputation of the would-be purchaser; and unless such a reasonable investigation shows that to a reasonable man no fraud is intended or likely to result, the sellers must refrain from the transfer of control.

## III.

In light of the facts and applicable law, plaintiffs' right to recover turns on whether Keebler had sufficient knowledge to foresee the likelihood of fraud so as to give rise to a duty to conduct a further investigation and to satisfy itself, by the test of a reasonable man, that no fraud was intended or likely to result before it consummated the sale of control. The district court identified essentially seven circumstances which "might have indicated [to Keebler] that Atlantic Services had no intention of operating Meadors * * *." 329 F.Supp. at 220. These factors were: (1) no one from Atlantic had any experience in the candy business, (2) at the time the contract was executed no one from Atlantic had inspected the "Meadors operation," (3) by the time of the closing, only Atlantic's accountant had examined Meadors to "any appreciable extent and he was interested principally in the books and inventory," (4) Meadors had no market of its own and the "profit as shown could not have been accepted at face value by an outsider," (5) prior to the closing Atlantic had no negotiations with Meadors' key employees concerning the continuation of the business, (6) the sale was consummated with dispatch, and (7) Atlantic had inquired as to the availability of Meadors' funds for payment of the purchase price. Although the district court concluded that the first five factors were "not necessarily inconsistent with a legitimate sale of a business the size of Meadors," it held that when coupled with facts six and seven, they "were more than sufficient to arouse the suspicion of Keebler."

We think that the findings of fact relied on by the district court to conclude that Keebler was liable to Meadors' debenture holders were insufficient to support that result. We will comment on them seriatim.

From Keebler's point of view, the fact that no one from Atlantic had any experience in the candy business should not have been suspicious. Atlantic was represented to Keebler as a holding and investment company which did business through subsidiaries. A conglomerate, which Atlantic professed to be aspiring, regularly acquires diverse businesses; and in any event, it is not unusual for any corporation to venture into a new business field. Meadors was an integrated functioning enterprise with management and equipment in place, and Keebler agreed, except with respect to Meadors' officers and directors, which were Keebler personnel, to use its best efforts to maintain intact other personnel of Meadors then on Meadors' payroll. As a result of Keebler's agreement to purchase candy for a nine-month period, Keebler could assume that Meadors would have, at least for the short run, a ready market for candy and an opportunity to recruit and train a sales force.

No suspicion should have been aroused from the fact that no one from Atlantic inspected the Meadors' operation prior to execution of the contract, and that at the time of closing, only Atlantic's accountant had examined Meadors to any appreciable extent. Atlantic's broker, Olen, who first telephoned Keebler's Burchsted, had some familiarity with Meadors, albeit apparently obtained from the broker retained by Keebler. Keebler made extensive warranties concerning the plant and its financial operations and were these warranties untrue, Atlantic might have rescinded the sale or sued for damages. A sufficient inspection prior to closing was made so that the parties agreed to a $5,000 reduction in the purchase price. From Keebler's point of view, Atlantic's reliance on its broker, on Keebler's warranties, and on Atlantic's accountant's inspections was hardly a circumstance indicative of an intention not to operate, much less of an intention to loot.

We see nothing suspicious in the fact that Meadors had no market of its own, and we do not agree that the profit as shown on Meadors' financial statements could not have been accepted at face value by an outsider. While Meadors' past profit history may have been somewhat questionable, its operation by Keebler was profitable, and Keebler warranted Meadors' balance sheet at the time of closing. There is no question but that Keebler's agreement to purchase candy provided Meadors with a substantial initial market, and Keebler could have reasonably assumed that during the period and with the financial support of its purchase of candy, Meadors could build up its own market. Keebler cannot be held liable as a result of its failure to sell Meadors to a company with a candy market already well developed. Only a small portion of the business community could live under such a restrictive rule with regard to the purchase and sale of business enterprises.

Nor do we find significant the fact that prior to closing, Atlantic conducted no negotiations with key employees then operating Meadors relative to their continuation of the business. Keebler contracted to use its best efforts to retain them as employees, and Atlantic did retain them after it took over. The wisdom of Atlantic's failure to negotiate with them prior to closing is not in issue—only its impact on Keebler as a "suspicious circumstance" is significant. Since Keebler owned Meadors, had full power to sell the company, and agreed to do its part in keeping the enterprise intact, we do not think that Keebler was confronted with a suspicious circumstance.

The dispatch with which the sale was consummated was not suspicious. In the first place, no reason to delay closing has been suggested. In any event, any haste was principally that of Keebler's making and not that of Atlantic. Keebler had been prepared to sell Meadors to Flora Mir Candy; active negotiations were being carried on and legal papers to consummate the transaction were in the course of preparation when Atlantic appeared on the scene. When agreement with Atlantic was reached, Keebler was pressing to consummate a more profitable transaction in lieu of a less profitable one before the latter was irrevocably lost.

The inquiries made by Atlantic with regard to the availability of Meadors' funds for payment of the purchase price were not such as to provide a basis on which Keebler could suspect how payment would be made, especially since Keebler made its position clear that Atlantic must consummate the purchase with its own funds. It is true that the record shows that Atlantic did not do so, but the record does not disclose an evidentiary basis to find, nor did the district court find, that Keebler knew or had reason to know of Atlantic's one-day loan and its immediate repayment with Meadors' funds. Whatever inkling Keebler may have had that Atlantic was interested in using Meadors' cash did not rise to a level sufficient to necessitate further investigation, especially in light of Atlantic's seemingly strong financial position and its apparent ability to finance the transaction with its own monies.

Overall, we conclude that the seven factors considered singly or in concert, were not sufficient to suggest to Keebler that Atlantic did not intend to operate Meadors, but rather intended to loot it. As our discussion of the findings relied on to support the contrary conclusion discloses, there were many positive indications that Atlantic intended to operate Meadors and to operate it profitably. In addition, Atlantic's guarantee of the payment of principal of and interest on Meadors' debentures was significant, especially in the light of Atlantic's apparent financial ability to fulfill that commitment. It follows, we think, that Keebler's obligation to conduct a further investigation sufficient to satisfy a reasonable man that no fraud was intended or likely to result, or to refrain from the transfer of control, did not arise. The obligation could not have been breached, so that there was therefore no basis to impose liability on Keebler.

Reversed.

### Note: Liability for Looting

Why should the *seller* rather than the buyer be liable if it is the buyer who engages in looting? In *Harris v. Carter*, 582 A.2d 222 (Del.Ch.1990), Chancellor Allen suggested that the principle of *Insuranshares*, on which the court relied in *Swinney v. Keebler Co.*, is grounded in tort law:

> [I]t does not follow from the proposition that ordinarily a shareholder has a right to sell her stock to whom and on such terms as she deems expedient, that no duty may arise from the particular circumstances to take care in the exercise of that right. It is established American legal doctrine that, unless privileged, each

person owes a duty to those who may foreseeably be harmed by her action to take such steps as a reasonably prudent person would take in similar circumstances to avoid such harm to others. While this principle arises from the law of torts and not the law of corporations or of fiduciary duties, that distinction is not, I think, significant unless the law of corporations or of fiduciary duties somehow privileges a selling shareholder by exempting her from the reach of this principle. The principle itself is one of great generality and, if not negated by privilege, would apply to a controlling shareholder who negligently places others foreseeably in the path of injury.

That a shareholder may sell her stock (or that a director may resign his office) is a right that, with respect to the principle involved, is no different, for example, than the right that a licensed driver has to operate a motor vehicle upon a highway. The right exists, but it is not without conditions and limitations, some established by positive regulation, some by common-law. Thus, to continue the parallel, the driver owes a duty of care to her passengers because it is foreseeable that they may be injured if, through inattention or otherwise, the driver involves the car she is operating in a collision. In the typical instance a seller of corporate stock can be expected to have no similar apprehension of risks to others from her own inattention. But, in some circumstances, the seller of a control block of stock may or should reasonably foresee danger to other shareholders; with her sale of stock will also go control over the corporation and with it the opportunity to misuse that power to the injury of such other shareholders. Thus, the reason that a duty of care is recognized in any situation is fully present in this situation. I can find no universal privilege arising from the corporate form that exempts a controlling shareholder who sells corporate control from the wholesome reach of this common-law duty. * * *

Thus, I conclude that while a person who transfers corporate control to another is surely not a surety for his buyer, when the circumstances would alert a reasonably prudent person to a risk that his buyer is dishonest or in some material respect not truthful, a duty devolves upon the seller to make such inquiry as a reasonably prudent person would make, and generally to exercise care so that others who will be affected by his actions should not be injured by wrongful conduct.

*Id.* at 234–35.

One question, of course, is in what circumstances "may or should [a selling shareholder] reasonably foresee danger to other shareholders?" In particular, does a purchaser's payment of a large premium trigger a duty to investigate? *Clagett v. Hutchison*, 583 F.2d 1259, 1262 (4th Cir.1978), held that payment of $34.75 per share for a majority interest in a race track corporation whose shares had been trading for $7.50 to $10.00 could "not be said to be so unreasonable as to place [the seller] on notice of the likelihood of fraud * * *." The court found it "farfetched" that a purchaser would pay a 400% premium to acquire control of a corporation simply to loot it. Do you agree?

It should be noted that computation of the liability of a shareholder who wrongfully sells control to a looter is consistent with a tort rationale. That is, the liability of the selling shareholder is equal to the loss suffered by the corporation, not merely to the premium she received.

# C.  SALE OF CORPORATE OFFICE

## ESSEX UNIVERSAL CORP. v. YATES

305 F.2d 572 (2d Cir.1962).

[Plaintiff contracted to purchase defendant's 28.3% interest in Republic Pictures for $8 per share, approximately $2 above the price at which the stock sold on the New York Stock Exchange. The contract required the seller to deliver resignations of a majority of Republic's directors and to cause the election of persons designated by the buyer. The seller refused to go ahead with this condition and claimed as a defense in a suit for breach of contract that to do so would be illegal.

The court unanimously reversed a judgment for defendant, but its decision is reflected in three separate opinions.]

LUMBARD, CHIEF JUDGE.

It is established beyond question under New York law that it is illegal to sell a corporate office or management control by itself (that is, accompanied by no stock or insufficient stock to carry voting control). The rationale of the rule is undisputable: persons enjoying management control hold it on behalf of the corporation's stockholders, and therefore may not regard it as their own personal property to dispose of as they wish. Any other rule would violate the most fundamental principle of corporate democracy, that management must represent and be chosen by, or at least with the consent of, those who own the corporation.

Essex was, however, contracting with Yates for the purchase of a very substantial percentage of Republic stock. If, by virtue of the voting power carried by this stock, it could have elected a majority of the board of directors, then the contract was not a simple agreement for the sale of office to one having no ownership interest in the corporation, and the question of its legality would require further analysis. Such stock voting control would incontestably belong to the owner of a majority of the voting stock, and it is commonly known that equivalent power usually accrues to the owner of 28.3% of the stock. For the purpose of this analysis, I shall assume that Essex was contracting to acquire a majority of the Republic stock, deferring consideration of the situation where, as here, only 28.3% is to be acquired.

Republic's board of directors at the time of the aborted closing had fourteen members divided into three classes, each class being "as nearly as may be" of the same size. Directors were elected for terms of three years, one class being elected at each annual shareholder meeting on the first Tuesday in April. Thus, absent the immediate replacement of directors provided for in this contract, Essex as the hypothetical new majority shareholder of the corporation could not have obtained managing control in the form of a majority of the board in the normal course of events until April 1959, some eighteen months after the sale of the stock. The first question before us then is whether an agreement to accelerate the transfer of management control, in a manner legal in form under the corporation's charter and by-laws, violates the public policy of New York.

There is no question of the right of a controlling shareholder under New York law normally to derive a premium from the sale of a controlling block of stock. In other words, there was no impropriety *per se* in the fact that Yates was to receive more per share than the generally prevailing market price for Republic stock.

The next question is whether it is legal to give and receive payment for the immediate transfer of management control to one who has achieved majority share control but would not otherwise be able to convert that share control into operating control for some time. I think that it is.

\* \* \*

A fair generalization from these cases may be that a holder of corporate control will not, as a fiduciary, be permitted to profit from facilitating actions on the part of the purchasers of control which are detrimental to the interests of the corporation or the remaining shareholders. There is, however, no suggestion that the transfer of control over Republic to Essex carried any such threat to the interests of the corporation or its other shareholders.

Given this principle that it is permissible for a seller thus to choose to facilitate immediate transfer of management control, I can see no objection to a contractual provision requiring him to do so as a condition of the sale. Indeed, a New York court has upheld an analogous contractual term requiring the board of directors to elect the nominees of the purchasers of a majority stock interest to officerships. San Remo Copper Mining Co. v. Moneuse, 149 App.Div. 26, 133 N.Y.S. 509 (1st Dept.1912). The court said that since the purchaser was about to acquire "absolute control" of the corporation, "it certainly did not destroy the validity of the contract that by one of its terms defendant was to be invested with this power of control at once, upon acquiring the stock, instead of waiting for the next annual meeting."

\* \* \*

The easy and immediate transfer of corporate control to new interests is ordinarily beneficial to the economy and it seems inevitable that such transactions would be discouraged if the purchaser of a majority stock interest were required to wait some period before his purchase of control could become effective. Conversely it would greatly hamper the efforts of any existing majority group to dispose of its interest if it could

not assure the purchaser of immediate control over corporation operations. I can see no reason why a purchaser of majority control should not
ordinarily be permitted to make his control effective from the moment of
the transfer of stock.

\* \* \*

Because 28.3 per cent of the voting stock of a publicly owned
corporation is usually tantamount to majority control, I would place the
burden of proof on this issue on Yates as the party attacking the legality
of the transaction. Thus, unless on remand Yates chooses to raise the
question whether the block of stock in question carried the equivalent of
majority control, it is my view that the trial court should regard the
contract as legal and proceed to consider the other issues raised by the
pleadings. If Yates chooses to raise the issue, it will, on my view, be
necessary for him to prove the existence of circumstances which would
have prevented Essex from electing a majority of the Republic board of
directors in due course. It will not be enough for Yates to raise merely
hypothetical possibilities of opposition by the other Republic shareholders to Essex' assumption of management control. Rather, it will be
necessary for him to show that, assuming neutrality on the part of the
retiring management, there was at the time some concretely foreseeable
reason why Essex' wishes would not have prevailed in shareholder
voting held in due course. In other words, I would require him to show
that there was at the time of the contract some other organized block of
stock of sufficient size to outvote the block Essex was buying, or else
some circumstance making it likely that enough of the holders of the
remaining Republic stock would band together to keep Essex from
control.

Reversed and remanded for further proceedings not inconsistent
with the judgment of this court.

CLARK, CIRCUIT JUDGE (concurring in the result).

Since *Barnes v. Brown*, 80 N.Y. 527, teaches us that not all contracts
like the one before us are necessarily illegal, summary judgment seems
definitely improper and the action should be remanded for trial. But
particularly in view of our lack of knowledge of corporate realities and
the current standards of business morality, I should prefer to avoid too
precise instructions to the district court in the hope that if the action
again comes before us the record will be generally more instructive on
this important issue than it now is. I share all the doubts and questions
stated by my brothers in their opinions and perhaps have some additional ones of my own. My concern is lest we may be announcing abstract
moral principles which have little validity in daily business practice other
than to excuse a defaulting vendor from performance of his contract of
sale. Thus for fear of a possible occasional contract inimical to general
stockholder interest we may be condemning out of hand what are more
often normal and even desirable business relationships. As at present
advised I would think that the best we can do is to consider each case on

its own facts and with the normal presumption that he who asserts illegality must prove it.

\* \* \*

FRIENDLY, CIRCUIT JUDGE (concurring).

Chief Judge Lumbard's thoughtful opinion illustrates a difficulty, inherent in our dual judicial system, which has led at least one state to authorize its courts to answer questions about its law that a Federal court may ask. Here we are forced to decide a question of New York law, of enormous importance to all New York corporations and their stockholders, on which there is hardly enough New York authority for a really informed prediction what the New York Court of Appeals would decide on the facts here presented.

I have no doubt that many contracts, drawn by competent and responsible counsel, for the purchase of blocks of stock from interests thought to "control" a corporation although owning less than a majority, have contained provisions like paragraph 6 of the contract\* *sub judice.* However, developments over the past decades seem to me to show that such a clause violates basic principles of corporate democracy. To be sure, stockholders who have allowed a set of directors to be placed in office, whether by their vote or their failure to vote, must recognize that death, incapacity or other hazard may prevent a director from serving a full term, and that they will have no voice as to his immediate successor. But the stockholders are entitled to expect that, in that event, the remaining directors will fill the vacancy in the exercise of their fiduciary responsibility. A mass seriatim resignation directed by a selling stockholder, and the filling of vacancies by his henchmen at the dictation of a purchaser and without any consideration of the character of the latter's nominees, are beyond what the stockholders contemplated or should have been expected to contemplate. This seems to me a wrong to the corporation and the other stockholders which the law ought not countenance, whether the selling stockholder has received a premium or not. Right in this Court we have seen many cases where sudden shifts of corporate control have caused serious injury. To hold the seller for delinquencies of the new directors only if he knew the purchaser was an intending looter is not a sufficient sanction. The difficulties of proof are formidable even if receipt of too high a premium creates a presumption of such knowledge, and, all too often, the doors are locked only after the horses have been stolen. Stronger medicines are needed—refusal to enforce a contract with such a clause, even though this confers an unwarranted benefit on a defaulter, and continuing responsibility of the former directors for negligence of the new ones until an election has been held. Such prophylactics are not contraindicated, as Judge Lumbard suggests, by the conceded desirability of preventing the dead hand of a former "controlling" group from continuing to dominate the board

---

\* Paragraph 6 provided for the resignation of the old board and the election of new directors designated by the purchaser.

after a sale, or of protecting a would-be purchaser from finding himself without a majority of the board after he has spent his money. A special meeting of stockholders to replace a board may always be called, and there could be no objection to making the closing of a purchase contingent on the results of such an election. I perceive some of the difficulties of mechanics such a procedure presents, but I have enough confidence in the ingenuity of the corporate bar to believe these would be surmounted.

Hence, I am inclined to think that if I were sitting on the New York Court of Appeals, I would hold a provision like Paragraph 6 violative of public policy save when it was entirely plain that a new election would be a mere formality—i.e., when the seller owned more than 50% of the stock. I put it thus tentatively because, before making such a decision, I would want the help of briefs, including those of *amici curiae*, dealing with the serious problems of corporate policy and practice more fully than did those here, which were primarily devoted to argument as to what the New York law has been rather than what it ought to be. Moreover, in view of the perhaps unexpected character of such a holding, I doubt that I would give it retrospective effect.

As a judge of this Court, my task is the more modest one of predicting how the judges of the New York Court of Appeals would rule, and I must make this prediction on the basis of legal materials rather than of personal acquaintance or hunch. Also, for obvious reasons, the prospective technique is unavailable when a Federal court is deciding an issue of state law. Although *Barnes v. Brown*, 80 N.Y. 527 (1880), dealt with the sale of a majority interest, I am unable to find any real indication that the doctrine there announced has been thus limited. True, there are New York cases saying that the sale of corporate offices is forbidden; but the New York decisions do not tell us what this means and I can find nothing, save perhaps one unexplained sentence in the opinion of a trial court in *Ballantine v. Ferretti*, 28 N.Y.S.2d 668, 682 (1941), to indicate that New York would not apply Barnes v. Brown to a case where a stockholder with much less than a majority conditioned a sale on his causing the resignation of a majority of the directors and the election of the purchaser's nominees.

Chief Judge Lumbard's proposal goes part of the way toward meeting the policy problem I have suggested. Doubtless proceeding from what, as it seems to me, is the only justification in principle for permitting even a majority stockholder to condition a sale on delivery of control of the board—namely that in such a case a vote of the stockholders would be a useless formality, he sets the allowable bounds at the line where there is "a practical certainty" that the buyer would be able to elect his nominees and, in this case, puts the burden of disproving that on the person claiming illegality.

Attractive as the proposal is in some respects, I find difficulties with it. One is that I discern no sufficient intimation of the distinction in the New York cases, or even in the writers, who either would go further in voiding such a clause. * * * When an issue does arise, the "practical certainty" test is difficult to apply. * * * Judge Lumbard correctly recognizes that, from a policy standpoint, the pertinent question must be the buyer's prospects of election, not the seller's—yet this inevitably requires the court to canvass the likely reaction of stockholders to a group of whom they know nothing and seems rather hard to reconcile with a position that it is "right" to insert such a condition if a seller has a larger proportion of the stock and "wrong" if he has a smaller. At the very least the problems and uncertainties arising from the proposed line of demarcation are great enough, and its advantages small enough, that in my view a Federal court would do better simply to overrule the defense here, thereby accomplishing what is obviously the "just" result in this particular case, and leave the development of doctrine in this area to the State, which has primary concern for it.

I would reverse the grant of summary judgment and remand for consideration of defenses other than a claim that the inclusion of paragraph 6 *ex mero motu* renders the contract void.

### Note: Selling Corporate Office

In *Carter v. Muscat*, 21 A.D.2d 543, 251 N.Y.S.2d 378 (1st Dept. 1964), the directors of Republic Corporation chose a new majority of the board in connection with the sale of 9.7 percent of the stock, by Republic's former management, at a price slightly above market. The sale occurred approximately nine months before the next regularly scheduled shareholders' meeting; an interim report on the board's action was furnished to shareholders. At their next meeting, the shareholders reelected the new directors. A dissident shareholder then petitioned to set the directors' election aside.

The court rejected the petition, remarking: "When a situation involving less than 50% of the ownership of stock exists, the question of what percentage of stock is sufficient to constitute working control is likely to be a matter of fact, at least in most circumstances." The interim notice and subsequent election establish that there was no deception of Republic's shareholders.

*Brecher v. Gregg*, 89 Misc.2d 457, 392 N.Y.S.2d 776 (1975), involved the sale by Gregg, the president of Lin Broadcasting Corporation, of his 4 percent stock interest to the Saturday Evening Post. Gregg also promised to resign and cause the Post's president and two others to be elected directors of Lin and the Post's president to be elected Lin's president.

A Lin shareholder sued to recover from Gregg and the other directors the premium paid by the Post. The court held Gregg, but not the other directors, liable, reasoning as follows:

> The Court concludes as a matter of law that the agreement insofar as it provided for a premium in exchange for a promise of control, with only 4% of the outstanding shares actually being transferred, was contrary to public policy and illegal.

In summary, an officer's transfer of fewer than a majority of his corporation's shares, at a price in excess of that prevailing in the market, accompanied by his promise to effect the transfer of offices and control in the corporation to the vendee, is a transaction which breaches the fiduciary duty owed the corporation and upon application to a court of equity; the officer will be made to forfeit that portion of his profit ascribable to the unlawful promise as he has been unjustly enriched; and an accounting made on behalf of the corporation, since it is, of the two, the party more entitled to the proceeds.

Since there has been no showing that the actions of any directors other than Gregg either led to any pecuniary loss to the corporation or to the realization of any personal profit or gain to themselves, it follows that they cannot be held liable jointly, or severally, with Gregg for the payment of the premium over to the corporation.

392 N.Y.S.2d at 779–82.

### Note: What Constitutes "Control"?

Claims of sale of office, almost by definition, are brought only against shareholders who possess the ability to transfer control. Do similar rules apply to a large shareholder, even a director, who is not a controlling person?

*Treadway Companies, Inc. v. Care Corp.*, 638 F.2d 357 (2d Cir.1980), involved a claim against Cowin, the largest shareholder and a director of Treadway Companies, Inc., who owned 14 percent of its stock. Treadway became the target of a takeover bid by Care Corporation. While negotiating with Care concerning sale of his stock, Cowin accepted renomination for election to Treadway's board. He also rejected an invitation to sell his stock back to Treadway because he did not think the company could afford the purchase and because he questioned whether it was proper for a director to resell his stock to the company at a premium price. Cowin subsequently sold his shares to Care for consideration having a present value of $8 a share, equal to a 35 percent premium over market.

Treadway sued to recover from Cowin his profits on the sale of his stock. The court rejected its claim:

We also conclude that Cowin breached no duty in selling his own shares to Care at a premium. Apparently Treadway's argument is that Cowin had a duty to afford the other shareholders an opportunity to participate in the sale, either because he was a director or because he was Treadway's "largest shareholder." We find both theories unpersuasive.

Treadway has pointed us to no case, and we know of none, in which a director was required, solely by reason of his status as director to account to the shareholders for profits earned on the sale of his shares.

> Ordinarily a director possesses the same right as any other stockholder to deal freely with his shares of stock and to dispose of them at such a price as he may be able to obtain, provided the director acts in good faith, since the corporation as such has no interest in its outstanding stock or in dealing in its shares among its stockholders.

3 Fletcher, [CYCLOPEDIA OF THE LAW OF PRIVATE CORPORATIONS at § 900]. There is no indication that Cowin acted other than in good faith toward Treadway and its shareholders. The district court found that Cowin did not misuse confidential information and that he did not usurp any corporate opportunity. Cowin's sale permitted Care to increase its stake in Treadway, but the district court found that neither Treadway nor its shareholders were thereby harmed in any way. Thus, we see nothing that would take this case outside the general principle that a director is free to sell his stock at whatever price he may obtain.

Nor do we find that Cowin's status as Treadway's "largest shareholder" carried with it a duty to share his premium with the other shareholders. It is true that in certain circumstances, a *controlling* shareholder may be required to account to the minority shareholders for the "control premium" he obtains upon selling his controlling shares. But Cowin was not a controlling shareholder. At the time of his sale, Cowin owned only 14% of Treadway's outstanding stock; the district court specifically found that Cowin did not have control of the corporation. Since Cowin therefore did not transfer control, he was under no duty to account for the premium he obtained.

See, also, In re Sea–Land Corporation Shareholders Litigation, 642 A.2d 792 (Del.Ch.), *aff'd* 633 A.2d 371 (Del.1993) (holding that shareholder that participated in purchase of 39.5% of Sea–Land through hostile takeover bid, but never exercised domination or control of Sea–Land, owed no fiduciary duty to Sea–Land's shareholders when it later sold its Sea–Land stock at premium price.)

## D.  SHAREHOLDER'S DUTY OF LOYALTY AND THE SALE OF CONTROL

### PERLMAN v. FELDMANN

219 F.2d 173 (2d Cir.1955), cert. denied 349 U.S.
952, 75 S.Ct. 880, 99 L.Ed. 1277 (1955).

CLARK, CHIEF JUDGE.

This is a derivative action brought by minority stockholders of Newport Steel Corporation to compel accounting for, and restitution of, allegedly illegal gains which accrued to defendants as a result of the sale in August, 1950, of their controlling interest in the corporation. The principal defendant, C. Russell Feldmann, who represented and acted for the others, members of his family [owning a total of 37%], was at that time not only the dominant stockholder, but also the chairman of the board of directors and the president of the corporation. Newport, an Indiana corporation, operated mills for the production of steel sheets for sale to manufacturers of steel products, first at Newport, Kentucky, and later also at other places in Kentucky and Ohio. The buyers, a syndicate organized as Wilport Company, a Delaware corporation, consisted of end-users of steel who were interested in securing a source of supply in a market becoming ever tighter in the Korean War. Plaintiffs contend that the consideration paid for the stock included compensation for the sale of a corporate asset, a power held in trust for the corporation by Feldmann as its fiduciary. This power was the ability to control the allocation of the corporate product in a time of short supply, through control of the board of directors; and it was effectively transferred in this sale by having Feldmann procure the resignation of his own board and the election of Wilport's nominees immediately upon consummation of the sale.

\* \* \*

The essential facts found by the trial judge are not in dispute. Newport was a relative newcomer in the steel industry with predominantly old installations which were in the process of being supplemented by more modern facilities. Except in times of extreme shortage Newport was not in a position to compete profitably with other steel mills for customers not in its immediate geographical area. Wilport, the purchasing syndicate, consisted of geographically remote end-users of steel who were interested in buying more steel from Newport than they had been able to obtain during recent periods of tight supply. The price of $20 per share was found by Judge Hincks to be a fair one for a control block of stock, although the over-the-counter market price had not exceeded $12 and the book value per share was $17.03. But this finding was limited by Judge Hincks' statement that "[w]hat value the block would have had if shorn of its appurtenant power to control distribution of the corporate product, the evidence does not show." It was also conditioned by his earlier ruling that the burden was on plaintiffs to prove a lesser value for the stock.

Both as director and as dominant stockholder, Feldmann stood in a fiduciary relationship to the corporation and to the minority stockholders as beneficiaries thereof. Although there is no Indiana case directly in point, the most closely analogous one emphasizes the close scrutiny to which Indiana subjects the conduct of fiduciaries when personal benefit may stand in the way of fulfillment of trust obligations. \* \* \*

In Indiana, then, as elsewhere, the responsibility of the fiduciary is not limited to a proper regard for the tangible balance sheet assets of the corporation, but includes the dedication of his uncorrupted business judgment for the sole benefit of the corporation, in any dealings which may adversely affect it. \* \* \*

It is true, as defendants have been at pains to point out, that this is not the ordinary case of breach of fiduciary duty. We have here no fraud, no misuse of confidential information, no outright looting of a helpless corporation. But on the other hand, we do not find compliance with that high standard which we have just stated and which we and other courts have come to expect and demand of corporate fiduciaries. In the often-quoted words of Judge Cardozo: "Many forms of conduct permissible in a workaday world for those acting at arm's length, are forbidden to those bound by fiduciary ties. A trustee is held to something stricter than the morals of the market place. Not honesty alone, but the punctilio of an honor the most sensitive, is then the standard of behavior. As to this there has developed a tradition that is unbending and inveterate. Uncompromising rigidity has been the attitude of courts of equity when petitioned to undermine the rule of undivided loyalty by the 'disintegrating erosion' of particular exceptions." *Meinhard v. Salmon, supra*, 249 N.Y. 458, 464, 164 N.E. 545, 546, 62 A.L.R. 1. The actions of defendants in siphoning off for personal gain corporate advantages to be derived from a favorable market situation do not betoken the necessary undivided loyalty owed by the fiduciary to his principal.

The corporate opportunities of whose misappropriation the minority stockholders complain need not have been an absolute certainty in order to support this action against Feldmann. If there was possibility of corporate gain, they are entitled to recover. * * *

This rationale is equally appropriate to a consideration of the benefits which Newport might have derived from the steel shortage. In the past Newport had used and profited by its market leverage by operation of what the industry had come to call the "Feldmann Plan." This consisted of securing interest-free advances from prospective purchasers of steel in return for firm commitments to them from future production. The funds thus acquired were used to finance improvements in existing plants and to acquire new installations. In the summer of 1950 Newport had been negotiating for cold-rolling facilities which it needed for a more fully integrated operation and a more marketable product, and Feldmann plan funds might well have been used toward this end.

Further, as plaintiffs alternatively suggest, Newport might have used the period of short supply to build up patronage in the geographical area in which it could compete profitably even when steel was more abundant. Either of these opportunities was Newport's, to be used to its advantage only. Only if defendants had been able to negate completely any possibility of gain by Newport could they have prevailed. It is true that a trial court finding states: "Whether or not, in August, 1950, Newport's position was such that it could have entered into 'Feldmann Plan' type transactions to procure funds and financing for the further expansion and integration of its steel facilities and whether such expansion would have been desirable for Newport, the evidence does not show." This, however, cannot avail the defendants, who—contrary to the ruling below—had the burden of proof on this issue, since fiduciaries always have the burden of proof in establishing the fairness of their dealings with trust property.

Defendants seek to categorize the corporate opportunities which might have accrued to Newport as too unethical to warrant further consideration. It is true that reputable steel producers were not participating in the gray market brought about by the Korean War and were refraining from advancing their prices, although to do so would not have been illegal. But Feldmann plan transactions were not considered within this self-imposed interdiction; the trial court found that around the time of the Feldmann sale Jones & Laughlin Steel Corporation, Republic Steel Company, and Pittsburgh Steel Corporation were all participating in such arrangements. In any event, it ill becomes the defendants to disparage as unethical the market advantages from which they themselves reaped rich benefits.

We do not mean to suggest that a majority stockholder cannot dispose of his controlling block of stock to outsiders without having to account to his corporation for profits or even never do this with impunity when the buyer is an interested customer, actual or potential for the corporation's product. But when the sale necessarily results in a sacrifice of this element of corporate good will and consequent unusual profit to the fiduciary who has caused the sacrifice, he should account for his gains. So in a time of market shortage, where a call on a corporation's product commands an unusually large premium, in one form or another, we think it sound law that a fiduciary may not appropriate to himself the value of this premium. Such personal gain at the expense of his coventurers seems particularly reprehensible when made by the trusted president and director of his company. In this case the violation of duty seems to be all the clearer because of this triple role in which Feldmann appears, though we are unwilling to say, and are not to be understood as saying, that we should accept a lesser obligation for any one of his roles alone.

Hence to the extent that the price received by Feldmann and his codefendants included such a bonus, he is accountable to the minority stockholders who sue here. And plaintiffs, as they contend, are entitled to a recovery in their own right, instead of in right of the corporation (as in the usual derivative actions), since neither Wilport nor their successors in interest should share in any judgment which may be rendered. Defendants cannot well object to this form of recovery, since the only alternative, recovery for the corporation as a whole, would subject them to a greater total liability.

The case will therefore be remanded to the district court for a determination of the question expressly left open below, namely, the value of defendants' stock without the appurtenant control over the corporation's output of steel. We reiterate that on this issue, as on all others, relating to a breach of fiduciary duty, the burden of proof must rest on the defendants. Judgment should go to these plaintiffs and those whom they represent for any premium value so shown to the extent of their respective stock interests.

The judgment is therefore reversed and the action remanded for further proceedings pursuant to this opinion.

SWAN, CIRCUIT JUDGE (dissenting).

With the general principles enunciated in the majority opinion as to the duties of fiduciaries I am, of course, in thorough accord. But, as Mr. Justice Frankfurter stated in *Securities and Exchange Comm. v. Chenery Corp.*, 318 U.S. 80, 85, 63 S.Ct. 454, 458, 87 L.Ed. 626, "to say that a man is a fiduciary only begins analysis; it gives direction to further inquiry. To whom is he a fiduciary? What obligations does he owe as a fiduciary? In what respect has he failed to discharge these obligations?" My brothers' opinion does not specify precisely what fiduciary duty Feldmann is held to have violated or whether it was a duty imposed upon him as the dominant stockholder or as a director of Newport. Without such specification I think that both the legal profession and the business world will find the decision confusing and will be unable to foretell the extent of its impact upon customary practices in the sale of stock.

The power to control the management of a corporation, that is, to elect directors to manage its affairs, is an inseparable incident to the ownership of a majority of its stock, or sometimes, as in the present instance, to the ownership of enough shares, less than a majority, to control an election. Concededly a majority or dominant shareholder is ordinarily privileged to sell his stock at the best price obtainable from the purchaser. In so doing he acts on his own behalf, not as an agent of the corporation. If he knows or has reason to believe that the purchaser intends to exercise to the detriment of the corporation the power of management acquired by the purchase, such knowledge or reasonable suspicion will terminate the dominant shareholder's privilege to sell and will create a duty not to transfer the power of management to such purchaser. The duty seems to me to resemble the obligation which everyone is under not to assist another to commit a tort rather than the obligation of a fiduciary. But whatever the nature of the duty, a violation of it will subject the violator to liability for damages sustained by the corporation. Judge Hincks found that Feldmann had no reason to think that Wilport would use the power of management it would acquire by the purchase to injure Newport, and that there was no proof that it ever was so used. Feldmann did know, it is true, that the reason Wilport wanted the stock was to put in a board of directors who would be likely to permit Wilport's members to purchase more of Newport's steel than they might otherwise be able to get. But there is nothing illegal in a dominant shareholder purchasing from his own corporation at the same prices it offers to other customers. That is what the members of Wilport did, and there is no proof that Newport suffered any detriment therefrom.

My brothers say that "the consideration paid for the stock included compensation for the sale of a corporate asset", which they describe as "the ability to control the allocation of the corporate product in a time of short supply, through control of the board of directors; and it was effectively transferred in this sale by having Feldmann procure the resignation of his own board and the election of Wilport's nominees immediately upon consummation of the sale." The implications of this are not clear to me. If it means that when market conditions are such as to induce users of a corporation's product to wish to buy a controlling block of stock in order to be able to purchase part of the corporation's output at the same mill list prices as are offered to other customers, the dominant stockholder is under a fiduciary duty not to sell his stock, I cannot agree. For reasons already stated, in my opinion Feldmann was not proved to be under any fiduciary duty as a stockholder not to sell the stock he controlled.

### Notes

1.  The Court of Appeals' opinion makes no reference to the following finding of fact contained in the District Court's opinion:

> Since the Wilport nominees took over the management of Newport on August 31, 1950, substantial improvements have been made in Newport's property and the corporation has enjoyed continued prosperity. Although the Wilport stockholders have purchased substantial quantities of steel from Newport, no sales were made at less than Newport's quoted mill prices. There is no evidence of any sort that Newport has suffered from mismanagement or inefficient management since August 31, 1950, or that it has suffered or is likely hereafter to suffer any harm whatever at the hands of its new management, or that its new management has in any way failed to do anything which should have been done for the good of the corporation.

129 F.Supp. 162, 175–76 (D.Conn.1952).

In light of this finding, which the appellate court did not find to be clearly erroneous, on what did the appellate court base its reversal of the trial court's decision?

2.  Robert Hamilton, *Private Sale of Control Transactions: Where We Stand Today*, 36 CASE W.RES.L.REV. 248, 275 (1985), argues that *Perlman* involves the wrongful appropriation of a corporate opportunity. Other commentators have interpreted *Perlman* to establish a duty to share a control premium with all of a corporation's shareholders. See, e.g., Andrews, 78 HARV. L. REV. at 514–15, 524–26. Professor Elhauge suggests the key to understanding *Perlman* lies in the existence of a market shortage created by the informal, Korean–War–period system of price controls. Wilport, once in control of Newport, could arrange to purchase more of the steel Newport was producing at the ethically fixed price. A Newport shareholder, however, would find it difficult to prove Newport was injured by such sales, since no court was likely to rule that

Newport had a duty to evade the wartime system of price controls. The court's ruling, viewed in this light, is based not on some general equal sharing principle, but represents a particularized holding that Feldmann, Newport's controlling shareholder, had a duty to share with Newport's other shareholders any premium attributable to the existence of these special market conditions. Elhauge, *supra*, 59 U.Chi.L.Rev. at 1516–17.

Elhauge's interpretation appears consistent with the Court of Appeals' ruling on damages. On remand, the District Court computed the investment value of Newport's common stock based on a capitalization of its earnings, and then ordered Feldmann to distribute to Newport's public shareholders their *pro rata* share of the amount by which the purchase price he received exceeded that figure. 154 F.Supp. 436 (D.C.Conn.1957).

3. Professors Easterbrook and Fischel, in contrast, critique *Perlman* as follows:

> The Second Circuit held in *Perlman* that the seller of the control block had a duty to share the control premium with the other shareholders. The court's holding * * * was based on a belief that the steel shortage allowed Newport to finance needed expansion via the "Plan," and that the premium represented an attempt by Wilport to divert a corporate opportunity—to secure for itself the benefits resulting from the shortage. The court stated that "[o]nly if defendants had been able to negate completely any possibility of gain by Newport could they have prevailed."

> There are several problems with this treatment. Foremost is the assumption that the gain resulting from the "Plan" was not widely reflected in the price of Newport's stock. Newport stock was widely traded, and the existence of the Feldmann Plan was known to investors. The going price of Newport shares prior to the transaction therefore reflected the full value of Newport, including the valued of advances under the Feldmann Plan. The Wilport syndicate paid some two-thirds more than the going price and thus could not profit from the deal unless (a) the sale of control resulted in an increase in the value of Newport, or (b) Wilport's control of Newport was the equivalent of looting. * * *

> Hence, the court's proposition that Wilport extracted a corporate opportunity from Newport—the functional equivalent of looting—has testable implications. Unless the price of Newport's outstanding shares plummeted, the Wilport syndicate could not be extracting enough to profit. In fact, however, the value of Newport's shares rose substantially after the transaction [even after adjusting for price increases in steel company shares generally]. The data refute the court's proposition that Wilport appropriated a corporate opportunity from Newport.

Easterbrook & Fischel, *supra*, 91 Yale L.J. at 718.

# JONES v. H.F. AHMANSON & CO.

1 Cal.3d 93, 81 Cal.Rptr. 592, 460 P.2d 464 (1969).

[Plaintiff, the owner of 25 shares of United Savings and Loan Association (Association) brought a class action on behalf of herself and all similarly situated stockholders. Defendants were H.F. Ahmanson & Co. (Ahmanson) and other persons who had controlled Association prior to transferring 85% of Association's stock to a holding company known as United Financial Corporation (United Financial), which defendants also controlled.

Association, originally organized as a mutual savings and loan company, became a stock corporation in 1956 when is issued 6,568 shares, including 987 shares (14.8%) purchased by plaintiff and other depositors. In May 1958, Ahmanson acquired a majority of Association's shares, and by May 1959 it owned 63.5% of Association's stock.

From 1958 to 1962, the price of stock in most publicly traded savings and loan companies increased sharply. Association stock did not participate in this trend, largely because the trading market in its stock was very thin. With a book value of more than $1,000 per share, a small number of shares outstanding, and little information about the company available because the federal securities laws as they then existed did not oblige Association to furnish periodic reports to shareholders, there was little investor demand for Association shares.

In 1959, Ahmanson and other defendants formed United Financial and transferred the 85% of Association stock that they owned to it, receiving 250 shares of United Financial stock (a "derived block") for each share of Association. Defendants did not offer Association's minority shareholders an opportunity to exchange their shares. Following the exchange, defendants controlled United Financial and, through it, continued to control Association.

In June 1960, United Financial raised $7.2 million through a public offering of units consisting of shares of its stock and a debenture. In connection with this offering, United Financial also acknowledged that it would need to rely on dividends from Association, which accounted for approximately 85% of United Financial assets, to service the debentures. Following the offering, United Financial distributed $6.2 million of the proceeds (an amount equal to $927.50 for each derived block) as a return of capital to defendants, who remained in control of United Financial. Eight months later, United Financial made a secondary offering of 600,000 shares of the derived stock, including 568,190 shares sold by defendants, for a total of $15,275,000. During this period, trading in Association stock declined from about 170 shares per year, prior to the formation of United Financial, to about 85 shares per year.

Shortly after United Financial's first public offering, at a time when Association stock had a book value of $1,411 per share and earnings of $301 per share, defendants caused United Financial to offer to purchase up to 350 shares of Association stock at $1,100 per share. By way of comparison, at that time a derived block of United Financial had a market value of $3,700, in addition to the $927.50 received as a return of capital. United Financial acquired an additional 130 Association shares through this offer.

Association had paid extra dividends of $75 and $57 per share in 1959 and 1960, but in December 1960, after United made its $1,100 per share offer, defendants caused Association to notify each of its minority stockholders that for the foreseeable future Association would pay only a regular $4 per share annual dividend.

United Financial thereafter proposed to exchange 51 shares of United Financial stock with each of the minority shares of Association. Association shares then had a book value of $1,700 per share and the earnings of $615 per share. Fifty-one United Financial shares had a market value of $2,400, a book value of $210 and earnings of $134. Defendant's derived blocks were then worth approximately $8,800 each. When Association's minority shareholders objected, United Financial withdrew its offer.

Plaintiff then brought suit, alleging that defendants had breached the fiduciary duty they owed as majority or controlling shareholders by rendering Association stock unmarketable and then refusing to purchase it at a fair price or to allow plaintiff to exchange it for United Financial stock on the same terms as had defendants. Defendants responded that they had "an absolute right to use and dispose of their stock as they saw fit so long as they violated no right of the corporation or the other stockholders." They asserted that they had no duty to permit minority shareholders to participate on an equal basis in the disposition of their stock.

The trial court ruled for defendants and an intermediate appellate court affirmed, observing: "To act in good faith one does not have to be a 'good neighbor' nor does the law demand of a fiduciary that he should in all matters do unto his beneficiary as he would be done by." *Jones v. H.F. Ahmanson & Co.*, 76 Cal.Rptr. 293, 297 (Cal.App.1969), *vacated* 1 Cal.3d 93, 81 Cal.Rptr. 592, 460 P.2d 464 (1969).]

TRAYNOR, J.

I

PLAINTIFF'S CAPACITY TO SUE

We are faced at the outset with defendants' contention that if a cause of action is stated, it is derivative in nature since any injury suffered is common to all minority stockholders of the Association. Therefore, defendants urge, plaintiff may not sue in an individual capacity or on behalf of a class made up of stockholders excluded from the United Financial exchange, and in any case may not maintain a derivative action without complying with Financial Code, section 7616.
* * *

It is clear from the stipulated facts and plaintiff's allegations that she does not seek to recover on behalf of the corporation for injury done to the corporation by defendants. Although she does allege that the value of her stock has been diminished by defendants' actions, she does not contend that the diminished value reflects an injury to the corporation and resultant depreciation in the value of the stock. Thus the gravamen of her cause of action is injury to herself and the other minority stockholders.

## II

### Majority Shareholders' Fiduciary Responsibility

Defendants take the position that as shareholders they owe no fiduciary obligation to other shareholders, absent reliance on inside information, use of corporate assets, or fraud. This view has long been repudiated in California. The Courts of Appeal have often recognized that majority shareholders, either singly or acting in concert to accomplish a joint purpose, have a fiduciary responsibility to the minority and to the corporation to use their ability to control the corporation in a fair, just, and equitable manner. Majority shareholders may not use their power to control corporate activities to benefit themselves alone or in a manner detrimental to the minority. Any use to which they put the corporation or their power to control the corporation must benefit all shareholders proportionately and must not conflict with the proper conduct of the corporation's business.

\* \* \*

Defendants assert, however, that in the use of their own shares they owed no fiduciary duty to the minority stockholders of the Association. They maintain that they made full disclosure of the circumstances surrounding the formation of United Financial, that the creation of United Financial and its share offers in no way affected the control of the Association, that plaintiff's proportionate interest in the Association was not affected, that the Association was not harmed, and that the market for Association stock was not affected. Therefore, they conclude, they have breached no fiduciary duty to plaintiff and the other minority stockholders.

Defendants would have us retreat from a position demanding equitable treatment of all shareholders by those exercising control over a corporation to a philosophy much criticized by commentators and modified by courts in other jurisdictions as well as our own. In essence defendants suggest that we reaffirm the so-called "majority" rule reflected in our early decisions. This rule, exemplified by the decision in *Ryder v. Bamberger*, 172 Cal. 791, 158 P. 753 but since severely limited, recognized the "perfect right [of majority shareholders] to dispose of their stock \* \* \* without the slightest regard to the wishes and desires or knowledge of the minority stockholders; \* \* \* " (p. 806, 158 P. p. 759) and held that such fiduciary duty as did exist in officers and directors was to the corporation only. The duty of shareholders as such was not recognized unless they, like officers and directors, by virtue of their position were possessed of information relative to the value of the corporation's shares that was not available to outside shareholders. In such case the existence of special facts permitted a finding that a fiduciary relationship to the corporation and other shareholders existed. (*Hobart v. Hobart Estate Co.*, 26 Cal.2d 412, 159 P.2d 958.)

\* \* \* The rule applies alike to officers, directors, and controlling shareholders in the exercise of powers that are theirs by virtue of their position and to transactions wherein controlling shareholders seek to gain an advantage in the sale or transfer or use of their controlling block of shares. Thus we held in In re Security Finance, 49 Cal.2d 370, 317 P.2d 1, that majority shareholders do not have an absolute right to dissolve a corporation, although ostensibly permitted to do so by Corporations Code, section 4600, because their statutory power is subject to equitable limitations in favor of the minority. We recognized that the majority had the right to dissolve the corporation to protect their investment *if* no alternative means were available *and* no advantage was secured over other shareholders, and noted that "there is nothing sacred in the life of a corporation that transcends the interests of its shareholders, but because dissolution falls with such finality on those interests, above all corporate powers it is subject to equitable limitations." (49 Cal.2d 370, 377, 317 P.2d 1, 5.)

\* \* \*

The increasingly complex transactions of the business and financial communities demonstrate the inadequacy of the traditional theories of fiduciary obligation as tests of majority shareholder responsibility to the minority. These theories have failed to afford adequate protection to minority shareholders and particularly to those in closely held corporations whose disadvantageous and often precarious position renders them particularly vulnerable to the vagaries of the majority. Although courts have recognized the potential for abuse or unfair advantage when a controlling shareholder sells his shares at a premium over investment value *(Perlman v. Feldmann*, 219 F.2d 173, 50 A.L.R.2d 1134) or in a controlling shareholder's use of control to avoid equitable distribution of corporate assets (*Zahn v. Transamerica Corporation* (3rd Cir.1947) 162 F.2d 36, 172 A.L.R. 495 [use of control to cause subsidiary to redeem stock prior to liquidation and distribution of assets] ), no comprehensive rule has emerged in other jurisdictions. Nor have most commentators approached the problem from a perspective other than that of the advantage gained in the sale of control. Some have suggested that the price paid for control shares over their investment value be treated as an asset belonging to the corporation itself (Berle and Means, THE MODERN CORPORATION AND PRIVATE PROPERTY (1932) p. 243), or as an asset that should be shared proportionately with all shareholders through a general offer (Jennings, *Trading in Corporate Control* (1956) 44 CAL.L.REV. 1, 39), and another contends that the sale of control at a premium is always evil (Bayne, *The Sale–of–Control Premium: the Intrinsic Illegitimacy* (1969) 47 TEX.L.REV. 215).

\* \* \* The case before us, in which no sale or transfer of actual control is directly involved, demonstrates that the injury anticipated by these authors can be inflicted with impunity under the traditional rules and supports our conclusion that the comprehensive rule of good faith and inherent fairness to the minority in any transaction where control of the corporation is material properly governs controlling shareholders in this state.

We turn now to defendants' conduct to ascertain whether this test is met.

### III

#### FORMATION OF UNITED FINANCIAL AND MARKETING ITS SHARES

Defendants created United Financial during a period of unusual investor interest in the stock of savings and loan associations. They then owned a majority of the outstanding stock of the Association. This stock was not readily marketable owing to a high book value, lack of investor information and facilities, and the closely held nature of the Association. The management of the Association had made no effort to create a market for the stock or to split the shares and reduce their market price to a more attractive level. Two courses were available to defendants in their effort to exploit the bull market in savings and loan stock. Both were made possible by defendants' status as controlling stockholders. The first was either to cause the Association to effect a stock split (Corp.Code, § 1507) and create a market for the Association stock or to create a holding company for Association shares and permit all stockholders to exchange their shares before offering holding company shares to the public. All stockholders would have benefited alike had this been done, but in realizing their gain on the sale of their stock the majority stockholders would of necessity have had to relinquish some of their control shares. Because a public market would have been created, however, the minority stockholders would have been able to extricate themselves without sacrificing their investment had they elected not to remain with the new management.

The second course was that taken by defendants. A new corporation was formed whose major asset was to be the control block of Association stock owned by defendants, but from which minority shareholders were to be excluded. The unmarketable Association stock held by the majority was transferred to the newly formed corporation at an exchange rate equivalent to a 250 for 1 stock split. The new corporation thereupon set out to create a market for its own shares. Association stock constituted 85 percent of the holding company's assets and produced an equivalent proportion of its income. The same individuals controlled both corporations. It appears therefrom that the market created by defendants for United Financial shares was a market that would have been available for Association stock had defendants taken the first course of action.

After United Financial shares became available to the public it became a virtual certainty that no equivalent market could or would be created for Association stock. United Financial had become the controlling stockholder and neither it nor the other defendants would benefit from public trading in Association stock in competition with United Financial shares. Investors afforded an opportunity to acquire United Financial shares would not be likely to choose the less marketable and expensive Association stock in preference. Thus defendants chose a course of action in which they used their control of the Association to obtain an advantage not made available to all stockholders. They did so without regard to the resulting detriment to the minority stockholders and in the absence of any compelling business purpose. Such conduct is not consistent with their duty of good faith and inherent fairness to the minority stockholders. Had defendants afforded the minority an opportunity to exchange their stock on the same basis or offered to purchase them at a price arrived at by independent appraisal, their burden of establishing good faith and inherent fairness would have been much less. At the trial they may present evidence tending to show such good faith or compelling business purpose that would render their action fair under the circumstances. On appeal from the judgment of dismissal after the defendants' demurrer was sustained we decide only that the complaint states a cause of action entitling plaintiff to relief.

Defendants gained an additional advantage for themselves through their use of control of the Association when they pledged that control over the Association's assets and earnings to secure the holding company's debt, a debt that had been incurred for their own benefit.[14] In so doing the defendants breached their fiduciary obligation to the minority once again and caused United Financial and its controlling shareholders to become inextricably wedded to a conflict of interest between the minority stockholders of each corporation. Alternatives were available to them that would have benefited all stockholders proportionately. The course they chose affected the minority stockholders with no less finality than does dissolution (In re Security Finance, *supra,* 49 Cal.2d 370, 317 P.2d 1) and demands no less concern for minority interests.

In so holding we do not suggest that the duties of corporate fiduciaries include in all cases an obligation to make a market for and to facilitate public trading in the stock of the corporation. But when, as here, no market exists, the controlling shareholders may not use their power to control the corporation for the purpose of promoting a marketing scheme that benefits themselves alone to the detriment of the minority. Nor do we suggest that a control block of shares may not be sold or transferred to a holding company. We decide only that the

---

**14.** Should it become necessary to encumber or liquidate Association assets to service this debt or to depart from a dividend policy consistent with the business needs of the Association, damage to the Association itself may occur. We need not resolve here, but note with some concern, the problem facing United Financial, which owes the same fiduciary duty to its own shareholders as to those of the Association. Any decision regarding use of Association assets and earnings to service the holding company debt must be made in the context of these potentially conflicting interests.

circumstances of any transfer of controlling shares will be subject to judicial scrutiny when it appears that the controlling shareholders may have breached their fiduciary obligation to the corporation or the remaining shareholders.

## IV

### DAMAGES

From the perspective of the minority stockholders of the Association, the transfer of control under these circumstances to another corporation and the resulting impact on their position as minority stockholders accomplished a fundamental corporate change as to them. Control of a closely held savings and loan association, the major portion of whose earnings had been retained over a long period while its stockholders remained stable, became an asset of a publicly held holding company. The position of the minority shareholder was drastically changed thereby. His practical ability to influence corporate decision-making was diminished substantially when control was transferred to a publicly held corporation that was in turn controlled by the owners of more than 750,000 shares. The future business goals of the Association could reasonably be expected to reflect the needs and interest of the holding company rather than the aims of the Association stockholders thereafter. In short, the enterprise into which the minority stockholders were now locked was not that in which they had invested.

Appraisal rights protect the dissenting minority shareholder against being forced to either remain an investor in an enterprise fundamentally different than that in which he invested or sacrifice his investment by sale of his shares at less than a fair value. Plaintiff here was entitled to no less. But she was entitled to more. In the circumstances of this case she should have been accorded the same opportunity to exchange her Association stock for that of United Financial accorded the majority.

Although a controlling shareholder who sells or exchanges his shares is not under an obligation to obtain for the minority the consideration that he receives in all cases, when he does sell or exchange his shares the transaction is subject to close scrutiny. When the majority receives a premium over market value for its shares, the consideration for which that premium is paid will be examined. If it reflects payment for that which is properly a corporate asset all shareholders may demand to share proportionately. (*Perlman v. Feldmann, supra,* 219 F.2d 173.) Here the exchange was an integral part of a scheme that the defendants could reasonably foresee would have as an incidental effect the destruction of the potential public market for Association stock. The remaining stockholders would thus be deprived of the opportunity to realize a profit from those intangible characteristics that attach to publicly marketed stock and enhance its value above book value. Receipt of an appraised value reflecting book value and earnings alone could not compensate the minority shareholders for the loss of this potential. Since the damage is real, although the amount is speculative, equity demands that the minority stockholders be placed in a position at least as favorable as that the majority created for themselves.

If, after trial of the cause, plaintiff has established facts in conformity with the allegations of the complaint and stipulation, then upon tender of her Association stock to defendants she will be entitled to receive at her election either the appraised value of her shares on the date of the exchange, May 14, 1959, with interest at 7 percent a year from the date of this action or a sum equivalent to the fair market value of a "derived block" of United Financial stock on the date of this action with interest thereon from that date, and the sum of $927.50 (the return of capital paid to the original United Financial shareholders) with interest thereon from the date United Financial first made such payments to its original shareholders, for each share tendered. The appraised or fair market value shall be reduced, however, by the amount by which dividends paid on Association shares during the period from May 14, 1959 to the present exceeds the dividends paid on a corresponding block of United Financial shares during the same period.

\* \* \*

### Note: Tender Offers and Sales at a Premium

SEC Rule 14d–10, which implements the "best price rule" established by § 14(d)(7) of the Securities Exchange Act of 1934, requires every person who purchases stock in a tender offer to pay to every person who tenders stock a price equal to "the highest consideration paid to any to any other security holder during such tender offer." This Rule constrains a person holding a large block of stock from selling at a price higher than that received by other shareholders by saddling the purchaser with a large potential liability if a court subsequently determines that the block was purchased *during [a] tender offer.*"

*Field v. Trump*, 850 F.2d 938 (2d Cir.1988), *cert. denied*, 489 U.S. 1012, 109 S.Ct. 1122, 103 L.Ed.2d 185 (1989), held that plaintiffs, public shareholders of Pay'n Save Corporation, could maintain an action for damages under Rule 14d–10. Plaintiffs alleged that Julius and Eddie Trump, four days after they had commenced a tender offer at $22.50 per share to acquire all the stock of Pay'n Save, "withdrew" the offer in order to arrange to purchase about 17% of Pay'n Save's outstanding stock from certain dissident directors. After acquiring an option to purchase the dissident directors' shares and agreeing to make a side payment to the dissident directors for "fees and expenses," the Trumps, later the same night, announced a "new" tender offer at $23.50 per share. Plaintiffs alleged that when the price of the option and the side payment were taken into account, the Trumps had paid the dissident directors $25.00 per share, and that, under Rule 14d–10, plaintiffs therefore were entitled to receive an additional $1.50 per share for their stock.

*Epstein v. MCA, Inc.*, 50 F.3d 644 (9th Cir. 1995), *rev'd on other grounds, Matsushita Elec. Indus. Co., Ltd. v. Epstein*, 516 U.S. 367, 116

S.Ct. 873, 134 L.Ed.2d 6 (1996), involved claims by the public shareholders of MCA. Matsushita Electrical Co., Ltd. ("Matsushita") had negotiated with Lew Wasserman, MCA's chairman and CEO, and Sidney Sheinberg, MCA's chief operating officer, a friendly acquisition of MCA at $71 per share, to be paid through a tender offer for all MCA stock. However, Matsushita also entered into a separate agreement with Wasserman, then age 77, pursuant to which he received preferred stock in a wholly-owned MCA subsidiary, in a tax-free transaction, in exchange for the roughly five million MCA shares he owned. In addition, shortly after the tender offer was announced, MCA agreed, with Matsushita's approval, to pay Sheinberg $21 million, pursuant to an amended employment agreement, if the tender offer succeeded.

The Ninth Circuit upheld plaintiffs' contention that Matsushita's agreement with Wasserman was part of the tender offer and remanded that portion of the case for a hearing on whether the consideration Wasserman received had a value greater than $71 per share. As concerned the payment to Sheinberg, the court reversed the trial court's decision granting summary judgment to defendants and remanded for a determination of whether the payment was part of the tender offer or was made to induce Sheinberg to relinquish his right to receive options to purchase 1,000,000 shares of MCA stock at $50 per share. The court noted that if the $21 million paid to Sheinberg was a premium for the 1,179,635 shares he had tendered, the damages owed to each tendering shareholder would be $17.80 per share, *see* 50 F.3d at 669, or a total of about $2 billion payable to the other tendering shareholders. The Ninth Circuit's subsequent opinion in *Epstein* is set forth in Chapter 20.

# Chapter 22

## PROTECTING CONTROL

### A. INTRODUCTION

Most changes in control are negotiated. One corporation "buys" another corporation. The managements of the two corporations bargain at arm's length over the terms, conditions, future management, and precise legal form of the transaction. If no deal is struck, that usually is the end of the matter.

In a negotiated transaction, shareholders' interests are represented by the managements of the companies involved. Although corporate law may require shareholder approval and federal securities law may require full disclosure to shareholders, the deal is the work of managers, directors and their advisers. In a truly arm's length transaction, the business judgment rule largely insulates directors from liability. As long as the board exercises due care and no self dealing is involved, directors have little to fear from a stockholder suit.

If the management of a corporation that another company wants to acquire (the *target* company) is unable to agree to terms with the would-be acquiror (the *bidder*) or is unwilling (or believed to be unwilling) to negotiate at all, the latter may launch a "hostile" takeover bid, seeking to gain control by going over the heads of management and appealing directly to the target company's stockholders. The bidder can select the form of challenge—either a proxy contest or a tender offer. The two have different economic consequences. If the bidder succeeds in a proxy contest, it will gains managerial control; if it succeeds through a tender offer, it will also obtain ownership control. The bidder's objectives will determine which it chooses; does it seek managerial control alone or does it want to own the target as well?

Proxy contests occur with less frequency than tender offers although, relatively speaking, they are much easier to mount. One explanation for this phenomenon is that bidders generally have found it more difficult to gain control of target companies through proxy contests than through tender offers. Not surprisingly, it is easier to convince investors to sell out at a premium price than to vote for a change in management. Moreover, proxy contests may ultimately prove to be more costly. If the bidder fails, it will not be able to recoup the expenses it incurred mounting the proxy contest, unless it can convince (or coerce) the target to buy it off. But a bidder in a tender offer, although it may spend a great deal more in an effort to purchase a control block of the target's stock, often will earn a large profit even if the bid falls short because it will be able to sell its stock to the successful bidder at a profit.

The focus of this chapter is not on bidders but on issues relating to the target management's efforts to fend off hostile takeover bids. However, it is difficult to appreciate those issues fully without some understanding of how proxy contests and tender offers are conducted and regulated. The next two sections deal with those questions.

## B.  PROXY CONTESTS

A proxy contest provides stockholders a choice in the selection of directors, and ultimately in management. Stockholders receive proxy statements and proxy voting forms from two different slates of candidates, one favored by the target's incumbent management and the other favored by the bidder. In addition, both sides may contact shareholders directly and run newspaper advertisements that make strenuous appeals for votes.

The goal of a proxy contest is to win the voting support of the stockholders, not to acquire their shares, although bidders often also seek to increase their own holdings of target company stock. A challenger must frame the issues and select its candidates. Traditionally, shareholders tend to vote in favor of management. Waging an effective campaign to overcome this tendency requires time. But time may be limited, due to the pendency of the target's annual meeting and the problems involved in calling a special meeting. In addition, management has some ability to manipulate the corporate machinery to its advantage. Recall Chapters 3 and 12. If state law and the target's articles of incorporation permit (*see* DGCL § 228), the challenger may simply solicit consents to remove incumbent directors without cause and replace them with its nominees. Bidders often combine such consent solicitations or the threat of a concurrent proxy contest with a hostile tender offer.

Although proxy contests are fought openly, challengers often hope to get organized before the target's management knows much about them or their plans. They want to contact potential supporters and to launch their effort before management can put takeover defenses in place. The SEC's rules, however, may make it difficult for a challenger to proceed secretly. As discussed in Chapter 14, Section 13(d) of the 1934 Act requires any "person" that acquired more than 5% of the stock of a public company to file a Schedule 13D within 10 days after reaching the 5% threshold. "Person" includes a "group" and the SEC rules state that a "group" is deemed to have "acquired" the shares of its members when the "group" is formed. Thus, although the proxy rules allow limited contact without any disclosure, under § 13(d) the same conduct may trigger a filing obligation.

Management begins a proxy contest with certain distinct advantages. We have already mentioned the shareholders' usual propensity to vote for management. In addition, management has a ready source of funds—the corporate treasury. The limits on how much corporate money managers may use are not very stringent. Although a bidder may be able to recover its expenses if it wins the contest, while the contest is in process, management usually has a substantial financial edge.

Management also maintains the shareholder list and thus knows who the shareholders are and how many shares they own. A bidder may have a right to obtain a copy of the list as a matter of state law. Recall Chapter 12. But even if the bidder has a proper purpose for seeking the list, management may question that purpose and force the bidder to sue, thereby delaying delivery of the list. If the proxy contest has already begun, delay can be very damaging.

Bidders often also have to deal with costly litigation, which frequently is financed on the target's side by the corporate treasury. SEC Rule 14a–9 prohibits false and misleading statements in connection with the solicitation of a proxy. In most proxy contests, each side closely reads the soliciting material of the other side and then tries to convince the staff of the SEC to seek to enjoin its opponent's solicitations as false and misleading. Failing that, the parties—especially the target's management—is likely to go to court on their own to seek injunctive relief.

Finally, bidders have to be prepared to engage in several rounds of soliciting activity. Proxies are revocable; a later executed proxy often revokes all earlier executed proxies. Hence, a bidder must be prepared to counter efforts by the target's management to wean away support the bidder has obtained, as well as to make second, third and fourth efforts to secure the votes of shareholders who have resisted the bidders' previous blandishments.

In the end, both sides are likely to target most of their efforts on large institutional investors, whose votes are likely to determine the outcome of most proxy contests. Here, too, proxy contests pose hazards greater than those posed by tender offers. An institution, especially one concerned about its own interests as well as those of its beneficiaries, may well find it easier to justify voting in favor of an incumbent management, even one whose performance has been poor, than to explain why it is not tendering shares it owns for a price that represents a substantial premium over market. Money talks.

## C.  TENDER OFFERS

In a tender offer, a bidder typically offers to buy stock in a publicly held target corporation at a price substantially above the price at which that stock currently is trading. The consideration offered may be cash, stock, other securities, or some combination. The offer may be for some portion of the target company's stock or for all the outstanding shares. Almost all tender offers contain one or more conditions that must be satisfied before the bidder will be obligated to purchase any tendered stock.

Notwithstanding the high probability of success, acquiring another company in a tender offer entails substantial risks for a bidder. One is surprise. In a negotiated purchase, a would-be acquiror generally can arrange to investigate fully the business of the proposed target company. In a tender offer, a hostile bidder often flies blind; it has no opportunity to learn about the target from the inside. Moreover, if a contest for control develops, a bidder may find itself overpaying for its prize. As in any auction, the party who prevails is the one who, rightly or wrongly, places the highest value on the company to be acquired.

A bidder contemplating a possible tender offer begins by selecting its prospective target which may be a company that has the potential to prosper under new and better management, a company whose business might efficiently be combined with that of the bidder, or a company whose stock the bidder believes is selling for less than the "true value" of the company's assets. Economists generally believe that the stock market is "efficient," that stock prices represent the most accurate available prediction of the present value of the future earnings or cash flow that a company will generate under its present management. Believers in efficient capital markets predict that targets will tend to be poorly managed companies, and that tender offers consequently have the potential to increase real wealth. Critics hotly dispute this point. They claim that the market places undue emphasis on short-term factors and that stock prices do not necessarily reflect a company's fundamental, or inherent value. They also point to evidence that targets of hostile tender offers have been well-managed companies, not deadwood.

Whatever the general merit of these competing arguments, it does seem clear that some targets have been the financial equivalent of an "attractive nuisance." That is, they had large pools of liquid assets which anyone who purchased those companies could use, after acquiring control, to pay off a large part of the purchase price. For example, some targets have had substantially overfunded pension plans, retirement funds with more in assets than actuarially necessary to pay pensions to all anticipated retirees. Bidders acquiring such companies terminated the pension plans, drew off the excess assets, and had enough left over to provide for the beneficiaries.

The bidder must arrange to finance the tender offer. This is perhaps the most critical aspect of planning; it is not uncommon for a takeover bid to exceed a billion dollars. Bidders sometimes are large well financed companies that do not require extensive outside financing. If the bidder needs outside funding, it often will turn to commercial banks or investment banks. Commercial banks generally charge commitment fees when they agree to provide financing for a takeover bid. Investment banks may have access to investors who are willing to finance takeover bids. In such cases, they can furnish potential bidders with letters stating that they are "highly confident" they can raise the funds needed to finance the offer. Since the bidder will need the funds only if and when its bid succeeded, proceeding on the basis of such a letter reduces a bidder's costs. At other times, investment banks will commit to providing "bridge loans" with their own funds to finance clients' takeover bids. At still others, investment banks ally themselves with their clients, becoming co-bidders with a view to participating as equity holders if the target is acquired.

A bidder typically forms a shell corporation to make the tender offer. If the bid is successful, the bidder often will merge the shell with the target company in a second step transaction designed to eliminate that company's remaining public shareholders. In part, the bidder's ability to cause the second step transaction helps to create an atmosphere in which shareholders of the target company feel compelled to tender their stock, even if they believe that present management best serves their long term interests, or that a better deal is possible given enough time. A tactic that effectively created such pressure was the so-called two-tier tender offer: a bidder offered $50 cash per share for 51% of the stock of a target company selling at $30 per share and simultaneously announced that if its bid succeeded, it would effectuate a second step merger in which the target's remaining shareholders would receive $40 per share in debt securities. The offer presented shareholders with a "prisoner's dilemma." Even if they would prefer to reject the offer entirely, believing the "blended" price of $45 per share to be inadequate, they would be unwilling to risk having other shareholders accept the $50 per share front end and being left with the $40 per share back end payment. Consequently, shareholders were forced to accept the front end offer, assuring both its success and the ensuing merger. This was the strategy used in *Unocal, infra*. After *Unocal*, however, the tactic fell into disuse.

Bidders' ability to put pressure on target shareholders has been reduced by the Williams Act governing tender offers and the implementing SEC rules discussed in greater detail in the next section. Shareholders may wait out the bid until the last minute without prejudice. Whether the offer is for any and all shares tendered or only for some of the shares, it must remain open for 20 business days (Rule 14e–1). Shares that are tendered may be withdrawn at any time during the offer (Section 14(d)(5) and Rule 14d–7) which gives the target about a month to come up with a better alternative. A new offer, or an increase in the price of the original offer, will extend the duration of the offer and the withdrawal period by ten business days. If the offer is for less than all the shares, acceptance must be on a pro-rata basis, not first-come, first-served. (Section 14(d)(6) and Rule 14d–8) An increase in the offer must apply retroactively. (Section 14(d)(7)) But even though these rules allow shareholders to take their time and change their minds, most sell unless a better deal is presented because they realize that if they do not, the market after the offer is likely to be inactive and the stock's price is likely to retreat to pre-offer levels. Many will not even wait for the offer period to end. Rather, they sell their shares soon after the offer is made, pocketing a sure profit rather than waiting to see if the offer succeeds.

During the time in which the tender offer is open, the dominant purchasers in the market are arbitrageurs, or "arbs," who are professional risk takers. Often they are brokers who purchase from the public at a price below the tender offer price (sometimes higher if the arbs are convinced that an auction is about to ensue), with the expectation that they will tender to the bidder at the higher price and make a profit on the spread. The reason for the spread is because of the risk that the target will be able to prevent consummation of the tender offer by some means and send the price back to its pre-tender offer level. The arbitrageur assumes the risk of failure of the offer in return for the expected profit.

Consequently, a large percentage of the shares tendered to most bidder are owned by arbs. This presents the misleading impression that tender offers mainly benefit the arbs, overlooking the fact that the arbs acquired their stock from shareholders who willingly sold to them at a discount rather than incur the risk that the offer would fail. Arbs will be alert to the possibility that a competing bidder may offer a higher price, providing them with an opportunity for a greater than expected profit. However, arbs lose money as well, and when they do, their losses are large. The game is not for the faint of heart or nerve.

Ultimately the tender offer will run its course. Several possible outcomes exist. First, the bidder may succeed on approximately the terms originally offered. Second, the target may have agreed to be acquired by a suitor of its choice, a "white knight." Shareholders will do at least as well under this arrangement as they would have under the original offer, and management may do considerably better. Third, the target's management may make a competing bid or may propose a financial restructuring, usually with the target financing a substantial distribution to its shareholders with borrowed funds. Fourth, the bidder and the target may reach a compromise, perhaps compelled by the strength of the target's defenses, whereby the bidder increases the price it is offering and, sometimes, provides some job security to the target's management. Finally, and least likely, the target will be able to thwart the bid entirely on some legal objection, or through its internal defenses, and remain largely intact.

## D. FEDERAL SECURITIES LAW PROVISIONS RELATING TO PROXY CONTESTS AND TENDER OFFERS

The Securities Exchange Act of 1934 always authorized the regulation of proxy solicitations and since 1954, the Securities and Exchange Commission has had special rules dealing with proxy contests. In 1968, Congress passed the Williams Act, which added provisions regulating tender offers to the Securities Exchange Act of 1934.

## 1. PROXY CONTESTS

All the provisions of the proxy rules, including Rule 14a–9 which prohibits materially false or misleading statements in proxy solicitations, apply to proxy contests as well as to the types of solicitations discussed in Chapter 14.

Rule 14a–7 provides that an issuer must make available to a shareholder who seeks to solicit proxies from the issuer's other shareholders an estimate of the number of record holders and beneficial owners whose shares are owned in street name, and an estimate of the cost of mailing proxy materials to those holders. If the shareholder defrays the reasonable costs of mailing, the issuer must promptly mail the shareholders' proxy materials to all other shareholders. In lieu of that mailing, an issuer may furnish the shareholder with a list that sets forth names and addresses of all shareholders, but that need not list the number of shares each shareholder owns. Because the issuer retains the choice and always elects to mail, the challengers rarely avail themselves of the Rule.

Rule 14a–11 is a special rule that deals with election contests, which are defined as solicitations in opposition to another candidate for director. Under that Rule 14a–11, all "participants" in an election contest—including the issuer, directors, nominees, committees or groups soliciting proxies or financing the solicitation must disclose in their proxy statement biographical information about the participant and any interest in the securities of the subject company.

## 2. TENDER OFFERS

Section 14(d)(1) prohibits the making of a "tender offer" (a term the statute does not define) for a class of securities registered under Section 12 of the 1934 Act, if the bidder would then own 5% of that class, unless certain information is filed with the SEC and sent to the target when the offer is first made. There are no pre-offer filing requirements. Schedule 14D–1, the required form, calls for information similar to that set forth in Schedule 13D, including the description of the bidder's purposes and plans for the target. In addition, when the bidder is a corporation and its financial condition is material to the target company shareholder's decision to accept the offer, certain financial information about the bidder is required.

Section 14(d)(5) permits a security holder to withdraw any shares she has tendered until seven days after the commencement of the tender offer and after 60 days from the commencement of the tender offer. Rule 14d–7 extends this right. A shareholder now can withdraw her shares any time a tender offer remains open. Rule 14e–1 requires that a tender offer be held open for a minimum of 20 business days. If a bidder increases the consideration or the soliciting dealer's fee, the offer must remain open for 10 business days after the increase.

Section 14(d)(6) provides that if a tender offer is for less than all of a class of securities and a greater number are tendered, then the bidder is required to purchase tendered shares on a pro-rata basis from all shareholders who tendered their shares within ten days of the date the offer was made. Rule 14d–8 effectively extends this pro rata period by providing that shares tendered while an offer was open must be purchased on a pro-rata basis.

Section 14(d)(7) provides that if a bidder increases the consideration offered before the offer expires, then the increased consideration must be paid to those who previously tendered their shares.

Rule 14d–9 requires certain persons to file a Schedule 14D–9 with the SEC when they publish or send a solicitation or recommendation with respect to a tender offer. These persons include the subject company, its management, affiliates, the bidder and persons acting on the bidder's behalf. Rule 14e–2 requires a target company to disclose its position with respect to a tender offer to its security holders in a statement no later than ten business days from the dissemination of a tender offer. The statement must include the reasons for the company's position. If the company takes no position on the offer, it must explain why. A target company may issue a "stop-look-and-listen" communication to security holders without filing a Schedule 14D–9, but it must then inform shareholders of a date by which it will advise them of its position on the tender offer.

Rule 14d–10 is known as the "all holders rule." It requires that a tender offer must be open to all security holders of the class subject to the offer and that the consideration paid to all holders must be the highest consideration paid to any other security holder of that class during the tender offer. The latter requirement does not prohibit offering a choice of form of consideration.

Section 14(e) makes it unlawful "for any person to make any untrue statement of a material fact or omit to state any material fact necessary in order to make the statements made, in the light of the circumstances under which they are made, not misleading, or to engage in any fraudulent, deceptive, or manipulative acts or practices, in connection with any tender offer or request or invitation for tenders, or any solicitation of security holders in opposition to or in favor of any such offer, request or invitation."

Rules 14e–1 and 14e–2, both noted above, have been issued under Section 14(e). Rule 14e–3 addresses the problem of persons who have advance knowledge of a pending tender offer, where the bidder has taken substantial steps to commence an offer. Except for the bidder and a few others, Rule 14e–3 declares it to be a fraudulent, deceptive or manipulative act or practice for a person possessing knowledge gained from the bidder, the issuer or an officer, director or employee of such person, to buy or sell shares of the target unless the information has been publicly disclosed a reasonable time before the purchase. The rule contains a number of detailed operational provisions.

# E. POLICY QUESTIONS

## 1. CORPORATE GOVERNANCE

Earlier chapters of the book presented some of the legal and corporate governance issues that tender offers raise, but it is well to review them at this point. The initial regulatory question is the extent to which federal law should control. *CTS Corporation v. Dynamics Corporation of America* (Chapter 4) suggests states have considerable, but not unlimited, scope to regulate takeover bids. It is also clear that Congress has the constitutional power to preempt state law affecting tender offers and defenses against them. Justice Scalia's concurring comment in *CTS* that "a law can be both economic folly and constitutional" may dictate the Court's deference to the legislature, but not Congress'. Thus, the issue is one of policy, not power. If both the federal government and the states are to retain jurisdiction in this field, is it desirable for them to pursue different objectives? If not, how should their objectives be harmonized?

The substantive issues of corporate governance arise in the context of responses to takeovers. Powerful defenses have been created to deter tender offers, or at least slow down the process. In countering takeover bids, targets have undertaken major corporate transactions, such as massive restructuring or recapitalization, that would not have occurred but for the tender offer. Corporations have incurred heavy debt to fend off a raid. Enhancing the power of the board of directors and management to defeat a bid may weaken the shareholders' ability to hold directors and managers accountable. This weakening is troublesome if one views takeover defenses as essentially self-serving. But if tender offers serve shareholders well, does resistance serve them even better? Courts have wrestled with the proper standard to apply to takeover defenses, whether it is the business judgment rule (or doctrine), intrinsic fairness or something in between. The legal question is related to the underlying economic issue of whether takeovers function as effective governors of management conduct, which in turn may be dependent upon empirical studies of which companies become targets of tender offers.

The ultimate question is how much freedom should a target company board have to resist a takeover bid that it determines is not in the best interests of the corporation? Should the board be denied all discretion, allowed to employ tactics designed to extract a higher price for shareholders, or empowered to decide that the company is "not for sale" to anyone regardless of price or the bidder's capabilities?

## 2. ECONOMIC THEORY

The fundamental issue is whether tender offers create or simply redistribute wealth. If wealth is created, what is the source? Economists Michael Jensen and Richard Ruback in *The Market for Corporate Control: The Scientific Evidence*, 11 J.FIN.ECON. 5 (1983), referring to stock prices, point to the great gains by shareholders of target companies and the slight gains by shareholders of bidder companies, and conclude that the evidence plainly demonstrates that tender offers have created wealth. Moreover, although Jensen and Ruback are uncertain as to the source, they believe that the gains do not result from monopoly profits. To them, the clear public policy implication is that no impediments to hostile takeover bids should be allowed.

However, the economic and political issues concern a broader spectrum of interests than shareholders. Even assuming the validity of Jensen and Ruback's conclusions, is the public policy directive so clear? Do the objectively measurable stock gains they find reflect the gains and losses of other with an interest in the corporation—the employees, the suppliers, the communities where the corporation operates? There is a political question as well: does a dollar of shareholder gain justify imposing a loss of 80 cents on employees, suppliers, customers and the community combined (assuming those figures are correct)? The marginal value of the added wealth to shareholders, given the demographics of that body, may not be as "important" as the marginal losses to the others.

Economists Andrei Shleifer and Lawrence Summers, in their paper *Hostile Takeovers as Breaches of Trust* (Feb. 20, 1987), contend that society *can* be worse off from a takeover bid that benefits shareholders. For example, bidders may be willing to terminate implicit long-term contracts with other stakeholders (employees, suppliers and the community) that existing management would honor. Sometimes these terminations result in benefits to the community as well as to stockholders, when the stakeholders can replace their old relationships without cost. In that event, assets have been moved to more productive users. The stock gains measure society's gain. In other situations, the stakeholders' losses may equal shareholder gains, in which event society has not gained, nor has it lost. But at times the stakeholder losses may exceed shareholder gains, if the consequences of job and supplier losses produce a ripple effect of further community losses.

## 3. MANAGEMENT DISCIPLINE

Are hostile takeovers a useful discipline for managers of publicly traded corporations? Does this discipline improve the efficiency of those corporations? No issue affecting tender offers has been debated more heatedly.

In Chapter 14, we saw that the market for corporate control plays a central role in the nexus-of-contracts theory of the corporation. Chapter 6 of the 1985 ECONOMIC REPORT OF THE PRESIDENT contains a good exposition of this theory. Focusing on maximizing shareholder wealth, the Report asserts that the market aligns management interests with those of the shareholders through the labor market for management services and through the external market for corporate control. There are important limits to the effectiveness of the labor market. Most notably, it allows poorly performing entrenched managers to remain in control if they believe they are performing efficiently. What is needed, therefore, is an objective means of measuring management performance. The stock market provides this function by its efficient pricing of corporate stock.

Management's best assurance that it will retain control is to keep the stock price high relative to outsiders' estimates of the potential value of the shares. By contrast, a low stock price attracts bidders who seek to gain control, displace management, and achieve the potential value. In this fashion, the market for corporate control disciplines managers who have failed to maximize share values.

The Report observes that available evidence indicates that target company shareholders gain from 16–34% over pre-bid stock values and bidder shareholders gain approximately 2% when tender offers are made. The Report presents five hypotheses concerning the source of these gains. First, there may be production and distribution economies. Second, acquisitions may permit technology transfers that would otherwise be unavailable. Third, there may be cost-reducing effects to companies that have larger market shares. Fourth, assets may be shifted to higher valued uses. Finally, gains may come from improved management. So as not to overstate the last point, the Report notes that not all targets are poorly managed, but that poor management is one motive for takeovers, and that restraints on takeovers can protect managers from the discipline of the marketplace.

In *A Guide to Takeovers: Theory, Evidence, and Regulation*, 9 YALE J. REG. 119 (1992), Professor Roberta Romano surveys the empirical evidence for explanations of takeovers. She finds that the data on returns from takeovers corresponds to those in the Economic Report of the President. Takeovers do create an overall gain when bidder and target returns are aggregated. Romano finds, however, that the data for bidder returns is more ambiguous than that in the Report, at least during the 1980's. She agrees with the Report that management discipline provides an explanation for takeovers, but argues that there are other explanations.

Romano divides the possible causes into two groups. First, there are value-maximizing sources in which the desire to increase the equity share price of the bidder motivates the acquisition. These explanations can be divided into efficiency, wealth transfer or expropriation, and market inefficiency categories. Second, there are non-wealth-maximizing explanations in which management's desire to maximize its own utility at the expense of shareholder wealth causes the takeover.

Romano finds the strongest empirical support for efficiency-enhancing value-maximizing causes of takeovers. Not surprisingly, there is more than one explanation of takeovers with strong empirical support, an indication that takeovers occur for a variety of reasons. She concludes that replacement of inefficient management has empirical support as one source of takeover gains. Statistics indicate that poorly managed corporations are often targets, and that targets typically have lower profitability relative to their industry peers prior to being acquired. Asset productivity, as measured by cash flow, improves after an acquisition regardless of whether the bidder and target are in related or unrelated industries. The absence of any difference in the rate of improvement suggests that the gains from takeovers do not rely solely on operating synergies, which should be higher when the bidder and target engage in related businesses.

Operating synergies provide another source of efficiency gains in takeovers. Economies of scale allow the bidder to spread overhead expenses across a bigger business. Economies of scope allow bidder and target to combine complementary assets to raise their productivity. The bidder's management expertise can be extended and transferred to the target. Finally, the takeover may lower the target's cost of capital, because it can use the bidder's internally generated funds to finance its capital expenditures rather than relying on more expensive external borrowings.

Romano does not find significant empirical support for other value-maximizing theories of takeovers based on either market inefficiency or expropriation. There is no evidence that the stock market consistently undervalues takeover targets nor that stock market myopia creates targets by penalizing long-term projects or research and development. She concludes that gains from takeovers cannot be traced to wealth transfers to target shareholders by labor, bondholders, consumers, or taxpayers. Although tax benefits from interest deductions may account for the premiums in going-private transactions, the net effect for taxpayers is ambiguous, because those benefits are offset by taxes paid by target shareholder on their gains. Consumers may fear that increasing industry concentration will raise prices, but Romano finds no support for this. Bondholders may suffer in takeovers as the value of bonds drop, because the target's indebtedness increases, but that loss in value does not account for gain to shareholders. Romano also sees no linkage between takeovers and employment levels except for top and middle managers.

Romano concludes that the data relied on to support theories that takeovers are not value-maximizing are ambiguous. Some data suggest that management may engage in takeovers to promote its own welfare at the expense of shareholder wealth. The fact, however, that the data show that there are net gains from takeovers demonstrates that takeovers do increase overall wealth. Therefore, non-value-maximizing theories cannot explain the majority of takeovers. Takeovers occur for a variety and combination of reasons. No single theory can explain all takeovers. Non-value-maximizing theories explain an isolated number of takeovers. In the majority of takeovers, Romano finds that efficiency-enhancing, value-maximizing theories of takeovers provide the best explanation for the gains created.

The wealth-creating nature of takeovers suggests to Romano that some takeover regulation should be reconsidered. Regulations that seek to protect employees or other constituencies in takeovers do not protect the public interest. Because the empirical support for claims that takeovers expropriate wealth from labor or other groups is weak, while the evidence does support claims that takeovers serve to eliminate inefficient management, such regulation may simply transfer wealth from shareholders to management. Similarly, restrictive state takeover laws have a negative stock price effect, harming shareholders with little benefit for other groups except management. Romano finds that regulations favoring auctions have an ambiguous impact. Auctions do raise premiums for target shareholders, but the increased competition may lower bidder returns and therefore make the threat of hostile takeovers a less effective disciplinary device. The data, however, do not make clear whether legal rules promoting auctions have a negative impact on the number of takeovers, and it is possible that by reducing search costs or allowing the highest valuing-bidder to acquire the target, those rules have a beneficial effect.

A related question is whether the rapid decline in takeover activity after 1989, which followed a long gradual increase that began in 1975, was caused by the proliferation in antitakeover defenses. By 1991, 87% of all New York Stock Exchange listed Corporations were protected against an uninvited takeover bid by either a poison pill, a business combination statute, a control share statute, or some combination of the three. Robert Comment & G. William Schwert, *Poison or Placebo? Evidence on the Deterrent And Wealth Effects of Modern Antitakeover Measures* 3 (NBER WORKING PAPER No. 4316 (1993). Despite the strong correlation between the proliferation of antitakeover defenses and the demise of takeover activity, Professors Comment and Schwert found no "direct evidence" that antitakeover measures caused the decline. *Id*. at 37. That led them to "conclude that the demise of the 1980s market for corporate control was caused by secular trends [i.e., "the 1990 recession and cash crunch"] and not the introduction, spread, and legal acceptance of poison pill rights plans, control share statutes, or business combination statutes." *Id*.

## F.  PROTECTION OF CONTROL

### PROBLEM
### GENERAL INDUSTRIES CORPORATION—PART I

General Industries Corporation (GIC) is a Columbia corporation whose stock is listed on the New York Stock Exchange. GIC's authorized capital is 100 million shares of common stock, of which 50 million shares are outstanding. GIC develops and produces high technology medical products. Its headquarters and principal laboratories are located in a medium size city in Connecticut, where GIC employs 3,000 people.

GIC has long been a research-oriented firm. It enjoys an excellent reputation for innovative, high quality work. Many of its employees are scientists, and GIC has always spent substantial amounts on research and development. R & D expenditures have grown in recent years, but few commercially successful products have been developed. GIC has reported losses for the last several years and its stock price has declined from a high of $90 to a current price of $34 per share.

GIC's 15 member board consists of seven management and eight non-management directors. The chairman of the board and chief executive officer is Abigail Andrews. Among the eight non-management directors is William Post, a partner in the company's outside law firm. Members of the board own a total of 5% of the outstanding stock.

Several months ago, GIC announced that it had negotiated a large contract with the National Institutes of Health (NIH) to work on development of new treatments for breast and prostate cancer. The contract calls for GIC to commit substantial resources to further investigate and test experimental technologies initially developed by NIH. Profits, if any, will come only if GIC develops commercially viable treatment technologies. Then, GIC will have exclusive rights to market any products it develops. GIC's board, after having been briefed on the contract and the potential impact of the technologies involved, unanimously approved the contract, even though in the short term its financial impact on GIC will be negative.

Charles Danton, a wealthy real estate investor, has owned 400,000 shares of GIC for several years and recently has become quite concerned about the company's declining earnings. After GIC announced the NIH contract, Danton decided the time had come to seek control of GIC. He is prepared to commit about $300 million of his personal funds and has been told by his investment bank, Merrill, Stanley & Co., that it can arrange a line of credit to provide the additional funds Danton would need to acquire 51% of GIC's stock at a price of up to $60 per share. Danton's plan is to make GIC more profitable by emphasizing consumer and industrial uses of its technology, eliminating some of the less profitable and riskier research, attempting to abrogate the NIH contract, and moving GIC's headquarters to Tucson, where his real estate investment firm is headquartered and where he is a trustee of the University Medical Center.

After receiving the commitment from Merrill, Stanley, Danton purchased an additional 600,000 shares of GIC stock on the open market at an average price of $32 per share, bringing his holdings to 2% of the outstanding stock. GIC's investment banker, First Prudential (First Pru), became aware of increased activity and managed to determine that Danton was the buyer. Through an intermediary, First Pru also learned about Danton's plans for GIC and also learned that he probably would be willing to sell his one million shares for $45 million, slightly more than his total cost for those shares.

First Pru has brought all this information to the attention of Ms. Andrews. It also has pointed out that to finance the purchase of Danton's stock, GIC probably would have to borrow $45 million at slightly over the prime rate. The GIC board has scheduled a meeting to consider how to proceed. Both Post and representatives of First Pru are scheduled to make presentations. Post has asked you, an associate in his law firm, to brief him on the following questions.

1. Can GIC purchase Danton's stock at an above market price? If the purchase is made, should GIC seek a commitment from Danton that he will not turn around and make another takeover bid?

2. If it decides not to buy Danton's stock, what other measures might GIC take in anticipation of the expected bid? What measures the board implement on its own and what measures require shareholder approval?

## 1. BUSINESS JUDGMENT OR SELF–DEALING?

### CHEFF v. MATHES

41 Del.Ch. 494, 199 A.2d 548 (1964).

CAREY, JUSTICE.

This is an appeal from the decision of the Vice–Chancellor in a derivative suit holding certain directors of Holland Furnace Company liable for loss allegedly resulting from improper use of corporate funds to purchase shares of the company. Because a meaningful decision upon review turns upon a complete understanding of the factual background, a somewhat detailed summary of the evidence is required.

Holland Furnace Company, a corporation of the State of Delaware, manufactures warm air furnaces, air conditioning equipment, and other home heating equipment. At the time of the relevant transactions, the board of directors was composed of the seven individual defendants. Mr. Cheff had been Holland's Chief Executive Officer since 1933, received an annual salary of $77,400, and personally owned 6,000 shares of the company. He was also a director. Mrs. Cheff, the wife of Mr. Cheff, was a daughter of the founder of Holland and had served as a director since 1922. She personally owned 5,804 shares of Holland and owned 47.9 percent of Hazelbank United Interest, Inc. Hazelbank is an investment vehicle for Mrs. Cheff and members of the Cheff–Landwehr family group, which owned 164,950 shares of the 883,585 outstanding shares of Holland. As a director, Mrs. Cheff received a compensation of $200.00 for each monthly board meeting, whether or not she attended the meeting.

The third director, Edgar P. Landwehr, is the nephew of Mrs. Cheff and personally owned 24,010 shares of Holland and 8.6 percent of the outstanding shares of Hazelbank. He received no compensation from Holland other than the monthly director's fee.

Robert H. Trenkamp is an attorney who first represented Holland in 1946. In May 1953, he became a director of Holland and acted as general counsel for the company. During the period in question, he received no retainer from the company, but did receive substantial sums for legal services rendered the company. Apart from the above-described payments, he received no compensation from Holland other than the monthly director's fee. He owned 200 shares of Holland Furnace stock. Although he owned no shares of Hazelbank, at the time relevant to this controversy, he was serving as a director and counsel of Hazelbank.

John D. Ames was then a partner in the Chicago investment firm of Bacon, Whipple & Co. and joined the board at the request of Mr. Cheff. During the periods in question, his stock ownership varied between ownership of no shares to ownership of 300 shares. He was considered by the other members of the Holland board to be the financial advisor to the board. He received no compensation from Holland other than the normal director's fee.

Mr. Ralph G. Boalt was the Vice President of J.R. Watkins Company, a manufacturer and distributor of cosmetics. In 1953, at the request of Mr. Cheff, he became a member of the board of directors. Apart from the normal director's fee, he received no compensation from Holland for his services.

Mr. George Spatta was the President of Clark Equipment Company, a large manufacturer of earth moving equipment. In 1951, at the request of Mr. Cheff, he joined the board of directors of Holland. Apart from the normal director's fee, he received no compensation from the company.

\* \* \*

Prior to the events in question, Holland employed approximately 8500 persons and maintained 400 branch sales offices located in 43 states. The volume of sales had declined from over $41,000,000 in 1948 to less than $32,000,000 in 1956. Defendants contend that the decline in earnings is attributable to the artificial post-war demand generated in the 1946–1948 period. In order to stabilize the condition of the company, the sales department apparently was reorganized and certain unprofitable branch offices were closed. By 1957 this reorganization had been completed and the management was convinced that the changes were manifesting beneficial results. The practice of the company was to directly employ the retail salesman, and the management considered that practice—unique in the furnace business—to be a vital factor in the company's success.

During the first five months of 1957, the monthly trading volume of Holland's stock on the New York Stock Exchange ranged between 10,300 shares to 24,200 shares. In the last week of June 1957, however, the trading increased to 37,800 shares, with a corresponding increase in the market price. In June of 1957, Mr. Cheff met with Mr. Arnold H. Maremont, who was President of Maremont Automotive Products, Inc. and Chairman of the boards of Motor Products Corporation and Allied Paper Corporation. Mr. Cheff testified, on deposition, that Maremont generally inquired about the feasibility of merger between Motor Products and Holland. Mr. Cheff testified that, in view of the difference in sales practices between the two companies, he informed Mr. Maremont that a merger did not seem feasible. In reply, Mr. Maremont stated that, in the light of Mr. Cheff's decision, he had no further interest in Holland nor did he wish to buy any of the stock of Holland.

None of the members of the board apparently connected the interest of Mr. Maremont with the increased activity of Holland stock. However, Mr. Trenkamp and Mr. Staal, the Treasurer of Holland, unsuccessfully made an informal investigation in order to ascertain the identity of the purchaser or purchasers. The mystery was resolved, however, when Maremont called Ames in July of 1957 to inform the latter that Maremont then owned 55,000 shares of Holland stock. At this juncture, no requests for change in corporate policy were made, and Maremont made no demand to be made a member of the board of Holland.

Ames reported the above information to the board at its July 30, 1957 meeting. Because of the position now occupied by Maremont, the board elected to investigate the financial and business history of Maremont and corporations controlled by him. Apart from the documentary evidence produced by this investigation, which will be considered *infra*, Staal testified, on deposition, that "leading bank officials" had indicated that Maremont "had been a participant, or had attempted to be, in the liquidation of a number of companies." * * *

On August 23, 1957, at the request of Maremont, a meeting was held between Mr. Maremont and Cheff. At this meeting, Cheff was informed that Motor Products then owned approximately 100,000 shares of Holland stock. Maremont then made a demand that he be named to the board of directors, but Cheff refused to consider it. Since considerable controversy has been generated by Maremont's alleged threat to liquidate the company or substantially alter the sales force of Holland, we believe it desirable to set forth the testimony of Cheff on this point: "Now we have 8500 men, direct employees, so the problem is entirely different. He indicated immediately that he had no interest in that type of distribution, that he didn't think it was modern, that he felt furnaces could be sold as he sold mufflers, through half a dozen salesmen in a wholesale way."

Testimony was introduced by the defendants tending to show that substantial unrest was present among the employees of Holland as a result of the threat of Maremont to seek control of Holland. * * * Moreover, at approximately this time, the company was furnished with a Dun and Bradstreet report, which indicated the practice of Maremont to achieve quick profits by sales or liquidations of companies acquired by him. The defendants were also supplied with an income statement of Motor Products, Inc., showing a loss of $336,121.00 for the period in 1957.

On August 30, 1957, the board was informed by Cheff of Maremont's demand to be placed upon the board and of Maremont's belief that the retail sales organization of Holland was obsolete. The board was also informed of the results of the investigation by Cheff and Staal. Predicated upon this information, the board authorized the purchase of company stock on the market with corporate funds, ostensibly for use in a stock option plan.

Subsequent to this meeting, substantial numbers of shares were purchased and, in addition, Mrs. Cheff made alternate personal purchases of Holland stock. As a result of purchases by Maremont, Holland and Mrs. Cheff, the market price rose. * * * On September 4th, Maremont proposed to sell his current holdings of Holland to the corporation for $14.00 a share. However, because of delay in responding to this offer, Maremont withdrew the offer. At this time, Mrs. Cheff was obviously quite concerned over the prospect of a Maremont acquisition, and had stated her willingness to expend her personal resources to prevent it.

On September 30, 1957, Motor Products Corporation, by letter to Mrs. Bowles, made a buy-sell offer to Hazelbank. Although Mrs. Bowles and Mrs. Putnam were opposed to any acquisition of Holland stock by Hazelbank, Mr. Landwehr conceded that a majority of the board were in favor of the purchase. Despite this fact, the finance committee elected to refer the offer to the Holland board on the grounds that it was the primary concern of Holland.

Thereafter, Mr. Trenkamp arranged for a meeting with Maremont, which occurred on October 14–15, 1957, in Chicago. Prior to this meeting, Trenkamp was aware of the intentions of Hazelbank and Mrs. Cheff to purchase all or portions of the stock then owned by Motor Products if Holland did not so act. As a result of the meeting, there was a tentative agreement on the part of Motor Products to sell its 155,000 shares at $14.40 per share. On October 23, 1957, at a special meeting of the Holland board, the purchase was considered. All directors, except Spatta, were present. The dangers allegedly posed by Maremont were again reviewed by the board. Trenkamp and Mrs. Cheff agree that the latter informed the board that either she or Hazelbank would purchase part or all of the block of Holland stock owned by Motor Products if the Holland board did not so act. The board was also informed that in order for the corporation to finance the purchase, substantial sums would have to be borrowed from commercial lending institutions. A resolution authorizing the purchase of 155,000 shares from Motor Products was adopted by the board. The price paid was in excess of the market price prevailing at the time, and the book value of the stock was approximately $20.00 as compared to approximately $14.00 for the net quick asset value. The transaction was subsequently consummated. The stock option plan mentioned in the minutes has never been implemented. In 1959, Holland stock reached a high of $15.25 a share.

On February 6, 1958, plaintiffs, owners of 60 shares of Holland stock, filed a derivative suit in the court below naming all of the individual directors of Holland, Holland itself and Motor Products Corporation as defendants. The complaint alleged that all of the purchases of stock by Holland in 1957 were for the purpose of insuring the perpetuation of control by the incumbent directors. The complaint requested that the transaction between Motor Products and Holland be rescinded and, secondly, that the individual defendants account to Holland for the alleged damages. Since Motor Products was never served with process, the initial remedy became inapplicable. Ames was never served nor did he enter an appearance.

After trial, the Vice Chancellor found the following facts: (a) Holland directly sells to retail consumers by means of numerous branch offices. There were no intermediate dealers. (b) Immediately prior to the complained-of transactions, the sales and earnings of Holland had declined and its marketing practices were under investigation by the Federal Trade Commission. (c) Mr. Cheff and Trenkamp had received substantial sums as Chief Executive and attorney of the company, respectively. (d) Maremont, on August 23rd, 1957, demanded a place on the board. (e) At the October 14th meeting between Trenkamp, Staal and Maremont, Trenkamp and Staal were authorized to speak for Hazelbank and Mrs. Cheff as well as Holland. Only Mr. Cheff, Mrs. Cheff, Mr. Landwehr, and Mr. Trenkamp clearly understood, prior to the October 23rd meeting, that either Hazelbank or Mrs. Cheff would have utilized their funds to purchase the Holland stock if Holland had not acted. (g) There was no real threat posed by Maremont and no substantial evidence of intention by Maremont to liquidate Holland. (h) Any employee unrest could have been caused by factors other than Maremont's intrusion and "only one important employee was shown to have left, and his motive for leaving is not clear." (i) The Court rejected the stock option plan as a meaningful rationale for the purchase from Maremont or the prior open market purchases.

The Court then found that the actual purpose behind the purchase was the desire to perpetuate control, but because of its finding that only the four above-named directors knew of the "alternative", the remaining directors were exonerated. No appeal was taken by plaintiffs from that decision.

\* \* \*

Under the provisions of 8 Del.C. § 160, a corporation is granted statutory power to purchase and sell shares of its own stock. The charge here is not one of violation of statute, but the allegation is that the true motives behind such purchases were improperly centered upon perpetuation of control. In an analogous field, courts have sustained the use of proxy funds to inform stockholders of management's views upon the policy questions inherent in an election to a board of directors, but have not sanctioned the use of corporate funds to advance the selfish desires of directors to perpetuate themselves in office. Similarly, if the actions of the board were motivated by a sincere belief that the buying out of the dissident stockholder was necessary to maintain what the board believed to be proper business practices, the board will not be held liable for such decision, even though hindsight indicates the decision was not the wisest course. *See Kors v. Carey*, Del.Ch., 158 A.2d 136. On the other hand, if the board has acted solely or primarily because of the desire to perpetuate themselves in office, the use of corporate funds for such purposes is improper. *See Bennett v. Propp*, Del., 187 A.2d 405, and *Yasik v. Wachtel*, 25 Del.Ch. 247, 17 A.2d 309.

Our first problem is the allocation of the burden of proof to show the presence or lack of good faith on the part of the board in authorizing the purchase of shares. Initially, the decision of the board of directors in authorizing a purchase was presumed to be in good faith and could be overturned only by a conclusive showing by plaintiffs of fraud or other misconduct. In *Kors*, cited *supra*, the court merely indicated that the directors are presumed to act in good faith and the burden of proof to show to the contrary falls upon the plaintiff. However, in *Bennett v. Propp*, *supra*, we stated:

> We must bear in mind the inherent danger in the purchase of shares with corporate funds to remove a threat to corporate policy when a threat to control is involved. The directors are of necessity confronted with a conflict of interest, and an objective decision is difficult. * * * Hence, in our opinion, the burden should be on the directors to justify such a purchase as one primarily in the corporate interest. (187 A.2d 409, at page 409).

\* \* \*

To say that the burden of proof is upon the defendants is not to indicate, however, that the directors have the same "self-dealing interest" as is present, for example, when a director sells property to the corporation. The only clear pecuniary interest shown on the record was held by Mr. Cheff, as an executive of the corporation, and Trenkamp, as its attorney. The mere fact that some of the other directors were substantial shareholders does not create a personal pecuniary interest in the decisions made by the board of directors, since all shareholders would presumably share the benefit flowing to the substantial shareholder. Accordingly, these directors other than Trenkamp and Cheff, while called upon to justify their actions, will not be held to the same standard of proof required of those directors having personal and pecuniary interest in the transaction.

Plaintiffs urge that the sale price was unfair in view of the fact that the price was in excess of that prevailing on the open market. However, as conceded by all parties, a substantial block of stock will normally sell at a higher price than that prevailing on the open market, the increment being attributable to a "control premium". Plaintiffs argue that it is inappropriate to require the defendant corporation to pay a control premium, since control is meaningless to an acquisition by a corporation of its own shares. However, it is elementary that a holder of a substantial number of shares would expect to receive the control premium as part of his selling price, and if the corporation desired to obtain the stock, it is unreasonable to expect that the corporation could avoid paying what any other purchaser would be required to pay for the stock. In any event, the financial expert produced by defendant at trial indicated that the price paid was fair and there was no rebuttal.

The question then presented is whether or not defendants satisfied the burden of proof of showing reasonable grounds to believe a danger to corporate policy and effectiveness existed by the presence of the Maremont stock ownership. It is important to remember that the directors satisfy their burden by showing good faith and reasonable investigation; the directors will not be penalized for an honest mistake of judgment, if the judgment appeared reasonable at the time the decision was made.

\* \* \*

\* \* \* [W]e are of the opinion that the evidence presented in the court below leads inevitably to the conclusion that the board of directors, based upon direct investigation, receipt of professional advice, and personal observations of the contradictory action of Maremont and his explanation of corporate purpose, believed, with justification, that there was a reasonable threat to the continued existence of Holland, or at least existence in its present form, by the plan of Maremont to continue building up his stock holdings. We find no evidence in the record sufficient to justify a contrary conclusion. The opinion of the Vice Chancellor that employee unrest may have been engendered by other factors or that the board had no grounds to suspect Maremont is not supported in any manner by the evidence.

As noted above, the Vice–Chancellor found that the purpose of the acquisition was the improper desire to maintain control, but, at the same time, he exonerated those individual directors whom he believed to be unaware of the possibility of using non-corporate funds to accomplish this purpose. Such a decision is inconsistent with his finding that the motive was improper, within the rule enunciated in *Bennett*. If the actions were in fact improper because of a desire to maintain control, then the presence or absence of a non-corporate alternative is irrelevant, as corporate funds may not be used to advance an improper purpose even if there is no non-corporate alternative available. Conversely, if the actions were proper because of a decision by the board made in good faith that the corporate interest was served thereby, they are not rendered improper by the fact that some individual directors were willing to advance personal funds if the corporation did not. It is conceivable that the Vice Chancellor considered this feature of the case to be of significance because of his apparent belief that any excess corporate funds should have been used to finance a subsidiary corporation. That action would not have solved the problem of Holland's over-capitalization. In any event, this question was a matter of business judgment, which furnishes no justification for holding the directors personally responsible in this case.

Accordingly, the judgment of the court below is reversed and remanded with instruction to enter judgment for the defendants.

### Note: Evaluating Defensive Tactics:
### An Introduction

Courts usually avoid inquiry into directors' motives for making corporate decisions. If no conflict of interest is shown, courts assume directors acted in good faith and that their decisions reflect valid business judgments. If a conflict is shown, courts assume directors were motivated by their personal financial interests and require that they demonstrate their decisions were fair. This analytic framework breaks down, however, with regard to decisions that have the effect of protecting control. On the one hand, a board must decide whether a change in control is in the corporation's best interest. On the other, management (especially inside directors and officers) has an interest in safeguarding its jobs. *See* Ronald J. Gilson, *A Structural Approach to Corporations: The Case Against Defensive Tactics in Tender Offers*, 33 STAN.L.REV. 819, 826–827 (1981).

One could argue that because of management's interest, the business judgment rule should not apply and that fairness must be proved. But Professor Gilson points out that fairness is not an effective standard to evaluate a decision to protect control. A transaction usually is considered "fair" if its terms are equivalent to those that disinterested parties would reach in an arm's-length transaction. When a defensive tactic such as a share repurchase is being evaluated, the real question is whether the decision to repurchase shares was justified, *not* whether the repurchase price was fair. Judicial review should focus on whether shareholders were better off after the repurchase than they were before. It is difficult to answer this question using a fairness standard, but a court also must examine "factors which the business judgment rule excludes from consideration." *Id*. at 827.

Professor Gilson suggests that the *Cheff* court attempted to deal with this problem by focusing on the Holland directors' motives for repurchasing Maremont's stock. He notes that courts are accustomed to examining motive in a variety of other contexts, which may have made the court comfortable with this approach. What the court actually held was that if Holland's directors had reasonable grounds to believe that Maremont's stock ownership threatened corporate policy and effectiveness, the court would not second guess the board's decision. The court further stated that it would treat the board's determination that a threat existed as a business judgment if it found the board had acted in good faith and after reasonable investigation. The board's showing that it had policy difference with Maremont satisfied this requirement.

*Cheff* can be read as implying that so long as a corporation's management can identify some policy difference between itself and a potential bidder, courts will not evaluate whether the tactics it employs to eliminate that "threat" are either reasonable or fair even though management has a conflict of interest. The rule is a little different than in a standard business judgment situation, in that directors have the burden of proving that their determination a threat existed was based on a reasonable investigation. But consider the scanty evidence on which the court relied to hold that Holland's directors had satisfied that burden.

### *Note: Corporate Defensive Tactics*

During the 1980s as the number of hostile takeovers rose, corporate boards adopted a variety of tactics to protect their shareholders and their corporations. Aided by corporate lawyers and investment bankers, companies implemented a variety of innovative defensive techniques including self-tender offers, defensive mergers, leveraged management-buyouts, poison pills, supermajority voting provisions, and corporate restructurings. No single technique created an absolute bar to hostile takeovers. Each one, however, helped deter a hostile transaction by slowing the process, raising the economic cost to the bidder, or providing shareholders with an attractive alternative to the takeover bid. In assessing the efficacy of the defenses outlined below, consider what the rationale is for each. Is it to maintain the independence of the target? Is it meant to produce negotiations with the bidder? Is it designed to initiate an auction? Or is it intended to bring about a business combination with another partner?

Further, in thinking about what view the law should take with respect to takeover defenses, consider the weight to be given to the market effects of each tactic. The Office of the Chief Economist of the SEC has studied different takeover defenses and has found that anti-takeover amendments, poison pills and targeted share repurchases (greenmail) reduce shareholder wealth as measured by their immediate impact on the market place of affected companies' stock. This conclusion is consistent with the argument advanced by Frank H. Easterbrook & Daniel R. Fischel, *The Proper Role of a Target Management in Responding to a Tender Offer*, 94 HARV.L.REV. 1161 (1981), that any resistance to takeovers injures shareholders' interests. A contrary view holds that shareholders are not so foolish as to approve takeover defenses that are injurious, and that certain defenses allow shareholders to act in a coordinated way, avoid the prisoner's dilemma and thereby improve their welfare. William J. Carney, *Shareholder Coordination Costs, Shark Repellents, and Takeout Mergers: The Case Against Fiduciary Duties*, 1983 AM.B.FOUND RES.J. 341.

#### a. *Poison Pills*

Probably the most common and effective defensive technique has been the shareholder rights plan or "poison pill." A rights plan grants to each shareholder, typically as a dividend, a contingent right to purchase stock or other securities at any time within a long time period, generally 10 years. Because the right is not exercisable until a triggering event occurs, it has little present value to the holder. The events that trigger poison pills typically are a tender offer for the company that the incumbent board of directors has not approved (a hostile tender offer) or the acquisition of common stock by a third party above a certain threshold, usually 20% or 30% of the outstanding common stock. Until the triggering event occurs, the board retains the power to redeem the rights for a nominal payment.

A poison pill can have "flip-over" rights, "flip-in" rights or both. A flip-over right issued by the target company allows the target company's shareholders (but not any bidder who purchases their stock) to purchase shares of the *bidder's* stock at half-price if the bidder (or a corporation controlled by the bidder) merges with the target after the tender offer. Such second-step mergers are common, and will be essential if the bidder plans to use the assets of the target to finance, or secure financing for, the cost of the acquisition. If a flip-over plan is in place and a substantial portion of the target's shareholders do not tender their stock, their ability to purchase shares in the merged entity at half price will have the effect of diluting the value of stock held by the bidder's other shareholders, often to the point where the overall cost of the acquisition will become prohibitive. However, a flip-over plan will not deter an acquiror who does not plan on effectuating a second-step merger. For example, even though Crown Zellerbach had a flip-over poison pill, it was never triggered because Sir James Goldsmith, who purchased the controlling interest, did not plan a second-step merger.

Flip-in poison pills were developed to overcome this problem. A flip-in pill allows a rights holder, other than the bidder, to purchase stock or other securities of the *target* company at a below-market price. When such rights are exercised, the overall cost of the takeover is raised to an uneconomic level.

Another variant of poison pills is a "back-end" plan. These plans allow target company directors to designate a "fair price" for target company stock and give shareholders the right to require the target to purchase their shares at that price if the bidder does not do so after it obtains control. A back-end plan protects shareholders from coercive two-tier tender offers in which a bidder offers a high price for a control block and then offers a lower price on the back-end to purchase the remaining shares. The back-end right ensures shareholders that they will not be penalized in the second step, and thus effectively eviscerates the coercive component of a two-tier bid.

A key element of all three types of poison pills is that the target company's board of directors retains the right to redeem the pill before a triggering event has occurred. This provides a powerful incentive for a potential bidder to negotiate with the target's board to have the poison pill redeemed. The board can use this bargaining leverage to seek a better deal for shareholders, or for other, arguably less legitimate purposes.

An increasingly popular form of poison pill is the continuing director pill that can be redeemed only by the directors who adopted the pill or their designated successors. The purpose of such a pill is to prevent the bidder from electing directors in a proxy contest and then removing the pill after they have assumed control. The validity of such a pill is discussed later in this section.

In *Moran v. Household International, Inc.*, 500 A.2d 1346 (Del.1985), Household's board adopted the pill out of concern that the company was vulnerable to a hostile bid although no bid had yet been made. Plaintiff sought to have the pill declared invalid on the grounds that it deprived shareholders of their right to receive a subsequent tender offer. The Delaware Supreme Court upheld the validity of the pill. The court found that DGCL § 157 authorized the board to issue rights to purchase the company's stock, although it acknowledged that § 157 had never been used to create the rights such as those Household had created. The court also noted that flip-over provisions were analogous to "anti-dilution" or "anti-destruction" provisions which were customary provisions of corporate securities that protect the security holder in a merger. The court rejected the argument that the poison pill precluded all future tender offers because a potential bidder could avoid triggering the pill by not effectuating a second-step merger, could condition its offer on redemption of the poison pill by Household's board of directors, or could seek to remove Household's board through a proxy solicitation and then have the new board redeem the rights. The court emphasized that it was only holding that adoption of the poison pill constituted legitimate corporate planning that was reasonable under the standard of Unocal Corporation v. Mesa Petroleum Co., 493 A.2d 946 (Del.1985), *infra*. It made clear, however, that a board's subsequent decision to redeem the pill also would be evaluated under *Unocal*.

For an interesting discussion of poison pills in the context of a proxy contest, *see* Randall S. Thomas, *Judicial Review of Defensive Tactics in Proxy Contests: When Is Using A Rights Plan Right?*, 46 VAND.L.REV. 503 (1993).

### b. Using the Corporate Machinery

There are measures that a board can take before a proxy contest or tender offer to make a hostile takeover bid less attractive. By amending its charter, a company can stagger the terms of its directors, so that only one-third are elected each year. A bidder then faces the prospect of having to win two successive proxy contests to gain control. Other charter amendments can make directors removable only for good cause; allow directors but not shareholders to call special shareholder meetings; or eliminate shareholder power to act without a meeting. These deterrents have the potential to slow down a bidder seeking control, but are unlikely to stop an aggressive bidder prepared to make an all-cash tender offer.

A supermajority voting requirement may constitute a more useful tender offer defense. A corporation's charter can be amended to require that all mergers be approved by 80 percent of the shares, instead of the usual majority, if the other party to the transaction owns more than 5% of the corporation's stock. For a bidder to gain complete control of the corporation, it thus will need to acquire the support of at least 80 percent of the stock. A supermajority provision can prove to be an especially effective deterrent if a company's insiders own enough stock to block a merger.

### c.  Corporate Restructuring

In some cases, companies have chosen to preempt bidders by restructuring the corporation so as to confer value on the shareholders in excess of the bidder's offer. In a restructuring, the potential target offers shareholders a package of securities (usually debt or preferred stock) and cash either as an extraordinary dividend, in which event shareholder approval is not required, or through an exchange offer, merger, corporate reclassification, or a spin-off that requires shareholder approval. After the transaction, shareholders will have received a payment of cash and/or debt securities and the company will have a more highly leveraged capital structure.

To finance a restructuring, a company often will take actions similar to those taken by a prospective bidder. It will borrow much of the money it needs, sell non-essential assets and attempt to streamline its remaining business. Management, to survive, will have to find a way to both service the debt and maintain the viability of the company's operations.

A restructuring undertaken in the face of a takeover may raise duty of loyalty problems. If management's equity interest in the restructured company will increase because shareholders are given a choice of receiving cash or securities for their stock and management plans to take additional equity, the possibility arises that management is enriching itself at shareholders' expense. The analysis is complicated by the difficulty of valuing precisely the securities to be issued as part of the restructuring.

### d.  Defensive Mergers

The "white knight" defense, in which the target searches for a more compatible merger partner, offers an alternative to restructuring the company. Shareholders still receive an attractive price for their shares, but managers are likely to keep their jobs. A friendly transaction often encourages closer communication between buyer and seller, which can increase the price. However, the haste with which the target seeks to attract an alternate suitor creates its own danger. Acquisitions require careful study to determine whether they make sense and how they should be priced. A hostile bidder may have studied the target for months before launching its bid. In contrast, the target may have only a few weeks to find a white knight and conclude an acquisition agreement. The white knight, caught up in the excitement of a battle for corporate control, may discover that the business it has acquired is not exactly the business it thought it was buying.

### e.  Issuance of Stock

A corporation's board of directors has authority to issue previously authorized stock to acquire assets, to effect a merger, to fund an employee stock ownership plan (ESOP), or in exchange for stock or cash. Issuance of stock to an investor friendly to management can have a decisive effect in a takeover contest. In simple terms, if enough additional shares are issued to persons friendly to management, the bidder will not be able to obtain control.

Judicial decisions as to the propriety of a stock issuance in the context of a takeover bid have been heavily influenced by the surrounding facts and circumstances. *Compare Condec Corp. v. Lunkenheimer Co.*, 43 Del.Ch. 353, 230 A.2d 769 (1967) (sale enjoined where primary purpose was to prevent transfer of control to a suitor who had acquired more than 50 percent of common stock in two tender offers) with *Cummings v. United Artists Theatre Circuit, Inc.*, 237 Md. 1, 204 A.2d 795 (1964) (sale not enjoined where "principal motive was not related to control, and the effect on control caused by the board's action is not of compelling significance").

The sale of a large block of stock to an ESOP has become a popular defensive tactic. ESOPs provide valuable business benefits to the corporation in the form of lower benefit costs due to special tax advantages and improved employee performance by aligning employee interests with those of shareholders. However, because management often controls the right to vote some or all of the shares in the ESOP, and since employees often vote with management in any event, a potential conflict of interest exists. *See Buckhorn, Inc. v. Ropak Corp.*, 656 F.Supp. 209 (S.D.Ohio 1987).

*Compare Shamrock Holdings, Inc. v. Polaroid Corp.*, 559 A.2d 257 (Del.Ch.1989), (in view of the timing of the ESOP, its structure and operation and its purpose and probable impact, the ESOP was fair to Polaroid and its shareholders because it did not constitute an insurmountable obstacle to Shamrock's takeover bid) with *NCR Corp. v. American Telephone & Telegraph Co.*, 761 F.Supp. 475 (S.D.Ohio 1991), (plan was an improper attempt by NCR management to perpetuate its control; the NCR directors were not protected by the business judgment rule because they had reached their decision to fund the ESOP on the basis of "grossly inadequate information."

### f. Share Repurchases and Greenmail

A corporation generally has the power to repurchase its own stock, so long as such action does not violate the applicable legal capital rules. Repurchases often serve valid financial purposes such as to fund the exercise of options and warrants, the conversion of convertible securities, the acquisition of assets, or a merger without diluting current stockholders.

When a contest for control is in progress, a stock repurchase also can be used to eliminate the bidder by paying a premium price. To prevent the bidder from using the proceeds of its resale to launch another bid, the target will require the bidder to enter into a standstill agreement—an agreement not to purchase or bid for the target's shares for a specified period of time.

The willingness of some companies to resolve takeover threats by repurchasing their shares at a premium made it attractive for entrepreneurial investors to acquire substantial blocks of stock in potential targets and then threaten a takeover bid in the hope that the target would offer to repurchase the stock instead. In the jargon of the takeover world, such payments became known as "greenmail" and investors who sought them became known as "greenmailers." *See Unocal, infra.*

Scholars are not of one mind on the propriety of greenmail. Most criticize it as self-serving, but some believe that greenmail often confers benefits on shareholders by facilitating an auction for the target's shares. It signals important information to the market place while at the same time enabling the company to rid itself of an unwanted suitor. Jonathan R. Macey & Fred S. McChesney, *A Theoretical Analysis of Corporate Greenmail*, 95 YALE L.J. 13 (1985). Studies by the Office of the Chief Economist of the SEC and by the Office of Management and Budget differ in their assessment of greenmail, with the former offering evidence that share prices significantly decline after a greenmail payment (Study dated September 11, 1984) and the latter contending that shareholders benefit. Memorandum from Douglas H. Ginsburg, dated September 13, 1984.

In any event, as a consequence of the development and judicial endorsement of a plethora of other takeover defenses, very few bidders have sought, and very few corporations have elected to pay, greenmail in recent years.

## 2. ENHANCED BUSINESS JUDGMENT RULE

### UNOCAL CORPORATION v. MESA PETROLEUM CO.
493 A.2d 946 (Del.1985).

MOORE, JUSTICE.

We confront an issue of first impression in Delaware—the validity of a corporation's self-tender for its own shares which excludes from participation a stockholder making a hostile tender offer for the company's stock.

The Court of Chancery granted a preliminary injunction to the plaintiffs, Mesa Petroleum Co., Mesa Asset Co., Mesa Partners II, and Mesa Eastern, Inc. (collectively "Mesa")[1] enjoining an exchange offer of the defendant, Unocal Corporation (Unocal) for its own stock. The trial court concluded that a selective exchange offer, excluding Mesa, was legally impermissible. We cannot agree with such a blanket rule. The factual findings of the Vice Chancellor, fully supported by the record, establish that Unocal's board, consisting of a majority of independent directors, acted in good faith, and after reasonable investigation found that Mesa's tender offer was both inadequate and coercive. Under the circumstances the board had both the power and duty to oppose a bid it perceived to be harmful to the corporate enterprise. On this record we

1. T. Boone Pickens, Jr., is President and Chairman of the Board of Mesa Petro- leum and President of Mesa Asset and con- trols the related Mesa entities.

are satisfied that the device Unocal adopted is reasonable in relation to the threat posed, and that the board acted in the proper exercise of sound business judgment. We will not substitute our views for those of the board if the latter's decision can be "attributed to any rational business purpose." *Sinclair Oil Corp. v. Levien*, Del.Supr., 280 A.2d 717, 720 (1971). Accordingly, we reverse the decision of the Court of Chancery and order the preliminary injunction vacated.

## I.

The factual background of this matter bears a significant relationship to its ultimate outcome.

On April 8, 1985, Mesa, the owner of approximately 13% of Unocal's stock, commenced a two-tier "front loaded" cash tender offer for 64 million shares, or approximately 37%, of Unocal's outstanding stock at a price of $54 per share. The "back-end" was designed to eliminate the remaining publicly held shares by an exchange of securities purportedly worth $54 per share. However, pursuant to an order entered by the United States District Court for the Central District of California on April 26, 1985, Mesa issued a supplemental proxy statement to Unocal's stockholders disclosing that the securities offered in the second-step merger would be highly subordinated, and that Unocal's capitalization would differ significantly from its present structure. Unocal has rather aptly termed such securities "junk bonds".

Unocal's board consists of eight independent outside directors and six insiders. It met on April 13, 1985, to consider the Mesa tender offer. Thirteen directors were present, and the meeting lasted nine and one-half hours. The directors were given no agenda or written materials prior to the session. However, detailed presentations were made by legal counsel regarding the board's obligations under both Delaware corporate law and the federal securities laws. The board then received a presentation from Peter Sachs on behalf of Goldman Sachs & Co. (Goldman Sachs) and Dillon, Read & Co. (Dillon Read) discussing the bases for their opinions that the Mesa proposal was wholly inadequate. Mr. Sachs opined that the minimum cash value that could be expected from a sale or orderly liquidation for 100% of Unocal's stock was in excess of $60 per share. In making his presentation, Mr. Sachs showed slides outlining the valuation techniques used by the financial advisors, and others, depicting recent business combinations in the oil and gas industry. The Court of Chancery found that the Sachs presentation was designed to apprise the directors of the scope of the analyses performed rather than the facts and numbers used in reaching the conclusion that Mesa's tender offer price was inadequate.

Mr. Sachs also presented various defensive strategies available to the board if it concluded that Mesa's two-step tender offer was inadequate and should be opposed. One of the devices outlined was a self-tender by Unocal for its own stock with a reasonable price range of $70 to $75 per share. The cost of such a proposal would cause the company to incur $6.1—6.5 billion of additional debt, and a presentation was made informing the board of Unocal's ability to handle it. The directors were told that the primary effect of this obligation would be to reduce exploratory drilling, but that the company would nonetheless remain a viable entity.

The eight outside directors, comprising a clear majority of the thirteen members present, then met separately with Unocal's financial advisors and attorneys. Thereafter, they unanimously agreed to advise the board that it should reject Mesa's tender offer as inadequate, and that Unocal should pursue a self-tender to provide the stockholders with a fairly priced alternative to the Mesa proposal. The board then reconvened and unanimously adopted a resolution rejecting as grossly inadequate Mesa's tender offer. Despite the nine and one-half hour length of the meeting, no formal decision was made on the proposed defensive self-tender.

On April 15, the board met again with four of the directors present by telephone and one member still absent. This session lasted two hours. Unocal's Vice President of Finance and its Assistant General Counsel made a detailed presentation of the proposed terms of the exchange offer. A price range between $70 and $80 per share was considered, and ultimately the directors agreed upon $72. The board was also advised about the debt securities that would be issued, and the necessity of placing restrictive covenants upon certain corporate activities until the obligations were paid. The board's decisions were made in reliance on the advice of its investment bankers, including the terms and conditions upon which the securities were to be issued. Based upon this advice, and the board's own deliberations, the directors unanimously approved the exchange offer. Their resolution provided that if Mesa acquired 64 million shares of Unocal stock through its own offer (the Mesa Purchase Condition), Unocal would buy the remaining 49% outstanding for an exchange of debt securities having an aggregate par value of $72 per share. The board resolution also stated that the offer would be subject to other conditions that had been described to the board at the meeting, or which were deemed necessary by Unocal's officers, including the exclusion of Mesa from the proposal (the Mesa exclusion). Any such conditions were required to be in accordance with the "purport and intent" of the offer.

Unocal's exchange offer was commenced on April 17, 1985, and Mesa promptly challenged it by filing this suit in the Court of Chancery. On April 22, the Unocal board met again and was advised by Goldman Sachs and Dillon Read to waive the Mesa Purchase Condition as to 50 million shares. This recommendation was in response to a perceived concern of the shareholders that, if shares were tendered to Unocal, no shares would be purchased by either offeror. The directors were also advised that they should tender their own Unocal stock into the exchange offer as a mark of their confidence in it.

Another focus of the board was the Mesa exclusion. Legal counsel advised that under Delaware law Mesa could only be excluded for what the directors reasonably believed to be a valid corporate purpose. The directors' discussion centered on the objective of adequately compensating shareholders at the "back-end" of Mesa's proposal, which the latter would finance with "junk bonds". To include Mesa would defeat that goal, because under the proration aspect of the exchange offer (49%) every Mesa share accepted by Unocal would displace one held by another stockholder. Further, if Mesa were permitted to tender to Unocal, the latter would in effect be financing Mesa's own inadequate proposal.

Meanwhile, on April 22, 1985, Mesa amended its complaint in this action to challenge the Mesa exclusion. A preliminary injunction hearing was scheduled for May 8, 1985. However, on April 23, 1985, Mesa moved for a temporary restraining order in response to Unocal's announcement that it was partially waiving the Mesa Purchase Condition. After expedited briefing, the Court of Chancery heard Mesa's motion on April 26.

On April 29, 1985, the Vice Chancellor temporarily restrained Unocal from proceeding with the exchange offer unless it included Mesa. The trial court recognized that directors could oppose, and attempt to defeat, a hostile takeover which they considered adverse to the best interests of the corporation. However, the Vice Chancellor decided that in a selective purchase of the company's stock, the corporation bears the burden of showing: (1) a valid corporate purpose, and (2) that the transaction was fair to all of the stockholders, including those excluded.

* * *

## II.

The issues we address involve these fundamental questions: Did the Unocal board have the power and duty to oppose a takeover threat it reasonably perceived to be harmful to the corporate enterprise, and if so, is its action here entitled to the protection of the business judgment rule?

Mesa contends that the discriminatory exchange offer violates the fiduciary duties Unocal owes it. Mesa argues that because of the Mesa exclusion the business judgment rule is inapplicable, because the directors by tendering their own shares will derive a financial benefit that is not available to *all* Unocal stockholders. Thus, it is Mesa's ultimate contention that Unocal cannot establish that the exchange offer is fair to *all* shareholders, and argues that the Court of Chancery was correct in concluding that Unocal was unable to meet this burden.

Unocal answers that it does not owe a duty of "fairness" to Mesa, given the facts here. Specifically, Unocal contends that its board of directors reasonably and in good faith concluded that Mesa's $54 two-tier tender offer was coercive and inadequate, and that Mesa sought selective treatment for itself. Furthermore, Unocal argues that the board's approval of the exchange offer was made in good faith, on an informed basis, and in the exercise of due care. Under these circumstances, Unocal contends that its directors properly employed this device to protect the company and its stockholders from Mesa's harmful tactics.

## III.

We begin with the basic issue of the power of a board of directors of a Delaware corporation to adopt a defensive measure of this type. Absent such authority, all other questions are moot. Neither issues of fairness nor business judgment are pertinent without the basic underpinning of a board's legal power to act.

The board has a large reservoir of authority upon which to draw. Its duties and responsibilities proceed from the inherent powers conferred by 8 Del.C. § 141(a), respecting management of the corporation's "business and affairs". Additionally, the powers here being exercised derive from 8 Del.C. § 160(a), conferring broad authority upon a corporation to deal in its own stock. From this it is now well established that in the acquisition of its shares a Delaware corporation may deal selectively with its stockholders, provided the directors have not acted out of a sole or primary purpose to entrench themselves in office.

Finally, the board's power to act derives from its fundamental duty and obligation to protect the corporate enterprise, which includes stockholders, from harm reasonably perceived, irrespective of its source. Thus, we are satisfied that in the broad context of corporate governance, including issues of fundamental corporate change, a board of directors is not a passive instrumentality.

Given the foregoing principles, we turn to the standards by which director action is to be measured. In *Pogostin v. Rice*, Del.Supr., 480 A.2d 619 (1984), we held that the business judgment rule, including the standards by which director conduct is judged, is applicable in the context of a takeover. *Id.* at 627. The business judgment rule is a "presumption that in making a business decision the directors of a corporation acted on an informed basis, in good faith and in the honest belief that the action taken was in the best interests of the company." *Aronson v. Lewis*, Del.Supr., 473 A.2d 805, 812 (1984). A hallmark of the business judgment rule is that a court will not substitute its judgment for that of the board if the latter's decision can be "attributed to any rational business purpose." *Sinclair Oil Corp. v. Levien*, Del.Supr., 280 A.2d 717, 720 (1971).

When a board addresses a pending takeover bid it has an obligation to determine whether the offer is in the best interests of the corporation and its shareholders. In that respect a board's duty is no different from any other responsibility it shoulders, and its decisions should be no less entitled to the respect they otherwise would be accorded in the realm of business judgment. *See also Johnson v. Trueblood*, 629 F.2d 287, 292–293 (3d Cir.1980). There are, however, certain caveats to a proper exercise of this function. Because of the omnipresent specter that a board may be acting primarily in its own interests, rather than those of the corporation and its shareholders, there is an enhanced duty which calls for judicial examination at the threshold before the protections of the business judgment rule may be conferred.

This Court has long recognized that:

We must bear in mind the inherent danger in the purchase of shares with corporate funds to remove a threat to corporate policy when a threat to control is involved. The directors are of necessity confronted with a conflict of interest, and an objective decision is difficult.

*Bennett v. Propp*, Del.Supr., 187 A.2d 405, 409 (1962). In the face of this inherent conflict directors must show that they had reasonable grounds for believing that a danger to corporate policy and effectiveness existed because of another person's stock ownership. *Cheff v. Mathes*, 199 A.2d at 554–55. However, they satisfy that burden "by showing good faith and reasonable investigation. \* \* \*" *Id.* at 555. Furthermore, such proof is materially enhanced, as here, by the approval of a board comprised of a majority of outside independent directors who have acted in accordance with the foregoing standards.

### IV.

### A.

In the board's exercise of corporate power to forestall a takeover bid our analysis begins with the basic principle that corporate directors have a fiduciary duty to act in the best interests of the corporation's stockholders. *Guth v. Loft, Inc.*, Del.Supr., 5 A.2d 503, 510 (1939). As we have noted, their duty of care extends to protecting the corporation and its owners from perceived harm whether a threat originates from third parties or other shareholders. But such powers are not absolute. A corporation does not have unbridled discretion to defeat any perceived threat by any Draconian means available.

The restriction placed upon a selective stock repurchase is that the directors may not have acted solely or primarily out of a desire to perpetuate themselves in office. *See Cheff v. Mathes*, 199 A.2d at 556; *Kors v. Carey*, 158 A.2d at 140. Of course, to this is added the further caveat that inequitable action may not be taken under the guise of law. *Schnell v. Chris–Craft Industries, Inc.*, Del.Supr., 285 A.2d 437, 439 (1971). The standard of proof established in *Cheff v. Mathes* and discussed *supra,* is designed to ensure that a defensive measure to thwart or impede a takeover is indeed motivated by a good faith concern for the welfare of the corporation and its stockholders, which in all circumstances must be free of any fraud or other misconduct. *Cheff v. Mathes*, 199 A.2d at 554–55. However, this does not end the inquiry.

### B.

A further aspect is the element of balance. If defensive measure is to come within the ambit of the business judgment rule, it must be reasonable in relation to the threat posed. This entails an analysis by the directors of the nature of the takeover bid and its effect on the corporate enterprise. Examples of such concerns may include: inadequacy of the price offered, nature and timing of the offer, questions of illegality, the impact on "constituencies" other than shareholders (*i.e.*, creditors, customers, employees, and perhaps even the community generally), the risk of nonconsummation, and the quality of securities being offered in the exchange. *See* Lipton and Brownstein, *Takeover Responses and Directors' Responsibilities: An Update*, p. 7, ABA NATIONAL INSTITUTE ON THE DYNAMICS OF CORPORATE CONTROL (December 8, 1983). While not a controlling factor, it also seems to us that a board may reasonably consider the basic stockholder interests at stake, including those of short term speculators, whose actions may have fueled the coercive aspect of the offer at the expense of the long term investor.[11] Here, the threat posed was viewed by the Unocal board as a grossly inadequate two-tier coercive tender offer coupled with the threat of greenmail.

Specifically, the Unocal directors had concluded that the value of Unocal was substantially above the $54 per share offered in cash at the front end. Furthermore, they determined that the subordinated securities to be exchanged in Mesa's announced squeeze out of the remaining shareholders in the "back-end" merger were "junk bonds" worth far less than $54. It is now well recognized that such offers are a classic coercive measure designed to stampede shareholders into tendering at the first tier, even if the price is inadequate, out of fear of what they will receive at the back end of the transaction. Wholly beyond the coercive aspect of an inadequate two-tier tender offer, the threat was posed by a corporate raider with a national reputation as a "green-mailer".[13]

In adopting the selective exchange offer, the board stated that its objective was either to defeat the inadequate Mesa offer, or, should the offer still succeed, provide the 49% of its stockholders, who would otherwise be forced to accept "junk bonds", with $72 worth of senior debt. We find that both purposes are valid.

However, such efforts would have been thwarted by Mesa's participation in the exchange offer. First, if Mesa could tender its shares, Unocal would effectively be subsidizing the former's continuing effort to buy Unocal stock at $54 per share. Second, Mesa could not, by definition, fit within the class of shareholders being protected from its own coercive and inadequate tender offer.

---

**11.** There has been much debate respecting such stockholder interests. One rather impressive study indicates that the stock of over 50 percent of target companies, who resisted hostile takeovers, later traded at higher market prices than the rejected offer price, or were acquired after the tender offer was defeated by another company at a price higher than the offer price. *See* Lipton, *supra* 35 BUS.LAW. at 106–109, 132–133. Moreover, an update by Kidder Peabody & Company of this study involving the stock prices of target companies that have defeated hostile tender offers during the period from 1973 to 1982 demonstrates that in a majority of cases the target's shareholders benefited from the defeat. The stock of 81% of the targets studied has, since the tender offer, sold at prices higher than the tender offer price. When adjusted for the time value of money,

the figure is 64%. *See* Lipton & Brownstein, *supra* ABA INSTITUTE at 10. The thesis being that this strongly supports application of the business judgment rule in response to takeover threats. There is, however, a rather vehement contrary view. *See* Easterbrook & Fischel, *supra* 36 BUS.LAW. at 1739–1745.

**13.** * * * The Chancery Court noted that "Mesa has made tremendous profits from its takeover activities although in the past few years it has not been successful in acquiring any of the target companies on an unfriendly basis." Moreover, the trial court specifically found that the actions of the Unocal board were taken in good faith to eliminate both the inadequacies of the tender offer and to forestall the payment of "greenmail".

Thus, we are satisfied that the selective exchange offer is reasonably related to the threats posed. It is consistent with the principle that "the minority stockholder shall receive the substantial equivalent in value of what he had before." *Sterling v. Mayflower Hotel Corp.*, 33 Del.Ch. 293, 93 A.2d 107, 114 (Supr. 1952). *See also Rosenblatt v. Getty Oil Co.*, Del.Supr., 493 A.2d 929, 940 (1985). This concept of fairness, while stated in the merger context, is also relevant in the area of tender offer law. Thus, the board's decision to offer what it determined to be the fair value of the corporation to the 49% of its shareholders, who would otherwise be forced to accept highly subordinated "junk bonds", is reasonable and consistent with the directors' duty to ensure that the minority stockholders receive equal value for their shares.

### V.

Mesa contends that it is unlawful, and the trial court agreed, for a corporation to discriminate in this fashion against one shareholder. It argues correctly that no case has ever sanctioned a device that precludes a raider from sharing in a benefit available to all other stockholders. However, as we have noted earlier, the principle of selective stock repurchases by a Delaware corporation is neither unknown nor unauthorized. The only difference is that heretofore the approved transaction was the payment of "greenmail" to a raider or dissident posing a threat to the corporate enterprise. All other stockholders were denied such favored treatment, and given Mesa's past history of greenmail, its claims here are rather ironic.

However, our corporate law is not static. It must grow and develop in response to, indeed in anticipation of, evolving concepts and needs. Merely because the General Corporation Law is silent as to a specific matter does not mean that it is prohibited. In the days when *Cheff, Bennett, Martin* and *Kors* were decided, the tender offer, while not an unknown device, was virtually unused, and little was known of such methods as two-tier "front-end" loaded offers with their coercive effects. Then, the favored attack of a raider was stock acquisition followed by a proxy contest. Various defensive tactics, which provided no benefit whatever to the raider, evolved. Thus, the use of corporate funds by management to counter a proxy battle was approved. *Hall v. Trans–Lux Daylight Picture Screen Corp.*, Del.Supr., 171 A. 226 (1934); *Hibbert v. Hollywood Park, Inc.*, Del.Supr., 457 A.2d 339 (1983). Litigation, supported by corporate funds, aimed at the raider has long been a popular device.

More recently, as the sophistication of both raiders and targets has developed, a host of other defensive measures to counter such ever mounting threats has evolved and received judicial sanction. These include defensive charter amendments and other devices bearing some rather exotic, but apt, names: Crown Jewel, White Knight, Pac Man, and Golden Parachute. Each has highly selective features, the object of which is to deter or defeat the raider.

Thus, while the exchange offer is a form of selective treatment, given the nature of the threat posed here the response is neither unlawful nor unreasonable. If the board of directors is disinterested, has acted in good faith and with due care, its decision in the absence of an abuse of discretion will be upheld as a proper exercise of business judgment.

To this Mesa responds that the board is not disinterested, because the directors are receiving a benefit from the tender of their own shares, which because of the Mesa exclusion, does not devolve upon *all* stockholders equally. However, Mesa concedes that if the exclusion is valid, then the directors and all other stockholders share the same benefit. The answer of course is that the exclusion is valid, and the directors' participation in the exchange offer does not rise to the level of a disqualifying interest. The excellent discussion in *Johnson v. Trueblood*, 629 F.2d at 292–293, of the use of the business judgment rule in takeover contests also seems pertinent here.

Nor does this become an "interested" director transaction merely because certain board members are large stockholders. As this Court has previously noted, that fact alone does not create a disqualifying "personal pecuniary interest" to defeat the operation of the business judgment rule. *Cheff v. Mathes*, 199 A.2d at 554.

Mesa also argues that the exclusion permits the directors to abdicate the fiduciary duties they owe it. However, that is not so. The board continues to owe Mesa the duties of due care and loyalty. But in the face of the destructive threat Mesa's tender offer was perceived to pose, the board had a supervening duty to protect the corporate enterprise, which includes the other shareholders, from threatened harm.

Mesa contends that the basis of this action is punitive, and solely in response to the exercise of its rights of corporate democracy. Nothing precludes Mesa, as a stockholder, from acting in its own self-interest. However, Mesa, while pursuing its own interests, has acted in a manner which a board consisting of a majority of independent directors has reasonably determined to be contrary to the best interests of Unocal and its other shareholders. In this situation, there is no support in Delaware law for the proposition that, when responding to a perceived harm, a corporation must guarantee a benefit to a stockholder who is deliberately provoking the danger being addressed. There is no obligation of self-sacrifice by a corporation and its shareholders in the face of such a challenge.

Here, the Court of Chancery specifically found that the "directors' decision [to oppose the Mesa tender offer] was made in the good faith belief that the Mesa tender offer is inadequate." Given our standard of review * * *, we are satisfied that Unocal's board has met its burden of proof. *Cheff v. Mathes*, 199 A.2d at 555.

## VI.

In conclusion, there was directorial power to oppose the Mesa tender offer, and to undertake a selective stock exchange made in good faith and upon a reasonable investigation pursuant to a clear duty to protect the corporate enterprise. Further, the selective stock repurchase plan chosen by Unocal is reasonable in relation to the threat that the board rationally and reasonably believed was posed by Mesa's inadequate and coercive two-tier tender offer. Under those circumstances the board's action is entitled to be measured by the standards of the business judgment rule. Thus, unless it is shown by a preponderance of the evidence that the directors' decisions were primarily based on perpetuating themselves in office, or some other breach of fiduciary duty such as fraud, over-reaching, lack of good faith, or being uninformed, a Court will not substitute its judgment for that of the board.

In this case that protection is not lost merely because Unocal's directors have tendered their shares in the exchange offer. Given the validity of the Mesa exclusion, they are receiving a benefit shared generally by all other stockholders except Mesa. In this circumstance the test of *Aronson v. Lewis*, 473 A.2d at 812, is satisfied. *See also Cheff v. Mathes*, 199 A.2d at 554. If the stockholders are displeased with the action of their elected representatives, the powers of corporate democracy are at their disposal to turn the board out. *Aronson v. Lewis*, Del.Supr., 473 A.2d 805, 811 (1984). *See also* 8 Del.C. §§ 141(k) and 211(b).

With the Court of Chancery's findings that the exchange offer was based on the board's good faith belief that the Mesa offer was inadequate, that the board's action was informed and taken with due care, that Mesa's prior activities justify a reasonable inference that its principle objective is greenmail, and implicitly, that the substance of the offer itself was reasonable and fair to the corporation and its stockholders if Mesa were included, we cannot say that the Unocal directors have acted in such a manner as to have passed an "unintelligent and unadvised judgment". *Mitchell v. Highland–Western Glass Co.*, Del.Ch., 167 A. 831, 833 (1933). The decision of the Court of Chancery is therefore RE-VERSED, and the preliminary injunction is VACATED.

## 3. CHANGES IN CONTROL

### PROBLEM

### GENERAL INDUSTRIES CORPORATION—PART II

### A

At the meeting anticipated in Part I, the GIC board adopted a Stock Rights Plan pursuant to which the holder of each share of GIC stock received a right to purchase one additional share of GIC stock for one-half the closing price of that stock on the New York Stock Exchange on the last trading day before the date on which any person became the owner of 20% or more of GIC's outstanding stock without the prior approval of GIC's board of directors. GIC can redeem the rights at any time, for $.01 per share. The board also asked First Pru to consider alternative transactions that GIC might pursue if Danton made a tender offer, including a defensive merger, but the board also stressed the importance of GIC's retaining its ability to continue its most important research projects. Finally, GIC advised Danton that it was not interested in entering into any transactions with him or any company that he controls.

One month later, First Pru advised GIC's management that Mercury Industries, Inc., a large diversified corporation, was interested in acquiring GIC in a friendly transaction because Mercury is extremely supportive of GIC's corporate goals. Mercury has acquired other companies in negotiated transactions, after which it usually has left existing management in place and has tried to avoid layoffs and relocations. But Mercury owes its success to a management system that requires managers of acquired companies to meet ambitious earnings targets and removes those who fail. Mercury has indicated that, subject to an opportunity to conduct a reasonable investigation of GIC, including an examination of budgets, forecasts, and certain other confidential information, it is prepared to offer $55 cash per share for all GIC stock in a tender offer and second step cash merger. First Pru has provided the GIC board with its opinion that the fair value of GIC stock is from $52 to $64 per share and, accordingly, that the Mercury offer is fair from a financial point of view.

1. Before announcing the Mercury transaction, what are GIC's obligations, if any, to negotiate with Danton or inquire further of First Pru as to whether any other company might offer a higher price for GIC? Are such obligations those of GIC's management? Its outside directors?

2. Assume that Mercury has proposed the following conditions to its offer:

(a) GIC will not make available to any other potential bidder the confidential documents that it will make available to Mercury (the "no shop" clause);

(b) GIC will pay Mercury $25 million if for any reason Mercury does not succeed in acquiring GIC (the "topping fee"); and

(c) GIC will grant Mercury an option to purchase 10 million shares of authorized but unissued GIC stock for $35 per share (the current price on the New York Stock Exchange) (the "option").

What obligations, if any, must GIC's management or outside directors meet before GIC can agree to these conditions?

### B

Assume that GIC agreed to all of Mercury's conditions and that Mercury made its offer to GIC as described above. In response, Danton announced a $60 per share cash tender offer, to be made by Danton Acquisition Corp. (Acquisition), for all outstanding GIC stock, subject to

(i) GIC redeeming the rights; (ii) the Mercury conditions being declared invalid; and (iii) at least 24 million shares being tendered. Danton also announced that if Acquisition's offer was successful, he intended to effect a second-step merger of GIC and Acquisition as soon as practicable, in which all remaining public shareholders of GIC would receive $60 per share in cash. He further disclosed that he plans to finance the proposed transactions with $300 million of his own funds and approximately $2.5 billion in bank loans and a line of credit for which he has firm commitments.

The day after Danton's announcement, the GIC board held an all-day meeting with counsel and First Pru to evaluate the offer and decide how to proceed. First Pru acknowledged that Danton's offer was at a fair price, but several members of the board questioned Danton's ability to manage a sophisticated, research-oriented company like GIC. They also made clear that they had no interest in negotiating a better deal with Danton.

1.  Advise the board as to its responsibilities concerning Danton's tender offer. In particular, does the board have any obligation to redeem the rights, negotiate with Danton to see if he will pay a higher price, or seek a higher bid from either Mercury or other third parties?

2.  What is the likely outcome of a suit by Danton or a GIC shareholder challenging the validity of the no shop clause, the topping fee, and the option?

C

Assume that, in response to Danton's bid, Mercury advised GIC that it would not raise the amount of cash that it would pay ($55), but that it also would issue a new class of stock to the GIC shareholders whose value would depend on GIC's performance after the acquisition. Mercury stated that if GIC met the projections that its management had given to Mercury, the stock would have a value of no less than $7 per share. However, First Pru and other investment bankers with whom GIC has consulted have advised GIC that the stock is not likely to have an initial market value of more than $3 per share.

1.  Can GIC support Mercury's offer by approving the acquisition of GIC stock by Mercury but not by Danton, thus leaving the rights in effect with respect to Danton's bid?

2.  What other responsibilities, if any, do GIC's management or its outside directors have with respect to the two competing bids?

## REVLON, INC. v. MACANDREWS & FORBES HOLDINGS, INC.

506 A.2d 173 (Del.1985).

[Revlon, Inc. (Revlon), a Delaware corporation, had a 14 member board of directors. Six directors held senior management positions and two others owned significant blocks of Revlon stock. Four of the remaining six directors had been associated with entities that had business relationships with Revlon.

In June 1985, Ronald O. Perelman, the chief executive officer of Pantry Pride, Inc. (Pantry Pride) met with Michel C. Bergerac, Revlon's chief executive officer to discuss a friendly acquisition of Revlon by Pantry Pride at a price in the $40–$50 range. Bergerac, who developed a strong personal antipathy toward Perelman, rejected the offer as being far below Revlon's intrinsic value. In mid-August, Perlman offered to acquire Revlon in a negotiated transaction at $42–$43 per share or in a hostile tender offer at $45. Again, Bergerac rejected any possible Pantry Pride acquisition.

On August 19, the Revlon board met with counsel and with Lazard Freres, its investment banker, to consider the impending hostile tender offer. The board voted to repurchase up to 5 million shares of its common stock and to adopt a Note Purchase Rights plan. The plan permitted the rights holders to exchange their stock for a $65 one-year note unless someone acquired all the Revlon stock at $65 per share.

On August 23, Pantry Pride made an all cash, all shares tender offer at $47.50 per share, subject to obtaining financing and to the redemption of the rights. On August 26, the Revlon board rejected the offer and, three days later, offered to exchange notes for 10 million shares of common stock. The notes contained various covenants, the most important of which was a covenant against incurring future debt. Ultimately Revlon accepted the full 10 million shares in the exchange offer.

On September 16, Pantry Pride announced a revised offer at $42 per share, conditioned on receiving 90% of the stock (or less, if Revlon removed the rights). Because of the exchange offer, the revised offer was the economic equivalent of Pantry Pride's earlier higher bid. Again the Revlon board rejected the offer. On September 27, Pantry Pride increased its bid to $50 per share, and on October 1 raised it again to $53.

Meanwhile, the Revlon board agreed to a leveraged buyout in the form of a merger with Forstmann Little (Forstmann) in which the Revlon shareholders would receive $56 per share, Forstmann would assume the debt incurred in the exchange offer, and Revlon would redeem the rights and waive the note covenants for Forstmann or any offer superior to Forstmann's. Immediately after the announcement of the merger, the market price of the notes fell substantially.

On October 7, Pantry Pride raised its bid to $56.25, subject to cancellation of the rights and the waiver of the note covenants. Two days later, it declared its intention to top any competing bid.

On October 12, Forstmann offered $57.25 per share and agreed to support the market price of the notes after the covenants were removed. The offer also required Revlon to grant Forstmann a lock-up option on two of its divisions at a price well below Lazard Frere's valuation if anyone else acquired 40% of the Revlon stock. Finally Revlon was to pay a $25 million cancellation fee if the merger agreement was terminated or anyone else acquired more than 19.9% of the Revlon stock. The Revlon board accepted the offer because the price exceeded Pantry Pride's bid, the noteholders were protected against a decline in the value of their notes, and Forstmann's financing was secure.

Pantry Pride promptly sued to invalidate the agreement and, on October 22, raised its bid to $58, conditioned upon the nullification of the rights, the waiver of the note covenants, and the granting of an injunction against the lock-up.]

MOORE, JUSTICE:

In this battle for corporate control of Revlon, the Court of Chancery enjoined certain transactions designed to thwart the efforts of Pantry Pride to acquire Revlon.[1] The defendants are Revlon, its board of directors, and Forstmann Little & Co. and the latter's affiliated limited partnership (collectively, Forstmann). The injunction barred consummation of an option granted Forstmann to purchase certain Revlon assets (the lock-up option), a promise by Revlon to deal exclusively with Forstmann in the face of a takeover (the no-shop provision), and the payment of a $25 million cancellation fee to Forstmann if the transaction was aborted. The Court of Chancery found that the Revlon directors had breached their duty of care by entering into the foregoing transactions and effectively ending an active auction for the company. The trial court ruled that such arrangements are not illegal *per se* under Delaware law, but that their use under the circumstances here was impermissible. We agree. *See MacAndrews & Forbes Holdings, Inc. v. Revlon, Inc.*, Del.Ch., 501 A.2d 1239 (1985). Thus, we granted this expedited interlocutory appeal to consider for the first time the validity of such defensive measures in the face of an active bidding contest for corporate control. Additionally, we address for the first time the extent to which a corporation may consider the impact of a takeover threat on constituencies other than shareholders. *See Unocal Corp. v. Mesa Petroleum Co.*, Del.Supr., 493 A.2d 946, 955 (1985).

In our view, lock-ups and related agreements are permitted under Delaware law where their adoption is untainted by director interest or other breaches of fiduciary duty. The actions taken by the Revlon directors, however, did not meet this standard. Moreover, while concern for various corporate constituencies is proper when addressing a takeover threat, that principle is limited by the requirement that there be some rationally related benefit accruing to the stockholders. We find no such benefit here.

Thus, under all the circumstances we must agree with the Court of Chancery that the enjoined Revlon defensive measures were inconsistent with the directors' duties to the stockholders. Accordingly, we affirm.

\* \* \*

---

**1.** The nominal plaintiff, MacAndrews & Forbes Holdings, Inc., is the controlling stockholder of Pantry Pride. For all practical purposes their interests in this litigation are virtually identical, and we hereafter will refer to Pantry Pride as the plaintiff.

## II.

*  *  *

### A.

We turn first to Pantry Pride's probability of success on the merits. The ultimate responsibility for managing the business and affairs of a corporation falls on its board of directors. 8 Del.C. § 141(a). In discharging this function the directors owe fiduciary duties of care and loyalty to the corporation and its shareholders. These principles apply with equal force when a board approves a corporate merger pursuant to 8 Del.C. § 251(b); *Smith v. Van Gorkom*, Del.Supr., 488 A.2d 858, 873 (1985); and of course they are the bedrock of our law regarding corporate takeover issues. *Pogostin v. Rice*, Del.Supr., 480 A.2d 619, 624 (1984); *Unocal Corp. v. Mesa Petroleum Co.*, Del.Supr., 493 A.2d 946, 953, 955 (1985); *Moran v. Household International, Inc.*, Del.Supr., 500 A.2d 1346, 1350 (1985). While the business judgment rule may be applicable to the actions of corporate directors responding to takeover threats, the principles upon which it is founded—care, loyalty and independence—must first be satisfied. *Aronson v. Lewis*, 473 A.2d at 812.

If the business judgment rule applies, there is a "presumption that in making a business decision the directors of a corporation acted on an informed basis, in good faith and in the honest belief that the action taken was in the best interests of the company." *Aronson v. Lewis*, 473 A.2d at 812. However, when a board implements anti-takeover measures there arises "the omnipresent specter that a board may be acting primarily in its own interests, rather than those of the corporation and its shareholders. * * * "*Unocal Corp. v. Mesa Petroleum Co.*, 493 A.2d at 954. This potential for conflict places upon the directors the burden of proving that they had reasonable grounds for believing there was a danger to corporate policy and effectiveness, a burden satisfied by a showing of good faith and reasonable investigation. *Id.* at 955. In addition, the directors must analyze the nature of the takeover and its effect on the corporation in order to ensure balance—that the responsive action taken is reasonable in relation to the threat posed. *Id.*

### B.

The first relevant defensive measure adopted by the Revlon board was the Rights Plan, which would be considered a "poison pill" in the current language of corporate takeovers—a plan by which shareholders receive the right to be bought out by the corporation at a substantial premium on the occurrence of a stated triggering event. By 8 *Del.C.* §§ 141 and 157, the board clearly had the power to adopt the measure.Thus, the focus becomes one of reasonableness and purpose.

The Revlon board approved the Rights Plan in the face of an impending hostile takeover bid by Pantry Pride at $45 per share, a price which Revlon reasonably concluded was grossly inadequate. Lazard Freres had so advised the directors, and had also informed them that Pantry Pride was a small, highly leveraged company bent on a "bust-up" takeover by using "junk bond" financing to buy Revlon cheaply, sell the acquired assets to pay the debts incurred, and retain the profit for itself. In adopting the Plan, the board protected the shareholders from a hostile takeover at a price below the company's intrinsic value, while retaining sufficient flexibility to address any proposal deemed to be in the stockholders' best interests.

To that extent the board acted in good faith and upon reasonable investigation. Under the circumstances it cannot be said that the Rights Plan as employed was unreasonable, considering the threat posed. Indeed, the Plan was a factor in causing Pantry Pride to raise its bids from a low of $42 to an eventual high of $58. At the time of its adoption the Rights Plan afforded a measure of protection consistent with the directors' fiduciary duty in facing a takeover threat perceived as detrimental to corporate interests. Far from being a "show-stopper," as the plaintiffs had contended in *Moran,* the measure spurred the bidding to new heights, a proper result of its implementation.

\* \* \*

### C.

The second defensive measure adopted by Revlon to thwart a Pantry Pride takeover was the company's own exchange offer for 10 million of its shares. The directors' general broad powers to manage the business and affairs of the corporation are augmented by the specific authority conferred under 8 Del.C. § 160(a), permitting the company to deal in its own stock. However, when exercising that power in an effort to forestall a hostile takeover, the board's actions are strictly held to the fiduciary standards outlined in *Unocal.* These standards require the directors to determine the best interests of the corporation and its stockholders, and impose an enhanced duty to abjure any action that is motivated by considerations other than a good faith concern for such interests.

The Revlon directors concluded that Pantry Pride's $47.50 offer was grossly inadequate. In that regard the board acted in good faith, and on an informed basis, with reasonable grounds to believe that there existed a harmful threat to the corporate enterprise. The adoption of a defensive measure, reasonable in relation to the threat posed, was proper and fully accorded with the powers, duties, and responsibilities conferred upon directors under our law. *Unocal,* 493 A.2d at 954.

### D.

However, when Pantry Pride increased its offer to $50 per share, and then to $53, it became apparent to all that the break-up of the company was inevitable. The Revlon board's authorization permitting management to negotiate a merger or buyout with a third party was a recognition that the company was for sale. The duty of the board had thus changed from the preservation of Revlon as a corporate entity to the maximization of the company's value at a sale for the stockholders' benefit. This significantly altered the board's responsibilities under the *Unocal* standards. It no longer faced threats to corporate policy and effectiveness, or to the stockholders' interests, from a grossly inadequate bid. The whole question of defensive measures became moot. The directors' role changed from defenders of the corporate bastion to auctioneers charged with getting the best price for the stockholders at a sale of the company.

III.

This brings us to the lock-up with Forstmann and its emphasis on shoring up the sagging market value of the Notes in the face of threatened litigation by their holders. Such a focus was inconsistent with the changed concept of the directors' responsibilities at this stage of the developments. The impending waiver of the Notes covenants had caused the value of the Notes to fall, and the board was aware of the noteholders' ire as well as their subsequent threats of suit. The directors thus made support of the Notes an integral part of the company's dealings with Forstmann, even though their primary responsibility at this stage was to the equity owners.

The original threat posed by Pantry Pride—the break-up of the company—had become a reality which even the directors embraced. Selective dealing to fend off a hostile but determined bidder was no longer a proper objective. Instead, obtaining the highest price for the benefit of the stockholders should have been the central theme guiding director action. Thus, the Revlon board could not make the requisite showing of good faith by preferring the noteholders and ignoring its duty of loyalty to the shareholders. The rights of the former already were fixed by contract. The noteholders required no further protection, and when the Revlon board entered into an auction-ending lock-up agreement with Forstmann on the basis of impermissible considerations at the expense of the shareholders, the directors breached their primary duty of loyalty.

The Revlon board argued that it acted in good faith in protecting the noteholders because *Unocal* permits consideration of other corporate constituencies. Although such considerations may be permissible, there are fundamental limitations upon that prerogative. A board may have regard for various constituencies in discharging its responsibilities, provided there are rationally related benefits accruing to the stockholders. *Unocal*, 493 A.2d at 955. However, such concern for non-stockholder interests is inappropriate when an auction among active bidders is in progress, and the object no longer is to protect or maintain the corporate enterprise but to sell it to the highest bidder.

Revlon also contended that by *Gilbert v. El Paso Co.*, Del.Ch., 490 A.2d 1050, 1054–55 (1984), it had contractual and good faith obligations to consider the noteholders. However, any such duties are limited to the principle that one may not interfere with contractual relationships by improper actions. Here, the rights of the noteholders were fixed by agreement, and there is nothing of substance to suggest that any of those terms were violated. The Notes covenants specifically contemplated a waiver to permit sale of the company at a fair price. The Notes were accepted by the holders on that basis, including the risk of an adverse market effect stemming from a waiver. Thus, nothing remained for Revlon to legitimately protect, and no rationally related benefit thereby accrued to the stockholders. Under such circumstances we must conclude that the merger agreement with Forstmann was unreasonable in relation to the threat posed.

A lock-up is not *per se* illegal under Delaware law. Its use has been approved in an earlier unpublished case. *Thompson v. Enstar Corp.*, Del.Ch. (1984). Such options can entice other bidders to enter a contest for control of the corporation, creating an auction for the company and maximizing shareholder profit. Current economic conditions in the takeover market are such that a "white knight" like Forstmann might only enter the bidding for the target company if it receives some form of compensation to cover the risks and costs involved. However, while those lock-ups which draw bidders into the battle benefit shareholders, similar measures which end an active auction and foreclose further bidding operate to the shareholders' detriment.

Recently, the United States Court of Appeals for the Second Circuit invalidated a lock-up on fiduciary duty grounds similar to those here. *Hanson Trust PLC, et al. v. ML SCM Acquisition Inc.*, et al., 781 F.2d 264 (2d Cir.1986). Citing *Thompson v. Enstar Corp.*, *supra*, with approval, the court stated:

> In this regard, we are especially mindful that some lock-up options may be beneficial to the shareholders, such as those that induce a bidder to compete for control of a corporation, while others may be harmful, such as those that effectively preclude bidders from competing with the optionee bidder.

In *Hanson Trust,* the bidder, Hanson, sought control of SCM by a hostile cash tender offer. SCM management joined with Merrill Lynch to propose a leveraged buy-out of the company at a higher price, and Hanson in turn increased its offer. Then, despite very little improvement in its subsequent bid, the management group sought a lock-up option to purchase SCM's two main assets at a substantial discount. The SCM directors granted the lock-up without adequate information as to the size of the discount or the effect the transaction would have on the company. Their action effectively ended a competitive bidding situation. The Hanson Court invalidated the lock-up because the directors failed to fully inform themselves about the value of a transaction in which management had a strong self-interest. "In short, the Board appears to have failed to ensure that negotiations for alternative bids were conducted by those whose only loyalty was to the shareholders."

The Forstmann option had a similar destructive effect on the auction process. Forstmann had already been drawn into the contest on a preferred basis, so the result of the lock-up was not to foster bidding, but to destroy it. The board's stated reasons for approving the transaction were: (1) better financing, (2) noteholder protection, and (3) higher price. As the Court of Chancery found, and we agree, any distinctions between the rival bidders' methods of financing the proposal were nominal at best, and such a consideration has little or no significance in a cash offer for any and all shares. The principal object, contrary to the board's duty of care, appears to have been protection of the noteholders over the shareholders' interests.

While Forstmann's $57.25 offer was objectively higher than Pantry Pride's $56.25 bid, the margin of superiority is less when the Forstmann price is adjusted for the time value of money. In reality, the Revlon board ended the auction in return for very little actual improvement in the final bid. The principal benefit went to the directors, who avoided personal liability to a class of creditors to whom the board owed no further duty under the circumstances. Thus, when a board ends an intense bidding contest on an insubstantial basis, and where a significant by-product of that action is to protect the directors against a perceived threat of personal liability for consequences stemming from the adoption of previous defensive measures, the action cannot withstand the enhanced scrutiny which *Unocal* requires of director conduct. *See Unocal,* 493 A.2d at 954–55.

In addition to the lock-up option, the Court of Chancery enjoined the no-shop provision as part of the attempt to foreclose further bidding by Pantry Pride. The no-shop provision, like the lock-up option, while not *per se* illegal, is impermissible under the *Unocal* standards when a board's primary duty becomes that of an auctioneer responsible for selling the company to the highest bidder. The agreement to negotiate only with Forstmann ended rather than intensified the board's involvement in the bidding contest.

It is ironic that the parties even considered a no-shop agreement when Revlon had dealt preferentially, and almost exclusively, with Forstmann throughout the contest. After the directors authorized management to negotiate with other parties, Forstmann was given every negotiating advantage that Pantry Pride had been denied: cooperation from management, access to financial data, and the exclusive opportunity to present merger proposals directly to the board of directors. Favoritism for a white knight to the total exclusion of a hostile bidder might be justifiable when the latter's offer adversely affects shareholder interests, but when bidders make relatively similar offers, or dissolution of the company becomes inevitable, the directors cannot fulfill their enhanced *Unocal* duties by playing favorites with the contending factions. Market forces must be allowed to operate freely to bring the target's shareholders the best price available for their equity. Thus, as the trial court ruled, the shareholders' interests necessitated that the board remain free to negotiate in the fulfillment of that duty.

IV.

Having concluded that Pantry Pride has shown a reasonable probability of success on the merits, we address the issue of irreparable harm. The Court of Chancery ruled that unless the lock-up and other aspects of the agreement were enjoined, Pantry Pride's opportunity to bid for

Revlon was lost. The court also held that the need for both bidders to compete in the marketplace outweighed any injury to Forstmann. Given the complexity of the proposed transaction between Revlon and Forstmann, the obstacles to Pantry Pride obtaining a meaningful legal remedy are immense. We are satisfied that the plaintiff has shown the need for an injunction to protect it from irreparable harm, which need outweighs any harm to the defendants.

V.

In conclusion, the Revlon board was confronted with a situation not uncommon in the current wave of corporate takeovers. A hostile and determined bidder sought the company at a price the board was convinced was inadequate. The initial defensive tactics worked to the benefit of the shareholders, and thus the board was able to sustain its *Unocal* burdens in justifying those measures. However, in granting an asset option lock-up to Forstmann, we must conclude that under all the circumstances the directors allowed considerations other than the maximization of shareholder profit to affect their judgment, and followed a course that ended the auction for Revlon, absent court intervention, to the ultimate detriment of its shareholders. No such defensive measure can be sustained when it represents a breach of the directors' fundamental duty of care. *See Smith v. Van Gorkom*, Del.Supr., 488 A.2d 858, 874 (1985). In that context the board's action is not entitled to the deference accorded it by the business judgment rule. The measures were properly enjoined. The decision of the Court of Chancery, therefore, is affirmed.

### *Note: Auctions*

In *Revlon*, the court held that the responsibility of the board of directors changes when the company is "for sale." Long-term considerations disappear; the short-term selling price becomes paramount. "The directors' role change[s] from defenders of the corporate bastion to auctioneers charged with getting the best price for the stockholders at a sale of the company." 506 A.2d at 182. Concerns over threats to corporate policy or shareholder interests from an inadequate bid become moot.

What does it mean to say that a company is "for sale?" In *Revlon*, a moment arrived when "it became apparent to all that the break-up of the company was inevitable," and at that moment an auction was required. The court's analysis is easiest to understand in the context of a hostile tender offer in which target management seeks to remain independent and undertakes extensive defensive measures to achieve that end. But does *every* acquisition transaction, even when voluntarily negotiated, constitute a "sale" that requires the selling corporation to conduct an auction before closing the transaction? If so, *Revlon* would have profound consequences for ordinary corporate acquisitions.

The most recent Delaware cases, *Paramount Communications, Inc. v. Time, Inc.*, 571 A.2d 1140 (Del.1989) and *Paramount Communications,*

*Inc. v. QVC Network, Inc. (QVC)*, 637 A.2d 34 (Del.1994), answer many of these questions, but some background to those cases is useful.

### a. Triggering the Auction

Two years after *Revlon*, in *City Capital Associates Limited Partnership v. Interco*, 551 A.2d 787 (Del.Ch.1988), the Court of Chancery noted that *Revlon* did not "require * * * that before every corporate merger agreement can validly be entered into, the constituent corporations must be 'shopped' or, more radically, an auction process undertaken, even though a merger may be regarded as a sale of the Company." *Id.* at 802. The court emphasized that a board must be informed as to possible alternatives and found that if it were in a position to act advisedly * * * the *Revlon* holding [does not require] it to turn to an auction alternative, if it has arrived at a good faith, informed determination that a recapitalization or other form of transaction is more beneficial to shareholders. *Id.* at 803. "Similarly, in *Barkan v. Amsted Industries, Inc.*, 567 A.2d 1279, 1287 (Del.1989), the court commented:

> * * * *Revlon* does not demand that every change in the control of a Delaware corporation be preceded by a heated bidding contest. *Revlon* is merely one of an unbroken line of cases that seek to prevent the conflicts of interest that arise in the field of mergers and acquisitions by demanding that directors act with scrupulous concern for fairness to shareholders. When multiple bidders are competing for control, this concern for fairness forbids directors from using defensive mechanisms to thwart an auction or to favor one bidder over another. When the board is considering a single offer and has no reliable grounds upon which to judge its adequacy, this concern for fairness demands a canvas of the market to determine if higher bids may be elicited. When, however, the directors possess a body of reliable evidence with which to evaluate the fairness of a transaction, they may approve that transaction without conducting an active survey of the market. As the Chancellor recognized, the circumstances in which this passive approach is acceptable are limited. "A decent respect for reality forces one to admit that * * * advice [of an investment banker] is frequently a pale substitute for the dependable information that a canvas of the relevant market can provide." The need for adequate information is central to the enlightened evaluation of a transaction that a board must make. Nevertheless, there is no single method that a board must employ to acquire such information.

### b. Best Price and the Conduct of the Auction

Another way to look at *Revlon* is as an elaboration of *Unocal*. Once it is clear that a company is for sale, the only reasonable actions a board can take are those directed at obtaining what the Delaware Supreme Court now terms the "best value reasonably available" for shareholders. *QVC, infra.* Moreover, because *Unocal* applies, directors' conduct of an auction will be scrutinized under *Unocal*'s enhanced business judgment rule. A board may rely on corporate officers, employees, and outside advisers who have been selected with reasonable care, but the board retains ultimate responsibility for ensuring the integrity of the auction. It cannot delegate this responsibility to others, although it can create a special committee of independent directors to conduct the auction. Indeed, if some board members have an interest in a potential transaction, use of an independent special committee of the board will increase materially the proof that a defensive tactic was reasonable.

In deciding what is the best value, the board must look at more than the asserted nominal value of the offer and may decide that the highest available price for shareholders is not the transaction with the highest nominal price. *See Citron v. Fairchild Camera and Instrument Corp.*, 1988 WL 53322 (Del.Ch.1988), *aff'd* 569 A.2d 53 (Del.1989) (decision to reject a seemingly higher offer in favor of an all-cash offer with an arguably lower value does not by itself constitute a breach of the duty of loyalty, absent evidence of a breach of duty in the decision-making process).

In order to obtain the best possible price, the board may negotiate with potential bidders, but need not negotiate with them on identical terms. The duties created by *Revlon* are owed by the board to shareholders and not to potential suitors. *Mills Acquisition Co. v. Macmillan, Inc.*, 559 A.2d 1261 (Del.1989), which involved an auction for control of Macmillan between KKR and Robert Maxwell, shows the limits of unequal treatment. During the auction, Macmillan's management and investment bankers provided KKR with significant assistance not offered to Maxwell. This assistance included greater access to confidential information, tipping KKR to the terms of Maxwell's bid, and giving additional bidding instructions to KKR on how to structure its bid to obtain board approval. In addition, despite Maxwell's stated willingness to increase his $89 all cash bid if it were not the highest bid for the company, Macmillan's advisers negotiated a lockup option with KKR which would allow KKR to purchase several of Macmillan's core assets if KKR's bid for the entire company was topped. In exchange for this lockup, KKR submitted a bid of $90.05 consisting of cash and securities. The terms of the lockup effectively terminated the auction.

The Delaware Supreme Court held that the Macmillan board had breached its fiduciary duties in the conduct of the auction by not "scrupulously [adhering] to ordinary principles of fairness." Fairness did not require equal treatment, but it did require that "stockholder interests are enhanced, rather than diminished, in the conduct of an auction for sale of corporate control." Because Macmillan failed to demonstrate that its special arrangements with KKR promoted stockholder interests or that they were done in good faith, the court enjoined the lock-up. *Id.* at 1285.

### Note: Poison Pills Revisited

1.   In the 1980s, the poison pill became a favorite defensive measure. Courts gave boards of directors considerable freedom to use poison

pills to delay a hostile takeover bids while they attempted to negotiate better deals from bidders or explored alternative transactions that had the potential to produce a higher value for shareholders. In *CRTF Corp. v. Federated Department Stores*, 683 F.Supp. 422 (S.D.N.Y.1988), the court described a poison pill as providing "the directors with a shield to fend off coercive offers and with a gavel to run an auction." *Id.* at 439. Accepting this rationale, Delaware courts held that a board may refuse to redeem a pill if the offer is inadequate, or because an auction for the company exists. See, e.g., *BNS, Inc. v. Koppers Company, Inc.*, 683 F.Supp. 458 (D.Del.1988).

*Moran* had made clear that a board did not have "unfettered discretion in refusing to redeem the Rights." and that the decision not to redeem the pill would be evaluated under *Unocal*. 500 A.2d at 1354. Bidders and target company shareholders both brought numerous suits, seeking to force boards to redeem poison pills after a tender offer had been made. The issue which caused the courts most difficulty was whether a target company board must provide shareholders with an alternative to the hostile bid, or whether a decision to "just say no" can ever be considered reasonable.

Analytically, the courts used *Unocal*'s enhanced business judgment test to examine decisions concerning the redemption of poison pills, focusing on whether a board's refusal to redeem was a reasonable response to a perceived threat to the corporation. In *AC Acquisitions Corp. v. Anderson, Clayton & Co.*, 519 A.2d 103 (Del.Ch.1986), the court held that management had breached its *Unocal* duty by precluding shareholders from considering a non-coercive hostile bid that represented an alternative to a management recapitalization plan. Other decisions, however, suggested that courts might give greater weight to business judgments not to redeem poison pills when hostile tender offers were coercive or inadequate. *See Ivanhoe Partners v. Newmont Mining Corp.*, 535 A.2d 1334 (Del.1987); John C. Coffee, Jr., *Proportionality after Pillsbury: The New Delaware Common Law on Defensive Tactics*, 1 M & A L.Rep. 982 (1989).

Two cases, however, suggested that a board cannot hide behind a pill indefinitely when faced with a non-coercive all-cash tender offer for all shares at an adequate price. In *City Capital Associates L.P. v. Interco, Inc.*, *supra*, the Rales brothers made a hostile $74 all-cash, all-shares offer for Interco, subject to the redemption of Interco's poison pill. The Interco board determined that the price was inadequate and, as an alternative, proposed a restructuring plan that would offer shareholders a package of cash and securities worth a minimum of $76 per share. Interco contended that its decision not to redeem the pill was necessary to guard the company and its shareholders from the threat posed by the inadequate offer and to protect the higher-valued restructuring. The court rejected this argument, finding that the offer was not coercive because it was an all-cash offer for all the shares. Although recognizing that such an offer could be a "threat" under *Unocal* if it was for an inadequate price, the court stated that the value of Interco's own plan was an "inherently * * * debatable proposition." *Id.* at 795. Thus, the court concluded that a shareholder might well prefer an immediate cash payment of $74 to receiving the package that might be worth $76. For the court, the shareholder's ability to make this choice—rather than the choice itself—was pivotal. The court held that the Rales offer did not pose a sufficiently significant threat to warrant preventing shareholders from accepting it if they so desired. In *Unocal* terms, the refusal to redeem the pill was not reasonable in relation to the threat presented by the offer.

In *Grand Metropolitan Public Ltd. Co. v. Pillsbury Co.*, 558 A.2d 1049 (Del.Ch.1988), the "just say no" defense arose more squarely. Grand Met made a $63 all-cash, all-shares offer for Pillsbury that the Pillsbury board determined was inadequate. In response, the board developed (or announced that it would develop) a restructuring plan involving the spin-off and sale of some of its assets in a time frame stretching from six months to five years. Pillsbury's investment bankers advised that, giving effect to such restructuring, Pillsbury had a present value of between $68 and $73 per share. The Court of Chancery found that the Grand Met offer was for a fair price and that, for a shareholder to realize the higher price, it would be necessary "to be patient and endure for a long time, perhaps until 1992 or 1993." *Id.* at 1057. Even then, the higher price would depend on economic conditions that were beyond Pillsbury's control. Thus the court held that the "threat" posed by Grand Met's offer did not justify the Pillsbury board's refusal to redeem the poison pill. Although the court did not directly address the question of whether a target company board could leave a pill in place simply because it believed a non-coercive offer was not in the best interests of the corporation or its shareholders, the court's decision seemed to imply that there comes a time in the life of every company when poison pills and other impediments to shareholder acceptance of a hostile tender offer must be swept away.

In *TW Services, Inc. v. SWT Acquisition Corp.*, 1989 WL 20290 (Del.Ch.1989), the Court of Chancery appeared to back away from this implication. SWT made an all-cash, all-shares offer for TW, subject to the somewhat unusual conditions that the TW board of directors redeem its poison pill, approve SWT's offer and enter into a merger agreement with SWT. TW argued that SWT's offer was simply an invitation to the board to enter into merger negotiations, not a bona fide offer to acquire the company. TW argued further that it was entitled to manage the corporation in the best long-range interests of the shareholder and was not required to come up with an alternative value-enhancing plan in opposition to an unsolicited offer. The court acknowledged this latter argument but found it unnecessary to resolve the issue. Rather, it held that because of SWT's conditions, the offer "involves *both* a proposal to negotiate a merger and a conditional tender offer precluded by a poison pill." *Id.* at *10. Insofar as the offer concerned merger negotiations, the refusal to negotiate was fully protected by the business judgment rule.

Because the board's actions were proper under such an analysis, the court refused to order the board to redeem the pill.

2. The validity of the continuing director pill remains an open question. In *Invacare Corp. v. Healthdyne Technologies*, 968 F.Supp. 1578 (N.D.Ga.1997), the District Court upheld the validity of such a pill under Georgia law. The court pointed to Georgia O.C.G.A. § 14–2–624(c) which provides that "nothing contained in [the equivalent of RMBCA § 8.01] shall be deemed to limit the board of directors authority to determine, in its sole discretion, the terms and conditions of the rights ... issuable pursuant to this Code section. Such terms and conditions need not be set forth in the articles of incorporation." The only limits on the directors are their fiduciary duties to the corporation which the court found had not been breached. *Id.* at 1580–81. Although not directly necessary to its decision, the court also noted that other Georgia law "embrace[d] the concept of continuing directors as part of a defense against hostile takeovers." *Id.* at 1580.

By contrast, the New York State Supreme Court invalidated a continuing directors pill on the ground that it restricted the power of the board of directors to manage the corporation under N.Y.B.C.L. § 701. *Bank of New York Co., Inc. v. Irving Bank Corp.*, 139 Misc.2d 665, 528 N.Y.S.2d 482 (1988). The court noted that the restriction on the board's power to redeem the pill was not contained in the certificate of incorporation as required by N.Y.B.C.L. § 620(b). The court stated that "the evil * * * is not that it deprives a Board of certain powers; it is that it is selective in the deprivation. In other words, the present Board members could have the powers, if they were re-elected to the Board, but the insurgents would not if they were elected by the same plurality. Those new members of the Board approved by the current Board would have the powers, but those not so approved would. not. This retention of authority is beyond the powers of the Board." *Id.* at 485.

The Delaware courts have not decided on the validity of a continuing directors pill, although it was used in two early contests for control. Nevertheless, it is unlikely that such a pill would be valid under the Delaware statutory and judicial regime. As one commentator has noted, the Delaware statutory structure is like that of New York. "These various statutory elements may be altered by the articles, or in some cases the bylaws, but a deadhand pill is unlikely to obtain shareholder approval as an articles amendment and, if adopted as a bylaw, would presumably be subject to both shareholder power and the power of a successor board to amend bylaws." Jeffrey N. Gordon, *"Just Say Never?" Poison Pills, Deadhand Pills, and Shareholder–Adopted Bylaws: An Essay for Warrent Buffett*, 19 Cardozo L.Rev. 511, 537 (1997). Moreover, such a pill would also face substantial difficulties under *Blasius* and *Unocal*.

### Note: Other Constituencies

Recall Chapter 5, in which we saw that constituency statutes often were enacted to give directors an additional weapon against hostile takeovers. These statutes permit directors to consider the effects of their actions (including the adoption of defensive techniques) on a broad range of non-shareholder constituencies and afford the protection of the business judgment rule to directors when they do so.

Lacking a constituency statute, the Delaware courts have taken a somewhat narrower view of the directors' power. In *Unocal*, the Delaware Supreme Court stated that the board of directors could consider other constituencies such as "creditors, customers, employees, and perhaps even the community generally" when selecting reasonable defensive measures to a takeover which threatens the corporation. In *Revlon*, *infra*, the court limited the consideration of these other constituencies to the extent that the directors' consideration is "rationally related to benefits accruing to the stockholders." Consideration of non-stockholder constituencies, in those circumstances, does not violate a director's duty of loyalty and will allow directors to retain the protection of the business judgment rule.

Generally, consideration of other constituencies will be rationally related to stockholder interests. Stockholders may have an interest in maintaining and increasing the long run value of the corporation even if its short run value may suffer. That value can often be improved when the board considers the interest of other constituencies. However, when the board reaches the decision to sell the company and terminate the interests of current stockholders, concern for the company's long run value disappears. The interests of stockholders is limited to obtaining the highest price possible for their shares. *Revlon* circumscribes a board's ability to consider the interests of other constituencies, although the factual contexts of *Unocal* and *Revlon* are clearly different.

*Herald Co. v. Seawell*, 472 F.2d 1081 (10th Cir.1972), which involved a struggle for control of the company that published the Denver Post newspaper, took a different approach. The Denver Post was a large metropolitan newspaper with a long tradition of local ownership. The Bonfils family had had a large ownership interest in the Post, and Helen Bonfils, the daughter of one of the Post's founders, was both an officer and director. In May 1960, Samuel Newhouse, the owner of one of the nation's largest newspaper chains purchased 18 percent of the outstanding common stock of the Denver Post with the intent of acquiring the newspaper. On July 7, 1960, the Post purchased 19,574 shares of its stock (about 21 percent of that outstanding) held by the U.S. National Bank as trustee for Children's Hospital at $260 per share. For several years prior to this purchase, the Post board of directors had contemplated establishing an employee stock ownership plan. After the purchase, the board implemented an employee stock trust plan, transferring approximately 3400 treasury shares to the trust. Helen Bonfils donated 1600 shares from her personal holdings. By December 1969, 415 of the eligible 1159 employees had purchased shares from the trust.

More than eight years after the purchase of the Children's Hospital stock, the Herald Company, which was owned by Newhouse, brought a derivative action on behalf of the Post against its officers and directors for misconduct, breach of trust and misuse of corporate assets. The plaintiff claimed that the board and the trustees of the employee stock trust had conspired to acquire sufficient shares of stock to vest control in Helen Bonfils. Among the numerous acts which the defendants allegedly committed was the creation of an "illusory stock trust" from which the defendants sold shares at prices which resulted in a decrease in the Post's surplus.

The district court determined that management's primary obligation was to earn profits for the company's shareholders, and ordered the public sale of several blocks of Post shares, including those remaining in the treasury from the Children's Hospital purchase and those transferred to the trust.

The Tenth Circuit reversed. The evidence established that the directors feared a Newhouse takeover would adversely affect the character and quality of the Post. The directors believed that local independent ownership was preferable and superior to chain ownership. They also knew that Newhouse had a reputation among his employees for having poor relations with labor. Significantly, the court noted that a newspaper had a threefold obligation—to the stockholders, to the employees, and to the public—that was greater than the duty to increase profits.

> * * * Such a newspaper is endowed with an important public interest. It must adhere to the ethics of the great profession of journalism. The readers are entitled to a high quality of accurate news coverage of local, state, national and international events. The newspaper management has an obligation to assume leadership, when needed, for the betterment of the area served by the newspaper. Because of these relations with the public, a corporation publishing a great newspaper such as the Denver Post is, in effect, a quasi-public institution.

*Id.* at 1095.

Because the board had the power to adopt the stock trust plan, the court refused to substitute its own judgment for that of the board and upheld the transaction.

## 4.  STRATEGIC TRANSACTIONS

The foregoing materials raise difficult conceptual and practical questions. Is a target company ever free to enter into a transaction that its management believes is in the best interest of the corporation without first being subject to *Revlon* duties? Put differently, can there be such a thing as a "friendly" deal without considering other potential or actual bidders? Are there circumstances under which the target's board can effectively preclude its shareholders from accepting a non-coercive tender offer? More succinctly, absent coercion, can directors "just say no?" Consider the extent to which the following cases answer these questions.

## PARAMOUNT COMMUNICATIONS, INC. v. TIME, INC.

571 A.2d 1140 (Del.1989).

[Time, Inc. (Time) was a Delaware corporation whose traditional business was the publication of magazines and books. It owned cable television franchises and provided pay television programming through its Home Box Office and Cinemax subsidiaries. In 1983, Time began to consider expanding into the entertainment industry and in 1987, a special committee of Time executives endorsed expansion into ownership and creation of video programming.

Some of Time's outside directors viewed such a move as a threat to the editorial integrity and journalistic focus of Time. Their primary concern was the preservation of the "Time Culture." They believed that Time was recognized as an institution built upon a foundation of journalistic integrity. To protect this reputation, Time's management had refrained from involvement in Time's editorial policy. The outside directors feared that a merger with an entertainment company would divert Time's focus from news journalism and would weaken the separation of the editorial policy from the business side of Time.

In June 1988, management distributed to the board a comprehensive long-range plan that examined strategies for the 1990s. The plan included Warner as potential acquisition candidate. J. Richard Munro, Time's chairman and CEO, and N.J. Nicholas, Jr., president and chief operating officer then met with each outside director to discuss long-term strategies and specifically a combination with Warner Communications (Warner) whose business complemented Time better than other potential merger candidates. After these discussions, Time's board approved in principle a strategic plan for expansion and authorized continuing merger discussions with Warner.

Talks between Time and Warner began in August, 1988. Although Time had preferred an acquisition involving all cash or cash and securities, it agreed to a stock-for-stock exchange so that Warner's stockholders could retain an equity interest in the new corporation. Time also insisted on control of the board in order to preserve "a management committed to Time's journalistic integrity." Negotiations broke down when the parties failed to agree on the top executives of the new corporation, and Time then pursued other merger alternatives.

In January, 1988, Time resumed its talks with Warner after the parties agreed on the governance issues. Many of the details of the original agreement remained intact, and on March 3, 1989, Time's board approved a stock-for-stock merger with Warner. The merger would give Warner shareholders 62% of the combined company. The new company would have a 24-member board with Time and Warner each initially represented by 12 directors. The board would have both an entertainment and editorial committee controlled respectively by Warner and

Time directors. The rules of the New York Stock Exchange (NYSE) required Time's shareholders to approve the merger, although, because the transaction was cast as a triangular merger (see Chapter 12), Delaware law did not.

At the March 3 meeting, Time's board adopted several defensive tactics. It agreed to an automatic share exchange with Warner which gave Warner the right to receive 11.1% of Time's outstanding common stock. Time also sought and paid for "confidence letters" from its banks in which the banks agreed to not finance a hostile acquisition of Time. Time agreed to a no-shop clause preventing it from considering any other consolidation proposal regardless of the merits. After the announcement of the transaction, Time publicized the lack of debt in the transaction as being one of its chief benefits. Time scheduled the shareholder vote for June 23 and sent out its proxy materials for the merger on May 24.

On June 7, Paramount Communications (Paramount) announced a $175 per share, all-cash, all-shares "fully-negotiable" offer for Time. Time's board found that Paramount's offer was subject to three conditions: that Time terminate its merger agreement and share exchange agreement with Warner; that Paramount obtain acceptable cable franchise transfers from Time; and that DGCL § 203 (the anti-takeover statute) not apply to any subsequent Time–Paramount merger. Time believed that it would take at least several months to satisfy these conditions.

Although, Time's financial advisors informed the board that Time's per share value was materially higher than Paramount's $175 offer, the board was concerned that shareholders would not appreciate the long-term benefits of the Warner merger if given the opportunity to accept the Paramount offer. Therefore, Time sought the NYSE's approval to complete the merger without stockholder approval. The NYSE refused.

On June 8, Time formally rejected Paramount's offer. Because it continued to believe that the offer presented a threat to Time's control of its own destiny and the "Time Culture", the board chose to recast the form of the Warner transaction. Under the new proposal, Time would make an immediate all-cash offer for 51% of Warner's outstanding stock at $70 per share. The remaining 49% would be purchased at some later date for a mixture of cash and securities worth $70 per share. Time would fund the acquisition of Warner by incurring $7–10 billion of debt, despite its original assertion that the debt-free nature of the combination was one of its principal benefits. Time also agreed to pay $9 billion to Warner for its goodwill. As a condition of accepting the revised transaction, Warner received a control premium and guarantee that the corporate governance provisions in the original merger agreement would remain. Time agreed to not employ its poison pill against Warner, and unless enjoined, to complete the transaction.

On June 23, 1989, Paramount raised its offer to $200 per share while continuing to maintain that all aspects of the offer were negotiable. On June 26, Time's board rejected the second offer on the grounds that it was still inadequate and that Time's acquisition of Warner "offered a greater long-term value for the stockholders and, unlike Paramount, was not a threat to Time's survival and its 'culture.' "

Two groups of Time shareholders ("Shareholder Plaintiffs") and Paramount sought to enjoin Time's tender offer. The Court of Chancery denied plaintiffs' motions. Plaintiffs appealed.]

HORSEY, JUSTICE.

\* \* \*

## II.

The Shareholder Plaintiffs first assert a *Revlon* claim. They contend that the March 4 Time–Warner agreement effectively put Time up for sale, triggering *Revlon* duties, requiring Time's board to enhance short-term shareholder value and to treat all other interested acquirers on an equal basis. The Shareholder Plaintiffs base this argument on two facts: (i) the ultimate Time–Warner exchange ratio of .465 favoring Warner, resulting in Warner shareholders' receipt of 62% of the combined company; and (ii) the subjective intent of Time's directors as evidenced in their statements that the market might perceive the Time–Warner merger as putting Time up "for sale" and their adoption of various defensive measures.

The Shareholder Plaintiffs further contend that Time's directors, in structuring the original merger transaction to be "takeover-proof," triggered *Revlon* duties by foreclosing their shareholders from any prospect of obtaining a control premium. In short, plaintiffs argue that Time's board's decision to merge with Warner imposed a fiduciary duty to maximize immediate share value and not erect unreasonable barriers to further bids. Therefore, they argue, the Chancellor erred in finding: that Paramount's bid for Time did not place Time "for sale"; that Time's transaction with Warner did not result in any transfer of control; and that the combined Time–Warner was not so large as to preclude the possibility of the stockholders of Time–Warner receiving a future control premium.

Paramount asserts only a *Unocal* claim in which the shareholder plaintiffs join. Paramount contends that the Chancellor, in applying the first part of the *Unocal* test, erred in finding that Time's board had reasonable grounds to believe that Paramount posed both a legally cognizable threat to Time shareholders and a danger to Time's corporate policy and effectiveness. Paramount also contests the court's finding that Time's board made a reasonable and objective investigation of Paramount's offer so as to be informed before rejecting it. Paramount further claims that the court erred in applying *Unocal*'s second part in finding Time's response to be "reasonable." Paramount points primarily to the preclusive effect of the revised agreement which denied Time shareholders the opportunity both to vote on the agreement and to respond to Paramount's tender offer. Paramount argues that the underlying motivation of Time's board in adopting these defensive measures was management's desire to perpetuate itself in office.

The Court of Chancery posed the pivotal question presented by this case to be: Under what circumstances must a board of directors abandon an in-place plan of corporate development in order to provide its shareholders with the option to elect and realize an immediate control premium? As applied to this case, the question becomes: Did Time's board, having developed a strategic plan of global expansion to be launched through a business combination with Warner, come under a fiduciary duty to jettison its plan and put the corporation's future in the hands of its shareholders?

While we affirm the result reached by the Chancellor, we think it unwise to place undue emphasis upon long-term versus short-term corporate strategy. Two key predicates underpin our analysis. First, Delaware law imposes on a board of directors the duty to manage the business and affairs of the corporation. 8 *Del.C.* § 141(a). This broad mandate includes a conferred authority to set a corporate course of action, including time frame, designed to enhance corporate profitability.[12] Thus, the question of "long-term" versus "short-term" values is largely irrelevant because directors, generally, are obliged to charter a course for a corporation which is in its best interests without regard to a fixed investment horizon. Second, absent a limited set of circumstances as defined under *Revlon,* a board of directors, while always required to act in an informed manner, is not under any *per se* duty to maximize shareholder value in the short term, even in the context of a takeover. In our view, the pivotal question presented by this case is: "Did Time, by entering into the proposed merger with Warner, put itself up for sale?" A resolution of that issue through application of *Revlon* has a significant bearing upon the resolution of the derivative *Unocal* issue.

## A.

We first take up plaintiffs' principal *Revlon* argument, summarized above. In rejecting this argument, the Chancellor found the original Time–Warner merger agreement not to constitute a "change of control" and concluded that the transaction did not trigger *Revlon* duties. The Chancellor's conclusion is premised on a finding that "[b]efore the merger agreement was signed, control of the corporation existed in a fluid aggregation of unaffiliated shareholders representing a voting majority—in other words, in the market." The Chancellor's findings of fact are supported by the record and his conclusion is correct as a matter of law. However, we premise our rejection of plaintiffs' *Revlon* claim on broader grounds, namely, the absence of any substantial evidence to conclude that Time's board, in negotiating with Warner, made the

---

**12.** In endorsing this finding, we tacitly accept the Chancellor's conclusion that it is not a breach of faith for directors to determine that the present stock market price of shares is not representative of true value or that there may indeed be several market values for any corporation's stock. We have so held in another context. *See Van Gorkom,* 488 A.2d at 876.

dissolution or breakup of the corporate entity inevitable, as was the case in *Revlon*.

Under Delaware law there are, generally speaking and without excluding other possibilities, two circumstances which may implicate *Revlon* duties. The first, and clearer one, is when a corporation initiates an active bidding process seeking to sell itself or to effect a business reorganization involving a clear break-up of the company. However, *Revlon* duties may also be triggered where, in response to a bidder's offer, a target abandons its long-term strategy and seeks an alternative transaction also involving the breakup of the company. Thus, in *Revlon*, when the board responded to Pantry Pride's offer by contemplating a "bust-up" sale of assets in a leveraged acquisition, we imposed upon the board a duty to maximize immediate shareholder value and an obligation to auction the company fairly. If, however, the board's reaction to a hostile tender offer is found to constitute only a defensive response and not an abandonment of the corporation's continued existence, *Revlon* duties are not triggered, though *Unocal* duties attach.[14]

The plaintiffs insist that even though the original Time–Warner agreement may not have worked "an objective change of control," the transaction made a "sale" of Time inevitable. Plaintiffs rely on the subjective intent of Time's board of directors and principally upon certain board members' expressions of concern that the Warner transaction *might* be viewed as effectively putting Time up for sale. Plaintiffs argue that the use of a lock-up agreement, a no-shop clause, and so-called "dry-up" agreements prevented shareholders from obtaining a control premium in the immediate future and thus violated *Revlon*.

We agree with the Chancellor that such evidence is entirely insufficient to invoke *Revlon* duties; and we decline to extend *Revlon*'s application to corporate transactions simply because they might be construed as putting a corporation either "in play" or "up for sale." The adoption of structural safety devices alone does not trigger *Revlon*. Rather, as the Chancellor stated, such devices are properly subject to a *Unocal* analysis.

Finally, we do not find in Time's recasting of its merger agreement with Warner from a share exchange to a share purchase a basis to conclude that Time had either abandoned its strategic plan or made a sale of Time inevitable.[16] The Chancellor found that although the merged Time–Warner company would be large (with a value approaching approx-

---

**14.** Within the auction process, any action taken by the board must be reasonably related to the threat posed or reasonable in relation to the advantage sought, *see Mills Acquisition Co. v. Macmillan, Inc.*, Del. Supr., 559 A.2d 1261, 1288 (1989). Thus, a *Unocal* analysis may be appropriate when a corporation is in a *Revlon* situation and *Revlon* duties may be triggered by a defensive action taken in response to a hostile offer. Since *Revlon*, we have stated that differing treatment of various bidders is not actionable when such action reasonably relates to achieving the best price available for the stockholders. *Macmillan*, 559 A.2d at 1286–87.

**16.** We note that, although Time's advisors presented the board with such alternatives as an auction or sale to a third party bidder, the board rejected those responses, preferring to go forward with its pre-existing plan rather than adopt an alternative to Paramount's proposal.

imately $30 billion), recent takeover cases have proven that acquisition of the combined company might nonetheless be possible. The legal consequence is that *Unocal* alone applies to determine whether the business judgment rule attaches to the revised agreement. * * *

**B.**

We turn now to plaintiffs' *Unocal* claim. We begin by noting, as did the Chancellor, that our decision does not require us to pass on the wisdom of the board's decision to enter into the original Time–Warner agreement. That is not a court's task. Our task is simply to review the record to determine whether there is sufficient evidence to support the Chancellor's conclusion that the initial Time–Warner agreement was the product of a proper exercise of business judgment.

We have purposely detailed the evidence of the Time board's deliberative approach, beginning in 1983–84, to expand itself. Time's decision in 1988 to combine with Warner was made only after what could be fairly characterized as an exhaustive appraisal of Time's future as a corporation. After concluding in 1983–84 that the corporation must expand to survive, and beyond journalism into entertainment, the board combed the field of available entertainment companies. By 1987 Time had focused upon Warner; by late July 1988 Time's board was convinced that Warner would provide the best "fit" for Time to achieve its strategic objectives. The record attests to the zealousness of Time's executives, fully supported by their directors, in seeing to the preservation of Time's "culture," i.e., its perceived editorial integrity in journalism. We find ample evidence in the record to support the Chancellor's conclusion that the Time board's decision to expand the business of the company through its March 3 merger with Warner was entitled to the protection of the business judgment rule. *See Aronson v. Lewis*, Del.Supr., 473 A.2d 805, 812 (1984).

The Chancellor reached a different conclusion in addressing the Time–Warner transaction as revised three months later. He found that the revised agreement was defense-motivated and designed to avoid the potentially disruptive effect that Paramount's offer would have had on consummation of the proposed merger were it put to a shareholder vote. Thus, the court declined to apply the traditional business judgment rule to the revised transaction and instead analyzed the Time board's June 16 decision under *Unocal*. The court ruled that *Unocal* applied to all director actions taken, following receipt of Paramount's hostile tender offer, that were reasonably determined to be defensive. Clearly that was a correct ruling and no party disputes that ruling.

In *Unocal*, we held that before the business judgment rule is applied to a board's adoption of a defensive measure, the burden will lie with the board to prove (a) reasonable grounds for believing that a danger to corporate policy and effectiveness existed; and (b) that the defensive measure adopted was reasonable in relation to the threat posed. *Unocal*, 493 A.2d 946. Directors satisfy the first part of the *Unocal* test by demonstrating good faith and reasonable investigation. We have repeatedly stated that the refusal to entertain an offer may comport with a valid exercise of a board's business judgment. *See, e.g., Macmillan,* 559 A.2d at 1285 n. 35; *Van Gorkom,* 488 A.2d at 881; *Pogostin v. Rice,* Del.Supr., 480 A.2d 619, 627 (1984).

*Unocal* involved a two-tier, highly coercive tender offer. In such a case, the threat is obvious: shareholders may be compelled to tender to avoid being treated adversely in the second stage of the transaction. In subsequent cases, the Court of Chancery has suggested that an all-cash, all-shares offer, falling within a range of values that a shareholder might reasonably prefer, cannot constitute a legally recognized "threat" to shareholder interests sufficient to withstand a *Unocal* analysis. AC *Acquisitions Corp. v. Anderson, Clayton & Co.,* Del.Ch., 519 A.2d 103 (1986); see Grand *Metropolitan, PLC v. Pillsbury Co.,* Del.Ch., 558 A.2d 1049 (1988); City *Capital Associates v. Interco, Inc.,* Del.Ch., 551 A.2d 787 (1988). In those cases, the Court of Chancery determined that whatever danger existed related only to the shareholders and only to price and not to the corporation.

From those decisions by our Court of Chancery, Paramount and the individual plaintiffs extrapolate a rule of law that an all-cash, all-shares offer with values reasonably in the range of acceptable price cannot pose any objective threat to a corporation or its shareholders. Thus, Paramount would have us hold that only if the value of Paramount's offer were determined to be clearly inferior to the value created by management's plan to merge with Warner could the offer be viewed—objectively—as a threat.

Implicit in the plaintiffs' argument is the view that a hostile tender offer can pose only two types of threats: the threat of coercion that results from a two-tier offer promising unequal treatment for nontendering shareholders; and the threat of inadequate value from an all-shares, all-cash offer at a price below what a target board in good faith deems to be the present value of its shares. Since Paramount's offer was all-cash, the only conceivable "threat," plaintiffs argue, was inadequate value. We disapprove of such a narrow and rigid construction of *Unocal,* for the reasons which follow.

Plaintiffs' position represents a fundamental misconception of our standard of review under *Unocal* principally because it would involve the court in substituting its judgment for what is a "better" deal for that of a corporation's board of directors. To the extent that the Court of Chancery has recently done so in certain of its opinions, we hereby reject such approach as not in keeping with a proper *Unocal* analysis. *See, e.g., Interco,* 551 A.2d 787, and its progeny; *but see TW Services, Inc. v. SWT Acquisition Corp.,* Del.Ch., WL 20290 (March 2, 1989).

The usefulness of *Unocal* as an analytical tool is precisely its flexibility in the face of a variety of fact scenarios. *Unocal* is not intended as an abstract standard; neither is it a structured and mechanistic procedure of appraisal. Thus, we have said that directors may consider, when evaluating the threat posed by a takeover bid, the "inadequacy of the price offered, nature and timing of the offer, questions of illegality, the impact on contingencies other than shareholders, the risk of nonconsummation and the quality of securities being offered in the exchange." 493 A.2d at 955. The open-ended analysis mandated by *Unocal* is not intended to lead to a simple mathematical exercise: that is, of comparing the discounted value of Time–Warner's expected trading price at some future date with Paramount's offer and determining which is the higher. Indeed, in our view, precepts underlying the business judgment rule mitigate against a court's engaging in the process of attempting to appraise and evaluate the relative merits of a long-term versus a short-term investment goal for shareholders. To engage in such an exercise is a distortion of the *Unocal* process and, in particular, the application of the second part of *Unocal*'s test, discussed below.

In this case, the Time board reasonably determined that inadequate value was not the only legally cognizable threat that Paramount's all-cash, all-shares offer could present. Time's board concluded that Paramount's eleventh hour offer posed other threats. One concern was that Time shareholders might elect to tender into Paramount's cash offer in ignorance or a mistaken belief of the strategic benefit which a business combination with Warner might produce. Moreover, Time viewed the conditions attached to Paramount's offer as introducing a degree of uncertainty that skewed a comparative analysis. Further, the timing of Paramount's offer to follow issuance of Time's proxy notice was viewed as arguably designed to upset, if not confuse, the Time stockholders' vote. Given this record evidence, we cannot conclude that the Time board's decision of June 6 that Paramount's offer posed a threat to corporate policy and effectiveness was lacking in good faith or dominated by motives of either entrenchment or self-interest.

Paramount also contends that the Time board had not duly investigated Paramount's offer. Therefore, Paramount argues, Time was unable to make an informed decision that the offer posed a threat to Time's corporate policy. Although the Chancellor did not address this issue directly, his findings of fact do detail Time's exploration of the available entertainment companies, including Paramount, before determining that Warner provided the best strategic "fit." In addition, the court found that Time's board rejected Paramount's offer because Paramount did not serve Time's objectives or meet Time's needs. Thus, the record does, in our judgment, demonstrate that Time's board was adequately informed of the potential benefits of a transaction with Paramount. We agree with the Chancellor that the Time board's lengthy pre-June investigation of potential merger candidates, including Paramount, mooted any obligation on Time's part to halt its merger process with Warner to reconsider Paramount. Time's board was under no obligation to negotiate with Paramount. *Unocal,* 493 A.2d at 954–55; *see also Macmillan,* 559 A.2d at 1285 n. 35. Time's failure to negotiate cannot be fairly found to have been uninformed. The evidence supporting this finding is materially enhanced by the fact that twelve of Time's sixteen board members were outside independent directors.

We turn to the second part of the *Unocal* analysis. The obvious requisite to determining the reasonableness of a defensive action is a clear identification of the nature of the threat. As the Chancellor correctly noted, this "requires an evaluation of the importance of the corporate objective threatened; alternative methods of protecting that objective; impacts of the 'defensive' action, and other relevant factors." *In Re: Time Incorporated Shareholder Litigation*, Del.Ch., 565 A.2d 281 (1989). It is not until both parts of the *Unocal* inquiry have been satisfied that the business judgment rule attaches to defensive actions of a board of directors. *Unocal*, 493 A.2d at 954.[17] As applied to the facts of this case, the question is whether the record evidence supports the Court of Chancery's conclusion that the restructuring of the Time–Warner transaction, including the adoption of several preclusive defensive measures, was a *reasonable response* in relation to a perceived threat.

Paramount argues that, assuming its tender offer posed a threat, Time's response was unreasonable in precluding Time's shareholders from accepting the tender offer or receiving a control premium in the immediately foreseeable future. Once again, the contention stems, we believe, from a fundamental misunderstanding of where the power of corporate governance lies. Delaware law confers the management of the corporate enterprise to the stockholders' duly elected board representatives. 8 Del.C. § 141(a). The fiduciary duty to manage a corporate enterprise includes the selection of a time frame for achievement of corporate goals. That duty may not be delegated to the stockholders. *Van Gorkom*, 488 A.2d at 873. Directors are not obliged to abandon a deliberately conceived corporate plan for a short-term shareholder profit unless there is clearly no basis to sustain the corporate strategy. *See, e.g.*, *Revlon*, 506 A.2d 173.

Although the Chancellor blurred somewhat the discrete analyses required under *Unocal*, he did conclude that Time's board reasonably perceived Paramount's offer to be a significant threat to the planned Time–Warner merger and that Time's response was not "overly broad." We have found that even in light of a valid threat, management actions that are coercive in nature or force upon shareholders a management-sponsored alternative to a hostile offer may be struck down as unreasonable and nonproportionate responses. *Macmillan*, 559 A.2d 1261; *AC Acquisitions Corp.*, 519 A.2d 103.

Here, on the record facts, the Chancellor found that Time's responsive action to Paramount's tender offer was not aimed at "cramming down" on its shareholders a management-sponsored alternative, but rather had as its goal the carrying forward of a pre-existing transaction in an altered form. Thus, the response was reasonably related to the

**17.** Some commentators have criticized *Unocal* by arguing that once the board's deliberative process has been analyzed and found not to be wanting in objectivity, good faith or deliberateness, the so-called "enhanced" business judgment rule has been satisfied and no further inquiry is undertaken. *See generally* Johnson and Siegel, *Corporate Mergers: Redefining the Role of Target Directors*, 136 U.Pa.L.Rev. 315 (1987). We reject such views.

threat. The Chancellor noted that the revised agreement and its accompanying safety devices did not preclude Paramount from making an offer for the combined Time–Warner company or from changing the conditions of its offer so as not to make the offer dependent upon the nullification of the Time–Warner agreement. Thus, the response was proportionate. We affirm the Chancellor's rulings as clearly supported by the record. Finally, we note that although Time was required, as a result of Paramount's hostile offer, to incur a heavy debt to finance its acquisition of Warner, that fact alone does not render the board's decision unreasonable so long as the directors could reasonably perceive the debt load not to be so injurious to the corporation as to jeopardize its well being.

* * *

CONCLUSION

Applying the test for grant or denial of preliminary injunctive relief, we find plaintiffs failed to establish a reasonable likelihood of ultimate success on the merits. Therefore, we affirm.

———

The *Time* decision triggered an avalanche of comment. Many believe *Time* endorses a "just say no" defense that allows a board of directors to ignore shareholder wealth maximization so as to pursue what the board believes are the corporation's interests. Consider the following excerpt:

> * * * The court appears to have been very impressed * * * with the effort Time's management had devoted to planning and negotiating the merger with Warner; with the Time outside director's determination * * * to stick to their original plan and resist the Paramount bid; and with the possibility that those directors reasonably believed Paramount, after disrupting the Time–Warner merger, would rely on the other conditions in its bid to abandon its bid and leave Time's shareholders holding the bag. Operating very much within the framework of the two-part *Unocal* test, the court was not willing to term unreasonable either the directors' belief that Paramount's offer threatened the well-being of Time and its shareholders, or the directors's decision to employ a non-coercive defense to counter that threat. In short, while *Time* may suggest that corporations have more latitude to respond to noncoercive bids than one might infer from *Revlon* and *Mills, Time* surely does not signify that the Delaware court has abandoned its effort to develop a principled approach that allows courts to meaningfully review corporations' responses to uninvited takeover bids.

Elliott J. Weiss, *Whose Rules Should Govern Takeovers: Delaware's, The ALI's, or Martin Lipton's?*, 33 ARIZ.L.REV. 761, 781–82 (1991).

## PARAMOUNT COMMUNICATIONS INC. v. QVC NETWORK INC.

637 A.2d 34 (Del.1994).

VEASEY, C.J.

In this appeal we review an order of the Court of Chancery * * * preliminarily enjoining certain defensive measures designed to facilitate a so-called strategic alliance between Viacom Inc. ("Viacom") and Paramount Communications Inc. ("Paramount") approved by the board of directors of Paramount (the "Paramount Board" or the "Paramount directors") and to thwart an unsolicited, more valuable, tender offer by QVC Network Inc. ("QVC"). In affirming, we hold that the sale of control in this case, which is at the heart of the proposed strategic alliance, implicates enhanced judicial scrutiny of the conduct of the Paramount Board under Unocal Corp. v. Mesa Petroleum Co., Del.Supr., 493 A.2d 946 (1985), and Revlon, Inc. v. MacAndrews & Forbes Holdings, Inc., Del.Supr., 506 A.2d 173 (1985). We further hold that the conduct of the Paramount Board was not reasonable as to process or result.

QVC and certain stockholders of Paramount commenced separate actions (later consolidated) in the Court of Chancery seeking preliminary and permanent injunctive relief against Paramount, certain members of the Paramount Board, and Viacom. This action arises out of a proposed acquisition of Paramount by Viacom through a tender offer followed by a second-step merger (the "Paramount–Viacom transaction"), and a competing unsolicited tender offer by QVC. The Court of Chancery granted a preliminary injunction. * * *

The Court of Chancery found that the Paramount directors violated their fiduciary duties by favoring the Paramount–Viacom transaction over the more valuable unsolicited offer of QVC. The Court of Chancery preliminarily enjoined Paramount and the individual defendants (the "Paramount defendants") from amending or modifying Paramount's stockholder rights agreement (the "Rights Agreement"), including the redemption of the Rights, or taking other action to facilitate the consummation of the pending tender offer by Viacom or any proposed second-step merger, including the Merger Agreement between Paramount and Viacom dated September 12, 1993 (the "Original Merger Agreement"), as amended on October 24, 1993 (the "Amended Merger Agreement"). Viacom and the Paramount defendants were enjoined from taking any action to exercise any provision of the Stock Option Agreement between Paramount and Viacom dated September 12, 1993 (the "Stock Option Agreement"), as amended on October 24, 1993. The Court of Chancery did not grant preliminary injunctive relief as to the termination fee provided for the benefit of Viacom in Section 8.05 of the Original Merger Agreement and the Amended Merger Agreement (the "Termination Fee").

Under the circumstances of this case, the pending sale of control implicated in the Paramount–Viacom transaction required the Paramount Board to act on an informed basis to secure the best value reasonably available to the stockholders. Since we agree with the Court of Chancery that the Paramount directors violated their fiduciary duties, we have AFFIRMED the entry of the order of the Vice Chancellor granting the preliminary injunction and have REMANDED these proceedings to the Court of Chancery for proceedings consistent herewith.

\* \* \*

## I.  FACTS

\* \* \*

Paramount is a Delaware corporation with its principal offices in New York City. Approximately 118 million shares of Paramount's common stock are outstanding and traded on the New York Stock Exchange. The majority of Paramount's stock is publicly held by numerous unaffiliated investors. Paramount owns and operates a diverse group of entertainment businesses, including motion picture and television studios, book publishers, professional sports teams, and amusement parks.

There are 15 persons serving on the Paramount Board. Four directors are officer-employees of Paramount [including] Martin S. Davis ("Davis"), Paramount's Chairman and Chief Executive Officer since 1983 [and] Donald Oresman ("Oresman"), Executive Vice–President, Chief Administrative Officer, and General Counsel \* \* \*. Paramount's 11 outside directors are distinguished and experienced business persons who are present or former senior executives of public corporations or financial institutions.

\* \* \* Viacom is controlled by Sumner M. Redstone ("Redstone"), its Chairman and Chief Executive Officer, who owns indirectly approximately 85.2 percent of Viacom's voting Class A stock and approximately 69.2 percent of Viacom's nonvoting Class B stock through National Amusements, Inc. ("NAI"), an entity 91.7 percent owned by Redstone. Viacom has a wide range of entertainment operations, including a number of well-known cable television channels such as MTV, Nickelodeon, Showtime, and The Movie Channel. Viacom's equity co-investors in the Paramount–Viacom transaction include NYNEX Corporation and Blockbuster Entertainment Corporation.

\* \* \* QVC has several large stockholders, including Liberty Media Corporation, Comcast Corporation, Advance Publications, Inc., and Cox Enterprises Inc. Barry Diller ("Diller"), the Chairman and Chief Executive Officer of QVC, is also a substantial stockholder. QVC sells a variety of merchandise through a televised shopping channel. QVC has several equity co-investors in its proposed combination with Paramount including BellSouth Corporation and Comcast Corporation.

Beginning in the late 1980s, Paramount investigated the possibility of acquiring or merging with other companies in the entertainment, media, or communications industry. Paramount considered such transactions to be desirable, and perhaps necessary, in order to keep pace with competitors in the rapidly evolving field of entertainment and communications. Consistent with its goal of strategic expansion, Paramount made a tender offer for Time Inc. in 1989, but was ultimately unsuccessful. See Paramount Communications, Inc. v. Time Inc., Del.Supr., 571 A.2d 1140 (1989) ("Time–Warner").

Although Paramount had considered a possible combination of Paramount and Viacom as early as 1990, * * * serious negotiations began taking place in early July [1993].

* * * After a short hiatus [because of a disagreement as to the terms of the transaction], the parties negotiated in earnest in early September, and performed due diligence with the assistance of their financial advisors, Lazard Freres & Co. ("Lazard") for Paramount and Smith Barney for Viacom. On September 9, 1993, the Paramount Board was informed about the status of the negotiations and was provided information by Lazard, including an analysis of the proposed transaction.

On September 12, 1993, the Paramount Board met again and unanimously approved the Original Merger Agreement whereby Paramount would merge with and into Viacom. The terms of the merger provided that each share of Paramount common stock would be converted into 0.10 shares of Viacom Class A voting stock, 0.90 shares of Viacom Class–B nonvoting stock, and $9.10 in cash. In addition, the Paramount Board agreed to amend its "poison pill" Rights Agreement to exempt the proposed merger with Viacom. The Original Merger Agreement also contained several provisions designed to make it more difficult for a potential competing bid to succeed. We focus, as did the Court of Chancery, on three of these defensive provisions: a "no-shop" provision (the "No–Shop Provision"), the Termination Fee, and the Stock Option Agreement.

First, under the No–Shop Provision, the Paramount Board agreed that Paramount would not solicit, encourage, discuss, negotiate, or endorse any competing transaction unless: (a) a third party "makes an unsolicited written, bona fide proposal, which is not subject to any material contingencies relating to financing"; and (b) the Paramount Board determines that discussions or negotiations with the third party are necessary for the Paramount Board to comply with its fiduciary duties.

Second, under the Termination Fee provision, Viacom would receive a $100 million termination fee if: (a) Paramount terminated the Original Merger Agreement because of a competing transaction; (b) Paramount's stockholders did not approve the merger; or (c) the Paramount Board recommended a competing transaction.

The third and most significant deterrent device was the Stock Option Agreement, which granted to Viacom an option to purchase approximately 19.9 percent (23,699,000 shares) of Paramount's outstanding common stock at $69.14 per share if any of the triggering events for the Termination Fee occurred. In addition to the customary terms that are normally associated with a stock option, the Stock Option Agreement contained two provisions that were both unusual and highly beneficial to Viacom: (a) Viacom was permitted to pay for the shares with a senior subordinated note of questionable marketability instead of cash, thereby avoiding the need to raise the $1.6 billion purchase price (the "Note Feature"); and (b) Viacom could elect to require Paramount to pay Viacom in cash a sum equal to the difference between the purchase price and the market price of Paramount's stock (the "Put Feature"). Because the Stock Option Agreement was not "capped" to limit its maximum dollar value, it had the potential to reach (and in this case did reach) unreasonable levels.

After the execution of the Original Merger Agreement and the Stock Option Agreement on September 12, 1993, Paramount and Viacom announced their proposed merger. In a number of public statements, the parties indicated that the pending transaction was a virtual certainty. Redstone described it as a "marriage" that would "never be torn asunder" and stated that only a "nuclear attack" could break the deal. Redstone also called Diller and John Malone of Tele–Communications Inc., a major stockholder of QVC, to dissuade them from making a competing bid.

Despite these attempts to discourage a competing bid, Diller sent a letter to Davis on September 20, 1993, proposing a merger in which QVC would acquire Paramount for approximately $80 per share, consisting of 0.893 shares of QVC common stock and $30 in cash. QVC also expressed its eagerness to meet with Paramount to negotiate the details of a transaction. When the Paramount Board met on September 27, it was advised by Davis that the Original Merger Agreement prohibited Paramount from having discussions with QVC (or anyone else) unless certain conditions were satisfied. In particular, QVC had to supply evidence that its proposal was not subject to financing contingencies. The Paramount Board was also provided information from Lazard describing QVC and its proposal.

On October 5, 1993, QVC provided Paramount with evidence of QVC's financing. The Paramount Board then held another meeting on October 11, and decided to authorize management to meet with QVC. Davis also informed the Paramount Board that Booz–Allen & Hamilton, a management consulting firm, had been retained to assess, inter alia, the incremental earnings potential from a Paramount–Viacom merger and a Paramount–QVC merger. Discussions proceeded slowly, however, due to a delay in Paramount signing a confidentiality agreement. In response to Paramount's request for information, QVC provided two binders of documents to Paramount on October 20.

On October 21, 1993, QVC filed this action and publicly announced an $80 cash tender offer for 51 percent of Paramount's outstanding shares (the "QVC tender offer"). Each remaining share of Paramount common stock would be converted into 1.42857 shares of QVC common stock in a second-step merger. The tender offer was conditioned on, among other things, the invalidation of the Stock Option Agreement, which was worth over $200 million by that point. QVC contends that it had to commence a tender offer because of the slow pace of the merger discussions and the need to begin seeking clearance under federal antitrust laws.

Confronted by QVC's hostile bid, which on its face offered over $10 per share more than the consideration provided by the Original Merger Agreement, Viacom realized that it would need to raise its bid in order to remain competitive. Within hours after QVC's tender offer was announced, Viacom entered into discussions with Paramount concerning a revised transaction. These discussions led to serious negotiations concerning a comprehensive amendment to the original Paramount–Viacom transaction. In effect, the opportunity for a "new deal" with Viacom was at hand for the Paramount Board. With the QVC hostile bid offering greater value to the Paramount stockholders, the Paramount Board had considerable leverage with Viacom.

At a special meeting on October 24, 1993, the Paramount Board approved the Amended Merger Agreement and an amendment to the Stock Option Agreement. The Amended Merger Agreement was, however, essentially the same as the Original Merger Agreement, except that it included a few new provisions. One provision related to an $80 per share cash tender offer by Viacom for 51 percent of Paramount's stock, and another changed the merger consideration so that each share of Paramount would be converted into 0.20408 shares of Viacom Class A voting stock, 1.08317 shares of Viacom Class B nonvoting stock, and 0.20408 shares of a new series of Viacom convertible preferred stock. The Amended Merger Agreement also added a provision giving Paramount the right not to amend its Rights Agreement to exempt Viacom if the Paramount Board determined that such an amendment would be inconsistent with its fiduciary duties because another offer constituted a "better alternative." Finally, the Paramount Board was given the power to terminate the Amended Merger Agreement if it withdrew its recommendation of the Viacom transaction or recommended a competing transaction.

Although the Amended Merger Agreement offered more consideration to the Paramount stockholders and somewhat more flexibility to the Paramount Board than did the Original Merger Agreement, the defensive measures designed to make a competing bid more difficult were not removed or modified. In particular, there is no evidence in the record that Paramount sought to use its newly-acquired leverage to eliminate or modify the No–Shop Provision, the Termination Fee, or the Stock Option Agreement when the subject of amending the Original Merger Agreement was on the table.

Viacom's tender offer commenced on October 25, 1993, and QVC's tender offer was formally launched on October 27, 1993. Diller sent a letter to the Paramount Board on October 28 requesting an opportunity to negotiate with Paramount, and Oresman responded the following day by agreeing to meet. The meeting, held on November 1, was not very fruitful, however, after QVC's proposed guidelines for a "fair bidding process" were rejected by Paramount on the ground that "auction procedures" were inappropriate and contrary to Paramount's contractual obligations to Viacom.

On November 6, 1993, Viacom unilaterally raised its tender offer price to $85 per share in cash and offered a comparable increase in the value of the securities being proposed in the second-step merger. At a telephonic meeting held later that day, the Paramount Board agreed to recommend Viacom's higher bid to Paramount's stockholders.

QVC responded to Viacom's higher bid on November 12 by increasing its tender offer to $90 per share and by increasing the securities for its second-step merger by a similar amount. In response to QVC's latest offer, the Paramount Board scheduled a meeting for November 15, 1993. Prior to the meeting, Oresman sent the members of the Paramount Board a document summarizing the "conditions and uncertainties" of QVC's offer. One director testified that this document gave him a very negative impression of the QVC bid.

At its meeting on November 15, 1993, the Paramount Board determined that the new QVC offer was not in the best interests of the stockholders. The purported basis for this conclusion was that QVC's bid was excessively conditional. The Paramount Board did not communicate with QVC regarding the status of the conditions because it believed that the No–Shop Provision prevented such communication in the absence of firm financing. Several Paramount directors also testified that they believed the Viacom transaction would be more advantageous to Paramount's future business prospects than a QVC transaction. Although a number of materials were distributed to the Paramount Board describing the Viacom and QVC transactions, the only quantitative analysis of the consideration to be received by the stockholders under each proposal was based on then-current market prices of the securities involved, not on the anticipated value of such securities at the time when the stockholders would receive them.[8]

The preliminary injunction hearing in this case took place on November 16, 1993. On November 19, Diller wrote to the Paramount Board to inform it that QVC had obtained financing commitments for its tender offer and that there was no antitrust obstacle to the offer. On November 24, 1993, the Court of Chancery issued its decision granting a preliminary injunction in favor of QVC and the plaintiff stockholders. This appeal followed.

**8.** The market prices of Viacom's and QVC's stock were poor measures of their actual values because such prices constantly fluctuated depending upon which company was perceived to be the more likely to acquire Paramount.

## II. Applicable Principles of Established Delaware Law

The General Corporation Law of the State of Delaware and the decisions of this Court have repeatedly recognized the fundamental principle that the management of the business and affairs of a Delaware corporation is entrusted to its directors, who are the duly elected and authorized representatives of the stockholders. Under normal circumstances, neither the courts nor the stockholders should interfere with the managerial decisions of the directors. The business judgment rule embodies the deference to which such decisions are entitled.

Nevertheless, there are rare situations which mandate that a court take a more direct and active role in overseeing the decisions made and actions taken by directors. In these situations, a court subjects the directors' conduct to enhanced scrutiny to ensure that it is reasonable. The decisions of this Court have clearly established the circumstances where such enhanced scrutiny will be applied. The case at bar implicates two such circumstances: (1) the approval of a transaction resulting in a sale of control, and (2) the adoption of defensive measures in response to a threat to corporate control.

### A. The Significance of a Sale or Change[10] of Control

When a majority of a corporation's voting shares are acquired by a single person or entity, or by a cohesive group acting together, there is a significant diminution in the voting power of those who thereby become minority stockholders. Under the statutory framework of the General Corporation Law, many of the most fundamental corporate changes can be implemented only if they are approved by a majority vote of the stockholders. Such actions include elections of directors, amendments to the certificate of incorporation, mergers, consolidations, sales of all or substantially all of the assets of the corporation, and dissolution. Because of the overriding importance of voting rights, this Court and the Court of Chancery have consistently acted to protect stockholders from unwarranted interference with such rights.

In the absence of devices protecting the minority stockholders, stockholder votes are likely to become mere formalities where there is a majority stockholder. For example, minority stockholders can be deprived of a continuing equity interest in their corporation by means of a cash-out merger. Absent effective protective provisions, minority stockholders must rely for protection solely on the fiduciary duties owed to them by the directors and the majority stockholder, since the minority stockholders have lost the power to influence corporate direction through the ballot. The acquisition of majority status and the consequent privilege of exerting the powers of majority ownership come at a price. That price is usually a control premium which recognizes not only

---

**10.** For purposes of our December 9 Order and this Opinion, we have used the terms "sale of control" and "change of control" interchangeably without intending any doctrinal distinction.

the value of a control block of shares, but also compensates the minority stockholders for their resulting loss of voting power.

In the case before us, the public stockholders (in the aggregate) currently own a majority of Paramount's voting stock. Control of the corporation is not vested in a single person, entity, or group, but vested in the fluid aggregation of unaffiliated stockholders. In the event the Paramount–Viacom transaction is consummated, the public stockholders will receive cash and a minority equity voting position in the surviving corporation. Following such consummation, there will be a controlling stockholder who will have the voting power to: (a) elect directors; (b) cause a break-up of the corporation; (c) merge it with another company; (d) cash-out the public stockholders; (e) amend the certificate of incorporation; (f) sell all or substantially all of the corporate assets; or (g) otherwise alter materially the nature of the corporation and the public stockholders' interests. Irrespective of the present Paramount Board's vision of a long-term strategic alliance with Viacom, the proposed sale of control would provide the new controlling stockholder with the power to alter that vision.

Because of the intended sale of control, the Paramount–Viacom transaction has economic consequences of considerable significance to the Paramount stockholders. Once control has shifted, the current Paramount stockholders will have no leverage in the future to demand another control premium. As a result, the Paramount stockholders are entitled to receive, and should receive, a control premium and/or protective devices of significant value. There being no such protective provisions in the Viacom–Paramount transaction, the Paramount directors had an obligation to take the maximum advantage of the current opportunity to realize for the stockholders the best value reasonably available.

### B. The Obligations of Directors in a Sale or Change of Control Transaction

The consequences of a sale of control impose special obligations on the directors of a corporation.[13] In particular, they have the obligation of acting reasonably to seek the transaction offering the best value reasonably available to the stockholders. The courts will apply enhanced scrutiny to ensure that the directors have acted reasonably. The obligations of the directors and the enhanced scrutiny of the courts are well-

---

**13.** We express no opinion on any scenario except the actual facts before the Court, and our precise holding herein. Unsolicited tender offers in other contexts may be governed by different precedent. For example, where a potential sale of control by a corporation is not the consequence of a board's action, this Court has recognized the prerogative of a board of directors to resist a third party's unsolicited acquisition proposal or offer. *See Pogostin,* 480 A.2d at 627; *Time–Warner,* 571 A.2d at 1152; *Ber-*

*shad v. Curtiss–Wright Corp.,* Del.Supr., 535 A.2d 840, 845 (1987); *Macmillan,* 559 A.2d at 1285 n. 35. The decision of a board to resist such an acquisition, like all decisions of a properly-functioning board, must be informed, *Unocal,* 493 A.2d at 954–55, and the circumstances of each particular case will determine the steps that a board must take to inform itself, and what other action, if any, is required as a matter of fiduciary duty.

established by the decisions of this Court. The directors' fiduciary duties in a sale of control context are those which generally attach. * * *

In the sale of control context, the directors must focus on one primary objective—to secure the transaction offering the best value reasonably available for the stockholders—and they must exercise their fiduciary duties to further that end. The decisions of this Court have consistently emphasized this goal. * * *

In pursuing this objective, the directors must be especially diligent. In particular, this Court has stressed the importance of the board being adequately informed in negotiating a sale of control: "The need for adequate information is central to the enlightened evaluation of a transaction that a board must make." *Barkan*, 567 A.2d at 1287. This requirement is consistent with the general principle that "directors have a duty to inform themselves, prior to making a business decision, of all material information reasonably available to them." *Aronson*, 473 A.2d at 812. Moreover, the role of outside, independent directors becomes particularly important because of the magnitude of a sale of control transaction and the possibility, in certain cases, that management may not necessarily be impartial.

*Barkan* teaches some of the methods by which a board can fulfill its obligation to seek the best value reasonably available to the stockholders. These methods are designed to determine the existence and viability of possible alternatives. They include conducting an auction, canvassing the market, etc. Delaware law recognizes that there is "no single blueprint" that directors must follow. [567 A.2d] at 1286–87.

In determining which alternative provides the best value for the stockholders, a board of directors is not limited to considering only the amount of cash involved, and is not required to ignore totally its view of the future value of a strategic alliance. Instead, the directors should analyze the entire situation and evaluate in a disciplined manner the consideration being offered. Where stock or other non-cash consideration is involved, the board should try to quantify its value, if feasible, to achieve an objective comparison of the alternatives. In addition, the board may assess a variety of practical considerations relating to each alternative, including:

> [an offer's] fairness and feasibility; the proposed or actual financing for the offer, and the consequences of that financing; questions of illegality; * * * the risk of non-consum[m]ation; * * * the bidder's identity, prior background and other business venture experiences; and the bidder's business plans for the corporation and their effects on stockholder interests.

*Macmillan*, 559 A.2d at 1282 n. 29. These considerations are important because the selection of one alternative may permanently foreclose other opportunities. While the assessment of these factors may be complex, the board's goal is straightforward: Having informed themselves of all material information reasonably available, the directors must decide which alternative is most likely to offer the best value reasonably available to the stockholders.

### C.   Enhanced Judicial Scrutiny of a Sale or Change of Control Transaction

Board action in the circumstances presented here is subject to enhanced scrutiny. Such scrutiny is mandated by: (a) the threatened diminution of the current stockholders' voting power; (b) the fact that an asset belonging to public stockholders (a control premium) is being sold and may never be available again; and (c) the traditional concern of Delaware courts for actions which impair or impede stockholder voting rights. * * *

The key features of an enhanced scrutiny test are: (a) a judicial determination regarding the adequacy of the decisionmaking process employed by the directors, including the information on which the directors based their decision; and (b) a judicial examination of the reasonableness of the directors' action in light of the circumstances then existing. The directors have the burden of proving that they were adequately informed and acted reasonably.

Although an enhanced scrutiny test involves a review of the reasonableness of the substantive merits of a board's actions, a court should not ignore the complexity of the directors' task in a sale of control. There are many business and financial considerations implicated in investigating and selecting the best value reasonably available. The board of directors is the corporate decisionmaking body best equipped to make these judgments. Accordingly, a court applying enhanced judicial scrutiny should be deciding whether the directors made a reasonable decision, not a perfect decision. If a board selected one of several reasonable alternatives, a court should not second-guess that choice even though it might have decided otherwise or subsequent events may have cast doubt on the board's determination. Thus, courts will not substitute their business judgment for that of the directors, but will determine if the directors' decision was, on balance, within a range of reasonableness.

### D.   Revlon and Time–Warner Distinguished

The Paramount defendants and Viacom assert that the fiduciary obligations and the enhanced judicial scrutiny discussed above are not implicated in this case in the absence of a "break-up" of the corporation, and that the order granting the preliminary injunction should be reversed. This argument is based on their erroneous interpretation of our decisions in *Revlon* and *Time–Warner*.

In *Revlon,* we reviewed the actions of the board of directors of Revlon, Inc. ("Revlon"), which had rebuffed the overtures of Pantry Pride, Inc. and had instead entered into an agreement with Forstmann Little & Co. ("Forstmann") providing for the acquisition of 100 percent of Revlon's outstanding stock by Forstmann and the subsequent break-up of Revlon. Based on the facts and circumstances present in *Revlon,* we held that "[t]he directors' role changed from defenders of the corporate bastion to auctioneers charged with getting the best price for the stockholders at a sale of the company." 506 A.2d at 182. We further held that "when a board ends an intense bidding contest on an insubstantial basis, * * * [that] action cannot withstand the enhanced scrutiny which Unocal requires of director conduct." *Id.* at 184.

It is true that one of the circumstances bearing on these holdings was the fact that "the break-up of the company * * * had become a reality which even the directors embraced." *Id* at 182. It does not follow, however, that a "break-up" must be present and "inevitable" before directors are subject to enhanced judicial scrutiny and are required to pursue a transaction that is calculated to produce the best value reasonably available to the stockholders. In fact, we stated in *Revlon* that "when bidders make relatively similar offers, or dissolution of the company becomes inevitable, the directors cannot fulfill their enhanced *Unocal* duties by playing favorites with the contending factions." *Id.* at 184 (emphasis added). *Revlon* thus does not hold that an inevitable dissolution or "break-up" is necessary.

The decisions of this Court following *Revlon* reinforced the applicability of enhanced scrutiny and the directors' obligation to seek the best value reasonably available for the stockholders where there is a pending sale of control, regardless of whether or not there is to be a break-up of the corporation. In *Macmillan,* this Court held:

> We stated in *Revlon,* and again here, that *in a sale of corporate control* the responsibility of the directors is to get the highest value reasonably attainable for the shareholders.

559 A.2d at 1288 (emphasis added).

Although *Macmillan* and *Barkan* are clear in holding that a change of control imposes on directors the obligation to obtain the best value reasonably available to the stockholders, the Paramount defendants have interpreted our decision in *Time–Warner* as requiring a corporate break-up in order for that obligation to apply. The facts in *Time–Warner,* however, were quite different from the facts of this case, and refute Paramount's position here. In *Time–Warner,* the Chancellor held that there was no change of control in the original stock-for-stock merger between Time and Warner because Time would be owned by a fluid aggregation of unaffiliated stockholders both before and after the merger:

> If the appropriate inquiry is whether a change in control is contemplated, the answer must be sought in the specific circumstances surrounding the transaction. Surely under some circumstances a stock for stock merger could reflect a transfer of corporate control. That would, for example, plainly be the case here if Warner were a private company. But where, as here, the shares of both constituent corporations are widely held, corporate control can be expected to remain unaffected by a stock for stock merger. This in my judgment was the situation with respect to the original merger

agreement. When the specifics of that situation are reviewed, it is seen that, aside from legal technicalities and aside from arrangements thought to enhance the prospect for the ultimate succession of [Nicholas J. Nicholas, Jr., president of Time], neither corporation could be said to be acquiring the other. *Control of both remained in a large, fluid, changeable and changing market.*

The existence of a control block of stock in the hands of a single shareholder or a group with loyalty to each other does have real consequences to the financial value of "minority" stock. The law offers some protection to such shares through the imposition of a fiduciary duty upon controlling shareholders. *But here, effectuation of the merger would not have subjected Time shareholders to the risks and consequences of holders of minority shares. This is a reflection of the fact that no control passed to anyone in the transaction contemplated.* The shareholders of Time would have "suffered" dilution, of course, but they would suffer the same type of dilution upon the public distribution of new stock.

Paramount Communications Inc. v. Time Inc., Del.Ch., No. 10866, Allen, C. (July 17, 1989), reprinted at 15 Del.J.Corp.L. 700, 739 (emphasis added). Moreover, the transaction actually consummated in *Time–Warner* was not a merger, as originally planned, but a sale of Warner's stock to Time.

In our affirmance of the Court of Chancery's well-reasoned decision, this Court held that "The Chancellor's findings of fact are supported by the record *and his conclusion is correct as a matter of law.*" 571 A.2d at 1150 (emphasis added). Nevertheless, the Paramount defendants here have argued that a break-up is a requirement and have focused on the following language in our *Time–Warner* decision:

However, we premise our rejection of plaintiffs' *Revlon* claim on different grounds, namely, the absence of any substantial evidence to conclude that Time's board, in negotiating with Warner, made the dissolution or break-up of the corporate entity inevitable, as was the case in *Revlon.*

Under Delaware law there are, generally speaking and *without excluding other possibilities*, two circumstances which may implicate *Revlon* duties. The first, and clearer one, is when a corporation *initiates an active bidding process seeking to sell itself* or to effect a business reorganization involving a clear break-up of the company. However, *Revlon* duties may also be triggered where, in response to a bidder's offer, a target abandons its long-term strategy and seeks an alternative transaction involving the breakup of the company.

*Id.* at 1150 (emphasis added) (citation and footnote omitted).

The Paramount defendants have misread the holding of *Time–Warner*. Contrary to their argument, our decision in *Time–Warner* expressly states that the two general scenarios discussed in the above-quoted paragraph are not the *only* instances where "*Revlon* duties" may be implicated. The Paramount defendants' argument totally ignores the phrase "without excluding other possibilities." Moreover, the instant case is clearly within the first general scenarios set forth in *Time–Warner*. The Paramount Board, albeit unintentionally, had "initiate[d] an active bidding process seeking to sell itself" by agreeing to sell control of the corporation to Viacom in circumstances where another potential acquiror (QVC) was equally interested in being a bidder.

The Paramount defendants' position that *both* a change of control and a break-up are *required* must be rejected. Such a holding would unduly restrict the application of *Revlon*, is inconsistent with this Court's decisions in *Barkan* and *Macmillan*, and has no basis in policy. There are few events that have a more significant impact on the stockholders than a sale of control or a corporate break-up. Each event represents a fundamental (and perhaps irrevocable) change in the nature of the corporate enterprise from a practical standpoint. It is the significance of each of these events that justifies: (a) focusing on the directors' obligation to seek the best value reasonably available to the stockholders; and (b) requiring a close scrutiny of board action which could be contrary to the stockholders' interests.

Accordingly, when a corporation undertakes a transaction which will cause: (a) a change in corporate control; or (b) a break-up of the corporate entity, the directors' obligation is to seek the best value reasonably available to the stockholders. This obligation arises because the effect of the Viacom–Paramount transaction, if consummated, is to shift control of Paramount from the public stockholders to a controlling stockholder, Viacom. Neither *Time–Warner* nor any other decision of this Court holds that a "break-up" of the company is essential to give rise to this obligation where there is a sale of control.

### III. Breach of Fiduciary Duties by Paramount Board

We now turn to duties of the Paramount Board under the facts of this case and our conclusions as to the breaches of those duties which warrant injunctive relief.

#### A. *The Specific Obligations of the Paramount Board*

Under the facts of this case, the Paramount directors had the obligation: (a) to be diligent and vigilant in examining critically the Paramount–Viacom transaction and the QVC tender offers; (b) to act in good faith; (c) to obtain, and act with due care on, all material information reasonably available, including information necessary to compare the two offers to determine which of these transactions, or an alternative course of action, would provide the best value reasonably available to the stockholders; and (d) to negotiate actively and in good faith with both Viacom and QVC to that end.

Having decided to sell control of the corporation, the Paramount directors were required to evaluate critically whether or not all material aspects of the Paramount–Viacom transaction (separately and in the aggregate) were reasonable and in the best interests of the Paramount stockholders in light of current circumstances, including:. the change of control premium, the Stock Option Agreement, the Termination Fee, the coercive nature of both the Viacom and QVC tender offers, the No–Shop Provision, and the proposed disparate use of the Rights Agreement as to the Viacom and QVC tender offers, respectively.

These obligations necessarily implicated various issues, including the questions of whether or not those provisions and other aspects of the Paramount–Viacom transaction (separately and in the aggregate): (a) adversely affected the value provided to the Paramount stockholders; (b) inhibited or encouraged alternative bids; (c) were enforceable contractual obligations in light of the directors' fiduciary duties; and (d) in the end would advance or retard the Paramount directors' obligation to secure for the Paramount stockholders the best value reasonably available under the circumstances.

The Paramount defendants contend that they were precluded by certain contractual provisions, including the No–Shop Provision, from negotiating with QVC or seeking alternatives. Such provisions, whether or not they are presumptively valid in the abstract, may not validly define or limit the directors' fiduciary duties under Delaware law or prevent the Paramount directors from carrying out their fiduciary duties under Delaware law. To the extent such provisions are inconsistent with those duties, they are invalid and unenforceable.

Since the Paramount directors had already decided to sell control, they had an obligation to continue their search for the best value reasonably available to the stockholders. This continuing obligation included the responsibility, at the October 24 board meeting and thereafter, to evaluate critically both the QVC tender offers and the Paramount–Viacom transaction to determine if: (a) the QVC tender offer was, or would continue to be, conditional; (b) the QVC tender offer could be improved; (c) the Viacom tender offer or other aspects of the Paramount–Viacom transaction could be improved; (d) each of the respective offers would be reasonably likely to come to closure, and under what circumstances; (e) other material information was reasonably available for consideration by the Paramount directors; (f) there were viable and realistic alternative courses of action; and (g) the timing constraints could be managed so the directors could consider these matters carefully and deliberately.

### B.   The Breaches of Fiduciary Duty by the Paramount Board

The Paramount directors made the decision on September 12, 1993, that, in their judgment, a strategic merger with Viacom on the economic terms of the Original Merger Agreement was in the best interests of Paramount and its stockholders. Those terms provided a modest change of control premium to the stockholders. The directors also decided at that time that it was appropriate to agree to certain defensive measures (the Stock Option Agreement, the Termination Fee, and the No–Shop Provision) insisted upon by Viacom as part of that economic transaction.

Those defensive measures, coupled with the sale of control and subsequent disparate treatment of competing bidders, implicated the judicial scrutiny of *Unocal, Revlon, Macmillan,* and their progeny. We conclude that the Paramount directors' process was not reasonable, and the result achieved for the stockholders was not reasonable under the circumstances.

When entering into the Original Merger Agreement, and thereafter, the Paramount Board clearly gave insufficient attention to the potential consequences of the defensive measures demanded by Viacom. The Stock Option Agreement had a number of unusual and potentially "draconian" provisions, including the Note Feature and the Put Feature. Furthermore, the Termination Fee, whether or not unreasonable by itself, clearly made Paramount less attractive to other bidders, when coupled with the Stock Option Agreement. Finally, the No–Shop Provision inhibited the Paramount Board's ability to negotiate with other potential bidders, particularly QVC which had already expressed an interest in Paramount.

Throughout the applicable time period, and especially from the first QVC merger proposal on September 20 through the Paramount Board meeting on November 15, QVC's interest in Paramount provided the opportunity for the Paramount Board to seek significantly higher value for the Paramount stockholders than that being offered by Viacom. QVC persistently demonstrated its intention to meet and exceed the Viacom offers, and frequently expressed its willingness to negotiate possible further increases.

The Paramount directors had the opportunity in the October 23–24 time frame, when the Original Merger Agreement was renegotiated, to take appropriate action to modify the improper defensive measures as well as to improve the economic terms of the Paramount–Viacom transaction. Under the circumstances existing at that time, it should have been clear to the Paramount Board that the Stock Option Agreement, coupled with the Termination Fee and the No–Shop Clause, were impeding the realization of the best value reasonably available to the Paramount stockholders. Nevertheless, the Paramount Board made no effort to eliminate or modify these counterproductive devices, and instead continued to cling to its vision of a strategic alliance with Viacom. Moreover, based on advice from the Paramount management, the Paramount directors considered the QVC offer to be "conditional" and asserted that they were precluded by the No–Shop Provision from seeking more information from, or negotiating with, QVC.

By November 12, 1993, the value of the revised QVC offer on its face exceeded that of the Viacom offer by over $1 billion at then current values. This significant disparity of value cannot be justified on the basis of the directors' vision of future strategy, primarily because the change of control would supplant the authority of the current Paramount Board to continue to hold and implement their strategic vision in any meaningful way. Moreover, their uninformed process had deprived their strategic vision of much of its credibility.

When the Paramount directors met on November 15 to consider QVC's increased tender offer, they remained prisoners of their own misconceptions and missed opportunities to eliminate the restrictions they had imposed on themselves. Yet, it was not "too late" to reconsider negotiating with QVC. The circumstances existing on November 15 made it clear that the defensive measures, taken as a whole, were problematic: (a) the No–Shop Provision could not define or limit their fiduciary duties; (b) the Stock Option Agreement had become "draconian"; and (c) the Termination Fee, in context with all the circumstances, was similarly deterring the realization of possibly higher bids. Nevertheless, the Paramount directors remained paralyzed by their uninformed belief that the QVC offer was "illusory." This final opportunity to negotiate on the stockholders' behalf and to fulfill their obligation to seek the best value reasonably available was thereby squandered.

IV. VIACOM'S CLAIM OF VESTED CONTRACT RIGHTS

Viacom argues that it had certain "vested" contract rights with respect to the No–Shop Provision and the Stock Option Agreement. In effect, Viacom's argument is that the Paramount directors could enter into an agreement in violation of their fiduciary duties and then render Paramount, and ultimately its stockholders, liable for failing to carry out an agreement in violation of those duties. Viacom's protestations about vested rights are without merit. This Court has found that those defensive measures were improperly designed to deter potential bidders, and that such measures do not meet the reasonableness test to which they must be subjected. They are consequently invalid and unenforceable under the facts of this case.

The No–Shop Provision could not validly define or limit the fiduciary duties of the Paramount directors. To the extent that a contract, or a provision thereof, purports to require a board to act or not act in such a fashion as to limit the exercise of fiduciary duties, it is invalid and unenforceable. Despite the arguments of Paramount and Viacom to the contrary, the Paramount directors could not contract away their fiduciary obligations. Since the No–Shop Provision was invalid, Viacom never had any vested contract rights in the provision.

As discussed previously, the Stock Option Agreement contained several "draconian" aspects, including the Note Feature and the Put Feature. While we have held that lock-up options are not per se illegal, no options with similar features have ever been upheld by this Court. Under the circumstances of this case, the Stock Option Agreement clearly is invalid. Accordingly, Viacom never had any vested contract rights in that Agreement.

Viacom, a sophisticated party with experienced legal and financial advisors, knew of (and in fact demanded) the unreasonable features of the Stock Option Agreement. It cannot be now heard to argue that it obtained vested contract rights by negotiating and obtaining contractual provisions from a board acting in violation of its fiduciary duties. As the Nebraska Supreme Court said in rejecting a similar argument in *ConAgra, Inc. v. Cargill, Inc.*, Neb.Supr., 382 N.W.2d 576, 587–88 (1986), "To so hold, it would seem, would be to get the shareholders coming and going." Likewise, we reject Viacom's arguments and hold that its fate must rise or fall, and in this instance fall, with the determination that the actions of the Paramount Board were invalid.

## V. CONCLUSION

The realization of the best value reasonably available to the stockholders became the Paramount directors' primary obligation under these facts in light of the change of control. That obligation was not satisfied, and the Paramount Board's process was deficient. The directors' initial hope and expectation for a strategic alliance with Viacom was allowed to dominate their decisionmaking process to the point where the arsenal of defensive measures established at the outset was perpetuated (not modified or eliminated) when the situation was dramatically altered. QVC's unsolicited bid presented the opportunity for significantly greater value for the stockholders and enhanced negotiating leverage for the directors. Rather than seizing those opportunities, the Paramount directors chose to wall themselves off from material information which was reasonably available and to hide behind the defensive measures as a rationalization for refusing to negotiate with QVC or seeking other alternatives. Their view of the strategic alliance likewise became an empty rationalization as the opportunities for higher value for the stockholders continued to develop.

It is the nature of the judicial process that we decide only the case before us—a case which, on its facts, is clearly controlled by established Delaware law. Here, the proposed change of control and the implications thereof were crystal clear. In other cases they may be less clear. The holding of this case on its facts, coupled with the holdings of the principal cases discussed herein where the issue of sale of control is implicated, should provide a workable precedent against which to measure future cases.

## 5.  CONTEMPORARY METHODOLOGY

### UNITRIN, INC. v. AMERICAN GENERAL CORP.

651 A.2d 1361 (Del.1995).

HOLLAND, JUSTICE.

This is an appeal from the Court of Chancery's entry of a preliminary injunction on October 13, 1994, upon plaintiffs' motions in two actions: American General Corporation's ("American General") suit against Unitrin, Inc. ("Unitrin") and its directors; and a parallel class action brought by Unitrin stockholders * * *

American General, which had publicly announced a proposal to merge with Unitrin for $2.6 billion at $50–3/8 per share, and certain

Unitrin shareholder plaintiffs, filed suit in the Court of Chancery, inter alia, to enjoin Unitrin from repurchasing up to 10 million shares of its own stock (the "Repurchase Program"). On August 26, 1994, the Court of Chancery temporarily restrained Unitrin from making any further repurchases. After expedited discovery, briefing and argument, the Court of Chancery preliminarily enjoined Unitrin from making further repurchases on the ground that the Repurchase Program was a disproportionate response to the threat posed by American General's inadequate all cash for all shares offer, under the standard of this Court's holding in *Unocal Corp. v. Mesa Petroleum Co.,* Del.Supr., 493 A.2d 946 (1985) ("*Unocal*").

### Unitrin's Contentions

Unitrin has raised several issues in this appeal. First, it contends that the Court of Chancery erred in assuming that the outside directors would subconsciously act contrary to their substantial financial interests as stockholders and, instead, vote in favor of a subjective desire to protect the "prestige and perquisites" of membership on Unitrin's Board of Directors. Second, it contends that the Court of Chancery erred in holding that the adoption of the Repurchase Program would materially affect the ability of an insurgent stockholder to win a proxy contest. According to Unitrin, that holding is unsupported by the evidence, is based upon a faulty mathematical analysis, and disregards the holding of *Moran v. Household Int'l, Inc.,* Del.Supr., 500 A.2d 1346, 1355 (1985). Furthermore, Unitrin argues that the Court of Chancery erroneously substituted its own judgment for that of Unitrin's Board, contrary to this Court's subsequent interpretations of *Unocal* in *Paramount Communications, Inc. v. QVC Network, Inc.,* Del.Supr., 637 A.2d 34, 45–46 (1994), and *Paramount Communications, Inc. v. Time, Inc.,* Del.Supr., 571 A.2d 1140 (1989)* * *.

### This Court: Ultimate Disposition

This Court has concluded that the Court of Chancery erred in applying the proportionality review *Unocal* requires by focusing upon whether the Repurchase Program was an "unnecessary" defensive response. *See Paramount Communications, Inc. v. QVC Network, Inc.,* 637 A.2d at 45–46. The Court of Chancery should have directed its enhanced scrutiny: first, upon whether the Repurchase Program the Unitrin Board implemented was draconian, by being either preclusive or coercive and; second, if it was not draconian, upon whether it was within a range of reasonable responses to the threat American General's Offer posed. Consequently, the interlocutory preliminary injunctive judgment of the Court of Chancery is reversed. This matter is remanded for further proceedings in accordance with this opinion.

### The Parties

American General is the largest provider of home service insurance. On July 12, 1994, it made a merger proposal to acquire Unitrin for $2.6 billion at $50–3/8 per share. Following a public announcement of this proposal, Unitrin shareholders filed suit seeking to compel a sale of the company. American General filed suit to enjoin Unitrin's Repurchase Program.

Unitrin is also in the insurance business. It is the third largest provider of home service insurance. The other defendants-appellants are the members of Unitrin's seven person Board of Directors (the "Unitrin Board" or "Board"). Two directors are employees, Richard C. Vie ("Vie"), the Chief Executive Officer, and Jerrold V. Jerome ("Jerome"), Chairman of the Board. The five remaining directors are not and have never been employed by Unitrin. * * *

The record reflects that the non-employee directors each receive a fixed annual fee of $30,000. They receive no other significant financial benefit from serving as directors. At the offering price proposed by American General, the value of Unitrin's non-employee directors' stock exceeded $450 million.

## AMERICAN GENERAL'S OFFER

In January 1994, James Tuerff ("Tuerff"), the President of American General, met with Richard Vie, Unitrin's Chief Executive Officer. Tuerff advised Vie that American General was considering acquiring other companies. Unitrin was apparently at or near the top of its list. Tuerff did not mention any terms for a potential acquisition of Unitrin. Vie replied that Unitrin had excellent prospects as an independent company and had never considered a merger. Vie indicated to Tuerff that Unitrin was not for sale.

* * * The parties agree that the Board's position in February [1994] was that Unitrin was not for sale. It was unnecessary to respond to American General because no offer had been made.

On July 12, 1994, American General sent a letter to Vie proposing a consensual merger transaction in which it would "purchase all of Unitrin's 51.8 million outstanding shares of common stock for $50–3/8 per share, in cash" (the "Offer"). The Offer was conditioned on the development of a merger agreement and regulatory approval. The Offer price represented a 30% premium over the market price of Unitrin's shares. In the Offer, American General stated that it "would consider offering a higher price" if "Unitrin could demonstrate additional value." American General also offered to consider tax-free "[a]lternatives to an all cash transaction."

## UNITRIN'S REJECTION

Upon receiving the American General Offer, the Unitrin Board's Executive Committee (Singleton, Vie, and Jerome) engaged legal counsel and scheduled a telephonic Board meeting for July 18. At the July 18 special meeting, the Board reviewed the terms of the Offer. The Board was advised that the existing charter and bylaw provisions might not effectively deter all types of takeover strategies. It was suggested that the Board consider adopting a shareholder rights plan and an advance notice provision for shareholder proposals.

The Unitrin Board met next on July 25, 1994 in Los Angeles for seven hours. All directors attended the meeting. The principal purpose of the meeting was to discuss American General's Offer.

Vie reviewed Unitrin's financial condition and its ongoing business strategies. The Board also received a presentation from its investment advisor, Morgan Stanley & Co. ("Morgan Stanley"), regarding the financial adequacy of American General's proposal. Morgan Stanley expressed its opinion that the Offer was financially inadequate.[4] Legal counsel expressed concern that the combination of Unitrin and American General would raise antitrust complications due to the resultant decrease in competition in the home service insurance markets.

The Unitrin Board unanimously concluded that the American General merger proposal was not in the best interests of Unitrin's shareholders and voted to reject the Offer. The Board then received advice from its legal and financial advisors about a number of possible defensive measures it might adopt, including a shareholder rights plan ("poison pill") and an advance notice bylaw provision for shareholder proposals. Because the Board apparently thought that American General intended to keep its Offer private, the Board did not implement any defensive measures at that time.

On July 26, 1994, Vie faxed a letter to Tuerff, rejecting American General's Offer.

AMERICAN GENERAL'S PUBLICITY: UNITRIN'S INITIAL RESPONSES

On August 2, 1994, American General issued a press release announcing its Offer to Unitrin's Board to purchase all of Unitrin's stock for $50–3/8 per share. The press release also noted that the Board had rejected American General's Offer. After that public announcement, the trading volume and market price of Unitrin's stock increased.

At its regularly scheduled meeting on August 3, the Unitrin Board discussed the effects of American General's press release. The Board noted that the market reaction to the announcement suggested that speculative traders or arbitrageurs were acquiring Unitrin stock. The Board determined that American General's public announcement constituted a hostile act designed to coerce the sale of Unitrin at an inadequate price. The Board unanimously approved the poison pill and the proposed advance notice bylaw that it had considered previously.

Beginning on August 2 and continuing through August 12, 1994, Unitrin issued a series of press releases to inform its shareholders and the public market: first, that the Unitrin Board believed Unitrin's stock was worth more than the $50–3/8 American General offered; second, that the Board felt that the price of American General's Offer did not reflect Unitrin's long term business prospects as an independent company; third, that "the true value of Unitrin [was] not reflected in the

---

**4.** Eric Daut, who prepared these materials for Morgan Stanley under extreme time pressure, had never prepared such in- formation previously and did not rely on firm figures. Morgan Stanley, in turn, did not investigate these figures.

[then] current market price of its common stock," and that because of its strong financial position, Unitrin was well positioned "to pursue strategic and financial opportunities;" fourth, that the Board believed a merger with American General would have anticompetitive effects and might violate antitrust laws and various state regulatory statutes; and fifth, that the Board had adopted a shareholder rights plan (poison pill) to guard against undesirable takeover efforts.

### UNITRIN'S REPURCHASE PROGRAM

The Unitrin Board met again on August 11, 1994. The minutes of that meeting indicate that its principal purpose was to consider the Repurchase Program. At the Board's request, Morgan Stanley had prepared written materials to distribute to each of the directors. Morgan Stanley gave a presentation in which alternative means of implementing the Repurchase Program were explained. Morgan Stanley recommended that the Board implement an open market stock repurchase. The Board voted to authorize the Repurchase Program for up to ten million shares of its outstanding stock.

On August 12, Unitrin publicly announced the Repurchase Program. The Unitrin Board expressed its belief that "Unitrin's stock is undervalued in the market and that the expanded program will tend to increase the value of the shares that remain outstanding." The announcement also stated that the director stockholders were not participating in the Repurchase Program, and that the repurchases "will increase the percentage ownership of those stockholders who choose not to sell."

Unitrin's August 12 press release also stated that the directors owned 23% of Unitrin's stock, that the Repurchase Program would cause that percentage to increase, and that Unitrin's certificate of incorporation included a supermajority voting provision. The following language from a July 22 draft press release revealing the antitakeover effects of the Repurchase Program was omitted from the final press release.

> Under the [supermajority provision], the consummation of the expanded repurchase program would enhance the ability of nonselling stockholders, including the directors, to prevent a merger with a greater-than–15% stockholder if they did not favor the transaction.

\* \* \*

Between August 12 and noon on August 24, Morgan Stanley purchased nearly 5 million of Unitrin's shares on Unitrin's behalf. The average price paid was slightly above American General's Offer price.

\* \* \*

### NATURE OF PROCEEDING: DETERMINES JUDICIAL REVIEW

In this case, before the Court of Chancery could evaluate the reasonable probability of the plaintiffs' success on the merits, it had to determine the nature of the proceeding. When shareholders challenge directors' actions, usually one of three levels of judicial review is applied: the traditional business judgment rule, the *Unocal* standard of enhanced judicial scrutiny, or the entire fairness analysis. * * * The Court of Chancery [concluded] that the Unitrin Board's actions should be examined under the standard of enhanced judicial scrutiny this Court set forth in *Unocal*

UNITRIN BOARD'S ACTIONS DEFENSIVE: UNOCAL IS PROPER REVIEW STANDARD

Before a board of directors' action is subject to the *Unocal* standard of enhanced judicial scrutiny, the court must determine whether the particular conduct was defensive * * *

According to the Unitrin Board, the Repurchase Program was enacted for a valid business purpose and, therefore, should not be evaluated as a defensive measure under *Unocal*. The Court of Chancery agreed that, had the Board enacted the Repurchase Program independent of a takeover proposal, its decision would be reviewed under the traditional business judgment rule. The Court of Chancery concluded, however, that the Unitrin Board perceived American General's Offer as a threat and, from the timing of the consideration and implementation of the Repurchase Program, adopted the Repurchase Program as one of several defensive measures in response to that threat. Unitrin does not dispute that conclusion for the purpose of this interlocutory appeal.

The Court of Chancery held that all of the Unitrin Board's defensive actions merited judicial scrutiny according to *Unocal*. The record supports the Court of Chancery's determination that the Board perceived American General's Offer as a threat and adopted the Repurchase Program, along with the poison pill and advance notice bylaw, as defensive measures in response to that threat. Therefore, the Court of Chancery properly concluded the facts before it required an application of *Unocal* and its progeny * * *

* * *

PARTIES' BURDENS SHIFT: JUDICIAL REVIEW STANDARDS
DIFFER: BUSINESS JUDGMENT RULE AND UNOCAL

* * * The ultimate question in applying the *Unocal* standard is: what deference should the reviewing court give "to the decisions of directors in defending against a takeover?" E. Norman Veasey, *The New Incarnation of the Business Judgment Rule in Takeover Defenses*, 11 DEL.J.CORP.L. 503, 504–05 (1986). The question is usually presented to the Court of Chancery, as in the present case, in an injunction proceeding, a posture which is known as "transactional justification." *Id*. To answer the question, the enhanced judicial scrutiny *Unocal* requires implicates both the substantive and procedural nature of the business judgment rule.

* * *

The litigation between Unitrin, American General, and the Unitrin shareholders in the Court of Chancery is a classic example of a transactional justification case. The Court of Chancery's determination that the conduct of Unitrin's Board was subject to *Unocal*'s enhanced judicial scrutiny required it to evaluate each party's ability to sustain its unique burden in the procedural context of a preliminary injunction proceeding. The plaintiff's burden in such a proceeding is to demonstrate a reasonable probability of success after trial.

In general, to effectively defeat the plaintiff's ability to discharge that burden, a board must sustain its burden of demonstrating that, even under *Unocal*'s standard of enhanced judicial scrutiny, its actions deserved the protection of the traditional business judgment rule. Thus, the plaintiff's likelihood of success in obtaining a preliminary injunction was initially dependent upon the inability of the Unitrin Board to discharge the burden placed upon it first by *Unocal*. Accordingly, having concluded that the Board's actions were defensive, the Court of Chancery logically began with an evaluation of the Unitrin Board's evidence.

### AMERICAN GENERAL THREAT: REASONABLENESS BURDEN SUSTAINED

The first aspect of the *Unocal* burden, the reasonableness test, required the Unitrin Board to demonstrate that, after a reasonable investigation, it determined in good faith, that American General's Offer presented a threat to Unitrin that warranted a defensive response. This Court has held that the presence of a majority of outside independent directors will materially enhance such evidence * * *

The Unitrin Board identified two dangers it perceived the American General Offer posed: inadequate price and antitrust complications. The Court of Chancery characterized the Board's concern that American General's proposed transaction could never be consummated because it may violate antitrust laws and state insurance regulations as a "makeweight excuse" for the defensive measure. It determined, however, that the Board reasonably believed that the American General Offer was inadequate and also reasonably concluded that the Offer was a threat to Unitrin's uninformed stockholders.

The Court of Chancery held that the Board's evidence satisfied the first aspect or reasonableness test under *Unocal*. The Court of Chancery then noted, however, that the threat to the Unitrin stockholders from American General's inadequate opening bid was "mild," because the Offer was negotiable both in price and structure. * * *

### PROPORTIONALITY BURDEN: CHANCERY APPROVES POISON PILL

The second aspect or proportionality test of the initial *Unocal* burden required the Unitrin Board to demonstrate the proportionality of its response to the threat American General's Offer posed. The record reflects that the Unitrin Board considered three options as defensive measures: the poison pill, the advance notice bylaw, and the Repurchase Program. The Unitrin Board did not act on any of these options on July 25.

The Court of Chancery analyzed each stage of the Unitrin Board's defensive responses separately * * * [and] concluded that Unitrin's Board believed in good faith that the American General Offer was inadequate and properly employed a poison pill as a proportionate defensive response to protect its stockholders from a "low ball" bid.

No cross-appeal was filed in this expedited interlocutory proceeding. Therefore, the Court of Chancery's ruling that the Unitrin Board's adoption of a poison pill was a proportionate response to American General's Offer is not now directly at issue. Nevertheless, to the extent the Unitrin Board's prior adoption of the poison pill influenced the Court of Chancery's proportionality review of the Repurchase Program, the Board's adoption of the poison pill is also a factor to be considered on appeal by this Court.

PROPORTIONALITY BURDEN: CHANCERY ENJOINS REPURCHASE PROGRAM

The Court of Chancery did not view either its conclusion that American General's Offer constituted a threat, or its conclusion that the poison pill was a reasonable response to that threat, as requiring it, a fortiori, to conclude that the Repurchase Program was also an appropriate response. The Court of Chancery then made two factual findings: first, the Repurchase Program went beyond what was "necessary" to protect the Unitrin stockholders from a "low ball" negotiating strategy; and second, it was designed to keep the decision to combine with American General within the control of the members of the Unitrin Board, as stockholders, under virtually all circumstances. Consequently, the Court of Chancery held that the Unitrin Board failed to demonstrate that the Repurchase Program met the second aspect or proportionality requirement of the initial burden *Unocal* ascribes to a board of directors.

\* \* \*

\* \* \* Therefore, the Court of Chancery held that the plaintiffs proved a likelihood of success on that issue and granted the motion to preliminarily enjoin the Repurchase Program.[18]

PROXY CONTEST: SUPERMAJORITY VOTE: REPURCHASE PROGRAM

Before the Repurchase Program began, Unitrin's directors collectively held approximately 23% of Unitrin's outstanding shares. Unitrin's certificate of incorporation already included a "shark-repellent" provision barring any business combination with a more-than–15% stockholder unless approved by a majority of continuing directors or by a 75% stockholder vote ("Supermajority Vote"). Unitrin's shareholder directors announced publicly that they would not participate in the Repurchase Program and that this would result in a percentage increase of ownership for them, as well as for any other shareholder who did not participate.

The Court of Chancery found that by not participating in the Repurchase Program, the Board "expected to create a 28% voting block to support the Board's decision to reject [a future] offer by American

---

**18.** We note that the directors' failure to carry their initial burden under Unocal does not, ipso facto, invalidate the board's actions. Instead, once the Court of Chancery finds the business judgment rule does not apply, the burden remains on the directors to prove "entire fairness."

General." From this underlying factual finding, the Court of Chancery concluded that American General might be "chilled" in its pursuit of Unitrin.

### Proportionality Test: Shareholder Franchise

This Court has been and remains assiduous in its concern about defensive actions designed to thwart the essence of corporate democracy by disenfranchising shareholders * * *

[R]ecently, this Court stated: "we accept the basic legal tenets," set forth in *Blasius Indus., Inc. v. Atlas Corp.,* Del.Ch., 564 A.2d 651 (1988), that "[w]here boards of directors deliberately employ * * * legal strategies either to frustrate or completely disenfranchise a shareholder vote, * * * [t]here can be no dispute that such conduct violates Delaware law." *Stroud v. Grace,* 606 A.2d at 91. * * *

This Court also specifically noted that boards of directors often interfere with the exercise of shareholder voting when an acquiror *launches both a proxy fight and a tender offer. Id.* at 92 n.3. We then stated that such action "necessarily invoked both *Unocal* and *Blasius*" because "both [tests] recognize the inherent conflicts of interest that arise when shareholders are not permitted free exercise of their franchise." *Id.* Consequently, we concluded that, "[i]n certain circumstances, [the judiciary] must recognize the special import of protecting the shareholders' franchise within *Unocal's* requirement that any defensive measure be proportionate and 'reasonable in relation to the threat posed.' "*Id.* (citation omitted).

### Takeover Strategy: Tender Offer/Proxy Contest

We begin our examination of Unitrin's Repurchase Program mindful of the special import of protecting the shareholder's franchise within *Unocal's* requirement that a defensive response be reasonable and proportionate. *Stroud v. Grace,* 606 A.2d at 92. For many years the "favored attack of a [corporate] raider was stock acquisition followed by a proxy contest." *Unocal,* 493 A.2d at 957. Some commentators have noted that the recent trend toward tender offers as the preferable alternative to proxy contests appears to be reversing because of the proliferation of sophisticated takeover defenses. Lucian A. Bebchuk & Marcel Kahan, *A Framework for Analyzing Legal Policy Towards Proxy Contests,* 78 Cal.L.Rev. 1071, 1134 (1990). In fact, the same commentators have characterized a return to proxy contests as "the only alternative to hostile takeovers to gain control against the will of the incumbent directors." *Id.*

The Court of Chancery, in the case *sub judice,* was obviously cognizant that the emergence of the "poison pill" as an effective takeover device has resulted in such a remarkable transformation in the market for corporate control that hostile bidders who proceed when such defenses are in place will usually "have to couple proxy contests with tender offers." Joseph A. Grundfest, *Just Vote No: A Minimalist Strategy for Dealing with Barbarians Inside the Gates,* 45 Stan.L.Rev. 857, 858

(1993). The Court of Chancery concluded that Unitrin's adoption of a poison pill was a proportionate response to the threat its Board reasonably perceived from American General's Offer. Nonetheless, the Court of Chancery enjoined the additional defense of the Repurchase Program as disproportionate and "unnecessary."

The record reflects that the Court of Chancery's decision to enjoin the Repurchase Program is attributable to a continuing misunderstanding, i.e., that in conjunction with the longstanding Supermajority Vote provision in the Unitrin charter, the Repurchase Program would operate to provide the director shareholders with a "veto" to preclude a successful proxy contest by American General. The origins of that misunderstanding are three premises that are each without record support. Two of those premises are objective misconceptions and the other is subjective.

### DIRECTORS' MOTIVES: "PRESTIGE AND PERQUISITES": SUBJECTIVE DETERMINATION

The subjective premise was the Court of Chancery's *sua sponte* determination that Unitrin's outside directors, who are also substantial stockholders, would not vote like other stockholders in a proxy contest, i.e., in their own best economic interests. At American General's Offer price, the outside directors held Unitrin shares worth more than $450 million. Consequently, Unitrin argues the stockholder directors had the same interest as other Unitrin stockholders generally, when voting in a proxy contest, to wit: the maximization of the value of their investments.

In rejecting Unitrin's argument, the Court of Chancery stated that the stockholder directors would be "subconsciously" motivated in a proxy contest to vote against otherwise excellent offers which did not include a "price parameter" to compensate them for the loss of the "prestige and perquisites" of membership on Unitrin's Board. The Court of Chancery's subjective determination that the *stockholder directors* of Unitrin would reject an "excellent offer," unless it compensated them for giving up the "prestige and perquisites" of directorship, appears to be subjective and without record support. It cannot be presumed.

\* \* \*

### WITHOUT REPURCHASE PROGRAM: ACTUAL VOTING POWER EXCEEDS 25%

The first objective premise relied upon by the Court of Chancery, unsupported by the record, is that the shareholder directors needed to implement the Repurchase Program to attain voting power in a proxy contest equal to 25%. The Court of Chancery properly calculated that if the Repurchase Program was completed, Unitrin's shareholder directors would increase their absolute voting power to 25%. It then calculated the odds of American General marshalling enough votes to defeat the Board and its supporters.

The Court of Chancery and all parties agree that proxy contests do not generate 100% shareholder participation. The shareholder plaintiffs argue that 80–85% may be a usual turnout. Therefore, *without* the

Repurchase Program, the director shareholders' absolute voting power of 23% would already constitute *actual voting power greater than* 25% in a proxy contest with normal shareholder participation below 100%.

### SUPERMAJORITY VOTE: NO REALISTIC DETERRENT

The second objective premise relied upon by the Court of Chancery, unsupported by the record, is that American General's ability to succeed in a proxy contest depended on the Repurchase Program being enjoined because of the Supermajority Vote provision in Unitrin's charter. Without the approval of a target's board, the danger of activating a poison pill renders it irrational for bidders to pursue stock acquisitions above the triggering level. Instead, "bidders intent on working around a poison pill must launch and win proxy contests to elect new directors who are willing to redeem the target's poison pill." [Grundfest, *supra*, at 859.]

As American General acknowledges, a less than 15% stockholder bidder need not proceed with acquiring shares to the extent that it would ever implicate the Supermajority Vote provision. In fact, it would be illogical for American General or any other bidder to acquire more than 15% of Unitrin's stock because that would not only trigger the poison pill, but also the constraints of 8 Del.C. § 203. If American General were to initiate a proxy contest *before* acquiring 15% of Unitrin's stock, it would need to amass only 45.1% of the votes assuming a 90% voter turnout. If it commenced a tender offer at an attractive price contemporaneously with its proxy contest, it could seek to acquire 50.1% of the outstanding voting stock.

### WITH SUPERMAJORITY VOTE: AFTER REPURCHASE PROGRAM: PROXY CONTEST APPEARS VIABLE

The assumptions and conclusions American General sets forth in this appeal for a different purpose are particularly probative with regard to the effect of the institutional holdings in Unitrin's stock. American General's two predicate assumptions are a 90% stockholder turnout in a proxy contest and a bidder with 14.9% holdings, i.e., the maximum the bidder could own to avoid triggering the poison pill and the Supermajority Vote provision. American General also calculated the votes available to the Board or the bidder with and without the Repurchase Program: Assuming no Repurchase [Program], the [shareholder directors] would hold 23%, the percentage collectively held by the [directors] and the bidder would be 37.9%, and the percentage of additional votes available to either side would be 52.1%. Assuming the Repurchase [Program] is fully consummated, the [shareholder directors] would hold 28%, the percentage collectively held by the bidder and the [directors] would be 42.9%, and the percentage of additional votes available to either side would be 47.1%.

American General then applied these assumptions to reach conclusions regarding the votes needed for the 14.9% stockholder bidder to prevail: first, in an election of directors; and second, in the subsequent vote on a merger. With regard to the election of directors, American General made the following calculations: Assume 90% stockholder turnout. To elect directors, a plurality must be obtained; assuming no abstentions and only two competing slates, one must obtain the votes of 45.1% of the shares. The percentage of additional votes the bidder needs to win is: 45.1% − 14.9% (maximum the bidder could own and avoid the poison pill, s 203 and supermajority) = 30.2%. A merger requires approval of a majority of outstanding shares, 8 Del.C. § 251, not just a plurality. In that regard, American General made the following calculations: Assume 90% stockholder turnout. To approve a merger, one must obtain the favorable vote of 50.1% of the shares. The percentage of additional votes the bidder needs to win is 50.1% − 14.9% = 35.2%.

Consequently, to prevail in a proxy contest with a 90% turnout, the percentage of additional shareholder votes a 14.9% shareholder bidder needs to prevail is 30.2% for directors and 35.2% in a subsequent merger. The record reflects that institutional investors held 42% of Unitrin's stock and 20 institutions held 33% of the stock. Thus, American General's own assumptions and calculations in the record support the Unitrin Board's argument that "it is hard to imagine a company more readily susceptible to a proxy contest concerning a pure issue of dollars."

The conclusion of the Court of Chancery that the Repurchase Program would make a proxy contest for Unitrin a "theoretical" possibility that American General could not realistically pursue may be erroneous and appears to be inconsistent with its own earlier determination that the "repurchase program strengthens the position of the Board of Directors to defend against a hostile bidder, but will not deprive the public stockholders of the 'power to influence corporate direction through the ballot.' " Even a complete implementation of the Repurchase Program, in combination with the pre-existing Supermajority Vote provision, would not appear to have a preclusive effect upon American General's ability successfully to marshall enough shareholder votes to win a proxy contest. A proper understanding of the record reflects that American General or any other 14.9% shareholder bidder could apparently win a proxy contest with a 90% turnout.

The key variable in a proxy contest would be the merit of American General's issues, not the size of its stockholdings. If American General presented an attractive price as the cornerstone of a proxy contest, it could prevail, irrespective of whether the shareholder directors' absolute voting power was 23% or 28%. In that regard, the following passage from the Court of Chancery's Opinion is poignant:

> Harold Hook, the Chairman of American General, admitted in his deposition that the repurchase program is not a "show stopper" because the directors that own stock will act in their own best interest if the price is high enough. Fayez Sarofim, one of the Unitrin directors that holds a substantial number of shares, "testified that 'everything has a price parameter.' "

Consequently, a proxy contest apparently remained a viable alternative for American General to pursue notwithstanding Unitrin's poison pill,

Supermajority Vote provision, and a fully implemented Repurchase Program.

### Substantive Coercion: American General's Threat

This Court has recognized "the prerogative of a board of directors to resist a third party's unsolicited acquisition proposal or offer."[*QVC* at 43 n.13]. The Unitrin Board did not have unlimited discretion to defeat the threat it perceived from the American General Offer by any draconian[34] means available. See *Unocal*, 493 A.2d at 955 ...

* * * Courts, commentators and litigators have attempted to catalogue the threats posed by hostile tender offers. [*Time*] at 1153. Commentators have categorized three types of threats:

> (i) *opportunity loss* * * * [where] a hostile offer might deprive target shareholders of the opportunity to select a superior alternative offered by target management [or, we would add, offered by another bidder]; (ii) *structural coercion*, * * * the risk that disparate treatment of non-tendering shareholders might distort shareholders' tender decisions; and (iii) *substantive coercion*, * * * the risk that shareholders will mistakenly accept an underpriced offer because they disbelieve management's representations of intrinsic value.

*Id.* at 1153 n. 17 (quoting Ronald J. Gilson & Reinier Kraakman, *Delaware's Intermediate Standard for Defensive Tactics: Is There Substance to Proportionality Review?*, 44 Bus.Law. 247, 267 (1989)).

* * *

The record appears to support Unitrin's argument that the Board's justification for adopting the Repurchase Program was its reasonably perceived risk of substantive coercion, i.e., that Unitrin's shareholders might accept American General's inadequate Offer because of "ignorance or mistaken belief" regarding the Board's assessment of the long-term value of Unitrin's stock. In this case, the Unitrin Board's letter to its shareholders specifically reflected those concerns in describing its perception of the threat from American General's Offer. The adoption of the Repurchase Program also appears to be consistent with this Court's holding that economic inadequacy is not the only threat presented by an all cash for all shares hostile bid, because the threat of such a hostile bid could be exacerbated by shareholder "ignorance or * * * mistaken belief."

### Range of Reasonableness: Proper Proportionality Burden

* * *

We have already noted that the Court of Chancery made a factual finding unsupported by the record, i.e., that the increase in the percent-

---

**34.** Draconian, adj. Of or pert. to Draco, an archon and member of the Athenian eupatridae, or the code of laws which is said to have been framed about 621 B.C. by him as thesmothete. In them the penalty for most offenses was death, and to a later age they seemed so severe that they were said to be written in blood. Hence, barbarously severe; harsh; cruel. Webster's New International Dictionary 780 (2d ed. 1951).

age of ownership by the stockholder directors from 23% to 28%, resulting from the completed Repurchase Program, would make it merely theoretically possible for an insurgent to win a proxy contest. That finding was based upon a hypothetical risk which originated from the Court of Chancery's attribution of subjective "prestige and perquisite" voting motives to Unitrin's outside shareholder directors. In addition, that factual finding was based upon two objective mathematically erroneous calculations regarding the relative voting strength of American General and the stockholder directors.

The Court of Chancery applied an incorrect legal standard when it ruled that the Unitrin decision to authorize the Repurchase Program was disproportionate because it was "unnecessary."

In *QVC*, this Court recently elaborated upon the judicial function in applying enhanced scrutiny, citing *Unocal* as authority, albeit in the context of a sale of control and the target board's consideration of one of several reasonable alternatives * * * The Court of Chancery did not determine whether the Unitrin Board's decision to implement the Repurchase Program fell within a "range of reasonableness."

The record reflects that the Unitrin Board's adoption of the Repurchase Program was an apparent recognition on its part that all shareholders are not alike. This Court has stated that distinctions among types of shareholders are neither inappropriate nor irrelevant for a board of directors to make, e.g., distinctions between long-term shareholders and short-term profit-takers, such as arbitrageurs, and their stockholding objectives. In *Unocal* itself, we expressly acknowledged that "a board may reasonably consider the basic stockholder interests at stake, including those of short term speculators, whose actions may have fueled the coercive aspect of the offer at the expense of the long term investor." *Unocal*, 493 A.2d at 955–56.

The Court of Chancery's determination that the Unitrin Board's adoption of the Repurchase Program was unnecessary constituted a substitution of its business judgment for that of the Board, contrary to this Court's "range of reasonableness" holding in *Paramount Communications, Inc. v. QVC Network, Inc.*, 637 A.2d at 45–46. Its decision to enjoin the Repurchase Program as an "unnecessary" addition to other complementary defensive mechanisms is also inconsistent with a similar analysis in *Shamrock Holdings, Inc. v. Polaroid Corp.*, Del.Ch., 559 A.2d 278 (1989). * * *

DRACONIAN DEFENSES: COERCIVE OR PRECLUSIVE: RANGE OF REASONABLENESS

An examination of the cases applying *Unocal* reveals a direct correlation between findings of proportionality or disproportionality and the judicial determination of whether a defensive response was draconian because it was either coercive or preclusive in character * * *

More than a century before *Unocal* was decided, Justice Holmes observed that the common law must be developed through its application and "cannot be dealt with as if it contained only the axioms and corollaries of a book of mathematics." Oliver Wendell Holmes, Jr., THE COMMON LAW 1 (1881). As common law applications of *Unocal*'s proportionality standard have evolved, at least two characteristics of draconian defensive measures taken by a board of directors in responding to a threat have been brought into focus through enhanced judicial scrutiny. In the modern takeover lexicon, it is now clear that since *Unocal*, this Court has consistently recognized that defensive measures which are either preclusive or coercive are included within the common law definition of draconian.

If a defensive measure is not draconian * * * because it is not either coercive or preclusive, the *Unocal* proportionality test requires the focus of enhanced judicial scrutiny to shift to "the range of reasonableness." [*QVC* at 45–46]. Proper and proportionate defensive responses are intended and permitted to thwart perceived threats. When a corporation is not for sale, the board of directors is the defender of the metaphorical medieval corporate bastion and the protector of the corporation's shareholders. The fact that a defensive action must not be coercive or preclusive does not prevent a board from responding defensively before a bidder is at the corporate bastion's gate.[38]

The *ratio decidendi* for the "range of reasonableness" standard is a need of the board of directors for latitude in discharging its fiduciary duties to the corporation and its shareholders when defending against perceived threats. The concomitant requirement is for judicial restraint. Consequently, if the board of directors' defensive response is not draconian (preclusive or coercive) and is within a "range of reasonableness," a court must not substitute its judgment for the board's. [*QVC* at 45–46]

THIS CASE: REPURCHASE PROGRAM: PROPORTIONATE WITH POISON PILL

\* \* \*

A limited nondiscriminatory self-tender, like some other defensive measures, may thwart a current hostile bid, but is not inherently coercive. Moreover, it does not necessarily preclude future bids or proxy contests by stockholders who decline to participate in the repurchase. A selective repurchase of shares in a public corporation on the market, such as Unitrin's Repurchase Program, generally does not discriminate because all shareholders can voluntarily realize the same benefit by selling. Here, there is no showing on this record that the Repurchase Program was coercive.

---

**38.** This Court's choice of the term draconian in *Unocal* was a recognition that the law affords boards of directors substantial latitude in defending the perimeter of the corporate bastion against perceived threats. Thus, continuing with the medieval metaphor, if a board reasonably perceives that a threat is on the horizon, it has broad authority to respond with a panoply of individual or combined defensive precautions, e.g., staffing the barbican, raising the drawbridge, and lowering the portcullis. Stated more directly, depending upon the circumstances, the board may respond to a reasonably perceived threat by adopting individually or sometimes in combination: advance notice by-laws, supermajority voting provisions, shareholder rights plans, repurchase programs, etc.

We have already determined that the record in this case appears to reflect that a proxy contest remained a viable (if more problematic) alternative for American General even if the Repurchase Program were to be completed in its entirety. Nevertheless, the Court of Chancery must determine whether Unitrin's Repurchase Program would only inhibit American General's ability to wage a proxy fight and institute a merger or whether it was, in fact, preclusive because American General's success would either be mathematically impossible or realistically unattainable. If the Court of Chancery concludes that the Unitrin Repurchase Program was not draconian because it was not preclusive, one question will remain to be answered in its proportionality review: whether the Repurchase Program was within a range of reasonableness?

\* \* \*

The Court of Chancery found that the Unitrin Board reasonably believed that American General's Offer was inadequate and that the adoption of a poison pill was a proportionate defensive response. Upon remand \* \* \*, the Court of Chancery may conclude that the implementation of the limited Repurchase Program was also within a range of reasonable additional defensive responses available to the Unitrin Board. In considering whether the Repurchase Program was within a range of reasonableness the Court of Chancery should take into consideration whether: (1) it is a statutorily authorized form of business decision which a board of directors may routinely make in a non-takeover context; (2) as a defensive response to American General's Offer it was limited and corresponded in degree or magnitude to the degree or magnitude of the threat, (i.e., assuming the threat was relatively "mild," was the response relatively "mild?"); (3) with the Repurchase Program, the Unitrin Board properly recognized that all shareholders are not alike, and provided immediate liquidity to those shareholders who wanted it.

\* \* \*

### REMAND TO CHANCERY

In this case, the Court of Chancery erred by substituting its judgment, that the Repurchase Program was unnecessary, for that of the Board. The Unitrin Board had the power and the duty, upon reasonable investigation, to protect Unitrin's shareholders from what it perceived to be the threat from American General's inadequate all-cash for all-shares Offer. *Unocal*, 493 A.2d at 958. The adoption of the poison pill and the limited Repurchase Program was not coercive and the Repurchase Program may not be preclusive. Although each made a takeover more difficult, individually and collectively, if they were not coercive or preclusive the Court of Chancery must determine whether they were within the range of reasonable defensive measures available to the Board.

If the Court of Chancery concludes that individually and collectively the poison pill and the Repurchase Program were proportionate to the threat the Board believed American General posed, the Unitrin Board's adoption of the Repurchase Program and the poison pill is entitled to review under the traditional business judgment rule. The burden will then shift "back to the plaintiffs who have the ultimate burden of persuasion [in a preliminary injunction proceeding] to show a breach of the directors' fiduciary duties." *Moran v. Household Int'l, Inc.*, Del. Supr., 500 A.2d 1346, 1356 (1985) (citing *Unocal*, 493 A.2d at 958). In order to rebut the protection of the business judgment rule, the burden on the plaintiffs will be to demonstrate, "by a preponderance of the evidence that the directors' decisions were primarily based on [(1)] perpetuating themselves in office or [(2)] some other breach of fiduciary duty such as fraud, overreaching, lack of good faith, or [(3)] being uninformed." *Unocal*, 493 A.2d at 958 (emphasis added).

\* \* \*

# WILLIAMS v. GEIER

671 A.2d 1368 (Del.1996).

VEASEY, CHIEF JUSTICE, for the majority:

In this appeal, we consider whether defendant below-appellee, Cincinnati Milacron ("Milacron"), may validly implement a recapitalization plan (the "Recapitalization") resulting from an amendment to Milacron's certificate of incorporation (the "Amendment"). The Amendment was recommended by resolution of the Milacron Board of Directors (the "Board") and approved by the requisite stockholder vote. Plaintiff below-appellant, Josephine L. Williams ("Williams"), an individual minority stockholder, brought suit in the Court of Chancery against Milacron and certain members of the Board, challenging the validity of the Amendment and Recapitalization.

The essence of the Recapitalization is to provide for a form of "tenure voting" whereby holders of common stock on the record date would receive ten votes per share. Upon sale or other transfer, however, each share would revert to one-vote-per-share status until that share is held by its owner for three years. The Recapitalization applied to every stockholder, whether a stockholder was a minority stockholder or part of the majority bloc. Williams argues that the Recapitalization disproportionately and invalidly favors stockholders who are part of the majority bloc and disfavors the minority stockholders. Williams further contends that the sole purpose of the Recapitalization was to entrench Milacron management in office and allow the majority bloc to sell a portion of its holdings while retaining control of the company.

The Court of Chancery granted summary judgment in favor of defendants, holding that Milacron's adoption of the Amendment and Recapitalization was valid. Specifically, the court held that *Unocal* [*v. Mesa Petroleum Corp.*] applied, and found that the Board had reasonable grounds to believe that a corporate threat existed and that the Recapitalization was a reasonable response to that threat, there being no improper action or motive. In this appeal, Williams claims that the Court of

Chancery erred in analyzing the Recapitalization under *Unocal* rather than *Blasius* [*Indus. Inc. v. Atlas Corp.*] Williams also contends that the trial court incorrectly found that the Board satisfied its burden under *Unocal*. Finally, Williams contends that the stockholder vote approving the Amendment does not validate the Amendment or the Recapitalization.

We AFFIRM the judgment of the Court of Chancery, but on the following grounds: (1) the instant factual situation implicates neither *Unocal* nor *Blasius*; (2) the business judgment rule applies to the action of the independent majority of the Board in recommending the advisability of the Amendment to the Milacron stockholders; and (3) since a fully informed majority of the stockholders voted in favor of the Amendment pursuant to the statutory authority of 8 Del.C. § 242 ("Section 242"), the stockholder vote is dispositive.

## I. FACTS

Milacron is a Delaware corporation that manufactures machine tools, plastics machinery, computer controls and various other industrial machinery and tools. During the time period relevant to this suit, the Board consisted of ten members—seven independent, disinterested directors who collectively owned less than 1 percent of the common shares outstanding, and three inside directors (deemed not to be independent or disinterested for this purpose) who collectively owned approximately 12.6 percent of the common shares outstanding. With regard to overall share ownership, the Geier family (including the two Geier directors, in-laws and family trusts), together with employee benefit plans owned or controlled in excess of 50 percent of the total voting power of Milacron. We assume, without deciding, therefore, that this group represents a controlling bloc for purposes of this decision. Hence, we will refer to the Geier family and the employees and benefit plans collectively as the "Family Group."[6]

Toward the end of 1985, Meyer [Milacron's Executive Vice–President of Finance and Administration] determined that it would be in Milacron's best interests to develop a recapitalization plan. With that goal in mind, he pursued talks with the First Boston Corporation ("First Boston"). On December 10, 1985, Meyer, along with Geier [Milacron's Chief Executive Officer] and several [other] Milacron officers, met with First Boston and Milacron's outside legal counsel, Cravath, Swain & Moore ("Cravath"), to communicate Milacron's goals and analyze its options. Another meeting followed on January 8, 1986, at which First Boston identified Milacron's objectives as follows:

● Maintain ability to maximize long-term value for shareholders.

---

**6.** According to the Proxy Statement for the April 22, 1986 Annual Meeting:

> Current and former employees and Directors, employee benefit plans, descendants of the Company's founder, their in-laws and trusts established by them, own or control in excess of 50% of the total

voting power of the Company's stock [and are expected to vote in in favor of the Recapitalization.] * * * Accordingly, approval of the Recapitalization at the meeting is virtually assured.

Cincinnati Milacron, Inc. Proxy Statement 21 (Mar. 24, 1986) (the "Proxy").

- Provide for ability to meet financing needs of corporation without impairing ability of management to maintain focus on long-term values rather than short-term business cycles.

- Protect long-term commitment to continued growth and investment in machine tool business.

- Reduce level of exposure to raiders seeking to capitalize on corporate vulnerability due to short-term business cycles.

- Continue process of diversification away from primary reliance on machine tool business to mix of 1/3 of revenue and income from machine tools and 2/3 from other sources.

- Provide Board of Directors with a corporate structure which gives the Board the best opportunity to fairly evaluate and negotiate, in the best interests of all shareholders, any proposal to acquire control of the Company.

In light of these goals, First Boston recommended pursuing a "tenure voting plan," * * * whereby all shares would be granted multiple votes which would be lost at transfer and then regained by the transferee after holding the shares for a certain period of time.

Pursuant to First Boston's recommendation, Article Fourth of Milacron's Restated Certificate of Incorporation would be amended so that all stockholders owning common stock on the effective date would be entitled to ten votes per share. Upon sale or other transfer of ownership, the voting rights of each share would revert to a single vote per share until such time as the new stockholder held the share for thirty-six consecutive months. If Milacron issued new shares after the effective date, these shares would be treated the same as pre-Recapitalization shares that had been sold or transferred—they would be entitled to only one vote until held for thirty-six consecutive months by the same stockholder. Milacron's officers ultimately decided to pursue the Recapitalization and instructed First Boston to prepare a presentation to be made to the Board.

On January 24, 1986, Milacron management and First Boston presented the Recapitalization to the Board at a special board meeting. First Boston provided the directors with detailed materials focusing on the benefits long-term investors would realize under the Recapitalization, as well as analyses of several other possible recapitalization plans. The Board decided to postpone action concerning the Recapitalization, and agreed to discuss the subject further at its next meeting on February 11, 1986. On March 21, 1986, the Board ultimately adopted a resolution proposing the Amendment and Recapitalization, determining that the Amendment and Recapitalization are "in the best interests of the Company and its shareholders" and recommending a favorable vote by stockholders at the April 22, 1986 Annual Meeting.

* * * [E]ffectuation of the Amendment required * * * the affirmative vote of a majority of the outstanding stock entitled to vote thereon. Accordingly, Milacron sent to stockholders a Notice of Annual Meeting of

Shareholders and accompanying Proxy Statement for the April 22, 1986 meeting. The Proxy explained that the Board believed the Recapitalization was in the best interests of the stockholders and had the threefold effect of: (1) providing existing and long-term stockholders with a greater voice in the company; (2) permitting issuance of additional shares of common stock with minimal dilution of voting rights; and (3) discouraging hostile takeovers.

In addition to informing the stockholders of the benefits of the Recapitalization, the Proxy also informed them of possible disadvantages: (1) if passed, the Recapitalization would "concentrate voting power in the hands of long-term shareholders" including the "descendants of the Company's founder, their in-laws and trusts established by them";[10] (2) "the Recapitalization may make [Milacron] a less attractive target for a takeover bid or share accumulation ..." and, as a result, "approval of the Recapitalization may deprive shareholders of an opportunity to sell their shares at a price higher than that prevailing in the market ..."; (3) "[i]f the Recapitalization is approved by the shareholders, the same shareholders who voted to approve the Recapitalization may have insufficient voting power to amend or repeal the Recapitalization at a future date"; and (4) if the Recapitalization is approved by less than a 66.7 percent majority, Milacron is likely to be delisted from the New York Stock Exchange (NYSE). As noted, the Proxy also informed the stockholders that the Family Group owned or controlled in excess of 50 percent of the total voting power, and that, accordingly, "approval of the Recapitalization at the meeting is virtually assured."

Over 72 percent of the outstanding common stock voted in favor of the Amendment. Assuming all the common stock held by the Family Group voted in favor, of the remaining (presumed unaffiliated) shares present or represented by proxy, approximately 5,858,777 voted in favor and 3,103,608 voted against or abstained. An additional 3,302,759 shares of common stock were not represented at the meeting. This means that there were approximately 6,406,367 presumed unaffiliated common shares that did not vote in person or by proxy or did not vote in favor, compared with approximately 5,858,777 which did vote in favor. Therefore, construing the record most favorably for Williams, the Amendment received less than 50 percent of the votes of all the unaffiliated shares outstanding.

**10.** Prior to the Recapitalization, the Family Group held over 50% of the outstanding Milacron shares, making it Milacron's controlling stockholder bloc. First Boston prepared an analysis of the relative control the Family Group could expect to exert under the Recapitalization. Assuming 30% of the minority shares were sold, the Family Group would control anywhere from 51.9% if they sold 30% of their own shares, to 59.1% if they held on to all of their shares for a period of three years. Their control would become even greater in the event of a mass minority share sell-off, such as in a hostile tender offer. For example, in a scenario where 70% of the minority shares are sold, the Family Group will control anywhere from 67.3% if they sell 30% of their own holdings, to 73.9% if they do not sell their own shares for a period of three years. Thus, the Recapitalization strengthened the Family Group's "veto" power over any proposed sale of Milacron, and perpetuated the Family Group's control over the election of future directors, even after substantial reduction of Family Group share holdings.

## II. Procedural History in Court of Chancery

In April 1986, Williams challenged the Recapitalization by bringing suit against Milacron and nine of its directors (collectively, the "Defendants") [challenging the Recapitalization. Defendants filed a motion to dismiss the complaint which was granted in part and denied in part. The Court of Chancery permitted Williams to pursue her claim that, in recommending the Recapitalization, Milacron management was motivated solely by a desire to entrench itself in office and her related claim that the Recapitalization was designed to allow the Family Group to liquidate a portion of its holdings and still retain control of Milacron.] * * *

After discovery was nearly complete, Williams moved for partial summary judgment as to liability. Defendants cross-moved for summary judgment. The Court of Chancery * * * granted Defendants' cross-motion. Analyzing the facts under *Unocal*, the trial court found that the Recapitalization was a reasonable defensive measure in light of the undisputed evidence that the Board carefully considered the Company's long-term needs and its potential vulnerability * * *.

\* \* \*

## IV. Inapplicability of *Unocal* and *Blasius*

Williams begins her attack on the grant of summary judgment by questioning the trial court's choice of the "more lenient standard of *Unocal*" to review the Board's actions, rather than the "heightened standard of scrutiny" used in *Blasius Industries v. Atlas Corp.*, Del. Ch., 564 A.2d 651 (1988). We hold that neither standard is implicated here because there was no unilateral board action. Here, there was stockholder approval of the Amendment. Accordingly, the Board action was not unilateral. The Board recommended that stockholders vote in favor of the Amendment. We must examine, therefore, both the Board action and the validity of the stockholder approval.

In *Blasius*, * * * [t]he Court of Chancery held that "when [a board] acts ... for the primary purpose of preventing or impeding an unaffiliated majority of shareholders from expanding the board and electing a new majority," its action "constitute[s] an offense to the relationship between corporate directors and shareholders that has traditionally been protected ..." Such disenfranchising actions are not, however, invalid per se. "Rather, ... in such a case, the board bears the heavy burden of demonstrating a compelling justification for such action."

*Blasius'* burden of demonstrating a "compelling justification" is quite onerous, and is therefore applied rarely. As this Court noted in *Stroud v. Grace*, Del.Supr., 606 A.2d 75, 92 (1992) ("*Stroud II* "), the application of the "compelling justification" standard set forth in *Blasius* is appropriate only where the " 'primary purpose' of the board's action [is] to interfere with or impede exercise of the shareholder franchise," and the stockholders are not given a "full and fair opportunity to vote."

We can find no evidence to support Williams' claim that the Defendants' primary purpose in adopting the Recapitalization was a desire to impede the Milacron stockholders' vote. The record does not rebut the business judgment rule presumption that the Board acted independently, with due care, in good faith and in the honest belief that its actions were in the stockholders' best interests. According to the Proxy, the directors were motivated by a desire to:

> promote long-term planning and values by enhancement of voting rights of long-term shareholders ... [;] permit the issuance of additional shares of common stock for financing or other purposes with minimal dilution of voting rights of long-term shareholders ... [; and] discourage hostile takeovers and put the Board of Directors in the best position to represent the interests of all shareholders.

Plaintiff has submitted no evidence to the contrary.

A *Unocal* analysis should be used only when a board unilaterally (i.e., without stockholder approval) adopts defensive measures in reaction to a perceived threat. *Unocal*, 493 A.2d at 954–55. *Unocal* is a landmark innovation of the dynamic takeover era of the 1980s. It has stood the test of time, and was recently explicated by this Court in *Unitrin, Inc. v. American General Corp.* Yet, it is inapplicable here because there was no unilateral board action.

The Court of Chancery did, however, apply a *Unocal* analysis here, finding that a threat to corporate policy and effectiveness existed and that the Recapitalization was a reasonable response to that threat. Specifically, the Court of Chancery found that:

> Milacron's directors were interested in long-term planning and, given the cyclical nature of Milacron's business, they were concerned that the company would be vulnerable during short-term market fluctuations. The reasonableness of the Recapitalization Plan as a defensive measure is established by the fact that the plan achieves Milacron's goals without preventing any stockholder from becoming a long-term stockholder and, thus, obtaining the super voting power.

The instant case does not involve either unilateral director action in the face of a claimed threat or an act of disenfranchisement. Rather, the instant case implicates the traditional review of disinterested and independent[19] director action in recommending, and the vote of the stockholders in approving, the Amendment and the resulting Recapitalization, Thus, neither *Blasius* nor *Unocal* applies. The Court of Chancery's finding does, however, support the conclusion that the director and

---

**19.** This Court has defined "disinterested directors" as those directors that "neither appear on both sides of a transaction nor expect to derive any personal financial benefit from it in the sense of self-dealing, as opposed to a benefit which devolves upon the corporation or all stockholders generally." *Aronson v. Lewis*, Del.Supr., 473 A.2d 805, 812 (1984) (citing *Sinclair Oil Corp. v. Levien*, Del.Supr., 280 A.2d 717, 720 (1971). Likewise, "independent" means that a "director's decision is based on the corporate merits of the subject before the board rather than extraneous considerations or influences." *Aronson*, 473 A.2d at 816. * * *

stockholder action which effectuated the Recapitalization here "can be attributed to [a] . . . rational business purpose."

### V. STANDARD OF JUDICIAL REVIEW OF BOARD ACTION RECOMMENDING THE AMENDMENT TO THE STOCKHOLDERS

The Board's action in recommending the Recapitalization to the stockholders pursuant to Section 242(b)(1) is protected by the presumption of the business judgment rule unless that presumption is rebutted.

\* \* \*

There was on this record: (1) no non-pro rata or disproportionate benefit which accrued to the Family Group on the face of the Recapitalization, although the dynamics of how the Plan would work in practice had the effect of strengthening the Family Group's control; (2) no evidence adduced to show that a majority of the Board was interested or acted for purposes of entrenching themselves in office; (3) no evidence offered to show that the Board was dominated or controlled by the Family Group; and (4) no violation of fiduciary duty by the Board.

\* \* \*

Based on the undisputed evidence in this record, we conclude that the Board's action in recommending the Amendment and Recapitalization to the stockholders for approval \* \* \* is protected by the business judgment rule. \* \* \*

### VI. THE EFFECT OF THE STOCKHOLDER VOTE

#### A. *General*

The recommendation by a board of directors of the advisability of a charter amendment is merely the first step under the organic, statutory scheme of 8 Del.C. § 242. which authorizes amendments to certificates of incorporation. The second step—the stockholder vote pursuant to which an amendment is approved—must be examined for compliance with the statute, the adequacy of the disclosures advanced to secure the stockholder approval, and compliance with fiduciary duty. In such a situation, "our standard of review is linked to the validity of the shareholder vote." *Stroud II*, 606 A.2d at 83.

\* \* \* The burden rests on the party relying on stockholder approval to establish that the approval resulted from a fully informed electorate and that all material facts relevant to the transaction were fully disclosed.

\* \* \*

*Stroud II* provides a useful example of the type of analysis required of this Court when presented with this type of organic, statutory change. In *Stroud II*, the board of Milliken Enterprises ("Milliken"), a privately held Delaware corporation, recommended to its stockholders that the certificate of incorporation be amended in certain respects and that certain bylaw amendments be approved. The minority-stockholder plaintiffs alleged that the amendments were defensive, served no legitimate purpose, were designed to entrench the majority, and were, therefore, invalid under *Unocal*. * * *

In *Stroud II*, this Court first determined that the directors' actions in recommending to the stockholders the charter and bylaw amendments were protected by the business judgment rule and that *Unocal* was inapplicable. Since the majority of the stockholders entitled to vote approved the changes, the issue confronting this Court was whether the stockholder vote was effective. While 78 percent of the shares entitled to vote approved the changes, the vast majority of these shares were controlled by four members of Milliken's board of directors. Turning to the validity of the stockholder vote, the Court concluded [that the presence of a controlling majority stockholder did not undermine the validity of the stockholder vote.]

### B. *Applicability of Existing Law to this Case*

* * *

In the instant case, like *Stroud II*, the Board recommended the advisability of the Amendment to the stockholders who voted in favor of the Amendment. On its face, therefore, the corporate action was authorized and regular. Stockholders (even a controlling stockholder bloc) may properly vote in their own economic interest, and majority stockholders are not to be disenfranchised because they may reap a benefit from corporate action which is regular on its face. * * *

The result here, as in *Stroud II*, is entirely in harmony with the broad policies underlying the Delaware General Corporation Law. At its core, the Delaware General Corporation Law is a broad enabling act which leaves latitude for substantial private ordering, provided the statutory parameters and judicially imposed principles of fiduciary duty are honored. Although directors are given much discretion in managing the business and affairs of the corporation, some fundamental measures require stockholder action. For example, when the statutory framework was altered in 1986 to permit some exemptions from personal liability for directors in 8 Del.C. § 102(b)(7), it was (and is) the legislative policy of this State that such exemptions could be enjoyed by directors only if stockholders approved such a provision in the certificate of incorporation. Further, all amendments to certificates of incorporation and mergers require stockholder action. Thus, Delaware's legislative policy is to look to the will of the stockholders in these areas.

Like the statutory scheme relating to mergers under 8 Del.C. § 251, it is significant that two discrete corporate events must occur, in precise sequence, to amend the certificate of incorporation under 8 Del.C. § 242: First, the board of directors must adopt a resolution declaring the advisability of the amendment and calling for a stockholder vote. Second, a majority of the outstanding stock entitled to vote must vote in favor. The stockholders may not act without prior board action. Likewise, the board may not act unilaterally without stockholder approval. Therefore, the stockholders control their own destiny through informed voting. This is the highest and best form of corporate democracy.

### C. No "Majority of Minority" Vote Required

\* \* \*

There is no requirement under the Delaware General Corporation Law that a majority of the outstanding minority shares must vote in favor of a transaction which benefits the majority. The issue of the role of a "majority of the minority" vote must be clearly understood. Where, as here, there is a controlling stockholder or a controlling bloc, there is no requirement under the Delaware General Corporation Law that the transaction be structured or conditioned so as to require an affirmative vote of a majority of the minority group of outstanding shares. In those parent-subsidiary situations where the circumstances call for an entire fairness analysis, the burden is normally on the defendants to show entire fairness, but if a majority of the minority votes in favor under certain circumstances, the burden shifts to the plaintiff to show unfairness. The converse does not apply, however—namely, the failure to obtain a majority of the minority does not give rise to any adverse inference of invalidity. Moreover, in a case such as the case at bar where entire fairness is not an issue, the question of whether a majority of the minority was obtained is simply irrelevant.

### D. Alleged Improper "Coercion"

Williams claims that the stockholder vote was rendered null and void because the vote was improperly coerced and the majority of stockholders voting to approve the Amendment were members of the Family Group. Williams' claim that the Recapitalization vote was wrongfully coerced is based on disclosures in the Proxy: First, the Proxy informed the stockholders that, due to the Family Group's voting control and the likelihood that the Family Group would favor the Recapitalization, "approval of the Recapitalization ... [was] virtually assured." The Proxy further disclosed that the then current NYSE rules "prohibit[ed] voting structures similar to that proposed by the Recapitalization." The Proxy went on to explain that, "[i]f the NYSE's current policy is modified in accordance with the NYSE subcommittee proposal, and if the Recapitalization is approved by the holders of shares entitled to cast two-thirds of the votes at the meeting, then it appears that the Common Stock could continue to trade on the NYSE." The effect of these two statements, Williams contends, was impermissibly to coerce the stockholders into voting for the Recapitalization. "[E]ven in light of a valid threat, management actions that are coercive in nature[,] ... force upon shareholders a management sponsored" proposal, or fail adequately to inform the stockholders of all material information, "may be struck down as unreasonable." *Time*, 571 A.2d at 1154.

Thus, a board of directors seeking stockholder approval of a transaction must walk a fine line between disclosures designed to inform and disclosures which may be seen as coercive. An otherwise valid stockholder vote may be nullified by a showing that the structure or circumstances of the vote were impermissibly coercive. Wrongful coercion may exist where the board or some other party takes actions which have the effect of causing the stockholders to vote in favor of the proposed transaction for some reason other than the merits of that transaction. In the final analysis, however, the determination of whether a particular stockholder vote has been robbed of its effectiveness by impermissible coercion depends on the facts of the case.

The simple answer to Williams' argument in this case is that the Proxy was merely stating facts which were required to be disclosed. These disclosures were neutrally stated and were not threatening in any respect. * * * The Milacron Board was required to disclose the reality of the situation (i.e., that the voting control of the Family Group makes passage of the Recapitalization "virtually assured" and that voting against the Recapitalization may harm the stockholders in that the failure to obtain two-thirds of the voting shares could risk NYSE delisting). The board could not couch these disclosures in vague or euphemistic language or in terms that would deprive the stockholders of their right to choose. The disclosures must be forthright and clear, and they were in this case.

* * *

The possibility of NYSE delisting, which could decrease share value, is certainly a fact that a reasonable stockholder would want to know before casting his or her vote. Likewise, the fact that the vote was candidly described as "virtually assured" was something that a reasonable stockholder would want to know. Neither statement could have been omitted or incompletely described. Moreover, inclusion of one fact without the other could have been misleading.

The tension between full disclosure and perceived coercion is clearly present in this case. The alternative of nondisclosure is obviously unacceptable and could have invalidated the vote. The other alternative, which would preclude an amendment which is otherwise valid because of the requirement of full disclosure, would be truly ironic and is likewise clearly unacceptable. Hence, we do not find improper coercion in the disclosures here.

### E.   Whether the Result of the Stockholder Vote was "Fair" to the Minority

Williams contends that the Family Group—due solely to their majority status—benefited from the Amendment and the Recapitalization to a disproportionately greater extent than the minority stockholders. Accordingly, she contends that the Family Group breached its duty of loyalty to the minority, thus requiring that the majority show entire fairness. But this argument is misplaced. * * * When the presumption of the business judgment rule is rebutted either because the board lacked independence (as in *Kahn v. Lynch* and *Nixon v. Blackwell*, for example) or because of lack of due care (as in *Technicolor*), the burden shifts to the defendants to show entire fairness (fair dealing and fair price). That is not the case here. The Milacron board was independent and acted with the requisite care. There were no disclosure violations. Therefore, the entire fairness inquiry articulated in *Technicolor* simply has no application here, and plaintiffs reliance thereon is misplaced.

As in *Stroud II*, the stockholder vote in favor of the Amendment "was fully informed, and in the absence of any fraud, waste, manipulative or other inequitable conduct, that should have ended the matter on basic principles of ratification." *Stroud II*, 606 A.2d at 92. Strict compliance with the statutory scheme laid out in 8 Del.C. § 242(b)(1) will not protect a corporate act if that act involved the excepted misconduct articulated in *Stroud II*. As we stated in *Schnell v. Chris–Craft Industries, Inc.*, for example. "inequitable action does not become permissible simply because it is legally possible." There is no basis for a finding here that the Amendment and Recapitalization involved waste, fraud, or manipulative or other inequitable conduct. Likewise, there is no showing either that the Recapitalization lacked a rational business purpose or that its sole or primary purpose was entrenchment. The burden is on the plaintiff to prove these outer limits on corporate behavior, and plaintiff has not sustained her burden.

## VI. Conclusion

This is an old case. In the nearly nine years this case has languished in the Court of Chancery, Williams has had ample opportunity to produce some proof of wrongdoing and has failed to do so. Conclusory allegations that the result of the Recapitalization was "unfair" to the minority are not a substitute for analysis or proper pleading and proof of violation of fiduciary duty. It is no answer to say that the statute should not permit the result obtained here even though the Amendment is within the broad powers of Section 242. The quarrel (if any) with the result is not with the application of the statutory authority in this case; it is with the breadth of the statutory authority itself. The remedy is not to ask this Court to fashion some ad hoc "relief" for Williams. If we were to engraft here an exception to the statutory structure and authority in order to accommodate Williams' objection to this result, we would be engaging in impermissible judicial legislation.[36]

**36.** In addition to the specter of impermissible judicial legislation, the relief requested by Williams, if granted, would introduce an undesirable degree of uncertainty into the corporation law. *See Nixon*. Directors and investors must be able to rely on the stability and absence of judicial interference with the State's statutory prescriptions. Nearly fifty years ago, this Court addressed a similar problem in the case of *American Hardware Corp. v. Savage Arms Corp.*, Del.Supr., 136 A.2d 690 (1957). In *American Hardware*, the Court was called upon to evaluate the validity of a corporate act taken pursuant to the corporation's bylaws. The board of Savage Arms accelerated the date of its annual meeting, arguably to thwart an unsolicited tender offer by American Hardware and assist the board in consummating a transaction with its preferred merger partner, Aircraft Armaments Corp. American Hardware contended that the change of the meeting date was impermissible despite compliance with the corporation's bylaws because it adversely impacted on American's tender offer. Chief Justice Southerland, focusing

Williams has failed to sustain her burden to show invalidity. The statutory procedure was followed and authorized the adoption of the Amendment. The Board's action in recommending the Recapitalization to the stockholders was the result of an independent business decision of the Board, protected by the presumption of the business judgment rule which was not rebutted. The fully informed stockholder vote approving the Amendment validly effected the Recapitalization. The fact that the Family Group voted in favor of the Amendment does not invalidate the vote, even if they benefited more than the minority. Plaintiff has not alleged or shown a violation of Section 242 or any proof of fraud, waste, manipulative or other inequitable conduct.

Accordingly, the judgment of the Court of Chancery granting summary judgment to defendants is AFFIRMED.

HARTNETT, JUSTICE, and HORSEY, JUSTICE (Retired), dissenting:

We respectfully dissent. The question is what is the appropriate standard of review to be employed by the Court of Chancery in reviewing the Milacron Recapitalization Plan that was approved by a vote of the shareholders pursuant to 8 Del.C. § 242, the effect of which will inevitably entrench the majority stockholders, to the ultimate detriment of the minority stockholders who did not approve the Plan. The members of the Geier Family Group, the intended and acknowledged beneficiaries of the Plan, "own or control in excess of 50% of the total voting power of the Company's stock and in excess of two-thirds of the Preferred Stock Outstanding." Under these circumstances, neither the business judgment rule nor the shareholder vote shift the burden of persuasion in the required judicial inquiry into the reasonableness of the Recapitalization Plan or its fairness to the minority shareholders.

Furthermore, the existence of controverted facts precluded the Court of Chancery from finding that the Plan was reasonable under the standard articulated in *Unocal* or that the standard articulated in *Blasius* was not applicable.

I.

We believe the action of the Milacron Board in instituting and recommending adoption of the Recapitalization Plan implicates the duty of loyalty and, therefore, must be subject to full judicial scrutiny, not to judicial deference because of the business judgment rule. The Board's stated reason for the Plan is not dispositive, given the Plan's conceded effect: to confer substantial benefits on the majority shareholders, the Geier Family Group, without conferring similar benefits upon the minor-

on the Savage board's compliance with the corporation's bylaws, held that "[i]t needs little consideration to realize that the adoption of [American Hardware's] ... view would import serious confusion and uncertainty into corporate procedure." *Id.* at 693. As we held in *American Hardware*, absent a showing of inequitable conduct on the part of the board, compliance with the applicable corporate governance regime (be it statute or bylaw) will generally shield corporate action from judicial interference. *Schnell* cited this principle with approval, but found inequitable conduct.

ity shareholders having equally legitimate, but differing, investment objectives.

The shareholders were informed by the Proxy that shareholder approval of the Plan was "virtually assured." We, therefore, do not believe that the Board's submission of the Recapitalization Plan to the shareholders, pursuant to 8 Del.C. § 242, and the approval of it by the same majority shareholders who are the beneficiaries of the Plan lessens judicial scrutiny into the reasonableness of the Plan and its fairness to the minority shareholders.

Even if the shareholder vote was voluntary (which it was not), it would have merely accorded the Plan a presumption of fairness. The Court of Chancery still had a duty to determine whether the power exercised by the Board was oppressive to the minority.

## II.

The majority's reliance on *Stroud II* to preclude or lessen judicial review of the Plan is misplaced. In the present case, the Geier Family Group are the controlling shareholders of a public corporation. The proposed Plan significantly alters shareholder voting rights to the detriment of those minority shareholders who have no interest in preserving the family ownership, or whose investment objectives may have a different time frame from the Family Group. *Stroud II* involved a private, closely held corporation that sought to have adopted a "right of first refusal" charter amendment commonly used by such corporations to preclude the transfer of shares to outsiders. Milacron's status as a public corporation does not permit the Court of Chancery to merely defer to the text of the Recapitalization Plan which has the ultimate effect of turning a public corporation into a de facto close corporation.

In *Stroud II* this Court relied upon a shareholder vote to cure otherwise suspect board actions involving charter amendments commonly adopted by close corporations. The court found that "[i]n the absence of fraud, a fully informed stockholder vote in favor of even a 'voidable' transaction ratifies board action and places the burden of proof on the challenger." *Stroud II*, 606 A.2d at 83.

In the present case, however, the charter amendments worked fundamental changes in the governance of Milacron, as the Proxy concedes. The Recapitalization Plan's ultimate effect will be to confer upon the Geier Family shareholders control not only over the future composition of the Board, but over the strategic long-term planning of the company. A coerced shareholder vote which received the approval of less than 50 percent of the votes of all the unaffiliated [non-Geier Family] shares outstanding cannot be deemed to be a shareholder approval that lessens judicial scrutiny as to the fundamental fairness of the Plan. In our opinion, for there to be a vote that cures a defect, two factors are implicated. First, there must be a full disclosure of the pertinent facts. Second, the vote must be free from coercion, that is, the shareholder action must be meaningful and voluntary. The legal imprimatur of a shareholder ratification cannot arise out of a staged and essentially meaningless vote.

Here the minority stockholders were faced with two significant disclosures in the Proxy: (1) the adoption of the Recapitalization Plan was "virtually assured" of approval because of the votes of the Geier Family (the proposers of, and the prime beneficiaries of the Plan), and (2) the adoption of the proposed Charter Amendment could result in a de-listing of Milacron stock from the New York Stock Exchange unless it was ratified by an affirmative vote of 2/3 of all the shares. The minority stockholders, therefore, had no real choice. Nor did a majority of the minority apparently vote for the Plan. Notwithstanding that the shareholder vote was legally sufficient to meet the requirements of 8 Del.C. § 242, the burden of persuasion to show the unfairness of the Plan was not shifted to the minority shareholders.

### III.

In our opinion, the Board's decision proposing and recommending the adoption of the Recapitalization Plan should be subject to a heightened level of judicial scrutiny, under the rationale of *Unocal* or *Blasius* or both. When the voting rights of minority stockholders are changed without their consent, there is the omnipresent specter of inherent conflict between a board's duty to all the stockholders and the desires of the block of stockholders holding a majority of the shares. This conflict is similar to the conflict that existed in *Unocal*.

Although an action diminishing a shareholder's vote is not invalid, per se, the right of an individual stockholder to exercise the voting rights of its shares is a fundamental corporate right. The right of franchise must not be diluted except where reasonably necessary to accomplish an appropriate corporate business policy.

If the Milacron Board's purpose was to reduce the voting power of the minority shareholders or to increase the voting strength of the Geier Family Group shares, then the Board's action must pass the "compelling justification" standard of scrutiny articulated in *Blasius*. As the majority concedes, the Board's duties were not fulfilled merely by blind compliance with the technical mandates of 8 Del. C. § 242.

The Court of Chancery's determination that the "compelling justification" standard of *Blasius* was not implicated was apparently based on its conclusory finding that "the recapitalization plan does not interfere with voting rights so as to preclude effective stockholder action." This, however, is contradicted by the Court of Chancery's finding that the Plan has an entrenchment effect. The Court of Chancery's finding of the inevitability of the entrenchment of the Geier Family shareholders in the control of Milacron's future is an indisputable fact fully supported by the record through the Proxy Statement, and acknowledged in the Majority's Opinion at p.___ and footnote 10. Hence, the Majority's conclusion to the contrary [later in its opinion] is not supported by the record. Because the primary issue is shareholder entrenchment, the directors' motivation and good faith are not dispositive.

From a review of the entire record, we are convinced that, notwithstanding the self-serving denials of the proponents of the Plan, its effect on shareholders' voting rights was clearly substantial rather than incidental. The Court of Chancery, in our view, should have held an evidentiary hearing to determine if the Recapitalization Plan has a negative effect on the minority shares and to determine whether the primary purpose of the Plan was to assure the continual control of the corporation by the Geier Family members while permitting them to sell some of their shares.

If the Court of Chancery found these factors existed, it should have reviewed the Plan under the *Blasius* compelling justification standard.

## IV.

In *Stroud II*, this Court described the relationship between the tests articulated in *Blasius* and *Unocal* and stated that these tests are not mutually exclusive. Although the Court of Chancery improperly, in our view, rejected the "compelling justification" standard of *Blasius*, unlike the majority, we believe that it correctly found that the action of the Board in adopting the Recapitalization Plan was subject to the heightened judicial scrutiny mandated by *Unocal*. A court must apply the enhanced scrutiny test set forth in *Unocal* whenever the board "adopts any defensive measure taken in response to some threat to corporate policy and effectiveness which touches upon issues of control."

If the purpose of the Recapitalization Plan was defensive, so as to eliminate challenges to control from hostile acquisition offers or proxy contests, as the Proxy suggests, the *Unocal* standard is triggered, as the Court of Chancery properly found. In conducting its *Unocal* analysis, however, the Court of Chancery failed to recognize that genuine issues of material fact existed that precluded its finding that the Recapitalization was a reasonable response to a perceived corporate threat.

From a review of the entire record, we are convinced that there are several disputed issues of fact that must be resolved before the *Unocal* heightened judicial scrutiny as to the proportionality and reasonableness of the Recapitalization Plan can be completed. Among them are: 1) whether the primary purpose of the Recapitalization Plan was to disenfranchise the non-Geier Family shares; 2) whether the Plan's purpose was to substantially reduce the value and marketability of those shares; and 3) whether the primary purpose of the Plan was to enable the Geier Family members to dispose of a substantial portion of their shares and still retain control of the corporation.

Lastly, we find nothing in the text of 8 Del.C. § 242(b)(1) that precludes the Court of Chancery from exercising judicial oversight over a Recapitalization Plan with such a disproportionate effect on the minority shares.

## V.

\* \* \*

It is clear from the record that the Recapitalization Plan will increase the relative voting power of the long-term holders of the common stock—who are likely to be Geier Family members. This fact mandates a factual inquiry into the purpose of the Board in adopting and recommending the Recapitalization Plan. If the change in shareholder voting power was an unintended byproduct of a defensive strategy, the heightened scrutiny standard in *Unocal* should be applied. If, however, the facts show that the Board's primary purpose was to dilute the franchise of the non-Geier Family shares, then, under *Blasius*, Defendants "[bear] the heavy burden of demonstrating a compelling justification for such action." *Blasius*, 564 A.2d at 661.

If the facts show that the purpose of the Recapitalization Plan was simply to favor the Geier Family at the expense of the other stockholders, then a breach of the duty of loyalty likely occurred.

* * *

We believe, therefore, that the case should be remanded to the Court of Chancery for a limited evidentiary hearing to resolve the remaining issues of material fact and for a meaningful review of the Recapitalization Plan in which the proponents of the Plan bear the burden of showing its fairness and reasonableness to the minority shareholders. After resolving the disputed factual issues, the Court of Chancery would be in a position to decide whether the review should be conducted under the enhanced standard of review of *Unocal* or *Blasius*.

### Note: A Post–Unitrin Approach

1. *Kidsco, Inc. v. Dinsmore*, 674 A.2d 483 (Del.Ch.1995), *aff'd* 670 A.2d 1338 (Del.1995) arose out of an attempt by SoftKey International to defeat a proposed merger between The Learning Company (TLC) and Broderbund Software and acquire TLC itself. As has become customary, SoftKey's effort took the form of a tender offer, proposed second-tier cashout merger, and a solicitation of consents to demand a special meeting of shareholders to replace the TLC board with SoftKey representatives who would remove the TLC poison pill. The unusual twist to this scenario was that the special meeting was to be held two days after the stockholder vote on the TLC–Broderbund merger.

TLC responded by amending its by-laws to extend the time for calling a shareholder-initiated special meeting from sixty to ninety days, thereby postponing the SoftKey meeting. TLC claimed that without the by-law amendment, the TLC "shareholders would be left in an exposed position if the Broderbund merger proposal were turned down" and the TLC board had little time to seek alternatives to the SoftKey transaction. The amendment was approved at a board meeting by four directors, two of whom were disinterested; the fifth director (also disinterested) who had been unable to attend the meeting subsequently consented to the amendment.

The Court of Chancery rejected SoftKey's claim that the amendment constituted a breach of fiduciary duty by the TLC board. The court found no evidence of entrenchment and that the amendment had been approved by a majority of disinterested directors. The court then concluded that *Unocal* rather than *Blasius* provided the proper framework for analyzing the board's actions. In so doing, the court limited the types of situations in which a pure *Blasius* analysis would be appropriate to circumstances which were unrelated to a tender offer. If a tender offer were involved, either by itself or combined with a proxy contest, either a *Unocal* or a combined *Unocal/Blasius* test would be used.

On the facts of the case, the court had little difficulty finding that *Blasius* was not implicated at all. The court found that the by-law amendment was designed to give the board more time to consider alternatives if the shareholders rejected the Broderbund merger. Thus, to the court, the case was "functionally indistinguishable from *Stahl*. * * * Here, as in *Stahl*, 'the franchise process [cannot] be said to be sufficiently engaged before the fixing of [the] meeting date to give rise to * * * [the possibility of inequitable manipulation]' " *Id.* at 496.

Taken together, *Stahl*, *Williams* and *Kidsco* represent a substantial diminution of the emphasis that *Blasius* places on the protection of shareholder voting rights. *Williams* stated that the *Blasius* test of "compelling justification" was "quite onerous and is therefore applied rarely." 671 A.2d at 1376. The court also found no evidence that the primary purpose of the recapitalization was to impede the Milacron stockholder vote, even though, in fact, that might be a consequence. And, as noted above, *Kidsco* limits *Blasius* to those situations in which a tender offer is not involved.

2. *In re Santa Fe Pacific Corporation Shareholder Litigation*, 669 A.2d 59 (Del.1995) was brought by Union Pacific Corp., the defeated bidder in an attempt to acquire Santa Fe. The challenged transaction was a stock-for-stock merger between Santa Fe and Burlington Northern, Inc. which had been approved by the shareholders of both corporations. Union Pacific alleged that the Santa Fe directors had breached their *Unocal* duties through the adoption of various defensive tactics as well as their *Revlon/QVC* duty to seek the highest value reasonably available. Union Pacific also alleged that Santa Fe's merger proxy statement was materially misleading in breach of a state law duty to disclose. The Court of Chancery dismissed the complaint for failure to state a claim for relief. The Supreme Court affirmed with respect to the disclosure and *Revlon* claims but reversed on the *Unocal* allegation.

The court first considered the effect of a fully-informed shareholder vote on the plaintiffs' claims. The court noted that *Unocal* rested in part on a concern about defensive actions that would disenfranchise shareholders. The court also observed that *Revlon* rested on "the overriding importance of voting rights." *Id.* at 68. Thus, the court found that "[p]ermitting the vote of a majority of stockholders on a merger to remove from judicial scrutiny unilateral Board action in a contest for corporate control would frustrate the purposes underlying *Revlon* and *Unocal*. Board action which coerces stockholders to accede to a transaction to which they otherwise would not agree is problematic." *Id.*

The court also rejected the argument that Santa Fe's board had breached its duty to seek the highest value reasonably available. Plaintiffs were unable to show facts that the Burlington–Santa Fe merger would constitute a sale of control, i.e., that control after the merger would not remain "in a large, fluid and changeable and changing market" as required by *QVC*. Thus, notwithstanding the existence of an arguably higher third-party bid, the target board had no duty to seek the highest value reasonably available.

Finally, the court refused to dismiss a well-pleaded *Unocal* claim. In so doing, the court strongly suggested that such claims, resting as they do on a determination of the reasonableness of the target board's response, generally raised fact questions that could not be decided on a defense motion attacking the pleadings.

3.    *Santa Fe* was followed by *Wells Fargo & Co. v. First Interstate Bancorp*, 1996 WL 32169 (Del.Ch.1996), a case that arose from Wells Fargo's unsuccessful attempt to acquire First Interstate in a friendly merger. Rather than deal with Wells Fargo, First Interstate entered into a stock-for-stock merger with First Bank System, Inc., a white knight. Wells Fargo announced its intent to make a higher offer than First Bank and to solicit proxies against the merger and consents to remove the First Interstate board. Wells Fargo claimed that First Interstate's failure to redeem its poison pill breached its *Unocal* duties. It also alleged that in accepting the First Bank merger, the First Interstate board had breached its *Revlon* duties by failing to obtain the highest value reasonably available for its stockholders.

The Court of Chancery held that Wells Fargo's complaint failed to state a claim for relief. Relying on *Santa Fe*, Chancellor Allen found that there were no *Revlon* duties where, as here, no change of corporate control was involved in the stock-for-stock merger. He noted that this finding did not preclude a claim of entrenchment, but held that the complaint did not allege sufficient facts to support such a claim.

Recognizing the difficulty of defining "*Revlon* duties," he stated:

What I take to be distinctive about this state of affairs [when "*Revlon*" duties apply] is three things principally. First, in this situation the board must seek to achieve greatest available current value; it may not, in effect, trade achievable current value for a prospect of greater future value, as it may normally do in the exercise of its good faith business judgment. Historically, one would say that courts would be slow to impose this limitation except in limited circumstances. And indeed despite the fact that commentators tended to treat the *Revlon* case as revolutionary, recent cases have made clear that it did not deviate from this tradition very greatly. Second, when in this situation, a board's duty to be informed will require it to fully consider alternative transactions offered by any responsible buyer. Third, in part "*Revlon* duties" are not distinctive duties at all, but a changed standard of judicial review. That is when "Revlon duties" are triggered a burden will shift to the directors and the court will undertake more active review of the traditional directorial duties of care and loyalty under a reasonableness standard.

*Id.* at *13, n.3.

The Chancellor also noted different uses of "control" in the Delaware takeover cases. Noting that *Unocal/Unitrin* applies when there are defensive measures that "touch[es] upon issues of control," he observed "that [t]he corporate control referred to in this context is apparently a different concept than the change in corporate control that triggers '*Revlon*' duties, as the holding in the recent *Santa Fe* case seems to demonstrate." *Id.* at *17.

4. *Moore Corp. Ltd. v. Wallace Computer Services, Inc.*, 907 F.Supp. 1545 (D.Del.1995) illustrates the apparent trend of increased judicial deference to target company boards with respect to various defensive tactics—in this case, the refusal of the Wallace board to redeem its poison pill. The case involved Moore's all cash, all shares offer for Wallace at a price which Wallace's board, after receiving an opinion from its investment banker, determined to be inadequate. The principal reason for the board's decision (although not the only one) was the board's belief that the offer did not give full effect to the future financial results that would result from past board decisions that were not fully reflected in the pre-offer stock price.

Applying the first prong of *Unocal*, the court found that the Moore offer did, in fact, pose a threat to Wallace and its shareholders. In reaching this conclusion, the court stated:

> This case presents a factual scenario different from that which normally occurs. In most cases, the target seeks to persuade the Court that the hostile tender offer posed a threat to the company's future plans and the company's shareholders which justified the defensive measures until the expected benefits of the plan come into fruition. Here, however, the directors seek to prove that the hostile tender offer poses a threat of a different nature. The favorable results from the board's *past* actions are now beginning to be translated into financial results which even surpass management and financial analyst projections, and the financial data which manifests these results are facts only known to them. Therefore, Moore's tender offer poses a threat that shareholders might tender their shares without appreciating the fact that after substantial capital investment, Wallace is actually witnessing the beginning of the pay-off of its business strategy. The Court therefore finds that Moore's tender offer poses a threat to Wallace that shareholders, because they are uninformed, will cash out before realizing the fruits of the substantial technological innovations achieved by Wallace.

*Id.* at 1560–61.

With respect to the second prong of the *Unocal* test, the court found that the failure to redeem the pill was a reasonable response. Relying heavily on *Unitrin* (a case which the court found to be "closely analogous"), the court held that the board's decision not to redeem the pill was neither coercive nor preclusive. The court noted that retention of the pill would not have a discriminatory effect on the shareholders and thus was not coercive. More important, such retention would have no effect on Moore's ability to conduct a proxy contest to elect a board that would redeem the pill. Having thus satisfied itself, the court then found that Wallace's actions fell within *Unitrin*'s "range of reasonableness" test. For the reasons that it found that the Moore offer constituted a threat, the court concluded that "the Wallace Board has demonstrated that its retention of the poison pill falls within the range of reasonableness required under *Unocal*." *Id.* at 1563.

The court's decision in *Moore* comes very close to accepting the validity of the "just say no" defense. The court does recognize that at some point the failure to redeem a poison pill may constitute a breach of fiduciary duty (citing *Interco*), but its use of the *Unitrin* "Draconian" and "range of reasonableness" tests suggests that that point will be very hard for a bidder to establish, even in an all cash, all shares offer. In that light, one might ask, although the court does not, why Wallace could not have disclosed the relevant facts and the board's opinion to the shareholders and allowed them to make the choice of whether to accept the Wallace offer.

5. The Delaware Supreme Court's citation of *American Hardware Corp. v. Savage Arms Corp.* in note 36 to *Williams v. Geier* suggests that *Moore* may be an accurate reflection of the court's current attitude. In *American Hardware*, the court placed great emphasis on the board's legal authority to take the action being challenged and gave short shrift to plaintiff's claim that that action was inequitable. As the court notes in *Williams*, it declined to follow *American Hardware* in *Schnell*. But what the court does not mention in *Williams* is that, in the 25 years between *Schnell* and *Williams*, no other Delaware decision has cited with approval this aspect of *American Hardware*. Thus, the *Williams* court's expression of concern about the dangers of "import[ing] serious confusion and uncertainty into corporate procedure" may portend that it is inclined to retreat from the more subjective modes of analysis suggested by *Schnell*, *Blasius* and *Unocal*.

6. *Hilton Hotels Corp. v. ITT Corp.*, 978 F.Supp. 1342 (D.Nev. 1997), reads Delaware's recent takeover jurisprudence quite differently. In response to a hostile tender offer by Hilton and a concurrent proxy contest, ITT had announced a "Comprehensive Plan" pursuant to which it would split its operations among three corporations, spin-off the stock of two of them to its shareholders, and adopt a poison pill that would trigger a $1.4 billion tax liability if Hilton's offer succeeded. Most important, all members of the current ITT board would become directors

of the largest of the new corporations—which would hold 93% of ITT's assets—and that corporation's board would be divided into three classes, only one of which would stand for election in any given year. As a consequence, even if Hilton gained the support of, or purchased, a majority of ITT's stock, it would not be able to elect a majority of the board of that new corporation for more than a year.

ITT, a Nevada corporation, claimed that under Nevada law its board had the authority to implement the Comprehensive Plan, without shareholder approval, because the spin-off and poison pill were structured as dividends. Hilton sued to enjoin the plan, claiming that it inequitably deprived ITT's shareholders of their right to elect ITT's board and vote on a transfer of substantially all of ITT's assets.

There is virtually no Nevada case law concerning the duties of target company directors. As a consequence, the court looked to Delaware law for "persuasive authority." The court determined that *Unocal* and *Blasius* set forth the appropriate legal standard. It noted that those cases hold a board's power "is limited by the right of shareholders to vote for the members of the board" and "fully endorse[d] the reasoning in * * * *Blasius* regarding the importance of the shareholder franchise to the entire scheme of corporate governance." *Id*. at 1347.

The court held that ITT had failed to satisfy the first prong of *Unocal* because it could not establish "reasonable grounds for believing that a threat to corporate policy and effectiveness exists." The court noted that ITT's board also had not made a reasonable investigation into the Hilton threat and had refused to meet with Hilton to discuss its offer. It also pointeed out that ITT had substantially adopted Hilton's business plan for running ITT. As a consequence, the sole legally cognizable threat was the alleged inadequacy of the price Hilton was offering, but the court found such inadequacy to be insufficient in light of the increased leverage flowing from ITT's own plan.

Applying *Unitrin*, the court found that ITT's plan was preclusive because the classified board provision would preclude ITT shareholders from exercising their existing right to determine the membership of the ITT board. "At the very minimum, ITT shareholders will have no choice but to accept the Comprehensive Plan and a majority of ITT's incumbent board members for another year." *Id*. at 1348.

The court noted that *Blasius* held that even though a board "had a good faith reason to act as it did, and it acted with appropriate care, the board could not lawfully prevent the shareholders from electing a majority of new directors." *Id*. Thus, if the primary purpose of the ITT plan was to disenfranchise ITT shareholders facing a tender offer and a proxy contest, it would be improper under *Blasius*.

The court recognized that ITT's board could not be expected to admit that its motive was entrenchment and proceeded to examine the circumstances surrounding ITT's adoption of the Comprehensive Plan to determine the board's purpose. In light of (1) the timing of the Plan, (2) the fact that the directors who approved the Plan would continue to serve as directors after the Plan was implemented, (3) the absence of any justification for not seeking shareholder approval of the Plan, and (4) the fact the Plan would preclude ITT's shareholders from electing Hilton's candidates as a majority of the the board at ITT's forthcoming annual meeting, the court had little trouble concluding that the plan was adopted for the primary purpose of entrenching ITT's current directors and should be enjoined.

# Chapter 23

# CASH OUT MERGERS

---

## A.  INTRODUCTION

The previous two chapters dealt with problems that arise when those who control a corporation decide to sell or use corporate resources or authority to protect that control. This chapter, in contrast, deals with the issues raised by transactions in which the person (or persons) who controls a corporation seeks to terminate, or *cash out*, other shareholders' equity interest in that corporation, usually by forcing those shareholders to accept cash for their stock.

At first blush, the very concept that a shareholder can be forced to sell her stock at all may seem strange. After all, a person who owns a '56 Chevy convertible or an heirloom gold watch cannot be compelled to sell it. Why should stock be different?

The answer derives from the fact that corporate stock, as much as the corporate entity itself, is a creature of state law. Its attributes are those that state law assigns to it. As we saw in Chapter 12, state corporation laws typically provide that a merger agreement approved by a majority of a corporation's shareholders is binding on all the other shareholders. Like it or not, this latter group must accept the consideration paid in the merger (unless they dissent and seek appraisal). And, in virtually every state, cash (or debt securities or stock of some other corporation) can constitute valid consideration. *See, e.g.*, RMBCA §§ 11.01(b)(3), 11.02; DGCL § 251.

Consequently, arranging to cash out unwanted shareholders in a controlled corporation is relatively straightforward. Typically, the person (P) who controls the corporation (S) organizes a new shell corporation (Newco) into which she transfers all her S stock. Next, P causes the boards of directors of S and Newco to enter into a merger agreement providing that, upon the merger of Newco into S, all the shareholders of S will receive cash for their S stock.* P then votes all the stock of Newco in favor of the merger. She also votes her S stock in its favor and, if

---

* The issues are substantially the same if S's non-controlling shareholders receive Newco debt or P stock in the merger rather than cash.

necessary, uses her control of S (generally through the proxy machinery) to obtain the support of enough shares to approve the merger. The S shareholders who are dissatisfied with the terms of the merger cannot remain as shareholders of S. Under most corporate statutes, their only option is to exercise dissenters' rights and demand payment in cash of the "fair value" of their stock.

Cash out mergers are fraught with potential for abuse. If P owns a majority of S stock, she can dictate the terms on which S's minority shareholders will be cashed out through her control of S's board of directors and her ability to vote sufficient S stock to ensure shareholder approval of the cash out merger. Unless S's non-controlling shareholders can induce a court to intervene on equitable grounds, they will be powerless to alter the terms of the merger or to retain their equity interest in S.

If P has *de facto* but not *de jure* control of S, she will need the support of other S shareholders to accomplish the cash out. But three factors limit their ability, other than by judicial means, to block cash out mergers that they believe are unfair: collective action problems, the absence of real bargaining between P and S's non-controlling shareholders, and the obstacles non-controlling shareholders would face were they to seek to oust P from control of S.

These problems are exacerbated by the fact that P usually will have a better understanding than other shareholders of S's business, the character and value of S's assets, and whether S's past performance accurately indicates its future potential. P also generally will have made or approved all of S's significant business policy decisions for many years and will be aware of how changes in those policies could affect S's earnings, cash flows, and distributions to shareholders. Finally, P often will be in a position to time a cash out so as to take advantage of shifts in interest rates, fluctuations in S's stock price, or changes in the value of S's assets.

The availability of appraisal does not significantly mitigate the potential for P's abuse, even if one assumes that non-controlling shareholders will be satisfied if they receive a higher price for their stock in an appraisal proceeding. Consider the position of the owner of 1,000 shares of S stock who receives a proposal for a cash out merger at $9 per share and who believes that her stock is worth $12. With a maximum potential gain of an additional $3,000, she is likely to be reluctant to incur the legal fees, expert witness fees, and other costs involved in pursuing her dissenters' rights. Moreover, even if most of the non-controlling shareholders of S similarly valued their stock at $12, collective action problems similar to those discussed in Chapter 14 will impede those shareholders in coordinating their efforts to pursue appraisal in an amount that might have been a significant deterrent to P when determining the initial terms of the transaction. In other words, if the fear of a substantial award in an appraisal proceeding were a cogent threat before P presented her initial offer to the minority shareholders, that offer would be higher than it will be where P knows that collective action problems will minimize the number of shareholders who actually seek appraisal. Silent, if resentful, acquiescence in the terms of the cash out seems more likely.

Despite the potential for abuse, a cash out merger is not inevitably exploitative or unfair. P may have *bona fide* reasons for such a transaction. P may believe that there will be operating efficiencies from combining P and S. P may wish to engage in concededly fair transactions with S without the threat of litigation (recall *Sinclair v. Levien* in Chapter 17). Or P may wish to eliminate the expense of having public shareholders, including S's compliance with the reporting requirements of the Securities Exchange Act of 1934. Finally, of course, whatever the business reasons for the cash out, P may, in fact, offer the minority shareholders a fair price for their stock.

All that said, a number of factors almost guarantee that litigation will occur in every cash out merger: the conflicts of interest and inherent potential for abuse; the very large stakes involved; and the likelihood that any attorney who successfully challenges a cash out merger will receive a substantial contingent fee. Faced with continuing litigation, courts are sensitive to the need to provide corporate planners with some degree of certainty when planning cash out mergers which, after all, are authorized by law. Consequently, when considering challenges to such mergers, courts have attempted to consider both the potential for abuse in the merger *and* the possibility that the challenge to the merger is driven more by an attorney's desire to generate a substantial fee than by truly unfair conduct.*

This chapter treats the most important issues that courts have considered. These are: (1) whether a control person must have a "proper purpose" before cashing out non-controlling shareholders and, if so, what constitutes such a purpose; (2) what other remedies, if any, a court should make available to a shareholder who has a statutory right to seek appraisal of her stock; (3) whether there are procedures that, if followed, make it more likely the terms of a cash out merger will be fair; (4) how, in the absence of market prices, a court can best determine whether the terms of a cash out are fair; and (5) what factors a court should consider to determine the "fair value" of a cashed out shareholder's stock. Because of the complexity of the subject, these issues are necessarily interrelated. Although separated here for organizational purposes, you should appreciate that each is a part of an integrated whole.

## PROBLEM
### PHILLIPS CORPORATION

Phillips Corporation (Phillips) is a diversified corporation, operating a wide variety of businesses directly and through subsidiaries. Phillips

---

* *See Lewis v. Celina Fin. Corp.*, 655 N.E.2d 1333 (Ohio App. 1995) (sanctions imposed against plaintiff and his counsel who had not read offer or other disclosure documents in cash-out merger prior to filing suit.

manufactures construction equipment, ball bearings, machine tools and computer equipment and operates retail stores, hotels and a travel agency. Its stock is listed on the New York Stock Exchange.

Phillips owns 12 million shares of common stock of Slick, Inc. (Slick), which operates a chain of supermarkets in a ten-state region. The remaining 8 million shares of Slick's stock are owned by about 22,500 public investors and are traded in the over-the-counter market on the NASDAQ system. Slick has a nine-member board of directors. Three directors also are officers and directors of Phillips and another two are officers but not directors of Phillips. Phillips acquired its holdings in Slick over a number of years in private transactions with members of the family that founded Slick and through purchases on the open market.

The price of Slick stock has declined from the $40–45 per share range at which it was selling three years ago to about $10–12 per share now. Slick's earnings also have declined from $4.00 per share three years ago to $2.40 per share last year. Analysts have attributed the decline to the fact that many of Slick's stores have become obsolete, are too small or have been managed inefficiently. Slick's shareholders have grown increasingly restive, especially because Slick's management appears to have done little to reverse these trends.

Phillips' board of directors became greatly concerned because Phillips' rate of return on its investment in Slick was lower than its return from any of its other divisions or subsidiaries. At the board's request, Phillips management commissioned Tolliver Brothers (Tolliver), an investment banking firm with expertise in the retail food industry, to conduct a study of the alternatives available to Phillips.

Tolliver prepared a report stating that Slick probably could be sold for $15 per share, but that Slick also could be made considerably more profitable if the following steps were taken:

    A.   About one-fourth of Slick's stores should be closed and the real estate sold because the real estate on which those stores sit is worth more than are the stores on an operating basis.

    B.   Slick could enhance the profitability of another one-fourth of its stores by enlarging and modernizing them. The cost would be substantial, but Slick could earn in excess of 20 percent per annum on the investment it would be required to make.

    C.   The remaining half of Slick's stores do not require major investments, but their performance could be improved by better management. In addition, most need new computerized equipment that would lower labor costs, provide valuable information, and link the stores to each other and to Slick's headquarters.

The total cost of the proposed program would be around $150 million. Tolliver opined that financing would be available on reasonable terms, and that in five years Slick's earnings would double. Tolliver also suggested that, if Phillips decided to go forward with the investment in Slick, it should consider cashing out Slick's minority shareholders before doing so. Tolliver estimated that, assuming Phillips caused Slick to implement the rest of its recommendations, Phillips could increase its overall return on its investment in Slick to 25 percent by buying out the minority shareholders at $18 per share, a price more than 50 percent above the current market price of Slick stock.

One month later, Phillips management submitted a report to the board in which it recommended that Phillips cash out Slick's minority shareholders at $18 per share and then make the recommended investment in, and changes at, Slick. The form of the transaction would be a merger of Slick into New Slick, a new subsidiary of Phillips. In the merger, the minority shareholders of Slick would receive $18 in cash, and New Slick would acquire all the assets and assume the liabilities of Slick. Finally New Slick would change its name to Slick. Management also reported that Tolliver was prepared to opine that $18 was a fair price for the Slick stock, in light of Slick's current market price and its book value of $17.86 per share.

The report also noted that, based on management's own studies, the proceeds from closing Slick's obsolete stores and selling the real estate probably would be greater than Tolliver had estimated. Management also estimated that if the board decided to liquidate Slick and sell its assets rather than do a cash out merger, the Slick shareholders probably would realize $20–21 per share.

After reviewing and discussing management's recommendations and the Tolliver report, a copy of which was given to all Phillips directors prior to the board meeting, the Phillips board unanimously endorsed the plan to cash out Slick's minority shareholders and take the actions recommended by Tolliver to revive Slick's business. Two days later, Doris Knight, Phillips' CEO and a director of both Phillips and Slick, presented Phillips' offer to the Slick board of directors. Knight, acting on the advice of counsel, also gave a copy of the Tolliver report to all Slick directors. She did not give them Phillips' internal report. She recommended that the Slick board appoint a committee consisting of three Slick outside directors who had no other affiliation with Phillips to review the offer and represent Slick in its dealings with Phillips. The Slick board accepted this recommendation and authorized the new Special Negotiating Committee (SNC) to retain advisors and counsel as necessary and to represent Slick in negotiating the proposed merger with Phillips.

The SNC retained Blanchard & Co., investment bankers, to help it assess Phillips' offer. After two weeks of intensive research and analysis, Blanchard submitted a report concluding that the fair value of Slick, considered as a whole, was between $500 million and $600 million, or $25 to $30 per share. The SNC then advised Phillips that it was prepared to recommend a merger of Slick and New Slick only if Slick's minority shareholders would receive $27.50 per share. Knight, on behalf of Phillips, replied that Phillips was not prepared to offer more than $18. The SNC responded that, after further consideration, it might be prepared to recommend a merger at $26 per share and suggested that, if Phillips was not prepared to pay that price, it consider soliciting bids for all Slick stock, including the stock it owned. If no bid came in above the $18 Phillips was offering, the SNC said, it would be prepared to reconsider Phillips' offer of $18 per share.

After consulting with the Phillips board, Knight responded that Phillips was not prepared to improve its bid and had no intention of selling its Slick stock. Negotiations then ended, with the SNC stating that it was not prepared to make any further concessions.

Knight has now asked your firm for advice as to how to proceed. More specifically, she has asked:

    1.   Does Phillips have any obligation to sell its Slick stock if some third party is prepared to offer more than the $18 per share Phillips is prepared to pay for the minority interest in Slick?

    2.   Can Phillips lawfully effectuate the proposed merger of New Slick and Slick at $18 per share without the consent of the members of the SNC? What risks would be involved in so proceeding?

    3.   Alternatively, should Phillips, by means of a tender offer or open market purchases, seek to acquire sufficient additional shares of Slick to become a more than 90% shareholder and then cash out Slick's minority shareholders in a short form merger? What risks would be involved in so proceeding?

## B.   FRAMING THE ISSUES

The Delaware Supreme Court's decision in *Weinberger v. UOP, Inc.*, reproduced below, addresses most of the major issues raised by cash out mergers. To adequately appreciate *Weinberger*, though, it is helpful to know something about that decision's antecedents.

Recall *Santa Fe Industries, Inc. v. Green* (Chapter 18), which involved a claim by cashed out shareholders of Kirby Lumber, a Delaware corporation, that they should be allowed to recover damages from Santa Fe, Kirby's majority shareholder, under Rule 10b–5. Plaintiffs claimed that a federal remedy was necessary because Delaware law did not adequately redress their injury. Specifically, plaintiffs contended that Delaware law (1) allowed Santa Fe to cash them out for any reason whatsoever, (2) provided that appraisal was their exclusive remedy, and (3) mandated an approach to determining fair value in an appraisal proceeding (known as the "Delaware block approach") that would not provide them with the fair market value of their stock. A number of Delaware decisions, including *Stauffer v. Standard Brands Inc.*, 187 A.2d 78 (Del.1962) and *David J. Greene & Co. v. Schenley Industries, Inc.*, 281 A.2d 30 (Del.Ch.1971), seemed to support plaintiffs' characterization of Delaware law. *See Santa Fe supra*, at n. 14.

The Second Circuit agreed that the inadequacy of Delaware's appraisal remedy, combined with Santa Fe's alleged lack of a business purpose for cashing out Kirby's minority shareholders, constituted constructive fraud and was actionable under Rule 10b–5. *Green v. Santa Fe Indus., Inc.*, 533 F.2d 1283, 1291 (2d Cir.1976), *rev'd and remanded* 430 U.S. 462, 97 S.Ct. 1292, 51 L.Ed.2d 480 (1977). The Supreme Court reversed on the ground that some evidence of deception or manipulation was necessary to make out a claim under Rule 10b–5. But the Court never questioned plaintiffs' claim that the merger involved "mismanagement" and a "breach of fiduciary duty." 430 U.S. at 479–80, 97 S.Ct. at 1304. Rather, the Court declined "to federalize the substantial portion of the law of corporations that deals with transactions in securities," observing that while "[t]here well may be a need for uniform federal fiduciary standards to govern mergers such as that challenged in this complaint * * * those standards should not be supplied by judicial extension of section 10(b) and Rule 10b–5 * * *." *Id.*

Three months later, the Delaware Supreme Court handed down its decision in *Singer v. Magnavox Co.*, 380 A.2d 969 (Del.1977), a case that it had taken under submission before *Santa Fe* was decided. North American Phillips Corporation (NAP) had acquired 84% of the stock of Magnavox through a $9 per share cash tender offer that Magnavox management had supported. NAP then sought to acquire the remaining 16% of Magnavox stock, again at $9 per share, through a cash out merger. The Singers sued to enjoin that merger, alleging that NAP's sole purpose was to cash out Magnavox's minority shareholders at a grossly inadequate price.

The Court of Chancery, relying on *Stauffer* and *Schenley*, dismissed the complaint. The Delaware Supreme Court reversed, overruling *Stauffer* and *Schenley*. It held that a merger "made for the sole purpose of freezing-out minority stockholders is an abuse of the corporate process" and that, in any event, under the rule of *Sterling v. Mayflower Hotel Corp.*, 93 A.2d 107 (Del. 1952), NAP, as Magnavox's majority shareholder, bore the burden of demonstrating the "entire fairness" of the proposed merger. 380 A.2d at 980.

In *Singer* and two subsequent decisions, *Tanzer v. International General Industries, Inc.*, 379 A.2d 1121 (Del.1977), and *Roland International Corp. v. Najjar*, 407 A.2d 1032 (Del.1979), the Delaware Supreme Court made clear that it wanted to provide minority shareholders with enhanced protection against unfair cash out mergers. These decisions, often referred to as the "*Singer* trilogy," established that a shareholder dissatisfied with the terms of a cash out merger would avoid being relegated to her appraisal remedy if she filed a complaint alleging that the sole purpose of the cash out merger was "to eliminate minority shareholders at a grossly inadequate price." However, the *Singer* trilogy provided little guidance as to when the court would consider a cash out merger to have a proper purpose or what criteria it would use to decide if such a merger was "entirely fair." Thus, the *Singer* trilogy served largely to make it substantially more likely that any given cash out merger would become the subject of extended litigation. An aggrieved shareholder could always allege that the merger had been effectuated "solely to cash out minority shareholders at an inadequate price," since one effect of cash out mergers always is to eliminate minority shareholders. The allegation would create an issue of fact as to whether the merger had a proper purpose. It would also shift to the majority shareholder the burden of proving that the terms of the merger were "entirely fair."

More importantly, an aggrieved shareholder generally would be able to challenge the cash out merger in a class action brought on behalf of all similarly situated shareholders, including those who had not objected to the merger. Such an action would eliminate the collective action problems that often make appraisal an unattractive remedy. The potential damages theoretically would be equal to the difference between the cash out price and whatever the plaintiff could establish to be the "fair value" of all shares previously owned by non-controlling shareholders. The potential for a large damage award would make it attractive for an entrepreneurial (or opportunistic) attorney to represent aggrieved shareholders on a contingency basis. Concern about this aspect of the *Singer* trilogy—the likelihood of increased litigation and the uncertainty that would result—led one member of the Delaware Supreme Court to criticize the *Singer* trilogy for creating an "unnecessary damage forum" and to suggest that the court should have sought to make appraisal a more effective remedy. *See Najjar*, 407 A.2d at 1040, n.12 (Quillen, J., dissenting).

## WEINBERGER v. UOP, INC.

457 A.2d 701 (Del.1983).

MOORE, JUSTICE.

This post-trial appeal was reheard en banc from a decision of the Court of Chancery. It was brought by the class action plaintiff below, a former shareholder of UOP, Inc., who challenged the elimination of UOP's minority shareholders by a cash-out merger between UOP and its majority owner, The Signal Companies, Inc. Originally, the defendants in this action were Signal, UOP, certain officers and directors of those companies, and UOP's investment banker, Lehman Brothers Kuhn Loeb, Inc. The present Chancellor held that the terms of the merger were fair to the plaintiff and the other minority shareholders of UOP. Accordingly, he entered judgment in favor of the defendants.

Numerous points were raised by the parties, but we address only the following questions presented by the trial court's opinion:

    1) The plaintiff's duty to plead sufficient facts demonstrating the unfairness of the challenged merger;

    2) The burden of proof upon the parties where the merger has been approved by the purportedly informed vote of a majority of the minority shareholders;

3) The fairness of the merger in terms of adequacy of the defendants' disclosures to the minority shareholders;

4) The fairness of the merger in terms of adequacy of the price paid for the minority shares and the remedy appropriate to that issue; and

5) The continued force and effect of *Singer v. Magnavox Co.*, Del.Supr., 380 A.2d 969, 980 (1977), and its progeny.

In ruling for the defendants, the Chancellor re-stated his earlier conclusion that the plaintiff in a suit challenging a cash-out merger must allege specific acts of fraud, misrepresentation or other items of misconduct to demonstrate the unfairness of the merger terms to the minority. We approve this rule and affirm it.

The Chancellor also held that even though the ultimate burden of proof is on the majority shareholder to show by a preponderance of the evidence that the transaction is fair, it is first the burden of the plaintiff attacking the merger to demonstrate some basis for invoking the fairness obligation. We agree with that principle. However, where corporate action has been approved by an informed vote of a majority of the minority shareholders, we conclude that the burden entirely shifts to the plaintiff to show that the transaction was unfair to the minority. But in all this, the burden clearly remains on those relying on the vote to show that they completely disclosed all material facts relevant to the transaction.

Here, the record does not support a conclusion that the minority stockholder vote was an informed one. Material information, necessary to acquaint those shareholders with the bargaining positions of Signal and UOP, was withheld under circumstances amounting to a breach of fiduciary duty. We therefore conclude that this merger does not meet the test of fairness, at least as we address that concept, and no burden thus shifted to the plaintiff by reason of the minority shareholder vote. Accordingly, we reverse and remand for further proceedings consistent herewith.

In considering the nature of the remedy available under our law to minority shareholders in a cash-out merger, we believe that it is, and hereafter should be, an appraisal under 8 Del.C. § 262 as hereinafter construed. We therefore overrule *Lynch v. Vickers Energy Corp.*, Del. Supr., 429 A.2d 497 (1981) (*Lynch II*) to the extent that it purports to limit a stockholder's monetary relief to a specific damage formula. But to give full effect to section 262 within the framework of the General Corporation Law we adopt a more liberal, less rigid and stylized, approach to the valuation process than has heretofore been permitted by our courts. While the present state of these proceedings does not admit the plaintiff to the appraisal remedy per se, the practical effect of the remedy we do grant him will be co-extensive with the liberalized valuation and appraisal methods we herein approve for cases coming after this decision.

Our treatment of these matters has necessarily led us to a reconsideration of the business purpose rule announced in the trilogy of *Singer v. Magnavox Co., supra; Tanzer v. International General Industries, Inc.,* Del.Supr., 379 A.2d 1121 (1977); and *Roland International Corp. v. Najjar,* Del.Supr., 407 A.2d 1032 (1979). For the reasons hereafter set forth we consider that the business purpose requirement of these cases is no longer the law of Delaware.

## I.

The facts found by the trial court, pertinent to the issues before us, are supported by the record, and we draw from them as set out in the Chancellor's opinion.

Signal is a diversified, technically based company operating through various subsidiaries. Its stock is publicly traded on the New York, Philadelphia and Pacific Stock Exchanges. UOP, formerly known as Universal Oil Products Company, was a diversified industrial company engaged in various lines of business, including petroleum and petrochemical services and related products, construction, fabricated metal products, transportation equipment products, chemicals and plastics, and other products and services including land development, lumber products and waste disposal. Its stock was publicly held and listed on the New York Stock Exchange.

In 1974 Signal sold one of its wholly-owned subsidiaries for $420,-000,000 in cash. *See* Gimbel v. Signal Companies, Inc., Del.Ch., 316 A.2d 599, *aff'd,* Del.Supr., 316 A.2d 619 (1974). While looking to invest this cash surplus, Signal became interested in UOP as a possible acquisition. Friendly negotiations ensued, and Signal proposed to acquire a controlling interest in UOP at a price of $19 per share. UOP's representatives sought $25 per share. In the arm's length bargaining that followed, an understanding was reached whereby Signal agreed to purchase from UOP 1,500,000 shares of UOP's authorized but unissued stock at $21 per share.

This purchase was contingent upon Signal making a successful cash tender offer for 4,300,000 publicly held shares of UOP, also at a price of $21 per share. This combined method of acquisition permitted Signal to acquire 5,800,000 shares of stock, representing 50.5% of UOP's outstanding shares. The UOP board of directors advised the company's shareholders that it had no objection to Signal's tender offer at that price. Immediately before the announcement of the tender offer, UOP's common stock had been trading on the New York Stock Exchange at a fraction under $14 per share.

The negotiations between Signal and UOP occurred during April 1975, and the resulting tender offer was greatly oversubscribed. However, Signal limited its total purchase of the tendered shares so that, when coupled with the stock bought from UOP, it had achieved its goal of becoming a 50.5% shareholder of UOP.

Although UOP's board consisted of thirteen directors, Signal nominated and elected only six. Of these, five were either directors or employees of Signal. The sixth, a partner in the banking firm of Lazard Freres & Co., had been one of Signal's representatives in the negotiations and bargaining with UOP concerning the tender offer and purchase price of the UOP shares.

However, the president and chief executive officer of UOP retired during 1975, and Signal caused him to be replaced by James V. Crawford, a long-time employee and senior executive vice president of one of Signal's wholly-owned subsidiaries. Crawford succeeded his predecessor on UOP's board of directors and also was made a director of Signal.

By the end of 1977 Signal basically was unsuccessful in finding other suitable investment candidates for its excess cash, and by February 1978 considered that it had no other realistic acquisitions available to it on a friendly basis. Once again its attention turned to UOP.

The trial court found that at the instigation of certain Signal management personnel, including William W. Walkup, its board chairman, and Forrest N. Shumway, its president, a feasibility study was made concerning the possible acquisition of the balance of UOP's outstanding shares. This study was performed by two Signal officers, Charles S. Arledge, vice president (director of planning), and Andrew J. Chitiea, senior vice president (chief financial officer). Messrs. Walkup, Shumway, Arledge and Chitiea were all directors of UOP in addition to their membership on the Signal board.

Arledge and Chitiea concluded that it would be a good investment for Signal to acquire the remaining 49.5% of UOP shares at any price up to $24 each. Their report was discussed between Walkup and Shumway who, along with Arledge, Chitiea and Brewster L. Arms, internal counsel for Signal, constituted Signal's senior management. In particular, they talked about the proper price to be paid if the acquisition was pursued, purportedly keeping in mind that as UOP's majority shareholder, Signal owed a fiduciary responsibility to both its own stockholders as well as to UOP's minority. It was ultimately agreed that a meeting of Signal's Executive Committee would be called to propose that Signal acquire the remaining outstanding stock of UOP through a cash-out merger in the range of $20 to $21 per share.

The Executive Committee meeting was set for February 28, 1978. As a courtesy, UOP's president, Crawford, was invited to attend, although he was not a member of Signal's executive committee. On his arrival, and prior to the meeting, Crawford was asked to meet privately with Walkup and Shumway. He was then told of Signal's plan to acquire full ownership of UOP and was asked for his reaction to the proposed price range of $20 to $21 per share. Crawford said he thought such a price would be "generous", and that it was certainly one which should be submitted to UOP's minority shareholders for their ultimate consideration. * * *

Thus, Crawford voiced no objection to the $20 to $21 price range, nor did he suggest that Signal should consider paying more than $21 per share for the minority interests. Later, at the Executive Committee meeting the same factors were discussed, with Crawford repeating the position he earlier took with Walkup and Shumway. Also considered was the 1975 tender offer and the fact that it had been greatly oversubscribed at $21 per share. For many reasons, Signal's management concluded that the acquisition of UOP's minority shares provided the solution to a number of its business problems.

Thus, it was the consensus that a price of $20 to $21 per share would be fair to both Signal and the minority shareholders of UOP. Signal's executive committee authorized its management "to negotiate" with UOP "for a cash acquisition of the minority ownership in UOP, Inc., with the intention of presenting a proposal to [Signal's] board of directors * * * on March 6, 1978". Immediately after this February 28, 1978 meeting, Signal issued a press release stating:

The Signal Companies, Inc. and UOP, Inc. are conducting negotiations for the acquisition for cash by Signal of the 49.5 per cent of UOP which it does not presently own, announced Forrest N. Shumway, president and chief executive officer of Signal, and James V. Crawford, UOP president.

Price and other terms of the proposed transaction have not yet been finalized and would be subject to approval of the boards of directors of Signal and UOP, scheduled to meet early next week, the stockholders of UOP and certain federal agencies.

The announcement also referred to the fact that the closing price of UOP's common stock on that day was $14.50 per share.

Two days later, on March 2, 1978, Signal issued a second press release stating that its management would recommend a price in the range of $20 to $21 per share for UOP's 49.5% minority interest. This announcement referred to Signal's earlier statement that "negotiations" were being conducted for the acquisition of the minority shares.

Between Tuesday, February 28, 1978 and Monday, March 6, 1978, a total of four business days, Crawford spoke by telephone with all of UOP's non-Signal, i.e., outside, directors. Also during that period, Crawford retained Lehman Brothers to render a fairness opinion as to the price offered the minority for its stock. He gave two reasons for this choice. First, the time schedule between the announcement and the board meetings was short (by then only three business days) and since Lehman Brothers had been acting as UOP's investment banker for many years, Crawford felt that it would be in the best position to respond on such brief notice. Second, James W. Glanville, a long-time director of UOP and a partner in Lehman Brothers, had acted as a financial advisor to UOP for many years. Crawford believed that Glanville's familiarity with UOP, as a member of its board, would also be of assistance in enabling Lehman Brothers to render a fairness opinion within the existing time constraints.

Crawford telephoned Glanville, who gave his assurance that Lehman Brothers had no conflicts that would prevent it from accepting the task. Glanville's immediate personal reaction was that a price of $20 to $21 would certainly be fair, since it represented almost a 50% premium over UOP's market price. Glanville sought a $250,000 fee for Lehman Brothers' services, but Crawford thought this too much. After further discussions Glanville finally agreed that Lehman Brothers would render its fairness opinion for $150,000.

During this period Crawford also had several telephone contacts with Signal officials. In only one of them, however, was the price of the shares discussed. In a conversation with Walkup, Crawford advised that as a result of his communications with UOP's non-Signal directors, it was his feeling that the price would have to be the top of the proposed range, or $21 per share, if the approval of UOP's outside directors was to be obtained. But again, he did not seek any price higher than $21.

Glanville assembled a three-man Lehman Brothers team to do the work on the fairness opinion. These persons examined relevant documents and information concerning UOP, including its annual reports and its Securities and Exchange Commission filings from 1973 through 1976, as well as its audited financial statements for 1977, its interim reports to shareholders, and its recent and historical market prices and trading volumes. In addition, on Friday, March 3, 1978, two members of the Lehman Brothers team flew to UOP's headquarters in Des Plaines, Illinois, to perform a "due diligence" visit, during the course of which they interviewed Crawford as well as UOP's general counsel, its chief financial officer, and other key executives and personnel.

As a result, the Lehman Brothers team concluded that "the price of either $20 or $21 would be a fair price for the remaining shares of UOP". They telephoned this impression to Glanville, who was spending the weekend in Vermont.

On Monday morning, March 6, 1978, Glanville and the senior member of the Lehman Brothers team flew to Des Plaines to attend the scheduled UOP directors meeting. Glanville looked over the assembled information during the flight. The two had with them the draft of a "fairness opinion letter" in which the price had been left blank. Either during or immediately prior to the directors' meeting, the two-page "fairness opinion letter" was typed in final form and the price of $21 per share was inserted.

On March 6, 1978, both the Signal and UOP boards were convened to consider the proposed merger. Telephone communications were maintained between the two meetings. Walkup, Signal's board chairman, and also a UOP director, attended UOP's meeting with Crawford in order to present Signal's position and answer any questions that UOP's non-Signal directors might have. Arledge and Chitiea, along with Signal's other designees on UOP's board, participated by conference telephone. All of UOP's outside directors attended the meeting either in person or by conference telephone.

First, Signal's board unanimously adopted a resolution authorizing Signal to propose to UOP a cash merger of $21 per share as outlined in a certain merger agreement, and other supporting documents. This proposal required that the merger be approved by a majority of UOP's outstanding minority shares voting at the stockholders meeting at which the merger would be considered, and that the minority shares voting in favor of the merger, when coupled with Signal's 50.5% interest would have to comprise at least two-thirds of all UOP shares. Otherwise the proposed merger would be deemed disapproved.

UOP's board then considered the proposal. Copies of the agreement were delivered to the directors in attendance, and other copies had been forwarded earlier to the directors participating by telephone. They also had before them UOP financial data for 1974–1977, UOP's most recent financial statements, market price information, and budget projections for 1978. In addition they had Lehman Brothers' hurriedly prepared fairness opinion letter finding the price of $21 to be fair. Glanville, the Lehman Brothers partner, and UOP director, commented on the information that had gone into preparation of the letter.

Signal also suggests that the Arledge–Chitiea feasibility study, indicating that a price of up to $24 per share would be a "good investment" for Signal, was discussed at the UOP directors' meeting. The Chancellor made no such finding, and our independent review of the record, detailed *infra*, satisfies us by a preponderance of the evidence that there was no discussion of this document at UOP's board meeting. Furthermore, it is clear beyond peradventure that nothing in that report was ever disclosed to UOP's minority shareholders prior to their approval of the merger.

After consideration of Signal's proposal, Walkup and Crawford left the meeting to permit a free and uninhibited exchange between UOP's non-Signal directors. Upon their return a resolution to accept Signal's offer was then proposed and adopted. While Signal's men on UOP's board participated in various aspects of the meeting, they abstained from voting. However, the minutes show that each of them "if voting would have voted yes".

On March 7, 1978, UOP sent a letter to its shareholders advising them of the action taken by UOP's board with respect to Signal's offer. This document pointed out, among other things, that on February 28, 1978 "both companies had announced negotiations were being conducted".

Despite the swift board action of the two companies, the merger was not submitted to UOP's shareholders until their annual meeting on May 26, 1978. In the notice of that meeting and proxy statement sent to shareholders in May, UOP's management and board urged that the merger be approved. The proxy statement also advised:

> The price was determined after *discussions* between James V. Crawford, a director of Signal and Chief Executive Officer of UOP, and officers of Signal which took place during meetings on February

28, 1978, and in the course of several subsequent telephone conversations. (Emphasis added.)

In the original draft of the proxy statement the word "negotiations" had been used rather than "discussions". However, when the Securities and Exchange Commission sought details of the "negotiations" as part of its review of these materials, the term was deleted and the word "discussions" was substituted. The proxy statement indicated that the vote of UOP's board in approving the merger had been unanimous. It also advised the shareholders that Lehman Brothers had given its opinion that the merger price of $21 per share was fair to UOP's minority. However, it did not disclose the hurried method by which this conclusion was reached.

As of the record date of UOP's annual meeting, there were 11,488,-302 shares of UOP common stock outstanding, 5,688,302 of which were owned by the minority. At the meeting only 56%, or 3,208,652, of the minority shares were voted. Of these, 2,953,812, or 51.9% of the total minority, voted for the merger, and 254,840 voted against it. When Signal's stock was added to the minority shares voting in favor, a total of 76.2% of UOP's outstanding shares approved the merger while only 2.2% opposed it.

By its terms the merger became effective on May 26, 1978, and each share of UOP's stock held by the minority was automatically converted into a right to receive $21 cash.

## II.

### A.

A primary issue mandating reversal is the preparation by two UOP directors, Arledge and Chitiea, of their feasibility study for the exclusive use and benefit of Signal. This document was of obvious significance to both Signal and UOP. Using UOP data, it described the advantages to Signal of ousting the minority at a price range of $21–$24 per share. Mr. Arledge, one of the authors, outlined the benefits to Signal:

PURPOSE OF THE MERGER

1) Provides an outstanding investment opportunity for Signal— (Better than any recent acquisition we have seen.)

2) Increases Signal's earnings.

3) Facilitates the flow of resources between Signal and its subsidiaries—(Big factor—works both ways.)

4) Provides cost savings potential for Signal and UOP.

5) Improves the percentage of Signal's "operating earnings" as opposed to "holding company earnings."

6) Simplifies the understanding of Signal.

7) Facilitates technological exchange among Signal's subsidiaries.

8) Eliminates potential conflicts of interest.

Having written those words, solely for the use of Signal it is clear from the record that neither Arledge nor Chitiea shared this report with their fellow directors of UOP. We are satisfied that no one else did either. This conduct hardly meets the fiduciary standards applicable to such a transaction * * *

The Arledge–Chitiea report speaks for itself in supporting the Chancellor's finding that a price of up to $24 was a "good investment" for Signal. It shows that a return on the investment at $21 would be 15.7% versus 15.5% at $24 per share. This was a difference of only two-tenths of one percent, while it meant over $17,000,000 to the minority. Under such circumstances, paying UOP's minority shareholders $24 would have had relatively little long-term effect on Signal, and the Chancellor's findings concerning the benefit to Signal, even at a price of $24, were obviously correct.

Certainly, this was a matter of material significance to UOP and its shareholders. Since the study was prepared by two UOP directors, using UOP information for the exclusive benefit of Signal, and nothing whatever was done to disclose it to the outside UOP directors or the minority shareholders, a question of breach of fiduciary duty arises. This problem occurs because there were common Signal–UOP directors participating, at least to some extent, in the UOP board's decision-making processes without full disclosure of the conflicts they faced.[7]

### B.

In assessing this situation, the Court of Chancery was required to:

examine what information defendants had and to measure it against what they gave to the minority stockholders, in a context in which "complete candor" is required. In other words, the limited function of the Court was to determine whether defendants had disclosed all information in their possession germane to the transaction in issue. And by "germane" we mean, for present purposes, information such as a reasonable shareholder would consider important in deciding whether to sell or retain stock.

* * *

* * * Completeness, not adequacy, is both the norm and the mandate under present circumstances.

---

**7.** Although perfection is not possible, or expected, the result here could have been entirely different if UOP had appointed an independent negotiating committee of its outside directors to deal with Signal at arm's length. *See, e.g., Harriman v. E.I. du Pont de Nemours & Co.*, 411 F.Supp. 133 (D.Del.1975). Since fairness in this context can be equated to conduct by a theoretical, wholly independent, board of directors acting upon the matter before them, it is unfortunate that this course apparently was neither considered nor pursued. *Johnston v. Greene*, Del.Supr., 121 A.2d 919, 925 (1956). Particularly in a parent-subsidiary context, a showing that the action taken was as though each of the contending parties had in fact exerted its bargaining power against the other at arm's length is strong evidence that the transaction meets the test of fairness. *Getty Oil Co. v. Skelly Oil Co.*, Del. Supr., 267 A.2d 883, 886 (1970); *Puma v. Marriott*, Del.Ch., 283 A.2d 693, 696 (1971).

*Lynch v. Vickers Energy Corp.*, Del.Supr., 383 A.2d 278, 281 (1977) (*Lynch I*). This is merely stating in another way the long-existing principle of Delaware law that these Signal designated directors on UOP's board still owed UOP and its shareholders an uncompromising duty of loyalty. \* \* \*

Given the absence of any attempt to structure this transaction on an arm's length basis, Signal cannot escape the effects of the conflicts it faced, particularly when its designees on UOP's board did not totally abstain from participation in the matter. There is no "safe harbor" for such divided loyalties in Delaware. When directors of a Delaware corporation are on both sides of a transaction, they are required to demonstrate their utmost good faith and the most scrupulous inherent fairness of the bargain. *Gottlieb v. Heyden Chemical Corp.*, Del.Supr., 91 A.2d 57, 57–58 (1952). The requirement of fairness is unflinching in its demand that where one stands on both sides of a transaction, he has the burden of establishing its entire fairness, sufficient to pass the test of careful scrutiny by the courts.

There is no dilution of this obligation where one holds dual or multiple directorships, as in a parent-subsidiary context. *Levien v. Sinclair Oil Corp.*, Del.Ch., 261 A.2d 911, 915 (1969). Thus, individuals who act in a dual capacity as directors of two corporations, one of whom is parent and the other subsidiary, owe the same duty of good management to both corporations, and in the absence of an independent negotiating structure (see note 7, *supra*), or the directors' total abstention from any participation in the matter, this duty is to be exercised in light of what is best for both companies. The record demonstrates that Signal has not met this obligation.

#### C.

The concept of fairness has two basic aspects: fair dealing and fair price. The former embraces questions of when the transaction was timed, how it was initiated, structured, negotiated, disclosed to the directors, and how the approvals of the directors and the stockholders were obtained. The latter aspect of fairness relates to the economic and financial considerations of the proposed merger, including all relevant factors: assets, market value, earnings, future prospects, and any other elements that affect the intrinsic or inherent value of a company's stock. However, the test for fairness is not a bifurcated one as between fair dealing and price. All aspects of the issue must be examined as a whole since the question is one of entire fairness. However, in a non-fraudulent transaction we recognize that price may be the preponderant consideration outweighing other features of the merger. Here, we address the two basic aspects of fairness separately because we find reversible error as to both.

#### D.

Part of fair dealing is the obvious duty of candor required by *Lynch I, supra*. Moreover, one possessing superior knowledge may not mislead any stockholder by use of corporate information to which the latter is not privy. Delaware has long imposed this duty even upon persons who are not corporate officers or directors, but who nonetheless are privy to matters of interest or significance to their company. *Brophy v. Cities Service Co.*, Del.Ch., 70 A.2d 5, 7 (1949). With the well-established Delaware law on the subject, and the Court of Chancery's findings of fact here, it is inevitable that the obvious conflicts posed by Arledge and Chitiea's preparation of their "feasibility study", derived from UOP information, for the sole use and benefit of Signal, cannot pass muster.

The Arledge–Chitiea report is but one aspect of the element of fair dealing. How did this merger evolve? It is clear that it was entirely initiated by Signal. The serious time constraints under which the principals acted were all set by Signal. It had not found a suitable outlet for its excess cash and considered UOP a desirable investment, particularly since it was now in a position to acquire the whole company for itself. For whatever reasons, and they were only Signal's, the entire transaction was presented to and approved by UOP's board within four business days. Standing alone, this is not necessarily indicative of any lack of fairness by a majority shareholder. It was what occurred, or more properly, what did not occur, during this brief period that makes the time constraints imposed by Signal relevant to the issue of fairness.

The structure of the transaction, again, was Signal's doing. So far as negotiations were concerned, it is clear that they were modest at best. Crawford, Signal's man at UOP, never really talked price with Signal, except to accede to its management's statements on the subject, and to convey to Signal the UOP outside directors' view that as between the $20–$21 range under consideration, it would have to be $21. The latter is not a surprising outcome, but hardly arm's length negotiations. Only the protection of benefits for UOP's key employees and the issue of Lehman Brothers' fee approached any concept of bargaining.

As we have noted, the matter of disclosure to the UOP directors was wholly flawed by the conflicts of interest raised by the Arledge–Chitiea report. All of those conflicts were resolved by Signal in its own favor without divulging any aspect of them to UOP.

This cannot but undermine a conclusion that this merger meets any reasonable test of fairness. The outside UOP directors lacked one material piece of information generated by two of their colleagues, but shared only with Signal. True, the UOP board had the Lehman Brothers' fairness opinion, but that firm has been blamed by the plaintiff for the hurried task it performed, when more properly the responsibility for this lies with Signal. There was no disclosure of the circumstances surrounding the rather cursory preparation of the Lehman Brothers' fairness opinion. Instead, the impression was given UOP's minority that a careful study had been made, when in fact speed was the hallmark, and Mr. Glanville, Lehman's partner in charge of the matter, and also a UOP director, having spent the weekend in Vermont, brought a draft of the "fairness opinion letter" to the UOP directors' meeting on March 6, 1978 with the price left blank. We can only conclude from the record that the rush imposed on Lehman Brothers by Signal's timetable contributed to the difficulties under which this investment banking firm attempted to perform its responsibilities. Yet, none of this was disclosed to UOP's minority.

Finally, the minority stockholders were denied the critical information that Signal considered a price of $24 to be a good investment. Since this would have meant over $17,000,000 more to the minority, we cannot conclude that the shareholder vote was an informed one. Under the circumstances, an approval by a majority of the minority was meaningless.

Given these particulars and the Delaware law on the subject, the record does not establish that this transaction satisfies any reasonable concept of fair dealing, and the Chancellor's findings in that regard must be reversed.

### E.

Turning to the matter of price, plaintiff also challenges its fairness. His evidence was that on the date the merger was approved the stock was worth at least $26 per share. In support, he offered the testimony of a chartered investment analyst who used two basic approaches to valuation: a comparative analysis of the premium paid over market in ten other tender offer-merger combinations, and a discounted cash flow analysis.

In this breach of fiduciary duty case, the Chancellor perceived that the approach to valuation was the same as that in an appraisal proceeding. Consistent with precedent, he rejected plaintiff's method of proof and accepted defendants' evidence of value as being in accord with practice under prior case law. This means that the so-called "Delaware block" or weighted average method was employed wherein the elements of value, i.e., assets, market price, earnings, etc., were assigned a particular weight and the resulting amounts added to determine the value per share. This procedure has been in use for decades. However, to the extent it excludes other generally accepted techniques used in the financial community and the courts, it is now clearly outmoded. It is time we recognize this in appraisal and other stock valuation proceedings and bring our law current on the subject.

While the Chancellor rejected plaintiff's discounted cash flow method of valuing UOP's stock, as not corresponding with "either logic or the existing law" (426 A.2d at 1360), it is significant that this was essentially the focus, i.e., earnings potential of UOP, of Messrs. Arledge and Chitiea in their evaluation of the merger. Accordingly, the standard "Delaware block" or weighted average method of valuation, formerly employed in appraisal and other stock valuation cases, shall no longer exclusively control such proceedings. We believe that a more liberal approach must include proof of value by any techniques or methods which are generally considered acceptable in the financial community and otherwise admissible in court, subject only to our interpretation of 8 Del.C. § 262(h), *infra*. This will obviate the very structured and mechanistic procedure that has heretofore governed such matters. *See Tri–Continental Corp. v. Battye*, Del.Ch., 66 A.2d 910, 917–18 (1949).

Fair price obviously requires consideration of all relevant factors involving the value of a ·company. This has long been the law of Delaware as stated in *Tri–Continental Corp.*, 74 A.2d at 72:

> The basic concept of value under the appraisal statute is that the stockholder is entitled to be paid for that which has been taken from him, viz., his proportionate interest in a going concern. By value of the stockholder's proportionate interest in the corporate enterprise is meant the true or intrinsic value of his stock which has been taken by the merger. In determining what figure represents this true or intrinsic value, the appraiser and the courts must take into consideration all factors and elements which reasonably might enter into the fixing of value. Thus, market value, asset value, dividends, earning prospects, the nature of the enterprise and any other facts which were known or which could be ascertained as of the date of merger and which throw any light on *future prospects* of the merged corporation are not only pertinent to an inquiry as to the value of the dissenting stockholders' interest, but *must be considered* by the agency fixing the value. (Emphasis added.)

\* \* \*

It is significant that section 262 now mandates the determination of "fair" value based upon "all relevant factors". Only the speculative elements of value that may arise from the "accomplishment or expectation" of the merger are excluded. We take this to be a very narrow exception to the appraisal process, designed to eliminate use of *pro forma* data and projections of a speculative variety relating to the completion of a merger. But elements of future value, including the nature of the enterprise, which are known or susceptible of proof as of the date of the merger and not the product of speculation, may be considered. When the trial court deems it appropriate, fair value also includes any damages, resulting from the taking, which the stockholders sustain as a class. If that was not the case, then the obligation to consider "all relevant factors" in the valuation process would be eroded. We are supported in this view not only by *Tri–Continental Corp.*, 74 A.2d at 72, but also by the evolutionary amendments to section 262.

\* \* \*

Although the Chancellor received the plaintiff's evidence, his opinion indicates that the use of it was precluded because of past Delaware practice. While we do not suggest a monetary result one way or the other, we do think the plaintiff's evidence should be part of the factual mix and weighed as such. Until the $21 price is measured on remand by the valuation standards mandated by Delaware law, there can be no finding at the present stage of these proceedings that the price is fair. Given the lack of any candid disclosure of the material facts surrounding establishment of the $21 price, the majority of the minority vote, approving the merger, is meaningless.

The plaintiff has not sought an appraisal, but rescissory damages of the type contemplated by *Lynch v. Vickers Energy Corp.*, Del.Supr., 429 A.2d 497, 505–06 (1981) (*Lynch II* ). In view of the approach to valuation that we announce today, we see no basis in our law for *Lynch II*'s exclusive monetary formula for relief. On remand the plaintiff will be permitted to test the fairness of the $21 price by the standards we herein establish, in conformity with the principle applicable to an appraisal— that fair value be determined by taking "into account all relevant factors" [*see* 8 *Del.C.* § 262(h), *supra* ]. In our view this includes the elements of rescissory damages if the Chancellor considers them susceptible of proof and a remedy appropriate to all the issues of fairness before him. To the extent that *Lynch II,* 429 A.2d at 505–06, purports to limit the Chancellor's discretion to a single remedial formula for monetary damages in a cash-out merger, it is overruled.

While a plaintiff's monetary remedy ordinarily should be confined to the more liberalized appraisal proceeding herein established, we do not intend any limitation on the historic powers of the Chancellor to grant such other relief as the facts of a particular case may dictate. The appraisal remedy we approve may not be adequate in certain cases, particularly where fraud, misrepresentation, self-dealing, deliberate waste of corporate assets, or gross and palpable overreaching are involved. Under such circumstances, the Chancellor's powers are complete to fashion any form of equitable and monetary relief as may be appropriate, including rescissory damages. Since it is apparent that this long completed transaction is too involved to undo, and in view of the Chancellor's discretion, the award, if any, should be in the form of monetary damages based upon entire fairness standards, i.e., fair dealing and fair price.

Obviously, there are other litigants, like the plaintiff, who abjured an appraisal and whose rights to challenge the element of fair value must be preserved. Accordingly, the quasi-appraisal remedy we grant the plaintiff here will apply only to: (1) this case; (2) any case now pending on appeal to this Court; (3) any case now pending in the Court of Chancery which has not yet been appealed but which may be eligible for direct appeal to this Court; (4) any case challenging a cash-out merger, the effective date of which is on or before February 1, 1983; and (5) any proposed merger to be presented at a shareholders' meeting, the notification of which is mailed to the stockholders on or before February 23, 1983. Thereafter, the provisions of 8 Del.C. § 262, as herein construed, respecting the scope of an appraisal and the means for perfecting the same, shall govern the financial remedy available to minority shareholders in a cash-out merger. Thus, we return to the well established principles of *Stauffer v. Standard Brands Inc.*, Del.Supr., 187 A.2d 78 (1962) and *David J. Greene & Co. v. Schenley Industries, Inc.*, Del.Ch., 281 A.2d 30 (1971), mandating a stockholder's recourse to the basic remedy of an appraisal.

### III.

Finally, we address the matter of business purpose. The defendants contend that the purpose of this merger was not a proper subject of inquiry by the trial court. The plaintiff says that no valid purpose existed—the entire transaction was a mere subterfuge designed to eliminate the minority. The Chancellor ruled otherwise, but in so doing he clearly circumscribed the thrust and effect of *Singer. Weinberger v. UOP*, 426 A.2d at 1342–43, 1348–50. This has led to the thoroughly sound observation that the business purpose test "may be * * * virtually interpreted out of existence, as it was in *Weinberger* ."[9]

The requirement of a business purpose is new to our law of mergers and was a departure from prior case law. *See Stauffer v. Standard Brands Inc.*, *supra; David J. Greene & Co. v. Schenley Industries, Inc.*, *supra.*

In view of the fairness test which has long been applicable to parent-subsidiary mergers, *Sterling v. Mayflower Hotel Corp.*, Del.Supr., 93 A.2d 107, 109–10 (1952), the expanded appraisal remedy now available to shareholders, and the broad discretion of the Chancellor to fashion such relief as the facts of a given case may dictate, we do not believe that any additional meaningful protection is afforded minority shareholders by the business purpose requirement of the trilogy of *Singer, Tanzer, Najjar,* and their progeny. Accordingly, such requirement shall no longer be of any force or effect.

The judgment of the Court of Chancery, finding both the circumstances of the merger and the price paid the minority shareholders to be fair, is reversed. The matter is remanded for further proceedings consistent herewith. Upon remand the plaintiff's post-trial motion to enlarge the class should be granted.

* * *

Reversed and remanded.

---

On remand, the Court of Chancery seemed unimpressed with the Delaware Supreme Court's finding that Signal had dealt unfairly with the UOP minority shareholders. *Weinberger v. UOP, Inc.*, 1985 WL 11546 (Del.Ch.1985). It interpreted the Supreme Court's holding as equating "to a finding that Signal was guilty of a misrepresentation," even though the court did not believe that Signal had committed deliberate fraud. Chancellor Brown stated that he felt free to make a damage award without reference to "the results of an appraisal of the value of a share of UOP stock either at the merger date or at some other date." Accordingly, he awarded $1 per share together with interest from

**9.** Weiss, *The Law of Take Out Mergers: A Historical Perspective*, 56 N.Y.U.L.Rev. 624, 671, n. 300 (1981).

the date of the Supreme Court's opinion. He declined to award rescissory damages because of the speculative nature of the offered proof.

### Note: Other Approaches

*Weinberger* left unresolved important details concerning what constitutes fair dealing, how fair price should be determined, and when collateral attacks on cash out mergers will be allowed, but set forth a basic approach to regulating cash out mergers that many other courts have embraced. Nevertheless, a few of those courts have continued to require that cash out mergers have a proper purpose.

*Alpert v. 28 Williams St. Corp.*, 473 N.E.2d 19 (N.Y. 1984), involved a cash out of minority shareholders in a corporation that owned a valuable building. After affirming that the merger was the product of fair dealing and involved a fair price, the court added:

> Fair dealing and fair price alone will not render the merger acceptable. As mentioned, there exists a fiduciary duty to treat all shareholders equally. * * * The fact remains, however, that in a freeze-out merger the minority shareholders are being treated in a different manner: the majority is permitted continued participation in the equity of the surviving corporation while the minority has no choice but to surrender their shares for cash. On its face, the majority's conduct would appear to breach this fiduciary obligation.

> \* \* \*

> In the context of a freeze-out merger, variant treatment of the minority shareholders—i.e., causing their removal—will be justified when related to the advancement of a general corporate interest. The benefit need not be great, but it must be for the corporation. For example, if the sole purpose of the merger is reduction of the number of profit sharers—in contrast to increasing the corporation's capital or profits, or improving its management structure—there will exist no "independent corporate interest." * * * What distinguishes a proper corporate purpose from an improper one is that, with the former, removal of the minority shareholders furthers the objective of conferring some general gain upon the corporation. Only then will the fiduciary duty of good and prudent management of the corporation serve to override the concurrent duty to treat all shareholders fairly. * * *

> \* \* \*

> Without passing on all of the business purposes cited by Supreme Court as underlying the merger, it is sufficient to note that at least one justified the exclusion of plaintiffs' interests: attracting additional capital to effect needed repairs of the building. There is proof that there was a good-faith belief that additional, outside capital was required. Moreover, this record supports the conclusion that this capital would not have been available through the merger had not plaintiffs' interest in the corporation been eliminated.

*Id.*, at 676–77, 473 N.E.2d at 27–29.

Similarly, in *Coggins v. New England Patriots Football Club*, 492 N.E.2d 1112 ( Mass. 1986), the court held that, "[u]nlike the [*Weinberger* ] court, * * * we believe that the 'business-purpose' test is an additional useful means under our statutes and case law for examining a transaction in which a controlling stockholder eliminates the minority interest in a corporation." *Id.* at 1117. The court then affirmed a trial court ruling that it was not proper for a controlling shareholder to effectuate a cash out merger solely to gain access to the corporation's assets for the purpose of repaying personal debts that he had incurred to finance his purchase of control. *Id.* at 1119.

The SEC advanced a disclosure-based approach to regulating certain cash out mergers by adopting Rule 13e–3, which applies to "going private transactions." Rule 13e–3(a)(3). The person effectuating such a transaction must file with the SEC and distribute to shareholders a Schedule 13E that discusses, *inter alia,* the purpose and fairness of the cash out. More specifically, Item 7 of Schedule 13E requires that person to state the purpose of the transaction, to describe briefly any alternative means to accomplish that purpose that she considered, to explain why she rejected those alternatives, and to explain her reasons for structuring the transaction as a cash out. Item 8 of Schedule 13E requires that person to state whether she believes the terms of the merger are reasonably fair to the shareholders who will be cashed out and to discuss "in reasonable detail the material factors upon which the belief * * * is based, and, to the extent practicable, the weight assigned to each factor" in a list of valuation factors.

In *Howing v. Nationwide Corp.*, 826 F.2d 1470 (6th Cir.1987) ("*Howing I*"), the Sixth Circuit held that a cashed out shareholder could maintain an implied private action for damages under § 13(e) of the 1934 Act and Rule 13e–3. The court also held that Rule 13e–3 requires a "reasonably detailed analysis of the various financial valuation methods discussed by the Rule and the weights attached thereto." *Id.* at 1479. In *Howing v. Nationwide Corp.*, 927 F.2d 263 (6th Cir.1991) ("*Howing II*"), the court further held that the instructions to Item 8 of Schedule 13E create a presumption that a reasonable investor would consider a discussion of book, going concern and liquidation value to be important and, consequently, that any proxy statement that omits such information will be presumed to be materially misleading. The Supreme Court granted certiorari, but subsequently vacated *Howing II* and remanded for reconsideration in light of its intervening decision in *Virginia Bankshares, Inc. v. Sandberg* (Chapter 18). The Sixth Circuit interpreted *Sandberg* to allow a plaintiff to establish causation in an action under Rule 13e–3 by proving that a defendant's misleading disclosures had caused her to lose a state law remedy. *Howing v. Nationwide Corp.*, 972 F.2d 700 (6th Cir.1992), *cert. denied* 507 U.S. 1004, 113 S.Ct. 1645, 123 L.Ed.2d 266 (1993). Plaintiffs had lost their right to seek appraisal under Ohio law, which led the court to remand the case for trial on the merits.

# C.  EXCLUSIVITY OF APPRAISAL

In *Weinberger*, the court stated that although appraisal was to be considered the exclusive remedy for a dissenting shareholder, it might "not be adequate * * * where fraud, misrepresentation, self-dealing, deliberate waste of corporate assets, or gross and palpable overreaching are involved." In such a case, equitable relief or monetary damages would be appropriate. States are similarly divided as to whether appraisal is the exclusive remedy available to a shareholder dissatisfied with a cash out merger or any other transaction that gives rise to dissenters' rights. *Yanow v. Teal Industries, Inc.*, 422 A.2d 311, 317–18 (Conn. 1979) interpreted Conn.Gen.Stat. § 33–373(f) as making appraisal exclusive. *In re Jones & Laughlin Steel Corp.*, 412 A.2d 1099, 1102–03 (Pa. 1980) gave a similar reading to the Pennsylvania statute, but added that an aggrieved shareholder also could seek to enjoin a transaction fraught with "fraud or fundamental unfairness." On the other hand, some statutes explicitly allow shareholders to challenge a merger if it involves self-dealing and is unfair, *see, e.g.*, Maine Bus. Corp. Act § 909(13); South Carolina Corporations, Partnerships and Associations § 33–11–270(k), and some courts have held that a shareholder entitled to seek appraisal nonetheless can maintain a collateral attack on an unfair transaction. *See Vorenberg, Exclusiveness of the Dissenting Stockholder's Appraisal Right*, 77 HARV.L.REV. 1189 (1964).

*Fleming v. International Pizza Supply Corp.*, 640 N.E.2d 1077 (Ind. App.1994), involved the sale of all the assets of a close corporation to another corporation partially owned by the close corporation's majority shareholder. The Indiana statute appeared to make appraisal the exclusive remedy for a shareholder challenging a sale of assets. However, the court held that the statute did not eliminate the right of the plaintiff, as a minority shareholder in the close corporation, to pursue a claim for breach of the fiduciary duty owed to him by the majority shareholder.

Calif. Corp.Code § 1312 makes appraisal the exclusive remedy unless: (1) the plaintiff alleges that the required number of shareholders did not vote to approve the challenged transaction or (2) the parties to that transaction were affiliated with each other (as is the case in a cash out merger). In *Steinberg v. Amplica, Inc.*, 729 P.2d 683 (Cal. 1986), a divided court held that appraisal was the exclusive remedy available to minority shareholders who claimed that their shares were undervalued in a merger that did not fall within the statutory exception. Analyzing the history of the merger and appraisal provisions of California corporation law, the court pointed out that one important benefit of the exclusivity provision was that it precluded obstructive "strike suits" by opportunistic minority shareholders.

Ohio's courts have adopted an approach that places even greater emphasis on certainty and predictability. *Armstrong v. Marathon Oil Co.*, 513 N.E.2d 776 (Ohio 1987), involved an appraisal proceeding brought by former shareholders of Marathon, which U.S. Steel had acquired in a two-tier takeover bid that Marathon's board had supported. U.S. Steel first acquired 51% of Marathon's stock by means of a $125 per share cash tender offer. It then effected a second-step merger in which it exchanged a bond with a projected market value of $88 for each Marathon share that had not been accepted in the tender offer. The dissenting Marathon shareholders claimed they were entitled to considerably more—at least the "blended value" of U.S. Steel's offer, or roughly $106 per share, and preferably a much higher price that reflected the estimated market value of Marathon's huge oil reserves.

The court held that where a corporation's stock was actively traded prior to a merger, the benchmark for determining the "fair cash value" of that stock—the term used in Ohio's appraisal statute—is the price at which the stock traded on the day before the merger. The court explained:

> By utilizing the stock market price as the beginning point of analysis in cases such as those before us now, a great many advantages will result to shareholders and corporations alike. One obvious benefit is that the scope of analysis is fairly narrowed such that the parties may, to a reasonable degree, predict the outcome of the proceedings. Pre-appraisal settlement then becomes the better alternative to litigation. The harassment potential inherent within an appraisal remedy as well as vexatious lawsuits (by those whose real goal is simply to receive more money for their stock) will, under the within clarified standard, become much more unlikely. Further, costs to all shareholders will be ultimately reduced by this more straightforward proceeding.

> The dissenting shareholder will bear fewer costs to exercise his legal rights since the scope of discovery and concomitant courtroom presentations will be lessened. Also, the costs to the majority shareholders will decrease since less corporate funds will go toward participation in the appraisal proceeding. Finally, a less complicated valuation proceeding will advance the goal of streamlining corporate reorganizations and, at the same time, protect the liquidity and value of the dissenting shareholder's stock.

*Id.* at 787–88.

The court further held that Ohio law required that the pre-merger market price of a company's stock be adjusted to eliminate the effects of a pending merger. Dissenting shareholders would not be entitled to any increase in value attributable to the pendency of the merger or any tender offer that has preceded it. Rather, if the pendency of the merger had caused the price of the company's stock to increase, a reduction from the pre-merger market price would be appropriate. Following this approach on remand, the trial court adjusted the pre-merger price of Marathon's stock, $75.75 per share, downward and found that its premerger "fair cash value" was $68.43 per share. *See Armstrong v. Marathon Oil Co.*, 583 N.E.2d 462 (Ohio App. 1990).

*Stepak v. Schey*, 553 N.E.2d 1072 (Ohio 1990) involved the question of when a shareholder can maintain a class action challenging a cash out merger as unfair because it allegedly involved self-dealing. A former shareholder of Scott & Fetzer charged that company's directors with having agreed to a cash out merger with Berkshire Hathaway Inc., at a price lower than other bidders might have been prepared to pay, in exchange for Berkshire Hathaway's agreement to allow those directors to receive $30 million in "golden parachute" payments. A three-judge plurality of the Ohio Supreme Court held that the plaintiff could not maintain this action because his objection to the merger essentially related to the price he had received for his stock. Citing *Armstrong*, the plurality continued: "The obvious benefit of this approach is that it makes more unlikely vexatious lawsuits by those whose goal is simply to receive more money for their stock." *Id*. at 1075. Two other justices concurred, reasoning that in the interest of promoting certainty and eliminating unnecessary litigation, a suit for breach of fiduciary duty of the kind alleged in the case should be allowed only if it was filed prior to the consummation of the merger. *Id*. at 1075–79.

Two justices dissented, arguing that the majority's decision confronted the minority shareholders with a Catch–22 situation:

> * * * If corporate management engages in a bid-rigging scheme which deprives shareholders of a premium over market price, a complaint cannot be made without challenging the price paid for the stock. But, dissatisfaction with the price paid does not automatically convert the action to a simple demand for the 'fair cash value' of a stockholder's shares. Here, the complaint clearly charges that the directors failed in their duty to obtain the best price possible for the sale of shares.

> * * * Had plaintiff pursued his action via appraisal, he would not have received any premium over market price. *Armstrong v. Marathon Oil Co.* (1987), 32 Ohio St.3d 397, 410, 513 N.E.2d 776, 788. Where the opportunity to obtain a premium price for sale of shares is destroyed by self-dealing officers of a corporation, there should be a remedy. Unfortunately, the majority's holding eliminates the possibility of remedy for that wrong.

*Id*. at 1079–80.

RMBCA § 13.02(b) essentially adopts *Weinberger*'s approach. It provides that appraisal is a dissenting shareholder's exclusive remedy "unless the action [giving rise to dissenters' rights] is unlawful or fraudulent with respect to the shareholder or the corporation." The Official Comment to RMBCA § 13.02(b) explains:

The theory underlying this section is as follows:

> * * * [W]hen a majority of shareholders has approved a corporate change, the corporation should be permitted to proceed even if a minority considers the change unwise or disadvantageous, and persuades a court that this is correct. Since dissenting shareholders

can obtain the fair value of their shares, they are protected from pecuniary loss. Thus in general terms an exclusivity principle is justified. But the prospect that shareholders may be "paid off" does not justify the corporation in proceeding unlawfully or fraudulently. If the corporation attempts an action in violation of the corporation law on voting, in violation of clauses in articles of incorporation prohibiting it, by deception of shareholders, or in violation of a fiduciary duty—to take some examples—the court's freedom to intervene should be unaffected by the presence or absence of dissenters' rights under this chapter. Because of the variety of situations in which unlawfulness and fraud may appear, this section makes no attempt to specify particular illustrations. Rather, it is designed to recognize and preserve the principles that have developed in the case law of Delaware, New York and other states with regard to the effect of dissenters' rights on other remedies of dissident shareholders.

*Rabkin v. Philip A. Hunt Chemical Corp.*, 498 A.2d 1099 (Del.1985) attempted to clarify *Weinberger*'s ruling as to when a cash out merger can be challenged as unfair. On March 1, 1983, Olin Corporation had purchased a 63.4% interest in Hunt, from Hunt's controlling shareholder, for $25 per share. As part of that transaction, Olin agreed to pay the same price if it sought to purchase the minority interest in Hunt within one year. Internal Olin documents made it clear that Olin always intended to acquire 100% of Hunt. However, Olin waited until three weeks after the one-year period had expired to propose a second-step merger in which the minority shareholder in Hunt would be cashed out at $20 per share.

Hunt's board created a special committee of three outside directors, which then hired an investment banker. The investment banker advised the committee that Hunt's stock had a fair value of between $19 and $25 a share and stated that Olin's offer therefore qualified as fair. The committee nonetheless sought an increase in the merger price. Olin declined to increase its offer and the committee then unanimously approved the merger as fair to Hunt's minority shareholders. All this was disclosed. Three Hunt minority shareholders then filed class actions challenging the merger as unfair.

The Court of Chancery dismissed those actions, ruling that, absent deception, *Weinberger* made appraisal the exclusive remedy available to dissatisfied minority shareholders. The Delaware Supreme Court reversed, stating that "the holding in *Weinberger* is broader than the scope accorded it by the trial court." *Id.* at 1100. The court continued:

> [W]e find that the trial court erred in dismissing the plaintiffs' actions for failure to state a claim upon which relief could be granted. As we read the complaints and the proposed amendments, they assert a conscious intent by Olin, as the majority shareholder of Hunt, to deprive the Hunt minority of the same bargain that Olin made with Hunt's former majority shareholder, Turner and Newall.

But for Olin's allegedly unfair manipulation, the plaintiffs contend, this bargain also was due them. In short, the defendants are charged with bad faith which goes beyond issues of "mere inadequacy of price." *Cole v. National Cash Credit Association*, Del.Ch., 156 A. 183, 187–88 (1931). In *Weinberger* we specifically relied upon this aspect of *Cole* in acknowledging the imperfections of an appraisal where circumstances of this sort are present.

Necessarily, this will require the Court of Chancery to closely focus upon *Weinberger*'s mandate of entire fairness based on a careful analysis of both the fair price and fair dealing aspects of a transaction. We recognize that this can present certain practical problems, since stockholders may invariably claim that the price being offered is the result of unfair dealings. However, we think that plaintiffs will be tempered in this approach by the prospect that an ultimate judgment in defendants' favor may have cost plaintiffs their unperfected appraisal rights. Moreover, our courts are not without a degree of sophistication in such matters. A balance must be struck between sustaining complaints averring faithless acts, which taken as true would constitute breaches of fiduciary duties that are reasonably related to and have a substantial impact upon the price offered, and properly dismissing those allegations questioning judgmental factors of valuation. Otherwise, we face the anomalous result that stockholders who are eliminated without appraisal rights can bring class actions, while in other cases a squeezed-out minority is limited to an appraisal, provided there was no deception, regardless of the degree of procedural unfairness employed to take their shares. Without that balance, *Weinberger*'s concern for entire fairness loses all force.

Id. at 1107–08. However, the minority shareholders' triumph in *Rabkin* proved to be short lived. On remand, the Court of Chancery found for Olin, concluding that it had not deliberately timed the merger to avoid its one-year price commitment. *Rabkin v. Olin Corp.*, 1990 WL 47648 (Del.Ch.1990).

*Cede & Co. v. Technicolor, Inc.*, 542 A.2d 1182 (Del.1988), also addressed the relation between the appraisal remedy and an action alleging a cash out merger was unfair. A cashed out shareholder who had exercised dissenters' rights filed a second suit challenging the fairness of the cash out merger on the basis of a later-discovered fraud. In a decision allowing the second suit to proceed, the Delaware Supreme Court stated:

An appraisal proceeding is a limited legislative remedy intended to provide shareholders dissenting from a merger on grounds of inadequacy of the offering price with a judicial determination of the intrinsic worth (fair value) of their stock. Value was traditionally arrived at by determining "the true or intrinsic value" of the shareholders' proportionate interest in the company, valued on a going-concern rather than a liquidated basis. *See Universal City Studios, Inc. v. Francis I. duPont & Co.*, Del.Supr., 334 A.2d 216

(1975); *Tri–Continental Corp. v. Battye*, Del.Supr., 74 A.2d 71, 72 (1950).

*Weinberger* broadens or liberalizes the process for determining the "fair value" of the company's outstanding shares by including all generally accepted techniques of valuation used in the financial community, thereby supplementing the previously employed rigid or stylized approach to valuation. *See* 457 A.2d at 712–13. *Weinberger* directs that this "liberalized approach" to appraisal shall be used to determine the value of a cashed-out minority's share interest on the day of the merger, reflecting all relevant information regarding the company and its shares. *Id.* at 713. This includes information concerning future events not arising solely "from the accomplishment or expectation of the merger," 8 Del.C. § 262(h), which, if made public, can affect the current value of the shares and "which are known or susceptible of proof as of the date of the merger.* * * *" 457 A.2d at 713; 8 Del.C. § 262(h).[8]

In contrast to appraisal, entire fairness—fair price and fair dealing—is the focal point against which the merger transaction and consideration arrived at can be measured. *See Rabkin*, 498 A.2d at 1106 (unfair dealing claims, based on breaches of the duties of loyalty and care, raise "issues which an appraisal cannot address"); *Weinberger*, 457 A.2d at 714 ("[t]he appraisal remedy * * * may not be adequate in certain cases, particularly where fraud, misrepresentation, self-dealing, deliberate waste of corporate assets, or gross and palpable overreaching are involved"). It is important to emphasize that "the test for fairness is not a bifurcated one as between fair dealing and price. *All aspects of the issue must be examined as a whole* since the question is one of *fairness*." Id. at 711 (emphasis added).

To summarize, in a section 262 appraisal action the only litigable issue is the determination of the value of the appraisal petitioners' shares on the date of the merger, the only party defendant is the surviving corporation and the only relief available is a judgment against the surviving corporation for the fair value of the dissenters'

**8.** Information and insight not communicated to the market may not be reflected in stock prices; thus, minority shareholders being cashed out may be deprived of part of the true investment value of their shares. *See generally* Robert Charles Clark, CORPORATE LAW 507 (1986); Fama, *Efficient Capital Markets: A Review of Theory and Empirical Work*, 25 J.FIN. 383 (1970). The issue we are addressing is not the manipulation of the transaction, see *Rabkin*, 498 A.2d at 1104–05, nor the suppression or misstatement of material information by insiders defrauding the market, *see Basic Inc. v. Levinson*, 485 U.S. 224, 108 S.Ct. 978, 99 L.Ed.2d 194 (1988). Instead, we recognize that the majority may have insight into their company's future based primarily on bits and pieces of nonmaterial information that have value as a totality. *See* Clark, *supra* at 508. It is this information that, if available in a statutory appraisal proceeding, the Court of Chancery must evaluate to determine if future earnings will affect the fair value of shares on the day of the merger. *See* 8 Del.C. § 262(h). To obtain this information the appraisal petitioner must be permitted to conduct a "detailed investigation into the facts that is warranted by the acute conflict of interest and the potential for investor harm that is inherent in freezeout transactions." Clark, *supra* at 508.

shares. In contrast, a fraud action asserting fair dealing and fair price claims affords an expansive remedy and is brought against the alleged wrongdoers to provide whatever relief the facts of a particular case may require. In evaluating claims involving violations of entire fairness, the trial court may include in its relief any damages sustained by the shareholders. *See Rabkin,* 498 A.2d at 1107; *Weinberger,* 457 A.2d at 713. In a fraud claim, the approach to determining relief may be the same as that employed in determining fair value under 8 Del.C. § 262. However, an appraisal action may not provide a complete remedy for unfair dealing or fraud because a damage award in a fraud action may include "rescissory damages if the [trier of fact] considers them susceptible of proof and a remedy appropriate to all issues of fairness before him." *Weinberger,* 457 A.2d at 714. *Weinberger* and *Rabkin* make this clear distinction in terms of the relief available in a section 262 action as opposed to a fraud in the merger suit.

*Id.* at 1186–88.

# STRINGER v. CAR DATA SYSTEMS, INC.

314 Or. 576, 841 P.2d 1183 (1992).

PETERSON, JUSTICE.

This case involves what courts and commentators have described as a "cash-out merger," a "squeeze-out merger," or a "freeze-out merger." In this opinion, we will use the term "cash-out merger." Under ORS 60.551 to 60.594, majority shareholders may eliminate minority shareholders of a corporation by merger procedures that allow dissenting minority shareholders to receive "fair value" for their shares.

Plaintiffs were minority shareholders in Consumer Data Systems, Inc. (CDS), an Oregon corporation. They filed this action, claiming a violation of various rights incident to a cash-out merger involving CDS and another corporation, Car Data Systems, Inc. (Car Data). Plaintiffs allege that other CDS shareholders and directors breached a fiduciary duty owed to plaintiffs as minority shareholders. They seek compensatory and punitive damages. The trial court dismissed their complaint for failure to state a claim, ORCP 21 A(8), and the Court of Appeals affirmed. *Stringer v. Car Data Systems, Inc.,* 108 Or.App. 523, 816 P.2d 677, *modified on reconsideration,* 110 Or.App. 14, 821 P.2d 418 (1991). We affirm the decision of the Court of Appeals, but on different grounds.

Before turning to the facts, a brief summary of cash-out mergers is appropriate.

At common law, each shareholder of a corporation was considered to have a "vested right" in the corporation. As a result, the rule in many jurisdictions was that a single shareholder could veto a proposed business combination.

Legislatures, courts, and commentators found that the right of a single shareholder to veto business transactions trammeled the concept of corporate democracy. The veto was therefore eliminated. The general rule today is that decision-making by the majority must take precedence over the objection of a lone dissenter. *See* Revised Model Business Corporation Act § 13.02 (1984) (the "Model Act"); ORS 60.554(1).

The rejection of a minority veto and the recognition of majority rule has not occurred without regard for the potential abuses of a majority's power directed against minority interests. The linchpin of a dissenter's protection in merger cases is found in the statutory appraisal remedy. This remedy is designed to provide statutory protection to those minority shareholders who do not concur with the decision of the majority shareholders.

One device commonly used to eliminate minority shareholders who disagree with the majority shareholders about corporate decision-making is the cash-out merger. * * * Undeniably, such mergers have a coercive element.

> "Freezeouts, by definition, are coercive: minority stockholders are bound by majority rule to accept cash or debt in exchange for their common shares, even though the price they receive may be less than the value they assign to those shares. But this alone does not render freezeouts objectionable. Majority rule always entails coercion. It is, nonetheless, an acceptable rule of governance if all members of the voting constituency share a common goal and if all will be identically affected by the outcome of the vote. In the ordinary arm's-length merger negotiated by the managements of two unrelated corporations, stockholders of the merged entity are properly viewed as having a common interest in maximizing the returns on their stock, whether through periodic dividends or through sale or liquidation of the firm. Once approved by a statutory majority, the terms of such a merger will apply equally to each of the merging company's stockholders, and the common decision will satisfy the principle that all members of the class be treated alike. Majority rule is thus an appropriate means of deciding whether an arm's-length merger should be allowed, and it is of course a universal feature of the corporate law. Despite the element of coercion, dissenters to such a merger are bound, or remitted to an appraisal proceeding, by vote of a majority of their class, because it is assumed that any disagreement among the stockholders involves nothing more than a practical judgment about the best way to achieve a common aim." Brudney & Chirelstein, *A Restatement of Corporate Freezeouts*, 87 YALE L.J. 1354, 1357–58 (1978).

Dissenters from a proposed merger have a right to demand payment for their shares. ORS 60.571. If they do so, the corporation is then required to pay each dissenter "the fair value of the shareholder's shares, plus accrued interest." ORS 60.577(1). If the parties do not agree as to fair value for the shares, the corporation "shall commence a proceeding * * * to determine the fair value of the shares and accrued interest." ORS 60.591(1). A court then determines the fair value of the shares. The appraisal procedure is the sole remedy for dissenting shareholders in the absence of "unlawful or fraudulent" conduct. ORS 60.554(2) provides: "A shareholder entitled to dissent and obtain payment for the shareholder's shares under ORS 60.551 to 60.594 may not challenge the corporate action creating the shareholder's entitlement unless the action is unlawful or fraudulent with respect to the shareholder or the corporation."

* * *

Plaintiffs' complaint alleges that plaintiffs Stringer and Schubert and two other shareholders owned 43 percent of the shares of CDS. Thirty-two individuals, including the six directors of CDS, owned the remaining 57 percent of CDS. According to the complaint, "[i]n late 1988 or early 1989, the CDS Directors and the larger CDS shareholders, Donald Smith, Mark Kallenberger and Lawrence Custer * * *, decided to squeeze the Minority Shareholders out of their ownership in CDS and to offer them a nominal sum for their stock, which sum was significantly below the fair market value of the stock." The directors and larger shareholders formed a new company that subsequently became Car Data, transferred their shares in CDS to Car Data in exchange for its stock, and solicited all the remaining shareholders, except for the four minority shareholders, to participate in their plan. A total of 32 CDS shareholders transferred their stock, amounting to 57 percent of the CDS shares, to Car Data. Car Data shareholders then voted for a merger between Car Data and CDS. Pursuant to the merger proposal, each CDS shareholder would receive $0.002 per share. As owner of 57 percent of CDS, Car Data voted for the merger. The merger was approved over the objections of plaintiffs and two other minority shareholders.

Plaintiffs claimed that their shares were worth at least $0.10 per share and refused to accept the $0.002 offered them. Car Data rejected plaintiffs demand for $0.10 per share and instituted an appraisal proceeding in the circuit court pursuant to ORS 60.591. Plaintiffs instituted this action in the circuit court against Car Data, CDS, the 32 individual former shareholders of CDS and the present shareholders of Car Data (the shareholder defendants), and the lawyers who represented both CDS and Car Data during the merger process. Plaintiffs' complaint contained * * * a claim for breach of fiduciary duty against all defendants, in which they prayed for rescission of the merger and appointment of a receiver, or, alternatively, for compensatory damages and an award of punitive damages against Car Data and the shareholder defendants * * *.

The circuit court stayed the proceedings in the present case pending trial of the appraisal case. The appraisal case was concluded, and this case then proceeded.*

* * *

---

* The court found that the fair value of       CDS stock, as of the merger date, was $0.07

As stated above, ORS 60.554(2) provides that a dissenting shareholder "may not challenge the corporate action creating the shareholder's entitlement unless the action is unlawful or fraudulent with respect to the shareholder or the corporation." The dispositive question here is whether plaintiffs have alleged facts that would establish that defendants' conduct was "unlawful or fraudulent" within the meaning of ORS 60.554(2).

We start with the observation that this court may not question the wisdom of the Legislative Assembly in enacting the Oregon Business Corporation Act. That law drew upon the Model Business Corporation Act and contains procedures for majority shareholders to "squeeze out" minority shareholders. The legislative decision involved considerations affecting both majority shareholders and dissenting shareholders. "The accompanying proposals as a whole are designed to benefit both minority shareholders and controlling shareholders. Minority shareholders benefit because the assertion of their rights is made easier, and penalties are introduced for vexatious obstruction by corporate management. Controlling shareholders benefit directly and indirectly. They benefit directly by the added incentives for dissenters to settle without a judicial appraisal. They benefit indirectly because the provision of an adequate appraisal right diminishes the justification for courts to enjoin or set aside corporate changes because of the absence of an 'adequate remedy at law,' or because the corporate action 'would operate as a fraud.'" Conard, *Amendments of Model Business Corporation Act Affecting Dissenters' Rights* (Sections 73, 74, 80, and 81), 33 Bus.Law. 2587, 2593 (1978).

\* \* \*

Plaintiffs' complaint in this case alleged neither fraud nor misleading representations that were relied upon by plaintiffs. From plaintiffs' complaint, one can infer only that the amount paid by CDS was unfair and unreasonably low, in an attempt to avoid paying fair value to plaintiffs for their shares.

Cases such as this are the very kind addressed by the statutory scheme. With the exception of punitive damages, every element of damages that plaintiffs seek herein is recoverable under ORS 60.551 to 60.594. The complaint contains no allegations of fact that, if proved, would support a punitive damages award. The legislative plan expressly provides for recovery of attorney fees and expenses and of expert fees and expenses for arbitrary or vexatious action, or actions "not in good faith" in connection with the cash-out merger. *See* 60.594(1) and (2). This provision suggests to us that the legislature intended that, even if the corporation offers too little money to the dissenters for their shares "arbitrarily, vexatiously or not in good faith," ORS 60.594(2), and if the disagreement is solely as to the value of the shares, statutory appraisal is the exclusive remedy.

per share. *Chrome Data Systems, Inc. v. Stringer*, 109 Or.App. 513, 820 P.2d 831 (1991).

The last clause of ORS 60.551(4) also is significant. To the extent, if any, that plaintiffs seek damages for "any appreciation or depreciation in anticipation of the corporate action," those damages can be considered if "exclusion would be inequitable." We agree with the Delaware Supreme Court that "there is a legislative intent to fully compensate shareholders for whatever their loss may be, subject only to the narrow limitation that one can not take speculative effects of the merger into account." *Weinberger v. UOP, Inc.*, 457 A.2d 701, 714 (Del.1983). * * *

Plaintiffs' complaint clearly alleges a disagreement as to valuation, and we also can infer payment by Car Data of an unreasonably low price. Where the allegations show only a disagreement as to price, however, with no allegations that permit any inference of self-dealing, fraud, deliberate waste of corporate assets, misrepresentation, or other unlawful conduct, the remedy afforded by ORS 60.551 to 60.594 is exclusive. That is true even if the majority shareholders acted arbitrarily or vexatiously or not in good faith. *Stepak v. Schey*, 51 Ohio St.3d 8, 553 N.E.2d 1072, 1075 (1990) (remedy for breach of fiduciary duty involving only the price that a shareholder receives is limited to appraisal statute); *Schloss Associates v. C & O Ry.*, 73 Md.App. 727, 536 A.2d 147, 158 (1988) ("What we have then is essentially a complaint over price—the amount and how it was established—for which the statutory appraisal right is a wholly adequate remedy."); *Green v. Santa Fe Industries, Inc.*, 70 N.Y.2d 244, 519 N.Y.S.2d 793, 800, 514 N.E.2d 105, 112 (1987) ("Here, * * * all of the actions with which defendant corporations are charged relate to price; there are no claims asserted against individual defendants based on dual representation; and it cannot be said that the 'defendants are charged with bad faith which goes beyond issues of "mere inadequacy of price". *Cole v. National Cash Credit Association* 18 Del.Ch. 47, 156 A. 183, 187–88 [1931]' ").

It may be that the $0.002 offer was insulting to plaintiffs, and it may even have been motivated by bad faith. But, because the facts alleged in the complaint, if established, support no claim for damages apart from the fair value of the shares, we believe that the legislature intended that dissenting shareholders in the position of plaintiffs be limited to their remedies under the appraisal statutes.

The decision of the Court of Appeals and the judgment of the circuit court are affirmed.

UNIS, JUSTICE, concurring in part, dissenting in part.

The issue in this case is whether plaintiffs' complaint states a claim for breach of fiduciary duty and civil conspiracy. I cannot agree with the majority's holding that plaintiffs' complaint fails to state a claim under either theory. I would hold that plaintiffs' complaint states a claim for breach of fiduciary duty and civil conspiracy against all defendants except defendant attorneys. * * *

Because plaintiffs' complaint was dismissed for failure to state a claim pursuant to ORCP 21 A(8), this court must accept the allegations in the complaint as "true." Moreover, as the majority recognizes, we must give plaintiffs the benefit of all favorable inferences that may be drawn from the allegations. Applying these principles, the following seems to be a fair summary of those pleaded "facts" and favorable inferences to be drawn therefrom.

Plaintiffs Stringer and Schubert and three others founded CDS in 1986. Stock was sold in the corporation until, in 1989, there were 36 shareholders. Stringer and Schubert, along with the two nominal defendants in this case, retained about 43 percent of the stock. The stock was sold at about 10 cents a share during this period.

According to the complaint, CDS was successful during this period, and revenues were increasing faster than expenses. In early 1989, again according to the complaint, a third party made a written offer to purchase CDS at a price substantially above what was subsequently offered during the "squeeze-out" merger at issue here. CDS, by vote of the majority of shareholders, rejected the third party's offer.

The complaint alleges the following: "In late 1988 or early 1989, the CDS Directors and the larger CDS shareholders, Donald Smith, Mark Kallenberger and Lawrence Custer (collectively referred to herein as the 'Controlling Shareholders'), decided to squeeze the Minority Shareholders out of their ownership in CDS and to offer then a nominal sum for their stock, which sum was significantly below fair market value of the stock (the 'Plan'). *The principal purpose of the Plan was to deprive the Minority Shareholders of most of the present value of their stock in CDS* and to deprive the Minority Shareholders of their share of the anticipated significant rise in the value of CDS stock over the next few years." (Emphasis added). * * *

The complaint also alleges that, in furtherance of the plan, the CDS directors and the "Controlling Shareholders" transferred all their CDS stock to Car Data and then solicited the participation of all CDS shareholders, except plaintiffs and the two nominal defendants. Once Car Data had obtained by these means a majority of the stock of CDS, a merger was proposed between CDS and Car Data.

As majority shareholder of CDS, Car Data approved the merger with a stock value of $0.002 per share, a price far below that previously offered by the third party. The stockholders of Car Data, i.e., the board of directors of CDS and all the former shareholders of CDS except plaintiffs and the two nominal defendants, also approved the merger. Plaintiffs allege that, as a result of this vote, the minority shareholders received $9,900 for stock with a fair market value of $290,000.

BREACH OF FIDUCIARY DUTY CLAIM

In plaintiffs' claim for breach of fiduciary duty, plaintiffs allege that the above acts by the directors, the collective majority of CDS shareholders and Car Data, constitute a breach of their fiduciary duty to the minority shareholders, including plaintiffs. Plaintiffs seek, inter alia, rescission of the merger or, in the alternative, damages equal to the fair market value of plaintiffs' proportionate share of defendant Car Data on the date of trial, plus punitive damages.

The majority['s] * * * conclusion, in my judgment, ignores allegations that we must accept on an ORCP 21 A(8) motion as "true" pleaded "facts," and it ignores inferences favorable to plaintiffs that may be drawn from those allegations.

* * *

The statutory provisions relating to the appraisal procedure are subject to ORS 60.554(2) and must be read in conjunction with that provision. ORS 60.554(2), which is taken from RMBCA section 13.02(b), provides that a dissenting shareholder "may not challenge the corporate action creating the shareholder's entitlement *unless the action is unlawful or fraudulent with respect to the shareholder or the corporation.*" (Emphasis added.) * * *

* * *

* * * [N]one of the fiduciary obligations owed by corporate directors and majority shareholders were satisfied in this case. Plaintiffs Stringer and Schubert alleged that the directors of CDS, acting with three certain larger CDS shareholders, developed a plan to squeeze out plaintiffs for a nominal sum, a sum significantly below the fair market value of plaintiffs' shares. The squeeze-out merger was implemented just after the majority shareholders had rejected a third-party offer to purchase substantially all of CDS assets at a price substantially greater than the $0.002 per share price set in the squeeze-out merger. The squeeze-out merger would have permitted the majority shareholders, which includes the six directors of CDS, to sell the CDS assets at this higher price without sharing any of the proceeds with the minority shareholders.

Such conduct by directors and the large shareholders does not meet duties of good faith and fair dealing imposed by Oregon law. *See, e.g.*, *Zidell v. Zidell, Inc.*, 277 Or. 413, 418, 560 P.2d 1086 (1977) ("those in control of corporate affairs have fiduciary duties of good faith and fair dealing toward minority shareholders"). With respect to the minority shareholders of CDS and, in particular, plaintiffs, the allegations of the complaint are, in my view, sufficient to permit an inference of self-dealing and gross, palpable, overreaching conduct—a violation of the fiduciary duty owed to plaintiffs by CDS directors and majority shareholders. As such, the case should not have been dismissed at the pleading stage for failure to state a claim.

* * *

The inference fairly drawn from the complaint is that there was no "merger" in this case to which one could apply an appraisal remedy. Car Data, the complaint alleges, was no more than the alter ego of CDS's own directors and several of its largest shareholders. Its purpose, again according to the complaint, was to create a majority voting block to devalue the corporation's stock.

Had the three larger majority shareholders ("Controlling Shareholders") conspired with the CDS directors to reject a legitimate purchase offer and then sold all CDS's assets to Car Data at far below market value so that they could resell Car Data at a windfall price, I do not believe that the majority would find it as difficult to find "overreaching." Yet, in this case, an allegation that certain shareholders and the directors of CDS created a paper corporation in order to accomplish the same result through a "merger" is considered insufficient. I do not believe that the drafters of the RMBCA or the Oregon legislature intended to create a vehicle for this kind of business practice simply because they wished to facilitate legitimate business mergers when there is a disagreement among shareholders over the wisdom of the merger.

\* \* \*

FADELEY, J., joins in this opinion.

---

Assuming plaintiffs had prevailed in *Stringer*, to what relief should they have been entitled, over and above the $0.07 per share they received in their appraisal action? Put differently, was the real issue here not whether appraisal was the exclusive remedy available to plaintiffs, but whether the valuation approach used in plaintiffs' appraisal action took account of all the factors that should have been considered in valuing plaintiffs' stock.

# D. FAIR DEALING

*Weinberger* suggests that a court assessing the fairness of a cash out merger should consider whether the merger was the product of fair dealing and whether it involved a fair price. Fair dealing requires inquiry into the process by which the transaction was negotiated and approved. Fair price involves a review of the substantive terms of the merger.

Courts often seem more comfortable dealing with issues of process than with issues of price, especially when there is no ready market for the product in question (the stock of S, in a cash out merger). In that context, determining a fair price often calls for a type of business judgment that courts traditionally are reluctant to make. On the other hand, if there has been fair dealing, it is easier for a court to conclude that the price is also fair. In other words, a fair process may well be indicative, if not dispositive, of a fair price. Thus, it would seem to follow that if the parties to a cash out merger employed a process that replicated (or better yet involved) the operation of market forces, a court should conclude that the requirements of fair dealing and fair price both have been satisfied.

## 1. USING MARKET FORCES TO ENSURE FAIR DEALING

Two fundamental characteristics of cash out mergers increase the potential that they will be exploitative. In most cash out situations, the control person knows more about the corporation involved—i.e., the property to be sold—than do the shareholders who will be cashed out; in other transactions, the person selling property often knows (or is a position to know) more about that property than does the buyer. In addition, in most cash out situations, the control person can block or obstruct bids by others, while in most other settings, a person interested in selling property can solicit bids from as many potential buyers as she wishes and can decide not to sell if none of the bids pleases her.

In concept, these characteristics largely could be eliminated by treating every proposal for a cash out merger as the equivalent of a decision to sell the company and by making the company's control person subject to a *Revlon* duty to get the best price for all the the stockholders. Courts, however, have rejected this approach in situations where a corporation has a majority shareholder. *Bershad v. Curtiss–Wright Corp.*, 535 A.2d 840, 845 (Del.1987), held that the proposition that a majority shareholder has "an affirmative duty * * * to auction the corporation when seeking to cash-out the minority" was "unsupported by any accepted principle of law." The court explained:

> Stockholders in Delaware corporations have a right to control and vote their shares in their own interest. They are limited only by any fiduciary duty owed to their shareholders. * * * Clearly, a stockholder is under no duty to sell its holdings in a corporation, even if it is a majority shareholder, merely because the sale would profit the minority.

*Id.*

In contrast, when a group that owns less than a majority of a company's stock seeks to cash out that company's public shareholders, an auction is possible and, under *Revlon*, would seem to be required. See *Paramount Communications, Inc. v. QVC Network, Inc.* (Chapter 22).

### Note: Mendel v. Carroll

In *Mendel v. Carroll*, 651 A.2d 297 (Del.Ch.1994), a special committee of outside directors of Katy Industries, Inc. (Katy) had agreed to support a cash-out of Katy's public shareholders by the Carroll family, which owned approximately 50% of Katy's outstanding stock. The cash out price was to be $25.75 per share. Pensler Capital Corp. (Pensler), an unrelated party, then made a bid to acquire all the stock of Katy for $27.80 per share, subject to Katy granting Pensler an option to acquire 20 percent of Katy's stock at the same price. The purpose of the option was to dilute the Carroll family's controlling interest so that Pensler could acquire sufficient stock from public shareholders to gain control of Katy. The board declined to grant the option to Pensler. Minority shareholders of Katy then sued to compel it to do so. The shareholders claimed that by agreeing to accept the Carroll's offer, the board had put Katy up for sale. Consequently, the shareholders argued, the board had a *Revlon* duty to take all reasonable actions, including granting the option, to secure the highest available price for Katy's shareholders.

Chancellor Allen declined to order the board to grant the option. He noted that, were this a case where the "controlling shareholder is abusing its power and is exploiting or threatening to exploit the vulnerability of minority shareholders, * * * the board might permissibly take such an action." *Id.* at 304. However, Chancellor Allen concluded, this was not such a case. The Carrolls already controlled Katy; consequently; they did not need to pay a "control premium." Pensler did. Consequently, the two transactions proposed by the Carrolls and Pensler were fundamentally different. Chancellor Allen continued:

> * * * There is nothing in the present record * * that suggests to me that the $25.75 price the Carroll Group proposed to pay for the public shares was an inadequate or unfair price for the non-controlling stock. For the reasons stated above, the fact that Pensler was willing to pay more for all of the shares does not, logically, support an inference that the Carroll proposal for the non-controlling public shares was not fair.

> * * *

> In my opinion, far from "*Revlon* duties" requiring such action, the Katy board could not, consistent with its fiduciary obligations to all of the stockholders of Katy Industries, have issued the dilutive option for the purpose sought in this instance. Therefore, that the board considered the matter and declined to do so could in no event be considered to constitute a breach of duty to the minority shareholders.

*Id.* at 306–07.

## ALI, PRINCIPLES OF CORPORATE GOVERNANCE (1994)

### § 5.15. Transfer of Control in Which a Director or Principal Senior Executive Is Interested

(a) If directors of principal senior executives of a corporation are interested in a transaction in control or a tender offer that results in a transfer of control of the corporation to another person, then those directors or principal senior executives have the burden of proving that the transaction was fair to the shareholders of the corporation unless (1) the transaction involves a transfer by a controlling shareholder or (2) the conditions of Subsection (b) are satisfied.

(b) If in connection with a transaction described in Subsection (a) involving a publicly held corporation:

(1) public disclosure of the proposed transaction is made;

(2) responsible persons who express an interest are provided relevant information concerning the corporation and given a reasonable opportunity to submit a competing proposal;

(3) the transaction is authorized in advance by disinterested directors after the procedures set forth in Subsections (1) and (2) have been complied with; and

(4) the transaction is authorized or ratified by disinterested shareholders (or, if the transaction is effected by a tender offer, the offer is accepted by disinterested shareholders), after disclosure concerning the conflict of interest and the transaction has been made;

then a party challenging the transaction has the burden of proving that the terms of the transaction are equivalent to a waste of corporate assets.

COMMENT:

\* \* \* No recourse to the market for corporate control for price protection is possible in connection with a freeze-out transaction because the presence of a controlling shareholder eliminates the possibility of a competitive bid. In the context of a management buyout, however, the market for corporate control is potentially available to police the fairness of the non-arm's-length division of the gain from the management buyout transaction. If the price to be paid for the corporation is too low, the possibility exists that it will evoke a competing bid, thereby creating an incentive for management to fairly price the transaction in the first place.

Under current circumstances, there is substantial reason to doubt that bids competing with the management-sponsored bid will be forthcoming with sufficient frequency. Although announcement of the terms of proposed management buyout often has given rise to a competing bid, a party that might contemplate bidding against a management-sponsored group suffers under significant information and timing disadvantages. Most important, the management-sponsored group, and its financing sources, have access to substantial, often non-public, information concerning the corporation at essentially no cost. Additionally, even if the potential competing bidder has the means to develop independent sources of information, the opportunity for the management-sponsored group to choose the moment when it makes its offer, and to act first, puts any potential competitor at a disadvantage.

Section 5.15 sets out governance rules that will allow the market for corporate control to operate as a realistic protection against non-arm's-length division of gains from a transaction in control of the corporation to which its directors or principal senior executives are parties. Section 5.15(b) provides a safe harbor for transactions that are subjected to an adequate market test of the fairness of their terms. \* \* \*

\* \* \*

Section 5.15(b) reflects two basic premises. The first is that a market review of the fairness of the terms of a management buyout is preferable to judicial review. Thus, when the requirements of § 5.15(b) are satisfied, judicial review is limited to a waste standard in contrast to the fairness review contemplated by § 5.15(a). The second is that before the market for corporate control can serve as a meaningful check on the pricing of management buyout transactions, and thus serve as a substitute for a judicial fairness review, the disadvantages under which potential competitive bidders currently operate must be significantly reduced. To this end, § 5.15(b) establishes three transactional requirements that must be met before market review can be substituted for judicial review.

## 2. FAIR DEALING IN THE ABSENCE OF A MARKET

*Weinberger* gives some guidance as to how fair dealing can be promoted in parent-subsidiary mergers. Footnote 7 states that "fairness, in this context, can be equated to conduct by a theoretical, wholly independent board of directors," and notes that "[a]lthough perfection is not possible, or expected," the result could have been better "if UOP had appointed an independent negotiating committee of its outside directors to deal with Signal at arm's length." The court also held that if a merger is "approved by an informed vote of a majority of the minority shareholders, * * * the burden entirely shifts to the plaintiff to show that the transaction was unfair to the minority." The court also held that those relying on a shareholder vote to shift the burden of proof must show that they fully disclosed all material facts. Issues relating to directors' and controlling shareholders' disclosure obligations are discussed in Chapter 18.

As might be expected, subsequent to *Weinberger* it became common for corporations involved in cash out mergers to create "independent negotiating committees of [their] outside directors" to negotiate with controlling shareholders and to condition such mergers on the approval of a majority of the minority shareholders. Recall *Virginia Bankshares, Inc. v. Sandberg* (Chapter 18). Post-*Weinberger* decisions have assessed the performance of such committees and have considered what weight to attach to shareholder approval.

*Rosenblatt v. Getty Oil Company*, 493 A.2d 929 (Del.1985) involved a challenge to the fairness of a merger between Getty Oil Company and its majority-owned subsidiary, Skelly Oil Company. Skelly had appointed a committee of unaffiliated directors to negotiate the merger. The committee and Getty's representatives differed sharply concerning the value of the two companies' assets. Finally, the negotiators asked DeGolyer & McNaughton, a highly respected petroleum engineering firm, to prepare an estimate of asset values. The two companies then agreed to a merger exchange ratio based on that firm's estimate.

A substantial majority of Skelly's minority shareholders subsequently approved the merger. As a consequence, the Delaware Supreme Court held, pursuant to *Weinberger*, that the shareholders challenging the merger bore the burden of proving the merger was unfair. But the court also held, without much explanation, that the standard applicable to the merger remained entire fairness, not waste.

*Rosenblatt* also addressed one procedural issue that had provoked controversy after *Weinberger*: the duty of the parent to disclose its own internal reports. In *Rosenblatt*, the plaintiffs argued that an internal Getty report, projecting reduced Getty earnings, was improperly withheld from Skelly, likening this action to the treatment of the Arledge–Chitiea report in *Weinberger*. The court cautioned, "While it has been suggested that *Weinberger* stands for the proposition that a majority shareholder must under all circumstances disclose its top bid to the minority, that clearly is a misconception of what we said there. The sole basis for our conclusions in *Weinberger* regarding the non-disclosure of the Arledge–Chitiea report was because Signal appointed directors on UOP's board, who thus stood on both sides of the transaction, violated their undiminished duty of loyalty to UOP. It had nothing to do with Signal's duty, as the majority stockholder, to the other shareholders of UOP." *Id.* at 939.

# KAHN v. LYNCH COMMUNICATION SYS., INC.

## 638 A.2d 1110 (Del.1994).

[Lynch Communication Systems, Inc. (Lynch), a Delaware corporation, designed and manufactured electronic telecommunications equipment, primarily for sale to telephone operating companies. Alcatel U.S.A. Corp. (Alcatel), a holding company, is a subsidiary of Alcatel (S.A.), a French company involved in public telecommunications, business communications, electronics, and optronics, which itself was a subsidiary of Compagnie Generale d'Electricitie (CGE), another French corporation.

In 1981, Alcatel acquired 30.6 percent of Lynch's common stock pursuant to a stock purchase agreement in which Lynch agreed to amend its certificate of incorporation to require an 80 percent affirmative vote of its shareholders for approval of any business combination. Alcatel also obtained proportional representation on the Lynch board of directors and the right to purchase 40% of any equity securities offered by Lynch to third parties. The agreement also precluded Alcatel from holding more than 45 percent of Lynch's stock prior to October 1, 1986.

In the spring of 1986, Lynch's management recommended that Lynch acquire Telco Systems, Inc. (Telco), which possessed fiber optics technology that Lynch needed to remain competitive in the rapidly changing telecommunications field. Because of the supermajority voting provision, Lynch needed Alcatel's consent to acquire Telco. Alcatel advised Ellsworth F. Dertinger ("Dertinger"), CEO and chairman of the board of directors of Lynch, that it opposed Lynch's acquisition of Telco. Alcatel proposed that Lynch acquire Celwave Systems, Inc. ("Celwave"), an indirect subsidiary of CGE that manufactured and sold telephone wire, cable and related products.

At a Lynch board meeting held on August 1, 1986, Dertinger said that Celwave would not be of interest to Lynch if Alcatel did not own it. The Lynch board, five of whose eleven members were designees of

Alcatel, nonetheless voted unanimously to establish an Independent Committee, consisting of Hubert L. Kertz ("Kertz"), Paul B. Wineman ("Wineman"), and Stuart M. Beringer ("Beringer"), to make recommendations concerning the appropriate terms and conditions of a combination with Celwave. Alcatel's investment banking firm, Dillon, Read & Co., Inc. ("Dillon Read") subsequently proposed to the Independent Committee that Lynch acquire Celwave in a stock-for-stock merger. After the Committee's investment bankers advised that Dillon Read's proposal overvalued Celwave, the Committee, on October 31, 1986, voted to reject Dillon Read's proposal and to oppose a merger of Celwave into Lynch.

Alcatel responded on November 4, 1986, by simultaneously withdrawing the Celwave proposal and offering to acquire the 56.7% of Lynch's outstanding stock that it did not own for $14 cash per share.

Three days later, the Lynch board authorized the Independent Committee to negotiate with Alcatel the terms of its cash merger offer. The Committee began that process by concluding that Alcatel's $14 per share offer was inadequate.

On November 12, 1986, Beringer, as chairman of the Independent Committee, made a counteroffer to Alcatel of $17 per share. Alcatel responded with an offer of $15 per share, which the Independent Committee's rejected $15 as insufficient. Alcatel raised its offer to $15.25 per share. which the Committee also rejected. Alcatel then made a final offer of $15.50 per share.

At a meeting on November 24, 1986 Beringer told the other two members of the Independent Committee that Alcatel was "ready to proceed with an unfriendly tender at a lower price" if the Independent Committee did not recommend and the Lynch board of directors did not approve Alcatel's $15.50 per share offer. Beringer also advised that alternatives to a cash-out merger had been investigated but were impracticable. The Independent Committee met with its financial and legal advisors and then voted unanimously to recommend that the Lynch board of directors approve Alcatel's proposal for a $15.50 cash merger. Later that day, the Lynch board approved the Committee's recommendation, Alcatel's nominees abstaining.]

HOLLAND, JUSTICE.

This Court has held that "a shareholder owes a fiduciary duty only if it owns a majority interest in or *exercises control* over the business affairs of the corporation." *Ivanhoe Partners v. Newmont Mining Corp.*, Del.Supr., 535 A.2d 1334, 1344 (1987) (emphasis added). With regard to the exercise of control, this Court has stated:

> [A] shareholder who owns less than 50% of a corporation's outstanding stocks does not, without more, become a controlling shareholder of that corporation, with a concomitant fiduciary status. For a dominating relationship to exist in the absence of controlling stock

ownership, a plaintiff must allege domination by a minority share-holder through actual control of corporation conduct.

*Citron v. Fairchild Camera & Instrument Corp.*, Del.Supr., 569 A.2d 53, 70 (1989) (quotations and citation omitted).

Alcatel held a 43.3 percent minority share of stock in Lynch. Therefore, the threshold question to be answered by the Court of Chancery was whether, despite its minority ownership, Alcatel exercised control over Lynch's business affairs. * * *

At the August 1 [Lynch board] meeting, Alcatel opposed the renewal of compensation contracts for Lynch's top five managers. * * * Christian Fayard ("Fayard"), an Alcatel director, told the board members, "[y]ou must listen to us. We are 43 percent owner. You have to do what we tell you." The minutes * * * recite that Fayard [also] declared, "you are pushing us very much to take control of the company. Our opinion is not taken into consideration."

* * *

At the same meeting, Alcatel vetoed Lynch's acquisition of the target company, which, according to the minutes, Beringer considered "an immediate fit" for Lynch. Dertinger agreed with Beringer, stating that the "target company is extremely important as they have the products that Lynch needs now." Nonetheless, Alcatel prevailed. The minutes reflect that Fayard advised the board: "Alcatel, with its 44% equity position, would not approve such an acquisition as ... it does not wish to be diluted from being the main shareholder in Lynch." * * *

The record [thus] supports the Court of Chancery's underlying factual finding that "the non-Alcatel [independent] directors deferred to Alcatel because of its position as a significant stockholder and not because they decided in the exercise of their own business judgment that Alcatel's position was correct." The record also supports the subsequent factual finding that, notwithstanding its 43.3 percent minority share-holder interest, Alcatel did exercise actual control over Lynch by domi-nating its corporate affairs. The Court of Chancery's legal conclusion that Alcatel owed the fiduciary duties of a controlling shareholder to the other Lynch shareholders followed syllogistically as the logical result of its cogent analysis of the record.

A controlling or dominating shareholder standing on both sides of a transaction, as in a parent-subsidiary context, bears the burden of proving its entire fairness. *Weinberger v. UOP, Inc.*, Del.Supr., 457 A.2d 701, 710 (1983). *See Rosenblatt v. Getty Oil Co.*, Del.Supr., 493 A.2d 929, 937 (1985). * * *

The logical question raised by this Court's holding in *Weinberger* was what type of evidence would be reliable to demonstrate entire fairness. That question was not only anticipated but also initially ad-dressed in the *Weinberger* opinion['s suggestion regarding the use of an independent negotiating committee of outside directors]. *Id.* at 709–10 n. 7. * * *

In this case, the Vice Chancellor noted that the Court of Chancery has expressed "differing views" regarding the effect that an approval of a cash-out merger by a special committee of disinterested directors has upon the controlling or dominating shareholder's burden of demonstrating entire fairness. One view is that such approval shifts to the plaintiff the burden of proving that the transaction was unfair. *Citron v. E.I. Du Pont de Nemours & Co.*, Del.Ch., 584 A.2d 490, 500–02 (1990); *Rabkin v. Olin Corp*, Del.Ch., C.A. No. 7547 (Consolidated), Chandler, V.C., 1990 WL 47648, *aff'd*, Del.Supr., 586 A.2d 1202 (1990). The other view is that such an approval renders the business judgment rule the applicable standard of judicial review. *In re Trans World Airlines, Inc. Shareholders Litig.*, Del.Ch., C.A. 9844 (Consolidated), Allen, C., 1988 WL 111271.

"It is often of critical importance whether a particular decision is one to which the business judgment rule applies or the entire fairness rule applies." *Nixon v. Blackwell*, Del.Supr., 626 A.2d 1366, 1376 (1993). The definitive answer with regard to the Court of Chancery's "differing views" is found in this Court's opinions in *Weinberger* and *Rosenblatt*. In [*Rosenblatt*], * * * this Court recognized that it would be inconsistent with its holding in *Weinberger* [abolishing the business purpose test imposed by the *Singer* trilogy] to apply the business judgment rule in the context of an interested merger transaction which, by its very nature, did not require a business purpose. *See Rosenblatt v. Getty Oil Co.*, 493 A.2d at 937. Consequently, in *Rosenblatt*, in the context of a subsequent proceeding involving a parent-subsidiary merger, this Court held that the "approval of a merger, as here, by an informed vote of a majority of the minority stockholders, while not a legal prerequisite, shifts the burden of proving the unfairness of the merger entirely to the plaintiffs." *Id*.

Entire fairness remains the proper focus of judicial analysis in examining an interested merger, irrespective of whether the burden of proof remains upon or is shifted away from the controlling or dominating shareholder, because the unchanging nature of the underlying "interested" transaction requires careful scrutiny. *See Weinberger v. UOP, Inc.*, 457 A.2d at 710 (citing *Sterling v. Mayflower Hotel Corp.*, Del.Supr., 93 A.2d 107, 110 (1952)). The policy rationale for the exclusive application of the entire fairness standard to interested merger transactions has been stated as follows:

> Parent subsidiary mergers, unlike stock options, are proposed by a party that controls, and will continue to control, the corporation, whether or not the minority stockholders vote to approve or reject the transaction. The controlling stockholder relationship has the potential to influence, however subtly, the vote of [ratifying] minority stockholders in a manner that is not likely to occur in a transaction with a noncontrolling party.

> Even where no coercion is intended, shareholders voting on a parent subsidiary merger might perceive that their disapproval could risk retaliation of some kind by the controlling stockholder.

For example, the controlling stockholder might decide to stop dividend payments or to effect a subsequent cash out merger at a less favorable price, for which the remedy would be time consuming and costly litigation. At the very least, the potential for that perception, and its possible impact upon a shareholder vote, could never be fully eliminated. Consequently, in a merger between the corporation and its controlling stockholder—even one negotiated by disinterested, independent directors—no court could be certain whether the transaction terms fully approximate what truly independent parties would have achieved in an arm's length negotiation. Given that uncertainty, a court might well conclude that even minority shareholders who have ratified a ... merger need procedural protections beyond those afforded by full disclosure of all material facts. One way to provide such protections would be to adhere to the more stringent entire fairness standard of judicial review.

*Citron v. E.I. Du Pont de Nemours & Co.*, 584 A.2d at 502.

Once again, this Court holds that the exclusive standard of judicial review in examining the propriety of an interested cash-out merger transaction by a controlling or dominating shareholder is entire fairness. *Weinberger v. UOP, Inc.*, 457 A.2d at 710–11. The initial burden of establishing entire fairness rests upon the party who stands on both sides of the transaction. *Id.* However, an approval of the transaction by an independent committee of directors or an informed majority of minority shareholders shifts the burden of proof on the issue of fairness from the controlling or dominating shareholder to the challenging shareholder-plaintiff. *See Rosenblatt v. Getty Oil Co.*, 493 A.2d at 937–38. Nevertheless, even when an interested cash-out merger transaction receives the informed approval of a majority of minority stockholders or an independent committee of disinterested directors, an entire fairness analysis is the only proper standard of judicial review. *See id.*

\* \* \*

The same policy rationale which requires judicial review of interested cash-out mergers exclusively for entire fairness also mandates careful judicial scrutiny of a special committee's real bargaining power before shifting the burden of proof on the issue of entire fairness. A recent decision from the Court of Chancery articulated a two-part test for determining whether burden shifting is appropriate in an interested merger transaction. *Rabkin v. Olin Corp.*, Del.Ch., C.A. No. 7547 (Consolidated), Chandler, V.C., 1990 WL 47648, *aff'd*, Del. Supr. 586 A.2d 1202 (1990). In *Olin*, the Court of Chancery stated:

The mere existence of an independent special committee \* \* \* does not itself shift the burden. At least two factors are required. First, the majority shareholder must not dictate the terms of the merger. *Rosenblatt v. Getty Oil Co.*, Del.Ch., 493 A.2d 929, 937 (1985). Second, the special committee must have real bargaining power that it can exercise with the majority shareholder on an arms length basis.

*Id.*, slip op. at 14–15. This Court expressed its agreement with that statement by affirming the Court of Chancery decision * * *.

### Lynch's Independent Committee

In the case *sub judice*, the Court of Chancery observed that although "Alcatel did exercise control over Lynch with respect to the decisions made at the August 1, 1986 board meeting, it does not necessarily follow that Alcatel also controlled the terms of the merger and its approval." This observation is theoretically accurate * * *. However, the performance of the Independent Committee merits careful judicial scrutiny to determine whether Alcatel's demonstrated pattern of domination was effectively neutralized so that "each of the contending parties had in fact exerted its bargaining power against the other at arm's length." *Id.* The fact that the same independent directors had submitted to Alcatel's demands on August 1, 1986 was part of the basis for the Court of Chancery's finding of Alcatel's domination of Lynch. Therefore, the Independent Committee's ability to bargain at arm's length with Alcatel was suspect from the outset.

The Independent Committee's original assignment was to examine the merger with Celwave which had been proposed by Alcatel. The record reflects that the Independent Committee effectively discharged that assignment and, in fact, recommended that the Lynch board reject the merger on Alcatel's terms. Alcatel's response to the Independent Committee's adverse recommendation was not the pursuit of further negotiations regarding its Celwave proposal, but rather its response was an offer to buy Lynch. That offer was consistent with Alcatel's August 1, 1986 expressions of an intention to dominate Lynch, since an acquisition would effectively eliminate once and for all Lynch's remaining vestiges of independence.

The Independent Committee's second assignment was to consider Alcatel's proposal to purchase Lynch. The Independent Committee proceeded on that task with full knowledge of Alcatel's demonstrated pattern of domination. The Independent Committee was also obviously aware of Alcatel's refusal to negotiate with it on the Celwave matter.

### Burden of Proof Shifted Court of Chancery's Finding

The Court of Chancery began its factual analysis by noting that Kahn had "attempted to shatter" the image of the Independent Committee's actions as having "appropriately simulated" an arm's length, third-party transaction. The Court of Chancery found that "to some extent, [Kahn's attempt] was successful." The Court of Chancery gave credence to the testimony of Kertz, one of the members of the Independent Committee, to the effect that he did not believe that $15.50 was a fair price but that he voted in favor of the merger because he felt there was no alternative.

The Court of Chancery also found that Kertz understood Alcatel's position to be that it was ready to proceed with an unfriendly tender offer at a lower price if Lynch did not accept the $15.50 offer, and that Kertz perceived this to be a threat by Alcatel. The Court of Chancery concluded that Kertz ultimately decided that, "although $15.50 was not fair, a tender offer and merger at that price would be better for Lynch's stockholders than an unfriendly tender offer at a significantly lower price." The Court of Chancery determined that "Kertz failed either to satisfy himself that the offered price was fair or oppose the merger."

In addition to Kertz, the other members of the Independent Committee were Beringer, its chairman, and Wineman. Wineman did not testify at trial.[7] * * * Beringer testified that at the time of the Committee's vote to recommend the $15.50 offer to the Lynch board, he thought "that *under the circumstances*, a price of $15.50 was fair and should be accepted" (emphasis added).

Kahn contends that these "circumstances" included those referenced in the minutes for the November 24, 1986 Independent Committee meeting: "Mr. Beringer added that Alcatel is 'ready to proceed with an unfriendly tender at a lower price' if the $15.50 per share price is not recommended to, and approved by, the Company's Board of Directors." * * *

The record reflects that Alcatel was "ready to proceed" with a hostile bid. This was a conclusion reached by Beringer, the Independent Committee's chairman and spokesman, based upon communications to him from Alcatel. Beringer testified that although there was no reference to a particular price for a hostile bid during his discussions with Alcatel, or even specific mention of a "lower" price, "the implication was clear to [him] that it probably would be at a lower price."[8]

According to the Court of Chancery, the Independent Committee rejected three lower offers for Lynch from Alcatel and then accepted the $15.50 offer "after being advised that [it] was fair and after considering the absence of alternatives." The Vice Chancellor expressly acknowledged the impracticability of Lynch's Independent Committee's alternatives to a merger with Alcatel: Lynch was not in a position to shop for other acquirors, since Alcatel could block any alternative transaction. Alcatel also made it clear that it was not interested in having its shares repurchased by Lynch. The Independent Committee decided that a stockholder rights plan was not viable because of the increased debt it would entail.

---

**7.** Based upon inferences from Kertz's testimony, the Court of Chancery noted that "Wineman apparently agreed" that $15.50 was a fair price. However, the record also reflects that it was Wineman who urged the other independent directors to yield to Alcatel's demands at the August 1, 1986 meeting. Wineman's failure to testify also permits both this Court and the Court of Chancery to draw the inference adverse to Alcatel, that Alcatel dictated the outcome of the November 24, 1986 meeting. As we have previously noted, the production of weak evidence when strong is, or should have been, available can lead only to the conclusion that the strong would have been adverse. *See* Smith v. Van Gorkom, Del. Supr., 488 A.2d 858, 878 (1985).

**8.** On the other hand, Dertinger, an officer and director of Lynch, testified that he was informed by Alcatel that the price of an unfriendly tender offer would indeed be lower and would in fact be $12 per share.

Nevertheless, based upon the record before it, the Court of Chancery found that the Independent Committee had "appropriately simulated a third-party transaction, where negotiations are conducted at arms-length and there is no compulsion to reach an agreement." The Court of Chancery concluded that the Independent Committee's actions "as a whole" were "sufficiently well informed * * * and aggressive to simulate an arms-length transaction," so that the burden of proof as to entire fairness shifted from Alcatel to the contending Lynch shareholder, Kahn. The Court of Chancery's reservations about that finding are apparent in its written decision.

*The Power to Say No, The Parties' Contentions,*
*Arm's Length Bargaining*

The Court of Chancery properly noted that limitations on the alternatives to Alcatel's offer did not mean that the Independent Committee should have agreed to a price that was unfair:

> The power to say no is a significant power. It is the duty of directors serving on [an independent] committee to approve only a transaction that is in the best interests of the public shareholders, to say no to any transaction that is not fair to those shareholders and is not the best transaction available. It is not sufficient for such directors to achieve the best price that a fiduciary will pay if that price is not a fair price.

(Quoting *In re First Boston, Inc. Shareholders Litig.*, Del.Ch., C.A. 10338 (Consolidated), Allen, C., 1990 WL 78836, slip op. at 15–16 (June 7, 1990)).

The Alcatel defendants argue that the Independent Committee exercised its "power to say no" in rejecting the three initial offers from Alcatel, and that it therefore cannot be said that Alcatel dictated the terms of the merger or precluded the Independent Committee from exercising real bargaining power. The Alcatel defendants contend, alternatively, that "even assuming that such a threat [of a hostile takeover] could have had a coercive effect on the [Independent] Committee," the willingness of the Independent Committee to reject Alcatel's initial three offers suggests that "the alleged threat was either nonexistent or ineffective." *Braunschweiger v. American Home Shield Corp.*, Del.Ch., C.A. No. 10755, Allen, C., 1991 WL 3920, slip op. at 13 (Jan. 7, 1991).

Kahn contends the record reflects that the conduct of Alcatel deprived the Independent Committee of an effective "power to say no." Kahn argues that Alcatel not only threatened the Committee with a hostile tender offer in the event its $15.50 offer was not recommended and approved, but also directed the affairs of Lynch for Alcatel's benefit in such a way as to make it impossible for Lynch to continue as a public company under Alcatel's control without injury to itself and its minority shareholders. * * *

* * * Unlike *Braunschweiger*, in this case the coercion was extant and directed at a specific price offer which was, in effect, presented in

the form of a "take it or leave it" ultimatum by a controlling shareholder with the capability of following through on its threat of a hostile takeover.

### Alcatel's Entire Fairness Burden Did Not Shift to Kahn

A condition precedent to finding that the burden of proving entire fairness has shifted in an interested merger transaction is a careful judicial analysis of the factual circumstances of each case. Particular consideration must be given to evidence of whether the special committee was truly independent, fully informed, and had the freedom to negotiate at arm's length. "Although perfection is not possible," unless the controlling or dominating shareholder can demonstrate that it has not only formed an independent committee but also replicated a process "as though each of the contending parties had in fact exerted its bargaining power at arm's length," the burden of proving entire fairness will not shift. *Weinberger v. UOP, Inc.*, 457 A.2d at 709–10 n. 7.

Subsequent to *Rosenblatt*, this Court pointed out that "the use of an independent negotiating committee of outside directors may have significant advantages to the majority stockholder in defending suits of this type," but it does not *ipso facto* establish the procedural fairness of an interested merger transaction. *Rabkin v. Philip A. Hunt Chem. Corp.*, Del.Supr., 498 A.2d 1099, 1106 & n. 7 (1985). * * * [T]his Court implied that the burden on entire fairness would not be shifted by the use of an independent committee which concluded its processes with "what could be considered a quick surrender" to the dictated terms of the controlling shareholder.[10] *Id.* at 1106. This Court concluded in *Rabkin* that the majority stockholder's "attitude toward the minority," coupled with the "apparent absence of any meaningful negotiations as to price," did not manifest the exercise of arm's length bargaining by the independent committee. *Id.*

The Court of Chancery's determination that the Independent Committee "appropriately simulated a third-party transaction, where negotiations are conducted at arm's-length and there is no compulsion to reach an agreement," is not supported by the record. * * * The record reflects that the ability of the Committee effectively to negotiate at arm's length was compromised by Alcatel's threats to proceed with a hostile tender offer if the $15.50 price was not approved by the Committee and the Lynch board. The fact that the Independent Committee rejected three initial offers, which were well below the Independent Committee's estimated valuation for Lynch and were not combined with an explicit threat that Alcatel was "ready to proceed" with a hostile bid, cannot alter the conclusion that any semblance of arm's length bargaining ended when the Independent Committee surrendered to the ultimatum that accompanied Alcatel's final offer.

---

**10.** A "surrender" need not occur at the outset of the negotiation process in order to deny a controlling shareholder the burden-shifting function which might otherwise follow from establishing an independent committee bargaining structure. * * *

*Conclusion*

Accordingly, the judgment of the Court of Chancery is reversed. This matter is remanded for further proceedings consistent herewith, including a redetermination of the entire fairness of the cash-out merger to Kahn and the other Lynch minority shareholders with the burden of proof remaining on Alcatel, the dominant and interested shareholder.

———

### William T. Allen, *Independent Directors in MBO Transactions: Are They Fact or Fantasy?*
45 Bus. Law. 2055–2058, 2060–2063 (1990).

* * * I want to inquire into the role of outside directors—special committees of outside directors—when the corporation is to be sold, and whether such committees can or do function adequately to protect appropriate interests in such a setting. Addressing that subject requires, as well, that one explore, a bit, the role of the investment bankers and lawyers who guide the board in a change of control transaction.

To relieve any suspense, I will report now that I am going to conclude that, as one who has reviewed in one way or another a fair number of special committees in a sale context, I remain open to the possibility that such committees can be employed effectively to protect corporate and shareholder interests. But I must confess a painful awareness of the ways in which the device may be subverted and rendered less than useful. I conclude, as well, that it is the lawyers and the investment bankers who in many cases hold the key to the effectiveness of the special committee.

Now, the foundation for an inquiry into whether special committees are worthy of respect by courts is the question whether outside directors can be expected to exercise independent judgment on matters in which the corporation's CEO has a conflicting interest—the paradigm case of such conflict and the one that I presently have in mind being the management affiliated leveraged buyout.

On this foundational question, there is a disturbing dichotomy of views. A prominent view is the view that outside directors serve a largely ornamental role in the month-to-month direction of the enterprise. * * *

Yet our statutory corporation law has long assumed that disinterested directors can exercise a business judgment unaffected by the fact that the CEO of the firm may be self-interested. Indeed, one of the principal threads in the development of corporation law over the past 20 years has been the emphasis on bringing more outside directors onto boards, and the creation of more board committees comprised of outside directors. * * *

What is going on here? How do we explain the dissonance between what the established organs of corporation law—statutes, court decrees, statements by the organized bar—imply, and what those who purport to be realists say, about the likelihood that outside directors will act as an effective constraint upon self-interested management?

\* \* \*

Consider the outside director who is asked to serve on a special committee to preside over a sale of the company. While he may receive some modest special remuneration for this service, he and his fellow committee members are likely to be the only persons intensely involved in the process who do not entertain the fervent hope of either making a killing or earning a princely fee. Couple that with the pressure that the seriousness and urgency of the assignment generate; the unpleasantness that may be required if the job is done right; and, the fact that no matter what the director does he will probably be sued for it, and you have, I think, a fairly unappetizing assignment.

Combine these factors with those mentioned earlier that create feelings of solidarity with management directors, particularly the corporation's CEO, and it becomes, I would think, quite easy to understand how some special committees appear as no more than, in T.S. Eliot's phrase, "an easy tool, deferential, glad to be of use."

Only one factor stands against these pressures towards accommodation of the CEO: that is a sense of duty. When special committees have appeared to push and resist their colleagues, it has been, I submit, because the men and women who comprised the committee have understood that as a result of accepting this special assignment, they have a new duty and stand in a new and different relationship to the firm's management or its controlling shareholder. \* \* \*

I fully appreciate that corrupt conduct does occur. But I believe—especially in the context of the larger public companies—that when outside directors serving on a special committee fail to meet our expectations, it is likely that they fail because they have not understood what was expected of them. Directors must know what is right before courts can expect them to do what is right.

Thus, I come to the role of the committee's advisors—the lawyers and investment bankers who guide the committee through the process of the sale of a public company. I regard the role of the advisors in establishing the integrity of this process as absolutely crucial. Indeed, the motives and performance of the lawyers and bankers who specialize in the field of mergers and acquisitions is to my mind the great, largely unexamined variable in the process. In all events, it is plain that quite often the special committee relies upon the advisors almost totally. It is understandable why. Frequently, the outside directors who find themselves in control of a corporate sale process have had little or no experience in the sale of a public company. They are in terra incognito. Naturally, they turn for guidance to their specialist advisors who will typically have had a great deal of relevant experience.

Thus, in my opinion, if the special committee process is to have integrity, it falls in the first instance to the lawyers to unwrap the bindings that have joined the directors into a single board; to instill in the committee a clear understanding of the radically altered state in which it finds itself and to lead the committee to a full understanding of its new duty.

Please don't mistake me. This is not a call to pay even greater attention to appearances; it is advice to abandon the theatrical and to accept and to implement the substance of an arm's-length process. To do this, the lawyers and the bankers must be independent of management. They must accept in their hearts that in the MBO or the auction context, their client is the committee and not management. They must clearly and emphatically remind their client that, at this juncture, the CEO and his associates are to be treated at arm's-length. And the lawyers and bankers must act on that view. That means that from the outset, the advisors must be prepared to forego future business. It comes to that.

\* \* \*

My intuition is that the jury is still out on the question whether the special committee device works well enough, often enough, for the law to continue to accord it weight. I am sure, however, of this: if the future leads us to view that that process does offer to shareholders protections that are consistent with justice, it will in large measure be because lawyers have been true to their professional responsibilities and have used their talent and power to see that outside directors understand and strive to satisfy their duty.

### 3.   FAIR DEALING IN TENDER OFFERS

As noted in Chapter 18, *Eisenberg v. Chicago Milwaukee Corp.*, 537 A.2d 1051, 1057 (Del.Ch.1987), held that a controlled corporation making a tender offer for its own stock had a duty to make full disclosure "even 'more onerous' than in a contested offer." *Barkan v. Amsted Industries*, 567 A.2d 1279 (Del.1989), appeared to curtail *Eisenberg*, interpreting its concerns as a mere "admonishment" that "courts be particularly mindful of the danger of omissions and misrepresentations in situations in which directors are confronted with conflicts of interest," 567 A.2d at 1288, and noting that, "a recognition of these dangers does not affect the definition of materiality." *Id.* But other courts have followed *Eisenberg*'s approach, asserting that judicial review of disclosures is "especially rigorous" in the case of management buyouts, where material information is often "exclusively within" the possession of management. *Plaza Securities v. Fruehauf Corp.*, 643 F.Supp. 1535, 1544 (E.D.Mich.1986).

Whatever the nature of a majority shareholder's disclosure duties, it remains unclear whether a majority shareholder also has a duty to offer minority shareholders a "fair price" in a tender offer. Recall *Bershad*'s holding that a majority shareholder has no duty to sell her shares, even if a third party will pay more for them than the majority shareholder is prepared to offer minority shareholders in a cash out merger. It would seem inconsistent with this holding to require the majority shareholder to offer a given price for the minority shareholders' stock, particularly in a tender offer where, unlike a cash out merger, minority shareholders are free to refuse to sell at all. On the other hand, as the court pointed out in *Citron*, minority shareholders who must approve a cash out merger are likely to feel coerced, even if no coercion is intended. The same is likely to be true when a majority shareholder makes a tender offer.

However, the Delaware Supreme Court recently held that in the case of "totally voluntary tender offers," minority shareholders do not have a right to receive a particular price. *Solomon v. Pathe Communications Corp.*, 672 A.2d 35, 39 (Del.Supr. 1996). The court continued:

> Delaware law recognizes that, as to allegedly voluntary tender offers (in contrast to cash-out mergers), the determinative factor as to voluntariness is whether coercion is present, or whether there is materially false or misleading disclosures made to shareholders in connection with the offer. A transaction may be considered involuntary, despite being voluntary in appearance and form, if one of these factors is present.* * *

> [I]n the absence of coercion or disclosure violations, the adequacy of the price in a voluntary tender offer cannot be an issue.

*Id.*

*Joseph v. Shell Oil Co.*, 1985 WL 150466 (Del.Ch.1985), aff'd on other grounds *Selfe v. Joseph*, 501 A.2d 409 (Del.1985) involved a claim that a majority shareholder does have a duty to offer a fair price in a tender offer. Royal Dutch Petroleum Company ("Royal Dutch") had for more than 60 years conducted most of its business in the United States through Shell Oil Company ("Shell"), a Delaware corporation. As of January 24, 1984, Royal Dutch controlled approximately 70 percent of Shell's stock. On that date, Royal Dutch proposed a cash out merger, at $55 per share, between Shell and a newly-created subsidiary, SPNV Holdings, Inc. ("Holdings"). The merger price was $2.00 per share more than the price that Morgan Stanley & Co., Royal Dutch's investment banker, on the basis of publicly available information, had opined was the fair value of Shell's minority stock It was also approximately $11 per share more than the price at which Shell stock was trading.

Shell's board of directors created a special committee, consisting of six outside directors, to evaluate Royal Dutch's merger proposal. The committee retained Goldman Sachs & Co., which estimated that the fair value of Shell stock was between $70.00 and $95.00 per share and that Shell had a liquidation value of $80.00 to $85.00 per share. Relying largely on this opinion, the special committee concluded unanimously that it would support a cash out merger only if the price was $75.00 per share.

Royal Dutch chose not to negotiate. Instead, it withdrew its merger proposal and, six days later, made a cash tender offer of $58.00 per share for the minority shares. It simultaneously announced that it would not make another tender offer for 18 months; that it intended eventually to acquire all the minority shares; that it would cash out any remaining minority shareholder at $58.00 per share in a short-form merger if after the tender offer it owned more than 90 percent of Shell's stock; and that if the tender offer did not result in its owning more than 90 percent of Shell, it might buy sufficient shares in the open market to reach the 90 percent level and then effect a short-form merger.

Shell's board of directors recommended that the minority shareholders not tender their stock. The board also circulated a Form 14D–9 to shareholders explaining its reasons for opposing the Royal Dutch offer and supporting a merger at $75.00 per share. Nonetheless, minority shareholders tendered more than 80 percent of the outstanding minority stock. Certain minority shareholders sought to enjoin Royal Dutch's tender offer and any subsequent short-form merger. They claimed that Royal Dutch had failed to disclose all material information and that Royal Dutch had breached its duty to deal fairly with the minority shareholders by offering a grossly inadequate price for their stock.

In Joseph v. Shell Oil Co., 482 A.2d 335 (Del.Ch.1984), the court enjoined consummation of the tender offer, ruling that it "did not satisfy the requirements of disclosure of all germane facts with complete candor." The court found that Royal Dutch had not disclosed (1) that it had denied Morgan Stanley access to information about Shell's probable oil reserves, (2) its internal estimates that Shell's going concern value was $91.00 per share, and (3) information about Shell's recent discovery of oil reserves potentially worth more than $3.90 per share. The court recommended that new valuation studies be undertaken and ordered Royal Dutch to circulate a supplemental disclosure document and afford all shareholders who had tendered an opportunity to withdraw their stock.

After this information, together with a letter from Morgan Stanley reiterating its earlier opinion as to the value of Shell stock, was circulated, the Shell shareholders withdrew only 363,000 shares, less than 0.5% of those that had been tendered. Through Holdings, Royal Dutch then purchased the remaining shares that had been tendered for $58.00 per share, increasing its ownership of Shell to 94.6%. About 17 million shares remained in the hands of public shareholders.

Litigation continued relating to the claim that Royal Dutch had violated its duty of fair dealing by offering a grossly inadequate price. Royal Dutch argued that its only duty was to disclose all material information it possessed, leaving the minority shareholders free to accept or reject its offer. The case was settled shortly before trial. Royal Dutch agreed to pay an additional $2.00 per share to all shareholders who had accepted its tender offer; to offer $58.00 per share in merger consideration, plus an additional $2.00 per share for agreeing not to seek an appraisal, to all remaining minority shareholders; and to pay $15 million in fees to plaintiffs' attorneys. In approving the settlement, the court found that there were serious questions as to the merit of plaintiffs' claims. The court also noted that it was unclear whether, even if plaintiffs prevailed, they would be entitled to any relief beyond being allowed to withdraw their shares, dissent from the planned short-form merger, and seek appraisal for their stock. Finally, the court pointed out that the proposed $190 million settlement was perhaps the largest recovery ever achieved in a shareholder class action.

## E.  FAIR PRICE

*Weinberger* recognized that price often is "the preponderant consideration" in a cash out merger and held that the determination of a fair price "requires consideration of all relevant factors involving the value of a company," including "proof of value by any techniques or methods which are generally considered acceptable in the financial community and otherwise admissible in court * * *." RMBCA § 13.01(3) is similarly open-ended, defining "fair value" for purposes of appraisal as "the value of the shares immediately before the effectuation of the corporate action to which the dissenter objects, excluding any appreciation or depreciation in anticipation of the corporate action unless exclusion would be inequitable."

The Official Comment to RMBCA § 13.01 states:

> The definition of "fair value" in section 13.01(3) leaves to the parties (and ultimately to the courts) the details by which "fair value" is to be determined within the broad outlines of the definition. This definition thus leaves untouched the accumulated case law about market value, value based on prior sales, capitalized earnings value, and asset value. It specifically preserves the former language excluding appreciation and depreciation in anticipation of the proposed corporate action, but permits an exception for equitable considerations. The purpose of this exception * * * is to permit consideration of factors similar to those approved by the Supreme Court of Delaware in *Weinberger v. UOP, Inc.*, 457 A.2d 701 (Del. 1983), a case in which the court found that the transaction did not involve fair dealing or fair price * * *. Consideration of appreciation or depreciation which might result from other corporate actions is permitted; these effects in the past have often been reflected either in market value or capitalized earnings value.

## 1.  SHARES OF STOCK OR INTEREST IN A COMPANY

### IN RE VALUATION OF COMMON STOCK OF MCLOON OIL CO.

565 A.2d 997 (Me.1989).

McKusick, Chief Justice.

Ten years ago we examined for the first time the principles to be applied in finding the "fair value" of a dissenting shareholder's stock under the recently enacted Maine Business Corporations Act. See *In re Valuation of Common Stock of Libby, McNeill & Libby*, 406 A.2d 54 (Me.1979). Libby involved a public corporation with common stock listed on the New York Stock Exchange. In the present appeal we revisit the fair value question in an appraisal proceeding involving three Maine corporations with untraded stock owned entirely by the members of a single family.

\* \* \*

### FACTS AND PROCEDURAL HISTORY

McLoon, Morse Bros., and T–M Oil Companies were closely held companies entirely owned by the members of the Pescosolido family under the leadership of Carl Pescosolido, Sr. Two of his sons, Carl Jr. and Richard, each held 475 shares in McLoon, 800 shares in Morse Bros., and 350 shares in T–M. The combined holdings of Carl Jr. and Richard constituted 50% of the McLoon common stock, 50% of the Morse Bros. common stock, and 14.3% of the T–M common stock.

In December 1975 Carl Sr. proposed to merge all family-held companies into Lido, over which he would exercise sole voting control. Carl Jr. and Richard (hereinafter "Dissenters") objected in writing to the proposed merger. On December 6, 1976, the parties executed a merger agreement in which the Dissenters expressly preserved their appraisal rights under 13–A M.R.S.A. § 909. On December 15, 1976, the Dissenters individually wrote to each of the three Maine companies and requested payment for their shares. On January 8, 1977, Lido responded by offering each Dissenter $128,685.55 for his combined interests in all three companies. Within a week, both Dissenters formally rejected that offer.

Pursuant to 13–A M.R.S.A. § 909(9)(B), the Dissenters on April 1, 1977, filed a Superior Court suit nominally in Lido's name for valuation of their stock in all three companies. \* \* \*

Ten years later, on May 22, 1987, acting pursuant to M.R.Civ.P. 53 and with the agreement of the parties, the Superior Court (Delahanty, J.) appointed Professor David P. Cluchey of the University of Maine School of Law to serve as referee to determine all issues in the case. \* \* \*

\* \* \*

### FAIR VALUE WITH NO MINORITY OR NONMARKETABILITY DISCOUNT

Ten years ago in the *Libby* case we ruled that a stock's fair value under section 909 could appropriately be determined by weighing three factors—the stock's market price, the company's net asset value, and the company's investment value—with the weight to be accorded each factor depending on its reliability as an indicator of fair value. See *In re Valuation of Common Stock of Libby, McNeill & Libby*, 406 A.2d at 60. We recognized that the reliability of each factor will vary with the particular facts and circumstances of each case, so that "[t]he weighing of these interdependent elements of fair value is more akin to an artistic composition than to a scientific process. A judicial determination of fair value cannot be computed according to any precise mathematical formula." *Id.* However, the court should in each case consider all three elements of fair value, even if only to find one or more of them unreliable in the circumstances. *Id.*

\* \* \*

[T]he referee held that the fair value of each Dissenter's stock was his proportionate share of the full value of each company, as determined from the expert appraisal testimony presented by the parties. The referee expressly rejected Lido's contention that he should discount the full value of each company because of the minority status and lack of marketability of the Dissenters' stock. On appeal Lido's only serious challenge to the referee's finding of fair value is directed at the referee's recognition of the Dissenters' full proportionate interest in the whole value of each company, free of any minority or nonmarketability discount. We find Lido's arguments for such discounts unpersuasive. In our view application of those discounts would run directly counter to our appraisal statute's purpose of protecting dissenting shareholders. The referee's finding of aggregate fair value of $334,925 for each Dissenter is fully supported by the evidence and by a correct application of legal principles.

The referee applied the three-factor valuation method used in *Libby* but noted that the method has come under some criticism since 1979, specifically citing *Weinberger v. UOP, Inc.*, 457 A.2d 701 (Del.1983), for the proposition that the modern approach to valuation "must include proof of value by any techniques or methods which are generally considered acceptable in the financial community, and otherwise admissible in court." *Id.* at 712–13. *Weinberger* by its own terms broadened rather than changed the basic method of stock valuation used in *Libby.* \* \* \*

Nothing in *Libby*, however, prevents the consideration and use of any other generally accepted and admissible valuation techniques. In the case at bar the evidence presented by the witnesses went toward establishing those same three criteria of value; even the discounted cash flow analysis used by Cooper deals essentially with investment value. Although Lido argues that the three-part test is outmoded, we find the approach as outlined in *Libby* entirely compatible with *Weinberger* and the broadening of the Delaware block method.

Lido tries to use *Weinberger* and its progeny as a basis upon which to introduce the use of minority and nonmarketability discounts as a generally accepted alternative method of valuation. As previously noted, however, *Weinberger* advocated the same definition of "fair value" of a single shareholder's stock as did *Libby*: "his proportionate interest in a going concern." 457 A.2d at 713. *Weinberger* stands for the simple proposition that the value of the business entity as a whole should be determined by the best available valuation methods. No one can quarrel with that proposition. It has nothing to do, however, with the critical issue raised by Lido's appeal, which arises only after completion of the valuation of the whole firm by the best available methods: Should the dissenting shareholder's proportionate part of that whole firm value as so determined be discounted because of the minority status and lack of marketability of his stock? The Delaware Supreme Court, the same court that decided *Weinberger*, has recently said no: Delaware emphatically rejects the application of those discounts in determining the fair value of a dissenting shareholder's stock. *See Cavalier Oil Corp. v. Harnett*, 564 A.2d 1137, 1141 (Del.1989) ("application of a discount to a minority shareholder is contrary to the requirement that the company be viewed as a going concern").

The appraisal remedy has deep roots in equity. The traditional rule through much of the 19th century was that any corporate transaction that changed the rights of common shareholders required unanimous consent. The appraisal remedy for dissenting shareholders evolved as it became clear that unanimous consent was inconsistent with the growth and development of large business enterprises. By the bargain struck in enacting an appraisal statute, the shareholder who disapproves of a proposed merger or other major corporate change gives up his right of veto in exchange for the right to be bought out—not at market value, but at "fair value." Methods used in valuing stock for tax, probate, ERISA, and like purposes in which market value is of the essence are inapposite to the determination of the fair value owed to dissenting shareholders. In the statutory appraisal proceeding, the involuntary change of ownership caused by a merger requires as a matter of fairness that a dissenting shareholder be compensated for the loss of his proportionate interest in the business as an entity. The valuation focus under the appraisal statute is not the stock as a commodity, but rather the stock only as it represents a proportionate part of the enterprise as a whole. The question for the court becomes simple and direct: What is the best price a single buyer could reasonably be expected to pay for the firm as an entirety? The court then prorates that value for the whole firm equally among all shares of its common stock. The result is that all of those shares have the same fair value.

Our view of the appraisal remedy is obviously inconsistent with the application of minority and nonmarketability discounts. Lido would have us discount the stock for minority status and lack of marketability in order to reflect what it calls the "real world" value of the stock to the Dissenters. * * * Especially in fixing the appraisal remedy in a close corporation, the relevant inquiry is what is the highest price a single buyer would reasonably pay for the whole enterprise, not what a willing buyer and a willing seller would bargain out as the sales price of a dissenting shareholder's shares in a hypothetical market transaction. Any rule of law that gave the shareholders less than their proportionate share of the whole firm's fair value would produce a transfer of wealth from the minority shareholders to the shareholders in control. Such a rule would inevitably encourage corporate squeeze-outs. As the Delaware Supreme Court stated recently in *Cavalier Oil Corp. v. Harnett*, to fail to accord to a minority shareholder the full proportionate value of his shares imposes a penalty for lack of control, and unfairly enriches the majority shareholders who may reap a windfall from the appraisal process by cashing out a dissenting shareholder, a clearly undesirable result.

*Cavalier Oil Corp. v. Harnett*, 564 A.2d at 1141. We agree.

————

As noted in the discussion of exclusivity, Ohio courts allow a dissenting shareholder only the pre-transaction market value of her stock. *Armstrong v. Marathon Oil Co.*, supra. Other courts also have held that, in certain circumstances, a minority discount should apply to avoid paying a dissenter as if she had a controlling interest. *See Hernando Bank v. Huff*, 609 F.Supp. 1124 (N.D.Miss.1985), *aff'd* 796 F.2d 803 (5th Cir.1986); *Perlman v. Permonite Mfg. Co.*, 568 F.Supp. 222 (N.D.Ind. 1983), *aff'd* 734 F.2d 1283 (7th Cir.1984); *Atlantic States Constr., Inc. v. Beavers*, 314 S.E.2d 245 (Ga.App.1984); *Stanton v. Republic Bank*, 581 N.E.2d 678 (Ill.1991); *Moore v. New Ammest, Inc.*, 630 P.2d 167 (Kan. App.1981); *Blasingame v. American Materials, Inc.*, 654 S.W.2d 659 (Tenn.1983).

A majority of courts, however, agree with *McLoon's* argument that to allow a minority discount would provide an inappropriate incentive for controlling shareholders to effectuate cash out mergers. *See, e.g., Woolf v. Universal Fidelity Life Ins. Co.*, 849 P.2d 1093 (Okl.App.1992); *MT Properties, Inc. v. CMC Real Estate Corp.*, 481 N.W.2d 383 (Minn.App. 1992); *Hunter v. Mitek Indus.*, Inc., 721 F.Supp. 1102 (E.D.Mo.1989); *Brown v. Allied Corrugated Box Co.*, (Cal.App.1979); *Walter S. Cheesman Realty Co. v. Moore*, 770 P.2d 1308 (Colo.App.1988); *Woodward v. Quigley*, 133 N.W.2d 38 (Iowa 1965), modified on other grounds 136 N.W.2d 280 (Iowa 1965); *Columbia Management Co. v. Wyss*, 765 P.2d 207 (Or.App.1988); *Charland v. Country View Golf Club, Inc.*, 588 A.2d 609 (R.I.1991).

In *Rapid–American Corp. v. Harris*, 603 A.2d 796 (Del.1992), the Delaware Supreme Court carried one step further the idea that a dissenting shareholder should receive her proportionate interest in the value of a company as a whole. Rapid–American was essentially a holding company with three operating subsidiaries. The Court of Chancery had valued Harris' Rapid American stock by estimating what the trading value of the subsidiaries' stock would have been if those subsidiaries had been public companies. Harris argued that Rapid–American could sell the subsidiaries at prices in excess of the projected trading value of their stock and that the "control premium" Rapid–American could receive should be counted in determining the "fair value" of Rapid American stock. On appeal, citing *Cavalier Oil*, the Delaware Supreme Court agreed. On remand, the Court of Chancery determined that the fair value of Rapid American stock, as of the date of the merger, was $73.29 per share, which was $22.29 per share more than the value the court had found without the control premium. *Harris v. Rapid–American Corp.*, 1992 WL 69614 (Del.Ch.1992).

### *Note: Value and the Form of the Transaction*

An interesting question in appraisal proceedings is whether the form of the transaction affects the extent to which the cashed out shareholders are entitled to share in any benefits that may arise from the change in control. As *Weinberger* makes clear, DGCL § 262 fixes the date of the merger as the date as of which fair value is to be determined and § 262(h) excludes from the determination of fair value "any element of value arising from the accomplishment or expectation of the merger." *Weinberger* read this as a "very narrow exception to the appraisal process" and held that "elements of future value including the nature of the enterprise, which are known or susceptible of proof as of the date of the merger and not the product of speculation may be considered."

The language of § 262 (h) and *Weinberger* are less clear than might appear at first reading and difficult interpretative questions arise when the form of the transaction is not simply a one step cash-out merger, as was true in *Weinberger*. In that connection, recall the litigation involving Cinerama's challenge to the sale of Technicolor discussed in Chapters 16 and 17 and this chapter. In that transaction, MAF acquired 82% of Technicolor stock on December 3, 1982. Upon acquiring control, it immediately began to seek to sell some of Technicolor's assets and to implement its own business plan. On January 24, 1983, MAF acquired the balance of the Technicolor stock in a cash-out merger to which Cinerama dissented.

One of the issues in the appraisal proceedings, as Chancellor Allen stated, was:

> * * * [W]hether in valuing Technicolor as of January 24, 1983, the court should assume the business plan for Technicolor that MAF is said by [Cinerama] to have had in place at that time or whether a proper valuation is premised upon ignoring such changes as [MAF] had in mind because to the extent they create value they are "elements of value arising from the accomplishment of expectation of the merger." 1990 WL 161084 at *17 (Del.Ch.1990).

The Chancellor acknowledged that under § 262(h) and *Weinberger*, Cinerama's argument seemed persuasive. Nevertheless, he declined to accept it, reasoning that the valuation process in an appraisal proceeding should not turn on whether the merger was accomplished in one or two steps.

The Delaware Supreme Court reversed. *Cede & Co. v. Technicolor, Inc.*, 684 A.2d 289 (Del.1996). The court laid great stress on the form of the transaction and the statutory language of § 262. Citing *Rapid–American*, the court stated that "in a two-step merger, to the extent that value has been added following a change in majority control before cash-out, it is still value attributable to the going concern, *i.e.*, the extant 'nature of the enterprise.' . . . [V]alue added to the going concern by the 'majority acquiror' during the transient period of a two-step merger accrues to the benefit of all shareholders and must be included in the appraisal process on the date of the merger.

*Id.* at 298–99.

The technical difference between Chancellor Allen and the Delaware Supreme Court concerns what constitutes "elements of value arising from the accomplishment or expectation of the merger." But the underlying debate is about the extent to which cashed out shareholders are entitled to share in the gains that will arise from the merger. In holding for Technicolor, Chancellor Allen took the position that MAF, as the acquiror, need not share the gains from its own strategy with those who are being cashed out. Such an approach is consistent with the view that changes in control are beneficial and should be encouraged if they will increase the value of the firm. The Delaware Supreme Court's approach is that cashed out shareholders are entitled to the benefit of the acquiror's plans because they were known on the date of the merger and could occur even if there were no merger. This approach is also consistent with what we saw in Chapter 12: subject to a fiduciary duty exception, the statute literally means what it says and the parties who choose to structure a transaction in a particular way must take the consequences of that choice.

## 2. THE RELATIONSHIP BETWEEN "FAIR DEALING" AND "FAIR PRICE"

### KAHN v. LYNCH COMMUNICATION SYS., INC.

669 A.2d 79 (Del.1995).

WALSH, JUSTICE:

[Review the facts in *Kahn v. Lynch Communication Sys., Inc., supra* ("*Lynch I*"), which remanded this case to the Court of Chancery for a "redetermination of the entire fairness of the cash-out merger to Kahn and the other Lynch minority shareholders with the burden of proof remaining on Alcatel, the dominant and interested shareholder." 638 A.2d at 1122. The Court of Chancery reexamined the cash-out merger, relying solely on the existing record, and once again held that the defendants had carried the burden of showing that the merger was entirely fair to Lynch's public shareholders. *Kahn v. Lynch Communication Systems, Inc.*, Del.Ch., 1995 WL 301403 (1995) (the "*1995 Decision*").

The Court of Chancery concluded that, despite Alcatel's coercion of the Independent Committee, defendants had met their burden of proving fair dealing because they had satisfied other relevant factors set forth in *Weinberger v. UOP, Inc.*, 457 A.2d 701 (1983)—specifically, the transaction's timing, initiation, structure and negotiation. On the issue of fair price, the Court of Chancery found the evaluation of the plaintiffs' expert flawed and concluded that the defendants had also met their burden of establishing the fairness of the price received by the stockholders. *1995 Decision* at 5–6. Thus, the Court of Chancery held for the defendants because they had established the entire fairness of the transaction.

Kahn again appealed. He contended that the finding of fair dealing was inconsistent with *Lynch I* and was not supported by the record. Specifically, he asserted that the coercion of the Independent Committee constituted a *per se* breach of fiduciary duty which strongly compels a finding that the transaction was not entirely fair. He also argued that the initiation, timing and negotiation of the merger were unfair and required a finding of unfair dealing. In addition, Kahn challenged the Chancery Court's determination that Lynch's shareholders received a fair price for their shares.]

## II

\* \* \*

## A.

At the outset we must confront the disagreement between the parties concerning the extent to which our decision in *Lynch I* limited the scope of the Court of Chancery's re-examination of the record on remand. \* \* \*

While we agree that our decision in *Lynch I* limited the range of findings available to the Court of Chancery upon remand, our previous review of the record focused upon the threshold question of burden of proof. Our reversal on burden of proof left open the question whether the transaction was entirely fair. *Lynch I*, 638 A.2d at 1122. Indeed, Kahn concedes that our ruling on burden shifting did not create *per se* liability, an obvious concession since we did not address the fair price element in *Lynch I*, except to note that the Independent Committee's ability to negotiate price had been compromised by Alcatel's threat to proceed with a hostile tender offer. The Court of Chancery correctly took as its premise on remand that Alcatel, as the dominant and interested shareholder bore the burden of demonstrating the entire fairness of the merger transaction. Its findings will be tested from that perspective.

As we noted in *Lynch I*, "a controlling or dominating shareholder standing on both sides of a transaction, as in a parent-subsidiary context, bears the burden of proving its entire fairness." *Id.* at 1115. The standard for demonstrating entire fairness is the oft-repeated one announced in *Weinberger*, 457 A.2d at 711: fair dealing and fair price. Fair dealing addresses the timing and structure of negotiations as well as the method of approval of the transaction, while fair price relates to all the factors which affect the value of the stock of the merged company. *Id.* at 711. An important teaching of *Weinberger*, however, is that the test is not bifurcated or compartmentalized but one requiring an examination of all aspects of the transaction to gain a sense of whether the deal in its entirety is fair. *Id.* In its most recent authoritative analysis of the subject, this Court held: "the board will have to demonstrate entire fairness by presenting evidence of the cumulative manner by which it ... discharged all of its fiduciary duties." *Cinerama, Inc. v. Technicolor, Inc.*, Del.Supr., 663 A.2d 1156, 1163 (1995).

B.

\* \* \* The record reflects that the Court of Chancery followed this Court's mandate by applying a unified approach to its entire fairness examination. *Lynch I*, 638 A.2d at 1115. In doing so, the Court of Chancery properly considered "how the board of directors discharged all of its fiduciary duties with regard to each aspect of the non-bifurcated components of entire fairness: fair dealing and fair price." *Cinerama, Inc. v. Technicolor, Inc.*, 663 A.2d at 1172.

In addressing the fair dealing component of the transaction, the Court of Chancery determined that the initiation and timing of the transactions were responsive to Lynch's needs. This conclusion was based on the fact that Lynch's marketing strategy was handicapped by the lack of a fiber optic technology. Alcatel proposed the merger with Celwave to remedy this competitive weakness but Lynch management and the non-Alcatel directors did not believe this combination would be beneficial to Lynch. Dertinger, Lynch's CEO, suggested to Alcatel that, under the circumstances, a cash merger with Alcatel will be preferable to a Celwave merger. Thus, the Alcatel offer to acquire the minority interests in Lynch was viewed as an alternative to the disfavored Celwave transaction.

Kahn argues that the Telco acquisition, which Lynch management strongly supported, was vetoed by Alcatel to force Lynch to accept Celwave as a merger partner or agree to a cash out merger with Alcatel. The benefits of the Telco transaction, however, are clearly debatable. Telco was not profitable and had a limited fiber optic capability. There is no assurance that Lynch's shareholders would have benefitted from the acquisition. More to the point, the timing of a merger transaction cannot be viewed solely from the perspective of the acquired entity. A majority shareholder is naturally motivated by economic self-interest in initiating a transaction. Otherwise, there is no reason to do it. Thus, mere initiation by the acquirer is not reprehensible so long as the controlling shareholder does not gain a financial advantage at the expense of the minority.

In support of its claim of coercion, Kahn contends that Alcatel timed its merger offer, with a thinly-veiled threat of using its controlling position to force the result, to take advantage of the opportunity to buy Lynch on the cheap. As will be discussed at greater length in our fair price analysis, infra, Lynch was experiencing a difficult and rapidly changing competitive situation. Its current financial results reflected that fact. Although its stock was trading at low levels, this may simply have been a reflection of its competitive problems. Alcatel is not to be faulted for taking advantage of the objective reality of Lynch's financial situation. Thus the mere fact that the transaction was initiated at Alcatel's discretion, does not dictate a finding of unfairness in the absence of a determination that the minority shareholders of Lynch were harmed by the timing. The Court of Chancery rejected such a claim and we agree.

## C.

With respect to the negotiations and structure of the transaction, the Court of Chancery, while acknowledging that the Court in *Lynch I* found the negotiations coercive, commented that the negotiations "certainly were no less fair than if there had been no negotiations at all" *1995 Decision* at 4. The court noted that a committee of non-Alcatel directors negotiated an increase in price from $14 per share to $15.50. The committee also retained two investment banking firms who were well acquainted with Lynch's prospects based on their work on the Celwave proposal. Moreover, the committee had the benefit of outside legal counsel.

It is true that the committee and the Board agreed to a price which at least one member of the committee later opined was not a fair price. *Lynch I*, 638 A.2d at 1118. But there is no requirement of unanimity in such matters either at the Independent Committee level or by the Board. A finding of unfair dealing based on lack of unanimity could discourage the use of special committees in majority dominated cash-out mergers. Here Alcatel could have presented a merger offer directly to the Lynch Board, which it controlled, and received a quick approval. Had it done so, of course, it would have borne the burden of demonstrating entire fairness in the event the transaction was later questioned. *See Weinberger*. Where, ultimately, it has been required to assume the same burden, it should fare no worse in a judicial review of the fairness of its negotiations with the Independent Committee.

Kahn asserts that the Court of Chancery did not properly consider our finding of coercion in *Lynch I*. Generally, as in this case, the burden rests on the party that engaged in coercive conduct to demonstrate the equity of their actions. *Lynch I*, 638 A.2d at 1121; *Unitrin, Inc. v. American General Corp.*, Del.Supr., 651 A.2d 1361, 1373, 1387 (1995) (holding that burden rests on board of directors which has taken draconian, e.g., coercive, measures in response to hostile tender offer). Kahn challenges the Court of Chancery's finding of fair dealing by relying upon the holding in *Ivanhoe Partners v. Newmont Min. Corp.*, Del.Ch., 533 A.2d 585, 605–06 (1987), *aff'd*, Del.Supr., 535 A.2d 1334 (1987), for the proposition that coercion creates liability *per se. Ivanhoe* makes clear, however, that to be actionable, the coercive conduct directed at selling shareholders must be a "material" influence on the decision to sell. *Id.*

Where other economic forces are at work and more likely produced the decision to sell, as the Court of Chancery determined here, the specter of coercion may not be deemed material with respect to the transaction as a whole, and will not prevent a finding of entire fairness. In this case, no shareholder was treated differently in the transaction from any other shareholder nor subjected to a two-tiered or squeeze-out treatment. *See, e.g., Unocal Corp. v. Mesa Petroleum Co.*, Del.Supr., 493 A.2d 946, 956 (1985). Alcatel offered cash for all the minority shares and paid cash for all shares tendered. Clearly there was no coercion exerted which was material to this aspect of the transaction, and thus no finding of *per se* liability is required.

### D.

As previously noted, in *Lynch I* this Court did not address the fair price aspect of the merger transaction since our remand required a reexamination of fair dealing at the trial level. * * *

In considering whether Alcatel had discharged its burden with respect to fairness of price, the Court of Chancery placed reliance upon the testimony of Michael McCarty, a senior officer at Dillon Read, who prepared Alcatel's proposal to the Independent Committee. He valued Lynch at $15.50 to $16.00 per share—a range determined by using the closing market price of $11 per share of October 17, 1988 and adding a merger premium of 41% to 46%. Dillon Read's valuation had been prepared in October, 1986 in connection with the Lynch/Celwave combination proposed at a time when Lynch was experiencing a downward trend in earnings and prospects. Subsequent to the October valuation, Lynch management revised its three year forecast downward to reflect disappointing third quarter results.

The Court of Chancery also considered the valuation reports issued by both Kidder Peabody and Thompson McKinmon who were retained by the Independent Committee at the time of the Celwave proposal in October. At that time both bankers valued Lynch at $16.50 to $17.50 per share. These valuations, however, were made in response to Alcatel's Celwave proposal and were not, strictly speaking, fairness opinions. When Lynch later revised downward its financial forecasts based on poor third quarter operating results both firms opined that the Alcatel merger price was fair as of the later merger date.

Kahn supported his claim of inadequate price principally through the expert testimony of Fred Shinagle, an independent financial analyst, who opined that the fair value of Lynch on November 24, 1986 was $18.25 per share. He reached that conclusion by averaging equally the values he derived from market price, book value, earning power and capitalization.

* * *

In addition to the testimony of his valuation expert, Kahn offered the view of Dertinger, Lynch's CEO at the time of the merger, who testified that he thought the fair value of Lynch at the time of the merger was $20 per share. Dertinger considered "two values of Lynch: Our marketing value—that is in the eyes of our customers—and the value of Lynch on Wall Street as exemplified primarily by the stock price. But I think that is definitely secondary to a company's potential." Board member Hubert Kertz also testified that in his opinion Lynch's value was well above the $14 merger price. Although conceding that "not being a financial man but being a manager" he thought that "even under almost the worst scenario, it ought to be somewhere in the high teens or $20 a share."

In its fair price analysis, the Court of Chancery accepted the fairness opinions tendered by Alcatel and found the merger price fair. The court rejected Kahn's attack on the merger price because it found the Shinagle valuation methodology to be flawed * * *.*

In resolving issues of valuation the Court of Chancery undertakes a mixed determination of law and fact. When faced with differing methodologies or opinions the court is entitled to draw its own conclusions from the evidence. So long as the court's ultimate determination of value is based on the application of recognized valuation standards, its acceptance of one expert's opinion, to the exclusion of another, will not be disturbed.

* * * Although the burden of proving fair price had shifted to Alcatel, once a sufficient showing of fair value of the company was presented, the party attacking the merger was required to come forward with sufficient credible evidence to persuade the finder of fact of the merit of a greater figure proposed. *See Cinerama, Inc. v. Technicolor, Inc.*, 663 A.2d at 1177; *Citron*, 584 A.2d at 508; *Rosenblatt*, 493 A.2d at 942. The Court of Chancery was not persuaded that Kahn had presented evidence of sufficient quality to prove the inadequacy of the merger price. We find that ruling to be logically determined and supported by the evidence and accordingly affirm.

* * *

---

In most cases where a court has concluded that a cash out merger was the product of fair dealing, it also has found that the merger price was fair. *See, e.g., Rosenblatt,* supra; *Citron,* supra. But that has not invariably been the case. *Kahn v. Household Acquisition Corp.*, 591 A.2d 166 (Del.1991), involved a challenge to a cash out merger of an 11.6% minority interest in Wien Air Alaska, Inc. at $6.00 per share. Household had previously purchased substantial blocks of Wien stock at $6.00 per share from Wien directors and a group of pilots and had acquired additional shares through tender offers at $6.00 and $6.50 per share. The court found that the cash out merger involved no unfair dealing, but, relying on expert testimony, concluded that Wien stock had a fair value of $7.27 per share.

In *Alabama By–Products Corp. v. Neal*, 588 A.2d 255 (Del.1991), the Delaware Supreme Court made clear that a court should not consider

---

* Shinagle estimated that Lynch had a capitalization value of $27.92 per share, which he calculated using the highest capitalization ratio of any comparable company. Had Shinagle used the average ratio of comparable companies, as he did in his other calculations, Lynch's capitalization value would have been $13.18 per share and its fair value would have been $14.44 per share. [Ed.]

claims of unfair dealing in connection with a cash out merger when determining the fair value of the dissenting shareholders' stock. However, a court properly can treat evidence of unfair dealing as a "relevant factor" when it is assessing the credibility of the corporation's evidence concerning fair value. The court distinguished breach of duty claims relating to the cash out merger from derivative claims for pre-merger breaches of fiduciary duty, noting that *Cavalier Oil* had held that the value of the latter should be considered in determining fair value in an appraisal proceeding.

*BNE Massachusetts Corp. v. Sims*, 588 N.E.2d 14 (Mass.App.1992), an appraisal action to determine the fair value of Charterbank stock, did not involve any claim of unfair dealing. Charterbank had retained Merrill Lynch to solicit acquisition offers in the context of a "controlled auction." Six substantial banking institutions made bids. Charterbank chose what it believed to be the best bid and agreed to be acquired by the Conifer/Essex Group, Inc. (Conifer) in a two-step transaction with a blended value of $95.35 per share—$101 in cash for 35% of Charterbank's stock and $92.25 in Conifer stock for the balance. Certain Charterbank shareholders dissented and sought appraisal pursuant to M.G.L.A. c. 156B, § 92.

At trial, expert witnesses retained by the shareholders testified that the fair value of Charterbank's stock was $118.78 or $120.00. Conifer's expert testified that the fair value of the stock was only $72.45. The trial judge, using the "Delaware block" method, concluded that the stock had a fair value of $101.75 per share. The appellate court reversed, pointing out that the trial court had not explained why he had assigned equal weight to market price, earnings value and asset value and had valued only the dissenters' minority interests rather than the value of Charterbank as a whole. The court then suggested that where shareholders dissented from an arm's-length transaction, a different approach should be used to value their stock.

Assuming the plaintiff's statements are an accurate description of the transaction—an arm's-length merger agreement which was the product of a "controlled auction" among six qualified bidders and approved by the officers and directors who were free of any conflicting interest and who sought and obtained the advice of experienced investment bankers—the trial judge could appropriately consider whether the blended value of the merger price should be binding upon both parties. The plaintiff argues that the dissenting shareholders should be required to accept $22.90 less than the blended value of the merger terms, but its brief is silent as to why § 92 requires that dissenting stockholders be penalized for having dissented. Similarly, the defendants claim that they are entitled to more than the merger terms, but they suggest no reason in their cross-appeal why § 92 requires that dissenting stockholders be rewarded for having dissented. Given the untainted nature of this merger transaction—if that is the fact of the matter—we are unable to perceive any sound reason why dissenting stockholders should receive any more or less than the amount received by all other stockholders in a transaction approved by the board of directors upon the advice of investment bankers. The purpose of § 92, as we have said, is to assure minority stockholders that those in control of the enterprise will not obtain unfair advantage. In this case, neither party has suggested that unfair advantage was sought or obtained. Section 92 was not designed to provide sellers with an opportunity for a windfall or to provide buyers with an opportunity for a bargain. * * * The opinion of experts, who have analyzed the experience of comparable institutions and extrapolated the results to the behavior of an hypothesized willing buyer, cannot match the reality experienced by this institution in setting the terms of the merger with the actual buyer who prevailed over five competing institutions.

On remand, the trial judge should determine the blended value in cash of the merger price (unless the value is agreed to by the parties), and he should determine whether the [dissenters] are prepared to place before the court an offer of proof that the merger transaction was either (i) tainted by conflicting interests at the officer or board level, or (ii) for some other identified reason, not the genuine product of an arms-length bidding process among qualified, informed and willing bidders. Absent such proof, the judge should consider whether judgment may appropriately be entered for the dissenters in the amount of the blended cash value of the Conifer payment, with interest. If there is an offer of proof satisfactory to the judge, he should proceed to trial on that issue. If, at the conclusion of the trial, he is not persuaded by a preponderance of the evidence that the financial terms of the merger agreement should prevail, he should proceed to a determination of the fair value of the shares of the dissenters based on the expert testimony already received.

*Id*. at 20–21. *See, also*, ALI Principles of Corporate Governance (1994) § 7.22, providing that when appraisal is sought in connection with a business combination not involving a controlling shareholder or other control person, "the aggregate price accepted by the board of directors of the subject corporation should be presumed to represent the fair value of the corporation * * *, unless the [dissenting shareholder] can prove otherwise by clear and convincing evidence."

Of course, when a court finds that a merger was not the product of arm's length bargaining, it has little choice but to rely on expert testimony to determine whether the merger price was fair. As the materials in Chapter 8 make clear, determining a corporation's value often requires many complex and highly subjective judgments. In a cash out merger, this determination is more difficult because plaintiffs and defendants can be expected to choose experts who will disagree sharply about the value of the corporation.

*In re Appraisal of Shell Oil Co.*, 607 A.2d 1213 (Del.1992), involved just such a situation. The dissenting shareholders' expert valued Shell stock at $89.00 per share; Shell's expert said it was worth only $55.00. The court, after affirming the vice chancellor's decision that Shell stock had a fair value of $71.20 per share, commented:

> [W]e take the occasion to comment upon a recurring theme in recent appraisal cases—the clash of contrary, and often antagonistic, expert opinion on value. The presentation of widely divergent views reflecting partisan positions in appraisal proceedings adds to the burden of the Court of Chancery's task of fixing value. * * * We impute no impropriety to the participants in this or other appraisal litigation in their efforts to advance their respective positions. That is to be expected in an adversarial system. But if the Court is limited to the biased presentation of the parties, it is often forced to pick and choose from a limited record without the benefit of objective analysis and opinion. To compensate for this handicap, the Court of Chancery should consider, in a proper case, appointing its own expert witness.

> \* \* \*

> We do not mandate the use of court appointed experts in any case, leaving such determination to the discretion of the trial judge, but we believe the time has come for the Court of Chancery to avail itself of such a practice whenever it believes that a more objective presentation of evidence is required, particularly in valuation matters. Finally, we suggest that the Court of Chancery consider adoption of a rule, modeled after Federal Rule[s of Evidence] 706, which will implement its inherent authority in this area.

Id. at 1222–23

In *Kleinwort Benson Ltd. v. Silgan Corp.*, 1995 WL 376911 (Del. Ch.1995), Vice Chancellor Chandler appointed a neutral expert to critique the valuations prepared by the parties' experts rather to conduct an independent valuation. The Vice Chancellor then relied on the neutral expert's critique to make upward adjustments to the discounted cash flow and market values used by respondent's expert, whose testimony the Vice Chancellor found more credible than that of petitioners' expert.

## 3. INTEREST IN APPRAISAL PROCEEDINGS

Whether dissenting shareholders are awarded interest on the fair value of their stock, what rate of interest they receive, and whether interest is compound or simple can have a major impact on the attractiveness of the appraisal remedy. Litigation involving a series of transactions in which Royal Dutch Petroleum cashed out the minority shareholders of Shell Oil (U.S.) makes this clear. Shareholders who accepted Royal Dutch's tender offer received a total of $60.00 per share for their stock; shareholders who did not tender but were cashed out in a subsequent short form merger and who waived their right to seek appraisal received $62.00 per share; shareholders who dissented and sought appraisal were awarded $71.20 per share. However, the vice chancellor awarded only simple interest to the dissenting shareholders, which reduced the economic value of the payment they received to the equivalent of approximately $61.13 per share paid at the time of the tender offer. *See In re Appraisal of Shell Oil Co.*, 607 A.2d 1213 (Del.1992) (affirming award). Thus, although those shareholders apparently were "right" to dissent, they ended up with little more than they would have received had they tendered their stock.

Decisions about whether to award interest and how it is to be computed generally are within the discretion of the trial court. A customary guideline is that dissenting shareholders should be compensated for their inability to use the money tied up in the stock being appraised, and that a defendant corporation should be required to pay a rate of interest equivalent to what it would have paid to borrow funds at the time of the transaction giving rise to the appraisal proceeding. In an appraisal proceed that grew out of a controlling shareholder's cash out of all public shareholders in the New England Patriots Football Club (Patriots), the corporation that owned the New England Patriots football team, the trial court found that Patriots stock was worth $80.00 per share at the time of the merger, but also awarded dissenting shareholders 9% compound interest—an award that the appellate court affirmed as "not an abuse of the judge's discretion." *See Sarrouf v. New England Patriots Football Club*, 492 N.E.2d 1122, 1129 (Mass.1986). As a consequence, the dissenting shareholders received a total of about $173.75 per share for their stock. In contrast, the majority shareholder agreed to pay another group of shareholders, who had won a class action alleging that the cash out involved a breach of fiduciary duty, an amount equal to $254.91 per share. However, because those shareholders were required to pay their attorneys' fees and expenses, they ended up with only about $158.64 per share.

In *McLoon Oil Co., supra*, the Supreme Judicial Court of Maine held that the trial court had abused its discretion in awarding dissenting shareholders simple rather than compound interest. It explained:

As a matter of law, interest under the appraisal statute is not a mere procedural incentive but is a substantive right, intended to reimburse the Dissenters for the lost use of their money during the pendency of the appraisal proceeding while the corporation retained control and use of it. One commentator has forcefully noted that in the absence of compound interest, the corporation could force the dissenter to sell his shares at less than fair value. If the corporation initially makes a low settlement offer, lengthy appraisal proceedings are inevitable. However, the allowance of only simply interest on the appraisal award could, in some cases, result in a situation where it would be more profitable for the shareholder to accept the settlement offer and invest the money in a savings account, drawing compounded interest quarterly, rather than go through the lengthy appraisal process. This result is clearly inconsistent with the purpose of the appraisal statutes which is to guarantee the dissenting shareholder fair value of his shares and to encourage the corporation to make a fair settlement offer. Compounding the 8% interest rate selected in this case is the only fair and equitable way to compensate the Dissenters for the lost use of their funds for nearly thirteen years.

565 A.2d at 1007–08.

The Delaware Supreme Court has followed a different approach. In *Rapid–American Corp. v. Harris*, supra, the parties agreed that the appropriate rate of interest, representing what Rapid–American would have paid to borrow funds, was 12.75 percent. The Court of Chancery accepted that figure, but then ruled, without further explanation, that it would not depart from its standard practice of awarding simple interest.

On appeal, Harris pointed out that Rapid–American had had the use of the funds due to him since the merger was consummated and that no prudent investor would make an investment during that period for simple interest. He also argued that awarding simple interest provided corporations with an incentive to delay the resolution of appraisal proceedings. The Delaware Supreme Court rejected Harris' argument. It first recognized "that no Delaware case has ever explicitly considered the factors which determine whether a court should award either simple or compound interest." 603 A.2d at 808. It then held that DGCL § 262(i) gave the trial court discretion to determine whether simple or compound interest should be awarded and concluded that it had not been an abuse of discretion to award only simple interest.

This decision significantly reduced Harris's ultimate recovery. Rapid–American had cashed out its minority shareholders in January 1981 for approximately $28.00 per share. Harris dissented and the Court of Chancery eventually determined his stock had a fair value, as of the merger date, of $73.29 per share. *Rapid–American Corp. v. Harris*, *supra*. Consequently, with 12.75% simple interest for approximately 11 1/2 years, Harris received roughly $187 per share. Had the court awarded interest compounded annually, Harris would have received 55% more, or approximately $292 per share, for his stock. *See also In re Appraisal of Shell Oil Co.*, *supra*.

As Yogi Berra once said, "It's never over 'til its over."

# Index

References are to Pages